Shakespeare

Shakespeare

AN OXFORD GUIDE

Edited by

Stanley Wells
Lena Cowen Orlin

OXFORD
UNIVERSITY PRESS

OXFORD
UNIVERSITY PRESS

Great Clarendon Street, Oxford OX2 6DP

Oxford University Press is a department of the Unversity of Oxford.
It furthers the University's objective of excellence in research, scholarship,
and education by publishing worldwide in

Oxford New York

Auckland Cape Town Dar es Salaam Hong Kong Karachi Kuala Lumpur
Madrid Melbourne Mexico City Nairobi New Delhi Taipei Toronto
Shanghai

With offices in

Argentina Austria Brazil Chile Czech Republic France Greece
Guatemala Hungary Italy Japan South Korea Poland Portugal
Singapore Switzerland Thailand Turkey Ukraine Vietnam

Oxford is a registered trade mark of Oxford University Press
in the UK and in certain other countries

Published in the United States
by Oxford University Press Inc., New York

A catalogue record for this book is available from the British Library

Library of Congress Cataloguing in Publication Data

Data available

ISBN-10: 0–19–924522–3 (Pbk)
ISBN-13: 978–0–19–924522–2

10 9 8 7 6 5 4 3

Typeset by RefineCatch Limited, Bungay, Suffolk
Printed in Great Britain by
CPI Bath

Preface

The aim of this volume is to present students and other readers of Shakespeare's plays and poems with a series of readily intelligible and well-informed essays which will enhance their understanding of and increase their store of knowledge on a wide range of relevant topics, both critical and scholarly. The volume is designed so that individual contributions may be read either on their own or in conjunction with others. In the sections on critical approaches, for instance, each essay is followed by an application of the method discussed to a particular play or poem, but this is not meant to imply that other approaches are not equally applicable to that work. Readers are encouraged to make their own connections between the topics explored and Shakespeare's plays.

The first readers for many of these essays were students in a Fall 2001 Shakespeare course at the University of Maryland, Baltimore County. For their recommendations for revisions and, especially, clarifications, the editors are indebted to Matthew Barth, Nicholas Brown, Ralph Corbitt, Lisa Cunningham, Austin Curtis, Teresa Eckles, Joe Ellis, Kim Le, Zach Luceti, Teresa McCarthy, Amanda Miracle, Raquel Rosa, John Sales, Michael Scheffler, Matt Smith, Stephanie Trickey, Alyssa Tuel, Kaela Victor, and Rachel Williams. Their careful evaluations were a guiding spirit for the entire volume. Lena Orlin thanks the National Endowment for the Humanities and the University of Maryland, Baltimore County, for a fellowship leave during which much of the work on this volume was completed. The editors are also grateful for the efficient and friendly co-operation of Matthew Cotton, Sarah Hyland, and especially Fiona Kinnear, who encouraged the enterprise from its earliest stages, at Oxford University Press.

Note on references

Quotations and references are to the Norton Shakespeare, based on the Oxford edition, General Editor Stephen Greenblatt (New York and London: Norton, 1997). One exception is that the titles employed for Shakespeare's plays are those in most common usage. Those that diverge in the Norton edition (listed to the right) are:

Henry VI Part Two: *The First Part of the Contention of the Two Famous Houses of York and Lancaster.*

Henry VI Part Three: *The True Tragedy of Richard Duke of York and the Good King Henry VI.*

Henry IV Part One: *The History of Henry the Fourth.*

King Lear: *The History of King Lear: the quarto Text; The Tragedy of King Lear: The Folio text; The tragedy of King Lear: A Conflated Text.* References are to the last-named unless otherwise stated.

Henry VIII: *All is True.*

Stanley Wells and Lena Cowen Orlin, September 2002.

Outline contents

Detailed contents

List of illustrations

List of contributors

Alan Armstrong Southern Oregon University

Emily C. Bartels Rutgers, State University of New Jersey

Michael Best University of Victoria

Michael Billington *The Guardian*

A. R. Braunmuller University of California, Los Angeles

Michael D. Bristol McGill University

William C. Carroll Boston University

David Crystal, OBE Writer, lecturer, broadcaster

Christy Desmet University of Georgia

Paul Edmondson Shakespeare Birthplace Trust

Gabriel Egan King's College, University of London

Lynn Enterline Vanderbilt University

Inga-Stina Ewbank University of Leeds

Reginald Foakes University of California, Los Angeles

Miriam Gilbert University of Iowa

John Gross *The Sunday Telegraph*

Jonathan Gil Harris Ithaca College

Terence Hawkes University of Wales, Cardiff

Ton Hoenselaars Utrecht University

Jean E. Howard Columbia University

Tony Howard University of Warwick

Martin Ingram Brasenose College, University of Oxford

David Kathman Freelance scholar

Margaret Jane Kidnie University of Western Ontario

Peter Lake Princeton University

Carole Levin University of Nebraska, Lincoln

Russ McDonald University of North Carolina, Greensboro

Lynne Magnusson Queen's University, Ontario

Laurie Maguire Magdalen College, University of Oxford

Lena Cowen Orlin University of Maryland, Baltimore County and Shakespeare Association of America

Lois Potter University of Delaware

Phyllis Rackin University of Pennsylvania

Kiernan Ryan Royal Holloway College, University of London

Leah Scragg University of Manchester

Jyotsna Singh Michigan State University

Bruce R. Smith Georgetown University

Patricia Tatspaugh Freelance writer

Michael Taylor Carleton University

Joan Thirsk, CBE St Hilda's College and Kellogg College, University of Oxford

Peter Thomson University of Exeter

Stanley Wells University of Birmingham and Shakespeare Birthplace Trust

Linda Woodbridge Pennsylvania State University

Georgianna Ziegler Folger Shakespeare Library

Part I

Shakespeare's life and times

Fig. 1.1 The title page of the First Folio of 1623, in which Shakespeare's plays first appeared in collected form, seven years after he died. This engraving, by Martin Droeshout, is one of the two best-authenticated portraits of Shakespeare (the other, the bust in Holy Trinity Church in Stratford-upon-Avon, is shown in Figure 4.4).

1 | Why study Shakespeare?

Stanley Wells

This question is open to interpretation. It could, for example, mean why study *Shakespeare?*—that is, Shakespeare rather than any other topic—or why *study* Shakespeare?—that is, why should it be necessary to study a writer whose works were written to give pleasure, any more than we must 'study' current films or pop music in order to enjoy them.

Let's take the first meaning first. Reasons for taking an interest in Shakespeare are given by all the contributors to this book, but it may be helpful to offer some general thoughts. Shakespeare is worth studying because reading his plays and poems, and experiencing the plays in performance, can enrich our lives in countless ways: by making us more sensitive to language and therefore more capable of expressing ourselves and of responding to experience; by involving us in the ethical dilemmas of the characters in the plays and thus increasing our moral sensibility; by allowing us entry to states of mind different from our own and thus enlarging our imaginative experience; by showing us, too, that other people may experience emotions that we find in ourselves, and thus giving us a sense of shared humanity. Shakespeare's sonnets articulate experiences of friendship and love in ways that none of us can rival. Look for example at the confident lyricism of Sonnet 18 ('Shall I compare thee to a summer's day'), at the expression of longing in the absence of the beloved in Sonnet 27 ('Weary with toil I haste me to my bed'), at the adoring self-abasement of Sonnet 57 ('Being your slave . . .'), and at the tormented struggle between love for a man and a woman in Sonnet 144 ('Two loves have I, of comfort and despair'). Within a single scene of *Measure for Measure* Shakespeare offers two of the most powerful expressions ever written of the fear of death (Claudio's 'Ay. but to die and go we know not where', 3.1.118–132) and of consolation for its terrors (the Duke's 'Be absolute for death', 3.1.5–41). Lear's desolation at the death of his daughter Cordelia (*King Lear*, 5.3.232 to the end), the mutual happiness of the twins Viola and Sebastian as they are reunited after believing each other dead (*Twelfth Night*, 5.1.224–255)—these and innumerable other episodes can work upon our emotions however distant they may be from our personal experience.

Shakespeare's plays can stimulate thought about abstract issues such as heroism, government, and war; friendship and love; sexuality and gender; personal and public responsibility; humankind's relationship to society and to the universe. They are packed full with wit and humour. Shakespeare had an extraordinary ability to observe, and to transmute into art, the quirks and oddities of the way people talk and behave—an enjoyment of eccentricity, a tolerance of unconventionality, a delight in clever answers and sparkling repartee, in sexual innuendo and robust, knockabout humour, both verbal and physical. And his plays give aesthetic pleasure, arousing admiration of their shapeliness and patterning, of the relationships of details to the whole, of their linguistic virtuosity and intellectual vitality, of their capacity to engage and entertain us in ways that enhance our appreciation of life.

To an extent these things are true of any good dramatist. What is special about Shakespeare? Partly it's the fact that his plays and poems cover an exceptional range of human experience. They range from the delicate comedy of *The Two Gentlemen of Verona* to the austerely passionate tragedy of *King Lear*; from the farcical complications of *The Comedy of Errors* to the sensuous eroticism of *Antony and Cleopatra*; from the violence and horror of *Titus Andronicus* and the early history plays to the fantasy and charm of *A Midsummer Night's Dream* and *The Tempest*. And they engage with the spiritual world, most obviously in the visions of late plays such as *Cymbeline*, *Pericles*, and *The Tempest*, but no less pervasively in, for instance, *Hamlet*, whose hero is charged with a task by a ghost, and in *Richard III* and *Macbeth*, where spirits externalize states of mind. Each of Shakespeare's plays is unique. This does not make them better in themselves, but does increase our sense of the achievement of the single mind from which they all proceeded. And it can be fascinating to look for and to think about links among the plays, as if they all formed one great work of art.

The range evident from one play to another is apparent too within the plays themselves. As soon as one tries to categorize any of them one realizes the inevitable inadequacy—discussed by many of our contributors—of attempts to do so. None of Shakespeare's plays is purely comic or purely tragic, each of them stretches the limits of its framework, inviting not singularity but multiplicity of response. Most of his comedies bring one or more characters close to death, the tragedy of *Hamlet* is shot through with comedy from beginning to end, *Macbeth* has its comic porter, and even *King Lear* can raise laughter. The plays' emotional complexity is a part of their richness. Shakespeare's creativity in the greatest of them is so profuse that like the night sky it can never be taken in all at once. The depth of characterization in figures such as Falstaff and Hamlet, Rosalind and Cleopatra, means that they can only be read or performed selectively. An actor who tried to give equal weight to every word and image in a role would clog the play's forward movement; a reader who tried to plumb the depths of every speech would lose sense of the shape of the whole.

The richness of Shakespeare's plays is a cause of great diversity of interpretation. Shakespeare himself was clearly aware that his actors, and their followers from one generation to another, would interact with what he wrote in creative ways, so that each performance of a role has its own uniqueness. Many of these roles remain among the greatest and most rewarding challenges ever offered to actors. As actors vary in response, so too do readers, according to their education and sensibility. The texts are fluid: none of them exists in a form that was finally approved by Shakespeare; some of them, such as *Hamlet* and *King Lear*, have come down to us in more than one version, each with its own claims to authenticity; and all of them are subject to change according to the circumstances in which they are performed. They release different energies each time they are acted. And they are essentially collaborative, calling on the skills of actors, musicians, directors, designers, dancers, costumiers, and property makers. These are among the reasons why we can gain pleasure and understanding by going on seeing the plays in varied interpretations, and why they reveal new facets of themselves in repeated re-readings.

An additional reason for studying Shakespeare is his pervasive influence on the English language and on Western and, increasingly, global culture. Many creative artists have been inspired by his plays to compose works of their own. If we have at least a degree of familiarity with his works we shall have a fuller understanding of some of the music by great composers such as Mendelssohn and Berlioz, Prokokiev and Britten, of paintings by Reynolds and Blake, of modern novels such as John Updike's *Claudius and Gertrude* (based on *Hamlet*) and Jane Smiley's *A Thousand Acres* (based on *King Lear*), of the thousands of popular films and television sitcoms that make allusions to Shakespeare, and of references to him by politicians and journalists, preachers and comedians. Awareness of Shakespeare has become part of the mental equipment expected of educated persons in many different countries.

There are, however, obstacles to an easy appreciation of Shakespeare which we cannot ignore. To think about this is to face the second interpretation of the question with which we opened—why we need to *study* Shakespeare. He wrote for theatres and theatre companies very different from our own (though many modern theatres attempt to capture features of the stages of his time, or even to replicate them, in order to accommodate his plays). We shall understand his stagecraft more fully—why, for example, he often writes short scenes, why action is not precisely located, why there are far fewer female than male roles, what is meant by terms such as 'above' and 'aside'—if we know something of the theatres for which he wrote. The fact that he wrote largely in verse, often deeply infused with rhetorical patterns and using classical and biblical allusions, may act as a deterrent in an age that is not accustomed to heightened language.

Even in Shakespeare's own time, the complexity and density of some of his writing must have challenged readers and listeners. Often he is expressing subtle and intellectually probing thoughts, and the swift shifts of his wordplay are not for lazy minds. This is more apparent in some plays than in others. While much of the language of, for example, *The Merchant of Venice* or *Julius Caesar, As You Like It* or *The Merry Wives of Windsor* is unproblematic, that of *Troilus and Cressida* or *The Winter's Tale*, *Cymbeline* and *The Two Noble Kinsmen* is, for one reason or another, often dense in its own right. Though *Romeo and Juliet* is appealing in its lyricism, the play also includes passages of elaborate rhetoric and wordplay that are often omitted in performance. And since Shakespeare's time the English language has changed. Some of the words that he uses have become archaic or obsolete; others, more deceptively, have shifted in meaning. Syntax has changed. Training in close reading, in Elizabethan vocabulary and grammar, in the proper use of edited and annotated texts, may help to overcome such obstacles. Having said this, one must also say that there are long sections of the plays that pose no problems to averagely literate readers, and that even in modern books we don't necessarily expect to understand every word. Beatrix Potter in a book for very young children could write that eating lettuces 'certainly had a very soporific effect upon the Flopsy Bunnies!' Writers popular with young people, such as J. R. Tolkien, Philip Pullman, and J. K. Rowling, use invented words with full confidence that they will form no obstacle to enjoyment. And in the theatre, where the language has already passed through the trained intelligences of the actors who speak it, much of the work of comprehension has already been done for us.

Enjoyment of Shakespeare also requires understanding of the dramatic and theatrical conventions with which he worked. Modern playgoers may be disturbed by the use of soliloquy and the aside, by conventions of disguise and obvious artificialities of plot. Why does Hamlet talk to himself? How can we be expected to believe that no one in *The Comedy of Errors* is intelligent enough to realize that twins must be around, or that Viola in *Twelfth Night* should not see that the only explanation for what is happening is that her brother has survived the shipwreck? In *As You Like It*, how is it possible that Rosalind's father should not recognize his own daughter until the moment that the plot requires him to do so? In *Twelfth Night*, if we can hear Sir Toby and Sir Andrew as they stand behind Malvolio, why can't he do so? Can anyone really believe that Iago would have been able so quickly to convince Othello of Desdemona's adultery? Acceptance of the conventions on which such episodes depend requires a submission of the imagination into which modern audiences may have to be educated.

Once such acceptance has been cultivated, there should be little difficulty in gaining much enjoyment from most of Shakespeare's plays, but they can offer deeper rewards when more intensively studied. To read books that Shakespeare read, such as Sir Thomas North's translation of Plutarch's *Lives of the Noble Grecians and Romans*, on which he based his Roman plays, or Thomas Lodge's *Rosalynde*, the source for *As You Like It*, gives us insights into his creative processes. There is no way in which we can turn ourselves into Shakespeare's contemporaries, but an understanding of the historical circumstances in which his plays were composed may illuminate aspects of them. When he writes of ancient Greece and Rome, he does so as an inhabitant of Elizabethan and Jacobean London. Poignantly depicting the abdication of Richard II, he must have been aware of its relevance at a time when the succession to the English throne was being hotly debated; and use of the play as an incentive to the rebellion plotted by the Earl of Essex in 1601 shows that his contemporaries saw this. Shakespeare lived at a time when religion held a far greater sway over the populace than it does now, when attitudes to superstition and witchcraft, magic and madness, differed greatly from those now prevalent at least in Western culture. His society was more hierarchical than ours, the monarchy and the aristocracy held easier sway, the gap between rich and poor was greater. Social attitudes to love and marriage, friendship, family and sex, the place of women in society, race and nationhood, have changed, and an understanding of what Shakespeare's contemporaries thought about them may broaden our understanding. Materialist criticism and other modern approaches have done much to explore relationships between Shakespeare and his time.

The fact that Shakespeare's plays have been read, performed, studied, and written about for centuries means that it is not always easy to come to them freshly. Traditions of performance and critical attitude that have accrued around them need to be reassessed. We have been accustomed, for instance, to thinking of certain characters— Shylock in *The Merchant of Venice*, Beatrice and Benedick in *Much Ado About Nothing*, even Falstaff in the *Henry IV* plays—as star roles, whereas the plays in which they appear might be better served if they were thought of as having been written for a more evenly matched company. Some plays—'Unfamiliar Shakespeare'—have built up a reputation as difficult or unrewarding, and need to be reassessed from time to time. Fresh understanding of the plays may proceed from, or be associated with, trends in social attitudes and in critical thought. A conspicuous example is *Troilus and Cressida*, which has progressed from virtually total neglect—we have no record of performance until the beginning of the twentieth century—to being a play whose profound concern with war and sex has come to seem especially relevant to modern audiences. One of the finest productions, Peter Hall's at Stratford-upon-Avon in 1962, gained in significance from coinciding with the Cuban Missile Crisis. Serious thought about Shakespeare's sonnets was for a long time inhibited by anxiety that they might reflect same-sex desire on Shakespeare's part; more recently it has been possible to discuss them more frankly. Advances in scholarship may affect our attitude to Shakespeare the man—the idea that in Stratford he could not have received education enough to read the plays has been scotched by investigations of what was taught in grammar schools; textual scholarship has shown that his texts were more fluid in early performance than had been suspected; and we have become more receptive to the idea that collaborative plays such as *The Two Noble Kinsmen* and even possibly *Edward III* are worthy of a place in the canon.

It has increasingly been realized that Shakespeare's plays shift in meaning according to the mental attitudes that people bring to them. 'Shakespeare', Terence Hawkes has said, 'does not mean; we mean by Shakespeare'. His works interact with the preoccupations of those who experience them, and can be appropriated for many different purposes. Much modern study attempts not only to illuminate the plays by applying to them a wide range of critical practices, but also to use reactions to the plays as a means of exploring the society of our and of other times. Investigation of Victorian attitudes to Shakespearian sexuality may teach us about the Victorians as well as about Shakespeare; we may be made more aware of modern attitudes to religion, economics, and cultural identity if we think about reactions to *The Merchant of Venice*, with its portrayal of Jews and Christians in a commercial relationship.

During the later part of the twentieth century Shakespeare criticism and scholarship became highly professionalized and institutionalized. He and his works became the object of an industry as never before. Larger and larger numbers of performances were given, on film and television as well as on stage, more journals were established, more books—many of them adapted from graduate dissertations—appeared, and new critical approaches were developed. This bears witness to Shakespeare's continuing appeal to the modern world, to the fact that his plays can go on provoking debate, arousing enjoyment, rewarding intellectual investigation. It also means that students may be overwhelmed by the sheer bulk of material available to them. We hope that this volume will act as a friendly guide, removing obstacles and enhancing its readers' understanding and, above all, enjoyment of Shakespeare.

2 | Shakespeare's life and career

Lois Potter

Shakespeare's home and family

The ordinariness of Shakespeare's background—even the fact that his parents' names were John and Mary—is part of its fascination. He was one of eight children and the oldest son. He was born some time between 21 and 24 April 1564; people like to think that it was the 23rd, the day devoted to celebrating St George, England's patron saint. His birthplace, the borough of Stratford-upon-Avon, lies in what is now called the Heart of England. With hindsight, one can see that it had the ideal conditions for a future actor-playwright. The nearby city of Coventry had a rich tradition of theatrical activity. Professional touring companies also visited Stratford. If Shakespeare attended the local grammar school, he received a rigorous, Latin-based education, which gave him access to famous classical myths and histories and trained him in oral presentation.

Both his parents had long lives for their time (John lived to at least seventy, Mary to her late sixties), but their children did not: Shakespeare died at fifty-two but he outlived all his younger siblings except his sister Joan, who lived to be seventy-seven. None of his brothers seems to have married. His father's career was also unusual. In 1564, John Shakespeare was a successful citizen (though of less distinguished family than his wife) who had already held a series of important Stratford offices. John Shakespeare went on to the town Council, then became Bailiff (the town's highest office) in 1568. At about this time, he applied for a coat of arms, which would give him the status of a gentleman. But the arms were not granted, and from about 1576 things changed for the worse. He borrowed money in 1578, and eventually lost part of his wife's land because he was unable to repay the loan. He sold other land in 1580. In 1587 he lost his post on the Council for failing to attend town meetings.

It used to be assumed that John Shakespeare had become incompetent, perhaps alcoholic. Now, some scholars argue that he was a victim of his religious beliefs. In 1591 he was listed among those who did not come to church because they were afraid of being arrested for debt. Those who think that this was a false excuse point to the eighteenth-century discovery, in his former Stratford home, of a Roman Catholic profession of faith in the name of John Shakespeare (it has since disappeared). There are connections to Roman Catholics in his biography—as Chapter 12 explains, almost everyone in England had been Roman Catholic only a generation earlier—but some of the actions in which John Shakespeare was engaged on behalf of the borough, early in Elizabeth I's reign, were militantly Protestant. He might have avoided church because he was a Puritan. But the late sixteenth century was in any case a time of severe economic depression, dangerous for anyone who took risks in business, as John Shakespeare seems to have done.

For whatever reason, the Shakespeare family had serious financial problems during William Shakespeare's early adolescence. They may have prevented him from obtaining the university degree that would have given him the status of gentleman. They may explain his numerous investments in property and his tendency to make the language of love interchangeable with that of money: 'Farewell—thou art too dear for my possessing', Sonnet 87 begins, with a typical double meaning. Shakespeare's early plays are obsessed with father-son relationships, though this is partly because so many of them deal with English history and succession through the male line. Some scholars have been tempted to see reflections of a lovable, alcoholic father in such characters as Falstaff (from the *Henry IV* plays) and Sir Toby Belch (from *Twelfth Night*). Others think that the poet shared his father's religious beliefs. In 1581, Alexander Houghton, a Lancashire Catholic, named a William Shakeshafte, one of his retainers, in his will. Was this Shakespeare, and had he been sent so far from home to escape punishment for subversive Catholic activities?[1]

Shakespeare's actions in this period could hardly have helped his family's financial position. In November 1582, aged eighteen, he made a hastily arranged marriage with the twenty-six-year-old Anne Hathaway; their daughter Susanna was born in May 1583. Anne gave birth to twins, a son and daughter (Hamnet and Judith), in 1585. After fathering three children while still a minor, Shakespeare spent a substantial amount of time away from home. This may have been an attempt at birth-control.

Early acting and writing career

The first references to Shakespeare as a writer and actor in London date from 1592, when he was nearly thirty, and his first published works date from still later. It seems likely that he began his theatrical career by joining a company of actors on tour in Stratford. He may have been young enough to play women's parts, as apprentices usually did.[2] The construction of the purpose-built theatres in London in 1576 created a competitive situation for actors (see Chapter 3). Shakespeare could have belonged to any one of the companies (all, as the law required, under the patronage of particular noblemen) that grew, declined, and re-combined during the 1580s. The strongest of these, the Lord Admiral's Men, merged with another company in about 1589 and successfully established itself in London for the next five years. If Shakespeare belonged to this group, he probably wrote at least some of his plays for the Rose

Theatre on the south side of the Thames. He would also have acted in plays by Christopher Marlowe and other highly respected dramatists of the period: Thomas Kyd, Robert Greene, and George Peele (see also Chapter 6). He may have collaborated with them too. Many Elizabethan plays had as many as five authors. This was particularly true when a play needed to appear quickly—to exploit a topical event or manipulate public opinion.

The first mention of Shakespeare, a very negative one, comes in a pamphlet called *Greene's Groatsworth of Wit* (1592). Robert Greene, a scholar and writer, died in poverty just after an outbreak of the plague had forced the closing of the London theatres. The pamphlet claims to be his life story, including a bitter deathbed farewell to Marlowe and two other scholar-dramatists. He warns them against an 'upstart crow'—an actor who, having become famous through speaking their lines ('beautified with our feathers'), is now showing that he has a 'tiger's heart wrapped in a player's hide'. This last phrase parodied the magnificent speech Shakespeare wrote for the Duke of York, who accuses Queen Margaret of having a 'tiger's heart wrapped in a woman's hide' (*Henry VI Part Three*, 1.4.138). It clearly pointed at Shakespeare.[3]

It is not clear whether Greene was accusing the actor-playwright of plagiarism, of cruelty, or simply of being too successful. If he had collaborated with Shakespeare, he may have recognized a shift in the balance of power from author to actor. The three *Henry VI* plays could have been the work of a team, but someone had to be in charge of any collaboration. One of Shakespeare's contemporaries was called 'our best plotter'. This seems to mean that he took overall responsibility for assigning the several tasks of each writer and assembling them into a coherent whole. Shakespeare's gift for plotting must already have been evident by the early 1590s. Greene may be warning the co-authors of the *Henry VI* plays against further collaboration with someone who not only had the nerve to rewrite the work of university graduates, but who was also making more money out of the plays than they were.

Poetry and the Earl of Southampton

Shakespeare's name spread still farther through the first publication that had his name on the title page. He probably wrote *Venus and Adonis* (1593), a fashionable erotic poem inspired by Ovid, while the theatres were closed during an epidemic of the plague. Dedicating it to the young Earl of Southampton was a wise move. Southampton, immensely rich, was a target for many dedications, but Shakespeare's seems to have been rewarded since the poet presented another poem, *The Rape of Lucrece*, to the same patron a year later. An early biographer records a tradition that Southampton gave Shakespeare £1,000 for some 'purchase', but the sum is unbelievably large.[4] Apart from cash, the poet may have received other equally important benefits, such as access to a good private library, at a time when public libraries did not exist. Two of his most important sources—Raphael Holinshed's *Chronicles* and Plutarch's *Lives of the Noble Grecians and Romans*—were large, expensive books. In the early 1590s he probably could not afford them.

What did Southampton get in return? The first poem describes the goddess of love, Venus, trying unsuccessfully to arouse the petulant young Adonis, who finally dies and becomes a flower. The second is a story of guilt—first that of the lustful rapist Tarquin, then that of his victim Lucrece, who is totally innocent but kills herself. Southampton probably did not take the poems too personally. Other readers clearly enjoyed them both, since they went through a number of editions. Many people think that at least some of Shakespeare's sonnets were also written to Southampton at this time. Some of them say what Venus had already said to Adonis: beautiful young men should put their beauty out to interest like money, or distil it like roses in perfume, or leave it behind in the form of a son. Southampton's mother and guardian were already urging him to wed (they were thinking specifically of his guardian's daughter, and the Earl eventually paid a huge fine for refusing to marry her). Other sonnets depict someone betraying and humiliating the writer, whose consolation is the thought that some day this person will be remembered only because of these very sonnets. Others address a woman whom the speaker lusts after but despises. Most of these sonnets, except two that were published in 1598, could have been written any time before their publication in 1609. They may be about Shakespeare's inner life, but many attempts have been made to connect them with an outer one (see Chapter 22).

The Lord Chamberlain's Men

By the time acting companies were able to perform again, in 1594, some of them had dispersed, or been ruined by the long period of inactivity in London during the plague. It was an opportunity to regroup. Shakespeare must by now have met the Burbages, an early 'theatre dynasty'. James Burbage is best known for building, in 1576, a purpose-built professional playhouse in London, called The Theatre (the word had classical associations at this period). His son Richard became his leading actor, but seems also to have been a painter; he was still making money from his art as late as 1616. The Burbages formed The Lord Chamberlain's Men, playing at the Theatre and other venues in north London (see Chapter 3). Within about a year, Shakespeare was a sharer (or shareholder) in the Chamberlain's Men. Buying a share was expensive, but Shakespeare was a desirable partner. The plays on the reigns of Henry VI and Richard III had been successful for several years. This was probably true also of *Titus Andronicus* (published in 1594), *The Taming of the Shrew*, and *The Two Gentlemen of Verona*.

If Shakespeare was living with Southampton during the plague, in comfortable working conditions (rather than with his family in his parents' overcrowded Stratford home), it would provide a neat explanation for the large number of first-class plays that appeared in the mid-1590s: the brilliant group of *Love's Labour's Lost*, *Romeo and Juliet*, and *A Midsummer Night's Dream*, then the new sequence of histories beginning with *Richard II* (published in 1597). The parts in which Burbage became famous—the deformed villain Richard III, the young lover Romeo, and presumably Prince Hal who grows from a wild young man into the hero King Henry V—indicate his range. A plausible-sounding anecdote (in the diary of a young law student, John Manningham) records that a London lady fell in love with Burbage as Richard III and invited him to an assignation. Shakespeare, overhearing the plan, got there first. When Burbage arrived, Shakespeare, now in the lady's arms, sent back the message that William the Conqueror reigned before Richard III.

The competition went on outside the bedroom, as the parts Shakespeare wrote for Burbage, usually much longer than those of any other actor, stretched the talents of both men to the limit and demanded an amazing range: the young prince Hamlet, the middle-aged Moor Othello, and King Lear, who says that he is over eighty years old. But Shakespeare usually wrote with particular actors in mind. Will Kempe the clown was as popular as Burbage, and his roles got steadily better, culminating in Falstaff and constable Dogberry in *Much Ado About Nothing*, just before he left the company in 1599. Robert Armin took over the role of clown (and perhaps inspired a different kind of comedy) while John Lowin, who arrived at about the same time, eventually became Falstaff. Shakespeare must have seen many Juliets and Rosalinds during his career, but we know nothing about the boys who played them and other women's and children's roles. Everyone would like to know which parts he played himself. Traditions link him with the ghost in *Hamlet* and Adam in *As You Like It*, and a contemporary wrote that he 'played some kingly parts in sport'.[5] It is pleasant to think of him as the Prologue to *Romeo and Juliet* or the Chorus in *Henry V*, characters who seem to speak for the author. But there is no evidence on this subject.

The first positive indication of Shakespeare's artistic and financial success dates from 1598. This is when his plays first began to be published with his name on the title page, obvious evidence that it was a selling-point. He is also mentioned in a survey of the literary scene as a reincarnation of Ovid in poetry and a dramatist who was equal to both Plautus and Seneca—that is, who excelled in both comedy and tragedy, as very few have done.[6] In 1596 John Shakespeare was finally awarded his coat of arms. It incorporates a falcon brandishing a gold spear and the motto *Non sans droit* (not without deserving). Whoever designed it, possibly his son, boldly punned on the family name that had embarrassed at least one earlier Shakespeare, a fifteenth-century Oxford scholar who changed it to Saunders.[7] In 1597, the younger Shakespeare bought New Place, a large house in Stratford with extensive grounds. Clearly, by this time, he was rich enough to be able to maintain another house. The early modern period did not have the copyright laws that now let an author make money from a play throughout its run and from later revivals and adaptations. But Shakespeare's position as an actor and sharer ensured him a part of all receipts earned by his company.

The success was a hollow one in one respect: Shakespeare's only son, Hamnet, died in 1596. Anne Shakespeare was about forty and unlikely to have more children; there would be no one after Shakespeare to enjoy the status of landed gentry. *King John*, the play which most pathetically depicts a parent's grief for an absent child, was probably written before this personal tragedy, while the plays written in the years immediately after it—*The Merchant of Venice*, *Henry IV Parts One and Two*, and *Much Ado About Nothing*—have a strongly comic element. When Shakespeare first wrote about twins, in *The Comedy of Errors*, the result (based on Plautus) was one of his funniest farces. In *Twelfth Night* (1601), the heroine, Viola, wrongly thinks that her twin brother is dead. Their reunion in the final scene is more moving than funny.[8]

The Globe

Increasingly, the major London companies wanted a permanent home. In the 1590s, the Lord Chamberlain's Men thought they had one. James Burbage bought part of Blackfriars priory, hoping to use it for an indoor theatre, which would have allowed a far longer acting season than the outdoor playhouses. After a last minute ban by the Queen's Privy Council, he rented it out to a children's company, which, because it performed less frequently, was more acceptable to the neighbours. Meanwhile, the actors moved between theatres in north London. After the death of James Burbage and a dispute with their landlord late in 1598, they decided to take advantage of the fact that they owned the Theatre, though not the land it was on. In two raids, they took it apart, carried the timbers across the river, and with them built the Globe. Perhaps because of his physical involvement with this new building, Shakespeare in this period seems particularly conscious of the theatre's double nature as both a material object and a source of imaginative experience. *Henry V*, his last Elizabethan history play, constantly draws attention both to the limitations of what it calls 'this wooden O' and to the epic scale of the events dramatized in it. Audiences at *As You Like It*, aware that they were in a building called the Globe, would find a special point in Jaques' famous speech beginning, 'All the world's a stage'. In *Julius Caesar* Brutus and Cassius imagine their murder of Caesar being reenacted; *Hamlet* imagines himself as an actor and advises visiting players in their craft.

Though Shakespeare complimented Queen Elizabeth ('a fair vestal thronèd by the west') in *A Midsummer Night's Dream* (2.1.158), her reaction to his work is unknown. Trying to fill the gap, a tradition says that she asked him to write about Falstaff in love, and got *The Merry Wives of Windsor*. Another reaction to Shakespeare's greatest comic character was very different. In *Henry IV Part One* (1597), Falstaff was instead called Sir John Oldcastle, but a descendent of the Oldcastles protested. Shakespeare changed the name to Falstaff and in the epilogue to *Henry IV Part Two* (1598) obligingly wrote that 'Oldcastle died a martyr, and this is not the man' (line 27). But, although he promised to bring the character back in *Henry V*, he decided instead to have him die offstage. In 1601, an earlier history play about Richard II, probably Shakespeare's, was involved in the unsuccessful rebellion of the popular but unstable Earl of Essex. The earl's followers attempted to rally public opinion, paying the Lord Chamberlain's Men for a special performance at the Globe. The play may have inspired Essex's friends but it did not lead to an uprising in his favour, and he was beheaded a month later for treason. Neither the author nor the actors were punished, but the young Earl of Southampton, a devoted follower of Essex, was one of those imprisoned afterwards. It was the last traumatic event of Elizabeth's reign.

The King's Men

The death of the queen herself in March 1603 was followed by the worst plague in ten years, which meant another period of theatre closings, but Elizabeth's cousin, James VI of Scotland, became James I of England without the civil war that some had feared. As a writer himself, the new ruler seems to have felt it important to associate himself with the performing arts. In May 1603 the Chamberlain's Men were honoured by becoming the King's Men, and other companies were renamed the Queen's and the Prince's Men (James also released Southampton from prison). As part of the royal household, the new company received an allowance of cloth to show their status at ceremonial events. James's wife and children enjoyed court entertainments, and records indicate that Shakespeare's plays were the ones most often given at court, far more than in Elizabeth's reign.

Shakespeare was now recognized as the leading playwright of the country's most famous dramatic company. Other dramatists complimented him with imitations, parodies, and even continuations of his work: for instance, John Fletcher wrote a continuation of *The Taming of the Shrew* (*The Tamer Tamed*) in which the tamer Petruchio, having buried the shrew Katherine at last, is then tamed by his second wife. In James's reign Shakespeare's plays became more self-conscious and classical than his earlier ones. *Othello* probably belongs to the Elizabethan period, whenever it was first performed, but *Measure for Measure* may have been inspired by James's intellectual reputation: he had asked for a repeat performance of *The Merchant of Venice*—an earlier comedy combining romance with the discussion of abstract issues—only two days after he first saw it. In writing a play about the division and reunion of the kingdom (*King Lear*) Shakespeare was echoing a theme that became prominent when James united the crowns of England and Scotland. James was more tolerant than Elizabeth of topical allusions, and Shakespeare's choice of a subject from Scottish history (*Macbeth*) was almost too appropriate for a king whose father had been murdered and whose own life had been threatened several times; the play even refers obliquely to the Catholic Gunpowder plot of 1605, which aimed to blow up the king and Parliament.

Not all Shakespeare's experiments were successful. *Timon of Athens* looks unfinished. Did the theme of generosity betrayed begin to look too much like condemnation of James I's habit of lavish gifts to his favourites, rather than a celebration of his generosity? *Antony and Cleopatra* and *Coriolanus* (which probably refers to another topical event, rioting in the Midlands) have deeply flawed heroes who do not make it easy for an audience to take their side. None of these plays has the obvious popular appeal of the Elizabethan ones, and none, apart from *King Lear*, was published before 1623 when, after Shakespeare's death, his colleagues collected all his available play-scripts in one large volume. The language of these later plays is sometimes complex to the point of being unintelligible, as if Shakespeare was trying, like his friend and rival Ben Jonson, to create a more élite drama. Even *Macbeth* seems to have been reworked, with more emphasis on music and spectacle. Thomas Middleton, a gifted writer of satiric comedy and tragedy, may have revised it along with *Timon* and (some think) *Measure for Measure*.[9] Perhaps Shakespeare was becoming too difficult for much of his audience. Even the publication in 1609 of *Shakespeare's Sonnets, Never Before Imprinted*, whether he authorized it or not, seems to have attracted surprisingly little attention.

One work from this period, however, was popular. *Pericles*, which dramatizes a medieval romance by John Gower, also appeared in 1609. Shakespeare uses Gower as a narrator, in a deliberately old-fashioned style. Shakespeare's next three comedies are usually called romances; like *Pericles*, they emphasize wide expanses of time and space that seem more appropriate to narrative than to drama. *Cymbeline, The Winter's Tale*, and *The Tempest* all involve story-telling and end with reunions of long-lost relatives and forgiveness of long-past crimes. They also exploit the theatre's musical and spectacular resources. Blackfriars, after ten years of occupation by children's companies, finally reverted to the King's Men in about 1607, giving them a winter as well as a summer playhouse. The plays that Shakespeare wrote could of course be performed in either place—or at court, or on tour—but the newer, better equipped theatre probably encouraged him to include such attractions as music, dance, and dream visions. *The Tempest* ends with the magician-hero, Prospero, saying farewell to his magic and asking forgiveness of the audience. Many readers have liked to think that they could hear Shakespeare's own voice speaking through him.

But *The Tempest* was not the end of Shakespeare's career. He wrote two more plays— perhaps three—with a younger dramatist, John Fletcher. While Fletcher, the son of a bishop, was of a higher social class than most playwrights of the period, Shakespeare's status as a gentleman gave them something in common; moreover, both men, as teenagers, had experienced the disgrace of their fathers and the financial decline of their families. They apparently collaborated on *Cardenio*, a play based on a story from Cervantes' *Don Quixote*. There are records of its performance in 1611 but the play itself has disappeared. Fletcher is not named as co-author of *Henry VIII* but the style and tone of the play make it likely that he helped to dramatize historical events that could not have been shown while Henry's daughter ruled England. In particular, the play's recreation of the divorce trial of Henry's first wife, Catherine of Aragon, must have exploited the fact that Blackfriars had been the original site of that trial. But the play was also performed at the Globe, where one of its spectacular effects, the firing of cannon, caused a fire that destroyed the theatre in 1613. The names of both Fletcher and Shakespeare appeared on the title page of *The Two Noble Kinsmen* when it was first published in 1634. It is based on *The Knight's Tale* by Chaucer, already an inspiration for *A Midsummer Night's Dream*.

Retirement and death

By the time of these last plays Shakespeare was based at Stratford, but continued to make frequent trips to London. The Globe fire was a financial disaster, though one from which the company rebounded quickly by building a new and larger outdoor playhouse. Its shareholders had to contribute large sums for this purpose. Shakespeare had just bought an expensive house in Blackfriars. The evidence points two ways: he may have sold his shares in the Globe rather than contribute to the cost of the rebuilding and kept the Blackfriars house (mentioned in his will) as an investment. Or he may have kept the shares (not mentioned in his will, but perhaps part of his estate in general) and intended to use the house during his periods of residence in London. The death of the last of his brothers in 1613 might have led to his decision to retire. He may have planned to collect his plays for publication. Perhaps he knew that Ben Jonson was doing the same thing: Jonson's *Works* appeared in 1616. Like Jonson, Shakespeare may have revised his plays: some that had already been published—particularly *Richard III*, *Hamlet*, *Othello*, and *King Lear*—look very different in the later versions. He may have intended to remove collaborations. This might explain the disappearance of *Cardenio* and perhaps *Love's Labour's Won*, which is mentioned in 1598 as a Shakespeare comedy.

His older daughter Susanna had married John Hall, a respectable and successful physician. Her younger sister Judith (the surviving twin) was less fortunate. When she became engaged in 1616 to Thomas Quiney, the son of an old friend and neighbour, Shakespeare drew up a carefully worded will that left a substantial estate to Susanna and her husband but tried to protect the rights of both daughters. It soon became apparent not only that Quiney was a bad risk financially but that he had fathered a child by another woman. Clearly aware that his death was approaching, Shakespeare revised the will to ensure, without disinheriting Judith, that his new son-in-law never got his hands on the family money. He left bequests to friends and fellow-actors, and to the poor of Stratford, but gave his wife Anne, apparently as an afterthought, only his second-best bed. This fact, and the impersonal tone of the document, indicate to some readers that Shakespeare died (on 23 April) an unhappy man. Others argue that Anne was already provided for, that the second-best bed (unlike the 'best' one kept for guests) might have been a meaningful bequest, and that wills are not the best place for expressions of feeling. Some think the verses on his gravestone, in Holy Trinity Church, Stratford, are such an expression:

> Good frend for Jesus sake forbeare,
> To dig the dust encloased heare:
> Bleste be ye [the] man yt [that] spares thes stones,
> And curst be he yt moves my bones.

That he was buried near the altar, with a monument nearby, is probably a tribute not only to his wealth but also his fame.

It took his colleagues, possibly with Jonson's help, seven years to publish his plays in the large volume now known as the First Folio. Its actual title was *Mr. William Shakespeare's Comedies, Histories, and Tragedies*. It included no poems and two plays were missing—*Pericles* was added in editions published after 1660 and *The Two Noble Kinsmen* even later. If Shakespeare had lived longer, the volume might have included a contemporary portrait rather than the present engraving, based on an earlier drawing or painting, by an artist who probably never saw him. Jonson wrote verses about this picture. He called it a good likeness, but ended by urging the reader to 'look/ Not on his picture, but his book'. It was, and is, good advice.

FURTHER READING

Duncan-Jones, Katherine. *Ungentle Shakespeare: Scenes from His Life* (London: The Arden Shakespeare, 2001). This book offers provocative re-readings of several episodes in the poet's life, with new information about, for instance, his purchase of a coat of arms.

Honan, Park. *Shakespeare: a Life* (Oxford: Oxford University Press, 1998). Rich in detail, this book is particularly good on the background of the period.

Honigmann, E. A. J. *Shakespeare: the Lost Years* (Manchester: Manchester University Press, 1995). Honigmann makes the case for Shakespeare's presence in largely Catholic Lancashire in about 1580.

Kay, Dennis. *William Shakespeare: His Life and Times* (New York: Twayne Publishers, 1995). This is the shorter of two biographies by this author; a lucid and balanced account of the basic facts.

Matus, Irvin Leigh. *Shakespeare, in Fact* (New York: Continuum Publishing Company, 1994). This is a detailed survey of the arguments and evidence in the 'authorship controversy', from a scholar who believes that Shakespeare wrote the works ascribed to him.

Michell, John. *Who Wrote Shakespeare?* (London: Thames and Hudson, 1996). This author's survey of past and present theories ends by suggesting some alternatives to Shakespearian authorship.

Schoenbaum, S. *Shakespeare: a Compact Documentary Life* (New York: Oxford University Press, 1977). This is the indispensable collection and evaluation of the documents that are the basis of all other biographies. To see photographs of the originals, consult Schoenbaum's earlier *Shakespeare: a Documentary Life* (New York: Oxford University Press and Scolar Press, 1975).

Schoenbaum, S. *Shakespeare's Lives* (New York: Oxford University Press, 1991). Schoenbaum surveys early biographical accounts, evaluating their reliability.

Southworth, John. *Shakespeare the Player: a Life in the Theatre* (Sutton, UK: Sutton Publishing, 2000). An actor speculates on Shakespeare's career from a theatrical perspective.

Wells, Stanley. *Shakespeare: the Poet and His Plays* (London: Methuen, 1997) (first published as *Shakespeare: a Dramatic Life*). Chapters 1 and 2 ('Who is Shakespeare?' and 'Shakespeare: Man of the Theatre') provide full but concise treatment of the issues. The same writer's *Shakespeare: For all Time* (London: Macmillan, 2002) discusses Shakespeare's life in Stratford and London.

NOTES

1. E. A. J. Honigmann. *Shakespeare: the Lost Years* (Manchester: Manchester University Press, 1995).

2. John Southworth. *Shakespeare the Player: a Life in the Theatre* (Sutton, UK: Sutton Publishing, 2000), pp. 20–2.

3. Quoted in S. Schoenbaum. *Shakespeare: a Compact Documentary Life* (New York: Oxford University Press and Scolar Press, 1977), p. 151 (hereafter cited as Schoenbaum).

4. Nicholas Rowe. 1709, in Schoenbaum, pp. 178–9.

5. John Davies. Epigram 159 in 'The Scourge of Folly' (1610), quoted in Schoenbaum, pp. 200–1.

6. Francis Meres. *Palladis Tamia* (1598), quoted in Schoenbaum, p. 190.

7. Katherine Duncan-Jones. 'Ungentle Shakespeare: Scenes from His Life' (London: *The Arden Shakespeare*, 2001), pp. 91–2; Schoenbaum, pp. 13, 324.

8. Richard P. Wheeler. 'Deaths in the Family: the Loss of a Son and the Rise of Shakespearean Comedy', *Shakespeare Quarterly*, 51 (2000), 127–53.

9. See the *Norton Shakespeare*, pp. 207–8, 2251, 2563.

3 | Theatre in London

Gabriel Egan

The rise of the London industry

For a thousand years after the departure of the Romans in the fifth-century AD no theatres were built in Britain, and Shakespeare's works are key texts in the rebirth of professional playing in the late sixteenth century. There were travelling troupes of players in the late medieval period, comprising on average four to six men, and some received royal patronage, but they lacked the element that characterizes professionalism: accumulated capital. Theatrical capital takes three forms—costumes, scripts, and venues—and the pressures placed upon informal troupes of players around the middle of the sixteenth century gave a strong competitive advantage to those troupes which acquired such capital.

Travelling players necessarily used whatever venues they found in the towns they visited, and they could rent costumes at need. The officers of the royal household who controlled costumes used in state pageants appear to have rented them to players as early as the 1520s. In 1550 the aldermen of the City of London prevented 'common' players (those without an aristocratic patron) from playing in the City, and in 1559 Elizabeth I issued a proclamation reminding patrons of their obligation to ensure that their players did not perform anything 'wherein either matters of religion or of the governance of the estate of the commonwealth shall be handled or treated'. It was clear that civic and royal authorities wanted players and their patrons to be held accountable, and casual troupes without a patron found life increasingly difficult.

An early and active theatrical patron was Robert Dudley, Earl of Leicester. Between 1582 and 1585 his hitherto well-recorded company seems to have disappeared; no provincial touring records name them. Just then a new company, perhaps Leicester's Men under a new name, was formed by two senior government officials, Sir Francis Walsingham and Edmund Tilney. This new troupe of Queen's Men under Elizabeth's direct patronage had the star performers of Leicester's Men (most famously the clown Richard Tarlton) and it soon overshadowed its rivals. The crown's policy was to take control of the playing companies and make them professional, profitable, and answerable. The Queen's Men were a touring troupe, but unlike their predecessors who stayed close to their patron's home they toured the entire country in the summer and settled in London for the winter. Over Christmas the players were invited to perform for the monarch at court, and reaching a state of preparedness for these festivities was, officially at least, the sole reason for the profession's existence; playing to the public was supposed to be mere practice.

In London permanent open-air, virtually circular amphitheatre playhouses were built in the suburbs; to the north were the Theatre in Shoreditch (1576) and the Curtain in Holywell (1577), and to the south on Bankside were the Rose (1587) and the Swan (1595). Playing companies visiting London moved between these venues, as though touring the city's outskirts. The players preferred to perform indoors and especially in the city inns close to the centres of population, but these were strictly controlled by the city authorities. In 1594 it was agreed by the Queen's Privy Council and the Lord Mayor of London that inns could no longer be used and just two companies, the Chamberlain's Men and the Admiral's Men, would be licensed to play at two designated suburban playhouses, the Theatre in Shoreditch and the Rose on Bankside respectively.

A touring company needed costumes and a variety of places to play, but it did not need many scripts since each new town could be shown the same fare as the last. In London, however, the enforced settlement of two companies at two playhouses brought a new capital requirement into the equation, since there was a great need for new playscripts to satisfy the ever-returning audiences. The state-enforced duopoly of the Admiral's Men and the Chamberlain's Men gave these two troupes pre-eminence in London, but to exploit this market required enormous expenditure on new playscripts. One of the beneficiaries of this increased demand was the Chamberlain's Men's actor William Shakespeare who, in the 1590s, became his fellows' main and most successful playwright. Being settled at a single suburban venue each, the star actors Richard Burbage (for the Chamberlain's Men) and Edward Alleyn (for the Admiral's Men) were able to build legions of dedicated fans who would come to see each new production.

The venues

The open-air amphitheatres of Shakespeare's time (like the Globe) dominate our thinking about the actors' venues, but men used to the vagaries of touring easily adapted to any performance space which might be available. A large inn at which coaches unloaded would have an enclosed yard within which a temporary stage might easily be mounted; the elevated galleries which provided access to the rooms around the yard offered further accommodation for spectators with the additional benefit of protection from the elements. Less capacious, but more comfortable and dependable, was a room inside the inn, and the final deciding factor might well have been the weather. The placing of a temporary stage within an innyard has been claimed as the origin of the open-air amphitheatre design, but the virtually circular structures of the Theatre, Curtain, Rose, Swan, and later the Globe were too unusual to be merely alterations of the innyard layout. Foreign visitors in London who saw the wooden amphitheatres commented on their likeness to the stone amphitheatres of Roman times, and indeed in naming his 1576 playhouse the Theatre James Burbage (father of star actor Richard) appears to have deliberately invoked this antecedent. A possible additional inspiration was the animal baiting arenas which had developed from simple circular wooden fences (animals within, spectators without) to become multi-storey structures containing many hundreds of spectators on staggered degrees, such as the Bankside bear-baiting ring called Paris Garden, which fatally collapsed upon its patrons in January 1583. Superficially, a temporary stage erected within an animal ring might seem much like an open-air amphitheatre, but the heavy fencing needed to keep the agonized animals from attacking the spectators would have made it difficult to see the stage. The first multi-use venue, suitable for both animal shows and plays, was the Hope, built in 1613, which was specially designed to reconcile the differing needs of the two kinds of entertainment.

The players always preferred to act indoors, but until 1608 most of the opportunities to do so were in temporarily adapted halls rather than permanent structures. An indoor theatre was built in St Paul's Church around 1575 and a room in the former Dominican monastery at Blackfriars was converted into a theatre in 1576. Both of these were used just once a week by boy actors who, the official excuse had it, were merely being tutored. Occasionally these indoor theatres are referred to as private theatres and the open-air amphitheatres are called public theatres, but this distinction is unhelpful since the public could attend either. High admission charges, not explicit exclusion, ensured that the indoor theatres attracted only the well-off. Indoor hall playhouses were considerably smaller than the open-air theatres (the St Paul's hall was probably about forty feet by twenty-three feet) which meant that they were more suitable for intimate domestic scenes than battles, and for the gentle music of oboes rather than the stern alarums of trumpets and drums. Lit by candles which needed periodic trimming, indoor theatres punctuated their performances with four act intervals (on the classical model) during which music played.

James Burbage's twenty-one year lease on the site of the open-air Theatre was due to expire on 13 April 1597. As a replacement venue for his son's troupe Burbage acquired the Blackfriars building which boy actors had used from 1576 to 1584 with a view to making it a permanent indoor venue in the heart of the city, playing to the select clientele there. However, the locals raised a petition which prevented the Chamberlain's Men from using the Blackfriars and it was again leased to a company of boy actors from 1600 to 1608. The Burbages stayed at the Theatre after their lease expired and the landlord continued to accept the rent, but by the autumn of 1598 they had moved to the nearby Curtain playhouse. Fearing the loss of their building by repossession, the Burbages secretly dismantled the Theatre over the Christmas holiday of 1598–9 and moved it to a new plot on Bankside, adjacent to the rival Admiral's Men's

Rose playhouse. The expedient of recycling the Theatre's timbers was necessary because Burbage had financially over-extended himself on the aborted Blackfriars project, and to fund the reassembly and furnishing of the new playhouse, the Globe, the Burbages brought the leading players of the Chamberlain's Men, including Shakespeare, into a syndicate of cost- and profit-sharing 'housekeepers'. Although it was not immediately apparent, this arrangement made the Chamberlain's Men a more tightly bound and economically stable organization than their rivals the Admiral's Men. So successful was this syndicate that when the Blackfriars became available again in 1608 the company (now under royal patronage as the King's Men) repeated the arrangement to manage the indoor theatre as a winter home while continuing to use the Globe in the summer. For at least a decade the King's Men performed the same plays in both venues, preferring a unified repertory and the luxury of keeping one venue empty at all times rather than staking their future on one kind of playhouse and audience over the other.

The family relationship whereby James Burbage, builder of the first playhouse (the Theatre), provided venues for the acting company led by his son Richard was somewhat mirrored in their chief rivals. The Admiral's Men's star was the physically and vocally imposing Edward Alleyn whose father-in-law, Philip Henslowe, built the Rose theatre in 1587 and extensively rebuilt it in 1592, adding a stage cover and a machine to lower an actor from its underside (the 'heavens') to the stage. Henslowe also acted as financier for the playing companies which used his theatre, and his 'Diary' provides detailed information about the finances of the theatre industry. In 1600, shortly after the Chamberlain's Men moved into the nearby Globe, Henslowe built a new theatre called the Fortune in the northern parish of St Giles without Cripplegate, and moved the Admiral's Men there, headed by Alleyn back from a brief retirement. Possibly Henslowe planned all along to build another playhouse, but it seems likely that the arrival of the Chamberlain's Men on his doorstep accelerated his departure.

We should not assume that the Globe was much more attractive than the Rose, although to judge from the foundations uncovered in 1989–90 it was larger: ninety-nine feet in diameter to the Rose's seventy-four feet. The standard amphitheatre configuration was three tiers of galleries rising to between thirty and thirty-five feet, and contemporary accounts indicate that as many as 3,000 people might squeeze into a playhouse. Even allowing for Elizabethans being 10 per cent smaller than us, it is clear that they demanded much less personal space than we do. The Fortune construction contract, which survives, required the builder to model it on the new Globe with the exception that instead of being virtually round, the Fortune was to have a square of galleries surrounding its yard. The Rose continued in use until its demolition in 1606. Henslowe and Alleyn had for a long time sought to monopolize the animal baiting shows as well as the theatre industry and in 1613 Henslowe had the Paris Garden bearbaiting ring torn down and the Hope theatre put in its place. The Hope had the innovations of a demountable stage and a cover cantilevered into the walls, leaving a clear circular space for animal shows.

The companies

The recorded history of playing companies in Shakespeare's time is dominated by professional troupes patronized by senior aristocrats or monarchs and existing to fulfil the entertainment needs of the monarch during the holidays. Can we call this an industry in the modern sense? The forces of aristocratic patronage on one hand and capitalist economics on the other combined to create a sudden explosion of dramatic activity at the end of the sixteenth century, and the sharers in the leading playing companies became rich men. Thirty years earlier such men were thought little better than vagabonds.

Theatre historians used to model London's theatre industry as an east-west divide: the Westminster-based monarchy and aristocracy, the defenders of cultural excellence, supported it, and the businessmen of the City of London to the east were Puritan anti-theatricalists. This is too simple, as is shown in Chapter 4. Political power was indeed polarized, but the players were alternately defended and attacked by each side as the need arose in the larger struggle which culminated in the English Civil War of the 1640s. The city authorities frequently objected that large gatherings at playhouses were a threat to public order, but seldom complained that the plays contained dangerous ideas. The court and church authorities who licensed performance and publishing, on the other hand, were concerned with subversive ideas and not the places of performance. If the court thought that plays might help promote official monarchical ideology, modern critics almost unanimously hold that they were mistaken: the best dramatic literature's meanings exceed simple propaganda. The closing of the theatres in 1642 represents not the final victory of anti-theatrical republican businessmen, but the rebels' nervous acknowledgement that either side (or indeed the extreme republican movement of ultra-egalitarian Levellers) might wrest the power of this medium to its own ends.

The city authorities regulated business activity via the guild system, which required that to learn a trade a man had to be apprenticed to a master who was 'free' of a trade organization or 'company'. The rules of companies determined the rates of pay and conditions of service, the arrangements by which products were made or exchanged, and regulated output to ensure that supply did not exceed demand. For example, the Stationers' Company, which controlled the printing industry, limited a standard edition to 1,250 copies of any one book. When the touring playing companies were encouraged to settle in London in the late sixteenth century there was no guild to regulate their industry; senior players usually had another official profession besides acting and belonged to that profession's company. Entry to a company was most commonly by apprenticeship, usually for seven years, after which one received the 'freedom' of the company (the right to practise its, or almost any other, profession) and entered the class of citizens (superior to mere labourers).

The internal structure of a playing company was essentially the same as the newly formed joint-stock companies which operated outside the guild structure and which allowed anyone with sufficient capital to buy a share. Playing company sharers held in common the physical capital of their company (costumes, properties, and books) and shared running expenses such as rent payments to the owner of their venue, fees to licensing authorities, and the hiring of casual labour. Sharers were almost always actors and they took the major roles in each play, the lesser roles being given to hired men. After the payment of expenses, whatever surplus remained from the takings was divided amongst the sharers. Unlike the regulated trades of the guild system, players had no protection against their losses but equally there was no brake upon profits in the event of success. When the Admiral's Men and the Chamberlain's Men were granted a state-imposed duopoly in London in 1594 the suppression of competition gave them the potential to make huge gains. Both companies made the most of this opportunity, although other London competitors operating semi-legally sprang up in the interstices between governmental and civic authority.

From 1594 the London market was divided north-south between two companies. The Chamberlain's Men had the advantage of sole access to the dramatic output of one of their sharers, William Shakespeare, who produced on average two plays a year which met with increasing success and fame. The Admiral's Men began their rise with the works of Christopher Marlowe, and after his death in 1593 they turned to freelance dramatists. In 1595 another playhouse, the Swan, was built on Bankside near the Rose, and in 1596 it was depicted in a sketch by Dutch tourist Johannes de Witt; this sketch provides our only view of the inside of an open-air playhouse of the period. The Swan was closed in 1597 when Pembroke's Men played *The Isle of Dogs* (now lost) by Thomas Nashe and Ben Jonson, which was highly critical of the government and landed the dramatists in jail. In the aftermath of this incident the city authorities attempted to close the Rose and the Theatre, too, but the Privy Council (the monarch's most senior advisers) engineered a mere suspension of playing and protected the Admiral's and Chamberlain's Men. These two companies were clearly more favoured than their competitors, and this became even more apparent when James I succeeded Elizabeth I in 1603.

In the first decades of the seventeenth century a blurred distinction arose between the northern amphitheatres (the Fortune was followed by the Red Bull in 1605) and the southern ones (the Rose, the Globe, and the Swan), and its basis was class. The northern playhouses developed clienteles of citizens and apprentices, and repertories deriving from Alleyn's physically aggressive 'roaring and stalking' style of perform-ance, while the southern ones were associated with the court and with Burbage's restrained and naturalistic acting. This dichotomy can easily be overstated and is less clear than the difference in decorum which obtained between the open-air theatres, which could exploit large sounds and light effects, and the indoor hall theatres where sound effects had to be restrained, musical instruments had to be less powerful, and scenes of intimacy were easier to create than scenes of battle. Until 1608 only boy companies regularly performed indoors, but when the King's Men got the Blackfriars back they chose to perform there in the winter and at the Globe in the summer. Possibly the chaotic beginning of Shakespeare's *The Tempest* was a deliberate shock tactic, throwing an amphitheatre-style spectacle of noisy chaos at a Blackfriars audience that had just been lulled by the soft harmonies of music and song from the Blackfriars' renowned consort of musicians who stayed at the playhouse when the boy company left.

However, Shakespeare and his company did not suddenly change their style to suit the indoor conditions. For at least ten or fifteen years there was no discernible division in the repertory, and plays had to be performable at both locations. To help with this, the King's Men regularized practices that had hitherto been different at the different venues. Prior to 1608 only indoor theatres observed act intervals with music, and the musicians of the Blackfriars were visible in a gallery set in the back wall of the stage. The Globe music room, however, was located out of sight within the back-stage area where the actors changed their costumes, known as the tiring-house. The King's Men moved the Globe music room to the back-wall gallery (also used when characters had to enter 'above', as at a window or balcony) and began to observe act intervals with music at both venues. The Blackfriars had a machine for the descent of supernatural figures from the 'heavens' (as the Rose had from 1595), but no play written for the Globe uses such a machine until Shakespeare's *Cymbeline* of 1610, so perhaps part of the bringing their two playhouses into alignment was the retro-fitting of a descent machine at the Globe.

Readying the script

The raw material of a playing company is its scripts, and when performing in one location to an audience made mostly of spectators who attend frequently, a great demand for new plays is generated. Apart from the amateurs, the dramatists were divided into two types: the attached men who worked exclusively for one company for a length of time and received a salary, and the freelancers who sold each play for a fixed fee of around £6 to £10. An attached dramatist such as Shakespeare would know the resources of his company (especially the kinds of roles in which each man excelled) and would write his material accordingly. A freelancer, on the other hand, might be asked to pitch his idea and possibly to read parts of the work-in-progress to the sharers, with payment being made by instalments if the writing proceeded satisfactorily. In addition to these fees, an incentive system operated whereby the dramatist received the profits from one of the performances, usually the second. Apart from writing plays, an attached dramatist probably had additional chores such as the alteration of old plays for revival and the writing of prologues, epilogues, and other framing devices. It appears that unless integrated with the action (as is the Induction to Shakespeare's *The Taming of the Shrew*), such devices were considered to be separate from the play they framed and might even be recycled for use with several plays. It is possible that prologues and epilogues, which frequently ask for the audience's indulgence, were spoken only at the first performance or first revival, and not on subsequent occasions.

When the dramatist had finished his play he passed a copy to the company. It is not clear whether this had to be a specially made 'fair' copy, free of authorial crossings-out and changes of mind, or whether the 'foul' authorial papers with all these untidy marks had also to be handed over. Certainly, as intellectual property the play was no longer the dramatist's once he had transferred it to the company, and our modern notions of author's copyright were invented much later. No company had enough actors to assign one to each part, so a certain amount of doubling was needed. The most senior actors took one major role each, while the hired men were given two or more roles of smaller size. Most companies had no more than two or three boys amongst whom the women's parts would be divided. The copying of manuscripts was expensive in labour and materials, so rather than providing each actor with a complete text, the play was divided into 'parts', each of which was a scroll containing the speeches of one character. Each speech was preceded by its 'cue': the few words which ended the previous speaker's speech, upon hearing which the next actor spoke. The mechanicals in Shakespeare's *A Midsummer Night's Dream* are given their parts by Peter Quince and implored to 'con [learn] them by tomorrow night' (1.2.82). Most preparation was indeed solitary, and there was little time for collective rehearsals before the first performance; probably these took place in the mornings, since live performance occupied the afternoons.

Before a play could be performed, its script had to be inspected by the state censor, the Master of the Revels, who worked within the office of the Lord Chamberlain and received from the players a fee for his work. The censor's remit was never precisely defined, but successive postholders took their responsibility to be the excision of material offensive to the church and state, broadly interpreted to include not only sedition and personal satire but also foul language and excessive sexuality. If the Master of the Revels allowed the play he would attach his licence (a signed statement of his approval) at the end of the manuscript. Often the licence would state conditions such as 'may with the reformations [i.e., changes] be acted' or '[with] all the oaths left out'. On 27 May 1606 an 'Act to Restrain Abuses of Players' was passed which made it an offence to 'jestingly or profanely speak or use the holy name of God, or of Christ Jesus, or of the Holy Ghost, or of the Trinity' in a stage play, on penalty of a £10 fine. As well as effectively censoring new works, this Act also required old plays to be expurgated if they were revived for the stage. The Act did not cover printing, however, and the 1623 Folio of Shakespeare's collected plays contained a mixture of expurgated and unexpurgated plays according to the provenance of the manuscript underlying each of them.

It might seem that the censor was inherently the enemy of dramatists and players, but what records we have suggest that both parties knew that they would benefit from mutual co-operation rather than antagonism. The Master, after all, received considerable fees from the playing companies, and the players received the seal of state approval that their works were harmless entertainment; each had good reason not to push the other too far. No doubt this symbiotic relationship promoted a form of self-censorship on the part of the dramatists, but we should not see this as simple artistic emasculation. The dramatists artfully encoded pressing political and social themes such as the organization of government and the status of women, creating works that were subtle and not overtly dangerous. This may well be one of the reasons that plays from this period have remained fascinating to scholars of textual and performative art.

Staging

Most of the world's theatres are now of the proscenium arch style which became popular in the centuries since the Restoration. The essential element of this arrangement is the placing of the actors in one room and the audience in an adjacent one, the separating wall between the rooms being replaced by a rising curtain. The open-air playhouses of Shakespeare's time, by contrast, had stages which projected into the mass of the audience who thus surrounded the actors on at least three sides. Moreover, performance by daylight meant that the actors could see the audience and the audience could see themselves; in such conditions it is impossible for actors to ignore the audience in the way they commonly do in the darkened auditoriums of proscenium arch theatres.

Whereas modern theatres generally charge the greatest admission fee for seats near the stage, the open-air theatres allowed those in the yard (who had paid least) to stand almost directly underneath the actors near the edge of the stage. The indoor hall theatres provided something like the modern conditions—seats nearest the stage were the most expensive, and lighting could be controlled—but throughout Shakespeare's working lifetime there was no possibility of writing exclusively for such conditions. The plays of Shakespeare and his contemporaries were written for daylight performance by actors standing on a platform 'island' within a 'sea' of upturned spectatorial faces. The word 'soliloquy' had no theatrical meaning to actors working in these conditions: if there were no other characters on the stage, the speech would be consciously directed towards the highly visible audience.

Apart from their playbooks, a company's greatest accumulation of capital was in their clothing stock, which might easily be worth more than the theatre in which they were performing. A typical theatrical doublet (a man's upper-body garment) cost about £3, most women's gowns were between £4 and £7, and skirts were about £2. To put these figures in perspective, the master of the Stratford Grammar School was at this time paid £20 per year. The high cost of costumes presumably reflected their importance within the theatrical event. The representation of characters of high social rank, especially monarchs, seems to have achieved a degree of naturalism by the use of appropriately luxurious clothing. When attempting to represent other times and other cultures, the players did not seek complete historical authenticity. Rather, they adapted Elizabethan dress with gestures towards the past or towards the foreign, so that a turban might indicate the countries of the east and a sash might suggest the Roman toga. Stage properties were minimal, usually confined to hand-held items (swords, crowns, torches) and small pieces of furniture such as tables and chairs. Bedroom scenes often began with a bed being 'thrust out' from one of the stage doors, usually with its occupant already in it.

The analogical thinking evidenced in naming the Globe theatre appears to have operated at all the playhouses: the main stage represented everyday earthly reality, the area under the stage, the 'hell', was the domain of devils and ghosts, and the underside of the cover over the stage was the 'heavens'. A trap door in the stage would provide a route for devils to enter the earthly realm, as with the rising of Asnath in Shakespeare's *Henry VI Part Two*,1.4, and another in the heavens would allow the descent by rope of supernatural beings such as Jupiter in Shakespeare's *Cymbeline*, 5.5. These visual effects and the lavish costuming which allowed the poorest spectator a close-up view of clothing hardly less sumptuous than that worn at the real court indicate that visual pleasure was an important part of playgoing. The remarkable poetry of the best writers, including Shakespeare, shows that playgoers could enjoy aural gratification too, and there really is no way to rank the two sensual pleasures. We can be sure, however, that playgoers came as much to see a play as to hear it, and indeed phrases such as 'see a play' occur ten times as often as phrases such as Hamlet's 'hear a play' (2.2.513) in the literature of the period.

Conclusion

Upon his succession James I took over as patron of Shakespeare's company, changing them from the Chamberlain's Men to the King's Men. His son Henry took over the Admiral's Men, transforming them into the Prince's Men. This declension marks the pre-eminence of Shakespeare's troupe: the King's Men performed at court more times than any other company (indeed, more often than Elizabeth had ever requested) and they toured more extensively than ever before, which might indicate that the new king saw his playing company as a travelling advertisement for the new reign. The power of royal patronage lies behind the King's Men's successful occupancy of the Blackfriars theatre in 1608, having been defeated by local opposition in 1596 when James Burbage bought the building. The company also learned from the success of the financial arrangements regarding the Globe—the leading players being also owners of the building—and formed a similar syndicate to bind common interests in the Blackfriars. Using the Globe in the summer and the Blackfriars in the winter was, however, a wasteful practice (one property being empty at all times) and is hard to explain. Perhaps nostalgia for their early 1590s habit of playing at an amphitheatre in the summer and an indoor venue (then, the city inns) in the winter got the better of them. The Globe had been a second-best option in 1599, but in the first part of the seventeenth century the company might have been surprised by its continued success. By retaining an outdoor theatre alongside their indoor one they continued to address the widest possible social spectrum of early modern Londoners. When the Globe burnt down in 1613 the King's Men immediately rebuilt it in the same style and on the same groundplan as before, which must indicate its continued profitability.

Shakespeare's output slowed down towards the end of the first decade of the seventeenth century and he began to collaborate with other dramatists. His first collaboration was with George Wilkins on *Pericles* in 1607, but Wilkins's petty criminality and habitual plagiarism (he published an unauthorized novella based on the play in 1608) probably did little to encourage Shakespeare in this direction. It was not until 1613 that Shakespeare again collaborated, this time choosing the rising star John Fletcher with whom he wrote *Henry VIII*, *The Two Noble Kinsmen*, and probably the lost play *Cardenio*. Fletcher already had a permanent collaborator in Francis Beaumont with whom he worked from 1608 or 1609 until 1613 or 1614 when the partnership was dissolved (Beaumont married a rich heiress and retired). In Shakespeare the King's Men had a dramatist who usually worked on his own, but Fletcher was more typical of the profession in bringing in Philip Massinger to take Beaumont's place as his collaborator for a number of hits throughout the 1610s and 1620s. Massinger himself became the attached dramatist of the King's Men from 1626 to 1639.

In its lineaments, Shakespeare would have recognized the theatre industry as it was when the theatres were closed almost thirty years after his retirement. Shakespeare lived through a period of extraordinarily rapid development of an entertainment industry which then changed little until the Civil War of the 1640s and was to re-emerge in the 1660 Restoration wholly unlike anything seen before (as described in Chapter 35).

FURTHER READING

Astington, John H. *English Court Theatre 1558–1642* (Cambridge: Cambridge University Press, 1999). Astington records everything known about the court performances which were the official raison d'être of playing companies. This book has detailed descriptions of the court venues (such as the Whitehall Banqueting Hall) used for plays and masques, and a comprehensive calendar of all known performances.

Bentley, Gerald Eades. *The Profession of Dramatist in Shakespeare's Time, 1590–1642* (Princeton: Princeton University Press, 1971). This is the best single-volume introduction to the daily work of a playwright, just as the next item is the best single-volume introduction to the daily work of an actor.

Bentley, Gerald Eades. *The Profession of Player in Shakespeare's Time, 1590–1642* (Princeton: Princeton University Press, 1984).

Dutton, Richard. *Mastering the Revels: The Regulation and Censorship of English Renaissance Drama* (London: Macmillan, 1991). Dutton takes the view that the censor was not simply the enemy of the dramatists and convincingly demonstrates how the Master of the Revels and the players worked together to promote their mutual interests.

Gurr, Andrew. *The Shakespearian Playing Companies* (Oxford: Clarendon Press, 1996). As well as outlining the relationship between playing companies and the forces of court and city authority, this scrupulously detailed scholarly work has a chapter describing the origins and career of each acting company.

Gurr, Andrew and Mariko Ichikawa. *Staging in Shakespeare's Theatres*, Oxford Shakespeare Topics (Oxford: Oxford University Press, 2000). This book explores what we know about the actual performance practices of companies in Shakespeare's time, including discoveries from the reconstructed Globe currently standing in south London.

Heinemann, Margot. *Puritanism and Theatre: Thomas Middleton and Opposition Drama under the Early Stuarts*, Past and Present Publications (Cambridge: Cambridge University Press, 1980). Heinemann's nuanced model of the relationship between early modern Christian fundamentalism and the theatres overturned a number of previous assumptions and gave the subject a modern historical grounding.

Ingram, William. *The Business of Playing: The Beginnings of the Adult Professional Theater in Elizabethan England* (Ithaca: Cornell University Press, 1992). This describes the forces which turned the late medieval casual troupes into professional playing companies, and traces the development of the industry within early capitalism.

Kastan, David Scott. *Shakespeare After Theory* (New York: Routledge, 1999), Chapter 11 ' "Publike Sports" and "Publike Calamities": Plays, Playing, and Politics'. Following Heinemann's lead, Kastan examines the closing of the theatres in 1642 and concludes that it was not simply the victory of anti-theatricalism.

Knutson, Roslyn Lander. *The Repertory of Shakespeare's Company 1594–1613* (Fayetteville: University of Arkansas Press, 1991). Knutson uses a combination of historical data and informed guesswork to reconstruct the likely repertory of the Chamberlain's/King's Men and argues that competition between the leading companies caused them to copy one another's successful productions and genres.

McMillin, Scott and Sally-Beth MacLean. *The Queen's Men and Their Plays* (Cambridge: Cambridge University Press, 1998). A company-centred study of a troupe whose early plays are of special interest for the origins of the history play genre in which Shakespeare first distinguished himself.

Stern, Tiffany. *Rehearsal from Shakespeare to Sheridan* (Oxford: Clarendon Press, 2000). This contains everything known about the essential process of rehearsal in early modern theatre, and shows that examination of the actors' parts (the individual scrolls, each of which contained one character's speeches) can reveal theatrical effects not immediately visible in the complete text.

4 | Shakespeare's audiences

Margaret Jane Kidnie

There is a long moment of silence towards the end of the film *Shakespeare in Love* (1998) as Romeo and Juliet lie dead on the stage of the Curtain Theatre. Eventually, a diverse mix of spectators, separated outside of the playhouse by gender, rank, and profession, break from their absorption in the drama's tragic events to burst into applause. When the Master of the Revels, Sir Edmund Tilney, abruptly marches onto the stage with his men to threaten the acting company with imprisonment for allowing a woman to play the part of Juliet, Elizabeth I reveals herself among the seated spectators in the galleries. Stepping onto the stage, she puts the authority and body of the Queen of England literally on display, meting out justice in place of Tilney and bringing to a comic resolution the film's confused identities and complexities of plot.

Although this scene today makes for entertaining viewing, the idea that the historical Elizabeth I might have attended a dramatic performance at the public amphitheatres is a fiction. The actors came to the monarchy, not the monarchy to the actors. This sort of disparity between historical evidence and filmic art is hardly surprising, but it brings to mind the question of who was, then, in those early London audiences—who might have paid to see drama performed at any time between 1567, when the first custom-made playhouse, the Red Lion, opened, and 1642, when the theatres were closed during the English Civil War? Moreover, what do we know of the popular response to the theatres? Clearly, public performances were a welcome diversion for some, but support for the players' enterprise was far from universal. The political controversies surrounding the early modern stage are suggested, and satirized, in *Shakespeare in Love* through the film's comic caricature of the Puritan who stands outside of the Curtain to warn passers-by of the evils of theatre—a character subsequently glimpsed among the play's spectators, wiping away a tear. This chapter considers what we know about the composition of Shakespeare's audiences before turning to examine, more generally, the cultural space occupied by the playhouses. Here the discussion will focus, in particular, on the moralists who attacked and defended the public stage between about 1578 and 1633.

Questions of evidence

Modern accounts of attendance at the commercial theatres depend on evidence which is relatively scant, and open to critical interpretation. This material includes such documents as private letters, diaries, published poetry, polemical pamphlets, legal records of the City of London, petitions to the Privy Council (a small group of powerful advisers to the monarch), and the plays themselves. These sorts of written accounts are imprecise and impressionistic. There is hardly any mention of tradesmen, for instance, attending theatrical performances in London in the ten years to 1600. As Andrew Gurr questions in *Playgoing in Shakespeare's London*, should we understand this absence of comment to imply that tradesmen did not visit the playhouses, or rather that their presence was so customary as to be entirely unremarkable? Attempts to characterize the composition of a supposedly typical audience are further complicated by the realization that the various London venues would attract different sorts of clientele, and that demographic profiles for particular theatres probably altered in their details over the years.

But with these reservations in mind, one can try to provide at least a preliminary indication of how accurately *Shakespeare in Love* portrays an early modern audience. Between 1590 and 1600—the period in which *Romeo and Juliet* was first staged—open-air amphitheatres like the Curtain and the Red Lion were the only commercial venues available to playgoers, and the acting companies seem to have drawn their audiences from across the social spectrum. Members of the gentry, foreign ambassadors, butchers, tailors, and leather-workers, students being trained as lawyers at the Inns of Court, apprentices, shopkeepers, and thieves all seem to have congregated at the playhouses on a more or less regular basis. There is also clear evidence that they were joined by women, whether ladies, citizens' wives, or prostitutes. The Epilogue to *As You Like It* (1600), delivered by the boy actor playing Rosalind, is premised on the presence of women in the audience: 'to beg will not become me. My way is to conjure you; and I'll begin with the women. I charge you, O women, for the love you bear to men, to like as much of this play as please you. And I charge you, O men, for the love you bear to women—as I perceive by your simpering none of you hates them—that between you and the women the play may please' (9–14).

In fact, the only people who can be said with any certainty to have been excluded from Shakespeare's audience during these years are those who could not afford the minimum price of a penny to stand crowded in the pit around the elevated stage. The people barred from plays for financial reasons increased in number, however, when the indoor, or hall theatres reopened in 1600 after a ten-year hiatus. These roofed, candle-lit playhouses could accommodate far fewer spectators than, for instance, the Globe. Providing space only for seated customers and with the cheapest places costing between three and six pence, theatres such as Blackfriars and later, the Cockpit, were priced beyond the means of the poorer members of the amphitheatre audience. The architectural distinctions between these two types of early modern playhouse, and what we know of the acting companies that performed in them, are discussed in this volume in Chapter 3.

The important point to note is that the reintroduction of the more expensive hall theatres did not immediately create firm distinctions between 'popular' and 'elite' theatre-going communities in London, although social boundaries between the indoor and open-air theatres became more apparent as the years progressed. Less wealthy customers were limited in their choice of venue by the price of admission, but there was little to prevent those with sufficient financial resources from moving freely between both the so-called public and private theatres. One could expect, then, that audiences at theatres such as the Rose, the Curtain, and the Globe represented a broad cross-section of the London populace.

The cultural space of Shakespeare's theatre

Expense was not, however, the only consideration. Other factors might have prevented potential spectators from attending a theatrical performance in London between the mid-1560s and 1642. The professional stage occupied a controversial cultural space that was defined by its unusual legal and moral status. The playing companies were licensed by the Crown, yet remained subject to the authority of the City of London. As early as 1574, the City passed an Act of Common Council attempting to control commercial theatrical practice. The Act insisted that professional players who resorted to the 'common collection of money of the auditory or beholders'—acting companies, that is, who charged admittance to their performances—should be allowed to perform only dramatic material that met with the approval of the Lord Mayor and Aldermen, and then never on Sundays, during Lent, or during the time of plague.[1]

The City's purpose was not to regulate performances that were taking place for the entertainment of invited guests in the private homes of noblemen or gentry. The 1574 Act of Common Council was expressly designed to set limits on 'common' playing, performances taking place for paying audiences at the amphitheatres and halls in the suburbs of London. The crowds making their way to the playhouses on a daily basis had apparently attracted the notice of the civic authorities. The City's concerns centred for the most part on the potential disturbances of public order to which large assemblies of people in one place gave rise: quarrels, sedition, increased rates of theft, the sexual corruption of unwary and underage girls, the dangers posed to audience members' personal safety either through building collapse or the use of weapons and gunpowder in performance, and the spread of disease. Significantly, however, the document, although lengthy and complex, had little bite. So long as the acting companies continued to enjoy the protection and patronage of the Crown, the City was in practice powerless to curtail either the frequency of, or the numbers in attendance at, public performances.

The strange relationship between the acting companies and the Lord Mayor and Aldermen of London resulted not solely from the companies' Court patronage, but also in part as a consequence of geographical location. The erection of the theatres 'within the liberties of this city' is emphasized repeatedly in the 1574 Act. The term 'liberty' referred to specific juridical areas, tracts of land often situated outside of the city walls and exempted from certain aspects of city control. The politically marginal relation of these areas to the urban centre coincided with a relative legal freedom from the constraints governing social behaviour in London to create a unique cultural space that both was, and was not, of the city. Getting to the theatres for potential customers who were not already resident in the liberties thus usually involved a journey beyond the city limits; when they reached their destination, they would find the playhouses situated cheek by jowl with bearbaiting and cockfighting pits, brothels, taverns, and gambling houses. The civic authorities might disapprove of such forms of entertainment as immoral and even illicit, but the deliberate decision to build the theatres just outside of the City's effective control gave the players a certain measure of practical independence.

The early modern moralists

This precarious independence from the City authorities did not, however, render the players immune to censure from contemporary moralists. Objections to the theatres began in earnest soon after the players took up fixed residence in what John Stockwood described during a sermon delivered in 1578 as 'the gorgeous playing place[s] erected in the fields'. The theatres came under sharpest criticism in these early years for performing on Sundays, transforming ministers' congregations into players' audiences. 'Will not a filthy play, with the blast of a trumpet', thundered Stockwood, 'sooner call thither a thousand, than an hour's tolling of a bell, bring to the sermon a hundred?' Even those who wrote in defence of the stage were in agreement that churches should not have to compete with the playhouses on the Sabbath. Thomas Lodge, one such apologist, conceded in about 1579 that such 'folly . . . makes those sin, which perhaps if it were not, would have been present at a good sermon'.[2] But even after Sunday playing was prohibited in the 1580s, the controversy surrounding the theatres continued.

The attack was particularly heated in the years between 1577 and 1583. Early polemicists such as John Northbrooke, Stephen Gosson, and Philip Stubbes were, at least at the outset, careful to differentiate between particular forms of theatre: while certain manifestations of the activity were condemned, others were deemed acceptable and even commendable. Northbrooke, for example, writing in *A Treatise wherein*

Dicing, Dancing, Vain Plays or Enterludes with other Idle Pastimes etc. Commonly Used on the Sabbath day, are Reproved (1577) considered that the occasional student production of a comedy, preferably in Latin and strictly for purposes of education, was permissible. Gosson, himself a reformed, albeit unsuccessful, playwright, expressed an even more tolerant view in *The School of Abuse* (1579). Here he not only excluded some actors from his attack whom he knew to be sober and discreet, but argued that there existed a few plays in the acting companies' repertory—one of his own creations among the number—which were above reproach.

The recurrent idea in these tracts is the 'abuse' of the profession. 'There is nothing so good, but it may be abused', wrote Stubbes in the Preface to his *Anatomy of Abuses* (1583).[3] The goal of the pamphleteers was to identify for their readers the variety of ways in which contemporary theatre deviated from good practice as a first step towards its amendment. These writers were spurred into print, not by an aversion towards theatrical representation in general, but, more specifically, by a mistrust, or even fear, of the commercial public theatres as an emergent social phenomenon in England in the third quarter of the sixteenth century.

The precise terms of the attack, however, soon shifted. Arguments guided by an ostensible desire to reform existing conditions were abandoned, with the rhetorical emphasis falling instead on categorical condemnations of the playhouses as 'the chapel of Satan'.[4] This transition is apparent in the first edition of Stubbes's *Anatomy of Abuses*. Although the Preface clarifies that plays, used with discretion, should meet with the approval of good Christians, this moderate view is contradicted in the chapter-length treatment of the subject. Here, asserting that every type of theatre has had a corrupting influence on players and spectators from the beginning of time, Stubbes calls for its immediate abolition. The Preface was omitted from the book's revised editions. The building of the playhouses 'in the fields' clearly unsettled some members of the Elizabethan public. The substance of the objections posed against the stage is worth exploring in some detail.

The antitheatricalists' complaints were numerous: religious plays abused the word of the Lord, secular plays tended to idolatry, all plays drew crowds away from sermons and offered a bad example to life, and actors, no better than beggars, dressed sumptuously in apparel above their rank. Above all, the theatres constructed by entrepreneurs such as James Burbage and John Brayne targeted Londoners with expendable income, and were unashamedly devoted to what was in effect a leisure activity. It was not just the apprentices—paying customers who, it was repeatedly asserted, could ill afford either the time or the money to see afternoon performances—about whom these writers were concerned. The widespread inclination to pursue frivolous entertainment and to neglect more sober forms of godly recreation such as Bible study and prayer signalled an intolerable moral laxity. Northbrooke's polemic, as the title of his treatise suggests, was directed not solely at the theatres, but at all forms of pastime which breed idleness.

And the consequences of such indolence were to be feared. Developing a syllogism in 1577 that was to become commonplace, 'T.W.' (probably Thomas White) preached that 'the cause of plagues is sin, if you look to it well: and the cause of sin are plays: therefore the cause of plagues are plays'.[5] Not just a matter for the next world, time misspent at the theatres resulted in sickness and death in our own. Evidence of God's wrath was similarly found in the calamities that occasionally befell the playhouses and their close cousins, the bearbaiting pits. The collapse on 13 January 1583 of Paris Garden, a pit located near the Rose Theatre on the south shore of the Thames, was frequently cited as a telling example of God's judgement. Five men and two women were killed instantly, and scores of other people were seriously wounded when the tiered galleries in which they were sitting fell to the ground, crushing the members of the audience below. The campaign reached perhaps its most extreme statement in 1633 with the publication of William Prynne's *Histriomastix*, a catalogue of argumentation and evidence against the theatres that ran to more than a thousand pages.

The conviction that playhouses provoked moral corruption was captured in an anecdote told by Richard Brathwait in *The English Gentleman* (1630), in which a desperately ill woman, enjoined on her deathbed to seek the Lord, cries out instead 'Hieronimo.' This account at once indicates the enduring popularity of *The Spanish Tragedy*, Thomas Kyd's hugely successful drama of the 1590s, and serves as a warning to Brathwait's readers of the compelling fascination exerted by the stage on spectators' imaginations. Such influence, however, as proponents of the stage were quick to note, need not be necessarily detrimental. In a story that, admittedly, does little to reassure opponents suspicious of the bewitching power of theatre, Thomas Heywood, in his *Apology for Actors* (1612), related the story of a woman driven to confess the murder of her husband as a direct result of the players' unwitting portrayal of a similar crime on stage. Her conscience troubled, she screamed out in the middle of the performance, 'Oh my husband, my husband! I see the ghost of my husband', and was subsequently apprehended, examined, and condemned.[6]

Although the suggestion that plays were as profitable as sermons was derided by many, the potential for moral improvement was one of the mainstays of defences mounted by advocates of the theatre. Thomas Nashe was thus merely repeating an argument advanced many times before when he asserted in *Pierce Penniless his Supplication to the Devil* (1592) that

In plays all cozenages, all cunning drifts overgilded with outward holiness, all stratagems of war, all the cankerworms that breed on the rust of peace, are most lively anatomized. They show the ill success of treason, the fall of hasty climbers, the wretched end of usurpers, the misery of civil dissension, and how just God is evermore in punishing of murder . . . [N]o play they have encourageth any man to tumults or rebellion, but lays before such the halter and the gallows; or praiseth or approveth pride, lust, whoredom, prodigality, or drunkenness, but beats them down utterly.[7]

Not only do the players set improving examples before their audiences, explained Nashe, but the exploits of English heroes, relived daily on the public stage, provided 'a rare exercise of virtue' and a necessary corrective to contemporary degeneracy. In what is almost certainly a reference to *Henry VI Part One*, written by Shakespeare and others (possibly including Nashe himself), Nashe drummed up patriotic fervour in support of the professional theatres: 'How would it have joyed brave Talbot, the terror of the French, to think that after he had lien two hundred years in his tomb he should triumph again on the stage, and have his bones new-embalmed with the tears of ten thousand spectators at least, at several times, who in the tragedian that represents his person imagine they behold him fresh bleeding!'[8] Anecdotal evidence was thus evoked by moralists positioned on either side of the debate. What is perhaps of particular interest to modern readers is the range of social preoccupations that might be inferred from the relation of such stories.

Promiscuity and the female spectator

In this respect, it is perhaps significant that Brathwait's anecdote about the corrupting influence of theatre involved a female spectator. Contemporary commentators focused at least as much on the actual experience of attending the theatre as on the content of the performance, and one of the features of the occasion to which their attention was repeatedly drawn was the presence of women in the audience. According to many of these writers, male spectators were entertained by the spectacle on offer in the galleries as well as by that provided by the actors on the stage. Gosson claims in *The School of Abuse* that at the theatres 'you shall see such heaving and shoving, such itching and shouldering, to sit by women . . . such ticking [dallying], such toying, such smiling, such winking, and such manning them home when the sports are ended that it is a right comedy to mark behaviour'.[9] Ignore for the moment that this supposedly eyewitness account in fact paraphrases the description of the Roman theatres found in Ovid's *Amores*. Such passages, even if—perhaps especially if—copied out of another book, indicate that what was particularly remarkable about the professional stage in early modern England was the extent to which it afforded unaccustomed opportunity for promiscuous behaviour. Recurrent in the antitheatrical tracts is the image of uncontrolled and uncontrollable sexual appetite.

The author of *A Second and Third Blast of Retreat from Plays and Theaters* (1580), probably Anthony Munday, asserts that 'harlots' who are past all shame make themselves at the playhouses the objects of men's eyes. If we are to believe this author, sexual intercourse actually took place during performance. Other pamphleteers, by contrast, tell us that the deals struck between prostitutes and their customers were concluded elsewhere. There seems little reason to doubt that prostitutes, whether taking an afternoon off or plying their trade, would number among the men and women in attendance at the theatres. But in a culture in which any woman who presented herself to the indiscriminate view of men was liable to be read as sexually available, one should be careful not to assume that the term 'whore' describes a professional who solicits clients for sex. As Gosson warns his gentlewoman citizen reader, 'Thought is free': it is not 'your modesty at home, that covereth your lightness, if you present yourselves in open theatres'.[10]

Allegations of bawdry in the antitheatrical tracts signal unease, not just with the potential for professional overlap between the theatres and the nearby brothels, but with the prospect of casual and unregulated interaction in the playhouses between men and women of all callings and ranks. This anxiety is voiced most memorably by Stubbes. He concludes his description of the theatrical event with the observation that when the play is ended, 'every mate sorts to his mate, every one brings another home-ward of their way very friendly, and in their secret conclaves (covertly) they play the sodomites, or worse'.[11] Stubbes's evocative phrasing seems to refer, at least to a modern ear, specifically to homosexual relations. But the ambiguities of the term 'sodomite' in the period, alongside the exclusive emphasis elsewhere in the book on transgressive sexual interaction between men and women, combine to suggest that lewd behaviour between men is here not of primary concern. The likelihood is that same-sex attraction was a feature of the public theatres. Stubbes, however, presents to his reader's imagin-ation a more inclusive and, for him, more frightening spectre: the vision of aroused members of the audience leaving the playhouse to have sex for fun with someone to whom they are not married.

A perhaps surprising point to note about Stubbes's otherwise comprehensive attack on the theatres is the fact that he never mentions the transvestite boy actor. The boy actors, assuming female dramatic roles and costumed in women's apparel, were char-acteristic of early modern performance. This stage convention, one we today tend to suppose was invisible because so commonplace, was vividly present to the eyes and judgements of the antitheatricalists. Not only does crossdressing transgress the Old Testament injunction forbidding one sex to wear the clothes of the other (Deut. 22:5), but such spectacles 'effeminate', or make womanish and therefore more susceptible to sexual desire and unmanly weakness, the male audience members. Thomas Heywood, in *An Apology for Actors*, tried to appeal to his reader's common sense, arguing that audiences were fully capable of grasping the concept of fictional impersonation: 'But to see our youths attired in the habit of women, who knows not what their intents be? Who cannot distinguish them by their names, assuredly knowing, they are but to represent such a lady, at such a time appointed?'[12] His defence, however, fell on hostile ears. The problem was not (or at least not simply) that spectators might not be able to discern the difference between the body of the actor and his enacted character. The larger issue, one made explicit in Gosson's *Plays Confuted in Five Actions* (1582), was that the boy actors—and not just they, but also the adult actors, commoners playing the roles of princes and kings—were performing a lie.

Religion and rhetoric

The attack on the theatres was thus something of a lightning conductor, drawing to itself wide-ranging anxieties about the blurring of boundaries of rank and gender only too apparent in other areas of early modern society. The visions of male and female licentiousness conjured up in these tracts are disturbing precisely to the extent to which they are emblems of social disorder. Chapters 9 and 13, on the political structure and ideological thought of early modern England, develop further in relation to Shakespeare's drama the impact and implications of disruptions to the hierarchy of degree. For a writer such as Stubbes, the stage was just one 'abuse' among many. The polemical treatises under study here assert the belief that a true relation should obtain at all times between personal identity and exterior appearance. Those who pretended to be something they were not, either by walking through the streets dressed in sumptuous clothing beyond their social rank, wearing cosmetics, or partaking in theatrical performance, were symptomatic of, and contributing to, the same perceived degeneracy.

It is not unusual to find the early modern antitheatricalists misleadingly caricatured as Puritan fanatics. This is the image projected in *Shakespeare in Love*, for instance, and it is a view that surfaces regularly in scholarly criticism of Shakespeare and the early modern stage. An avowed opposition to the theatres, however, did not necessarily imply solidarity with writers and political agitators, more accurately described as Puritan, who were determined to effect further reform of the English church after the Elizabethan religious settlement of 1559. Gosson, far from advocating such reform, opposed it. Stubbes, for his part, numbered religious innovators in *The Second Part of the Anatomy of Abuses* as a fault of Elizabethan society comparable in magnitude to absent landlords and neglect of the Sabbath.

Modern use of the label 'puritan' to refer to figures perhaps better described as kill-joys probably arises from a similar colloquial usage in early modern England. The drama of the period, in particular, presented the supposed connection between puritanism and (hypocritical) moral objections to dancing, May games, and the theatre as commonplace. Think, for instance, of *Twelfth Night*, and Maria's description of Malvolio, Olivia's austere steward, as 'a kind of puritan' (2.3.125). To adopt too easily such rhetoric in our own day, however, is not just wrongly to assume that religious conviction necessarily motivated each of the antitheatricalists, but to flatten out the nuances at play in the contemporary political debates. The ideological complexities surrounding the subject of religion in post-Reformation England are addressed further in Chapter 12.

The complex factors that led individual writers to oppose the stage in print are probably impossible to recover in their entirety. It seems unlikely, however, that a godly desire for social reform was the sole impetus behind all of the tracts. There is some evidence to suggest that Gosson's *School of Abuse*, in a manner similar to *A Second and Third Blast of Retreat from Plays and Theatres*, was commissioned by the City. Anthony Munday, the likely author of this anonymous sequel to Gosson's *School*, thereafter returned to the theatres as a playwright, giving credibility to the view that his pamphlet was the work of a professional hack. There is even a chance that Philip Stubbes, an author well-known to Shakespeare scholars for his moral piety and apoplectic condemnation of sin, carefully cultivated what was, in effect, a literary persona. The antitheatricalists wrote within what were, at the time, recognizable literary conventions, drawing on genres as various as satire, complaint, and the news pamphlet, and they incorporated into their own work, usually in an unattributed form, lengthy passages 'borrowed' from classical sources and each other.

The moralists in perspective

So how useful to theatre historians are the printed attacks and defences of Shakespeare's stage? These polemical tracts provide a striking indication of the personal and political anxieties occasioned by times of cultural, economic, and religious transition. Their importance rests in the construction of an intellectual framework through which early modern society attempted to make sense of itself. But for that very reason, any evidence they offer about the theatres must be interpreted with care. Most importantly, the antitheatricalists probably represented the opinions of a relatively small, but highly visible, proportion of the London populace. All the more reason, then, to remind ourselves that to remain commercially viable, the theatres must have in fact appealed to a wide variety of people, neither particularly sinful nor godly. The lawyer John Manningham, for instance, provides us with the first known record of *Twelfth Night* in performance. His diary entry from 1602, recounting the stratagem practised by Maria and the others on the gullible Malvolio, summons up not just the plot of Shakespeare's comedy, but in its very detail, the pleasure it afforded its Elizabethan audience:

At our feast we had a play called 'Twelve Night, or What You Will' . . . A good practice in it to make the steward believe his lady widow was in love with him by counterfeiting a letter as from his lady, in general terms, telling him what she liked best in him, and prescribing his gesture in smiling, his apparel, &c., and then when he came to practise, making him believe they took him to be mad.[13]

It is difficult to tell from the extant evidence who paid to see the earliest performances of *Romeo and Juliet* and *Twelfth Night*, and the fact is that we have trouble knowing with any certainty what the vast majority of Londoners who never put their opinions into print thought of the playhouses in the fields. The realization, however, that so much basic information is no longer available about the cultural space within which early modern theatre-going found its meaning, only makes more valuable such voices as

Manningham's and the moralists', anecdotal and compromised though they may be, that have survived.

FURTHER READING

Barish, Jonas. *The Antitheatrical Prejudice* (Berkeley: University of California Press, 1981). This book offers an informed and readable study of opposition to the theatres stretching from Plato to the present day. Chapters 4–6 are of particular relevance to the early modern English stage.

Chambers, E. K. 'Documents of Criticism' and 'Documents of Control'. *The Elizabethan Stage*. Vol. 4 (Oxford: Clarendon Press, 1923), pp. 184–345. An essential, and relatively easily accessible, collection of extracts. The first section samples the attacks and defences of the stage, while the second reprints official material pertaining to the theatres generated by the central and local authorities.

Cook, Ann Jennalie. *The Privileged Playgoers of Shakespeare's London, 1576–1642* (Princeton: Princeton University Press, 1981). The first book-length study to interrogate ill-founded assumptions about early modern audiences. Cook's central thesis is that the privileged playgoers of her title dominated not just the hall theatres, but also the open-air amphitheatres.

Gurr, Andrew. *Playgoing in Shakespeare's London*, 2nd edn. (Cambridge: Cambridge University Press, 1996). This book, now revised and reprinted, assembles and interprets a wide range of evidence relevant to the experience of attending the commercial theatres in early modern London. It is currently the standard text on Shakespeare's audiences.

Howard, Jean E. *The Stage and Social Struggle in Early Modern England* (London: Routledge, 1994). This book relates the moralists' emphasis on the commercialization of culture and theatricalization of identity to more widespread concerns about the disorder of rank and gender in early modern England. A powerful and enlightening study of the attacks and defences of the stage, and their relation to the drama.

Levine, Laura. *Men in Women's Clothing: Anti-Theatricality and Effeminization, 1579–1642* (Cambridge: Cambridge University Press, 1994). The opening essay in this book analyzes the antitheatricalists' rhetoric, and argues that a lack of a sense of fixed identity coincided with a belief in magic to generate the notion that 'doing' what another person does inevitably leads to 'being' that person. The argument is marred by claims, central to the thesis, that Philip Stubbes addresses in his tract the crossdressed boy actors.

Mullaney, Steven. *The Place of the Stage: License, Play, and Power in Renaissance England* (Chicago: University of Chicago Press, 1988). An important and fascinating discussion of the geographical and cultural situation of the theatres.

Ringler, William. 'The First Phase of the Elizabethan Attack on the Stage, 1558–1579', *Huntington Library Quarterly*, 4 (1942), 391–418. A classic piece of scholarship that argues that the attack began quite suddenly at the end of the 1570s as a direct response to the newly constructed public playhouses. The claim that Gosson's first antitheatrical pamphlet was commissioned by the City has since been challenged by A. F. Kinney in *Markets of Bawdrie: The Dramatic Criticism of Stephen Gosson* (Salzburg: Institut für Englische Sprache und Literatur, Universität Salzburg, 1974).

Somerset, Alan. 'Cultural Poetics, or Historical Prose? The Places of the Stage', *Medieval and Renaissance Drama in England*, 11 (1999), 34–59. This informative and wide-ranging essay reconsiders the available evidence to argue that early modern entrepreneurs located the public theatres in the liberties of London, not out of fear of City hostility, but primarily for reasons of longer leases, cheaper rents, and minimal taxation.

NOTES

1. As quoted in E. K. Chambers. 'Documents of Control', *The Elizabethan Stage*, Vol. 4 (Oxford: Clarendon Press, 1923), pp. 275–6.

2. John Stockwood. *A Sermon Preached at Paul's Cross on Bartholomew Day, being the 24. of August, 1578* (London, n.d.), sigs. I7v, B8. Thomas Lodge, quoted in E. K. Chambers, 'Documents of Criticism', *The Elizabethan Stage*, Vol. 4 (Oxford: Clarendon Press, 1923), p. 206.

3. Philip Stubbes. *The Anatomy of Abuses* (London, May 1583), sig. ¶ 7.

4. Anglo-phile Eutheo [Anthony Munday?]. *A Second and Third Blast of Retreat from Plays and Theatres* (London, 1580), sig. G3.

5. T. W. [Thomas White]. *A Sermon Preached at Paul's Cross on Sunday the Third of November 1577 in the Time of the Plague* (London, 1578), sig. C8.

6. Richard Brathwait. *The English Gentleman* (London, 1630), sig. Cc2. Thomas Heywood. *An Apology for Actors* (London, 1612), sig. G1v.

7. Thomas Nashe. *Pierce Penniless his Supplication to the Devil* (London, 1592), in *Thomas Nashe*, ed. Stanley Wells (London: Edward Arnold, 1964), pp. 65–6.

8. Ibid., pp. 64–5.

9. Stephen Gosson. *The School of Abuse* (London, 1579), ed. A. F. Kinney, *Markets of Bawdrie: The Dramatic Criticism of Stephen Gosson* (Salzburg: Institut für Englische Sprache und Literatur, Universität Salzburg, 1974), sig. C1v.

10. Ibid., sig. F2.

11. Stubbes. *Abuses*, sig. L8v.

12. Heywood. *Apology*, sig. C3v.

13. *The Diary of John Manningham*, ed. Robert Parker Sorlien (Hanover, NH: The University Press of New England, 1976), p. 48 (fol. 12b).

5 | Conventions of playwriting

Peter Thomson

Above all with the monumental figure of Shakespeare in mind, we tend to view play-writing as an art. Shakespeare, whether or not he had himself in mind, viewed it as a craft. Just as an Elizabethan shipwright undertook to shape his raw material (wood) into an artefact (a ship), an Elizabethan playwright undertook to shape his raw material (a story or stories) into an artefact (a play). The parallel can be carried further. A shipwright who set about fashioning a ship on the offchance that a purchaser might be found for the finished article might begin as an optimist but would certainly end as a pauper. For shipwrights and playwrights, men whose artefacts took time to pro-duce, the law of the market required a commission; and the final product, though distinguished throughout by the individual craftsman's 'signature', was necessarily affected by the preferences (and the deadlines) of the commissioning agent. Further-more, the shipwright/playwright who elected to work alone could do so only if the commission carried a generous deadline *and* if he could afford to maintain himself in the interim between obtaining the commission and completing it. It is easy to see why so many early modern playwrights (and shipwrights) chose to collaborate with fellow-craftsmen to hasten the completion of their commissioned artefacts.

In the emergent professional theatre of the late sixteenth century, the commission-ing agents were actors. A few of them, like Shakespeare, were also playwrights. Fewer still were the actor/playwrights who, like Shakespeare, established themselves in the management of London's major theatrical companies. It is important to recognize that Shakespeare, in this respect, was not a 'typical' playwright for the majority of his working life. The rules of the job were different for professional writers whose whole livelihood was dependent on the successful purveying of their wares. If they chose to write plays, it must have been because they believed that they could provide theatre-goers with the entertainment they relished, but they could reach that public only if they first convinced the actors.

There were probably no hard-and-fast rules of procedure, applied to proven crafts-men and debutants alike, but there were distinct phases in the preparation of a play for performance. The writer's first useful contact was with a senior member of the acting company. He had an idea for a comedy. Was it the sort of thing that would suit the current season? If the actor's answer was 'yes', our writer might have been asked to prepare a plot: a short account of the intended conduct of the dramatic narrative. He might even have been paid £1 for it in token of the company's interest. The ability to shape stories into drama was a recognized skill (in *Palladis Tamia* (1598), Francis Meres called Anthony Munday 'our best plotter'), but would-be playwrights needed also to know the range of skills in the acting companies they were hoping to impress. There had to be something for the specialist clown, no more female roles than boys available to play them, nothing too extravagant in the way of scenic demand—and the company members had to be sure that the unwritten play would suit the occasion and be ready on time. It would, after all, be their profits that were on the line. They would pay the writer no less than £6 for the completed commodity (comparable with the annual wage of an artisan), and there would be further outlays on costume, perhaps on properties and scenic units, and on the licence fee due to the Master of the Revels. The play now belonged to the company. There was no author's right of intellectual ownership. As the modern scholar Jeffrey Masten points out, this was 'a period that lacked, but did not see itself as lacking, authorial copyright'.[1] Just how the completed manuscript had been put together would not normally concern the company. If the commissioned writer worked in collaboration, it was for him to determine the just apportionment of his £6.

There was nothing holy about a playscript and nothing lofty about the status of its author, who generally functioned as the virtually anonymous shaper of a commodity for playhouse use. For those with high cultural aspirations, the composition of plays was tainted. John Marston, for example, apologized in the quarto of *The Malcontent* 'that Scenes invented, merely to be spoken, should be enforcively published to be read'. Drama straddled established cultural boundaries between high and low, literary and oral, history and fiction, city and court, but it paid most of its dues to the burgeoning entertainment industry. There is little of artistic merit in the text of *Mucedorus and Amadine*. We do not even know who wrote it. Yet this is a piece that not only held its place in the theatre for over thirty years, but also ran through more editions (nine) than any other play of the period. With Shakespeare as our only model, we get a distorted picture of the playhouse-culture that he fed off and into. We do well to adjust it by reference to the licence granted to a company by Henry Herbert, Master of the Revels from 1622, to 'add scenes to an old play, and give it out for a new one', that is, present it as if it were new. What place do we ascribe to any author in that decision?

Establishing the conventions

In 1576, when the first successful purpose-built playhouse, the Theatre, opened in London, there was no great stock of plays awaiting public exposure. By virtue of the fact that it was never long in one place, a touring company needed only a handful of production-ready pieces at any one time, but the position changed radically as soon as that company took up residence in a playhouse. The demands of a regular audience had now to be met, and that could not be achieved by the mere recycling of a limited repertoire. We have no reliable knowledge of the early history of the Theatre and its immediate successor, the Curtain, but we know a lot about the conduct of the Rose in the 1590s, and can reasonably surmise that, during the intervening years, ambitious companies came to see the value of attaching themselves to and identifying themselves with particular playhouses.

The socio-economic principles and the artistic policy of the professional theatre that emerged during the 1580s developed in response to the new presence of playhouses in, or immediately outside, the city of London. A resident company had somewhere to store props and costumes, to rehearse, to build scenery and install machinery, to shelve the manuscripts of purchased plays, and to ensure that those who came to see any of those plays in performance had paid the admission-price. It made sense for members of such a company to live close to the playhouse, to become, in fact, citizens of London rather than the 'rogues and vagabonds' of earlier years. These were substantial men, possessed of the symbol of substance, purchasing power. They were in the market for plays and, because the theatregoing public clamoured for novelty, they wanted them in a hurry. However, when we read the curiously ordered papers of Philip Henslowe during his managerial tenure of the Rose and the Fortune, it is clear that a resident company would risk losing audiences if it failed to bring on a new play after two weeks.

Commercial imperatives led to the creation, over the forty years from 1580 to 1620, of what can be seen in retrospect as a national repertoire of still-stageworthy plays. Almost all of these plays were written against deadlines and in pursuit of quick financial returns. Anyone who writes under that kind of pressure will write 'conventionally'. That is to say that playwrights tailored their writing to meet the expectations of the theatre because they were employed by actors to do just that. This is very obvious in the case of one of the first conventions to be established, that of length. A poem need not be longer than four lines but may stretch out to the epic length of Milton's 'Paradise Lost', and a novel may, like Samuel Richardson's *Clarissa*, run to over a million words, but a play that lasts much more than two hours is liable to be cut for performance. There were good reasons for this in 1580: the legs of a standing audience got tired, daylight faded, dramatic tension could not be sustained indefinitely by actors dealing with a hastily compiled or imperfectly memorized text.

The young men, many of them straight from university, who supplied plays to the first professional companies, had no difficulty with this convention. If the story had to be compressed, they compressed it; if the story was too short, they added a sub-plot, probably drawn from a quite different source. Control rested with their employers, the theatre companies. Stage directions, not necessarily but quite possibly authorial, from the work of Robert Greene, one of the first-generation playwrights, give some insight into the ethos: 'Exit Venus. Or if you can conveniently, let a chair come down from the top of the stage, and draw her up' (*Alphonsus of Aragon*); 'After a solemn service, enter from the widow's house a service, musical songs of marriages, or a masque, or what pretty triumph you list [desire]' (*James IV*).

It was not until the new century that playwrights began publicly to dispute with actors for control of their texts, and then only those who were concerned to establish a literary status for their work. Ben Jonson famously published *Sejanus* in order to deliver the *real* text, unblemished by theatrical intervention. (However, the earlier quarto of his *Every Man Out of His Humour* refers only to length. According to the title page, it contains 'more than hath been Publicly Spoken or Acted'.) The title page of the 1623 quarto of John Webster's *The Duchess of Malfi* is even more explicit in its promise that this is 'the perfect and exact copy, with diverse things printed that the length of the play would not bear in presentment'. The important point here is that it seems to have been a theatrical convention, though not a dramatic one, that plays that were too long, like *Richard III* and *Hamlet*, should be cut in performance. This is something that Humphrey Moseley takes for granted in his address to the readers at the opening of the 1647 collection of plays by Francis Beaumont and John Fletcher. It is far too readily assumed that the published texts that have come down to us, Shakespeare's and others', represent the play as originally performed.

The convention that plays could, even should, accommodate a mixture of styles was recognized from the start. Elizabethan dramatists found their source material in a variety of places, in the Latin classics, in the Bible, in popular chapbooks and ballads, in 'true' accounts of squalid murders. A purist theatre would have demanded that the 'high' language of poetry be used throughout in plays that warranted it. There were English precedents for a wholly poetic drama, but the new theatre wished also to preserve the kind of boisterous comedy which served as a playground for specialist clowns and seasonal romps. Over time, it became conventional to divide dramatic dialogue into verse for characters of high social status and demotic prose for common-ers. The iambic pentameter, to be sure, carries poetic speech as close to the rhythm of normal conversation as formal verse can hope to get, but it also invites an indulgence in the fanciful imagery in which Renaissance poets delighted. Poets were highly esteemed in early modern England, and the literary aspirations of the new young playwrights escaped into the drama, where they were largely disregarded by the arbiters of taste. Broadly speaking, Shakespeare followed the conventional verse/prose division. He was one of many contemporary playwrights with a separate reputation as a poet. When three of them, Ben Jonson, George Chapman, and John Marston, teamed up to write a play set among London tradesmen (*Eastward Ho!*, 1605), they voluntarily confined themselves to prose.

As a corollary to the promotion of a mixed drama, the convention of building a play on a principle of stylistically contrasting scenes, sometimes through an alternation of main- and sub-plot, was quickly established. A scene began with the entrance of one or more of its participants and ended when the last of its participants left the stage (crossing, if the actors got their timing right, those of their colleagues who would begin the next scene). The encouragement to the performers was to play each scene for maximum effect. The scenic unit was responsible only to itself. Dramaturgical convention rated contrast above consistency.

Established conventions

By the 1590s, when the Elizabethan drama reached maturity and Shakespeare confirmed his promise, some of the essential conventions of playwriting were, as we have seen, already in place:

(1) that, since the company repertoires called for a new piece every other week, plays should generally be written quickly (for the Admiral's Men at the Rose, this was sometimes in as little as three or four weeks).

(2) that plays should be of a length approximating to the 'two hours traffic' cited in the Prologue to *Romeo and Juliet*.

(3) that a mixture of 'high' and 'low' styles in general, and of verse and prose in particular, should be seen as not only acceptable but even preferable.

(4) that the building block should be the scene, nothing larger (the idea of what we now call an 'Act' was in dispute).

(5) that successive scenes should be stylistically contrasted (perhaps alternating main- and sub-plot).

We need constantly to remind ourselves that this was not a theatre in which actors endeavoured to delude audiences into believing that they were not acting. Lines spoken 'aside' were addressed to people wholly visible (and most of them very close) in the afternoon light. Nor should the poetic splendours of Marlovian or Shakespearian soliloquies blind us to their function as props to the dramatic narrative. Actors favoured (they still do) playwrights who kept them in touch with the audience.

The attention paid by literary critics to the work of Shakespeare and his contemporaries has disguised the historical priorities that governed their writing. Many playwrights in the modern theatre write in the *hope* of performance: professional playwrights in the early modern period wrote only on the *promise* of performance. Many of the plays that were staged during those years have not survived, but there is no lost store of unperformed masterpieces. It was in the interest of the acting companies to present to the public the commodities that they had purchased. The implication is clear: it was the material condition of the theatre that determined which plays would be written and, to a considerable extent, how they would be written. The professional playwright could not afford to specialize: if the commissioning company wanted a bloody tragedy to give variety to a comedy-dominated repertoire, a tragedy was what he wrote.

Playwrights needed to know how to work *with* the actors they were working *for* if a second commission was to follow the first. We have no reliable record of the interaction between players and writers, but it is no more than a commonsense assumption that the relationship was intrinsic to any effective theatrical enterprise. Playwrights were in no position to demand that the players should speak the words, and only the words, that they had written. Any theatrical event is the outcome of negotiation, and the controlling authority here was the players'. A tactful playwright (and there is presumptive evidence that Shakespeare was supremely tactful) would know when to concede and, unlike Ben Jonson, would avoid public recrimination in the wake of performance. We cannot identify the collaboration between writers and actors in the speaking of the text in the playhouse because we have only the published versions to hand, but we can be sure that such collaboration was taken for granted at the time. A scribal copy of the actor Edward Alleyn's title-role in Robert Greene's *Orlando Furioso* survives, with alterations in Alleyn's handwriting. It is unlikely that the actor felt obliged to seek the author's approval. The buyer had every right to tinker with the object he had bought. A proprietorial playwright in search of malleable actors was more likely to find them in the boys' companies, a fact which may go some way towards explaining why some of the proudest poets of the period sold their plays to them rather than to their adult counterparts.

Collaboration between writers has been much more often the subject of critical discourse than the elusive collaboration between writers and actors. Inasmuch as it speeded composition, and enabled reckless livers like Thomas Dekker to take on three or four commissions at a time, it was a logical response to market forces. G. E. Bentley has calculated that up to half of the plays produced by professional dramatists between 1590 and 1642 'incorporated the writing at some date of more than one man'.[2] These playwrights would have been intrigued by the efforts of later scholars to determine who exactly wrote what, having themselves so little sense of intellectual ownership in the provision of plays. Collaboration has its pitfalls (the character Francis Quicksilver is only nominally the same man throughout *Eastward Ho!*), but its objective was to produce a seamless artefact. Once sold to the players, that artefact rarely settled into fixity. Henslowe's papers are dotted with references to payments made to writers to add new scenes to old plays, not their own, and modern editors (of Shakespeare in particular) are confronted with new and newer questions about the nature of a dramatic text. Which of the versions of Christopher Marlowe's *Doctor Faustus* and Shakespeare's *King Lear* should take precedence? Which came first, Shakespeare's *The Taming of the Shrew* or the shorter and generally cruder play published anonymously in 1594 as *The Taming of a Shrew*? These are not, in themselves, matters that touch on convention, but they open the way to an appreciation of the early modern playwrights' attitudes to their own work and that of others.

What we would call originality was neither sought nor admired by Shakespeare's contemporaries. Fine writing was 'fine' by virtue of its proximity to classical models. The imitation of best practice was a writer's trade, and it was conventionally acceptable to copy. Whole passages of *Julius Caesar*, for example, display a compositional method that would lead today to accusations of plagiarism. Shakespeare wrote them with a copy of Thomas North's translation of Plutarch's *Lives of the Noble Grecians and Romans* propped open beside him, converting North's prose to iambic pentameters with the minimum of necessary adjustment. John Webster kept a commonplace book in which he noted, for future redeployment, striking excerpts from anything he read, or perhaps even heard in the playhouse. Both linguistically and structurally, playwrights set out to write like other admired playwrights. The popularity of Thomas Kyd's *The Spanish Tragedy* inspired a sequence of emulative Senecan revenge plays; Marlovian rhetoric was imitated by lesser poets; Ben Jonson's *Every Man In His Humour* established a new fashion in the creation of comic types. In following where theatrical success led, the dramatists acknowledged the conventional authority of imitation at the same time as they gratified their playhouse masters.

Dramatists knew the playing companies they were writing for, and it is, on the face of it, strange that virtually all the plays of the period call for several more characters than there were actors to play them. This had, of course, been a feature of the small household troupes (four men and a boy) earlier in the sixteenth century, but the professional companies were larger, probably twelve (ten men and two boys) to begin with, rising to sixteen. It might reasonably be expected that a convention matching the number of characters to the number of available actors would have been quickly established. That it was not is among the best evidence we have that actors and audiences enjoyed the alternative convention, that of doubling. It became a requirement that plays be so plotted as to allow time for costume changes among the lesser roles. If the playwright's manuscript was deficient in that respect, and he could not always know which parts would be doubled, the actors would arrange for an insertion of some kind; a soliloquy was a likely favourite. Surviving cast-lists are too fragmentary to confirm the intelligent supposition that, rather than being hidden, doubling was often made conspicuous. Audiences enjoyed hunting for significance—a murderous Casca doubling with the murdered Cinna in *Julius Caesar*, the murdered Duncan doubling with Banquo's mysterious third murderer in *Macbeth*. If the playwright did not make the connections himself, the actors would do it for him.

It should also be noted that doubling drew attention to theatrical costume at a time when distinctions of clothing were of real social significance. Sumptuary laws, until they were relaxed by James I, stipulated strictly what could or could not be worn by the different ranks in society, and it was only by virtue of their profession that actors were enabled to flout the regulations when they were on stage. In general, playwrights could rely on the audience's acceptance of the convention that a well-known and easily recognized actor's change of costume signified a change of role. There was, though, a significant exception to this general rule. Disguise is an integral feature of so many plays that it required a convention of its own. There is no mystery about the fact that, whilst all the members of the audience can recognize the 'true' character behind the disguise, none of the actors can: the impenetrability of disguise is defiantly a convention. It is as if the costume is all that is visible to define the person.

This is a convention that has extra resonances when the disguised actor is a boy playing a woman pretending to be a man. There can be no resolution to speculations about the erotic charge released into the playhouse by this sexually ambiguous figure. It is noticeable, though, that Shakespeare goes to great lengths to draw attention to the transvestite fiction when he wishes the audience to respond to it, and the sexual innu-endoes that exploit it in the drama of the period are heavily underlined. We cannot, of course, recover the impact of the physical presence of the boy/girl in the intimate location of the playhouse, where eyes and gestures can augment the activity of the words; even so, it may be that, accepting the convention unquestioningly, Elizabethan audiences read the gender in the costume and found no difficulty in ignoring the contradictory person wearing it.

Costume served a further purpose in guiding the audience's understanding of the disposition of power within the play. If we are to follow the intricate plots and counter-plots, the interaction of sub-plots and main-plots, the options open to characters, it is vital that we know where the authority lies. There was no cast-list to offer prior warning to the wary spectator. Dramaturgical convention ensured that each entering character should declare himself, or be declared, very quickly, but immediately recognizable distinctions of costume were spectacular aids to dramaturgy, and playwrights knew that they could rely on them. Not always careful with their dramatists, the acting companies were meticulous about costume.

The new drama declared its English heritage by its unruliness. The Aristotelian uni-ties of action, time, and place had informed the drama of classical Rome, to which many playwrights looked as a model, but the native narrative tradition proved more powerful in the long run. The unfolding of a single action over two hours had little appeal to an audience hungry for variety, and the young writers responded to their appetite by providing them with dramatic narratives that were profuse even when they were not diffuse.

The professional theatre's standing was enhanced in 1583, when Elizabeth I agreed to become the patron of a company of players. It might have been expected that the Queen's Men would favour the kind of chaste, neo-Platonic drama advocated in Philip Sidney's *Apology for Poetry* (published posthumously in 1595, but circulating in manuscript in the early 1580s), but this seems never to have been the intention. At the centre of the company was the charismatic clown, Richard Tarlton, and opportunistic playwrights provided material that mixed clowns and kings in just the way that Sidney abhorred. The few plays that survive from the repertoire of the Queen's Men valorize spectacle and admit a multiplicity of action.

Whilst unity of action could be silently disregarded, the preparedness to make the passage of time a feature of dramatic narrative called sometimes for a justifying con-vention. At its simplest, as in the prologue to Act Four of *The Winter's Tale*, convention permitted the interruption of the narrative flow in order that the audience be fully informed of the amount of time that has passed since the end of the previous scene, but there are many plays in which time is a physical presence almost as palpable as the actors. From the moment when Doctor Faustus pledges his soul to Mephistopheles to his excruciating final soliloquy, time is a character in Marlowe's play. This, it is fair to say, is artistry beyond convention, but the ease with which Shakespeare handles the passage of time in plays as various as *A Midsummer Night's Dream* and *Macbeth* is the outcome of a conventional agreement that the playwright would communicate to the audience anything about time that was essential to their understanding.

Much the same applies to issues of place. On a bare stage, with only rare assistance from free-standing scenic units, the actors had to carry the audience with them from, say, Duke Frederick's court to the Forest of Arden in *As You Like It*. Most of the successive scenes in Shakespeare's plays involve a change of location. The convention was that, at the opening of each scene, the characters brought the new place on with them, but where there was special significance in the location, dramatists would conventionally alert the audience to it. Only exceptionally did locations change in mid-scene. An odd example occurs in *The Pinner of Wakefield*, in which Robert Greene may have had a hand. There, Jenkin risks a beating from the Shoemaker of Bradford, and attempts to prevaricate by pointing out the inappropriateness of their present location. The subsequent exchange reads as follows:

> SHOEMAKER: Come, sir, will you go to the town's end now, sir?
> JENKIN: Aye, sir, come—
>   Now we are at the town's end, what say you now?
>
> (916-18)

The two actors ask the audience to believe that, simply by walking a few paces across the platform, they have reached the far end of the town. There can be little doubt that the intended effect was comic, but, to make a joke out of the breaking of a convention, the joker needed to be confident of the normative stability of that convention.

The opening lines of Shakespearian scenes are full of necessary information: Petruccio begins Act One Scene Two of *The Taming of the Shrew* with 'Verona, for a while I take my leave / To see my friends in Padua' (1–2); Richard II tells us, at the opening of Act Five Scene Five, that 'I have been studying how I may compare / This prison where I live unto the world' (1–2); we know we are in a graveyard at the start of Act Five of *Hamlet* because two clowns enter carrying spades and one of them asks, 'Is she to be buried in Christian burial that wilfully seeks her own salvation?' (1–2). These are random examples plucked from a rich store.

Scene-endings are equally indicative of theatrical conventions on the curtainless open stage. Actors could not conclude a scene *in medias res*. They needed the playwright's help to motivate the long walk to the upstage door. These are the closing words of four of the first scenes of *Coriolanus*: 'Let's along'; 'Farewell'; 'Well then, farewell'; 'Let's fetch him off, or make remain alike'. The actors are given a simple opportunity to tell the audience that they are now about to leave this place and go to another one.

Locational conventions are more strictly theatrical than dramatic, but a working playwright needed to be familiar with the liberties and constraints of the playhouse. The popular support for sprawling, large-scale historical chronicles was contingent on the conventional choreography of battle scenes. Stage deaths relied on conventions of performance, not least in the disposal of the corpses (did all the dead bodies at the end of *Hamlet* get carried off or did all but Hamlet himself simply stand up and walk away?) Playwrights would not have written crowd-scenes unless the companies had a system for staging them. The innumerable tropes of madness indicate the existence of a traditional style of presenting mental distraction that excited theatregoers. The crowd-pleasing tricks of witches, magicians, devils, conjurors, and sprites would not have been proposed by playwrights if the acting companies could not pull them off.

Shakespeare was as ready as any of his contemporaries to make hay in the playhouse sun. As a shareholding member of London's leading company, he was in a peculiarly privileged position. Unlike a freelance writer like Thomas Dekker, who might feel the need to contribute to as many as eight plays in a single year, Shakespeare seems rarely to have written more than two. Under less pressure from deadlines, he could afford to write alone, something which has fed the bardic myth of the lonely genius. The myth is fatally flawed by its neglect of theatrical collaboration. We cannot know, but may at least wonder, whether Shakespeare would have created the great tragic roles without Richard Burbage to play them, or the great female roles in the absence of one or two uncommonly talented boys. The point being made here is that Shakespeare was as much the servant of the playhouse as he was its master. The conventions outlined here informed his work as fully as that of his contemporaries. It was through respect for the conventions that playwrights confirmed their respect for the audience. To break them was to risk making fools of the public.

FURTHER READING

Bentley, Gerald Eades. *The Profession of Dramatist in Shakespeare's Time, 1590–1642* (Princeton: Princeton University Press, 1971). The most lucid and comprehensive study of the working conditions of professional playwrights.

Carson, Neil. *A Companion to Henslowe's Diary* (Cambridge: Cambridge University Press, 1988). A careful investigation of the enigmatic papers of Philip Henslowe, detailing his interest in the operation of the Admiral's Men at the Rose and Fortune playhouses.

Dent, R. W. *John Webster's Borrowing* (Berkeley and Los Angeles: University of California Press, 1960). A work of detailed detection revealing the compositional method of a playwright who may have copied from other writers more comprehensively than his contemporaries.

Knutson, Roslyn L. *The Repertory of Shakespeare's Company, 1594–1613* (Fayetteville: University of Arkansas Press, 1991). A study which places the choice of plays by the Chamberlain's/King's Men firmly in its commercial context.

McMillin, Scott and Sally-Beth MacLean. *The Queen's Men and their Plays* (Cambridge: Cambridge University Press, 1998). A pioneering study of England's premier touring company and the plays they performed.

Masten, Jeffrey. 'Playwrighting: Authorship and Collaboration'. In *A New History of Early English Drama*, ed. J. D. Cox and D. S. Kastan (New York: Columbia University Press, 1997), pp. 357–82. A well-informed essay that challenges traditional attitudes to collaboration. This is one of a number of relevantly informative essays in this excellent collection.

Rutter, Carol C. *Documents of the Rose Playhouse* (Manchester: Manchester University Press, 1984). A collection of documents with informative editorial commentary. This book usefully complements Neil Carson's and fills out available knowledge of the practices of the Admiral's Men, chief rivals of Shakespeare's company, the Chamberlain's Men.

Styan, J. L. *Shakespeare's Stagecraft* (Cambridge: Cambridge University Press, 1987). A highly readable, if cautious, approach to Shakespeare's plays in performance. Styan's concern is with theatrical conventions.

Thomson, Peter. *Shakespeare's Professional Career* (Cambridge: Cambridge University Press, 1992). This book charts Shakespeare's career as actor and playwright against the cultural and historical background of his time.

NOTES

1. Jeffrey Masten. 'Playwrighting: Authorship and Collaboration', in *A New History of Early English Drama*, ed. J. D. Cox and D. S. Kastan (New York: Columbia University Press, 1997), p. 375.
2. G. E. Bentley. *The Profession of Dramatist in Shakespeare's Time, 1590–1642* (Princeton: Princeton University Press, 1971), p. 199.

6 | Shakespeare's fellow dramatists

A. R. Braunmuller

Public theatre buildings appeared in England in the late 1560s, and professional performances in those buildings continued until September 1642, when Parliament 'ordained. . .public stage plays shall cease' because 'public sports do not well agree with public calamities'. Officially sanctioned theatrical performance did not resume until 1660, when the 'public calamities' of civil war had ended. During the seventy-five years between the building of the Red Lion theatre (1567), the first specially constructed London public theatre, and Parliament's ordinance, English-language professional theatre had its first great era. William Shakespeare's career spanned about two decades of that extraordinary period. Had he never written a word an actor spoke, many plays written by his predecessors, contemporaries, and successors would still rank among the finest in the English language.

This chapter offers a sketch of what those other playwrights accomplished and emphasizes (1) what Shakespeare might have learned or imitated from his 'fellow dramatists'; and (2) how their plays differ from his.

'Shakespeare's fellow dramatists' were not precisely his fellows, if we think of fellows as people who do the same sort of work we do and like and dislike it in the same degrees. Some fellows drank with him; some acted with him; some praised and envied him; some attacked him; some rewrote what he had written; some wrote what he rewrote; some taught him craft; some borrowed his skills, his characters, and his theatrical inventions; some probably knew him little at all except as a contemporary competitor; some eventually knew him only as a dead, sometimes still-potent commercial rival.

These fellow dramatists can be understood as a succession of artistic 'generations'. That is one way to shape an analysis of their once lived, once lively past. Other analytic models exist—competition, emulation, imitation, divergence, for example. Nor does such an analysis have to base itself in individual dramatists; it can look at theatrical commerce (competition among theatre companies, for example), varieties of dramatic language, or types of plots, kinds of subject matter, issues of gender or class. These models are all different ways to organize a narrative about the theatrical past. Several, including the generational one, are employed here. But any critical history, any story, remains one among many possible tales.

The uses of theatrical tradition

John Ford's *'Tis Pity She's a Whore* (1632 or thereabouts) imitates, rewrites, and re-conceives many plays first written and performed in the reigns of Elizabeth I (1558–1603) and James I (1603–25). *'Tis Pity* is, probably, a play first performed in a still later reign, Charles I's (1625–49). So far as we can tell, most of Ford's plays reached the stage after Shakespeare died in 1616, and Ford was a member of the generation that knew Shakespeare's plays as powerful commercial presences, but also as theatrical has-beens rather more popular with a nostalgic court-audience than with the *avant-garde* commercial theatregoing public, who sought theatrical novelty. For understandable financial reasons, Ford hoped to displace Shakespeare's plays and everyone else's with his own.

Ford's plays have been portrayed as 'decadent', tired remnants of a glorious theatrical past which Ford cynically pillages. And at first glance that characterization might seem accurate because his plays recall so much that came before. In *'Tis Pity*, Ford's incestuous hero, Giovanni, almost quotes phrases from and nearly re-enacts episodes from Christopher Marlowe's two *Tamburlaine* plays and his *Dr. Faustus*; Shakespeare's *Hamlet, Romeo and Juliet*, and *Julius Caesar*; John Fletcher's *A King and no King* and *The Maid's Tragedy*; John Webster's *Duchess of Malfi*; and various other plays from the preceding decades.

Despite first appearances, these imitations and echoes are Ford's answer to a serious dramatic problem. Rewriting *Romeo and Juliet* as a love-tragedy of brother-sister incest, Ford undertook a difficult task in winning his audience's sympathy for the central couple. One effect of his and his characters' frequent quotation and allusion is to make the play seem part of a known dramatic fabric even while Ford also stresses his play's divergence from almost every play that had come before. Ford seeks to make his deviant subject matter both familiar *and* strange. The aura of other plays in *'Tis Pity* makes the increasingly hysterical and dangerously melodramatic speeches and behaviour of the lovers—Annabella and Giovanni—seem appropriate to a world already 'theatrical'. Ford's artistic purpose would be advanced if his audience spotted at least some of his borrowings from his 'fellow dramatists'.

One of the play's many revenge-obsessed characters, Vasques, outmanipulates a woman, Hippolita, who will eventually become a victim: 'Work you that way, old mole? then I have the wind of you'—a conflation of two phrases from *Hamlet*. One phrase is from Hamlet's conversation with his father's ghost, the other from his angry attack on Rosencrantz and Guildenstern. That *Hamlet*, dating from the middle of Shakespeare's career (performed 1601 or 1602), should be quoted in a play so many years later and in a completely changed dramatic context shows its popularity and its memorableness.

Shakespeare's *Hamlet* was indeed an instantly influential play. Allusions appear in John Marston's *The Malcontent* (1604 or earlier) and *The Dutch Courtesan* (1603–4).

Yorick's skull caught Thomas Dekker's imagination in *The Honest Whore Part One* (c.1603–4), and Thomas Middleton revisits it a few years later in *The Revenger's Tragedy* (1606). Yet, Shakespeare was not the first English dramatist to write a *Hamlet*. Allusions and purported quotations of a now-vanished *Hamlet*, possibly by Thomas Kyd, exist about a decade before Shakespeare's version. One inference is that the story itself has power and fascination enough to command audiences over many years. Less obvious, perhaps, is how this instance of what one might think Shakespeare's best-known, even his most characteristic play, illustrates the density and sophistication of the theatrical world he joined when he came to London about 1590. Yes, there would be his celebrated *Hamlet* to come and, yes, Ford would imitate it many years later, but there was a popular *Hamlet* already on stage when Shakespeare arrived.

Young Shakespeare and his fellows

When Shakespeare, then in his late twenties, came to London, many talented men already wrote for the acting companies and others soon joined them. (All the period's professional dramatists—that is, those who were paid for their work—were male.) A too-tidy term for this founding group is 'the University Wits' because many of the best-remembered were graduates of the universities of Oxford or Cambridge. They are Robert Greene, Thomas Lodge, John Lyly, Christopher Marlowe, Thomas Nashe, and George Peele. One popular story explains the quality of the period's drama by noting the arrival of well-educated people who wrote for the theatre only because they could not find more conventionally dignified jobs that suited their training. And some individuals throughout the era—Lyly, Francis Beaumont, Ben Jonson, and John Marston, for instance—sought and sometimes achieved positions that allowed, or would have allowed, them to abandon professional playwriting for more secure livelihoods and more socially honoured positions. Yet Thomas Kyd, who inaugurated an entire subgenre, revenge tragedy, with his immensely popular *Spanish Tragedy* (c.1587), and Robert Wilson, who wrote highly individual plays for the Queen's Men in the 1580s and later, were successful contemporary dramatists who (like Shakespeare) did not happen to be university graduates. A few years after Shakespeare came to London, Jonson and George Chapman, neither of them university-educated, but both learned, began long and glittering careers in professional theatre.

Two dramatic genres—romantic comedy and historical drama—dominated box-office success in the 1590s when Shakespeare first made his mark. Greene, Lyly, and Peele were especially inventive and prolific in romantic comedy, while various 'fellow drama-tists'—Greene (again), Kyd, Lodge, Marlowe, and Peele (again)—wrote plays based on English, French, Spanish, Roman, Middle-Eastern, Asian, and other fanciful 'histories'.

Lyly wrote almost all his plays for companies of 'boy' actors—young men, some in their mid- or even late-teens, who were trained singers and whose voices had not yet broken at puberty. This combination of talent and material meant that Lyly could write plots ingeniously exploiting sexual and gender ambiguities. In the adult professional theatre, boy actors played most, perhaps all, women's roles. Western theatre depends upon illusion—someone pretending to be someone else for our pleasure. A company entirely of boys could develop this basic deceit far indeed. Every male actor was not merely pretending to be someone else, some other male character, but could be pretending to be a male pretending to be a female. If so, then why not a male pretending to be a female pretending to be a male? And why end the pretence there, or anywhere? Operatic composers and their libretto writers from Monteverdi to Mozart to Richard Strauss have seen the possibilities for plot complication, amorous confusion, comic dismay, and surprise. Lyly saw the possibilities, too. His dramatic insight is most enjoyably complex in *Gallathea* (c.1583–5), where two fathers attempt to save their beautiful daughters from rape (as females) and death by disguising them as boys, only to have the boys-who-are-playing-girls-who-are-playing-boys fall in love and quite explicitly recognize the likelihood that they are of the same (whichever) sex. They nonetheless affirm their love and devotion, whatever the gods, chance, fate, or fathers decide. Shakespeare's *As You Like It* and *Twelfth Night* echo the same delicious possibilities, but not more delicately than Lyly's play.

Gallathea takes place in a fully realized English county, Lincolnshire, and rejoices in local folklore. Vivid memories of the county's historical invasion by the Danes haunt the play, but it is also thoroughly populated by the gods of Greece and Rome. So, too, Shakespeare's comedies, tragedies, and tragicomedies occur in Illyria, northern Italy, Athens, Sicily, Bohemia, Roman Britain, and the eastern Mediterranean. Shakespeare's foreign countrysides also seem oddly English, their cities Londonish. Lyly invents his Humberside and infuses it and his other plays, such as *Endymion* (1588), with English references and the classical knowledge he learned at Oxford. Just so Shakespeare invents Herne and his oak in *The Merry Wives of Windsor*, a very local Windsor that also includes folk oddly knowledgeable about classical myth, or an Illyrian *Twelfth Night* that alludes to sixteenth-century English tourist attractions like the Elephant Inn in London and the Great Bed in Ware.

More obviously than Shakespeare, Greene, Marlowe, and Peele ranged far in time and space for their plays. Peele wrote an adventure-drama, *The Battle of Alcazar* (c.1589), about European warfare in North Africa; it is notable for its even-handed portrayal of black characters. Greene made a romantic history from early sixteenth-century Anglo-Scottish conflict (*The Scottish History of James IV*, c.1590) and turned his hand to *Alphonsus*, *King of Aragon*, unhistorical even by the loose standards of most Elizabethan history plays and no less a romantic fiction. Romanticized 'history' also appears in Greene's *Orlando Furioso* (c.1591), an exceedingly unhistorical account of Ludovico Ariosto's Italian romantic epic hero, Roland ('Orlando'). Roland—so the stories went—fought nobly in the medieval struggles between Christianity and Islam and also went mad for love. Violent chivalric acts and 'furious' (insane) amatory ones became staples of popular Elizabethan theatre.

Christopher Marlowe's two-part *Tamburlaine* (c.1587–88) probably initiated and certainly propagated a dramatic combination of violence, love, and exotic lands and peoples. World-conquering Tamburlaine proposed a hero no one could resist and all might admire. Marlowe's invention spawned many others—especially George Chapman's much later French intriguer-heroes (in *Bussy D'Ambois* and *The Revenge of Bussy*) and some of the inhabitants of John Fletcher's fantasized Mediterranean city-states, for example, but also the marvellously wicked Vindice ('Vengeance'), the clever criminal-hero of Middleton's *The Revenger's Tragedy*. Vindice brought the East closer to 'home' (England) in a fantastic 'Italy', or the Italianate England that dramatists invented to deflect their wild imaginings onto Another Place that was and was not their own country and their own and their audience's feared and desired place.

One way to understand what Lyly, Greene, and the others were doing is to say that they were making local and known to their audiences a rich native and foreign literary and historical past. Another way is to say that they participated in a cultural change that imposed a national, local present upon a long ago past. In so doing they contributed to a cultural shift that made their London, their England, a fit competitor with the greatest western, classical, past civilizations the audience and the writers knew.

Dramatic languages

Tamburlaine arrived in print with a defiant prologue. It accurately describes the hero as 'Threat'ning the world with high astounding terms'—a previously unknown magniloquence for a dramatic speaker. Those 'astounding terms' are conveyed in a mellifluous iambic pentameter blank verse, full of pomp and classical allusion, which the prologue indirectly praises by scorning 'jigging veins of rhyming mother wits' and offering to 'lead' the audience 'to the stately tent of war'. Deciding to attack the Persian emperor, Tamburlaine asks his followers:

> Is it not brave to be a king, Techelles?
> Usumcasane and Theridamus,
> Is it not brave to be a king,
> And ride in triumph through Persepolis?

Ambition, bravery, exoticism are all here, mostly conveyed through the wonderful use of exotic proper nouns—Techelles, Usumcasane, Theridamus, Persepolis. What Ben Jonson admiringly called 'Marlowe's mighty line' was instantly imitated, and his iambic pentameter—used dramatically as long before as Thomas Sackville and Thomas Norton's by-the-classical-rules *Gorboduc* (1565)—became the standard for serious plays and others, partly because Marlowe's work was so successful (see also Chapter 8). Marlowe's style was new and individual, but it was only one of many Elizabethan innovations in the way dramatic speech was written. In both drama and prose fiction,

Lyly popularized a highly artificial style, euphuism (named after his proto-novel, *Euphues*, 1578), which uses elaborate similes, often from imaginary natural history, combined with lots of repeated verbal sounds and structured by antithesis and parallelism. Here, a speaker in *Gallathea* explains how woes first came to Lincolnshire:

fortune, constant in nothing but inconstancy, did change her copy as the people their custom, for the land being oppressed by Danes, who instead of sacrifice committed sacrilege, instead of religion, rebellion, and made a prey of that in which they should have made their prayers, tearing down the temple even with the earth, being almost equal with the skies, enraged so the god who binds the winds in the hollows of the earth that he caused the seas to break their bounds, sith men had broke their vows, and to swell as far above their reach as men had swerved beyond their reason.

Falstaff parodies this distinctive style in *Henry IV Part One* (c.1597), presumably because it sounded laughable and old-fashioned by the end of the 1590s:

Harry, I do not only marvel where thou spendest thy time, but also how thou art accompanied. For though the camomile, the more it is trodden on, the faster it grows, yet youth, the more it is wasted, the sooner it wears. . . . For Harry, now do I not speak to thee in drink, but in tears; not in pleasure, but in passion; not in words only, but in woes also.

(2.5.364-80)

George Peele, too, ranged through a remarkable number of different verse forms in his plays and created an effective prose for *The Old Wives Tale* (c.1593) where country characters and courtly ones and fantastic magician figures—not to mention a talking bear—mingle their distinctive ways of speaking.

Peele's play, like *Gallathea* and Greene's magic-filled *Friar Bacon and Friar Bungay* (c.1589) and others, is set in recognizably English countryside, or one imaginary version of such a countryside. Plays about present-day localities, filled with ordinary Elizabethan events and ordinary Elizabethan people, though they sometimes mixed with disguised royalty and some preposterous events, formed a popular strand of entertainment in the 1590s and continued into the next century. Like plays about English history, these plays presumably responded to and satisfied an audience that wished to see itself and to learn where its present originated.

Dramatic London and its audiences

Showing the audience itself could become much more precise than the antics in a play by Lyly, Peele, or Greene. Early in the seventeenth century there appeared 'city comedy', a series of plays seemingly precise in their representation of London's commercial elite, who lived and traded in the 'City' of London, as distinct from Westminster and other locales outside the city's medieval walls. Some of the greatest English comedies—by Ben Jonson, George Chapman, and Thomas Middleton, for example—explore this proto-capitalistic, mercantile milieu with savage delight in the crassness and class-ambition of City dwellers and depict them as cheats who are themselves cheated and humiliated. Like their often complex plots, the record of daily life in London the plays offer is highly artificial and can produce, as in Jonson's *The Alchemist* (1610) and *Bartholomew Fair* (1614) or Middleton's *A Chaste Maid in Cheapside* (1613) or the collaborative *Eastward Ho!* (1605), complications so fantastic even their perpetrators sometimes lose track. More benign in its satire, Francis Beaumont's *The Knight of the Burning Pestle* (c.1607), a multi-layered comedy, parodies citizens' old-fashioned romantic taste and cultural ambition while also allowing them some pointed remarks about purportedly sophisticated cultural norms.

Comic complications produce delighted laughter, but the satire, cheerful or otherwise, in these plays may testify to a deep anxiety over an erosion of (imaginary?) 'old' values when they encountered commercial greed, social ambition, and, the dramatists suggest, the inevitable drive to destroy others in order to create one's self.

In the first decade of the seventeenth century and after, comedy and tragicomedy began to address more stringently than earlier the way social interactions generate individual identities and sense-of-self. This process could be represented as benign and reconciling, as it is in many romantic comedies of the 1590s and explicitly so in the blue-collar London of Thomas Dekker's *The Shoemaker's Holiday* (1599), a fantasia on a commonwealth where good things happen to good people, kings honour virtue be it never so humble, and every one knows and cheerfully accepts his or her social place. Grimmer analyses appear in Thomas Heywood's *A Woman Killed with Kindness* (1603) and George Chapman's *The Widow's Tears* (c.1605). Heywood's title plays upon the ambiguity of the Elizabethan senses of *kindness*—both our modern sense and a now-lost sense of 'naturalness'—and his drama depicts a husband, John Frankford, who destroys his adulterous wife Anne by simultaneously depriving her of her social, matrimonial place as his spouse and treating her with the utmost 'kindness'. Neither violent nor overtly abusive, Frankford effectively denies his repentant wife an identity. She dies, and he has acted 'naturally', has been 'kindly', in a way that lets us understand how unnatural human nature can be. The play's prologue warns, 'Look for no glorious state; our muse is bent / Upon a barren subject, a bare scene'. Charles Lamb called Heywood 'a sort of prose Shakespeare', and his unadorned play about 'a barren subject' has great power without Marlovian or Shakespearian 'high' characters, grand political events, or rousing rhetoric.

The Widow's Tears, Chapman's innovative two-plot play, displays a yet more terrible view of human sexual and social identities. Unlike other multiple-plot plays from the era, *The Widow's Tears* does not present its two plots in (roughly) alternating scenes. Rather, it presents them successively, completing the first at mid-play and then turning to the second. The first plot involves poor-but-aristocratic Tharsalio in successful pursuit of the young, beautiful, and rich Countess Eudora, a widow who has vowed never to remarry. So far, her situation has a general similarity to Olivia's in *Twelfth Night*, and the results are approximately the same: it is foolish to resist love and sex; life is for living; beautiful people deserve each other. And so Eudora and Tharsalio wed at the play's mid-point, just as Olivia and Sebastian (with help from Viola-Cesario) do at the end of Shakespeare's comedy.

Chapman's play has not ended. He now turns to Tharsalio's elder brother, Lysander (whose name literally means 'loose man' and may mockingly recall Leander, the mythical Greek lover who died for Hero). Long married to the famously devoted Cynthia, Lysander takes inordinate pride in his wife's reputation. Indeed, her devotion *is* his identity. Lysander has extracted and Cynthia has given a vow never to remarry should he die. Provoked by his brother's smug complacency, Tharsalio nastily suggests 'May be you trust too much' and accurately observes, 'Your only way to be resolved is to die and make trial of her'. Lysander spirals so far into paranoia and doubt that he decides to 'rise again', that is, to fake his own death and 'return' (a parody resurrection) to observe how his 'widow' behaves.

Her behaviour is just as his maniacal jealousy would demand, but Lysander goes further and (in disguise) successfully seduces his own 'widow'. Enraged at having cuckolded himself, Lysander drops his disguise and denounces his wife. Tharsalio has warned Cynthia of the trick, and she professes to have known her husband-seducer all along, as indeed she may have—the play is quite deliberately silent on the point. Trust, faith, and marriage are all wrecked; yet the marriage must continue. This ending mixes disillusionment with resignation. From some perspectives—perhaps Puck's 'What fools these mortals be!'—this sequence might be 'comic', though painful. The audience has been tricked into believing that the two plots will somehow identically and comically show silly human vanities rebuked and the now clear-eyed couples living happily ever after—as of course Eudora and Tharsalio conventionally will, and Cynthia and Lysander cannot.

New heroes

Heywood's and Chapman's plays illustrate an important trend in early seventeenth-century London theatre—the increasing centrality of female characters. Female *characters*, that is, though not yet female actors, who did not appear publicly until after 1660. The trend also appears in some of Shakespeare's post-1600 tragedies (Lady Macbeth, Cleopatra) and tragicomedies (Hermione in *The Winter's Tale*, Innogen in *Cymbeline*). The range of characterizations among his fellow dramatists' plays is large. In particular, John Webster, Thomas Middleton, and John Fletcher created unusually rewarding female roles which typically differed from many Shakespearian roles in that these dramatists' adult women are sexually active and bluntly forthright about their physical and emotional needs.

Webster's two tragic heroines, Vittoria Corombona (*The White Devil*, c.1612) and the Duchess in *The Duchess of Malfi* (c.1614), struggle against various forms of social, specifically masculine, resistance to their desires. Vittoria seeks adulterous pleasure outside a socially prominent but otherwise unsatisfying marriage. She eventually joins her paramour, the Duke of Bracciano, in a marriage first engineered and then destroyed by his political opponents. The widowed Duchess of Malfi—she has no personal name, only a political title—secretly marries her honest though non-aristocratic steward, Antonio. Her two brothers oppose the marriage for selfish, even incestuous, reasons, and employ a fascinating figure, Bosola, as their spy and eventually, their assassin.

The Duchess's principled resistance to her brothers and her calm acceptance of death eventually cause Bosola, a man who

> Would be as lecherous, covetous, or proud,
> Bloody, or envious, as any man,
> If he had the means to be so:—

to seek to save the Duchess's remaining family. A series of ironic reversals, what he calls 'direful misprision', leads to disaster for Bosola and those he would save. Similarly, the fifth act of *The White Devil* reveals a sequence of political schemers falling one after another to successively more devious schemers. In each case, disaster and failure follow what seems to be triumph. In both plays, there remains only an existential shrug of despair. One heroine dies saying, 'I am Duchess of Malfi still', a proud but futile remark. Vittoria's brother Flamineo claims,

> I do not look
> Who went before, nor who shall follow me;
> No, at myself I will begin and end.
> While we look up to heaven we confound
> Knowledge with knowledge.

His sister dies as ignorantly and intransigently: 'My soul, like to a ship in a black storm, / Is driven I know not whither'.

Fletcher created strong-willed and blunt enough heroines, but generally preferred to write titillating scenes where physical violence on female characters, incest, and sexual assault hover as never-quite-realized possibilities. Evadne, the king's mistress and Amintor's contemptuous wife in *The Maid's Tragedy* (1610 or 1611), eventually decides to kill her lover as a strained way to restore her honour. She ties the king to his bed in what he thinks is erotic play and then stabs him to death. As she sneaks away from the bedroom, two gentlemen of the king's retinue plan a future rape: ' 'Tis a fine wench; we'll have a snap at her one of these nights as she goes from him'.

As this nasty remark and, more important, Evadne's regicide and eventual death indicate, sex and politics are deeply intertwined in early seventeenth-century plays. In Thomas Middleton's *Women Beware Women* (c.1621) and Middleton and Thomas Rowley's *The Changeling* (1622), patriarchal assumptions and demands are both marital and political. The dramatists locate their tragic conflicts in the contradictions between those patriarchal assumptions and the central female characters' demand for freedom of choice and personal happiness. Beatrice-Joanna (*The Changeling*) and Bianca

(*Women Beware Women*) have numerous flaws. They are egotistical, selfish, impolitely outspoken, mistaken, and materialistic—just like Tamburlaine, or Hamlet, or Bussy D'Ambois. Those 'heroes' have many of the same weaknesses and make many of the same disastrous errors. The important difference? Female characters are here granted the will and independence once given only to male characters. At the same time, Bianca and Beatrice-Joanna seek their happiness, however mistakenly or madly defined, in a social and political world that resists and constricts them not only as individuals but as women.

The Changeling may be the early seventeenth century's finest tragedy following those of Shakespeare and Webster. Like many plays throughout the English Renaissance, it is a collaborative work, as many earlier plays had been. Here the known collaborators are the authors, but their colleagues in performance were also always collaborators. John Fletcher, who collaborated with Shakespeare and then succeeded him as principal dramatist for the King's Men, collaborated with many other 'fellow' dramatists— Francis Beaumont and Massinger and Middleton among them—and it is not always possible to specify Fletcher's contribution. He seems, however, to have introduced or at least very characteristically marked a new kind of tragicomedy. That new form emphasizes sexual situations and portentous political and psychological confusions, only to conclude happily and, usually, through unexpected and sometimes rather fallacious plot devices. By contrast, Shakespearian tragicomedies emphasize wrongs, suffering, and penitence, often in explicitly Christian terms. Later playwrights tended to follow Fletcher's formulae, but their differences from Shakespeare's practice late in his career can be exaggerated. Both Shakespeare and Fletcher favour sensational situations, often omit or just sketch important plot links, and rely on eye-popping coincidences. Even in terms of sexual explicitness Fletcher is not always so much franker or coarser than Shakespeare, as a comparison of the (female) brothel scenes in *Pericles* (c.1609) with the (male) brothel scenes in Fletcher and Massinger's *The Custom of the Country* (c.1619) shows.

John Dryden, the great Restoration dramatist and critic, spoke for his later 'fellow dramatists' and their audiences when he praised Beaumont and Fletcher for their writing's polite refinement. They wrote, he says, plots designed more closely on classical rules than Shakespeare did, and 'they understood and imitated the conversation of gentlemen much better'. Whether Dryden is correct about how gentlemen conversed half a century before, he is certainly right when he distinguishes the *way* Fletcher writes from the ways Jonson and Shakespeare write.

As any adept writer does, Fletcher uses verbal contrivance, but he tends to hide his dialogue's many rhetorical structures where Shakespeare, Peele, Kyd, and Marlowe emphasized them as part of the theatrical pleasure they sought to provide. Similarly, Fletcher's verse-syntax more often follows common prose word-order than does the verse of his predecessors. Fletcher's scansion is usually much less strict than all but the latest and loosest in Shakespeare's tragicomedies, and he rarely approaches Shakespeare's dense use of metaphor and other figurative writing.

A concluding example

This chapter began with Parliament's temporary ending of English professional theatre. Just before that end in 1642, James Shirley succeeded Philip Massinger as the 'house' dramatist for the King's Men, the premier theatrical company. Shirley and Massinger followed John Fletcher and William Shakespeare as London's most important dramatists. Norton, Sackville, Lyly, Marlowe, Peele, Kyd, Greene, and Lodge were all dead before 1600 or had abandoned the theatre. All this before many of Shakespeare's best-known plays were performed. Chapman, Jonson, Marston, Middleton, Heywood, and Dekker succeeded them as Shakespeare's 'fellows'. Many of them wrote for many more years and were joined by Beaumont and Fletcher, Webster and Massinger, Ford and Shirley.

This chapter concludes, as several of these stories ended, with dramatic language, female heroes, James Shirley, and a London play, *The Lady of Pleasure* (1635). Shirley wrote the play for Queen Henrietta Maria's Men, who performed at the Cockpit, then the main competitor for the King's Mens' indoor theatre, the Blackfriars. The 'lady' of *The Lady of Pleasure* is Aretina, Sir Thomas Bornwell's wife and an eager consumer of London's expensive pleasures—dicing, coaches, dancing, gowns, jewels, fancy food and drink, and suitors. Unlike Jacobean 'citizen comedies', this Caroline play has a socially elevated cast, mostly gentlemen, gentry, and minor aristocrats. The Bornwells have come to London from the country; he reluctantly, she happily. Conventionally enough, the play contrasts country virtue and city vice. Shirley satirizes conspicuous consumption well, but the nub of the play is Aretina's consumerist decision to take a lover, the insubstantial Alexander Kickshaw. His is a speaking name; he is a *quelque chose*, a cheap or trivial ornament, a gewgaw. A high-level bawd, Madam Decoy, helps Aretina (successfully disguised as an ancient crone-witch) to sleep with Kickshaw. Ignorant, Kickshaw then boasts about his night of love to Aretina, ' 'Twas a she-devil, too: a most insatiate, abominable devil with a tail thus long'. Appalled at this version of her acts, Aretina soliloquizes, 'I am more deformed. What have I done? My soul is miserable'. As so often, Shirley is borrowing here. In *The Changeling*, Beatrice-Joanna rejects the term 'whore': 'It blasts beauty to deformity . . . you have ruined / What you can ne'er repair again'. Unlike Middleton and Rowley, who follow the horror and tragic glory of illicit love through to death, Shirley has Aretina and Bornwell patch up adultery in an off-stage conversation.

Like John Ford's *'Tis Pity She's a Whore*, with which this chapter began, *The Lady of Pleasure* would not be as it is had not many other plays, Shakespeare's included, been written and performed over the preceding decades. Ford's play is quite an explicit response to, and divergence from, the theatrical tradition he knew so well. Shirley's play uses past plays less explicitly, but no less profoundly. Shakespeare's plays were deeply important in the making of Ford's and Shirley's plays and the plays of other playwrights. So were many plays by their many 'fellow dramatists'.

FURTHER READING

Bluestone, M. and N. Rabkin (eds.). *Shakespeare's Contemporaries*, 2nd edn. (Englewood Cliffs, N.J.: Prentice-Hall, 1970). Collection of previously published essays on non-Shakespearian plays, c.1560–1642. Useful bibliographies.

Braunmuller, A. R. and M. Hattaway (eds.). *The Cambridge Companion to English Renaissance Drama*, 2nd edn. (Cambridge: Cambridge University Press, 2002). Original essays (revised from 1st edn., 1990) on Elizabethan, Jacobean, and Caroline professional, private, and occasional drama and masques. Useful chronology, bibliographies, and bio-bibliographies.

Brown, J. R. and B. Harris (gen. eds.). *Elizabethan Theatre* (London: Edward Arnold, 1966). Essays and bibliographies on plays to 1603.

Brown, J. R. and B. Harris (gen. eds.). *Jacobean Theatre*. Essays and bibliographies on plays to 1625.

Ellis-Fermor, U. *Jacobean Drama*, 4th edn. (London: Methuen, 1958). Influential early study.

Farley-Hills, D. *Jacobean Drama: A Critical Study of the Professional Drama, 1600–25* (Basingstoke: Macmillan, 1988). Chapters devoted to single playwrights.

Ford, B. *The Age of Shakespeare*, rev. edn. (Harmondsworth: Penguin, 1982). Chapters on drama and other writings. Extensive bibliographies and short biographies by B. Vickers, with some annotation.

Forsythe, R. S. *The Relations of Shirley's Plays to the Elizabethan Drama* (1914, rep. New York: Blom, 1965). Comprehensive listing of stock characters and incidents treated as sources and analogues for James Shirley's Caroline plays.

Hunter, G. K. *English Drama, 1586–1642* (Oxford: Clarendon Press, 1997). The most recent synoptic study (see also Wilson's volume, below). Valuable chronology (of theatres, companies, and plays), biographies, selected bibliography.

Kastan, D. S. and P. Stallybrass (eds.). *Staging the Renaissance: Reinterpretations of Elizabethan and Jacobean Drama* (New York: Routledge, 1991). Collection of previously published essays that extends Bluestone and Rabkin's volume (see above).

Klein, D. *The Elizabethan Dramatists as Critics* (New York: Philosophical Library, 1963). Generous anthology of original discussions of many theatrical and literary topics.

Spencer, T. J. B. and S. W. Wells (eds.). *A Book of Masques: In honour of Allardyce Nicoll* (Cambridge: Cambridge University Press, 1964). Editions of numerous masques by Shakespeare's contemporaries with commentary; important critical essay by I. Ekeblad-Ewbank.

Stevens, D. *English Renaissance Theater History: a Reference Guide* (Boston: G. K. Hall, 1982). Comprehensive annotated bibliography of theatre and performance-oriented studies.

Wickham, G., H. Berry, and W. Ingram (eds.). *English Professional Theatre, 1530–1660* (Cambridge: Cambridge University Press, 2000). Large, annotated collection of original documents concerning governmental control, players and playwrights, theatres.

Wilson, F. P. *The English Drama: 1485–1585* (Oxford: Clarendon Press, 1969). Synoptic study of pre-Marlovian drama. Useful bibliography and biographies (by G. K. Hunter).

7 | The language of Shakespeare

David Crystal

You would expect a chapter on language near the beginning of a volume on Shake-speare. After all, that is what you hear and see, as soon as you open a book or watch a play. But that first encounter is deceptive in its apparent ease and obviousness, for we all bring to the book and the theatre our own language; and therein lies the problem. Reading a text is a meeting of minds; and when the minds are separated by 400 years of linguistic change, we must expect some difficulties.

Sometimes the difficulties are immediately apparent: we see a word and have no idea what it means. Sometimes they are hidden: we see a word and, because it looks familiar, we *think* we know what it means. 'False friends', as words of this second type are called, are one of the biggest causes of error when learning a foreign language: we see *demander* in French and think it means 'demand', when actually it means 'ask'. And they are a major source of error in getting to grips with Shakespeare's language too. 'The Duke is humorous', we hear Le Beau say about Duke Frederick (*As You Like It*, 1.2.233) and wonder why such a jocular person should be treating Orlando so nastily; only when we learn that *humorous* in this context means 'moody, tempera-mental, capricious', does the line begin to make some sense.

The discrepancy between Shakespeare's intuitions about language and our own applies to all aspects of language. There are 'false friends' in pronunciation and grammar, too, as well as in the way characters talk to each other. Quite clearly all of this needs to be considered if we are to understand what is going on; and there are really only two ways of doing so. The traditional way is on a 'case by case' basis, using an editor's textual notes to identify the language problems as they turn up in a poem or play. Useful as this approach is, it has several limitations when it comes to developing an awareness of Shakespearian English. No edition has space to explain all the linguistic points, and some editions (because of the thematic approach they have chosen) may actually give very limited information. Also, because our study of individual plays and our theatre visits are usually separated by significant periods of time, it proves difficult to build up an intuition about what is normal in the language of the period in which Shakespeare was writing—Early Modern English.

The second approach offers a more systematic alternative, deriving as it does from the way we learn a foreign language. This is to place Early Modern English in the centre of our attention as early as possible, and try to develop a sense of what the norms of

Shakespearian usage are. It is important to do this, because it is the only way to arrive at a conclusion about Shakespeare's linguistic creativity. As the twentieth-century poet Robert Graves once said, 'a poet . . . must master the rules of English grammar before he attempts to bend and break them'. This principle applies to pronunciation, vocabulary, and discourse too, and to all authors (not just male poets). It also applies to anyone attempting to understand what happens when people are being linguistically creative. To appreciate what Shakespeare did to the language of his time, we must also appreciate the language of his time. This is an old insight, but it is surprisingly still much neglected.

Levels of familiarity

Learning to 'speak Elizabethan' is actually much easier than learning to speak a foreign language, because there are so many continuities between Early Modern English and Modern English. Several linguistic differences can be seen in this exchange between Romeo and Juliet, but none of them poses a serious problem of understanding:

> JULIET: What o'clock tomorrow
>   Shall I send to thee?
> ROMEO: By the hour of nine.
> JULIET: I will not fail; 'tis twenty year till then.
>   I have forgot why I did call thee back.
> ROMEO: Let me stand here till thou remember it.
> JULIET: I shall forget, to have thee still stand there,
>   Rememb'ring how I love thy company.
> ROMEO: And I'll still stay, to have thee still forget,
>   Forgetting any other home but this.
> JULIET: 'Tis almost morning. I would have thee gone—
>   (2.1.212-21)

The two recurrent features, *'tis* and *thou/thee/thy*, still have resonance today: *'tis* may look strange in writing, but it is common in modern English colloquial speech; and *thou* forms are still encountered in some religious and regional expressions. *Forgot* is used for modern standard English *forgotten*, but as the two forms are so close, and as *forgot* is still heard in several non-standard dialects today, there should be no problem. Likewise, though the phrasings *what o'clock* and *by the hour of nine* feel slightly old-fashioned, we can readily interpret them. They too, like *twenty year* (for *twenty years*), are common enough regionally. The only possible difficulty is the sense of *still*, 'constantly'; but as this is so close to one of the modern meanings of the word, 'now as before' (the sense in which I used it three sentences ago), any potential for mis-interpretation is minor. In sum, a modern intuition encountering this dialogue would understand it without special help.

At the opposite extreme, there are extracts such as the following, where the difficulty is evident. Friar Laurence is advising Juliet how to escape from her dilemma. It is a crucial part of the plot, with the mood urgent, so the language needs to be grasped quickly; but the unfamiliar words and phrasing can produce a dip in the level of comprehension just when we do not want it.

> Take thou this vial, being then in bed,
> And this distilling liquor drink thou off,
> When presently through all thy veins shall run
> A cold and drowsy humour; for no pulse
> Shall keep his native progress, but surcease.
> (4.1.93-7)

Every line has at least one word which needs some glossing, and the result is a temporary uncertainty—temporary, because later in the speech there are clearer passages which make it plain what is to happen.

> And in this borrowed likeness of shrunk death
> Thou shalt continue two-and-forty hours,
> And then awake as from a pleasant sleep.
> (4.1.104-6)

People who argue that Shakespeare is unintelligible and inaccessible tend to quote the difficult bits and ignore the easier ones. We should always read the whole of a speech before worrying about the difficulties found in a part of it.

The impression that Elizabethan English is a foreign language is of course reinforced when we find the difficult words used in the expression of a complex thought, or in an extended piece of figurative expression. The situation is not helped by changes in educational practice since Shakespeare's day. Few students now are familiar with the mythology of Classical Greece or Rome, so the use of such names as *Phoebus* and *Phaeton* increases the alien impression of the language. But this is an encyclopedic not a linguistic difficulty—a lack of knowledge of the world (as it existed in Classical times), rather than a lack of knowledge of how to talk about the world. There is no linguistic problem in the sentence which Paris uses to explain why he has not mentioned his feelings to the grieving Juliet: 'Venus smiles not in a house of tears' (4.1.8), but it make no sense until you know who Venus is. She turns out to be the same goddess of love today as she was 400 years ago. This is not a matter of language change. And the same educational point applies to those parts of Shakespeare's text which are indeed in a foreign language—French, Latin, Spanish, and Italian, along with some mock-foreign expressions. In the days when most people learned French and Latin in school, those passages (such as the scenes in *Henry V* where a great deal of French is used) would have posed no problem. Today, they often do.

We should note a third type of difficulty, intermediate between these two extremes, where at one level we understand well enough, and at another level we do not. In

Kent's harangue of Oswald in *King Lear*, so much of the vocabulary is alien that a newcomer to Shakespeare's language can do no more than catch the drift.

A knave; a rascal; an eater of broken meats; a base, proud, shallow, beggarly, three-suited, hundred-pound, filthy worsted-stocking knave; a lily-livered, action-taking knave; a whoreson, glass-gazing, superserviceable, finical rogue; one-trunk-inheriting slave; one that wouldst be a bawd in way of good service . . .

(2.2.13-17)

But newcomers *do* catch the drift, very easily, as they will in all instances of insulting language. At the level of personal interaction, we sense that each of these phrases is demeaning in some way, and we appreciate the cumulative effect, even though at the level of vocabulary there is a lot we may not understand at all. The effect will be unavoidable when we see the speech performed on stage.

No-one would begin the task of learning to speak French by trying to understand passages of complex language first, and the same principle should apply to Shakespearian English. We need to work systematically, disentangling the types of difficulty we find there, so that we leave the really obscure issues (such as the phraseology of Elizabethan property law) until later, and deal with more everyday concerns earlier. When we do this, several major themes emerge.

Old and new within Early Modern English

A crucial part of this perspective is to recognize that this period of the language—as all other periods—is not linguistically homogeneous. In Modern English we sense that some words are current, some old, and some new. People refer to the older usages as 'obsolete words' or 'archaisms', the new usages as 'coinages' or 'neologisms'. It is easy to spot an arriving usage, because its novelty is noticed and usually attracts some degree of comment. Usages which are becoming obsolete are rarely commented upon, and tend to pass away in dignified silence.

Early Modern English was a period of extraordinarily dynamic change. The consequences of the Renaissance were sweeping through the language, and causing not a little consternation among people unsure of how they should react to the thousands of new words being introduced, especially from Latin and Greek. There was a great deal of self-consciousness about usage, and the period is remarkable for its lexical inventiveness and experimentation, to which Shakespeare made his own major contribution.

From a modern perspective, it is difficult to develop an intuition about the archaisms and neologisms of the past; but they are always there. In Shakespeare several can be found in the introductory remarks of Gower to the various scenes in *Pericles*, where we find *iwis* ('indeed') and *hight* ('called'), as well as such older verb forms as *speken* ('speak') and *y-clad* ('clothed'). Other examples include *eyne* ('eyes'), *shoon* ('shoes'), *wight* ('person'), and *eke* ('also'). All of these would have been considered old-fashioned or archaic by the Shakespearian audience. Several take us all the way back to Middle, or Medieval, English.

For neologisms, we are helped by the fact that some of Shakespeare's characters actually tell us that they are dealing with new words and usages. Biron describes the Spanish visitor to court, Don Armado, as 'A man of fire-new words' (*Love's Labour's Lost*, 1.1.176), and Armado himself is well aware of the way language is needed to keep the classes apart: 'the posteriors of this day, which the rude multitude call the afternoon' (5.1.75–76). In *Romeo and Juliet*, Mercutio thinks of Tybalt in the same way:

The pox of such antic, lisping, affecting phantasims, these new tuners of accent! 'By Jesu. a very good blade, a very tall man, a very good whore'.

(2.3.25-7)

Evidently Mercutio is irritated by the use of *very* as an intensifying word with a positive adjective, a linguistic trend which was emerging at the end of the sixteenth century. Also coming into fashion at that time was *accommodate*, which makes Bardolph reflect (*Henry IV Part Two*, 3.2.70–3), the sexual sense of *occupy* ('fornicate') noticed by Doll Tearsheet in an earlier version of the same play, and various new senses of *humour* ('mood', 'whim') which are obsessively used by Nym in *The Merry Wives of Windsor* and elsewhere.

That there was a level of style in which 'hard words' were the norm is plain from the many mistaken attempts at these words—malapropisms—put into the mouths of ordinary people, such as Mistress Quickly/Hostess, Dogberry, and various clowns. Lancelot says to Bassanio, 'the suit is impertinent to myself'—by which he means 'pertinent' (*The Merchant of Venice*, 2.2.122–3). Shakespeare seems not to have much liked pompous language, for several of his major characters poke fun at linguistic affectation—such as Hamlet at Osrick (*Hamlet*, 5. 2) or Kent at Oswald (*King Lear*, 2.2. 102), the latter 'going out of his dialect' in order to do so. A whole conversation can be summed up in a single parodic moment. In *Love's Labour's Lost*, after taking part in an erudite conversation with Armado and Nathaniel, the schoolteacher Holofernes turns to constable Anthony Dull:

HOLOFERNES: . . . Thou hast spoken no word all this while.
DULL: Nor understood none neither, sir.

(5.1.126-8)

Language variety in Early Modern English

It is a commonplace that Shakespeare gives us a remarkable picture of the range of social situations in Elizabethan England. What is less often remarked is that each of these situations would have been linguistically distinctive. Just as today we have scientific, advertising, and broadcasting English, so then there was legal, religious, and courtly English—to name just a few of the styles which are to be found. In addition to archaisms and neologisms, hard words and easy words, there is speech representing different degrees of formality, intimacy, social class, and regional origins. In short, we encounter in the plays most of the language *varieties* of Early Modern English.

Because we are totally reliant on the written language, apart from the occasional observation by a contemporary commentator, we shall never achieve a complete picture of the spoken stylistic variation of the past. But the plays quite often give us clues from the way in which characters are portrayed. We need to note, for example, that when Fluellen (in *Henry V*) and Evans (in *The Merry Wives of Windsor*) are talking, utterances such as *how melancholies I am* are not normal Early Modern English, but a humorous representation of Welsh dialect speech. A distinctive pronunciation is seen in the spellings: *pless* for *bless* and *falorous* for *valorous*. And the famous stereotype of Welsh speech, *look you*, is also used—though whether it had any greater reality then than now (Welsh people do not actually say *look you* very much) is a moot point. There is certainly a strong element of pastiche in the way these speakers persistently get their grammar wrong—*this is lunatics, a joyful resurrections*.

In these two plays we also hear hints of Scottish in Macmorris and Irish in Jamy, as well as foreign (French) accents in Caius and Katherine; disguised Edgar slips into West Country speech in *King Lear*. But regional variation is not as strongly represented in Shakespeare as social variation, especially distinctions in class. People may hide their faces but not their voices. Orlando, encountering disguised Rosalind in the forest, notices her speech: 'Your accent is something finer than you could purchase in so removed a dwelling' (*As You Like It*, 3.2.310–11). And Edmund notices the disguised Edgar's, 'thy tongue some say of breeding breathes' (*King Lear*, 5.3.142). Grammar and vocabulary is also affected. Prince Hal affirms to Poins, after drinking with the tavern staff, 'I am so good a proficient in one quarter of an hour that I can drink with any tinker in his own language during my life' (*Henry IV Part One*, 2.5.15–17). The upper classes had their own language, too, full of 'holiday and lady terms', as Hotspur puts it (*Henry IV Part One*, 1.3.45).

Many of the markers of class difference are to be found in the way people address each other—the titles they use, their terms of endearment, their insults, and their oaths. It is important to keep a careful eye on the way such forms as *sirrah*, *wench*, *master*, and *gentle* are used, for they are a sensitive index of personal temperaments and relationships. Variations in swearing habits, for example, are identified by Hotspur:

> HOTSPUR: Come, Kate, I'll have your song too.
> LADY PERCY: Not mine, in good sooth.
> HOTSPUR: Not yours, in good sooth! Heart, you swear like a comfit-maker's wife: 'Not you, in good sooth!' and 'As true as I live' and 'As God shall mend me!' and 'As sure as day!'
>
> (*Henry IV Part One*, 3.1.241-6)

He prefers 'A good mouth-filling oath', with expressions like *in sooth* left 'To velvet-guards and Sunday citizens' (3.1.250–2).

Manipulating Early Modern English rules

There is an intimate relationship between Early Modern English and Shakespeare. The more we understand the linguistic norms of his age, the more we will be able to appreciate his departures from these norms; at the same time, his linguistic ear is so sharp, and his character portrayal so wide-ranging, that much of what we know about the norms comes from the plays themselves. We therefore always need to focus on the interaction between these two dimensions. We should not try to study Early Modern English and *then* study Shakespeare. Rather, we should study Early Modern English alongside and through the medium of Shakespeare. Examining the way an author manipulates ('bends and breaks') linguistic rules gives us insights into the nature of the rules themselves.

At all times, we need to ask *why* rule-manipulation takes place. If language work is to be illuminating, we must go beyond 'feature-spotting'. To say, 'I spy an instance of neologism (metaphor, alliteration, etc.) in this line' is only a first step. We have to take a second step and ask: 'What is the neologism (metaphor, alliteration, etc.) doing there?' This is much more interesting, for it makes us reflect on the issue as it must have presented to Shakespeare himself. Why did he choose to do what he did? What effect would have been conveyed if he had made a different choice? It is always a matter of choice: to use or not to use a linguistic form—that is the crucial stylistic question.

This notion of choice lies behind the use of the label *pragmatic* for a stylistic approach which focuses on the reasons for an author's use of a linguistic form, and three examples follow—from grammar, vocabulary, and pronunciation—to illustrate this perspective in operation.

Grammar: thou vs. you

Social and attitudinal differences between people are so important that they affect some of a language's most frequently used forms, notably the pronouns *thou* and *you*. In Old English, *thou* was singular and *you* was plural. But during the thirteenth century, *you* began to be used as a polite form of the singular—probably because people copied the French manner of talking, where *vous* was used in that way. English then became like French, which has *tu* and *vous* both possible for singulars. So now there was a choice. The usual thing was for *you* to be used by inferiors to superiors—such as children to parents, or servants to masters; and *thou* to be used in return. But people would also use *thou* when they wanted special intimacy, such as when addressing God;

and *thou* was also normal when the lower classes talked to each other. The upper classes used *you* to each other, as a rule, even when they were closely related.

So when someone changes from *thou* to *you* (or vice versa) in a conversation, it must mean something. The change will convey a different emotion or mood. The new meaning could be virtually anything—affection, anger, distance, sarcasm, playfulness. To say *thou* to someone could be an insult: in *Twelfth Night*, Toby Belch actually advises Andrew Aguecheek to put down his enemy by calling him *thou* a few times (3.2.37–8). The way in which characters switch from one pronoun to the other therefore acts as a barometer of their evolving attitudes and relationships.

We find an important illustration in the opening scene of *King Lear*, where the king sets about dividing his kingdom among his daughters. We would expect Lear to use *thou* to them, and they to use *you* in return, which is how the interaction begins:

> GONERIL: Sir, I love you more than words can wield the matter . . .
> LEAR: Of all these bounds, even from this line to this . . .
>   We make thee lady. . . .
> REGAN: I . . . find I am alone felicitate
>   In your dear highness' love. . . .
> LEAR: To thee and thine hereditary ever
>   Remain this ample third of our fair kingdom.

But when Lear turns to his favourite daughter, he uses *you*:

> LEAR: . . . what can you say to draw
>   A third more opulent than your sisters?
>
> (1.1.53-85)

Plainly, if *thou* is for 'ordinary' daughters, *you* is here being used as a special marker of affection. But when Cordelia does not reply in the way he was expecting, Lear abruptly changes back:

> LEAR: But goes thy heart with this?
> CORDELIA: Ay, good my lord.
> . . .
> LEAR: Let it be so! Thy truth, then, be thy dower!
>   (1.1.104-8)

Now the *thou* forms are now being used not as a marker of fatherly affection, but of anger.

Vocabulary

The pragmatic approach makes us ask why an author has decided on a particular choice of language, and this is especially important in relation to vocabulary. Not all words present an author with a choice, of course. Many of Shakespeare's unfamiliar words are there simply because they reflect the culture of the time—for example, the vocabulary of clothing, body-armour, weapons, and sailing ships (*doublet* and *hose, casque* and *gauntlet, halberd* and *pike, maintop* and *topgallant*). In such cases, once Shakespeare made a decision to talk about a particular subject area, the terms would automatically follow; a doublet is a *doublet*, and there an end. If we are to understand such words, all we can do is learn about the Elizabethan world.

However, most of the vocabulary we would think of as distinctively Shakespearian is not like this, but involves a choice between one word and another. The Chorus puts a question to the audience, at the very beginning of *Henry V*:

> Can this cock-pit hold
> The vasty fields of France? Or may we cram
> Within this wooden O the very casques
> That did affright the air at Agincourt?
> (Prologue, 11-14)

There are two distinctive words in the first sentence, both of which have their first uses assigned to Shakespeare by the *Oxford English Dictionary*—*cockpit*, in its sense of 'theatre pit', and *vasty*, meaning 'vast'. *Cockpit* had been used before by other authors in other senses; but *vasty* is a new word, and probably (because we can see similarly constructed words elsewhere in the plays, such as *plumpy* and *brisky*) a Shakespearian creation. But why did Shakespeare find it necessary to invent a new word here? *Vast* already existed in the language, and indeed Shakespeare uses it himself, as in *Romeo and Juliet*: 'that vast shore washed with the farthest sea' (2. 1. 125). The answer has to lie in the value of the extra syllable to make the word suit the rhythm of the poetic line (the *metre*), which at this point in the speech is proceeding in a very regular manner, ten syllables at a time. (For more on metre, see Chapter 8.) To have written 'The vast fields of France' would have caused an unwelcome jerkiness in this steady progression.

Let us imagine the problem as it might have appeared to Shakespeare: we have a line beginning 'The—fields of France', and we need a two-beat adjective to fill the gap, expressive of great size. *Vast* is the obvious word, but it will not do, because it has only one syllable. So we need to think of other words in Early Modern English which might work. *Large, huge,* and *great* are available, but have the wrong rhythm—and are in any case hardly imaginative ways of capturing the enormity of the dramatic scene the Chorus is painting. *Immense* and *enormous* are also available; but the first of these has the strong syllable in the wrong place, and the second has too many syllables. *Massive* also exists—which does have the right rhythm, but unfortunately the wrong meaning, for it expresses the idea of concrete size upwards—as in a *massive building*—not the idea of a flat expanse. *Vast* seems to be the only word which has the right meaning, and to be sufficiently unusual (its first recorded usage is 1575) for it to have some poetic appeal. Adding an adjective-forming suffix, *-y*, is an attractive way of solving the metrical problem—and a perfectly acceptable one, in an era when the creation of new words was common practice, and when *-y* had previously been used in this way with many other words.

Pronunciation: the importance of rhythm

Metrical demands were a major influence on vocabulary formation, and they also affected choices in grammar. In the present tense, for example, there were two endings still in use: *-th* and *-s*, as in *readeth* and *reads*, the *-th* often adding an extra syllable to the word. The *-th* form was dying out, though it was still routine in *doth* and *hath*; but with most verbs there was still a choice. So, what would lead Shakespeare to choose one form and not the other? One factor is that *-s* seems to have conveyed a more colloquial tone (it is the normal form in prose), whereas *-th* was more formal (it is often used in the 'official' language of stage directions). But that explanation will not do for the many cases in the poetry where we find both endings. Once again it is the presence or absence of the extra syllable which can motivate the choice—as in this example from *Henry VI Part Two*, where the usages are juxtaposed, and only the sequence as shown preserves the regular rhythmical beat:

> For Suffolk, he that can do all in all
> With her that hateth thee and hates us all . . .
> (2.4.52-3)

The role of the extra syllable is seen in several types of construction. A parallel case with the past forms of verbs is seen in *Romeo and Juliet*, where the first usage has *-ed* as a separate syllable, and the second usage does not: 'Hence banishèd is banished from the world' (3.3.19). And a parallel case with adjectives is in *Henry IV Part One:*

> Why, Harry, do I tell thee of my foes,
> Which art my near'st and dearest enemy?
> (3.2.122-3)

Here the elision of the *-e* in *-est* gives the required flexibility. The same reasoning can also explain why an adjective goes after the noun—as in this example from *Antony and Cleopatra*:

> For he hath laid strange courtesies and great
> Of late upon me
> (2.2.162-3)

Here, 'strange and great courtesies' would not work.

All metrical patterns can be analysed from a pragmatic point of view. The aim is to find reasons for any differences in line length, changes in rhythm, or alterations in the way lines run together. The dramatic effect of even a brief pause can be considerable. In the following extract from *Macbeth*, Ross knows that Macduff's family has been killed, and he has to break the news. Faced with Macduff's direct questions, a pair of lies leap into his mouth. But there is a pause (conveyed by the missing metrical beat) before his second reply. We can almost hear his silent gulp.

MACDUFF: How does my wife?
ROSS: Why, well.
MACDUFF: And all my children?
ROSS: Well, too.
                    (4.3.177-8)

By contrast, the extra-long line which results from this intervention of Hotspur's, interrupting a sequence of regular ten-syllable lines, reinforces our impression of his impatient character, and in its urgency contrasts with the measured tones of Worcester's:

WORCESTER: Your son in Scotland being thus employed,
    Shall secretly into the bosom creep
    Of that same noble prelate well-beloved,
    The Archbishop.
HOTSPUR: Of York, is't not?
WORCESTER: True, who bears hard
    His brother's death at Bristol, the Lord Scrope.
                    (*Henry IV Part One*, 1.3.261-5)

Conclusion

People talk a lot about Shakespeare's 'linguistic legacy', saying that he was a major influence on the present-day English language, and citing as evidence his coining of new words (such as *assassination* and *courtship*) and idiomatic phrases (such as *salad days* and *cold comfort*). But when we add all of the coinages up, we do not get very large numbers. No-one has carried out a precise calculation; but the Shakespearian words that still exist in modern English can be counted in hundreds, not thousands, and there are only a few dozen popular idioms. Those who assert that huge numbers of words in modern English come from Shakespeare are seriously mistaken.

A 'counting words' approach to the assessment of Shakespeare's language is not enough, because it ignores his contribution to other domains of language use—such as grammar and pronunciation—and the way these domains creatively interact with vocabulary. It is in any case naive to think that quantity could ever be a guide to quality. The Shakespearian linguistic legacy is not in the number of words he used, but in the way he used them.

From Shakespeare we learn how it is possible to explore and exploit the resources of a language in original ways, displaying its range and variety in the service of the poetic imagination. In his best writing, we see how to make a language work so that it conveys the effects we want it to. Above all, Shakespeare shows us how to dare to do things with language. In a Shakespearian master-class, we would observe an object-lesson in the bending and breaking of rules.

FURTHER READING

Brook, G. L. *The Language of Shakespeare* (London: Deutsch, 1976). This book is a compilation of 450 descriptive observations about Shakespeare's language, grouped into eight broad thematic areas: vocabulary, syntax, accidence, word-formation, features of pronunciation and writing, metre, rhetoric, and language varieties.

Crystal, David and Ben Crystal. *Shakespeare's Words: A Glossary and Language Companion* (Harmondsworth: Penguin, 2002). This book is an alphabetical compilation of the Early Modern English vocabulary found in Shakespeare, interspersed with a thematic treatment of selected language topics.

Hulme, Hilda M. *Explorations in Shakespeare's Language* (London: Longmans, 1962). This book provides a further interpretation of some 200 of the more difficult items in Shakespeare, seen within the context of the language of his time.

Kermode, Frank. *Shakespeare's Language* (Harmondsworth: Penguin, 2000). This is an investigation of the development of Shakespeare's language over time, considering the period around 1600 as pivotal, and illustrating the argument through the detailed analysis of critical passages.

Quirk, Randolph. 'Shakespeare and the English language'. In R. Quirk, *The Linguist and the English Language* (London: Edward Arnold, 1974). This essay illustrates Shakespeare's personal use of English and his linguistic interests, seen against the backdrop of the language of his time.

Ronberg, Gert. *A Way with Words: The Language of English Renaissance Literature* (London: Edward Arnold, 1992). This is an introduction to Early Modern English illustrated from a wide range of authors of the period, but with copious illustration and analysis from Shakespeare.

Salmon, V. and E. Burness (eds.). *Reader in the Language of Shakespearian Drama* (Amsterdam/ Philadelphia: John Benjamins, 1987). This is an anthology of over thirty essays on aspects of Shakespearian dramatic language published in the twenty years between 1965 and 1985.

Williams, Gordon. *A Glossary of Shakespeare's Sexual Language* (London: Athlone, 1997). This is an alphabetical account of the sexually allusive words and phrases in Shakespeare, placed within their historical perspective.

8 | Shakespeare's verse

Russ McDonald

Shakespeare composed multiple forms of poetry, or verse, for different kinds of dramas and a wide range of characters and plots. In taking up the topic of prosody, the study of the kinds of poetic composition, this chapter will show how his predominant verse form contributes to the theatrical effectiveness and meaning of his plays. But first a broad definition may be helpful: 'Verse may be defined as a succession of articulate sounds regulated by a rhythm so definite, that we can readily foresee the results that follow from its application. Rhythm is also met with in prose, but in the latter its range is so wide, that we can never anticipate its flow, while the pleasure we derive from verse is founded on this very anticipation'.[1]

Although composed nearly 200 years ago, this formulation offers a clear distinction between ordinary language and most types of poetry. It is especially useful in identifying the sense of expectation that poetic form stimulates in the perceiver. In most English poetry, a listener hears the reiterated rhythm, presumes and desires that it will continue, and notices when it changes or fails. A simple illustration of such an aural design is found in *Macbeth*:

> Eye of newt and toe of frog,
> Wool of bat and tongue of dog,
> Adder's fork and blind-worm's sting,
> Lizard's leg and owlet's wing,
> For a charm of powerful trouble,
> Like a hell-broth boil and bubble.
> (4.1.14-19)

Here the patterns depend upon both rhythm and rhyme. While Shakespeare works in a variety of poetic forms, some rhymed and some unrhymed, all his verse is rhythmic. The particular rhythms derive from the chosen *metre*, the measured arrangement of sounds in the poetic line, or, simply, the 'beat'.

Metre in verse creates meaning, as a modern critic explains: 'First, all meter, by distinguishing rhythmic from ordinary statement, objectifies that statement and impels it toward a significant formality and even ritualism   The second way a meter can "mean" is by varying from itself: . . . departures from metrical norms powerfully reinforce emotional effects'.[2] First the pattern, and then variation of the pattern: these are the two central concepts required for an understanding of Shakespeare's poetic style. For the original audiences, such patterning was one of the principal attractions of the theatrical experience. Today, however, we tend to prefer what Gertrude in *Hamlet* calls 'more matter with less art' (2.2.96). In other words, we like theatre to look and sound 'natural' or 'realistic', suspecting that artifice or obvious ornament is pretentious or at least inauthentic. Too many modern actors and directors disregard the rhythmic structure of dramatic speech, instead pausing for effect when it suits them, or perhaps lingering indulgently over favourite words. Their aim is to make the language sound more 'natural', the character's speech more psychologically credible. But Shakespeare and his audience delighted in patterns and forms, and to neglect the rhythm of the lines is to deprive the listener of vast resources of pleasure and significance.

The pattern of blank verse

The verse form that Shakespeare favoured for dramatic speech, what we might call his default metre, is unrhymed iambic pentameter, or blank verse. An iamb is a two-syllable unit of sound, with the first syllable unstressed and the second stressed (˘/). A good example of a natural iamb is the word *because*, which never varies in pronunci-ation: the first syllable is always soft, the second hard (an alternative description to 'unstressed' and 'stressed'). Other kinds of poetic units are available, each known as a poetic 'foot': the most common are the trochee (as in 'essay'), the dactyl (as in 'care-fully'), and the anapest (as in 'interrupt'), and virtually all poets occasionally enlist these feet for particular dramatic purposes. But the iamb is by far the dominant unit in English poetry from the middle ages to the modern period, and some writers attribute its centrality to its correspondence with 'the natural rhythm of the language'.[3] The structure of blank verse, with its alternation of unstressed and stressed syllables, creates a pulsating rhythm that is predictable, reliable, and thus comforting in its regularity. It is said that the alternation of unstressed and stressed sounds approximates the 'lub-dub' rhythm of the human heartbeat, and that since this rhythm is slightly faster than the heartbeat, it quickens our pulse and thus impels us to match the slightly faster pace. Metre first creates a relation between speaker and listener. As it does so, it also unites an audience in the perception of the rhythmic pattern, affording them what has been called 'the experience of simultaneity'.[4]

In most of Shakespeare's verse, five iambs are joined together to form a poetic line of iambic pentameter. We might begin by 'scanning' two well-known lines, i.e. noticing (and marking) the number of feet and the stresses within them:

But soft, what light through yonder window breaks?
(*Romeo and Juliet*, 2.1.44)

Her father loved me, oft invited me
(*Othello*, 1.3.127)

The number of feet is significant because it is not too few and not too many. Lines containing two feet (dimeter) or three (trimeter) or four (tetrameter) sound brief and somehow naive, an effect Shakespeare exploits for the parodic tragedy that ends *A Midsummer Night's Dream*:

> And farewell friends,
>   Thus Thisbe ends.
> Adieu, adieu, adieu.
>   (5.1.332-4)

Children's poems or nonsense rhymes understandably employ such metre, in which the rhymes or stops come so close together. On the other hand, lines extending longer than five feet frequently split in half, a problem apparent in a passage from *The Arraignment of Paris*, a play written in the early 1580s by George Peele:

> OENONE: False Paris, this was not thy vow, | when thou and I were one,
>   To range and change old love for new: | but now those days be gone.
>   But I will find the goddess out, | that she thy vow may read,
>   And fill these woods with my laments, | for thy unhappy deed.
>   (3.3 585-6)

By contrast with these two extreme cases, the five-syllable line is just right: long enough not to sound inane, and short enough not to fracture.

The adjective 'blank' in 'blank verse,' signifying an absence or lack, establishes one of the defining characteristics of the form, the absence of rhyme. Until the middle of the sixteenth century, all English poetry was composed to rhyme in some fashion, whether in couplets or alternating lines or some other scheme: prominent examples are the ten-syllable rhyming lines of Geoffrey Chaucer's *The Canterbury Tales* or the lyric poems of the early Renaissance, such as Thomas Wyatt's sonnets. But apparently poets perceived a need for an alternative verse form appropriate for serious narrative poems.

The first known example of blank verse written in English was a translation by Henry Howard, Earl of Surrey, of part of Books II and IV of Virgil's great epic, the *Aeneid*. Surrey was perhaps prompted to his formal experiment by an Italian translation of Virgil published in 1539; it was composed in an unrhymed eleven-syllable line known as *versi sciolti*, or 'freed verse', i.e. freed from the constraints of rhyme.[5] Although Surrey probably completed his translation in the 1540s, it first appeared in *Tottel's Miscellany*, an important collection of 271 poems published in 1556. The expressive possibilities inherent in the form apparently struck other writers fairly quickly. It was taken up by Roger Sackville and Thomas Norton for their drama *Gorboduc* (performed in 1559), and within a mere three decades it had become the dominant medium for serious English playwrights.

To establish a kind of base line against which to measure later developments, especially Shakespeare's distinctive handling of the form, it is useful to listen to an example of early Elizabethan blank verse so as to observe its rhythmic properties in a relatively uncomplicated state. In the second act of *Gorboduc*, Sackville and Norton stage the dangers of political division by setting two brothers, Ferrex and Porrex, against each other. Here Porrex declares his unwillingness to communicate further with his treacherous sibling:

> PORREX: In mischiefs such as Ferrex now intends,
>   The wonted courteous laws to messengers
>   Are not observed, which in just war they use.
>   Shall I so hazard any one of mine?
>   Shall I betray my trusty friends to him,
>   That have disclosed his treason unto me?
>   Let him entreat that fears, I fear him not.
>   Or shall I to the king, my father, send?
>   Yea, and send now, while such a mother lives,
>   That loves my brother and that hateth me?
>   (2.2.42-51)

This is what an uncomplicated, standard version of blank verse sounds like. The ear immediately registers the uniformity of the iambic structure, the almost unvaried succession of similar units of sound, unstressed-stressed. No line lacks a syllable; no line contains an eleventh syllable (i.e., no line is 'hypermetrical'); no line displays a feminine ending (i.e., a case in which the final word has an added, unstressed syllable). Units of thought tend to correspond to units of poetry: in other words, phrases and clauses are apt to fall into ten-syllable segments. Every line but one is end-stopped, and even when the stop is only a pause, the speech unfolds in regular measures of five iambs. Only rarely do the poets depart from their firm rhythmic structure. In the third line, a double accent calls attention to the phrase 'just war'. And, most noticeably, at the head of the next-to-last line, the stress falls on 'Yea', the syllable that would normally be unstressed, as a trochee ('Yea, and') is substituted for an iamb.

Such simple variation opens a window onto the potential complexity of the medium. A generation later Christopher Marlowe, Thomas Kyd, George Peele, George Chapman, and other poets and playwrights began to explore these possibilities in earnest, developing the sound of dramatic speech and making it suitable for the representation of complex human problems. Marlowe in particular adopted certain strategies to 'colour' the verse, to make certain words and phrases stand out in relief from the regularity of the line: in particular he liked to end a line with an impressive sounding proper name which, while conforming to the metrical pattern, finished the phrase definitively and advertised the poet's virtuosity, nouns such as 'Persepolis', 'Zenocrate', 'Tripoli', and 'Tamburlaine'. When Shakespeare appeared on the scene around 1590, he began by imitating Marlowe and his contemporaries, and the blank verse of his earliest theatrical efforts, while not without interest and occasional brilliance, is not much more structurally complicated than the lines from *Gorboduc.*

Shortly, however, the young Shakespeare began to exploit the potential variables. Over the course of his career he utterly transformed the sound of the pentameter line. The sophistication of his mature verse, particularly its distance from the uncomplicated lines from *Gorboduc*, is audible in almost any passage from one of his last plays, as in the fourth act of *Cymbeline*, when the heroine awakens from a drugged sleep:

> Yes, sir, to Milford Haven. Which is the way?
> I thank you. By yon bush? Pray, how far thither?
> 'Od's pitykins, can it be six mile yet?
> I have gone all night. 'Faith, I'll lie down and sleep.
> (4.2.293-6)

This is still blank verse, but it is the work of a writer who has been experimenting with the form for twenty years. The remoteness from the early versions of iambic pentameter, including Shakespeare's own, could hardly be more striking. Regularity is maintained, but only barely, because the poet has admitted numerous variations and challenges to the sovereignty of the pentameter line.

The animating factor in Shakespeare's poetry, as in most English blank verse, is the tension between the iambic pattern and opposition to its regularity. The process of fitting English sentences into the pentameter frame generates a series of rhythmic variations, violations of the underlying scheme that range from the practically imperceptible to the fiercely arresting. The most efficient way of understanding Shakespeare's achievement is to survey some of these major deviations, identifying and illustrating the way the poet modifies the basic rhythm for the purposes of music and meaning.

Variations of the pattern

Although every line of iambic pentameter resembles every other, thanks to the similarity of structure, nevertheless some form of acoustic variation touches every line. Consider two famous cases. First, the Prince of Denmark's very first utterance:

> A little more than kin and less than kind.
> (*Hamlet*, 1.2.65)

Strictly speaking, the line offers no irregularities, no variations in the iambic beat. And yet there are audible differences among the degrees of stress given to each hard syllable; the first syllable of 'little', even though it occupies a stressed position and is crucial to the meaning of the statement, probably receives less emphasis than the nouns 'kin' or 'kind'. No two actors speaking the line will give it precisely the same inflection. Second, the opening line of *Twelfth Night*:

Ĭf mŭsĭc bĕ thĕ fŏod ŏf lŏve, plăy ŏn
(*Twelfth Night*, 1.1.1)

Here 'play on' is technically an iamb, although it is often spoken as a spondee, a foot in which equal stress is given to both syllables: plăy ŏn. Even if the actor slavishly obeys the iambic structure, giving less weight to the technically unstressed 'play' and more to the stressed 'on', still 'play' will receive a stronger hit than any of the other four unstressed syllables in the line (*If, ic, the,* and *of*).

Thus, in every line of Shakespearian iambic pentameter the regularity of the stressed and unstressed sounds is present but not absolute. And in no two lines will the pattern be identical. Each line is distinctive, varying according to the semantic sense of the words and the delivery of the actor.

A major variant that appears infrequently in the early plays and becomes more prominent as the poet matures artistically is the practice of dividing a line of iambic pentameter between two speakers—and sometimes more than two. Earlier dramatists tended to write fairly long speeches for their characters, but as they gained experience their scenes became increasingly dialogic, making the sharing of a line seem natural:

CASSIUS: Whŏ ŏffĕrĕd hĭm thĕ crŏwn?
CASCA: Whў, Ăntŏny.
(*Julius Caesar*, 1.2.233)

Such dovetailing of half-lines and even shorter segments makes the dialogue more conversational, less oratorical: characters seem to be talking with one another, not just at one another. The division of lines also accelerates the tempo of a conversation or a group scene. As characters trade off phrases in a rhythmic fashion, the listener may intuit a growing agitation or increasingly intimate engagement. This is especially true of argumentative characters such as Petruccio and Katherine in *The Taming of the Shrew*, or Richard III and his adversaries.

Sometimes multiple effects attend such sharing of lines, as in the scene from *Troilus and Cressida* where Cressida is presented to the Grecian army:

ULYSSES: Măy Ĭ, swĕet lădў, bĕg ă kĭss ŏf yŏu?
CRESSIDA: Yŏu măy.
ULYSSES: Ĭ dŏ dĕsĭre ĭt.
CRESSIDA: Whў, bĕg tŏo.
. . .
DIOMEDES: Lădў, ă wŏrd. I'll brĭng yŏu tŏ yŏur făthĕr.
NESTOR: Ă wŏmăn ŏf quĭck sĕnse.
ULYSSES: Fĭe, fĭe upŏn hĕr!
(4.6.48-9, 54-5)

The poet intended the rhythm to be heard, thus framing the moment in a kind of touchy formality. Also, the splitting of these lines creates a flirtatious repartee, an exchange presumably troubling to spectators who have just witnessed the amorous parting of Cressida from Troilus.

In the previous passage, Ulysses' line contains eleven syllables: a common Shakespearian variant is to allow an extra syllable, or sometimes two or three, making what is called a *hypermetrical* or *extrametrical* line. Usually, although not always, the extra syllable hangs off the end of the line. In fact, the most famous line in all of world drama is hypermetrical. Whether scanned as

To be or not to be, that is the question,

or

To be or not to be, that is the question,

Hamlet's opening line has eleven syllables.

Early on Shakespeare assigns these extra syllables specific tasks, such as the elucidation of character. For example, when Richard III awakens from a dream just before the final battle at Bosworth Field, the flaccid line endings connote irresolution and self-doubt:

> All several sins, all used in each degree,
> Throng to the bar, crying all, 'Guilty, guilty!'
> I shall despair. There is no creature loves me,
>
> . . .
> Methought the souls of all that I had murdered
> Came to my tent, and every one did threat
> Tomorrow's vengeance on the head of Richard.
> (5.5.152–4, 158–60)

Regret and fear, emotions new to Richard, require accentuation, and the extra syllables effectively perform such labour. Furthermore, they are supported in this task by other corruptions of the familiar beat. In the early plays, with their poetic uniformity, hypermetrism is relatively rare, so that an overcrowded line occurs only about ten per-cent of the time. As Shakespeare's career progressed, however, he became increasingly tolerant of the additional syllable, so that by the end of his career every third line is hypermetrical. The result is a deliberately complex, challenging metrical scheme appropriate for ambiguously represented characters and actions.

The more he begins to play with the form, the more Shakespeare seems to enjoy cutting off a speaker or stopping a sentence in the middle of a line. This mid-line pause is known as a *caesura*, from the Latin word for 'cut', *caedere*. Such a hesitation or halt is by no means a Shakespearian innovation: from Surrey forward every poet who wrote blank verse either pauses, changes direction, or ends a sentence in the middle of the line. But the frequent use of mid-line pauses, even of several stops in a single line, is characteristic of a much more sophisticated form of poetry, a style of verse written for a more acoustically sensitive audience. Elizabethan dramatic poets, the young Shakespeare among them, tended to stop after the fourth or the sixth syllable, i.e. after the second or third foot.[6] This is especially true in speeches where the previous line is enjambed (when the phrase is allowed to run into the next line without an end-stop), as in this passage from one of the earliest histories, *Henry VI Part Two*:

Sometime he talks as if Duke Humphrey's ghost
Were by his side; sometime he calls the King,
(3.2.375–6)

A more adventurous use of the pause occurs in Isabella's passionate plea to Angelo in *Measure for Measure*:

ISABELLA: . . . How would you be
    If He which is the top of judgement should
    But judge you as you are? O, think on that,
    And mercy then will breathe within your lips,
    Like man new made.
ANGELO: Be you content, fair maid,
    It is the law, not I, condemn your brother.
(2.2.77-82)

Such rhythmic complexity is typical of Shakespeare's work from mid-career, i.e. from *Hamlet* forward.

The most complicated kind of stop is that known as an 'epic caesura': the pause comes after the unstressed half of an iambic foot; sometimes this soft beat is an extra syllable; and usually the next syllable is unstressed as well. That doubling of unstressed syllables, with a stop between them, serves to isolate the two parts of the thought and thus to sharpen the thematic contrast, as after the murder in *Macbeth*:

Wake Duncan with thy knocking.| I would thou couldst.
(2.2.72)

Holes in the line make a strong impression, but their effect depends entirely on the listener's familiarity with the normally seamless verse.

Frequently the poet disrupts the metrical structure by inverting the stresses in the iambic foot, that is, substituting a trochee for an iamb. *Richard III* famously begins with a soliloquy in which the villain seizes the audience's attention and announces his monstrous plan. The speech, and therefore the play, begins with an inverted foot:

Now is the winter of our discontent
Made glorious summer by this son of York
(1.1.1-2)

After the initial trochee the line rights itself and finds its regular rhythm, but the first stressed syllable proclaims Richard's individualism and audacity. *Antony and Cleopatra* also begins with such an outburst. An argument is apparently in progress, and the first speaker contradicts his partner:

Nay, but this dotage of our General's
O'erflows the measure.
(1.1.1-2)

One explanation for Shakespeare's attraction to syllabic inversion is that such an acoustic reversal is a contrast to a contrast, an antithesis to an antithesis: the normal opposition, unstressed-stressed, is reversed to stressed-unstressed. And obviously the iambic feet before and after the trochee are affected because the normal alternating relation is violated.

The emphatic function of such a metrical tool soon became clear to Shakespeare. A speaker who forcefully breaks the regular pattern accentuates the word or phrase that causes the rupture and thus gives special prominence to the inverted foot. Such transpositions often occur in moments of exceptional tension or crisis:

> O that this too too solid flesh would melt,
> Thaw, and resolve itself into a dew
>> (*Hamlet*, 1.2.129-30)

> Bring me no more reports. Let them fly all.
>> (*Macbeth*, 5.3.1)

> HERMIONE: . . . You, my lord,
>   Do but mistake.
> LEONTES: You have mistook, my lady—
>> (*The Winter's Tale*, 2.1.82-3)

In this last exchange the double violation of the iambic pattern acoustically conveys the emotional violence of the struggle between suspicious King and blameless wife. Because the poetry of *The Winter's Tale*, like that of all the late plays, is notoriously irregular, it is not always possible to find specific meanings in particular poetic turns. But here the value of the disrupted pattern is indisputable.

Sometimes both syllables in the foot receive equal stress. This variation, known as the spondee, is often used like the trochee, to underscore a particular moment by signalling the importance of a word or phrase.

> Cry 'havoc!' and let slip the dogs of war
>> (*Julius Caesar*, 3.1.276)

> And that which should accompany old age
>> (*Macbeth* 5.3.25)

There is room for variation in the speaking of a spondaic phrase: two different Mark Antonys or Macbeths might give slightly different (rather than identical) weight to each syllable of his spondee. But more important than such slight differences is the power of the foot to derail the momentum of the iambic beat.

Shakespeare has many other tricks up his metrical sleeve. To mention only a few: the headless line, in which the initial unstressed syllable is eliminated; the short line, in which the omission of two or three feet brings the speaker to an emphatic halt; the alexandrine, a line with six full feet. Another major consideration is location—where in the line the irregularity occurs. A trochee beginning a line, for example, makes a vastly different impact from a trochee in the final position.

Sentence and line

All these variations arise from the poet's need to superimpose English sentences onto the dominant acoustic system, to fit the character's apparently spontaneous utterances into the metrical frame. Thus the constant, most potent threat to the regularity of the iambic pentameter is the unpredictable energy of sentences formed into verse. Sometimes the phrases or clauses lie nicely in their five-foot beds, ending where the line ends, and causing no real trouble (as in the excerpt from *Gorboduc*), while others resist arrangement by running past the end of the line, or stopping in the middle, or posing syntactical difficulties that subvert or contradict the metrical scheme (as in Imogen's speech from *Cymbeline*).

In all but his earliest plays Shakespeare exhibits a technical proficiency that allows him to match or not match sentence to line, as he sees fit. In Othello's narrative of his military past, sentences happily conform to the underlying pattern:

> Wherein I spoke of most disastrous chances,
> Of moving accidents by flood and field,
> Of hair-breadth scapes i'th' imminent deadly breach,
> Of being taken by the insolent foe
> And sold to slavery, of my redemption thence,
> And portance in my traveller's history
>
> (1.3.133-8)

Here the phrases are long, most of them just as long as the pentameter line; and those that do outrun the end of the line, i.e., that are enjambed, come to a graceful pause in the middle of the next line ('And sold to slavery'). There is little to counteract the uniformity of the iambs, and the pleasure of the persistent rhythm is reinforced by other poetic repetitions, such as the reiterated prepositional phrases beginning with 'Of', the alliterating pairs of words ('flood and field'), and other instances of assonance and consonance. Although there is little variation in the rhythm, variety and excitement derive from the diverse vocabulary, the combination of long and short words, the verbal crowding of line 135, and other such poetic strategies.

In the middle of *King Lear*, by contrast, language strains to escape the confines of the pentameter line:

> Rumble thy bellyful! Spit, fire! spout, rain!
> Nor rain, wind, thunder, fire, are my daughters.
> I tax not you, you elements, with unkindness;
> I never gave you kingdom, called you children,
> You owe me no subscription. Then let fall
> Your horrible pleasure. Here I stand, your slave,
> A poor, infirm, weak, and despised old man.

But yet I call you servile ministers,
That have with two pernicious daughters joined
Your high engendered battles 'gainst a head
So old and white as this. O! O! 't is foul!

(*King Lear*, 3.2.13-23)

This mad plea to the heavens displays, formally speaking, the same iambic structure as the lines from Othello's self-justification, but the acoustic effect—and therefore the meaning—is entirely different. In the first lines of Lear's outburst, the multiple stops and starts noticeably retard the tempo and communicate the bewilderment and self-division that have begun to rule Lear's consciousness. The bombastic inversions of the first line create a dactylic rhythm, a tripping measure that communicates Lear's state of madness. The simple clauses and the absence of conjunctions fix a grammatical pattern that competes with the metrical design. At last, in the second half of the speech, a kind of poetic momentum is achieved. But its speed and power make the lines seem almost ungoverned, as if they are not under control and likely to crash into something, which they do with the mid-line stop and the concluding 'O! O! 't is foul!'

In addition to the length and shape of clauses, the diction chosen may alter the metrical effect of a passage. One source of fruitful conflict in English poetry—according to some poets it is the primary conflict—is verbal origins, i.e. Latinate and Anglo-Saxon. Words descending from Anglo-Saxon tend to be monosyllabic, whereas those derived or borrowed from romance languages are more likely to be polysyllabic. When these two different kinds of words are combined, the resulting phrase can be especially arresting, as in Hamlet's 'incestuous sheets', or 'precious diadem stole', or 'rank corruption'.

Often Shakespeare makes music from such combinations, but he sometimes takes special care to limit himself in a particular passage to long words or to short words, and such a limitation has metrical consequences. At the beginning of the last scene of *Othello*, for example, the hero delivers a soliloquy over the sleeping body of Desdemona, whom he has come to murder. He begins simply, with monosyllabic words that convey the gravity of his mood:

It is the cause, it is the cause, my soul.
Let me not name it to you, you chaste stars.

(5.2.1-2)

As the speech becomes more passionate, his vocabulary becomes more flamboyant: 'monumental alabaster', 'flaming minister', 'cunning'st pattern of excelling nature', 'Promethean heat'. And then as he draws to a close, the diction changes markedly again:

One more, one more.
Be thus when thou art dead, and I will kill thee
And love thee after. One more, and that's the last.

(5.2.17-19)

A group of words similar in length creates yet another counter-rhythm, another aural scheme that is superimposed upon, or set against, the fundamental beat. Shakespeare often uses such a tactic at moments of reverence, as at the end of Titania's speech about the birth of the Indian boy (*A Midsummer Night's Dream*, 2.1.121–42), or in parts of Henry V's Saint Crispin's Day oration (*Henry V*, 4.3.40–67).

Music and meaning

What remain to be considered are the implications of this metrical system, the musical effects and even the symbolic value of blank verse employed as a dramatic instrument. The actor must respect the rhythmic structure of the lines, but must at the same time transmit to the audience the meaning of the sentences being spoken and make the language sound spontaneous, as if the character were inventing the words. It is this tension between rhythmic pattern and syntactic and semantic variety that makes the verse invigorating to hear. Commenting on the 'clotted, irregular rhythms and mis-accents' spoken by Leontes in *The Winter's Tale*, the great theatre director Sir Peter Hall insists that

[t]hese irregularities only make emotional sense and can only affect an audience, if the actor knows the underlying regularity beneath them. He must revel in the cross-rhythms, ride the irregularities and use the bumps in the smoothness for emotional purposes. He must not give up forcing the line to scan. . . . But it is the tension between that regularity and the irregularity of the speech which expresses the emotional turmoil.[7]

Hall goes on to compare the Shakespearian speaker to a jazz player who improvises but always keeps the beat. Some critics propose that we think of the iambics as the rhythm of a musical piece, and of the sentences as constituting the tune. Others compare these opposing claims to the interplay of the left- and right-hand lines in a piano piece. 'Counterpoint,' 'countercurrent,' 'cross-rhythms'—these familiar descriptions effectively convey the generative tension that animates Shakespeare's dramatic poetry.

The metrical structure and its controlled deviations also function symbolically. Every single iamb, we recall, is founded on an acoustic contrast (unstressed/stressed). This opposition makes blank verse an especially appropriate medium for Shakespeare to have taken up, since contrast or antithesis is perhaps his most pervasive artistic technique. Dark and light, court and commons, men and women, Egypt and Rome, crowd scenes and duets, poetry and prose, good and evil—the plays are saturated with oppositions and conflicts and antitheses within contrasts.

The difference between the two syllables of an iamb is yet another example, albeit a microscopic one, of Shakespeare's favourite method. Just as all these thematic antitheses depend upon each other to shape an audience's evaluation of the play's characters and actions—the contrast between, for example, Desdemona's virtue and Iago's villainy—so the antithetical relation between sounds is thematically meaningful. The competition between sounds is as vital in its own sphere as the contest between characters. For example, words or phrases that threaten to play havoc with the iambic pentameter may be seen as offering the same kind of rebellion in the acoustic sphere as a political or social rebel does in the realm of court politics. Similarly, the struggle between an idiosyncratic phrase and the normal acoustic order that governs the sound of the line is a tiny version of the conflict between a character like Hamlet and the apparently ordered, conventional world he feels obliged to resist. Such a contest informs virtually every speech with meaning.

It is worth reminding ourselves that it is mainly through language that we come to know the thoughts and actions of Shakespeare's characters. Their initial claim on our attention is physical. We receive from them sensible impressions that our minds then interpret—or, in the vulgar, they speak and we hear—and how they speak is as important as what they say. The English director Harley Granville-Barker, who in his productions at the beginning of the twentieth century swept away the visual spectacle of the Victorian theatre and replaced it with renewed attention to the aural dimension, stresses the priority of Shakespeare's poetry in bringing character to life. The Shakespearian play offers the audience

a strange surpassing of this modern work-a-day world. . . . We must have a beauty of speech that will leave us a little indifferent to the sense of the thing spoken. . . . The actor, in fine, must think of the dialogue in terms of music; of the tune and rhythm of it as at one with the sense—sometimes outbidding the sense—in telling him what to do and how to do it, in telling him, indeed, what to *be*.[8]

FURTHER READING

Attridge, Derek. *The Rhythms of English Poetry* (London: Longman, 1982). Attridge's study is a readable, mostly up-to-date survey of prosody and its importance in various kinds of poetry over several centuries.

Booth, Stephen. *An Essay on Shakespeare's Sonnets* (New Haven: Yale University Press, 1968). Although concerned with many different poetic features, Booth is attentive to the operation and value of iambic pentameter and offers numerous insights into the musical and significational contributions of rhythm.

Fussell, Paul. *Poetic Meter and Poetic Form* (New York: Random House, rev. edn. 1979). The standard work on metrics and stanzaic arrangement in English verse, this compact book is clear, lively, and illustrated with pertinent examples from a wide range of Anglo-American poetry.

McDonald, Russ. *Shakespeare and the Arts of Language* (Oxford: Oxford University Press, 2001). This introduction contains chapters on Renaissance rhetoric, on the major poetic properties of Shakespeare's language, and on the playwright's changing attitudes towards his medium. See especially the chapter entitled 'Loosening the Line'.

Preminger, Alex and T. V. F. Brogan, *et al.* (eds.). *The Princeton Encyclopedia of Poetry and Poetics* (Princeton: Princeton University Press, rev. ed. 1993). This immense volume, its topics alphabetically arranged and its entries written by numerous experts, is indispensable to anyone interested in Shakespeare's (or anyone else's) poetry.

Saintsbury, George. *A History of English Prosody from the Twelfth Century to the Present Day*. 3 vols.

(London: Macmillan, 1923 [1906–1910]). Although written a century ago, this is a standard work on English metrics—comprehensive, authoritative, and still valuable.

Steele, Timothy. *All the Fun's in How You Say a Thing: An Explanation of Meter and Versification* (Athens: Ohio University Press, 1999). This recent introduction to the subject of prosody is witty, wide-ranging, and readable, with an excellent bibliography and notes.

Wright, George T. *Hearing the Measures: Shakespearean and Other Inflections* (Madison: University of Wisconsin Press, 2002). This collection of essays extends the metrical interests of *Shakespeare's Metrical Art* (see below), dealing not only with Shakespeare but with some modern poets as well.

Wright, George T. *Shakespeare's Metrical Art* (Berkeley: University of California Press, 1988). Wright's is the most comprehensive recent study of Shakespeare's poetic instruments. The early chapters put the dramatist's practice in the context of sixteenth-century poetry; the later chapters are especially suggestive about how the playwright creates meaning with poetic metre.

NOTES

1. Edwin Guest. *A History of English Rhythms*, 2 vols. (London: William Pickering, 1836–38), I, 1. Guest's definition does not apply, of course, to such twentieth-century innovations as 'free verse', or other kinds of irregularly patterned language.

2. Paul Fussell. *Poetic Meter and Poetic Form* (New York: Random House, rev. edn. 1979), p. 12.

3. Raymond Chapman. *Oxford Companion to the English Language*, ed. Tom McArthur (Oxford: Oxford University Press, 1992), p. 496.

4. Bruce Smith. *The Acoustic World of Early Modern England: Attending to the O-Factor* (Chicago: University of Chicago Press, 1999), p. 218.

5. See the entry for 'blank verse' in *The Princeton Encyclopedia of Poetry and Poetics*, ed. Alex Preminger and T. V. F. Brogan, *et al.* (Princeton: Princeton University Press, rev. edn. 1993).

6. See George T. Wright. *Shakespeare's Metrical Art* (Berkeley: University of California Press, 1988), *passim*, and the initially daunting graphs in Ants Oras, *Pause Patterns in Elizabethan and Jacobean Drama: An Experiment in Prosody* (Gainesville: University of Florida Press, 1960), pp. 46–52.

7. *Exposed by the Mask: Form and Language in Drama* (New York: Theatre Communications Group, 2000), p. 48.

8. Quoted in Richard David. 'Actors and Scholars: A View of Shakespeare in the Modern Theatre', *Shakespeare Survey 12* (1959), p. 81.

9 | The society of Shakespeare's England

Carole Levin

Medieval laws, which dictated how people of different social groups should dress by regulating fabrics, colours, and styles, were still in existence in sixteenth- and seventeenth-century England. These 'sumptuary' laws were part of an attempt to keep people in their places and to mark those who tried to move out of them, for England was still a hierarchical, highly structured society with careful delineations of status. Yet by the reign of Elizabeth I (1558–1603) and her successor, James I (1603–25), a number of people broke these clothing laws with impunity. There was more fluidity and mobility than in previous centuries, and for some people, especially those who were ambitious and literate, there was a possibility to move beyond the social rank to which they had been born. Shakespeare is the most famous example of those who saw playwriting as one means to success. In the process of achieving his private ambitions, he transformed theatrical experience for his contemporaries—and theatrical history for all time.

We can imagine a whole range of different statuses and backgrounds when we consider audiences at the public theatres of the London suburbs in the late sixteenth and early seventeenth centuries. This chapter will examine not only the variety of people who attended Shakespeare's plays but also people of the royal court and of the countryside. In addition to differences of social status, it will consider differences of gender and will also look at those social groups that were perceived to be 'outsiders' in early modern English culture. It is important to recognize that although there were parallels and confluences between the fictional societies of Shakespeare's plays and those of his world, we cannot read one for the other.

The court

The very top of the social scale was held by the monarch at court. It certainly seems to be significant that when Shakespeare began to write and have his plays performed the monarch at that court was a woman, thus destabilizing the structure of a society that had always expected a king who would be father of his people as well as, it was hoped, father of the son who would be the next king. Elizabeth, an unmarried woman, did not fulfil either of these objectives. Moreover, intense changes in the structure of the church in the mid-sixteenth century had already caused deep fractions and insecurities (see Chapter 12). While the court was often kept in one of the palaces in the capital, it also moved to wherever the monarch happened to be. Because Elizabeth wanted to see and be seen by her subjects not only in London but throughout England, she often took the court on 'progresses' throughout the countryside.

Before Elizabeth became queen in 1558 England had broken with Rome under her father Henry VIII (1509–47), become more Protestant in her brother Edward VI's reign (1547–53), and returned to Catholicism under her older sister Mary I (1553–58). Those who did not accept the official religion of the moment faced horrific consequences; men and women were martyred in the reigns of both Henry VIII and Mary I. Indeed, Mary came to be known as 'Bloody Mary' because of the 300 Protestants burned during her brief reign. Elizabeth, restoring a Church of England separate from Rome, tried for a religious settlement that would be broad enough to satisfy most of her subjects. She looked for outward conformity, not, she said, 'wanting to make windows into men's souls'. Changes in religion and an unmarried queen caused anxiety; Elizabeth was also greatly loved, however, and she certainly shaped the society that was to take her name. Her forty-five year reign brought stability to England after the short and difficult reigns of her brother and sister. Until her death in 1603, Shakespeare had never known another ruler.

Unlike many monarchs, Elizabeth claimed, really boasted, that she was 'mere English' (meaning pure, unmixed English). Elizabeth was not only the daughter of Henry VIII; her mother, instead of being a foreign princess, was Anne Boleyn, a lady at court. Henry broke with the Church of Rome when the Pope refused to grant him an annulment from his first wife, the Spanish Princess Catherine of Aragon, in order to marry Anne Boleyn in his frantic attempt to beget a legitimate son. Though Elizabeth's maternal grandmother was Elizabeth Howard, niece of the third Duke of Norfolk, and from one of the oldest noble families in England, her maternal grandfather was Thomas Boleyn, the grandson of Sir Geoffrey Boleyn, a wealthy merchant and Lord Mayor of London. Sir Geoffrey's success had allowed him to buy Hever Castle, but he was not of the hereditary nobility, as were dukes, earls, marquises, viscounts, and barons. Anne Boleyn's personal story was tragic; she was executed in 1536 on a charge of committing adultery. Nonetheless, the success of the Boleyn family in having one of its members become queen consort demonstrated how status and structures were becoming more permeable in sixteenth-century England. One of Shakespeare's last plays, *Henry VIII*, dramatized the events of Elizabeth's parents' marriage, with the play ending in the triumphant celebration of Elizabeth's birth.

Elizabeth had become queen at the age of twenty-five after the deaths of both her brother Edward VI (1553) and her older sister Mary (1558). The court, which had traditionally been a male preserve, was now headed by a woman who enjoyed being 'courted' in the romantic sense, and used courtship and romantic games to keep her power over her people and as a political negotiating tool with other countries.

Elizabeth's way of ruling had a number of innovations. While some of the old nobility did have power and influence at her court, it was the new men, such as her closest adviser and principal secretary and later Lord Treasurer, William Cecil (eventually Lord Burghley), her spy master Sir Francis Walsingham, and her favourite, Robert Dudley, eventually Earl of Leicester, who had more sway. The power of these 'upstarts' did not sit easily with certain groups. By the late 1560s, though some of the grievances and concerns of the conservative older nobility differed, they were united in their distrust of Cecil and the direction in which Elizabeth's government was moving. Several of the older nobility were upset that the 'new men' in government were gaining power and prestige, and saw as a result a growing rift with the traditional ally Spain and too many ecclesiastical innovations instituted by committed Protestants. A number of conservative Catholic nobles rebelled in 1569.

One goal of this 'Northern rebellion' was to have Cecil pushed out of power and to force Elizabeth to rule under the control and direction of the old nobility. Other rebels, such as the Earls of Northumberland and Westmoreland, went further. They wanted to replace Protestant Elizabeth with her Catholic cousin Mary Stuart, who had been compelled to abdicate her Scottish throne in 1568 and who was an enforced resident in England. Mary Stuart was the granddaughter of Henry VIII's older sister Margaret; some Catholics perceived her as the legitimate heir to the English throne. Elizabeth's cousin, Thomas Howard, fourth Duke of Norfolk, hoped to marry Mary Stuart and rule with her. This rebellion was put down and eventually resulted in the life-long exile of the Earl of Westmorland in Flanders and, in 1572, the executions of the Earl of Northumberland and the Duke of Norfolk. Fifteen years later Mary Stuart was also executed as a result of her various plots against the queen. In the *Henry IV* and *Henry V* plays, Shakespeare's audiences would have recognized parallels to some of Elizabeth's painful decisions about how to deal with traitorous nobles.

By the 1590s there was a burst of cultural development with the plays of Marlowe and Shakespeare. At the same time, the court was changing as the queen aged; it was becoming dangerously factionalized. Many of the advisers and courtiers on whom Elizabeth had depended were gone. Her dearest favourite the Earl of Leicester died in 1588 and Sir Francis Walsingham, whose spy system had kept her safe during the long threat of Mary Stuart's imprisonment in England, died in 1590. Though her closest adviser, William Cecil, Lord Burghley, was still with her, he was getting elderly, and had handed over some of his work to his son Robert. In the early 1590s, Leicester's stepson, Robert Devereux, the Earl of Essex, and Robert Cecil battled for control of the Privy Council and influence over Elizabeth. Elizabeth loved to flirt with the glamorous and warlike Essex; Robert Cecil was a hardworking hunchback. The two younger Roberts, Cecil and Essex, went head to head fighting for control of the court. Though Essex was the popular hero, he was the one who lost not only the struggle for power but, as a result of his failed 1601 rebellion, his life.

The situation changed in a number of ways when Elizabeth died in 1603. She was succeeded by her Scottish cousin James, son of the executed Mary Stuart. Though many in the last years of Elizabeth's reign had waited impatiently for her death and looked forward to a male successor, the behaviour of James—along with his foreignness—disturbed many people. Those at court were irritated because of his laziness and extravagance, but those beyond the court, who heard exaggerated rumours of what was happening, were far more frightened. This intensified the divide between the court and the rest of the country. Mistrust of the court would have violent repercussions by the middle of the seventeenth century, when members of Parliament rebelled against their king; in 1649 Charles I was publicly tried and executed for treason.

The city of London

A wide range of people lived in the city of London: wealthy merchants, artisans, servants, the poor, and criminals, as well as some of the country nobility who kept town houses. Many of these Londoners met regularly at St Paul's Cathedral, which was not only a place of worship but also a social centre. People met their friends there; both employers and those people looking for work knew that they could find each other at St Paul's. Stalls were set up during the week so that people could buy a variety of items; books were especially cherished. But people there also had to be careful, as pickpockets knew that the crowd at St Paul's was a particularly fertile ground for them as well. Recognizing that merchants and tradesmen played an important role in the prosperity of the city, Elizabeth and her advisers proposed policies to further help them. For example, enforced meatless days on Fridays and during the entire period of Lent not only had religious significance but also aided the fishing industry and the trades that supported it: fishmongers and shipbuilders.

There were a number of significant guilds or trade companies in the city and each group had its own personality; each also occupied a particular district of London. These included Mercers (who dealt with expensive cloth), Grocers, Drapers (less expensive cloth), Fishmongers, Goldsmiths, Skinners, Merchant-Taylors, Haberdashers (sellers of hats and small articles relating to dress such as thread and ribbons), Salters (makers or dealers), Ironmongers, Vintners, and Clothworkers. London merchants owned or leased the buildings in which they had their various shops. These houses would be quite crowded. Usually the ground floor was the place of business and the goods for sale would be displayed there. The merchant, his family, the servants, and apprentices lived above the shop. There might also be lodgers if the house was large enough. Shakespeare was an example of someone who lived in lodgings when he first moved to London; he boarded with the Mountjoy family.

Most young people, both male and female, left their family homes and went into service or were apprenticed. A number of them came from the countryside to London to learn their trade. Sometimes the younger sons of landholders became apprentices; if they were clever or skilful enough, a career as a merchant or in the professions allowed them as much if not more status than that of the eldest son who was the family heir. The audiences of Shakespeare's plays had many young people in them. A number of the characters of *The Merry Wives of Windsor* reflected this class of Shakespeare's contemporaries; the cleverness of Mistress Page and Mistress Ford also paralleled the many competent women who were wives or widows of merchants. Widows and single women paid taxes and parish assessments to provide for the poor. Those who headed households performed, as did their male counterparts, their civic obligations.

All this commerce and business also required legal advice, and London had its share of lawyers. Most attorneys had trained as clerks for older attorneys and came from landholding classes. Another group of lawyers with even higher status specialized in pleading before the courts. The serjeants-at-law were the only lawyers who could argue before the Court of Common Pleas, which had jurisdiction over almost all civil litigation; usually judges had previously been serjeants-at-law. Just as we have different courts today, civil and criminal, so too did society in the age of Shakespeare: common law and equity courts, prerogative courts, civil law courts, and church courts. On the western edge of the city were the Inns of Court. The Inns served many functions: law school, graduate school, dormitory, library, dining hall, office building, and legal centre. The Inns also served as a social club, where plays and revels were performed. In the sixteenth century, as today, lawyers were necessary though they were not necessarily loved. In *Henry VI Part Two*, the rebel Jack Cade approves of the suggestion, 'The first thing we do let's kill all the lawyers' (4.2.68), when he and his men plan a kingdom ruled by the people.

Though London was thriving for many people in the late sixteenth and early seventeenth centuries, there were also many poor men and women whose lives were miserable. Many of those who fought for England and their queen in 1588 against the Spanish Armada were never paid, and in the 1590s they suffered lives of poverty. The war with Spain and problems with Ireland were an enormous cost at the end of Elizabeth's reign. To pay for the wars Elizabeth sold off crown lands, but this short-term solution cut down on her capital. She lost rents and other incomes those lands had provided. Elizabeth and her government had to rely more and more on her subjects for financial support. This meant not only a steep increase in Parliamentary taxation but an even steeper increase in the other ways the crown raised money, such as through the awarding of monopolies. To make matters worse, the harvests of 1596 and '97 yielded little: thus, prices were high while food supplies were scarce. There was certainly some private giving of charity, and those in need from some classes did better than others. While widows of some guild members received pensions and residences in the companies' almshouses, those of lower social status often found their situations bleak.

The Poor Laws passed by Parliament at the end of the sixteenth century attempted to distinguish between those who could work and instead chose to be idle and to beg or to steal and those who were truly in need and thus deserving of help. While vagrants were punished, the disabled poor received aid that was financed by compulsory poor rates. Those who refused to pay these assessments were supposed to be arrested. Those poor who were caught breaking the law were severely punished. Stealing could lead to being whipped, branded, or even executed, depending on the value of the goods stolen. Some juries, however, deliberately undervalued goods so that the crime could be punished as petty rather than grand larceny. Those in debt were sent to prison; since they were charged for their room and board there, their debt only increased.

Life in the countryside

Though London was the commercial centre of England, some of the villages and towns also had a variety of commercial emphases, and some people in country towns were extremely successful and built large new houses. There were a number of large land-holders who, though they held no hereditary title, did have some means to wealth and power. But much of the land in a given parish was still owned by the lord of the manor, who received either cash or goods for its use. Effectively, however, such property was held in common, and those who worked the land also managed it. The arable land for a village was divided into three sections that were rotated each year: rye or wheat cultivated for bread was grown on one third, and crops such as barley, oats, and beans on another third. The last third was allowed to lie fallow. Each villager had a six-acre portion in each third; of course that meant using only twelve, not eighteen, acres a year. While villagers often had long walks to reach their acreage, all thus got some of the best land as well as that which was less choice. Some villagers provided more specialized crafts or services. These included wheelwrights, smiths of all kinds, millers, possibly carpenters and masons, and often brewers.

Women as well as men worked in the fields when it was deemed necessary, such as during the planting season or the harvest. And this was beyond the regular jobs of the country woman, who worked as hard as the men of her family. She would bake bread, make butter and cheese, gather wood for the fire, tend the household garden, spin yarn, and then make clothes out of the cloth she had woven. She would also make candles and other tools, all while taking care of her children. Indeed, young children of every social rank in their early years were reared by their mothers. While aristocratic and wealthy women usually delegated the harder and less pleasant tasks to nurses or maidservants, they too took seriously the importance of training their children properly.

Just as there was more social mobility in the sixteenth century than formerly, so too was there more geographic mobility as some people left their towns and villages to make their fortune in London (as Shakespeare himself did). This movement, which coincided with changes in the church structure and thus different attitudes toward charity and neighbourliness, made it difficult for those on the edges of society. There was less of a sense of community, and thus less of a sense of obligation to help those in need. Along with the villagers who were part of the societal structure, there were others who were poor and on the margins, and they fared badly.

Those on the margins: witches, Jews, and Africans

Coinciding with poverty and the passage of strict poor laws, the 1590s saw the highest incidence of witchcraft accusations in Elizabeth's reign. A number of those accused of witchcraft were poorer women. The first statute against witchcraft in England had been passed in 1542 and repealed five years later. Early in Elizabeth's reign (1563) a more severe act against witchcraft was passed. This act was repealed in 1604 and under James I the most severe statute yet was passed, one that would not be repealed until 1736.

In the sixteenth and early seventeenth centuries there were a variety of ways that someone, almost always a woman, could be found to be a witch. Though it is disturbing that any person could be killed because of these beliefs, it is important to point out that the number of accusations and executions were far fewer in England than in Scotland or on the continent. Witchcraft prosecutions were only a small percentage of the indictments for crime in the Elizabethan era. The great fear people of the Elizabethan Age had of witches was that they would use their magic to harm their neighbours. It was not until the Act of 1604 that a pact between a witch and the devil was defined as part of the crime of witchcraft. One very common aspect in English trials was the charge of 'mischief following anger'. If a poor woman came to someone's door to beg and was turned away and if she then muttered some curse, this could be used as evidence against her if something tragic was later to befall the person who had refused help. Scholars such as Keith Thomas have suggested that the breakdown of community and guilt over refusing to help the needy caused some people to accuse poor women of witchcraft unjustly.

Shakespeare's audiences would have easily recognized this kind of evidence in an interchange the witches have in Act One of *Macbeth*, written and performed early in the reign of King James. When one witch asks the other where she has been, the reply is a clear example of mischief following anger:

> A sailor's wife had chestnuts in her lap,
> And munched, and munched, and munched. 'Give me,' quoth I.
> 'Aroint thee, witch,' the rump fed runnion cries.

> (1.3.3-5)

To punish the sailor's wife the witch explains that 'Her husband's to Allepo gone, master o' th' Tiger' (1.3.6). The other witches offer her winds to shake up his ship but she plans to go even further with her revenge. She will 'drain him dry as hay', and he will 'Sleep . . . neither night nor day' (1.3.17, 18). Her magic will make him dwindle and pine away. A woman feeling guilty over refusing to share food could easily believe the storm that rocked her husband's ship or his illness came because of a witch who had been begging and had been refused.

Just as some poorer women were targeted in the sixteenth and seventeenth centuries, so too was there concern both about Jews and Africans in England. There had been Jews in England in the earlier Middle Ages, but they were expelled in 1290. Despite, or because of, their banishment, by the thirteenth century the term 'Jew' had become part of the English vocabulary as a general term of abuse, often directed at other Christians. But though Jews were not allowed legally to return to England until the 1650s, in the early sixteenth century a number immigrated to England and outwardly practised Christianity. By the reign of Henry VIII there was a secret Jewish community in London with a secret synagogue, financial support, and business connections with Antwerp. In the late 1530s and 1540s this community consisted of about 100 people. The records also hint at the importance of Jewish women in cooking ritual meals and helping to maintain the religion in secret. A number of the musicians who played for the king were also Italians of Jewish origin. Henry VIII employed nineteen of these musicians at court. This group assimilated quickly and intermarried with the English so that their children and grandchildren were practising Christians, only partially aware of their Jewish origins. There were also some secretly observant Jews in Bristol and some connections between the London community and the one in Bristol. In the late 1540s and early 1550s in Bristol the community held religious services in the house of Henrique Nuñez, and Yom Kippur was observed as well as the Sabbath and festivals. Nuñez's wife, Beatriz Fernandes, taught new Jewish immigrants prayers and baked unleavened bread for Passover. Nuñez, like other members of the community, was outwardly a member of the Anglican Church, but continued to practise his faith in secret.

Despite the attempts of Jewish immigrants to live outwardly as Christians, there was still public Jew-baiting and hysteria which reached a high point in the early 1590s when a prominent converted Jewish physician, Dr Roderigo Lopez, was found guilty of planning to poison the queen on what may have been problematic evidence. Christopher Marlowe's play, *The Jew of Malta*, which was composed about 1589–90, was frequently performed in the last decade of the sixteenth century and the first decade of the seventeenth century. During the week of Lopez's execution in 1594 Philip Henslowe noted in his diary six performances of the play. Its renewed popularity probably led to the composition of Shakespeare's *The Merchant of Venice* and the creation of the character of the Jewish money lender Shylock. Though Shylock demanded his 'pound of flesh', Shakespeare created him as more than simply a one-sided villain.

Just as Jews were presented on the English stage, so too were Africans. In Shakespeare's early play *Titus Andronicus*, the villain Aaron is a Moor who is presented as a black man, though the term 'Moor' had a multiplicity of meanings in that time. In spite of his villainy, Aaron is also given human feelings and pride in his blackness:

> Coal-black is better than another hue
> In that it scorns to bear another hue
> (4.2.98-9)

By the time Shakespeare composed *Othello*, his title character was a much more textured character, even though he ended up a murderer. In the 1560s some seamen actively participated in the slave trade, and African slaves were brought to England from the 1570s onward in small numbers. In the late sixteenth century they were used in England in three capacities. Most of them were household servants, but some also were prostitutes for wealthy English and Dutch men, and we have records of a few as court entertainers.

By the end of the century, in fact, Queen Elizabeth had begun to be 'discontented' that a number of Africans were in England. She issued an edict in 1601 explaining that since Africans were taking jobs away from needy Englishmen, they were to be expelled from the country. The 1601 edict was the same year as the passage of the Poor Laws. But while the end of the 1590s was a time of inflation, bad harvests, and destitution for many of the English, expelling the few blacks who were in England at the time would hardly solve these serious problems. Despite this order, some blacks stayed in England, and in the seventeenth century more were brought in. Moreover, the drama of the Elizabethan/Jacobean era signified a greater blend of cultural experiences than ever before.

The harsh problems of the late sixteenth and early seventeenth centuries—the horrors of war and the ill treatment of soldiers, as well as the fear of witches, Jews, Africans, and other foreigners—were transformed by Shakespeare into plays of great power and eloquence as well as popularity. People of different classes and backgrounds met more than almost anywhere else in the theatre. The plays were not only presented in the London suburbs and at court; they were also played in the countryside when the companies went on tour, so that this cultural experience was shared by people of the many different backgrounds in Renaissance England. Despite the charming scene in *Shakespeare in Love*, Elizabeth I did not go the public theatre, but a whole range of different people, both men and women, did (see also Chapter 4). Groundlings paid but a pittance to stand while the wealthy sat in the galleries. And though Elizabeth I did not go to the plays, the plays came to her, as drama from the public theatre was performed at court. Thus members of the court had the opportunity to view not only the plays but also the monarch viewing the plays. If one were a ruler and enjoyed a play, on order of the monarch the play would be presented again. In 1605 *The Merchant of Venice* was performed before the king. Only a few days later James I ordered it performed a second time. We do not know if James fell asleep before the first performance was over—James I did drink heavily—and so wanted to learn the ending, or if he found the story of Portia, Antonio, and Shylock so compelling that he desired to see it again.

Centuries before the video recorder allowed us to repeat favourite television pro-grammes, how lucky it was to have the power of monarchy, the very top of society in Shakespeare's England.

FURTHER READING

Hall, Kim. *Things of Darkness: Economies of Race and Gender in Early Modern England* (Ithaca: Cornell University Press, 1995). This book discusses ideas about Africans and about 'blackness' in early modern English culture and literature. It also includes discussion of this issue in several of Shakespeare's plays.

Mendelson, Sara and Patricia Crawford. *Women in Early Modern England* (Oxford: Clarendon Press, 1998). This fascinating text examines many aspects of women's lives from the cradle to the grave for all levels of society.

Shapiro, James. *Shakespeare and the Jews* (New York: Columbia University Press, 1995). This useful study describes cultural and social ideas and attitudes toward Jews in early modern England. Shapiro discusses both the lives of actual Jews and the fear of Jews in the dominant culture.

Sharpe, J. A. *Early Modern England: A Social History, 1550–1760* (London and New York: Edward Arnold, reprinted with corrections, 1988). This very useful text on family life, towns and villages, and social hierarchy is also helpful on the mental life of early modern people.

Slack, Paul. *Poverty and Policy in Tudor and Stuart England* (London and New York: Longman, 1988). This book contains a useful discussion of the Poor Laws and ideas about the poor in early modern England.

Thomas, Keith. *Religion and the Decline of Magic* (Oxford and New York: Oxford University Press, 1971). This classic in the field discusses beliefs about witchcraft, ghosts, astrology, and other aspects of the mental world of people of all social and economic levels of society.

Wrightson, Keith. *English Society, 1580–1680* (London: Hutchinson, 1982). This book examines social stratification as well as social mobility and the consequences of the Reformation and social change.

10 | Daily life in town and country

Joan Thirsk

This chapter aims to give a picture of everyday life in Shakespeare's England. Any one of us going back in time would at first be struck by the familiarity of the scene, showing people doing the same things as us, getting up, snatching food before going about their daily tasks, talking with others along the road, muttering all the stock phrases and clichés in hurried conversations, switching from one mood to another, complaining, arguing, laughing and joking, pondering thoughtfully on life in general, and sharing deep sorrows in death. But we would also soon notice behind the many basic similarities in these doings a host of different assumptions.

People accepted the discipline of routines that are no longer imposed on us, and a whole world of background knowledge and conventional behaviour was taken for granted that is quite alien in our lives. At quite grand feasts men belched openly, and drunken men urinated freely without getting up from the table. The church bell that rang through villages and across the fields not only marked hours of the day and times to attend services in church, but spread news by its doleful tolling whenever someone had died. Children who attended small parish or dame schools skipped out at will to do errands, and did not turn up at all if they had to help with harvest in autumn. Women working in the fields took their babies with them and laid them to sleep beside the hedges. Pledges were deemed solemn and enduring if they were concluded in a church porch or within the church itself, so that was a serious place to do business. Time was unregulated by clocks; informally and carelessly, work mingled with leisure; you had a rough sense of the time by looking at the sky and the position of the sun. Thus the king judged one fit moment in Hamlet: 'The sun no sooner shall the mountains touch, / But we will ship him hence' (*Hamlet*, 4.1.28–9).

Country and town life

Most people in Shakespeare's day lived in the countryside, ever conscious of the changing seasons, and taking for granted the different routines, foods, outdoor activities, and travelling habits that changed between spring, summer, autumn, and winter. Short hours of daylight in winter meant long hours by candlelight, at home, or in the alehouse, gossiping rather than doing much, though the women could spin in semi-darkness. In summer everyone was outside, labouring hard in the fields, or roaming in the wilder parts of the neighbourhood, on the commons, in woodland or fen, picking up green plants and fruits for food, joining in sport, romping and rollicking with neighbours and friends.

Town life was different. But all country people had some taste of it, though not necessarily until their teenage years, and after that, only intermittently. Everyone lived in some sort of community which required them to turn up in town, sell produce, testify in court, buy something in the market, or just enjoy themselves at the fair. The amount of movement between town and country varied greatly between classes of people and at different stages in their lives, but most, including Shakespeare himself, had enough regular contact with the countryside to be as familiar as any villager with the plants, birds, animals, good and bad weather, and all the countryman's skills in getting food for free.

Shakespeare in Stratford-on-Avon lived in a town with about 250 households; he soon walked to the end of the streets and was out in the fields. Whenever he visited his grandparents, he was on farms in a nearby village. One author has written of Shakespeare's 'dyed-in-the-wool ruralism', for country associations are effortlessly captured again and again: in *Henry VI Part Three*, King Edward notes how 'The sun shines hot, and, if we use delay, / Cold biting winter mars our hoped-for hay' (4.10.28–9); more graphically, the Fool in *King Lear* deduces that 'Winter's not gone yet, if the wild-geese fly that way' (2.4.45); and none but an observant countryman could write of Beatrice eavesdropping, and liken her to a lapwing: 'look where Beatrice like a lapwing runs / Close by the ground to hear our conference' (*Much Ado About Nothing*, 3.1.24–5). So much knowledge of gardening shows in Shakespeare's lines that one could easily imagine he worked sometime as a gardener.

But the truth is, our imagination is stunted by a world dominated nowadays by town styles; we cannot enter into the life of people in the sixteenth century who moved freely across the frontiers between town and country. In town streets they watched the baker pushing bread into his ovens; the dyer, down by the river, stirring his smelly dye vats; or the miller grinding flour in mills on the outskirts. Yet in a matter of minutes they were wandering in the fields, learning how to trap animals, catch fish, pick up birds' eggs in spring, helping the women to milk the cows out in the open, sometimes with snow falling around (no wonder that milk came 'frozen home in pail'), gathering herbs for the pot, picking crab apples to make verjuice, that tasty vinegar of the past. Town and country gave equal but different pleasures in a balanced life that kept everyone in contact with the natural world.

In London, of course, life was something apart. It was far bigger than any other town, thronged with strangers from distant, scattered places. They arrived on foot, on horseback, occasionally by coach, from Wales or Scotland, by sea voyage from Ireland, the continent of Europe, Arabia, Asia, and the New World. Not all had pale skins; if they were Moors from Spain, driven out by religious persecution, they had brown skins;

Othello, remember, was a Moor. Some gentlemen brought back native Indians as servants from a visit to the New World. All sorts came together in alehouses, at foodstalls, in lodging houses, bedding down two and more in a room, jostling and chatting in narrow streets.

Privacy was not valued as it is today. Rather, people relished a world in which everyone was in sight of others, felt free to watch everyone else's doings, and talked readily to every stranger. Devout Protestants were learning to value private prayer, private reading, and private writing, but it was a luxury of the few. Most people looked for face-to-face encounters, and in London that offered newcomers some memorable experiences. On the dockside watermen, merchants, and mariners jostled with women stocking vessels with victuals and bedding. In Westminster Londoners gazed on the houses of rich noblemen, catching a glimpse of famous courtiers. They marvelled at the throng of people buying in fish and meat markets or stood outside shops catering only for the well-to-do buying expensive silks, velvet, gold and silver thread, lace and ribbons. In church parishoners saw the same privileged people again in a different context, and they would still stand apart in the forward pews. Did the rich wear their finery in church without a qualm, one wonders? Who can know?

But most people are adaptable and they met such experiences in a cheerful, positive frame of mind, content after a time to go home to their villages and drop back into their country ways. Their routine of life at home together with their religious faith in the world to come left them intrigued by London without any strong hankering or fretting to lead that life forever. They accepted the contrasts and enjoyed recounting their adventures to their friends. They accepted the conventions which kept most of them fixed in one locality for a lifetime. Alternatively, some found another kind of living as actors in roving companies, politicians, ambassadors, or cattle drovers, or pedlars following a roaming life. Pedlars wandered into the remotest country spots, laden with trinkets, ribbons and lace, crying their wares: 'Come buy of me, come, come buy, come buy, / Buy, lads, or else your lasses cry' (*The Winter's Tale*, 4.4.224–5). Ballad singers, actors, pipers, and fiddlers turned up surprisingly often to perform at places like the Shuttleworths' manor houses near Bolton and Burnley, in the northern county of Lancashire. Even people in that neighbourhood can never have felt remote from the world.

Young people's choice of career was frequently explained by their family's history; they generally followed the trades of their fathers, though it did not happen in Shakespeare's case. His father lived a settled life in Stratford, but like many other parents, he may have welcomed different opportunities for his son, and that meant William leaving home for a life that led him to London. Even then, London was only one of a host of town and country experiences that ended with his return to his native heath of Stratford, where his kin belonged.

Homes and home life

The scene in the ordinary home, as described for us by contemporaries, contained many features that are neither strange nor unexpected, even though modern technology has added a gloss to our basic routines that enlarges expectations and practical possibilities. To make the most of daylight, people got up earlier in summer than in winter, but they dressed amid a familiar scurrying search for the right clothes to suit the work and the day. Fancy choices were available to the rich, and servants were expected to have the right clothes laid out and ready to put on. But the labourer wore the same clothes day after day, long-lasting garments of leather, sheepskin, or canvas, and did not reckon on owning more than one change of clothing.

Clothes washing was difficult in the depth of winter, and in any case outer garments were never washed and were handed on as heirlooms. But from springtime onwards, shirts and stockings, whether made of cloth or handknitted, went into the wash from time to time, and were hung on hedges to dry. Thus Falstaff's ragged soldiers were expected to 'find linen enough on every hedge' (*Henry IV Part One*, 4.2.42). Thefts of such clothing brought people into court, and the burning or buying of wood-ashes to make a lye for soap were common events, telling us indirectly about the wash days in every household. When gentry travelled, they paid local women to wash their clothing, and the bills survive in our archives. But still, smells in town streets from decaying food, industrial processes, animals, unwashed people, what Shakespeare called 'the mutable rank-scented meinie [multitude]' (*Coriolanus*, 3.1.70), were disagreeable, and people sprinkled sweet-smelling substances wherever they could. They might wear a nosegay in the street, but indoors they often trod sweet-smelling herbs like thyme and rosemary underfoot, or sniffed them on the windowsills. Great men in the land expected more: dining elegantly after a session of judicial hearings in the Court of Star Chamber (the poor man's lawcourt), Elizabeth's chief ministers sat down in a room sprinkled with rosewater perfume (it cost twelvepence for one day, more than an average labourer's daily wage of ninepence), and ate at a table strewn with herbs and flowers. They rinsed their hands between courses in rosewater. In the country you could offer a paler version of the same amenity at no expense, simply gathering fragrant herbs at your door.

The way of making household linen smell sweet is described in a book on living the healthy life which shows how carefully one household task was performed when servants had time for elaborate procedures. Old people today remember muslin bags of lavender laid in the closet to sweeten the smell of linen. An Italian author, Alexis of Piedmont, gave a method which was translated (1558) for English readers and reprinted at least five times in Shakespeare's lifetime: you took an airtight chest, laid household linen in it along with lemons, oranges, or rose leaves, and added civet (a strongly scented substance imported from Africa). A container of warm coals was inserted (something like a warming pan), and it was left for days. Obviously, you took care to preserve a gentle warmth that did not burn everything. But people were past masters at regulating heat; otherwise they could never have cooked day after day on an open fire.

Sleeping quarters varied greatly in comfort between classes, but generally standards were rising, and contemporaries remarked admiringly on the improvements. The rich owned carved wooden beds, lay on goose-feather mattresses, were covered with sheets of linen, even fine cambric, laid their heads on goose-feather bolsters and pillows, with pillowcases, and kept warm under woollen blankets. The best quality blankets were made in Witney, Oxfordshire, and were still being bought in the 1930s; the Earl of Leicester sent specially to Witney for thirty blankets for Kenilworth Castle in 1584. Working people lay on truckle beds or straw palliasses, or at worst just mats, covering themselves with hardwearing hempen sheets and adding a thicker piece of woollen cloth for more warmth. One serving lad in a wealthy house in Worcestershire slept under a sack. Many wandering poor spent the night in barns, in the straw. Ordinary folk, however, reckoned to sleep on firm bedsteads, and lie on flock mattresses, filled with waste wool; women were paid sometimes 'to pick wool for mattresses', two of them earning in 1574 twopence a day for five days. You had a store of sheets and pillow cases which you handed on to your children as heirlooms, for they lasted many years. Over the generations families built up a considerable quantity of possessions by inheritance.

Furniture in the ordinary home was simple and spare, but it was being improved in quantity, with more benches, stools, and some chairs, though you might still prefer to sit on the floor on a cushion. Tables were replacing boards on trestles, and some living rooms might have an extra side-table or folding table. A dishboard or cupboard shelved plates that were of wood or pewter, for it was becoming more usual to eat food off plates rather than serve it on one or two thick slices of bread laid directly on the table. In big houses a woodturner came around occasionally to cut out a couple of dozen wooden plates at very small cost.

Bedrooms generally contained no more than beds and a chest to keep clothing. But they also stored miscellaneous possessions. Herbs were laid out to dry in chambers, and a resourceful widow might well malt barley in a corner, and earn some cash selling it. Purple-hued malt worms were evidently a risk, and that phrase was used by Shakespeare as a term of abuse for idling rogues (*Henry IV Part One*, 2.1.69–70).

Houses did not have many rooms, and so the household crowded into the main one, 'the hall', where food was cooked and the fire warmed everybody. Even then, what with draughts and doors opening and closing, the temperature in winter probably never reached above 60 degrees Fahrenheit (15 Centigrade) and was often nearer 50 (10 Centigrade). Sitting on upright chairs or at a bench without a back, you faced a solid wooden table to work, eat, and chat, or you pulled up a stool to perform operations nearer floor and fire, a posture that we see in illustrations of women, stirring the cooking pot.

Standards of domestic cleanliness varied with people, and the construction of the house. Floors often consisted of beaten earth, so fresh straw was strewn, on which rubbish fell and lay inconspicuously in the interstices until a fresh layer was added or the whole lot was swept out to the manure heap for fertilizing the fields. Herbs strewn on top gave off a sweet fragrance when trodden in, and signalled to visitors that a fastidious housekeeper was in charge of that house. But some women were overly fastidious and houseproud, and were criticized for cleaning too much. At the same time, archaeologists dig up old kitchen floors nowadays where plainly no one bothered about treading rubbish underfoot and leaving it there for evermore.

Some houses had painted cloths on their walls, giving a warm feeling to the rooms. Indeed, it is surprising how many modest farmhouses had painted cloths, not just in the hall but in the kitchen and bedchambers as well, thus hiding rough wall surfaces. Who painted the cloths, you may ask? When we look in the records of custom officials, we do not find them as imports. Most were probably produced in England, and some no doubt in the home, for artistry and the urge to paint and decorate lurk everywhere. Despite all the hard toil in growing food in fields and gardens, getting water from wells and springs, keeping a ready store of wood for the fire, brewing ale and beer, making bread, and gathering greenstuff and fruit promptly in season, people took time and trouble to improve and adorn their homes in distinctive ways. Canvas suitable for hangings was woven from home-grown hemp, and vegetable dyes were used to colour fabrics. We can readily picture some women painting their own cloths and doing more for their neighbours. Few of these cloths have survived, of course, for the smoky atmosphere in the house rotted and faded the home-made fabric. Tapestries, which were expensive imports from Brussels and France, lasted longer, but even they could become 'smirched' and 'worm-eaten' (*Much Ado about Nothing*, 3.3.120).

A more enduring improvement, which we can inspect today and date in some surviving houses, was the new-fangled chimney. It was added along one wall of the hall, and greatly reduced the smoke which normally swirled around the room from the open cooking hearth, escaping only through a hole in the roof. This change encouraged some to put a ceiling over the hall, and so create a storage loft above, called 'a cock loft', reached by a ladder, or 'a chamber' reached by a staircase. The loft stored cheese, apples, hemp, and wool. The chamber became a bedroom but a storeplace too. Another chamber downstairs next to the hall, soon to be called a parlour, gave the master and mistress of the house a purer air to sleep in at night. When the master died leaving a widow, he often ordained that she should continue to live in the parlour, sometimes also in the chamber above, and have access to the kitchen and the well for water.

Service rooms at the other end of the hall gave a dairy, brewhouse, and boulting house where flour was sifted and where the kneading trough could hold a bread mixture that would be left to rise overnight. More outbuildings clustered nearby, housing unthreshed grain in the barn, and animals in cowhouse and oxhouse; servants often slept above the animals for warmth and company.

Spending on luxuries

Comforts in the home crept in erratically, but in southern England at least they impressed contemporaries who saw London life at close quarters and recognized that a small consumer revolution was under way. Consumer goods reached the towns first, and instantly stirred covetous desires among the rich. But sharp-eyed, ingenious young people were caught in the consumer trap as well. They found ways of getting the same alluring goods at second-hand, for cast-offs were soon thrown out by careless spendthrifts. Alternatively, the young persuaded skilful friends to make copies; a young apprentice in London is said to have seen an Italian wearing knitted stockings of fine worsted and persuaded someone to copy them. A whole new industry grew out of that initiative.

From the pens of contemporary writers came mixed words of disapproval and wonder at all this consumerism. But nothing could stop the contagion spreading, infecting young and old alike with the desire for lace for a petticoat, gold or silver thread for stitching on a jerkin (a short coat), a pair of gaily coloured knitted stockings, or fancy buttons. Gorgeous buttons were made by the button-makers at this time; hence Guildenstern's exclamation: 'On Fortune's cap we are not the very button' (*Hamlet*, 2.2.224). Some gentlemen actually fed these desires for luxury among their servants, by paying out for clothes in the latest fashion for them. After all, well-dressed servants enhanced their masters' reputations; the epidemic of consumerism spread under many influences.

Food and health

Epidemics of a different kind, of plague, smallpox, measles, influenza, and typhoid concentrated minds on ways to preserve health and long life and encouraged much fresh thinking in Shakespeare's day about food, medicine, and how to survive to a ripe old age. Some people who fell sick decided it was God's will and would do nothing to cheat death. But this age saw a veritable library of new books assembled on health, on identifying plants and explaining their uses as medicine and food, and on ways of cooking all foodstuffs. They show us the full variety of animals, fish, and plants that was normally eaten.

Food and medicine were synonyms, fed into 'the store-house and the shop / Of the whole body', as Shakespeare called the stomach (*Coriolanus*, 1.1.22–3). Every part of almost every animal, apart from rats, was deemed edible, and practically every plant, except those known by experience to be poisonous. Fungi lingered in the uncertain category, but mushrooms were soon to be accepted and relished. Some herbs attracted fresh notice when Dutch immigrants were seen eating whole dishes of herbs like chervil. New fancies took hold among the well-to-do, like eating sage butter for break-fast to clear the brain. Among ordinary folk the main food, apart from bread, was a nourishing stew or pottage, containing everything that lay to hand, cereals, beans, peas, green stuff, roots, flavourings like mustard seed and salt, whatever foreign spices the family could afford, plus a slice of bacon, cut from a flitch hanging in the roof, a sheep's head, or a bone with a fragment of meat clinging to it. Only modest firing was needed for the pot to cook gently for hours on end; 'meals in minutes' were unheard of. Scottish and Irish people of the older generation still remember the appetizing smell and flavour of the stewpot, always simmering in the kitchen. Pottage was the same nourishing food in Shakespeare's day, and most ingredients came into the house of countrymen, if not of townsmen, without any money spent. They grew in fields, woods, and gardens.

Rich people ate pottage too, but for them it was one dish among several other varied meats or fish. Quantities of meat and fish at sumptuous tables were immense, but it did not mean that overeating was the rule. The books all urged moderate eating for health. Moreover, every groaning table had to feed many more servants down the line as well as the poor at the gate. Gentry regularly fed fifty and more people each day, counting visitors from afar, locals invited for charity's sake, and homeless vagrants waiting hope-fully outside. As for drink, the debate between ale or hopped beer continued, beer being the latest fashionable drink from Holland (and accounting for the 'swag-bellied Hollander—drink, ho!' (*Othello*, 2.3.68–9)), while ale was the drink of conservative country folk. Milk was appreciated, especially in winter in warm gruel and possets, but on the roads in summer you might be offered milk to drink, as happened to some foreigners, arriving from the continent and journeying through Kent. It would have been rich, full-cream milk straight from the cow, but whey, the liquid left after cheesemaking, was also a good food and thirst-quencher, so little valued by the dairymen that they gave it away free to the poor.

In printed books botanists classified and listed plants with increasing expertise, and physicians now quarrelled with traditional lore about plants for medicinal use; they insisted they knew better. In practice, though, they learned from each other. John Gerard, the herbalist, told readers of his *Herbal* how he offered free help to a labourer who had accidentally scythed his leg down to the bone. The labourer rejected the specialist's advice in favour of his own plant poultice, and he so impressed Gerard with the result that Gerard used the poultice himself thereafter.

Work and training

Problems of unemployment and poverty loomed large in the Tudor age, after the monasteries, where the poor had formerly found food and charity, were abolished (between 1536 and 1539). In consequence, the government legislated to ensure that everyone below the wealthy worked for a living. The old, the very young who became orphans, and the sick were helped in their parishes with weekly doles to stay in their own homes, to be sheltered in almshouses, or boarded with a local family. This meant that householders with sufficient means made regular weekly payments to relieve their poor. In your parish, you knew the people you were paying to help.

Young people went to school if their town or village offered the chance, but standards varied greatly. New schools were being founded by moneyed men who valued education. But only boys received this much attention. A village or single parish in a town might find a woman teacher, or sometimes a parson used space in the church to teach elementary reading, learning by heart, and writing. Then girls might be included. Otherwise, children stayed at home, learning practical skills by watching their elders in the kitchen, in craft workshops that were part of the home, or out in the fields. Around the age of twelve or thirteen they were apprenticed to a trade or went into farming, the apprentice promising to remain for between five and seven years.

You can imagine the homesickness of young people sent away, sometimes to London far from their homes in the north or south-west of England. It could become a liberating and agreeable experience, but might be an unhappy one from which the youngster fled, but was caught and punished. When apprenticeships were completed, young people made their own way in the world, becoming perhaps successful masters themselves and in due course dignitaries in their craft guilds. For young men serving apprenticeships, their careers were always helped if they managed to marry the master's daughter.

Some crafts flourished exceedingly if fashion successfully expanded their business. But some, like capmaking, went into decline as fashions changed. Caps were knitted, and so capmakers moved over to a related trade making knitted stockings. This new fashion superseded hose of fabric cut on the cross. Malvolio's yellow stockings in *Twelfth Night*, therefore, touched on two topics in current gossip. Brightly coloured stockings were desirable possessions, and knitting was a new way for womenfolk to earn money.

After training in farming, sons worked on their family's land, expecting to take it over themselves in due course, or they waited for vacant land to rent. They built up farmholdings slowly from small beginnings, receiving bequests from their relatives of a ewe-in-lamb, a cow-in-calf, a plough, a cart—every little helped. Sons of country craftsmen similarly learned their trade by following their fathers without the formalities of guild training.

For many young people, however, their livelihoods remained uncertain for many years, especially in the bigger towns. London was full of young men with a grammar school education, sprung from parents of yeomen, merchants, or parish gentry stock, watching for openings through influential kin ties, or just through gossip in the taverns. They might go abroad; one job-seeker agreed to go to Spain for a supply of *barilla* for making glass (copying the fine Venice glass which was an expensive fashion item in London circles). Hence, Falstaff's exclamation, 'Glasses, glasses is the only drinking' (*Henry IV Part Two*, 2.1.131). Two younger sons of gentry investigated tobacco-growing, learning the method in Holland. Other jobless hopefuls heard of James I's plan in 1607 to survey all Crown lands, and knew that many surveyors would be needed; they offered their services without prior training, and, helped by friends, some would indeed be taken on. 'Projects' of any and every kind were the order of the day, inventing a host of new and sometimes dubious ways of earning a living. The very word 'project' had a wealth of meaning; Hamlet seems to capture its association with chicanery and risk when saying 'this project / Should have a back or second that might hold / If this should blast in proof' (*Hamlet*, 4.7.124–6).

Gentlemen's sons were expected to keep themselves occupied in their teens, even though they would one day inherit land. Routinely they went to serve in the households of other gentry or nobility. Somehow they fitted these stints around and between school and university, and for parents it was a relief to occupy a teenager's difficult years in this way. Gentlemen learned to manage horses, hunt and hawk, wait politely on visitors, and converse intelligently with them.

Serving in other men's households was an old tradition suffering strain in Elizabeth's reign, for lords were learning to save every penny on their retinues in order to spend it on other kinds of display. Their earlier generosity, nay extravagance, to their servants faded; they became sharply aware of rising prices, for the sixteenth century saw rapid inflation from the 1540s onwards. Their stewards kept accounts more carefully and their masters adopted a new attitude towards money and the management of property. As an economy, lords even took into their retinues yeomen's sons who had had no training, whose fathers actually pleaded for this opportunity and paid for it, so enabling their sons to escape serving in the war and probably being killed. Cantankerous, cheese-paring lords became a byword among gossiping serving men, some of whom said they never knew in the morning if they would still be employed and sleeping in the same bed in the evening!

Thus, in early manhood, many young men lived precariously, waiting and watching for something to turn up. Whole families and family names stayed put for generations, but individuals in their twenties were highly mobile in both town and country. It was one way by which manners, news, and fashions spread with astonishing speed. Other means were promoted by trade and socializing. Women walked to London to sell fruit and vegetables. Diaries show all members of gentle families and servants cheerfully embarking on physically tough journeys to stay for a spell with relations or in London. They reduced their households at home, prompting a royal proclamation discouraging residence in London. They should stay in the country, it was argued, keep local life running smoothly, and maintain hospitality. But gadding about continued regardless.

If you lived in London in Shakespeare's day, you might well think it a magnetic centre of lively commerce and conviviality. But country people had their own satisfying lifestyle, bound together by networks of mutual exchange, borrowing, lending, praying, and protesting, regularly joining with neighbours to rejoice and feast as the seasons changed. The scenes in Shakespeare's plays slip effortlessly between town and countryside, telling us how much he knew of both worlds.

FURTHER READING

Alcock, N. W. *People at Home. Living in a Warwickshire Village, 1500–1800* (Chichester: Phillimore, 1993). Explanatory chapters about one Warwickshire village, Stoneleigh, are coupled with original documents, matching houses with sixteenth- and seventeenth-century owners, their wills, and their inventories listing possessions at death. House plans and photographs of houses surviving today bring past and present together.

Brown, J. Howard. *Elizabethan Schooldays. An Account of the English Grammar Schools in the Second Half of the Sixteenth Century* (Oxford: Blackwell, 1933). Written by a schoolmaster asking the right questions, this book gives a vivid and persuasive picture of school life, with illustrations of schoolrooms, the playground, etc.

Byrne, Muriel St Clare. *The Elizabethan Home* (London: Methuen, 1949). This book is a text of the time, reprinting dialogues that were used by two Huguenot refugees teaching French for a living in sixteenth-century London. They were texts for translation by their pupils, and are vivid and extremely informative on the ordinary routines of life.

Dodd, Arthur H. *Elizabethan England* (London: Batsford; New York: Putnam's Sons, 1961, 1973). This is an absorbing description of everyday life, supported by a large number of contemporary illustrations.

Garrett, George P., 'Daily Life in City, Town, and Country'. In *William Shakespeare. His World, His Work, His Influence*, ed. John F. Andrews, Vol. I (New York, 1985), pp. 215–32. This essay also describes ordinary life in Shakespeare's England.

Harrison, William. *The Description of England*, ed. Georges Edelen (Washington: The Folger Shakespeare Library and New York: Dover Publications, 1994). This is an early modern text describing English life, written by a clergyman living near London in Elizabeth's reign. It offers insights and very candid and sardonic comments on life and the changes seen by the author in his lifetime. The titles of the twenty-five chapters guide the reader.

Judges, A. V. *A Health to the Gentlemanly Profession of Serving Men, 1598* (Shakespeare Association, Facsimile No. 3, 1931). Nowadays this contemporary tract is confidently ascribed to Gervase Markham who was himself a serving man in a lordly household in the 1590s. Gives a lively, credible picture of the life.

Massingham, H. J. 'William Shakespeare of Warwickshire', Chapter I in Massingham, *Where Man Belongs* (London: Collins, 1946). Massingham was a true countryman with a keen appreciation of all the accurate detail on country ways found in Shakespeare's writings.

Nicoll, Allardyce (ed.). *Shakespeare in his own Age* (Cambridge: Cambridge University Press, 1976). Three writers in this book offer vivid illustrations on relevant themes: W. G. Hoskins, on 'Provincial Life', pp. 13–20; F. N. L. Poynter, on 'Medicine and Public Health', pp. 152–66; Katharine M.Briggs, on 'The Folds of Folklore', pp. 167–79.

Rothschild, J. A. de. *Shakespeare and his Day. A Study of the Topical Element in Shakespeare and in the Elizabethan Drama* (London: Arnold, 1906). This is an old book but a most sympathetic account, readable and well-informed. Chapter III from p. 105 onwards is especially relevant.

Stow, John. *The Survey of London* (London: Dent, 1945) (but many other editions). This is a much-used early modern text about London, published in 1598 by a Londoner, born c.1525. He never rode a horse, he walked everywhere, collected information from all and sundry, observed keenly, and conjures up a rich picture of traders, noble housekeepers, skilled craftsmen, and beggars. The index is no help; you must leaf through the book.

11 | Love, sex, and marriage

Martin Ingram

Love, sex, and marriage have been among the mainsprings of drama and literature in many cultures, but there were particular reasons why these themes should feature so strongly in the works of Shakespeare and his contemporaries. In Elizabethan and Jacobean England, the 'family'—a term most commonly used at this time to denote a household, including servants as well as those united by ties of blood and marriage—was an institution of exceptional social importance. Not only was it the matrix of procreation and the education of the young, it was also at all social levels an important focus of economic activity, of production as well as consumption, and above all was the site for the exercise of patriarchal authority and the reproduction of age and gender hierarchies at a time when the law regarded women as 'either married or to be married'.[1] Sex, power, and money were thus intimately connected. The family household was also seen as the nursery of religion, while it was imagined by statesmen as a vital political institution. Referring to 'private families', an official document of around 1600 stated as simple fact that 'on their good government the commonwealth depends'.[2]

It followed that courtship and marriage formation were not only of emotional and personal significance, nor were they simply a family matter of great moment: they were also of prime public importance. By the same token, personal relationships within the household, above all between husband and wife, were seen as the key not only to personal happiness but also to good citizenship. 'Necessary it is', wrote the moralist William Gouge shortly after Shakespeare's death, 'that good order be first set in families: . . . good members of a family are like to make good members of church and commonwealth'.[3]

The relationship between these pious principles and the foibles and frailties of human nature was inevitably problematic, and there was much scope for tension and conflict between the generations and between the genders. Moreover, although in general the importance of family and household was universally accepted, on particular issues there was debate and disagreement. Many of these controversies originated in or were fuelled by the Reformation, but they were given added urgency by economic and demographic pressures that, peaking in the decades around 1600, made governors and governed alike think hard about the social implications of sexual morality and the ethics of marriage. Problems were most acute, and the responses most elaborate, in

Courtship.

Couple embracing.

A wedding.

Fig. 1.2

towns and cities, above all in the rapidly growing metropolis. Moreover, the additional freedom and wider circle of acquaintance that London society offered wives and husbands, daughters and sons, created temptations that tested sexual and social *mores* to their limits. Shakespeare's London audiences must have been particularly attuned to the problems and controversies surrounding family, sex, and marriage, and were absorbed by them even though, in practice, the married state was not for everyone. Demographic calculations indicate that at any given moment in this period up to forty-five per cent of women were either not yet married or widowed, while the proportion of women who never married was on the increase and was to exceed one in five shortly after Shakespeare's death.[4]

Spousals and the law of marriage

Entry into the married state was less rigidly controlled than the importance of marriage and household might lead us to expect. Despite efforts to change the law in the sixteenth century, females could contract a valid marriage at the age of twelve and males at fourteen. Indeed it was possible for girls and boys to be betrothed from the age of seven, albeit with safeguards that allowed them the right to repudiate the union before they came of age. Although the practice was on the wane, such 'child marriages' did occasionally still take place in Shakespearian England. Teenage marriage, especially for girls, was certainly still commonplace among the nobility and gentry and other wealthy groups in Elizabeth's reign, though marriage ages tended to rise thereafter. It is true that most people married much later than the legal minimum, on average in the mid-late twenties. However, the mean conceals numerous local and individual variations, and it was by no means unusual for women to be married by the time they were twenty. Marriage at Juliet's tender age—not quite fourteen (*Romeo and Juliet*, 1.2.9, 1.3.11–19)—was at least imaginable in real life: writing in 1615, Alexander Niccholes reported with disapproval that the 'forward virgins' of the age claimed that thirteen or fourteen was the best time to marry.[5]

In *The Taming of the Shrew*, Lucentio's servant tells him 'I knew a wench married in an afternoon as she went to the garden for parsley to stuff a rabbit' (4.5.23–4). Ecclesiastical law, which governed matrimonial matters, allowed a couple to contract a valid and binding union by means of a simple pledge made to each other in words of the present tense. The marriage did not depend on the consent of parents, the presence of witnesses, the participation of a clergyman, or a ceremony in church. Admittedly, the authorities had always recognized that this situation created enormous potential for confusion, deceit, and ill-advised action. So for centuries they had tried to insist that couples contemplating matrimony should secure the consent of parents or other relatives, publicize their intentions beforehand by the calling of 'banns' (an announcement in church), and duly solemnize the marriage in the church in the presence of a priest. While licences could be issued to dispense couples from some of these requirements, those who wilfully evaded them were subject to punishment: their unions were in contravention of the law while being at the same time valid and binding.

Luther and other reformers regarded this situation as scandalous and ungodly as well as confusing, and in most parts of Europe the law of marriage was clarified in the sixteenth century. Despite powerful calls for similar reforms in England, the law remained in essence unchanged. What did happen was that, as Elizabeth's reign progressed, the Church insisted more and more rigorously on safeguards to ensure publicity, due regard for parental consent, and the necessity of solemnization. Detailed regulations were codified in the ecclesiastical canons (ordinances) of 1604. Moreover, the church courts—which represented a powerful system of justice separate from the secular courts, dealing with a wide range of religious and moral issues as well as matrimonial matters—became increasingly reluctant to recognize unsolemnized unions. In any case common lawyers had long regarded the church ceremony as necessary to secure the right of a wife to dower (maintenance) after her husband's death. The impact of these changes is seen in the fact that lawsuits over disputed marriage contracts, which had been frequent in earlier centuries and were still quite numerous in many areas in the late sixteenth century, declined in number quite sharply after about 1600. By this time there is abundant evidence that the overwhelming majority of couples, whatever promises they entered into beforehand, intended ultimately to solemnize their union. When people spoke of 'marriage' they normally meant marriage in church; and it is apparent that Shakespeare's characters always seem to envisage some kind of religious ceremony.

But this did not solve all problems. Eloping couples could resort to what were called 'clandestine' marriages, which were conducted by a minister and normally took place in a church or chapel in the presence of witnesses, but which happened at irregular times and evaded other formalities designed to ensure adequate publicity. While it was not until the late seventeenth century that this practice became a national problem on a huge scale, it was already a growing trend in London and some other localities by 1600. Many of the matrimonial intrigues of Shakespeare's plays feature precisely such a ceremony. In *The Taming of the Shrew* Lucentio hears that 'The old priest at Saint Luke's church is at your command *at all hours*' (4.5.13–14; emphasis added).

It was also still common (though the custom was declining) for couples to make themselves 'sure' in advance of the church wedding, in a ritual of 'handfasting' or 'spousals'. In their most elaborate form, these ceremonies were the culmination of weeks or months of negotiation between the partners and their families. Such 'treaty and communication of marriage', in which go-betweens (like Viola/Cesario in *Twelfth Night* (1.4.12–41)) not infrequently played an important part, was commonly punctuated by mutual visits and the giving of such gifts or 'tokens' of marriage as gloves, scarves, trinkets, pieces of money, and rings. Discussions over the bride's 'portion' and other exchanges of land and goods were often conducted simultaneously. The ceremony of handfasting might be presided over by a respected figure, perhaps even a priest, and family members were often present as witnesses and to give their blessing to the match. However, as the church wedding became ever more firmly established as the final step in the progress towards marriage, spousals tended to lose some of their ritual character and many, it would appear, were hardly more than promises to marry. The sheer diversity and ambiguity of practice—which inevitably led to dispute—is reflected not only in contemporary court records but also in Shakespearian drama, most notably in *Measure for Measure* (1.2.122–6; 3.1.210–12).

Courtship, consent, and constraint

Historians agree that simple models of 'arranged' or 'free' or 'individualistic' marriage are inapplicable to Shakespearian England. The far more subtle reality, that gave ample scope for dramatic treatment, encompassed a variety of circumstances in which flexibility and negotiation were more in evidence than rigid rules; and if few were married with no say in the matter, at the other end of the spectrum not many had a truly untrammelled choice. One constraint that bore hardly on the lower ranks was the principle that couples should have sufficient economic resources to maintain a household. This was among the reasons why marriage was forbidden to those in apprenticeship, and why, more generally, the marriage of the young was often viewed with disfavour. Even for those above the poverty line, accruing the means to finance a new household—whether through the inheritance of land or goods, the marriage portions that young women received from parents or other relatives, or careful savings of wages gained through service—was crucial to matrimonial calculations. A gradual increase in the size of dowries in the period may have made marriage increasingly difficult to attain for middling to poor women; at a different level of economic expectations, the inflation of portions among the aristocracy, gentry, and wealthy merchant classes made marriage a weighty matter for families with daughters to provide for.

At the highest social levels, marriage was important for not only financial but also dynastic and, sometimes, political reasons, and it was in these ranks that family influence in matchmaking was most powerful. Inevitably young girls were subject to the greatest pressures; as they grew older they were apt to develop not only minds of their own but also the means to exercise their will: hence the advice of the Isle of Wight gentleman Sir John Oglander to 'marry thy daughters betimes, lest they marry themselves'.[6] Sons had more freedom of movement than daughters, if not freedom of action, and when they were of age were often expected to take an active part in marriage negotiations on their own account, albeit with due consultation with parents or other family members. Whatever the age or sex of the child, accepted wisdom held that they must be given at least some say in the choice of marriage partner, if only a veto on someone who was utterly repugnant. The idea of voluntary acceptance was at the heart of the law of marriage, and it was widely accepted that a sound and happy union depended on the free consent of the couple.

Contemporary moralists inveighed against the wickedness of forced marriages, and it was proverbial that such unions led to ruin. In 1606 George Wilkins, Shakespeare's sometime collaborator, dramatized the issue in *The Miseries of Enforced Marriage*. Yet some parents insisted on their authority to the utmost—Sir Edward Coke, a leading common law judge, was reputed to have bullied his daughter into marrying the mentally unstable John Villiers by tying her to a bedpost and whipping her into submission. Against this background of conflicting social imperatives, Egeus's attempt to force his daughter Hermia to marry to his liking in *A Midsummer Night's Dream* (1.1.22–45) was a scene fraught with moral tension.

Lower down the social scale it was likewise accepted that children had a duty to consult their parents about their marriage plans. Polixenes' insistence in *The Winter's Tale* that a father

> . . . should hold some counsel
> In such a business
> (4.4.397-8)

was conventional wisdom. Seeking the 'good will' or 'blessing' of father or mother was a matter of prudence as well as courtesy and morality if the couple hoped to receive money, land, or goods to enable them to set up a household, or even expected an inheritance after their parents' or other relatives' deaths. On the other hand, practicalities tended to limit parental or other family influence. Men and women of the lower middling groups and labouring poor were often of mature age before they could reasonably hope to marry, by which time one or both parents might well be dead. Their late teens and early twenties were characteristically spent as apprentices, household servants, or servants in husbandry. As such they were under the quasi-parental authority of masters and mistresses—who themselves frequently took a part in marriage negotiations, sometimes assuming a role *in loco parentis*. But they were often remote from the direct influence of their natural families, and very much in contact with other young people in household, workshop, street, fair, and market. Inevitably they often took the initiative in finding partners and made what were essentially their own choices.

Whatever the social level, there was no *necessary* conflict between the matrimonial aspirations of young people and the wishes of their families. The contemporary ideal, expressed in numerous sermons and conduct books, was marriage with the multilateral consent of all the parties involved. All-round satisfaction was no doubt achieved in many cases, if necessary after some give and take on both sides. But the tensions implicit in this situation did sometimes explode into conflict. Church court lawsuits over disputed marriage contracts reveal many cases where parents reacted angrily on discovering that their offspring had attached themselves to partners of whom they disapproved, and used all the means in their power, including moral pressure, financial inducements, and the threat of disinheritance to bring them back into line. The outcome of such suits suggests that parents were often successful in re-asserting their control in contests of this sort, and the same is indicated by an interesting set of cases reported by the astrological physician Richard Napier.[7] To this extent parental and other family influence should not be underestimated. The vindictive rage of Polixenes when he discovers the marriage of his son Florizel to Perdita in *The Winter's Tale* directs the audience's sympathy towards the young couple. But his exercise of parental authority was basically in tune with contemporary expectations.

Yet Florizel's stance, or Hermia's for that matter in *A Midsummer Night's Dream*, would have likewise come as no surprise to the audience, because some individuals did defy their families. In a typical Wiltshire case in 1584, Emma Harrolde said that she would marry Richard Browne 'though all her friends would say nay thereunto and [they] should go a-begging together'.[8] Defiance was sometimes aided by the fact that family and 'friends' were by no means always of one mind. While parents, especially fathers, normally had the greatest say, uncles and aunts, brothers and sisters, and even more distant relatives sometimes meddled in matchmaking, and might play a major role if one or both the parents were no longer alive. But the lack of any clear rules to govern the role of kinsfolk provided fertile ground for dispute and the possibility of playing off one against the other. Even husband and wife were not always in agreement on choice of marriage partner for their offspring. Thus in *The Merry Wives of Windsor* Anne Page was able to slide between the preferences of her parents to secure a clandestine ceremony—''twixt twelve and one', that is outside the canonical hours—with her true love Master Fenton (4.6.47–50).

The suitors favoured by Anne Page's parents were preposterous. In real life parental choices could be quixotic or self-serving, which is why contemporaries could on occasion be sympathetic to defiant youngsters. But mostly, when parents objected to a match, it was because they were convinced that their offspring had made foolish choices that flew in the face of normal expectations. The most common complaint was that the individual in question was too poor or too lowly. Probably the most important factor that made youngsters themselves blind to material interests or family concerns was the power of love.

Admittedly the contemporary connotations of this term were different from those of today, and certainly emotion was only one element in a complex calculus. Thus men and women were often asked (or asked themselves) whether they could 'find in their heart to love' the other person; being 'in love' was not always expected. Nonetheless the rich vocabulary of emotion that is found in contemporary sources—'love', 'fantasy', 'fancy', 'delight', 'dalliance', 'gestures of lovely liking'—indicates that love could indeed be a powerful, active force in real life as well as poetry and drama. If a union was in other respects satisfactory, love could be accepted as a positive sentiment that parents were willing to accommodate. In 1586, for example, a Wiltshire gentleman gave approval to his daughter's choice of spouse to secure her 'well bestowing . . .

to live in the world as also the satisfaction of her own fantasy, seeing the same so firmly fastened'.[9] On the other hand, such sentiments could be regarded as destructive or 'diseased' if they were seen to override prudential considerations. Some contemporaries believed that an unrequited lover might sicken or die of love: Rosalind's statement in *As You Like It*, that 'men have died from time to time, and worms have eaten them, but not for love' (4.1.91–2), was more controversial than it sounds.

Honour, honesty, and illicit sex

In *Much Ado About Nothing*, when Hero is at the very point of being married to Claudio, he denounces her 'with public accusation, uncovered slander, unmitigated rancour' as no maid, an 'approvèd wanton', a 'rotten orange' (4.1.30, 42, 302–3). A confrontation of such compelling cruelty is the stuff of drama, not ordinary life. Yet in Shakespearian England people of all social ranks often found their sexual honour or 'honesty' called in question.

Women, defamed as 'whores'—a term used of any sexually transgressive female, not just of prostitutes—were particularly vulnerable to sexual slander because of the powerful operation of the double standard. But men were not altogether immune, and faced biting accusations of 'whoremonger' or 'whoremaster'. Of course such epithets were often employed as vulgar abuse, exploited for their emotive power in quarrels and disputes that were not primarily about sexual reputation. But the context—the counterpart of the stress on the sanctity of family and household—was a society in which sexual morality was of immense social importance and sexual transgressions were subject to legal penalty. The main agents of discipline, the church courts, could not touch life, limb, or property but could punish by means of public penance: characteristically dressed in a white sheet and carrying a white rod, penitents had to confess their fault before the local church congregation. (Near the end of Shakespeare's life, his son-in-law Thomas Quiney was ordered to do public penance for fathering an illegitimate child, though in the event the sentence was commuted into a money payment.)[10] Secular agents, in the form of constables and justices of the peace, were involved too; and many towns and cities claimed special powers to deal with sexual offenders. This was among the functions of the London Bridewell, established in 1553: culprits were whipped and incarcerated for short periods with hard labour. By ancient custom, moreover, the Lord Mayor and Aldermen could order 'strumpets', 'whores', and 'bawds' (males as well as females) to be carted through the city of London. These powers were used primarily against the professionals of the sex trade—vividly evoked in Shakespeare's plays by figures such as Doll Tearsheet and Mistress Overdone—but could be extended also to ordinary sex offenders. Fears of the 'pox' (syphilis) and other diseases sharpened civic concerns.

Attempts to regulate sexual expression inevitably created tensions, reflected in bawdy humour and sexual horseplay. Richard Fisher of Ely was reported around 1616 'for abusing of himself in the church upon midsummer day in setting himself in the lap of Margaret Woode, a maid, and most immodestly and unseemly . . . did pull up . . . [her] clothes . . . to her great shame: . . . [and] did call unto . . . the clerk saying unto him, "You see nothing" '[11]—the same bawdy pun as Hamlet makes when, lying with his head in Ophelia's lap, he cruelly teases her with 'country matters' (*Hamlet*, 3.2.101–9).

Inevitably things did not always stop at words, and large numbers of actual sexual transgressions came before the courts. They were not treated with equal severity, not least because the complexities of marriage law blunted moral disapproval in certain cases. Some people believed, or purported to do so, that a binding marriage contract licensed sexual relations because the couple were 'man and wife before God'. Thus, in *Measure for Measure*, the Duke can plausibly if tendentiously assure Mariana that Angelo

> . . . is your husband on a pre-contract.
> To bring you thus together 'tis no sin
> (4.1.68-9)

Others seem to have felt that, at most, such circumstances did but 'extenuate the forehand sin' as Claudio puts it in *Much Ado About Nothing* (4.1.48). In any case, it is clear that for many couples, whether contracted or not, restraints on sexuality crumbled when marriage was in sight. Parish register analysis indicates that at least a fifth of all brides in Shakespearian England were pregnant when they came to be married in church, though the pre-nuptial chastity of women in the upper ranks of society was more closely guarded. Though common, bridal pregnancy was becoming less acceptable as time went on. In the closing years of the sixteenth century the church courts began to prosecute couples for this transgression, and the trend intensified after 1600.

There was a thin line between sex in anticipation of marriage and simple fornication, that is, sexual relations between people who did not intend or had no realistic hope of marriage; and, in a society in which contraceptive and abortifacient techniques were not universally known and haphazardly employed, illegitimate births were the inevitable result. The extent of illegitimacy varied regionally and over time. More common in the 'highland zone' of western and north-west England, in the south-east the ratio of bastard births peaked at about three per cent in the decades around 1600. Coinciding with and partly conditioned by the harsh economic conditions of those years, which frustrated the marriage plans of many poor people and dislocated courtships to an unusual extent, illegitimacy raised the fears of local communities who experienced poor bastard births as yet another charge on the rates that parishes had to levy to relieve the poor. Economics thus sharpened moral concerns. Already subject to church court censures, and sometimes carted or whipped in the towns, by an act of 1576 the parents of poor bastard children could be punished by the Justices of the Peace, while in 1610 it was laid down that the mothers of bastard children should be incarcerated for a year in the local house of correction.

There were calls for harsher punishments yet, for this and other sexual transgressions. In this period the most severe punishment was reserved not for heterosexual offences but for 'buggery committed with mankind [sodomy] or beast [any intercourse with an animal]'. However, prosecutions for either activity were few, and particularly rare in the case of sodomy. The fact is that, though the erotic charge of same-sex relationships crackles through some of the literature of the period, evidence from which to gauge the extent of actual practice is meagre in the extreme. Sodomy—which was not necessarily thought to be inconsistent with heterosexual behaviour—might be execrated as the ultimate 'sin against nature', but the other sexual transgressions were generally of more immediate and practical concern to contemporary moralists and provoked the loudest demands for punitive action. In 1583 the Puritan popularizer Philip Stubbes suggested that 'the man or woman who are certainly known . . . to have committed the horrible fact of whoredom, adultery, incest, or fornication, either should drink a full draught of Moses' cup, that is, taste of present death . . .; or else, if that be thought too severe . . . then would God they might be cauterized and seared with a hot iron on the cheek, forehead, or some other part of their body'.[12] This was by no means a lone voice. By this period there was a long tradition of calling for the death penalty, especially in the case of adultery. Not only had this offence been singled out for severe treatment in Old Testament law; in contemporary eyes it was particularly abhorrent as a cause of strife and disruption of households, and (when committed by women) as an act that might pervert the inheritance of property. *Measure for Measure* must be understood in the light of these debates.

Marital relations and marriage breakdown

Divorce in the modern sense, with the right to remarry, did not exist in Shakespearian England, though the matter was controversial: the fact that unions could be broken only by death gave added weight to the importance of marital relations. While such relations were a less central theme of Shakespeare's plays than courtship and the marriage quest, they were important nonetheless, and there are also some poignant evocations of the ties between parents and small children, as in *Macbeth* (4.2.30–85) and *The Winter's Tale* (1.2.121–211; 2.1.1–34). The long-cherished notion that family relations were for the most part cold and severely authoritarian has now been discarded by historians. Letters, diaries, wills, and legal records provide abundant evidence of warm and loving sentiments both between husbands and wives and parents and children; they indicate that wives expected to be treated fairly and kindly; and they testify to the often powerful feelings of grief that were experienced when these relationships were prematurely ruptured by death.

Yet things could easily go wrong, in part as a corollary of some of the characteristics of contemporary courtship and matchmaking. The emphasis on marriage as an economic union cut both ways: while it could ballast the relationship, troubles could ensue if material expectations were disappointed. Prevailing patriarchal prescriptions, moreover, imposed strains on both sides. Churchmen denounced wife-beating as irrational and unmanly, but the repetition of this message suggests that many husbands thought differently: indeed the law itself allowed that 'the husband hath dominion over his wife, and may keep her by force within the bounds of duty, and may beat her'. Although such 'correction' was not to be administered in 'a violent and cruel manner', it was inevitable that the husband's authority sometimes degenerated into cruel tyranny enforced by fist, cudgel, and rope. Wives who were severely mistreated could sue for separation on the grounds of cruelty. In practice few did so, but the cases that did come before the courts bear witness to the hell that some women must have experienced.

On the other hand, men feared, but were also fascinated by, the sharpness of women's tongues. It was proverbial that 'Every man may tame a shrew but he who hath her'; and there was an extensive literature on the theme of scolding women, of which Shakespeare's *The Taming of the Shrew* was a sophisticated example. A man who so failed to live up to patriarchal expectations that he allowed himself to be beaten by his wife was even more abject. This was the signal for a 'riding' or 'skimmington ride': a mocking demonstration by the neighbours of the topsy-turvy couple, who in person, in effigy, or by proxy were paraded on a horse or ridden on a 'cowlstaff' (carrying pole) to the 'rough music' of pots and pans, drums and pipes, or even gunfire. While this motif is never directly represented in Shakespeare, there are echoes in plays as diverse as *The Merry Wives of Windsor* (3.3.115–24) and *The Winter's Tale* (2.3.75–6, 91–3).

More fully explored are the permutations—tragic and comic, psychological and situational—on the much more common fate of cuckoldry. In this patriarchal society, a man whose wife had been unfaithful—implying not only sexual inadequacy but also inability to govern his household—was commonly the object of contempt and derision. He might find horns, the ancient symbol of cuckoldry, hung on his gate or gable; in any event he was liable to be taunted by neighbours or street urchins, joking at his expense or making horn signs with their fingers. Yet no doubt some wore their horns philosophically enough, though Lavatch's *apologia* for the cuckold's state in *All's Well that Ends Well* (1.3.37–48) is a shade too paradoxical. The best way of deflecting the sting of cuckoldry was to take firm action. A wife's adultery was grounds for separation, and the Earl of Northumberland's robust view was that 'there can no dishonour rise to a man by a woman's whoredom, being separated'.[13] Separation suits were not numerous, but they did occur; and one of the attractions of proposals that adultery should be made a capital offence was that it would enable men not only to get rid of unfaithful wives but also leave them free to marry again. In 1604 a bill was actually introduced into the Lords 'for the better repressing of the detestable crime of adultery', which got as far as a second reading but was abandoned because it was found 'rather to concern some particular persons than the public good'.[14] Leontes' tyrannical arraignment of Hermione in *The Winter's Tale* (3.2.1–121) was no means complete fantasy.

Conclusion

Matters to do with courtship, sex, and marriage were well adapted to appeal to the whole range of Shakespeare's audiences—from the court itself through the well-heeled clientele of the hall theatres to the varied social scene of the Theatre or the Globe. Shot through with ambiguities of attitude and expectation, these themes were, in a time of rapid legal and social change, the subject of intense debate; and, spiced with mordant, often bawdy wit, Shakespeare's prose and poetry deftly yet relentlessly explored the dramatic confrontations and psychological tensions inherent in these subjects. While many of the issues still have enormous resonance in the present day, they can be fully understood only in the very different cultural context of Shakespeare's own time.

FURTHER READING

Adair, Richard. *Courtship, Illegitimacy and Marriage in Early Modern England* (Manchester: Manchester University Press, 1996). This study of regional variations in illegitimacy rates suggests that they may be related to differences in courtship and marriage practices.

Amussen, Susan Dwyer. *An Ordered Society: Gender and Class in Early Modern England* (Oxford: Basil Blackwell, 1988). This pioneering study of gender relations, based on Norfolk materials, emphasizes the political role of the family in relation to contemporary concerns with social order.

Archer, Ian. *The Pursuit of Stability: Social Relations in Elizabethan London* (Cambridge: Cambridge University Press, 1991). Sex, marriage, and the family are tangential to its main themes, but this book provides a valuable account of prostitution and the impact of Bridewell.

Carlson, Eric Josef. *Marriage and the English Reformation* (Oxford: Blackwell, 1994). This work is notable in linking law, theology, and popular practice, drawing on a wide range of sources including church court records.

Cressy, David. *Birth, Marriage, and Death: Ritual, Religion, and the Life-Cycle in Tudor and Stuart England* (Oxford: Oxford University Press, 1997). This richly detailed survey of the ritual and ceremonies associated with the rites of passage includes much material relevant to the themes of courtship, sex, marriage, household, and family.

Gowing, Laura. *Domestic Dangers: Women, Words, and Sex in Early Modern London* (Oxford: Clarendon Press, 1996). This gender-based study approaches church court records in terms of narrative, concentrating on sexual slander, marriage contract cases, and separation suits.

Griffiths, Paul. *Youth and Authority: Formative Experiences in England, 1560–1640* (Oxford: Clarendon Press, 1996). This ground-breaking study of an important topic covers courtship and sexual behaviour together with other aspects of the lives of servants and apprentices.

Houlbrooke, Ralph. *The English Family, 1450–1700* (London: Longman, 1984). This offers a reliable and wide-ranging introduction, based on a rich variety of sources.

Ingram, Martin. *Church Courts, Sex and Marriage in England, 1570–1640* (Cambridge: Cambridge University Press, 1987). Focusing mainly on Wiltshire, this study deals with the work of the church courts, with particular attention to suits over disputed marriage contracts, separation and divorce, prosecutions for sexual transgressions, and sexual slander.

Stone, Lawrence. *The Family, Sex and Marriage in England, 1500–1800* (London: Weidenfeld and Nicolson, 1977). This seminal work has been much criticized for its over-schematic account of changes in the family and for under-estimating the role of affective relationships in the sixteenth and early seventeenth centuries, but is nonetheless still worth reading, especially for its account of upper-class experiences.

NOTES

1. T.E. *The Lawes Resolutions of Womens Rights* (London: 1632), p. 6.

2. *Calendar of State Papers, Domestic, 1598–1601*, ed. Mary Anne Everett Green (London: 1869), p. 519.

3. William Gouge. *Of Domesticall Duties* (London: 1622), Epistle, sig. 2v.

4. Judith Bennett and Amy M. Froide (eds.). *Singlewomen in the European Past, 1250–1800* (Philadelphia: University of Pennsylvania Press, 1999), p. 237; Keith Wrightson. *Earthly Necessities: Economic Lives in Early Modern Britain* (New Haven and London: Yale University Press, 2000), p. 223.

5. Alexander Niccholes. *A Discourse, of Marriage and Wiving* (London: 1615), p. 11.

6. *A Royalist's Notebook: The Commonplace Book of Sir John Oglander*, ed. Fancis Bamford (London: Constable, 1936), p. 235.

7. Michael MacDonald. *Mystical Bedlam: Madness, Anxiety and Healing in Seventeenth-Century England* (Cambridge: Cambridge University Press, 1981), pp. 88–96.

8. Quoted in Martin Ingram. *Church Courts, Sex and Marriage in England, 1570–1640* (Cambridge: Cambridge University Press, 1987), p. 203.

9. Ibid., p. 142.

10. E. R. C. Brinkworth. *Shakespeare and the Bawdy Court of Stratford* (London and Chichester: Phillimore, 1972), pp. 79–80, 143.

11. Quoted in Richard Adair. *Courtship, Illegitimacy and Marriage in Early Modern England* (Manchester: Manchester University Press, 1996), p. 165.

12. *Philip Stubbes's Anatomy of the Abuses in England in Shakspere's Youth, A.D. 1583*, ed. Frederick J. Furnivall, 2 vols. in three parts (New Shakspere Soc., 6th series, Nos. 4, 6, 12, London, 1877–82), Vol. I, p. 99.

13. *Advice to his Son by Henry Percy, Ninth Earl of Northumberland (1609)*, ed. G. B. Harrison (London: Ernest Benn, 1930), p. 95.

14. *Journals of the House of Lords*, ii. 271–3.

12 | Changing attitudes towards religion

Peter Lake

England under Elizabeth I and James I was a Christian country. Not only were all English persons taken to be baptized Christians, they were assumed (indeed legally required) to be baptized members of the national church. That national church had been created relatively recently by Elizabeth's father Henry VIII when he broke with Rome in the 1530s. In theory, the new English church was a remarkably centralized and hierarchical institution, with the monarch as the supreme governor at the apex of power, appointing the bishops who governed the church in the monarch's name. The church had one liturgy—the Book of Common Prayer—that was to be used in every parish. The ideal was uniformity, order, and obedience to monarchical authority. However, precisely the same event that had created this church, the English Reformation, had also rendered what it meant to be a Christian newly problematic. There developed a number of rival versions of true Christianity and of what a true church should look like. To appreciate the nature of this emergent Protestant national church, we need to set the situation under Elizabeth and James in its historical context.

Late medieval Catholicism

It used to be thought that the religious changes started by Henry VIII had deep social and cultural roots; that the Reformation was a widely supported, even popular, movement of reform. In this view, the late medieval Catholic church was thoroughly superstitious and corrupt and, as such, increasingly unable to meet the spiritual needs of the more literate and sophisticated of the laity.

Of late, however, historians have produced a very different view of the causes and nature of the English Reformation. It has become clear that the late medieval English church was in fact a vibrantly healthy institution well able to meet the spiritual and social needs of the mass of the population, both élite and popular, noble and plebeian. This was a church which right up to the moment that Henry VIII took it over continued to attract the devotion and donations of the people. Through an elaborate series of liturgical practices, the church defined not only the calendrical and farming years but also the life cycle of the individual and the social life of the community. Here was a form of religion based as much on ritual observance as it was on individual belief. The rituals and sacraments of the church were designed to address both worldly and other-worldly purposes. The presence and power of God was taken to be contained in, shown forth and indeed distributed and manipulated by the church and clergy.

The central, paradigmatic instance of the immanent presence of God in his church was, of course, the mass, during which the priest was deemed actually to be able to change ('transubstantiate') the bread and wine into the body and blood of Christ. Thus he was understood to perform a literal repetition of Christ's sacrifice on the cross for the sins of the world. This capacity was of immense significance and power. It was a basic Christian belief that since the fall of Adam all humans were so riven with sin as to be incapable, through their own pious acts and virtues, of achieving salvation. Only God's mercy, which had achieved its highest and most potent form in the sacrifice of His Son, opened up the possibility of salvation for fallen humanity. But it was through the church and its sacraments that the resulting grace and merit were to be distributed. The church, its clergy, and its saints interceded between sinful humanity and a God both just and merciful. Through their intercession, salvation could be achieved and divine grace and power be controlled and distributed for beneficent purposes through the world. Of course, God could and did intervene directly through miracles, but for the ordinary Christian it was through the services, ceremonies, and sacraments of the church that salvation was to be won.

During their time on earth Christians were supposed to confess to priests who would assign a variety of penitential acts (prayers, pilgrimages, fasts, etc.) designed to wipe away the otherwise damning effects of their sins. For all but the most holy, this cycle of confession and penitence was never enough. The weight of sin was always too great. Only saints and near saints went straight to heaven. That was where purgatory came in. Purgatory was a place between heaven and hell to which most normally sinful persons were sent, to be purged of their sins through a series of torments quite the equal of anything they might experience in hell. The only difference was that the damned stayed in hell for ever, while the inmates of purgatory were there only for a while until they had been rendered fit for heaven.

The torments of purgatory were portrayed in terrifying terms; one might, depending on the number and seriousness of one's sins, spend hundreds of years there. It was, however, possible to shorten one's sentence. First, while one was alive, one might perform a range of religious works. Second, after death, one might benefit from prayers said by friends, family members, and a variety of groups (like trade-guilds, confraternities, or the wider parish community itself). But the most potent form of intercession was a mass said for the soul of the departed. For masses one needed priests, and priests cost money. Huge amounts of emotional energy, material resources, and money were poured into the task of getting through purgatory as quickly as possible.

The result, historians have argued, was a vision of a community of Christians, which included the living as well as the dead, now all incorporated, through the sacrifice of Christ on the cross and the intercessory activities of the church, into the mystical body of Christ. This body was created and sustained by the (seven) sacraments of the church, and particularly by the mass, that central event in which the consecrated elements (the bread and wine) were transformed, by the priest's performance of the correct liturgical forms, into the body and blood of Christ. Through the seemingly simple act of reception, these were literally incorporated into the body of the believer who was, in turn, incorporated thereby into the mystical body of Christ.

Protestantism

The ideological position that came to be known as Protestantism represented a self-conscious assault upon and break with this view of religion. Juxtaposing the authority of the scriptures against that of the church, Protestants used what they took to be the central tenets of biblical Christianity to criticize the position outlined above. Let us start with what was in many ways the foundational Protestant doctrine, that of justification by faith alone. This belief took the standard Christian tenet that held that fallen humanity was so sunk in sin that it could be saved only through the mercy of God and the intercessory sacrifice of Christ and, as it were, pushed it to the limit. According to Protestants there was nothing that anyone could do to render themselves just in the sight of God. If sinners were to be saved it was God alone who must save them. Christians who wanted to be saved had to acknowledge the depth of their own sin, and recognize their complete impotence in the face of the justice of God, and thus their complete reliance for salvation on God's mercy in Christ. Only through faith in Christ could Christians hope to be saved. Once they were united with Christ through a true saving faith, Christ's righteousness would be imputed to them, and when a just God came to judge them he would see not their sins but Christ's sacrifice.

Faith, then, was of the essence, and faith itself, rather than being the product of any act of an always already corrupt human will, was a gratuitous gift of God. To place any faith in one's own actions or virtues, or indeed in the intercessory claims and practices of any other group or institution, was a snare and a delusion; a sure sign, in fact, that one was not saved. Justification was thus a once-and-for-all divine act, not a long and tormented process of purification. Accordingly, there were only two places (heaven and hell) to which the souls of the departed would be sent and only two groups—the justified and the damned, the elect and the reprobate. There was thus no intermediate status and hence no purgatory, and all the intercessory powers claimed by the church were false.

Such a view of justification undercut the whole intercessory structure of Catholic religion. It emptied almost all of the external practices and ritual performances of late medieval Catholicism of their saving power or spiritual necessity. Instead of being essential routes to salvation, necessary means for sinful humanity to appease the wrath of God and speed its way through purgatory to divine bliss, they became tricks played on the populace by a grasping clergy, desperate to part a credulous laity from its money. Indeed, worse than that, the outward observances of Catholicism became spiritually destructive, potentially fatal forms of superstition and idolatry. They were forms of false worship distracting the believer's attention away from the true God towards delusory substitutes—often satanic illusions and stand-ins—which offered entirely false routes to salvation. Thus were simple Christians led to worship images and pictures, old bones and highly painted images in a devilish mockery of true reverence and religion. Catholicism was in fact 'popery', a false religion, designed to lead humanity into destruction by Satan. Satan had used as his agent Antichrist, a Biblical figure whom Protestants habitually identified as the Pope, to mislead Christians and hijack the church for his malign purposes.

Politics, dynastic and religious

If we take seriously the vision of the 'popularity' of the late medieval Catholicism evoked in recent scholarship, then it seems the origins of the Reformation were not in any longstanding popular dissatisfaction with the status quo; still less in any widespread adherence to the sorts of Protestant opinions summarized above. Rather, the origins of the Reformation in England lay in high politics and in particular in Henry VIII's desire for a divorce from Katherine of Aragon. This was a divorce the Pope, as head of the Catholic Church, was not willing to grant him. Henry's confrontation with the Pope eventually led to his desire to arrogate the very considerable authority and property of the church in England to the crown. Of course, if we take this view of the Reformation then the subsequent course of religious change and even more the 'triumph of Protestantism' seem less about faith than about power and wealth.

The Church of England created by Henry VIII was never Protestant. There was a change of authority at the top, but not a full-scale reformation of religious practice. Protestantism had to wait for the accession of Henry's son Edward VI, during whose brief reign England received its first Protestant vernacular liturgy and formulary of faith. But Edward died young (in 1553) without having produced an heir, and he was succeeded by his sister Mary Tudor. As the daughter of Katherine of Aragon, Mary not unnaturally regarded the Reformation and all those associated with it with loathing. She was anxious to return England to the embrace of Rome as quickly as possible. Accordingly, she overthrew the religious changes made by her father and brother and married a foreign Catholic prince, Philip II of Spain. She failed, however, to produce an heir. Mary died in 1558 and was succeeded by her sister Elizabeth. Henry VIII had broken with the Church of Rome and abandoned Katherine of Aragon to marry Elizabeth's mother, Anne Boleyn. Since the Church of Rome had never accepted the annulment of Henry's marriage to Katherine as valid and thus regarded Anne Boleyn as a whore and her daughter Elizabeth as a bastard, Elizabeth was unlikely to view

Catholicism with anything other than distaste. Accordingly, she returned the country to Protestantism.

Between 1530 and Elizabeth's accession in 1559, England had thus experienced at least four changes of religion; from traditional Catholicism, to the various versions of Henrician reform, to Protestantism under Edward VI, back to Papalist Catholicism under Mary, and now back to Protestantism again. Because of the peculiar marital and gynaecological histories of Henry VIII, his various wives and progeny, Henry bequeathed a situation to his successors in which the immediate heir to the throne was of the opposite religious persuasion to the reigning monarch. Nor did the accession of Elizabeth necessarily bring this crazy dynastic and religious switchback ride to a close. If Elizabeth were to die without issue the most plausible claimant to the throne was Mary Stuart ('Mary Queen of Scots'). Mary was the product of a marriage between Henry VIII's sister and the king of Scotland. She was now the regnant queen of Scotland, and a Catholic who, because of her own marital history, had very close links with Catholic France.

As it turned out (but as contemporaries in the 1560s and 1570s could not predict) Elizabeth never married and thus did not produce an heir of her body. And so, throughout the period from the 1540s until the execution of Mary Stuart in 1587, the religious and political situation was entirely dependent on the life of the reigning monarch. Both Protestants (under Edward VI) and Catholics (under Mary Tudor) had very good reason to remember what the sudden death of a ruler could mean. Religious settlements and political establishments whose hold on power seemed utterly safe and secure could crumble overnight to be replaced by regimes of exactly the opposite political and religious colouring.

The Elizabethan settlement

This then was the situation the Elizabethan regime confronted in the 1560s—a potentially unsettled political and dynastic situation, a church destabilized by two decades of constant change, and a largely conservative people. Elizabeth responded by restoring a version of the church established by her brother. The Book of Common Prayer (only slightly amended from the second Edwardian book of 1552) and the Thirty-Nine Articles (a position statement somewhat modified from the Forty-Two Articles of 1553) provided the liturgical and doctrinal spine for her church. Church government remained largely unreformed—its administrative and jurisdictional structures generally unchanged from the period before the Reformation. The same could not be said of its personnel—at least at the top. To a man, the bishops appointed by Mary Tudor refused to serve under Elizabeth, and so Elizabeth was forced to appoint a new bench of bishops. Many of these men had gone into exile on the continent under Mary, where they had been exposed to the latest models of reformed Protestant worship, church government, and spiritual discipline. When they returned to England, they were far more zealously evangelical than the Queen. The same was not true of the lesser clergy, most of whom had been ordained under some form of Catholic regime and then conformed their way through the subsequent religious changes. Those changes had rendered the clerical profession a much less inviting career than it had once been; there were severe shortages of manpower in many dioceses at the outset of the reign and no great untapped reserves of educated or qualified men available to fill them.

And then there was the mass of the people, many (perhaps even most) of whom hankered after the old ways, if only because many of them had never been exposed to the Protestant doctrine imparted by someone who either understood or believed it. Indeed, precisely because of this, it might be best to see the Elizabethan period not as the second but as the first age of the Reformation in England, not so much constituting part of the consequences of that event as, at the level of social and cultural change, comprising its course.

Puritans and conformists

In hindsight, of course, we know that Elizabeth lived until 1603 and that the settlement of the church achieved in 1559 was passed on unchanged to James I. But to contemporaries all that was far from clear. Indeed, just as no one in 1559 would have expected the Queen to remain unmarried, so relatively few contemporaries would have expected the settlement to remain unchanged. For hot Protestants it was an opening bid, a first move in a process of further reformation. For conservatives and Catholics, of course, it was another temporary setback likely to be removed if the Queen came to her senses, married a Catholic or was replaced by Mary Stuart.

Only the Queen and an emergent faction of conformist bishops saw the settlement as the last word on the subject. From the point of view of the Queen, the settlement had purged the church of popish idolatry, removed the power of the Pope from England, and staked out a firmly Protestant, even moderately reformed, doctrinal position. As for the government of the church and its liturgical structures these were 'things in-different' (i.e. things upon which scripture was silent and thus left by God to the discretion of the monarch), and she had spoken. With these principles established, the disruptive part of the Reformation was over. All that remained was to allow the people to accommodate themselves to the new dispensation, in the process ceasing to be Catholics and becoming, through force of habit as much as anything else, members of a Protestant national church united under the power of the Queen. Elizabeth had no wish to force her Catholic or conservative subjects to choose between their obligations to their sovereign and country and their religion. She also hoped to pose before foreign Catholic powers as a moderate; someone with whom they could do business, who indeed, under certain circumstances, they might even lure back to the Catholic fold. The result was a politique Protestantism, dominated by the issues of order, obedience, and loyalty to the person and authority of the Queen.

This was not the view taken by many early Elizabethan bishops or privy councillors and still less by the more commitedly Protestant members of the laity and clergy (still at the start of the reign a distinct minority). For them the church was a proselytising machine; its job was to convert people to true religion by spreading (ideally by preaching) the word of God. By true religion, these people did not mean the routinized conformity to the ceremonies and practices of a formally Protestant national church, at the centre of the Queen's strategy, but rather a religion (and style of rule) based on a strenuously personal understanding and application of the core Protestant doctrines of justification by faith alone and predestination and of a properly anti-papal under-standing of idolatry. From the hot Protestant perspective, the calming sense of continuity at the centre of Elizabeth's vision of the church, the hope of doing good gradually by stealth, was not merely mistaken, it seemed all but certain to lure people into a false sense of security, encouraging them in the (entirely false) assumption that they could be good Christians, that is, that they could be saved, even while still holding on to central elements of their old attitudes and practices. In fact, the more advanced Protestant critics of the settlement ('Puritans') came to think that some of the 'remnants of popery' strategically placed in and around the Book of Common Prayer (like kneeling to receive the communion or the use of the sign of the cross in baptism) were actually encouraging the people into fatal spiritual errors. Thus, they believed that the church was not telling the people how they could be saved, or showing what was damningly erroneous about the old ways. Instead, it was actively conniving in sending many of its weaker members to hell.

Out of the clash between these different priorities and perspectives developed the claims, arguments, and campaigns for further reform, first of the liturgy and then of the government of the church, that have come collectively to be known as Puritanism. At first, many of the major proponents of change were in the establishment. However, the longer Elizabeth's reign went on and the clearer it became that the Queen was not having any truck with further reformation, the more oppositional 'Puritanism' seemed. The men who became prominent within the ecclesiastical and then the political establishments were men who were happy to take the Queen's side in these disputes. That meant characterizing all such Puritan attempts to foster change as subversive challenges to royal authority and preference.

On the one hand, it is possible to write the history of Elizabethan Puritanism as a story of defeat; as a conservative queen defended her church from the aggressive attempts of radical Protestants, many of whom took their models of church govern-ment and worship, and indeed their standards of doctrinal purity, from the foreign reformed churches (most notably from Calvin's Geneva). There would, of course, be a good deal of truth in such an account. But on the other hand, the reign also saw the spread of Puritanism throughout the social, political, and ecclesiastical structures of England. How can this paradox be explained? The answer lies first in the nature of Puritanism, which became more than a list of changes to be made to the government and liturgy of the church. It was emerging as a distinctive style of belief and practice that set apart the most committed Protestants from their contemporaries. The answer also lies, as ever, in the political circumstances of the regime, and, in particular, in contemporary perceptions of the popish threat.

As we have seen, for the best part of her reign Elizabeth's most likely successor was Mary Stuart. After 1568 Mary was safely under house arrest in England, but she remained politically active. Tied by links of blood and religion to the most Catholic factions in France and by ties of political convenience and religion to the most powerful country in the world, Spain, Mary remained until her execution (in 1587) the object of incessant Catholic plotting. In the period after 1570, with Elizabeth excommunicated by the Pope, the regime's geo-political situation deteriorated sharply. England seemed ringed by actual and potential Popish enemies. There was a long cold war with Spain, which lasted throughout the 1570s and early 1580s. There were incessant fears of the imminent collapse of the Protestant cause in France and the Low Countries. After the outbreak of war with Spain in 1585 these anxieties were compounded by the prospect of foreign invasion. Always there was fear of Catholic conspiracy and assassination from within England, especially in the conservative Northern counties.

In this situation, Protestant zeal could often pass for political loyalty, and hatred of Catholicism could do duty as devotion to the Queen. And, of course, the Puritans were devoted to Elizabeth. However much they might disagree with her about reform of the church, about what to do with Mary Stuart (the Puritans wanted her dead and Elizabeth did not), about how beastly to be to English Catholics or how directly to intervene on the continent, Elizabeth was all that stood between Puritans and either religious civil war or the return of popery. Conversely, it was the Puritans who were likely to be the most active defenders of the regime against Catholic plotting and the most enthusiastic prosecutors of a war against popery and Spain. All of this ensured that Puritans retained friends in high places throughout the reign. By the end of the 1580s Puritan campaigns to reform the church had gone quiet. But the godly had in the interim quietly insinuated themselves into the power structures of provincial England. Nor did they ever lack friends at court. When James I came to the throne in 1603, the Puritans were to be found making their old pitch for further reformation to a new king.

Catholics under Elizabeth and James

But what of the Catholics? It could be argued that it was simply the Queen's longevity that killed off traditional Catholicism in England. As we have seen, traditional Catholicism was a religion of communal ritual observance, centred on the parish church and a range of liturgical and para-liturgical practices, of feasts and fasts and holy days, that suffused the social and cultural life of the people. It was a religion centred on sacraments and rites of passage—baptism, the last rites, confession and, centrally, of course, the mass—which only Catholic priests could perform. Seize the priesthood and churches of the national church for Protestant purposes, wait for the last of Mary Tudor's clergy to die out, and Catholicism would disappear. Arguably, Elizabeth's approach to religious change had been designed to have just such an effect. Up to a point it worked. Traditional Catholic religion, as the English had experienced it before the Reformation and then briefly again under Mary, did disappear. Like the spread of hot Protestantism, the change occurred more quickly in some places than in others. But that did not mean that English Catholicism vanished entirely.

From the 1570s the efforts of renegade priests ordained under Mary or Henry were supplemented by the arrival of English priests trained in seminaries on the continent. This ensured that English Catholicism would not wither away altogether. But what would it mean to be a Catholic in Elizabethan England? Could one continue to attend one's parish church, while doing Catholic things on the side, thus meeting the state's minimum requirements for membership of the national church, but retaining or reserving one's real religious identity as a Catholic? Many thought so. By the same token, some Catholic zealots—mostly priests but also some laity—claimed that such contact with the heretical services of the national church was a polluting sin. For them, to be a true Catholic was also to be a recusant, someone who refused to go to church and who paid the penalty. From the early 1570s onwards there were increasing numbers of such recusants, in part because the government, alarmed by the continued existence of English Catholicism, started to enforce the law more stringently. But throughout the reign, the enforcement of the recusancy laws was never better than haphazard and what came to be called the 'church papist' option (that is, Catholics who attended parish churches) remained very popular. People and families slid from conformity to recusancy and back again. In some areas—parts of Yorkshire and Lancashire in the north for instance—Catholicism remained something like the communal norm for decades. For the most part, however, Catholicism became an underground sect centred on certain households and social and kinship networks. Priests were shuttled between them to service what was becoming a distinct English Catholic community.

As English Catholicism refused to die out, so the regime passed more and more stringent laws against it. The fines imposed for recusancy were raised to solvency-threatening levels and certain central Catholic acts were equated with treason. By the mid 1580s it was a felony to harbour a Catholic priest and treason to exercise the functions of Catholic priest in England. The regime denied that such laws constituted persecution, for, they claimed, the Catholics were being punished not for religion but for their actually or potentially treasonable political beliefs and activities. Not only did Catholics refuse to acknowledge the God-given powers of the Queen as supreme governor of the church, they also owed allegiance to a foreign power, the Pope, who claimed to be able not only to excommunicate but to depose secular rulers and thus to free subjects from their obligations to their natural prince. This was to declare open season on heretical princes as fit objects for the assassination attempts of their Catholic subjects.

Many Catholics, of course, replied that they were loyal subjects of the Queen. Their refusal to attend church and eschew the services of Catholic priests was based on the promptings of conscience. They happened to think that the Queen was in error and would pray for her conversion. In the interim they asked only to be left alone to save their souls. Priests came to England not to plot sedition but to minister to the flock of Christ. Indeed, some Catholics went so far as to claim that should the King of Spain invade they would rush to defend their queen and country from the foreigner, as some of them in fact did in 1588 as the Armada approached.

Just like their Protestant contemporaries, then, English Catholics were divided: some were rigid recusants, more were church papists. Until she was executed in 1587, some looked to Mary Stuart to save them. Others looked to Spain. Most were politically 'loyal' or at least quiescent. Some claimed to believe that the Queen herself was benign, that she was merely being misled by a faction of evil self-seeking heretic or politique counsellors. Others said, and presumably still more thought, that she was a persecuting tyrant. A very small number actively plotted against her. By the 1590s there was a major division amongst English Catholics between those who were prepared to bargain some sort of profession of political loyalty for formal toleration (the appellants) and those who were not.

James I

By the end of Elizabeth's reign in 1603, for all the official talk of unity and uniformity, of hierarchy and obedience, a complex multiplicity of religious opinions and practices existed in England. In part this was a function of the complicated and ambiguous legacy of the English Reformation(s) of the sixteenth century; in part a function of the political exigencies and anxieties facing the Elizabethan regime throughout most of its existence; and in part a function of the limitations of the Tudor state, which found it easier to legislate unity and uniformity, to lay down set forms and clear chains of command, than to turn such laws and schemes into reality.

By the 1590s it was clear that Mary Stuart's son, James VI of Scotland, would succeed to the English throne. Taken as a babe in arms from his mother, James had been raised as a Protestant in Presbyterian Scotland. By providing an impeccably Protestant male ruler, with legitimate heirs, James's accession promised to resolve, at a stroke, some of the thorniest problems of Elizabeth's reign. His arrival was all the more enthusiastically anticipated because a range of English religious groupings thought they might have something to gain from his rule. Puritans saw in James a likely sponsor of further reformation. Defenders of the ecclesiastical status quo saw someone who had learned first hand of the subversive anti-monarchical leanings of Presbyterians and Puritans. Catholics saw Mary Stuart's son. In Scotland James had been sympathetic to Catholics and in England he was likely to be grateful for past loyalty directed to his mother, who (Catholics believed) had been the victim of a judicial murder at the hands of the regime James was about to take over. On this basis, many Catholics hoped for formal toleration or, at the very least, a suspension of the recusancy laws.

James did nothing to discourage any of these hopes; he wanted for political purposes to be all things to all men. Once safely ensconced on the throne, he went through the motions of reform, hearing, in council, court, and Parliament, the case for change from a variety of groups. In the end he did nothing much, producing a revamped and rejigged version of the Elizabethan status quo ante, articulated around his own version of divine right monarchy (and episcopacy) and his understanding of the threats posed thereto by extreme Puritans and jesuited papists alike. He then proceeded for the rest of his reign to play both sides against the middle.

Claiming always to want unity and order, presenting himself as the Solomonic apostle of moderation and peace, James offered patronage and preferment to men from any and all groups who would talk his language and distance themselves from opinions that in his view threatened monarchical rule. These variously included both Puritanism and popery. James enjoyed remarkable short-term success. He exploited the Gunpowder Plot, an attempted assassination, to gain a large grant of taxation from Parliament without giving in to inevitable demands that he persecute all Catholics with renewed vigour. Indeed, he responded with the Oath of Allegiance, a typically subtle attempt to exploit the existing divisions amongst English Catholics while posing as a moderate and peace-loving figure. He pursued a similar policy towards the Puritans, integrating a good many 'moderates' into the church while taking a virulently anti-Puritan game against 'extremists'.

It was not until the late 1610s and early 1620s that events in central Europe, events that were in origin entirely beyond his control, exposed the limitations of his policies. But in this he was in many ways the victim of the religious diversity and interconfessional conflict bequeathed to him (and indeed to the states of Christian Europe) by the Reformation and its aftermath.

FURTHER READING

Collinson, P. *The Elizabethan Puritan Movement* (London: Jonathan Cape, 1967). This standard account provides a wonderful depiction of the inner workings of the Elizabethan regime.

Duffy, E. *The Stripping of the Altars* (New Haven: Yale University Press, 1992). This is a classic account of late medieval Catholic piety as an integrated, emotional, spiritual, and cultural system and of the destructive impact of the Reformation upon it.

Fincham, K. (ed.). *The Early Stuart Church* (London: Macmillan, 1993). This is a very useful collection of essays on various aspects of early Stuart religion and politics.

Lake, P. and M. Questier. *The Antichrist's Lewd Hat: Protestants, Papists and Players in Post-Reformation England* (New Haven: Yale University Press, 2002). This book attempts to sketch the complex cultural scene of post-Reformation England using cheap print, religious polemic, performance (both judicial and theatrical), and drama.

McCulloch, D. *The Later Reformation in England, 1547–1603* (London: Macmillan, 1990). This is the best short overview of the period.

Thomas, K. V. *Religion and the Decline of Magic* (Harmondsworth: Penguin Books, 1970). This classic account of the popular effects of the Reformation offers a very different view from Duffy of late medieval religion and the impact of the Reformation.

Walsham, A. *Providence in Early Modern England* (Oxford: Oxford University Press, 1999). A classic account of a central Protestant (indeed Christian) doctrine and its application through a range of texts both popular and elite, this book usefully compares and contrasts with Thomas, Duffy, and Lake and Questier.

13 | Ideas of order

Lena Cowen Orlin

Certain ideas about the design of the cosmos, the nature of mankind, the necessity of government, the organization of society, and the inferiority of women were widely promulgated in Shakespeare's time. These basic elements of early modern English political thought emphasized divine order, human fallibility, monarchic rule, hierarchical relationships, and patriarchal doctrine. Political thought created a common language for the conduct of everyday life in Shakespeare's time. It was a language that the playwright understood and that he could expect his audiences to understand.

This is not to say that everyone in early modern England agreed with or acted upon generally promulgated notions. Just like today, people could know what the common cultural beliefs were without subscribing to them in full or practising them at all. Among intellectuals, for example, there was consensus that monarchy was the best form of government even while there were vigorously argued differences of opinion about the precise extent of the monarch's authority. Elsewhere in society, people who similarly accepted a monarchic government could nonetheless challenge an incumbent ruler by fomenting rebellion, plotting assassination, scheming to deflect the recognized lines of royal succession, or just speaking disrespectfully of the head of state. When it came to the organization of private life, there were fewer formal controversies, with the exception of some heated disagreements on the role of women in society. But honest citizens who accepted cultural values in principle could still violate them in practice, just by going about their daily business. This was because the officially prescribed standards for political order and obedience did not always match up with social realities and economic necessities. There were, moreover, dishonest tradesmen, thieving neighbours, runaway servants, and assertive wives who more deliberately broke the conventional rules. Shakespeare had a wealth of real-life examples for the royal usurpers, strong-willed women, and disobedient children in his plays.

In Elizabethan and Jacobean England, the situation with respect to ideology was not unlike that of religion (as described in Chapter 12). While individuals may have held a wide variety of personal beliefs, they nonetheless knew what the authorized beliefs were. In fact, there were many points of connection between political thought and religion. For this chapter which outlines the most familiar precepts of social order, it is useful to begin with these connections.

The religious cast of political thought

There are at least five reasons why politics and religion were difficult to disentangle in Shakespeare's time. First, early modern England was a Christian country. All political arguments referenced the Christian God and cited passages and precedents from the Christian Bible. Thus, those who subscribed to what has been called the 'divine right' of kings depicted the monarch not as a God himself but as the Christian God's deputy on earth. Two of the foundational narratives for popular political thought were the accounts of the fall of Lucifer from heaven and the fall of man in the Garden of Eden. These were politicized as allegories of disobedience. Political writers also used various other stories and verses from the Christian bible to 'prove' their partisan points.

Second, much political conceptualization in the sixteenth century was occasioned by religious upheavals. People of faith were asked to adapt to the abrupt break with the Roman Catholic Church effected by Henry VIII (1534), then to a more radical Protestantism inaugurated under Edward VI (1547–53), next to the enforced restoration of Roman Catholicism by Mary I (1553–8), and finally to a moderate (Protestant) Anglicanism under Elizabeth I (1558–1603). Because every reorganization of religion was caused by a change of political leadership, it was often defended or attacked in terms of political loyalty or political resistance.

Third, the eventual ascendancy of Protestantism in England can be correlated to a developing political consciousness, a new nationalism and a suspicion of foreigners. Many religious practices did not themselves alter a great deal over time, no matter the dictates of a particular regime. While there were urgent doctrinal controversies, what sometimes seemed to matter most of all was whether the English church was headed by an English monarch or by a Roman Pope. People who were happy to worship in the old, Catholic ways under Mary I could still distrust her fealty to a foreign power (the Pope) and her marriage to a foreign king (Philip II of Spain). People who clung to Catholic beliefs under Elizabeth I could nonetheless protest their loyalty to the English queen. Elizabeth's restoration of an English form of Protestantism was compatible with widespread convictions about England's political sovereignty.

Fourth, as the sixteenth century wore on, the church became the monarchy's most effective instrument for spreading political propaganda. Literacy was far from universal in early modern England, and so royal messages were most reliably disseminated orally, through church sermons. During Elizabeth I's reign, for example, approved ideology was represented not only in the Book of Common Prayer used by parish priests but also in a collection of *Homilies*, or state-authored sermons, which priests were required to read to their congregants on successive Sundays. Each of the parish churches Shakespeare attended, like all other churches in England, would have had an English-language Bible, the Book of Common Prayer, and the official *Homilies*. A twelve-sermon set of *Homilies* was published in 1547; this was reprinted in 1559; a new version of twenty-one sermons appeared in 1563; and in 1570 the six-part *Homily Against Disobedience and Wilful Rebellion* was added to the collection.

Fifth, as head of the established church, the monarch had many weapons to ensure that churchmen toed the party line. These included punishing, even executing, priests and pastors who made heretical statements or who enacted unauthorized forms of worship. With the power to name bishops, the monarch could also reward those who were more conforming. Henry VIII and his successors on the throne were the most important ecclesiastical patrons in the country. This could ensure that, for career reasons alone, many churchmen were self-censoring in matters both religious and political. The number of martyrs executed by Henry and 'Bloody' Mary demonstrated that there were men and women of conscience in this age, but there were also more adaptable members of the clergy who recognized that religion was sometimes a matter of politics.

Order and degree in the universe

Ideas of order in the Renaissance were patterned on notions of how the cosmos was organized. These notions were, like most things, religiously informed, but they also had important political implications. It was believed that God had created the universe as a system of multiple, corresponding hierarchies. The planets in the sky, the angels in heaven, all kingdoms on earth, each individual family, even the human body were constituted of ranked elements, each element subordinated to the one above it. In Shakespeare's *Troilus and Cressida*, the character Ulysses gives what is often recognized as the most concise description of the premise that the world is organized on the principle of hierarchy:

> The heavens themselves, the planets, and this centre
> Observe degree, priority, and place,
> Infixture, course, proportion, season, form,
> Office and custom, in all line of order.
>
> (1.3.85-8)

Despite the difficult terms in this passage—'centre' refers to the earth, 'infixture' means 'fixity', and 'office' is used in the sense of 'function'—the general theme is clear. Every element of the cosmos was believed to have a proper place which was defined by its relationship to other elements in their places. All social forms of organization were understood to follow along similar lines: 'communities . . . schools, and brotherhoods in cities', as well as 'The primogenity and due of birth' and 'Prerogative of age, crowns, sceptres, laurels' (1.3.103–7).

A key term was 'degree', a step or stage in the scale of order and rank. To occupy one's place in the hierarchy was to respect the mandates of degree. 'Take but degree away', Ulysses continues,

> And hark what discord follows. Each thing meets
> In mere oppugnancy. The bounded waters
> Should lift their bosoms higher than the shores
> And make a sop of all this solid globe;
> Strength should be lord of imbecility,
> And the rude son should strike his father dead.
>
> (1.3.109-15)

Here, the theme of discord is played out in terms of a total antagonism ('mere oppugnancy') and radical inversion (solid made saturated, 'imbecility' or weakness overruling strength, and child murdering father). The various hierarchies were believed to be so closely interrelated in their analogous structures that a violation of degree in any one sphere resonated in all. Thus, when Shakespeare described Macbeth killing a king, he imagined a corresponding disorder in the cosmos, as the skies darkened at midday, and in the natural world, with horses making 'war with mankind' (*Macbeth* 2.4.18).

The founding Christian myth of the origin of evil involved a violation of degree as well as an act of disobedience. In his ambition, Lucifer dared to challenge his place in the hierarchy of God's angels. In consequence, he and his compatriots were cast out from heaven. From then on, Lucifer was known by his fallen name, Satan.

Obedience and the law of nature

Like every other object in the universe, man was believed to have his degree, or place. He was ranked between angels and beasts in what was known as the 'Great Chain of Being'—a concept to which Hamlet alludes (2.2.294–97). Man's earthly situation was thought to have been defined in the moment when Adam and Eve were seduced by Satan. For eating the forbidden fruit of the tree of knowledge, they were exiled from Paradise. In consequence, all mankind was subjected to sin, fallibility, infirmity, and mortality. The biblical account of Adam and Eve took on cogent political meanings when it was explained as a story of their disobedience to God.

Lucifer, Adam, and Eve featured largely in the *Homily Against Disobedience and Wilful Rebellion*: 'Thus became rebellion, as you see, both the first and greatest, and the very root of all other sins, and the first and principal cause both of all worldly and bodily miseries—sorrows, diseases, sicknesses, and deaths—and, which is infinitely worse than all these, as is said, the very cause of death and damnation eternal also'. Jesus was understood to have redeemed the sin of Adam and Eve by means of a contrasting act of obedience to God, his willingness to die on the cross. 'Obedience', said the *Homily*, 'is the principal virtue of all virtues, and indeed the very root of all virtues, and the cause of all felicity'.

Man's ability to recognize virtue, even despite his fallen state, was understood to be an endowment from God. This gift, known as the 'law of nature', was sometimes described as imprinted in man's mind, sometimes as inscribed in his heart. Natural law was consistent with the biblical Ten Commandments. It was thought to be 'natural' that children should honour their parents, that families should be headed by fathers, and that countries should have kings.

A sovereign monarchy

All authorized political theory had two aspects. Whether it was concerned with the relations between God and man, king and subject, husband and wife, parent and child, or master and servant, political order was founded in an unequal distribution of power. In its first aspect, then, mainstream political theory sought to explain why it was right and necessary—that is, 'natural'—for power to be concentrated in inequitable, hierarchical ways. In its second aspect, political thought exhorted obedience to all those higher in the hierarchy.

It was universally agreed that government was necessary to thwart the chaos, savagery, and cannibalism that would otherwise prevail. This was to prevent mankind from descending on that Great Chain of Being to the level of beasts. The overwhelming consensus was that the best form of government was monarchic. All the hierarchies bore out and thus 'naturalized' this conclusion: as the cosmos was commanded by God, as the church was headed by Christ, as the body was ruled by its head, as the family was led by a father, so the kingdom was governed by a king. Because the system of hierarchies was understood to have been created by God, Renaissance political theorists could argue that the king received his power from God. In other words, he did not require the consent of the people to govern. A king who did not derive power from his people was ultimately not accountable to them. He was accountable only to God.

For this reason, early modern men and women were told that they owed loyalty even to a bad king. They were warned that it could be part of God's plan to punish a country for its sins by placing a tyrannical king on the throne. *The Homily Against Disobedience and Wilful Rebellion* argued this point vigorously:

What shall subjects do then? Shall they obey valiant, stout, wise, and good princes, and condemn, disobey, and rebel against . . . undiscreet and evil governors? God forbid. For first, what a perilous thing were it to commit unto the subjects the judgment which prince is wise and godly, and his government good, and which is otherwise. As though the foot must judge of the head, an enterprise very heinous, and must needs breed rebellion. . . . For subjects to deserve through their sins to have an evil prince, and then to rebel against him, were double and treble evil, by providing God more to plague them. Nay, let us either deserve to have a good prince, or let us patiently suffer and obey such as we deserve.

It was said that there was but one reason for a citizen to resist his sovereign: when a royal command conflicted with God's moral law. God's law would always take precedence over that of his deputy. However, even when such an eventuality was imagined, only passive disobedience could be countenanced. A subject caught in this hypothetical dilemma was authorized to resort to tears, prayer, and flight. The most frequently repeated political statement in Shakespeare's time was that force must never be used against the monarch.

Political dissent and rebellion

Authorized treatises like the *Homily Against Disobedience and Wilful Rebellion* were clear and vehement in their messages about the prerogatives of the monarch and the duties of the subject. But there were historical events and other views that made the discourse of authority and resistance far more complicated than these treatises indicated. The most radical manifestation of political opposition was rebellion. Each Tudor monarch weathered at least one major rebellion during his or her reign; there were eleven in total between 1485, when Henry VII established the Tudor dynasty, and 1603, when Elizabeth I died as the last of the Tudors.

In the Battle of Bosworth (1485), the Tudor royal line was itself created by an act of rebellion. Henry Tudor seized the throne from Richard III and created himself Henry VII. Almost immediately, there were Yorkist Risings against Henry VII (1486–87), but they failed to displace him. Later, his son, Henry VIII, commissioned authors to rewrite history, to portray Richard III as evil, murderous, himself a usurper. According to what has been called the 'Tudor myth', Henry VII enacted a merciful deliverance for the nation in overthrowing Richard III. Political writers subsequently developed an inventive theory that the sin of usurpation could burn itself out over time, so that descendants of a usurper were entitled to the full prerogatives of legitimate monarchy. Henry VIII and his son Edward VI each put down two significant uprisings for economic and religious causes; Henry executed 216 men who joined the Pilgrimage of Grace (1536).

The failure of male heirs in the Tudor line brought Mary I to the throne in 1553. When, a year later, she wed Philip II of Spain, there was widespread concern that the 'natural' order of marriage, which required a woman to yield authority to her husband, would result in a Spanish king interfering in English affairs. Four thousand men marched on London in Wyatt's Rebellion (1554), a vain attempt to prevent the foreign marriage. Fifteen years later, Elizabeth confronted the Northern Rebellion (1569), when a group of earls plotted to replace her with her cousin Mary Stuart, Queen of Scots. Mary Stuart was finally beheaded in 1587, although it was said that the order of execution was taken by Elizabeth's councillors and against her will. As a ruler, Elizabeth had cause to defend the principles of political sovereignty, and she was reluctant to authorize the death of a fellow monarch, no matter how potent a threat Mary might be. Meanwhile, for much of Elizabeth's reign there was acute distress that she had not produced an heir. Her childlessness helped motivate the Essex Rebellion (1601), led by a former favourite, the Earl of Essex.

The only successful uprising of the Tudor age was the originating one of 1485. There were many other symptoms of dissent, though, and these exerted a moderating influence on the actions of the Tudor monarchs. Elizabeth I, for example, was a practical politician rather than an absolutist theorist. Many of her Anglican clergy had fled England during the reign of her sister Mary I. In Europe, they developed an active polemic on citizens' right of resistance, and this dialogue did not entirely die out when they returned. Such issues of consent and dissent were recurrently represented on the Elizabethan stage, which itself constituted an important alternative site for political discourse.

Shakespeare's histories and tragedies, deeply engaged with issues of sovereignty and authority, were thus played out in a climate of authoritarian rhetoric, political turmoil, and continued religious controversy. *Richard III* subscribed to the Tudor myth, celebrating the virtue of Henry VII while making Richard unredeemably—if intriguingly—evil. Others of Shakespeare's plays were ideologically more complex, however. *Richard II* demonstrated that the weakness of this king led to his overthrow, but it also showed his usurper stricken by remorse: 'I'll make a voyage to the Holy Land / To wash this blood off from my guilty hand' (5.6.48–9). Modern critics known as 'New Historicists' have argued that plays like *Richard II* served conservative cultural functions by working to contain transgression (see Chapter 32). But Shakespeare's audiences undoubtedly took away varied messages. Elizabeth I, for one, seemed to think that any analogy between herself and a deposed king was seditious. The men who joined Essex in his rebellion of 1601 prepared themselves for insurgency by commissioning a performance of *Richard II* shortly beforehand. 'I am Richard II', Elizabeth recognized, 'Know you not that?'

The patriarchal family

One of the conceptual challenges for orthodox political theory was that the biblical Ten Commandments (Exodus 20:3–17), understood to summarize God's moral laws, were largely apolitical. They required honour to God: 'Thou shalt have no other gods before me'; 'Thou shalt not make unto thee any graven image'; 'Thou shalt not take the name of the Lord thy God in vain'. They also included prohibitions important for social order: 'Thou shalt not kill'; 'Thou shalt not commit adultery'; 'Thou shalt not steal'; 'Thou shalt not bear false witness'. In the early modern period, the Commandment that could most easily be reinterpreted to take on political meanings was the Fifth: 'Honour thy father and thy mother'.

The key to expanding the significance of this commandment was the theory of correspondences, by which the spheres of cosmos, kingdom, church, family, and corporeality were interrelated through a process of analogical thinking. If God had ordained that parents were to be honoured in their families, then it followed that monarchs were also to be honoured in their kingdoms. In fact, the Fifth Commandment was specifically invoked to enjoin deference not only of child for parent but also of citizen for king, servant for master, and student for teacher.

The early modern family was most often described as a political institution. In their *Godly Form of Household Government for the Ordering of Private Families According to the Direction of God's Word* (1598), John Dod and Robert Cleaver repeated a familiar conceptualization: 'A household is as it were a little commonwealth, by the good government whereof, God's glory may be advanced; the commonwealth, which standeth of several families, benefited; and all that live in that family may receive much comfort and commodity [advantage]'. The state overtly portrayed each household as a small commonwealth. This was in the interest of social welfare: good order in any household advanced good order in the kingdom. But the state also, more covertly, depicted the commonwealth as a large family. This was in the interest of self-justification: the monarchy borrowed credibility from a social institution, the family, that seemed more 'natural' than any other. Analogizing the commonwealth to a household, the state found yet another way to naturalize political organization.

For the family to naturalize the monarchic form of political organization, however, some fancy conceptual footwork was necessary. As indicated, the commandment to 'Honour thy father and thy mother' was taken to refer to heads of state as well as heads of household. But in early modern England the monarch had only one domestic analogue, the father. To advance its figurative meaning, then, a literal meaning of the commandment, its dualism, had to be suppressed. Other biblical passages were cited to justify an elevation of the father over the mother. St Paul, for example, was frequently quoted: 'Let women be subject to their husbands, as to the Lord, for the husband is the head of the woman, as Christ is the head of the Church'. In effect, the Fifth Commandment was read politically as an exhortation to 'Honour thy father'.

The intellectual appeal of the theory of correspondences was its apparent completeness. Any sphere that was out of step with the others threatened the entire belief system. In a kingdom committed to the monarchic, it was thus necessary for the family to be conceived as patriarchal.

Contested authority in the household

The ancient Greek philosopher Aristotle, who wrote the first great treatise on *Politics*, described multiple forms of government. In addition to monarchy, there were democracy and aristocracy, but these alternatives received little attention in early modern England despite Aristotle's enormous influence then. In fact, Aristotle's aristocratic model, a form of 'shared' rule, was ideal for the household commonwealth. In practical terms, the Fifth Commandment had it right: the family benefited from the joint governorship of father and mother.

The early modern household was a social and economic institution as well as a political one. It was a centre for production and consumption, as much a small business as a petty commonwealth. In this regard, the wife had essential responsibilities, as John Dod and Robert Cleaver recognized:

The duty of the husband is to get goods, and of the wife to gather them together and save them. The duty of the husband is to travel abroad [outdoors] to seek living, and the wife's duty is to keep the house. The duty of the husband is to get money and provision, and of the wives, not vainly to spend it. . . . The duty of the husband is to be Lord of all, and of the wife to give account of all. The duty of the husband is to dispatch all things without door, and of the wife to oversee and give order for all things within the house.

Dod and Cleaver were thoroughly persuaded that the husband should be 'lord of all' in his household. Even so, they could not help but admit that wives frequently had occasion to 'oversee and give order', as well. The *Homily of the State of Matrimony* was similarly reluctant to acknowledge that children and servants were generally supervised by wives. The result was contradictory logic and tortured syntax: 'For thus doth St Peter preach to them: "Ye wives, be you in subjection to obey your own husband". To obey is another thing than to control or command, which yet they may do to their children and to their family. But as for their husbands, them must they obey and cease from commanding and perform subjection'.

In 1622, the Puritan preacher William Gouge published a collection of his sermons, *Of Domestical Duties*. The preface recalled a sermon that had outraged his parishioners. No one objected to statements of the husband's supremacy when it was expressed in the usual, abstract terms. But when Gouge projected this political ideal into the tangible matters of daily life, there was mutiny: 'much exception was taken against the application of a wife's subjection to the restraining of her from disposing the common goods of the family without or against her husband's consent'. Gouge tried to explain that he had outlined the consequences 'in case her husband will stand upon the uttermost of his authority'. Ideally, he said, husbands would be more liberal. Practically, most had to be.

Early modern social critics lamented the number of domineering wives and contentious marriages. Troubled domestic relations were not caused solely by personality conflicts and political disobedience, however. Larger structural problems resulted from the way the domestic sphere was conceptualized to suit political ends. The priorities of the state forced a disconnect between ideology and social reality. Again, the stage was a social laboratory to explore some of the faultlines. There were impertinent servants in *The Comedy of Errors* and *The Taming of the Shrew*, disobedient daughters in *A Midsummer Night's Dream* and *King Lear*, and assertive women in nearly all Shakespeare's plays.

The place of women

Like all tenets of orthodox political theory in the early modern period, the inferiority of women could be 'proved' with passages from the Christian bible. St Paul was quoted with particular frequency, as was the historical basis for his misogyny. According to this rationale, all women deserved punishment because Eve had been the first to eat the forbidden fruit in the Garden of Eden.

For Eve's sin, it was argued, women were subjected to marriage and suffered pain in childbirth. Thus, the *Homily on the State of Matrimony* described wedlock as a penalty: 'Truth it is, that they [women] must specially feel the griefs and pains of their matrimony in that they relinquish the liberty of their own rule, in the pain of their travailing [labour in childbirth], in the bringing up of their children, in which offices they be in great perils and be grieved with great afflictions, which they might be without if they lived out of matrimony'.

While women had more social, economic, and religious freedom than the ideological literature would lead us to believe, they also had comparatively few political and legal rights. Subsumed by marriage into the identities of their husbands, they could be denied the ability to own property, write wills, or take part in civic government. While provision was made for boys to learn to read, write, and do sums, girls were more often taught to read and sew. As discriminatory as this distinction seems, it also gave many women a means to support themselves with their needle. Political ideology, being family-based, did not acknowledge that almost half the adult women in early modern England were single at a given moment—either unmarried or widowed—and thus responsible for their own livelihoods.

The famous speech that closes Shakespeare's *The Taming of the Shrew*—in which the formerly rebellious Kate declares submissively that 'Thy husband is thy lord, thy life, thy keeper, / Thy head, thy sovereign'—conforms almost literally to Dod and Cleaver's outline of preferred gender roles. The husband 'commits his body / To painful labour both by sea and land', says Kate, 'Whilst thou', the wife, 'liest warm at home, secure and safe' (5.2.150–55). Some who read or watched the play may have observed that Kate's husband Petruccio had done no painful labour to 'maintain' his new wife; instead, he had secured her dowry to support him.

Others, however, would have responded to the 'taming' of Kate less analytically and more approvingly. The extensive popular literature on the nature of women was thoroughly contradictory. There were collections of misogynistic tales, defences of women's rights, advice books about proper female behaviour, and sensational pamphlets about women who dressed in men's clothes, practised witchcraft, committed adultery, and murdered their husbands and children. Plays like *The Taming of the Shrew*, polemics like *The Arraignment of Lewd, Idle, Froward, and Inconstant Women* (1615), and pamphlets like *The Women's Sharp Revenge* (1640) testified to men's continuing preoccupation with the persistant and resistant power of women.

Triumphs of disorder

All early modern notions of cosmic order, natural law, absolute monarchy, patriarchal structure, and gender hierarchy were interrelated in an authorized political thought that purported to be comprehensive and logical. It was virtually impossible, however, for any ideological system to be both. The theory of correspondences sought to incorporate every sphere in order to be comprehensive, but there was no single logic that applied to every sphere. Inevitably, there were internal contradictions and conceptual gaps.

Even to identify these discrepancies, however, is to think inside the box that ideology worked to create. The everyday world of early modern England seemed often to exist outside this box of established political theory—familiar with it, certainly, but fundamentally unconcerned with it. For example, women were told repeatedly that they were expected to be chaste, silent, and obedient. Many were nonetheless brought to trial for having committed adultery, slander, and blasphemy. The various legal courts of early modern England were kept busy with widespread rebellion, crime, and disorder. And, while many of the Elizabethans who experienced the religious switchbacks of the sixteenth century diligently converted from Protestantism to Roman Catholicism and back again, others, almost untouched by doctrinal and ecclesiastical controversy, clung to their own belief systems. These included folk practices, inherited superstitions, astrological prognostication, and occult experimentation that co-existed more or less uneasily with orthodox Christian faith.

The priority of most political thought was to naturalize and authorize the monarchy. This, too, eventually failed. In 1603, Elizabeth I was succeeded by Mary Stuart's son James, who reigned in England until 1625. James I tried to close the conceptual gaps in political discourse. A political theorist in his own right, he authored such important treatises as *Basilikon Doron, Or His Majesty's Instructions to His Dearest Son* (1594) and *The True Law of Free Monarchies, Or the Reciprock and Mutual Duty Betwixt a Free King and His Natural Subjects* (1598). In these texts, James proved himself a more extreme absolutist than any Tudor had dared to be. Although he said that any good king would act with restraint, he nonetheless insisted that, in principle, kings had supreme authority, even over their subjects' lands and properties. His son Charles I, who similarly maintained the king's absolute prerogatives, was more brazen in exacting them.

In 1642, a new act of rebellion finally succeeded. In a development that no Elizabethan could have imagined, Charles I was replaced not by another king but by a Lord Protector, Oliver Cromwell. The monarchy was not restored until 1660, and it would never again have the power and authority it had enjoyed, by general consent, under Elizabeth and James. There had been cultural value, it seems, in the Elizabethan way of making some allowances for the differences between political theory and lived experience. The early modern world was never as orderly as was projected in authorized thought.

FURTHER READING

Dollimore, Jonathan. *Radical Tragedy: Religion, Ideology and Power in the Drama of Shakespeare and his Contemporaries* (Brighton: Harvester Press, 1984). This important book emphasizes the gaps and inconsistencies in the 'Elizabethan world view' and shows how stageplays interrogated and challenged conventional ideology.

Fletcher, Anthony and John Stevenson (eds.). *Order and Disorder in Early Modern England* (Cambridge: Cambridge University Press, 1985). Especially useful in this collection are D. E. Underdown's 'The Taming of the Scold: The Enforcement of Patriarchal Authority in Early Modern England' (pp. 116–36) and S. M. Amussen's 'Gender, Family, and the Social Order, 1560–1725' (pp. 196–217).

Guy, John. *Tudor England* (Oxford: Oxford University Press, 1988). This is a comprehensive and authoritative review of Tudor history. The book's main themes are religious and political events and changes between 1460 and 1603.

Henderson, Katherine Usher and Barbara F. McManus (eds.). *Half Humankind: Contexts and Texts of the Controversy about Women in England, 1540–1640* (Urbana: University of Illinois Press, 1985). The excerpts and reprints in this volume are from some of the most important tracts in the so-called 'pamphlet wars' about women in early modern England. There is also a helpful introduction.

Kinney, Arthur (ed.). *The Cambridge Companion to English Literature, 1500–1600* (Cambridge: Cambridge University Press, 2000). In this collection of essays, see especially Richard Helgerson's 'Writing Empire and Nation' (pp. 310–29), on the emergence of English national identity, and Lena Cowen Orlin's 'Chronicles of Private Life' (pp. 241–64), on private life and the ideologies of marriage and householding.

O'Day, Rosemary. *The Family and Family Relationships, 1500–1900* (London: Macmillan, 1994). This book reviews the structure and population of the early modern English household, the ideology of the family, and social conditions and kinship relations. A comparative perspective is provided with reference to the early modern family in France.

Pocock, J. G. A., Gordon J. Schochet, and Lois G. Schwoerer (eds.). *The Varieties of British Political Thought, 1500–1800* (Cambridge: Cambridge University Press, 1993). In active circulation in early modern England were political theories that took issue with the authorized ideas outlined in this chapter. The first three essays in this volume develop this more complicated picture of political discourse.

Sommerville, J. P. *Politics and Ideology in England, 1603–1640* (London: Longman, 1986). The first chapter of this book, 'The Divine Right of Kings', offers especially clear and concise accounts of natural law, patriarchalism, and absolutism. Although the focus is on the first half of the seventeenth century, political ideas are traced back to their medieval and Elizabethan roots.

Tillyard, E. M. W. *The Elizabethan World Picture: A Study of the Idea of Order in the Age of Shakespeare, Donne, and Milton* (New York: Vintage Books, 1959). This classic book is still the best and most concise review of topics like the Great Chain of Being and the theory of correspondences.

Wootton, David (ed.). *Divine Right and Democracy: An Anthology of Political Writing in Stuart England* (Harmondsworth: Penguin Books, 1986). Despite the title, this collection looks back to the Elizabethan years to include excerpts from the *Homily Against Disobedience and Wilful Rebellion* and James's *True Law of Free Monarchies*. The guide to 'Further Reading', pp. 127–8, puts additional bibliography in historiographic perspective.

14 | Shakespeare's view of the world

Emily C. Bartels

To survey the corpus of Shakespeare's plays, especially those that engage historical events, is to see England as the organizing centre of the universe. In Shakespeare's *Richard II* (1595), John of Gaunt eulogizes that 'little world' as an 'earth of majesty', a 'seat of Mars', a 'fortress built by nature for herself' (2.1.41–45). In the early part of his career, Shakespeare turned repeatedly to England, English history, and English kings as highly marketable theatrical subjects and traced over 100 years of the English monarchy, from the reign of Richard II (1367–1400) to the reign of Richard III (1483–85). Yet during Shakespeare's lifetime (1564–1616), England's conception of the world, and its place in that world, was expanding radically. In the theatre, from the 1580s onward, dramatists such as Shakespeare were seizing on 'all the world' as an important subject and setting.

Shakespeare's emergence as a playwright followed closely on the heels of Christopher Marlowe (1564–93). Marlowe revolutionized English theatrical practices by introducing blank verse as an unusually versatile medium for dramatic expression and by bringing the world to the theatre, the theatre to the world. Like the extraordinary conqueror about whom he wrote, Tamburlaine the Great, Marlowe seemed obsessed with 'measuring the limits' of his dramatic 'empery / By east and west' (*Tamburlaine Part One* 1.2.35–36), setting his scenes in such distant domains as Persia, Egypt, and Arabia, filling his stage with the exotic artefacts of imagined elsewheres, and luxuriating in a dream of worldly domination.[1] On Marlowe's stage, Tamburlaine is determined to become not only the king of Persia, lord regent of Africa, and emperor of the East, but also the indomitable 'terror of the world' (*Tamburlaine Part One* 3.3.45) and ruling 'monarch of the earth' (*Tamburlaine Part Two* 5.3.217). Marlowe's Jew of Malta traffics in 'Spanish oils' and 'wines of Greece' and lusts for the gold, pearl, and precious gems that the 'wealthy Moor' and 'merchants of the Indian mines' enjoy in alluring excess (*The Jew of Malta* 1.1.5, 19–21). Even within a secluded study in Germany, Marlowe's Doctor Faustus revels in the seductive fantasy of having his conjured spirits 'fly to India for gold, / Ransack the ocean for orient pearl, / And search all corners of the new-found world / For pleasant fruits and princely delicates' (*Doctor Faustus* 1.1.81–84).

Shakespeare's vision is, by no means, this geographically wide-ranging, this preoccupied with global conquest and commodities. Yet Shakespeare too looks outward to 'the world', even as he keeps his eye on England. His English history plays show an England struggling to gain or reclaim land or power just outside its borders, in France, Ireland, Scotland, and Wales. In *Richard II*, for example, the English crown is threatened by wars in Ireland; in *Henry IV Part One* (1596–7), by wars in Scotland and Wales. In *Hamlet* (1600–1), the Danish king, Claudius, expects aid from the English crown, and England stands alongside France and Germany, Paris and Wittenberg, as a place a Dane might travel to for refuge and relief.

In comedies and tragedies, Shakespeare seems to leave England far behind as he turns to Mediterranean regions and beyond. His settings include such places as Bohemia, Cyprus, Sicily, classical Egypt, and Troy, as well as the 'brave new world' (5.1.86) of *The Tempest* (1611). Embedded in these landscapes are figures who represent other cultures still. *A Midsummer Night's Dream* (1595–6) is set in classical Athens and also in a fairy world that is defined and disturbed by the absent presence of an Indian 'changeling' boy. The population of Shakespeare's Venice includes the Jew in *The Merchant of Venice* (1596–7) and the Moor in *Othello* (1604), and the population of classical Rome, in *Titus Andronicus* (1594), has both Moor and Goth. In *The Winter's Tale* (1610–11), Hermione, the dispossessed Sicilian queen, also claims a royal Russian heritage.

In addition, across his plays Shakespeare incorporates exotic images, costumes, and props. In *The Comedy of Errors* (1592), for example, Dromio of Syracuse 'find[s] out countries' in the 'kitchen wench' who 'haunts' him (3.2.82, 94, 113–14) and locates the Indies on her nose, 'all o'er embellished with rubies, carbuncles, sapphires' (3.2.132–3). In *The Merry Wives of Windsor* (1597), Falstaff depicts his would-be lovers, Mistress Page and Mistress Ford, as his 'East and West Indies' (1.3.61). French lovers in *Love's Labour's Lost* (1594–95) dress as Muscovites. And Othello stakes his marriage on a handkerchief that, he insists, came from an Egyptian 'charmer' (3.4.55), while his wife recalls that her mother 'had a maid called Barbary' (4.3.25) (the name of a region in northern Africa).

Shakespeare's plays do not indulge in dreams of world-wide outreach, power, and possession with the scope and obsession set by the Marlovian precedent. Even the plays that examine the effects of cross-cultural conquest are removed in time or space from the immediate pressures and geographies of ongoing explorations. The 'Roman' plays—*Titus Andronicus*, *Troilus and Cressida* (1601–2), *Antony and Cleopatra* (1606–7), and *Coriolanus* (1607–8)—produce territorial contests as part of a classical past that the English, who imagined London as 'New Troy', claimed, but did not experience, as their own. If Shakespeare's *Tempest* addresses England's early efforts at New World colonization, his vision is significantly detached from the contemporary events that may have inspired it, as we shall see.

Still, if Shakespeare is not Marlowe, if his plays do not reach out with the expansive and acquisitive energies that had already appeared on the Renaissance stage, it is precisely because they do not that they speak so aptly to the time. For although the English had long been implicated in foreign politics, especially though not exclusively in northern Europe, as other countries ventured beyond their own horizons and changed the global picture England fell behind. The 'little world' that Shakespeare produced and inhabited was thus poised tentatively on the brink of an enlarging geographical and ideological domain, sitting on the sidelines of 'all the world', only beginning to map a new way in.

The Mediterranean centre

During Shakespeare's lifetime, economic and cultural exchange was centred in Mediterranean regions—notably not in England or Europe. It was in the Mediterranean that the trades and traders of Europe, northern and sub-Saharan Africa, the Levant, and the East all converged, there that multinational alliances formed, and there that cultures crossed and clashed.

In 1578, for example, Morocco provided the battlefield for international politics, as the leaders of North Africa, Turkey, Portugal, and Spain, along with the Pope and one renegade Englishman, Thomas Stukeley, chose sides and either made or broke their political fortunes on African soil. Although this conflict started as a Moroccan civil war, it ultimately paved the way for Portugal to fall to Spain and so determined the balance of European power for decades to come. Ten years later, George Peele reanimated the event on the English stage in *The Battle of Alcazar* (1588–9). That play not only initiated a dramatic interest in the Moor that would carry through the seventeenth century; it also presented Morocco as a theatre for 'all the world', one that English audiences would want to understand.[2]

By the sixteenth century, the English had already established economic connections in the Mediterranean. A century before, the crown chartered a company of merchants (the Merchant Adventurers) to handle England's export of cloth to the Netherlands and northern Europe. During Elizabeth's reign, however, new companies formed in the early 1580s to regulate trade, largely of goods imported from the Levant (the Eastern regions of the Mediterranean) and from Venice. In addition, starting in the 1550s, England began to explore and develop new opportunities in Morocco for trading such goods as sugar, dates, and arms.

Yet the English were by no means the dominant players in the Mediterranean; neither were the Spanish, Venetians, or other Europeans with interests there. Rather, from the fourteenth century on, the trade and politics within this lucrative region were governed primarily by the Turks, whose extensive Ottoman empire absorbed a substantial number of Mediterranean ports and peoples. During the Elizabethan era, the Turks advanced significantly west and laid claim to pivotal territory in the eastern Mediterranean and North Africa, including Cyprus in 1571 and Tunis in 1574. In response, the Spanish, the Venetians, and the Pope formed a league to challenge these imperialist advances. But while the league's efforts climaxed with the famous Turkish defeat at Lepanto in 1571, the political and cultural tentacles of the Ottomans continued to reach across the Mediterranean and into Europe until the seventeenth century.

If the Turks were feared across Europe for their aggressive imperialism and adherence to Islam, Christianity's professed 'other', they were also admired for their military strength, their political organization, and their rich material resources. Moreover, the Ottoman empire was never simply Turkish. Years of imperialist conquest meant that Ottoman subjects included Africans, Egyptians, Indians, Armenians, and even Europeans, to name only a few—some of them Muslims or Muslim converts, some not.

In England, Queen Elizabeth negotiated repeatedly with the 'Great Turk' for safe passage of English venturers in the Levant and used the similarities between the Christian and Muslim faiths (their shared rejection of idolatry, their worship of a prophet, and their belief in a single God) to forge an alliance. Notably, too, it became commonplace in the sixteenth century to imagine an English citizen 'turning Turk', something conversion narratives bore out as a real possibility even as the phrase was also used pejoratively to connote an absolute turn for the worse. In Shakespeare, Hamlet worries that his fortunes might 'turn Turk' (*Hamlet* 3.2.254). In *Much Ado About Nothing* (1598–99), Margaret accuses the love-resistant Beatrice of having 'turned Turk' (3.4.47) when Beatrice finally acknowledges her desire for Benedick.

At the same time, although the Turks never invaded England, English dramatists, including Shakespeare, treated Turkish conquests in the Mediterranean as a pressing concern. In the opening scenes of *Othello* (1604), the crisis that most concerns the Venetian state and its Moorish general is the Turkish advance on the island of Cyprus (which was still a Turkish colony at the time Shakespeare wrote the play). Shakespeare erases this conflict from his story by having the Turks vanquished by a sea storm before they ever reach Cyprus. Still, the Turkish presence darkens the play's Mediterranean vision—so much so that when Othello finally stabs himself, he imagines killing 'a malignant and a turbaned Turk' who had once 'beat a Venetian and traduced the state' (5.2.361–2).

Although Turkish imperialism thus haunts the edges of Othello's story, Shakespeare's exploration of the Mediterranean tends to focus instead on Italy, and especially Venice, a place defined by its ethnically and religiously diverse population as well as by its seemingly unlimited access to global trades. Take away the Turks, as *Othello* does, and what emerges as the centre of controversy is a Moor's embrace of a Venetian senator's daughter and Venice's embrace of the Moor. In *The Merchant of Venice*, Venice becomes the obvious place to find Antonio, the merchant whose ships and fortunes have been cast as far east as India and as far west as Mexico. Like Marlowe's Mediterranean island of Malta, Venice is also the obvious place to find the Jew, a figure then without a homeland, defined rather by his unbounded interest in capitalist exchange with anyone—Christian or Jew—who can pay. In addition, although the scenes in *The Merchant of Venice* that take place in the nearby site of Belmont have the feel of a fairy tale, they nonetheless emphasize the cultural diversity and material basis of the Mediterranean world. In Belmont, Portia entertains suitors from such places as Morocco, Germany, Aragon, and England, and has them weigh their worth in lead, silver, or gold. In *The Taming of the Shrew* (1593–94), suitors from Verona and Pisa come to Padua to win a bride (Kate), and they attempt to enhance their chances by displaying their worldly connections. Lucentio, for example, promotes himself by marketing his father as 'a merchant of great traffic through the world' (1.1.12), while Gremio offers as dowry 'Tyrian tapestry', 'Turkey cushions bossed with pearl', 'ivory coffers', and 'cypress chests' as well as other eastern exotica (2.1.334–45).

It may be true that the revenge drama which came in vogue in the Jacobean period, in the hands of playwrights such as John Webster, popularized Italy as the site of unspeakable domestic and political scandal, immorality, and crime. But in Shakespeare's plays, what makes Italy, and especially Venice, stand out as a provocative setting is what made the Mediterranean such a vital hub: its cosmopolitan worldliness and centrality to economic and cultural exchange.

Overseas expansion

At the same time as Europeans conceived of the Mediterranean region as a centre of global activity, they also looked further afield, to areas and resources they imagined as relatively untapped. The voyages of Christopher Columbus to the New World in 1492 and of Vasco da Gama to India in 1498 mark the beginning of what has come to be known as the age of European expansion, a period when Spain, Portugal, France, and England, as well as the Dutch, devoted their energies, as never before, to exploring and developing markets overseas. While the discovery of the New World provided the impetus, Europe's outreach was not directed solely towards the West; it extended also southward to the west and east coasts of Africa, eastward to Asia, and northward primarily to Russia ('Muscovy').

The English were notoriously late in joining this larger global enterprise. The Spanish had established significant footholds in the Caribbean, Mexico ('New Spain'), Central and South America by the 1550s. By then, too, the Portuguese had secured a number of colonies and trading outposts along the coasts of Brazil and Africa, and eastward, from Arabia and India, all the way to the Moluccas (the 'Spice Islands') and even China. In the next two decades, the French also began their move to create settlements in North America. Yet as England's European rivals were making headway as colonial powers, the English were concentrating on gaining or holding territory closer to home, as Shakespeare's histories suggest, in Ireland, Scotland, Wales, and France.

English activity overseas only *started* to gain momentum in the 1550s, when figures such as Thomas Wyndham, William Towerson, and John Lok began to lead the drive to western Africa; Walter Raleigh, John Hawkins, and Francis Drake to the New World;

Martin Frobisher to Newfoundland and a northwest passage; and Anthony Jenkinson to Russia. The English had long imagined the East as a place of extraordinary wealth, but by the time they were ready to explore its markets, the Portuguese had already monopolized so much of the trade that securing access proved almost impossible. Although there was enough trade to the north to warrant the creation of the Muscovy Company in 1555, to regulate the exchange of English cloth for Russian fur, through much of the sixteenth century most of England's foreign trade and overseas ventures were limited to Euro-Mediterranean domains.

Moreover, English activities overseas, unlike those of Portugal or Spain, were neither unified nor sustained by an official nationalist policy or imperialist vision. English expeditions were propelled instead by individual entrepreneurs, looking for new markets or new ways to old markets, and were supported only reluctantly and sporadically by the crown. Even then, English 'privateers' could make a relatively quick and easy profit by stealing booty from Spanish ships. Not only did English seamen prefer to put their energy into these activities rather than into the more risky project of developing new trade routes or overseas settlements; England had been at war with Spain since the 1570s, and the crown itself sanctioned privateering.

In the 1570s, John Dee coined the phrase, 'British Empire', but Ireland was the only target of England's colonial projects at that time. England would not officially become Great Britain, or the English monarch the ruler of Scotland, Ireland, and Wales, until 1603, under James I, whose references to the British 'empire' meant only the territory we now know as the British Isles.

In the years when Shakespeare was crafting his early plays, however, laying a claim to overseas territory was becoming increasingly important to national identity and power. In 1589 Richard Hakluyt produced the single most important collection of travel narratives to appear in England, *The Principal Navigations, Voyages, Traffics & Discoveries of the English Nation*, an early landmark of nationalist and imperialist propaganda. His stated purpose was to document all of England's activities 'made by Sea or Over-land to the Remote and Farthest distant Quarters of the Earth at any time within the compass of these 1600 Years'. Motivating his effort was the fear that the English would fall behind the 'monstrous' Spanish in establishing their own hold on the world. According to Hakluyt, the *Navigations* would provide clear testimony that England, 'in compassing the vast globe of the earth more than once', not only *had* 'excelled' but also *could* excel 'all the nations and people of the earth'.[3]

With propagandists such as Hakluyt leading the ideological charge, the English did begin a push towards colonization in the New World in the 1580s, starting in Roanoke, Virginia, where the settlers of one colony (the 'lost colony') disappeared without a trace. In 1607, Jamestown became the first permanent English settlement in the Americas. These early ventures to Virginia clearly captured the public interest. Hakluyt's *Principal Navigations* included a full section of travel accounts documenting recent voyages to the Americas. John White produced extraordinary drawings of New World subjects, and these illustrations were published with Thomas Hariot's *Brief and*

True Report of the New Found Land of Virginia (1590). Sir Walter Raleigh created a lasting dream of finding abundant wealth, and especially gold, in the West in his *Discovery of the Large, Rich and Beautiful Empire of Guiana* (1596). And Shakespeare's ground-breaking play *The Tempest* (1611) brought a colonial encounter between Europeans and the inhabitants of a 'new world' to centre stage for the very first time.

Even though the revolutionary prospect of establishing colonies in the West began to be an imaginable, if not also realizable, goal, a colonial future was neither given nor foreseeable at this early stage in England's experimentation overseas. Despite the success at Jamestown, the early settlers faced huge obstacles, partly because they continued to rely on English goods and agricultural practices for survival. It was not until the 1620s that they begin to develop a plantation economy based on indigenous crops, and not until the 1660s that they began to import slaves from west Africa as a labour force, in numbers large enough to sustain the plantations. The English setting up stakes in the New World in the early 1600s were like the Americans landing on the moon in the 1960s in that no one could predict where that one small step of 'man' might lead.

The signs of that uncertainty are written all over Shakespeare's *Tempest*, which takes its cues from an English shipwreck in the Bermudas, documented by William Strachey's *A True Reportory of the Wrack and Redemption of Sir Thomas Gates, Knight* (1610). The play traces the course of a European, Prospero, who appoints himself master over a remote and unnamed island and turns the inhabitants, Ariel and Caliban, into his slaves. The geographical and ideological signposts of this dramatic colonial history, however, are obscured by ambiguity. For while the source suggests the Bermudas as the setting of *The Tempest*, the geographic references within the play hover around the coasts of Africa and the Mediterranean. Moreover, Shakespeare neither fully endorses nor fully critiques Prospero's artful control over the island, but leaves us hanging somewhere in between, to question both the intentions and the consequences of his colonizing actions. Because Prospero returns to his native Milan the first chance he gets, his moves towards colonization appear therefore more expedient than strategic, more accidental than planned, more tenuous than secure. If Shakespeare's *Tempest* provides a representative measure of popular sentiment and concern, it suggests that England's vision of empire was unsteady as late as 1611, the hopes for overseas colonization as shaky—though simultaneously as inviting—as the prospects (see also Chapter 33 on this subject).

Racial and ethnic 'others'

Given England's relative distance from the Mediterranean centre of 'the world' and its belated entry into the expansionist scene where its European rivals were charting their empires, for the English to position themselves literally or figuratively, as Hakluyt fantasized, above 'all the nations and people of the earth', for them to advance an English nationalist self over and against an ethnic 'other', a Prospero over an Ariel or Caliban, was no easy matter. Nor was it necessarily a desirable one. For what is striking about Shakespeare's era is that English representations of non-European cultures were drawn in two contradictory directions as they attempted, on the one hand, to highlight the differentness of other peoples and, on the other, to embrace their sameness. It was a period, that is, when the impulse to discriminate along racial or ethnic lines, to script the Turk or the Moor as distinctively unlike 'us', emerged in competition with the conflicting impulse to integrate, to understand a 'Moor of Venice', such as Othello, as a subject as legitimately 'of Venice' as would be a Florentine, merchant, or Jew.

Historically, England was no stranger to strangers. Since the twelfth and thirteenth centuries European immigrants came to England as agents ('factors') of trade or as Protestant refugees from Catholic states. When Shakespeare came to London, he himself may have lodged with a family of Huguenot refugees from France. A growing part of the English population, foreigners could gain limited or, in rare cases, full rights of citizenship. Attitudes towards such immigrants appear to have been mixed. In a passage Shakespeare may have contributed to one version of the play *Sir Thomas More* (1603–4), Thomas More tries to quell the hostility of certain English citizens against foreign residents. He insists that if England sent 'the wretched strangers, / Their babies at their backs, with their poor luggage / Plodding to th' ports and coasts for transportation', the English would set a regrettable precedent, and, in the end, citizen would turn against citizen and 'men like ravenous fishes / Would feed on one another'.

Whenever it was politically or economically expedient, the crown did regulate or restrict immigrant populations through taxation, tightened requirements for citizenship, and even deportation. Every year between 1571 and 1574, for example, the state ordered the expulsion of all immigrants, religious refugees excepted. At the turn of the century, Queen Elizabeth herself announced that 'too many' 'blackamoors' had come into the realm and were consuming the jobs and resources that her 'own liege people' needed.[4] Consequently, she attempted (with limited success) to deport a small number of those blacks to Spain, in exchange for English prisoners there. Yet England's only sustained and full-scale discrimination against a delineated population occurred with the expulsion of the Jews, initiated by Edward I in 1290. Arguably, even though Jews remained officially unwelcome in England throughout Shakespeare's lifetime, there was enough intellectually motivated philo-Semitism brewing within England by the early seventeenth century to support a serious consideration of their readmission in 1655.

To be sure, the religious, social, political, and imaginative discourses of the late sixteenth and early seventeenth centuries give shape to a variety of cultural stereotypes. The Jew was a popular stock figure on the English stage, a predictable representative of a distinctively greedy, deceptive, or murderous 'tribe'. Even Shylock, whom Shakespeare places beside the merchant of Venice as a comparable entrepreneur, was probably dressed in a red wig and beard, the requisite costume for the 'stage Jew'. In

Henry IV Part One, the Welsh leader, Owen Glendower, is tagged as 'irregular and wild', and certain Welsh women are accused of acts 'as may not be / Without much shame retold or spoken of' (1.1.40, 45–6). As well, other Europeans, including the Irish, the French, and the Dutch, were also categorically maligned.

Significantly, however, many of the subjects that came under such attack were the non-Europeans whom the English were encountering overseas. In Hakluyt's *Principal Navigations*, for instance, New World and west African natives at times stand out as savages, cannibals, and sodomites. In George Whetstone's *English Mirrour* (1586), Turks appear as a 'barbarous infidel people', and in Marlowe's *Tamburlaine*, the Turkish emperor Bajazeth presents himself as a blood-thirsty imperialist, eager to 'let thousands' of his own soldiers 'die' so that he can use their 'slaughter'd carcasses' for 'walls and bulwarks to the rest'.[5] In *Lust's Dominion* (c.1599), Thomas Dekker presents Eleazar the Moor as a 'black Devil', whose 'barbarous' career of lust, murder, and usurpation of the Spanish throne ultimately causes the newly crowned king to banish all Moors from Spain.[6] In *Titus Andronicus*, Shakespeare's irredeemably villainous Moor, Aaron, caps off his career of deception, adultery, murder, and joyous mutilation with the boast that he has 'done a thousand dreadful things, / As willingly as one would kill a fly' (5.1.141–2); he regrets only that he cannot perform 'ten thousand worse than ever yet [he] did' (5.3.186). And in 1601, in order to justify deporting selected 'blackamoors' from England, Queen Elizabeth categorically declares them 'infidels, having no understanding of Christ or his Gospel'.

Despite the appearance of stereotypes such as these, clear lines of ethnicity and race were not easy to draw in this period. For starters, the early modern idea of 'race' carried a wide range of connotations—including, on Shakespeare's stage alone, lineage, family, species, status, and disposition. In *Richard III* (1592–3), for example, the ghosts of two young princes murdered by Richard III direct his heroic adversary, Richmond, to 'live, and beget a happy race'—or line—'of kings!' (5.5.106). In *Antony and Cleopatra*, Antony chastizes the alluring Cleopatra for drawing him away from Rome and 'the getting of a lawful race', a family line, with his Roman wife, Octavia (3.13.107). Timon of Athens imagines that 'his hate may grow / To the whole race'—or species—'of mankind, high and low' (*Timon* 4.1.39–40). In *The Merchant of Venice*, Lorenzo celebrates music's seductive power to tame 'a wild and wanton herd / Or race of youthful and unhandled colts', with race here standing in explicitly for 'herd' (5.1.70–1). Additionally, in *Measure for Measure* (1604), Angelo uses race to point to his internal nature when he warns Isabella that he means to give 'the rein' to his 'sensual race' (2.4.160). In Renaissance England, to identify someone by 'race' meant to point to Romans as well as Egyptians, Europeans as well as non-Europeans, whites as well as blacks.

Renaissance writers were particularly interested in knowing what produced 'blackness', however, whether the cause was overexposure to the sun, an act of God (a curse against one of the sons of Noah), an excessive internal heat or passion or some other predictable factor. These speculations provided useful justification for colour-coding 'white' Europeans as superior and darker, non-Europeans, especially

Africans, as inferior. Yet darkness was also figuring within the imagery of the period, especially in representations of women, as an alluring alternative to 'fairness'. Shakespeare's sonnets, for example, idealize a 'dark' lady along with a rival poet, representing both as the unorthodox but nonetheless desired and desirable objects of the speaking poet's gaze. Thus, the colour-coded discriminations that were being used to set non-Europeans apart were as much a part of England's iconography as, say, of Africa's.

The Moor

If one thing is clear, it is that Renaissance representations of non-Europeans were not constrained by any single geography, ideology, or code. Take, for example, the case of the Moor, who stands out in Shakespeare's oeuvre as the non-European 'other' residing, literally and figuratively, closest to home. Etymologically, the term 'Moor' indicated a native of Mauritania, a region in ancient Morocco; historically, the Moors' homeland was North Africa, Morocco, or what the Renaissance called 'Barbary'. Yet within representations of Africa and the Moor, this geographic specificity is lost at least as often as it is affirmed. In some cases, Moors are blurred into the broader category of 'Africans', with 'Africa' denoting both a part and a whole of the African continent; in others, Moors are grouped with non-African peoples, Arabians, Turks, and Spaniards among them. In addition, geography and ethnicity often serve to register moral or behavioural traits. The travel narratives in Hakluyt's *Principal Navigations*, for example, uphold a fairly consistent distinction between North African Moors and west African 'negroes'. That distinction pivots on the assumption that Moors are more 'civilized' and the negroes more 'savage'—and unwittingly paves the ideological way for what followed much later, as west Africans (and not North Africans) were subjected to New World slavery. Elsewhere, on the Renaissance stage, *The Battle of Alcazar* sets the villainous Muly Mahamet apart from his noble uncle, the 'Moor' Abdelmelec, by designating Muly uniquely as a 'Negro-Moor', though both figures share a common Moroccan as well as Arabian, but not west African, ancestry.

Further, while Renaissance writers used skin colour to locate, differentiate, and define African subjects, colour was no sure guide in the case of Moors. Moors could be 'tawny', 'black', or 'coal black' as well as other hues, giving modern critics leeway to describe upperclass Moors, such as Shakespeare's Prince of Morocco (in *The Merchant of Venice*), metaphorically as 'white'. Even the designation of 'blackamoors' provided no guarantee: all black Moors were not necessarily blackamoors, nor were all blackamoors necessarily Moors. In *Titus Andronicus*, for example, Shakespeare's 'raven-coloured' (2.3.83) Aaron is always a Moor and never a blackamoor, while the stage directions describe the scandalously black baby he fathers adulterously with the ultra-white Gothic queen, Tamora, as a 'blackamoor child' (4.2.51). Tellingly too, Queen Elizabeth refers to the black subjects she would deport as 'blackamoors' even though all other historical documents identify them as 'negroes', who most likely originated in west Africa.

To complicate the question of racial and ethnic identity further, 'Moor' could also signal religious rather than regional or geographical affiliations. Moors had long been associated with Islam, and in a number of prominent English texts, to be a Moor means simply to be a Muslim. In 1600, John Pory translated into English *The History and Description of Africa*, the most authoritative and popular account of Africa to appear in England during the early modern period, written first in Arabic by the Moor 'Leo Africanus'. Africanus, who claimed both Africa and Granada (in Spain) as his homeland, had already converted to Christianity by the time he wrote the history and had taken the name of a Pope ('Leo'). Still, in order to entice the audience to read the Moor's account, Pory first addresses Africanus's Islamic past. Pory apologizes for the fact that Africanus was '*by birth a* Moor, *and by religion for many years a Mohammedan*' and insists that the history nonetheless is 'not altogether . . . unworthy to be regarded'—as if the converted Moor was indelibly suspect as Muslim.[7] At the same time, however ingrained or automatic the association was between Moor and Muslim, other texts represent Moors as Christian converts, non-believing 'infidels', or as assimilated subjects who speak the language of Christianity whether or not they believe.

It is no wonder, then, that since the seventeenth century Othello has been depicted as an African and an Arabian, a black representative of the 'dark continent' to the south and a tawny figure from the exotic lands to the east. It is no wonder that critics disagree about Othello's religious predilections, uncertain of what his invocation of a Christian vocabulary actually means. Nor does it seem a coincidence that in one of the signal moments when Othello imagines himself in culturally specific terms, different manuscripts of the play provide different terms: 'base Indian' or 'base Judean' (5.2.356). For while stereotypical Moors, such as Shakespeare's Aaron, were indeed taking shape within Renaissance discourse, the Moor emerged simultaneously as a highly complex subject, unlikely to fit any single mould, more likely to carry the signs of a number of cultural traditions. Othello not only tells stories of 'antres [caves] vast and deserts idle, / Rough quarries, rocks, and hills whose heads touch heaven' (1.3.139–40), of 'cannibals' and 'Anthropophagi, and men whose heads / Do grow beneath their shoulders' (1.3.142–4), all familiar subjects within classical descriptions of Africa. He also produces as his family's legacy an Egyptian handkerchief, made from silkworms and 'dyed in mummy' (3.4.72), compares his tears to the 'medicinable gum' that drops from 'Arabian trees' (5.2.359–60), and imagines himself as both Venetian and Turk. That Shakespeare would assign the Moor such a wide-reaching cultural vision suggests the awareness that emerges in other Renaissance texts as well: that the Moor was a multi-dimensional subject, vitally connected to the 'world' in ways that England could neither codify nor commodify.

Conclusion

Thus, if the uncertainties within the Renaissance vision of the Moor are any measure, they testify not to a lack of knowledge about non-European peoples and places, although, admittedly, some of those places and peoples were relatively 'new' to England. Rather, they suggest the range and flexibility of knowledges that taking stock of 'all the world' at once required and engaged. In Shakespeare's *The Tempest*, Caliban may be the 'misshapen knave' (5.1.271), 'demi-devil' (5.1.275), and 'thing of darkness' (5.1.278) that Prospero derogates and forces into slavery, Caliban's penchant for curses, drink, maybe rape, and violence giving him away. But he is also an articulate survivalist, who claims feelings of love and loyalty, understands the power of books, dreams of riches, and appreciates the 'sweet airs' of the island (3.2.131). Shakespeare's Cleopatra may be Egypt, as she asserts, surrounded as she is by perfumes, gold, barges, monuments, eunuchs, asps, and other 'Egyptian' exotica. But according to Antony, who can see only through Roman eyes, she is also indescribably more than the sum of these parts, like the crocodile, which is 'as broad as it hath breadth', 'just so high as it is', and 'shaped' finally 'like itself' (*Antony and Cleopatra* 2.7.39–40). If England's increasing stake in overseas expansion and colonization made the need to clarify and classify cultural others more urgent, during Shakespeare's lifetime and within Shakespeare's plays that desire intersects with a competing recognition that England was not the only one setting the terms.

To think then about Shakespeare's 'view of the world' is to think about a picture that is constantly, though gradually, changing shape, as new sites and subjects come to define the centre of world-wide interest and exchange. We can see a subtle shift in geographical focus lying within the chronology of the Shakespearian canon. The Elizabethan plays are grounded heavily in English history and England, that 'dear dear land' that John of Gaunt would glorify as 'dear for her reputation through the world' (*Richard II*, 2.1.57–8). Mixed within these works are plays—*The Taming of the Shrew*, *The Two Gentlemen of Verona* (1594), *Romeo and Juliet* (1595–6), *A Midsummer Night's Dream*, *The Merchant of Venice*—that turn to the Mediterranean, to Verona, Venice, Padua, and classical Rome. Within them are Indian boys, Turkish carpets, and other icons of the East, as if more and more within the dreams, if not also the reach, of England. By the seventeenth century, Shakespeare's comedies and romances—*Twelfth Night* (1601–2), *Pericles* (1607–8), *The Winter's Tale*, and *The Tempest*—begin to look even further overseas, not only to fantasy islands, where distanced families could find and restore themselves, but also to landscapes that evoke the perils and particulars of contemporary voyages. As well, during the Jacobean period Shakespeare chooses non-European figures, the Moor and the Egyptian, as central subjects of his tragedies.

The further Shakespeare's plays venture outward, the more they speak to their time, responding and contributing to the pressure against isolation. If England was to leave its mark as an influential nation, it had first to make its mark in the world. It had to come to terms with diverse interests and populations and, like King Lear, 'see better' (*King Lear* 1.156) to keep in step with the times. Yet what makes Shakespeare's era, and Shakespeare's plays, so fascinating is that there was no one or clear way of seeing. Neither England nor Shakespeare had *a* view of the world—only a series of views, being constantly tested, asserted and questioned, formed and reformed in answer to a dynamic global marketplace in which cross-cultural negotiations were as unpredictable as they were crucial. If we are to understand how Shakespeare imagined the 'other' as he turned his gaze away from 'dear, dear' England, we must do it not only culture by culture, but also play by play.

FURTHER READING

Alexander, Catherine M. S. and Stanley Wells (eds.). *Shakespeare and Race* (Cambridge: Cambridge University Press, 2000). This collection of essays comes at the issue of race in Shakespeare from a variety of perspectives, with particular attention being given to *Othello*, *The Merchant of Venice*, and *The Tempest*.

Bartels, Emily C. *Spectacles of Strangeness: Imperialism, Alienation, and Marlowe* (Philadelphia: University of Pennsylvania Press, 1993). This study offers sustained readings of the plays of Christopher Marlowe and of the cultural stereotypes his plays at once animate and overturn as a response to a growing English interest in imperialist activity.

Braudel, Fernand. *The Mediterranean and the Mediterranean World in the Age of Philip II*. 2 vols. Sian Reynolds, trans. (New York: Harper and Row, 1972). This book offers an extensive, well-indexed history of the Mediterranean across the early modern period.

Cohen, Walter. 'The Undiscovered Country: Shakespeare and Mercantile Geography'. In *Marxist Shakespeare*, ed. Jean E. Howard and Scott Cutler Shershow (London: Routledge, 2001), pp. 128–58. This essay provides an excellent overview of the relation between Shakespeare's plays and England's overseas outreach.

'Constructing Race: Differentiating Peoples in the Early Modern World'. Special Issue of *The William and Mary Quarterly: A Magazine of Early American History and Culture* 54 (1997). The essays in this special journal issue look at the construction of race and racism in the early modern period, in the old world and the new, from both historical and literary critical perspectives.

Hall, Kim F. *Things of Darkness: Economies of Race and Gender in Early Modern England* (Ithaca: Cornell University Press, 1995). This study traces the ways English conceptions of race and 'blackness' intersected with constructions of gender within the early modern period. It includes a particularly useful discussion of the emergence of the fair/dark dichotomy in representations of female beauty, as well as a chapter on *The Tempest* and *Antony and Cleopatra*.

Helgerson, Richard. *Forms of Nationhood: The Elizabethan Writing of England* (Chicago: University of Chicago Press, 1992). This book looks at England's attempts to define itself as a nation across a variety of discourses, including legal, historical, cartographic, dramatic, and ecclesiastical writings as well as the writing of romance. It also provides a sustained interrogation of the construction of nationhood within Richard Hakluyt's *Principal Navigations*.

Hendricks, Margo and Patricia Parker (eds.). *Women, 'Race', and Writing in the Early Modern Period*

(London: Routledge, 1994). This collection of essays focuses on the intersection of race and gender within early modern discourse and includes a number of explorations of *Othello*.

Hulme, Peter. *Colonial Encounters: Europe and the Native Caribbean, 1492–1797* (New York: Methuen, 1986). This study provides an energetic account of the colonial discourse that took shape around the New World, and offers an in-depth reading of Shakespeare's *Tempest*.

Joughin, John J. (ed.). *Shakespeare and National Culture* (Manchester: Manchester University Press, 1997). This essay collection includes a number of essays on England's construction of a national identity as well as the ways Shakespeare, in his own time and after, figures in the process.

Matar, Nabil. *Turks, Moors, and Englishmen in the Age of Discovery* (New York: Columbia University Press, 1999). This book interrogates Anglo-Islamic relations in the Elizabethan and early Stuart periods. It pays special attention to the histories and representations of Turks and Moors and how those histories and representations intersected with the 'discovery' of New World Indians.

Pagden, Anthony. *Lords of All the World: Ideologies of Empire in Spain, Britain and France c.1500–c.1800* (New Haven: Yale University Press, 1995). This historical study traces the roots and ideas of empire across Europe from the sixteenth to the eighteenth century.

Williamson, James A. *A Short History of British Expansion* (New York: Macmillan, 1931). This historical study offers an extensive but beautifully signposted survey of English expansion from the Norman conquest in 1066 through the eighteenth century.

Yungblut, Laura Hunt. *Strangers Settled Here Amongst Us: Policies, Perceptions and the Presence of the Alien in Elizabethan England* (London: Routledge, 1996). This book offers an accessible historical study of the foreigners, and especially the European immigrants, living in Elizabethan England.

NOTES

1. All quotations from Marlowe's plays are from Christopher Marlowe. *The Complete Plays*, ed. J. B. Steane (1969; London: Penguin Books, 1986).

2. George Peele. *The Battle of Alcazar*, in *The Works of George Peele*, Vol. 1, ed. A. H. Bullen (1888; Port Washington, N. Y.: Kennikat Press, 1966), 1.1.27.

3. Richard Hakluyt. *The Principal Navigations, Voyages, Traffiques & Discoveries of the English Nation*, 12 vols. (Glasgow: James Maclehose and Sons, 1903–5), I, xx.

4. The three documents that contain Elizabeth's proclamations (referenced again below) appear in *Acts of the Privy Council of England* n.s. 26 (1596–97), ed. John Roche Dasent (London: Mackie & Co, 1902), pp. 16–17, 20–1, and in Eldred D. Jones. *The Elizabethan Image of Africa* (Charlottesville: University of Virginia Press, 1971), pp. 20–1.

5. George Whetstone. *The English Mirrour* (London, 1586), p. 70; Marlowe, *Tamburlaine Part One* (3.3.138–9).

6. *Lust's Dominion; or, the Lascivious Queen* (2.4.1129, 5.5.3812), ed. J. Le Gay Brereton, in *Materials for the Study of Old English Drama*, ed. Henry de Vocht (Louvain: Librairie Universitaire, 1931).

7. *The History and Description of Africa and of the Notable things Therein Contained . . .*, trans. John Pory, ed. Dr. Robert Brown (London: Hakluyt Society, 1896), p. ii.

Part II

Shakespearian genres

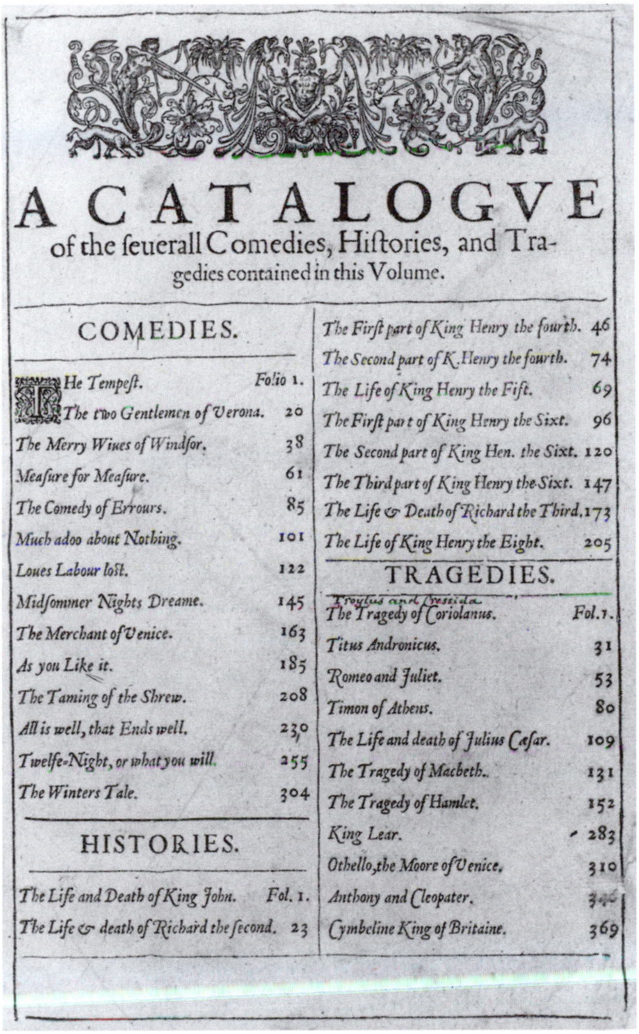

A CATALOGVE
of the ſeuerall Comedies, Hiſtories, and Tragedies contained in this Volume.

COMEDIES.

The Tempeſt. Folio 1.
The two Gentlemen of Verona. 20
The Merry Wiues of Windſor. 38
Meaſure for Meaſure. 61
The Comedy of Errours. 85
Much adoo about Nothing. 101
Loues Labour loſt. 122
Midſommer Nights Dreame. 145
The Merchant of Venice. 163
As you Like it. 185
The Taming of the Shrew. 208
All is well, that Ends well. 230
Twelfe-Night, or what you will. 255
The Winters Tale. 304

HISTORIES.

The Life and Death of King John. Fol. 1.
The Life & death of Richard the ſecond. 23
The First part of King Henry the fourth. 46
The Second part of K. Henry the fourth. 74
The Life of King Henry the Fift. 69
The First part of King Henry the Sixt. 96
The Second part of King Hen. the Sixt. 120
The Third part of King Henry the Sixt. 147
The Life & Death of Richard the Third. 173
The Life of King Henry the Eight. 205

TRAGEDIES.

Troylus and Cressida
The Tragedy of Coriolanus. Fol. 1.
Titus Andronicus. 31
Romeo and Juliet. 53
Timon of Athens. 80
The Life and death of Julius Cæſar. 109
The Tragedy of Macbeth. 131
The Tragedy of Hamlet. 152
King Lear. 283
Othello, the Moore of Venice. 310
Anthony and Cleopater. 346
Cymbeline King of Britaine. 369

Fig. 2.1 The contents page of the First Folio, of 1623. An early owner has written in the title of *Troilus and Cressida*, omitted from the Catalogue because it was a late addition to the volume.

Lena Cowen Orlin

What do we know about William Shakespeare? We might begin by saying that he wrote thirty-eight plays, a sequence of 154 sonnets, two long narrative poems, and various short poems. This is to think about his literary career in terms of both numbers of things and names for things. But nearly every subject connected with Shakespeare allows room for interpretation, even numbers and names.

The total of thirty-eight plays, for example, includes at least two that were co-authored with fellow playwright John Fletcher (*Henry VIII or All is True*, and *The Two Noble Kinsmen*) and omits two that were referred to in Shakespeare's lifetime but that have not come down to us (*Love's Labour's Won* and the Shakespeare–Fletcher collaboration *Cardenio*). The total further excludes a play for which Shakespeare evidently wrote some passages (*Sir Thomas More*). Because so many texts and so much information have been lost over time, we also lack an accurate catalogue of Shakespeare's shorter poetry. But the process of establishing his complete canon is no more challenging than is the practice of characterizing the plays and poems that have survived. Part Two of this *Guide* is about the sometimes difficult business of naming or labelling Shakespeare's works. It is about how these names can help us begin to interpret the works, to analyse what effects they are trying to create, and to understand the ideas and emotions they seek to provoke in us. It is also about the ways in which Shakespeare sometimes exceeds our efforts to put labels on him.

Literary genres

We organize most knowledge by creating categories. This is as true for literature as it is for zoology or botany. We begin to know an object by comparing it with other objects or by contrasting it with still more. Names give us ways of thinking about things; in the case of literature, they also give us ways of appreciating them and arguing about them. For literature, the principal term used in systems of classification is *genre*.

The major literary genres are prose narrative (novels), drama (plays), and non-dramatic verse (poetry). Thus, we can begin to position Shakespeare in the history of world literature by saying that as far as we know he did not write prose narratives, but he did write plays and poems. However, the categories of 'plays' and 'poems' are too large to be as useful as we might wish. It may seem easy to tell the difference between *Macbeth* and a sonnet, but then we might also want a name for referring to the difference between *Macbeth* and *A Midsummer Night's Dream*. Most of the chapters in this section of the *Guide* deal with the ways in which we group Shakespeare's plays in smaller categories, noting, for example, that *Macbeth* has more in common with *Hamlet*, as a tragedy, and that *A Midsummer Night's Dream* has more in common with *The Two Gentlemen of Verona*, as a comedy. Although these are technically subgenres, comedy and tragedy are often loosely called genres themselves.

Literary criticism essentially began with these very distinctions. In his treatise, *Poetics*, the ancient Greek philosopher Aristotle outlined the differing origins of comedy and tragedy and described their contrasting effects. His remarks on the history and theory of drama were highly influential in the Renaissance. We know that Shakespeare and his contemporaries were conscious of genre because they often made generic identifications in the titles of their plays. Thus, the full title of *Othello* is *The Tragedy of Othello, the Moor of Venice*. When, after his death, Shakespeare's former colleagues assembled his plays in one large volume, they called it *Master William Shakespeare's Comedies, Histories, & Tragedies Published according to the True Original Copies* (1623). We usually refer to this book as the 'First Folio', because it was the first collection of Shakespeare's plays and because it was printed in a large (folio-sized) volume. But it should not be forgotten that the First Folio's original collectors thought the book contained three different kinds of things. This principle is carried out in the table of contents, which is presented as a 'Catalogue' and in which the plays are divided into three groups, fourteen of them represented as 'Comedies', ten as 'Histories', and eleven as 'Tragedies'. (There are only thirty-five titles because *Pericles, Prince of Tyre* and *The Two Noble Kinsmen* were omitted from the First Folio, and, while the playtext for *Troilus and Cressida* was included, it was not listed in the Catalogue. See Figure 2.1.)

Shakespeare's comedies, histories, and tragedies

Genre identification carries with it certain burdens or expectations. A work given a generically specific name, like *The Comedy of Errors*, is usually expected to behave like other specimens of that genre and to adhere to conventions traditionally associated with it. Aristotle seems to have worked as a historian, detailing such generic practices as he observed, but later readers of Aristotle followed his observations as if they were rules. Thus, in his *Apology for Poetry*, Sir Philip Sidney complained that some English playwrights mingled kings, the proper subjects of tragedies, with clowns, the characters thought suitable only for comedy. Although the *Apology for Poetry* was not published until 1595, it was written by 1586, the year Sidney died. One of the most important Renaissance theoretical treatises on literature was composed, in other words, before Shakespeare had staged his first play. We don't really know what Sidney would have thought had he lived to see Shakespeare's tragedies, with clowns like *Macbeth*'s Porter.

In fact, few playwrights in Elizabethan and Jacobean England were strict in observing ancient social regulations about the genres. No matter how familiar they were with Aristotle, they responded to other influences, including native traditions from medieval England and their own innovations and fads. The Elizabethan and Jacobean theatre was a commercial business, and it adapted to, catered to, and also expanded the tastes and interests of its audiences. In practice, the comedies and tragedies of Shakespeare's time were differentiated more in terms of plot resolution than of social status. Comedies ended with characters pairing off for marriage, and tragedies concluded with many dead bodies on the stage (see Chapters 16 and 18).

'Histories', meanwhile, was a term that Aristotle never employed to define a dramatic genre. It was an Elizabethan invention, used with reference to a dramatic subject matter rather than a dramatic mode *per se*. Prose writing about the history of England was popular in Renaissance England as a medium through which a national identity was created and refined. Shakespeare was one of a number of playwrights who recognized the good source material available in the English chronicles and who turned this well-liked subject matter into dramatic form that was sometimes comic and sometimes tragic. The fashion for English history plays was especially strong in the 1590s, when Shakespeare first made his name as a playwright (see Chapter 17).

The three-part 'Catalogue' of the First Folio may seem to imply that the boundaries between tragedy, comedy, and English history were meticulously maintained in the Renaissance, but that is misleading. Some plays were given different generic identifications at different times. While the First Folio was printed after Shakespeare's death, many of his plays were published during his lifetime in small, single-volume editions known as quartos (see Chapter 38). We think of both *Richard II* and *Richard III* as English history plays, and both were catalogued that way in the First Folio. But in their earlier, quarto versions they were called *The Tragedy of King Richard the Second* (1597) and *The Tragedy of King Richard the Third* (1597).

In quarto, *Hamlet* was made inclusive of two genres, as *The Tragical History of Hamlet, Prince of Denmark* (1603 and 1606). Renaissance books were generally sold as a loose collection of pages, and purchasers could bind them if or as they wished. That means that title pages were, essentially, advertisements for the contents of books. Booksellers seem to have recognized the commercial value of appealing to as many interests as possible. Thus, in quarto *King Lear* was titled *Master William Shakespeare his True Chronicle History of the Life and Death of King Lear and his Three Daughters, with the Unfortunate Life of Edgar, Son and Heir to the Earl of Gloucester and his Sullen and Assumed Humour of Tom of Bedlam As It Was Played before the King's Majesty at Whitehall upon St. Stephen's night in Christmas Holiday by his Majesty's Servants Playing Usually at the Globe on the Bankside* (1608). This title page touches on history ('true chronicle history'), tragedy ('life and death'), and comedy ('sullen and assumed humour'). For good measure, it also borrows on the prestige of James I. The fact that Shakespeare is featured so prominently shows that his name had also become highly marketable by 1608.

In the First Folio, this play is simply *The Tragedy of King Lear*. The Folio generally confined itself to such short titles, perhaps because it was not trying to market any play individually. In consequence, the Folio suppressed some of the generic ambiguities of earlier printed versions of the plays. Despite the regularizations it imposed in both its play titles and its Catalogue, however, the Folio did not eliminate all generic controversy for Shakespeare's readers. *Cymbeline* is catalogued in the First Folio as a tragedy and given the name *The Tragedy of Cymbeline*, but today we think of it as a comedy. The play called *The Famous History of Troilus and Cressida* in quarto, where it was published with a preface that also praised it as 'passing full of the palm comical', was titled *The Tragedy of Troilus and Cressida* in the First Folio. Modern readers are not convinced that the Folio solution is the right one.

Dramatic variations and modern categorizations

If in his own time the labelling of Shakespeare's plays was sometimes variable, this is not evidence of his confusion or his publishers' incompetence. Instead, it testifies to a large and inclusive generic vision. Every Shakespearian tragedy included elements of comedy, like the gravediggers in *Hamlet*. And every comedy included threats of tragedy, like the apparent death of Hero in *Much Ado about Nothing*.

Mixing these modes, Shakespeare flouted strict generic distinctions with bravado. He thought outside the box in other ways, too. The idea that plays should observe severely restrictive unities of time and place, while not Aristotle's own, was generally attributed to him in the Renaissance. Sir Philip Sidney was particularly censorious of plays so wide-ranging as to have 'Asia of the one side, and Afric of the other'. But in Shakespeare's *Antony and Cleopatra*, the standard five acts are subdivided into an extraordinary number of scenes. The play careens between Rome and Egypt more extravagantly than Sidney could have imagined. By contrast, *Othello* comes close to observing a strict unity of time, with its action unfolding over the course of just a few days. The play is nonetheless anything but respectful of literary convention. It begins as a one-act comedy, in which two lovers succeed in making their match despite parental opposition, and ends with a four-act tragedy, as this blissful marriage plunges toward spouse-murder. Shakespeare seems to have posed himself the challenge of trying to make credible an astonishingly rapid alteration of genres and effects.

At the other temporal extreme lies *The Winter's Tale*. Three acts into this play, a choric figure called 'Time' enters to tell us that we should imagine that sixteen years have passed in the course of his thirty-two-line speech. The willingness to engage such a protracted narrative is one feature of plays Shakespeare wrote late in his career. *Pericles*, *Cymbeline*, *The Tempest*, and *The Winter's Tale* were all catalogued as comedies in the First Folio, but they seem sufficiently unlike earlier examples of the genre that modern critics have searched for a way of naming the difference. Today these plays are generally called 'romances', a term that was never applied to them in their own time, but one also adopted in this *Guide* (see Chapter 20). Shakespeare's romances are also closely related to dramas known in Renaissance England as 'tragicomedies' for their mingling of genres. While full of hazard and tragic possibility, tragicomedies succeed finally in recuperating happy endings from their harsh storylines. Shakespeare's particular variation on this form is infused with a sense of miracle, as if these joyous resolutions to tragic plots could be achieved only by means of literary magic.

Shakespeare also wrote plays that have been known as 'problem plays' or 'problem comedies'. The principal 'problem' with these plays is generic. *Troilus and Cressida*, variously associated with history, comedy, and tragedy in its own time, seems almost impossible to label, so profound is its participation in all these modes. Critics have also hesitated to call *Measure for Measure* and *All's Well that Ends Well* comedies. Neither play ends with multiple deaths, and both close on the subject of marriage. But the marriage proposal advanced in *Measure* is not necessarily accepted, and the marital union reconfirmed in *All's Well* seems a far from happy one. While the collectors of the First Folio were content to place these plays in the same category as *As You Like It* and *Twelfth Night*, most modern readers think they are sufficiently distinctive to constitute a kind of generic exploration that standard labels cannot capture (see Chapter 21).

Critics have proposed other refinements to the First Folio's tripartite system. In a group of tragedies, for example, Shakespeare dramatized stories from ancient Rome. Their concerns seem to be sufficiently similar that *Titus Andronicus*, *Julius Caesar*, *Antony and Cleopatra*, and *Coriolanus* are often grouped together as 'the Roman plays' (see Chapter 19). This was a subject matter to which Shakespeare turned also for his long non-dramatic poem, *The Rape of Lucrece*.

Some of the more particularized labels that have been employed for Shakespeare's plays derive less from his own corpus than from his engagement with the theatre of his time. For instance, *The Spanish Tragedy*, a play by Thomas Kyd, inaugurated a subgenre that has been called 'revenge tragedy'. Other plays on this popular theme, including one transparently titled *The Revenger's Tragedy*, held the stage for decades. Shakespeare wrote a revenge tragedy, too. It is interesting to think of *Hamlet*, a literary work of enormous and unrivalled cultural importance, as Shakespeare's contribution to a generic fad.

The missing genres

There were many literary trends to which Shakespeare did not subscribe. One was a subgenre that modern critics have called the 'domestic tragedy'. These plays refused to reserve tragic emotions for kings and queens, dealing instead with passion and violence in ordinary English households. *Othello* concerns murder in a marriage, but, as with others of Shakespeare's plays, it is domestic tragedy with a difference. The play is set in Venice and Cyprus, and its title character, while not royal, is an important man, a war hero. Other playwrights of Shakespeare's time wrote what have since been termed 'city comedies', scripts full of the exuberant commercial life of Elizabethan and Jacobean London. *The Merry Wives of Windsor* has much of the feel of a city comedy, but it is set in a small town rather than in England's great metropolitan centre.

In this way, the story of Shakespeare and genre is also a story of those genres he did not practise. He composed a great sonnet sequence, as did Sir Philip Sidney (*Astrophel and Stella*), Edmund Spenser (*Amoretti*), and Lady Mary Wroth (*Pamphilia to Amphilanthus*), but he did not write pastoral romance, as did Sidney (*Arcadia*) and Wroth (*Urania*; for Shakespeare's poetry, see Chapter 22). Shakespeare wrote two long narrative poems (*Venus and Adonis* and *The Rape of Lucrece*), but no epic poem to compare with those of Spenser (*The Faerie Queene*) and John Milton (*Paradise Lost*). There were minor fads in poetry, too, like the so-called 'country-house' or topographical poem, which was practised by Aemelia Lanyer (*The Description of Cooke-ham*) and Ben Jonson (*To Penshurst*) but not by Shakespeare. He authored historical chronicles neither in prose, like Sir Thomas More (*The History of King Richard the Third*) and Raphael Holinshed (*The Chronicles of England*), nor in poetry, like Samuel Daniel (*The Civil Wars*) and Michael Drayton (*Poly-Olbion*). While John Lyly and Thomas Lodge produced prose fiction (*Euphues* and *Rosalynde*, respectively), Shakespeare did not. He developed no English metrical versions of the biblical Psalms, as did Thomas Sternhold and Mary Sidney, nor did he accomplish any of the great translations from classical and continental literature, like Sir Thomas North's anglicization of Plutarch's *Lives of the Noble Grecians and Romans* and George Chapman's versions of Homer's *Iliad* and *Odyssey*. Unlike Shakespeare, playwrights Ben Jonson, Thomas Dekker, Anthony Munday, and Thomas Heywood wrote court masques, news pamphlets, civic pageants, and literary criticism.

Most of these other genres, though, inform Shakespeare's dramatic writing. There are elements of pastoral romance in *As You Like It* and *The Winter's Tale*. In *Richard II*, the character John of Gaunt speaks a poignant elegy on the threatened 'demi-paradise' of England that is like a topographical poem for the kingdom rather than for a single country estate (2.1.40–66). Prose chronicles were sources for Shakespeare's history plays, as were Plutarch for his Roman tragedies and Homer for *Troilus and Cressida*. *The Tempest* gives us a glimpse of a court masque, complete with music, elaborate costumes, and stylized representation. Interweaving so many modes and moods into his stageplays, Shakespeare demonstrated a supple and powerful range of generic knowledge.

The art of naming

When we recognize the genres within which Shakespeare worked, we come closer to knowing what his original audiences would have expected from him and also how he both satisfied and exceeded expectation. Shakespeare often pushed the edges of generic envelopes. He pressed conventional forms to see what unconventional effects he could achieve.

Because generic names so often imply generic rules and traditions, there are also hazards to the business of labelling Shakespeare's plays and poems. If we first define *Measure for Measure* as a comedy and then fault it for not ending as happily as other examples of that genre, the very act of naming inhibits us from appreciating its rich interplay of tones and topics. Much of Shakespeare's genius lies in the great variety of ideas and emotions we experience in any of his plays. The chapters in this section of the *Guide* show that generic naming is not a strict science but an art of interpretation.

FURTHER READING

Bamber, Linda. *Comic Women, Tragic Men: A Study of Gender and Genre in Shakespeare* (Stanford: Stanford University Press, 1982). This important early work of feminist criticism correlates the masculine 'Self' and the feminine 'Other' to the differing concerns and values of comedy and tragedy.

Bluestone, Max. *From Story to Stage: The Dramatic Adaptation of Prose Fiction in the Period of Shakespeare and his Contemporaries* (The Hague: Mouton, 1974). As he discusses the ways in which Shakespeare turned fiction into drama, Bluestone has enlightening things to say about the differences between these genres.

Colie, Rosalie L. *The Resources of Kind: Genre-Theory in the Renaissance*, ed. Barbara K. Lewalski (Berkeley: University of California Press, 1973). Erudite but readable, this slim book includes examples from European literature as well as some remarks on Shakespeare's sonnets and *King Lear*. Colie says that genres or 'kinds' of literature provide 'frames' or 'fixes' on the world and have an intrinsic connection to subject matter and thought.

Danson, Lawrence. *Shakespeare's Dramatic Genres*, Oxford Shakespeare Topics (Oxford: Oxford University Press, 2000). This is the best short introduction to the genres of Shakespeare's plays. In addition to chapters on genre in theory and as performed on stage, there are also three separate chapters on the comedies, the histories, and the tragedies.

Doran, Madeleine. *Endeavors of Art: A Study of Form in Elizabethan Drama* (Madison: University of Wisconsin Press, 1954). Of the books listed here, this is the most expansive, as Doran provides a learned and imaginative review of the generic heritage and innovations of Elizabethan drama. Shakespeare's experiments and achievements are seen in the context of those of other dramatists of the period.

Dubrow, Heather. *Genre* (London and New York: Methuen, 1982). This slender volume describes the historical development of genre theory, with one chapter covering 'Aristotle to [Matthew] Arnold' and another covering the twentieth century. Because Dubrow is a scholar of

Renaissance literature, there is considerable attention to Shakespeare, but drama is not her first concern.

Fowler, Alastair. *Kinds of Literature: An Introduction to the Theory of Genres* (Cambridge, Ma.: Harvard University Press, 1982). In this comprehensive handbook, Fowler argues that literary genres undergo constant processes of transmutation under the influences of social change, variations in taste, and also the inventiveness of individual works. Many but not all of his examples are from early modern English literature.

Lewalski, Barbara Kiefer (ed.). *Renaissance Genres: Essays on Theory, History, and Interpretation*, Harvard English Studies (Cambridge, Ma.: Harvard University Press, 1986). This collection of essays includes work by both theorists of genre and scholars of Shakespeare. Editor Lewalski emphasizes that concepts of genre are 'instruments of communication', not just systems of classification.

Snyder, Susan. *The Comic Matrix of Shakespearean Tragedy* (Princeton: Princeton University Press, 1979). Snyder reviews Renaissance theories of comedy and then shows how comic themes are introduced into Shakespeare's tragic plays. This is an important demonstration of Shakespeare's generic flexibility and innovation.

16 | Romantic comedies

William C. Carroll

When Shakespeare's colleagues assembled the collection of his works known as the First Folio in 1623, seven years after his death, they divided the plays into three genres, or categories of drama: 'Comedies', 'Histories', 'Tragedies'; these are largely still the genres modern critics invoke (though *Cymbeline* is no longer considered a tragedy, as it was in the Folio). For Shakespeare's contemporaries, a 'comedy' could be recognized by a relatively simple formula: comedies end in marriage, while tragedies end in death. Yet Shakespeare's comedies, as we shall see, radically complicate this formula in a variety of ways.

Since the late nineteenth century, critics and scholars have further subdivided the sixteen 'comedies' (including *Cymbeline*) which were printed in the Folio, plus *Pericles*, which was not. The 'romantic comedies' comprise the ten plays written (in roughly the order listed below) from the beginning of Shakespeare's career up to about 1601: *The Comedy of Errors*, *The Two Gentlemen of Verona*, *The Taming of the Shrew*, *Love's Labour's Lost*, *A Midsummer Night's Dream*, *The Merchant of Venice*, *Much Ado About Nothing*, *The Merry Wives of Windsor*, *As You Like It*, and *Twelfth Night*. In the years 1601 to 1604, he wrote three comedies now referred to as 'problem plays' or 'late comedies' (*Troilus and Cressida*, *Measure for Measure* and *All's Well That Ends Well*, discussed in Chapter 21). The remainder of his 'comedies'—*Pericles*, *Cymbeline*, *The Winter's Tale*, and *The Tempest*—are now classified as 'romances' (discussed in Chapter 20). This chapter will consider the origins and nature of the 'romantic comedies'.

The romantic comedies are termed 'romantic' in part because their plots and major themes involve love and desire. They are related to the so-called 'romances' in that both types of play have similar plots, typically involving some frustration of true love, a journey by a lover, improbable or even magical events, and a resolution in marriage or the promise of marriage arising from some discovery about identity. The difference between the two types of play is partly a matter of degree: in the romances, the journeys are more difficult and strange, gods may enter the action, deaths may in fact occur (though not to major characters and not at the end of the play), and plot and character improbabilities are often much greater than in the romantic comedies.

If we think of the period up to roughly 1601 as the first phase of Shakespeare's dramatic career, several trends are evident. By 1601, Shakespeare had written perhaps twenty-two plays: the ten romantic comedies listed above, nine plays about English history (*Henry VI Parts One, Two, and Three*; *Richard III*; *Richard II*; *Henry IV Parts One and Two*; *Henry V*; *King John*), but only three tragedies, *Titus Andronicus*, *Romeo and Juliet*, and *Julius Caesar* (and perhaps beginning *Hamlet*).[1] After 1601, Shakespeare never wrote another comedy like the ones we will be examining here. In the period roughly from 1601 to 1608, he wrote his major tragedies: *Hamlet*, *Othello*, *King Lear*, *Macbeth*, *Antony and Cleopatra*, *Timon of Athens*, and *Coriolanus*, in addition to the problem plays. Toward the end of his career, he turned away from tragedy altogether.

The dates of composition of his plays are often uncertain, but the large outlines of the pattern above are considered valid by most scholars: Shakespeare seems to have been interested in certain *types* of plays at different periods in his career. It's as if he took up a particular genre and worked his way through its possible permutations, and then went on to something different; certainly, there are other aspects of Shakespearian drama which seem to continue no matter what the genre (conflicts between parents and children, for example, particularly fathers and daughters). Still, Shakespeare mastered the writing of romantic comedy during a certain phase of his writing career, and before he fully turned his attention to tragedy.

If Shakespeare had died in 1601, before writing *Hamlet* and the other tragedies, he would still be remembered as the greatest writer of comedies (and histories) in early modern England; only two playwrights could rival him in the genre of comedy—Ben Jonson and Thomas Middleton—and none could rival him in romantic comedy.

Theories of comedy

For Shakespeare's contemporaries, comedy was considered a 'lower' genre than tragedy, just as tragedy was thought 'lower' than epic. The popularity of comedies on the early English stage, however, was enormous. There was little in the way of theory of comedy available to early writers, though, which probably stemmed from the fact that Aristotle's *Poetics* concerned itself largely with tragedy, his work on comedy having been lost. George Whetstone's definition of comedy in the Prologue to *Promos and Cassandra* (1578) is typical of the period: 'grave old men should instruct: young men should show the imperfections of youth: strumpets should be lascivious: boys unhappy: and clowns should speak disorderly: intermingling all these actions, in such sort, as the grave matter may instruct: and the pleasant, delight'. This prescription, as a glance at any of Shakespeare's comedies will show, was surely more honoured in the breach than in the observance. Many Elizabethan playwrights, Shakespeare foremost among them, ignored the boundaries between the serious and the playful, blurring the supposed lines of genre between tragedy and comedy. As a result, some writers, such as Sir Philip Sidney, complained about the infiltration of comic elements into higher genres such as tragedy: English playwrights, he said, 'thrust in clowns by head and shoulders to play a part in majestical matters', so that 'all their plays be neither right tragedies nor right comedies'. And conversely, Shakespeare's comedies are infiltrated by tragic elements, increasingly so after 1600.

Although the distinctions between comedy and tragedy were unstable in practice, still certain features of each genre can be distinguished. It may be safer to speak of *Shakespeare's* comedies, however, than of *Shakespearian* comedy, implying a clearly definable general concept, since the ten plays we will consider here are very different from one another.

First, to return to the cliché: Shakespeare's romantic comedies do *try* to end in marriage, or the promise of it; the expectation of such traditional endings was so great that when Shakespeare violated the principle in *Love's Labour's Lost*, one of the characters, Biron, commented on the oddity:

> BIRON: Our wooing doth not end like an old play.
>   Jack hath not Jill. These ladies' courtesy
>   Might well have made our sport a comedy.
> KING: Come, sir, it wants a twelvemonth an' a day;
>   And then 'twill end.
> BIRON: That's too long for a play.
>   (5.2.851-5)

And, a year or two later in *A Midsummer Night's Dream*, Puck invoked the same fairy tale to mark the promise that *this* play would end properly:

> Jack shall have Jill,
> Naught shall go ill . . .
> . . . and all shall be well.
>   (3.3.45-7)

The primary force behind the comic plots of the romantic comedies is erotic desire, and the primary action is the overcoming of obstacles to the fulfilment of such desire. Thus all of these comedies show lovers initially unable to fulfil their 'natural' desires for a particular lover: either the destined characters are separated by some external event (shipwreck, banishment) or one of them suffers from some internal bar (melancholy, anxiety). These 'blocking' conditions (a term used by the critic Northrop Frye to indicate forces that frustrate the satisfaction of desire) must be overcome, at which point the 'right' characters can come together happily—or, as in *Love's Labour's Lost*, the possibility is deferred. In a number of plays, the blocking action is embodied in a harsh or rigid law (as in *The Comedy of Errors* or, comically, in the compact sworn to by the lords in *Love's Labour's Lost*), often associated with a rigid and arbitrary father (as in Egeus in *A Midsummer Night's Dream*); this law will be softened, or simply set aside, by the end of the play. In *Twelfth Night*, there is such a law (Antonio the sea-captain is under sentence of death if he is captured), but most of the difficulties in love come from within the characters themselves: thus, Orsino is too fascinated with the role of melancholy lover to see clearly, and Olivia has shut out the world in continuing to grieve the death of her brother.

The marriages toward which the romantic comedies move are both the actual cere-monies, in the modern sense—in *As You Like It*, not one but four couples are to be married at the end of the play—and in some cases a restoration of a sundered marriage or love (Egeon and Emilia, husband and wife, are reunited at the end of *The Comedy of Errors*; Ford's jealousy vanishes in *The Merry Wives of Windsor*; Claudio and Hero come back together in *Much Ado About Nothing*). There are also social analogues to marriage, in which strained family relationships are healed, as in the reconciliation of the brothers in *As You Like It* or the general forgiveness of Falstaff at the end of *The Merry Wives of Windsor*.

A 'comedy' is a play with a certain kind of plot, then; there may be *comical* elements—moments of humour—in a play, but humour alone does not produce a comedy. The happy (or promised) ending, after the characters overcome obstacles, does. As many critics have noted, Dante's *Divine Comedy* is not a comedy because of its humour (of which there is virtually nil), but because its ending is 'happy', in heaven.

At the same time, Shakespeare is notorious for his disruptions of generic expec-tations: from the abortive ending of *Love's Labour's Lost*, as we have seen, to the shocking forgiveness of Proteus by Valentine in *The Two Gentlemen of Verona* and the forced conversion of Shylock in *The Merchant of Venice*. The comedies also often include satiric voices, at times self-directed, in figures like Jaques in *As You Like It* and Malvolio in *Twelfth Night*, and the mood at the very end of the comedies can be reflective, as in the epilogues at the end of *A Midsummer Night's Dream* and *As You Like It*, or even melancholic, as in the song at the end of *Twelfth Night*.

One other aspect of the plots of the romantic comedies needs to be mentioned here: namely, that there is never just a single focus in these plays, on a single relationship, but multiple tracks of interest followed in detail. Every set of lovers is surrounded by characters and situations that mirror their own: ageing parents, clowns and fools, parodic versions of romantic lovers (Silvius in *As You Like It*, Sir Andrew Aguecheek in *Twelfth Night*), extremes of comic celebration (Feste and Sir Toby Belch in *Twelfth Night*) and comic denial (Jaques in *As You Like It* and Malvolio in *Twelfth Night*). In some of the plays there are full-fledged secondary plots or even a play-within-the-play (*Love's Labour's Lost*, *A Midsummer Night's Dream*) that reflect on the actions of the main plot. Shakespeare's romantic comedies are of no simple or consistent type.

Some of the comedies are associated with particular occasions of ritual festive activity: *A Midsummer Night's Dream* is associated both with Midsummer Night's Eve, the time of the summer solstice, and with May Day, while *Twelfth Night*'s title comes directly from the day that marks the Feast of the Epiphany, January 6. These plays, along with *Love's Labour's Lost*, *The Merchant of Venice*, and *As You Like It*, were described by the critic C. L. Barber as Shakespeare's 'festive comedies' because of their associations with such holidays specifically, and more generally with the *values* of festivity, which seem central to comedy. Barber argued that after an initial conflict with an anti-festive blocking mechanism, these plays move, through an encounter with a festive world or values, from 'release' of inhibitions to 'clarification'. Northrop

Frye had at the same time noted that the comedies usually include an actual or symbolic journey, often to what he called a 'green world', a place associated with nature (by contrast with a corrupted court or city), where a healthy confusion of values and relationships might occur, leading to a restoration of a community to harmony and peace. These structural conceptions of comedy have been enormously useful in criticism, though they have also at times made the comedies seem more alike than they are, and they have passed over or masked other elements.

Contexts of comedy

After many years of interpreting the romantic comedies through the categories of structure, character, or theme, critics have in recent years also begun to situate these plays in terms of their historical and cultural contexts. For example, the romantic comedies are now seen to be in part concerned with tyranny and the nature of patriarchal rule, particularly within the family, as the histories and tragedies are in more obvious ways. The romantic comedies have also been seen to reflect early modern concerns about such material matters as the enclosure of common fields (*As You Like It*), the social and economic plight of younger brothers under the current rules of succession and inheritance (*As You Like It*), the nature of theatre in the early modern period (*Love's Labour's Lost*, *A Midsummer Night's Dream*), the Elizabethan encounter with religious otherness (*The Merchant of Venice*), the early modern subject's relation to Queen Elizabeth (*A Midsummer Night's Dream*, *The Merry Wives of Windsor*), and, above all, anxieties about gender and theatre.

Many critics have noted that while Shakespearian tragedies tend to centre on the actions of a single male protagonist (with notable exceptions like Juliet and Cleopatra), the comedies more often present the figure of a young woman as embodying the plays' central themes or values. Some critics following Northrop Frye simply asserted that tragedy was largely gendered masculine, while comedy was gendered feminine, not only because of such female characters, but also because the comedies seemed to work toward ideals such as reunion, birth or rebirth, marriage, 'natural' harmony, happiness—values which were (without much self-analysis) characterized as stereotypically 'female'; an opposite set of values, associated with tragedy, were stereotyped as 'male'.

There is certainly no denying the fact that Shakespeare's romantic comedies stage some of the most articulate, forceful, self-possessed female characters in all of drama, from figures in the early plays like Silvia in *The Two Gentlemen of Verona*, Kate in *The Taming of the Shrew*, and the four ladies in *Love's Labour's Lost*, through the brilliant wit of Beatrice in *Much Ado About Nothing* and the colder but powerful intelligence of Portia in *The Merchant of Venice*, to the youthful maturity and energy of Rosalind in *As You Like It* and Viola in *Twelfth Night*. Much of the early feminist criticism of the

1970s and 1980s analyzed these characters as examples of either Shakespeare's pre-liberationist ideology, or as his compromised reinscription of feminine independence into a confining patriarchal society. Whichever position one took, the result was a usefully heightened attention to these powerful and interesting characters; as a complement to this trend in analysis, moreover, critics began to devote attention to other women in the comedies, the Jaquenettas (*Love's Labour's Lost*) and Marias (*Twelfth Night*) who had not previously seemed worthy of much critical attention (see also Chapter 29).

In the past two decades or so, critical attention to gender issues has shifted away from character analysis to certain material facts of the early modern stage: namely, that the women's parts were played by boy actors, since female actors were prohibited from the public stages in England until the later seventeenth century. The consequences of this fact have been widely explored in contemporary criticism, particularly in two areas. First, under the rubric of metadramatic self-consciousness, critics noted that Shakespeare does not attempt to conceal the boy actor, but often acknowledges his existence (as in, for example, the epilogues to *A Midsummer Night's Dream* and *As You Like It*). What might have seemed a theatrical limitation, in the sense that stage realism was impossible, became instead a strength, an opportunity to suggest multiple layers of meaning in the plays, which turned out to be even more complex than previously thought. Secondly, and more recently, the fact of the boy actor has led to productive new emphases on the complex erotics of such performance—particularly the effect on the audience of the plays' frequent invocation of homoerotic desire—and the ways in which Shakespeare's blurring of what had seemed secure lines of gender identification calls into question many other supposedly fixed categories of identity.

The romantic comedies were once called, in an influential work of criticism published in 1962, 'Shakespeare's Happy Comedies'. The plays were considered almost entirely apart from their material and cultural contexts, largely in terms of themes such as forgiveness, love's wealth, and so on. In the past two decades, as the comedies have been historically contextualized, they have come to be seen as not nearly as 'happy' as once thought. The happy ending in marriage is now also seen as a cultural fantasy, and the origins of that fantasy have been sought in terms of psychoanalytic, cultural, and political discourses.

Origins

The plots, characters, and themes of Shakespeare's comedies can be traced with some completeness; Shakespeare's originality as a playwright lay not so much in his invention of something out of nothing, as in taking something familiar and making it new. With the comedies, Shakespeare's sources may be broadly defined into two categories, the classical and the popular, which will be examined in that order.

In *Hamlet*, Polonius notes that the travelling troupe of actors relies on classical precedents: 'Seneca [for tragedy] cannot be too heavy, nor Plautus [for comedy] too light' (2.2.382–3). The plays of the Roman playwright Plautus were very well-known in early modern England, both through the grammar school curriculum, where they were read and translated, and through early imitations and re-tellings, mostly Italian, of Plautine stories. A thorough study of Plautus's plays allows one to see his influence in all of Shakespeare's comedies, but four of them in particular are indebted to Plautus as an initial model: *The Comedy of Errors*, *The Taming of the Shrew*, *The Merry Wives of Windsor*, and *Twelfth Night*. One very perceptive theatre-goer in 1602, John Manningham, related that he had seen a performance of *Twelfth Night*, and it was 'much like the Comedy of Errors, or Menechmi in Plautus, but most like and near to that in Italian called *Inganni*'. Manningham was right on all counts: as in *The Comedy of Errors*, many of the plot devices and character types in *Twelfth Night* could be traced back to Plautus's farcical play about the Menechmi brothers, one of the best-known plays in Europe, and to Secchi's *Gl'Inganni* ['The Deceits'], but more likely to an earlier play, *Gl'Ingannati* ['The Deceived'], both of which were adapted and retold in Italian, French, and English collections of stories. *The Taming of the Shrew* derives in part from George Gascoigne's play, *Supposes*, which is a translation of Ariosto's *I Suppositi* ('The Supposes'), which itself looks back to Plautus. All of these plays' plots turn on transformations of identity, through trickery and deceit rather than magic; each involves multiple disguises, and each features largely ordinary citizens. A typical character-type from Plautine comedy is the witty, often deceitful servant.

Other comedies derive their stories, in part, from Shakespeare's readings in prose romances, such as *The Two Gentlemen of Verona* (from Jorge de Montemayor's *Diana*) and *As You Like It* (from Thomas Lodge's *Rosalynde*. For this, see Chapter 27). Some of the comedies derive from the same source stories as the tragedies; for example, *Much Ado About Nothing* and *Othello* both echo Giraldi Cinthio's collection of novellas, *Hecatommithi*, while *The Two Gentlemen of Verona* and *Romeo and Juliet* both include elements from Arthur Brooke's poem, *Romeus and Juliet*. Shakespeare's reading, as should be obvious, was extensive, and much scholarly energy has been expended on identifying and tracing his use of classical sources.

The heritage of the romantic comedies can also be traced back to materials of what we would now call popular culture, some of them unwritten, in contrast to the works mentioned above. The comedies (and all the other plays, in fact) owe much to the native tradition of medieval drama, such as the Morality plays.[2] The tricky servants from Plautine comedy, for example, are frequently fused with characteristics from the Vice figure of the late-medieval Morality plays. Some scholars, such as Robert Weimann, have also pointed out that Elizabethan actors' relations to their audience (and to different elements in it) derive from the popular drama, in which the Vice figure, for example, would directly address the audience, establishing a bond with it while breaking the illusion of realism.

Humour

The popular tradition also included a certain amount of unscripted, improvisatory humour, which found its way, often indirectly, into Elizabethan playtexts. Hamlet complains about the clown's mugging, and scorns those, like Polonius, who exhibit a taste for such low matter: 'He's for a jig or a tale of bawdry, or he sleeps' (*Hamlet*, 2.2.480–1). A jig was a dance, usually loud and boisterous, which followed the performance of a play, even at the end of a tragedy; elements of such boisterous action infiltrated the plays, just as the company's actors were the dancers in the jigs.

The Elizabethan period witnessed the rise of three of the greatest clown/actors in theatrical history: Richard Tarlton, Will Kemp, and Robert Armin. Tarlton (who died in 1588) was a kind of travelling entertainer, some of whose jests and quips were written down and printed in his lifetime, but also as late as 1611. He was a founding member of one theatrical company, the Queen's Men; wrote a comedy, *Seven Deadly Sins*; and became a cult figure for many years after his death. Will Kemp was in several different theatrical companies from 1585, and joined the Chamberlain's Men, Shakespeare's company, around 1593–4. Famous for his jigs and songs, Kemp with his unruly talents provided Shakespeare a unique comic talent, and soon parts were written specifically for Kemp to perform—Lance in *The Two Gentlemen of Verona*, Costard in *Love's Labour's Lost*, Bottom in *A Midsummer Night's Dream*, Dogberry in *Much Ado About Nothing*, perhaps even Falstaff in *Henry IV Parts One* and *Two* (as well as the servant Peter in *Romeo and Juliet*). In late 1599, Kemp left Shakespeare's company, striking out on his own; his first enterprise was his famous feat of dancing from London to Norwich, which he described in *Kempe's Nine Days' Wonder* (1600). Kemp was succeeded in Shakespeare's company by a different kind of clown, Robert Armin, already by 1600 a well-known actor and writer of anecdotes, and eventually a playwright himself. Armin's acting talents were evidently much different from Kemp's, with the result that Shakespeare no longer wrote parts like Bottom (though Armin may well have played the part in any revival); instead, Shakespeare began writing roles for the jester, such as Touchstone in *As You Like It*, Feste in *Twelfth Night*, Lavatch in *All's Well That Ends Well*, Thersites in *Troilus and Cressida*, and, perhaps most memorable, the Fool in *King Lear*, all of which Armin probably performed.

Shakespeare's plays have sometimes been criticized, even by his immediate contemporaries, for their willingness to indulge in what is said to be 'low' humour—the humour of the clown, which is often bawdy, full of bad jokes and awful puns, dependent on physical humour, almost slapstick. Yet the clowns are never irrelevant to the plays they are in, for they often serve to parody the themes of the main plots: Bottom falls in love with the Fairy Queen in *A Midsummer Night's Dream*, for example, Dogberry unearths the sinister plot in *Much Ado About Nothing*, and Lance and his dog Crab reflect his master Proteus in *The Two Gentlemen of Verona*. But in the shift from Tarlton to Armin, we can also see, as Robert Weimann has demonstrated, a shift from an often unscripted, improvisatory popular humour, in some ways literally outside the play (as in the jig), to the scripted inclusion of such humour within the play and a growing sophistication, as evident in Touchstone and Feste.

This 'low' humour, which Shakespeare seemed to love, puzzled some of his contemporaries—the rival playwright Ben Jonson offered several criticisms of Shakespeare's dramaturgy—and offended most of Shakespeare's editors and critics in the eighteenth century. Shakespeare's fondness for the pun, Samuel Johnson wrote in 1765, was his 'fatal Cleopatra'. Some Restoration and eighteenth-century authors rewrote his plays to 'improve' them, adding or deleting scenes, characters and dialogue, even changing the endings to suit a different moral or aesthetic vision. Low humour was especially disparaged, often dismissed as a commercial playwright's stooping to 'play to the groundlings' (those who paid the least, to stand on the 'ground' at the Globe).

However, the theoretical writings of Mikhail Bakhtin and Michel Foucault, among others, have taught critics in recent years new ways to read what seem to be marginal elements and connect them to traditionally central concerns. For example, Bakhtin's emphasis on the comedy of the body, particularly its most physical urges and manifestations, has helped readers connect such seemingly irrelevant moments as the report of the dog Crab's urinating on Silvia (in *The Two Gentlemen of Verona*) to Proteus's warped desires, or the puzzling letter which Malvolio reads (in *Twelfth Night*), with its obscene reference to the female genitals, to other issues of erotic desire and gender confusion in the play; at the same time, attention to such elements of the plays helps link Shakespeare's romantic comedies to other Renaissance literature, such as the work of the French writer, François Rabelais (who died in 1553).

Desire

Shakespearian romantic comedy, at its core, is fuelled by desire. The central plots as well as the low, reflecting humour of the clowns and fools are driven by erotic energies which cross the spectra from heteroerotic to homoerotic, from platonic and elevated to openly sexual and low, from Petrarchan clichés to innovative surprises (see also Chapter 30). The plays feature brilliant young women (who are actually male actors) and not-so-brilliant young men, stereotyped conventional lovers and fresh, inventive characters who are given an astonishing illusion of interiority.

The suggestive layerings of the plays' representations of romantic love are perhaps best encapsulated in *As You Like It*. The character Rosalind, performed by a boy actor, has put on a male disguise as 'Ganymede', who pretends to be 'Rosalind' in order to woo the love-sick Orlando as a way of 'curing' his love. In the following quotation, 'Rosalind' responds to Orlando's clichéd response to the news that his beloved will not have him ('Then in mine own person I die'):

No, faith; die by attorney. The poor world is almost six thousand years old, and in all this time there was not any man died in his own person, videlicet, in a love-cause. Troilus had his brains dashed out with a Grecian club, yet he did what he could to die before, and he is one of the patterns of love. Leander, he would have lived many a fair year though Hero had turned nun if it had not been for a hot midsummer night, for, good youth, he went but forth to wash him in the Hellespont and, being taken with the cramp, was drowned; and the foolish chroniclers of that age found it was Hero of Sestos. But these are all lies. Men have died from time to time, and worms have eaten them, but not for love.

And a few lines later, when he promises to love his beloved 'For ever and a day', Rosalind (still in disguise) replies,

Say a day without the ever. No, no, Orlando; men are April when they woo, December when they wed. Maids are May when they are maids, but the sky changes when they are wives.

(4.1.80-92, 123-7)

Rosalind's comic wisdom here works hard to puncture poetic hyperbole ('For ever and a day') and romantic clichés—the great Renaissance retellings of the stories of legendary lovers such as Troilus and Cressida, and above all Hero and Leander (the subject of a famous poem by that name by Christopher Marlowe, Shakespeare's contemporary), are in the end, she says, 'all lies'. That is, they are fictions which the culture has accepted. But then 'Rosalind' herself is also one of those 'lies'; somewhere beneath all the layers of performance is the boy actor, and the play's representation of a maturing heterosexual love is at the same time wonderfully complicated by the suggestions of homoerotic desire: is Orlando attracted to Rosalind or to her disguise as 'Ganymede' (which was a slang term for a young male homosexual)?

Shakespeare staged his own version of such tragical romantic stories as that of Hero and Leander in *Romeo and Juliet*, where the lovers' lives and deaths followed the same course as the legendary classical lovers, Pyramus and Thisbe; as sombre and tragic as *Romeo and Juliet* is, though, Shakespeare parodied his own romantic plot in *A Midsummer Night's Dream*, when he has his mechanicals put on a truly wretched performance of 'A tedious brief scene of young Pyramus / And his love Thisbe: very tragical mirth' (5.1.56–7). The exact same plot of young lovers, in frustration and despair, who take their own lives, can be either tragic or comic—as you like it, or what you will, it depends on how you look at it. Comic death, as seen in the play-within-the-play in *Dream*, is linked to real death through the Elizabethan pun on the verb 'to die', which meant both the physical extinction of the body but also sexual intercourse.

Rosalind points out that every April is followed by a December: there is a springtime of romantic love, but there is also always winter to follow. Mutability and death are facts of nature, but romantic comedy aspires to transcend such mundane facts even as it acknowledges their inescapable reality.

FURTHER READING

Bakhtin, Mikhail. *Rabelais and His World* (Bloomington: Indiana University Press, 1984). This book is the classic study of the carnivalesque in relation to society and literature.

Barber, C. L. *Shakespeare's Festive Comedy: A Study of Dramatic Form and Its Relation to Social Custom* (Princeton: Princeton University Press, 1959). This book relates the comedies to specific occasions of social festivity in early modern England.

Carroll, William C. *The Metamorphoses of Shakespearean Comedy* (Princeton: Princeton University Press, 1985). This book considers the comedies in relation to ideas of metamorphosis, particularly through Ovid's works.

Elam, Keir. *Shakespeare's Universe of Discourse: Language-Games in the Comedies* (Cambridge: Cambridge University Press, 1984). This book, with special emphasis on *Love's Labour's Lost*, closely examines language in the comedies.

Freedman, Barbara. *Staging the Gaze: Postmodernism, Psychoanalysis, and Shakespearean Comedy* (Ithaca: Cornell University Press, 1991). This book examines the comedies through various aspects of psychoanalytic theory.

Frye, Northrop. *A Natural Perspective: The Development of Shakespearean Comedy and Romance* (New York: Columbia University Press, 1965). This book is the classic formulation of the typical structures of Shakespearean comedy.

Salingar, Leo. *Shakespeare and the Traditions of Comedy* (Cambridge: Cambridge University Press, 1974). This book provides the most detailed examination of the origins—more than just 'sources'—of comedy in the period, especially as relates to Shakespeare.

Weimann, Robert. *Shakespeare and the Popular Tradition in the Theater* (Baltimore: Johns Hopkins University Press, 1978). This book is the complement to Salingar's, examining the 'popular', non-classical tradition of performance in early modern England.

NOTES

1. Some of the history plays were classified as 'tragedies' on their original title pages or by the editors of the First Folio.
2. Morality plays staged personified abstractions, such as the vices and virtues, to teach moral and religious lessons; the most famous Morality play is probably *Everyman*.

READING: *Twelfth Night, or What You Will*

Twelfth Night, or What You Will is the last of Shakespeare's ten romantic comedies, and arguably the best of them. The play is a culmination of virtually every aspect of the comedies that come before it, yet it also manages to look forward to the tragedies to follow. Probably written around 1601, the play recapitulates Shakespeare's recurring interest in mistaken identity, thwarted romantic love, sexual disguise, folly, marriage, metamorphosis, and vision, among other topics.

The play's title refers to the Twelfth Night after Christmas, January 6, the Feast of the Epiphany (marking the visit of the three kings to Bethlehem to worship the Christ child) in the Christian calendar. In Elizabethan England, the time between Christmas and Twelfth Night was one of celebration, revels, and festivity during which the overturning of traditional hierarchical rule was permitted. Whether the play's title was linked to an actual specific event is uncertain; on Twelfth Night 1601, Shakespeare's company performed at the court of Queen Elizabeth, whose guest was the Italian duke Orsino, but it is unknown whether the play was performed on that occasion.

The first reference to the play was by John Manningham, who saw a performance in February 1602 'at our feast' (see the quotation on page 181), so the play's association with festivity is marked early. Perhaps the most obvious link to festivity in the play is evident in the subplot with Sir Toby Belch, Maria, and the Fool, whose name, appropriately, is Feste. On the other hand, the play's subtitle, *What You Will*, seems at first to be dismissive, like *As You Like It* or *Much Ado About Nothing*; each of these titles, however, has been shown to relate closely to themes of their respective plays, and the phrases 'what you will' and 'what you would', which recur in *Twelfth Night*, are part of the play's investigations of identity.

What may have been Shakespeare's first romantic comedy, *The Comedy of Errors*, founded its plot on a shipwreck which divided a family and led to an often farcical plot of mistaken identity, and in *Twelfth Night* Shakespeare revisited this plot, which derived from the plays of Plautus. But rather than two sets of twin brothers, as in *Errors*, Shakespeare now created a single set, a twin brother and sister (mirroring Shakespeare's own children, the twins Hamnet, who had died in 1596, and Judith). This shift in gender between the two plays suggests how Shakespeare's interests had developed over the course of writing his comedies, for the roles of his female characters had become markedly more complex and substantial. *Twelfth Night*'s Viola follows in the line of active comic heroines—from Julia (*The Two Gentlemen of Verona*) and Portia (*The Merchant of Venice*) to Rosalind (*As You Like It*)—who disguise themselves, play roles in relation to their lovers, and take over large parts of their plays.

As it is extremely rare to have an eyewitness account of one of Shakespeare's plays during his own lifetime, it is worth returning to John Manningham's account. After remarking the play's resemblance to Plautine and Italian forerunners, Manningham notes only a single element of the plot: 'A good practice in it to make the steward believe his Lady widow[1] was in love with him, by counterfeiting a letter, as from his Lady, in general terms, telling him what she liked best in him, and prescribing his gesture in smiling, his apparel, etc., and then when he came to practise, making him believe they took him to be mad'. The plot which gulls Malvolio, in short, made the greatest impression on Manningham, who otherwise fails to mention Viola and her disguises, Orsino, or the spectacular 'natural perspective' at the end when the lost twins confront one another. Certainly Malvolio (whose name means 'ill-will') is one of Shakespeare's great comic creations. According to Maria, 'sometimes he is a kind of puritan', but then she qualifies the accusation: 'The dev'l a puritan that he is, or anything constantly but a time-pleaser, an affectioned ass that cons state without book and utters it by great swathes; the best persuaded of himself, so crammed, as he thinks, with excellencies, that it is his grounds of faith that all that look on him love him' (2.3.125–36). It is through this 'vice' of self-love that the comic trick against him will work. A less biased witness than Maria, Olivia also tells Malvolio that he is 'sick of self-love . . . and taste with a distempered appetite' (1.5.77–8).

Malvolio's 'self-love' is a kind of illness, comically taken to be a form of madness later, leading to Malvolio's imprisonment in the 'dark' house (in 4.2) and the attempted exorcism by Feste (playing the role of Sir Topas, the curate). The point is that Malvolio has always been imprisoned—'this house is as dark as ignorance' (4.2.40)—by his own inability to 'see' himself. He is described as a 'kind of puritan' because he opposes festivity: that is, life itself, with all its noise, excess, festivity, and grossness. When he confronts the loud, drunken singers late at night, Malvolio is challenged by the aptly named Sir Toby Belch in one of the most memorable lines in Shakespeare: 'Dost thou think because thou art virtuous there shall be no more cakes and ale?' (2.3.103–4). As a modern joke has it, a puritan is a man who worries that somewhere, somehow, someone else is having fun. As much as Shakespeare seems to mock Malvolio's behaviour, though, he also shows that Toby's festivity crosses the line from mere exuberance into disorderly excess, and he too is cautioned by Olivia. Still, at the end of the play, Malvolio is the one figure who refuses to take part in the general reconciliation. Olivia notes that 'He hath been most notoriously abused', which is true enough, but his parting line—'I'll be revenged on the whole pack of you' (5.1.365–6)—strongly suggests that his (self-)alienation will not be cured. As interesting as he is, however, Malvolio is by no means the main character in the play, though some nineteenth-century critics tried to make him into a tragic hero.

Malvolio's plot-line serves to some extent as a kind of ultimate parody of the lovers in the rest of the play. His love is narcissistic, turned entirely inward; others suffer similar debilities, though not to the same degree. Malvolio's mistress Olivia, for example, has committed to mourning her dead brother—or, as Valentine ambiguously states it, 'A brother's dead love, which she would keep fresh / And lasting in her sad remembrance' (1.1.30–1)—for seven more years, an unusually long time, which Toby (her uncle) less elegantly notes: 'What a plague means my niece to take the death of her brother thus? I am sure care's an enemy to life' (1.3.1–2). In terms of comic convention, then, Olivia has to be brought from this denial of life—a 'dead love'—to another kind of love. Similarly, Orsino suffers yet another kind of love-sickness, as he gorges himself emotionally in the play's opening lines: 'If music be the food of love, play on, / Give me excess of it that, surfeiting, / The appetite may sicken and so die' (1.1.1–3). His unrequited love for Olivia manifests itself in a self-indulgent melancholy nearly as crippling as Malvolio's own. Still another unrequited lover in the play is Sir Andrew Aguecheek, who also pines for Olivia, and who will be tricked into fighting a laughably cowardly duel for her sake. Finally, there is Viola, who like Olivia has lost a brother (she believes) to shipwreck, and must suffer an unrequited (indeed, totally unrecognized) love herself as she pines for Orsino.

'Cesario' is the name Viola assumes when she disguises herself as a male—in fact, as a 'eunuch' (1.2.52)—to serve Orsino. Viola quickly falls in love with Orsino, in spite of his infatuation with the idea of Olivia, and in an ironic situation already explored with Julia's disguise in *The Two Gentlemen of Verona*, Orsino commissions Cesario/Viola to woo Olivia on his behalf. Viola can only be true to herself by doing her best for Orsino, thereby doing the worst to her own chances for Orsino's love—or so she thinks. Malvolio's delusion, we were told, is his belief 'that all that look on him love him', but that description more nearly describes Cesario's position, for Olivia falls in love with Cesario rather than with 'his' master, and Orsino will discover, at the end of the play, that he has also fallen in love with Cesario.

Here Shakespeare plays with the artificiality of gender definitions in a highly sophisticated way. Behind the part of 'Viola' is the boy actor at the Globe Theatre; 'Viola' then disguises 'herself' as 'Cesario', a young man but, as we saw, also a 'eunuch'. Hence Cesario's sexuality is ambivalent—or perhaps, erased. So Olivia can fall in love with Cesario's 'masculine' characteristics (through which the constancy and fidelity of 'female' love manifests itself), while Orsino is attracted to the 'female' aspects of the 'male', Cesario. The androgynous figure of Cesario is thus 'what you will': the object of desire suitable for either sex.

The Orsino-Olivia-Viola triangle (even their names seem to be anagrams for one another) could, in a tragedy, lead to disaster, but Shakespeare engineers a different kind of ending. In Plautine comedy, and in Shakespeare's earlier comedies such as *The Comedy of Errors* and *Much Ado About Nothing*, the cases of mistaken identity were resolved in a predictable moment of unmasking, literally or figuratively: the twin Antipholus brothers finally come on stage at the same time in *Errors*, and Hero removes her veil in *Much Ado*. In *Twelfth Night*, though, the moment of discovery is also a moment of gender division. When Viola's brother Sebastian, whom she thought dead, appears in the final scene, the figure of Cesario is in effect split in two: Orsino sees

> One face, one voice, one habit, and two persons,
> A natural perspective, that is and is not
>
> (5.1.208-9)

A 'perspective' was a distorting glass which, by optical illusion, could make one picture or object appear like two or more, but the same effect, Orsino says, is here created naturally. But what exactly has been seen here? The 'two persons' are not finally, as Orsino thinks, identical, since one is a woman; yet Shakespeare is also here playing on several layers of performance, since Viola is dressed as a male and is, beneath all the costumes, a male actor playing the part. So what one sees 'is and is not' male. 'Cesario' disappears into two figures: the male Sebastian, who had encountered an amorous Olivia and married her earlier, and Viola, who as a 'female' now can serve as a permissible object of Orsino's desire. Yet Viola never quite shifts back to being a female, either, for 'she' remains in male clothing through the end of the play, and Orsino addresses her still as Cesario:

> Cesario, come—
> For so you shall be while you are a man;
> But when in other habits you are seen,
> Orsino's mistress, and his fancy's queen.
> (5.1.372-5)

Clothes thus make the man—or woman, or both.

The 'natural perspective' of the ending, when one sees what is and what is not at the same time, can serve as a paradigm for the ways in which the various characters see, or fail to see, both themselves and others throughout the play. On the simplest level, Sebastian and Cesario/Viola are seen as what they are not, until the final scene, with both comic and erotic consequences, while Antonio, Sebastian's friend, nearly comes to grief over the confusion. More frequently, however, a character is transformed or deformed by vision that is shaped by the power of desire. Orsino says,

> O, when mine eyes did see Olivia first
> Methought she purged the air of pestilence;
> That instant was I turned into a hart,
> And my desires, like fell and cruel hounds,
> E'er since pursue me.
> (1.1.18-22)

Like the mythological figure of Actaeon pursued by his own hounds, Orsino is, he says, destroyed by his own desires. Using the same language of the pestilence, Olivia remarks on her first sight of Cesario:

> Even so quickly may one catch the plague?
> Methinks I feel this youth's perfections
> With an invisible and subtle stealth
> To creep in at mine eyes.
> (1.5.265-8)

All the characters who are in love suffer from some kind of disease; even one name, Aguecheek (who loves Olivia), derives from 'ague', a fever.

The character most notoriously afflicted by a deforming vision and figurative sickness is Malvolio, 'sick of self-love'. The scene in which he reads Maria's counterfeit letter is one of Shakespeare's greatest comic moments. A somewhat similar scene occurs in *Much Ado About Nothing*, when counterfeited letters are read aloud so that they will be overheard by Benedick and Beatrice, who will be tricked into admitting their love for one another. But the scene in *Twelfth Night* is more spectacularly comic because Malvolio does all the damage to himself. The letter has been written, supposedly in Olivia's handwriting, by Maria, and it seems to be Olivia's invitation to Malvolio to approach her as a lover.

The mere possibility releases in Malvolio long-suppressed fantasies of power and sexuality. His dreams rest as well on a desire to transcend his class status: 'To be Count Malvolio!' he muses (2.5.30), and he recalls another instance of social climbing, when 'The Lady of the Strachey married the yeoman of the wardrobe' (34–5). This dream of upward social mobility leads to an imagined scenario in which Toby and his friends (who are eavesdropping and comically commenting on Malvolio's words) will pay for their indiscretions: 'And then to have the humour of state and—after a demure travel of regard, telling them I know my place, as I would they should do theirs—to ask for my kinsman Toby . . . Seven of my people with an obedient start make out for him. I frown the while, and perchance wind up my watch, or play with my—[*touching his chain*] some rich jewel. Toby approaches; curtsies there to me. . . . I extend my hand to him thus, quenching my familiar smile with an austere regard of control' (47–60) and so forth, until he discovers the counterfeit letter.

Here Malvolio professes to recognize Olivia's handwriting: 'These be her very c's, her u's, and her t's, and thus makes she her great P's. It is in contempt of question her hand', to which Sir Andrew wonders in an aside, 'Her c's, her u's, and her t's. Why that?' (78–81). The answer is that Malvolio has unwittingly spelled out c-u-t, a slang word for the female genitals (or possibly Malvolio's *and* was pronounced as *n*, thus making the word unmistakable), with the further joke on urination. Malvolio, in other words, *thinks* he recognizes Olivia's desire in the letter, but his failure to hear his own sexual reference indicates that he doesn't know what he is saying or reading. Olivia's sexuality is thus visible but not legible, or intelligible, as far as he is concerned.

What follows in Malvolio's reading of the actual letter inverts what has just happened with c-u-t. Now, in the famous riddle in the letter—'M.O.A.I. doth sway my life' (97)—Malvolio strains to read the text as relating to him: 'If I could make that resemble something in me' (107–8). Of course, he manages to connect the riddle to himself: 'and yet to crush this a little, it would bow to me, for every one of these letters are in my name' (123–4). This remarkable scene, which can take a very long time to perform while the actor milks every moment for its full comic potential, concludes with Malvolio's embrace of the letter's instructions to wear yellow stockings, dress cross-gartered, put himself 'into the trick of singularity' (i.e., to cultivate eccentricity, as if any more were needed) and in Olivia's presence 'still smile'. Malvolio thus becomes a paradigm, or rather a parody, of the transformed lover, for whom every sign seems to point to his lady's love, and who is himself utterly changed by the power of love. Absurd as he is, Malvolio is not that different from the figures of Orsino and Olivia as the play opens.

Twelfth Night ends, as we have seen, with the 'natural perspective' revealing the confused identities of Sebastian and Cesario/Viola, and this revelation also leads Orsino to see himself and his own desires more clearly. But though the play looks forward to the wedding of Orsino and Viola, the mood is darkened by Malvolio's call for revenge, and the play actually ends with Feste's poignant song,

> When that I was and a little tiny boy,
> With hey, ho, the wind and the rain,
> A foolish thing was but a toy,
> For the rain it raineth every day.
> (5.1.376-95)

This five-stanza song describes a kind of Four Ages of Man (cf. Jaques's famous 'seven ages' of man speech in *As You Like It*, 2.7), when man is a 'boy', when in 'man's estate', when he comes 'to wive', and when he comes 'unto my beds' (either drunk, or in old age). Each stage represents a disappointment or disillusioning of some kind, and the whole trajectory is an anti-romantic account of a man's growth, sexuality (the 'foolish thing' or phallus is only a 'toy' in youth), marriage, and ageing. With its refrain reminding the audience that 'the rain it raineth every day', the song is a philosophical, even melancholy reminder of the 'every day' realities of life.[2] Yet these realities, 'the wind and the rain', can also be temporarily set aside within the imaginative space of the theatre:

> But that's all one, our play is done,
> And we'll strive to please you every day.

FURTHER READING

Elam, Keir. 'The Fertile Eunuch: *Twelfth Night*, Early Modern Intercourse, and the Fruits of Castration', *Shakespeare Quarterly* 47 (1996), 1–36. Relating the play to its many sources in European literature, Elam considers the implications of Viola's claim to disguise herself 'as an eunuch'.

Greenblatt, Stephen. 'Fiction and Friction', in *Shakespearean Negotiations: The Circulation of Social Energy in Renaissance England* (Berkeley: University of California Press, 1988). This essay places the play in the context of early modern theories of sexuality and gender.

Hollander, John. '*Twelfth Night* and the Morality of Indulgence', *Sewanee Review* 68 (1959), 220–38. This classic essay reads the play as a 'moral comedy' that counters the moralizing comedy of Ben Jonson.

Malcolmson, Cristina. ' "What You Will": Social Mobility and Gender in *Twelfth Night*', in *The Matter of Difference: Materialist Feminist Criticism of Shakespeare* (Ithaca: Cornell University Press, 1991). This essay reads the play through the cultural context of early modern England, particularly in terms of social rank and social mobility.

NOTES

1. Olivia is not a widow in Shakespeare's play, though she is in one of the sources.
2. A related stanza of this song is sung, or quoted, by the Fool in *King Lear*, 3.2.73–6: 'He that has and a little tiny wit— / With hey, ho, the wind and the rain— / Must make content with his fortunes fit, / Though the rain it raineth every day'.

17 | English history plays

Phyllis Rackin

The first collected edition of Shakespeare's plays, known as the First Folio, divided the plays into three categories—Comedies, Histories, and Tragedies. Although many of the plays listed as tragedies were based on historical subjects, plays that depicted late medieval English history, whether the stories they told were comic or tragic, received a classification of their own.

The category of Histories may seem strange to a modern reader, and it was by no means clearly defined at the time Shakespeare wrote. Some of the plays listed as 'Histories' in the First Folio had been identified previously as tragedies, both on the title pages of earlier editions and in Francis Meres's survey of Elizabethan literature, *Palladis Tamia* (1598). At the end of the sixteenth century, 'history', whether dramatic or nondramatic, was not yet identified as a distinct genre. Edmund Spenser's prefatory letter to *The Faerie Queene* (1590), while insisting upon the difference between his work as a 'Poet historical' and that of a 'historiographer', still referred to his allegorical romance as a 'History'. Shakespeare's *The Merchant of Venice*, although listed in the Folio's Table of Contents as a comedy, was identified in the title of the earlier quarto edition as a 'history'. Nonetheless, Shakespeare's fellow actors, who published the First Folio seven years after his death, designated ten of the plays—almost a third of that first collected edition—as 'Histories'. Perhaps they did so because at the end of the sixteenth century, plays about English history had been extremely popular on the London stage.

The history play seems to be the vehicle by which the young Shakespeare first made his mark as a playwright. Three plays dealing with the reign of King Henry VI are among Shakespeare's earliest surviving works, and they are also the subject of the first references we have to Shakespeare as a London playwright. In *Greene's Groatsworth of Wit*, published in 1592, the university-trained playwright Robert Greene complained about 'an upstart crow, beautified with our feathers'. The 'upstart crow' was probably William Shakespeare because, Greene continued, 'with his *Tiger's heart wrapped in a Player's hide*, [he] supposes that he is as well able to bombast out a blank verse as the best of you: and being an absolute *Iohannes fac totum*, is in his own conceit the only shake-scene in a country'. The identity of Greene's target is indicated, not only by the epithet 'shake-scene', but also by 'his *Tiger's heart wrapped in a Player's hide*', which echoes a line—'O tiger's heart wrapped in a woman's hide' (1.4.138)—from

Shakespeare's *Henry VI Part Three*. This play, which was probably written for the 1590–1 theatrical season, was first published in 1595 in a version entitled *The True Tragedy of Richard Duke of York and the Good King Henry the Sixth*. Greene must have assumed the play would be well-known among his readers; otherwise the insulting barb could not have found its mark. And the play must have been successful: otherwise it would not have provoked Greene's animosity.

Additional, more favourable, notice of Shakespeare's early success as a writer of English histories appeared in another 1592 publication, Thomas Nashe's *Pierce Penniless his Supplication to the Devil*, which claimed that 'ten thousand spectators (at least)' had wept at the theatrical representation of John Talbot's death. Nashe was probably referring to the first part of *Henry VI*. Although some scholars believe that Nashe had a hand in writing this play, his account of its popularity seems to be accurate, because it is corroborated by the records of the theatre manager, Philip Henslowe, which indicate that the receipts for its initial run were greater than those from all but one of the many other plays Henslowe produced.

The uses of history

It is not surprising that the young Shakespeare turned to English history for his subject matter. The plays he wrote were commercial products, designed to draw the largest possible audiences to the playhouse, and his dramatizations of English history were designed to appeal to the same interests that had already attracted a wide readership for books on that subject. One of the first books printed by William Caxton after he established the first printing press in England was *The Chronicles of England* (1480), and by 1530, the book had been published thirteen times. John Stow's *Summary of English Chronicles*, published in 1565, had nineteen editions by 1618. William Warner's *Albion's England*, published in 1586, went through seven editions during the next twenty years. Fabyan's *Chronicles*, which traced English history from the time of the Roman conquest to the end of the Wars of the Roses in the fifteenth century, had seven editions in fifty years. Many other historical works enjoyed comparable popularity among a large and diverse readership.[1]

A number of reasons have been suggested for this widespread interest in English history. For one thing, the study of history was highly esteemed by humanist scholars. Sir Thomas Elyot, for instance, made it the centre of his educational programme: 'there is no study or science . . . of equal commodity and pleasure' for a noble man, he wrote. It includes 'all things that is necessary to be put in memory'.[2] The need for a specifically English history was also recognized by the Tudor monarchs, who used it to legitimate their rather dubious claim to the throne. The Tudors were a new dynasty whose founder, Henry VII, had acquired his crown, not by inheritance, but by defeating his predecessor, Richard III, in battle. Henry turned to various historical figures to authorize his monarchy. He claimed descent from the Trojan Brut, the legendary founder of Britain; he incorporated the red dragon of the ancient Welsh king Cadwallader in the royal arms; and he named his first son after the legendary British King Arthur. Henry VII also sponsored the work of the Italian historian, Polydore Vergil, whose *Anglica Historia* traced Henry's ancestry to Cadwallader and suggested that his ascent to the throne was divinely ordained. Edward Hall's 1548 chronicle went even further in constructing a story of ancient descent and providential purpose that reached its validating conclusion in the Tudor dynasty. Hall's chronicle was entitled *The Union of the Two Noble and Illustrious Families of Lancaster and York Being Long in Continual Dissension for the Crown of this Noble Realm, with all the Acts Done in Both the Times of the Princes, Both of the One Lineage and of the Other, Beginning at the Time of King Henry the Fourth, the First Author of this Division and so Successively Proceeding to the Reign of the High and Prudent Prince King Henry the Eighth, the Indubitable Flower and Very Heir of Both the Said Lineages*. In Hall's account, Henry IV's deposition of Richard II sowed the seeds for the Wars of the Roses, a prolonged dynastic struggle that was resolved only when the blood of Lancaster and York was finally united in the marriage of Henry VII to Elizabeth of York and in the person of their second son Henry VIII. (Henry VIII succeeded his father Henry VII as king, since his elder brother Arthur had died before their father).

But humanist scholarship and royal sponsorship alone could not account for the widespread interest in history in Tudor England. The writing of English history not only helped to legitimate Tudor sovereignty and to define an emergent nation-state; it also served to validate the status and identity of individual subjects. Having a history was equivalent to having a place in the status hierarchy. As Hall remarked in the prefatory letter to his chronicle, 'What diversity is between a noble prince and a poor beggar if after their death there be left of them no remembrance or token?' Moreover, the use of history to ratify personal claims to a place in an increasingly unstable social hierarchy was not confined to noble princes. The hereditary nobility could look for the names of their ancestors in the Tudor chronicles, but ambitious men born without hereditary titles (William Shakespeare's father among them) provided a thriving business for the College of Heralds, who were empowered to create coats of arms that authorized new money in genealogical fictions of privileged ancestry.

Nostalgia for a lost past

The historical past was also an object of sentimental veneration. Living in a time of rapid and often bewildering social, political, and economic change, Shakespeare's contemporaries looked to history, the study of change itself, to rationalize their changing world and to discover foundational narratives that could legitimate innovative cultural structures. As a result, England's medieval past was often idealized as a time of stable values and national glory. The nostalgic appeal of this imagined medieval world gave rise to a variety of cultural productions, ranging from the deliberate archaisms in the poetry of Edmund Spenser to the elaborate reconstructions of medieval tournaments staged each year in celebration of Queen Elizabeth's Accession Day. It also constituted one of the chief attractions of the English history play. According to Thomas Nashe, in plays based on 'our English Chronicles',

our forefathers' valiant acts (that have lain long buried in rusty brass and worm-eaten books) are revived, and they themselves raised from the Grave of Oblivion, and brought to plead their aged Honours in open presence, than which, what can be a sharper reproof to these degenerate, effeminate days of ours?[3]

In Shakespeare's history plays, this nostalgic longing for a better past is expressed in various ways, large and small. It even seems to inform the structural links that bind the plays together into a connected story. In the First Folio, the plays were printed in the order in which the kings for which they are named reigned, starting with *King John* and ending with *Henry VIII*. The eight intervening plays tell a connected historical story, beginning with the deposition and murder of Richard II, proceeding through the troubled reign of Henry IV to the triumphs of Henry V, the disastrous reign of his son Henry VI and the bloodbath of Richard III, and ending with the accession of the first Tudor monarch, Henry VII. However, this is not the order in which the plays were first produced.

The exact order of composition—and indeed the extent of Shakespeare's author-ship—of the three plays dealing with the reign of Henry VI has long been a subject of scholarly debate, and some editors consider that *Part One* was written last (an early version of *Part Two* was published in 1594 as *The First Part of the Contention of the Two Famous Houses of York and Lancaster*, and an early version of *Part Three* was published in 1595 as *The True Tragedy of Richard Duke of York and the Good King Henry the Sixth*).[4] There is no doubt, however, that the plays designated in the First Folio as the three parts of *Henry VI* are linked together in a sequence that ends with *Richard III*. *Henry VI Part One*, for instance, ends with the introduction of Margaret and the plan to marry her to Henry, *Part Two* with Clifford's promise to revenge himself upon the house of York, even including its children, and *Part Three* with Richard of Gloucester's resolution to obtain the crown. Moreover, there is no doubt that all four of those plays—*Henry VI Parts One, Two* and *Three*, and *Richard III*—were composed before the other history plays.

Because those four plays were composed earlier and because they can be read as a connected sequence, scholars often refer to them as the first tetralogy. The four plays that deal with the reigns of Richard II, Henry IV, and Henry V are known as the second tetralogy because they were composed later, but although they too can be read as a connected sequence, the historical events they depict actually preceded those depicted in the earlier plays. The sequence in which the plays were composed, then, replaces the order of history moving forward in time with the order of memory or nostalgia, moving backward to recapture a lost and better past.

Although the reasons for this order of composition are unknown, the final Chorus of *Henry V* defines it as a story of loss. Predicting Henry's premature death and the disastrous reign of his son, the Chorus ends by reminding the audience that the subsequent history has been already shown on their stage:

> Henry the Sixth, in infant bands crowned king
> Of France and England, did this king succeed,
> Whose state so many had the managing
> That they lost France and made his England bleed,
> Which oft our stage hath shown—and, for their sake,
> In your fair minds let this acceptance take.

The reference here to the Henry VI plays bends the linear progress of the history Shakespeare took from the Tudor Chronicles into a theatrical cycle, beginning and ending with Henry's death; for just as *Henry V* ends by predicting Henry's impending death, the first part of *Henry VI* begins with his funeral. The circle is joined at the point that represents the moment of loss—the death of the most heroic of Shakespeare's English kings. The opening Chorus of *Henry V* had already described the playhouse as a 'wooden O', inadequate to contain the magnitude of Henry's achievements. Like the image of the empty 'wooden O', the final Chorus of the play also marks an absence— the heroic past that the name of Henry V denotes.

The opening speech of the first part of *Henry VI*, like the final Chorus of *Henry V*, both announces Henry's death and reminds the audience that what they are watching is a theatrical representation:

> Hung be the heavens with black! Yield, day, to night!
> Comets, importing change of times and states,
> Brandish your crystal tresses in the sky,
> And with them scourge the bad revolting stars
> That have consented unto Henry's death—
> King Henry the Fifth, too famous to live long.
> England ne'er lost a king of so much worth.

In reading, Bedford's speech might seem hyperbolic, demanding as it does that the very heavens take part in the mourning for the lost king, but his reference to the heavens also had a very literal meaning in the playhouse since the actors in Shakespeare's time hung black draperies from the roof over the stage when a tragedy was to be performed, and the name for that roof was 'the heavens'.

The image of an empty circle also appears in the first part of *Henry VI*, with a significance very similar to that of the 'wooden O' in the opening chorus of *Henry V*. Near the beginning of that earlier play, Joan of Arc predicts,

> Glory is like a circle in the water,
> Which never ceaseth to enlarge itself

> Till, by broad spreading, it disperse to naught.
> With Henry's death, the English circle ends.
> Dispersèd are the glories it included.
>
> (1.3.112-16)

Here too the circle encloses an absence, and here too it is associated with Henry's death and the erasure of England's heroic past.

Shakespeare's early history plays

Just as Joan predicts, the three plays depicting the reign of Henry's son Henry VI portray the destruction of the father's legacy. Human exemplars of the heroic, chivalric, civic, patriotic, and ethical virtues associated with the reign of Henry V (such as John Talbot and the dead king's venerable brothers, Bedford and Gloucester) are clearly marked as representatives of an older, better world, and as they die, the virtues they exemplify seem to die along with them. The *Henry VI* plays have often been faulted by critics for their loose, episodic structure, variously explained as a result of authorial collaboration, as the product of the youthful playwright's inexperience, as imitative of the episodic quality of his chronicle sources, or as expressive of the disorderly state of the world they depict. There is, however, a persistent theme of degeneration in all three plays as the England they depict sinks increasingly into chaos and barbarity. Yorkists and Lancastrians compete with each other in treachery and atrocity, authority is effaced, power becomes an end in itself, and the crown becomes a prize of war, tossed from one head to another at the whim of brute force and blind fortune.

Thomas Nashe had celebrated the history play as offering a 'reproof to these degenerate, effeminate days of ours' by reviving on stage the martial valour of England's medieval 'forefathers', but the *Henry VI* plays depict the reign of 'an effeminate prince' (*Henry VI Part One*, 1.1 35), where the best warriors are often women. Talbot is unable to defeat Joan in single combat (*Henry VI Part One*, 1.7), and Queen Margaret is always a better soldier than her husband. The idealized medieval England that was an object of sentimental veneration in Shakespeare's time is notably absent in these plays, but the disordered realm they depict is framed by two emblems of royal perfection, English triumph, peace, and prosperity—Henry V at the beginning and Henry VII at the end. Although we see his funeral at the beginning of *Henry VI Part One*, Henry V never appears on stage in any of these early plays, and Henry VII appears only at the end of *Richard III* and only as Henry Tudor, Earl of Richmond, not as the ideal king he will become. Both, therefore, serve to mark the absence of the idealized England that is always already lost in all these early plays.

Shakespeare's later history plays

In the second tetralogy, Shakespeare moves back in time to trace the succession of kings from Richard II to Henry V, but even here the idealized England of nostalgic longing continues to elude dramatic representation. *Richard II*, the opening play in that sequence, depicts the deposition and murder of the last of the medieval kings who could trace their succession back to William the Conqueror. A secular analogue to the Biblical Fall, Richard's deposition is staged as the end of the idealized feudal world that constituted the object of sixteenth-century nostalgia. The opening scene, set in Richard's court, is replete with ceremonial gestures and elaborately rhymed speeches that give it the air of a medieval tableau. Even the play's opening line—'Old John of Gaunt, time-honoured Lancaster'—exploits this nostalgia, reminding the audience that they are about to enter the world of Chaucer's patron, John of Gaunt (1340–99), who was indeed 'time-honoured' by the time the play was produced. And before the first act ended, the audience was treated to all the formal preliminaries to a medieval trial by combat, complete with trumpets, two heralds, a Marshal, and armed combatants. The spectacle must have had enormous appeal for Shakespeare's original audiences, many of whom would have also flocked to see Queen Elizabeth's Accession Day tilts, which were open to the general public. In *Richard II*, the nostalgic appeal of the spectacle would have been reinforced by the fact that it was a trial by combat, a ritual that evoked an imagined medieval world where divine providence legitimated earthly justice.

Shakespeare loads enormous emphasis on the trial by combat, deferring it and emphasizing its importance in the represented action. The opening scene depicts Richard's attempt to resolve the quarrel between Bolingbroke and Mowbray about who was responsible for the murder of Richard's uncle, the Duke of Gloucester. Richard is eager to lay the dispute to rest, since the responsibility was ultimately his, but he cannot persuade the disputants to give it up, so the scene ends with his order that they meet in a formal trial by combat where divine justice will determine who is telling the truth. Next comes an invented scene between John of Gaunt and the Duchess of Gloucester, aged holdovers from an earlier world where power and legitimacy were united. The Duchess pleads with Gaunt to avenge her husband's murder, but Gaunt argues that there is no way a good subject can avenge the crime without opposing the will of God, since Richard, the culprit, is God's anointed king. Faced with this irresolvable dilemma, Gaunt and the Duchess finally agree to await the trial by combat. 'God's is the quarrel', Gaunt argues (1.2.37), and only God can resolve it.

The trial itself, however, never takes place. Richard himself aborts the proceedings, cheating the playgoers of the spectacle they have been led to anticipate from the end of the opening scene, when it was first announced. Here, as in much of the play, Richard is depicted as the destroyer of the idealized medieval England he inherited, and the object of nostalgic desire is pushed even further back into the past, into the time of

Richard's glorious predecessors, who are recalled to mark the extent of Richard's shortcomings.

The most powerful and explicit expression of that nostalgic ideal comes in the famous set speech delivered by John of Gaunt just before he dies in the opening scene of Act Two, which invokes the glory of this lost England to mark the present degradation he attributes to the misrule of the youthful King Richard. Gaunt calls his idealized England 'This other Eden', associating it with the archetypal focus of nostalgia, the perfect original home that is always already lost. However, he describes it not as a garden but as a 'fortress', the sea that surrounds it as 'a moat defensive to a house'—in short, as an idealized medieval landscape. Equally idealized, its rulers are described as medieval crusader-kings,

> Renownèd for their deeds as far from home
> For Christian service and true chivalry
> As is the sepulchre, in stubborn Jewry
> Of the world's ransom, blessèd Mary's son
> (2.1.53-6)

After Gaunt dies, his aged brother, the Duke of York, now the last surviving son of Edward III, explicitly details the contrast between Richard and his royal progenitors, whom he glorifies as heroic warriors abroad and ideal rulers at home:

> In war was never lion raged more fierce,
> In peace was never gentle lamb more mild. . . .
> . . . when he frowned it was against the French,
> And not against his friends. His noble hand
> Did win what he did spend, and spent not that
> Which his triumphant father's hand had won.
> His hands were guilty of no kindred blood,
> But bloody with the enemies of his kin
> (2.1.174-84)

Replicating and reduplicating the nostalgia that drew the audience to the playhouse, the historical figures represented on stage repeatedly look back to an even more distant past as a lost time when things were better. Living kings can never live up to the ideals represented by their dead predecessors. Even Richard II, although he never manages to emulate his heroic forefathers' example, imagines at the end of the play, after he has been deposed and shortly before he is murdered, that he too will be transmuted by death into a focus for nostalgic recollection. 'Think I am dead', he tells his queen:

> In winter's tedious nights, sit by the fire
> With good old folks, and let them tell thee tales
> Of woeful ages long ago betid;
> And ere thou bid goodnight, to quit their griefs
> Tell thou the lamentable fall of me,
> And send the hearers weeping to their beds
> (5.1.40-5)

Despite the evidence throughout the play of Richard's inadequacies as a ruler, his death will transform his deposition and murder into a melancholy tale of a lost and lamented past.

Here, as in all of Shakespeare's history plays, the focus for nostalgia is the reign of a dead monarchical figure. Those kings, like the Edenic England they ruled, are always already lost in Shakespeare's history plays. In *King John*, Richard the Lionheart never appears on stage, but his death and divided legacy initiate the contention between his son John and his grandson Arthur for a throne which no longer has a clear and undisputed occupant. In *Richard II*, both Richard's grandfather, Edward III, and his heroic father, Edward the Black Prince, are dead before the action begins, but both are invoked as ideal figures from the past to mark the nature and extent of present degradation. In *Henry VIII*, the only one of the history plays written during the reign of James I, the absent object of nostalgic desire is Queen Elizabeth. Represented as Henry's most important achievement ('Never before / This happy child did I get anything' (5.4.64–5)), Elizabeth appears in the play only in the final scene and only as a newborn infant. Cranmer's prophecy depicts her reign as an ideal time, but it also extends beyond her death, reminding Shakespeare's Jacobean audience that she was as inaccessible to them as she had been to the Henrician characters represented on stage ('few now living can behold that goodness' (5.4.21)). The reign of Henry VII occupies a similar position in Richmond's speech at the end of *Richard III*—the object of the characters' hopes for the future but also of the audience's nostalgia for a halcyon time that lies just beyond the bounds of dramatic representation.

The most persistent focus for nostalgic idealization in Shakespeare's history plays is the figure of Henry V. His image hovers just beyond the frame of both tetralogies. Henry is the lost heroic presence that the entire historical project seems designed to recover. The *Henry VI* plays depict the losing struggle to preserve his legacies of French conquest and national unity. The figure of Henry V hovers behind the entire second tetralogy as well. Always elusive, he is first mentioned in *Richard II* when his newly crowned father demands, 'Can no man tell of my unthrifty son? / 'Tis full three months since I did see him last' (5.3.1–2), but the audience does not see him either until the *Henry IV* plays, and even there he plays a series of roles designed, as he tells the audience from the beginning, to conceal his true nature.

'I know you all', he says in a soliloquy early in *Henry IV Part One*, 'and will a while uphold / The unyoked humour of your idleness' (1.2.173–4). Within the represented action, the 'you' refers to the disreputable crew of lowlife characters with whom the prince consorts in the Eastcheap tavern; but it also refers to the playgoers themselves, the idle crowd who have come to the playhouse to be entertained. Prominent among those entertainments, as advertised on the title page of the play's first published edition, were 'the humorous conceits of Sir John Falstaff'. The Prince we see in the first part of *Henry IV* spends more time with Falstaff than with his father, adopting a variety of disreputable but entertaining disguises, including those of a robber and a serving-man in a tavern. He plays a prominent part in the fictional comic subplot peopled by a cast of anachronistically modern characters, which repeatedly interrupts and parodies the historical action. While Hotspur and the other historical rebels are plotting to rob the crown from Henry IV on the grounds that he has himself robbed it from Richard II, the Prince and Poins plot to rob Falstaff and his companions of the spoils from their robbery of the travellers. Before the King meets with the Prince in *Part One* to chastise him about his dissolute behaviour, Falstaff and the Prince rehearse that interview in the tavern, acting, as the Hostess says, 'as like one of these harlotry players as ever I see!' (2.5.361–2). At the end of the mock interview, the Prince promises that he will 'Banish plump Jack, and banish all the world' (2.5.438), but he does not keep his promise until the final scene in *Part Two*.

The character in the *Henry IV* plays who most closely approximates the nostalgic ideal of chivalric honour is not Prince Hal but Hotspur, and both the Prince and the playwright subject that ideal to considerable irony. Literalized and parodied in his obsession with horses, Hotspur's single-minded devotion to chivalric (*cheval*ric) honour makes him an ambivalent figure—the nostalgic ideal of honour, but, since that ideal is outmoded in the modern world invoked in the tavern scenes, the object of sophisticated ridicule as well. The Prince mocks Hotspur as a provincial lout (2.5.94–101), and Hotspur himself is depicted as a kind of glorious but funny adolescent, more devoted to his horse than his wife and unable to control either his anger or his tongue (1.3.92–284). At the end of *Part One* Hal appears to appropriate Hotspur's chivalric honour, paying tribute to his rival's honours, killing him in single combat, and then completing Hotspur's dying speech to speak in his 'behalf' (5.4). Here, as in his opening soliloquy, the Prince recalls the heroic figure denoted by the name of Henry V, but in *Part Two*, the first time we see him, he is again consorting with his low companions, acknowledging that 'these humble considerations make me out of love with my greatness' (2.2.11–12). His apotheosis is again deferred until the end of the play, where he announces that he has 'turned away my former self' along with his lowlife companions in dissolute pleasure (5.5.56–7).

Just as the first tetralogy looks back to Henry V as an emblem of lost glory that shows up the inadequacy of his son's failed reign, the second looks forward to his glorious accession, the anticipated reward that will compensate for his father's crimes and justify his own riotous behaviour as Prince Hal. But when Shakespeare finally turns in the last play in the second tetralogy to the glorious reign of this once and future king, all that longingly remembered and eagerly anticipated glory evaporates in ambiguity, as the heroic words of the Chorus are repeatedly contradicted by the events enacted on stage and challenged by the irreverent voices of vulgar theatrical clowns. Even in the play that bears his name, Henry V is never fully present. The progress of the two tetralogies is a progress back in time to a dead hero and a lost heroic age that evaporate in ambiguity as soon as they are reached.

FURTHER READING

Calderwood, James L. *Metadrama in Shakespeare's Henriad: 'Richard II' to 'Henry V'* (Berkeley: University of California Press, 1979). With perceptive close readings of the plays in the second tetralogy, this book argues that they depict a progressive secularization of language and a developing conception of the playwright's art.

Howard, Jean E. and Phyllis Rackin. *Engendering a Nation: A Feminist Account of Shakespeare's English Histories* (London: Routledge, 1997). This book examines the changing conceptions of gendered identity in the nine history plays Shakespeare wrote during the reign of Queen Elizabeth. Topics emphasized include the relevance of these plays to Elizabethan and modern controversies about gender.

Leggatt, Alexander. *Shakespeare's Political Drama: The History Plays and the Roman Plays* (London and New York: Routledge, 1988). Written in clear, accessible language, this book contains perceptive close readings of all the English history plays except for *King John*.

Levine, Nina S. *Women's Matters: Politics, Gender, and Nation in Shakespeare's Early History Plays* (Newark: University of Delaware Press and London: Associated University Presses, 1998). This book offers clear, insightful feminist analysis of the plays in the first tetralogy and *King John*.

Levy, F. J. *Tudor Historical Thought* (San Marino, Calif.: The Huntington Library, 1967). Written by a historian, this book provides a detailed account of the development of historiography in Shakespeare's England.

Ornstein, Robert. *A Kingdom for a Stage: The Achievement of Shakespeare's History Plays* (Cambridge: Harvard University Press, 1972). Ornstein offers close readings of all of Shakespeare's history plays, arguing from a liberal humanist perspective that they transcend their own historical moment to express universal human themes.

Rackin, Phyllis. *Stages of History: Shakespeare's English Chronicles* (Ithaca: Cornell University Press and London: Routledge, 1990). This book sets Shakespeare's English history plays in the historical and theatrical context in which they were originally produced. Topics emphasized include Renaissance conceptions of history, the plays' use of anachronisms, and their representations of female characters and of common men.

Ribner, Irving. *The English History Play in the Age of Shakespeare* (Princeton: Princeton University Press, 1957). A useful introduction to history plays written by Shakespeare's contemporaries, this book includes a chronological list of the English history plays written betwen 1519 and 1563.

Saccio, Peter. *Shakespeare's English Kings: History, Chronicle, and Drama* (London and New York: Oxford University Press, 1977). With chapters on each of the kings depicted in Shakespeare's English history plays, this book summarizes their stories as understood by modern historians, and the ways they differ both from the versions Shakespeare found in his own historical sources and those he depicted in his plays.

Tillyard, E. M. W. *Shakespeare's History Plays* (New York: Collier Books, 1962, first published 1944). A pioneering study of Shakespeare's English history plays, this book was highly influential among conservative mid-century critics but later widely attacked for its monolithic conception of Shakespeare's history plays as governed by what Tillyard believed was a universally accepted political theology, which regarded medieval English history as governed by God's providence, culminating in the divinely ordained advent of the Tudor dynasty.

NOTES

1. Levy, F. J. *Tudor Historical Thought* (San Marino, Ca.: The Huntington Library, 1967), Chap. 6, 'The Popularization of History', pp. 202–36. See also David Scott Kastan, 'Shakespeare and English History', in *The Cambridge Companion to Shakespeare*, ed. Margreta de Grazia and Stanley Wells (Cambridge: Cambridge University Press, 2001), pp. 167–82.
2. *The Boke Named the Governour*, edited from the edition of 1531 by Henry H. S. Croft (London: Kegan, Paul, Trench, 1883), 1:91; 2:387–400.
3. *Pierce Penilesse his Supplication to the Divell* (1592), in E. K. Chambers, *The Elizabethan Stage* (Oxford: Clarendon Press, 1951), IV: p. 238.
4. See Stanley Wells and Gary Taylor. *William Shakespeare: A Textual Companion* (Oxford: Clarendon Press, 1987), pp. 111–13.

READING: *Henry V*

Critical responses to *Henry V* have been sharply divided. At one extreme, the play has been viewed as a kind of epic drama designed to celebrate Henry as the 'mirror of all Christian kings'. More recently, it has been read as an ironic deconstruction of the patriotic mythmaking that surrounds him. Both views can be supported by evidence from the playtext, for it offers not only opposed interpretations but also opposed accounts of the action, one in the discourse of the Chorus and the other in the dramatic representation staged for the audience. The two accounts not only differ from each other but also insist upon each other's inadequacies. Moreover, instead of reconciling the opposed accounts or discarding one for the other, Shakespeare lets both of them stand. In this last of his Elizabethan history plays, he seems to suggest that the entire project of bringing the past back to life on stage is finally impossible. He offers a poignant image for its inaccessibility when the Archbishop of Canterbury promises the king early in Act I that his conquest of France, like the heroic deeds of his predecessors, will make his 'chronicle as rich with praise / As is the ooze and bottom of the sea / With sunken wrack and sumless treasuries' (1.2.163–5).

The player who speaks the opening Chorus of *Henry V* begs the playgoers to use their imaginations, since it will be impossible to represent the magnificence of Henry's story on stage. He wishes for 'a muse of fire . . . / A kingdom for a stage, princes to act, / And monarchs to behold the swelling scene'. Instead, he has an 'unworthy scaffold', a 'cock-pit' that cannot possibly 'hold / The vasty fields of France'. Accordingly, he asks the audience to 'Piece out our imperfections with your thoughts'—to use their own imaginations to make up for the deficiencies of the spectacle they are about to see. Many readers, and scholarly critics, have taken the Chorus at his word, assuming it is designed to help the audience to imagine all that the players cannot present, but a minute's reflection will call this assumption into question. At the time this play was written, the Chorus was already an old-fashioned device. Far from activating the dramatic illusion, it can only disrupt it, foregrounding the present theatrical occasion and reminding the audience that what they are about to see performed on 'this unworthy scaffold' is totally inadequate to present the historical events and persons. Even the representation of Henry's greatest triumph, his victory at Agincourt, is disparaged by the Chorus at the beginning of Act Four:

> And so our scene must to the battle fly,
> Where O for pity, we shall much disgrace,
> With four or five most vile and ragged foils,
> Right ill disposed, in brawl ridiculous,
> The name of Agincourt. Yet sit and see,
> Minding true things by what their mock'ries be.
> (4.0.48-53)

The running conflict between the words of the Chorus and the actions represented on stage raises a disquieting question about the reliability of historical knowledge. The Chorus summarizes the received version of Henry's history and emphasizes that theatrical representation is inadequate to reproduce the past accurately, but just as the Choruses seem determined to discredit the represented action, the represented action often seems designed to subvert the heroic words of the Choruses. At the beginning of each act, the Chorus advertises the historical business to come, but never acknowledges the existence of the comic scenes that increasingly intrude to interrupt and retard the progress of the historical plot and parody the heroic action (two in Act Two, three in Act Three, and so on).

Many of these fictional comic scenes feature lowborn characters who had no precedents in Shakespeare's historical sources, suggesting, perhaps, that the official history is radically incomplete. At the beginning of Act Two, for instance, the Chorus promises to take us first to Southampton and then to France

> The King is set from London, and the scene
> Is now transported, gentles, to Southampton.
> There is the playhouse now, there must you sit.
> (2.0.34-6)

In the scene that follows, however, we are taken not to Southampton but to London, where the ragtag crew from Eastcheap who were Prince Hal's companions in the *Henry IV* plays are occupied with a quarrel between Pistol and Nim resulting from Pistol's marriage to Hostess Quickly, and where we hear of Falstaff's illness, his heart broken by his separation from the King. The promised scene at Southampton follows, depicting the exposure of the three traitors and ending with Henry's rousing couplet, delivered in the triumphant idiom of the Chorus:

> Cheerly to sea, the signs of war advance:
> No king of England, if not king of France.
> (2.2.188-9)

But we don't go to France, at least not yet. Another London scene intrudes, where we hear the Hostess mangle the king's English in a poignant account of Falstaff's death and Pistol's antiheroic echo to the glorious patriotic rhetoric of King and Chorus. The Chorus celebrates Henry's expedition to France as a glorious quest for honour. 'Now all the youth of England are on fire', he proclaimed at the beginning of Act Two, 'and honour's thought / Reigns solely in the breast of every man' (2.0.1–4). Pistol directly contradicts this heroic claim when he declares,

> Let us to France, like horseleeches, my boys,
> To suck, to suck, the very blood to suck!
> (2.3.46-7)

Henry stakes his claim to a place in history on the success of his French conquest, but here too Pistol implicitly undermines his project. In addition to calling Henry's glorious conquest of France into question, Pistol also reminds the audience that claims to battlefield triumphs can be misleading. Before the Battle of Agincourt, Henry promises his soldiers that they will be remembered for their heroism 'from this day to the ending of the world'. He envisions the soldiers feasting their neighbours, showing their scars, and boasting, 'These wounds I had on Crispin's day' (4.3.41–59). At the end of the play, however, Pistol resolves to turn the scars he got from his ignominious beating by Fluellen to good advantage: he will take up the trades of bawd and cutpurse, he says,

> And patches will I get unto these cudgelled scars,
> And swear I got them in the Gallia wars.
>   (5.1.79-80)

Before he embarked, Pistol had seen the French expedition as an opportunity to steal. In retrospect, he sees it as another opportunity for dishonest profit when he tells heroic lies about his experience there. Just as his initial resolve discredited the Chorus's proud claims about Henry's French expedition, his final resolution to lie about his own history in France suggests that the glorious history that Henry envisions may be equally unreliable.

In the first tetralogy, the heroic Henry V and the England he ruled were recalled with nostalgic longing as the world of his son sank into chaos. Never seen on stage, Henry was projected in unproblematic terms as a perfect image of lost perfection. In the second tetralogy, however, Shakespeare complicates that image by showing the process of its creation. From his first appearance on stage, in *Henry IV Part One*, Henry is characterized as a kind of playwright or actor, engaged in the process of creating his royal image. In his first soliloquy, he announces that he will 'imitate the sun' (1.2.175). Prince Hal can only promise to 'imitate' that cosmic image of royalty, like a player planning to perform the role of king on a stage. At the end of *Henry IV Part Two*, he is ready to play the role. Crowned as King Henry V, he immediately banishes Jack Falstaff. 'I know thee not, old man', he says to Falstaff at the beginning of the banishment speech (5.5.45), and the royal king who appears in *Henry V* never acknowledges the existence of the disreputable characters who were his constant companions in both parts of *Henry IV*. His former companions still speak of him, but he never mentions their names. When Fluellen reports (3.6.92–7) that one of the Duke of Exeter's men 'is like to be executed for robbing a church, one Bardolph, if your majesty know the man. His face is all bubuncles and whelks and knobs and flames o' fire', the King does not admit that he knows the man. He replies, 'We would have all such offenders so cut off', ignoring the vivid corporeality of Fluellen's description and his own previous association with Bardolph, disposing of the whole messy issue (and of Bardolph's life) by consigning him to the abstract category of 'such offenders'.

Like the Chorus, Henry seems oblivious to everything in the represented action that threatens to complicate the celebratory account of his reign. He seems, in fact, to be engaged throughout in a strenuous act of repression. 'We are no tyrant', he declares in a tellingly ambiguous simile, 'but a Christian king, / Unto whose grace our passion is as subject / As is our wretches fettered in our prisons' (1.2.241–3).

A similar repression characterizes Henry's attempts to deal with the question of the morality of his French invasion. Much of Act Two, Scene One, is devoted to a series of long speeches in which the Archbishop of Canterbury gives the desired response to Henry's request to tell him whether his claim to France is justified. Canterbury provides a long, involuted rationalization for the French conquest, which would be difficult or impossible to follow in the playhouse, interjecting at one point in a line that would surely draw a laugh that his argument is 'as clear as is the summer's sun' (1.2.86). When he finally finishes, Henry asks again, 'May I with right and conscience make this claim?' and Canterbury replies, 'The sin upon my head, dread sovereign' (1.2.96–7). The issue at stake is no laughing matter. Henry has already warned the Archbishop to 'take heed' of what he 'shall incite us to' because guiltless blood will undoubtedly be shed in the ensuing war (1.2.22–8). Now 'well resolved' to invade France and either 'bend it to our awe, / Or break it all to pieces', Henry orders that the waiting messengers from the French Dauphin be called in (1.2.221–5). The messenger brings the insulting gift of tennis balls, which provides the king with a second opportunity to lay off the guilt for the ensuing war: 'tell the pleasant Prince', he says, 'this mock of his / Hath turned his balls to gunstones, and his soul / Shall stand sore chargèd for the wasteful vengeance / That shall fly from them—for many a thousand widows / Shall this his mock mock out of their dear husbands, / Mock mothers from their sons' (1.2.281–6).

The only place in the play where Henry confronts a direct challenge to the heroic story told by the Chorus is on the night before the Battle of Agincourt, when he disguises himself as a common soldier for whom he invents the name Harry le roi. The name he chooses looks backward to the youthful 'Harry' who mingled with the lowlife characters in Eastcheap in the Henry IV plays, but it also looks forward to the historical title that he hopes to win in France: in the represented action, it conceals the King's true identity from the common soldiers he meets, but it also reminds the audience of his double nature as historical king and theatrical entertainer. The scene is a kind of play-within-the play that the player king 'Harry le roi', as a kind of surrogate for the playwright himself, invents for the night before the battle that will constitute the historical climax of the play. In it, both the King and the audience hear an eloquent challenge to the official version of events and a powerful case against war itself. The character who makes the case is an invented theatrical creation, a common soldier for whom William Shakespeare invented the name of Williams.

Williams is not at all certain that the King has a good cause for his French war; and, he points out,

if the cause be not good, the King himself hath a heavy reckoning to make, when all those legs and arms and heads chopped off in a battle shall join together at the latter day, and cry all, 'We died at such a place'—some swearing, some crying for a surgeon, some upon their wives left poor behind them, some upon the debts they owe, some upon their children rawly left.

(4.1.128-34)

Williams charges that the dismembered bodies of the forgotten casualties of Henry's great historical enterprise will be re-membered at the last judgement to recall the nameless soldiers lost in battle and the wives and children left poor by their sacrifice. The king, however, avoids Williams's challenge. After the battle, he arranges for Fluellen to take his place in the unresolved quarrel between Harry le roi and Williams, then enters in his own person to resolve the quarrel by presenting Williams with a gift of money.

The encounter with Williams is the only place in *Henry V* where the king is confronted with a challenge to the official version of events, but the audience is reminded repeatedly of that version's inadequacy. In what is probably the most famous speech in the play, Henry promises his soldiers before the Battle of Agincourt that

> . . . Crispin Crispian shall ne'er go by
> From this day to the ending of the world
> But we in it shall be rememberèd,
> We few, we happy few, we band of brothers.
> For he today that sheds his blood with me
> Shall be my brother; be he ne'er so vile,
> This day shall gentle his condition.
>
> (4.3.57-63)

Henry's promise to his soldiers denies social distinctions to identify England as a place where all men are brothers, united in their willingness to die for the national ideal. He identifies the decisive Battle of Agincourt as a communal enterprise, the triumph of a ragged band of Englishmen over a well-equipped French enemy obsessed with the accoutrements that mark their place in a hierarchical culture. After the battle, however, when Henry reads the list of the dead, he gives the full names and titles of the gentlemen who were killed, but when he comes to the common soldiers, all he can offer is a body count:

> Edward the Duke of York, the Earl of Suffolk,
> Sir Richard Keighley, Davy Gam Esquire;
> None else of name, and of all other men
> But five-and-twenty.
>
> (4.8.97-100)

The opening Chorus to Act Four anticipates Henry's idealized exhortation to his soldiers, telling how the king would visit 'all his host' and call 'them brothers, friends, and country-men', so 'every wretch, pining and pale before,/ Beholding him, plucks comfort from his looks' (4.0.32–42). It does not anticipate, or ever acknowledge, the encounter with Williams or the fate of the twenty-five English soldiers who died.

Henry's efforts to construct himself as 'the mirror of all Christian kings' (2.0.6) celebrated by the Chorus and recalled in the earlier plays as a paragon of English royalty are too apparent to be fully successful. Henry attempts to define the Battle of Agincourt as a kind of trial by combat that will prove the legitimacy of his claim to the British throne. 'No king of England, if not king of France', he declares (2.2.189) as he sets out for France. After the battle, he refuses to accept credit for the victory, insisting that it is God's alone. He threatens his soldiers, 'be it death proclaimèd through our host / To boast of this, or take that praise from God / Which is his only' (4. 8.108–10). The severity of the threatened punishment undermines the claim to heavenly warrant that the king attempts to enforce by the exercise and mystification of earthly force. Even more ruthless is his order during the battle for his soldiers to kill their prisoners. He first gives the order at the end of Act Four, Scene Six, motivated, he says, by the fact that 'the French have reinforced their scattered men'

(4.6.36); but he gives it a second time in the following scene, justified this time as a response to the news that the French have killed the boys who were guarding the English luggage. The intervening dialogue, an exchange between the fictional soldiers Gower and Fluellen, points up the ironic discrepancy between the heroic image of Henry and his action here. The king, Gower declares, learning about the slaughter of the boys and the theft of the luggage, 'most worthily hath caused every soldier to cut his prisoner's throat. O 'tis a gallant king' (4.7.7–8). Calling the order 'gallant' invokes exactly the standard that condemns it. Fluellen replies with his own celebration of Henry, comparing him to Alexander the Great. However, Fluellen's Welsh accent, which pronounces 'B' as 'P', renames the ancient hero 'Alexander the Pig' (4.7.10).

The many unresolved contradictions of *Henry V* seem to mark the dead end of the project of nostalgic recuperation. The action the players perform contradicts the story the Chorus tells. The king's actions contradict his celebratory image as the perfect embodiment of English royal authority. The Chorus urges the playgoers to suppose that the historical persons and events the play represents are actually present, but constantly reminds them that what they are watching is a theatrical representation that threatens to disgrace the historical reality it attempts to imitate. At the end of the play, the final Chorus echoes these contradictions even as it attempts to deny them. The final Chorus is a sonnet, and it uses the conventional sonnet rhetoric of verbal antithesis and paradox to paper over the contradictions it cannot resolve. It reiterates the nostalgic image of Henry V as an image of lost perfection, 'this star of England', even as it insists yet again that the dramatic action was inadequate to show him.

> Thus far with rough and all-unable pen
>   Our bending author hath pursued the story,
> In little room confining mighty men,
>   Mangling by starts the full course of their glory.
> Small time, but in that small most greatly lived
>   This star of England. Fortune made his sword,
> By which the world's best garden he achieved,
>   And of it left his son imperial lord.
> Henry the Sixth, in infant bands crowned king
>   Of France and England, did this king succeed,
> Whose state so many had the managing
>   That they lost France and made his England bleed,
> Which oft our stage hath shown—and, for their sake,
> In your fair minds let this acceptance take.

Perhaps most revealing of all is the final appeal for the audience's acceptance of the play, which conflates the disastrous future reign of Henry VI with the successful plays that had already shown it. The unresolved contradictions of *Henry V* implicate Shakespeare's entire historiographic project. Beginning with a desire to recover a glorious historical past, it ends by calling attention to the impossibility of representing that past and the play's compromised status as a commercial, theatrical entertainment.

FURTHER READING

Berman, Ronald (ed.). *Twentieth Century Interpretations of 'Henry V'* (Englewood Cliffs, New Jersey, Prentice Hall, 1968). This anthology offers a useful collection of selections from the older criticism of the play.

Dollimore, Jonathan, and Alan Sinfield. 'History and ideology: the instance of *Henry V*'. In *Alternative Shakespeares*, ed. John Drakakis (London and New York: Methuen, 1985), pp. 206–27. Dollimore and Sinfield analyse the ideological functions served by Shakespeare's play both in its own time and in ours, focusing on the contradictions that challenge the related ideals of imperial conquest and national unity.

Goddard, Harold C. *The Meaning of Shakespeare* (Chicago: University of Chicago Press, 1951), Vol. I, pp. 215–68. Goddard argues that Shakespeare deliberately contrived the actions the play depicts to contradict the celebratory words of the Chorus.

Howard, Jean E. and Phyllis Rackin. *Engendering a Nation: A Feminist Account of Shakespeare's English Histories* (London: Routledge, 1997), pp. 3–10, 186–227. Howard and Rackin focus on the roles of the female characters in the play, especially Katherine of France, to argue that Henry V has served as a prototype for the modern ideal of masculinity proved in heterosexual conquest.

Ornstein, Robert. *A Kingdom for a Stage: The Achievement of Shakespeare's History Plays* (Cambridge: Harvard University Press, 1972), pp. 175–202. Ornstein offers a sympathetic close reading of the play and its hero, with special emphasis on Henry's actions and character and the morality of war.

Rabkin, Norman. 'Rabbits, Ducks, and *Henry V*', *Shakespeare Quarterly*, 28 (1977), 179–96. This important and influential essay documents and analyses the ambivalences that have long divided critical accounts of *Henry V*.

Rackin, Phyllis. *Stages of History: Shakespeare's English Chronicles* (Ithaca: Cornell University Press and London: Routledge, 1990), pp. 225–47. Rackin argues that the play uses invented fictional characters and incidents of forgetting to mark the absence of common people from official history.

Saccio, Peter. *Shakespeare's English Kings: History, Chronicle, and Drama* (London and New York: Oxford University Press, 1977), pp. 64–89. Saccio summarizes the story of Henry V as it is understood by modern historians and notes some of the ways it differs both from the versions current in Shakespeare's time and the version depicted in his play.

18 | Tragedies

Linda Woodbridge

That strange genre, Shakespearian tragedy, challenges our belief that we read literature or watch plays out of enjoyment. Why would we enjoy watching suffering and death? Even those who see literature as educational usually offer some version of the sugar-coated pill metaphor—a coating of pleasure will induce us to swallow good lessons that are sometimes bitter medicine. But where is the sugar coating in this bleak and bloody genre?

Is the blood itself the sugar? Does the appeal of Shakespearian tragedy lie in its very sensationalism? Or does Shakespearian tragedy offer not exactly pleasure but a deep satisfaction, in that it tells the plain truth about death and human misery? Unlike genres which gloss over death and misery with false and saccharine happy endings, do Shakespearian tragedies pay us the compliment of assuming we are tough enough to bear reality? Another question: is the misery of tragedy offset by some good that it does? Is tragic suffering redemptive, and thus ultimately a pleasing rather than horrific spectacle? And if so, is this good? By regarding suffering as redemptive, do we evade constructive action in this world by tolerating suffering and those who cause it? Or *can* suffering lead to improvement of man's lot? After all, King Lear learns greater compassion through his suffering, and develops a sense of social justice, and even though he dies without having a chance to put these qualities to use, we as audience are able to learn what he learned without having to suffer as he suffered. Is it this kind of growth that makes Shakespearian tragedy tolerable? And if so, what happens if the tragic hero doesn't grow, as many don't?

So many questions—tragedy provokes questions, and takes on big issues. Among the biggest is one that philosophers since ancient times have grappled with, the 'problem of evil': if a benevolent and powerful force rules the universe, how do we account for the existence of evil and suffering? Milton tackled that problem in *Paradise Lost*, trying to 'justify the ways of God to man'. Tragedy is one of many human efforts to explore the problem of evil. And it is typical of tragedy to explore questions rather than to propound answers: if sermons explain evil in the declarative mood and legal statutes prohibit evil in the imperative mood, tragedy is an interrogative genre, full of questions. One question it nearly always asks is 'why?' Tragedy's central question is the one that often springs to people's lips when any terrible event occurs: why did this have to happen?

Causes of disaster

When we try to answer tragedy's 'why', we often think in terms of the 'tragic flaw'—something in the tragic hero's character accounts for the terrible things that happen to him. Beloved of English instructors to this day, the notion of the tragic flaw goes back to the inventors of tragedy, the ancient Greeks, who spoke of it in terms of *hamartia*, a mistake in judgement leading to calamity, and of *hubris*, some outstanding quality or conspicuous behaviour that brings one to the attention of the jealous gods, who are thereby provoked to inflict disaster. In the Renaissance, the idea of *hubris* got entangled with notions of guilty pride, giving the tragic flaw a moral tinge it hadn't had in ancient Greek times.

Overemphasis on the tragic flaw can narrow our vision of a Shakespearian tragedy. For one thing, it blames the victim for his or her misery, and so undercuts our sympathy, marring the pity that Aristotle thought was one of tragedy's two major emotional effects (the other was terror). And overemphasizing the tragic flaw also neglects the complexity of evil in these plays. Tragic disaster is brought on not only by flawed heroes like Titus Andronicus, Othello, Hamlet, and Lear, but also by villains like Aaron in *Titus Andronicus*, Iago in *Othello*, Claudius in *Hamlet*, or Goneril, Regan, and Edmund in *King Lear*. Especially in Shakespeare's early and middle tragedies, deliberate villainy and human malice often work against the protagonist. Sometimes rather than being particularized in one villain, human malice is distributed among members of a group, such as the feuding factions in *Romeo and Juliet*.

Another cause of disaster in tragedies is what we might loosely call Fate—the gods, the stars, the Goddess Fortune, chance, accident—all forces beyond the protagonist's control. In fact, the original meaning of 'dis-aster' was 'under the malign influence of the stars'—the first-mentioned cause of the undoing of Romeo and Juliet, those 'star-crossed lovers'. Today we have different notions of deterministic forces outside a person's control—the class system, global capitalism, oppressive governments, even a capricious stock market that can make or break an individual—but we can still appreciate the sense of helplessness and lack of personal control over events that the Renaissance called Fate. Chance and accident, too, are pervasive in tragedy, and often seem to play into the hands either of human villains or an evil destiny, as when a messenger detained in a plague quarantine can't deliver his crucial message telling Romeo that Juliet isn't really dead, or when Desdemona's dropping her handkerchief plays into Iago's hands, helping him destroy her and her husband. In a larger sense, the ethos of a protagonist's culture might work against him: racism bubbles under the surface of the Venetian culture in which Shakespeare's only black protagonist, Othello, makes his home, and the macho militarism of Rome turns Coriolanus into a killing machine unable to adapt to civilian life.

To explain everything by some flaw in a tragedy's protagonist (over-sensitivity in Hamlet, pride in Othello, sensuality in Antony and Cleopatra) is simplistic, and does violence to the complexity of evil whose multiple causes are intricately interwoven in every tragedy. But the idea of a tragic flaw makes sense at least in that it attributes *some* blame to the protagonist. Where Shakespeare parts company with Aristotelian notions of tragedy is that while Aristotle declared that tragedy involves *unmerited* misfortune, Shakespeare, over the course of his career, makes protagonists more and more responsible for their own catastrophes, moving from the largely innocent Romeo and Juliet to heroes more clearly responsible for setting in motion the forces that destroy them (King Lear, Antony and Cleopatra, Coriolanus), occasionally even casting outright villains as heroes (the Macbeths).

Granting protagonists some agency, some control over their own lives even if it means fatally harming themselves, at least alleviates our sense of depression at seeing a blameless person crushed by outside forces. But this move also returns us to the blaming-the-victim problem, and it runs the risk of damaging audience sympathy. Do we need audience sympathy to have a tragedy? Most would agree that we do: rubbing our hands gleefully together when someone exceedingly wicked meets his doom is not a tragic response. But can we sympathize with a tragic hero who is an outright criminal? Aristotle thought we couldn't. Shakespeare, apparently, thought we could.

Across the sweep of his ten tragedies, Shakespeare makes increasing demands on audience sympathy, choosing as his later tragic heroes—and therefore inviting some measure of audience identification with—such unpromising tragic figures as the murderous Macbeths; the stubborn, wrathful, self-centred old power abuser King Lear; the ageing sensualists Antony and Cleopatra; and the pugnacious mama's boy Coriolanus. How could he have expected audience empathy with such a sorry crew of social misfits?

Tragic scapegoats

One theory is that tragic heroes serve as scapegoats: the ills of a whole society, heaped on their shoulders, seem to disappear magically when the protagonists are killed. This is supposed to account for our getting something like pleasure out of this strange, bleak genre. Romeo and Juliet are the innocent sacrifice familiar to Greek tragedy: in Euripides' tragedies, for example, young people are often sacrificed to save a family, city, or nation from some grave crisis. The deaths of Romeo and Juliet, though not a religious rite as in Greek tragedy, have a kind of religio-magical effect: the feud ends, and Verona is saved. Innocence here is crucial: to dismiss the lovers' feelings as puppy love is to miss a vital emotional effect: precisely because it *is* puppy love, we respond to Romeo and Juliet as virtual children, innocent victims.

Some think that scapegoats *must* be innocent, but in cultures which practise forms of scapegoating—including the popular magic of Renaissance England with its sacrifice of warty toads and ritual bludgeoning to death of tied-up roosters—the victim is often spotted or tainted in some way. Do Shakespeare's 'guilty' tragic heroes serve some scapegoat function as well? It is true that Scotland's woes are pronounced cured upon the death of the Macbeths. But again, overemphasis on guilt is distorting: the killing of a scapegoat often, in Shakespeare, cures evils much more extensive than can be accounted for by any flaw in the scapegoated protagonist himself. Coriolanus exacerbates but does not solely cause Rome's class tensions, yet when he is banished, tensions cease, in 'a happier and more comely time / Than when these fellows ran about the streets, / Crying confusion'(4.6.29–31). At the end of a tragedy or a history play with a 'tragic ending', society's troubles are judged to be cured now that an offending protagonist is dead, as happens in *Macbeth*, *Coriolanus*, and *Richard III*; but a thinking audience is often left uneasy by this blaming of the victim. These plays often leave the impression that the troubles temporarily cured by sacrificing a scapegoat are deeply rooted in their society, and will recur.

Scapegoating is a troubling phenomenon, leaving us with a sense of its futility in the long run, and the melancholy recognition that in the fallen world of civic and national strife, every generation will need its scapegoats. It is partly our recognition that scapegoating is only a piece of wishful thinking, of magical thinking, that helps us sympathize with even a guilty protagonist, whose disaster most often outweighs his or her offence. We forgive, because the protagonist is (in King Lear's words) 'more sinned against than sinning'.

We would also forgive, if we were a good Renaissance Christian audience, because God commanded us to, and because we were sinners too, and shouldn't judge. Shakespeare's radical demand, going far beyond Aristotle, that we sympathize, that we understand, even a protagonist who brought all this on himself, is ultimately the demand of a Christian culture.

Tragedy and other genres

Tragedy as a genre comes from classical Greece and Rome. Shakespeare and his contemporary dramatists knew little about the great Greek tragic writers (Aeschylus, Sophocles, and Euripides), but they knew some classical theory from Aristotle's *Poetics*, and they were very familiar with the Roman tragic writer Seneca, on whom they drew for such sensational elements as bloodiness, revenge, ghosts, prophecies, and the supernatural. Seneca's plots were bloodthirsty, but he always kept the gore offstage and left bloody violence to be described by a messenger. Shakespeare and his fellow dramatists put it all right up there onstage—Queen Margaret stabbing a child to death in *Henry VI Part Two*, Gloucester's two eyes being gouged out with the nauseating comment 'Out, vile jelly!' (*King Lear*, 3.7.86), Macbeth's bleeding severed head stuck up on a pole. Some think that the Renaissance had developed a tolerance (or even a taste) for sensational gore from watching public executions; whatever the reason, gore was a hallmark of tragedy.

Shakespeare and his contemporaries were also influenced, in creating the tragic genre, by medieval stories of the 'fall of princes'—dismal tales about rulers such as Alexander the Great and Julius Caesar who died at the height of their power. Such tales were originally supposed to teach the brevity and uncertainty of life and the unwiseness of worldly ambition, but Renaissance tragedy uses the 'fall from a great height' motif much less preachily. Figures of evil in tragedies are sometimes influenced by the Vice figure in medieval morality plays—a wicked tempter who was originally an allegorical representative of Evil. Characters such as Richard III and Iago show signs of descent from the Vice, and they also owe something to the influence of the Italian Renaissance writer Machiavelli, who advocated an amoral will to power, seen in England not so much as politically expedient as downright demonic.

Shakespeare and his fellow dramatists were not fussy about keeping their genres and influences pure—they picked up traditions, plots, and characters as indiscriminately as magpies, and the boundaries of Renaissance dramatic genres are gloriously messy. Some plays can be considered either tragedies or history plays: *Richard II* and *Richard III* belong to cycles of history plays, but like tragedy, they feature a strong central protagonist and a tragic ending. In the First Folio, *Richard II* and *Richard III* are included with history plays, but both were called tragedies when first published in quarto versions. The plots of *King Lear* and *Macbeth* come from Holinshed, source of most of Shakespeare's English history plays. A deeply tragic figure like Shylock appears in a comedy, and the comedy *Love's Labour's Lost* ends with a death and the postponement of all its weddings. Scenes of clowning appear at dark moments in tragedies—just after Macbeth kills King Duncan and just before Cleopatra commits suicide. Shakespeare's greatest comic figure, Falstaff, occurs in history plays *and* a comedy, and meets a lonely, scapegoated death reminiscent of tragedy. Scapegoatings occur in history plays as in tragedies—Henry V and his Chief Justice ask us to believe that Henry IV's usurped crown and a violent civil war can all be cured by the rejection and expulsion of the seedy old drunk Falstaff, along with a few tavern-keepers and prostitutes.

Still, despite fascinating overlaps, tragedy can be distinguished from other genres at least broadly. Shakespearian tragedy differs from comedy in its unhappy ending, its more intense degree of suffering and evil, its more fully developed protagonists, the higher social class of its major characters, a higher percentage of blank verse, and in the fact that it is usually male-oriented.

Shakespeare identifies women with fertility (one reason their roles are central in comedy); by destroying them in tragedy, he stresses a triumph of sterility. Most tragic heroes are sterile in having no children: Hamlet tells his potential bride to become a nun; Othello and Desdemona, Romeo and Juliet, Richard III, and probably the Macbeths die childless; Lady Macbeth imagines baby-murder; Macbeth has a 'fruitless crown', a 'barren sceptre'; Lear curses his daughter with sterility, and his line perishes. Since neither Romeo nor Juliet has siblings, the fact that their death ends the feud is a

Pyrrhic victory: death both reconciles the families and wipes them out. Old Capulet will not sire more heirs, and Romeo's mother dies the same night as her son. Her gratuitous last-minute demise seems part of a campaign to leave no women alive onstage at a tragedy's end. Except in the Roman plays, Shakespeare kills off every woman prominent enough to have appeared in a tragedy's last scene: Lavinia, Tamora, Portia, Ophelia, Gertrude, Desdemona, Emilia, Ladies Macbeth and Macduff, all three daughters in *Lear* (a play with no other women). Most of these deaths are ill-prepared for and thinly explained—they have less to do with individual circumstance than with the anti-fertility agenda of Shakespearian tragedy, a direct contrast with the world-peopling action of comedy.

Tragedy differs from history plays first in emphasizing the private person, where histories emphasize the public person: even when tragic heroes are politically powerful, tragedies are more interested in their moral, ethical, and emotional dimensions than in their political dimension. Though the political and the domestic interpenetrated in this age (comparisons were often drawn between a nation's ruler and a family's father, as discussed in Chapter 13), the emphasis still falls, in tragedy, more heavily on the domestic than on the national role. Second, history plays muffle moral issues in favour of political realism, and it is common to find in history plays no clear-cut set of heroes and villains, but ambiguous collections of partly good, partly bad characters drawn in shades of grey. Third, except perhaps for *Julius Caesar* and *Antony and Cleopatra*, each tragedy stands alone, while Shakespeare's English history plays are linked in continuous historical sequence throughout a total of eight plays. Fourth, history plays often feel cut off arbitrarily at the end of Act Five, with unfinished actions left for the next play in the cycle; each tragedy, however, has a pronounced, even resounding climactic fifth act featuring spectacular violence and a stage strewn with corpses. Finally, history plays paint on a broader, less focused canvas crowded with characters vying for attention; tragedies focus on one or two prominent central protagonists. And a protagonist, a tragic hero, possesses distinctive features.

The tragic figure usually possesses an exalted social and/or political status: some are monarchs or princes (Hamlet, Lear, Macbeth, Cleopatra); some are generals or military heroes (Titus Andronicus, Othello, Coriolanus). The exceptions—Romeo and Juliet and Timon of Athens—if not politically or militarily powerful, are at least well-placed socially. The literary decorum of the period demanded that tragic figures speak with dignity befitting their high rank, in blank verse or other high-caste verse form, while those of lower social rank, populating comedies or the subplots of tragedies, might jingle along in tetrameter couplets or sink to prose. In cases when a hero is a scapegoat whose death is supposed to purge his or her society, the tragic hero's royal, noble, or heroic stature enables him or her to represent the entire society.

In keeping with tragedy's focus on the private person, however, nearly all tragic heroes are in some way alienated from their public, political roles. Hamlet has not succeeded his father as king; Lear has resigned his kingdom; the Macbeths have usurped the crown; Cleopatra ignores her kingdom in favour of private infatuation;

Titus is rejected by an ungrateful emperor; Othello is a foreign mercenary and racial outsider; Timon of Athens loses contact with senators and influential citizens when he goes bankrupt; Coriolanus, unable to bring himself to play his society's political games, is banished from the country he has valiantly defended. Where comedies bring people together in community, the tragic hero grows increasingly isolated—not only from the public life to which his high rank entitles him, but from the people closest to him. Romeo and Juliet get separated from each other and at fatal moments are abandoned by their closest confidantes, Friar Laurence and Juliet's nurse. Hamlet becomes disgusted with his mother and estranged from Ophelia. Othello is driven apart from his bride and discovers he didn't know his best friend very well after all. King Lear banishes his most trusted adviser and his most loved daughter, and his other two daughters reject him.

The tragic hero

It is no accident that it is in this bleak genre, where isolation is a prelude to death, that we find some of Shakespeare's most individualized characters. Shakespeare's age newly valued, but was also suspicious of, idiosyncratic and individualized personality, and therefore situated it in villains like Iago in *Othello*, in the tragic figures sometimes found in comedies, like Shylock in the *Merchant of Venice*, in the comic figures of history plays who may find themselves scapegoats, like Falstaff in *Henry IV Part Two*, and in the doomed protagonists of tragedy. Lovers in Shakespearian romantic comedies are often interchangeable—in *A Midsummer Night's Dream*, who can remember whether it was Demetrius or Lysander who was first in love with Helena—or was it Hermia? Relative flatness of character in Shakespeare's comedies is not an artistic blot: it expresses a sense of community, where beautiful young lovers find other beautiful young lovers pretty much like themselves, and together propagate a new generation of beautiful young-sters, thus peopling the world. Even death doesn't seem so drastic in the context of a comedy, since we know life will go on—in the community and in the next generation.

But in tragedy, a tragic figure is cut off from community, and her individuality makes her so irreplaceable that we cannot be consoled by any prospect of human continuity: 'Cordelia, Cordelia! stay a little! . . . Thou'lt come no more, / Never, never, never, never, never' (*King Lear*, 5.3.270, 306–7). Highly individualized personality in Shakespeare is often connected with defeat and death, as if it were something best stamped out; but it is also individuality that heightens the tragedy, that makes the action tragic at all. Tragedy affirms, by the intensity of its mourning for the dead hero, the value of what has been lost—the irreplaceable, unique human life.

The tragic hero is individualized by complexity of personality—Hamlet is by turns sensitive and brutal, suicidally melancholy and manically elated, broodingly lyrical and scorchingly satirical, a faithful friend to Horatio and a fatal friend to Rosencrantz and Guildenstern; he is scholar, fencer, soldier, lover, poet, theatre buff, joker, prince.

His speech is distinctive. He asks lots of questions and he rapidly repeats words and phrases: 'Very like, very like'; 'Thrift, thrift, Horatio'; also—unusual among exalted tragic figures—he speaks a lot of prose. Othello speaks in rolling, eloquent, musical blank verse, swelling with huge geographic images arising out of his life as a world-travelling soldier. The verbs of the early King Lear are almost entirely imperative; later, his speech resolves itself into curses, and only gradually do polite requests creep in: 'Pray you, undo this button'—his changing speech patterns track his changing character.

Tragic figures are also given individualized treatment in that each tragedy seems designed for the hero, or vice versa: each hero is placed in the tragic circumstances with which he is least equipped to cope, almost like a test (which, tragically, he always fails). King Lear, who defines his whole identity in terms of being 'a royal king' and 'so kind a father', gives away his kingdom and becomes estranged from all of his children—that is his testing situation, and it drives him mad. The same circumstances would hardly bother Coriolanus at all. If two tragic heroes swapped plays, Hamlet would never be vulnerable to Iago's insinuations—he would devise some mousetrap test to check on the authenticity of the handkerchief, and dally along with so many soliloquies that Iago's plot, which depends on speedy action and lack of close scrutiny, would come to light and the whole situation be saved. Conversely, Othello would never stand about, listening to Claudius praying and debating with himself whether to kill him: that robust man of action would smother Claudius first and ask questions later. The very absurdity of such hero-swapping brings into focus just how individualized the plots are: each protagonist is confronted with exactly the situation which will most severely test his unique individual qualities.

The tragic hero also possesses an uncompromising character, very unlike the flexible, resilient comic hero. The tragic hero doesn't go around obstacles but runs straight into them. Would King Lear ever, under any circumstances, answer Cordelia's 'Nothing, my lord', with a conciliatory 'well, let's all have some supper and talk this over later, when we've had a chance to rest up from a hard day'? Is Romeo likely to talk Juliet over with papa Montague or consider travelling around Europe with Benvolio for a while to see if he gets over his infatuation with this most unsuitable girl? Would Othello consider discussing his marital problems with a clergyman? Offered what looks like an easy face-saving compromise, 'The price is to ask it kindly' (*Coriolanus* 2.3.69), which would ultimately prevent civil war and avert his own death, Coriolanus can't bring himself to utter one civil sentence. The very uncompromising cussedness that dooms such tragic heroes is inseparable from the spirited integrity that makes them great.

One can evade trouble in a comedy, where running away is not considered reprehensible. Orlando in *As You Like It*, young lovers in *A Midsummer Night's Dream*, the hero of *Pericles*, Camillo in *The Winter's Tale*, and many other comedic figures escape from danger or intolerable situations simply by running away to a forest or to sea. But most tragic figures, with their blinkered, straight-ahead approach to life, don't even consider running away: they march head-on into catastrophe. The few who do try to run away—like Romeo and Juliet—can't get away with it. Shakespearian tragedy is deeply claustrophobic: characters are boxed into situations and incapable of seeing their way out. Again, we should not be too quick to blame the victims: their inability to escape is only partly attributable to their inflexible personalities; it also reflects circumstances beyond their control.

Radical tragedies

In Shakespearian tragedy we confront at every turn the issue of individual agency versus circumstances beyond one's control, and since most such circumstances are political or cultural, a question arises about whether Shakespearian tragedy might be politically radical. For several decades in the mid-twentieth century, Shakespeare was judged politically conservative, an upholder of monarchy, aristocracy, and the Church of England; a believer in unchangeable social hierarchy, and a proponent of obedience to authority, in the family and in the state. Beginning in the 1980s, however, books such as Jonathan Dollimore's *Radical Tragedy* started making claims for Shakespearian tragedy as a politically dissident genre. Sir Philip Sidney had, after all, given as one of tragedy's excellences that it 'maketh kings fear to be tyrants'; and quite a lot of the misery in Shakespeare's tragedies arises from the repressive behaviour of tyrants—Saturninus in *Titus Andronicus*, Claudius in *Hamlet*, the Senate oligarchs in *Coriolanus*, Macbeth, Lear, possibly Julius Caesar. Those who pronounce Shakespeare radical don't find in such images of repressive government any evidence of devotion to authority and political hierarchy at any cost. They think Shakespeare might have been reading some sixteenth-century resistance literature, which justified principled (even violent) resistance to unjust political authorities. *King Lear* is deeply concerned about social justice and the creation of a compassionate society: Lear himself is forced to live in a hovel and witness dire poverty, and comes to realize that he himself is responsible for these wretched economic conditions:

> You houseless poverty . . .
> Poor naked wretches, wheresoe'er you are,
> That bide the pelting of this pitiless storm,
> How shall your houseless heads and unfed sides,
> Your looped and windowed raggedness, defend you
> From seasons such as these? O, I have ta'en
> Too little care of this! Take physic, pomp;
> Expose thyself to feel what wretches feel,
> That thou mayst shake the superflux to them.
> (3.4.27-36)

The famous 'belly' speech in *Coriolanus* used to be interpreted as Shakespeare's statement of belief in an inflexible class system: a patrician justifies the privilege of his own class by lecturing the plebeians on the importance of the belly (metaphor for the patricians) in storing and distributing food to the whole body (metaphor for society as a whole). More recently, however, radical-minded readers have noted that the plebeians have been rioting because they are hungry, while the patricians are hoarding up corn in their warehouses, which exposes the hollow illogicality of the 'belly' speech: even granted their 'right' to store and distribute food supplies, the patricians have abused their position by storing but not distributing. Even in the 'belly speech's' own terms, the plebeians' grievances are justified. And this play was written during a time of famine in England, when the rich were being accused of hoarding grain and the poor were rioting in protest, clearly suggesting that this tragedy was making a radical political comment on its own society.

Those who see the plays as radical, as interventions in the politics of their day, tend to be very sceptical of the tragic flaw. Jonathan Dollimore locates the 'fatal flaw' not in the individual but in the state and the social order it upholds. Once again, here in a political context, overemphasizing the role of the individual in producing the tragic outcome obscures the crucial role of society and culture, not only in influencing what happens to the individual, but in forming that individual in the first place.

And might Shakespearian tragedy be religiously radical? Religion in the period had a good deal to say about individual responsibility versus outside control. One influential strain of contemporary Protestant thought, Calvinism, granted individual free will *no* influence on events, which were seen as entirely predestined by God. Re-enter the problem of evil: if God predetermined all that happens, is he responsible for evil? How could he be, if he is benevolent? This question keenly interests characters in Shakespearian tragedy. Macduff demands on behalf of Macbeth's murder victims, 'Did heaven look on / And would not take their part?' (4.3.225–6). In our own time, people have asked where God was during the Holocaust, and the same question is provoked by Shakespearian tragedy, with its deeply unfair universe, full of undeserved suffering and death. 'I have not deserved this', cries Desdemona; and 'A guiltless death I die' (*Othello* 4.1.236, 5.2.132); 'I am a man / More sinned against than sinning', declares Lear (3.2.57–8).

Although the Shakespearian tragic figure does set in motion the chain of events culminating in disaster and death, the punishment is nearly always in excess of the fault—yes, King Lear was arrogant, unperceptive, and insensitive, but are these capital offences? Did he deserve to be abandoned by his children and to die miserably, for these shortcomings? Did Cleopatra deserve death for being strong-willed and loving sex and wine? And what about the host of lesser characters swept to their doom in tragedy's general catastrophe—did Paris in *Romeo and Juliet*, or Roderigo in *Othello*, or Lady Macduff in *Macbeth* deserve to die? There is no balance and reasonableness about what happens in tragedy. That, in large part, is what makes it tragic.

But this is hard to accept, and it makes tragedies painful to read and to watch. People often resist this unfair tragic world, doggedly trying to make it fair, by depicting Desdemona as an undutiful daughter and rather flirty with Cassio, Othello as a braggart, Romeo and Juliet as impatient and oversexed, Coriolanus as snooty about the plebeians—all, by this view, had death coming to them. We have all heard such reactions to these disturbing plays, from students and from professional critics. They are understandable reactions, like the response of Job's so-called comforters to his tribulations: 'Who ever perished, being innocent? Or where were the righteous cut off? If thou wert pure and upright, surely now [God] would awake for thee, and make the habitation of thy righteousness prosperous'; or in other words, you must have done something to deserve this.

Overemphasis on the tragic flaw, to the neglect of the pervasive role of malice, an unjust society, chance, accident, and pure bad luck in nearly every tragedy, is part of a wistful desire to find the hero guilty of something serious enough to merit extreme suffering and death, and thus to preserve our sense that life is fair. But the profoundness of Renaissance tragedy is that at its best, it takes a steady look at a world where no just higher authority ensures that every person gets a square deal—not political authority, not divine authority. If fairness in this world is to be achieved, we must achieve it ourselves. As a tragedy ends, we realize that like the tragic hero, we are on our own. To weep for a tragic hero is to weep for ourselves.

FURTHER READING

Belsey, Catherine. *The Subject of Tragedy: Identity and Difference in Renaissance Drama* (London and New York: Methuen, 1985). This influential study challenges the widespread notion that Shakespearian tragedy offers insights into a timeless or universal 'human nature' and argues that a more modern sense of individual subjectivity did not even exist in Shakespeare's time.

Braden, Gordon. *Renaissance Tragedy and the Senecan Tradition: Anger's Privilege* (New Haven and London: Yale University Press, 1985). A rich background study of what Renaissance tragedy owes to the tragedies of ancient Rome.

Bradley, A. C. *Shakespearian Tragedy* (London: Macmillan, 1904). The book that inaugurated twentieth-century criticism of Shakespeare's tragedies, contributed the idea of tragic waste, and set up *Hamlet*, *Othello*, *King Lear*, and *Macbeth* as the greatest Shakespearian tragedies. Long under fire for treating dramatic characters as real people, as if they had lives beyond the page or stage, the book is still something that serious students of Shakespearian tragedy need to know about.

Cartwright, Kent. *Shakespearian Tragedy and Its Double: The Rhythms of Audience Response* (University Park: Pennsylvania State University Press, 1991). This book examines the way audiences sometimes engage closely with and sometimes are distanced from the action and characters of tragedies, and how Shakespeare manipulates these responses to gain tragic effects.

Dollimore, Jonathan. *Radical Tragedy: Religion, Ideology and Power in the Drama of Shakespeare and his Contemporaries*, 2nd edn. (Brighton: Harvester Wheatsheaf, 1989. 1st edn. 1984). This is an influential argument maintaining the political, social, religious, and intellectual radicalism of Renaissance tragedy as a genre.

Garner, Shirley Nelson, and Madelon Sprengnether, eds. *Shakespearian Tragedy and Gender* (Bloomington: Indiana University Press, 1996). This book consists of twelve essays on women and gender in Shakespearian tragedy; useful introduction.

Liebler, Naomi Conn. *Shakespeare's Festive Tragedy: The Ritual Foundations of Genre* (London and New York: Routledge, 1995). Liebler argues that Shakespearian tragedy celebrates community survival and that not only the protagonist but the community are tragedy's subject. The book also focuses on disasters that occur when a community violates or neglects the central rituals that hold it together.

Neill, Michael. *Issues of Death: Mortality and Identity in English Renaissance Tragedy* (Oxford: Clarendon, 1997). Neill explores the many cultural meanings of Renaissance tragedy's preoccupation with death.

Reiss, Timothy J. 'Renaissance Theatre and the Theory of Tragedy', in *The Cambridge History of Literary Criticism, III: The Renaissance*, ed. Glyn P. Norton (Cambridge, England: Cambridge University Press, 1999), pp. 229–47. This is a solid introduction to classical, medieval, and Renaissance theory of tragedy, with examples from across Europe.

Young, David. *The Action to the Word: Structure and Style in Shakespearian Tragedy* (New Haven and London: Yale University Press, 1990). This book contains sensible, readable discussions of the interplay of action and eloquence in *Hamlet*, *Othello*, *King Lear*, and *Macbeth*.

READING: *Macbeth*

If 'why did this have to happen?' is tragedy's great question, why do the evil events happen in *Macbeth*? As in most Shakespearian tragedies, the sources of evil are complex.

As for a tragic flaw, Macbeth is ambitious, of course; more interestingly, he is abnormally imaginative and sensitive, for a murderer. Far from having the poker face necessary for keeping secret murders quiet, he shows everything in his face. 'Why do you make such faces?' demands his wife (3.4.66). 'Your face . . . is as a book where men/ May read strange matters', she tells him, advising him instead to 'look like the innocent flower, / But be the serpent under't' (1.5.60–4). Macbeth suffers for a crime before he even commits it, because he imagines it so thoroughly. He imagines murdering the King, and the 'horrid image doth unfix [his] hair / And make[s] [his] seated heart knock at [his] ribs'. Even a hideous reality disturbs him less than do 'horrible imaginings', and although murder is as yet only a fantasy, it shakes his psyche to the foundations, until he can no longer distinguish between fantasy and reality: 'nothing is / But what is not' (1.3.134–41). Lady Macbeth is less imaginative and doesn't start suffering until after a crime; but she is fully as sensitive as Macbeth (she is the one who relives details of the murder nightly in her sleepwalks and sees blood on her hands forever). The fatal combination of lack of imaginative foresight and hypersensitive visual memory drive her to insanity and suicide.

Villains are normally part of the 'outside forces' against which a hero contends; but in this tragedy Shakespeare collapses the villain role into the protagonist role: the Macbeths are villains-as-heroes. *Macbeth* is the clearest example of a Shakespearian departure from Aristotle's dictum that tragedy involves *unmerited* misfortune, since the Macbeths fully deserve their misery. But by putting them in the role of tragic heroes, Shakespeare seems to invite us to sympathize with them, guilty or not. Unlike a murder mystery, in which we see through the eyes of the law, here we view crime through the criminals' eyes, with a corresponding demand put upon us to understand how those criminals feel.

Though they are criminal, we can't heap all blame on the Macbeths: outside forces are at work as well, in forging the evil of the play. Was murder the Macbeths' destiny? The three witches bring the Three Fates to mind; the play's main source, Holinshed's *Chronicles*, offers two interpretations of these witches—they may just be malicious old women, or they may be 'the goddesses of destiny'. Shakespeare often calls them the weird sisters, and 'weird' comes from the Anglo-Saxon *wyrd*, meaning Fate. There's clear evidence in the play that the Macbeths have discussed murdering the King before Macbeth ever met the three sisters.[1] But the presence of these supernatural agents in the play still suggests a complex interaction between human agency and a malign destiny.

The protagonists' culture, too, offers hostile elements: it apparently valorizes violence and ambition over more humane values. Between the evil gore of murder and the 'good' gore of

Fig. 2.2 'Macbeth hath murdered sleep': as depicted in *The Illustrated Shakespeare* of 1840.

battle described so graphically in the opening scenes there is a very fine line: the latter in some ways seems merely to set the stage for the former.

The prominence of Lady Macbeth as co-protagonist is unusual in tragedy, normally a male-oriented genre. She joins only two other genuinely powerful female figures in Shakespearian tragedies (Cleopatra in *Antony and Cleopatra* and Volumnia in *Coriolanus*), and all three are powerful at the expense of the man to whom they are closest, whom they help to ruin. Like most other female tragic figures, Lady Macbeth loses her personal power and dies before Act Five.[2]

The play's four temptresses—three witches and Lady Macbeth—have prompted many to regard *Macbeth* as a misogynistic play which ascribes evil to a female principle; but the play destabilizes simplistic thinking about men and women or about 'masculine' or 'feminine' character traits. Macbeth himself challenges—at least initially—Lady Macbeth's definition of manliness as innately violent, ambitious, and murderous; he argues that gentleness and compassion are basic human values, not flaws of the effeminate. She taunts him, 'When you durst do it [commit the murder], then you were a man', and tempts him with the prospect of becoming, if he murders the king, 'so much more the man' (1.7.49–51); but he declares, 'I dare do all that may become a man; / Who dares do more is none' (1.7.46–7). When Macduff is advised (upon the slaughter of his family) to 'let grief / Convert to anger', to sing a 'manly' tune by committing himself to revenge, he agrees that he must 'dispute it like a man'; however, he insists, 'I must also feel it as a man'; emotion, tears, are again not 'feminine' but human (4.3.221–31). It is possible to read the play's opening image of hermaphroditic bearded women as a horrific forecast of the protagonists' violation of their own 'natural' masculine or feminine characters, but it is also possible to argue that evil in the play results in part from a *failure* of wholesome hermaphrodism, from a suppression of 'feminine' pity and compassion in *both* the Macbeths.

Macbeth's two tragic heroes give us special opportunities to observe what a tragic hero is like. Both the Macbeths, like other tragic heroes, possess strongly individualized characters. Lady Macbeth displays a unique blend of murderous toughness, delicate squeamishness, and fear of her own tenderness. Macbeth possesses a complex individuality, suffering for a deed before he even does it, imagining actions in such vivid pictorial detail that it often verges on hallucination, and speaking in highly individualized, associative speech patterns, as in his 'tomorrow, and tomorrow, and tomorrow' soliloquy (5.5.16–27), where 'tomorrow' makes him think of 'yesterdays', which he personifies as fools carrying candles in a tomb, which leads to a metaphor of life as a candle, which reminds him of a shadow, which (because of another meaning of 'shadow') makes him think of actors, which reminds him of storytellers, all in the space of a very few lines, and all imagined visually, or in terms of sound—Macbeth's senses are abnormally vigilant. He carries the rhetorical figure of personification almost to the lengths of hallucination, so visual is his mode of thinking: a man whose imagination can turn a personified abstraction like Pity into a 'naked new-born babe' in a storm, or a personified abstraction like Ambition into a spurred rider vaulting onto a horse (1.7.21–8), may sooner or later clutch at daggers hanging in the air.

Typically of tragedy, the Macbeths are seen more in their private than their public character: even in this play of political ambition, the emphasis falls on what ambition does to the soul more than on what it does to the state. We witness here the complete unravelling of two strong personalities. Lady Macbeth, initially the stronger partner, who pushes her husband to action and holds him together when he keeps threatening to crack, ultimately breaks down first, driven to madness and probable suicide by nightmares in which she relives the murder. And that preternaturally sensitive man Macbeth grows brutalized, hardened almost beyond recognition. The man who once stared aghast at his murdered king's blood upon his hands now confesses he has 'almost forgot the taste of fears' (5.5.9). His senses, once honed to a razor edge, are now so dulled he can barely respond when he hears women shrieking in the castle:

> The time has been my senses would have cooled
> To hear a night-shriek, and my fell of hair
> Would at a dismal treatise rouse and stir
> As life were in't.
>
> (5.5.10-13)

But now horror is merely 'familiar' amidst his 'slaughterous thoughts'. He can hardly even respond when he learns that the women are crying at the death of his wife: 'She should have died hereafter. / There would have been a time for such a word' (5.5.16–17).

The horror of their own deeds which destroys their individual personalities also destroys their marriage. The Macbeths, ironically one of the most close-knit of Shakespeare's married couples as the play begins, find that one of crime's lessons is that partners can't stay together in it. Macbeth doesn't tell Lady Macbeth about his plan to murder Banquo and Fleance: 'Be innocent of the knowledge, dearest chuck, / Till thou applaud the deed' (3.2.46–7). Nor does he consult her on his barbaric plan to exterminate Macduff's wife, children, and servants; we are left to infer that she identifies with this poor murdered wife, as she murmurs in her sleep, 'The thane of Fife had a wife. Where is she now?' (5.1.36–7).

In comedies, and in plays by some of Shakespeare's contemporaries, dramatic characters do not change gradually—either they are relatively static in their behaviour, or they undergo instantaneous character reversals such as Duke Ferdinand's religious conversion in *As You Like It*. One of the hallmarks of Shakespearian tragedy is that characters change over time, in believably gradual modulations. Sometimes they grow, as King Lear grows from a petulant, egomaniacal old tyrant into a humane man who worries about the poor and whose gaze has turned outward: he dies not justifying himself, but thinking only of Cordelia. Sometimes they shrink, as Othello dwindles from a magnificent, heroic, self-possessed general into a cramped, suspicious wife-abuser, shrivelled of soul. The Macbeths are among those who shrink.

Like other tragic heroes, the Macbeths suffer from isolation: each is left alone at the moment of greatest agony. The crime alienates the Macbeths from each other, and from the very society they had sought the honour of leading. Before this happens, the two spouses together form a complex whole, so in tune with each other (in early scenes) that they echo each other's words and thoughts even when they are apart. Lady Macbeth in soliloquy, planning Duncan's murder, invokes night so that she will figuratively not have to see what she is doing:

> Come, thick night . . .
> That my keen knife see not the wound it makes,
> Nor heaven peep through the blanket of the dark.
> (1.5.48-51)

Macbeth in soliloquy, planning Banquo's murder, invokes night for exactly the same reason: 'Come, seeling night, / Scarf up the tender eye of pitiful day' (3.2.47–8). These wishes are uttered in soliloquy—it is themselves the Macbeths are trying to blind. To render their evil intentions relatively invisible to themselves, both use euphemisms to avoid having to say 'murder', such as the 'business' (1.5.66, 1.7.31, 3.1.126), 'his taking-off' (1.7.20), and 'I have done the deed' (2.2.14).

Even 'business' and 'deed', though having a much higher invisibility quotient than 'murder', are still nouns, and the Macbeths prefer pronouns, as in the oft-repeated 'do it', or 'he is about it' (2.2.4)—the latter, uttered by Lady Macbeth at the moment Macbeth is killing Duncan, causes 'Macbeth' to disappear into 'he' as well as 'murder' into 'it'; the victim disappears entirely. Often a pronoun's antecedent is unspecified, as in Lady Macbeth's opening soliloquy, which begins Act One, Scene Five. Tellingly for their close relationship, she begins by speaking in Macbeth's voice, reading aloud a letter from him: 'They met me in the day of success, and I have learned by the perfect'st report they have more in them than mortal knowledge'. Here the weird sisters' identity disappears into two 'they's and a 'them' (Macbeth has never asked their names, anyway). As Lady Macbeth's soliloquy begins *in medias res*, Macbeth two scenes later begins a closely analogous soliloquy in mid-meditation; like hers, it features a pronoun whose antecedent noun has been suppressed: 'If it were done when 'tis done, then 'twere well / It were done quickly' (1.7.1–2). Here again the pronoun 'it' replaces the noun 'murder', and even 'it' is contracted to ''t' in ''tis' and ''twere', diminishing the crime almost to invisibility (that tiny 't') or inaudibility (only a little click of the tongue against the teeth).

One of Lady Macbeth's favourite grammatical disappearing-devices is the substitution, for a noun, of a noun clause introduced by a relative pronoun. The first time she does this, it is to avoid saying 'king': 'Glamis thou art, and Cawdor, and shalt be / What thou art promised' (1.5.13–14). Presently she does it again: 'What thou wouldst highly, / That wouldst thou holily' (1.5.18–19) is an invisible way of saying 'You want to be king but you'd rather not do it by murdering the man who is king now'. Next she produces almost a self-parody of her own 'its', 'dos', 'undones', and disappearing-act noun clauses: 'Thou'dst have, great Glamis, / That which cries, "Thus thou must do" if thou have it, / And that which rather thou dost fear to do / Than wishest should be undone' (1.5.20–3). This passage is hard to follow, and deliberately so: Lady Macbeth's diction is designed to cover her tracks. Macbeth too sometimes uses the evasive noun clauses introduced by relative pronouns which are hallmarks of Lady Macbeth's speech; for example: 'let that be / Which the eye fears, when it is done, to see' (1.4.53–4); 'that which the eye fears', again, is murder.

The witches parody the Macbeths' grammar of invisibility, their terror of naming, when Macbeth visits them to demand 'How now, you secret, black, and midnight hags, / What is't you do?' Flinging his weasle-verb 'do' and his miniaturized ''t' in his face, they reply in Macbeth-speak: 'A deed without a name' (4.1.64–5). It is fitting that actors' superstitions have preserved for this play the fear of naming something frightful: it is supposedly bad luck, even now, to refer to 'the Scottish play' by its true title.

The Macbeths talk uncannily alike, even when apart. Writing at the height of his creative powers, Shakespeare creates speech patterns perfectly expressive of character and situation. In the Macbeths' language of evasion, we find two people determined not to look squarely at what they are doing. Unlike *King Lear*, whose characters are forced to 'see better' as the tragedy progresses (1.1.58), *Macbeth* gives us protagonists who start out seeing the situation and themselves pretty clearly: 'I am his kinsman and his subject, / Strong both against the deed; then, as his host, / Who should against his murderer shut the door, / Not bear the knife myself' (1.7.13–16), Macbeth reminds himself, when contemplating regicide. But they know their own sensitivity well enough to realize that to go through with their ruthless drive for power, they must commit murders with averted face: 'Stars, hide your fires, / Let not light see my black and deep desires; / The eye wink at the hand; yet let that be / Which the eye fears, when it is done, to see' (1.4.50–3). 'To know my deed', Macbeth acknowledges, ''twere best not know myself' (2.2.71).

Their shared language of euphemism and evasion expresses this situation, but it also reminds us how close they are to each other, how perfectly in tune their two minds are. A couple who can accurately read each other's suppressed nouns is a very intimate couple. The tragic waste of the play lies not only in their deaths, nor even in the probable loss of their immortal souls, but also in the destruction of a marriage, in the tragic estrangement of two lost souls who have loved each other.

FURTHER READING

Jorgensen, Paul. *Our Naked Frailties: Sensational Art and Meaning in 'Macbeth'* (Berkeley, Los Angeles, and London: University of California Press, 1971). Detailed, accessibly written reading of the play's dense language, set in the context of Renaissance beliefs, fears, and practices.

Nostbakken, Faith. *Understanding 'Macbeth': A Student Casebook to Issues, Sources, and Historical Documents* (Westport, Conn.: Greenwood, 1997). Valuable compilation of the play's sources, treatises on political ambition, kingship, witchcraft; also includes stage history and makes links with modern issues.

Stallybrass, Peter. '*Macbeth* and Witchcraft', in *Focus on 'Macbeth'*, ed. John Russell Brown (London: Routledge and Kegan Paul, 1982), pp. 189–209.

NOTES

1. Lady Macbeth reminds Macbeth that he first suggested 'this enterprise' (the regicide) to her, on some previous occasion when neither time nor place offered them opportunity for murder; but now, time and

place have 'made themselves' because the king has arrived at their castle (1.7.48–55). As staged in the play, the conversation wherein the Macbeths decide on murder takes place after they know Duncan is coming to the castle (1.5), and therefore Lady Macbeth's reminder must allude to a conversation that took place before the encounter with the witches, since the Macbeths have not been together in the interim.

2. The exceptions again are Cleopatra and Volumnia, both in Roman tragedies. We have seen in this chapter three good reasons for putting Shakespeare's Roman tragedies in a separate category from his other tragedies (as in Chapter 19): in the Roman tragedies the women sometimes survive where in non-Roman plays they are wiped out; *Julius Caesar* and *Antony and Cleopatra* form a pair while each of the non-Roman tragedies stands alone; and Cleopatra and Volumnia are unlike any other strong women in the tragedies in keeping their power until the end or very near the end of Act Five. Further, the dual emphasis on public and private life, politics and domesticity, war and love is more nearly in balance in the Roman plays; in other tragedies the emphasis tilts strongly toward the 'private' side of the hero's existence. But Roman tragedies are still Shakespearian tragedies, with their high-ranking, individualized, uncompromising heroes, claustrophobic situations, and spectacular deathly denouements. Examples drawn from the Roman plays in this chapter indicate significant continuity with non-Roman Shakespearian tragedies.

19 | Roman plays

Alexander Leggatt

The story of Rome

Rome was for Shakespeare and his contemporaries a collection of legends, a body of history, a set of values, and a still-living culture. Shakespeare tapped into the story of Rome throughout his career, in the narrative poem *The Rape of Lucrece* (1593–4); in the tragedies *Titus Andronicus* (c.1589–92), *Julius Caesar* (1599), *Antony and Cleopatra* (1606–7), and *Coriolanus* (c.1608); and in the late romance *Cymbeline* (c.1608–10). Throughout these works he examines Roman values, institutions, and political conflicts; the place of women in Rome; and the relationship between Rome and the world outside.

Rome presented to Shakespeare a finished story with a beginning, a middle, and an end; and in reading that story he and his contemporaries did not distinguish as sharply as a modern reader would between legend and verifiable history. The story begins with the legend, enshrined in Virgil's *Aeneid*, that Rome was founded by descendants of Aeneas, who after the fall of Troy (on the west coast of modern-day Turkey) journeyed to Italy. The story of Troy was part of the story of Rome—and of Britain, for there was a similar myth about Britain's founding. In the aftermath of her rape, Shakespeare's Lucrece studies a painting that depicts the sack of Troy, and for her and for the reader the acts of military and sexual violence are connected. Violence touches the story of Rome at key moments throughout. The legend of its founder Romulus includes his murder of his brother Remus and his gaining women for the new city by the abduction or 'rape' of the Sabines; while Shakespeare does not use either story directly, his Rome is a place that makes and re-makes itself through violence, and rape, whether it is defined as sexual assault or as abduction, is a recurring motif.

A crucial turning point in early Roman history was the ending of the monarchy, figured in legend as the expulsion of the royal family, the Tarquins, in retaliation for the rape of Lucrece. A mistrust of kingship runs through Roman history from this point on, and the institutions of the republic of Rome were designed to avoid the concentration of power in any one individual. For example, the two consuls, the state's most important officers, were elected for a single year, and shared power between them. Rome saw its success as depending not on the achievements of great individuals but on shared ideals of moral virtue, patriotism, and civic duty.

However, as Rome's sphere of influence became an empire that expanded through Italy and eventually through the rest of the Mediterranean world, internal dissension and the self-seeking of important men threw the republic into crisis and made its institutions unworkable. Julius Caesar, after defeating his rival Pompey the Great, began to consolidate something like kingly power for himself. His assassination in 44 BC by a conspiracy led by Brutus and Cassius did not restore the republic; the conspirators were in turn defeated by Caesar's successors, the Triumvirate of Octavius Caesar (Caesar's adopted heir), Lepidus, and Mark Antony. Then the victors turned on each other. Octavius quickly disposed of Lepidus. Antony tried to consolidate his power in the east through an alliance with the Egyptian queen Cleopatra. Octavius's victory over them at the battle of Actium led to their suicide and left their conqueror as the supreme authority in the Roman world. Octavius, re-named Augustus, though he used constitutional forms that were nominally republican, was in effect Rome's first emperor. His political mastery ushered in a great age of Roman culture exemplified by the poets Virgil, Horace, and Ovid, and a political stability that lasted, with occasional setbacks, for many generations to come. Eventually the empire collapsed, undone by internal division and succumbing to barbarian invasions. In AD 410 Rome was sacked by the Visigoths, and in AD 476 the last Roman emperor was deposed.

Rome lived on, however, in language and culture that pervaded later European civilization. Even now Latin survives on coins and public buildings, and in medicine and botany. Quasi-Roman architecture is found in capital cities, and capital is a Roman term. In Shakespeare's time, to go to school was to learn Latin. Shakespeare's *The Merry Wives of Windsor* includes a scene in which a schoolboy called (coincidentally?) William is drilled in Latin. Shakespeare's interest in Rome was not an antiquarian's interest: the stories, images, and language of Rome were a living part of his world.

Shakespeare and Rome

Shakespeare turned to Roman history more sporadically than he turned to English history, however; and his Roman plays stand apart from each other in a way that makes them unlike his English history sequences. He begins with *Titus Andronicus*, whose characters and action are fictions unknown to history, but whose period is evidently the late empire, when the barbarians were at the gate: the Goths become powerful in Rome when the emperor Saturninus marries the Gothic queen Tamora, and his successor Lucius enters Rome at the head of an army of Goths. Saturninus, at once villainous and ineffectual, embodies in his own person the decadence of Rome. Anachronistic Christian references in the dialogue, in a Rome that is still nominally pagan, project us beyond the end of the empire. Yet *Titus Andronicus*, possibly Shakespeare's most bookish play, is steeped in Roman literature. The rape and mutilation of Titus's daughter Lavinia—the rapists cut off her hands and cut out her tongue—draw on the myth of Philomela in Ovid's *Metamorphoses*, and the ensuing revenge action, in which Titus bakes the rapists in a pie and serves them to their mother, recalls the *Thyestes* of Seneca, the Roman tragedian whose works were widely read in the sixteenth century. Familiar Latin phrases and mythological references abound, and Lavinia, denied language, tells her family what happened to her by pointing to a page in Ovid. *Titus Andronicus* is the work of a young writer who is making his mark by displaying his schooling in Roman literature, more self-consciously than he will ever do again.

The Rape of Lucrece returns to the theme of rape, but locates it this time early in the story of Rome, ending with the expulsion of the Tarquins and the founding of the republic. It too is a writer's conscious bid for literary standing through the handling of a classical theme. In *Julius Caesar* Shakespeare turns for the first time to his principal Roman source, Plutarch's *Lives of the Noble Grecians and Romans* as translated by Thomas North (1579, revised 1595). In this play and *Antony and Cleopatra* we see the death of the republic as the assassination of Caesar produces the chaos from which Octavius emerges. Here Shakespeare is closest to the actual history of Rome. Yet though *Antony and Cleopatra* in historical terms follows along from *Julius Caesar*, their relations are not like those of, say, *Henry IV Parts One* and *Two*. They were written roughly eight years apart, in very different styles: tense and concentrated in *Julius Caesar*, relaxed and expansive in *Antony and Cleopatra*. Of the three characters who appear in both plays, the coldly efficient Octavius and the ineffectual Lepidus are recognizably the same; but Antony, a cynical manipulator in the first play and a magnanimous, doomed hero in the second, is completely re-drawn.

Still using Plutarch, but depicting a period shadowy to modern historians, *Coriolanus* returns to the early republic: Rome is a young city still sorting out its political institutions and fighting with its neighbours. Its very existence is in question when Coriolanus, a Roman hero cast out by his own city, returns with a Volscian army and threatens to annihilate it. Finally, *Cymbeline* takes us to the early empire, with Britain falling under Roman domination; but this is history filtered through legend. It imagines a fictional invasion under Augustus, and its chronology is scrambled. Its tale of lost princes and a husband who tests his wife's fidelity is pure romance. Yet *Cymbeline* has affinities with *Antony and Cleopatra*, showing the expanding empire encountering, in Britain as in Egypt, a life very different from its own.

Roman values

Most of Shakespeare's Roman characters have a sharp sense of what that life is, of what it is to be a Roman. The words 'Rome' and 'Roman' are evocative of a range of values, including virtue, honour, integrity, and public service. Justifying the murder of Caesar, Brutus asks the crowd, 'Who is here so rude that would not be a Roman?' and they call back, 'None, Brutus, none' (3.2.28–32). He tells his fellow conspirators there is no need to swear an oath because they are 'secret Romans, that have spoke the word / And will not palter' (2.1.124–5). To praise a dead hero, it is enough to call him a Roman; Brutus pays the ultimate tribute to Cassius: 'The last of all the Romans, fare thee well' (5.3.98). In *Cymbeline* the Roman commander Lucius, captured and threatened with death, declares, 'A Roman with a Roman's heart can suffer' (5.6.81). Antony's way of rejecting public responsibility in favour of a life of pleasure with Cleopatra is to cry, 'Let Rome in Tiber melt, and the wide arch / Of the ranged empire fall' (1.1.35–6). Cleopatra's way of noting that serious business is claiming him again is, 'He was disposed to mirth, but on the sudden / A Roman thought hath struck him' (1.2.72–3).

This sense of what it means to be a Roman is less clear in *Coriolanus*, where, as befits the early republic, the idea of Rome is still under negotiation. In the class conflict between patricians and plebeians that opens the play, the patricians claim that *they* are Rome. Menenius, whose role it is to pacify the people with his outward amiability, nonetheless warns them it is futile to oppose 'the Roman state' (1.1.60), clearly implying they are not part of it. He is even blunter when he declares 'Rome and her rats are at the point of battle' (1.1.151). Rome is not a set of values; Rome is simply, for Menenius, his side. The plebeians seem to take the point, since the word 'Rome' appears to have no evocative power for them: they are more inclined to speak of 'the commonalty' (1.1.24), the commons; they talk of their enemy Caius Martius (the war hero who will later be named Coriolanus) as one who has done good service for 'his country' (1.1.25–6), implying it is not their country; and their rallying cry is 'The people are the city' (3.1.200). If 'Rome' means the patricians, they want a city of their own that does not yet have a name.

In the decadent Rome of *Titus Andronicus*, Titus at first clings to the evocative power of his city's name as his family turns against him. When his son Mutius defies him, Titus cries, 'What, villain boy, / Barr'st me my way in Rome?' (1.1.286–7), and kills him. The fact that they are in Rome, *his* city, gives him the right to do this, and he is outraged not just to be dishonoured but 'To be dishonoured by my sons in Rome' (1.1.382). But what is Roman, and who has the right to invoke the name, are matters in dispute. The family quarrel is over Bassianus's seizure of Titus's daughter Lavinia; Bassianus was betrothed to her but Titus has tried to give her as a trophy to the emperor. Her uncle Marcus defends Bassianus's claim by invoking Roman law over imperial power, with a Latin tag: '*Suum cuique* [to each his own] is our Roman justice. / The prince in justice seizeth but his own' (1.1.280–1). When Titus refuses Mutius burial in the family tomb, Marcus insists there are Roman values that transcend his patriarchal authority: 'Thou art a Roman; be not barbarous' (1.1.375). Titus relents.

Decent acknowledgement in death is one Roman value. Even the villainous Saturninus is buried in his father's tomb, by order of Lucius, who killed him. *Julius Caesar* is full of funeral tributes, and the contrasting orations of Brutus and Antony over Caesar have in common their praise of the dead man. Antony pays tribute to Brutus in death as 'the noblest Roman of them all' (5.5.67). The play's orations are self-conscious rhetorical set-pieces, careful displays of language and argument. This too is

Roman: even Lucrece, pleading for her chastity, builds her argument like an orator making a case before a public body.

If the oration is a characteristic Roman mode, suicide is a characteristic Roman act, the last way to defeat an enemy. Macbeth refuses to 'play the Roman fool, and die / On mine own sword' (5.10.1–2), and many in Shakespeare's audience would have seen this refusal as disgraceful. Lucrece, Brutus, Cassius, and Antony all take this way out, and in every case there is a sense of heroic self-assertion. Antony calls himself 'a Roman by a Roman / Valiantly vanquished' (4.16.59–60)—though it is a sign of how far the play is going beyond Rome that his death is not like the swift, clean suicides of *Julius Caesar*. He bungles it, pleads for someone to finish him off (no one will), and dies not on the battlefield but in Cleopatra's arms. Lucrece's death is problematic in a different way. She sees it as a necessity for the 'dishonour' of her rape, and there was a tradition of admiring her for it; but Brutus (ancestor of Caesar's assassin), who foments the rebellion that avenges her, dismisses it: 'Thy wretched wife mistook the matter so / To slay herself, that should have slain her foe' (1826–7). The republic of Caesar's assassins, and the romantic heroism of Antony, are dying, and they die with them. But the Brutus of *Lucrece*, bent on driving out the Tarquins, is building a new Rome, and to him suicide seems pointless.

Political institutions

That new Rome will have no king. Tarquin's attack on Lucrece, triggered by her husband Collatine's praise of her, is given a political edge by the narrator's comment, 'Perhaps his boast of Lucrece' sov'reignty / Suggested [tempted] this proud issue of a king' (36–7). His royal pride can tolerate no rival claims. Lucrece, appealing to his better nature, calls 'for exiled majesty's repeal' (640), associating kingship with virtue; but the overall effect is that kingship is associated with Tarquin, and his crime leads to its abolition. The impact of this on the Roman collective memory is suggested in *Coriolanus* when a messenger equates Rome's relief at the news that Coriolanus will spare the city to its joy over the expulsion of the Tarquins (5.4.37–8). In *Julius Caesar* Cassius calls on Brutus to remember his great ancestor's role in that event (1.2.160–2). Caesar's ambition threatens a new monarchy. With an acquiescent senate and a republican faction that cannot consolidate its victory, the spirit of Caesar is unchecked even after death, when Antony imagines him calling for ruin 'with a monarch's voice' (3.1.275).

In *Antony and Cleopatra* Pompey, explaining why he opposes Caesar's successor Octavius, declares that like Brutus and Cassius he 'would / Have one man but a man' (2.6.18–19). But in that play the traditional institutions of the republic are even more shadowy than in *Julius Caesar*, and it comes down to a power struggle between two men, Octavius and Antony, in which the more skilled and ruthless player wins. In *Titus*

Andronicus the office of emperor has become a prize to fight over, like the crown in Shakespeare's English history plays. The play begins with the sons of the late emperor competing to succeed him, Bassianus appealing to virtue and nobility, Saturninus to the fact that he is the eldest son. Given the power to choose, Titus picks Saturninus. Technically this would be the right way to pick an English king, but here it is a disastrous blunder.

Roman political institutions are most acutely examined in *Coriolanus*. Menenius tries to suppress the citizens' revolt by telling them a fable of the other body parts rebelling against the belly. The point of the story for him is not that each member has an important role to play in the body but that only the belly does—by which he means the patricians. But the rebellion gains the citizens at least a vicarious role in Rome through the creation of tribunes to defend their interests, and while this seems a novelty, they have other rights that are long-standing and traditional. To be elected consul Coriolanus must plead for the people's votes, wearing a gown of humility. He does it, but under protest and with an ill grace: 'What custom wills, in all things should we do't, / The dust on antique time would lie unswept' (2.3.108–9). In the face of the people's traditional rights he is a radical; and he goes on to argue that if there are two centres of authority in the state the result is bound to be chaos (3.1.110–15).

In *Julius Caesar* the mob is fickle, swayed one way by Brutus's oratory and the opposite way by Antony's; once roused they are murderous. In *Antony and Cleopatra* the people are unseen, but described as 'slippery' (1.2.169). Something of their fickleness survives in *Coriolanus*, but there they have a greater desire for a real role in the state, and a more concentrated political will. In the give-and-take of politics the patricians unbend a little by granting them tribunes, and they unbend a little more by acknowledging Coriolanus's heroism as a claim to the consulship. But in the last analysis he is their enemy, and goaded by the tribunes they drive him into exile. Their triumph is short-lived: when he returns to destroy Rome they panic, disclaim responsibility—'though we willingly consented to his banishment, yet it was against our will' (4.6.152–4)—and turn on the tribunes who led them into this fix. In a play acutely critical of all sides—the patricians are blinkered by partisanship, Coriolanus is inhumanly arrogant—the judgement on the people seems to be that power is a toy too dangerous for them to play with.

Men and gods

Just as dangerous in their own way are the charismatic great men who rise above the institutions of Rome. The gods of Rome are not much in evidence. There are general invocations of 'the gods' and of particular deities for their standard attributes. But when in *Titus Andronicus* the hero sends messages to the gods for justice the only reply he gets is the entrance of a clown who thinks Jupiter is a gibbet- or gallows-maker

(4.3.79–80). Jupiter himself, powerful and intimidating, finally appears in *Cymbeline*, but that is under the conventions of romance. Yet *Julius Caesar* has a strong supernatural dimension centred on Caesar himself: his death is preceded by a storm and by weird sights in the streets of Rome; the Soothsayer and the augurers foretell it with deadly accuracy. Though its political analysis is realistic and acute, the play allows Caesar an air of magic that anticipates his later deification. In *Antony and Cleopatra* the depiction of Octavius's skill and Antony's ineptitude is equally realistic, but an Egyptian soothsayer sees another dimension, warning Antony,

> Thy daemon, that thy spirit which keeps thee, is
> Noble, courageous, high, unmatchable,
> Where Caesar's is not. But near him thy angel
> Becomes afeard, as being o'erpowered.
>
> (2.3.17-20)

Behind the life-sized political figures we see, projected like giant shadows on a wall, a battle of angels. No god appears in *Antony and Cleopatra*, but a god disappears; soldiers on sentry duty hear a mysterious music, which one of them interprets: ''Tis the god Hercules, whom Antony loved, / Now leaves him' (4.3.14–15). Antony's defeat has a supernatural dimension, and Octavius seems puzzled and disappointed that no omens mark his death (5.1.14–17).

In *Coriolanus*, a play as free of the supernatural as any of Shakespeare's, the hero's arrogance leads one of the tribunes to accuse him, 'You speak o'th' people as if you were a god / To punish, not a man of their infirmity' (3.1.85–6). His unstoppable violence in battle and his refusal to compromise in peace make Coriolanus seem hardly human. His pathological dislike of praise shows he cannot be beholden even to his friends. Though a patrician, he takes no interest in his ancestry, as though he were indeed, as he later claims to be, 'author of himself' (5.3.36). His reaction to banishment is to turn on the people and declare 'I banish you' (3.3.127), as though he himself is the city. When he returns with the Volsces to destroy Rome, the Romans no more think of resisting him than they would of fighting the sea, and as for the Volsces 'He is their god' (4.6.94). Shakespeare seems to be using him as a test case: is there a kind of man on whom society has no claim? The answer comes when the hero's family pleads with him to spare Rome, and he surrenders: 'I melt, and am not / Of stronger earth than others' (5.3.28–9). He is human after all, and the Volsces kill him for it.

Bodies on display

Shakespeare used Rome as a laboratory to try out the strength and weakness of political institutions, the relation of the individual to society, the power and the limits of charisma. Some of the power he sees resides in the human body itself, which is regularly on display. In life Julius Caesar can be argued about; in death he seems an unstoppable force, and one of the signs of this is the power of his corpse. As Calpurnia dreams of his statue running blood, Antony imagines his wounds as pleading mouths (3.1.262–4), and when towards the climax of his oration he uncovers Caesar's body the mob goes berserk. Coriolanus appears on the battlefield so covered in blood his own friends do not recognize him, and this sight too has charismatic power. It is a power he wants to husband and use on his own terms; a part of the election routine he particularly resents is the requirement to show his scars to the people. Scars are a joke in *Antony and Cleopatra*: 'I had a wound here that was like a T, / But now 'tis made an H' (4.8.4–5). Light-hearted though the moment is, it still uses wounds as tokens of valour, with a touch of allegory: the soldier who speaks is called Scarus.

Wounded female bodies have an equivalent power. Lucrece's corpse is paraded through the streets of Rome, and the rebellion against the Tarquins starts from there; her body has a power like that of Caesar's body. In *Titus Andronicus* the silent, mutilated Lavinia dominates every scene in which she appears, as she never did when she had speech; the sheer sight of her drives Titus first to grief and then to revenge. Part of the impact Coriolanus's family makes when they come to plead with him is, in the words of his mother Volumnia, 'our raiment / And state of bodies' (5.3.95–6).

Roman women

Women's bodies can have such impact in Shakespeare's Roman plays because in an intensely patriarchal society women have a special role and stand for a special set of values. They are values convenient to Roman men: chastity, domesticity, and silence. In the first act of *Coriolanus*, while the men are off fighting, the women '*set them down on two low stools and sew*' (1.3.0.2). Antony's Roman wife Octavia is, according to his friend Enobarbus, 'of a holy, cold, and still conversation'; Menas responds, 'Who would not have his wife so?' (2.6.120–1) (the answer in this case is, not Antony). Returning from the war, Coriolanus greets his wife Virgilia as 'My gracious silence' (2.1.161). When his wife and mother come to plead with him to spare Rome they are joined by Valeria, who is there not just to make up the magic number three but to stand for Roman womanhood in general. Coriolanus greets her as 'chaste as the icicle' that 'hangs on Dian's temple' (5.3.65–7).

These women take their value from their men: they are mothers, wives, daughters. In *Julius Caesar* Brutus's wife Portia virtually apologizes for being a woman, but asserts a dignity that comes from her marriage, and from a father renowned for his integrity: 'I grant I am a woman, but withal / A woman well reputed, Cato's daughter' (2.1.293–4). Coriolanus's mother Volumnia pours her considerable energy into celebrating the military achievements of her son and promoting his political career; she virtually lives through him. She is hardly a model of silence and withdrawal; those qualities are exemplified by Virgilia, who refuses, despite Volumnia's bullying, to leave the house until her husband has returned from the war. The women have opposite ways of honouring Coriolanus; the common factor is that they are both intensely focused on him.

The men in turn tend to use their women as trophies, and this can lead to trouble: Collatine in *The Rape of Lucrece* and Posthumus in *Cymbeline* both boast of their wives' chastity, provoking Tarquin and Giacomo to assault that chastity. So important is female chastity to a patriarchal state that in *Lucrece* the attack on the Roman matron is an attack on Rome. Tarquin's lust drives him 'To make the breach and enter this sweet city' (469). In the first act of *Titus Andronicus*, Saturninus and Bassianus compete for the empery, and then for Lavinia, implicitly equating her with Rome. This means that when in Act Two the Gothic princes Chiron and Demetrius rape her they are symbolically attacking Rome. Volumnia makes a similar equation when she tells Coriolanus that to attack Rome would be to tread on his mother's womb (5.3.123–6).

Beyond Rome

The attacks on Lucrece and Lavinia take place in symbolic wildernesses, as though the city they stand for, the city that protects them, has vanished. Lucrece is literally in her bedchamber, but finds herself pleading 'in a wilderness where are no laws' (544). Lavinia is attacked in a literal wilderness, a wood outside Rome. As the play's atrocities mount, the line between city and wood seems to dissolve and Titus complains, of the city he has served all his life, 'Rome is but a wilderness of tigers' (3.1.53). He has served Rome by fighting the Goths; now Saturninus has married the Gothic queen Tamora and the Goths are a power in Rome. Tamora, who is cuckolding Saturninus with her attendant Aaron the Moor, and who encourages her sons' rape of Lavinia, is the opposite of the chaste Roman matron. And yet her vengefulness has a cause. In the first act she pleaded with Titus and his family not to kill her first-born son, and she called them 'Roman brethren' (1.1.104), appealing to a shared set of values: 'O, if to fight for king and commonweal / Were piety in thine, it is in these' (1.114–15). Titus refuses the plea, and Tamora turns revenger. But we have seen that the division between Roman and outsider is not so clear-cut as we might have thought, and it is further weakened when Titus's son Lucius comes to clean up Rome at the head of a Gothic army, the Goths making common cause with him against their own queen.

The division between Rome and Other seems firmer in *Antony and Cleopatra*, where Rome is a place of political business and Egypt a place of luxury and pleasure. The Roman matron Octavia is opposed by Cleopatra: witty, voluble, hot-blooded, with a colourful sexual history. While Latin was everywhere in Shakespeare's England, Egyptian hieroglyphics had not yet been decoded, and were thought to conceal arcane mysteries. The greatest mystery is Cleopatra herself, whose infinite variety defies analysis, and who lives so totally in the moment that to ask at any point what her motives are, whether she is telling the truth or lying, is to pose unanswerable questions. She challenges conventional gender roles (of the sort Octavia exemplifies) by playing transsexual cross-dressing games with Antony (2.5.22–3). We have noted the Roman suspicion of monarchy; Cleopatra, in her tantrums no less than in her pride, is every inch a queen, and she dies robed and crowned, on a bed that seems transformed into a throne. Tamora insinuates herself into Rome, calling herself 'a Roman now adopted happily' (1.1.460). Cleopatra goes one better, co-opting a key Roman value for her own use, determined to commit suicide 'after the high Roman fashion' (4.16.89). In death she defies the Romans not just as the Queen of Egypt but as the noblest Roman of them all.

Antony and Cleopatra shows the consolidation of the Roman empire in the east. *Cymbeline* turns to its western frontier, but what it shows is not a simple victory of Rome over a foreign nation. For one thing, Britain is already to some degree Romanized. Its king, Cymbeline, though he provokes a Roman invasion by refusing to pay tribute to Caesar, is on friendly personal terms with the Roman ambassador and recalls with gratitude his early training under Caesar (3.1.67–70). Posthumus's father Sicilius fought the Romans, but the Roman Filario was Sicilius's friend, and when Posthumus is exiled from Britain, Filario takes him in. Posthumus returns to Britain as part of the Roman invasion, then switches sides to fight as a Briton, and then turns Roman again. This shuttling of national identities serves the plot, but also suggests Posthumus's double nationality as a Romanized Briton.

In *Cymbeline*, Rome is part classical Rome, part decadent modern Italy. The latter is exemplified by Giacomo, who is provoked by Posthumus's boasts of his wife Innogen's chastity to test that chastity. Invading her bedchamber, he compares himself to 'Our Tarquin' (2.2.12). Innogen is asleep; her bedtime reading was the story of Philomela, the story that lies behind the rape of Lavinia (*Titus Andronicus*, 2.3.44–6). History, or myth, seems about to repeat itself. But all Giacomo does is note the details of Innogen's chamber and steal a bracelet from her arm, to convince Posthumus he has succeeded. As Cleopatra dies in the high Roman fashion, Innogen—whose reading is Roman and whose chamber is decorated with stories from Roman myth and history—is a British Lucrece whose chastity remains inviolate.

The British defeat the Romans in battle; yet Cymbeline submits in the end to Caesar and agrees to pay tribute. His command, 'A Roman and a British ensign wave / Friendly together' (5.6.480–1) suggests a reconciliation of the two powers. But the Roman soothsayer's vision of an eagle vanishing into western sun could go beyond that, predicting (though the soothsayer is too loyal a Roman to read it this way) that Britain in the future will absorb Rome into its own life, as it has already absorbed its stories and emulated its valour. Shakespeare's Roman plays stand as one fulfilment of that prophecy.

FURTHER READING

Adelman, Janet. *The Common Liar: An Essay on 'Antony and Cleopatra'* (New Haven and London: Yale University Press, 1973). This detailed reading of *Antony and Cleopatra* concentrates on problems of interpretation and belief in a play that offers multiple perspectives on its action.

Cantor, Paul A. *Shakespeare's Rome: Republic and Empire* (Ithaca and London: Cornell University Press, 1976). Through a close analysis of *Coriolanus* and *Antony and Cleopatra*, Cantor argues that Shakespeare had an acute understanding of Rome at different stages of its political development.

Charney, Maurice. *Shakespeare's Roman Plays: The Function of Imagery in the Drama* (Cambridge, Ma.: Harvard University Press, 1961). Charney uses the imagery of *Julius Caesar*, *Antony and Cleopatra*, and *Coriolanus* to analyse the special character and atmosphere of each play.

Kahn, Coppélia. *Roman Shakespeare: Warriors, Wounds, and Women* (London and New York: Routledge, 1997). This feminist analysis, which includes *Lucrece*, *Titus Andronicus*, and *Cymbeline*, examines the importance of gender in constructing the idea of Rome.

MacCallum, M. W. *Shakespeare's Roman Plays and their Background* (London: Macmillan, 1910). This pioneering work is still valued for its thorough discussions of *Julius Caesar*, *Antony and Cleopatra*, and *Coriolanus* in relation to the source material.

Miles, Geoffrey. *Shakespeare and the Constant Romans* (Oxford: Clarendon Press, 1996). Miles traces the Roman value of constancy, stressing its ambiguity—is it virtue or role-playing?—through classical and Renaissance literature, concluding with discussions of *Julius Caesar*, *Coriolanus*, and *Antony and Cleopatra*.

Miola, Robert S. *Shakespeare's Rome* (Cambridge: Cambridge University Press, 1983). This is the first book to discuss the full range of Shakespeare's Roman work, including *Lucrece*, *Titus Andronicus*, and *Cymbeline*. It provides detailed commentary on Shakespeare's affinities with Roman literature, including Virgil, Ovid, and treatises on oratory.

READING: *Julius Caesar*

The road to assassination

Julius Caesar deals with Rome at a crucial turning point in its history. The republic, whose institutions were designed to keep any one person from getting too powerful, seems about to collapse in the wake of the victories of Julius Caesar, who is gathering for himself a power like that of a king. The last kings of Rome, the Tarquins, had been expelled centuries ago; now the monarchy seems on the brink of revival. There are pockets of resistance to Caesar; in the first scene the tribunes Flavius and Murellus rebuke the commoners for parading through the streets celebrating Caesar when they should be in their shops working. In the next scene we hear that as punishment for the gesture of removing the decorations from Caesar's images the tribunes have been 'put to silence' (1.2.280). Caesar is building the sort of regime we recognize all too well, one that brooks no opposition.

The resistance of the tribunes is short-lived; more serious is the conspiracy led initially by Cassius, whose aim is to assassinate Caesar on the assumption that only death can stop him. Cassius sees the growing power of Caesar as a sign of the degeneracy of Rome: 'he would not be a wolf / But that he sees the Romans are but sheep' (1.3.103–4), and Cassius goes on to call Rome 'trash' (1.3.107). Though he wants to preserve Roman liberty, his own language suggests that Rome is incapable of liberty. Yet the notion of restoring the monarchy seems stillborn. Casca reports a charade acted out by Caesar and his friend Mark Antony on the feast of Lupercal: Antony offers Caesar a crown three times, and each time (though, as Casca claims, with increasing reluctance) Caesar refuses it. This seems designed as an ostentatious display of Caesar's lack of ambition; it may even be designed to provoke the crowd into begging Caesar to take the crown. If this is the plan it misfires; every time Caesar refuses, the crowd cheers (1.2.235–70). Casca seems a bit vague about the kingly symbol in question, ''twas not a crown neither, 'twas one of these coronets' (1.2.237–8), as though the signs of monarchy, long out of use, are unfamiliar and do not register clearly. For Shakespeare's audience, used to thinking of monarchy as hereditary, the fact that his wife Calpurnia is barren would bode ill for Caesar's kingship (1.2.8–11).

Rome's problem, then, is to be caught between a dying republic and a stillborn monarchy. With no workable political institutions, what matters now is the pride and power of individual men. We see this when Cassius enlists Brutus in his conspiracy. He appeals to Brutus's family tradition, reminding him that one of his ancestors was a key figure in the expulsion of the Tarquins (1.2.160–2). But this is part of an appeal to Brutus's personal pride. Cassius does not present a political argument in favour of preserving the republic: rather he tells Brutus to weigh his name against Caesar's: 'Brutus and Caesar: what should be in that "Caesar"? / Why should that name be sounded more than yours?' (1.2.143–4).

He projects on to Brutus the personal jealousy he himself feels when he contemplates Caesar's power.

Rome is a place where men eye each other suspiciously. They are given to close analysis of each other's characters, weighing political advantage and political danger. Caesar has taken the measure of Cassius: 'Yon Cassius has a lean and hungry look. / He thinks too much. Such men are dangerous' (1.2.195–6). The cynical shrewdness of this judgement reveals one of the sources of Caesar's power; he knows people. Brutus tries his hand at analysing Caesar, but his touch is less sure. In soliloquy he argues that he should kill Caesar not because Caesar is showing any signs of tyranny now but because he might become a tyrant if he were crowned (2.1.10–34). Yet the signs of Caesar's incipient tyranny are everywhere.

Once he joins the conspiracy Brutus immediately becomes its leader, and his way of doing so is to disagree with any proposal that comes from someone else. Such is his standing with his fellows that he always prevails. Cassius proposes adding the famous orator Cicero to their number, and Metellus supports this, claiming Cicero will increase their prestige. It seems a plausible argument, but Brutus contradicts it with a brisk piece of character analysis: 'he will never follow anything / That other men begin' (2.1.150–1). Cassius urges that Antony be killed as well as Caesar; Brutus counters that Antony is so dependent on Caesar that without him he will be harmless. He gains his point, over Cassius's protests. The result is disaster, as Antony's funeral oration turns the mob against the conspirators, and they have to flee the city they thought to liberate. In Brutus's contrariness we see Shakespeare's own character analysis at work: Brutus needs to be right, he needs to be the leader, and all the ideas have to come from him. Cassius was the leader until Brutus joined; Brutus overrules him at every turn, here and in the war that follows; and events always prove Brutus wrong.

The assassination itself is both a success and a failure; it kills Caesar but not his power. It is presented self-consciously, by both the playwright and the characters, as a famous event. There is a sense in which, even from the beginning of the play, it has already happened: the audience's knowledge of what is coming colours the early scenes, and the Soothsayer's warning, 'Beware the ides of March' (1.2.20), fixes the date. On the morning of the event, Brutus's wife Portia hears 'a bustling rumour, like a fray, / And the wind brings it from the Capitol' (2.4.19–20). She hears it before it happens, as though it projects itself backward in time. It also projects itself forward. Caesar dies speaking Latin: '*Et tu, Bruté?* [And you, Brutus?]' then returns to English to make his death an act of his own will: 'Then fall Caesar' (3.1.76). He seems to be fixing his own death as a memorable moment, an image of a great man struck down by ingratitude and treachery. His speaking in Latin makes the moment a past action breaking through time and re-creating itself in the present.

When the conspirators stoop and wash in Caesar's blood, an action that suggests a primitive ritual beneath the assassination, they project themselves forward in time:

> CASSIUS: . . . How many ages hence
>   Shall this our lofty scene be acted over,
>   In states unborn and accents yet unknown!

> BRUTUS: How many times shall Caesar bleed in sport,
>   That now on Pompey's basis lies along,
>   No worthier than the dust!
> CASSIUS: So oft as that shall be,
>   So often shall the knot of us be called
>   The men that gave their country liberty.
>   (3.1.112-19)

They are right about the event, wrong about the interpretation. If we can imagine them for the moment as their historical counterparts, they speak these words in a language that does not yet exist, and (in the first production) on a stage in a country that for them would be an obscure northern island (and long after Shakespeare's death, the prophecy continues to resonate, in theatres and languages unknown to him). To that extent the conspirators are right about the fame of their deed, and their prediction is confirmed every time the play is acted.

The spirit of Caesar

But they are not remembered as the men who gave their country liberty. In his carefully crafted funeral oration Brutus pays tribute to Caesar's virtues, outlines the reasons for his death, and concludes, 'The question of his death is enrolled in the Capitol' (3.2.34–5). The matter is now on public record, written down, fixed, and finished. But the story is coming to us as living theatre, not as written history, and it is not finished at all. Half the play is still to come, and while Brutus wins the crowd's assent at first, Antony wins them back with oratory more dazzling, emotional, and cynically manipulative than his. The result is that Caesar becomes more powerful dead than living.

Even when living he seems to be something greater than the character we see on stage. What the actor plays is a man with a certain shrewdness and charm, but with a boastfulness that masks the insecurity we glimpse in his suspicion of Cassius. Cassius dwells on Caesar's physical frailty, and Caesar himself admits to being deaf in one ear. Yet his charisma is extraordinary: all eyes are on him, all conversations are about him. Brutus wishes he could kill Caesar's spirit without killing Caesar (2.1.167–71). In fact he and his fellows do just the opposite: killing Caesar they release his spirit and make it more powerful than ever. Antony, with Caesar's body lying before him, predicts what will happen:

> . . . Caesar's spirit, ranging for revenge,
> With Ate by his side come hot from hell,
> Shall in these confines with a monarch's voice
> Cry 'havoc!' and let slip the dogs of war . . .
>   (3.1.273-6)

Ate was the goddess of discord, and the final image is of animals unleashed. Antony himself unleashes the mob, whipping them up into a murderous rage, seeming not to care about the consequences: 'Mischief, thou art afoot. / Take thou what course thou wilt' (3.2.249–50).

We seem to have gone from the spirit of Caesar to a generalized force of chaos. But it was Antony's tribute to Caesar, his display of Caesar's body, and his reading of Caesar's will, that whipped the mob to frenzy. In the later scenes Caesar seems not just a memory to be fought over but a living presence. His ghost appears to Brutus, identifying itself as Brutus's evil spirit (4.2.333), as though he and Brutus—we remember that climactic '*Et tu, Bruté?*'—are now closer than ever. Not only has Brutus failed to free Rome from Caesar; Caesar is now part of him. In defeat Cassius and Brutus both take the Roman way out, suicide; but as Brutus reads the death of Cassius it is Caesar's act, not his own:

> O Julius Ceasar, thou art mighty yet.
> Thy spirit walks abroad, and turns our swords
> Into our own proper entrails.
>
> (5.3.93-5)

Cassius dies addressing the man he killed: 'Caesar, thou art revenged, / Even with the sword that killed thee' (5.3.44–5). So does Brutus: 'Caesar, now be still. / I killed not thee with half so good a will' (5.5.50–1). It is as though they imagine Caesar with them as they die. Even the risk Shakespeare takes with the play's structure, killing the title character when the play is only half over, shows the continuing impact of Caesar beyond death.

Breakdown

No state, however, can be governed for long by the spirit of a dead man. At a political level Rome remains unsettled. Antony, having with flaming rhetoric unleashed Caesar's spirit, cools into ordinary political cynicism. The climax of his appeal to the mob, hitting them with something close to home, is to read Caesar's will, in which every Roman citizen is to get seventy-five drachmas and Caesar's estates are to become public parks (3.2.231–40). But the will having served its purpose, Antony consults with Caesar's successor Octavius and their colleague Lepidus about reducing the legacies (4.1.7–9).

Lepidus having left the stage, Antony argues with Octavius over whether such a 'slight, unmeritable man' (4.1.12)—the character analysis continues—is fit to share power with them. Octavius insists he is, and the dispute is unresolved. The fractiousness Brutus introduced into the conspiracy by contradicting every proposal put by someone else now affects Caesar's party. As they prepare for battle Antony tells Octavius to take the left side of the field, Octavius insists on taking the right, and when Antony asks 'Why do you cross me in this exigent?' Octavius replies, 'I do not cross you, but I will do so' (5.1.19–20). If the spirit of Caesar lives, so does the spirit of contradiction. At the end of the play the conspirators are dead, and to that extent the action is resolved; but we are projected into a future in which Antony and Octavius will turn on each other.

The first three acts take place in a fully conceived Rome: on the locationless stage of Shakespeare's Globe the language of the play evokes the streets, houses, and shops of the city; we are in Brutus's orchard, then in the Capitol, then in the Forum. There is a clear sense of place. In the last two acts Rome has vanished, along with most of the characters from the first part of the play, and armies march across landscapes that are virtually featureless. We are at Sardis, then at Philippi. The one is in Asia Minor (modern Turkey), the other in Greece; but we have to look that up. There is no local atmosphere, no sense of place. In this empty space Roman gestures continue to be acted out—the suicides of the losing generals, the funeral tribute in which Antony calls Brutus 'the noblest Roman of them all' (5.5.67)—but they seem to be the last echoes of a Rome that has vanished, and that survives as gesture alone. A young man appears on the battlefield proclaiming himself heir to a famous Roman family: 'I am the son of Marcus Cato, ho!' (5.4.4). He is killed at once. The new Rome Octavius will build (under his new name, Augustus) lies beyond the ending of this play and is only hinted at in *Antony and Cleopatra*. It will be a very different place. Here Shakespeare shows only the old Rome emptying out.

Private lives

There is also in this play a curious emptiness at the personal level. Brutus and Cassius constantly, and with increasing desperation on Cassius's part, appeal to each other's friendship. But while there is occasional passion between them, the passions we see are anger and need. There is no warmth, no hint of a private life; the matters they discuss are political and military. Once they touch on philosophy: Cassius asks Brutus what he will do if they are defeated, and Brutus replies by arguing against suicide in one speech and for it in the next (5.1.95–113). There is no meeting of minds here, as in the Roman ideal of intellectual friendship: Cassius puts a question, and Brutus replies with contradict- ory gestures. In his last moments Cassius describes Titinius, not Brutus, as his best friend (5.3.35). After Cassius's death Brutus, though certainly touched, declares he has not yet time to mourn properly and adds, 'His funerals shall not be in our camp, / Lest it discomfort us' (5.3.104–5). Is he covering up feeling, or lack of feeling? We see Brutus at his most human in a small domestic scene with his servant Lucius (4.2.303–23). Here for once he is off guard, not trying to impress anyone, and we see an attractive courtesy and gentleness. With his fellow public figures he is always in competition, always on display.

Of all Shakespeare's Roman plays *Julius Caesar* gives the smallest role to women. Caesar makes public reference to Calpurnia's barrenness, and in private takes her dreams of his coming murder seriously only when they are alone together. Decius Brutus, appealing to Caesar's pride and his fear of being laughed at, wins him round easily, and he goes to the Capitol and to his death. Calpurnia has dreamed true, her concern for Caesar is real, but the play leaves her behind as Caesar does. We see how Rome takes Caesar's death; but at this point Calpurnia has vanished.

Brutus's wife Portia has a more prominent role; she too is concerned for her husband, disturbed at the signs of trouble she sees in him and at his attempt to hide this trouble from her. She makes an eloquent appeal to be taken seriously as his wife, asking if she is only 'To keep with you at meals, comfort your bed, / And talk to you sometimes?' (2.1.283–4). He is moved, and offers to share his secrets with her—but she has to wait, because there has just been a knock on the door (2.1.301–8). It is clear that she knows of the coming assassination; but the impression given in performance is that like Calpurnia, though more gently, she is put aside.

Her appeals to be taken seriously are appeals for a role in a male-dominated world: she argues that though she is a woman, she is Brutus's wife and Cato's daughter (2.1.291–4). She has proved her constancy by giving herself 'a voluntary wound / Here in the thigh' (2.1.299–300), an attack on her own body that comes close to genital mutilation. It is the closest she can come to the honourable wounds of a soldier. The last we hear of her is Brutus's report of her terrible death. Grieving at her husband's absence and at the growing power of Antony and Octavius, Portia, 'her attendants absent, swallowed fire' (4.2.208). Elsewhere Shakespeare makes the damaged body of the Roman woman, Lucrece in *The Rape of Lucrece* and Lavinia in *Titus Andronicus*, a public spectacle and a call to action. Caesar dies in public, on a crowded stage, Antony makes a public display of his body, and his spirit resonates through the rest of the play. The loneliness of Portia's death is compounded by the way Brutus uses it as an occasion to display Roman self-control by concealing his feelings (or his lack of feelings?) about it. This draws the admiration of his colleague Messala, who has told him to bear the news 'like a Roman': 'Even so great men great losses should endure' (4.2.240, 245). In a world in which men watch each other closely, Brutus has displayed his Roman virtue. But in Cassius's comment 'my nature could not bear it so' (4.2.247) there may be a touch of rebuke. With the republic dead and the empire not yet born, the idea of Rome survives in gestures such as these, held up for admiration. But we may wonder if as something of Rome survives, something of humanity is lost.

FURTHER READING

Berry, Ralph. *Tragic Instance* (Newark: University of Delaware Press; London: Associated University Presses, 1999). This collection of essays on Shakespearian tragedy includes an account of the special character of Roman society in *Julius Caesar*.

Granville-Barker, Harley. *Prefaces to Shakespeare* (Princeton: Princeton University Press, 1952). 2 vols. Written by one of the pioneers of twentieth-century Shakespeare production, this collection of prefaces includes an account of the way *Julius Caesar* works in performance.

Liebler, Naomi Conn. *Shakespeare's Festive Tragedy: The Ritual Foundations of Genre* (London and New York: Routledge, 1995). This work includes an essay on the importance of communal rituals in *Julius Caesar*.

Paster, Gail Kern. ' "In the Spirit of Men, there is no Blood": Blood as a Trope of Gender in *Julius Caesar*', *Shakespeare Quarterly*, 40 (1989), 284–98. This essay explores the gender significance of the play's blood imagery.

Ripley, John. *'Julius Caesar' on Stage in England and America, 1599–1973* (Cambridge: Cambridge University Press, 1980). This detailed stage history shows how productions of *Julius Caesar* have reflected changing theatrical and political conditions.

20 | Romances

Reginald Foakes

The term 'romance' provides a convenient label for a group of Shakespeare's late plays, *Pericles*, *Cymbeline*, *The Winter's Tale*, and *The Tempest*. Although Shakespeare never used the word in his plays, it usefully suggests the idea of fictions that are unrealistic, works that create a world dominated by chance rather than character or cause and effect, and plays in which we are attuned to delight in and wonder at the unexpected. Such fictions may involve sudden tempests or disasters, separations between parents and children or between friends or lovers, wanderings and shipwrecks, wives and children lost and found, strange accidents and coincidences, encounters with the marvellous, and eventual reconciliations and reunions.

The English word 'romance' was derived from French, and at first associated with long French poems, such as the *Chanson de Roland* or *The Romance of the Rose*, translated by Chaucer. In his *Art of English Poesy* (1589), George Puttenham thought of romances as 'Stories of old time', such as *Bevis of Southampton*, *Guy of Warwick*, and 'such other old Romances or historical rhymes'. In Shakespeare's age the word was chiefly identified with old chivalric verse narratives and folk tales, and there were many like Puttenham who regarded these with a certain disdain, if only to differentiate them from the more sophisticated kinds of romance that were widely read by educated readers, such works as Edmund Spenser's long unfinished poem *The Faerie Queene* (1590–9), and Sir Philip Sidney's prose *Arcadia* (1590). By this time simpler prose romances had become very popular, and Shakespeare used one, Robert Greene's *Pandosto* (1588 and many later editions) as his main source for *The Winter's Tale*.

The word 'romance' is only as old as French, but fictions containing romance motifs are, of course, much older, perhaps as old as literature itself, a notable example being Homer's tales of the wanderings of Odysseus in the *Odyssey*. Prose Greek romances, written mostly in the second and third centuries AD, began to appear in translation in the later sixteenth century, beginning with the *Aethiopica* of Heliodorus, translated into English in 1569. These had a considerable impact on the literature, especially prose fiction, of Shakespeare's age. He used only one as a direct source, the story of Apollonius of Tyre, as retold in John Gower's *Confessio Amantis*, first printed in 1493, and published again in 1554, which forms the basis for *Pericles*, but he probably knew others. He also seems to have been acquainted with more recent European forms of romance, such as the sprawling *Amadis de Gaul*, partly translated from the Spanish into

French in 1577, and Italian epic romances such as Torquato Tasso's *Jerusalem Delivered*, translated by Edward Fairfax in 1600. Shakespeare certainly knew well the work of Spenser and Sidney's *Arcadia*, from which he borrowed material for the subplot of *King Lear*.

Romances tend to spin one fiction out of another, and have no particular shape, indeed, may go on, as it seems to modern readers, interminably. They demand that their readers take pleasure in the telling of the tale rather than in neatness of plot or characterization. Romances tend to take place in far-off or invented places or times, such as the 'deserts of Bohemia' in Act Three of *The Winter's Tale* and the imaginary island of *The Tempest*. They opened up imaginative vistas for Shakespeare's age when most people, like the playwright himself as far as we know, had no opportunity for travel overseas.

Romance and tragicomedy

It is helpful to relate the idea of Shakespeare's late plays as romances to another perspective: they are also tragicomedies, for it is the nature of romance to be inclusive, to mingle episodes of misery or grief with incidents of joy and triumph. Sir Philip Sidney had poured scorn on what he called 'mongrel tragi-comedy' in his *Apology for Poetry* (1586), and the term only gained wider currency and approval after 1600. Those who collected Shakespeare's plays in the First Folio of 1623 arranged them under the headings Comedies, Histories, and Tragedies. They placed *The Tempest* at the beginning of the volume as the first of the comedies, and *The Winter's Tale* as the final comedy, while *Cymbeline* was included among the tragedies. *Pericles, Prince of Tyre* was left out of the Folio, and survives in a dubious text, published in 1609. It was perhaps partly written by George Wilkins, with whom Shakespeare may have collaborated (see below, p. 254). So these late plays were not called tragicomedies when printed, any more than they were called romances.

Tragicomedy, however, became increasingly modish during the early years of the seventeenth century, as a form given definition notably by Giambattista Guarini in his *Compendium of Tragicomic Poetry* (1601). He describes tragicomedy as follows:

He who composes tragicomedy takes from tragedy its great persons but not its great action, its verisimilar plot but not its true one, its movement of the feelings but not its disturbance of them, its pleasure but not its sadness, its danger but not its death; from comedy it takes laughter that is not excessive, modest amusement, feigned difficulty, happy reversal, and above all the comic order.

Guarini was anxious to define a mode of drama that would not offend against the 'decorum of a well-bred man', and that would appeal to an upper-class audience. Shakespeare and other dramatists writing for the King's Men, such as John Fletcher, with whom Shakespeare collaborated later in *Henry VIII* and *The Two Noble Kinsmen*, were increasingly attracted to tragicomedy from about 1609. Their plays were much in demand at times when the royal court required entertainment, and they were also, from this date onwards, catering for the higher class of spectator frequenting their more expensive indoor Blackfriars theatre, as well as for the crowds at the Globe (see Chapter 3). Tragicomedy seems to have appealed to a well-bred audience by allowing them to stay relaxed, and by not demanding a strong emotional engagement while offering a pleasant variety of entertaining incidents which could be enjoyed for their own sake.

A point of great importance made by Guarini is his concern that tragicomedy must reveal 'above all the comic order'. The overall development of romance and tragicomedy is towards recognitions and reconciliations, leading to some kind of final harmony. Tragicomedy is in the end a form of comedy, and the Folio editors were right to place *The Tempest* and *The Winter's Tale* among Shakespeare's comedies. They may have been uncertain where to place *Cymbeline*, set, like *King Lear*, in ancient Britain, and so left it to the end and placed it last in the volume. Some of Shakespeare's earlier comedies exploit romance motifs, as, for example, do *The Comedy of Errors* and *Twelfth Night*, in both of which plays twins separated by shipwreck are eventually joyfully reunited by chance after various adventures.

Shakespeare had also written serious tragicomedies, often called the 'dark' comedies, roughly between 1602 and 1605, when he was influenced by the new satirical plays of John Marston and Ben Jonson, written for the companies of boy actors playing at St Paul's and Blackfriars. The dark comedies, *Troilus and Cressida*, *All's Well that Ends Well*, and *Measure for Measure*, also have a satirical edge (as discussed also in Chapter 21). Heroes are diminished in figures such as Troilus, prostrated by infatuation; in Bertram, a tetchy adolescent; and in Angelo, who cannot control his lust. Heroines too are unconventional, the Trojan Cressida seduced and handed over to become a plaything for the Greeks; Helena singlemindedly pursuing the unpleasant Bertram; and Isabella almost fanatical in her self-discipline. Each of these plays also has a scurrilous jester (Thersites, Parolles, Lucio) who undermines the earnestness of others, and each is concerned directly with sexual drives rather than with the course of true love.

Once the satirists made sexuality rather than romantic love the focus of their plays, it was there to stay. Satire, however, was not best suited to a well-bred or courtly audience, and as a new mode of tragicomedy emerged in the late plays of Shakespeare and the early works of Beaumont and Fletcher, it developed in tandem with the court entertainment called a masque (see below p. 252). Romance as tragicomedy was developed by John Fletcher in ways that would perhaps have pleased Guarini, whose work he knew and emulated in his play *The Faithful Shepherdess* (c.1608) which invited comparison with Guarini's *Il Pastor Fido* or *The Faithful Shepherd* (1589).

Fletcher and his collaborator Francis Beaumont had a first great success with their play *Philaster* (c.1609), which uses conventions of romance drawn from prose works such as Sidney's *Arcadia* in a dramatic action set in a mythical Sicily. The play was better known by its subtitle, *Love lies a-bleeding*, referring to the sensational moment when the hero, Philaster, supposing Arethusa, the princess he loves, has betrayed him by having an affair with his page, Bellario, stabs her in the breast. The woodcut frontispiece to the 1620 quarto shows Arethusa costumed in the fashion of the period, with full breasts exposed and spouting blood. A 'country fellow' who tries to intervene is rebuked by Arethusa: 'What ill-bred man art thou, to intrude thyself / Upon our private sports, our recreations?' (4.5.91–2). The country fellow does not understand her, but the well-bred audience might have seen her 'sport' as a daring sexual encounter, a kind of symbolic deflowering. The whole situation seems contrived for this effect. Arethusa would have been played by a boy, as would Bellario, the page who turns out to be a disguised girl in love with Philaster, who later stabs him/her too. Guarini had defined tragicomedy as dealing with danger but not death, and here Beaumont and Fletcher created a situation designed to titillate a Jacobean audience by staging an act that suggests a kind of sexual penetration, seems very dangerous, but has no lasting consequences. Arethusa's wound is soon forgotten, and she is united with Philaster in marriage.

Tragicomedy, theatricality, and the court masque

The aristocratic characters in *Philaster* seem to be consciously performing their roles, and may be compared with figures in the masques that were a prominent feature of the court of King James and Queen Anne. A masque typically begins with an anti-masque of witches or other forces symbolizing evil, who might be played by professional actors, as in Ben Jonson's *Masque of Queens* (1609). These were suddenly dismayed by the stunning revelation of the House of Fame, in which sat twelve legendary queens famous for their virtue. After driving out the witches, the queens, among them the real Queen Anne, consort of James I, 'took out the men', or chosen spectators, in a dance.

The witches were masked, but the aristocrats who played the queens did not wear vizards, and everyone knew who they were. The audience was conscious of the performer within the role, and the masque projected an image of the monarch and his courtiers as representing virtue, light, and order, overthrowing and dispelling forces of darkness and disorder. Jacobean ideals of royalty and rule were staged in such performances. Being king or courtier meant looking and behaving in certain ways, consciously acting out the part.

Beaumont and Fletcher combine theatricality, a sense of characters consciously playing roles, as in a masque, with an emphasis on sexual assault or deviation designed to shock or titillate their well-bred audience. Shakespeare's genius can be seen in the very different way these influences affected him. His romances also deal with sexual violence (incest in *Pericles*, rape in *Cymbeline*, adultery in *The Winter's Tale*, and threatened rape in *The Tempest*) but not in ways that are merely sensational and have no consequences. Each of these plays has a prominent role for fathers and daughters in a dramatic world where the rule of a kingdom or dukedom is at stake.

In all but *The Tempest*, the daughter (Marina, Innogen, Perdita) is separated from her parent(s) by force of circumstances, and they are reunited only at the end of the play. The heroines are somewhat idealized, as characters who have the courage, strength of will, and virtue to withstand and overcome whatever sexual threats they face. Marina, confined to a brothel in *Pericles*, almost puts it out of business by her 'peevish chastity', as the bawd Boult calls it. In *Cymbeline*, Innogen escapes from threatened rape and murder by setting off for Wales in disguise. Perdita has a charmed life in *The Winter's Tale*, in which play it is her mother, Hermione, who survives charges of adultery, brutal imprisonment, and the threat of death to be reunited eventually with husband and daughter. In *The Tempest*, Miranda is under her father's protection on a fictitious island where Caliban desires to rape her. Whereas sexual penetration is a 'sport' in *Philaster*, in Shakespeare's plays it is an aspect of life that the heroines have to face in a rough world, and a threat to be rejected by firm adherence to an idea of virtuous conduct. The daughters seem by nature innocent and determined to preserve their virginity until they can marry.

Shakespeare's romances are also consciously theatrical, and each of them contains a masque or masque-like elements. Here again the difference from Beaumont and Fletcher illustrates Shakespeare's distinction as a dramatist. Whereas they exploit their artifice by contriving a series of situations in which characters strike attitudes in ways that ensure the action cannot be taken very seriously, Shakespeare invites audiences to experience new ways of understanding the human predicament through the theatrical self-awareness of his romances. The action of *Pericles* is framed and commented on by the chorus of the medieval poet John Gower, who presents it as an old story, a fiction which he partly relates and partly shows on stage. *Cymbeline* begins with a gentleman narrating to an incredulous visitor the improbable story of the king being unable in twenty years to trace the loss of his children, assuring him,

> Howsoe'er 'tis strange,
> Or that the negligence may well be laughed at,
> Yet is it true, sir.
>
> (1.1.66-8)

The title *The Winter's Tale* literally suggested an implausible old tale such as might be told by the fireside on a winter's night. *The Tempest* begins with a storm at sea and with Prospero's fantastic tale of being usurped in Milan, thrust out to sea in a rotten boat (sea at Milan?), and coming ashore on a fabulous island.

A sense of strangeness or estrangement from ordinary expectations is established in three of these plays, which represent events as strange yet true, to be apprehended as facts, not in terms of causes and motives or as occasions for moralizing. Things happen fortuitously and without warning, and at any moment, it seems, someone may cry, 'Thou metst with things dying, I with things new-born' (*The Winter's Tale*, 3.3.104–5).

In the last play, *The Tempest*, Prospero shapes the action by magic, so that we are always conscious of his artifice.

The characters in these last plays inhabit imagined worlds in which they are at the mercy of external forces (such as storms and shipwrecks) or internal pressures (such as the sudden jealousy of *The Winter's Tale*'s Leontes) over which they have little or no control. The action of each play concerns the effects events have over a period of time, roughly the span of a generation, about sixteen years in *Pericles*, twenty in *Cymbeline*, sixteen in *The Winter's Tale*, twelve in *The Tempest*. The theatrical self-consciousness of these plays and the distancing of the action enabled Shakespeare to portray his characters in relation to a pattern that is revealed only in a long time-span, and which remains inscrutable to the characters. They are not presented, so to speak, in close-up, or as burdened with choices, anxious like Hamlet whether to be or not to be, or like Macbeth whether to do or not to do, but rather as figures distanced in a large canvas, where their deeds and sufferings are in the end small matters in a world subject to the whims of Fortune and of Time. A winged figure representing Time appears as a chorus to Act Four in *The Winter's Tale*, announcing his indifference as far as humans are concerned:

> I that please some, try all: both joy and terror
> Of good and bad; that makes and unfolds error . . .
>
> (4.1.1-2)

Time in the larger perspective, like fortune in its immediate shifts and changes, brings joy and terror to good and bad alike, with no moral concern. Even suffering and death in these plays become happenings, details in the larger picture, to be accepted as part of existence.

Pericles

The first of Shakespeare's romances, *Pericles*, was published in a quarto in 1609, as performed at the Globe according to the title-page, and had been reprinted three times by 1619. The first nine scenes are prosaic and may have been contributed by George Wilkins, author of the novel, *The Painful Adventures of Pericles*, which appeared in 1608. Shakespeare's characteristic verse and complex imagery are found mainly in the later scenes. The textual problems of the play remain unsolved. Nevertheless, it was evidently popular and may have seemed very innovative when it was first played in 1607 or 1608. It is the most sensational of Shakespeare's romances, if anything overstuffed with action.

The play opens with the Chorus, Gower, drawing attention to a row of severed heads, not such an extraordinary image of violence as it would be today, since the heads of executed traitors were to be seen mounted on spikes on London Bridge, but still a striking display on stage. The heads once belonged to the many men who lost their lives in a failed attempt to explain the riddle of the king Antiochus in order to win his daughter as their bride. The heads are not merely emblems of cruelty, for they serve also to teach Pericles a lesson, to recognize his 'frail mortality':

> For death remembered should be like a mirror
> Who tells us life's but breath, to trust it error.
>   (1.88-9)

If life cannot be trusted, as frail and subject to chance, it is easier to understand why men should be drawn to take risks, and why Pericles himself has a go at solving the riddle. Pericles, of course, succeeds, making an enemy of Antiochus by revealing that the King has been practising incest with his daughter, and so Pericles is forced to escape and set off on his travels.

The play is full of incident, spectacle, and non-stop action, as Fortune alternately oppresses and favours Pericles. He enters 'wet' in Scene Five, cast ashore after his ship is wrecked. In Scene Eleven he is 'a-shipboard' in another storm, apparently about to be shipwrecked again, with a new-born daughter Marina and a wife, Thaisa, he supposes is dead. In Scene Sixteen Marina, now full-grown, walks on the sea-shore, where she is threatened with murder and is rescued by a band of pirates who suddenly arrive. Scene Twenty-one begins on board the ship of Pericles, whose voyages finally bring him to the temple of Diana at Ephesus. The first scenes follow the adventures of Pericles as he travels from Antioch to Tyre, pursued by a murderer, goes on to Tharsus, and thence to Pentapolis, where he fights in a tournament to win the hand of Simonides' daughter Thaisa, and arrives back in Tyre. The action then switches to Marina, now grown up, who is rescued from a murderer only to find herself traded to a brothel-keeper. Add the several dumb-shows that intervene in the choric speeches of Gower, and there is enough going on for several plays.

Whenever something good or bad happens, 'fortune's mood / Varies again' (10.46–7). There seems no reason why Pericles has to suffer so much, losing, as he thinks, both wife and daughter before they are restored to him at the end, in a reunion he sees as 'this great miracle' (22.81). In the course of his wanderings he accepts what happens: 'We cannot but obey / The pow'rs above us' (13.9–10), but those powers remain inscrutable, as his 'courses' are 'orderèd / By Lady Fortune' (18.41–2). At the end, when the winds blow his ship to Ephesus, and the ailing Pericles, King of Tyre, who has not spoken for three months, is restored to health and speech by reunion with Marina and with his wife Thaisa, Gower finally rounds off the play by finding a pattern in what we have 'seen':

> In Pericles, his queen, and daughter seen,
> Although assailed with fortune fierce and keen,
> Virtue preserved from fell destruction's blast,
> Led on by heav'n, and crowned with joy at last.
>   (22.110-13)

Only in retrospect do events that appear to have been random begin to make some sense and allow the possibility that the gods or heaven have some care for human affairs, as marked in the very moving reunion of Pericles with his daughter and his wife after being separated for years.

Cymbeline

A denser and richer play in which several actions are interwoven, *Cymbeline* (c.1609–10) involves varied conventions, as if to enhance the sense of contrivance. At first the play seems to be about the adventures of Posthumus and his wife Innogen, daughter of Cymbeline, King of Britain. The banished Posthumus goes off to what appears to be Renaissance Rome, and shockingly bets that Giacomo, an Italianate villain, can't seduce his wife. In a powerful scene of visual rape, Giacomo succeeds in establishing plausible evidence that he has won the bet. Threatened with death by her husband, and with rape by the Queen's son Cloten, Innogen sets off in disguise for Wales. At the same time, ancient Romans arrive to claim tribute in the name of the emperor Augustus; when it is denied they promise war. In a series of extraordinary coincidences, Innogen makes her way towards Milford Haven, encountering on the way the long-lost sons of Cymbeline. There she runs into the Roman general Lucius, who for no obvious reason has invaded Britain at the same port, and who promptly takes Fidele (Innogen disguised as a page) into his service. In the final act the king's sons, their mentor Belarius, and Posthumus win the battle, but Posthumus is arrested and gaoled when he puts on Roman costume, while Giacomo, who has fought with the Romans, and Lucius are taken prisoner. A whole series of discoveries is needed to unravel the complications of the plots. Among them are the sudden death of the Queen; the revelations that a 'Roman' prisoner is really Posthumus, that Fidele is really Innogen, that Belarius is really Morgan, and that his two 'sons', Polydore and Cadwal, are really the King's lost sons Guiderius and Arviragus; and Giacomo's confession of the dirty trick he played on Posthumus.

This final scene brilliantly resolves with an overt theatrical cleverness all the complications of the intricate plotting of the play. Again chance and fortune are prominent in human affairs, in which, as Innogen famously says, mistaking the body of Cloten for that of her husband Posthumus, 'Our very eyes / Are sometimes like our judgements, blind' (4.2.303–4). Although the play is nominally set in the reign of Cunobellus (Cymbeline) during the period when Jesus Christ was born, it contains no reference to this event. The gods are represented by Jupiter, who unexpectedly descends sitting on an eagle in a spectacular stage effect, only to announce to a group of apparitions of Posthumus's family (and to the audience),

> Whom best I love, I cross, to make my gift,
> The more delayed, delighted.
>
> (5.5.195-6)

Jupiter is hardly to be distinguished from fortune if he thwarts those he best loves.

As in *Pericles*, only in retrospect, when all is resolved, everyone pardoned, and harmony restored, does it appear that some larger dispensation may be at work, so that Cymbeline can cry, 'Laud we the gods' (5.6.476). Virtue finally wins out, though uneasily, as Posthumus strikes the page Fidele when Fidele interrupts Posthumus' confession that, as he thinks, he killed his wife Innogen, only for him to discover that the page is Innogen, alive after all, and in disguise. This incident is unlike the wounding of Arethusa in *Philaster*, in that it marks a final humbling of Posthumus, a recognition of his own blindness, preparing for the joy of his reunion with her.

A final twist in the action is the restoration of peace, and the resubmission of Cymbeline, in spite of winning the battle, to Rome; but then as Lucius says,

> Consider, sir, the chance of war. The day
> Was yours by accident.
>
> (5.6.75-6)

No one is concerned for the slaughter on the battlefield, as described by Posthumus (5.5.5–51), or for the death of Cloten, casually decapitated by Guiderius, or the death of the Queen. Such things happen, and are accepted in the recognition shown in the great dirge sung by Guiderius and Arviragus when they think Innogen is dead,

> Fear no more the heat o'th' sun,
>   Nor the furious winter's rages;
> Thou thy worldly task hast done,
>   Home art gone and ta'en thy wages.
> Golden lads and girls all must,
> As chimney-sweepers, come to dust.
>   (4.2.259-64)

If there is a pattern, death is part of it, as is seen also in the more powerful play *The Winter's Tale* (1611) in which Antigonus is notoriously pursued off stage and killed by a bear. *The Winter's Tale* has a different structure, the first part set in Sicily, the second part in Bohemia sixteen years later. It also has less incident and, in its special way, a greater development of character, but in this play too judgement is often blind, accidents and chance greatly affect human activities, and events unfold 'Like an old tale still' (5.2.55, 5.3.118).

The Tempest

Old tales may, as Shakespeare's do, embody wisdom and rich insights about the human condition. They may also have immediate social and political relevance, as seems true, for instance, of *Cymbeline*, in which Romans land at Milford Haven, where Henry VII landed to establish the Tudor dynasty; in which the terms 'Briton' and 'Britain' are much used, and could allude to the effort by King James to unify England,

Scotland and Wales as 'Great Britain'; and which ends in a surprising peace agreement, possibly relating to James's proclaimed motto, 'Beati pacifici', blessed are the peacemakers. But if this play seems to invite such speculations, it also teasingly unsettles them.

The same may be said of *The Tempest*, which was staged at court in November 1611, and again in 1613 as part of the celebrations for the wedding of King James's daughter Princess Elizabeth to Frederick, the Elector Palatine. In the play Prospero, effectively king of the island he controls, is concerned to bring about the betrothal of his daughter Miranda to Ferdinand, son of the King of Naples, which he celebrates with a splendid masque. So *The Tempest* may have seemed topical. The arrival of Prospero, the exiled Duke of Milan, on the island possessed by Caliban, an anagram of cannibal, is also certainly connected to Shakespeare's reading in narratives of voyages to the new world, the Bermudas and Virginia, where Jamestown was founded in 1608. Prospero has been seen as a colonial governor exercising authority over the natives of the island (see also Chapter 33 on this subject).

The Tempest too, however, unsettles any attempt at a consistent topical reading, while raising issues relating to slavery and freedom, to the idea of the savage as opposed to civilization, as well as to morality, education, colonial government, and the uses of power. *The Tempest* is a very complex play, although its action is simpler than that of the other romances. Prospero, landing on an imaginary island in the Mediterranean (though linked through Caliban also to the West Indies), at once seizes power and makes its residents, Caliban, a savage, and Ariel, a spirit, his slaves (1.2.272, 311). He imports into the island the social and moral order he was used to in Italy (or, as it might be, London). When by magic he contrives to have a party of his old enemies and friends from Italy shipwrecked on the island, he treats the young Ferdinand as a usurper or spy (1.2.457–60), as well he might, since most of those who have landed on the island, and Caliban too, want to become king over it in his place, and are willing to murder to gain power.

Even the good counsellor Gonzalo's vision of an ideal commonwealth begins from the idea of 'plantation' or colonization and, as Sebastian mockingly notices, 'he would be king on't' (2.1.157). The desire to be king, to claim possession and gain power, is related to two concepts that are central in the play, namely slavery or servitude and freedom. Power for rulers requires subservience in the ruled: Prospero's rule is dependent on maintaining Caliban as a slave to fetch in wood (1.2.314) and do menial tasks, and Ariel as a spy to keep the humans on the island under surveillance.

Freedom for most of the humans on the island is equated with gaining power for themselves, but a much finer idea of freedom emerges in the relation between Ferdinand and Miranda. In order to test him, Ferdinand is humiliated by Prospero and forced to take on a slave's job as log-bearer, and this scene, where we see him pitied by Miranda, defines both the limits of her father's power and the richest idea of freedom in the play. Miranda disobeys Prospero in revealing her name to Ferdinand, and, more startlingly, in offering to marry him: 'I am your wife, if you will marry me' (3.1.83). Ferdinand can endure slavery for her sake:

> The very instant that I saw you did
> My heart fly to your service; there resides
> To make me slave to it. And for your sake
> Am I this patient log-man.
>
> (3.1.64-7)

Slavery is transfigured, for in this higher voluntary 'service' of love is found true freedom. The willing acceptance of the service of love in the bond of marriage constitutes a noble conception of freedom. Prospero, who desired this outcome, is nonetheless 'surprised with all' (3.1.94), by her audacity presumably. The climax of the play comes with the splendid masque in Act Four, which marks the betrothal of Ferdinand and Miranda, and blesses their anticipated marriage.

Prospero's enemies have, in the meantime, been terrified by a kind of anti-masque in 3.3, in which Ariel appears as a harpy, a mythical bird with wings and claws but a woman's head, to denounce them. The reconciliations at the end prepare for a return to Italy and the completion of Prospero's plan, which has always been to return to Milan. In an epilogue he speaks of his 'project' as if he were the author, and it is not implausible to see in him a surrogate for Shakespeare the artist. However, it also seems possible that the jostlings for power among the Italian aristocrats, and their readiness to resort to usurpation or even murder, may resurface once they are back home. As always, Shakespeare offers multiple viewpoints, and no single interpretation does justice to any of his romances.

FURTHER READING

Bettelheim, Bruno. *The Uses of Enchantment. The Meaning and Importance of Fairy Tales* (New York, Random House, 1975). The account in this book of the way fairy tales work and their value has relevance for an understanding of romance and old tales.

Brown, John Russell and Bernard Harris (eds.). *Later Shakespeare* (London: Edward Arnold, 1966). This collection contains several important essays on the late plays, including 'Shakespeare and Romance' by Stanley Wells, and '*The Tempest*: Conventions of Art and Empire' by Philip Brockbank.

Edwards, Philip. 'Shakespeare's Romances: 1900–1957', in *Shakespeare Survey 11* (1958), 1–18. This is a searching examination of approaches that have had great influence on later interpretations of the romances.

Jordan, Constance. *Shakespeare's Monarchies: Ruler and Subject in the Romances* (Ithaca and London: Cornell University Press, 1997). She sees the late plays in their political aspect as concerned with ideas of rule and government.

Knight, G. Wilson. *The Crown of Life* (Oxford: Oxford University Press, 1947). This book established for decades a way of reading the romances as Christian allegories or *myths of immortality*.

Ryan, Kiernan (ed.). *Shakespeare. The Last Plays*, Longman Critical Readers (London and New York:

Longman, 1999). This collection of essays illustrates the impact of feminism, new historicism, cultural materialism, and deconstruction on interpretation of the romances.

Warren, Roger. *Staging Shakespeare's Last Plays* (Oxford: Clarendon Press, 1990). This analysis of productions by Peter Hall and the National Theatre in London deals with issues relating to performance.

READING: *The Winter's Tale*

Interpretation of Shakespeare's romances keeps changing with the times. For some decades from the 1940s a reading of the plays in religious, usually Christian, terms as concerned with atonement or redemption, seemed persuasive. Some critics sought, not very successfully, to find explanation of the plays in allusions to contemporary events and the court of James I. More recently psychoanalytic and feminist approaches have enlarged our understanding of Shakespeare's late works. New historicist readings have changed our perception of power relations in the plays, and deconstructionist criticism has raised questions about how we arrive at meanings and what, if any, relation these have to reality. Performance criticism is also beginning to show how much can be learned by studying the plays as acted in the theatre. The short list of further reading at the end of this section includes examples of these various modes of critical reading.

The following account of *The Winter's Tale* seeks to show how Shakespeare uses the conventions of romance to create a complex and moving work that speaks to the human condition. All is calm at the beginning of the play. Polixenes, King of Bohemia, has come to the end of a nine-month visit to his lifelong friend Leontes, King of Sicilia, and is taking his leave. Leontes cannot make him stay longer, and at his request his Queen Hermione presses Polixenes, who yields as she takes his hand and then his arm and leads him offstage to the 'garden' (1.2.179). Her actions here provoke a sudden, shocking change in Leontes, who is overwhelmed with a jealous rage and conviction that she has committed adultery with his friend. Hermione is with child, and vividly eight months or more pregnant, which makes the instantaneous change in Leontes even more inexplicable.

Leontes' tortured language now makes convincing his jealous anguish as he broods aloud to his uncomprehending young son Mamillius. At one point he seems momentarily to realize that he is making something out of nothing:

> Can thy dam?—may't be?—
> Affection, thy intention stabs the centre,
> Thou dost make possible things not so held,
> Communicat'st with dreams—how can this be?—
> With what's unreal thou coactive art,
> And fellow'st nothing. Then 'tis very credent
> Thou mayst co-join with something . . .
> (1.2.139-45)

'Affection' could overlap in meaning with 'lust', the 'vile affections' Paul refers to in Romans 1,26 (King James Bible, 1611). Leontes has a nightmare vision of sexual violence and adultery, focused in the phrase 'stabs the centre', which also suggests the wounding of his heart. Yet at the same time he glimpses the possibility that it is all fantasy, a bad dream, 'unreal'. A little later, imaging himself as a cuckold, he dismisses the boy: 'Go play, boy, play.

Thy mother plays, and I / Play too; but so disgraced a part . . .' (1.2.188–9). So he is also briefly aware of himself and also sees others as playing roles. The passion is terrible, but at the same time he is not totally absorbed by it as Othello is, but can sense it as nightmare, as role-playing and, in addition, as a disease for which there is no cure: 'Physic for't there's none' (1.2.201). These images suggest an affliction that does not surface from inside like a volcano erupting, but rather is the result of external forces, dreams, roles he cannot help playing, or a sickness for which he is not responsible.

This is how the court sees him. His closest counsellor, Camillo, attempts to cure Leontes of his 'diseased opinion' (1.2.299), but cannot shake 'the fabric of his folly' (1.2.429). Indeed, the more Leontes broods on adultery, the more suspicion turns into certainty, and he is quickly ready to order Camillo to poison Polixenes. Camillo's secret departure in company with Polixenes only serves to confirm Leontes' belief in Hermione's adultery. The disease grows worse, as he puts Hermione on trial as an adulteress and traitor, in spite of the protests of some of his courtiers, notably Antigonus, whose aside at the end of 2.1 emphasizes what he sees as the absurdity of Leontes' behaviour in sending Hermione to prison:

> LEONTES: We are to speak in public; for this business
>   Will raise us all.
> ANTIGONUS: To laughter, as I take it,
>   If the good truth were known.
>
> (2.1.199-201)

By the time Leontes encounters Paulina, wife of Antigonus, who proclaims herself his 'physician' (2.3.54), her 'medicinal' words (2.3.37) are useless to control his 'tyrannous passion'. His obsession extends to all the court, which becomes for Leontes 'A nest of traitors' (2.3.82). He is ready to burn Paulina, his new-born daughter, and Hermione as if they were witches. He has indeed, as Paulina says, descended into madness (2.3.72). Leontes has absolute power, and no-one can stop him putting Hermione on trial for adultery and conspiracy to murder him.

In the moving trial scene, Hermione has no defence against the nightmare fantasies of her husband, other than her honour, in the sense both of her probity and her reputation, which she values more than life. This is marked in the courage and dignity with which she faces him down when he threatens her with death: 'Sir, spare your threats. / The bug which you would fright me with, I seek' (3.2.89–90). Imprisoned, disgraced, separated from her children, life means little to her, and she can only hope that 'powers divine' (3.2.26) may somehow intervene. Leontes momentarily relents when the spectacle of the entire court on their knees influences him to let his baby live; but his notion of 'justice' (2.3.180) is to make Antigonus swear to deposit the 'bastard' in some 'remote and desert place'—in other words to get rid of it.

From his skewed point of view the evidence is overwhelming, but to satisfy the 'ignorant credulity' of others (2.1.194) Leontes has sent messengers to the oracle of Apollo, who return in time to stop the trial by proclaiming the 'good truth' that Hermione is chaste and Leontes has acted tyrannically. At the same time a servant reports the death of Mamillius. Good news and bad come together. The effect on Leontes is instantaneous; he at once sheds his fantasies, and is cured of his madness. As he was suddenly and without warning afflicted with jealous passion, so now with equal suddenness he is restored, but at great cost. His son is dead, which he takes to be a punishment on himself; his daughter is cast out and lost to him; and Paulina will shortly brings news that Hermione too, carried off stage in a faint, has died. If the obsessive rage of Leontes seemed absurd as it erupted out of dreams, fantasies, or sickness of the mind, it has terrible consequences.

There seems no reason why it happened, or why the innocent child Mamillius should die, or why Antigonus, having deposited Leontes' baby on a desert shore in the following scene, should be chased off the stage and killed by a bear. These deaths are presented as events which happen without warning and are accepted as part of life. Antigonus had agreed to the charge of Leontes concerning his baby daughter:

> As by strange fortune
> It came to us, I do in justice charge thee,
> On thy soul's peril and thy body's torture,
> That thou commend it strangely to some place
> Where chance may nurse or end it.
>
> (2.3.179-83)

'Strange' could mean 'foreign', and here Leontes alludes to Polixenes as the supposed father; but strange fortune and chance are at work in a larger sense in the play's action. Leontes wants the baby to die, but cannot control events. It turns out that the baby survives and Antigonus dies by the strangest fortune of all, the sudden intervention of a stage bear, probably an actor miming in a bearskin. The strangeness of this incident, which also has a grotesque aspect, distracts attention from the unexpected death of Antigonus, who was only trying to do some good.

To add to the strangeness, Leontes rules in Sicilia, the legendary home of pastoral poetry, though the action of the first part of the play takes place in his court, and Polixenes and Camillo escape from the 'city' (1.2.439) because Camillo has the keys of all the gates to it. The second part of the play is set nominally in Bohemia, which is imagined as having a sea-coast on which the ship of Antigonus is wrecked, with the loss of all the crew, and which opens up a pastoral world as the Shepherd and his son discover and save the baby Perdita. The restoration of Leontes to sanity coincides with 'things dying', with the death of Mamillius and apparent death of Hermione. The deaths of Antigonus and the entire crew of his ship coincide with 'things new-born', the finding of Perdita. We see the end of Antigonus and the crew through the eyes of the Clown, the Shepherd's son, who treats these events as spectacles to be wondered at, as rather exciting, much as television commentators now present the carnage in notable accidents on the roads.

The settings of the play are imaginary and remote; the time of the action also is ostensibly the remote past, when it might be appropriate to refer to classical deities and consult the oracle of Apollo. Yet the play wonderfully conveys a sense of life continuing from one generation to another, from the time when Leontes and Polixenes were small boys, 'twinned lambs that did frisk i'th' sun' (1.2.69), through their adult troubles, to the growing up of their children. It presents a cycle of birth and death, disaster and recovery, loss and renewal.

In a dramatic world where chance and strangeness are so important, Shakespeare is able to create characters whose behaviour is inconsistent and shaped by events. Camillo promised Leontes that he would poison Polixenes, but he at once forswears himself to rescue Polixenes and escape himself. Their actions only serve to confirm their guilt in the eyes of Leontes. Antigonus swears to carry out the task of depositing Perdita in a desert, and loses his life in doing so. Paulina swears that Hermione is dead: 'I say she's dead. I'll swear't' (3.2.201), but expectation that the 'good truth' will prevail might have led early spectators to feel she must be lying. If oaths may be broken and good characters tell lies, what are oaths and the truth worth? The answer seems to lie in the circumstances, as characters have to adapt to what happens, and do not control their destinies. Only time will show, so it is appropriate that Time appears as Chorus to Act Four, Time that 'makes and unfolds error' for good and bad alike in a kind of moral indifference. As in *Cymbeline* human judgements may be blind, and only in retrospect can understanding and the unfolding of error come.

The tone of the scenes in Bohemia is set by Autolycus, the lovable rogue named after the son of Mercury, god of pick-pockets, and 'snapper-up of unconsidered trifles', whose songs and dances mark his 'merry heart' (4.3.24–6, 115), and burst with life and energy, making at once a strong impact on stage. He is a liar, a cheat, and a thief, but those he robs seem none the poorer, there is no malice in him, and he works by taking advantage of what fortune throws in his way. He is adept at deceptions and appears in various disguises. His last one, resulting from the exchange of clothes with Florizel forced on him by Camillo, makes him appear a courtier. He ends by doing good, since it happens to be to his advantage to help the Shepherd and his son get audience at the court and reveal the origins of Perdita. He is the one character who addresses the audience directly to engage their sympathy and who is free from care: 'for the life to come, I sleep out the thought of it' (4.3.28–9). Autolycus is a subversive force, a kind of fool mocking the solemnity of the court, though he has served Florizel (4.3.13) and, when we last see him in 5.2, he is hoping to get his old job back.

The Shepherd's son, called simply 'Clown', also contributes to the gaiety of the sheep-shearing feast, with its masque-like elements in more songs and dances, and Autolycus peddling trinkets and ballads. The gaiety is disrupted by Polixenes, who has come to the feast with Camillo in disguise to spy on his son Florizel. Florizel himself is in disguise as the shepherd Doricles, making love to Perdita, dressed as the goddess Flora, as if she were in a masque. These two are set off from the other shepherds and shepherdesses not only by their costumes, but by their habit of speaking in verse rather than prose. Perdita has somehow acquired an education above her station as a shepherd's daughter, or else her 'robe' as a goddess changes her 'disposition' (4.4.134–5). She holds her own in debate with Polixenes about nature and art. He defends the practice of grafting:

> You see, sweet maid, we marry
> A gentler scion to the wildest stock,
> And make conceive a bark of baser kind
> By bud of nobler race. This is an art
> Which does mend nature—change it rather; but
> The art itself is nature.
>
> (4.4.92-7)

Perdita agrees, 'So it is', but still rejects the idea of meddling with nature. This sequence establishes, so to speak, Perdita's credentials as a princess, as well as her charm and innocence. It is also deeply ironic, for Polixenes is about to intervene to prevent his son from mending nature in this way, while Perdita, 'pranked up' as Flora, has the art to speak above her station as shepherdess. At the same time, her art reveals her true nature, for she is in fact a princess.

Art is nature in so far as inventiveness is natural to humans. Polixenes, Florizel, and Perdita are all in disguise in this scene, practising a more refined mode of deception than is habitual with Autolycus. Polixenes recognizes Florizel in an angry outburst that recalls in a much slighter way the rage of Leontes. Here, though, it is a ripple on the surface of the play. Camillo at once devises a scheme for Florizel and Perdita to sail off in yet another disguise to Sicilia. Art comes to their rescue, as Perdita changes her role as goddess by altering her appearance: 'I see the play so lies / That I must bear a part' (4.4.638–9). Camillo's aim is to get Polixenes to follow, so that he can see his homeland again; and to this end he betrays Florizel just as he had betrayed Leontes. As Paulina lied to Leontes, so Florizel lies when he reaches Sicilia, hoping to deceive the king into believing his voyage is sanctioned by his father. Art functions by kinds of deception, which can change the perception of time. Florizel would freeze Perdita ever as if she were a sort of mobile sculpture, wishing her a wave of the sea, having 'no other function' (4.4.143). The play ends with yet another playlet, orchestrated by Paulina, when at last she brings Leontes to see Hermione apparently turned into a work of art, and calls for music to mark the 'marvel' of her coming to life again. It is a deeply moving scene, and fittingly displays art turning into nature on stage to bring about restoration and reconciliation.

Throughout the play characters may lie, deceive, forswear an oath, betray, play roles, cheat, and disguise themselves for various purposes. The aims may be good, as when Camillo breaks his promise to Leontes to poison Polixenes, and Paulina by art brings Hermione back to life for Leontes; the aims may be bad, as Autolycus always looks to make a profit; or the aim may be unclear, as when Florizel deceives his father without knowing what the outcome may be. Only time will show the effects, and in that span of time, sixteen years (5.3.31), some things have worked out well, some badly, as in 'an old tale'. Mamillius is dead, and so are Antigonus, his followers, and the crew of his ship, as we are reminded at 5.2.55–66. There has been much anger and much suffering, but romances end happily, and if 'fortune, visible an enemy', as Florizel thinks of it (5.1.215), can frustrate or bring disaster, the Oracle speaks true, and it seems finally that some higher powers may have a beneficent influence on human affairs. Paulina's art creates the satisfying resolution of the play, the reunion of Hermione with her husband and daughter, which takes place in her chapel, with a sense almost of religious awe, and in the context of the repentance of Leontes for his sin (5.1.171). The 'good' queen and Leontes have to learn to be patient, 'Rejoicing in hope, patient in tribulation' (Romans 12.12, 1611 version).

Sin and patience invoke Christian values, and in some sense goodness prevails in a final harmony that transcends fortune and all the artifice and errors of humanity. The play invites us to share the 'notable passion of wonder' (5.2.13–14) Camillo and Leontes feel at the discovery that Perdita is alive, and the 'wonder' marked in the silence when the 'statue' of Hermione is unveiled (5.3.21). It is wonder at the mystery that what seems unlikely or even incredible can happen to bring suffering and sorrow (as for Mamillius and Antigonus), but also, in romance if not always in life, to bring restoration and joy.

FURTHER READING

Bartholomeusz, Dennis. *'The Winter's Tale' in Performance in England and America 1611–1976* (Cambridge: Cambridge University Press, 1982). An account of ways in which the play has been interpreted in stage productions.

Barton, Anne. 'Leontes and the Spider: Language and Speaker in Shakespeare's Last Plays', in *Essays, Mainly Shakespearean* (Cambridge: Cambridge University Press, 1994), pp. 161–81. On the fictional mode of the play, and what makes it richer and more powerful than legend and fairy tale.

Frey, Charles. *Shakespeare's Vast Romance: a Study of 'The Winter's Tale'* (Columbia: University of Missouri Press, 1980). Shows that the play's complexities cannot be reduced to a single perspective.

Hunt, Maurice (ed.). *'The Winter's Tale'. Critical Essays* (New York and London: Garland Publishing, Inc., 1995). A wide-ranging selection of essays and reviews of performances from the early nineteenth century through the twentieth century.

Neely, Carol Thomas. *'The Winter's Tale*: Women and Issue', in *Broken Nuptials in Shakespeare's Plays* (Urbana: University of Illinois Press, 1993), pp. 191–209. A feminist reading concerned especially with Hermione as wife and mother.

Nuttall, A. D. *William Shakespeare. 'The Winter's Tale'*. Studies in English Literature 26 (London: Edward Arnold, 1966). An intelligent reading of the play that seeks to reconcile its mythic aspects with a psychological analysis.

Orgel, Stephen (ed.). *The Winter's Tale*. Oxford Shakespeare (Oxford: Clarendon Press, 1996). The Introduction provides an excellent account of recent critical concerns in relation to this play.

Comical and tragical

Paul Edmondson

In Michael Almereyda's 2000 film of *Hamlet*, the 'To be or not to be' soliloquy takes place as Ethan Hawke's Hamlet is walking through a video store. He is surrounded by generically ordered shelves labelled 'action', a stingingly ironic contrast to the state of his mind. Using a similar example at the end of his book, *Shakespeare's Dramatic Genres*, Lawrence Danson asks 'What has become of genres? I go to my video store and find a whole section called Comedy. But none called Tragedy or Satire or History or Tragicomedy. Instead there's a huge undifferentiated section called Drama. For tragedies I have to look in a small section called Classics: mostly what I find are Shakespeare's tragedies, mixed up with some of his comedies and some BBC adaptations of Victorian novels'.[1] Generic classifications at the beginning of the twenty-first century are no less unsatisfactory than at the beginning of the seventeenth. With an indeterminacy similar to Hamlet the modern reader, both in the study and in the theatre, feels the tension inherent in deciding whether a particular play is to be or not to be pigeon-holed into one category or another.

Seeking to understand the genres of *Troilus and Cressida*, *All's Well That Ends Well*, and *Measure for Measure* is rather like Hamlet's question of being. Indeed, these three plays have often been grouped together because of their generic indeterminacy. Labels seem like an acute compromise in the light of critical investigation. Determining the genre of a play is a two-way process. It is determined partly by the content of the drama itself and partly by the drama's reception by the reader or audience. This process is enabled by an underlying sense that there are definite kinds of genre to be identified in the first place, but how appropriate is a generic consensus for these three plays? How helpful are questions of genre in relating these plays to the rest of the Shakespearian canon and his development as a dramatist? Furthermore, how far is genre something which limits the responses of a reader, as well as being established by performance choices in a theatre?

Edward Dowden was the first to consider these plays as a separate group in a biographical context (1875). Having divided the earlier comedies into the 'Rough and boisterous' and the 'Joyous, refined, romantic', he lists the three plays as 'serious, dark, ironical'. Dowden's popular study secured the grouping of the plays and influenced Frederick S. Boas in 1896 to include *Hamlet* and label them 'problem plays'. This term was applied to the plays of Henrik Ibsen (the contemporary Norwegian dramatist) as he portrayed individuals struggling with problems caused by the social pressures of his time.

The three plays contain similar features of dramatic narrative, artistry, and scope which have led to their being considered together as a subgenre of 'Comedy'. To some extent, all of them are fascinated by anti-heroism which complicates any notion of a dominant hero or heroine. Each play presents its audience with a morally complex and frustrated universe through which no direct course of action can be taken and in which no satisfying choices can be made. *All's Well* and *Measure* each use the plot device of the bed-trick, by which under cover of darkness a man is tricked into sleeping with a woman who is not the person he believes her to be. *Troilus* shows that one effect of war is to cause the Trojan Cressida to betray her lover Troilus in favour of the Greek Diomede. In this play, dramatic frustration among the characters is matched by frustrated narrative progression and conclusions. War continues to rage and destroy any lasting human achievement. The marriage in *All's Well* between the virtuous Helen and the caddish Bertram is decidedly not based on mutual trust and understanding, and *Measure* presents a series of endings with varying degrees of fairness and moral satisfaction. Justice and closure in all of the plays are depicted in a problematic relationship and one that allows for much interpretative freedom in the course of dramatic representation.

However, Shakespeare mixed genres throughout his career. Both Dowden and Boas represent the work of critics who seek formal characteristics within the plays in order to define and justify definite generic classification. William Witherle Lawrence wrote the first full-length study of *Troilus*, *All's Well*, and *Measure* in 1931, labelling them 'problem comedies'; the influential study by E. M. W. Tillyard, which also reconsidered *Hamlet* as a 'problem-play', appeared in 1950. The fact that subsequent studies have also seen *Timon of Athens*, *Julius Caesar*, and *Antony and Cleopatra* as 'problematic' testifies to the critical disagreements prompted by the exclusion and re-accommodation originally proposed by Boas and Dowden. This is a far cry from the more inclusive generic categories suggested in the First Folio of 1623.

The difficulty comes when genre critics are tempted to over-regularize the particularities of each play in their quest to provide a descriptive label. The heading 'Late Comedies' is not wholly satisfying, neither is the phrase 'Dark Comedies', nor even 'Tragi-comedies'. All of these terms make unhelpful assumptions about Shakespeare's development as a writer. 'Late Comedies' should also include *The Winter's Tale* and *The Tempest*, if not *Cymbeline*, *Pericles*, and *The Two Noble Kinsmen*. Similarly 'Dark Comedies' and 'Tragi-comedies' imply that Shakespeare did not include dark or tragic elements in his earlier comedies. Proteus attempts to rape Silvia in *The Two Gentlemen of Verona*; the death of the King of France prevents the comic ending of marriage at the end of *Love's Labour's Lost*; Katherine undergoes severe tribulations in the course of marriage in *The Taming of the Shrew*; the threatened deaths of Hermia and Egeon pervade *A Midsummer Night's Dream* and *The Comedy of Errors*; Shylock is cruelly treated in *The Merchant of Venice*; Hero in *Much Ado About Nothing* is supposed dead; Rosalind is grieving the banishment of her father in *As You Like It*; Olivia and Viola mourn the death (or supposed death) of their brothers in *Twelfth Night*; the world is torn apart by war in *Troilus and Cressida*; the Countess, Bertram, and Helen are bereaved at the beginning of *All's Well*; and Claudio is sentenced to death in *Measure for Measure*. Only *The Merry Wives of Windsor* seems genuinely to avoid darker moods, but not in its qualitative assessment of marriage. By these criteria all of Shakespeare's comedies might be staged as problem plays.

Attempts to identify and determine genre have preoccupied academics more than performers. Some of the finest productions of these plays were directed between 1967 and 1976 for the Royal Shakespeare Company by John Barton. Interviewed about them, he does not ask whether they are tragedies or comedies, but explains how he tried to make decisions about the plays' ambiguities in rehearsal.[2] His comments make provisional any generic expectation inherent in merely reading these plays. Where critics might simplify and reduce the plays' complexities in the search for a consistent interpretation, the theatre might surprise and contradict. There are, of course, aspects of the three plays which will remain broadly intelligible as comic, however pitiable, in performance: the flattery of Ajax in *Troilus and Cressida*, the loquacity of Paroles and Lavatch in *All's Well*, and the portrayals of Mistress Overdone, Pompey, and Elbow in *Measure*. Similarly, it is difficult to conceive that the death of Hector, the mourning at the beginning of *All's Well*, and the impending death of Claudio could evoke anything other than a broadly tragic tone.

Content, interpretation, and reception all contribute to generic understanding, which itself is developed and challenged by new readings and theatre productions. Here, the terms 'problem', 'late' and 'darker' will be provisionally rejected. Instead, the plays will be read to analyse how Shakespeare reaches out to the intersection where comedy borders tragedy. To return to Hamlet wondering about the purpose of existence, the only consensus profferable is a question: in what ways do these plays eschew what is dead to encourage an appreciation of life?

Troilus and Cressida

The genre of *Troilus*, probably written in 1602, was rendered problematical from its earliest appearance in two quarto versions in 1609. One refers to it as a 'History', the other as a 'Famous History', and also includes a letter addressed to an 'Ever Reader' which unequivocally presents the play as a comedy, 'passing full of the palm comical . . . as well as the best comedy in Terence or Plautus'. How *comic* is it? In the Folio it is entitled a tragedy and appears between *The Life of King Henry the VIII* and *The Tragedy of Coriolanus*. It is not surprising that critical opinion has been divided. The Romantic poet Samuel Taylor Coleridge found it the hardest to characterize of all the plays, and he is not alone in that. Whether or not it is meant to be cruelly satirical, in the end,

Troilus resists straightforward categorization. For a long time, this caused it to be neglected: there is no evidence that *Troilus* was ever performed in Shakespeare's lifetime, and it remained one of his least popular plays until its emergence on stage in the early twentieth century (as discussed also in Chapter 23). On the other hand, it is precisely its complexity of tone and difficulty of genre that have made it especially popular with modern audiences living through, and in the wake of, two world wars, Vietnam, the Cold War, the struggle for a Northern Ireland settlement, all manner of terrorist attacks, and ongoing hostility in the Middle East.

Troilus and Cressida comes between *Romeo and Juliet* and *Antony and Cleopatra* as plays in which pairs of lovers are depicted against the backdrop of political conflict. However, this play is decidedly less concerned with its hero and heroine than with the war which surrounds them. Its very title toys with its audience's generic expectations, and anyone approaching the play for the first time as a potential love story is likely to be sorely disappointed. Romance seems to be promised in the first two scenes as Pandarus begins his work of bringing the two lovers together. All this is irrevocably interrupted from 1.3 until 3.2 (well over a thousand lines), as Shakespeare introduces the bitter conflict of the Trojan War as his main dramatic interest. Later, a lover, Cressida, will be exchanged for a soldier, Antenor. The play in the theatre makes more demands on the company of actors as an ensemble than on any of its individual roles. The shifting generic tones make any attempt at lasting achievements in both war and love at worst extremely difficult, at best pathetically vulnerable. This is compounded with the play's interest throughout in the wasteful effects of time and the language of disease which infects the dialogue at every level.

Shakespeare's satirical and generic reworking of heroic myth is apparent when the play is considered alongside its chief sources, Homer's *The Iliad* and Chaucer's *Troilus and Criseyde*. Shakespeare suppresses key narrative features from Homer such as the predominating wrath of Achilles, the war amongst the gods and their divine intervention, the nobility of a hero's death and funeral, the killing of Patroclus by Hector, and Patroclus's ghost visiting Achilles to prompt the final single-armed combat between Achilles and Hector. These omissions show Shakespeare playing fast and loose with Homer. He is subverting any generic expectations his audience or readers might have of the classical epic. Similarly, Shakespeare changes crucial details from Chaucer's version and depicts, for example, a more embittered Pandarus. In Chaucer, after bringing the two lovers together, Pandarus enjoys Cressida for himself. Shakespeare's Pandarus is rewarded only vicariously—'How now, how now, how go maidenheads?' (4.2.25)—and is there later only to commiserate with his niece over her enforced leaving (4.3).

Shakespeare's wholesale debunking of gargantuan mythological heroes is achieved on many levels and uses a range of dramatic devices. 'After so many hours, lives, speeches spent' (2.2.1)—seven years of tired siege and war—the heroes, whose names ring like great cities and palaces through time, Agamemnon, Ulysses, Nestor, Diomedes, Menelaus (the Greeks) and Priam, Hector, Aeneas, Paris, and Helenus (the

Trojans) can do no more than argue about what they should be doing. Well might Agamemnon ask, 'Princes, what grief hath set the jaundice on your cheeks?' (1.3.1). The two great council scenes (1.3 and 2.2) present an intense philosophical and discursive drama of a kind not found anywhere else in Shakespeare. Ulysses's long speech on universal order (1.3.74–137) attempts to elucidate the reason for the military stalemate but is itself symptomatic of that stalemate. His remedy is to stir into action Achilles, who remains in his tent with Patroclus slandering, mocking, and pageanting Ulysses and other debating heroes (1.3.142–84). Ulysses himself manipulates the council's perception of heroism by spoiling the reputation of 'blockish Ajax' and 'Achilles' plumes' (1.3.368, 379).

In many of his plays, Shakespeare frames a dramatic event with comments from onstage observers designed to guide and question the audience's reactions to what is happening. In *Measure for Measure*, for example, Isabella's passionate pleas to Angelo on behalf of her condemned brother, Claudio (2.2), are framed with encouraging remarks from Lucio. So complex is the response required by *Troilus and Cressida* that there are many such remarks. These tend to be spoken more for the benefit of the audience than for the onstage characters. In 2.3.197–212 the heroes are shown as fractured and yet united in their mockery of Ajax. These seem less like heroes than schoolboys and Shakespeare is thoroughly skewering their reputations.

Plot devices such as Achilles idling 'Upon a lazy bed the livelong day' (1.3.147) with Patroclus, later rumoured to be 'Achilles' male varlet' (5.1.14), provide further satire and encourage interest in the play's presentation of fragile masculinity. Troilus describes himself as 'weaker than a woman's tear' in the first scene (1.1.9). Performance will determine where the love interest in this play is most effectively located. A reviewer of the 1981 Royal Shakespeare Company production wrote that Achilles and Patroclus portrayed 'the only physically convincing relationship in the whole play'.[3] There is, too, the debunking of Helen of Troy as the prime reason for the war in the first place. The Greeks want her back (she is Menelaus's wife, not Paris's) and the Trojans are divided about whether she should stay. Hector wants to 'Let Helen go' (2.2.16–24); Troilus believes she is worth all the fighting: 'a pearl / Whose price hath launched above a thousand ships' (2.2.80–1). Her appearance is Shakespeare's supremely satirical anti-climax. Christopher Marlowe had depicted her memorably in *Dr Faustus*: a glimpse of the most beautiful woman in history just before eternal damnation. Helen's one scene in *Troilus* presents her as little more than a prose-speaking harpy, self-absorbed and banal in her response to Pandarus's vacuous love song (3.1). The Greek Diomedes will later condemn her as 'bitter to her country', nothing more than a bringer of death (4.1.70–6).

There are two clowns in the roles of Pandarus and Thersites. Each contributes differently to the humour of the play. Pandarus is obsessive with his interference in Troilus and Cressida's potential love affair (1.1 and 2). His protracted joke with Troilus on the making of wheat cake (1.1.13–24) is similar to his joke with Cressida about Helen's opinion of Troilus (1.2.88–156). Later, he will instigate sex between the two lovers, wants them to press to death the bed he provides (3.2.195) and assumes they have been lovemaking all night (4.2.33–4). Sex, like his obsessive brand of humour, should be 'a great while going by' (1.2.156). The other comic instigator is Thersites, who functions more explicitly as a chorus but is often invited to interact with other characters. Patroclus invites him to 'come in and rail'; Achilles refers to him as 'my cheese, my digestion' (2.3.19–20, 36). Thersites provides a series of protracted, bitter, and scornful invectives (most notably in 2.3.1–18; 5.1.43–58 and 80–9; 5.2.189–94; 5.4.1–14) against war and the lechery (rather than heroism) he sees all around him. In the end, his comic vision saves his life and ensures a pitiful survival in the war-torn world (5.8). Simon Russell Beale, who played Thersites in the 1990 Royal Shakespeare Company production, discovered to his surprise that the role was genuinely funny and complex.[4] Thersites's comic voice, however, is only one contributor to the babble that makes up the play's generic mosaic.

Troilus and Cressida themselves are depicted as marginal figures in Shakespeare's theatre of war and raillery, but speak some of the most moving, tender, and affecting speeches of love in all of his plays. Initially 'bereft [. . .] of all words' on first meeting, their tender prose eventually reaches for versification (3.2.52–183). They articulate their vulnerable inarticulacy as lovers: 'Why have I blabbed?' says Cressida as she tentatively asks Troilus to kiss her (3.2.106–22). Together with Pandarus they occupy a special place in the drama and inscribe their identities as performance and prayer, heightening their own significance with reference to their future reputations: ' "As true as Troilus" ', ' "As false as Cressid" ', 'call them all panders.' All three of them respond with 'Amen' (3.2.167–93).

Shakespeare is ambiguous about whether his Cressida is unfaithful, and performances of the play must decide the degree to which the audience is called upon to judge her immorality, or be sympathetic to her pragmatism. Act Five Scene Two is one of Shakespeare's most complicated scenes. The device of framing a scene with onstage comments reaches its most complex form as Ulysses comments on Troilus with whom he is watching Cressida and Diomedes; Thersites watches and comments on all of them; and Calchas might even be watching the action too, possibly from an upper level. Shakespeare complicates an audience's response to the lovers in a scene of concentric observation and interpretation. It is comparable in complexity only to the eavesdropping scene in *Love's Labour's Lost* (a comedy, 4.3) and to that in *Othello* (a tragedy, 4.1). Shakespeare excels in frustrating any would-be straightforward response: 'This is and is not Cressid' (5.2.146).

There is no satisfying narrative closure: how do you conclude a play so complex and fraught? It is sometimes important to realize that there are two alternative endings to *Troilus*. One is heroic, with Troilus going into battle to fight Diomedes (as in the Oxford Complete Works); the other bitterly comic, with a speech from Pandarus about whores, brothels, and disease. Two Royal Shakespeare Company productions have played both ways within two years of each other. In 1996, Pandarus concluded the play; the 1998 production had Troilus at the very end. Often chilling in performance, Pandarus's closing couplet:

> Till then I'll sweat and seek about for eases,
> And at that time bequeath you my diseases

can be both moving and sour, both utterly distasteful and desperately funny. The obsessive sexual comedian is now the butt of his own humour and the victim of venereal disease. He has become a tired joke, but he is still clutching at the straws of life and laughter in a war-weary wasteland in which he alone grants the audience the relief of applause. The audience is reminded of death throughout this comedy, and Pandarus challenges us, and himself, to go on coping with the world as he knows it, and as Shakespeare has presented it. In seeking to be several things at once, *Troilus and Cressida* eliminates any sense of a moral, generically ordered universe and presents one where laughter is often alienating, and tragedy absurd.

All's Well That Ends Well

The main source of narrative inspiration for *All's Well* was the straightforward tale of human initiative told in the collection of stories known as the *Decameron* by the Italian author Giovanni Boccaccio (1313–75). Shakespeare's considerable adaptations of the scope and mood of his source include introducing the Countess and several comic roles (Paroles, the Clown, Lafeu). He probably wrote the play in 1602, which chronologically associates it with *Hamlet* and *Troilus*.

All's Well is expressive of the theatrical taste of its day. It combines narrative elements of the Griselda story (about a desperately faithful wife) and the prodigal son play (based on the biblical parable about a son who realizes the errors of his dissipated lifestyle and returns to his father). Together with its elements of domestic infidelity, *All's Well* relates to the interests of other contemporaneous plays performed by the King's Men (the theatre company for which Shakespeare wrote), for example: *Measure for Measure*, *Othello*, *The Fair Maid of Bristol* (anonymous), and *The London Prodigal* (anonymous). Its title proffers proverbial wisdom, potentially patronizing inclusivity, philosophical interrogation (*do the ends always justify the means?*), and a determinate sense of a happy ending.

Critical opinion, however, is mixed, and the title which promises narrative satisfaction has been thoroughly unpicked as appreciation of the play has deepened. The playwright George Bernard Shaw (1856–1950), himself a passionate defender of women's rights, emphasized the deeply serious aspects of the drama when he compared it to Ibsen's strongly feminist play *A Doll's House*. Joseph G. Price, a modern critic who has written illuminatingly about the play's effect in performance, explains how *All's Well* might be categorized by at least six generic interpretations: 'farcical comedy [emphasizing Paroles], sentimental romance [emphasizing Helena], romantic fable [emphasizing the intrigue and fairy-tale elements], serious drama [emphasizing the various philosophical strands and the basis of the marriage], cynical satire [emphasizing disease, old age, and contempt between the characters], and a thematic dramatization [emphasizing the roles as symbolic of moral absolutes]'.[5] Susan Snyder, a recent editor, conveys the gamut of moods and narratives as comprising unheroic war, class-conscious marriage, an abuse of royal wardship, and a world where human relationships are based on money.[6] The play by its very nature is irreconcilable to any determinate generic patterning, and with it Shakespeare takes his audiences and readers to the profound limits of comedy.

Three deaths affect the course of the drama. Two of them are real and happen before the action begins. The third death will be Helen's own, feigned to enable her disguise and planned bed-trick with Bertram (4.3.50–62; 4.4.10–14). At the play's opening, the Countess is mourning her husband and Bertram his father (1.1.1–4); Helen's father, too, has recently died, but her sadness is bound up with her deep affection for Bertram. The performance of her first soliloquy is crucial to an audience's sympathy for, and therefore allegiance to, Helen. Her words are direct and uncomplicated, and might even seem calculating:

> I think not on my father,
> And these great tears grace his remembrance more
> Than those I shed for him. What was he like?
> I have forgot him. My imagination
> Carries no favour in't but Bertram's.
> I am undone.
>
> (1.1.74-9)

Shakespeare provides ample space for the actor to present a dual dramatic perspective and take the emotions in both directions. 'What was he like? / I have forgot him' can be delivered with any length of pause at the end of the line and with any degree of relief, pity, regret, and grief.

The exposition of this opening scene unravels generic complexities and emphasizes their performative ambiguities. The 1981 Royal Shakespeare Company production portrayed an autumnal mood rich with Chekhovian-like subtext. The BBC television version of 1980 captures the happy melancholy of paintings by the Dutch artist Jan Vermeer (1623–75), which are echoed in the film's designs. Throughout that production there is a joy of movement as comedy reaches out from the parameters of muted colours and restrained light. A commentator within the play, partially determining the audience's response to the events, remarks: 'the web of our life is of a mingled yarn, good and ill together' (4.3.69–70). Through the course of the play, it is Helen who unmingles the threads of the main narrative which she has instigated. In the BBC version the camera adopts her perspective as she enters the King's court (5.3.301.1), skilfully showing the onlookers' mixed range of emotions. Helen's appearance at the end of the play is one of redemption and comedy regained, but she is only one part of the web. Redemption and comedy are not easily won in this play, and are always offset by the context in which they occur.

Whether critics like her or not is irrelevant. Most of those who do not are male. What is most important is the acceptance of her complexity. Dogged by the fatalism which demands her exaggerated pursuit of love for Bertram—'a bright particular star' (1.1.81)—Helen, perhaps more than any other of Shakespeare's comic heroines, utterly believes in her own self-sufficiency to control events: 'my intents are fixed and will not leave me' (1.1.212). Julia in *The Two Gentlemen of Verona*, Viola in *Twelfth Night*, and Rosalind in *As You Like It* interplay more crucially with circumstance. Helen leaves nothing to chance and her control includes several generic threads. She articulates her intense obsession with Bertram (1.1.87–93), tells the Countess of her lover (1.3.175–201), and commands a mystical, fairy-tale power in her healing of the King, which some critics, oversimplifying Helen's language in 2.1.159–67, have seen as primarily sexual.

Her physical investment in the narrative takes her across Europe, and the bed-trick is possible only through her powerful, material dependence on money. If Diana acquires Bertram's ring and arranges to sleep with him, Helen will pay her dowry (3.7). This is a heroine who is driven by an overriding knowledge of what she truly desires. She will get what she wants, whatever the cost, and whatever the effect on her reputation. Ultimately she is the physical expression of new life, at the end of the drama bearing in her body Bertram's child. She has ensured that her own status has become irrevocably unambiguous, and it is the presentation of this new self that relates her to the way genre is perceived and, literally, conceived. Helen stakes the largest generic claim as both instigator and concluder in this drama.

There is also a war raging, and Bertram (whom most critics, both male and female, dislike) is in pursuit of honour (2.1.1–58), 'Seeking the bubble reputation / Even in the cannon's mouth' (*As You Like It*, 2.7.151–2). The stakes are every bit as serious as in any war, but a production will have to decide just how high it wants to raise them. There is the comic braggartism of Paroles (for example, 2.1.39–44), and there is the sense that honour, as in *Henry IV Part One*, can easily be tainted by the cruelty of experience. Unwittingly, the army has killed some of its own men. 'There was excellent command: to charge in with our horse upon our own wings and to rend our own soldiers!' says Paroles; 'a disaster of war that Caesar himself could not have prevented' comes the apology (3.6.42–4, 46–7). In John Barton's 1967 Royal Shakespeare Company production, possibly influenced by the controversial *Oh! What A Lovely War!* (a satirical and playful series of vignettes about the First World War), battles were fought with toy weapons to emphasize irony over empathy. In contrast, the 1981 production presented a more tragic context, evocative of Crimea and foreshadowing the First World War.

Shakespeare provides overt comic potential in the roles of Paroles, Lavatch, and to some extent Lafeu, the senior and often contemptuous lord in the King's court. Paroles was usually highly comic in eighteenth-century performances. During the Romantic period, the play became more of a sentimental comedy, diminishing the clown figures. There are shades of Malvolio and *Twelfth Night* in the jest played on Paroles by Bertram and his fellow lords. The BBC production presents Paroles as cruelly pushed to the limits of torture and honestly believing he is about to die. Who would not confess under such conditions (4.3.116–288)? Shakespeare accommodates both acute sympathy for the role and the possibility of comic realization with Paroles's lines: 'Simply the thing I am / Shall make me live . . . There's place and means for every man alive' (4.3.310–11, 316). In some productions, Paroles has been utterly deflated at this point; in others fighting fit and ready to embrace life afresh. However this moment is played, Paroles will betray Bertram to the King later, for real (5.3.257–63). Similarly, Lavatch's humour is open to a variety of interpretations. Geoffrey Hutchings, who played the part in 1981, based his interpretation of the role on the relationship Lavatch has with the Countess. Hutchings decided to play him as an old and faithful servant of the former Count. The comedy was gentle and one of profound, long-established understanding, rather than Lavatch being played as the licensed fool, like Feste in *Twelfth Night*, or the Fool in *The Tragedy of King Lear*.

Finally, there is the issue of closure in a play whose title explicitly proclaims that all shall be well, and associates itself with the satisfaction of an ending. The play's conclusions are extremely problematic. As well as Helen's triumph, there are the strands of ending for everyone else, most notably Bertram and Diana. How far does Bertram repent? He is given only one conditional rhyming couplet with which to do so: 'If she, my liege, can make me know this clearly / I'll love her dearly, ever ever dearly' (5.3.312–13). Has Diana's reputation been ruined once and for all, or can the confusion of intentions that frustrate this moment be resolved?

> All yet seems well; and if it end so meet,
> The bitter past, more welcome is the sweet.
> (5.3.329-30)

The King's last words end the play and demand a pause for retrospective consideration. The degree of 'seeming' will depend on how crucial aspects of the play's genre are interpreted and performed. Of all the three plays, *All's Well* succeeds the most in eschewing death in favour of life. As, however, three deaths make considerable impact on the play, the life and comedy it gains are fraught with complicated questions and the threat of terminal sadness.

This consideration of *Troilus* and *All's Well* began with a glance at Ethan Hawke's 'To be or not to be' soliloquy. It closes with a speech of Lafeu's from *All's Well*:

They say miracles are past, and we have our philosophical persons to make modern and familiar things supernatural and causeless. Hence is it that we make trifles of terrors, ensconcing ourselves into seeming knowledge when we should submit ourselves to an unknown fear

(2.3.1-5)

Lafeu is pleading the case of the irrational, of making strange any sense of secure control, a submission to the unknown. From 'the chance of war' (*Troilus*, Prologue, 31)

to 'the web of our life' (*All's Well*, 4.3.69), Shakespeare is exploring ways in which to complicate the pursuit of life and happiness: ways of writing comedy. If you think you have found a single generic key, if you think *Troilus* and *All's Well* can conveniently be labelled as 'problem plays', then think again, and re-submit. You may be making 'trifles of terrors'.

FURTHER READING

Bevington, David (ed.). *Troilus and Cressida*, Arden 3 (Walton-on-Thames: Thomas Nelson and Sons, 1998), pp. 87–117. This edition provides a very long introduction which includes a detailed discussion of performance history.

Boas, Frederick S. *Shakespeare and His Predecessors* (London: John Murray, 1896). The study which first included *Hamlet* as a 'problem play'.

Danson, Lawrence. *Shakespeare's Dramatic Genres*, Oxford Shakespeare Topics (Oxford: Oxford University Press, 2000). This is a useful and short book which conducts a well-written and ample debate about the main critical issues at stake in discussing genre.

Dowden, Edward. *Shakespeare: A Critical Study of His Mind and Art*, 8th edn. (London: Kegan Paul, Trench and Company, 1886). The first study to group the three plays together and imply a subgenre.

Foakes, R. A. *Shakespeare: the Dark Comedies to the Last Plays: From Satire to Celebration* (London: Routledge and Kegan Paul, 1971). Foakes importantly emphasizes the comic life of the plays and considers them as part of Shakespeare's artistic development.

Foakes, R. A. (ed.). *Troilus and Cressida* (Harmondsworth: Penguin, 1987). Foakes's introduction is incisive and his edition is altogether more manageable than Bevington's, though not as full.

Jackson, Russell and Robert Smallwood (eds.). *Players of Shakespeare 3* (Cambridge: Cambridge University Press, 1993). This volume, in a worthwhile and fascinating series, includes an essay by Simon Russell Beale on playing Thersites (pp. 160–173) and one by Roger Allam on playing the Duke in *Measure for Measure* (pp. 21–41). Volume 1 in the series contains an essay on Lavatch by Geoffrey Hutchings (pp. 77–90), and there is another essay on the Duke in volume 2 by Daniel Massey (pp. 13–31).

Moshinsky, Elijah (dir.). *All's Well That Ends Well* (BBC Television, 1980). This is one of the best television versions in an uneven series. Sensitively shot and beautifully acted, it is a highly worthwhile illumination of the play.

Muir, Kenneth (ed.). *Shakespeare Survey 25* (Cambridge: Cambridge University Press, 1972). This annual publication includes six useful articles on the three plays, including a very interesting one on performance: 'Directing Problem Plays: John Barton talks to Gareth Lloyd Evans' (pp. 63–71).

Price, Joseph G. *The Unfortunate Comedy: A Study of 'All's Well That Ends Well' and Its Critics* (Liverpool: Liverpool University Press, 1968). This is one of the best books on the performance history of any play and combines a chronological development of criticism as well as a personal interpretation.

Snyder, Susan (ed.). *All's Well That Ends Well* (Oxford: Oxford University Press, 1993; repr. 1998). This is an excellent single-volume edition of the play.

Thomas, Vivian. *The Moral Universe of Shakespeare's Problem Plays* (London: Routledge, 1987). A thorough consideration of why and how these plays might be considered similar.

Tillyard, E. M. W. *Shakespeare's Problem Plays* (London: Chatto and Windus, 1950). This is now considered a classic of its kind.

NOTES

1. Lawrence Danson. *Shakespeare's Dramatic Genres* (Oxford: Oxford University Press, 2000), p. 142.
2. John Barton, 'Directing Problem Plays: John Barton talks to Gareth Lloyd Evans', in *Shakespeare Survey 25* (1972), 63–71.
3. David Bevington (ed.). *Troilus and Cressida*, Arden 3 (Walton-on-Thames: Thomas Nelson and Sons, 1998), p. 105.
4. Russell Jackson and Robert Smallwood (eds.). *Players of Shakespeare 3* (Cambridge: Cambridge University Press, 1993), p. 61.
5. Joseph G. Price. *The Unfortunate Comedy: A Study of 'All's Well That Ends Well' and Its Critics* (Liverpool: Liverpool University Press, 1968), p. 133.
6. Susan Snyder (ed.). *All's Well That Ends Well* (Oxford: Oxford University Press, 1993; repr. 1998), pp. 5–6.

READING: *Measure for Measure*

> *'I swear I will not die today, for any man's persuasion'*
> (4.3.52)

In *Measure for Measure*, Shakespeare takes his characters as close to death as he dares. A central, if brief, role is that of the drunken murderer Barnardine. He has slept and drunk out nine years of his life on death row. Pompey, a bawd now forced to learn how to chop off heads (4.2.1), has just approached Barnardine's cell with the executioner, Abhorson, to wake the condemned man: 'You must be so good, sir, to rise and be put to death' (4.3.23–4), but the prisoner defiantly declares: 'I swear I will not die today, for any man's persuasion' (4.3.52). It is a moment of grotesque comedy of a kind in which *Measure* excels. Here is Shakespeare trying to find comedy in the face of death. Behind Barnardine's firm refusal is the willingness to celebrate life, however desperate the existence (here perpetual inebriation and shuttered sleep), rather than surrender to death. The response of a condemned man, like Falstaff in the midst of the bloody Battle of Shrewsbury, serves as a fitting epigraph and opening into Shakespeare's drama of decidedly mixed genres: 'Give me life, which if I can save, so' (*Henry IV Part One*, 5.3.58).

In the eighteenth century, Samuel Johnson believed that genres exist to enable writers to innovate and subvert established rules and practices. *Measure* has long attracted critical appreciation for its complex intersections of tragedy and comedy. Branded a 'problem-play', along with *Troilus*, *All's Well* and *Hamlet* by Frederick S. Boas in 1896, *Measure* fell into an unhelpful, critically grey area of generic criticism. This is most readily exemplified by the work of E. M. W. Tillyard and runs the risk of blunting the edge of the plays' particularities by seeking primarily to discuss their similarities. Shakespeare's friends and colleagues decided that *Measure* was a comedy in publishing the First Folio.

To break it away from their liberal groupings of plays inevitably raises awkward questions about the plays which are left behind. How far are any of Shakespeare's plays purely comic? Certainly, as Lawrence Danson observes, in the light of performance, 'all Shakespeare's plays become problem plays, even if some seem in certain eras to be more insistently problematic than others'.[1] This chapter explores further the heterogeneity of *Measure* and uses performance choices to illustrate how far the many generic moods of this play are dependent on reception and interpretation, rather than determinate categorization.

James I saw a performance of *Measure for Measure* at Whitehall on St Stephen's night (26 December) 1604; it was probably written that same year. Shakespeare was to some extent conforming to fashion in writing a play employing the classical device of a disguised authority figure. Plays written around the same time, such as Thomas Middleton's *The Phoenix*, John Marston's *Parasitaster* and *The Malcontent*, and the anonymous *The London Prodigal* (the latter two performed by the King's Men, the company for which

Shakespeare was writing) all provide similar fare. The story was a widely known and taught European morality tale. Giraldi Cinthio's *Hecatommithi* (1565) provided Shakespeare with a complicated and compelling Italian source narrative. Cinthio asks his readers to decide whether justice or mercy is for the greater good. Other influences include George Whetstone's visions of moral laxity, his Puritan drama, *Promos and Cassandra* (1578), and his moral indictment *A Mirror for Magistrates of Cities* (1584). Works such as Philip Stubbes's *Anatomy of Abuses* (1581) suggest outrageous punishments for moral misdemeanours and also provide useful contextual material. So, the parameters for Shakespeare's exploration of personal and institutionalized morality were determined for him prior to composition. Within these he mapped his drama of sex, fear, and death, all bound together during the course of the play by religion and measured against an irrepressible will to live. After all, as R. A. Foakes has suggested, a 'measure' was also a term for a dance in Shakespeare's day.

Joyously, the play's title means 'a time to dance'; grimly it implies justice and taking 'an eye for an eye'. Shakespeare's title is also biblical in origin. Judaic tradition is saturated with measurements of all kinds, not least in its instructions for revenge. The new tradition, proposed by Christianity, re-measures and weighs up the old. Matthew 7:1–2, Mark 4:24, and Luke 6:38 irrevocably locate Shakespeare's title in the sayings of Christ: do not judge, for you will be treated the same way as you treat others. Shakespeare, like Cinthio, forces his audience to weigh up, judge, and consider for themselves. Pain is meted out in sufficient measure, and mercy follows. There are no encounters with enforced death throughout the duration of the play, though death is made to seem all too real. Ragusine conveniently dies of a fever and his head is brought on stage (4.3.62–96). How satisfying the events of the play prove to be, how comic or tragic the outcomes, will largely depend on performance that must make decisions about Shakespeare's difficult generic multiplicity.

Life and comedy are synonymous with commerce among the brothels of Vienna. Shakespeare presents the physical reality, and mutual acceptance, of those who make their money through sex: Mistress Overdone, Pompey, Froth, and Elbow. Lucio is glad to profit from vice and pay for his sexual pleasures. They live in a grotesque world of commodified sex and, in the theatre, often disgusting physicality: 'How now, which of your hips has the most profound sciatica?' an anonymous gentleman asks of Mistress Overdone (1.2.52–3).

Between them, Pompey and Lucio function as fools in the drama. Like Pandarus and Thersites (in *Troilus*), and Paroles and Lavatch (in *All's Well*), they are utterly caught up in the serious narrative drive and immediacy of events and, through their jesting, provide stringent moments of ridiculing insight on the world around them. Their presence, like Barnardine's, demands a comic acceptance of life. 'I am a poor fellow that would live' (2.1.199), says Pompey when arrested for being a bawd. He goes on to criticize the nonsensical legal restrictions on fornication: 'Does your worship mean to geld and spay all the youth of the city?' (2.1.205–6). Sex saturates the comic dialogue throughout. Pompey unashamedly provides intensely bawdy explications in the face of his judicial examination before Escalus (2.1.82–104). Lucio mentions 'the rebellion of a codpiece' (3.1.358–9) to make human Claudio's crime and to ridicule Angelo's death sentence. Here is an irrepressible taste for sex and comedy struggling in an all-infecting environment of unnatural repression.

The director of the 1987 Royal Shakespeare Company production encouraged his cast to visit Pentonville Prison in London, which like all jails symbolizes the ultimate power of any state to control, and usually impoverish, individual integrity. In the play, much of Viennese society outside the court is being imprisoned because of the strict moral clampdown. It can be grotesquely comic, pathetic, or both when Pompey remarks that he is the prisoner to many of his former acquaintances, Mistress Overdone's 'customers' (4.3.3). Peter Brook chose to celebrate this moment as comedy in 1950 with the grimly treated but irrepressible prisoners processing across the stage. In the 1998 Royal Shakespeare Company production Pompey's prisoners appeared like pitiful Beckettian heads, peering up out of several trapdoors. The containment of comedy and potent life-forces is of immense generic interest, and a production must decide on the degree of emphasis. The Provost's summation of events for the disguised Duke provides a useful touchstone for the severity of the situation:

> She is with child,
> And he that got it, sentenced—a young man
> More fit to do another such offence
> Than die for this.
>
> (2.3.12-15)

One of the play's original performance spaces, the Globe Theatre, would automatically have been on the side of the play's comic life. It stood on the south side of the river, out of the city of London's jurisdiction, among the brothels and gambling arena, and as a theatre was a focus for puritanical attack.

It is precisely this tension of atmosphere that measures against the serious drama of the absent Duke, his appointed deputy, Angelo, and the personal tragedies of Isabella, Claudio, and Juliet. The flipside of this comedy of sex and commerce is tragedy and punishment. In *Measure* both aspects are mutually inclusive. In a sound recording of the play, directed by the scholar and theatre practitioner George Rylands, as part of his audio production of the entire Shakespearian canon (1957–64), Rylands himself plays both Angelo and Mistress Overdone. The doubling, unlikely in live theatre, captures beautifully the coalescence of genres. The idea behind Rylands's performance provides a useful way of considering the pervasive control and damage of the establishment (the court, law, and religion) to the overtly comic world, as well as to itself.

The main bridge between the two worlds of the play is the Duke, Vincentio, who moves freely among his people disguised as a figure of religious authority. The fish rots at the head and Shakespeare's ruler is in every way responsible for the state his people are in: 'Which for this fourteen years [he has] let slip' (1.3.21). The interpretation of the Duke is crucial to the overall generic underpinning. One director made him aloof and awe-inspiring. He was a lively conjuror, while looking like Christ, in another production. The allegorical interpretation of the Duke as a deity is common in literary criticism. However, in some productions he has been insecure, even neurotic. In another he was morally active, ready for the social and pastoral care demanded of him. Sometimes he is perceived as Machiavellian, a callous puppeteer of lives, but whilst this emphasizes his desire to control (witness his extraordinary series of tetrametric spell-like rhyming couplets in 3.1.481–502), such a reading oversimplifies Shakespeare's essential generic complexity.

Angelo and Isabella are also propelled by a desire to control. Oddly, while the Duke erases his identity by adopting the disguise of the Friar, they are both striving to secure firm public identities for themselves. Angelo is only a deputy, Isabella a novice. Both obey and propagate a rigid fundamentalism to control the world in relation to themselves: Angelo with the law, Isabella with her religious order. Lucio explains that Angelo lacks any kind of naturally induced feeling 'But doth rebate and blunt his natural edge / With profits of the mind, study, and fast' (1.4.59–60). Likewise Isabella is searching for 'a more strict restraint / Upon the sisterhood, the votarists of Saint Clare' (1.4.4–5). They are both morally absolute in their outlook and seem able to measure the world only in stark terms of life and death, right and wrong. They are, to use Isabella's words, 'At war 'twixt will and will not' (2.2.33). It is this clash of personality which provides their electrifying dialogue during their confrontations: a sister pleading for her brother's life, a man intent on maintaining his authority and the law at all costs, terrified of being 'the very cipher of a function' (2.2.39). Fear of themselves and of each other is fringed with comedy, however, and Shakespeare frames the intensity of their first encounter with the distancing interjections of the comic Lucio.

Fear of sexuality and death breathes through every line of this play like an all-pervasive subtext; religion and law seek to silence it. Angelo's fear is exacerbated by intense masochistic sexual frustration. His realization, 'For I am that way going to temptation, / Where prayer is crossed' (2.2.163–4), is indicative of a mind terrified of what it truly desires. His soliloquy of sexual self-censure (2.2.167–91) ends with glimmers of a new, almost comic self-awareness of his own folly: 'Ever till now / When men were fond, I smiled, and wondered how'. He does not know what it is to love, and his recriminations become even more intense by the beginning of 2.4. Here, Isabella begins to articulate her own view of sex. She would rather die than sleep with Angelo to save her brother's life (2.4.99–109), she says, in a scene which culminates in a soliloquy that often complicates a modern audience's sympathy for her:

> Then Isabel live chaste, and brother die:
> More than our brother is our chastity.
> (2.4.184-5)

However, Isabella is not offered sex, she is offered rape. Angelo fails to realize that she is unobtainable and that any sex at all would destroy her religious and personal integrity.

Fear, sex, and death all accrue around Claudio in his condemned cell. Shakespeare's sense of location becomes an intensifying crucible for the complexities of genre, the joys of life, and the mysteries of death. The Duke's 'Be absolute for death' speech (3.1.5–41) offers comfort and reconciliation to the dying, only to be shatteringly juxtaposed against Isabella's entrance which, for Claudio, brings with it the hope of life. A London production in 1981 swapped these two episodes around. Claudio was comforted by the Friar after being made to fear the worst. Shakespeare's ordering, however, is starkly unsentimental. At this scene's cold climax is the growing fear and distrust between a brother and a sister and Claudio's agnostic articulations about death itself: 'To lie in cold obstruction, and to rot' (3.1.119). Religion and law provide no answers in the face of death.

An important direction in the overall generic patterning is Mariana and the planned bed-trick as revenge on Angelo. Removed and inhabiting a totally different social world in her 'moated grange' (3.1.254), Mariana seems to enjoy a distinct generic existence. She is presented in a contrasting, pastoral, and fertile space. Associated with music, and a song of unrequited love, to ease her pain (4.1.1–13) she lives in world of waiting (like Tennyson's poetic recreation of her two centuries later). Mariana is waiting for her genre to be determined, hopefully in the form of a comic ending, to shape and make comfortable her own imprisoned life. She is eventually granted the closure of marriage to Angelo as her reward— Angelo who, like Bertram in *All's Well*, had sex with her in the belief she was someone else.

Endings, as in *Troilus* and *All's Well*, are not easy in *Measure*, but they are latent in the text and it is up to productions to give them life and decide their generic form. As in *Much Ado About Nothing*, *All's Well*, and *The Winter's Tale*, the comic closure ultimately depends on the supposed dead coming to life again. One of the pleasures of watching a performance of *Measure* is waiting to see how it will all end. Shakespeare constructs many tightropes for his audience in the long final scene. There are several fates to be decided which rely on the Duke, as reinstated centre of authority, and on Isabella's moral integrity. Four people are sentenced to death: Claudio, Barnardine, Angelo, and Lucio. Angelo's life depends on Isabella pleading for him before the Duke (5.1.435–46). Why should she do so? In Peter Brook's famous 1950 production the actress held as long a pause as the audience could take before begging mercy for the man who believes he has had her brother executed. Performance must decide on what the text leaves silent. Juliet and Claudio's baby often appears as the new life at the end of productions. Claudio has nothing to say once he has been revealed as alive again and Shakespeare scripts silence between him, Juliet, and Isabella.

Moreover, Shakespeare is ambiguous about the fate of Isabella. There are three certain marriages: Claudio to Juliet, Angelo to Mariana, and Lucio to a whore. The Duke makes Isabella three fairly vague proposals of marriage (5.1.373–7, 486–7, and 527–30). Whether she accepts or not will depend on the production. Until the advent of feminist criticism it was always assumed that she would marry the Duke. Why should she? The Duke has trifled with her emotions and lied to her. She wants only to be a nun and no longer a novice. Breaking her vow of chastity would make that impossible, and Angelo has virtually raped her. So much for 'heavenly comforts' (4.3.102). John Barton's 1970 Royal Shakespeare Company production had her remain on stage, self-possessed, alone at the end; the BBC production ends with definite, exultant acceptance. There are many options between these two extremes.

However the final moments are played, Isabella's moment of decision can provide a stunning dramatic pause—a gift to any director, actress, and audience. Comedy, in the final scene, hovers on the intersection of tragedy. Shakespeare stares death in the face and looks away again. For all concerned, sex—that formerly robust and vital expression of Viennese society—will forever after be associated with the threat of death. If Isabella does marry the Duke, then she has died to her former life. If a production shows this is forced upon her, then the closure of *Measure* actually conjures up a sort of living death: a painful compromise for someone who, above all else, wants to be a nun.

Reconciliation is not to be expected from a world where justice corrupts and changes, and where notions of human value vary so widely. Readers and directors can provide any number of solutions: Shakespeare's play will always measure us as much as we measure it. For a final impression of the aesthetic impact of *Measure* try the following. Imagine standing in front of three paintings: a gritty social scene by Pieter Bruegel (1525–69), a dimly lit conversation by Rembrandt (1606–69), and a calmly austere religious scene by Piero della Francesca (1410/20–92). That combination of artists is similar to the dramatic and tonal effect achieved in *Measure*. All three painters are masters of focal complexity; together they provide the comic grotesque, darkening depths, and a frighteningly precise exploration of religious perspective. If *Troilus* seeks life amid its ruins and *All's Well* presents a multidirectional web of life, then *Measure* finds life and death to be purely coincidental and makes no apologies for either. In all three plays it is as if Shakespeare is trying to write about death but is too fascinated with life, however desperate it might be. These plays will continue to resist easy categorization, but should no longer be perceived as problems. Rather, they are highly individual comedies of a distinctly radical kind.

FURTHER READING

Bloom, Harold (ed.). *William Shakespeare's 'Measure for Measure'* (New York: Chelsea House, 1988). This is a useful anthology of critical essays.

Gibbons, Brian (ed.). *Measure for Measure* (Cambridge: Cambridge University Press, 1991; repr. 1999). This is an excellent single-volume edition. Gibbons presents a full introduction and comprehensive glosses.

Hawkins, Harriett, '*Measure for Measure*', Harvester New Critical Introductions to Shakespeare (Brighton: Harvester Wheatsheaf, 1987). A challenging and useful survey of some modern critical approaches.

Knight, G. Wilson. '*Measure for Measure* and the Gospels.' In *The Wheel of Fire: Essays in Interpretation of Shakespeare's Sombre Tragedies* (London: Oxford University Press, 1930). A creative and engaged account which has become a classic of its kind.

Wilders, John. 'The Problem Plays'. In Stanley Wells (ed.), *Shakespeare: a Bibliographical Guide*, rev. edn. (Oxford: Clarendon Press, 1990). This is a useful, short account of the main issues at stake.

NOTE

1. Lawrence Danson, *Shakespeare's Dramatic Genres* (Oxford: Oxford University Press, 2000), p. 14.

Lynne Magnusson

Venus and Adonis and *The Rape of Lucrece*, narrative poems published in 1593 and 1594, were Elizabethan bestsellers, running respectively through at least ten and six editions in Shakespeare's lifetime. Surprisingly, what first made Shakespeare a celebrity were these early poems, not the 'Sonnets' printed in 1609, in which, for later generations, Shakespeare seemed to have 'unlocked his heart',[1] nor his more famous plays. The narrative poems and the lyrical sonnets represent two poles of his poetic output, the former marked by a full explicitness at the level of story, language, and context and the latter by an elusive suggestiveness. This chapter will begin with a look at Shakespeare's early venture into print poetry, considering his abortive fashioning as a famous poet and the life of his poems in their own day. Then it will offer critical introductions to the major narrative poems and the sonnets, exploring shared features as well as differences. The narrative poems and the sonnets share, first, an interest in mental states arising within intense personal interactions. Often they give voice to a divided self-consciousness engendered as the inward experience of power relations, especially conceived as the forceful and afflicting action of one person upon another rather than as mutual or reciprocal interaction. Second, as with the classical Roman poet Ovid, whose verse Shakespeare emulates, the poetry offers vivid explorations of sexuality and eroticism which transpose, invert, and challenge stereotypical gender relations and sexual arrangements. And, third, whether explicit or suggestive in their manner, whether 'sweet' and 'honey-tongued' or 'salty' and sharp-tongued or satirical in their wit, each of Shakespeare's poems, like his plays, takes linguistic ingenuity to a new level.

Poetry and prestige

The 'honey-flowing vein' of Shakespeare's *Venus and Adonis* and *Rape of Lucrece* put Shakespeare's 'name in fame's immortal book', according to the contemporary poet, Richard Barnfield, and early tributes and imitations abounded.[2] John Weever wrote that 'thousands' vowed 'subjective duty' to Venus, Adonis, and Lucrece, 'burn[ing] in love' for the mythical characters he called Shakespeare's 'children'. Sonnets written early on by Shakespeare and circulating in manuscript shared some praise with the printed narrative poems in Francis Meres's 1598 tribute: 'the sweet witty soul of Ovid lives in mellifluous and honey-tongued Shakespeare, witness his "Venus and Adonis", his "Lucrece", his sugared Sonnets among his private friends'. Yet it is surprising that when the collected 'Sonnets', the 154 short lyric poems today almost universally prized more highly than the narrative poems, came to be printed in 1609 together with *A Lover's Complaint*, they drew no surviving tributes and were not even reprinted until 1640. Less has been claimed, either now or then, for other non-dramatic poems that have been attributed to Shakespeare, which include *The Phoenix and Turtle*, a fascinating but puzzling poem printed in a 1601 collection with others on the same subject, and a handful of occasional poems whose authorship has been subject to debate, most of them comic or serious epitaphs on people's deaths.

Shakespeare might not even have ventured into print poetry had not the plague in 1592 to 1594 closed down London theatres and, thus, his livelihood as a player and commercial playwright. The small fees a publisher might pay for a verse manuscript or a patron for a dedication must have been incentives, yet clearly money was not all he set his sights on in switching from theatre to print. On the title page of *Venus and Adonis* was set out a motto from Ovid, Shakespeare's favourite classical poet. It is a big Latin boast borrowed from the 'Amores'—a boast that, however the vulgar crowd might be pleased with cheap things, 'for me golden Apollo serves up full cups from the Castalian spring'. With this first printed poem, Shakespeare and his publisher, Stratford-born Richard Field, show a practical savvy learned, perhaps, from writers like Spenser about taking an active role in shaping poetic fame. In two short lines, the quoted Latin couplet lays a claim to poetic distinction, identifying the new English poet with the honey-tongued Roman poet Ovid. Claiming superior taste also solicits a level of social recognition for the new poet, a kind of prestige not associated with theatre ventures.

After the learned classical boast, a dedicatory letter makes a modest petition to an important young nobleman, the Earl of Southampton. In the self-deprecating tones of an Elizabethan suitor's plea, it begs support and protection for *Venus and Adonis*. Nonetheless, the modest epistle is just as much a self-consciously managed performance as the boastful motto. Shakespeare signs his full name to the letter, securing—at a time when contemporary writers, and especially playwrights, were usually treated as anonymous labourers—a clear identification of this poetic work with its author's name. Furthermore, casting *Venus and Adonis* as 'the first heir of my invention', the dedication raises expectation of 'some graver labour' to follow from the genius of this emerging poet. Given that Shakespeare is not known to have arranged for the printed preservation of any of his playtexts, it is remarkable that he contrived so successfully his emergence in print as a poet destined for lasting fame.

Not all acts of self-assertive risk-taking pay off, but how sweet it must have felt for him to read the tributes in which the learned and the literati so frequently played back to him his own identification with the honey tongue and sweet soul of Ovid. The language of praise and even of mild criticism echoed his own inventions, with Weever on Shakespeare's 'children', for example, picking up his metaphor of poetic heirs. When a 'Parnassus' play performed by Cambridge undergraduates gently satirized admirers of *Venus and Adonis* who were stimulated by its eroticism, it reiterated Shakespeare's own mention of 'graver' work to imagine what power this new poet's 'heart throbbing line[s]' would have if he took on 'a graver subject'. The learned Gabriel Harvey amplified Shakespeare's implicit distinction between first efforts and mature accomplishment in claiming that 'Venus' suited 'the younger sort', 'but his Lucrece, & . . . Hamlet . . . have it in them, to please the wiser sort'.

This grand narrative of a poetic vocation having evidently been so carefully constructed, after *The Rape of Lucrece* it would seem to have been as casually abandoned when the playhouses reopened and Shakespeare's energies became reabsorbed in his theatrical enterprises. Even though the poet-speaker of the Sonnets eventually published in 1609 brags of preserving his young male friend's beauty in his enduring verse, there are no clear signs that Shakespeare either controlled, or sought to control, how these poems came to circulate in print or how they were received. The fortunes of sonnets written by Shakespeare during his own lifetime suggest instead how a poet's reputation may be subject to the profits and interests of others. In 1599, for example, the printer William Jaggard capitalized on Shakespeare's early poetic fame by publishing a rag-bag collection of sonnets and lyrics by various writers, some about Venus and some fairly salacious, under the title *The Passionate Pilgrim* 'by W. Shakespeare'. It did include two Shakespearian sonnets later to appear as numbers 138 and 144 in the 1609 edition along with three poems taken from Shakespeare's comedy *Love's Labour's Lost*. In the play, the three embedded poems are represented as mawkish amateur verses 'written' by besotted noblemen, which end up accidentally circulating outside of their control to their mockery and shame. The irony of seeing these verses circulate as specimens of his own poetic artistry cannot have been lost on Shakespeare, however much any distinction between authentic and inauthentic 'Shakespeare' must have been lost on those who purchased *The Passionate Pilgrim*.

Many details remain obscure about the publication and contemporary reception of the 1609 Sonnets, the text invariably relied upon for Shakespeare's 'authentic' sonnets. Scholars still debate whether Shakespeare authorized the edition or whether the publisher Thomas Thorpe merely pursued his own advantage and profit. Like the narrative poems, they are prefaced by a dedication, but one—as we shall see later—that has caused endless speculation over the centuries about its details and meaning. Readers also speculate about the identities of the characters addressed within the poems and whether or not they are pure fictions or allude to historical persons. These mysteries and uncertainties about the life of Shakespeare's 'Sonnets' in their own time are part of the indeterminacy that contributes to their open-ended interpretation and endless fascination for modern readers.

Venus and Adonis

Imitating and striving to outdo Ovid as the poet of desire and sweet verse, Shakespeare makes two essential changes to the story of Venus and Adonis as it is told in Book X of *The Metamorphoses*. In Ovid's brief account, the goddess's youthful mortal lover comes to grief when he resists her advice and hunts the deadly boar. After he dies, Venus mourns, and makes a short-lived flower spring up out of Adonis's blood. In Shakespeare's poem, it is Venus's love itself that Adonis resists, and the brief tale is amplified, mainly by Venus's repeated and cleverly varied persuasions that Adonis's rejection of her love motivates, into a long poem of heightened verbal display. At this relatively early stage in his writing career, both in poetry and in dramatic verse, the ideal of language that Shakespeare pursues is *copia* or abundance of speech. Almost all Elizabethan schoolboys would have read the humanist scholar Erasmus's textbook on this subject, which he introduced with this claim: 'Just as there is nothing more . . . splendid than a speech with a rich copia of thoughts and words overflowing in a golden stream, so it is, assuredly, such a thing as may be striven for at no slight risk'.[3] The risk of wordiness, for the word-loving poet, is surprisingly similar to the risk Venus tries to anticipate and correct when she offers thousands of kisses—that is, satiety, or too much of a good thing: 'I'll smother thee with kisses, / And yet not cloy thy lips with loathed satiety, / But rather famish them amid their plenty, / Making them red, and pale, with fresh variety; / Ten kisses short as one, one long as twenty' (18–22). In this poem, the economies of language and eroticism, copia and copulation, are closely allied. The price of what is on plentiful offer must be kept high through ingenious variations.

Some of Shakespeare's strategies for amplification are imaginative ways to translate classical myth into an English context and to domesticate it as erotic epyllion (or mini-epic). For example, epic similes flesh out descriptions and situations, the extended comparisons often being introduced with 'Look', as if the words are drawing visual pictures: 'Look how a bird lies tangled in a net, / So fastened in her arms Adonis lies' (67–8) or 'Look when a painter would surpass the life / . . . So did this horse excel a common one' (289, 293). In these comparisons as in the physical descriptions of setting, Shakespeare transports Venus and her story from her Mediterranean haunts to a vividly realized rural English landscape. However sophisticated the poem's wit and sexual politics, it seems very much through a country-boy's eyes and leisurely observation that the plant and animal life of the rural setting are sympathetically and appreciatively viewed. A wonderful example occurs when Venus tells Adonis to hunt something less dangerous than the boar and then describes the erratic movements of a hare in flight 'to overshoot his troubles', how 'he cranks and crosses with a thousand doubles. / The many musits [hedge gaps] through the which he goes / Are like a labyrinth to amaze his foes' (680–4). As Venus elaborates the evasive tactics of the hunter's prey, the reader comes almost to taste the grief and fear of 'poor Wat' [the hare] (697).

In a mythologizing spirit, Shakespeare further animates and personalizes the poem's natural world by representing everyday occurrences as caused by gods and goddesses. The morning dew, for example, comes of the dawn-goddess's weeping when the sun leaves her bed (1–2), and the blazing mid-day heat that burns Adonis's cheek is caused by Titan's veering close to take a lustful look at the courting pair, 'Wishing Adonis had his team to guide / So he were like him, and by Venus' side' (179–80). The 'storying' of the natural world also deploys myths of 'origin', from the tale of how Adonis got his 'pretty dimple' (242) to Venus's own interpretation of the overall story, as a tale of how love's pleasure would henceforth be interlaced with frustration and misery (1135–64). In this world of speaking pictures, if Adonis's horse trots, rears, and leaps for his beloved mare, it is 'As who should say, "Lo, thus my strength is tried, / And this I do to captivate the eye / Of the fair breeder that is standing by"' (280–2). Shakespeare has created a fully languaged world, where signs luminously yield up their significations, as where the 'dumb play' of Venus's petitionary kneeling to Adonis 'had his [its] acts made plain / With tears which, chorus-like, her eyes did rain' (359–60). This lucid eloquence is enhanced by the formality of the six-line stanza, with its regular iambic pentameter measures and rich rhymes (*ababcc*).

Despite the artistry of the descriptions, what, above all, animates the poem's language is the vibrancy of its unorthodox speech interactions, together with the power and gender reversals they involve. Indeed, Venus's extended talk, motivated by the unresponsiveness of her interlocutor, supplies the poem's main action. Guides to rhetoric and poetic technique will not tell the whole story about the verbal tactics of this poem. Its wit calls upon the reader's own tacit knowledge of how conversation is supposed to work in various contexts and how people might be expected to address one another across different power relations. Shakespeare sets it all up in a kind of intertextual dialogue between his own preliminary speech acts and Venus's surprising speech acts within the poem. Just as the poet has put himself and his goods on offer, first boastfully and then playing the deferential suitor for his patron's favour, so Venus is positioned to play the role of 'bold-faced suitor' (6). At the outset, when she offers herself up to Adonis, she has every reason to expect ecstatic acceptance and little need for extended pleas. The power, anyone would assume, is all in Venus's court. She is, after all, not only a goddess but the love goddess; the sun-god Titan is dying to be in her arms. Even the behaviour of Adonis's horse, she tells him, should teach him how normal it is to take up such a glorious offer, 'To take advantage on presented joy' (405). The wit is in the reversal of conversational expectations, as the goddess experiences the risk of rejection that less powerful mortals experience when they make verbal offers. This stalemate opens up, in a comic way, the whole issue of how relationships can encompass the desires and wants of both parties. How can couples negotiate mutuality in their interactions, rather than just confront situations where one takes and the other gives? Sexual desire may be very self-centred, but en route to its fulfilment is an encounter with dialogue. Venus's speech plight and incompetence at dialogue highlight the problem, for she both wants Adonis's acquiescence and does not want to contend with his independent will: 'Speak, fair', she directs him, 'but speak fair words, or else be mute' (208).

Thus Venus becomes the frustrated petitioner, a 'suitor' in both Elizabethan senses of the word, which includes both the subordinate's courtier-like pleading for hard-to-obtain 'suits' or rewards and also sexual courting. The poem reverses sex as well as power roles, with the woman playing seducer and the young man 'coy maiden'. Whereas, in traditional love verse, the poetic devices of the male suitor objectify a silent female beloved, cataloguing her body parts or casting him as colonizer of her body as his new-found-land, *Venus and Adonis* surprises these conventions in the imaginative and sensuous ways that Venus tropes her own body. Most often quoted in Shakespeare's own time and ours is the deer park metaphor:

> I'll be a park, and thou shalt be my deer.
> Feed where thou wilt, on mountain or in dale;
>> Graze on my lips, and if those hills be dry,
>> Stray lower, where the pleasant fountains lie.
>>> (231-4)

Down lower, the erotic temptations include 'Sweet bottom-grass' (236) and 'Round rising hillocks' (237).

However tempting Venus's offer, her extreme persistence catches her up in what in modern-day terms is the 'no-means-no' dilemma: that is, the issue of when persuasion crosses over into coercion. Shakespeare, on the one hand, signals with a metaphor about the 'blindfold fury' of the foraging 'vulture' when Venus's impulses turn dark and violent (547–54). On the other hand, he exploits the physical comedy of the female sexual predator for all it is worth: when 'He on her belly falls, she on her back' (594), Venus, hot to 'clip Elysium', still 'lack[s] her joy' (600) due to 'The warm effects which she in him finds missing' (605).

But the sexual role reversals at the heart of the poem do not merely provide a clever variation on the dynamics of male–female eroticism. Once the reversals at the heart of this erotic epyllion are considered in relation to the activating of desire in the poem's anticipated readers, one effect is to create a spillage of desire outside of conventional gendered boundaries. For the Cambridge undergraduates (all male at this time), who are said to have kept the poem under their pillows, it offered fantasies of both Venus's 'bottom-grass' and Adonis's loveliness. Even perhaps for female readers, who in the 1590s were increasingly being wooed by sexual fictions in print, there was some choice of object amidst the poem's temptations.

The Rape of Lucrece

The Rape of Lucrece develops the 'graver' subject of Shakespeare's second printed poem, amplifying to 1,855 verse lines the terse, 131-line account in Ovid's *Fasti*, a poetic calendar of Roman festivals and related legends. In Ovid's telling, as in the related short versions most likely known to Shakespeare from Livy's *History of Rome* and Chaucer's *Legend of Good Women*, the Roman lords, at the youthful Tarquin's suggestion, seek recreation late one night from the slow work of besieging Ardea with a quick trip to Rome to check whether their wives are still thinking about them. While the thoughtless court ladies are found to be drinking and frolicking, at Lord Collatine's house his chaste wife's thoughts are on her husband's comfort: Lucrece is spinning wool with her maids to make him a warm coat. Tarquin's lust is stirred by Lucrece's beauty and virtue. Returning secretly the next night, the king's son is received hospitably by Lucrece, but, once the house is asleep, Tarquin forcefully ravishes her, after threatening to shame her as an adultress by depositing a murdered slave in her bed. Once morning comes, a mournful Lucrece summons her father and husband. Tarquin's deed made known, her relatives and friends exonerate Lucrece, and yet she stabs and kills herself. Proud Tarquin pays with exile and eventual death, and the political order of the day is overturned, the sway of tyrant kings replaced by a republican government.

A succinct prose Argument provides a political frame for Shakespeare's poem, telling how—before the rape—Lucius Tarquin (the protagonist's father) had violently seized possession of the kingdom without 'the people's suffrages' and how—after the rape— 'with one consent' the people exile the Tarquins and change the state government 'from kings to consuls'. Focusing almost exclusively on the interpersonal encounter the night Tarquin rapes Lucrece and the next morning's aftermath, Shakespeare's copious poem covers a smaller slice of action than its sources or its frame. Frame and poem, the political and the interpersonal, are nonetheless interwoven by the themes of possession and consent. Both in usurpation and in rape, the Tarquins' crimes are read as the wilful seizure (without social consent) of another's property. Modern readers may find it strange to think of chaste Lucrece as her husband Collatine's treasured 'possession' (18), and to think of the injury of rape as the theft of *his* property, but this patriarchal idea is the intertextual lynchpin between the personal and political on which the 'graver' import of Shakespeare's poem depends.

The full-languaged style repeats many of the verbal ornaments of *Venus and Adonis*, with highly embellished schemes of word and sound repetition and extended comparisons prominently displayed. Images of claustrophobic interiors dominate over the genial outdoor imagery of the earlier poem, and draw as much upon the stylized representational practices of heraldry as directly from nature. The habit of parallelism and antithesis is sharpened into oxymoron, the verbal meeting of opposites which has been recognized as the poem's most characteristic trope.[4] Tarquin, for example, led by the 'lightless fire' (4) of his lust, goes forth to prey upon Collatine's marital happiness, 'cancelled ere well begun' (26); he departs from the ravished Lucrece as 'A captive victor that hath lost in gain' (730).

In opening out its copiousness, the poem explores the emotional phases of the unfolding encounter, its point of view fixed on Tarquin before the rape and Lucrece after. It also provides a running moral commentary on Tarquin's actions, which distinguishes it from *Venus and Adonis* and, indeed, from most of Shakespeare's other works. As in *Venus*, a flawed dialogue between the two central characters is at the heart of the poem, but the governing speech genre here is deliberative oratory or formal debate rather than conversation. If Lucrece resembles *Titus*'s Lavinia and *Cymbeline*'s Innogen in her injured innocence, she resembles *Measure for Measure*'s Isabella in her skilful display of oratory and logic. Copious speech and feminine modesty are usually said to be entirely at odds in early modern cultural ideology, but Shakespeare characterizes this faithful wife, piteously wordless in Chaucer's *Legend* both when threatened with and when grieving her violation, in terms of her 'modest eloquence' (563). Elizabethan readers would have likely heard another oxymoron in this expression.

The narrative of the rape is highly stylized. At one level, the drama seems to be unfolding at a glacial pace, hundreds of verse lines each occupied by the minor plot stages in which Tarquin withdraws into his chamber, disputes within himself, lights a torch by sparking his sword against stone, moves through the castle to Lucrece's bedchamber, reveals his will to Lucrece, hears her oration against his action—and, then, quite astonishingly, in two lines the rape is done. But at another level, dominated by a flood of metaphors, many animated dramas seem to be unfolding, the poem exploding with actions.

These actions are loosely guided or connected by a larger recurring metaphor of conquest and usurpation, a metaphor that again connects the interpersonal and political. Lucrece is represented as a territory or unconquered world, securely possessed throughout its history by its one rightful lord, and having at its centre a fortified city. Tarquin is represented as the foul usurper, whose army pitilessly assails, conquers, and destroys. Yet only occasionally is this governing metaphor brought into focus. The reader's attention is more often being caught up with an animated action or conflict amongst the divided qualities or parts of one or other character: disputation ''Tween frozen conscience and hot-burning will' (247) in Tarquin, for example; or his veins 'like straggling slaves for pillage fighting' (428) until 'his beating heart, alarum striking, / Gives the hot charge, and bids them do their liking' (433–4).

Although the basic encounter of the poem is between two persons and two bodies, Shakespeare defamiliarizes this encounter by shaking up such familiar categories as the body and the person as integrated and individual agents. Recent studies of everyday metaphors that sustain familiar categories that people take for granted and live by have emphasized how prevalent is the metaphor of body as container.[5] That is, the human body is imagined as bounded, unitary, containing and integrating its various passions and parts; this contained body helps to reinforce the concept of the person as an individual and autonomous agent. But in *Lucrece* the body is fractured or divided and its parts become the primary actors and agents in the poem's quick-paced mini-dramas. At times these representational techniques resemble predictable conventions of allegory—with Tarquin's inner conflict figured in a debate of his personified parts and the ravished Lucrece in turn berating the personifications Night, Opportunity, and Time.

On the whole Shakespeare's tactics are more dynamic, specifically and creatively adapted to the intersubjective encounter at the poem's centre, with an important relation established between the frustrated dialogue and fractured identities. The act or interaction at the centre of this poem is neither mutual nor consensual, and yet it is depicted as inescapably social and radically affecting the selfhood of each party. This is reflected in Tarquin's quite literal discomposure into multiple agents advancing upon Lucrece. Her oration works to summon and recompose her interlocutor. Her guiding theme is her insistence that he collect himself and govern his unruly parts: 'Thou are not what thou seem'st, and if the same, / Thou seem'st not what thou art, a god, a king, / For kings like gods should govern everything' (600–2). This is evident in the form of her address to him, insisting on 'Thou' and 'thee' over the third persons that exert agency over him: 'Hast *thou* command?' (624), she asks, and pleads, 'To *thee*, to *thee* my heaved-up hands appeal, / Not to seducing lust, thy rash relier' (638–9, emphasis added).

Equally striking, given how much readers and Lucrece's hearers might wish to assert that the ravished Lucrece is the same Lucrece still, is the poem's representation of her discomposure after the encounter, when he leaves behind his 'load of lust' (734). Her fractured self-consciousness is perhaps initiated by his first words spoken in her chamber, which insinuate the complicity of her parts with his crime when she asks 'Under what colour he commits this ill' (476): 'The colour in thy face . . . Shall plead for me . . . Thy beauty hath ensnared thee to this night' (477–80, 485). The dividing practices in this rejoinder draw upon the poetic tradition of the 'blazon', a convention of listing and advertising the attractive physical parts of a beloved that has been much critiqued in recent years as misogynist. It was, indeed, by means of a bragging anatomy of his wife's features that Collatine unwittingly aroused Tarquin's lust. But Lucrece's 'mutiny' 'with herself' (1153) that is an outcome of the encounter is also caught up with her lived confusion in a pre-Cartesian world about how the contamination of the body can coexist with the purity of the mind or soul. It is very difficult to give a satisfactory answer to why Lucrece feels the need to kill herself, but it is surely caught up with this complex apprehension of the affliction of rape as self-alienating.

Shorter narrative poems

Two shorter narrative poems also focus on relationships as impaired dialogue, the one frustrated by the finality of death, the other by desertion. *The Phoenix and Turtle*, appended together with other poets' work on the same subject to Robert Chester's *Love's Martyr* (1601), is an elegy, in an abstract or philosophical tone, for the ideal love of two birds. It consists of three movements: a summons, in which mourners are called together and such undesirables as the screech owl and 'treble-dated crow' (17) warded off; an anthem, which celebrates the wondrous mutuality and consent of the two birds—'Single nature's double name / Neither two nor one was called' (39–40); and a *threnos*, or mourning song, in which Reason laments their passing. Obscure though this poem is generally agreed to be, read in relation to Shakespeare's other poems it registers what all the other love relationships lack: a fully mutual communion or dialogue.

A Lover's Complaint, appended in 1609 to the Sonnets, bears out Shakespeare's fascination with exploring how the complex interiority of a desiring subject is caught up with the negotiation of an unequal power relation. The poem begins with a deserted woman's grief and clamours of complaint, like a 'double voice' echoing or 're-worded' off the concave surface of a hill (1–3); the rime royal stanza (*ababbcc*), also used in *Lucrece*, emphasizes the theme of repeated sounds. Next a human listener, an aged and 'reverend man' 'desires to know / In brief the grounds and motives of her woe' (57, 62–3); then she finds language for her pain, figuring her youthful seducer's attractive power as giving rise to a false assurance of consensual dialogue:

> Consents bewitched, ere he desire, have granted,
> And dialogued for him what he would say,
> Asked their own wills, and made their wills obey
> (131-3)

As in *Lucrece*, the woman's encounter with the powerful other is self-alienating. As in *Venus and Adonis*, the young man's beauty is calculated to arouse both men and women, summoning up or spilling desire outside of the ostensibly heterosexual boundaries depicted. And, as in Sonnets such as 'They that have power to hurt but will do none' (S. 94), the love object's chilly lack of affect registers his power: 'Harm have I done to them, but ne'er was harmèd; / Kept hearts in liveries [i.e. in subjection], but mine own was free' (194–5).

Shakespeare's sonnets

The publication circumstances of *Shakespeare's Sonnets* (1609) contribute to uncertainties about how to read the 154 short poems, most of them addressed by an unidentified 'I' to an unidentified 'thee' or 'you'. The textual apparatus includes a dedication, not by the poet but by T. T., evidently the publisher Thomas Thorpe, 'To the only begetter of these ensuing sonnets Mr. W. H'. 'Begetter' has been taken to point towards any one of the following: the writer, the provider of the manuscript, a patron, or the primary love object of the sonnets. In the latter two categories, conjectures have often landed either on Shakespeare's early poetic patron, Henry Wriothesley, Earl of Southampton, or William Herbert, Earl of Pembroke, although it has never been clear why either nobleman would be addressed by the inappropriate title, 'Master'.

To what extent these identifications matter depends, in part, on the much-debated issue of whether or not the poems' situations of address have links to Shakespeare's own life and relationships. Not only is the overall period of composition uncertain (the Oxford editors suggest 1593 to 1603), but it is also unclear whether Shakespeare authorized the eventual printing of the Sonnets. Do the 154 printed poems, then, constitute an organized sequence planned by the poet? If the debate about the dedication raises uncertainty about relevant biographical or historical contexts for reading the Sonnets, the question about authorization raises uncertainty about how to read individual sonnets in relation to a larger composition or textual narrative.

Whereas the narrative poems make background information explicit, the individual sonnets often leave to the readers' inference-making the questions, who is speaking? to whom? and in what situation? Yet no one comes without assumptions to the reading of sonnets by a cultural icon like William Shakespeare. Modern-day texts usually cue readers to construct the sequence as a loose story of four 'characters': a poet-speaker (in some views identified with Shakespeare, in some carefully separated from him); a fair high-born young man, the idealized beloved of Sonnets 1–126; a dark and sexually active lady, the denigrated beloved of Sonnets 127–54; and, as a secondary character, a rival poet.

As the reader begins interpolating from individual sonnets to a larger narrative, some surprising reversals of conventions from earlier love poetry, such as the Petrarchan sonnet tradition, come into view. Instead of wooing an idealized female beloved, the male speaker of Sonnets 1–126 woos a younger man. First, he urges him, apparently disinterestedly, to preserve his beauty by finding a wife and producing children, until at Sonnet 20 he brings out the contradictions of his own position in relation to 'the master-mistress' he is wooing, a man 'pricked . . . out for women's pleasure' and yet the object of his own passion. The next hundred or so sonnets directly cultivate, celebrate, or seek to repair and maintain an achieved love bond between the two men. On the one hand, the youth is idealized and made an object of the poet's skill at memorializing (without, paradoxically, ever being named). On the other hand, he is found at times to disappoint, whether by absence, lack of attention, sexual straying, aloof self-containment, the speaker's own self-doubts, or the lovers' disparity of social status. Sonnets 78–86 complicate the situation when a 'rival poet' competes for the youth's attentions.

The second major surprise of the sonnet story is the woman courted in Sonnets 127–54. Again the conventional poetic beloved is jettisoned, but now for a woman who seems moulded to be her opposite: not fair in hair or complexion, but dark; not chaste, but sexually promiscuous ('the bay where all men ride' [S. 137], including, apparently, the fair young friend); not epitomizing truth, but full of lies; not worthy of devotion, but the unworthy object of sexual obsession. In each relation, how the speaker imagines himself is closely related to how he imagines the other, so that the later sonnets are as marked by cynical self-loathing as the early sonnets are by hopeful idealism.

Recently, the self-evident presence within the sonnet sequence of this, or any, unified story line has been radically challenged. The late-eighteenth-century editor, Edmond Malone, for example, has been credited with setting up his text and commentary in such a way as to construct and regularize this conventional narrative and, so, in a way, to 'invent' our modern-day Shakespeare together with the rich and recognizable interior life read out of the sonnets. Critics also charge that interpretations of the sonnet relationships—for example, a longstanding tendency to deny homosexual aspects of the male 'friendship'—have as often been touchstones of their times, encoding the interpreters' cultural biases, as reflecting an objective sonnet story. Furthermore, some critics have proposed jettisoning even the assumed bipartite division at Sonnet 126 altogether, to rediscover what individual sonnets might potentially mean if readers dropped set assumptions about any continuous story and admitted how ambiguous are the situations of address in many individual sonnets.[6] Impossible though it may be to read and interpret without bringing background assumptions into play, the indeterminateness of the sonnet story must be acknowledged.

Despite these uncertainties, general agreement remains that the sonnets develop and vary such key themes of Renaissance literature and humanist thought as time, death, art, and fame. Sonnets 1 to 17 most closely approximate the narrative poetry's aesthetic of amplification, repeatedly arguing with copious variation that time's assault on the beloved's beauty can be forestalled by reproducing heirs. Other sonnets displace this cure for time and death, elaborating the poet's brag about the immortalizing power of his writing—that 'As [time] takes from you, I engraft you new' (S. 15). The sonnets give astonishingly potent expression to the theme of time's devastations, personifying time at one moment as tyrant, at another as defacing graffiti artist (S. 64), imaging time's power as the 'hungry' ocean's erosion of the shore (S. 64), or the reaper's scything (S. 12), or the predator's devouring (S. 19). No less potent are observations about lust as 'Th' expense of spirit in a waste of shame', a vanishing pleasure 'Enjoyed no sooner but despisèd straight' (S. 129) or about love as sometimes beyond 'the breath of words' and elaborate praise, known in 'dumb thoughts, speaking in effect' (S. 85).

Beyond these compelling general themes and their rich linguistic realizations, the sonnets have been most highly valued for their evocation, both complex and immediate, of inner experiences. It is almost as if sonnets like 'When to the sessions of sweet silent thought' (S. 30) invent or give language to mental experiences their readers could not have described but nonetheless recognize, or feel they inhabit, and then appropriate and quote the words almost as their own thoughts. Of course, readers can always practise reading strategies to resist, but the lyric 'I' of these poems seems to summon these identifications. It may seem paradoxical that these poems evidently unfolding private subjectivity are almost all addressed to a second person, to 'thou' or to 'you'. Although no one ever answers, the poems imagined as speech acts or utterances are strongly dialogic, in that the other's responses or reactions are always being constructed and anticipated, as with sonnets beginning 'Is it thy will?' (S. 61), 'Say that thou didst forsake me for some fault' (S. 89), 'Accuse me thus' (S. 117), or 'That you were once unkind befriends me now' (S. 120). Some of the most powerful emotions of the sonnets—shame, self-recrimination, different shades of desire, longing, and loathing—depend upon this realization of individual interiority as social dialogue, usually played out, as in the narrative poems, across power differences.

There may be a quality of voyeurism to reading Shakespeare's narrative poems, as one gazes from outside at a scene exquisitely and fully rendered for one's pleasure and grazing. The pleasure of Shakespeare's sonnets is much more caught up with the activity of reading and meaning-making, as one works with suggestions and gaps to situate the 'I' and 'thou' and bring the inner scene into intelligible focus.

FURTHER READING

Bate, Jonathan. *Shakespeare and Ovid* (Oxford: Clarendon Press, 1993), pp. 1–100. The classical poet Ovid provides the source or inspiration for many of Shakespeare's poems, and this book examines what Ovid meant within Renaissance culture and schooling and how Shakespeare's poetry emulates and amplifies Ovid's.

Belsey, Catherine. 'Tarquin Dispossessed: Expropriation and Consent in "The Rape of Lucrece"', *Shakespeare Quarterly*, 52 (2001), 315–35. A clear exposition of how personal and political themes intersect, with particular attention to the construction of rape as theft of property.

de Grazia, Margreta. 'The Scandal of Shakespeare's Sonnets', *Shakespeare Survey 46* (1994), 35–49. Rpt. Schiffer, 'Shakespeare's Sonnets', pp. 89–112. Against the view that eighteenth-century editors covered up the 'scandal' of homosexuality associated with Shakespeare in the sonnets, this essay argues that the uncontrollable passion for the 'dark lady' is more likely to have seemed shameful to Renaissance readers.

Dubrow, Heather. *Captive Victors: Shakespeare's Narrative Poems and Sonnets* (Ithaca and London: Cornell University Press, 1987). The book offers sustained readings of Shakespeare's major poems, intertwining formal questions with psychological questions.

Duncan-Jones, Katherine (ed.). *Shakespeare's Sonnets* (London: Arden Shakespeare, 1997). This edition provides an interesting account of the early publication history of the sonnets, arguing that the 1609 quarto was authorized by Shakespeare.

Kolin, Philip C. (ed.). *Venus and Adonis: Critical Essays* (New York and London: Garland Publishing, 1997). This book offers a good view of the overall critical tradition, including a wide range of perspectives from Samuel Taylor Coleridge to present-day critics.

Maus, Katharine Eisaman. 'Taking Tropes Seriously: Language and Violence in Shakespeare's "Rape of Lucrece"', *Shakespeare Quarterly*, 37 (1986), 66–82. A close reading of *The Rape of Lucrece* focusing in detail upon rhetoric and drawing attention to the close connection between metaphor and the characters' decisions, between language and psychological states.

Schiffer, James (ed.). *Shakespeare's Sonnets: Critical Essays* (New York and London: Garland Publishing, 1999). This volume collects recent essays representing a wide range of current critical approaches to the Sonnets, including both theoretical overviews and critical readings.

Smith, Bruce R. *Homosexual Desire in Shakespeare's England: A Cultural Poetics* (Chicago: University of Chicago Press, 1991), pp. 228–70. A key work for understanding the love sonnets addressed to the young man in relation to the history of homosexuality in Renaissance England.

Vickers, Nancy. ' "The blazon of sweet beauty's best": Shakespeare's "Lucrece" '. In *Shakespeare and the Question of Theory*, ed. Patricia Parker and Geoffrey Hartman (New York and London: Methuen, 1985), pp. 95–115. This feminist essay explores the role of poetic blazon in *Lucrece*, explaining the relation between male rivalry and descriptive occasions for anatomizing and praising admired features of female beauty. It also considers the related importance of heraldic imagery in the poem.

NOTES

1. William Wordsworth, 'Scorn not the sonnet' (1827).
2. Contemporary allusions are quoted from E. K. Chambers, *William Shakespeare: A Study of Facts and Problems*, 2 vols. (Oxford: Clarendon Press, 1930), 2: 194–201. Spelling has been modernized.
3. 'On Copia of Words and Ideas', trans. Donald B. King and H. David Rix (Milwaukee, Wis.: Marquette University Press, 1963), p. 11.
4. Or, more technically, syneciosis (the cross-couple). See Heather Dubrow, *Captive Victors*, pp. 80–168 and Joel Fineman, 'Shakespeare's *Will*: The Temporality of Rape', *Representations* 20 (1987), 25–76.
5. See George Lakoff and Mark Johnson, *Metaphors We Live By* (Chicago and London: Chicago University Press, 1980). It is equally important in reading Tarquin's variable passions to recognize that Elizabethan bodily perception was to some extent still linked to the humoral materialism of Galenic physiology, which might ascribe agency and affective capacity to body parts. See Gail Kern Paster, *The Body Embarrassed* (Ithaca: Cornell University Press, 1993), pp. 6–17.
6. For details of these arguments, see the reprinted essays in James Schiffer's *Shakespeare's Sonnets* by Peter Stallybrass, Margreta de Grazia, and Heather Dubrow.

READING: *Shakespeare's sonnets*

Structures and their complication

In reading some representative Shakespeare sonnets, this brief chapter develops a set of ten questions, grouped into general topic areas, that might enrich the activity of reading other sonnets. Two questions about overall structure can provide a fruitful starting point. *(1) How do stanzaic structure, syntactic structure, and movement of thought fit together? (2) Looking more closely, what complicates the simple trajectory of the thought?*

Let's take Sonnet 12 as a test case.

> When I do count the clock that tells the time,
> And see the brave day sunk in hideous night;
> When I behold the violet past prime,
> And sable curls ensilvered o'er with white;
> When lofty trees I see barren of leaves,
> Which erst from heat did canopy the herd,
> And summer's green all girded up in sheaves
> Borne on the bier with white and bristly beard:
> Then of thy beauty do I question make
> That thou among the wastes of time must go,
> Since sweets and beauties do themselves forsake,
> And die as fast as they see other grow;
> > And nothing 'gainst time's scythe can make defence
> > Save breed to brave him when he takes thee hence.

Most Shakespeare sonnets conform to what has come to be called the English or Shakespearian sonnet stanza, with fourteen iambic pentameter lines, rhyming *abab cdcd efef gg*—as illustrated in Sonnet 12. While stanza patterns are formal structures—constraining repetitive arrangements of unaccented and accented syllables and of end-rhymes—they also set up patterns of expectation for how the thought of a poem might be developed. Paul Fussell long ago made the useful suggestion that the English sonnet promotes a 'balloon-and-pin-prick' pattern of problem development and resolution.[1] That is, the invitation is to build up and develop a problem through the twelve lines comprising the three quatrains marked off by alternating rhymes—as if slowly blowing air into a balloon-like vessel and giving it shape—and then to produce a quick turn or witty conclusion in the chiming final couplet—as if to suddenly burst the bubble. Of course, the sequence of three quatrains within the stanza provides for alternative ways to divide the thought, with a turn or shift also easily made and formally marked at line 5 or 9.

In Sonnet 12, the large-scale syntactic framework operates to demarcate the thought trajectory. We see it in the logic of the 'When (1) . . . When (3) . . . When (5) . . . Then (9) . . . And (13)', which marks off clear steps in the thinking process. These co-ordinate with the quatrains-and-couplet units demarcated by rhyme words. Here the subordinate 'When' clauses build up a problematic observation about short-lived phenomena within the natural world, heralding at 'Then' the thought's arrival in its principal clause at the problem applied to what the speaker particularly prizes, the beloved's transient beauty. The couplet succinctly supplies a solution to time's onslaught in the word 'breed'. Thus, stanza form, syntax, and logical development orient readers to grasp readily the overall shape of the sonnet's meditation. Often, a cluster of poems varying a shared theme also provides orientation, as in this case with Sonnets 1 to 14, which all recommend dynastic continuation accomplished by marriage and children as the solution to the ephemerality of the beloved young man's beauty.

A complex texture of thought and rhetorical figuration unfolds within the simple overall structure of Sonnet 12. Differences, even contradictions, stand out amidst a structural frame that sets up expectations of parallelism or sameness. This pattern of likeness is set up not only by the overall 'When . . . When' development, but also by the enforced *isocolon* (equal length) and *parison* (parallel structure) of the pentameter line units. The poem builds, as do Shakespeare's narrative poems, on the principle of rhetorical *copia*, elegantly restating and varying its similar expressions. Line after line, it piles up images of how time's passing registers within a physical scene or setting, most of them natural—the day's sinking, the violet's fading, the trees dropping leaves, the summer's growth finished. Difference-making amidst this accumulated and reinforced sameness of things enters with an occasional pattern that conflates nature's process with human progression.

The poem's first measure of time is the human clock, but when the measure shifts to nature's setting sun, a slightly incongruous note enters with the human descriptor 'brave'—as if the sun wore fine clothes or even showed defiance in moving towards 'hideous' night. Human descriptors start to colour and even distort perceptions of a sadness to the natural process, with lofty trees incongruously 'barren' in fall, though we know they will produce new leaves in spring; and autumn's fresh produce or grain carried on a 'bier', as if like an old white-bearded man to his burial. The 'When . . . Then' shape of the poem makes us expect the beloved's situation to be emotionally coloured by what the speaker has taken in from the natural scene, but this is complicated by how the speaker's human sympathies have already pre-coloured or even falsified his perception of natural processes, which are cyclical and renewable. These surprises culminate in the surprising word choice—'breed'—of the defence against time's ruin the poet recommends to his beloved friend. The word choice signals, as 'children' would not, the non-human aspect of this solution. It forecasts, in a way, why, after thirteen or fourteen repetitions in separate sonnets, this solution may come to seem unsatisfactory and be discarded, how one might want for one's beloved a solution that distinguishes human aspirations and potential from plant and animal process. In a sense, the poem deconstructs its own resolution, even as it loudly brays it out in the abrasive 'br' sounds of 'breed to brave him'

Figures

Four additional questions about rhetorical figures can help to shift attention from overall structures to detailed texture. *(3) Where do rhetorical figures come into play? That is, where does the language show a certain strangeness or depart from common usage? (4) What role do schemes play? (5) What role do tropes play? (6) What different fields of discourse do Shakespeare's metaphors bring into association?*

In Sonnet 12, one can readily see how some simple rhetorical figures of sound make the poem's incongruities stand out. *Isocolon* (units of equal length), *parison* (units of parallel structure), and *anaphora* (the same word repeated at the beginning of a series of clauses, as illustrated by 'When') set up a background sameness, which in turn foregrounds the interruptions by the alliterative repetitions of the *b*s and *br*s at 'brave' (l. 2), 'barren' (l. 5), then crowded together in assorted patterns at '*B*orne on the *b*ier with white and *b*ristly *b*eard' (l. 8), and reinvoked as climactic finale at '*br*eed to *br*ave him' (l. 14).

George Puttenham, Shakespeare's contemporary, described figures of speech as ornaments in language, which are 'also in a sort abuses or rather trespasses in speech' in that they 'pass the ordinary limits of common utterance'; they draw the ear and mind away from 'plainness and simplicity to a certain doubleness'.[2] Against Puttenham, it is possible to argue (as Shakespeare himself, with a dramatist's keen interest in the eloquence of conversation, was aware) that everyday speech has its metaphors, its word and sound repetitions that correspond to recognized figures. Nonetheless, the basic question—Where does the language show a certain strangeness or depart from common usage?—even without the equipment of Greek or Latin names for figures of speech, will permit a reader to recognize and enjoy much of the figurative density of the sonnets. Consider, for example, the opening quatrain of Sonnet 64, a poem with the same 'When . . . When' structure as 12:

> When I have seen by time's fell hand defaced
> The rich proud cost of outworn buried age;
> When sometime-lofty towers I see down razed,
> And brass eternal slave to mortal rage. . . .

Some points of strangeness here include: the abstract 'time' attributed a human hand and its action of destruction figured as the vandalism of graffiti wreckage; 'cost', rather than material objects like statues or monuments, as what is defaced by time, generalizing and broadening the perception of how human expense or expenditure of energy on memorializing is wasted; the doubleness to the ear of the phrase 'down razed', which means obliterate but, sounding like 'down raised', captures in its contradiction the poem's long-term view of how proudly built-up towers are inevitably brought down by time; the doubleness to the mind of line 4, where one is caught by the sliding syntax between thinking of 'brass [as] eternal' and as 'eternal slave to mortal rage'.

Nonetheless, in discovering the pleasures and verbal surprises arising from rhetorical figures in Shakespeare's sonnets, it is helpful to be aware of a traditional distinction between *schemes* and *tropes*. Schemes are figures of sound, which create ornamental patterns with words through repeating or transforming letters, syllables, or words. The 'br' repetitions in Sonnet 12 exemplify the scheme, as does the expansion of 'silvered' into 'ensilvered' (l. 4) or syllabic reduction of 'against' in ''gainst' (l. 13), as well as the *anaphora*, *isocolon*, and *parison* previously described. While such devices contribute to the placid formality of the meditation in Sonnet 12, they also create the high-tension reversals which, juxtaposing before and after, create the vanishing present of lust as portrayed in Sonnet 129:

> Mad in pursuit and in possession so,
> Had, having, and in quest to have, extreme;
> A bliss in proof and proved, a very woe;
> Before, a joy proposed; behind, a dream.
> (ll. 9-12)

In contrast to schemes, tropes are defined as figures of thought, which 'translate' words from their normal sense or usage. For example, through personification, 'time's scythe' (12, l. 13) translates the abstraction into something like a human agent, the mower. Most potent of the figurative devices in the sonnets is metaphor, which Puttenham calls the 'figure of transport', aptly in that Shakespeare's metaphors seem to transport words from one realm or field of discourse in which they are commonplace, to a fresh field, where they may come as a surprise. Take, for example, Sonnet 4, where words relating to moneylending and usury are transported into the love poetry, where they are used to question the young man's resistance to reproducing his beauty through marriage and children:

> Unthrifty loveliness, why dost thou spend
> Upon thyself thy beauty's legacy?
> Nature's bequest gives nothing, but doth lend,
> And being frank, she lends to those are free.
> Then, beauteous niggard, why dost thou abuse
> The bounteous largess given thee to give?
> Profitless usurer, why dost thou use
> So great a sum of sums yet canst not live?
> (ll. 1-8)

Here, as at the start of *Measure for Measure*, Nature is imagined as a moneylender who expects a return on the loan of assets like the young man's beauty. The metaphorical accusation, 'Profitless usurer', might be particularly startling to readers of *The Merchant of Venice*, where usury for profit is condemned by the Christian characters, as it also was in many tracts circulating in Shakespeare's day. The economic metaphors transported into this and other Shakespearian love sonnets may catch up the proto-capitalist tensions within Elizabethan society, where the reputation of usury was in transition, both widely practised and widely criticized. Thus, the doubleness of metaphor in the poem, captured, for example, in the charge of double meaning the verb 'use' acquires in this overall figurative context, brings into the small space of the sonnet a larger world's anxieties about value and responsibility in changing economic circumstances.

Speech acts

The readings thus far have emphasized the reflective or meditative cast of some of the sonnets. It is as if the evanescence of thought is brought together with the formality of the sonnet structure with such art that the sonnet seems a small memorial to a thought event, an event that can be called back to life by the reader's inward or outward speaking of the verse. But many of Shakespeare's sonnets come across less as private inward meditations than as speech acts, as if the words themselves could do something or even effect change within a particular situation of address. Four final questions can help to illuminate the nature of a particular sonnet as a speech act. *(7) What is the speech act being performed by the sonnet? (8) Who is speaking and to whom? (9) What is the power relation set up between the 'I' and the 'you' or 'thou'? (10) How is deixis used to invoke a context of situation?*

Sonnet 58 strongly evokes the sense of someone speaking on a specific occasion and actively using his words to get his lover to do something or to change.

> That god forbid, that made me first your slave,
> I should in thought control your times of pleasure,
> Or at your hand th'account of hours to crave,
> Being your vassal bound to stay your leisure.
> O let me suffer, being at your beck,
> Th'imprisoned absence of your liberty,
> And patience, tame to sufferance, bide each check,
> Without accusing you of injury.
> Be where you list, your charter is so strong
> That you yourself may privilege your time
> To what you will; to you it doth belong
> Yourself to pardon of self-doing crime.
>   I am to wait, though waiting so be hell,
>   Not blame your pleasure, be it ill or well.

In this sonnet, the speech act is complaint or recrimination, though the accusations are made obliquely. Strongly foregrounded is the direct address of the speaker's 'I' to a much more powerful 'you'. It can be debated whether this sonnet is imagined as something that might actually be uttered to the beloved or whether it is 'silent speech',[3] the workings of the speaker's mind made vivid as he formulates so vigorously what he wished he dare say.

In the first line, the language of heated interaction comes alive through Shakespeare's estranging of a colloquial expression for disavowal: '*God forbid* I should have any say in what you choose to do' is reshaped to 'That god forbid, that made me first your slave'—presumably the god of love, who, in the metaphors of conventional love poetry, turns men to slaves. The power dynamics of the relationship are front and centre in this poem, with the speaker's strong pent-up emotions of frustration and neglect arising out of his sense of powerlessness. In an odd way, it is difficult to determine whether the 'serving-man' self-representation of the speaker is metaphorical or literal. Here is where the 'standard story' of the Sonnets as background knowledge for interpretation comes into play. In at least one version of the standard story, there is a huge difference of social status between the 'you' and the 'I' of Sonnets 1 to 126, with the 'you' imagined as a young nobleman and the 'I' a common theatre player. There were certainly historical circumstances in which play-actors functioned as serving-men for aristocratic patrons, forming part of their entourage, for example, on formal occasions such as coronations. Some such situation might be alluded to in Sonnet 125: 'Were't aught to me I bore the canopy' (l. 1).

Sonnet 58 uses and distorts the social speech scripts for Renaissance master-servant relations: a good serving-man 'waits' upon his master's 'pleasure' ('If it please you'), leaving aside direct imperatives or any considerations or demands about his own needs as he attends to the wishes, decisions, and even the whims of the other. To the resentment that might well arise in any such situation of subordination, Shakespeare adds the element of desire, to create the exquisite painfulness of this situation of having no say about the absences of a beloved and powerful other. Once again the rhetorical doubleness of a sliding syntax characterizes the contradictions of this asymmetrical dependence relation, as the speaker prays, deferentially but probably also sarcastically, 'O let me suffer . . . Th'imprisoned absence of your liberty' (ll. 5–6). Logically, imprisonment is synonymous with 'absence of liberty'; but here the surprises of the language deliver the contradiction that the beloved's 'liberty' is felt by the speaker as the imprisonment of separation.

It is virtually a defining feature of any speaking in a Shakespeare sonnet, however strongly it demands an answer, that it doesn't get one: the 'I' who speaks, at least in the 'standard story', is 'ever the same' (76, l. 5). The Adonis of the sonnets, the speaker's 'lovely boy' (126), 'Lord of my love' (26), 'master-mistress' (20), or, in Sonnet 58, more simply his master, does not respond. These are dialogues, then, of one self, and yet they strongly anticipate or project the responses or the reactions of the other. Sonnet 58 readily evokes the nonchalance of an aristocratic beloved, his failure to see how what is normal behaviour for him can have consequences of such inward pain for his faithful lover, his readiness to deny anyone, however dear, the right to stand in judgement over him. As in the narrative poems, subjectivity is strongly caught up with social dialogue.

The power dynamics within the primary sonnet relationship are not, however, static. In Sonnet 81 (among others) the poet draws attention to the variable measures of power and worth, in a poem that turns upon literary or poetic uses of linguistic *deixis*.

> Or *I* shall live *your* epitaph to make,
> Or *you* survive when *I* in earth am rotten.
> From *hence your* memory death cannot take,
> Although in *me* each part will be forgotten.
> *Your* name from *hence* immortal life shall have,
> Though *I*, once gone, to all the world must die.
> The earth can yield *me* but a common grave
> When *you* entombèd in men's eyes shall lie.
> *Your* monument shall be *my* gentle verse,
> Which eyes not yet created shall o'er-read,
> And tongues to be *your* being shall rehearse

> When all the breathers of *this* world are dead.
> *You* still shall live–such virtue hath *my* pen–
> Where breath most breathes, even in the mouths of men.
>
> (deictics emphasized)

Deictics are indexical or pointing words that bridge between a speaker's utterance and the world or referent of its imagined context. In addition to the pronominal deictics, 'I' and 'you', speakers and writers rely on spatial and temporal deictics such as 'here' and 'now', or the demonstratives 'this' and 'that'. Deictics might be considered the key words in Sonnet 81. Without giving proper names to the characters or supplying the kind of background information the narrative poems provide, it demands, with its alternating repetitions of 'you' and 'I', that we construct imaginary characters related in such a way as to make sense of these forms of address. The pronouns and the reiterated 'from hence' invite us to set in contrast a 'you', whose memory in the mortal world he inhabits will be sustained by elaborate funeral monuments, and an 'I', who, buried in a commoner's grave, will be quickly forgotten. In other words, it invokes the version of the standard story that reads 'you' as a nobleman, 'I' as a commoner with a gift for writing very much like the poet, William Shakespeare. Indeed, the near-autobiographical association is abetted by the fact that most of the poems attributed to Shakespeare which have not been directly discussed above are epitaphs.

The poem's turn of thought depends on the doubleness of deictics, which can point either to a context outside a text or to a context within a text. Thus, 'from hence' *could* mean 'from this worldly world of Elizabethan England' or 'from hence' *could* mean 'from these lines', 'from this poem'. The surprising claim of the finale is that the lines of this sonnet are what have the power to give the 'you' continuing life. Monuments become inconsequential, and the poet holds the power, as has been anticipated by his own elevation to 'gentle' status through the agency of his verse in line 9. The subject of deixis is an appropriate place to end this discussion of reading strategies for Shakespeare's sonnets, because deictics are one important source of the indeterminacy that separates the sonnets from the narrative poems. They demand that the reader become an active collaborator in creating the world to which their pointers give imagined reference.

FURTHER READING

Booth, Stephen. *An Essay on Shakespeare's Sonnets* (New Haven: Yale University Press, 1969). A classic on close reading of selected sonnets, with particular attention paid to their various levels of structural patterning—'formal, logical, ideological, syntactic, rhythmic, and phonetic' (p. ix).

Booth, Stephen (ed.). *Shakespeare's Sonnets* (New Haven and London: Yale University Press, 1977). An edition with analytical commentary that explores in detail for each sonnet how Shakespeare exploits the verbal and rhetorical resources available within early modern English language and culture.

Fineman, Joel. *Shakespeare's Perjured Eye: The Invention of Poetic Subjectivity in the Sonnets* (Berkeley: University of California Press, 1986). A complex but influential study, based upon Lacanian theory, which argues that Shakespeare's sonnets develop the poetics of praise to invent a new form of poetic subjectivity.

Kerrigan, John (ed.). *The Sonnets and 'A Lover's Complaint'*, New Penguin Shakespeare (Harmondsworth: Penguin, 1986). This edition considers seriously the sonnets and 'A Lover's Complaint' as an integrated whole, arguing that the two parts can be more productively understood in relation to each other.

Magnusson, Lynne. ' "Power to Hurt": Language and Service in Sidney Household Letters and Shakespeare's sonnets', *ELH* 65 (1998), 799–824. Argues that in sonnets exploring unequal power relations such as 57 and 58 outward social scripts (for example, for the Elizabethan language of service) supply the emotional contours for inward subjective states.

Marotti, Arthur F. ' "Love is Not Love": Elizabethan Sonnet Sequences and the Social Order', *ELH* 49 (1982), 396–428. An important essay that initiated attempts to depart from purely formalist readings to explore how the sonnets interrelate with various Elizabethan social practices, including client–patron relationships.

Schalkwyk, David. *Speech and Performance in Shakespeare's Sonnets and Plays* (Cambridge and New York: Cambridge University Press, 2002). Schalkwyk's reading of the sonnets is based on speech act theory and links their imagined contexts to situations of address found in the plays. It explores unequal power relations, interiority, gender, and the issue of proper names.

Schiffer, James (ed.). *Shakespeare's Sonnets: Critical Essays* (New York and London: Garland Publishing, 1999). This volume collects recent essays representing a wide range of current critical approaches to the sonnets, including both theoretical overviews and critical readings.

Vendler, Helen. *The Art of Shakespeare's Sonnets* (Cambridge, Mass. and London: Belknap Press of Harvard University Press, 1997). This book offers a detailed reading analysing the poetic artistry of each sonnet, with particular attention to language, formal structures, and psychological process.

Wright, George T. 'The Silent Speech of Shakespeare's Sonnets'. In *Shakespeare and the Twentieth Century*. Jonathan Bate, Jill A. Levenson, and Dieter Mehl (eds.) (Newark: University of Delaware Press, 1998). Rpt. Schiffer, 'Shakespeare's Sonnets', pp. 135–58. This essay considers the interiority of the sonnets in relation to unsounded inner speech and speculates about the historical development of consciousness conceived as a 'continuous wordstream'.

NOTES

1. Paul Fussell. *Poetic Meter and Poetic Form* (New York: Random House, rev. 2nd edn. 1979), p. 128.
2. George Puttenham. *The Arte of English Poesie* (1589), intro. Baxter Hathaway (Kent, Ohio: Kent State University Press, 1970), p. 166.
3. See George T. Wright. 'The Silent Speech of Shakespeare's Sonnets'. In *Shakespeare and the Twentieth Century*, Jonathan Bate, Jill A. Levenson, and Dieter Mehl (eds.) (Newark: University of Delaware Press, 1998).

23 | Unfamiliar Shakespeare

Alan Armstrong

For a variety of reasons over the past four centuries, some of Shakespeare's plays have become more equal than others. In our time, familiarity with Shakespeare implies knowledge of such plays as *A Midsummer Night's Dream, Romeo and Juliet, Henry IV Part One, Henry V, Much Ado About Nothing, Twelfth Night, Hamlet, Macbeth, King Lear, The Tempest*. But nearly a third of the playwright's work lies outside the scope of the ordinary reader or playgoer who 'knows' Shakespeare. At the beginning of the twenty-first century, this realm of unfamiliar Shakespeare includes several of the histories, most notably *King John, Henry VIII*, the three *Henry VI* plays, and the disputed *Edward III*; romances such as *Pericles Prince of Tyre* and *The Two Noble Kinsmen*; troubling comedies such as *All's Well that Ends Well* and *Troilus and Cressida*; and tragedies such as *Titus Andronicus* and *Timon of Athens*.

Changing tastes

Are unfamiliar plays deservedly less well-known? Every era seems to think so, but every era's list of neglected plays is different. Clearly, particular Shakespeare plays from time to time are either cast into outer darkness or rescued from oblivion by dynamic historical processes that do not simply measure artistic merit. Changing tastes can throw whole genres out of fashion. Of the three categories into which the 1623 Folio divides Shakespeare's plays, the comedies and tragedies generally remain more widely read and regularly seen than the histories that constituted roughly half the young playwright's output at mid-career. Although later ages continue to discover in the histories parallels to present-day political issues and events, such connections scarcely rival the immediate relevance that Shakespeare's representations of recent English history held for audiences in the 1590s, at the height of the short, intense vogue of the English history play. The *Henry VI Part One* that stirred the hearts of ten thousand playgoers, according to Thomas Nashe in 1592, never since has enjoyed such popularity. By the eighteenth and nineteenth centuries, time had dimmed the glories of all three of Shakespeare's *Henry VI* plays, dismissed now as a merely episodic succession of noisy battles and impenetrably complex genealogical claims to the crown—the apprentice work of an immature playwright, if his at all.

Today, the *Henry VI* plays are better known and better appreciated again partly because of a post-Second World War phenomenon: the conception of Shakespeare's histories as a cycle of plays, divided into two tetralogies (sequences of four plays) and telling one continuous story of the English kings from Richard II to Henry VI (1398–1485). *Richard II*, *Henry IV Part One*, *Henry IV Part Two*, and *Henry V* make up one tetralogy; *Richard III* and the three *Henry VI* plays, the other. The rising influence of this view in both the theatre and the academy privileged eight of Shakespeare's ten English history plays, and especially the more popular tetralogy which chronicles the development of the prodigal Prince Hal into the hero-king Henry V, while leaving two odd men out: *King John* and *Henry VIII*.

King John had remained a familiar, oft-performed play in the eighteenth and nineteenth centuries, partly for the rousing patriotic sentiment of its conclusion ('Come the three corners of the world in arms / And we shall shock them. Naught shall make us rue, / If England to itself do rest but true'). As late as 1899, the noted actor/manager Beerbohm Tree's elaborate production of *King John* commanded a run of 114 performances, but with the repackaging of the histories into cycles the play faded rapidly into obscurity. Changing taste played a part in this decline, too. Victorian audiences loved the play for Constance's flights of maternal passion and the pathos of young Arthur's pleading with his appointed executioner. Our age's much-diminished interest in *King John* focuses rather on the cynical opportunism exhibited by the play's great ones and enunciated by the blunt-spoken character known simply as the Bastard. The earlier appeal of *King John* had been partly antiquarian, too, as reflected in historically accurate theatrical reproduction of costumes and settings of the play's era.

For quite similar reasons, Shakespeare's *Henry VIII* is largely neglected by readers, actors, and scholars today. When the theatres closed by the Puritans in 1642 were re-opened in the Restoration era (following the restoration of the English monarchy at the return of the theatre-loving Charles II to the throne, in 1660), *Henry VIII* was still, however, one of the dozen Shakespeare plays that held the stage regularly. To underscore the spectacular rises to greatness and subsequent tragic falls of Buckingham, Wolsey, and Queen Katherine, in succession, *Henry VIII* presents pageant after pageant, from the appearance of the King and court 'as masquers, habited like shepherds' to the christening of Elizabeth and ceremonial prophecy of her future greatness. The pomp and circumstance with which Shakespeare marked the heights of greatness in *Henry VIII* answered better to the nineteenth-century taste for scenic extravagance than to later theatrical values.

Sumptuous spectacle is a feature also of the new kind of comedy, derived from Greek romances, that Shakespeare attempted late in his career, the period to which *Henry VIII* also belongs. The most familiar of these late romances in our time is *The Tempest*, but in the early seventeenth century it was *Pericles* that became a byword for theatrical success, provoking the envious disparagement of Ben Jonson, Shakespeare's friend and rival playwright, who complained that audiences preferred 'a mouldy Tale,/Like *Pericles*' to his own new work. *Pericles* was reprinted four times before the theatres closed in 1642 and appears to have been the first Shakespeare play revived when they reopened after the Restoration, but, along with its fellow *The Two Noble Kinsmen*, *Pericles* virtually disappeared from the stage after the seventeenth century. In addition to spectacular pageantry and stately ritual, such as the display of severed heads, the 'triumph' of the six knights bearing their heraldic devices, and the vision of the goddess Diana in *Pericles*, or the chivalric tournament and the ceremonious appearances of the three queens in *The Two Noble Kinsmen*, these plays rest on miraculously improbable coincidences and jump startlingly from one place or time to another to tell the stories of their emblematic characters. The generic innovations responsible for the plays' popularity with Jacobean audiences prove challenging to modern readers and playgoers better accustomed to the naturalistic conventions and seemingly three-dimensional characters of Shakespeare's tragedies and romantic comedies.

During the same period in which he wrote his great tragedies, Shakespeare produced three other plays that have endured a long history of neglect: *All's Well That Ends Well*, *Troilus and Cressida*, and *Timon of Athens* (the first two are discussed also in Chapter 21). Unlike *Pericles*, there is no evidence that any of these dark, disconcerting works answered to popular taste in Shakespeare's own time, and all three were almost completely ignored by theatrical producers for more than three centuries. Critics and editors, too, have scarcely known what to make of these plays, or how to classify them. *Troilus and Cressida*, variously titled both a history and a tragedy in Shakespeare's time and placed ambiguously at the junction of the two categories in the 1623 Folio, has since been labelled also a tragicomedy or a satire. The 1623 Folio sets among Shakespeare's tragedies the play identified less decisively by its title page as *The Life of Timon of Athens*, but even *Timon* has been treated since as a comedy by some editors. Modern scholars have appropriated the term 'problem play' to register the distinctive qualities of *All's Well That Ends Well* and *Troilus and Cressida* (along with the more familiar *Measure for Measure*).

However we label them, these three plays share common traits that have threatened to render them off-putting, distasteful, and unpopular not just for an age but for all time. All three have a strong element of cynical, deflating social satire; an unsettling juxtaposition of disturbing psychological realism with the plot conventions of fairy tale and romance; and problematic endings which potentially put their heroes and heroines in an unflattering light, leading readers to disagree vehemently in the awarding of their sympathies. Is Cressida the legendary epitome of woman's infidelity, or an innocent victim sacrificed to the self-indulgent romantic and chivalric delusions of Troilus and his fellow warriors? Is Timon a benevolent saint eventually poisoned by the disloyalty of friends, or a fool who must earn an enlightened misanthropy through suffering the loss of everything, even his life? Is Bertram (in *All's Well That Ends Well*) the unfortunate victim of a determined social climber, or the shallow, unworthy husband that a virtuous Helena disappointingly achieves?

In the second half of the twentieth century, the bitter irony of these plays at last found fit audience, though few. The disillusioned eye that *Troilus and Cressida* casts on the failed love of its title characters and on the spurious epic grandeur of the Trojan War ('All the argument is a whore and a cuckold', 2.3.65) seems strikingly modern. Similarly, the bleak, despairing critique of a money-driven society in *Timon of Athens* speaks strongly to present-day concerns about the corrosive effect of material prosperity on moral values and social bonds. *All's Well that Ends Well* appeals to contemporary audiences with its satirical depiction of a feeble, enervated ruling establishment reinvigorated by an enterprising heroine who defeats conventional restrictions of class and gender to achieve her ends.

An even less familiar work, *Titus Andronicus*, belongs to a much earlier period in Shakespeare's career. In Shakespeare's day, *Titus Andronicus* achieved a degree of popularity comparable to that which its kindred revenge tragedy, *Hamlet*, enjoys in our time. The play was printed several times, inspired the only surviving contemporary sketch of a Shakespeare play in performance, and held the stage into the 1620s before disappearing into a centuries-long oblivion. One need not look far for an explanation. Next to the earlier *Titus Andronicus*, even such bloody tragedies as *Hamlet* or *Macbeth* look tame. When Titus, a Roman general, appeases the battlefield deaths of twenty-one of his sons by sacrificing the son of Tamora, the conquered queen of the Goths, he unleashes a cycle of grotesquely violent vengeance that leaves most of the play's main characters dead. The play ends horrifically with the fatal stabbing of Titus, after he has killed his dishonoured daughter Lavinia and served the treacherous queen Tamora a meat pie made of her two murdered sons, before slaying her as well. Even the play's stage directions ('*Enter the Empress' sons*, [CHIRON *and* DEMETRIUS,] *with* LAVINIA, *her hands cut off and her tongue cut out, and ravished*') are gruesome. Theatrical conventions pleasing and familiar to Elizabethan audiences helped to assure the popular reception of *Titus Andronicus* in Shakespeare's time, but succeeding ages found the play's over-the-top horrors either distasteful or ludicrous. In the past decade, however, increasing scholarly attention to the play and strong stage and film productions indicate a new readiness to look beyond the play's exaggerated violence and respond to its poetry and contemporary political relevance.

Authorship

Changing literary fashions and aesthetic principles made *Hamlet* a cultural icon but *Titus Andronicus* a bizarre curiosity. It is useful to remember that such alterations of taste made virtually all of Shakespeare's plays unfamiliar to playgoers in the century following the Restoration, in the sense that literary and theatrical adaptations replaced the scripts preserved in the 1623 Folio. Even such well-known plays as *Romeo and Juliet*, *Richard III*, *Macbeth*, *King Lear*, and *The Tempest* survived on stage in thoroughly revised versions which aimed to improve upon what a neoclassical age saw as the crude works of Shakespeare's untutored genius. Such adaptations repaired perceived defects of language and action and freely refashioned the plays to suit contemporary tastes. In 1679, for instance, John Dryden, in his adaptation *Troilus and Cressida, or Truth Found Too Late*, restored heroic stature to the title characters by having a faithful, betrayed Cressida commit suicide and a tragically deceived Troilus nobly avenge her death before being killed in turn by the Greeks. The year before, Thomas Shadwell's revision of *Timon of Athens* added two female characters to the play (Timon's false and faithful mistresses) and Edward Ravenscroft's *Titus Andronicus* invented the earlier sacrificial murder of Titus's son by the pitiless Tamora, to justify Titus's subsequent sacrifice of her son Alarbus.

These theatrical adaptations remind us forcibly that our acquaintance with any of Shakespeare's plays has depended ultimately upon the faithful transmission of their original texts. The least familiar Shakespeare plays of all would be those that have not survived. Some scholars believe that we can identify by title two lost Shakespeare plays—that is, plays that were performed in Shakespeare's time but subsequently disappeared because their scripts were never printed. Two Elizabethan documents attribute to Shakespeare, in lists of his works, a play called *Love's Labour's Won*, perhaps a lost companion to *Love's Labour's Lost* but perhaps also merely a different title for a Shakespeare play we have. Contemporary records show that Shakespeare's company, the King's Men, performed in 1613 a play called *Cardenio* (probably based on an episode in Cervantes' *Don Quixote*, which had been translated into English the year before). In 1653 a publisher claimed to possess a manuscript of the play attributing its authorship to Shakespeare and his sometime collaborator, the playwright John Fletcher, and in 1727 an early editor of Shakespeare's works published an adaptation of the play said to be based on manuscripts in his possession. Given the absence of any trace of these manuscripts after the early eighteenth century, we are unlikely now ever to know this play, let alone resolve the issue of Shakespeare's possible authorship.

Because Shakespeare himself took few pains to preserve his scripts for posterity, other Shakespeare plays might easily have met the fates of *Love's Labour's Won* and *Cardenio*—not merely unfamiliar but unknown, because lost. The 1623 Folio collection edited by his fellow actors John Heminges and Henry Condell, seven years after the playwright's death, preserved eighteen Shakespeare plays which had never before been published, and which might otherwise have vanished entirely. The 1623 Folio thus helped to ensure that the texts of most of Shakespeare's plays remained potentially available in the long run to readers, even though they were supplanted for a time in the theatre by sometimes almost unrecognizable adaptations. The publication of the Folio, however, did not guarantee that all the plays would be equally prized and read. Indeed, one of the more potent determinants of which plays we are most likely to read, see, and study has been their canonical status, as authentically Shakespeare's. Had Shakespeare overseen the publication of his own collected plays—an atypical behaviour for a playwright of the time, but one undertaken by his contemporary Ben Jonson—we should know with certainty which plays Shakespeare wrote and whether we possessed them all today. The circumstances surrounding the printing of plays in Shakespeare's time, however, have left these issues problematic, with the result that some plays of uncertain authorship, perhaps written wholly or in part by Shakespeare, have been pushed to the margins of the Shakespeare canon or excluded altogether. As succeeding ages came to exalt Shakespeare's individual genius over his participation in the fundamentally collaborative enterprise of producing plays, plays of doubtful provenance suffered a disproportionate risk of neglect.

Consider, for example, *Edward III*, an anonymous play first printed in 1596 and first attributed to Shakespeare only some sixty years later, in a list that mistakenly credited him also with plays known to have been written by Marlowe and Heywood. Scholars continue to disagree about whether Shakespeare wrote all or part (or any) of *Edward III*. For four centuries this interesting play has gone essentially unread and unperformed, excluded from the Shakespeare canon. In 1998, however, an important scholarly edition of Shakespeare's plays for the first time included *Edward III* as a canonical work. The almost inevitable consequence of this step is that, eventually, the play will be better known to readers and playgoers of the twenty-first century than to any other audience since its composition, simply because the now-powerful name of William Shakespeare has been applied to it.

Edward III is reminiscent of Shakespeare's chronicle history plays at many points. The play begins, like the far better known *Henry V*, with the English king's assertion of a hereditary claim to the crown of France and goes on to depict a series of glorious offstage English victories over the French, punctuated by moralizing vignettes that illustrate the valour and chivalry of the English King Edward and his son, and the pride, callousness, and dishonour of the French. The scenes that most readily have earned attribution to Shakespeare, however, belong to an earlier part of the play. They focus on a 'true English lady', the beautiful and courageous Countess of Salisbury, who is besieged first by the rebellious, ignoble King David of Scotland, and then by her rescuer King Edward. Depraved by his sudden infatuation to the point of seeking the murders of the Countess's husband and his own queen, King Edward is finally brought to his senses by the resourceful Countess, who threatens suicide rather than compromise her honour.

Scholars are in greater agreement about Shakespeare's limited contribution to another unfamiliar play that lies outside the canon: *Sir Thomas More*. The play, believed to have been written by Anthony Munday and Henry Chettle, survives in a manuscript also bearing comments by Sir Edmund Tilney, the Master of the Revels (a Court official with the authority of a censor, who in this case refused permission to perform the play), along with later additions to the play in several other hands. One of these additions, a scene in which More as Sheriff of London eloquently calms the rioting commoners, is generally held to have been written by Shakespeare's own hand. The three-page scene is prized accordingly as the only existing autograph Shakespeare script, but the play itself never saw the light of day until the twentieth century, with its first professional performance in 1954.

Paradoxically, the same logic that recently has elevated the status of *Edward III* and *Sir Thomas More*, because they may after all have been written *partly* by Shakespeare, has also contributed in the past to the neglect of other plays in the canon, because they may not have been written *entirely* by Shakespeare. Collaborative authorship has helped to consign both *Pericles* and *The Two Noble Kinsmen* to a long oblivion. When *The Two Noble Kinsmen* first appeared in print in 1634, the title-page listed Shakespeare and John Fletcher as authors, and beginning in 1679 the play was regularly published as the work of Fletcher and his frequent partner Francis Beaumont rather than Shakespeare. Even without so specific an indication of collaborative authorship, editors of Shakespeare's plays from Alexander Pope on denigrated the suspect *Pericles* as at least partly the work of an inferior playwright and dropped it from the canon.

It is no accident that the plays most widely believed to have been written collaboratively by Shakespeare and others—*Sir Thomas More*, *Edward III*, the three *Henry VI* plays, *Titus Andronicus*, *Timon of Athens*, *Pericles*, *Henry VIII*, and *The Two Noble Kinsmen*—make up the greater part of unfamiliar Shakespeare territory today. Centuries of Bardolatry have constructed the false perspective that makes us see Shakespeare retrospectively as a giant among pygmies, with the corollary implication that Shakespeare's words are more valuable than others'—gold among dross. Readers and playgoers, with considerable encouragement from scholars and editors, have come to assume that a play written partly by Shakespeare is intrinsically 'worse' than one written entirely by him, and that the parts written by Shakespeare are intrinsically 'better' than the parts that may have been contributed by a George Peele, a Thomas Middleton, or a John Fletcher.

The injury to the reputations of plays suspected of collaborative authorship has been compounded at times by the topsy-turvy conviction that the 'bad' parts of a Shakespeare play (often merely those that we do not like or understand) must therefore have been written by someone else. This curiously circular logic is evident as early as the second scholarly edition of Shakespeare's plays, in 1725, when Alexander Pope derogated to the bottom of the page passages which he found 'excessively bad' and therefore not Shakespeare's. Confidently asserting their ability to discern, by virtue of aesthetic judgement as much as external evidence, where Shakespeare ended and a lesser writer began, a long succession of scholars and editors have helped to perpetuate indifference to some neglected plays by imputing their mediocrity to their inauthenticity, and *vice versa*, in an unbreakable chain of disparagement. Such denigration of collaborative plays peaked in the late nineteenth and early twentieth centuries when the new, rudimentary tools of critical bibliography lent a scientific colour to the game of reassigning 'bad' Shakespeare virtually line by line to other playwrights.

This vogue for 'disintegration', as it came to be called, was at bottom another expression of an age's tendency to see its own reflection in Shakespeare's plays and to value them according to its peculiar standards of taste, preferring some before others. Just as Alexander Pope expunged or demoted the passages of florid rhetoric, the vulgar and clownish characters, or the scenes depicting riotous commoners that to his mind were blemishes, other editors well into the nineteenth century saw fit to prune the plays according to contemporary principles of taste and decorum. The disintegrators were unusual in the extremity of their response to parts of the plays that failed their criteria for literary excellence, in that they simply (and sometimes correctly) denied Shakespeare's authorship of these parts. Editors today are not free to inflict their political, social, and aesthetic prejudices on the texts of Shakespeare's plays as directly, aggressively, and unselfconsciously as did their predecessors.

For Victorian readers, the category of unfamiliar Shakespeare might include those lines and scenes considered unseemly by a well-intentioned editor such as Thomas Bowdler, whose ten-volume *Family Shakespeare* (published in 1818) stripped the plays of profane language, as well as characters and actions, deemed unsuitable for the ears of children and ladies. Victorians found distasteful such plays as *Pericles*, with its incest-riddle and brothel scenes; *All's Well That Ends Well*, whose heroine takes another woman's place to trick her estranged husband into impregnating her; and *Troilus and Cressida*, in which the heroine's sexual degradation is abetted by her uncle and her lover. Their aversion expressed itself practically through censorship which helped to marginalize these plays for succeeding ages as well as their own. The forms in which the texts of Shakespeare's plays get transmitted constitute just one of these mechanisms, with scholarly complete editions operating as a kind of democratic safeguard to ensure that no play disappears entirely.

Rediscovering Shakespeare

Despite the odds against them, such plays are not necessarily doomed forever to constitute the unknown territory of Shakespeare's works. The explosive growth of the Shakespeare industry in our time has made **all** Shakespeare's plays potentially more familiar than ever before, and so has afforded to the less well-known plays unprecedented opportunities to have their merits rediscovered. The international proliferation of theatre companies devoted more or less exclusively to Shakespeare has vastly increased the possibility of our seeing his less familiar plays performed. Even half a century ago, only a heroic few playgoers or actors could dream of completing the Shakespeare canon; today, it is an accomplishment, especially for audiences, much more easily achieved. David Garrick's Shakespeare Jubilee, a lavish three-day celebration of the playwright held in his native Stratford-upon-Avon in 1769, is the original ancestor of the Shakespeare festivals that today have made performances of Shakespeare's plays so much more regularly and widely available. Surprisingly, Garrick's Jubilee included costume balls, parades, feasts, speeches, and fireworks, but not performances of the plays, which did not find their way into Stratford celebrations until 1830. Not until the late nineteenth century, with the building of the Shakespeare

Memorial Theatre, did the community festival feature regular annual performances, and decades more passed before Garrick's original idea achieved its present incarnation in the shape of the Royal Shakespeare Company.

A recent international census counted more than 150 Shakespeare festivals and companies, not only in Great Britain, the United States, Australia, Canada, and other English-speaking countries, but in France, Germany, Spain, Japan, and China. Although many are ephemeral, and only a few begin to approach the pre-eminently large impact of the Royal Shakespeare Company, the total number of such companies and of Shakespearian performances continues to rise. The Royal Shakespeare Company attracts millions of playgoers and tourists every year to its complex of theatres in Stratford-upon-Avon and extends its reach even further through touring productions, film, and television. More than 600,000 playgoers each year see Shakespeare performed at the Stratford Festival in Canada, and nearly 400,000 each year attend the Oregon Shakespeare Festival, the oldest in North America, founded in 1935. In Britain and the United States especially, dozens of smaller festivals and new companies devoted to Shakespeare continue to sprout up like mushrooms—a phenomenon that has increased exponentially since the mid-twentieth century both the number of Shakespearian performances and the number of playgoers.

Although in absolute terms the first effect of such growth is an ever-greater frequency of performance for favourites such as *A Midsummer Night's Dream* or *Hamlet*, the greater beneficiaries of the insatiable appetite for Shakespeare may well be, ultimately, the lesser-known plays. Given the eventual commitment of the successful Shakespeare companies and festivals to playing through the entire canon, the seemingly inevitable result is that plays such as *Timon of Athens*, *Titus Andronicus*, *Pericles*, and *Henry VI Part Two* are virtually always on stage somewhere, sooner or later in productions that render them fresh and newly inviting to us. Gone are the days when years might pass between isolated productions of minor plays.

The international scope of these burgeoning theatrical productions calls attention to another phenomenon that in a different respect has increased familiarity with Shakespeare's plays—the globalization of Shakespeare. Cassius's lines in *Julius Caesar* ('How many ages hence / Shall this our lofty scene be acted over, / In states unborn and accents yet unknown!') offer a rare hint that Shakespeare imagined the possibility of his plays enduring longer than marble or the gilded monuments of princes, disseminated throughout the globe. Just as later ages have made these Elizabethan and Jacobean plays peculiarly their own, readings and productions generated by other cultures can defamiliarize Shakespeare's plays, revealing them to us in new lights, as the rich history of Latin American reinterpretations of *The Tempest* has done. In this arena, too, the odds favour the transmission of the best-known plays, spawning Japanese *Macbeth*s, German *Othello*s, Spanish *Richard III*s, and *Hamlet*s everywhere. But global Shakespeare always contains the promise of a new perspective that may discover what is vital in a neglected play. In the annals of German Shakespeare, for example, *Coriolanus* holds an unexpectedly large place, partly because its exploration of the conflict between martial and democratic values addressed pressing national political issues in a long line of productions stretching throughout the twentieth century. A lesser known Shakespeare play may also benefit from the fact that producers and audiences in other countries and languages are less intimidated by its particular unfamiliarity. *Titus Andronicus*, for instance, was the play chosen to open the first China Shakespeare Festival, in Shanghai, in 1986, and not long after, three different productions of the same play, in English, French, and Italian, might have been seen in Paris within a space of fifteen months.

The global audience for performances of Shakespeare's plays today was built largely by the rapid, worldwide dissemination of the plays in print, both in English and in translation, and by the inclusion of Shakespeare in educational curricula outside his native England. Now another medium, film, has demonstrated its capacity to overleap barriers of space, language, and culture and to create an audience of a previously unimaginable magnitude for the performance of a Shakespeare play. Even in the cinema's earliest days, before the technology of sound recording could lend voice to Shakespeare's language, the producers of silent films looked on the Shakespeare canon as a treasure trove of material, churning out abbreviated versions of *King John* (1899) and *Henry VIII* (1911) as well as the better-known plays.

The resurgent popularity of Shakespeare movies beginning in the 1990s, like the prodigious growth of Shakespeare festivals and companies, resulted first and foremost in the replication of favourite plays, not only as full-length feature-film performances such as the movie versions of *Hamlet* directed by Franco Zeffirelli, Kenneth Branagh, and Michael Almereyda, but in appropriations of *Hamlet* ranging from glancing allusions to full-blown parodies, in films such as *Renaissance Man*, *The Last Action Hero*, Steve Martin's *L. A. Story*, Disney's *The Lion King*, and Branagh's *A Midwinter's Tale*. Precisely because recent internationally distributed feature films of better known plays such as *Othello*, *Romeo and Juliet*, *Much Ado About Nothing*, *Richard III*, and *Henry V* have become box-office hits, however, the movies may be the medium best positioned to restore unfamiliar Shakespeare plays to a larger audience. Branagh's turning to a film production of the minor comedy *Love's Labour's Lost* before the seemingly more likely subject of *Macbeth* underscores the potential freedom of successful film directors to undertake the less familiar plays. Director Julie Taymor's *Titus*, one of three film versions of Shakespeare's *Titus Andronicus* produced between 1999 and 2000, is likely to make the play better known than ever before in its history, not only because of the millions of moviegoers directly introduced to the play, but also because the mere existence of the film will cause the play to turn up with greater frequency in the repertories of theatrical Shakespeare companies and festivals and in the syllabi of university Shakespeare courses.

Powerful cultural engines are always at work to privilege some plays and obscure others. For centuries, the theatre has both created and reflected the changing tastes of playgoers. As the plays we know and like best come to define 'Shakespeare' for us, the plays we know and like less well are kept at arm's length, pushed offstage and out of the classroom, omitted from standard textbooks and selected volumes of best-known plays, neglected by scholars, and divorced from the mainstream of popular culture, where catchphrases and characters from favoured plays live on in endlessly recycled familiarity. Readers, playgoers, actors, students, and scholars are always necessarily involved in a process of evaluation that finds them conceiving of some parts of Shakespeare's work as more essentially, maturely, representatively Shakespearian than other parts. Such judgements, deeply influenced by reigning tastes and values, operate on many fronts to help determine how Shakespeare's plays will be passed on to succeeding generations. Nevertheless, the coming years will bring nearer to us some Shakespeare plays now relatively unappreciated, while relegating others to the category of unfamiliar Shakespeare.

FURTHER READING

Bate, Jonathan, and Russell Jackson (eds.). *Shakespeare: An Illustrated Stage History* (Oxford: Oxford University Press, 1996). This book surveys four centuries of changing approaches to and receptions of Shakespeare's plays in the English theatre.

Charney, Maurice (ed.). *Bad Shakespeare: Revaluations of the Shakespeare Canon* (London: Associated University Presses, 1988). This collection of essays challenges traditional, hierarchical evaluations of the Shakespeare canon which assume that certain plays (and kinds of plays) are self-evidently better than others.

Curren-Aquino, Deborah (ed.). *'King John': New Perspectives* (Newark: University of Delaware Press, 1989). This collection of essays on the play, spanning a variety of critical approaches, maps out the recent resurgence of interest in *King John*.

Dessen, Alan. *'Titus Andronicus'*, Shakespeare in Performance (Manchester: Manchester University Press, 1989). This book examines the performance history of *Titus Andronicus*, specifically discussing the problems that this early tragedy poses for contemporary theatrical productions.

Dobson, Michael. *The Making of the National Poet: Shakespeare, Adaptation, and Authorship, 1660–1769* (Oxford: Oxford University Press, 1992). This book provides a historical account of Shakespeare's canonization as the British national poet during the Enlightenment. In the process, the author shows how individual plays came to be perceived and valued differently in the light of this new construction of Shakespeare.

Marsden, Jean I. (ed.) *The Appropriation of Shakespeare: Post-Renaissance Reconstructions of the Works and the Myth* (Hemel Hempstead: Harvester Wheatsheaf, 1991). Although many of the essays in this collection focus on better known plays, the volume's focus on changing cultural perceptions and uses of Shakespeare can be applied instructively to the less familiar plays.

Melchiori, Giorgio (ed.). *King Edward III*, The New Cambridge Shakespeare (Cambridge: Cambridge University Press, 1998). This volume marks the first inclusion of the play in a multi-volume edition of Shakespeare's works. The introduction contains a full discussion of the play, its authorship, and its performance history.

Saccio, Peter. *Shakespeare's English Kings: History, Chronicle, and Drama* (Oxford: Oxford University Press, 1977, rev. edn. 2000). This book combines historical accounts of their royal protagonists with discussions of all of Shakespeare's English history plays, including chapters on the three *Henry VI* plays, *King John*, and *Henry VIII*.

Schoenbaum, Samuel. *Internal Evidence and Elizabethan Dramatic Authorship: An Essay in Literary History and Method* (Evanston, Ill.: Northwestern University Press, 1966). This book tells the story of literary scholarship's mixed progress toward a scientific rather than merely subjective analysis of stylistic evidence to identify the authors of disputed Elizabethan and Jacobean plays, with reference to many of the unfamiliar Shakespeare plays discussed in this chapter.

Part III

Shakespeare criticism

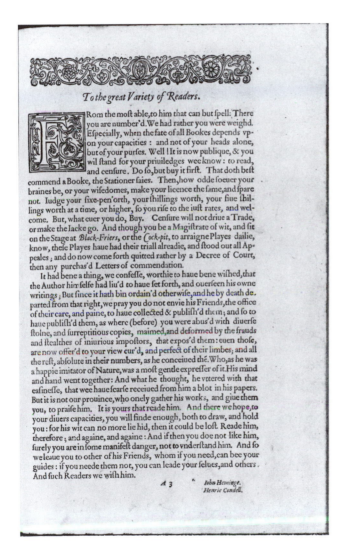

Fig. 3.1 One of the earliest critical appraisals of Shakespeare is this address to the readers in the First Folio of 1623. Shakespeare's colleagues John Heminges and Henry Condell, who were responsible for its publication, also had a commercial message: 'whatever you do, buy'.

24 | The critical tradition

Michael Taylor

If the history of famous literary prognostications were ever to be written, there's no doubt that Ben Jonson's prediction for the longevity of his friend Shakespeare's reputation—not of an age but for all time—would have to be given pride of place. Ever since the publication in 1623 of the celebratory Folio of Shakespeare's (more or less) complete plays, the consuming interest in Shakespeare—critical and general, philosophical and biographical, adulatory and scornful—has maintained an upward beat and curve that have defied gravity, other market forces, and—some would say—common sense. We are now awash in writings on Shakespeare, and this phenomenal degree of attention to a single author has scandalized a number of commentators. In 1923 C. H. Herford reeled under 'the number and variety of the minds at work, and especially in the extent and closeness of their scientific grip upon their subject-matter'. In 1939 Ivor Brown and George Fearon recoiled from the spectacle of the Bard's popularity. 'Really there's no escaping William Shakespeare now' was their exasperated conclusion. By the 1990s one professional Shakespearian, Gary Taylor, was prepared to throw in the towel: 'Even for hard-core Shakespearians, lifers, it is impossible to digest the hundreds of books and thousands of articles published on the subject in any year'. Many lifers, needless to say—myself included—don't find the fare quite so indigestible. One of the great pleasures of today's critical smorgasbord, in fact, lies in the opportunity it offers for the discriminating palate to sample a large variety of exotic dishes.

It wasn't always like this, of course. And one way of encapsulating the history of the Shakespeare critical tradition is to think of it in terms of a process of increasingly ferocious professionalization and specialization. (It is hard to imagine anyone today having the temerity or the naivety to write a piece, as Johnson did in 1745, called *Miscellaneous Observations on the Tragedy of 'Macbeth'*.) In the eighteenth and nineteenth centuries the notion of a hard-core Shakespearian, a lifer, would have been difficult to understand. No one, for example—then or since—would accuse a critic like Samuel Johnson in the eighteenth century of a life-long subservience to a single critical enthusiasm, despite his love for and enthusiastic promotion of Shakespeare's works. He had plenty of time for other critical and philological adventures as well as for periods of self-confessed—and candidly lamented—indolence. The Shakespeare industry, you might say, was still a cottage one at this time, not yet given over to the mass production of Shakespeare criticism characteristic of an age of universal suffrage and literacy, with an institute of higher education on practically every corner and within reach of everyone's pocket. Even now, though, the critical tradition can throw up the occasional critic with Johnson's omnivorous literary appetite, a William Empson, a T. S. Eliot, or a Harold Bloom, say, generalists to a man, whose work on Shakespeare has all the advantages (and some of the disadvantages) of not being narrowly professionalized. Like Shakespeare himself they range freely over a variety of terrains, the critical counterparts of Othello's 'antres vast and deserts idle, / Rough quarries, rocks, and hills whose heads touch heaven' (*Othello* 1.3.139–40).

From the seventeenth century to the end of the nineteenth the critical tradition in Shakespeare studies was dominated by professional writers of literature who would now be considered amateur Shakespearians. They were the precursors of an undying breed, as nearly all major European writers then and since, by no means professional Shakespearians, have at some time in their careers felt compelled to record their sometimes ambivalent feelings about the world's master writer. At first, however, especially in the late sixteenth and early seventeenth centuries, Shakespeare criticism (if it can be called that) was hardly ambivalent—it was little more than the kind of thing we find on the dust-jackets of today's best-sellers: high praise for the writer and exhortations to buy his work. The model for both these promotional activities can be found in the first Shakespeare best seller, the above-mentioned 1623 Folio of Shakespeare's Works, in which the compilers, John Heminges and Henry Condell, urge the bookshop browser to buy this book—'But whatever you do, buy'—while the likes of Ben Jonson and Leonard Digges compete with each other (in verse no less) to justify the buyer's purchase (see Figures 3.1 and 4.1). The two poet-publicists do this by praising Shakespeare to the skies, literally in Jonson's case: 'I see thee in the hemisphere / Advanced, and made a constellation there!'

One possible way to divide the subsequent history of Shakespeare criticism is between the work of those who want to bring Shakespeare back down to earth and the bardolatry of those who want to keep him, like Isabella in *Measure for Measure*, 'enskied and sainted' (1.4.33). The division is frequently chimerical as individual and age alike often demonstrate both tendencies at the same time. This is especially the case with the eighteenth century and the latter half of the seventeenth, whose writers heaped praise on Shakespeare as the poet *au naturel* whose rule-flouting beauties of expression *almost* justified his deplorable lack of a proper morality, regularity, and correct grammar. However honey-tongued, the sweet swan of Avon needed the civilized graces of the finishing school of the late seventeenth century (or so its literary masters thought), and one way to enforce his attendance—at one remove and posthumously—was to take his offspring, the plays, and give them the discipline their father conspicuously lacked. As a consequence, Volume 2 of Brian Vickers' indispensable six volume compilation of Shakespeare criticism, stretching from 1623 to 1801, is more or less devoted to a criticism that takes the form of rewriting Shakespeare's plays to the 'higher' standards of the time: hence Nahum Tate's now infamous adaptation in 1681 of *King Lear* which omits the Fool, keeps Lear and Cordelia alive, and dismisses Cordelia to happiness in a marriage with Edgar. Those native woodnotes warbled wild by Shakespeare that Milton praised were clearly not acceptable without some rearranging in a period which liked its nature tamed and laid out in gardens of a geometric design.

Shakespeare criticism in the nineteenth and twentieth centuries also seesaws between denigration and idolatry. In the nineteenth century the Victorian poet and critic, Matthew Arnold, like Johnson before him (not to mention John Dryden in the late seventeenth century and Alexander Pope in the eighteenth), thought Shakespeare's linguistic flamboyance a pernicious influence on the language poets use while at the same time (and sometimes in the same sentence) arguing for its transfiguring excellence. On the one hand, Shakespeare has the gift of 'happy, abundant, and ingenious expression, eminent and unrivalled' ('Preface to First Edition of Poems 1853'); on the other, this very gift 'leads him astray, degenerating sometimes into a fondness for curiosity of expression, into an irritability of fancy . . .' Arnold responds to the waywardness of Shakespeare's linguistic gift with an irritability of judgement: 'how extremely and faultily difficult Shakespeare's language often is'. Arnold echoes here Johnson's famous charge in his 1765 edition of Shakespeare's works that Shakespeare's language was 'ungrammatical, perplexed and obscure', affecting a 'disproportionate pomp of diction and a wearisome train of circumlocution'. Wearisome trains of circumlocution continue to bother critics in the twentieth century. At the beginning of the century, for instance, in 1904, the Shakespeare of Shakespeare critics, A. C. Bradley, objected to Shakespeare's occasional lapses into a language that was 'obscure, inflated, tasteless, or "pestered with metaphors"' (*Shakespearian Tragedy*). And at the century's end Frank Kermode is as Johnsonian as Bradley in reproving Shakespeare for using words that unnecessarily obscure meaning. In too many places in Shakespeare there is complexity in excess of value, so Kermode believes, and he quotes Shakespeare against himself: 'O, it is excellent / To have a giant's strength, but it is tyrannous / To use it like a giant' (*Measure for Measure*, 2.2.109–11).

One line of denigration that has always been popular, but perhaps never so popular as in the twentieth century, involves casting a cold and censorious eye on Shakespeare as a man of business: 'But whatever you do, buy'. It is as though it were beneath our greatest writer to be so mundanely concerned with bread-and butter issues; he should, perhaps, live like Hamlet's chameleon, eating the air promise-crammed. This critical tradition goes back at least to Pope's sneer that Shakespeare 'for gain, not glory, winged his roving flight'—as though gain and glory were necessarily incompatible (and as though Pope as a professional poet didn't do the same thing himself)—but the tradition really winged its own roving flight in the twentieth century, when not just the plays and the poems but all pieces of documentary evidence concerning Shakespeare seem to have been scrutinized with a puritan zeal for evidence of an unbecoming parsimony. Hence the number of recent critics who have looked askance at Shakespeare's hoarding of eighty bushels of malt in 1598, at a time of great malnutrition in Stratford, seeing this as evidence for him as a hard-hearted entrepreneur. And other critics have seized upon Shakespeare's last piece of writing, his will, as further evidence that, even beyond the grave, Shakespeare continued to exercise a fiendish ingenuity in money matters, unfair and selfish, at the expense, in particular, of a long-suffering wife who gets only his second-best bed as a resting-place for her pains. (There are, of course, counter-arguments to these censorious interpretations of the documents, as there are to similar ones prised out of Shakespeare's works.)

These critical voices are drowned out by the chorus of praise that has always accompanied Shakespeare studies. From the other side of their mouths, the fault finders themselves pay expansive homage. And so for Johnson Shakespeare was the most profound investigator of human passions, revealing 'the real estate of sublunary nature'. For Arnold Shakespeare, unlike other writers, is simply too much for us; 'outtopping knowledge', he does not abide our question. When Keats sits down to read *King Lear* again, such is the purgative power of Shakespeare's poetry that he must 'burn' through, rather than read, 'the fierce dispute / Betwixt damnation and impassion'd clay'. Indeed the English and European Romantic poets in the early part of the nineteenth century, all of them inflammatory readers of Shakespeare, threw off the shackles of eighteenth-century respectability and conventionality (or so they thought) in their rapturous response to what Keats's fellow poet and literary theorist Samuel Taylor Coleridge described as Shakespeare's 'organic form', the way 'he goes on kindling like a meteor through the dark atmosphere'. Since Coleridge, the notion of organic form has continued and will no doubt continue to be a source of inspiration in the study of Shakespeare, producing book after book that discovers networks of affinities and correspondences in and among all of Shakespeare's works. ('Organic form' could describe the corpus of Shakespeare criticism.) And Johnson's image of Shakespeare-as-constellation and Coleridge's of Shakespeare-as-meteor become in the twentieth century Shakespeare-as-the-sun, radiant, awe-inspiring, but also, in a typically twentieth-century development, destructive, blinding, and castrating.

I would not like to give the impression that Shakespeare criticism before the end of the nineteenth century was unscholarly. Dr Johnson was not *Dr* Johnson for nothing. His 1765 edition of Shakespeare's plays marks the end of the amateur tradition in the editing of Shakespeare and anticipates the extraordinary intensity of the editorial scholarship in the following centuries. It was he and other eighteenth-century editors, for example, who first attempted the hugely important task of distinguishing between the texts of the quartos and the text of the Folio. Which are the more authentically Shakespearian? The earlier single editions of Shakespeare's plays, the quartos? Or the posthumously compiled and edited Complete Works, the Folio? We are still fighting their turf wars. With Johnson, Edward Capell (1713–81), Lewis Theobald (1688–1744), and Edmond Malone (1741–1812), the modern 'professional' editing of Shakespeare began. Pride of scholarly first place must be given to Lewis Theobald, who issued his seven-volume edition of Shakespeare, based on Pope's, in 1733. It is with him that the writing of scholarly and critical notes became a significant feature of the editor's duty, and one has only to turn to any current scholarly edition of any of Shakespeare's plays—the Oxford, the Arden, or the Cambridge, say—to see how important Theobald's innovation has become. Too important, some critics argue, and a glance at any of the New Variorum editions of Shakespeare (begun in 1871, not yet completed but still appearing, and so named because they record voluminous notes by a variety of editors and commentators), where the text of the play almost gets shouldered off the page by a verbose commentary, might support such criticism. Even now, especially now, we can respond to Johnson's magnanimously self-defeating injunction: 'Read every play from the first scene to the last, with utter negligence of all his commentators'.

The cultural history of the Shakespeare note has not, I believe, ever been undertaken, at least not directly. But when we examine the kind of information that an eighteenth-century or nineteenth-century editor thought important to illuminate Shakespeare's lines we notice just how foreign and superfluous much of what they said now seems to be. Do we, for instance, really need to know, or want to know, that the omission of the final *d* in the participle passive is most common in verbs derived from the passive participle of Latin verbs of the first conjugation? (I take this pretty well verbatim from a note in the Variorum *Macbeth*.) In 1873 when the New Variorum edition of *Macbeth* first appeared, much serious scholarly notation concerned itself with picayune matters of philology and etymology—or so we might judge today. A note in a twenty-first-century edition of *Macbeth* would be more interested in semantic, stylistic, theatrical, and cultural curiosities in its attempt to explain Shakespeare's dramatic practice. In other words, the history of the Shakespeare note plays out in miniature the cultural history of Shakespeare criticism, as each editor and critic speaks in complicated ways from his or her cultural circumstances. Which does not mean to say, of course, that modern-day editors of *Macbeth* speak with one voice: there are interesting differences between the kind of attention the Arden editor of *Macbeth* brings to the play from that brought to it by the Oxford or the Cambridge.

The Shakespeare critical tradition has always kept an eye on what is going on in the theatrical presentation of Shakespeare's plays. Often warily, to be sure. There is a history of critical aversion to the very idea of Shakespeare on the stage, as though taking him out of the sanctity of the study is a kind of contamination, even though he did not write for the study and would no doubt have found the notion incredible. In the eighteenth century, as we have already seen, a kind of contamination was at work in the manner in which eighteenth-century writers felt obliged to render Shakespeare worthy of the 'superior' taste of eighteenth-century theatregoers by rewriting his plays. Perhaps the tradition of aversion to the theatre originated at a time when what theatregoers were watching was not really Shakespeare at all but a ghostly simulacrum of him. But this argument does not apply to the nineteenth century which, by and large, re-discovered a delight in a Shakespeare recognizably himself. And yet we find in the work of the essayist, Charles Lamb (1775–1834), an almost pathological hatred of Shakespeare on the stage, bitingly expressed, for instance, in an essay with the outrageous title, 'On the Tragedies of Shakspeare, considered with reference to their fitness for stage representation' (1811). (Although we find on reading the essay that

Lamb thinks it more a question of the nineteenth-century actors not being fit for the tragedies than the tragedies not being fit for the stage.) Lamb's view of the actors' 'low tricks upon the eye and ear' has some resonance in the twentieth century even though it was a time when the theatre became a dominant force in the critical reception of Shakespeare. Few critics nowadays would, for example, offer an interpretation of a play like *Othello* without drawing upon and interpreting from the conflicted history of its performance. Yet someone like Martin Buzacott in *The Death of the Actor: Shakespeare on Page and Stage* (1991), outdoing even Lamb in the rhetoric of contemptuous dismissal, considers the modern Shakespearian stage 'a battleground where jealous and ambitious men and women struggle and rage to fill the vacuum of the sublime with the activity of their own bowels and egos'.

Bowels and egos. The phrase may have more application to critics than to actors. And even more perhaps to eighteenth-century editors whose bilious attacks on each other belie the notion of the 'gentlemanly' standard of debate ('gentlemanly' because there were hardly any women editors of Shakespeare before the twentieth century). In the nineteenth and twentieth centuries Shakespeare became such a cultural icon, so much was invested in having him on your side, that interpretative conflicts over his works became part of the larger struggle to possess him ideologically. And while it is difficult to imagine a play like *The Two Gentlemen of Verona* ever becoming a cause célèbre for this or that faction in the current ideological debates—though even here its theme of the superiority of male friendship over heterosexual love offers interesting possibilities—this is clearly not the case for plays like *The Tempest*, *Othello*, *Coriolanus*, and *The Merchant of Venice*. On the contrary, these plays—by no means the only ones— are fodder for the politically minded. Issues of race, sex, colonialism, and (even) participatory democracy have colonized discussion of them. Dominating their critical agendas these days are the themes of anti-Semitism in *The Merchant*, racial difference in *Othello*, colonial exploitation in *The Tempest*, political tyranny in *Coriolanus*.

From the very beginning, then, from Hemings's and Condell's determined advocacy of their friend's excellence in 1623, urging Shakespeare's readers to read him again and again, the critical tradition has been well aware of the value of its supreme object of attention. But that value (in every sense of the word) was given an extraordinary fillip and a new outlet by the huge cultural shift that began at the end of the nineteenth century, continued into and through the twentieth, and has by no means finished running its course in the twenty-first. I refer, of course, to the explosive growth of education at the secondary and post-secondary levels with Shakespeare the irresistible star attraction in liberal arts programmes in the UK and the United States. In Britain in the latter half of the nineteenth century, with the establishment of universal compulsory education, the Shakespeare industry discovered the value of children and provided them with a Shakespeare sanitized sexually and popularized as a great British patriot. In the twentieth century the large increase in the number of institutions of post-secondary education encouraged, indeed demanded, a professoriate trained to propagate Shakespeare as a respectable object of study, which involved reading him in ways he no doubt would have found astonishing. Hence the famous squib in *Punch* in 1926 in which Shakespeare's ghost did very badly on the questions on *King Lear* because he hadn't read his A. C. Bradley.

Making Shakespeare (or any other literary artist) academically respectable entailed a way of reading him that could compete with the 'scientific' procedures of other disciplines. As early as 1885 R. G. Moulton wrote a book on Shakespeare whose title, *Shakespeare as a Dramatic Artist: A Popular Illustration of the Principles of Scientific Criticism*, perfectly captures for its own and later ages their obsession with a technique of reading both democratic and scientific. We now find writings on Shakespeare with vocabularies borrowed from the languages of science, social science, politics, philosophy, and other academic disciplines. But it is not the case that the scientific language of criticism has remained 'popular' in Moulton's sense of the word. Instead, its probings into Shakespeare's works have tended to reveal, as science always tends to, heretofore unexamined areas of complexity, instability, and uncertainty. The more narrowly phenomena are scrutinized the more perplexing they often appear, and this seems to be the case with the phenomenon of Shakespeare's plays and poems. Criticism of Shakespeare often seems to be at work in a mysterious subatomic world with critical vocabularies as strange (but not usually as attractive) as the one dealing with the physics of neutrinos, hadrons, and quarks.

The etymology of 'quark' throws light on a curious paradox at the heart of the Shakespeare critical tradition. The word was invented in the 1960s by Murray Gellmann, an American theoretical physicist, but first took the form 'quork'. It was then changed by its association with the line 'Three quarks for Muster Mark' in James Joyce's *Finnegans Wake* (1939)—a work that could compete for bloody-minded opacity with a book of the most esoteric scientific theorems. And so one of the most famous (and most likeable) terms in modern science took its final form through an inspired merger of literature and physics. Such a merger reverberates for the critical tradition. Shakespeare criticism in the seventeenth century, as we have seen, often appeared as poetry, and this tradition has continued to the present day (though we would not now call it Shakespeare criticism). In the eighteenth and nineteenth centuries the pre-scientific essay on Shakespeare was as much an exercise in fine writing as any other piece of occasional prose. And the advent of a scientific criticism of Shakespeare in the twentieth century frequently seems to have stimulated its practitioners to write with someone like James Joyce in mind. Nowadays postmodern Shakespeare criticism often reads like an intellectual poem (though not of the rhyming kind) and even earlier in the century it has often been remarked that A. C. Bradley wrote *Shakespearian Tragedy* with a narrative thrust that resembled the novel's.

Writing criticism in competition with who you are writing criticism about returns us, I suppose, to the world of bowels and egos. It is certainly true that much contemporary criticism of Shakespeare is directed at other pieces of contemporary criticism of Shakespeare or takes umbrage with the criticism of the past. This critical merry-go-round has not gone unnoticed. For Haines in James Joyce's *Ulysses* 'Shakespeare is the happy hunting ground of all minds that have lost their balance', and even as early as the end of the nineteenth century Oscar Wilde could contemplate writing an essay called 'Are the Commentators on *Hamlet* Really Mad, Or Only Pretending to be?' In his engagingly written book *Criticism and Literary Theory 1890 to the Present* (1996), Chris Baldick talks of twentieth-century criticism as 'a cut-throat intellectual bazaar of contending critical "schools" whose only point of agreement is that the critical methods of twenty years ago are too shop-soiled to be put on sale at all' (p. 7). Of course Baldick exaggerates. Shakespeare critics in fact often take pleasure in making their obligations clear to a criticism that has gone before, and much (perhaps most) twentieth-century criticism of Shakespeare does what it does regardless of fashion and change. We may see the history of modern criticism in D. J. Palmer's book *The Rise of English Studies* (1965) as a constant reconstitution of traditional elements—the new always defines itself against the established.

But there is no doubt that some of the most interesting contemporary criticism of Shakespeare continues in the polemical tradition established by Dryden and Thomas Rymer (the latter notorious, we may remember, for his attack on *Othello* in 1693 as a 'bloody farce, without salt or savour'). Twentieth-century Shakespeare criticism hinges on a number of countervailing tendencies, each proclaimed by its advocates as the century's most representative one. The formalists, for instance, at their crudest, deny the value of seeing Shakespeare's work in historical terms. Instead they posit a critical methodology which seals itself off from what they consider the distracting influences of the untidy culture beyond the plays. There is more than enough to work on, they would argue, within the parameters of the plays themselves, and they advocate a disciplined attention to the plays' formal elements as the be-all and end-all of Shakespeare criticism. It would probably be true to say that this way of reading Shakespeare has dominated twentieth-century criticism; the production of books and articles on the formal properties of Shakespeare's works (including the characters in the plays) shows no signs of diminishing. Extreme formalists tend to read a Shakespeare play as though it were an intricately intertwined Metaphysical poem from the school of John Donne (c.1571–1633). *Macbeth*, for instance, is particularly and rewardingly receptive to the kind of reading a formalist critic like Cleanth Brooks gives it in his famous essay, 'The Naked Babe and the Cloak of Manliness', as he follows the course of those powerful, strange, binding images of the naked babe and the ill-fitting clothes as they recur in various guises throughout the play.

Many critics, however, including some formalists, are properly outraged at formalism's cavalier disregard of history and culture. A navel-gazing Shakespeare positioned smugly above the turbulence of his or any other times does not strike us now as either adequate or true. Although he was in real life much less noticeable than someone like Jonson or Marlowe, fellow dramatists who managed to get themselves in the news by their provocative public behaviour, he clearly lived a full life in the turbulent world of gain-getting and litigation. From all we know of him (which is more than people think) he seems to have been one of those gregarious writers like a Keats, say, rather than a

J. D. Salinger, moodily aloof from the social world. More importantly, as many modern critics point out, his plays engage the world, past and present (and predict the future too, some would argue), with an intense and irrepressible curiosity. Shakespeare and history are as intricately intertwined as the formal elements in any Metaphysical poem (or any *Macbeth*), and in the latter half of the twentieth century criticism has swung away from a narrow focus on form for form's sake to larger, less redundant combinations: form for politics' sake, perhaps, or for religion's sake, or for feminism's sake, or for the sake of any number of other concerns from the world of historical circumstance. So a book like Leonard Tennenhouse's *Power on Display: The Politics of Shakespeare's Genres* (1986) asks questions once deemed purely aesthetic (why is *Henry VIII* so different from *Richard II*, *Henry IV Part One*, or *Henry V*?—why did Shakespeare write no romantic comedies after 1600/02?) and answers them in terms of the politics of the time, the politics of Shakespeare's genres, in the belief that 'political imperatives were also aesthetic imperatives'.

Formalism had also in the twentieth century to contend with Shakespeare criticism's enormous interest, despite some strident nay-sayers, in a Shakespeare taken off the printed page and thrust rudely into the commercial world of boards and screens. Charles Lamb must be turning in his grave. At no other time have the contributions of stage, film, and television directors been examined by academic writers (and others) with such a respectful scrutiny. It is greatly to the credit of Shakespeare criticism in the twentieth century that Shakespeare has been restored to the boards on which he himself trod (though only in minor roles). Even the editorial process has got into the act, so to speak. The 1986 Oxford edition of the *Complete Works of Shakespeare*, the most interesting edition of Shakespeare since the First Folio (as John Carey remarked in the *Sunday Times*), chooses the playhouse versions of Shakespeare's plays over any other as representing Shakespeare at his most professionally authentic. In the editors' words: 'Performance is the end to which they were created, and in this edition we have devoted our efforts to recovering and presenting texts of Shakespeare's plays as they were acted in the London playhouses which stood at the centre of his professional life'.

Despite the reservations of the critics with which this essay began, as they recoiled in alarm and despondency from the spectacle of Shakespeare's status as the most written-about of all writers, it does not seem likely (or desirable) that things will change much in the foreseeable future. The centre of Shakespeare's professional life has a tendency to shift to different planes. The simple facts of a complicated matter are that, first of all, Shakespeare was so marvellous a writer that he has a built-in inexhaustibility for inspiring new things to be said about him. And secondly, and just as importantly, the times are always changing: in other words, there will always be new things to say about Shakespeare because there will always be new people living in changed historical circumstances who will look on his works with new eyes. For that matter, the times in which Shakespeare himself lived will always be changing as new research reveals the inadequacies of previously held paradigms about the nature of his society. The only paradigm that perhaps will always hold for the future of the Shakespeare critical tradition is the scientific one that believes in a world of restless indeterminacy, a world in which even particles as minute as neutrinos, hadrons, and quarks may not be the last word in the quest for the basic building blocks of the universe.

FURTHER READING

Bate, Jonathan (ed.). *The Romantics on Shakespeare*. The Penguin Shakespeare Library (London: Penguin Books, 1992). An important anthology of essays on Shakespeare by some of the leading writers in Europe in the nineteenth century. Bate's introductory essay makes impressive connections between the book's extracts and the political circumstances of the times in which they were written.

Eastman, Arthur M. *A Short History of Shakespearian Criticism* (New York: Random House, 1968). A workmanlike introduction to Shakespeare criticism from the eighteenth century to the 1960s. Eastman manages to pack in a large number of critics both major and minor.

Halpern, Richard. *Shakespeare among the Moderns* (Ithaca and London: Cornell University Press, 1997). A rewardingly provocative account of the Modernist reading of Shakespeare with a particular emphasis on T. S. Eliot. Shakespeare's modernity and that of the twentieth century are interestingly paralleled.

Jardine, Lisa. *Reading Shakespeare Historically* (London and New York: Routledge, 1996). An impressive attempt to see Shakespeare in terms of a mutual animation between his own historical time and ours.

Pechter, Edward. *What Was Shakespeare? Renaissance Plays and Changing Critical Practice* (Ithaca and London: Cornell University Press, 1995). A highly readable book about Shakespeare criticism that concentrates on making connections between different schools of criticism, and in particular (and very usefully) subjecting their claims of innovation to a friendly scepticism.

Stavisky, A. Y. *Shakespeare and the Victorians; Roots of Modern Criticism* (Norman, Oklahoma: University of Oklahoma Press, 1969). This is a book that helpfully links modern Shakespeare criticism primarily with the criticism of Shakespeare in the middle and late nineteenth century. But Stavisky also shows how the strength of modern criticism lies in the fusion of Victorian method with Romantic insight.

Taylor, Gary. *Reinventing Shakespeare: A Cultural History from the Restoration to the Present* (London: Hogarth Press, 1989). A lively, irreverent, contentious account of Shakespeare's interactions with his own and later cultures. Taylor pays rewarding attention to the life of the plays in the various theatres of the world.

Taylor, Michael. *Shakespeare Criticism in the Twentieth Century* (Oxford: Oxford University Press, 2001). An introductory book on the major critics and movements of the late nineteenth and twentieth centuries. Taylor points out connections, parallels, and echoes between and among the diverse critical approaches.

Vickers, Brian. *Shakespeare: The Critical Heritage*, 6 vols. (London and Boston: Routledge and Kegan Paul, 1974–81). An indispensable collection of critical essays on Shakespeare covering the period 1623 to 1801.

25 | Humanist interpretations

Michael D. Bristol

What is 'humanism'?

Humanism is a word with too many meanings. It can mean simply the state of being human, or, more commonly, a concern for the welfare of human beings. In this sense being humanistic means more or the less the same as being humanitarian. But humanism refers specifically to an educational programme based on the study of Greek and Latin classical literature that originated in Italy in the fourteenth century. These early humanists were also Christians, and they saw their task partly as reconciling great literary works by pagan writers like Virgil and Ovid with the teachings of the Church. In a larger sense humanism can also mean any philosophy with a focus on human nature and human action. In contemporary society some conservatives have opposed the influence of 'secular humanism' as an orientation that weakens the authority of religious institutions. And in a way these critics are quite right, since humanistic interpretations, even of sacred scripture, are strongly distinguished from any type of theological exegesis. Humanism is committed to a strong view of human freedom and autonomy, as expressed in the *Oration on the Dignity of Man* by the early Italian humanist Pico della Mirandola. 'Like a free and sovereign artificer, you might mold and fashion yourself into that form you yourself shall have chosen'.[1] On this view the state of being human cannot be achieved through obedience to the authority of a revealed truth. What is fundamental to any form of humanism is a belief in the liberating potential of human reason and human creativity.

In Latin the word *liber* means free; it also means a book. In a way humanism is really all about this connection between human liberation and the library. Humanists think that men and women are best able to enjoy their freedom through careful study of the great written traditions as they have been preserved in poetry, philosophy, rhetoric, and even in political writings. These traditions provide the basis for a common or 'universal' literature. The Russian philosopher Mikhail Bakhtin believed that 'great works of literature' collectively reveal a 'complex unity of human cultures'.[2] What makes these works great is their enduring saliency in the evolving context of historical difference and social change. Humanistic interpretation is motivated by an interest in the encyclopedic aspects of literary works, their capacity to reveal something about a common human nature, shared and understood throughout historically diverse cultures. This aim is best achieved, according to any humanistic philosophy, through the careful study and teaching of languages, viewed as the defining characteristic that distinguishes human beings from all other animals. *Incipit philologia, incipit philosophia*—philosophical understanding begins with the consideration of human utterance. In this broad sense all the disparate forms of interpretation discussed in this section of *Shakespeare: An Oxford Guide* may be described as specialized variants of humanism. However, several elements distinguish contemporary humanist interpretation of Shakespeare's plays from other approaches.

Taking things literally

In an important sense humanistic criticism is simply the art of taking things literally. Humanism is deeply concerned with the figurative uses of language, but any consideration of metaphor and other rhetorical elaborations begins with an understanding of the literal meaning of words. When Macbeth wonders if 'th'assassination / Could trammel up the consequence' (1.7.2–3), it's extremely helpful to know that a 'trammel' means fishnet, or a rope used to hobble a horse. When Macduff realizes that all his children have been killed in 'one fell swoop' (4.3.220) he's thinking about the grim [fell] dive of a hawk as it attacks its helpless prey. Part of the fascination of Shakespeare's use of language is his capacity for 'unmetaphoring' common usages.[3] Unmetaphoring is a way to make conventional expressions or other figurations of language flow in a 'reverse direction' and transform themselves into actual intended behaviour. Shakespeare as a writer is really interested in getting back to the literal sense of the various linguistic and narrative conventions he is using. He looks at a conventional notion like 'falling in love at first sight' and tries to show us what that would be like if it were to happen in real life. No one really falls in love at first sight, it just seems that way in retrospect. But *Romeo and Juliet* actually shows us two people who fall deeply in love the minute they set eyes on each other.

   If a literary work seems to tell a story, then humanist interpretation will be interested in understanding that story by reflecting on the words and the actions of its fictional characters. This reflection is based on the view that fictional characters represent actual people, and that we can think about literary figures in more or less the same way that we think about the people we know in real life. Humanistic interpretations adopt a robust picture of human agency—people act purposefully and they know what they are doing. The specific deeds performed by individual human selves are not viewed simply as local effects of impersonal social forces; in an important sense they are evidence of personal autonomy and a capacity for self-determination. On this view what a person 'has in mind' is important as the motive for what that person actually does. However, as Duncan says, 'There's no art / To find the mind's construction in the face' (1.4.12–13). It's never easy to really know what is in someone else's heart. But humanist interpretation also adopts a robust picture of the expressive power of the individual utterance. It's not that people can always be counted on to say just exactly what they mean. Nevertheless, a person's utterances can be used very effectively as a way to get at their thoughts and feelings.

Folk psychology

Humanist readings focus on Shakespeare's characters by applying what might be called a folk psychology to the interpretation of dramatic language and action. Folk psychology is based on the assumption that people have reasons for what they do, and that those reasons can generally be inferred from what they say. The 'reasons' for an action can be analysed in terms of beliefs and desires, along with more complex states of mind such as purposes, intentions, and strategic calculations. So, for example, if we ask 'why did Macbeth kill Duncan' it seems obvious that the answer must be 'because he wanted to be king.' This interpretation seems feasible because the text of Shakespeare's *Macbeth* wouldn't really make any sense otherwise. But in fact Macbeth doesn't explicitly say 'I want to be king and so I guess I should kill Duncan'. His state of mind is based on the interpretative inferences we can make about his desires [*I want to be king*] and his beliefs [*being a king would be really great and if I kill Duncan the other thanes will agree to place me on the throne*]. And these inferences are based partly on what he does actually say along with what the other characters say about him. But they are also based on what the interpreter knows about how the world works, and more specifically about how people generally are prompted to act in particular ways. In this sense folk psychology can also be talked about as common-sense psychology.

What makes the example of *Macbeth* particularly interesting for humanistic interpretation, however, is the psychological complexity of its hero. Macbeth is not just a bloody-minded and ruthless killer who is willing to do anything to get what he wants. He does have a belief that killing Duncan will clear the way for him to become king. But he has other beliefs that conflict with what appears to be his primary motive or ruling passion. For one thing he isn't really sure he can get away with it. 'If th'assassination / Could trammel up the consequence, and catch / With his surcease success / . . . We'd jump the life to come' (1.7.2–7). Macbeth realizes that there will be consequences, that his actions will 'teach / Bloody instructions which, being taught, return / To plague th'inventor' (1.7.8–10). And he also has a belief in a moral order that tells that killing the king is wrong. Macbeth reminds himself that 'He's here in double trust' (1.7.12). Duncan is his friend, his kinsman, and his guest. Macbeth believes in honour, duty, and obligation; he really is 'full o'th' milk of human kindness' (1.5.15), in the sense that Duncan is one of his own kind, one of the noble people who keep their word and who are true to themselves. Duncan and Macbeth are both gentlemen; therefore Macbeth decides that he should not kill Duncan, all things considered.

Of course Macbeth acts against his better judgement and he kills Duncan anyway. Humanist interpretation is interested in understanding just how and why he is able to do this. Macbeth commits the murder despite his careful estimates of possible success [*I probably won't get away with this*] and despite his serious assessment of the morality of his intended action [*killing the king is bad*]. It's clear that his reasons do not have a sufficient motivational force to determine his actual deeds. This is the ethical problem described by Aristotle as *akrasia*—incontinence or weakness of the will. 'The continent man is identical with one who tends to abide by his estimate of what it is right to do, and the incontinent man with one who tends to depart from it. The incontinent man does wrong because he feels like it, although he knows that it is wrong'.[4] The key thing in this discussion is knowledge in the sense of lucid self-awareness—I know what I'm doing is wrong—for me—but I do it anyway. The point is not only that Macbeth acts against his own better judgement, but with the full knowledge that his actions will seriously harm exactly what he holds most dear in himself.

Philosophers have often had trouble understanding how weakness of the will could even be possible: 'when a man has knowledge in him it is impossible that something else should overmaster it and drag it about like a slave . . . nobody acts consciously against what is best—only through ignorance'.[5] Aristotle's idea is that real self-knowledge is incompatible with incontinent action; something prevents the incontinent man from really knowing himself. In Macbeth's case this 'something' is a ruling passion; his desire to be king, exacerbated by various fantasies of the kind suggested by the witches or by Lady Macbeth, turns out to be stronger than his own better judgement. In a way this looks like saying the 'devil made me do it'. It's similar to the notion that actions, motives, dispositions, and so forth are caused by malevolent 'outside influences'—by the evil eye, for example, or by witches, or space aliens, except that the idea of a 'ruling passion' is more like an unconscious and irresistible drive. If our actions are caused by our reasons then the strongest reason should be the strongest cause. But Macbeth's actual deed is not motivated by his reason, and therefore he must be driven by some powerful but unacknowledged irrationality. 'Why did Macbeth kill Duncan?' On this view the answer seems to be that he had no reason. Macbeth knows what he thinks and he thinks carefully enough to explore a range of ethical alternatives. But it is not really clear that he knows what he feels, or recognizes that his feelings are his own in some unique and special way. And when, towards the end of his life, he declares that life 'is a tale / Told by an idiot' (5.5.25–6), it is evident that he is talking about his own life and his own failure to care enough about who he really is.

It's important for humanist critics to use common sense psychology with caution and not to expect it to do too much. After all, Shakespeare lived in a world very different from our own where, for example, people believed in the existence of witches and were quite preoccupied with the behaviour of the spirits of the dead. What seems like psychological common sense to us might not seem the least bit obvious to someone who lived at the time Shakespeare was writing. Humanist interpreters understand the importance of knowing the historical context for reading Shakespeare's plays. But for a humanist it is important for people to enjoy Shakespeare's plays without requiring any special academic qualifications as a pre-condition for that enjoyment. And, as the example of Macbeth's motives for killing Duncan should suggest, interpretations based on common-sense psychology are quite effective in bringing out the complexity of the material. They also possess an immediacy for readers that is otherwise lacking with interpretations that insist too narrowly on historical contexts.

The role of the emotions

Humanist interpretation is concerned with dramatic action not only as a way to represent the motives for specific acts, but also more broadly as a way to explore human feeling. *Romeo and Juliet* is about two teenagers who fall in love. But what is this feeling really like?

> ROMEO: If I profane with my unworthiest hand
> This holy shrine, the gentler sin is this:
> My lips, two blushing pilgrims, ready stand
> To smooth that rough touch with a tender kiss.
> JULIET: Good pilgrim, you do wrong your hand too much,
> Which mannerly devotion shows in this.
> For saints have hands that pilgrims' hands do touch,
> And palm to palm is holy palmers' kiss.
> ROMEO: Have not saints lips, and holy palmers, too?
> JULIET: Ay, pilgrim, lips that they must use in prayer.
> ROMEO: O then, dear saint, let lips do what hands do:
> They pray; grant thou, lest faith turn to despair.
> JULIET: Saints do not move, though grant for prayers' sake.
> ROMEO: Then move not while my prayer's effect I take.
> *[He kisses her]*
>
> (1.5.90-103)

This is a sonnet, a poetic form often used to express love. In most sonnets only one voice is speaking, either praising the beloved or complaining about her coldness. Typically the sonnet is a monologue that imagines courtship as a one-sided game of pursuit, resistance, and evasion. Romeo and Juliet compose their sonnet in the form of a dialogue. This establishes that their courtship is a participatory format in which the partners can explore the possibility of reciprocal desire. Romeo and Juliet change the purpose of the game here; instead of a negotiation of erotic power and domination, they explore the possibility of reaching mutual consent through shared communication. The sonnet is a brilliant poetic condensation of the larger experience of courtship and of falling in love. What Shakespeare has done here is to substitute a single, poetically dense verse form for the more long-winded and elaborate negotiations of a real courtship.

A close analysis of this passage could usefully focus on gesture and the forms of bodily self-expression. The first rhyme word in the first line is 'hand' and the language of the hand will turn out to be one of the most important forms of expression not only for the sonnet, but also for the larger shape of the play. The hand is a primary organ of human communication—it can be extended in greeting, it can establish contact even at a distance, and it can reach out to touch another. Hand-holding is a primary form of personal intimacy. The hand also has larger symbolic valences as a kind of metonymy for ideas of consent. We shake hands to signify an agreement we will later come to recognize as morally—and even legally—binding. And of course we refer to matrimony itself by talking about the giving of someone's hand in marriage. The hand also refers to the capacity for writing, another way that the hand is extended toward others and participates in the social acknowledgement of personal responsibility and consent, as in the signing of a letter, a contract, or legal agreement. When we speak of someone's hand in the sense of their handwriting we're referring to ideas of unique individuality, as in the concept of signature.

What happens in the scene literally or unmetaphorically is that Romeo takes Juliet's hand, at the same time placing that taking into a discursive context of offering or giving, as when we speak of the giving of one's hand in friendship. The crucial turning of this figure happens a few lines later when Juliet says ' . . . saints have hands that pilgrims' hands do touch, / And palm to palm is holy palmers' kiss'. When you 'take' someone's hand the palm usually grasps the back of the other person's hand and the fingers curl around the edge. Or you may grasp the other person's hand around the fingertips. What Juliet does here is to shift the position of her [left] hand to press against Romeo's [right] hand in a matching of symmetrical shapes. The gesture here is a 'mirroring' of similar shapes. This is the 'holy palmers' kiss', the chaste kiss of religious pilgrims that substitutes for the more sensual form of amatory kiss. The touching of hands—as opposed to the meeting of lips—would then represent a more spiritual aspect of love. But at the same time the hands are held together in a form that can also signify a more immediately physical form of intimacy. The hand can be understood as a metonymy for the whole body, and specifically for the way we differentiate between the front regions and the back regions. The pressing together of the palms then would be a metonymy for the face-to-face meeting of bodies in sexual intimacy.

The sonnet turns when Romeo withdraws his hand and makes the gesture of prayer. Hands are joined in prayer to represent the attitude of requesting. What Romeo communicates to Juliet here is not that he wants to kiss her, or even that he wants her to kiss him, but that he wants a kiss to be given. This is an act of deep recognition, the full and unqualified acknowledgement of another's separate and autonomous personhood, which is the real purpose of courtship, at least as it is articulated by Shakespeare in this remarkable passage. The process of courting someone obviously begins with a decision to express certain intentions, as when I take someone's hand, but this taking is not the ultimate aim. The immediate intention of this gesture of taking is a wish to learn or to discover the other person's intentions. The initial or interim goal is achieved in a joining or matching or mirroring of intentions with a view to establishing the possibility of reciprocal desire. But mutual acceptance does not complete the trajectory of courtship. Each of the partners has to move away from joining or mirroring back towards a sense of the separateness of self. It is only from the attitude of faith, where we are most in touch with ourselves, that we come to sense another's presence not as the representation or the object of our own desire, but as an altogether separate person capable of intending, desiring, touching, mirroring, and requesting, all in ways that must remain at least partially opaque. I can only give myself to someone if my self is mine to give *and* if the other's self is capable of receiving such a gift.

The centrality of ethics

The humanist's interest in the poetic elaboration of human feelings in Shakespeare's plays is closely tied to the exploration of ethical questions. Aristotle believed that as human beings we feel a sense of fellowship with other human beings, we are by nature social animals, and that no matter how varied our specific ideas of justice or of friendship may be, there is some point in seeing them as overlapping expressions of the same family of shared human needs.[6] A dramatic narrative represents the way a person is oriented by ethical dispositions and beliefs in a space of moral questions. The contemporary philosopher Alasdair McIntyre says that characters are the 'masks worn by moral philosophies'.[7] In this sense, then, characters just like those represented in a Shakespeare play really exist in this world, their forms of appearance are not arbitrary literary conventions, and their speech no less than their actions is roughly similar to that of ordinary men and women we know from our own social experience. Shakespeare's characters are a mirror of human nature because they are represented as fully embedded in the concrete particularity of everyday life.

It is because Shakespeare has so much insight into both the desires and the moral sources that direct all human agency, that his works are so richly instructive. One of the more culturally significant and influential explanations for Shakespeare's durable importance begins from the conviction that everyday life has an overriding priority as a moral source. This view assigns moral pre-eminence to the regime of intimate personal relations, to the family, and to the lives of ordinary unprivileged people engaged in their everyday social activities. The moral supremacy of everyday life is then taken up as an evaluative standard for literature and art. Within this framework, Shakespeare has been seen not only as satisfying this criterion but also and more importantly as a powerful source for articulating the moral pre-eminence of ordinary life. The moral philosophy represented in Shakespeare's characters is realistic knowledge about how one might act in concrete social circumstances. The moral force of these depictions arises from an immediate sympathy between the dramatic character and the spectator. What makes such sympathy possible is a shared background in the complex and contradictory experience of everyday life. Shakespeare's characters are non-heroic, and even at times anti-heroic, but it is precisely the modest human scale of their depiction that makes them morally significant.

King Lear is a play about civil war, the politics of dynastic succession, and the tragic contradictions of monarchy. And yet many people have seen in King Lear something that reminds them of their own ageing and difficult parents. The king is interesting not because he is 'royal Lear' but because he is an emotional tyrant whose behaviour may be all too familiar to those who see in him a resemblance to their own father. And when Lear asks his daughters 'which of you shall we say doth love us most?' (1.1.49) we may feel an immediate sympathy with the awkward feelings the situation creates for them. What Lear asks of his daughters is a public and ceremonial expression of love, something he may indeed be entitled to as king and father. But there's something about this moment that makes us squirm, something obscene and creepy in the old man's needy emotional demands. How can anyone possibly respond to this kind of behaviour in a parent? As a practical matter most people would prefer to say something a bit dishonest and insincere, just for the sake of peace in the family. And while it may not be advisable to engage in wilful deception, kind words are seldom regretted, especially in a domestic context.

Lear's older daughters, Goneril and Regan, both reply to his question according to a perfunctory and expedient morality. They give him what he wants because they don't want any fuss. But if we ask 'what did Cordelia say that made her father so angry?' the answer, paradoxically, is 'nothing'. 'Nothing' is naught, and her refusal to co-operate makes Cordelia a 'naughty girl' for refusing to give her father what he asks for. 'Nothing will come of nothing' (1.1.89), he says, 'mend your speech a little, / Lest it may mar your fortunes' (1.1.93–4). It appears to Lear that naughty Cordelia wants to get something—maybe a whole lot of something—for nothing. But what does Cordelia actually feel when she refuses to bid for her father's bounty? She says 'I love your majesty / According to my bond; nor more nor less' (1.1.91–2). This may be truthful, but in a way it is not very polite and this is why we might think Cordelia is being naughty. The point here is that communicating with other people is not just conveying information about our current state of mind. In our speech we try to avoid hurting someone else's feelings. We don't say everything that might be in our hearts because we need to maintain the emotional ties that bind us together. This is exactly what Cordelia means when she refers to the 'bond' between a father and a daughter. In this sense it seems that the standards of politeness have already been suspended when Lear asks 'which of you shall we say doth love us most'. Given the circumstances of the bidding it is hard to see how the requirements of tact, or modesty, or even real generosity can be satisfied, except perhaps by saying 'nothing, my lord'. But Lear is unwilling to understand the real meaning of silence here. It may be that politeness is just incompatible with the family, since it appears that politeness is really about respecting personal boundaries. Lear ignores the boundary between private and public, he extends the borders of his emotional needs in a way that invades the human dignity of his daughters, and he forces them to defend those borders in ways that conflict with their sense of personal integrity. The family, seen in this way, turns out to be about hurt feelings, resentment, and the circulation of guilt.

Profound relationships

Thinking about *King Lear* as a narrative of ordinary domestic life requires some careful thinking about the exact nature of family obligations. What are the specific kinds of things we owe to loved ones? In *Reciprocity*, Lawrence Becker begins with the suggestion that 'families are potent' and then goes on to consideration of what he calls 'profound relationship'. Here the idea of 'profound' refers both to depth and to obscurity. The sense is that interactions within families are so frequent and so dense that it is not possible to achieve any kind of balance in the give and take of everyday life. Our obligations are 'incalculable'—so much is going on that we can never know everything that we have given and everything we have received. Ordinary reciprocity that says 'I did the laundry so now you must vacuum the rugs' is simply inadequate as a way to express love. According to Becker, 'Love stands as an implicit rebuke to the business of reciprocating. That business is crass by comparison—simplistic, superficial, single-minded, overly concerned with obligations and with getting even'.[8] Most people sense something like this about Lear's determination to measure the amount of his daughters' love. There is something false and dishonest in the assumption that love can be expressed in terms of real estate.

Cordelia risks everything by saying nothing, because she wants to put an end to the practice of family bargaining and to replace it with more genuine forms of reciprocal acknowledgement. What Cordelia actually says when she says 'nothing' is 'I love your majesty according to my *bond*'. 'Bond' comes from the verb 'to bind', and the past participle of 'bind' is 'bound', a word that refers both to obligation—what I am bound to do—and to boundary—where I stand as a separately embodied self in the sense of a limit, or bourne. A bond is also a pledge or a promise. And in the sense that a bond represents some kind of material value the idea is related to the notion of a 'boon' or a 'bounty', which is Lear's word for his gift to his daughters. This constellation of words captures much of the complexity of the family dynamic and why Cordelia evidently feels she must decline to participate in the bidding for her father's bounty. 'Bid' is a condensation of two Old English words: *beodan* 'to stretch out, reach out, offer, present', hence 'to communicate, inform, announce, proclaim, command', and *biddan* 'to ask pressingly, beg, pray, require, demand, command'. This is exactly what Cordelia wants to avoid when she says she lacks a 'still soliciting eye,' an eye that watches the other person's face and calculates the effects of every word. For Cordelia, there is no shame in speaking 'according to my bond'; shame is attached only to speech that begs, or bids, or solicits approval.

One way to see what Cordelia might have in mind when she says 'according to my bond' is to think about Immanuel Kant's maxim of 'the end in itself'—'So act as to treat humanity, whether in thine own person or in that of any other, in every case as an end withal, never as means only'.[9] Cordelia thinks well enough of her own personhood to insist on maintaining her own dignity. She won't 'sell out' to her father or to her sisters by making some kind of bid for love and property. In other words she is committed to maintaining her own bounds or psychological boundaries, her own separateness as a person from the emotionally needy and exploiting parent. What we see in Cordelia looks something like Aristotle's *philautia*, which means 'self-love' or more precisely 'self-respect'. It is precisely this aspect of her character that makes her 'naughty Cordelia'. Women have traditionally been expected to function according to an ethics based on self-sacrifice, taking responsibility only for the needs of others. Cordelia will not be bound in a life of self-deception; her bond with Lear is a covenant, undertaken in the freedom and dignity of full personhood.

Humanist interpretation is governed by certain normative commitments, most notably to ideas of human freedom, rational autonomy, and the acknowledgement of human diversity. Because of this, humanistic criticism is open to a wide range of interpretive methods and orientations. Close reading, psychoanalysis, historicism, and myth criticism are all fully compatible with humanist interpretation. It is possible to be a Christian humanist or a Marxist humanist or a Feminist humanist. Contemporary humanism rejects the view that people are all alike, nor does it pursue the illusory goals of codifying an abstract or totalizing universality. There are no generic or interchangeable 'humans'; people acquire identities in terms of their religious affiliations, métiers, ethnic communities, race, gender, sexuality, and social class. At the same time, however, humanistic criticism seeks out the possibility for convergence, dialogue, and mutual recognition across these differences.

FURTHER READING

Berger, Jr., Harry. *Making Trifles of Terrors: Redistributing Complicities in Shakespeare* (Stanford: Stanford University Press, 1997). Berger's work combines disciplined attention to textual detail with a profound understanding of human psychology.

Bradley, A. C. *Shakespearean Tragedy*, 3rd edn. (London: Macmillan, 1992). This influential study is the culmination of a long tradition of character-based criticism of Shakespeare's plays.

Cavell, Stanley. *Disowning Knowledge in Six Plays by Shakespeare* (Cambridge: Cambridge University Press, 1986). Stanley Cavell is a philosopher who has written extensively on the problem of scepticism and its complex function in modern society.

Parker, Patricia. *Shakespeare from the Margins: Language, Culture, Context* (Chicago: University of Chicago Press, 1996). Parker's treatment of figurative language reveals the dense and complicated weaving of ideas through the body of Shakespeare's work.

Taylor, Charles. *Sources of the Self: The Making of the Modern Identity* (Cambridge, Massachusetts: Harvard University Press, 1989). The political philosopher Charles Taylor turns his attention here to a comprehensive history of 'self' and 'subjectivity' since the early modern period.

NOTES

1. Pico della Mirandola, Giovanni. *Oration on the Dignity of Man*, trans. A. Robert Caponigri (South Bend, Indiana: Regnery Gateway, 1956), p. 27.
2. Bakhtin, Mikhail M. *Speech Genres and Other Late Essays*, ed. Caryl Emerson and Michael Holquist, trans. Vern McGee (Austin: University of Texas Press, 1986), p. 27.
3. Colie, Rosalie. *The Resources of Kind; Genre-Theory in the Renaissance*, ed. Barbara K. Lewalski (Berkeley: University of California Press, 1973), pp. 118–19.
4. Aristotle. *Nichomachean Ethics* (Harmondsworth: Penguin Books, 1968), Bk. VII, p. 211.
5. Ibid., p. 214.
6. Martha Nussbaum. 'Non-Relative Virtues: An Aristotelian Approach'. In *The Quality of Life*, ed. Martha Nussbaum and Amartya Sen (Oxford: Clarendon Press, 1993), pp. 261 ff.
7. McIntyre, Alasdair. *After Virtue*, 2nd edn. (South Bend: University of Notre Dame Press, 1984), p. 28.
8. Becker, Lawrence. *Reciprocity* (Chicago: University of Chicago Press, 1986), p. 186.
9. Kant, Immanuel. *Foundations of the Metaphysics of Morals*, ed. Robert Paul Wolff, trans. Lewis White Beck (Indianapolis: Bobbs-Merrill, 1969), p. 58.

READING: *King Lear*

The application of humanist interpretation to a reading of *King Lear* begins from the intuition that there is something immediately recognizable and familiar in the play's dramatic situation. For many readers *King Lear* is a story of ordinary domestic life, parents and children, family bargaining, hurt feelings, and unrequited love. *King Lear* is about an ageing parent whose excessive demands for love annihilate the basic elements of trust, openness, and mutual forbearance that constitute the minimum conditions for any kind of genuine social existence. The play dramatizes a power struggle between parents and children, in which the basic interactions of family life simply become intolerable. Central to this struggle are issues of truth, sincerity, and deception. Humanist interpretations of *King Lear* privilege the domestic sphere as the space of our moral being. *King Lear* reminds people of the seriousness of everyday moral problems, like trying to care for an ageing and difficult parent. The play represents as powerfully as any cultural artefact we possess the dignity and the pathos of moral agents in the ethical space of everyday life.

The play starts off quietly enough. Two old men gossip about politics while a younger man listens:

> KENT: I thought the king had more affected the Duke of Albany than Cornwall.
> GLOUCESTER: It did always seem so to us; but now, in the division of the kingdom, it appears not which of the dukes he values most; for equalities are so weighed, that curiosity in neither can make choice of either's moiety.

(1.1.1–6)

Each duke worries that the king might value the other one more, but they really can't be sure. But would the king bestow more affection on one of these dukes rather than another, especially if they are equal in rank and nobility? The question of the king's affection looks like trivial court gossip, but we should perhaps reflect more seriously on just what it is to favour someone. Why should anyone prefer one person to another? The court politics of royal favour and advancement may seem remote and alien for us today, but we should recognize the more general and immediate importance of partiality—because partiality is simply what we call love. We are partial to loved ones; we favour those we care for over others not for any particular reason, but just because we love them. And we expect to be loved, not because we are especially deserving, but because grandma, or dad, or our lover recognize and prefer the singular special person each of us is. But this wish can have a dark side when we consider the possibility of rivalry among family members, as when we say to a sibling 'mom always liked you best'. Each of the dukes wonders if he is to be favoured. But in Lear's England 'equalities are so weighed' that even the minutest curiosity cannot help the dukes determine who stands first in the king's affection. And this creates suspicion, rivalry, and mistrust, because the dukes don't know where they stand.

Curiosity implies a 'desire to know' and this desire will prove central to the situation that begins to unfold in the first scene of *King Lear*. A bit more of the importance of this 'desire to know' in the context of family politics is evident in what Gloucester tells Kent about his son Edmund:

> GLOUCESTER: But I have, sir, a son by order of law, some year elder than this, who yet is no dearer in my account. Though this knave came something saucily into the world before he was sent for, yet was his mother fair; there was good sport at his making, and the whoreson must be acknowledged.
>
> (1.1.18-22)

Gloucester's 'acknowledgement' of Edmund has the narrow legal sense here of assuming responsibility for someone, and additionally of making a public declaration of that responsibility. And since he holds his legitimate son Edgar 'no dearer', he may well intend to leave Edmund with an extremely generous settlement. Again, the conditions for rivalry are already present in the Gloucester family, just as they are in Lear's 'royal family' and in the court. Gloucester's apparently fair-minded impartiality towards his bastard masks a deeper and more dangerous partiality; his love for Edmund reflects his own self-satisfaction over the 'sport at his making' rather than a sense of family obligation. Gloucester 'knew' Edmund's mother, and therefore he 'knows' he is Edmund's father. But his 'acknowledgement' seems to mean something rather different from the kind of 'knowledge' that would satisfy 'curiosity'. Curiosity here seems more closely related to the problematic of scepticism as it is articulated by Stanley Cavell in *Disowning Knowledge*. 'We cannot know the world exists, and hence that perhaps there isn't one . . . since we cannot know the world exists, its presentness to us cannot be a function of knowing. The world is to be accepted, as the presentness of other minds is not to be known, but acknowledged'.[1]

The tragedy of Lear is that he is incapable of acknowledging Cordelia's love, because he is incapable of acknowledging himself. All three of his daughters know 'he hath but slenderly known himself'. And so he decides to ask 'which of you shall we say doth love us most?' What happens when Lear asks Cordelia to say how much she loves him? She says 'nothing, my lord' and then insists 'I love your majesty / According to my bond; nor more nor less' (1.1.91–2). Edmund starts the trouble in the Gloucester family with the same phrase. Some people suggest that Cordelia is somehow at fault here for saying what is perhaps true, but socially inappropriate. But it is hard to see how Cordelia is responsible for Lear's darker purpose in the division of his kingdom or his decision to 'unmake' the family in response to her 'nothing'. Lear's extreme response to Cordelia's silence irreversibly extends the chain of harmful consequences.

> LEAR: Let it be so! Thy truth, then, be thy dower!
> For, by the sacred radiance of the sun,
> The mysteries of Hecate, and the night;
> By all the operation of the orbs
> From whom we do exist and cease to be;
> Here I disclaim all my paternal care,
> Propinquity and property of blood,

> And as a stranger to my heart and me
> Hold thee, from this, for ever.
>
> (1.1.108-16)

Nothing is naught, and in her response to Lear we can say that Cordelia has been naughty. Nothing is also nihil, the void out of which God creates the world *ex nihilo*. The basic paradox is this, that Lear has been 'all', but now that he has given 'all' to his daughters he is himself become nothing. And hearing that nothing from his naughty daughter, he decides to annihilate his bond, disaffiliating himself from his only loving daughter and from his only real friend.

Lear's 'darker purpose' amounts to a deliberate refusal to accept even the minimum conditions for ordered social life. The king renounces his kingdom; the father disowns his daughter. Institutional authority, shared patterns of mutual obligation give way to wilful partiality. Lear is no longer a king, but rather a tyrant in the sense that he feels himself no longer bound by any traditional bonds, obligations, or laws. He is determined to have what he wants, whether it is a lavish display of affection from his youngest daughter, or simply having his supper served whenever he wants it. He wants everything, but what he gets is nothing and even less than nothing when he is driven out into a violent storm by Regan and Goneril.

In the scenes on the heath Lear wants to 'outface' the elements, to see in the storm some kind of sympathetic expression of his own towering rage. Lear is convinced that the storm means something—he is now more and more living inside his own narrative of self-pity and vindictive rage.

> LEAR: Blow, winds, and crack your cheeks! rage! blow!
> You cataracts and hurricanoes, spout
> Till you have drenched our steeples, drowned the cocks!
>
> (3.2.1-3)

Lear's reading of the storm is a manifestation of the dreadful folly that was always implicit in the darker purpose with which he began. It's important to recognize the storm as a powerful metaphor for Lear's out-of-control rage, for his derangement and alienation, for his complete lack of self-awareness. But it is just as important to recognize the storm 'unmetaphorically' as the destructive indifference of the natural world. Kent and the Fool realize that the storm is something much more terrible than a symbol. It can do real harm; people die of exposure if they are deprived of shelter. Even bears, and lions, and wolves stay in their dens to 'keep their fur dry'. The storm's indifference is matched by the savagery of Lear's daughters. But the Fool realizes that refusing shelter when the weather is so bad may in fact be a greater evil than even the unkindness of Goneril and Regan.

The central scenes on the heath can be read as a procession of 'liminary outcasts'—the mad king, the fool, Tom o' Bedlam, and Caius, the masterless man, who is really the Earl of Kent in disguise. In a sense these tattered fools and madmen are exemplary figures of the carnivalesque, with Lear himself as the Lord of Misrule who is expelled at the end of carnival. Here we are able to see what happens to him in his exile. The fool's response to the storm is the single verse from a song, the same song that was sung by Feste at the end of *Twelfth Night*.

FOOL: He that has and a little tiny wit—
 With hey, ho, the wind and the rain—
 Must make content with his fortunes fit,
 Though the rain it raineth every day.
    (3.2.72-5)

Fools must learn to be content with whatever fortune brings. But of course in this sense everyone is a fool because people have only a little tiny wit at their disposal. But this storm blows with an 'eyeless rage'—it is blind and indifferent to the humanity of its victims. It 'makes nothing' of Lear's white hairs, both in the sense that it doesn't care about Lear's age or his dignity and in the sense that it can literally make something—a human being let's say—into nothing.

Lear himself is, of course, aware both of the blind indifference of the storm as a physical reality and of the equally blind social indifference that ignores the human suffering of deprivation and homelessness. The heavens—in the sense of the sky or the weather—are, of course, neither just nor unjust. Only human institutions can be either of these things. What's being suggested here, among other things, is that there is finally nothing in the natural world that even remotely corresponds to any ideas of justice or even divine providence. And the absence or disappearance of justice from both the natural and the social landscape is figured with even more terrifying literalness in the scenes of Gloucester's blinding. Gloucester tried to help Lear, and for this act of kindness he is seized, and accused of treason. It's difficult to imagine how this scene can actually be performed as it's written, because the intent here is to force members of the audience to witness mutilation and torture. The gouging out of the eyeball takes place in full view of the audience. And in addition, Shakespeare injects an element of black comedy into the scene when Regan demands that the other eye be destroyed. 'One side will mock another. The other too' (3.7.72). This is a grotesque parody of the idea of a retributive justice that demands 'an eye for an eye'. The only rebuke to this breathtaking and incomprehensible deed comes from one of the servants, who tries to resist and is killed by Regan, who then orders that he be thrust out the gates of his own home so he can 'smell his way to Dover'.

Gloucester didn't see through Edmund's malicious deception, but somehow his punishment seems completely out of proportion to the fault of his credulity. Edmund is the worst kind of liar in the way his 'inventions' make it virtually impossible to know the truth. But Gloucester's folly in believing Edmund's lies was in thinking he didn't really know the truth about Edgar. This is what he finally realizes when he meets an old man who tries to help him:

OLD MAN: O, my good lord, I have been your tenant, and your father's tenant, these fourscore
 years.
GLOUCESTER: Away, get thee away! Good friend, be gone.
 Thy comforts can do me no good at all;
 Thee they may hurt.
OLD MAN: Alack, sir, you cannot see your way.
GLOUCESTER: I have no way, and therefore want no eyes;
            (4.1.13-19)

Stanley Cavell suggests that both Gloucester and Lear have an unwarranted scepticism about their own children. There are some things we cannot know about our loved ones, but we cannot insist on ever-more-palpable demonstrations of their love and concern for us. Gloucester was all too ready to believe that Edgar would betray him. And Lear was so irritated with naughty Cordelia that he couldn't see that she was the one who really loved him.

King Lear is a story about three sisters where the youngest, who is at first despised and rejected by her father, eventually saves him from the treachery of the older daughters. In a way this is a variation on a simple fairy tale, like Cinderella. But why is it the youngest child, the naughty and unpromising one, the dirty and dejected Fool, who comes to be revealed at the end as a redemptive hero? The burden of obligation and indebtedness in families falls more heavily on the first-born. The naughty one, the youngest, the one who is foolish, is somehow shielded from the full force of patriarchal domination. Coppélia Kahn has noticed that these three sisters have no mother; and the mother is also absent from the story of Gloucester and his two sons. When Lear first arrives at Gloucester's home he is looking for Regan, hoping she will turn out to be 'kind and comfortable' to him, something he badly needs after the unkindness he has experienced at the hands of Goneril. But instead he finds his servant in the stocks, and he takes this humiliation very personally.[2]

> LEAR: O, how this mother swells up toward my heart!
> *Hysterica passio*, down, thou climbing sorrow;
> Thy element's below!
>
> (2.4.54-6)

Hysterica passio, or 'the mother', is the wandering womb, and Kahn has argued that the 'absent mother' is somehow inscribed in Lear's own body at this point of the narrative. Her reading is an effort 'to uncover the hidden mother in the hero's inner world. . . . Lear's very insistence on paternal power, in fact, [suggests] its shakiness; similarly the absence of the mother points to . . . his repressed identification with and also his rage against the mother'. Lear's rage, on this view, reflects his agonized feeling over the deprivation of the mother's presence, a loss his daughters were supposed to make good.[3]

Lear is finally rescued by Cordelia, but there is no happy ending in view for either of them. The armies of France are defeated by Edmund, who has Cordelia and Lear led away to prison. The king is asked if he wants to see his other two daughters, but he refuses:

> LEAR: No, no, no, no! Come, let's away to prison.
> We two alone will sing like birds i' the cage,
> When thou dost ask me blessing, I'll kneel down,
> And ask of thee forgiveness. So we'll live,
> And pray, and sing, and tell old tales, and laugh
> At gilded butterflies,
>
> (5.3.8-13)

The metaphor of the temporal world as a prison is part of the stoic tradition which suggests that the spirit is most free when the body acknowledges its bonds, and that temporal power is just an illusion when viewed from the perspective of eternity. But this is a real prison, just like the storm was a real storm and what happens there had nothing to do with imagery of spiritual freedom. Lear still doesn't grasp what is really happening. He clings to the infantile fantasy that he can be secure against suffering and evil, that Cordelia will always take care of him, that they can always be together and love each other.

The story of Lear is like a fairy tale that has been unmetaphored and rendered literally. It doesn't show us the world as we wish it could be. Instead it presents a spectacle of vulnerability, suffering, and disintegration that seems endless. In the eighteenth century people found Shakespeare's ending so unbearable that it was changed so that Lear lived and Cordelia was married to Edgar. It has been said of the play that if Cordelia dies, then there is no justice in the universe. Well Cordelia does die, but why should anyone expect justice to come from the universe? Justice is about being together in the world with other people, it is about the ordinary everyday work of maintaining the shared fabric of social life. This is what Lear was willing to risk when he divided his kingdom and banished the only one of his children who really cared about him. But because the death of Cordelia seems so extreme a form of retribution, some readers want to see in Lear's last moments some kind of spiritual insight, some compensatory gain for the irreparable loss of his daughter. And so they try to find in his final words an indication of a belief in the soul's redemption after death. What does he think he sees just at the moment of his own death? Perhaps the last thing he sees is some kind of hope that Cordelia is still alive. But she isn't and we're left in the end only with the dreadful echoing of 'never, never, never, never, never' (5.3.307). This is an image of the finality of death and it is presented without any consolation, either for Lear or for anyone watching the story of his suffering. This goes beyond acceptance or reconciliation with the idea of my own death or the death of someone I love. It also means that the deep recognition or acknowledgement of the people we love is necessarily a deep recognition that we are destined to lose them or else to be lost to them.

King Lear is a work of immense complexity. The more closely it is studied the more it reveals new potentialities of meaning. And yet in some ways it is really very simple. An old man loved his daughter but he felt betrayed and angry when she hurt his feelings. He sent her away but then he suffered terribly without her. And when they were at last reconciled, she was killed. The story is painful and impossibly sad, but it reveals a truth about the human condition that everyone can understand.

FURTHER READING

Barber, C.L. and Richard Wheeler. *The Whole Journey: Shakespeare's Power of Development* (Berkeley: University of California Press, 1986). This book will provide its readers with a clear and sympathetic treatment of the plays from a psychoanalytic perspective.

Berger, Jr., Harry. '*King Lear*: The Lear Family Romance'. In *Making Trifles of Terrors: Redistributing Complicities in Shakespeare* (Stanford: Stanford University Press, 1997). Berger's essay discusses the play against the familiar background of family interaction, using a sophisticated version of common-sense psychology.

Booth, Stephen. *'King Lear', 'Macbeth', Indefinition, and Tragedy* (New Haven: Yale University Press,

1983). Stephen Booth's essays on *King Lear* and *Macbeth* represent the critical practice of close reading by one of its most gifted practitioners.

Bradley, A. C. *Shakespearean Tragedy*, 3rd edn. (London: Macmillan, 1992). Originally published in 1903, this work remains among the most influential examples of character study.

Colie, Rosalie. *Shakespeare's Living Art* (Princeton: Princeton University Press, 1974). Rosalie Colie's work stresses the formal and aesthetic complexity of Shakespearian drama.

Danby, John F. *Shakespeare's Doctrine of Nature: A Study of 'King Lear'* (London: Faber, 1949). Danby's approach emphasizes social history and elements of class conflict in the play's dramatic structure.

Mack, Maynard. *'King Lear' in Our Time* (Berkeley: University of California Press, 1965). Mack shows that the play is both a parable of the meaning of human suffering and at the same time an example of stark realism.

NOTES

1. Cavell, Stanley. 'The Avoidance of Love: A Reading of *King Lear*'. In *Disowning Knowledge in Six Plays by Shakespeare* (Cambridge: Cambridge University Press, 1986), p. 43.

2. Kahn, Coppélia. 'The Absent Mother in *King Lear*'. In *Rewriting the Renaissance: The Discourses of Sexual Difference in Early Modern Europe*, ed. Margaret W. Ferguson, Maureen Quilligan, and Nancy Vickers (Chicago: University of Chicago Press, 1986), p. 33.

3. Ibid., pp. 35–6.

Character criticism

Christy Desmet

Introduction: the rise and fall of Shakespearian character criticism

Character criticism of Shakespeare, the analysis of his characters as individuals worthy of close scrutiny and strong feelings of identification, is both a manifestation of bardolatry and a mode of reading. Character criticism rose with the reputation of Shakespeare as an author in the Restoration and eighteenth century; reached its high point as a critical genre during the Romantic and Victorian periods, as Shakespeare appreciation intensified into Shakespeare worship or bardolatry; and declined after the 1930s, when formalism and the New Criticism took hold in universities on both sides of the Atlantic. As an informal practice, however, character appreciation has survived repeated attacks from literary theorists who think that empathizing with literary characters encourages shallow thinking and sentimentalized responses to Shakespeare's plays.

Shakespeare as author and the origins of character criticism

Shakespearian character criticism, as we understand it today, would have seemed alien to a Renaissance audience. The term 'character', which derives from the Greek word for a graphic 'mark' or alphabetical letter, indicates a sharply drawn fictional figure, based on social, psychological, or moral stereotypes. In Renaissance England, the type of short prose essay known as the 'character' became a popular, if minor, literary genre. Sir Thomas Overbury's book of *Characters* (1616), for instance, collected together portraits of social types that are made vivid, even larger-than-life, by lavish descriptive detail. We can find evidence of such social types in some dramatic characters from Shakespeare's plays. For instance, Jaques of *As You Like It* resembles the 'type' of the disaffected courtier; so does Hamlet, although his character is much more complex.

But readers and spectators have long felt that Shakespeare's characters exceed the stereotypes that may be recognized in them. In a commendatory poem attached to *Poems Written by William Shakespeare* (1640), Leonard Digges offers the first praise for

Shakespeare's characters, both as individuals and as members of a dramatic ensemble. The earliest full-scale character portrait, however, is the brief vignette describing Caliban that appears in John Dryden's essay, 'The Grounds of Criticism in Tragedy' (1679). Dryden attributes Caliban's bad qualities not only to his condition as a slave on Prospero's island, but also to the genetic influence of his supposedly devilish father and witch-mother. In the larger context of Dryden's essay, the portrait is intended to illustrate Shakespeare's superiority as an author and the worth of English literature in general.[1] But on a more local level, Dryden establishes the criteria by which later writers will judge Shakespeare's dramatic persons. Caliban has verisimilitude—he seems real to us—because Shakespeare made his character understandable in terms of his supposed 'background' and psychological makeup.

Debate over Shakespeare's literary virtues soon became, in itself, a critical industry that encouraged further efforts at character analysis. Samuel Johnson's *Preface* to Shakespeare (1765), the best-known assessment of his plays from the eighteenth century, weighs Shakespeare's artistic merits against his faults, using characterization as one pertinent measure. Shakespeare excels in creating 'just representations of *general* nature'; while 'in the writings of other poets a character is too often an individual', in Shakespeare 'it is commonly a species'. But Shakespeare also 'holds up to his readers a faithful *mirror* of manners and of life' (emphasis added); his characters are, para-doxically, also particularized.[2] In Johnson's view, Shakespeare sees the 'general' in the 'particular' and thus makes readers perceive in individuals such as Hamlet, Iago, and Falstaff the general qualities of human nature that they, ostensibly, share with the rest of mankind.

The *Preface* does not discuss particular figures from Shakespeare's plays, but in the notes to his Shakespeare edition, Johnson offers compact character assessments that often prompt further critical debate. These sketches juxtapose sharply the merits of various Shakespearian characters against their demerits, without trying to reconcile one with the other; for this reason, Johnson's attitude toward the characters can seem paradoxical, even self-contradictory. His account of Falstaff from the two *Henry IV* plays, for instance, balances admiration for Falstaff's power to elicit affection from both Hal and Shakespeare's readers with moral distaste for his many faults. 'Falstaff, unimitated, unimitable Falstaff', Johnson begins, 'how shall I describe thee? Thou compound of sense and vice; of sense which may be admired but not esteemed, of vice which may be despised, but hardly detested'. Johnson's delicately balanced syntax, always on the verge of being upset by paradox, imitates the back-and-forth movement of his response to Falstaff. Admittedly, the fat knight is 'loaded' with faults: 'He is a thief, and a glutton, a coward, and a boaster, always ready to cheat the weak, and prey upon the poor; to terrify the timorous and insult the defenceless'. To his credit, how-ever, Falstaff possesses that 'most pleasing of all qualities, perpetual gaiety' and 'an unfailing power of exciting laughter'.[3] With its abrupt syntactic twists and semantic turns, Johnson's paragraph works its way through a richly layered response to Falstaff as a character.

In the period between Johnson's *Preface* and A. C. Bradley's *Shakespearian Tragedy* (1904), character criticism outstripped its original function—the praise of Shakespeare as poet or author—to become a self-contained exercise in critical appreciation. Writers take Johnson's understanding that Shakespeare finds the *general* in the *particular* in different directions. Psychological critics examine the characters 'scientifically' for general principles of human nature. Belletristic writers produce playful sketches of Shakespeare's characters as individuals, mining the plays for particulars of their fictional biographies.

Shakespeare and the psychology of human nature

William Richardson, Professor of Humanity at the University of Glasgow from 1773 to 1814, exemplifies the quasi-scientific approach to character analysis. Drawing on empiricist psychology (specifically, the *Elements of Criticism* by Henry Home, Lord Kames), Richardson distinguishes between the experience of a Shakespearian play as a vivid and pleasurable 'waking dream' and analysis of Shakespeare's characters after the fact. Reflecting on the motivation of fictional characters helps us to understand the general principles of human nature, which Richardson considers to be stable and universal, and in this way, promotes moral improvement.

Because Richardson looks for general principles, he moves quickly through Shakespeare's plays, discovering the 'ruling passion' of each character. Richard III is a portrait of inner and outer deformity. King Lear illustrates how 'mere sensibility, undirected by reflection', leads to violent expressions of feeling and irresolute conduct.[4] His character sketch of Falstaff, emphasizing vice mingled with an ability to please, resembles that of Johnson, but aims at simplicity rather than complexity. Richardson concludes that Falstaff is a 'voluptuary, cowardly, vain-glorious, with all the arrogance connected with vain-glory, and deceitful in every shape of deceit; but injurious, incapable of gratitude or of friendship, and vindictive'.[5] Once Richardson has recited this litany of bad qualities, who could remember Falstaff's wit, humour, and skill with people?

For Richardson, Shakespeare's collected plays are a useful encyclopedia of human nature; for Maurice Morgann, they offer opportunities for mental exercise and literary play. In 'An Essay on the Dramatic Character of Sir John Falstaff' (1777), Morgann offers a long, counter-intuitive, essay in praise of Falstaff's courage that relies on dramatic 'Impressions'—the term comes from empiricist philosopher David Hume—rather than on literary rules or psychological principles.

Previous writers argued about Falstaff's virtues and vices, but before Morgann no one had seriously challenged the common-sense notion that Falstaff is a coward. To make his argument, Morgann weighs first the apparently overwhelming dramatic evidence of Falstaff's cowardice—the testimony of others, his flight from the Prince and Poins after the robbery of the Canterbury pilgrims, the act of counterfeiting death at Shrewsbury, and finally, the damaging lies that Falstaff himself tells—but arrives at a conclusion exactly opposite to that of Richardson. While we can rationally list all of Falstaff's faults, Morgann insists, our strong first 'impression' of his character is favourable: 'We all like *Old Jack*; yet, by some strange, perverse fate, we all abuse him, and deny him any single good or respectable quality'.[6]

Morgann exonerates Falstaff from charges of cowardice at Gadshill on the grounds that he was setting up an elaborate jest and calls into question Prince John's harsh words against Falstaff on the battlefield by characterizing John as a shady 'politician'. By his own admission, Morgann is more interested in the 'exercise' of his critical faculties than in deeper 'truths' of a moral or philosophical kind. He practises a maddeningly literal-minded form of biographical reading, pursuing tangential arguments until the amused reader is provoked to concede Morgann's improbable thesis: that, far from being inherently cowardly, Falstaff is a prudent old soldier, a military freethinker. Morgann places, side by side, a portrait of the vicious Falstaff and one of likeable 'Old Jack'. Making no attempt to reconcile them, he celebrates the multiplicity of Shakespeare's fat knight rather than his moral unity.

Romantic bardolatry and Shakespearian readers

The Romantics turned bardolatry, the praise of Shakespeare as an author and creator of characters, into an art form. In an essay of 1818, Romantic poet John Keats coined the now-familiar term 'negative capability' to describe Shakespeare's ability to have no central identity of his own. According to Keats, the poetical character is 'not itself—it has no self—it is every thing and nothing—it has no character—it enjoys light and shade—it lives in gusto, be it foul or fair, high or low, rich or poor, mean or elevated'.[7] The poet has no distinguishing 'character' of his own, in Keats's view, because he becomes the characters he creates; in the Romantics' lexicon, he is a 'chameleon'.

Keats's vocabulary and perspective are shared by other Romantic writers, such as Samuel Taylor Coleridge and William Hazlitt. In his lectures and private marginalia, Coleridge offers brief character portraits of Shakespearian individuals, but he is more interested in how Shakespeare creates, and how readers respond to, his characters. For Coleridge, Shakespeare is a 'Proteus' who spins characters out of his own universalized nature. These 'fragments' of the 'divine Shakespeare' embody the deepest and most basic truths about human nature because Shakespeare himself is a 'myriad-minded' genius whose own self encompasses and embraces the widest range possible of human experience.[8] As Coleridge sees it, Shakespeare's ability to imagine himself as the 'other' gives to his characters' speech and actions a sense of authenticity lacking from the work of other dramatists. But in this view the act of identification, for both the poet and readers who aspire to follow in genius's tracks, has a dark side precisely because Shakespeare's understanding of human nature is universal. While at different times

Coleridge insists that Shakespeare 'kept always the high road' and that he never represented viciousness, Shakespeare, at least in theory, can 'become' a 'motiveless malignity' such as Iago as well as the noblest among his tragic heroes.[9] A genius such as Shakespeare knows both good and evil.

For Coleridge, the poet's engagement with his characters provides the ideal model for imaginative reading. Shakespeare's characters are a 'divine Dream' whom we can help to create from ourselves.[10] Yet if Shakespeare becomes Iago, can we do so also without moral danger? In his more abstract statements about dramatic illusion, Coleridge stresses that we are never truly 'deluded' by the 'waking dreams' of poetry. Nightmares cannot be distinguished from reality; artistic 'dreams' can. Coleridge is best-known, perhaps, for the phrase 'the willing suspension of disbelief', which describes the way in which readers actively suspend their rationality and therefore fight against a natural tendency to disbelieve in fictional worlds and their populace.[11] The positive exertion of will and the necessity of conquering disbelief, both implied by Coleridge's compact phrasing, suggest that readers and spectators will not fall prey to destructive illusions. The process of seeing oneself in fictional others is, nevertheless, tinged with eeriness and danger because the ideal reader of Shakespeare resembles most closely the genius-poet, whose knowledge of all things human takes him beyond ordinary experiences and moral standards. Thus, the creation and reception of Shakespeare's characters remains, for Coleridge, a complex and emotionally charged process.

While Coleridge is the principal theorist of Shakespearian character in the Romantic period, his contemporary William Hazlitt is the best practical analyst of Shakespeare's dramatic persons. Hazlitt shares with Coleridge a sense that Shakespeare's characters are larger than life, but insists more strenuously on their individuality. Taking issue with Samuel Johnson's belief that Shakespeare represents 'species' or classes of characters in the Preface to *Characters of Shakespear's Plays* (1817), Hazlitt cites, instead, Alexander Pope's belief that 'every single character in Shakespear[e], is as much an individual, as those in life itself'.[12] Not only is Shakespeare a Proteus who produces fictional persons from the creative depths of his own nature, as Coleridge claimed, but he creates characters who stand independent of their author, 'as if they were living persons, not fictions of the mind'.[13]

Characters of Shakespear's Plays gives us a composite portrait of Shakespeare the poet through a thoughtful catalogue of his characters, collected together as a useful handbook to the plays. Hazlitt often is grouped with Charles Lamb as favouring the page over the stage, but he was, in fact, a practising theatre critic, and *Characters* incorporates observations from his many theatre reviews and notices. Nevertheless, the kind of sympathetic imagination that makes identification with Shakespeare the poet possible seems to occur most forcibly in acts of solitary reading. In his *Characters*, therefore, Hazlitt models for his own audience one reader's response to the emotional logic of Shakespeare's plays.

Hazlitt shows how the main characters' emotional vicissitudes both reflect and shape their dramatic worlds. *Macbeth* the play, for instance, 'is alike distinguished for the lofty imagination it displays, and for the tumultuous vehemence of the action'. The character Macbeth, in turn, 'appears driven along by the violence of his fate like a vessel drifting before a storm: he reels to and fro like a drunken man; he staggers under the weight of his own purposes and the suggestions of others; he stands at bay with his situation; and from the superstitious awe and breathless suspense into which the communications of the Weird Sisters throw him, is hurried on with daring impatience to verify their predictions, and with impious and bloody hand to tear aside the veil which hides the uncertainty of the future'.[14] Through the vivid rhythm of his own prose, Hazlitt recreates the fits and starts of Macbeth's career and mind. Building his metaphors on images and episodes from the plays—in this case, the ship 'tempest-tossed' by the Witches and the drunken Porter—Hazlitt delineates general passions as they succeed one another in the highly individualized trajectory of a single tragic hero: Macbeth.

Hazlitt is also sensitive to the differences between plays and their heroes. Hazlitt sees *Othello*, for instance, as governed not by tempests of passion but by a slow, inexorable process in which Othello, a 'noble, confiding, tender, and generous man', succumbs to a destructive jealousy that finally 'breaks out into open fury'.[15] *King Lear*, Hazlitt believes, is Shakespeare's 'great master-piece in the logic of passion'. In this play, we see the 'ebb and flow' of passion, 'its impatience of opposition, its accumulating force when it has time to recollect itself, the manner in which it avails itself of every passing word or gesture, its haste to repel insinuation, the alternate contraction and dilatation of the soul . . . in this mortal combat with poisoned weapons, aimed at the heart, where each wound is fatal'.[16]

William Hazlitt uses 'character' as a key to understanding Shakespeare's plays in their totality. His greatest heir in the late Victorian period, who shares with Hazlitt a sense of passion's vicissitudes, as well as an interest in character, is A. C. Bradley.

Heroic Shakespeare

A. C. Bradley's *Shakespearian Tragedy* (1904) has remained influential long after character criticism generally fell out of fashion, in part because the book appeals to a wide range of readers. As a professor, Bradley addresses himself specifically to university undergraduates and leads them, in an orderly way, through the Shakespearian texts to their central passions. In published form, the lectures also became a hefty, but penetrable, armchair guide for ordinary readers ensconced at home with their *Complete Works of Shakespeare*.

Bradley frames his gallery of Shakespearian heroes with an account of how drama works on audiences and, in particular, readers. Bradley insists, as does Aristotle's *Poetics*, that Shakespearian tragedy is 'the story' of one person, the hero, who is defined by his deeds—not those things done ''tween asleep and wake', in a fit of absence of mind, but actions and omissions that are 'thoroughly expressive of the doer'. Thus, Bradley defines Shakespearian tragedy as 'action issuing from character' or 'character issuing in action'.[17]

Through the hero's sufferings, we experience vicariously the titanic upheavals of Shakespeare's moral universe. A system that aims for perfection, this moral order nevertheless engenders from within itself evil, which it can expel only at the price of great agony and senseless waste. Bradley's approach, mixing Hegelian philosophy (which posits that existence is structured around the struggle between opposing forces) with Aristotelian aesthetics (which makes the individual hero the centre of tragedy), sounds quite abstract. But Bradley emphasizes that this system serves a human purpose; Shakespearian drama educates readers morally through their emotions. Shakespeare, for instance, never lets us off the hook by attributing the hero's downfall to definite causes, such as inscrutable fate or the even-handed calculus of poetic justice. Shakespearian drama confronts us, instead, with the self-destruction of a moral order that, paradoxically, in striving for perfection, becomes the source of its own undoing. When we understand this inexorable process, we can feel the full pathos of the hero's position.

Bradley's conception of the 'substance of Shakespearian tragedy' provides readers with a simple, but powerful, master-plot against which he measures individual plays. Othello's fault, for instance, is a sexual jealousy so intense that it 'converts human nature into chaos, and liberates the beast in man'. In Othello's fall, we see the noblest of human passions, love, recoiling upon itself, producing in a man who is 'great of heart' a 'tortured mixture of longing and loathing'. Othello becomes increasingly mired in jealousy, 'the animal in man forcing itself into his consciousness in naked grossness, and he writhing before it but powerless to deny it entrance, grasping inarticulate images of pollution, and finding relief only in a bestial thirst for blood'. Iago is the diabolical artist behind this drama in self-destruction; in one sense Othello's tragedy is equally Iago's, since Iago also yields to evil forces within himself and 'is at once destroyed'. The tragedy's most heartbreaking victim, however, is Desdemona, 'the sweetest and most pathetic of Shakespeare's women' who nevertheless lacks the 'independence and strength of spirit' that might help her rise above suffering.[18] In Othello, evil destroys itself, but not before taking down all goodness with it.

In a similar vein, Macbeth's ambition is constitutional, but not inherently evil. Yet in the bloody, tempest-tossed world that confronts the hero—where supernatural forces join with his own wife against his better self—even Macbeth's characteristic ability to imagine the horrific consequences of his deeds cannot save him. We watch in awe as Macbeth grows inhuman and as his wife, equally sublime in her courage and commitment to murder, descends into madness. In Bradley's somewhat unusual equation, Macbeth and Lady Macbeth destroy both the good within themselves and within each other. Once again, good produces evil and, tragically, ensures its own destruction.

With the professionalization of English literature as a university subject and a scholarly discipline in the early twentieth century, Bradley's style of character criticism came under attack. In 'How Many Children Had Lady Macbeth?' (1933), L. C. Knights satirizes the excesses of character criticism, such as Bradley's attempt to decide whether Lady Macbeth really fainted upon hearing the news of Duncan's murder or whether Macbeth and Lady Macbeth were young enough still to anticipate children; but he also critiques the literary assumptions behind the entire practice. Knights complains that Bradley treats Shakespeare's plays as if they were second-rate novels. Knights argues, instead, that the Shakespearian play is a poem, whose words and patterns of words must be read attentively if readers are to recover their full emotional significance. Yet outside academia, both before and after Knights dealt his decisive blow to Bradley's style of critical analysis, other writers have continued to practise character criticism and so have kept alive the tradition.

Feminism and reading character from the margins

While writers from Coleridge to Bradley attempted to define a heroic, masculine model of Shakespearian greatness, feminist critics, in particular, have found that performing character criticism allows them to look at Shakespeare's plays from new perspectives. In her *Girlhood of Shakespeare's Heroines* (1850), nineteenth-century writer and editor Mary Cowden Clarke invents fictional biographies for Shakespeare's women characters that chronicle their lives prior to the beginning of the plays and therefore supplement our knowledge of them in those plays. In the case of Portia from *The Merchant of Venice*, for instance, Cowden Clarke begins with an imagined match between Portia's angelic, yet poor, mother and Count Guido of Belmont, attributing Portia's courtroom eloquence to a legal education acquired at the feet of her uncle Bellario, a man barely mentioned in Shakespeare's play but now fleshed out, in true Shakespearian manner, as a faithful friend to Guido, devoted brother to the elder Portia, and mentor to their orphaned daughter. Although in Cowden Clarke's story young Portia has a full complement of womanly arts and virtues, she also possesses a traditionally masculine body of professional knowledge and an independent understanding of legal ethics.

Cowden Clarke elaborates on Shakespeare's plots with her own fictions, but she does not write formal Shakespearian criticism. It was Anna Jameson, a travel writer and chronicler of Italian art and museums, among other things, who published the first feminist literary criticism of Shakespeare. Originally titled *Characteristics of Women* (1832) but later published as *Shakespeare's Heroines*, the book was read largely because of its character portraits.

Familiar with the male Romantic writers and their commentaries, Jameson often responds directly to their lack of interest in or strictures against Shakespeare's women. While Hazlitt argues that Lady Macbeth is 'a great bad woman, whom we hate, but whom we fear more than we hate', Jameson writes, by way of contradiction, that Lady Macbeth, although terrifying, is never beyond our sympathy.[19] While Hazlitt blames

Lady Macbeth for her husband's downfall, Jameson reverses the charge and shows that Lady Macbeth, far from being overly masculine, has a strong enough conscience to drive her to suicide. Hazlitt, to give a second example, is appalled by Isabella's choice of her chastity over her brother in *Measure for Measure*. Jameson argues that she is both principled and strong, weathering the assault on her chastity as if she were a stately cedar tree buffeted about by storms.

Jameson also celebrates Shakespeare's comic heroines, particularly those whom she calls 'characters of intellect'. *Characteristics of Women* opens with a discussion of Portia from *The Merchant of Venice*. In Jameson's account as in Cowden Clarke's later novella, Portia has all the requisite womanly charms, plus an unusual degree of intelligence and eloquence. But for Jameson, Portia's intelligence is predominantly moral; she analyses at length the trial scene, taking pains to show that Portia appeals desperately to Shylock's higher sentiments and produces the legal quibble only as a last resource. The entire essay treads delicately a difficult path between accepting the prevailing cultural position that women are less intellectual than men and defining a new, and perhaps superior, kind of feminine intellect. For eighteenth- and nineteenth-century critics, character analysis is sometimes a moral exercise, sometimes a political gesture. In either case, reading Shakespeare's plays from the margins has long proved to be not only edifying, but also fun and liberating.

Playwrights, actors, and the persistence of character criticism

An interest in dramatic character has often been linked to a disregard for the integrity of drama as an artistic medium. But playwrights, directors, and actors themselves have done much to sustain interest in Shakespearian character. In one radical, twentieth-century rewriting of Shakespeare's *The Tempest*, Caribbean playwright Aimé Césaire depicts Caliban as a heroic, eloquent freedom fighter who triumphs at last over the colonialist Prospero (*A Tempest*, 1969). Patrick Stewart, although best-known for his role in the *Star Trek* television series, is also one of the Royal Shakespeare Company's most articulate spokesmen about the process of creating drama for an audience. Discussing his portrayal of Shylock in *The Merchant of Venice*, for example, Stewart draws on the venerable language of character criticism. To Stewart, Shylock's appeal lies in his universality; although to a post-Holocaust audience the anti-Semitism of Shakespeare's Venice will be palpable, Shylock's character reflects not his own particular Jewishness, but the commercialism and love of money that govern his whole world. Given a choice between race and religion, on the one hand, and business on the other, Shylock always chooses his financial interests. Convinced that Shylock has a private self that the audience glimpses only briefly, Stewart sees Shakespeare's Jew as a man who is truly himself only at home, where he is revealed as a 'man deeply unhappy and embittered, a man from whose life love had been removed'. Stewart is quick to admit that Shylock's character is complex, but believes that the 'jigsaw puzzle' of his character can be solved by finding a 'dominant motivation' that makes sense of Shylock's many inconsistencies.[20]

Conclusion: the motives of Shakespearian character criticism

Within the academy, Shakespearian character analysis has fallen prey to shifts in critical ideology that have favoured explorations of language over plot and character. But still, Shakespearian character criticism persists, and its resilience suggests some motivation more profound than a 'low-brow' tendency to sentimentalize fiction within popular culture. A 'character'—from the Renaissance to the present—is a figure whom spectators or readers recognize as both similar to and different from themselves. Liberal humanists have always celebrated literature's power to provide contact with distant times and places; opponents of humanism, by contrast, fear the human tendency to assimilate all experience to familiar patterns, which can become a refusal to acknowledge historical and cultural difference. But while character criticism has often served dominant ideologies and conservative political attitudes, it need not do so.

In 1887, at the height of character criticism's popularity, *The Girl's Own Paper* sponsored an essay contest asking its readers to analyse their favourite Shakespearian heroine. The contest organizers were chagrined to find that their young readers much preferred Portia, the 'female lawyer', and the energetic, successful heroines of Shakespeare's comedies to his more 'exquisite' but doomed tragic heroines, such as Ophelia, Juliet, and Desdemona. Who should be surprised that girls of any century prefer long life and happiness to literary fame? Now as in 1887, Shakespearian character criticism provides readers and spectators of all ages and dispositions with a forum for analysing their own experiences. This is, often has been, and always should be, the function of Shakespearian character criticism.

FURTHER READING

Bradley, A. C. *Shakespearean Tragedy*, 3rd edn., with an introduction by John Russell Brown (New York: St. Martin's, 1992). As a venerable and important work of Shakespearian character criticism, Bradley's collected lectures continue to influence criticism and classroom pedagogy. Bradley defines Shakespearian tragedy in terms of its heroes, who both shape and reflect the moral nature of their dramatic worlds.

Coleridge, Samuel Taylor. *Coleridge's Criticism of Shakespeare*. Ed. R. A. Foakes (Detroit: Wayne State University Press, 1989). A handy, modern compilation of Coleridge's writings on Shakespeare, which places his theories about character and readers' responses to Shakespeare within the general context of his literary and philosophical concerns.

Desmet, Christy. *Reading Shakespeare's Characters: Rhetoric, Ethics, and Identity* (Amherst: University of Massachusetts Press, 1992). This book studies identification as a key to the cultural function of Shakespearian character. Chapter 1 considers the theory of character, Chapter 2 the history of Shakespearian character criticism.

Hazlitt, William. *Characters of Shakespear's Plays*. In Vol. 4 of *The Collected Works of William Hazlitt*. Ed. P. P. Howe (London: Dent, 1930), pp. 165–361. Hazlitt's lectures are useful to this day, as a complete introduction to Shakespeare's plays and their major characters. Hazlitt uses Shakespeare's metaphorical language and his own vibrant prose style to communicate a sense of the individualized passion that drives each play.

Jameson, Anna Brownell Murphy. *Shakespeare's Heroines* (London: E. P. Dutton, n.d.). Originally published as *Characteristics of Women* (London, 1832). The first feminist literary criticism of Shakespeare's plays, Jameson's work remained popular throughout the nineteenth and twentieth centuries and is mentioned approvingly by Bradley. Jameson's collected essays, which are notable for their subtle and thorough assessment of Shakespeare and his female characters, are available in libraries and soon will be made available in a contemporary student edition.

Knights, L. C. 'How Many Children Had Lady Macbeth? An Essay in the Theory and Practice of Shakespeare Criticism'. In *Explorations: Essays in Criticism, Mainly on the Literature of the Seventeenth Century* (London: Chatto and Windus, 1946), pp. 1–39. Originally published as *How Many Children Had Lady Macbeth?* (Cambridge: Minority Press, 1933). In this influential essay, Knights mocks Bradley's tendency, especially noticeable in his long endnotes, to think about textual detail in Shakespeare's plays from a literal-minded perspective. Knights argues that the plays are 'dramatic poems', not novels, and that we can understand them only by attending carefully to patterns of words that suggest thematic oppositions.

Morgann, Maurice. 'An Essay on the Dramatic Character of Sir John Falstaff'. In *Shakespearian Criticism*, ed. Daniel A. Fineman (Oxford: Clarendon Press, 1972), pp. 141–215. Morgan offers an elaborate, ingenious defence of Falstaff's courage and moral character that takes the assessments of his contemporaries in a bold new direction. Bradley admired Morgann's essay and gave it renewed importance in the history of Shakespearian character criticism.

Richardson, William. *Essays on Shakespeare's Dramatic Characters of Richard the Third, King Lear, and Timon of Athens* (1784; reprint New York: AMS Press, 1974); and *Essays on Shakespeare's Dramatic Character of Sir John Falstaff, and on His Imitation of Female Characters* (1789; reprint New York: AMS Press, 1973). Although these are rare books, both are available in facsimile reprint. Richardson exemplifies the scientific approach to Shakespeare's characters, seeking general principles of human nature by analysing 'ruling passions', particularly those governing the behaviour of his male heroes.

NOTES

1. John Dryden. ' "Preface, The Grounds of Criticism in Tragedy", Prefixed to *Troilus and Cressida*', in *'Of Dramatic Poesy' and Other Critical Essays*, Vol. 1, ed. George Watson (London: Dent, 1962), pp. 252–3.

2. Samuel Johnson. 'Preface', in *Johnson on Shakespeare*, ed. Arthur Sherbo, *The Yale Edition of the Works of Samuel Johnson*, Vol. 7 (New Haven and London: Yale University Press, 1968), pp. 61, 62.

3. Samuel Johnson. 'Notes on Shakespeare's Plays', in *Johnson on Shakespeare*, ed. Arthur Sherbo, *The Yale Edition of the Works of Samuel Johnson*, Vol. 7 (New Haven and London: Yale University Press, 1968), p. 523.

4. William Richardson. *Essays on Shakespeare's Dramatic Characters of Richard the Third, King Lear, and Timon of Athens* (1784; reprint, New York: AMS Press, 1974), p. 83.

5. William Richardson. *Essays on Shakespeare's Dramatic Character of Sir John Falstaff, and on His Imitation of Female Characters* (1789; reprint, New York: AMS Press, 1973), p. 18.

6. Maurice Morgann. 'An Essay on the Dramatic Character of Sir John Falstaff'. In *Shakespearian Criticism*, ed. Daniel A. Fineman (Oxford: Clarendon Press, 1972), p. 148.

7. John Keats. 'Letter to Richard Woodhouse', 27 October 1818, reprinted in *The Romantics on Shakespeare*, ed. Jonathan Bate (London: Penguin, 1992), p. 199.

8. Samuel Taylor Coleridge. *Lectures, 1808–1819: On Literature*, ed. R. A. Foakes, Vol. 5 of *The Collected Works of Samuel Taylor Coleridge* (Princeton: Princeton University Press, 1987), Part 1, p. 225; Samuel Taylor Coleridge. *Coleridge's Miscellaneous Criticism*, ed. Thomas Middleton Raysor (London: Constable & Company, 1936), p. 44; Coleridge. *Lectures, 1808–19*, ed. R. A. Foakes, Vol. 5 of *The Collected Works of Samuel Taylor Coleridge* (Princeton: Princeton University Press, 1987), Part 2, pp. 480, 112.

9. Coleridge. *Lectures, 1808–1819*, ed. R. A. Foakes, Vol. 5 of *The Collected Works of Samuel Taylor Coleridge* (Princeton: Princeton University Press, 1987), Part 1, pp. 520, 319; Part 2, p. 315.

10. Samuel Taylor Coleridge. *The Notebooks of Samuel Taylor Coleridge*, ed. Kathleen Coburn (New York: Bollingen Foundation, 1957–73), Vol. 2, Entry 2086.

11. Samuel Taylor Coleridge. *Biographia Literaria*, ed. James Engell and Walter Jackson Bate, Vol. 7 of *The Collected Works of Samuel Taylor Coleridge* (Princeton: Princeton University Press, 1983), Vol. 7, Part 2, Chap. 14, Section 6.

12. William Hazlitt. *Characters of Shakespear's Plays*. In Vol. 4 of *The Collected Works of William Hazlitt*, ed. P. P. Howe (London: Dent, 1930), p. 171.

13. Hazlitt. 'On Shakespeare and Milton'. In Vol. 4 of *The Collected Works of William Hazlitt*, ed. P. P. Howe (London: Dent, 1930), p. 50.

14. Hazlitt. *Characters*. In Vol. 4 of *The Collected Works of William Hazlitt*, ed. P. P. Howe (London: Dent, 1930), p. 187.

15. Ibid., pp. 201, 203.

16. Ibid., p. 259.

17. Ibid., p. 7.

18. Ibid., pp. 151, 187, 174.

19. Hazlitt. *Characters of Shakespear's Plays*. In Vol. 4 of *The Collected Works of William Hazlitt*, ed. P. P. Howe (London: Dent, 1930), p. 188; Anna Jameson, *Shakespeare's Heroines* (London: E. P. Dutton, n.d.), p. 291.

20. John Barton. *Playing Shakespeare* (New York: Random House, 1984), pp. 216–17.

READING: *Hamlet*

Introduction

Hamlet—both the play and the prince—have long held a privileged place in the popular and scholarly imagination. A spoof such as Tom Stoppard's *Fifteen-Minute Hamlet*, a radical condensation of the Shakespearian text that produces hilarious nonsense as famous lines follow one another at a dizzying pace, plays off our reverence for the Prince and his text, but depends also on our cultural intimacy with Hamlet's every utterance.[1] In Mark Twain's *Huckleberry Finn*, the duke offers his own memory of 'To be or not to be', which begins:

> To be or not to be; that is the bare bodkin
> That makes calamity of so long life;
> For who would fardels bear; till Birnam Wood do come to Dunsinane,
> But that the fear of something after death
> Murders the innocent sleep . . .[2]

We laugh at the duke's ability to exploit Shakespeare's reputation while butchering his poetry because we, too, have memorized—however imperfectly—Hamlet's most celebrated flight of thought.

Identifying (with) Hamlet

Neither Hamlet nor *Hamlet* has always enjoyed such reverence among critics, playgoers, and students. Early commentary on Shakespeare showed more interest in figures such as Falstaff from the *Henry IV* plays and Richard III. In fact, many writers considered *Hamlet* a faulty play because its hero was not only morally and emotionally inconsistent, but also excessively histrionic. In the eighteenth and nineteenth centuries, a series of great actors—David Garrick, John Philip Kemble, Edmund Kean, and William Macready, for example—brought Hamlet before the public by raising the prince above his play. It remained for literary criticism, however, to make *Hamlet* the test case for Shakespeare's supposed intellectual and moral superiority. Such a phenomenon depends on the public's ability to identify with Hamlet as a character. Philosopher-rhetorician Kenneth Burke defines 'identification' as a balance between identifying *with* a person (whether psychologically, emotionally, or politically) and identifying that person *as* something (by labelling his or her moral nature, behaviour, and motives). Explaining literary characters goes hand in hand with empathy for them.[3]

As *Hamlet* grew in popularity, the troubled prince became an emotional icon for many spectators and readers. In 1709, Sir Richard Steele wrote admiringly of how Hamlet's speeches 'dwell strongly upon the Minds of the Audience'. Even a young cousin, attending a performance with Steele, could participate vicariously in the 'Affections and Passions of Manhood' through his concern for Hamlet's fate.[4] By 1827, Samuel Taylor Coleridge could say casually that 'I have a smack of Hamlet myself' and expect others to understand his meaning.[5] Nineteenth-century readers and playgoers understood Hamlet's character primarily through his soliloquies, which for them mirrored the Prince's most private thoughts. In 'On the Tragedies of Shakspeare' (1811), Charles Lamb wrote that 'nine parts in ten of what Hamlet does, are transactions between himself and his moral sense, they are the effusions of his solitary musing, which he retires to holes and corners and the most sequestered parts of the palace to pour forth'. No wonder, then, that a 'gesticulating actor' who 'mouths' these sentiments 'before an audience, making four hundred people his confidants at once', should fail to do justice to 'the shy, negligent, retiring Hamlet'.[6]

The psychology of Hamlet and *Hamlet*

Lamb's image of a 'shy, negligent, retiring Hamlet' conflates two distinct 'Hamlets' who emerged in the Romantic period and came to dominate discussion of that character in the nineteenth century. Romantic Hamlet is slow to act; but what causes his delay? According to one reading, Hamlet, as a poet-philosopher and a sensitive soul, is incapable of action. Although the German poet Johann Wolfgang von Goethe invented and English poet Samuel Taylor Coleridge popularized the image, in *Characters of Shakespear's Plays* (1817), William Hazlitt fleshes out more fully this portrait of Hamlet: 'The character of Hamlet stands quite by itself. It is not a character marked by strength of will or even of passion, but by refinement of thought and sentiment. Hamlet is as little of the hero as a man can well be: but he is a young and princely novice, full of high enthusiasm and quick sensibility'. In Hazlitt's view, Hamlet's philosophical predilections disable him as a revenger: 'because he cannot have his revenge perfect, according to the most refined idea his wish can form, he declines it altogether'.[7]

The second 'Hamlet' is a somewhat more pathological, but also more universalized figure. The Viennese psychologist Sigmund Freud constructed Hamlet as an Everyman who is driven by common unconscious desires. In *The Interpretation of Dreams* (1899), Freud uses Hamlet, along with Sophocles' King Oedipus from the play *Oedipus Rex*, to illustrate his theory of the Oedipus complex, in which the infant—usually male—child seeks to displace the father and supplant him in the mother's affections.[8] Although in *Dreams*, Freud's discussion of *Hamlet* is restricted to a long footnote, in 1910 the American psychoanalyst Ernest Jones elaborated upon Freud's observations about the Oedipus complex to conclude that Hamlet could not bring himself to murder Claudius because the uncle had accomplished two deeds—killing Hamlet's father and possessing sexually his mother—that were desired by the infant Hamlet himself: 'In reality [Hamlet's] uncle incorporates the deepest and most buried part of his own personality, so that he cannot kill him without also killing himself'.[9] Claudius, in other words, is Hamlet's double.

Most of us, however, understand Hamlet's delay from the unscientific version of his psychology that A. C. Bradley offers in *Shakespearian Tragedy* (1904). Bradley contradicts Coleridge's Romantic belief that Hamlet delays his revenge on Claudius because he is too sensitive, too poetical, too philosophical, and therefore incapable of action. Bradley also critiques Goethe's 'sentimental' view that Hamlet has such a pure moral nature that he sinks under the burden of the Ghost's command. Hamlet mentions his conscience only once, reacts with indifference to Polonius's death, casually betrays his old school friends Rosencrantz and Guildenstern, and, finally, dispatches Claudius with savage decision.

According to Bradley, Hamlet *is* morally superior, but he is also betrayed from within by his own psychological temperament. In Elizabethan terms, Hamlet is 'melancholic'—that is, 'inclined to nervous instability, to rapid and perhaps extreme changes of feeling and mood' and 'disposed to be, for the time, absorbed in the feeling or mood that possessed him, whether it were joyous or depressed'.[10] When faced with Claudius's drunkenness and Gertrude's sensuality, Hamlet's moral nature recoils and he sinks melancholically into lethargy. The tendency to dissect his own actions settles into a pathology, and Hamlet, by now weary of life, faces Ophelia's death with gloomy resignation; his address to the corpse of Ophelia, 'I loved you ever; but it is no matter', really means that '*nothing* matters' (emphasis in original).[11] Because according to Bradley's view both virtue and vice, character and pathology derive from the same source, in *Hamlet*, as in other Shakespearian tragedies, goodness tragically destroys itself.

In the early parts of the twentieth century, critics began to reject not only Bradley's explanation of Hamlet's motives, but also the underlying assumption that this fictional Prince of Denmark has a coherent psychology that can be subjected to analysis and definition. In a famous criticism of the play that was published in 1919, T. S. Eliot argues that *Hamlet* lacks an 'objective correlative', which means that Prince Hamlet is dominated by an emotion that is 'in *excess* of the facts as they appear' (emphasis in original). Although in Eliot's view Hamlet's disgust 'is occasioned by his mother', for him Gertrude's character is too insignificant to account for such a strong emotion in her son. This disparity between feelings and facts baffles both Hamlet and his creator, Shakespeare. According to Eliot, 'we must simply admit here that Shakespeare tackled a problem which proved too much for him'.[12]

But while Eliot saw both hero and play as flawed, the long tradition of audience identification with Hamlet encouraged Shakespearians of the earlier twentieth century to extend Bradley's observations even as they attacked his concept of the tragic hero. G. Wilson Knight, for instance, develops Bradley's brief statement that Claudius 'takes good care of the national interests'. Acknowledging Claudius' good stewardship and tracing thematic patterns through Shakespeare's imagery, Wilson Knight reaches the surprising conclusion that Hamlet, rather than Claudius, is the source of the disease that makes Denmark a prison.[13] In this critical transformation of received wisdom, Hamlet, not Claudius, becomes the villain of the piece.

The woman in Hamlet and the women in *Hamlet*

Despite the fact that theorists of the twentieth century have attacked character criticism, psychoanalytic readings of Hamlet and the male psyche continue to flourish, focusing more sharply on how the Prince's need to idealize his father depends on the denigration of woman. As David Leverenz writes, when Hamlet idealizes the father, he tries to replace feeling with duty, repressing the 'woman' in himself and lashing out at both Ophelia and Gertrude. In this reading, 'Ophelia's suicide becomes a little microcosm of the male world's banishment of the female, because "woman" represents everything denied by' men.[14] In her chapter on *Hamlet* from *Suffocating Mothers* (1992), Janet Adelman follows Lacanian psychoanalysis by re-situating the mother at the centre of the family romance. While Freud's analysis of *Hamlet* focused on the father, Adelman sees the mother as crucial to Hamlet's experience. She argues that the Gertrude Hamlet sees or imagines is a larger-than-life figure. More precisely, this Gertrude is the mother of Hamlet's pre-Oedipal fantasies: 'Hamlet initiates the period of Shakespeare's tragedies' because it deals not with the son-hero's search for autonomy, but with the location of masculine identity in the child's ambivalent relation to the mother's body, a threatening body that stands at once for birth and death.[15]

Critical focus on the role of the feminine in male psychology has also renewed interest in women characters from *Hamlet*, about whom Bradleian character criticism had little to say. In his chapters on *Hamlet*, for instance, Bradley describes Ophelia as merely young and inexperienced. Gertrude is 'dull', 'shallow', and 'sensual' rather than evil: 'she loved to be happy, like a sheep in the sun; and to do her justice, it pleased her to see others happy, like more sheep in the sun'.[16] Dating back to the nineteenth century, however, there exists an alternative tradition of criticism that focuses on Shakespeare's female characters and argues for their importance to the plays in which they appear.

In the nineteenth century, performances by actresses such as Sarah Siddons, Fanny Kemble, and Harriet Smithson raised interest in Shakespeare's women and often affected interpretations of them. Political debates over such topics as women's education, woman's nature, and women's rights also informed critical study of Shakespearian heroines. Anna Jameson, Shakespeare's first truly feminist critic, was interested in both theatre and gender politics. Her *Characteristics of Women* (1832), reprinted many times as *Shakespeare's Heroines*, devotes a chapter to Ophelia. As a character of 'passion' and 'imagination', Jameson writes, Ophelia is 'too soft, too good, too fair, to be cast among the briers of this working-day world, and fall and bleed upon the thorns of life!' A young girl brought too early from her private life to court, Ophelia is like a dove caught in a storm—frightened, bewildered, and ultimately destroyed.[17] Jameson, admittedly, sounds a bit like Bradley as she extols the tragic innocence of Ophelia, but she also argues that Ophelia's love for Hamlet, although it proves her undoing, is simple but 'true'. Jameson's Ophelia is neither negligible nor pathological, nor is she a mere victim of circumstance. She has an admirable 'character' of her own that makes Ophelia worthy of any reader's empathy. Twentieth-century critical and theatrical practice often emphasizes as well that *Hamlet* narrates the tragedy of Ophelia as well as that of its titular hero. In the Franco Zeffirelli film of *Hamlet* (1991), for instance,

Kate Winslet as Ophelia sings bawdy songs and makes lewd advances toward a stoic palace guard, but she also struggles heroically with a madness that is brought on not by Ophelia's own frailty but rather, by her father's death and Hamlet's betrayal—serious tragedies rather than feminine weakness. Still other readers have commented on Ophelia's unacknowledged intellectual powers and eloquence, which become evident in moments such as the speech concluding the nunnery scene, in which Ophelia laments Hamlet's descent into 'madness' (3.1.149–60).

Middle-aged Gertrude has fewer partisans among readers of the last two centuries. Rebecca West, even more so than A. C. Bradley, shows unbridled contempt for Gertrude when she writes that 'the Queen is one of the most poorly endowed human beings which Shakespeare ever drew. Very often he created fools, but there is a richness in their folly, whereas Gertrude is simply a stately defective. The whole play depends on her not noticing, and not understanding'. Even Gertrude's eloquent account of Ophelia's drowning, which contrasts with the 'empty rotundity' of her other speeches, contains rhetorical errors and other evidence of the Queen's 'stupidity'.[18] Harry Levin's influential, and very scholarly, analysis of the Player's speech compares Gertrude unfavourably to the classical figure of Hecuba, the loyal wife, mother, and queen from Troy who is left to lament piously the death of her family and nation.[19] Gertrude the 'widow/wife/mother' looks quite bad by comparison to a moral exemplar such as Hecuba.

Defences of Gertrude tend to take two different approaches. In an essay published in 1980, Rebecca Smith analyses Gertrude in terms of sixteenth-century theories of companionate marriage and depicts her as a positive version of Bradley's unexcitable queen-mother. Smith's Gertrude is a rather 'traditional' woman who has at heart the best interests of both her son and her new husband; rather than a monster, Gertrude is a normal Renaissance woman caught in a nightmare situation.[20] Dorothea Kehler, by contrast, examines the Queen as she appears in the first quarto of *Hamlet*, where Gertrude learns directly from Hamlet about Claudius's perfidy and pledges to take her son's part in revenging the father's murder. Strong in a rather archaic sense, the first-quarto Queen is both knowledgeable and utterly focused on goals that derive ultimately from classical tragedy. Far from being a 'traditional' woman from any time and place, this Gertrude herself acquires the status of a revenger.[21] Finally, Canadian novelist Margaret Atwood satirizes traditional assessments of Gertrude by writing for her an imaginative two-page response to Hamlet's wild and whirling words in the closet scene (3.4); in this monologue, the Queen points out patiently her son's lapses in manners and finally informs him that she, not Claudius, had murdered the elderly, boringly puritanical King Hamlet.[22]

Characterizing Hamlet and *Hamlet*

Analysing *Hamlet* after three centuries of venerable Shakespearians have had their say may seem like a daunting task. How can one be more intelligent than Sigmund Freud, more eagle-eyed than A. C. Bradley, or more poetic than Samuel Taylor Coleridge? *Hamlet*, however, is a play that rewards close and frequent reading; analysing *Hamlet* and its characters, as an intellectual exercise, never grows old or stale. Furthermore, as the historical record shows, any literary character is no more than a metaphor, a construction that reflects the reader's or playgoer's personal, historical, and cultural orientation. Thus, performing character criticism can tell us as much about ourselves as it does about the fictional Prince of Denmark. For this reason as well, characterizing Hamlet and *Hamlet* seems to be a worthwhile endeavour.

Where should one begin in this long play, full as it is with speeches, diatribes, riddles, confidences, and secrets? First, we might start where the Romantics did, with Hamlet's speeches. When Hamlet speaks to others, his motives seem unclear. For instance, Hamlet follows a long speech in praise of the earth and its inhabitants by telling Rosencrantz and Guildenstern that 'man delights not me' (2.2.298); but these 'friends' have already confessed that they have been sent for by the King. Their friendship, and Hamlet's sincerity, must come into question. Hamlet's outburst against Ophelia, and women generally, in the nunnery scene (3.1.58–148) *may* be heartfelt, but his verbal and physical violence toward Ophelia may also be a misleading performance aimed at the King and Polonius, who in several film versions can be glimpsed hiding behind curtains and doors. Grappling with Laertes in Ophelia's grave (5.1), Hamlet seems to be in the throes of grief, but even here he performs before an audience of mourners. Finally, in the closet scene (3.4), where Hamlet seems most desperate to show his mother the dark spots within her soul, he also warns her not to pass on in bed to the enemy Claudius the (debatable) fact of Hamlet's sanity. Hamlet is on a mission of revenge and shortly will be sent to England; because he is always and already in danger, we cannot take any of his outbursts or interactions at face value.

But the Prince of Denmark also has no fewer than six soliloquies, speeches spoken aloud to no one in particular, which by dramatic convention are accepted as representations of the speaker's thoughts (1.2.129–59; 1.5.92–113; 2.2.526–82; 3.1.58–92; 3.3.73–96; and scene 9.22–56 on pp. 1729–30 of the Norton Shakespeare, a speech that appears only in the second quarto of *Hamlet*). Even if we isolate these passages and scrutinize them carefully, however, logistical problems arise. First, emotions seem to be out-of-synch with their causes. Hamlet, for instance, contemplates 'self-slaughter' (1.2.132) significantly before he learns from the ghost that his father was murdered by Claudius. In fact, Hamlet's loathing of the world and misogyny seem to be constant throughout the play. Furthermore, Hamlet's world view has more in common with that of the ghost than it does with any other inhabitant of Denmark. Does this mean that he has a wider range of insight than the other characters or that his imagination is diseased by an apparition that comes to him in a very 'questionable' shape? What could it mean that only the ghost and Hamlet refer to Gertrude's marriage to Claudius as adulterous?

Second, like earlier commentators we might look closely at the relationship between Hamlet's words and deeds, and discover to our dismay that Hamlet himself, as writers in the nineteenth century first noticed, does not match his words with actions. Hamlet swears to 'remember' his father in 1.5. (1.5.112–13). In 2.2, he accuses himself of cowardice (2.2.554) and finally comes up with a plan to 'catch the conscience of the King' (2.2.582). A few lines later, however, Hamlet digresses into a soliloquy on the question of whether 'to be, or not to be' (3.1.58), but after the Mousetrap play recovers his sense of purpose, vowing melo-dramatically to 'drink hot blood' and do 'such bitter business as the day / Would quake to look on' (3.2.360, 361–2). What has happened in the meantime? Hamlet has killed Polonius in error and passed up a splendid chance to kill Claudius while he is at prayer. It takes two full acts longer for Hamlet finally to exact his revenge on Claudius, and by that point the body count in Denmark has risen sharply.

Third, we might consider that while Hamlet enjoys a lion's share of stage space and time, other characters also have important speeches. Claudius himself has a long soliloquy detail-ing his crime and expressing intelligently the sad theological truth that a murderer who will not give up his ill-gotten gains cannot repent, no matter how humble his posture and how sincere the desire to cleanse his soul (3.3.36–72). Gertrude, often silent when she appears on stage and reduced to cries for help at the beginning of the closet scene, nevertheless offers a tender, poetic, and moving description of Ophelia's death by drowning (4.7.137–54). From this speech, she gains both moral and emotional stature. Ophelia herself is assigned a small eulogy for Hamlet, who is, as she perceives it, 'blasted' with 'ecstasy' or madness (3.1.159). Her words, not Hamlet's, conclude the nunnery scene. Even a minor character such as a gravedigger can produce with Hamlet a joint meditation on death that functions as a symbolically resonant and rhetorically sensational set piece (5.1.1–200).

Finally, we might consider the disturbing possibility that Hamlet's character simply cannot be wrestled into a comprehensible pattern because he performs not for any particular pur-pose, but for the inherent pleasure that performance itself gives to actors and audiences. Hamlet may be the unfortunate son of a murdered father, but he is also a player on the stage of the world who acts 'in a fiction' or a 'dream of passion' that finally may be 'all for nothing' (2.2.529, 534).

FURTHER READING

Adelman, Janet. 'Man and Wife is One Flesh: *Hamlet* and the Confrontation with the Maternal Body'. In *Suffocating Mothers: Fantasies of Maternal Origin in Shakespeare's Plays, 'Hamlet' to 'The Tempest'* (New York and London: Routledge, 1992), pp. 11–37. Arguing that from *Hamlet* forward, Shakespeare's plays resemble Oedipal dramas without the father figure, Adelman explores the problematic role of the wife/mother in Shakespeare's later plays. In this reading, Hamlet attributes to the mother a malevolent power over both husband and son, so that Gertrude, even more so than Claudius, assumes the blame for the murder of Hamlet's father. Confronted by the feminine body, which is at once maternal and disturbingly sexualized, Hamlet retreats into himself, then attempts unsuccessfully to 'save' Gertrude from the taint of sexuality. But the problematic female body can be neither contained nor excluded, and Hamlet's masculine identity remains fragmented.

Armstrong, Philip. *Shakespeare in Psychoanalysis* (London: Routledge, 2001). A succinct and well-written literary history that discusses Shakespeare's character Hamlet as a psychological case study and the play *Hamlet* as a textual model for psychoanalysis, this book contains substantial chapters on Freud and Lacan that explain the assumptions and critical methods underlying these two important schools of thought.

Bradley, A. C. *Shakespearean Tragedy*, 3rd edn., with an introduction by John Russell Brown (New York: St. Martin's, 1992). Although now unfashionable, Bradley's chapters on Hamlet as hero remain influential. Bradley debunks the Romantic notion that Hamlet is too sensitive to act by stressing his cruelty, his disregard for human life, and his eagerness to accept the Ghost's version of events. Bradley then defends Hamlet's actions by stressing that he has a finely tuned moral nature that sinks into inactivity under the influence of a psychological predisposition to melancholy. Thus, Bradley offers us a moral hero who nonetheless helps to destroy his own world.

Erickson, Peter. 'Maternal Images and Male Bonds in *Hamlet*, *Othello*, and *King Lear*'. In *Patriarchal Structures in Shakespeare's Drama* (Berkeley: University of California Press, 1985), pp. 66–122. In a wide-ranging analysis of male bonding in Shakespeare's plays, Erickson argues that Hamlet finally evades both the Ghost's efforts to usurp his identity and his own agonized relations with Gertrude and Ophelia and enters into a safe, calm, self-sufficient relationship with the stoic Horatio. Male–male friendship provides an alternative to the fraught relations between parents and child and between man and woman.

Hawkes, Terence. 'Telmah'. In *Shakespeare and the Question of Theory*, ed. Patricia Parker and Geoffrey Hartman (New York and London: Methuen, 1985), pp. 310–32. A post-structural and political development of L. C. Knights's argument against treating Shakespeare's plays as a 'little world of persons', this essay discusses *Hamlet* and its hero as improvisational creations of language and argues, further, that literary and social concerns interact with one another. In the case study offered here, twentieth-century English editor and critic J. Dover Wilson defends the unity of Hamlet's personality within a context of nationalistic concerns over the rise of Bolshevism. Thus, cultural context takes precedence over and shapes our understanding of literary character.

Kerrigan, William. *Hamlet's Perfection* (Baltimore and London: Johns Hopkins University Press, 1994). This pugnaciously old-fashioned book returns to the concerns of nineteenth-century character criticism, with a new twist. Instead of addressing the question of Hamlet's delay, Kerrigan focuses on psychoanalytic examinations of both the father's and mother's roles in the son's development. Challenging the premises of much recent *Hamlet* criticism, Kerrigan concludes that Hamlet, unable to recover the idealized father and mother figures of infancy, can resolve the inevitable splitting of the psychological self only by embracing action-as-suicide.

Lanham, Richard A. 'Superposed Plays: *Hamlet*'. In *The Motives of Eloquence: Literary Rhetoric in the Renaissance* (New Haven: Yale University Press, 1976), pp. 129–43. As part of a larger study of rhetorical culture in Renaissance England, this chapter on *Hamlet* contrasts Laertes, who plays the revenge hero in earnest, with Hamlet, who engages in sophisticated rhetorical display and histrionic play for their own sake. Thus, Hamlet fails to achieve his revenge efficiently because he is only too aware that life is a play and that all action involves speechifying and the enactment of social roles. Drama and rhetoric shape even our inner selves and our moral choices.

Leverenz, David. 'The Woman in Hamlet: An Interpersonal View'. In *Representing Shakespeare: New Psychoanalytic Essays*, ed. Murray M. Schwartz and Coppélia Kahn (Baltimore and London: Johns Hopkins University Press, 1980), pp. 110–28. In the nineteenth century, actresses sometimes took on the role of Hamlet. In this psychoanalytic essay, Leverenz analyses critically the 'woman' within the character of Hamlet. While Goethe was right to say that Hamlet was part woman, Freud was wrong to equate 'woman' with weakness and disease and man with noble reason. Hamlet's acceptance of the Ghost's charge means dissociating the head from the heart, so that Hamlet experiences the same self-division that is forced upon the play's women, who face an intolerable contradiction between love and duty. Hamlet's quest for self-knowledge, a laudably 'womanish' impulse, is repressed by the demands of masculine roles that no longer have any social use.

Levin, Harry. *The Question of 'Hamlet'* (New York: Oxford University Press, 1959). A key text focusing on the language of *Hamlet*, this small book analyses how rhetorical interrogations, formulations of doubt, and irony structure Hamlet's world and how he uses those same available resources to construct a façade of 'madness'. In an appendix, Levin discusses the importance of Hecuba, a classical figure who appears in the Player's speech, as an archetype of maternal woe and queenly suffering who exemplifies proper mourning and therefore contrasts with Gertrude.

Smith, Rebecca. 'A Heart Cleft in Twain: The Dilemma of Shakespeare's Gertrude'. In *The Woman's Part: Feminist Criticism of Shakespeare*, ed. Carolyn Ruth Swift Lenz, Gayle Greene, and Carol Thomas Neely (Urbana: University of Illinois Press, 1980), pp. 194–210. The first wave of contemporary feminist Shakespearian criticism in the 1980s often revised existing assessments of Shakespeare's women. Challenging the idea that Gertrude, at best, is sensual and passive, at worst a collaborator in her husband's death, Smith defines the Queen's character through her own speech and actions, which contrast strikingly with the assessments of her made by Hamlet and the Ghost. Although not the sexual monster perceived by Hamlet, Smith's Gertrude does fit another traditional stereotype: the nurturing, submissive wife and mother who is destroyed by her divided loyalties to husband and son.

States, Bert O. *'Hamlet' and the Concept of Character* (Baltimore and London: Johns Hopkins University Press, 1992). This useful book is divided into two parts. The first gives an extensive overview of critical frameworks and vocabulary for analysing literary character; the second examines exhaustively the 'Hamlet family'. Rather than focusing on the figures in this play as individuals, States discusses issues that arise from their function as 'satellite' characters, whose relations to Hamlet himself contribute to the effect of depth in the hero's character.

NOTES

1. Tom Stoppard. *The Fifteen-Minute Hamlet* (London: Samuel French, 1976).
2. Mark Twain. *The Adventures of Huckleberry Finn*, ed. Justin Kaplan with a foreword and addendum by Victor Doyno (New York: Random House, 1996), p. 186.
3. Kenneth Burke. *A Rhetoric of Motives* (1950; reprint, Berkeley: University of California Press, 1969), pp. 19–20.
4. Sir Richard Steele. *Tatler*, No. 71 (20 September 1709); reprinted in *Shakespeare: The Critical Heritage*, ed. Brian Vickers, 6 vols. (London and Boston: Routledge and Kegan Paul, 1974), Vol. 2, pp. 207–8.
5. Samuel Taylor Coleridge. *Table Talk* (24 June 1827); cited in R. A. Foakes. *Hamlet versus Lear: Cultural Politics and Shakespeare's Art* (Cambridge: Cambridge University Press, 1993), p. 15.
6. Charles Lamb. 'On the Tragedies of Shakespeare' (1811), excerpted in *The Romantics on Shakespeare*, ed. Jonathan Bate (London: Penguin, 1992), p. 115.
7. William Hazlitt. *Characters of Shakespear's Plays*, excerpted in *The Romantics on Shakespeare*, ed. Jonathan Bate (London: Penguin, 1992), p. 325.
8. Sigmund Freud. *The Interpretation of Dreams*, trans. Joyce Crick with an Introduction and Notes by Ritchie Robertson (Oxford: Oxford University Press, 1999), p. 204n.
9. Ernest Jones. *Hamlet and Oedipus* (New York: W. W. Norton & Company, 1949), p. 88.
10. A. C. Bradley. *Shakespearean Tragedy*, 3rd edn, with an introduction by John Russell Brown (New York: St. Martin's, 1992), p. 91.
11. Ibid., p. 123.
12. T. S. Eliot. 'Hamlet and His Problems'. In *Selected Essays, 1917–1932* (New York: Harcourt, Brace, & Company, 1932), pp. 125, 126.

13. Bradley. op. cit., p. 143; G. Wilson Knight. *The Wheel of Fire: Interpretations of Shakespearian Tragedy* (London: Methuen, 1930), pp. 17–46.

14. David Leverenz. 'The Woman in Hamlet: An Interpersonal View'. In *Representing Shakespeare: New Psychoanalytic Essays*, ed. Murray M. Schwartz and Coppélia Kahn (Baltimore and London: Johns Hopkins University Press, 1980), p. 121.

15. Janet Adelman. 'Man and Wife is One Flesh: *Hamlet* and the Confrontation with the Maternal Body'. In *Suffocating Mothers: Fantasies of Maternal Origin in Shakespeare's Plays, 'Hamlet' to 'The Tempest'* (New York and London: Routledge, 1992), p. 30.

16. Bradley. op. cit., p. 141.

17. Anna Brownell Murphy Jameson. *Shakespeare's Heroines* (London: E. P. Dutton, n.d.), pp. 111, 112.

18. Rebecca West. *The Court and The Castle: Some Treatments of a Recurrent Theme* (New Haven: Yale University Press, 1957), p. 24.

19. Harry Levin. *The Question of 'Hamlet'* (New York: Oxford University Press, 1959), pp. 157–64.

20. Rebecca Smith. 'A Heart Cleft in Twain: The Dilemma of Shakespeare's Gertrude'. In *The Woman's Part: Feminist Criticism of Shakespeare*, ed. Carolyn Ruth Swift Lenz, Gayle Greene, and Carol Thomas Neely (Urbana: University of Illinois Press, 1980), pp. 194–210.

21. Dorothea Kehler. 'The First Quarto of *Hamlet* Reforming Widow Gertred', *Shakespeare Quarterly*, 46 (1995), 398–413.

22. Margaret Atwood. 'Gertrude Talks Back'. In *Good Bones and Simple Murders*, 1st edn. (New York: Doubleday, 1994), pp. 16–19.

Whereas for the modern reader the study of Shakespeare's sources tends to suggest a species of archaeological investigation, designed to explore the range of the dramatist's reading rather than elucidate the plays, for Shakespeare's contemporaries the recognition of the material used in the construction of a literary work afforded a significant element of the pleasure afforded by the text. The creative process during the Renaissance was rooted in the concept of imitation, a methodology wholly at odds with the emphasis placed on originality today. Children were trained to write during this period through the study and adaptation of literary models, and thus to appreciate the fresh meanings produced by the deft alteration of a source. As a product of this educational system, Shakespeare was not aloof from these mental habits but turned naturally to the literary stock in the construction of his plays. Rather than inventing his own plots or dramatic situations, he shaped inherited stories to his own ends, implicitly inviting the more discerning of his audience, in some instances, to reflect on novel departures from familiar motifs.

By exploring the use that Shakespeare makes of the materials on which he draws—that which he adds, changes, or chooses to omit—the modern reader is afforded an insight into the shifting preoccupations that shaped his work and the new meanings that he elicits from old tales. Contemporary source studies are thus not primarily directed to establishing the breadth and nature of the dramatist's literary tastes. They exhibit the degree to which Shakespeare's works are enmeshed in their own culture, contribute to the construction of meaning, and provide a means of access to the process of artistic decision-making itself.

Amplification

Though Shakespeare conforms to the intellectual habits of his age in his use of literary models, the ways in which he adapts his inherited materials vary very considerably from play to play. Among the most straightforward of the range of strategies that he employs is the amplification of an existing work. In *The Comedy of Errors* (1592–4), for example, which is structured on the *Menaechmi* (a comedy by the Roman dramatist

Plautus), he enhances the humour of the situation by doubling the basic elements of the borrowed plot. In Plautus' play, confusion is created by the arrival of one member of a pair of identical twins in a city in which his brother, from whom he was parted in childhood, is a prominent member of the community—neither twin being aware of the other's presence. Shakespeare expands the comic potential of this basic situation by partnering his identical brothers with identical servants, thus significantly widening the scope for mis-identification. He further broadens the implications of the story by enfolding the confusion between the two sets of siblings within the history of an older generation, also parted in the storm in which the twins were initially separated. Plautus' comedy of mistaken identity is thus transformed into both a funnier and a richer work, turning not simply on a series of humorous misconceptions, but on the severance of family ties across two generations, and the erosion of the sense of selfhood that arises from the radical fracturing of the social group.

A different species of amplification involves the conflation of plot motifs from previously unrelated sources. The main plot of *King Lear* (1604–5), for example, is drawn from an anonymous play, *The True Chronicle Historie of King Leir* (c.1590), whereas the sub-plot derives from an episode in the *Arcadia*, a prose romance written by Sir Philip Sidney and published posthumously in 1590. Though the two have little in common generically, both turn upon a father's rejection of a loving child and his misplaced trust in an ungracious offspring. By bringing these two stories together and augmenting the parallels between them, Shakespeare is able to broaden a personal history into a wider exploration of sibling rivalry and generational conflict. Lear's treatment at the hands of his daughters thus becomes both an idiosyncratic experience, the product of his own actions, and part of a larger phenomenon, the problematic nature of the transfer of power in both the public and private (parent/child) spheres. The correspondences between the events of the two plots serve, moreover, to clarify their significance. The mental blindness of Lear, for example, which is derived from the conduct of the old king of the chronicle play, is paralleled by the physical blindness of Gloucester, which again looks back to the source, the link that the dramatist establishes between them enforcing the imperative to 'see', in the fullest sense of the word, that is a prime concern of the play.

In *The Taming of the Shrew* (1592), by contrast, in which historically unrelated material is also brought together, it is dissimilarity rather than likeness that the dramatist exploits. The two major plot strands again derive from very different literary traditions, one (the Bianca/Lucentio plot) rooted in the world of courtly love, and the other (the Kate/Petruccio plot) in folk tale. Whereas the amatory relationship for one couple is defined in terms of service to an ideal mistress, for the other it is an economically motivated arrangement in which the female is commodified and subjugated by the male. In this instance, it is not merely the inherited stories that the dramatist draws on but the cultural baggage that they bring with them, in that each carries with it a set of assumptions about the nature of the relationship between the sexes. By bringing the two stories together, Shakespeare is able to explore different kinds of wooing and wedding and to question the presuppositions and expectations that surround them. Significantly, neither action leads to the outcome predicated by the inherited story. The breakdown of the Bianca/Lucentio relationship at the close of the play functions as a critique of a code of courtship (worship of an idealized lady) divorced from the actualities of day-to-day life, while the accommodation finally achieved between Kate and Petruccio is ambivalent, capable of construction either as an endorsement of an oppressive patriarchy or as promoting a species of partnership that rejects both the Petrarchan (Bianca/Lucentio plot) and misogynistic (inherited shrew plot) models.

Revising expectations

A more radical process of adaptation involves the reversal of audience expectation through the unexpected variation of a familiar plot motif. *Henry IV Part One* (1596–7), for example, looks back to the biblical story of the prodigal son (Luke 15, 11–31) a well-known text during the period, and one that had attached itself at an early date to the wild young prince who was to become the embodiment of English military prowess as Henry V. The tale is evoked from the outset of Shakespeare's play by the regret that Henry IV expresses at his son's behaviour (defined in terms of 'riot and dishonour', 1.1.84) in comparison with that of Northumberland's son, Hotspur ('the theme of honour's tongue', 1.1.80). The dissolute nature of the prince is confirmed in the following scene, in which he is introduced in a tavern, the traditional site of the corruption of youth, participating in the pursuits of inappropriate companions, including the beguiling but degenerate Falstaff. The subsequent conduct of the Prince conforms, moreover, to the pattern of the familiar parable. Repenting of his dissolute conduct in terms that encourage the audience to relate his progress to that of the biblical prodigal (cf. 'I do beseech your majesty may salve / The long-grown wounds of my intemperature', 3.2.155–6), he is reconciled to his father (3.2.160–1), attracts wonder at his reformation (4.1.98–111), and redeems himself in battle with the defeat of Hotspur (5.4.57ff.). The career of the Prince is thus placed in the context of a pattern familiar to a Christian audience, enacting the eternal verities of the Christian faith (i.e. the relationship between repentance, forgiveness, right conduct, and divine approbation).

Though Shakespeare conforms in large measure, however, to the pattern of the traditional story, he adapts it in one significant respect. At the close of 1.2 the Prince reveals to the audience that his dissolute behaviour is merely a pretence—that he is not, in fact, a prodigal son, but a son pretending to be a prodigal, in order to harvest the public esteem that will inevitably follow his supposed reformation. The revelation that he is consciously constructing a degenerate identity for pragmatic purposes serves to locate the action in a very different world from that of the exemplary story to which his conduct looks back. Rather than evoking a universe in which right conduct leads inexorably to reward, it draws the spectator into the world of realpolitik, in which religion is deployed as an instrument of power. Shakespeare's prince is thus far from the wild, but potentially able, young man of the Henry V legend. He is a cynical politician in the Machiavellian mould, consciously engaged in exploiting deeply rooted religious beliefs in order to strengthen an uncertain claim to the throne with the aura of divine sanction.

The overturning of the assumptions implicit in an inherited text is also at work in *Measure for Measure* (1603), but in this instance Shakespeare draws on more than one familiar story in order to explore the considerable distance between the exemplary world of the traditional tale and the grim realities of day-to-day life. The main plot looks back to the story of the monstrous sacrifice, exemplified by Whetstone's *Promos and Cassandra* (1578), in which a woman is required by a corrupt official to sacrifice her chastity in order to preserve the life of a male relative. The story depends upon the supposition, deeply embedded in patriarchal societies, that female virtue is exemplified through self-abnegation, and by the dutiful promotion of the wishes and well-being of the male. In Shakespeare's play, however, the central female character, Isabella, declines to participate in the proposed exchange, mounting an argument that calls in question the value systems implicit in the inherited story. Where the imprisoned brother in Whetstone's drama persuades his sister to consent to the proposition on the grounds that she would be universally condemned if she refused to sacrifice her chastity for a male relative, thus bringing about the downfall of their house, Shakespeare's Claudio is roundly condemned by his sister for failing to resist the proposal (3.1.137–48), which she expects him, at first, to reject (2.4.177–83). Isabella's trenchant resistance arises not from indifference to her brother, for whom she is ready to sacrifice her life (cf. 3.1.103–5), but from her acute awareness of the spiritual implications of the action, both for herself (2.4.107–9) and any man prepared to save his life by such means (cf. 3.1.137–41). Here, Shakespeare might be said to be engaging in a dialogue with the text on which he draws, constructing an alternative version of female virtue from that implicit in his source.

A similar process is at work in his use in the same play of the disguised ruler motif, a popular device in romance literature (e.g., Barnaby Riche, *The Adventures of Brusanus, Prince of Hungaria*, 1592), and one frequently deployed on the Elizabethan-Jacobean stage. The story turns on the decision of a ruler, the embodiment of moral authority in the state, to temporarily forsake his throne and go disguised among his people in order to assess their spiritual condition. Though the Duke in *Measure for Measure* belongs to this tradition, his plan to discover 'what our seemers be' (1.3.54) by ostensibly absenting himself from his realm does not follow the conventional pattern, in that the depth of corruption he discovers not only exceeds his expectation but almost evades his ultimate control. His difficulty in exercising his expected quasi-divine function serves, like the unconventional handling of the monstrous sacrifice motif, to destabilize audience assumptions, combining with the Isabella/Claudio story to evoke a world in which expectations are constantly subverted, the outcome of actions cannot be predicted, and the rightness of any decision, however well-intentioned, is far from clear-cut.

Self-borrowing

The readiness of Shakespeare's audience to reflect on the relationship between a new work and the sources on which it was built is attested by the comments of contemporary playgoers. Among the most well-known is an observation by John Manningham, a student at the Middle Temple, who attended a performance of *Twelfth Night* in 1602. Manningham wrote:

At our feast we had a play called *Twelfth Night or What You Will*, much like *The Comedy of Errors* or *Menaechmi* in Plautus, but most like and near to that in Italian, called *Inganni*.

While bearing witness to the writer's interest in the dialogue between the Shakespearian play and other literary texts, Manningham's note also highlights one of the most interesting features of Shakespeare's attitude to the literary stock, his habit of drawing on his own compositions. Not only did he conform to contemporary practice in adapting the work of other writers, he turned back throughout his dramatic career to his own earlier plays, constantly reworking situations that he had previously employed. No less than seven of his female characters, for example, disguise themselves as youths, while a supposed death is a recurrent device in both comedy and tragedy (e.g., *Romeo and Juliet*, *Much Ado About Nothing*, *Antony and Cleopatra*, *The Winter's Tale*). It is this habit of composition that has given rise to one of the most rewarding branches of contemporary source study. By comparing the dramatist's use of recurrent situations as they make their way through a succession of plays, critics have shown the changing preoccupations that shaped his work at different points in his career, and the very different meanings that he elicits from the same inherited stories and motifs.

One of the most striking examples of his re-use of a borrowed plot is his return in *Twelfth Night*, noted by Manningham, to the sibling confusion device. Like *The Comedy of Errors*, *Twelfth Night* looks back to the *Menaechmi*, in that it too turns on the misunderstandings created by the arrival of one member of a pair of identical twins in a place in which the other is an established member of the community. As Manningham observed, however, in constructing the later play Shakespeare was influenced by an Italian version of the story, in which the separated siblings are of different sexes, and the confusion between them arises not from their inherent likeness but from the decision of the more vulnerable female twin to disguise herself as her brother. Nevertheless, though Shakespeare clearly drew on this version of the story (cf. Viola's decision to disguise herself as Sebastian), there is also considerable evidence that he looked back to his own earlier treatment of the motif in *The Comedy of Errors* in the course of constructing his new play. A number of incidents are common to both comedies (like the denial of a purse, and the claiming of one twin as an amatory partner by an unknown lady). There are also some striking verbal parallels between the Antipholus of Ephesus/Egeon plot of *The Comedy of Errors* and the Antonio/Sebastian plot of *Twelfth Night*, both of which involve the repudiation by a younger man of an older man whose life is at stake (cf. *The Comedy of Errors*, 5.1.283–330 and *Twelfth Night*, 3.4.305–18 and 5.1.54–95).

For all the similarities between the two plays, however, *Twelfth Night* is not merely *The Comedy of Errors* under a new name. Whereas the emphasis in the earlier work is on the humour of the situations to which the confusion between the siblings gives rise, in *Twelfth Night* the dramatist explores the psychological effects of the mis-understandings, and the emotional problems that the mistaken assumptions of the characters pose. Rather than taking place in the public arena (e.g., before the Abbey or in the street), the events are set in more private, enclosed spaces (e.g., the garden of Olivia's residence), implying more inward concerns, while the Italianate location and aristocratic characters suggest a refined, courtly environment, very different from the middle-class world of commerce evoked in the earlier play. An increased use of soliloquy and aside encourages the audience not merely to sit back and laugh at the escalating disorder but to participate in the characters' inner confusion and the growing discomfort to which it leads. While turning on the same initial situation as *The Comedy of Errors*, the later play thus ushers the audience into a new world, engaging a wider range of emotions, and offering the spectator a different kind of dramatic experience.

The Comedy of Errors and *Twelfth Night* belong to different periods of Shakespeare's career, the former an early work, and the latter generally classed as the last of the middle comedies. *All's Well That Ends Well* (1604–5) and *Measure for Measure*, by con-trast, which also share a borrowed plot, are chronologically close (though the order in which they were composed is disputed), and thus offer an even more striking example of Shakespeare's tendency to rework his own material. The main plot of *All's Well That Ends Well* is ultimately derived from Boccaccio's *Decameron*, in which the heroine is required to fulfil two impossible conditions; she must bear her husband a child and obtain a ring from his finger before he will consummate their marriage and acknowledge her as his wife. The tasks are accomplished by means of a deception, the nocturnal substitution of the virgin bride for another woman, whom the husband is attempting to seduce. It this device, commonly known as the 'bed trick', that forms a link with *Measure for Measure*. As noted above, the plot of the latter play involves the proposed exchange of the virginity of the heroine, Isabella, for the life of her brother, Claudio, and the situation is resolved when a legitimate sexual partner, Mariana, is substituted for Isabella. That Shakespeare was drawing, in part, on his own version of the bed trick in constructing the second of the two plays is indicated by a number of features common to both. The circumstances in which the substitution takes place, for example, are markedly similar. The men are asked in both cases to agree to a number of conditions—that the encounter should take place in silence, for example, and that the stay should be brief (cf. *All's Well That Ends Well*, 4.2.55–9, and *Measure for Measure*, 3.1.238–9). More significantly, the stratagem is employed in both instances not simply to salvage the predicament of a female character, a traditional function of the device, but to allow a male character to commit a grossly transgressive act that is nevertheless capable of forgiveness, in that it is notional rather than real.

Once again, however, Shakespeare does not simply transpose the story, with a change of names, into a new context. In *Measure for Measure* the transgressive conduct of the seducer, Angelo, is greater: the dramatist follows the tale of the monstrous bargain in making him the authority figure within the play world but transforms Isabella, the target of Angelo's predatory intentions, into a woman who has dedicated her life to God. The implications of the two tricks, for all their superficial similarity, are thus radically different. In *All's Well That Ends Well* the device is constructive in that it allows the consummation of a marriage and saves a thoughtless young man from dishonouring both an innocent person and himself, while in *Measure for Measure* it is a desperate expedient, designed to frustrate sexual blackmail and avert a gross abuse of judicial power.

Dramatic conventions: revenge

Though the main plot of *All's Well That Ends Well* ultimately derives from the *Decameron*, in all probability Shakespeare did not draw directly on Boccaccio's version of the bed trick, but on an English adaptation of the story in Painter's *Palace of Pleasure* (third edition, 1575). The relationship between Boccaccio's story, Painter's, and the two Shakespearian plays is indicative of the way in which Shakespeare's plots are embedded in literary traditions, and of their dependence upon a set of conventions (e.g., that women are interchangeable in the darkness of the bedchamber) to which the audience lends its assent. It is not merely the assumptions underlying particular plot motifs, however, that Shakespeare draws on in constructing his plays, but the conventions that govern the larger literary/dramatic genres within which those tales or motifs are themselves located.

The story of Hamlet, for example, originated in the *Historiae Danicae* of Saxo Grammaticus, published in 1514, but it became known to the Elizabethan public through a French version, in the fifth volume of Belleforest's *Histoires Tragiques* (first published 1570). By the time that Shakespeare came to compose his play, the story had already been transposed to the English stage, dramatized, in all probability, by Thomas Kyd, in the 1580s. A number of references to this lost play, known as the *Ur-Hamlet*, survive, including a description of the way in which the ghost called upon Hamlet to revenge his death. The evidence indicates that the work belonged to the revenge tradition, a form popular in England throughout the Elizabethan-Jacobean period. The similarities between the little that we know of this play and *Hamlet* suggest that Shakespeare drew on this earlier play (compare his use of *King Leir*, discussed above), and a host of correspondences between his treatment of the story of the Danish prince and other Elizabethan revenge dramas confirms that he was self-consciously operating within this dramatic genre.

The foundations of the revenge tradition in England were laid by Kyd's *The Spanish Tragedy* (c.1587), a hugely successful work to which numerous later writers looked back. The plot turns on a murder by a powerful figure within the play, which drives a relative of the victim to near-madness as he agonizes over a slow vengeance, finally exacted through a play-within-a-play. This central vengeance is located within a number of other revenge actions, all of which reflect in some way on the predicament of the principal figure and the issues raised by his situation, such as the legitimacy of private retribution. All the ingredients of Kyd's plot found their way into later plays, including Shakespeare's *Hamlet*, with its murderous king, anguished son, delayed revenge, multiple revengers (Hamlet, Laertes, Fortinbras), and play-within-the-play. For Shakespeare's initial audience, familiar with the genre, the experience afforded by the drama would thus have been very different from that of a modern reader or spectator experiencing the work in isolation. The interest offered by the storyline would inevitably be less, while a large part of the pleasure offered by the work would spring from the anticipation of traditional incidents (e.g., the appearance of the ghost), and the surprise afforded by the innovative use of stock motifs (e.g., the systematic correspondences Shakespeare sets up between his avenging sons—Hamlet, Laertes, and Fortinbras).

Literary conventions: pastoral

While *Hamlet* remains accessible to a modern audience unfamiliar with the conventions of the genre to which it belongs, some plays rely much more heavily on the capacity of the audience to decipher a system of signification encoded within the literary form. A number of plays depend, for example, on the pastoral tradition, so named for the Latin *pastor* or shepherd. This convention, which reaches back to the third century BC and the work of the Sicilian poet, Theocritus, ultimately depends upon an equation between shepherd and poet/lover. It developed into a highly sophisticated form, embraced not only by poets but by romance writers and dramatists. Though ostensibly concerned with rustics, the pastoral is remote from the harsh realities of rural life, presenting an idealized countryside, free from the corruption of civilized society. Conventional elements of the genre include refined states of feeling, some species of courtship, and lengthy 'complaints' (i.e. laments) by unrequited lovers, while the concept of shepherds piping to their flocks finds expression in an emphasis on music and song.

As You Like It (1599–1600), discussed more fully below, approximates most closely to the conventional form. Once banished from the court by the usurping Duke, Rosalind and Celia elect to disguise themselves as rustics, and to pursue the life of a shepherd and shepherdess in the forest of Arden. Their activities within the forest, however, have little to do with the pragmatic processes of earning a living. The removal to the pastoral location signals a movement into a different mental landscape from that of the usurper's court, and an engagement with amatory experience, including the pain of unrequited love. To an audience familiar with the convention, the cousins' choice of disguise functions as a species of dramatic shorthand, triggering a set of expectations that are borne out in the course of the play. For a reader or spectator with no knowledge of the form, by contrast, the significance of the entry into the pastoral world is lost, and with it the pleasure afforded by the handling of such stock motifs as the debate between Corin and Touchstone on the virtues of court and country (3.2.11–74).

Though *As You Like It* conforms most fully to the pastoral mode, it is not the only play in the canon in which Shakespeare makes use of the genre's conventions. The forlorn Henry VI, for example, in an early play, compares his troubled state with that of a shepherd when he laments the cares of the crown (*Henry VI Part Three*, 2.5.1–54), describing a life that, with its peaceful tending of flocks and time for sport and contemplation, has little bearing on the realities of rural existence in either his own or Shakespeare's day. It is in the plays of his last period, however, that Shakespeare draws most extensively on the pastoral mode. In *Cymbeline* (1609–10), the sons of the king, stolen in infancy, are reared in the wilds of Wales, becoming the embodiment of princely virtue in an environment divorced from the corruption of the court, while the daughter of Leontes in *The Winter's Tale* (1609), repudiated by her father at birth, is reared by shepherds in Bohemia and is firmly associated through that upbringing with the beauty and innocence of the natural world (cf. 4.4.1–146).

Though superficially different, in that it is set in an all-but-uninhabited island, *The Tempest* (1610–11) represents Shakespeare's most innovative use of the genre. The mode is explicitly evoked in the masque that takes place in Act Four, when Ceres (the goddess of the earth and agriculture) is invoked to bless the marriage of the play's lovers (4.1.60ff.), and a variety of aspects of the tradition are utilized elsewhere in the play. Gonzalo, seeking to distract Alonso from the loss of his son, for example, enters into a dialogue with the pastoral ideal in describing a utopian society that rejects cultivation while relying on the bounty of nature (2.1.143ff.)—his reflections forming part of a larger debate between nature and nurture that informs the drama as a whole. While drawing on a convention that has its origins in the third century BC, however, Shakespeare brings the tradition into contact with the concerns of his own day. A principal source of *The Tempest* is a group of pamphlets concerned with a shipwreck that took place in the Bermudas in 1609, in particular a letter by William Strachey, written in 1610, detailing the circumstances of the event. The wrecked fleet was carrying five hundred colonists to Virginia, and by bringing the story of their shipwreck and his inherited genre together, the dramatist endows the convention with a striking modernity, fusing the mental landscape of the pastoral and the new world encountered in the Americas in a complex exploration of the concept of the natural. In this instance the recognition of the contemporary materials exploited in the play is vital to an understanding of the resonances that the work carried for a seventeenth-century spectator and the topical issues it addressed, such as colonization.

Uses of source study

An assumed chronology of the Shakespearian corpus, implicit in the previous discussion, has been intrinsic to critical investigation since the late eighteenth century. The canon is conventionally divided for purposes of comparison into early, middle, and late periods, while studies of the repeated use of particular plot motifs depend upon a knowledge of the order in which the plays were written. The chronology of the work, however, is itself a product of scholarly enquiry, in that no contemporary record of the order of composition exists. The study of Shakespeare's sources has, from the outset, played a major part in this area of critical investigation. *As You Like It*, for example, which is known to have been in existence by 1600, draws on a number of works published in 1598, confirming the probability that it was written circa 1599. *The Tempest* provides a particularly striking example of the value of this kind of investigation. The play was once held to be an early work, revived at a later date, but the discovery of its indebtedness to the Bermuda pamphlets has helped to confirm that it was written in late 1610 or early 1611 (i.e., at the close of Shakespeare's career), sanctioning comparison with other late works.

No text exists in isolation from other texts. Its form is determined by a set of conventions familiar to its expected audience, and its subject matter arises from a complex set of interactions between contemporary concerns and the literary stock. In electing to write, the artist is self-consciously positioning his work amidst a host of other texts, and the study of the dialogue in which he engages with the materials on which he draws, and the traditions to which those materials belong, contributes to the sum of meanings adducible from his work. It is the proximity that source studies afford to the creative process, the insight that they allow into the dramatist's changing strategies and concerns, and the recognition that they bring of the collaborative nature of all cultural activity, that make this field of investigation one of the most exciting areas of contemporary Shakespearian study.

FURTHER READING

Bate, Jonathan. *Shakespeare and Ovid* (Oxford: Clarendon Press, 1993). This book is among the most important of those studies devoted to a single influence on Shakespeare's work.

Bullough, Geoffrey. *Narrative and Dramatic Sources of Shakespeare*, 8 vols. (London and New York: Routledge and Kegan Paul, 1957–75). The foundation of modern source study, this comprehensive work prints and discusses the major sources and analogues of the Shakespearian corpus. It also includes a history of source scholarship and substantial bibliographies.

Hunter, G. K. 'Shakespeare's Reading'. In *A New Companion to Shakespeare Studies*, ed. Kenneth Muir and S. Schoenbaum (Cambridge: Cambridge University Press, 1971), pp. 55–66. This essay offers an accessible introduction to the range of Shakespeare's reading.

Latham, Agnes (ed). *As You Like It* (London: Methuen, 1975). A volume in the Arden series, this edition includes a very detailed account of the sources of the play.

Miola, Robert S. *Shakespeare's Reading* (Oxford: Oxford University Press, 2000). A lucid exploration of Shakespeare's reshaping of sources.

Muir, Kenneth. *The Sources of Shakespeare's Plays* (London: Methuen, 1977). This study considers the use that Shakespeare makes of the material on which he draws and the ways in which his work is informed by his reading.

Scragg, Leah. *Shakespeare's Mouldy Tales* (London: Longman, 1992). This book, designed for the student or general reader, locates Shakespeare's use of inherited material within the context of Renaissance attitudes to the creative process and explores the dramatist's repeated use of a number of plot motifs.

Scragg, Leah. *Shakespeare's Alternative Tales* (London: Longman, 1996). A companion volume to *Shakespeare's Mouldy Tales* and also designed for the student or general reader, this study prints a number of the stories that Shakespeare draws on in his plays and exhibits the ways in which he interrogates their traditional meanings.

READING: *As You Like It*

As You Like It offers a useful example of the kinds of insight that may be achieved through an exploration of the relationship between a Shakespearian play and its principal source. The play is directly indebted to *Rosalynde* (1590), a prose romance by Thomas Lodge, a new edition of which appeared on the bookstalls in 1598, immediately prior to the composition of Shakespeare's play. The storylines of the two works have much in common. In both an eldest son withholds an inheritance from a younger brother, subjecting him to a series of abuses that drive him to seek shelter in a forest environment, remote from the corruption of the court. A lady, with whom the wronged man has fallen in love at a wrestling match, is subjected to similarly unjust treatment by a usurping duke, and she too flees to the country-side, disguised as a boy, accompanied by her devoted friend, the duke's daughter. The women embrace the life of a shepherd and shepherdess, attracting the notice of an arrogant maiden who falls in love with the seeming youth, disdaining the extravagant devotion of a rustic suitor. An encounter between the disguised heroine and the fugitive hero leads to a proxy courtship which results in a mock marriage, while the arrival of the hero's elder brother in the forest precipitates a reconciliation when the younger man rescues his former abuser from a lioness. The newly arrived brother falls in love with the heroine's friend, and the couples eventually return to the court with the reinstatement of the true duke.

The similarity between the stories makes it hard to resist the suggestion that the two works are closely related, and Shakespeare's choice of nomenclature serves to confirm his dependence on the romance. Like the central figure of Lodge's story, the heroine of *As You Like It* is named Rosalind, and she adopts the same pseudonym (Ganymede) when disguised as a boy. In both instances, the misguided shepherdess who falls in love with the heroine's masculine persona is called Phoebe, while the hero is attended by a faithful retainer, whose links to an older social order are signalled by the name Adam. More broadly, both composi-tions operate within the pastoral tradition (as discussed above), a mode made popular in the late sixteenth century by such works as Edmund Spenser's *The Shepheardes Calendar* (1579) and Sir Philip Sidney's *Arcadia* (1590). Both Lodge's story and Shakespeare's play share the pastoral's concern with unrequited love, explore the contrast between court and country, and embrace opportunities for song.

Nevertheless, for all their obvious similarities, *As You Like It* is not simply Lodge's *Rosalynde* transferred to the stage, and the differences between the two works offer a perspective on the issues explored in the Shakespearian play. One of the most significant features of *As You Like It*, for example, is the emphasis placed by the dramatist upon family ties. Whereas in Lodge's narrative the true and false dukes are unrelated, in the Shakespearian play the two men are brothers. This seemingly minor adaptation is highly significant, both in terms of the contrasting environments in which the action is located and the resolution achieved at the close of the play. By paralleling the conflict between Oliver and Orlando with the fraternal discord between the true and usurping dukes, Shakespeare opens his play in a universe characterized by the fracturing of family bonds, and this situation is heightened by the fact that in banishing Rosalind, the duke is expelling not simply his daughter's friend, as in the source, but his own niece.

The destruction of the family unit is also implicit in the emblematic wrestling match which takes place before the duke. Whereas two brothers in *Rosalynde* meet their deaths at the hands of the duke's man, three brothers are killed in *As You Like It*. Their grieving father, moreover, is broken-hearted at their loss, rather than receiving the news of their deaths with stoical resolve. In placing their love before their fathers' hatred, Celia and Rosalind are thus asserting the primacy not merely of friendship, as in the source, but the bonds of kinship, and their journey to Arden denotes a shift to an environment in which family ties are fostered and equated with the natural. The true duke, for example, salutes those who share his misfortunes as his 'co-mates and brothers in exile' (2.1.1), while Orlando, on arriving in the forest, likens his care of Adam to that of a 'doe' anxious 'to find my fawn / And give it food' (2.7.127–8). Positive relationships of a variety of kinds abound, including Adam's devotion to Orlando and Touchstone's to Celia and Rosalind, serving to locate Orlando's rescue of Oliver in a context in which affection triumphs over hardship. By making his true and false dukes brothers, moreover, Shakespeare is able to achieve a resolution that knits his society together not only through marriage but through the reconstitution and strengthening of the family unit. Rosalind is reunited with her father, Celia with her uncle, the three sons of Sir Rowland de Bois with one another (counterbalancing the three brothers killed in the opening act), while the marriages made between Orlando and Rosalind, Oliver and Celia join all six characters (the duke, his daughter, his niece, and the sons of Sir Rowland de Bois) in a web of intermeshing relationships.

In a further adaptation of the source, the usurping brother is not killed in battle, but converted on the outskirts of the forest, his repentance and decision to embrace a spiritual life endowing the positive stances of the central characters with supernatural approval. The harmony achieved at the close of the play is thus not simply a product of the fulfilment of amatory desires. As in many Shakespearian comedies, including *The Comedy of Errors* and *Twelfth Night*, the happiness envisaged beyond the close of the play depends upon a much more complex set of relationships, seen as the basis of a kind of society favourable to the security of the individual.

It is not merely the changes that Shakespeare makes to his source, however, that offer an insight into the concerns of his play—equally illuminating is that which he adds or chooses to omit. Though *Rosalynde* is a relatively lengthy work, inviting pruning rather than amplification, a number of the characters who appear in Shakespeare's play have no counterpart in the romance. Touchstone, for example, does not appear in Lodge's work, and his introduction is indicative of the wider social and intellectual scope that distinguishes *As You Like It* from its source. As the devoted follower of Celia and Rosalind, he functions as a parallel to Orlando's servant, Adam, contributing (as noted above) to the network of positive relationships that link the characters of the Shakespearian play, but he differs from the older retainer in that he adopts a much more sceptical stance towards the activities of his superiors—for example in his less than enthusiastic attitude to their flight to the forest.

The contrast that Touchstone offers to Adam in this respect is the gateway to a series of further oppositional positions, the most notable of which involves his attitude to love. Lodge's romance traces the courtship of three couples, all of whom, regardless of social position, experience the same emotions when in the grip of amatory passion, are equally at ease with complex poetic forms, and express their feelings in much the same terms. Shakespeare, by contrast, presents four pairs of lovers whose attitudes are sharply distinguished. Celia and Oliver fall in love at first sight, and their love is untested at the close of the play; Rosalind and Orlando grow in understanding both of one another and the nature of love; while Silvius and Phoebe operate within the realm of the never-never-land of romance. For all these couples, however, love implies spirituality and total commitment, as it does for the inhabitants of Lodge's pastoral world. Touchstone, by contrast, brings with him a set of attitudes that find no place in the romance, in that he is keenly aware of both the physicality and transient nature of sexual attraction. By adding his relationship with Audrey to the varieties of love experienced by his principal figures, Shakespeare broadens the exploration of amatory experience undertaken in the course of the play, offering his audience an 'anatomy', or examination, of the range of forms that love may take.

While Silvius, for example, expresses his undying devotion to Phoebe in the most lyrical of terms, and asserts his willingness to subsist on the slightest indication of her favour, Touchstone indicates, in the most down-to-earth language, the compelling physical needs that drive his suit towards Audrey, and his firm expectation that his interest in his marriage will be short-lived. Silvius declares:

> So holy and so perfect is my love,
> And I in such a poverty of grace,
> That I shall think it a most plenteous crop
> To glean the broken ears after the man
> That the main harvest reaps. Loose now and then
> A scattered smile, and that I'll live upon
>
> (3.5.100-5)

This can be compared with the following exchange between Touchstone and Jaques:

> JAQUES: Will you be married, motley?
> TOUCHSTONE: As the ox hath his bow, sir, the horse his curb, and the falcon her bells, so man hath his desires; and as pigeons bill, so wedlock would be nibbling.
> JAQUES: And will you, being a man of your breeding, be married under a bush, like a beggar? Get you to church, and have a good priest that can tell you what marriage is. This fellow will but join you together as they join wainscot; then one of you will prove a shrunk panel and, like green timber, warp, warp.
> TOUCHSTONE: I am not in the mind but I were better to be married of him than of another, for he is not like to marry me well, and not being well married, it will be a good excuse for me hereafter to leave my wife.
>
> (3.3.65-77)

While the addition of Touchstone to the list of the play's lovers allows for a more comprehensive analysis of amatory experience than that afforded by the source, it also serves as a pointer to the broader society evoked by the play. Though Lodge's central characters disguise themselves as a shepherd and shepherdess and diligently lead their flocks out to graze, the rustics they encounter prove as polished in their speech as the members of the court, and are equally refined in terms of understanding. In the Shakespearian play, by contrast, Touchstone's rustic partner, Audrey, another addition to the source, is far from the rural maiden of the pastoral idyll. Rather than composing songs and sonnets, she is unable to comprehend what poetry is, and while she repudiates the term 'slut', she is so far from the sophistication of the source that she thanks God she is 'foul' (3.3.31).

Audrey does not stand alone, moreover, in embodying an entirely different concept of rural life from that presented in the romance. Though Corin, the shepherd through whom Celia aquires her farm, has his origins in Lodge's work, he functions not merely to introduce the central figures into rustic society, but to offer a view of peasant life that contrasts sharply with the concern with love and poetry that the term 'shepherd' in a literary context conventionally evokes. He talks of hands greasy from contact with sheep, skin hardened and tarred with administering physic (3.2.46ff.), and of basic needs, such as money and good pasture (3.2.22–4). The representation of a system of life markedly different from that of both the court and the pastoral convention is heightened, moreover, by the addition of yet another character with no counterpart in the romance—Audrey's rustic suitor, William. His encounter with Touchstone in 5.1 exhibits a stolid slow-wittedness wholly at odds with the mental refinement and classical knowledge of Montanus and Corin, the shepherds encountered by Lodge's heroine, and exposes the social gulf between courtiers and rustics that in the real world prevents any meaningful communication between the two.

The addition of characters whose existence is firmly rooted in the day-to-day realities of the countryside is indicative of the dialogue that Shakespeare sets up with the assumptions that are encoded in Lodge's text. Whereas on the one hand the dramatist superficially conforms to the pastoral convention, in that he places his action in a rural location in which refined states of feeling are explored, on the other he gently mocks the tradition on which he draws, exposing the harsh realities of rustic life. While Lodge's shepherds and shepherdesses are untroubled by adverse weather, for example, the true duke in *As You Like It* comments on the biting of the winter wind and on the bitter cold, and Touchstone is in no doubt of the superiority of courtly life.

While the addition of Touchstone, Audrey, and William contributes to the dialogue that Shakespeare sets up between what might be called two versions of the conventions of pastoral life, Jaques, another character who has no counterpart in Lodge's work, interrogates a wider set of assumptions. In contrast to the inhabitants of Lodge's Arden, who propound a common set of values once the world of the court is left behind (notably the prime value of heterosexual love), the inhabitants of Shakespeare's forest find their suppositions constantly challenged. In 2.1, for example, the First Lord reports Jaques' negative response to the killing of the deer, an event celebrated by the true duke's courtiers in that it affords them sustenance, but mourned by Jaques as a species of tyranny. Similarly, in 3.2

Jaques counters the central characters' commitment to love with the assertion that being in love is Orlando's principal vice, while in 2.7 he announces his wish to become a professional fool in order to be free to satirize society as a whole. In the final scene, rather than embracing 'pastime' he elects to withdraw from the social group, sustaining the play's presentation of a variety of stances by prioritizing reflection over participation.

The additions that Shakespeare makes to his source material serve to transform the inherited narrative into a much more interrogative text. The nature of love, the validity of the pastoral convention, the idealistic positions that the characters propound are all subjected to scrutiny, inviting the audience to think about the issues raised. An examination of those aspects of the source that Shakespeare chooses to omit, moreover, confirms his concern with the exploration of emotions and ideas. For all the elegance of its style and its emphasis upon amatory experience, *Rosalynde* contains a significant number of violent incidents, the majority of which find no place in Shakespeare's work. The physical abuses that Rosader (Orlando's counterpart) suffers at the hands of his brother, for example, are far more fully documented, while the wrestling match in which the unnamed brothers are killed is much more graphic than the comparable incident in the Shakespearian play. Alinda, Celia's antecedent, is attacked by kidnappers who plan to offer her up to the lascivious embraces of the usurping duke, thus introducing the threat of incest and rape, while the action culminates in a battle in which the usurper is killed. An element of physical violence is thus a constant thread running through the work, contrasting with the serenity that prevails in Shakespeare's Arden. The reduction of the element of physical danger faced by the characters contributes to the shift of emphasis from circumstances to mental states, in that the problems facing Shakespeare's characters subsequent to their arrival in Arden are internal rather than external, arising from mistaken attitudes or assumptions. Orlando, for example, has little understanding of the way that relationships change with time, Phoebe's arrogance blinds her to the fact that her hopes of happiness lie with Silvius, Jaques' negativity is all-corroding, and Touchstone's understanding of human relationships is radically incomplete.

In conformity with the pastoral convention, Lodge's work contains a substantial number of poetic effusions, and an examination of Shakespeare's treatment of this aspect of his source also sheds light on his own idiosyncratic concerns. Lodge's many sonnets, madrigals, and eclogues are uniformly concerned with the pains and pleasures of love, typified by the first verse of Rosalynde's madrigal:

> Love in my bosom like a bee
>   Doth suck his sweet;
> Now with his wings he plays with me,
>   Now with his feet.
> Within mine eyes he makes his nest,
> His bed amidst my tender breast,
> My kisses are his daily feast,
> And yet he robs me of my rest.
>   Ah wanton, will ye?

Less than half of the many lyrics of the Shakespearian play, by contrast, are composed by the play's lovers, and of these all are either ludicrous in themselves or derided by others. Orlando's verses to Rosalind, quoted in 3.2, for example, are instantly parodied by Touchstone, while both Celia and Rosalind laugh at the poetic limitations of the lines Celia reads in the same scene. Touchstone slips briefly into verse after arranging his suspect marriage to Audrey, undermining the lyricism of the poetic form by his own attitudes, while Phoebe's verses to Rosalind in 4.3 are delivered in a context that renders them both cruel and misdirected. Rather than reinforcing a romantic idyll, the songs thus contribute to the play's exhibition of the multifaceted nature of love, exposing its humorous, touching, and destructive dimensions. This broadening of perspective is also evident in the remainder of the songs, which touch on social rather than amatory issues. Amiens's songs in 2.5 and 2.7, for example, contrast the hardships faced in the forest with the greater ills present in human society, while the song that follows Hymen's joining of the lovers celebrates marriage as the foundation of the social unit (cf. ''Tis Hymen peoples every town', 5.4.132).

The relationship between *Rosalynde* and *As You Like It* explored in this chapter illustrates just some of the many ways in which source studies may contribute to an understanding of Shakespeare's work. The close correlation between the storylines of the two texts exhibits the way in which Shakespeare's play is embedded in sixteenth-century culture, and its reliance upon literary modes with which contemporary audiences were familiar. At the same time, the discrepancies between the two works affords the modern reader a means of access to the concerns that shaped the play, and the means by which its multifacetedness is crafted. Above all, perhaps, an investigation of the changes that *Rosalynde* undergoes in its transfer to the stage offers an insight into Shakespeare's response to Lodge's text, and thus a glimpse of a creative mind at work.

FURTHER READING

Barber, C. L. *Shakespeare's Festive Comedy: A Study of Dramatic Form and its Relation to Social Custom* (Princeton: Princeton University Press, 1959). This book, which relates comedy to social rituals, has had a significant impact on the study of Shakespeare's work.

Belsey, Catherine. 'Disrupting Sexual Difference: Meaning and Gender in the Comedies'. In *Alternative Shakespeares*, ed. J. Drakakis (London: Methuen, 1985), pp. 166–90. This important essay discusses the disruption of gender in Shakespeare's plays in the context of definitions of the family in the sixteenth and seventeenth centuries.

Brissenden, Alan (ed.). *As You Like It* (Oxford: Oxford University Press, 1993). A volume in the World's Classics series, this edition includes a full discussion of the sources of the play.

Erickson, Peter. 'Sexual Politics and the Social Structure in *As You Like It*.' In *Shakespeare's Comedies*, ed. G. Waller (London: Longman, 1991), pp. 155–67 (reprinted from P. Erickson, 'Patriarchal Structures in Shakespeare's Drama' (Berkeley: University of California Press, 1985)). This essay explores gender roles in *As You Like It* and affords an interesting contrast to Jackson's essay, below.

Frye, Northrop. *A Natural Perspective: The Development of Shakespearian Comedy and Romance* (New York: Columbia University Press, 1965). A highly influential study, this book illuminates the entire spectrum of Shakespeare's comedies.

Jackson, Russell. 'Perfect Types of Womanhood: Rosalind, Beatrice, and Viola in Victorian Criticism and Performance', *Shakespeare Survey 32* (1979), 15–26. This relatively brief essay offers an interesting insight into the changing reception of Shakespeare's heroines.

Jenkins, Harold. 'As You Like It', *Shakespeare Survey 8* (1955), 40–51. Elegantly written and perceptive, this celebrated essay exhibits the subtlety of Shakespeare's art of comic juxtaposition.

Leggatt, Alexander. *Shakespeare's Comedy of Love* (London: Methuen, 1974). One of the most valuable surveys of Shakespearian comedy, this book includes an illuminating chapter on *As You Like It*.

28 | Close reading

Inga-Stina Ewbank

When, seven years after his death, Shakespeare's colleagues John Heminges and Henry Condell put together the first collected edition of his plays, the 1623 Folio, they prefaced it with an address 'To the great Variety of Readers'. As good businessmen, they begin with sales talk—'whatever you do, buy!'—but as literary advisers they have but one thing to say to Shakespeare's readers: 'Read him, therefore; and again, and again'. They are thinking in early-seventeenth-century terms when they define the 'variety' of readers of the volume as a range 'from the most able, to him that can but spell', but the point of their advice is just as valid for the twenty-first-century reader. Serious students of Shakespeare—meaning by 'Shakespeare' the corpus of plays that bears his name—have always been, and will always be, close readers; and close reading as a critical practice[1] has meant and means reading 'again, and again' in order to acquire an understanding and appreciation of the words on the page, of how and why they function in the work of which they are part. To read closely means to summon up questions about context as well as text—and this is the theme of this chapter.

'Again and again' has special relevance as an encouragement to the modern reader who may well come to Shakespeare with a fear of his language as old, strange, and complex. It is all those things; but close reading can turn fear into familiarity, and strangeness into wonder. For of course Shakespeare's language teems with complexities and ambiguities: exploring these offers the excitement of discovering how Shakespeare moulds the English language to serve his own purposes. In our increasingly visual culture it may be more appealing to watch a video than to read the text of a play. These two activities can certainly be cross-illuminating; and both are forms of reading, in so far as 'reading' means, in its widest sense, constructing meanings from signs presented—signs that don't have to be printed on a page. A visual sign can be more revealing than words, as Lady Macbeth knows when she first meets her husband after his encounter with the witches: 'Your face, my thane, is as a book where men / May read strange matters' (*Macbeth*, 1.5.60–1). But—as in this scene—it is the words that articulate and communicate the interpretation of what is seen; and the marvel of Shakespeare's language will fully open itself to appreciation only in close reading of texts. The words on the page are inextricably part of the life of the plays, and as such they need to be approached with the level of engagement which Warwick attributes to the wayward Prince Hal when, identifying language with a way of life, he assures the

King that 'The Prince but studies his companions, / Like a strange tongue, wherein, to gain the language, / 'Tis needful that the most immodest word / Be looked upon and learnt' (*Henry IV Part Two*, 4.3.68–71).

This chapter does not aim to be prescriptive—to say 'this is how to do it'—but to suggest what happens when you read closely: in other words, to explore the responsibilities and rewards of the practice of close reading. While most of what follows is in one way or another about rewards, it is as well to remember at this stage the responsibility of being as open-minded and as informed a reader as possible. Within the plays themselves (where characters are forever reading each other's words, rightly or wrongly) there is a great deal about such responsibility. 'God forbid', says King Henry V, 'That you should fashion, wrest, or bow your reading' (*Henry V*, 1.2.13–14). He is addressing the Archbishop of Canterbury, asking for a close reading of his own claims to the 'crown and seat of France', fully aware that the possible consequences of the reading are war and its bloody 'waste in brief mortality'. Ironically, the Archbishop then produces a formidable amount of data through which he strains and bends his explication of the Salic Law on which Henry's claim is based, to actualize all those consequences.

In real life the effects of a biased reading are rarely as tragic as this, nor as comic as when, in *Twelfth Night*, Malvolio's self-love makes him read a fake letter as a love missive to himself from Olivia. But it is as well to remember that we are all conditioned in our reading of texts by our own backgrounds and circumstances, by preconceptions—conscious and unconscious—that may make us read not so much what is there as what we want or expect to be there. And that for modern readers of texts that were created four hundred or more years ago there is always the danger of misreading through sheer ignorance. We meet words that may have changed meanings, like the very word 'modern', which in Shakespeare always has the derogatory sense of 'everyday' or 'commonplace' (see Chapter 7). We meet puns, 'immodest' words whose bawdy meaning may be obscure, and allusions—topical, proverbial, classical, and biblical—that may seem meaningless to us. And the texts are bound to contain data and embody assumptions—social, political, and religious—that are unfamiliar. All this points to the importance, in reading 'again and again', of having access to the kinds of information—linguistic, historical, and so on—provided by a good annotated edition of Shakespeare's works.

Reading texts in context

Close reading of Shakespeare begins and ends with the words on the page but, to be effective, cannot take place in a vacuum. The text is inalienably rooted in a context. Shakespeare's words are part of dramatic texts, written to be spoken from a stage and apprehended by an audience as a continuous process in time. The members of early modern audiences were used to listening to sermons that lasted for hours and, whether literate or not, were attentive to structured discourses and verbal details, as we tend not to be. Close reading of what Shakepeare and his contemporaries would have called 'the book of the play' puts us in one sense more on a par with them, in that we can stop the flow and go back over details in the text (some of which may well have been missed by members of Shakespeare's original audience, too). Yet, in another, and crucial, sense we cannot read the Shakespeare text as we would a novel or a poem: first because it is a play, and second because it is a play for the theatre, and a particular kind of theatre at that.

Dramatic as well as narrative fiction tells stories, and like poems Shakespeare's plays use devices such as metre and rhyme as well as charged, often metaphorical, language. But because they are plays, they unroll in time ('the two-hours' traffic of our stage') as neither a novel nor a poem does. Structure is crucial, and *where* in that structure something is said may be as important as *what* is said. Semantically, the word 'see' is the same in the first and the last scene of *King Lear*, but does it mean the same when spoken by the dying Lear, poring over Cordelia's face and asking bystanders to look at her lips, as it did when he swore that he had no such daughter, 'nor shall ever see / That face of hers again' (1.1.264–5)? There is an ironic echo across five acts, the irony turned to tragedy by all the seeing and blindness, literal and metaphorical, in between.

Again, in a play it crucially matters *who* is speaking, and *to whom*. 'Common' means something different spoken by Gertrude, assuring Hamlet that his father's death is in the natural order of things (or commonplace), from the word thrown back at her—'Ay, madam, it is common' (that is, crude)—by Hamlet (1.2. 72–4). The difference measures the gulf between two attitudes. Hamlet also has perhaps the most shifting register of all Shakespeare's characters; he speaks, as it were, different languages to different people. But so also does Prince Hal, who uses one language to his father, King Henry IV, and—until he himself becomes king—another to Falstaff and his Eastcheap tavern companions. The interaction of characters can effect transformations, as when the hero Othello's language appropriates the imagery of the villain Iago, or when Enobarbus, the staunch Roman, is moved by the memory of the Egyptian queen, Cleopatra, at Cydnus to deliver the barge speech (*Antony and Cleopatra*, 2.2.196–224). But if the relation of language to character is important, we also need to be aware that the aesthetic or thematic needs of the play as a whole may override characterization.

Theatrical contexts

Shakespeare's plays were written for the theatre, and as in any text for performance, what is heard (or read) cannot be separated from what is (or is intended to be) seen. Clearly, words are variously prominent agents. They can give us the emotional impact of a scene which we don't witness at all, like Gertrude's description of the drowning of

Ophelia (*Hamlet*, 4.7.137–54), and they can be a powerful means of creating something which both is and is not seen, as in Edgar's description of the non-existent cliff on whose top Gloucester believes he is poised for suicide (*King Lear*, 4.6.1–27). The context can give the simplest phrase the greatest load of power and meaning. In *King Lear* words may sometimes need to point only to what is before us: 'a head / So old and white as this' (3.2.22–3). To articulate his experience of watching the meeting of the mad Lear and the blinded Gloucester, Edgar need only say that it *is*: 'I would not take this from report. It is, / And my heart breaks at it' (4.6.138–9). Elsewhere it is 'report' that builds the dramatic situation. *Antony and Cleopatra* opens with ten highly suggestive lines by Philo on what Antony has allowed his love of Cleopatra to do to him. And then the two lovers enter, and we have to weigh what we actually see and hear against the image that Philo's words have built and are building: 'The triple pillar of the world transformed / Into a strumpet's fool' (*Antony and Cleopatra*, 1.1.12–13).

In Hamlet's soliloquies the language, imitating the movement of thought in the character's mind, *is* the action. But there are also times, as in Leontes's wordless wonder at his wife's 'resurrection' in the last scene of *The Winter's Tale*, when silence communicates more than words. The fatal moment when Coriolanus allows his will to be broken by his mother is held in a stage direction: '[*He*] *holds her by the hand, silent*'; and yet, a few lines earlier, spoken language acts as stage direction when Volumnia creates a tableau of supplication: 'Let us shame him with our knees' (*Coriolanus*, 5.3.183, 170).

Close reading involves awareness of how the particular conditions and conventions of the theatres for which Shakespeare wrote (see Chapter 3) have helped shape his texts. The perception that 'all the world is a stage' is behind the name and motto of the theatre for which he wrote his greatest plays; it also pervades much of what he wrote. In *Julius Caesar*, which was probably the first tragedy played at the Globe, we watch the murder of Caesar and also hear it become, in the words of Cassius, a 'lofty scene' to be 'acted over, / In states unborn and accents yet unknown' (*Julius Caesar*, 3.1.113–14). Metatheatrically, Cleopatra voices her dread of being brought in triumph to Rome and having to watch, in a play about herself, 'Some squeaking Cleopatra boy my greatness / I'th' posture of a whore' (*Antony and Cleopatra*, 5.2.216–17). Like all pre-Restoration dramatists Shakespeare wrote his women's parts for boy (or men) actors—*and* gloried in the way the speeches of his cross-dressed heroines could subvert gender expectations, as in Rosalind's battles of wit with Orlando in *As You Like It*, or Viola's plangent duologue with Orsino in *Twelfth Night*, 2.4.

There was no scenery in the modern sense in Shakespeare's theatres; such sense of place as is necessary for the play is provided by the language: an Ephesus 'full of cozenage' in *The Comedy of Errors* (1.2.97), an 'isle . . . full of noises, / Sounds, and sweet airs' in *The Tempest* (3.2.130–1). Each of the Roman plays establishes by verbal style its particular sense of Rome (and in *Antony and Cleopatra* also of Egypt), and the Forest of Arden (in *As You Like It*), Illyria (in *Twelfth Night*), and Venice (in *The Merchant of Venice* and *Othello*) all have thematic importance. But this is not the same as geographical or historical authenticity. Nor is Shakespearian climate as much meterological as emotional and moral. The condition of Denmark is established within the first few lines of *Hamlet*: ''Tis bitter cold, / And I am sick at heart' Francisco tells us. Plays were acted in natural daylight at the Globe, but the language has its own lighting effects. Following immediately on Lady Macbeth's invocation, 'Come, thick night, / And pall thee in the dunnest smoke of hell', the arrival of King Duncan at Macbeth's castle becomes a halcyon moment of stillness and light: 'This castle hath a pleasant seat. The air / Nimbly and sweetly recommends itself' (1.5.48–9 and 1.6.1–2). But darkness dominates the internal and external worlds of the Macbeths. When he asks 'seeling night' to 'Cancel and tear to pieces that great bond / Which keeps me pale', then 'Light thickens, and the crow / Makes wing to th' rooky wood', and by the next line the landscape is explicitly a moral one: 'Good things of day begin to droop and drowse, / Whiles night's black agents to their preys do rouse' (3.2.47–54).

The text needs to be read with an awareness of how it may have been affected by the social and political realities of performance. As the King's Men's leading playwright, Shakespeare seems to have been uncannily able to internalize external pressures and vice versa. Some of the play texts show cuts, revisions, and additions between an early and a later version (see Chapter 38). Some of these suggest the imposition of censorship from outside, others suggest playhouse experience of what does and does not work. In the case of *Hamlet*, for example, Shakespeare seems to have decided that, as the Oxford editors put it, 'the play as a whole would be better without' the Prince's last soliloquy, 'How all occasions do inform against me'. Unlike any modern playwright, Shakespeare would not have regarded his texts as his own spiritual property; they belonged to the company. But where we can assume that Shakespeare was himself responsible for revisions of his texts—as many do in regard to *King Lear*—we have a genuine marriage of external and internal impulses.

Similarly, overall changes in Shakespeare's style can be seen as both the effect and the cause of a change in acting styles in the Elizabethan and Jacobean theatre, from a more formal to a more natural mode. The language in an early tragedy such as *Titus Andronicus* asks for a declamatory delivery; in the mature plays it seems moulded to the thoughts and voices of characters. Shakespeare mocks obtrusive rhetoric in the Pyramus and Thisbe play in *A Midsummer Night's Dream* and elsewhere, and has Hamlet instruct the players in speaking and acting that 'hold as 'twere the mirror up to nature' (*Hamlet*, 3.2.20). The text can become such a mirror, enabling us to follow—to take just a few examples—the very different ways a mind moves towards the act of murder in a Brutus, an Othello, or a Macbeth. Shakespeare was fortunate to have, in Richard Burbage, a great actor to speak those parts—but then who is to say that it wasn't speaking these parts that made him a great tragic actor?

Close reading will not turn us all into Burbages, but it will give access to the world of Shakespeare's art. Accepting the need to understand at least some of the many external and internal determinants that condition the text, what then does it mean to read closely the words on the page of any one play?

Shakespeare's ways with words

A grasp of context is still needed in order fully to appreciate Shakespeare's creativity in dealing with his raw material. A great borrower (and adapter) of plots, he also often negotiated with the language of his source, transforming it to serve his own purposes. An obvious example is Enobarbus's description of Cleopatra on her barge, where Shakespeare follows in close detail his chief source text for the Roman plays, Thomas North's translation of Plutarch's *Lives of the Noble Grecians and Romans*, and yet gives the scene a life that the source does not have. Where out of North's barge 'there came a wonderful passing sweet savour of perfumes', Shakespeare translates the adjectives—'A strange invisible perfume'—and makes the perfume an agent: 'Purple the sails, and so perfumèd that / The winds were love-sick with them'. North has people running 'out of the city to see [Cleopatra] coming in'; in Shakespeare 'The city cast / Her people out upon her' (2.2.197–220). Words that in themselves are not particularly remarkable are in the context charged with the energy of the unexpected, to make the whole scene, Cleopatra's appearance and Enobarbus's perception of it, *felt*.

Shakespeare's real raw material was of course the English language. If there is a source text for Macbeth's lines when he despairs of washing Duncan's blood off his hands, it is remote, in classical drama; and here Shakespeare gains his effect from the very etymology of English words. In the schizoid state where Macbeth's own hands don't seem to be his, the language itself splits into Latin and Anglo-Saxon roots: 'No, this my hand will rather / The multitudinous seas incarnadine, / Making the green one red' (2.2.59–61). Thus, even as the words on the page suggest a unique verbal imagination, they also remind us that this imagination had, in the English of the late sixteenth and early seventeenth century, a uniquely expanding and flexible medium to operate in.

Thanks to scholars who have compiled dictionaries and concordances, we have statistical proof of Shakespeare's ever-expanding vocabulary: of the number of words in any one play which were new to Shakespeare, or new to the English language, or invented for a particular play and never to be used by him again. *Hamlet* is particularly high in all these categories but is only one illustration of what the statistics mean: that each of Shakespeare's plays demanded its own vocabulary, and that new experiences needed new words. Unless the dramatic context requires it—as with 'the mobbled queen' in *Hamlet* (2.2.452–4)—it is not a question of newness for newness' sake. *Love's Labour's Lost* laughs at the affectation of newfangledness and pedantry. But when the otherwise ribald Lucio tells Isabella 'I hold you as a thing enskied and sainted' (*Measure for Measure*, 1.4.33), the new word 'enskied' marks the shift from his normal tone and so, by this almost literal elevation of Isabella, it also marks the gulf that separates her from other girls and that is so central to the play as a whole.

Treating vocabulary and grammar as malleable, Shakespeare redirects the energy of verbs by adding prefixes and shifts the function of words, turning verbs into nouns and vice versa. Edgar's expression of feeling not only *for* but *with* Lear, 'He childed as I fathered' (*King Lear*, 3.6.103), does things to the language which are abnormal but appropriate in a play in which parents and children do abnormal things to each other, and in which Cordelia is soon to beg the gods to cure 'this child-changéd father' (4.7.17).[2] Whether her words mean that Lear is changed into a child or that he is changed by his children, or both, may be a deliberate ambiguity. Compounding words, as here, to make out of the combination of two something which is more than the sum of both, serves Shakespeare all the way from the solemn, as in Cleopatra's death-scene ('Now from head to foot / I am marble-constant', 5.2.235–6), to the abusive, as when Leontes calls his wife Hermione 'A bed-swerver' (*The Winter's Tale*, 2.1.95).

On the page, the category of words which perhaps most clearly shows Shakespeare's moulding of language is that of words beginning with an *un-*. He uses more than 600 different words with that prefix, about a fourth of which were new to the language, and about half of which he uses only once. Behind these statistics lies his extraordinary fondness for expressing negatives as contradictories of the corresponding positive terms. Richard II is 'unkinged', Lady Macbeth asks spirits to 'unsex' her, Mark Antony comes 'smiling from / The world's great snare uncaught' (*Antony and Cleopatra*, 4.9.17–18). In each case the *un*-word sets up a tension between the negative and the positive and so creates a sense, within what is, of what could have been. Vocabulary, it seems, is to Shakespeare something not only malleable but also inherently dramatic.

Shakespeare wrote in an age of intense concern, in practically all spheres of social and cultural life, with what language is and what it can do (see Chapter 7); and across the corpus we constantly come across signs of such concern. His characters discuss language, play with it, reflect on it. All these things are done superbly by Hamlet, for one, and Falstaff, for another. Falstaff has an inimitable 'catechism' on the meaning—or, rather, non-meaning—of the word 'honour' (*Henry IV Part One*, 5.1.127–39). At one extreme Hamlet voices the possibility that 'words, words, words' may be merely false; at another they are his chief weapon. As he goes to confront his mother, he 'will speak daggers to her', and indeed Gertrude finds that 'These words like daggers enter in mine ears' (3.2.366, 3.4.85). Ears and tongues in the plays tend to be both literal and metaphorical. Speech is both a physical and a moral act. Obsessed with Isabella, Angelo tries to pray but finds that his words are empty: 'God in my mouth, / As if I did but only chew his name' (*Measure for Measure*, 2.4.4–5).[3]

To Shakespeare's characters, then, speech can be both performative and utterly inadequate. Paradoxically, some of Shakespeare's most powerful language, such as Angelo's speech just quoted, is about the emptiness of words, and the dialogue between Angelo and Isabella which follows on his monologue is one of the most stunning examples of what people can do to each other with words. In expressing Angelo's self-division as a division between language and meaning, Shakespeare the dramatist shows the power of language to persuade us of the human realities of a situation. His interest in words is functional, and sometimes their function is to point to their own slipperiness, to the gap between language and truth. Angelo is not a professional hypocrite, but Richard III is, and Macbeth struggles to be one: 'False face must hide what the false heart doth know' (1.7.82). In *King Lear*, Goneril draws on the very topic of language's inadequacy to profess (falsely) to her father Lear: 'Sir, I love you more than words can wield the matter' (1.1.53). Like many of the statesmen in the English history plays, Claudius in his long first speech in *Hamlet* (1.2.1–39) is adept at manipulating his onstage audience into accepting his version of the state of affairs, public and private.

Shakespeare's ways with rhetoric

Elaborate rhetoric, like Claudius's, can be a sign of insincerity, but it need not be. In theory and practice—both exemplified in the period's numerous books on rhetoric—Shakespeare's age was fascinated with the tropes and figures into which language can be structured, and with the effect of these on a reader or an audience. Shakespeare, grammar-school trained in the arts of language, moved into acting and playwriting in a context assured of the dramatic potential and audience appeal of formally patterned language. He inherited conventions such as rhetorical laments and the rapid-fire, alternate-lines dialogue known as *stichomythia*. In so far as rhetoric is about the control of structures and audiences, Shakespeare was a rhetorician throughout his career. Nor did he ever abandon the structuring principles behind the most popular figures of rhetoric: repetition, parallelism or contrast, and antithesis. But he soon became more flexible in his use of such figures, bending them, as he bent vocabulary, to his own needs for dramatic expressiveness. They are deeply and movingly functional when Romeo and Juliet meet and progress to a kiss on the shared lines of a formal sonnet (1.5.90–103), or when Richard II resigns his crown in an inverted coronation ceremony (*Richard II*, 4.1.191–212). *Stichomythia* finds searingly ironic uses in *Hamlet* (3.4.9–10):

> GERTRUDE: Hamlet, thou hast thy father much offended.
> HAMLET: Mother, you have my father much offended.

As early as in *Love's Labour's Lost*, a play much dependent on artificial modes of speech, we find its most eloquent character (Biron) prompted by a 'real' death to criticize such modes: 'Honest plain words best pierce the ear of grief' (5.2.735). Much later in Shakespeare's career Timon of Athens cuts short the effusions of the Poet, who cannot find words large enough to 'cover / The monstrous bulk' of Athenian ingratitude, with a blunt 'Let it go naked; men may see't the better' (5.1.61–4). Going naked is also what Edgar finds himself doing in the closing speech of *King Lear*: 'The weight of this sad time we must obey; / Speak what we feel, not what we ought to say' (5.3.322–3).[4] This is the rhetoric of non-rhetoric. But speaking what you feel should not, in mature Shakespeare, be equated with the naturalism of 'plain words': more often than not it is a matter of intricately woven rhetoric, as any one of the tragedies or the romances will demonstrate.

Nor, the reader will find, should levels of rhetorical artifice be equated with the difference between verse and prose. Shakespeare largely conformed to the stylistic conventions of the drama of his period by giving prose to speakers of an inferior class—servants or clowns—and blank verse (unrhymed iambic pentameter) to their betters. In *Twelfth Night*, which is 61 per cent prose, the carnivalesque world round Sir Toby Belch is marked by the absence of verse. Yet, as we can see in *Much Ado About Nothing* and *As You Like It*, or in the structured spontaneity of Falstaff's language, Shakespeare's comic prose often utilizes and adapts highly artificial rhetorical patterns. What is more, he moulded the prose/verse convention to his own needs by using shifts from one mode to another to mark a change in a situation or character. Hamlet's rapid shifts of moods and attitudes—and not only in and out of an 'antic disposition'—are thus marked. Lady Macbeth's prose when sleepwalking (5.1) marks her loss of control of her mind; and Othello breaks down into near-inarticulate frenzy: 'Noses, ears, and lips! Is't possible? Confess? Handkerchief? O devil!' (4.1.40–1).

The growth of obsessive jealousy in Leontes happens in verse, but in a flexible medium that could accommodate the broken syntax of his disordered thinking: 'Inch-thick, knee-deep, o'er head and ears a forked one!— / Go play, boy, play. Thy mother plays, and I / Play too' (*The Winter's Tale*, 1.2.187–9). To set his speeches (or any speech in the great tragedies) alongside an early Shakespeare play is to note how Shakespearian blank verse developed to admit the rhythms of the speaking voice, without losing the advantages of metre (see Chapter 8). When Titus Andronicus reacts to finding his daughter raped and mutilated, emotion is held in rigidly end-stopped lines with a mid-line caesura (pause for breath): 'It was my dear, and he that wounded her / Hath hurt me more than had he killed me dead' (3.1.91–2).

Wordplay

Though separated by almost all Shakespeare's playwriting years, the just-quoted lines of Titus Andronicus and Leontes are alike in pivoting on a play of words: 'dear' and 'play'. In the case of Titus, one feels, it is Shakespeare who cannot resist squeezing the dear/deer homophone for what it is worth, whereas it is Leontes's self-engendered suspicion that is mirrored in the leap from the boy's innocent play to the implied sexuality of the mother's, and so on to the disgrace of the father's. Wordplay—linking disparate thoughts and images through a word with two or more meanings—is endemic in Shakespeare's corpus and forms one of the great challenges (and rewards) to the close reader. Certain words—like 'dear', 'lie', 'act', 'state', or 'grace', let alone all those capable of signifying sexual organs or functions, of which 'will' and 'die' are only the most obvious—are almost certain to signal a pun, comic or serious; but Shakespeare can wring multiple meanings out of apparently safe words, like 'satisfy' in *The Winter's Tale* (1.2.233–6). Wordplay is operative in comic (not least bawdy) wit and central to the embattled wooing of the great couples: Katherine and Petruccio, Rosaline and Biron, Beatrice and Benedick. But it also has darker sides: the malapropisms of clown-ish Dogberry are pure fun, but Feste, the Fool in *Twelfth Night*, proclaims himself a 'corrupter of words', and his wordplay, like the Fool's in *King Lear*, goes straight to the thematic centre of the play. In the tragedies puns can be obvious and deliberate, as when the mortally wounded Mercutio declares himself 'a grave man' (*Romeo and Juliet*, 3.1.94) or Hamlet is 'too much i'th'sun' (1.2.67). But they also tend to grow into extended playing on ambivalent key-words: this happens to words like 'nature' and 'kind' in *King Lear*, or 'fortune' in *Timon of Athens*.

Characters play with words, and with or against or around them the author plays with language itself. A deep sense of the ambivalence of words—their range of meanings, which at one extreme topples into no meaning—penetrates the mature plays. The texts of individual plays hammer away at certain words as if to crack them open: 'honest' in *Othello*, for example, or 'value' in *Troilus and Cressida*. The action of each play is intertwined with an action in the language itself, and this is reflected not just in the semantics but in the grammar and syntax of the text. The language of *Antony and Cleopatra* abounds in superlatives. Time is a central concern of *Macbeth*; and Macbeth moves from a state marked by the future tense and the subjunctive mood ('If it were done when 'tis done' (1.7.1)) to one of eternal, meaningless present: 'Tomorrow, and tomorrow, and tomorrow / Creeps in this petty pace from day to day / To the last syllable of recorded time' (5.5.18–20). *Hamlet* is dominated by questions. Lear goes from bold imperatives to utterly basic questions and a humble request for a button to be undone.

Imagery

The close reader, then, will find in each play its own particular language, its idiolect. Perhaps the element of that language which most determines its tone and colour, its range, and even its cohesiveness, is metaphor. It is understandable that, for several decades in the twentieth century, one of the major ways into Shakespeare was through his imagery, since such an approach could both demonstrate the associative power of the poet's imagination and reveal the important dramatic functions of single and recurrent metaphors. A wealth of insights awaits the close reader here. Take the way Macbeth's argument in the 'If it were done when 'tis done' speech is carried forward by a chain of images, linked by rapid association, and the way those images bring whole other spheres of reference into the play (most memorably 'pity, like a naked new-born babe'). Or the way earlier plays are more given to extended comparisons—similes which tell a whole illustrative story—while later a sudden brief image will measure the intensity of an experience, as when Lear is 'bound / Upon a wheel of fire' (4.7.46–7), or bring in an analysis and evaluation of it, as when Hamlet thinks this world 'an unweeded garden' (1.2.135). Metaphors will irrupt into action, and vice versa, as with poison in *Hamlet* or eyesight in *King Lear*. And more and more Shakespeare developed a unique art of making iterative images not only create the dominant mood of a play but also form a kind of subtext of signs and their meanings, whereby the emotive texture and the intellectual structure of the play is sustained and enriched.

Exploring this aspect of the words on the page may well form the ultimate reward of close reading, if only because it so keenly suggests that Shakespeare's texts are the product of an extraordinary coming together of verbal and dramatic creativity, one which can be defined only by borrowing his own words from 'The Phoenix and Turtle': 'Single nature's double name' (39).

FURTHER READING

Adamson, S., Hunter, L., Magnusson, L., Thompson, A., and Wales, K. (eds.). *Reading Shakespeare's Dramatic Language: A Guide* (London: Thompson Learning, for the Arden Shakespeare, 2001). This is a collection of essays which together form a comprehensive guide to the study of Shakespeare's language, with particular emphasis on its dramatic and theatrical qualities.

Crystal, David and Crystal, Ben. *Shakespeare's Words: A Glossary and Language Companion* (London: Penguin Books, 2002). This companion to Shakespeare's language is particularly useful for the student who wants to look up unfamiliar words.

Edwards, P., Ewbank, I.-S., and Hunter, G. K. (eds.). *Shakespeare's Styles* (Cambridge: Cambridge University Press, 1980). This collection of essays provides a guide to the various ways in which Shakespeare's stylistic techniques may be discussed. Each essay proceeds from close reading of a particular passage in a play, ranging from *Henry VI Part Two* to *The Tempest*.

Empson, W. *The Structure of Complex Words* (London: Chatto & Windus, 1951; Penguin Books, 1995). This is a book for the student who wants to think about the multiple meanings of words. The chapters on 'Fool in *Lear*', 'Timon's Dog', 'Honest in *Othello*', and 'Sense in *Measure for Measure*' deal specifically with Shakespeare.

Kermode, F. *Shakespeare's Language* (London: Allen Lane, 2000). This book provides both a comprehensive introduction to the study of Shakespeare's language and a subtle analysis of the writing in individual plays.

Mahood, M. *Shakespeare's Wordplay* (London: Methuen, 1957; University Paperback, 1968, 1979). This book remains the most comprehensive guide to Shakespeare's use of words with double or multiple meanings. The analysis and discussion move across the entire corpus of plays.

Spevack, M. *The Harvard Concordance to Shakespeare* (Cambridge, Mass.: Harvard University Press, 1973). This is a complete one-volume concordance to all the plays and poems of Shakespeare. Detailed statistical analysis of neologisms, etc. can be found in Spevack's multi-volume *Complete and Systematic Concordance to the Works of Shakespeare* (Hildesheim, 1968–70).

Vendler, H. *The Art of Shakespeare's Sonnets*. This book deals specifically with the *Sonnets*, but, as an outstanding example of close reading of Shakespeare's poetry, can also guide the reading of the plays.

Vickers, B. *The Artistry of Shakespeare's Prose* (London: Methuen, 1968). This book provides a comprehensive guide to the study of Shakespeare's prose, including his use of formal rhetoric.

Wright, G. *Shakespeare's Metrical Art* (Berkeley: University of California Press, 1988). This is a comprehensive survey of Shakespeare's metrical techniques. The discussion focuses on how his use of iambic pentameter adds to the expressiveness of his characters' stage language.

NOTES

1. In the history of literary criticism, the *term* 'close reading' has come to be associated with particular mid-twentieth-century critical agendas ('New Criticism' in the US, 'Practical Criticism' in the UK) which—in reaction against a tradition of reading Shakespeare's works as revealing Shakespeare the man—insisted on revealing the art of each work by disciplined attention to the words on the page. However mistakenly, the *critical term* 'close reading' sometimes refers to an anti-historical approach concerned with the text as a self-sufficient object, severed from author and reader and from its context in time and place. This chapter, on the other hand, is about close reading as a *critical practice* which begins with the words on the page but endeavours to see them in their full context.

2. Edgar's soliloquy is in the 1608 quarto only, whereas Cordelia's 'child-changéd' is in both Q and F.

3. This reading assumes that when *Measure for Measure* was first printed, in the 1623 Folio, an original 'God' had been replaced by 'Heaven', as a consequence of the 1606 Act to Restrain Abuse of Players, which ordered the censorship of profane oaths and had the effect of more or less removing the name of God from dramatic texts.

4. In the 1608 quarto this speech is given to Albany.

READING: *Richard III*

Close reading of *Richard III* may at first seem a formidable task. Here is a long play—longer than any other Shakespeare play except *Hamlet*—with a huge and bewildering array of historical characters, many of whom are related to each other in complicated and significant ways, some of whom even have the same name, and nearly all of whom speak a highly stylized language. But here is also a play known to have been very popular in its own time, both as text and in performance; and a play that has been a stage and screen success in our time. To discover why this is not a paradox is probably the main challenge to the close reader, for here is a text whose qualities of language and style are inseparable from its dramatic and theatrical energies.

Text and history

The editors of the 1623 Folio naturally put *Richard III* among the histories, but they titled it *The Tragedy of Richard III*. In this dual genre identity lies a peculiar strength. It is both a play about England—the culmination of a tetralogy of plays about the Wars of the Roses—and a play about the rise to and fall from kingship of a character of extraordinary evil energy, and as such a poetic drama in its own right. The memory of events dramatized in the three *Henry VI* plays rests heavy on *Richard III*, and for background the close reader is well advised to look back at least to *Henry VI Part Three*, to the murder of young Rutland, Queen Margaret's taunting of York, and the killings of Prince Edward and Henry VI. In the closing speech of *Richard III* the new King Henry VII announces the end of an age when 'England hath long been mad, and scarred herself'. The figure of Richard Gloucester, who becomes King Richard III, embodies and enacts that madness and scarring, but before meeting him in his own play, the reader would do well to refer to his self-defining monologue after stabbing King Henry VI: 'I am myself alone' (*Henry VI Part Three*, 5.6.61–94).

The stretch of history that Shakespeare dramatizes was only just over 100 years old. His ultimate source was Sir Thomas More's *History of Richard III*, which was transmitted into the *Chronicles* of Edward Hall and Raphael Holinshed, where Shakespeare encountered it. In real life More had absorbed virulent anti-Richard attitudes from his patron, who appears in the play as the Bishop of Ely. On the throne as Shakespeare wrote was Elizabeth I, the granddaughter of Henry VII, the conquering hero of the play. No wonder that the play can be read as a piece of Tudor propaganda. But read as a dramatic structure, it can be seen to telescope events into a dynamic process from one 'Now' to another: from Richard's opening speech, 'Now is the winter of our discontent / Made glorious summer by this son of York', to King Henry's closing, 'Now civil wounds are stopped; peace lives again. / That she may long live here, God say "Amen" '. There is no physical violence on stage between the murder of Clarence in the first act and the battle in the last; the violence is in the language, and the dynamism is in what people do to themselves and each other through words. To achieve this, Shakespeare transforms his source texts. For example, Holinshed's account of Henry VI's bleeding corpse, 'The dead corpse . . . laid on a bier or coffin bare-faced, the same in the presence of the beholders did bleed', becomes Lady Anne's attack on Richard Gloucester, the murderer whose presence provokes the bleeding:

> O gentlemen, see, see! Dead Henry's wounds
> Ope their congealèd mouths and bleed afresh.—
> Blush, blush, thou lump of foul deformity,
> For 'tis thy presence that ex-hales this blood
> From cold and empty veins where no blood dwells.
> (1.2.55-9)

And the dialogue over the coffin which follows, a battle of words by the end of which Richard has persuaded Anne to marry him, is Shakespeare's invention altogether. So also are the appearances of Henry VI's widow, Queen Margaret, whose prophecies and curses bring the past into the play's present and establish a retributive pattern. There is no chronicle source for Clarence's dream the night before he is murdered (1.4.3–63); here is an opportunity to see Shakespeare bringing together materials from a number of classical and native English sources and re-moulding them to create a dramatic narrative of nightmarish fear and guilt.

Textual history

The reader exploring the text needs to be aware that *Richard III* has a complex textual history. The first edition of the play, a 1597 quarto, was followed by five more quartos, all derivative from the first, before the First Folio was printed. The Folio has more than 200 lines not in the quarto, but the quarto has passages not in the Folio; and there are hundreds of variants in vocabulary, sentence structure, stage directions, and so on. In some cases the differences may suggest theatrical cuts, as when the quarto lacks fifty-four lines of Richard's rhetorical ingenuity in the wooing of Queen Elizabeth for the hand of her daughter (after 4.4.273). But, for reasons too complex to go into here, the quarto cannot in its entirety be a revision of the Folio, nor the Folio of the quarto. We are, then, reading a text which is in some ways unreliable, but this is no excuse for not reading closely. On the contrary, where there is a possibility of an alternative reading, this becomes a stimulus to sharper thinking about the words on the page. Besides, none of these possibilities alters the overall and dominant characteristics of the text.

Theatricality

Those characteristics are above all theatrical: not the spectacular theatricality of pageants and processions, but a fearful symmetry of bodies in space, and of their language. Twice—in 2.2 and 4.4—a chorus of women (and in 2.2 also children) lament their losses, either in a crescendo of parallel single lines (*stichomythia*), as in 2.2.72–8, or in a cross-fire which turns history into a pattern of gruesome parallels:

> QUEEN MARGARET: I had an Edward, till a Richard killed him;
> I had a husband, till a Richard killed him.
> (*To Elizabeth*) Thou hadst an Edward, till a Richard killed him;
> Thou hadst a Richard, till a Richard killed him.
> DUCHESS OF YORK [*rising*]: I had a Richard too, and thou didst kill him;
> I had a Rutland too, thou holpst to kill him.
>
> (4.4.40-5)

Twice—in 1.2 and 4.4—Richard woos and wins (though the second time the winning may be only apparent) where he has killed a woman's nearest and dearest. But the symmetry of parallelisms and contrasts catches up with him in the night before the battle of Bosworth. Unlike Clarence's narrated nightmare, this is a double dream, staged like an embodied and extended antithesis. On one side of the stage is Richard's tent, on the other Richmond's, as the ghosts of all those whom Richard has murdered enter, each to rehearse his (or, in the case of Lady Anne, her) grievance and to curse Richard, wishing that he may 'Despair and die', and then to bless Richmond and wish him victory.

The reader soon becomes aware that the theatricality rests not only in the patterning of scenes but in the explicit self-consciousness that the author has given to the characters. To announce the death of King Edward, his Queen enters appropriately dishevelled, '*with her hair about her ears*' (Folio stage direction), and when her mother-in-law, the Duchess of York, questions her wailing—'What means this scene of rude impatience?'—she responds in the same theatrical terms: 'To mark [or, in both Quarto and Folio, make] an act of tragic violence' (2.2.34–9). Her grief is genuine, but often the theatrical references point to pretence. Richard enters upon his 'cue' (3.4.26) and stages a macabre scene, accusing Hastings of 'devilish plots'. To justify the sudden execution of Hastings, Richard and Buckingham appear costumed '*in rotten armour, marvellous ill-favoured*' (Folio stage direction) and, challenged by Richard on his ability to act and speak as if 'distraught and mad with terror', Buckingham insists that he 'can counterfeit the deep tragedian' and proceeds to describe his repertoire of body languages (3.5.1–11). In Act Three Scene Seven the entire scene—in which Richard ('*aloft, between two bishops*') is nearly too clever at pretending unwillingness to become king—is elaborately stage-managed.

To make the audience in the theatre so aware of what the stage audience does not grasp is clearly an ironic technique with comic potential, and no one practises it more than Richard himself. He is not only the most accomplished actor within the play but is also forever drawing the attention of the audience to his artistry. He blatantly reviews his performance: 'And thus I clothe my naked villainy / With odd old ends, stol'n forth of Holy Writ, / And seem a saint when most I play the devil' (1.3.334–6). He even tells us what is, quite literally, his role model:

> RICHARD GLOUCESTER (*aside*): So wise so young, they say, do never live long.
> PRINCE EDWARD: What say you, uncle?
> RICHARD GLOUCESTER: I say, 'Without characters fame lives long'.
>   (*Aside*) Thus like the formal Vice, Iniquity,
>   I moralize two meanings in one word.
>
> (3.1.79-83)

The 'formal'—here meaning 'conventional'—Vice, a favourite character in sixteenth-century morality plays, was an intriguer who, while embodying all the evils of the world, was also a showman-comedian, master both of duplicity and of the art of drawing the audience into a conspiratorial relationship with him. That Shakespeare's Prince Hal, acting the part of the King, refers to Falstaff as 'that reverend Vice, that grey Iniquity' (*Henry IV Part One*, 2.5.413) may remind us of the amoral pull towards anarchy which the Vice figure exerts. Richard Gloucester's demonic gusto gives him just that pull. Even without his sinister chuckle—'Was ever woman in this humour wooed? / Was ever woman in this humour won?' (1.2.215–16)—it is impossible not to enjoy the perverse logic with which his language captures Anne:

> RICHARD GLOUCESTER: It is a quarrel most unnatural,
>   To be revenged on him that loveth you.
> LADY ANNE: It is a quarrel just and reasonable,
>   To be revenged on him that killed my husband.
> RICHARD GLOUCESTER: He that bereft thee, lady, of thy husband,
>   Did it to help thee to a better husband.
>
> (1.2.134-9)

Patterns of language and structure

The pattern which the language displays here, of repetitions which produce inversions or reversals of meaning, is also the play's dominant pattern of dramatic construction. We see it in details: the two murderers of Clarence, true to convention, speak prose with each other, but in the encounter with their victim they move into a stichomythic verse pattern pitching 'royal' against 'loyal' (1.4.154–9). We see it in the play as a whole, in that reversals in the action are expressed as ironic reversals of characters' apprehension of words spoken earlier. Anne recalls, word for word, her initial curse on Richard ('If ever he have wife'; 1.2.26–8), every word of which has now come to apply to herself (4.1.65–86). Buckingham on his way to execution (5.1.12–29) sees himself caught both by the prophecy of Margaret which he once scorned as a meaningless curse (1.3.295–302) and by his own vow to King Edward (2.1.32–5): punished as he asked to be if he broke it.

The antithesis of false and true, which we see played out in the lines of *stichomythia* as

Anne begins to capitulate, is equally a structuring principle of language and action in the play as a whole:

> LADY ANNE: I would I knew thy heart.
> RICHARD GLOUCESTER: 'Tis figured in my tongue.
> LADY ANNE: I fear me both are false.
> RICHARD GLOUCESTER: Then never man was true.
> (1.2.180-3)

Richard may claim that he is as he is because he is 'Cheated of feature by dissembling nature, / Deformed, unfinished' (1.1.19–20), but it is also clear that he is only an extreme, and often extremely funny, example of the 'dissembling' public morality in his world. He does not have a monopoly on devious uses of language. Moralizing two meanings in one word, Catesby tells Hastings that 'The Princes both make high account of you' and then, in an aside, hands the audience the other meaning: 'For they account his head upon the bridge'. Hastings's complacent response to the line he did hear—'I know they do, and I have well deserved it' (3.2.66–8)—ironically gains its own double meaning from the image of his head mounted high on London Bridge, as decapitated traitors' heads were. Richard is brilliant at wordplay, from the pun on the 'son' of York in his very first line. But so are other characters, not least his young namesake, the ominously 'parlous [that is, shrewd] boy' (3.1.153).

Language and truth, it becomes clear, have parted company in the political world of the play. As the Scrivener says, who has copied out the indictment of Hastings (and who is clearly brought on just to say this): 'Who is so gross / That cannot see this palpable device? / Yet who so bold but says he sees it not?' (3.6.10–12). It is doubly ironic that, when the dying King Edward urges the warring factions in the court to be reconciled, he insists that they 'do it unfeignedly' (2.1.22). It is in this scene of apparent sincerity that Buckingham swears the oath of loyalty to the King's side that he will violate and that Richard Gloucester has his most cringingly insincere speech, at once—like Dickens's Uriah Heep—a hypocrite and a Pharisee: 'I thank my God for my humility' (2.1.73). Whereupon he springs the bomb of the death of Clarence (2.1.80), and the scene culminates in the King's conscience-stricken lament. These words—Edward's last in the play—are no less 'unfeigned' for extending over thirty formally structured lines. Rhetoric does not equal insincerity in this play; moulded according to context it is the play's idiom, its vernacular. At this relatively early stage in his career Shakespeare is drawing freely on rhetorical models, such as the set speeches of Senecan tragedy. Recognizing his models helps us to recognize his re-modelling of them to create the world of the play.

If the language of *Richard III* is more in the service of the play as a thematic whole than of characterization, this does not exclude psychological insight. Queen Margaret, whose contribution to the whole might seem the most ritualized, also has lines of acute perception. 'What?' she asks, in words which catch the temporary shifting of allegiances in a group faced with a common enemy, 'Were you snarling all before I came, / Ready to catch each other by the throat, / And turn you all your hatred now on me?' (1.3.185–7). The women of the play function, like the women of devastated Troy, as a chorus of mourners; but they are also the ones who are made to question the very use and function of language. Queen

Elizabeth, mourning the death of her young sons, turns to Margaret for help: 'My words are dull. O quicken them with thine!', and is assured that suffering translates directly into language: 'Thy woes will make them sharp and pierce like mine'. At that point the Duchess of York throws in a radical question: 'Why should calamity be full of words?' (4.4.124–6).

This provokes Elizabeth into thinking what words are for. In one of the textually most debated passages of the play (which therefore needs particularly close reading), she attempts to define the gap between words and reality. Words are insubstantial: 'Windy attorneys to their client woes'. *But* they are therapeutic: 'Though what they will impart / Help nothing else, yet do they ease the heart'. The Duchess of York seizes on this point:

> If so, then be not tongue-tied; go with me,
> And in the breath of bitter words let's smother
> My damnèd son, that thy two sweet sons smothered.
> (4.4.127-34)

The fact that Richard has literally had the two young princes 'smothered' (as described by Tyrrell in 4.3.1–22) makes the smothering by 'the breath of bitter words' both more and less of a metaphor. Less, because the sheer rhetorical parallelism enforces a retributive logic: a smother for a smother. More, because the logic of Elizabeth's preceding lines enforces the metaphorical status of words, their inability to *do* anything other than 'ease the heart'. They do, of course, do a great deal more in the play as a whole; and the impotent women's position is not the author's. The passage points his interest in the nature and function of language, and in what can be achieved by figures—the physical shaping and structuring of language—and by tropes: image-making devices like metaphor and allegory.

Images in *Richard III* are rarely the rapid associative metaphors that we find in later Shakespeare, where characters seem to think in images. Here they are mostly deliberate rhetorical tools, used to convey feelings and/or a state of affairs, as Queen Margaret does in an inversion of Richard's opening speech: 'So now prosperity begins to mellow / And drop into the rotten mouth of death' (4.4.1–2). They often lengthen into mini-allegories, as when Richmond refers to Richard as 'The wretched, bloody, and usurping boar' and then expounds how this 'foul swine' is disembowelling the country and its people (5.2.7–11). The identification of Richard with his heraldic badge (a white boar) tends, as here, to become a jumping-off point for articulating his beastliness: the 'sty' of his regime (4.5.2), the 'abortive, rooting hog' that he is (1.3.225). Other animal imagery crowds around him, turning his physical deformity into a moral one: he is a 'toad', a 'foul bunch-backed toad', a 'bottled spider'; in relation to the young princes he is a 'wolf' or a 'dog' that preys on 'lambs'. Infernal imagery intensifies the sinister aura: he is 'hell's black intelligencer' and a 'hell-hound that doth hunt us all to death' (4.4.71, 48).

For all the suggestive power of these metaphors, the reader might often find the simple words of a literal statement even more powerful, made so by context and juxtaposition. Again and again this happens to family nomenclature, as in the scathing ironies of Queen Elizabeth asking 'Under what title' she should woo her daughter for Richard:

> What were I best to say? Her father's brother
> Would be her lord? Or shall I say her uncle?
> Or he that slew her brothers and her uncles?[1]
>
> (4.4.273, 50-3)

It happens to the first person pronoun in the speech which results from Richard's dream:

> What do I fear? Myself? There's none else by.
> Richard loves Richard; that is, I am I.
> Is there a murderer here? No. Yes, I am.
> Then fly! What, from myself? Great reason. Why?
>
> (5.5.136-9)

The tyrant and Vice has become a schizophrenic whose 'I' is split into two; no 'I am I'[2] can contain both a murderer and a moral conscience. Shakespeare was later to articulate such a split more subtly, in Macbeth. Here the choppy rhetoric of Richard's agony has its own peculiar power as a version of the play's idiom of repetition and inversion. And, finally, in this play that so lives in and by speech, it is peculiarly appropriate that Richard's conscience is embodied in a chorus of *tongues*:

> My conscience hath a thousand several tongues,
> And every tongue brings in a several tale,
> And every tale condemns me for a villain.
>
> (5.5.147-9)

FURTHER READING

Brooke, N. *Shakespeare's Early Tragedies* (London: Methuen, 1968). The chapter on *Richard III* in this book remains a sympathetic and also challenging discussion of genre, seeing the play in its own right and not merely as a prelude to the 'great tragedies'.

Bullough, G. *Narrative and Dramatic Sources of Shakespeare*, Vol. 3 (*Earlier English History Plays*) (London: Routledge and Kegan Paul, 1966). This collection of sources—complete texts, excerpts, and analogues—is indispensable for the student who wants to know how Shakespeare used and adapted his raw material.

Clemen, W. *A Commentary on Shakespeare's 'Richard III'* (London: Methuen, 1968). This is the most exhaustively thorough study, scene by scene, of Shakespeare's handling of language in the play, particularly useful for the student interested in the dramatic function of rhetorical devices.

Jowett, J. (ed.). *William Shakespeare: 'Richard III'* (Oxford: Oxford University Press, 2000). One section of the Introduction to this edition focuses helpfully on textual problems; other sections provide a useful guide to how the play, has been, and can be, read on the page and on the stage.

Kermode, F. *Shakespeare's Language* (London: Allen Lane, 2000). This book provides both a comprehensive introduction to the study of Shakespeare's language and a subtle analysis of the writing in individual plays, and includes an analysis of the language of *Richard III*.

Mahood, M. *Shakespeare's Wordplay* (London: Methuen, 1957; University Paperback, 1968, 1979). This book remains the most comprehensive guide to Shakespeare's use of words with double or multiple meanings. The analysis and discussion move across the entire corpus of plays, including *Richard III*.

Miner, M. M. ' "Neither Mother, Wife, nor England's Queen": The Roles of Women in *Richard III*'. In

Lenz, C., Greene, G., and Neely, C.T. (eds.). *The Woman's Part* (Urbana: University of Illinois Press, 1980), pp. 35–55. This essay studies Richard's employment of women as scapegoats.

Rossiter, A. P. 'The Unity of *Richard III*'. In *Angel With Horns* (London: Longmans, 1961), pp. 1–22. An influential essay which has not dated, this remains a model for the study of Shakespeare's blending of historical and moral themes and of his creation of a hero who is a 'diabolic humorist'.

NOTES

1. These lines are in the Folio but not in the quartos.
2. The first quarto reads 'I and I', which points the two 'I's even more strongly.

| **Feminist criticism**

Jean E. Howard

What is feminist criticism?

Shakespeare's plays are full of puzzling occurrences. At the beginning of *The Winter's Tale*, one of Shakespeare's last plays, the main character, King Leontes, suddenly becomes extremely jealous of his wife and, though lacking any evidence, decides she must be having an affair with his oldest friend. In *Hamlet*, probably Shakespeare's most famous tragedy, Prince Hamlet is ordered by the ghost of his father to take revenge on the uncle who has murdered him. But for much of the play the Prince delays his revenge and instead turns his anger against his mother, Gertrude, even though the Ghost has commanded him to leave her alone. Why does Hamlet do this? And why does Leontes suddenly grow suspicious of his wife? There is no one answer to either question, but feminist criticism is a mode of analysis that helps make sense of dilemmas such as these in which gender issues seem to lie at the heart of a play's mystery.

Gender refers to the distinctions cultures make between people and things based on the idea of sexual difference. In contemporary culture we assume that there are two sexes, men and women, and that biology, at least in part, dictates the attributes associated with each. But biology alone cannot explain the elaborate and varied systems cultures have employed in distinguishing masculine and feminine domains and qualities. In some times and places women have been associated with the body and men with reason; but the reverse is also true. Similarly, in some cultures women perform domestic work only, and the feminine is associated with the home and family. In other cultures, however, women perform paid work and are religious leaders, healers, and warriors in the public sphere. The infinite variety of gender definitions and roles suggests that gender distinctions are not so much securely based on innate biological differences as they are constructed, or built, by human effort as part of specific historical conditions. Though gender systems vary, however, what does not change from culture to culture, period to period, is the persistence of gender difference as a central system for organizing society. In every culture known to human beings, gender codes and expectations help to determine what different kinds of work men and women do, how much status they have, what cultural benefits they enjoy, as well as distinguishing valued from less valued activities and skills.

Fig. 3.2 With its images of widow, wife, and maid, this illustration from 1609 shows the most common categorization of women in the early modern period.

Feminist literary criticism attempts to understand the role literary texts play in helping to construct, to reflect, and sometimes to undermine the gender categories, codes, and expectations unique to a given culture. Shakespeare, for example, lived in a patriarchal culture, by which historians mean a culture in which authority and privilege is particularly invested in the hands of the father, or patriarch, of a family. Wives are subordinate to the father, and so are children. In Shakespeare's Christian culture, the authority for this family structure was predominantly Biblical. The official sermon on matrimony read in Protestant churches throughout England in the sixteenth century cites St Paul's injunction: 'Wives, submit yourselves unto your own husbands, as unto the Lord. For the husband is the head of the wife, even as Christ is the head of the church' (Ephesians 5: 22–3). This patriarchal family structure, in turn, was the model for governmental structures. The king was assumed to be the supreme authority in the land, as was the father in the family (see Chapter 13).

This does not mean, however, that there were no contradictions in this gender system. Women, while subordinate to men, were also given authority over children and servants in their households, even when those children and servants might be male. Moreover, women were expected to have primary control of the domestic arena including the preparation of food, the care and education of young children, oversight of the laundry and gardens, and primary responsibility for the medical needs of the family. Wives often prepared remedies from the herbs they themselves grew. Moreover, childbirth was almost always the domain of women, and only gradually were female midwives replaced by male doctors in the birthing chambers of early modern England.

Thus, while the father in theory had control over every aspect of the household, in practice authority over particular matters was ceded to women. Many ministers enjoined husbands to give wives autonomy in their own spheres. In one of Shakespeare's comedies, *The Merry Wives of Windsor*, we are given a comic picture of a husband, Master Ford, who does not trust his wife to retain proper control over her household. Irrationally jealous, Ford barges into his house looking for his wife's supposed lover, and in one hilarious scene he seeks this man by emptying out the huge laundry basket that his wife has just got ready to be taken to the stream for washing. All the neighbours admonish Ford for the inappropriateness of his behaviour. This suggests that in practice there were informal limits to the authority a patriarch was supposed to wield.

Feminist criticism investigates how Shakespeare's plays relate to the codes and conventions of the gender system specific to the early modern period. For example, in Renaissance England women were generally defined in relation to their marital status. That is, they were maids (understood as women who were preparing to marry), wives (women who had made it to the married state), or widows (women who had been married but whose husbands had died). The only other category was for whores (women assumed to be forever outside the marriage state). While maids and widows were supposed to be sexually chaste and married women sexually faithful to their husbands, whores, by definition, were unchaste and performed for money what wives supposedly performed for love.

The power of this system of classifying women, and its influence on literary texts, cannot be overestimated. All of Shakespeare's comedies, for example, are motivated by the imperative to get maids to the altar, that is, to position them to make the successful transition to wives. With marriage as the goal, the interest of the comedies lies largely in the way blocks to marriage are overcome. Sometimes, as in *As You Like It*, a bad ruler mistreats his own family—a brother and niece—so that the niece is forced to dress as a man and flee his court in order, finally, to be reunited with her father and married to the man she loves. In *A Midsummer Night's Dream*, a father prevents a daughter from marrying her beloved; but there is the added complication that two young men love one young woman while ignoring a second marriageable female. In this instance, all four young people flee to the woods outside Athens and there undergo a night of magical transformations and encounters before the power of the father is set aside and the affections of the lovers alter in such a way that each man has a different mate.

Feminist criticism of the comedies, noting the fact that marriage is so insistently the goal of every comedy, has explored its different consequences for men and women. For the men of Shakespeare's comedies, marriage is *one* of the social roles they will perform. It in no way precludes their continuing as public figures in the world of work and diplomacy, learning and commerce. At the end of *A Midsummer Night's Dream*, the two male lovers talk at length with the Duke of Athens on the eve of their mutual nuptials. The two female lovers, significantly, say not a word through all of Act Five. Their social destiny has been achieved with their marriage. For the men there is marriage—and then more, the play hints, a whole world of public achievement and courtly service.

Feminist critics have also observed that in the middle portion of Shakespeare's comic plays the female protagonists—before they actually head to the altar—enjoy an unusual degree of freedom. In *A Midsummer Night's Dream* the young women run away from their families and spend the night in a wood with their lovers. In *As You Like It* and several other of Shakespeare's plays the female heroines dress for a time as men, and when they do, they have many of the freedoms men enjoy. In *The Merchant of Venice* the crossdressed heroine argues a case in a court of law; in *Twelfth Night* the crossdressed female protagonist attends a duke and is wooed by a great lady; in *As You Like It* the disguised heroine travels great distances, sets up a household of her own, and educates her chosen mate on how he should woo and how he should love a woman.

Many feminist critics have argued that in the middle portion of his comedies Shakespeare offers a 'world upside down' in which women have powers not usually granted to them in the 'real world' of Elizabethan England. When his female heroines successfully perform roles usually reserved for men, these plays may have changed and expanded assumptions about what men and women could do. Even though at the end of most comedies the hierarchical gender system is typically restored and women returned to their subordinate roles, for a time the plays offer a holiday world of expanded possibility. This is one of the cultural functions of early modern drama. It not only reproduces the values and beliefs of the culture that produces it; it also can alter them.

In other genres, such as the tragedies, women's position is more troubled. In these plays, wives and mothers, rather than maids, are more often at centre stage, and questions about the chastity of wives are the source of intolerable anxiety in the plays' male protagonists. In *Hamlet*, for example, the young Prince is fixated on the fact that his mother quickly remarried after the death of her husband, old Hamlet. Worse yet, she married Hamlet's uncle, the man the ghost of old Hamlet identifies as his murderer. In the imagination of the young Prince, a wife should be faithful to the memory of her first husband. If not, she becomes an example of unrestrained lust, rather like a whore, and not a proper wife. So powerful is Hamlet's obsession with his mother's sexuality and her 'infidelity' to his dead father that he cannot focus on the punishment of his father's murderer. His fixation on his mother's 'crimes' has another effect, as well. It makes him unable to trust other women, in particular Ophelia, the maid whom he seems to have intended to marry. But in his mind Ophelia becomes confused with his mother and his distrust of his mother's sexuality; consequently, Hamlet at times treats Ophelia as if *she* were a prostitute. This play does not end, like comedy, with a marriage; but rather with the deaths of most of its major characters, including Hamlet, Ophelia, and Gertrude. The causes of this tragedy are multiple, but one is certainly masculine expectations concerning female sexuality and the straitjacket in which men would contain that sexuality.

In yet another genre, Shakespeare's history plays, the position of women is different from both comedy and tragedy. Plays about English history are above all about the men who wore the crown and ruled the nation. Although women characters appear in these plays, their primary role is to help reproduce the legitimate male heirs who ensure that one king is followed on the throne by his own progeny. The chastity of these wives is especially important because on their faithfulness depends the legitimacy of the royal offspring. But, again, the gender system in these plays never works seamlessly. Occasionally, as in *Henry VI Part One*, one of Shakespeare's earliest histories, a strong woman emerges who challenges masculine authority. In this play, it is Joan of Arc, a French warrior woman who says it is her mission from God to drive the English army from France and who challenges gender roles by being more successful in battle than most of the men around her, whether French or English. Here, the supreme authority of God is pitted against the authority of earthly men. One of the chief ways in which Shakespeare discredits Joan's claim to be God's ambassador is to connect her with unchastity. When captured by the English, Joan tries to save her life by saying she is with child by one Frenchman and then another and another. Despite her prowess in battle, she is demonized as a whore.

A different case is posed by Margaret, the wife of Henry VI, who attains enormous power because her husband is a weak man and a weak ruler. In this case it is a failure of a man to uphold his place in the gender system that allows the world temporarily to be turned upside down and for female rule to ensue. Henry is presented as a pious man, but an ineffectual ruler and a complete failure as a military leader. Margaret herself becomes a warrior, consequently, in order to protect Henry's throne and the claims of their son to that throne. Taking over her husband's place in battle and at the council table, Margaret successfully rules until finally defeated by the forces of the English rebels. In one way Margaret is perfectly conventional, especially in her desire to see her son rule in the place of his father. In another way, however, she is utterly unconventional and a threat to patriarchal order in her insistence on assuming the roles typically reserved for men, and, tellingly, in her adultery with an English courtier named Suffolk. Despite her strengths, she is vilified as a monster. In this instance, unlike the comedies, the inversion of gender roles produces a nightmare world, not one of expanded possibilities.

Feminist criticism tries, above all, to understand the impact of gender norms and expectations on the narrative structures and on the creation of character in Shakespeare's plays. As a mode of analysis, its primary goal is to bring to light information that will allow more adequate interpretation of those plays. Sometimes that information comes from inside the plays themselves. Feminist critics, for example, often focus on dramatic elements that other critics overlook, such as the women characters in Shakespeare's histories. Or they examine issues such as female friendship or the kinds of pleasure female audience members might have taken in Shakespeare's plays. A number have explored the consequences of the fact that on the early modern stage all women's parts were played by male actors.[1] In each case, the goal is to reveal something new and unexpected about the drama, something that could not be discerned without looking at the plays from a feminist perspective.

Feminist literary criticism is, of course, part of a larger social movement whose aim is to produce a world of greater gender equity. In this regard, within English departments feminists have asked that women writers be included in the curriculum. They have also asked for greater equity in discussing aspects of literary works dealing with women, with sexuality, and with the domestic sphere, so that attention is not given solely to the domains of politics and public life from which women have often been excluded. Feminists aim to expand understanding of the full range of human experience represented in literary form.

The purpose of most feminist criticism, moreover, is not to indict Shakespeare for failing to hold the gender values of the early twenty-first century. As a person of his era, it would have been an historical impossibility for Shakespeare to replicate the views of modern-day feminists. Instead, their aim is to understand just how thoroughly and in what specific ways Shakespeare shared the gender assumptions of his own time and the ways, as well, in which his plays may have disrupted those assumptions.

But it is one thing to be aware of historical difference and the ways in which Shakespeare was of his time, and not ours, and another to *endorse* the gender norms found in his plays. Enormous cultural cachet attaches to the name of Shakespeare, and his works have been equated with truth itself. Feminists, however, have criticized the idea that any writer has access to universal truths, even Shakespeare. When his plays reproduce ideas that perpetuate gender inequality, feminists call attention to that fact. By placing Shakespeare firmly in his own time and pointing to the ways in which his plays seem at odds with many contemporary assumptions about men and women's roles, feminists are able to 'denaturalize' Shakespeare's texts—that is, show that they are not a mirror of nature, but a reflection of man-made ideas and concepts, concepts that other ages can question and even discard.

Feminist approaches to *The Taming of the Shrew*

Shakespeare's controversial early comedy, *The Taming of the Shrew*, offers a good example of the multiple responses Shakespeare's representations of gender can evoke over time. The main plot involves the 'taming' of a strong willed woman, Katherine, by Petruccio, the fortune hunter who seeks her hand. While Katherine's younger sister, Bianca, is beloved by all the young men of Padua, the older sister is feared because of her sharp tongue and independent spirit. Bianca can get married only if her older sister is wed first; therefore, Katherine's father assents to the plan to give Kate, and a large dowry, to Petruccio. Petruccio, in turn, develops a plan to transform the wilful maid into a compliant wife by being more wilful and unconventional than Katherine herself. He appears, for example, at their wedding in ragged clothes, and refuses to stay for the wedding feast. Having taken Katherine away from her family and friends and off to his country house for their honeymoon, Petruccio then refuses to let her sleep or to eat, all the while proclaiming that love for her motivates all he does. In order to be allowed to return to Padua, Katherine has to prove her obedience by proclaiming the sun the moon and an old man a young virgin. Even after they do return to the city, Petruccio demands further public signs of Katherine's obedience. He requires that she come when he commands, trample her fashionable hat underfoot, and lecture other women on the duties of an obedient wife. Kate complies.

In the twentieth and twenty-first centuries, this play has been controversial, and feminist criticism has helped to raise the discussion of it to new levels of sophistication. Once it was fairly routine to argue that the taming of Katherine is a good thing since this wilful outsider, by working in partnership with Petruccio, successfully makes the transition from maid to wife and in doing so wins a position of cultural centrality from which she can even lecture other women about their improper behaviour. Feminists, however, have pointed to the violence involved in Kate's taming. In the upside down world of the farmhouse she is transformed through techniques akin to modern forms of brainwashing. While Shakespeare's play is less violent than many of his source stories (Petruccio, for example, never strikes Katherine), nonetheless the hero achieves his victory over the shrew by confining her and causing her a good deal of bodily discomfort. As feminists have pointed out, even in the early modern period there was a spirited debate about whether a husband should be able to beat a wife who displeased him and the degree to which her compliance with his wishes should be coerced. Consequently, they have argued that in its own time the play might have raised questions in the minds of the audience about the appropriateness of Petruccio's tactics. Almost uniformly, feminists have wanted to query the play's central premiss: namely, that a headstrong woman should be forced by whatever means to transform herself, at least outwardly, into a compliant wife.

Feminists have also spent a good deal of effort considering how the play might be staged in a way that would call in question the assumption that the taming of Kate (1) was a good thing or (2) was successful. If a standard way to perform the play depicts an unhappy Kate gradually being transformed into a happy bride who has seen the error of her ways, feminists have suggested at least two different approaches. One is to stress the play's latent brutality and Kate's disoriented terror in the farmhouse so that audience members have to feel uncomfortable with 'the happy ending'. Alternatively, feminists have argued that Kate should always be more than a match for Petruccio. Often this has meant improvising new stage action for Kate to perform, such as snatching food from servants when Petruccio isn't looking, saying her speeches of compliance with exaggerated irony, or even repeatedly catching Petruccio in judo holds from which he cannot escape. The first set of performance choices asks the audience to consider the possibility that if Kate is really 'tamed', it is through violent and unjust means. The second queries whether the patriarchal order is really powerful enough to quell a spirit as strong as Katherine's. In both cases the intent has not been to indict Shakespeare for being politically incorrect, but rather to use the interpretive or performative moment to call attention to what—for our age—seems troubling or alien in the Shakespearian play or to offer a performative alternative to the dominant ideology of the written script.

The history of feminist criticism of Shakespeare

Clearly, feminist criticsm takes many forms, and a brief history of its development within Shakespeare studies in the last few decades will underscore this diversity. In the 1970s and early 1980s, the first goal was to change the questions one could ask of Shakespeare's plays and to put issues such as gender and sexuality on the critical agenda. Early feminists analysed, in particular, the portrayal of women characters in each genre, focusing on the patriarchal norms and gender stereotypes that shaped these representations. Simultaneously, they examined the ways in which Shakespeare's plays 'stretched the envelope', that is, created female characters, especially in the comedies, who successfully challenged normative gender roles.

Some of this work was psychoanalytic in nature, that is, it focused on formative moments in family life as the key to a character's gendered behaviour, and, in some cases, read in the plays traces of Shakespeare's own psychic development. An excellent example of such work is provided by Janet Adelman's early essay on *Coriolanus*.[2] This play's tragic protagonist is a fierce Roman warrior who cannot bear to be dependent on anyone except his mother Volumnia, to whom he is excessively deferential. Adelman argues that Volumnia effectively created her son's rigid, self-punishing personality by teaching him in childhood to scorn sustenance—meat and milk—in order to prove himself a self-sufficient warrior who does not have the needs of other men. At the same time, he desperately craves the approval of his demanding mother, whose only route to public acclaim lies in the military and political successes of her son. In her subsequent book, *Suffocating Mothers*, Adelman argues that especially in the second half of his career Shakespeare was working through a deep ambivalence toward the figure of the mother. This ambivalence sometimes expressed itself in the creation of monsters such as Volumnia, and at other times led to an at least partial reconciliation with the mother figure.

This kind of feminist criticism continues. The 1980s, however, saw a new emphasis on *historicizing* the particular gender system within which Shakespeare lived. If some early feminist work tended to be ahistorical, focusing on invariant family structures or on supposedly timeless stereotypes of women, much of the later work looked instead at the particular way in which male and female behaviour was structured in a culture in some ways unlike our own. Some of the most provocative work of that decade grew out of research suggesting that in the early modern period, men's and women's bodies were not assumed to be anatomically different in any fundamental way. Instead of two sexes with different bodies, many early modern scientific and medical writers saw only one sex and one kind of body. Men and women were not assumed to be innately different, but rather were viewed as more perfect and less perfect versions of the same prototype. In this model, derived from the classical writer Galen, women differed from men primarily in having cooler, more humid bodies and, consequently, being less rational and more guided by their passions. During the sexual act that led to the conception of a woman, sufficient heat was lacking to produce a perfect creation, a man. The woman resulting from this imperfect act of generation was believed to have the same genitalia as men, but they had not been pushed outside the body. Stories exist from the early modern period recording cases in which, when women supposedly became overheated in running or jumping, male genitalia would erupt from inside their bodies.

The implications of this view of male-female difference are far-reaching. For one thing, it highlights the volatility of the masculine-feminine binary in early modern culture. If women might under certain conditions become men, might men not also sink to the level of women? In the sophisticated crossdressing comedies in which boy actors play the parts of women who in turn dress as men, there is a dizzying but by-and-large benign play with gender categories as women turn themselves into the men they have always, in terms of the sex of the boy actor, been. In other genres the mannish woman and the womanish man are more problematic and threatening. A

Volumnia destroys all before her, while the irresolute Henry VI loses his wife, his kingdom, and his son.

In a culture in which gender difference is not guaranteed by bodily difference, moreover, other marks of distinction become especially important in enforcing gender divisions. For example, England had sumptuary regulations governing the kinds of clothing that could be worn by people of each class. Rank was proclaimed by the colours, texture, and value of one's clothes. Similarly, preachers and moralists warned against women dressing in the clothes of men, or men in the clothes of women. This fact alone makes the idea of an all-male stage potentially disruptive of gender norms since on that stage men assumed female clothing as part of their daily performance practice, while the plots of many disguise narratives require that women characters crossdress as men. These things suggest that the early modern public theatre in which Shakespeare worked was a place of considerable experimentation with gender roles and behaviours.

Two more developments within feminist criticism deserve mention. One is the expansion of feminist studies in the 1980s and 1990s to include critical examination of men and masculinity as well as women and femininity. Feminist work now often takes place under the larger rubric of gender studies, which examines both poles of the male-female binary and the relationship of the one to the other. Second, much recent feminist work has argued that gender categories cannot be understood in isolation from other categories of difference, such as race, class, and sexuality. 'Difference feminism', as it is sometimes called, starts from the premiss that neither men nor women form a homogeneous group. A female servant and her mistress inhabit different class positions that cause their femininities to diverge, while a tawny Egyptian queen such as Shakespeare's Cleopatra will be constructed quite differently from a 'white' woman such as Desdemona, the female protagonist in Shakespeare's *Othello*.

Some of the most interesting recent feminist work, consequently, has considered gender in conjunction with race, class, and/or sexuality as they together influence the construction of female characters and fissured and complex notions of femininity. Kim Hall, for example, has argued that Shakespeare shares with many of his contemporaries a 'beauty discourse' in which the 'fairness' of many of his heroines implicitly helps to create an idea of England as a white nation.[3] By contrast, a dark or tawny woman such as Cleopatra is exoticized and sexualized, as a way of marking her non-European identity. The queen is variously described as a 'gipsy', as 'a triple-turned whore', and a 'witch', all terms of opprobrium that suggest her negative effect on the Roman general, Mark Antony, who becomes her lover and gradually loses his ability to dominate the Roman world. This trope of the seductive Eastern woman who draws European men from their public duty has continued to have currency to the present day.

Attention has also shifted to women's erotic life and the ways in which early modern women may have differed from one another in their experience of erotic relations with men or with other women. Early modern England, as far as we can tell, did not assign people sexual identities or classify them in terms of a supposedly exclusive erotic commitment to one sex or the other. That is, no one was labelled a homosexual or a heterosexual; those terms were inventions of the nineteenth century. In the early modern period, sexual practices seem to have been fluid and did not necessarily occur only with members of one sex. For men, there were erotic friendships between men of equal status as well as a variety of eroticized relationships which involved power, age, and status differentials between the partners (see Chapter 30).[4]

For women the situation is more complex, as there are few textual traces of their erotic friendships, so centrally did marriage figure in their lives. As has been suggested, in Shakespeare's plays, women's relation to marriage is foregrounded. Recently, however, critics have focused, variously, on female friendship in the plays and on the anomaly posed by the never-married or mature virgin figure.[5] In *As You Like It*, when Rosalind flees her evil uncle's court, her cousin and dear friend, Celia, goes with her, abandoning her father for the sake of Rosalind's friendship. The two of them set up housekeeping together at the edge of the forest of Ardenne, and Celia is repeatedly annoyed with Rosalind during Rosalind's subsequent courtship of a man. In the friendship of these two women it is possible to read the contours of an homoerotic friendship that, as in most of Shakespeare's comedies, is eventually displaced by the imperative of marriage.

In later plays, such as the so-called 'problem comedies' composed early in the seventeenth century, the marriage plot is more vexed (see Chapter 21). In *Measure for Measure* the heroine, Isabella, wants to become a nun and eschew the company of men. Drawn back into society because her brother gets into trouble with the law for impregnating a woman before they are legally married, Isabella eventually finds herself made an offer of marriage by the Duke of Vienna. But the text does not tell us if Isabella accepts the proposal. In this play there are no untroubled marriages, and sexual excess holds sway in the brothels of Vienna. In such a context, Isabella might well prefer the company of women.

In focusing on female homoeroticism and female friendship, and on the intersections of race, gender, and class, feminists have found new ways to extend the lines of feminist inquiry first laid down in the 1970s. At the dawning of the new century, feminists are as likely to work on men and masculinity as on women and femininity; and they are very likely to consider their work on women within the context of other systems of stratification in the plays. Given the openness of Shakespeare's plays to reinterpretation, one can be fairly certain that the twenty-first century will continue to find new and productive ways to approach the question of gender in Shakespeare's dramatic canon.

FURTHER READING

Adelman, Janet. *Suffocating Mothers: Fantasies of Maternal Origin in Shakespeare's Plays* (London: Routledge, 1992). This book is an example of feminist psychoanalytic criticism focusing on the figure of the mother in Shakespeare's plays.

Dolan, Frances (ed.). *The Taming of the Shrew* (Boston: Bedford Books, 1996). Dolan's contextual edition brings together selections from a wide range of early modern texts dealing with gender issues relevant to *The Taming of the Shrew* such as the duties of man and wife in marriage and the permissibility of a husband's using violence to discipline his wife.

Howard, Jean E. and Phyllis Rackin. *Engendering a Nation: A Feminist Account of Shakespeare's English Histories* (London: Routledge, 1997). This book offers a feminist reading of the nine history plays Shakespeare wrote in the 1590s.

Kahn, Coppélia. *Roman Shakespeare: Warriors, Wounds, and Women* (London: Routledge, 1997). Kahn offers a feminist analysis of the concept of 'Roman virtue' in the plays and poems which Shakespeare set in ancient Rome.

Laqueur, Thomas. *Making Sex: Body and Gender from the Greeks to Freud* (Cambridge, Mass.: Harvard University Press, 1990). Laqueur's book usefully explains the Galenic view of the body, prevalent in Shakespeare's time, in which men and women were not considered to be inherently different but were imagined as more or less perfect examples of a single bodily prototype.

Mendelson, Sara and Patricia Crawford. *Women in Early Modern England* (Oxford: Clarendon Press, 1998). This book offers an account of women's daily lives in early modern England with special attention to the differences between women from different classes.

Orgel, Stephen. *Impersonations: The Performance of Gender in Shakespeare's England* (Cambridge: Cambridge University Press, 1996). Orgel asks why boys played women's parts on the early modern English stage and explains what this practice tells us about early modern gender ideology.

Parker, Patricia. *Shakespeare from the Margins: Language, Culture, Context* (Chicago: University of Chicago Press, 1996). This book is particularly concerned with the relationship between language, politics, and power in early modern England, with special attention to how rhetoric affects understandings of gender.

Paster, Gail Kern. *The Body Embarrassed: Drama and the Disciplines of Shame in Early Modern England* (Chicago: University of Chicago Press, 1993). This book offers a feminist account of the way in which early modern men and women experienced their bodies and of how understandings of the early modern body differ from current beliefs.

Traub, Valerie. *The Renaissance of Lesbianism in Early Modern England* (Cambridge: Cambridge University Press, 2002). Traub examines the evidence for various forms of female homoeroticism in early modern texts.

NOTES

1. There is a great deal of scholarship on the effects on the gender system of the boy actors playing women's parts and of female characters assuming male disguises. I summarize this literature in 'Power and Eros: Crossdressing in Dramatic Representation and Theatrical Practice', Chapter V of *The Stage and Social Struggle in Early Modern England* (London: Routledge, 1994), pp. 93–128.

2. Janet Adelman. ' "Anger's My Meat": Feeding, Dependency, and Aggression in *Coriolanus*'. In *Representing Shakespeare: New Psychoanalytic Essays*, ed. Murray M. Schwartz and Coppélia Kahn (Baltimore: The Johns Hopkins University Press, 1980), pp. 129–49.

3. See Kim Hall. *Things of Darkness: Economies of Race and Gender in Early Modern England* (Ithaca: Cornell University Press, 1995), pp. 62–122.

4. For crucial work in this area see especially Bruce Smith. *Homosexual Desire in Shakespeare's England* (Chicago: University of Chicago Press, 1991); Jonathan Goldberg. *Sodometries* (Stanford: University of Stanford Press, 1992); and Mario DiGangi. *The Homoerotics of Early Modern Drama* (Cambridge: Cambridge University Press, 1997).

5. Valerie Traub. *Desire and Anxiety: Circulations of Sexuality in Shakespearean Drama* (London: Routledge, 1992) and Theodora A. Jankowski. *Pure Resistance: Queer Virginity in Early Modern English Drama* (Philadelphia: University of Pennsylvania Press, 2000).

READING: *Othello*

Othello is one of Shakespeare's most unusual tragedies. If tragedies are typically about people of elevated social rank, this one stars a Moorish soldier in the employ of the Venetian state and the 'white' daughter of a Venetian senator. They are neither European royalty nor aristocrats. Moreover, the play is not primarily about affairs of state, though Venice, a Mediterranean maritime power, is threatened briefly by a possible invasion of some of its territories by the Ottoman Turk. Rather, like *Romeo and Juliet*, *Othello* is above all a love story about two people whose love ends tragically. In trying to figure out why, feminists have increasingly insisted that satisfactory answers depend on simultaneously probing the gender and the racial dimensions of the play as they unfold in the charged arena of Renaissance Venice.

At first, differences in background and skin colour do not seem to affect Desdemona's and Othello's exceptionally powerful passion for one another. Desdemona has rejected all the 'curlèd darlings' (1.2.69), that is, the fashionable young men of Venice, and fastened her heart on Othello because of his deeds. As she proclaims, 'I saw Othello's visage in his mind' (1.3.251), meaning that his inward qualities of courage, martial prowess, and leadership drew her love, not the superficiality of outward looks. Othello, in turn, loves Desdemona because of her responsiveness to him and to the tales he tells of his life and exploits. A professional soldier, he seems to find in Desdemona the singular passion of his life. In the first act the two live out a classic comic narrative in miniature. Overcoming the objections of her angry father, the maid, Desdemona, is transformed into a wife, one set to follow her husband on his posting to Cyprus.

But *Othello* is far from a comedy, and the play daringly challenges gender and racial stereotypes only, in the end, to acknowledge and so to some extent yield to their force. Desdemona at first seems to be that rare thing in tragedy, a strong outspoken woman who is also unquestionably good. Her initial actions are strikingly bold. Not only does she steal away from her father's house to marry Othello, but she also appears in the Venetian Senate chamber to testify to her love and to ask to accompany her husband on his military mission. She is afraid neither of public speech nor of declaring her own mind. Many early modern texts, however, enjoined women to silence and to obedience. Much in Desdemona's bold behaviour allows for sinister interpretation if one reads her with the intent to find fault. Iago, Othello's lieutenant, is just such a reader, a walking encyclopedia of gutter thoughts. He assumes his own wife has been unfaithful to him, though there is no evidence in the play that that is true; and he tells Othello that because Desdemona defied her father in marrying him, she will in turn deceive him with other men (3.3.197–212). Because she married a man not of her own country, Iago further assumes—not that she sees Othello's inner virtues— but that she has perverse erotic tastes and excessive sexual desire (3.3.232–43). Similarly, he urges Othello to mistrust Desdemona's opinions, such as her belief that Cassio, Othello's lieutenant, should not be dismissed from his post for getting drunk on the night watch. When Desdemona advocates for Cassio, Iago leads Othello to believe it is a sign of her love for the ensign.

Why does Othello accept Iago's readings of his wife? Partly the answer lies in the way Iago adopts the voice of worldly common sense, speaking about 'women' as if everyone knows what he says to be true. Reading through an anti-feminist lens, he turns Desdemona's unusual attributes of courage, clearsightedness, and verbal dexterity into marks of whoredom. Bianca's role in the play reveals the deep structure of the fantasy Iago induces in Othello. Bianca, one of the play's three women, is not a wife, but an unmarried woman in Cyprus who has developed a powerful affection for Cassio. Though Cassio and Iago laugh and make jokes at her expense, treating her as a courtesan, there is no textual indication that Bianca is attached to a number of men simultaneously, and her loyalty to Cassio is unswerving. When he is wounded in the last act, Bianca rushes out to help him and in so doing opens herself to the charge that she herself is the would-be assassin. Nonetheless, despite her unusual qualities, in the play's gender economy Bianca stands for the non-wife, the sexually unchaste whore. In one of the key symbolic scenes of the play, Othello confuses his wife with Bianca (4.1.72–202). Iago places Othello where he can supposedly hear Cassio and Iago discussing Desdemona. In actuality, they are talking of Bianca who comes on stage as their conversation ends. Othello is completely deceived. Having come to doubt his wife's chastity, he assumes that when Cassio and Iago make jokes about Cassio's mistress, they must be speaking of Desdemona.

This confusion of wife and whore is compounded by Iago's skilful manipulation of what is perhaps the key symbolic object found in *Othello*, namely, the handkerchief Othello once gave to Desdemona. The trajectory of this handkerchief is crucial to the play's meaning. Desdemona tries to use it in Act Three to ease the pain of Othello's jealously throbbing head, but he casts it aside dismissively (3.3.290–2). Momentarily ignored by Desdemona, the castaway handkerchief is retrieved by Emilia, who gives it to Iago, who drops it in Cassio's chamber. Cassio then picks it up and gives it to Bianca so she can copy out the strawberry pattern with which it is embroidered. Hence it is that Othello's jealousy is compounded when in Act Four, during the eavesdropping scene just discussed, Bianca enters carrying the handkerchief.

Feminists have probed the multiple significances of this object. As a gift from Othello to Desdemona, it can symbolize the bond between them. He accuses her of destroying the bond (by sexual infidelity and by losing the handkerchief), but in actuality he is the one who destroyed their bond (by mistrusting her and by thrusting aside the handkerchief she is trying to use to help him). But the handkerchief is important not only as a sign of an abstract bond, but as a material object in its own right. It is, for instance, the kind of household object over which a good wife was to exercise managerial control. Women were, in this period, expected to spin and weave cloth, embroider and do needlework, and tend to the washing and bleaching of all household linens. When Othello accuses Desdemona of losing the handkerchief, he is accusing her, in essence, of ceasing to be a good housewife and so of becoming a sexually and economically improvident whore.

But the strawberry design on the handkerchief makes it significant in other ways as well. The red design on white linen can symbolize the blood from the hymen shed when Desdemona and Othello first consummated their marriage. It would thus be a reminder that Desdemona came to the marriage as a virgin. This may also be what she wishes Othello to recall when, on the eve of her murder, she orders Emilia to lay her wedding sheets on the bed, since wedding sheets were frequently inspected to be sure that they showed evidence of blood on the morning after the wedding night.

Finally, it is not just the handkerchief itself that is important, but also the stories Othello tells of its origins. He gives two accounts of these, once saying simply that the handkerchief was a gift from his father to his mother (5.2.223–4), once claiming that the handkerchief had magical properties and was given to his mother by an Egyptian sorceress (3.4.53–73). For a wife to lose it is to forfeit her power over her husband. This second account has been read as a sign that the rational Othello, under the pressure of jealousy, is degenerating into a superstitious barbarian.

This account of the handkerchief's origins is one of the many points where an analysis of the gender and racial dimensions of the play must proceed together, for *Othello*'s tragic outcome depends on more than the deep-seated misogyny that lies at the heart of Iago's duping of Othello. It also depends on the hero's own outsider status in Venice, and the way in which both Iago and the play itself manipulate ideas of Othello's exotic origins. Not content with disparaging women, Iago also introduces a pernicious racism into the play.

Othello's place in Venice is apparently an honoured one. A proven soldier, he has been employed to help defend Venetian shipping from attacks by the Turks. But he is also a Moor, and Moors on the early modern stage, and in other kinds of texts, were often depicted as treacherous, cruel, and sexually rapacious. By contrast, Othello seems to be a noble Moor of proven courage who speaks in some of the most beautiful poetry in any of Shakespeare's plays. Nonetheless, his Moorishness makes him vulnerable, as Desdemona is vulnerable, to sinister interpretation. In the play's first scene, Iago and Roderigo stand outside Desdemona's father's house flinging out racial slurs against Othello and the sexual union of a white woman and a Moorish man. They tell Desdemona's father that 'an old black ram / Is tupping your white ewe' (1.1.88–9) and that he and Desdemona are 'making the beast with two backs' (1.1.118) This coarse language reduces both Desdemona and Othello to animals, and it plays on the fear that there is something dangerous and outrageous about the sexual union of a black man and a 'fair' woman. From the start her 'whiteness' is privileged as something precious that can be sullied by the touch of the 'lascivious Moor'.

The calm and poised Othello who enters the play soon thereafter, however, bears little resemblance to the crazed sex-fiend of Iago's diatribe. But by the middle of the play, Iago has so thoroughly disoriented Othello's equilibrium that he can insinuate to Othello's face that that there is something unnatural in Desdemona's affection for him. Of her he says:

Not to affect many proposèd matches
Of her own clime, complexion, and degree,

> Whereto we see in all things nature tends.
> Foh, one may smell in such a will most rank,
> Foul disproportions, thoughts unnatural!
> But pardon me. I do not in position
> Distinctly speak of her, though I may fear
> Her will, recoiling to her better judgement,
> May fall to match you with her country forms
> And happily repent.
>
> (3.3.234-43)

Here Iago reads Desdemona as a creature of excessive will or sexual appetite who has unnaturally chosen a man not of her own complexion or skin colour. Like a tragic version of the jealous husband Master Ford in *The Merry Wives of Windsor*, Othello begins to doubt his wife's chastity and also his own worth, wondering aloud whether his blackness, his age, and his lack of Venetian manners make him unattractive (3.3.267–71). The tragedy is thus powerfully fuelled, first, by the assumption that every outspoken woman is potentially unchaste and, second, by Iago's skilful insinuation that the union of black and white is unnatural. Desdemona's passion for that union becomes yet more evidence of her aberrant, lawless will.

As the tragedy unfolds, the play creates a stark juxtaposition between a Desdemona increasingly represented as an icon of purity and martyred virtue and an Othello who becomes ever more irrational and cruel. Race and gender are set, horrifyingly, at odds, and from a feminist perspective even the vindication of Desdemona is deeply problematic in that Desdemona is also, in the second half of the play, increasingly stripped of agency. No longer the initiator of action, she patiently endures Othello's wrath, even when he strikes her in public. In one particularly moving scene, she talks with her waiting woman, Emilia, as she prepares for bed. Entertaining thoughts of her own death, Desdemona expresses them by singing an old song about a woman abandoned by her lover. Through the line 'Let nobody blame him, his scorn I approve' (4.3.50), Desdemona seems to express her own acceptance of Othello's cruelty to her. Later, after Othello has strangled Desdemona, she momentarily revives, declaring herself guiltless of any crime but also assuming responsibility for her own murder. When Emilia asks who has killed her, Desdemona responds: 'Nobody, I myself. Farewell' (5.2.133).

In a trenchant essay, Lisa Jardine has argued that 'good' women in Renaissance tragedy are often represented as long-suffering martyrs.[1] This is a longstanding version of acceptable femininity. The Desdemona of the play's early acts is not such a martyr, but toward the end of the play she conforms more closely to the stereotypical picture of the good wife as one who is chaste, silent, and obedient. Desdemona's absolute purity is especially emphasized in the scene where she prepares for bed and sings the song about the woman abandoned by her lover. At one point in the scene Desdemona asks Emilia if she would, for all the world, sleep with a man not her husband. Desdemona declares she would not, but Emilia, more pragmatic, exclaims:

Marry, I would not do such a thing for a joint ring, nor for measures of lawn, nor for gowns, petticoats, nor caps, nor any petty exhibition; but for all the whole world? Ud's pity, who would not make her husband a cuckold to make him a monarch?

(4.3.71-5)

Emilia shows herself an astute judge of the relative value of things. She would not be seduced for the small items of clothing or the trinkets young men use as gifts for their girlfriends, but the whole world is a different matter. Emilia goes on to declare that women have appetites and affections just as men do, and that if men mistreat women, women will learn from men how to satisfy themselves outside of marriage.

Desdemona is clearly the heroine of the play, but some feminists have preferred the earthy pragmatism of the waiting woman to the idealized virtue of the martyred heroine. Certainly the two women are strongly contrasted in this scene, inviting the audience to compare their values and their attitudes toward men, though in the end Emilia dies in a way that shows she has a capacity for heroism as well as cynical pragmatism. Realizing that her husband has been responsible for Othello's jealousy, Emilia refuses to obey him when he commands her silence. Instead, she reveals his crimes and dies by his hand. In the end, her friendship with and loyalty to Desdemona win out over her bond to her husband.

If the play ends up strongly vindicating the purity of Desdemona and the courage of Emilia, this is done in counterpoint to the gradual transformation of Othello into a stereo-typically jealous, irrational, and murderous Moor. In the play's final acts, Othello strikes his wife in public, orders the murder of Cassio, strangles Desdemona in her bed, and kills himself, an act which within a Christian framework is taboo, a mark of despair rather than trust in God's providential care. These acts represent the obverse of the confident and poised general who in the first scene of the play faced down a crowd of armed men with the confident comment: 'Keep up your bright swords, for the dew will rust 'em' (1.2.60). All tragic heroes to some degree disintegrate, before the moment of death allows for a partial restitution of former greatness.

What is horrifying about Othello's disintegration, however, is that it conforms to derogatory discourses that delineated the Moor as bestial in his lack of reason, uncontrolled passion, and potential for jealousy. As a consequence, Othello's disintegration can seem to follow, not from his assent to Iago's twisted beliefs, but from his status as a 'barbarian', a thinly civilized black Moor whose primitive and destructive impulses are unleashed by Iago's skilful manipulations. Even at the moment of his death, Othello identifies with the Venetian state as the bulwark of civilization and the seat of justice, while locating criminality with 'outsiders' like the Turk and the Moor. As he stabs himself he says:

> . . . in Aleppo once,
> Where a malignant and a turbaned Turk
> Beat a Venetian and traduced the state,
> I took by th' throat the circumcisèd dog
> And smote him thus.
>
> (5.2.361-5)

In re-enacting this story, Othello divides himself. He is both the defender of the Venetian state and also the turbaned Turk and circumcised dog who must be killed. Nobly accepting responsibility for his crimes, Othello tragically locates their origins in his own 'otherness' rather than in his complex encounter with the Venetian racism and misogyny embodied in Iago.

For contemporary feminists it has become important to understand how the 'fair' Desdemona is constructed in relation to the 'black' Othello and how the gender and racial ideologies of the play intersect to destroy both the Moorish general and his Venetian wife. The unjust suffering of Desdemona, the wife falsely accused of the linked crimes of bad housewifery and sexual promiscuity, reveals how easily an early modern woman could lose the title 'good wife' and be vilified as a whore. Equally horrific is that in *Othello* the wronged wife's persistence in virtue requires both her increasing passivity and ultimately her death, and this martyrdom coincides with the play's escalating emphasis on Othello's barbarity. To the extent that *Othello* enables the fantasy of victimized white womanhood imperilled by black masculinity, it circulates stereotypes still being combated today.

FURTHER READING

Callaghan, Dympna. 'Looking Well to Linens: Woman and Cultural Production in *Othello* and Shakespeare's England'. In *Marxist Shakespeares*, ed. Jean E. Howard and Scott Shershow (London: Routledge, 2000). This essay explores the role of needlework and the care of linen as part of female housewifery in early modern England and in *Othello*.

Callaghan, Dympna. *Shakespeare Without Women: Representing Gender and Race On the Renaissance Stage* (London: Routledge, 2000). This book examines the absence of women and racial others as actors on Shakespeare's stage. There is a chapter on *Othello*.

D'Amico, Jack. *The Moor in English Renaissance Drama* (Tampa: University of South Florida Press, 1991). D'Amico provides an overview of positive and negative representations of Moors in early modern English stage plays.

Hall, Kim F. *Things of Darkness: Economies of Race and Gender in Early Modern England* (Ithaca: Cornell University Press, 1995). Hall looks at the way exploration and early colonialism affected racial thinking in early modern England, including ideas of 'whiteness' particularly connected to English women.

Loomba, Ania. *Gender, Race, Renaissance Drama* (Manchester: Manchester University Press, 1989). Loomba provides one of the first extended explorations of the interconnections between race and gender in early modern drama, with special attention to *Othello*.

Neely, Carol Thomas. *Broken Nuptials in Shakespeare's Plays* (New Haven: Yale University Press, 1985). Neely explores how the marriage plot affects the representation of women in Shakespeare's plays. There is a chapter on *Othello*.

Neill, Michael. 'Unproper Beds: Race, Adultery, and the Hideous in *Othello*', *Shakespeare Quarterly*, 40 (1989), 383–412. Neill explores the submerged fear of miscegenation in Shakespeare's tragedy.

Newman, Karen. *Fashioning Femininity and English Renaissance Drama* (Chicago: University of Chicago Press, 1991). Newman examines the historical contexts within which early modern drama created its representations of femininity. There is a chapter on *Othello*.

Orlin, Lena Cowen (ed.). *New Casebooks 'Othello': Contemporary Critical Essays* (Houndmills: Palgrave, 2003). This collection focuses on gender and race with essays by Denise Albanese, Emily C. Bartels, Harry Berger, Lynda E. Booso, Michael D. Bristol, Elizabeth Hanson, Barbara Hodgdon, Alan Sinfield, and Jyotsna Singh.

Parker, Patricia. 'Fantasies of "Race" and "Gender": Africa, *Othello* and Bringing to Light'. In *Women, 'Race', and Writing in Early Modern England*, ed. Margo Hendricks and Patricia Parker (London:

Routledge, 1994), pp. 84–100. Parker explores the discourse of the monstrous in *Othello*, linking fears of feminine sexuality with Othello's African origins.

Vitkus, Daniel. 'Turning Turk in *Othello*: The Conversion and Damnation of the Moor', *Shakespeare Quarterly*, 48 (1997), 145–77. Vitkus examines the religious meanings of Othello's Moorish background, discussing the hero's ambiguous status as a converted Christian and fears that such a convert might lapse again into barbarism.

NOTES

1   Lisa Jardine. ' "She sat like Patience on a monument, / Smiling at grief": The saving stereotypes of female heroism'. In *Still Harping on Daughters: Women and Drama in the Age of Shakespeare* (Brighton: Harvester Press, 1983), pp. 169–98.

30 | **Studies in sexuality**

Bruce R. Smith

Shakespeare's contemporaries give us very good reasons for starting an investigation of his plays and poems with stirrings of feeling in the genitals. Philip Stubbes is probably the best known of these witnesses. In his attack on 'Stage Plays and Interludes, with Their Wickedness' in *The Anatomy of Abuses* (1583) Stubbes makes no bones about it: the fundamental appeal of stage plays is to incite lust. 'Do they not induce whoredom and uncleanness?' he begins. 'Nay, are they not rather plain devourers of maidenly virginity and chastity?' As instances he cites two public playhouses, The Theatre and The Curtain, just outside London's city walls to the north, where the young William Shakespeare was soon to cast his lot with the players. 'For proof whereof, but mark the flocking and running to Theatres and Curtains, daily and hourly, night and day, time and tide, to see plays and interludes. Where such wanton gestures, such bawdy speeches, such laughing and fleering, such kissing and bussing, such clipping and culling, such winking and glancing of wanton eyes and the like is used as is wonderful to behold'. What such sights inspire, according to Stubbes, includes rather more than the devouring of maidenly virginity and chastity. 'Then, these goodly pageants being done, every mate sorts to his mate, everyone brings another homeward of their way, very friendly, and in their secret conclaves [covertly] they play the sodomites, or worse'.[1]

Contemporary readers found Shakespeare's nondramatic poems no less seductive. Francis Meres, surveying the current state of English letters in *Palladis Tamia* (1598), declares that 'the soul of Ovid lives in mellifluous and honey-tongued Shakespeare, witness his *Venus and Adonis*, his *Lucrece*, and his sugared sonnets among his private friends'.[2] For Renaissance writers and readers, Ovid was the consummate poet of love, witness his how-to manual (*Ars Amatoria*), his love lyrics (*Amores*), and his encyclopedia of violent transformations wrought by lust (*Metamorphoses*). Shakespeare's two narrative poems are pages out of Ovid's book: *Venus and Adonis* tells how the love goddess's attempted seduction of a nubile young man ended in his violent death, gored in the groin by a boar, while *The Rape of Lucrece* recounts the brutal violation of a Roman matron in her bed and her subsequent suicide. Equally inspired by Ovid, so Meres implies, are the diverse passions played out in Shakespeare's sonnets. The 'sugar' in those poems comes from the writer's 'honeyed tongue', suggesting that the circulation of the poems in manuscript among Shakespeare's 'private friends' was like the passing around of confits or kisses (see also Chapters 22 and 31).

Passion as a starting point for criticism

How should we categorize the responses described by Stubbes and Meres? The first word that comes to mind may well be *sexual*. For us, *bodily* desire is *sexual* desire. There are problems, however, in applying this word to the bodily experiences of Shakespeare and his contemporaries. For a start, the English word *sexuality* and its cognates in other European languages date only from the 1830s and 1840s, when the term was coined to denote reproductive activity involving biological apparatus classified as male and as female. In fact, the earliest application of the word in English referred specifically to the reproductive processes of plants. *Sexuality* as the internal experience of bodily desire dates from much later, from the publication of Sigmund Freud's work in the early twentieth century. The word *sex* occurs in Shakespeare's plays twenty-one times, but only to refer to the biological difference of females from males.

The word that Shakespeare and his contemporaries would have applied to the phenomenon that Stubbes and Meres describe is *passion*. Freud's notion of desire is based on an energy-transfer model derived ultimately from eighteenth-century ideas about the human body as a machine; Shakespeare's notion of desire, on a biochemical model derived ultimately from the Greek physician Galen (first century AD). What did a person in 1600 imagine was happening when he or she felt the desire to conjoin his or her body with another person's body? Thomas Wright explains the process in *The Passions of the Mind in General*, published in 1604, the same year Shakespeare's company was acting *Othello*. Writing a quarter of a century before Descartes convinced most European intellectuals (and their successors down to our own day) that they could think without their bodies, Wright assumes instead that thinking starts with sense experience. First the viewer's eyes are pierced by light rays that convey the shape and colours of another person's body. Then an aerated fluid called *spiritus* carries the sensation to the phantasy or imagination, which in turn sends the image to the heart. The heart, once it apprehends the object presented by the imagination, 'immediately bendeth either to prosecute it or to eschew it, and the better to effect that affectation draweth other humours to help him'.[3]

According to Galen and his early modern disciples, there are four of these 'humours'—blood, choler, phlegm, and black bile—each sited in a separate organ but capable of changing into one another and circulating all over the body. Each of the 'humours' has different physical qualities—blood is hot and moist, choler hot and dry, phlegm cold and moist, black bile cold and dry—that can change a person's body in radical ways. If the heart decides to 'prosecute' an object presented by the imagination, the 'humour' that is drawn into action is blood. A person experiences this hot, wet rush of blood as a *passion*. If the quantity of blood is great enough, reason can be overwhelmed entirely. Reading Aristotle in his treatise *On the Soul* (*De Anima*), Wright and his contemporaries came to think of this state of desire as 'appetite' (*orexis*). To have the faculty of sensation, Aristotle says, is to have appetite: 'whatever has a sense has the capacity for pleasure and pain and therefore has pleasant and painful objects present to it, and wherever these are present, there is desire, for desire is appetition of what is pleasant' (414b.1–5).[4] Othello is drawing on the Galenic/Aristotelian model of desire when he asks the Duke to allow Desdemona to accompany him to Cyprus:

> I therefor beg it not
> To please the palate of my appetite,
> Nor to comply with heat—the young affects
> In me defunct—and proper satisfaction,
> But to be free and bounteous to her mind. . . .
> (1.3.260-4)

Othello had reason to be apologetic: his Venetian compeers would have expected a dark-skinned Moor, a denizen of the hot, moist climes of the southern Mediterranean, to be dominated by blood, at the expense of the other three 'humours', and to the detriment of reason. In strictly historical terms, Othello cannot be said to possess sexuality; what he was believed to possess instead is a 'sanguine', or bloody, temperament that predisposes him to lust.

Sexuality as a starting point for criticism

Be that as it may, sexuality inescapably remains a possession of actors, audiences, readers, and critics today. After Freud's *Three Essays on the Theory of Sexuality* (1905), after Frantz Fanon's *Black Skin, White Masks* (1952), after Michel Foucault's *A History of Sexuality* (1976–84), it is neither possible nor desirable to view a character like Othello exclusively in terms of Aristotelian ethics and Galenic medicine. What is needed is a strategy that deploys the term *sexuality* with full awareness of its present-day specificity, that recognizes the difference of bodily experience in the past from what it is today, and that bridges the gap between the two by putting past and present into dialogue. We may begin with our own concepts, but we must allow the historical record to critique those concepts, just as we use our concepts to critique the historical record. Along at least three lines of enquiry—interiority, socialization, and epistemology—the idea of *sexuality* stands as a major signpost in contemporary critical thought.

Interiority

In psychological terms, first of all, sexuality figures as a fundamental component in our sense of personal interiority. Since Freud, libido has been imagined to provide the very energy of ego-formation. If psychoanalytic critic Joel Fineman is correct, the historical beginnings of this sense of self are to be found in Shakespeare's sonnets. Certainly there are scenes in Shakespeare's plays that seem to reinforce the modern conviction that sexuality forms part of a person's core identity. Shakespeare's Troilus, for example, defines himself totally in terms of his desire for Cressida: 'Why should I war without the walls of Troy / That find such cruel battle here within?' he asks in his very first speech. 'Each Trojan that is master of his heart, / Let him to field—Troilus, alas, hath none' (*Troilus and Cressida*, 1.1.2–5). So strong is his desire, so much is the world shaped in the image of his desire, that when he sees Cressida betray him he literally cannot believe his eyes: 'This is and is not Cressid' (5.2.146). The implied sexuality of Achilles seems equally strong in determining who he *is*. Achilles refers in passing to his female concubine Briseis, but the reason for his refusal to leave his tent is his comrade-in-arms Patroclus. Thersites, never one to spare an insult, taunts Patroclus as 'Achilles' male varlet', his 'masculine whore' (5.1.14, 16). It is Patroclus's death on the battlefield that finally spurs Achilles into heroic action. Sexuality seems no less constitutive of Achilles' identity in the play than Troilus's, even as it challenges modern assumptions about how gender is aligned with sexual identity.

In the two hundred years or so since popular imagination began to isolate men who engage in sexual acts with other men as a distinct social type and to identify that social type with effeminacy, British and North American culture has attempted to enforce a rigid distinction between male friendship and male homosexuality. No such distinction was made in Shakespeare's time. Instead, the rhetoric used to exalt male bonds was charged with erotic imagery. Thus Aufidius embraces his archenemy Coriolanus using just the terms he might use in embracing his wife: 'that I see thee here, / Thou noble thing, more dances my rapt heart / Than when I first my wedded mistress saw/ Bestride my threshold' (4.5.114–17).

Shakespeare anticipates Katharine Phillips, a poet of the 1660s, in applying the same sort of rhetoric to the friendship of women. Helena in *A Midsummer Night's Dream* chides her friend Hermia's betrayal by reminding her that, as children, 'we grew together, / Like to a double cherry: seeming parted, / But yet an union in partition' (3.2.209–11). More passionate still are Emilia's memories of her friendship with Flavinia in *The Two Noble Kinsmen*. Emilia's rehearsal of all the things she shared with Flavinia—the same flower in each other's bosom, the same headgear, the same adornments to their clothing, the mutually favourite tunes that Emilia, sharing the same bed, could hear Flavinia sing 'in her slumbers'—concludes with this declaration: 'the true love 'tween maid and maid may be / More than in sex dividual' (1.3.78, 81–2).

Helena and Emilia, like Aufidius in *Coriolanus* or Shakespeare's persona in the sonnets, could speak in such blatantly physical terms in part because early modern understandings of genital passion were, by our standards, so narrow. Sodomy was against the law, but in practice prosecutions were limited to adult males who used force to engage in anal intercourse with under-aged boys, in effect making sodomy a species of rape. In both sodomy and rape, the offence was damage to another adult male's property (his wife, his marriageable daughter, his sons), not damage to the victim's personhood. Physical relations between women do not figure in the statutes or in the legal commentaries precisely because no 'real' acts of intercourse could be committed between women. In the eyes of the law at least, genital desire was of interest only when it ended in certain physical acts. No clearer case could be found in which our own concepts of sexuality need to be differentiated from early modern concepts of passion. The experience of desire may give these characters, on the stage, an illusion of interiority. What it does not give them is an identity based on object choice.

Socialization

The ambiguous place of homoeroticism in early modern culture points up the second line of inquiry in which sexuality is, for us, centrally important: as a site of socialization. Sexuality, in Foucault's analysis, is the very place where ideology intersects with the individual body. We can witness that intersection not only in prohibitions against certain physical acts but in positive inducements to feel certain feelings. Power and knowledge, the two components in Foucault's social analysis, circulated in early modern England not only through laws against male/male intercourse but through celebrations of male/male passion in the speeches of Aufidius and in the sonnets addressed to the man right fair. We also witness that circulation of knowledge and power in the position of marriage as the end toward which Shakespeare's comedies inevitably move.

In this respect *The Two Gentlemen of Verona*, arguably Shakespeare's first surviving script, sets a pattern that the later comedies all follow. Two friends, Valentine and Proteus, fall out with one another over a woman. Through all its twists and turns of plot *The Two Gentlemen of Verona* plays out the tensions between male bonds and married bonds, until a compromise of sorts is reached in the play's last scene. Valentine acquires a wife-to-be of his own, and the play ends with Valentine proclaiming to Proteus and Julia, 'our day of marriage shall be yours, / One feast, one house, one mutual happiness' (5.4.169–70). Numerous modern critics have commented on the weighty social issues that are negotiated in these flimsy lines: nothing less than the patriarchal distribution of power in early modern society versus the biological necessity of chaste and trustworthy wives in maintaining that system.

What happens in *The Two Gentlemen of Verona* is not just a matter of ideology; it is a matter of dramatic tension, of energy that builds and reaches a climax in the impending double marriages at the end. For the original audience, that tension derived in no small part from the facts of early modern social life. Other than scions of the aristocracy, whose marriages might be arranged quite early in their lives, most men and women in early modern England could not expect to be married until their mid to late twenties, when they had finished their apprenticeships or household service and had saved up enough money to establish households of their own. The legal age of marriageability for boys was fourteen and for girls twelve, fairly approximate with the ages at which boys and girls reached sexual maturity. In Galenic medicine the teens and the early twenties were deemed to be the hottest and the moistest times in the entire life cycle, and hence the most prone to excitations of blood. What happened to these blood-induced passions between puberty and marriage?

Shakespeare's comedies chart a course through the veins of the body as well as the pathways of the mind. We can feel that mounting energy with special keenness in *The Taming of the Shrew*, as Petruccio interrupts his own wedding festivities and hails Kate away from the banquet and the ceremonial putting of bride and groom to bed that usually followed the public pledging of vows in sixteenth- and seventeenth-century marriages. Petruccio, however, refuses to bed his bride until he has tamed his bride. He tells the audience so, in no uncertain words: 'some undeservèd fault / I'll find about the making of the bed, / And here I'll fling the pillow, there the bolster, / This way the coverlet, another way the sheets' (4.1.180–3). As a result, 'she shall watch [or stay awake] all night' (4.1.186). It is, perhaps, the long deferred pleasures of the marriage bed (or is it just sleep deprivation?) that explain Kate's capitulation in the play's last scene. Petruccio rewards her forty-four-line declaration of wifely deference with a one-line quip: 'Come, Kate, we'll to bed' (5.2.188). To his friends Vincentio and Lucentio he then jokes, 'We three are married, but you two are sped' (5.2.189). 'To speed' in sixteenth-century English meant 'to attain one's purpose or desire'. By Act Five, Vincentio and Lucentio have already consummated their marriages; Petruccio will succeed them in an imagined Act Six—that is, just after the audience's applause. Or perhaps during, in, and through their applause.

Read against the facts of demographic history, Shakespeare's comedies shape up as devices for arousing passions and managing them toward socially acceptable ends. Valentine and Sylvia, Proteus and Julia lead off a long procession to the altar that includes Lysander and Hermia and Demetrius and Helena in *A Midsummer Night's Dream*, Bassanio and Portia in *The Merchant of Venice*, Master Fenton and Anne Page in *The Merry Wives of Windsor*, Benedick and Beatrice and Claudio and Hero in *Much Ado About Nothing*, Orlando and Rosalind in *As You Like It*, and Orsino and Viola in *Twelfth Night*. But in performance plays did not end just there.

Audiences at The Theatre or The Curtain in the early 1590s may not have been able to participate directly in the bedding down of Petruccio and Kate, but they would have enjoyed a good substitute in the music, the dancing, and the cynical sentiments of a jig. Eyewitnesses like the Swiss traveller Thomas Platter testify that performances of plays in London's public playhouses, even tragedies, customarily ended with one of these danced and sung jests. The subject of most surviving jigs is anything but a celebration of marriage. Typically, the chief dancer—in Shakespeare's company through the 1590s he was the clown Will Kemp—succeeds in seducing someone else's wife. If Stubbes is to be believed, the play did not end even there. On paper Shakespeare's comedies, with their teleological drive toward marriage, may look like instruments of the patriarchal state apparatus, but in performance they gave passion wide room for play.

With or without a jig, with or without members of the audience bringing one another homeward to play the sodomites or worse, several of Shakespeare's comedies, especially the later ones, seem calculated to question marriage as an efficient means of socialization through sexuality. In contrast to Shakespeare's earlier comedies, the plots of *Measure for Measure* (1604) and *All's Well That Ends Well* (1605) turn on sexual unions that take place well before the end of the play. The Vienna of *Measure for Measure* is a city of brothels. Claudio has impregnated Juliet before the play even begins. Three-quarters through the play Angelo is tricked into consummating his promised marriage to Mariana. A similar substitution of one woman for another, at a similar point well before the play's last scene, seals Bertram's unwanted marriage to Helen in *All's Well That Ends Well*. It is partly as a result of these premature climaxes that each play ends on a decidedly uneasy note.

Still more subversive of marriage are the polymorphous desires that receive free play in *A Midsummer Night's Dream*, *As You Like It*, and *Twelfth Night*. In the forest outside Athens, if not in the city itself, it is possible for two women to feel as close in body as two cherries with one stone, for a king to take a man-hating Amazon as his bride by force, for a king and a queen to fall out over possession of a slave boy, for a queen to fall in love with an ass. In the Forest of Arden, if not in Duke Frederick's court, it is possible for a woman, much to the consternation of her bosom friend, to take on the disguise of Jupiter's catamite and flirt outrageously with her boyfriend. In Illyria, if not in Messaline, it is possible for a sea captain to risk his very life to pursue the young man he loves and for that young man's female twin to dress up in his likeness and enflame the desires of both a duke and a lady who has sworn off love.

Venus and Adonis presents the same dizzying array of sexual possibilities. As the story of Venus's desire for Adonis, the poem offers the reader a female subject position for contemplating a male object of desire—or rather an object of desire who combines male and female features in his white, unbearded beauty. The specific body parts that are fetishized in Shakespeare's poem—flashing eyes, rosy lips, smooth chin, white neck, ripe buttocks—are attributes of both maidens and prepubescent boys. A taste for such androgyny can be explained in part by early modern ideas of anatomy. Galen encouraged Shakespeare and his contemporaries to see one sex where we see two. Women's sexual organs were imagined to be the inverse of men's, the neck of the womb corresponding to the penis and the ovaries to the testicles. It is the greater heat of men's bodies, reached at puberty, that causes the male organs to be externalized and enlarged.

Adonis seems to occupy an ambiguous status somewhere between male and female. The position of the desiring subject with respect to this desired object could hardly be more graphic: it is Venus who does the hand-holding, the embracing, the kissing: 'Her lips are conquerors, his lips obey' (549). When Venus sees Adonis's fatal wound by a boar, the reader, along with Venus, is put in the position of a rapist: 'nuzzling in his flank, the loving swine / Sheathed unaware the tusk in his soft groin' (1115–16). Despite the female subject position implied by the narrative, the prime reader of the poem is specified in Shakespeare's dedication to be Henry Wriothesley, Earl of Southampton. Furthermore, *Venus and Adonis* belongs to a genre of lascivious Ovidian narrative poems that was associated specifically with young men who were students at the Inns of Court, London's centres of legal training. The gender of the desiring subject remains as ambiguous as the gender of the desired object. In terms of our own nomenclature, the passions played out in Shakespeare's plays and poems are not heterosexual, not homosexual, not bisexual, but *pan*sexual.

Epistemology

The third line of inquiry in which sexuality occupies a centrally important place is epistemology, the branch of philosophy that deals with what we can know and how valid our knowledge is. Sexuality exposes the limits of language as a way of knowing the world and knowing oneself. The Greeks recognized that bodily desire works against the power of the mind to name, to classify, to think. In Hesiod's *Theogony* (8th century BC) *erōs* figures as the opposite of reason. Along with Earth and Chaos, Eros is named by Hesiod as a primordial god. Among human beings it 'overpowers the intelligence in the breast, and all their shrewd planning'.[5] Earth and *erōs*, if not chaos, were likewise linked in early modern thinking. Christian adaptations of the Great Chain of Being ranged all of creation along a continuum that descended from pure spirit at the top to gross materiality at the bottom. Mankind was situated precisely at the middle. The location of the genitals on the human body, below the head, below the heart, made it easy to associate sexual activity with mankind's lower, bestial half.

One particular word that Shakespeare and his contemporaries habitually associated with the body's genital region was 'filth', a reminder that the human body was created by God out of earth. 'The Lord God also made the man of the dust of the ground', goes the account in Genesis 2:7, 'and breathed in his face the breath of life'. Especially after the fall of Adam and Eve from innocence, sexual desire could be regarded as the very essence of mankind's fleshliness, the very essence of body untempered by divine breath. What this meant in practice is that sexual behaviours of diverse sorts— behaviours to which we would attach the separate labels of 'gay', 'lesbian', 'masturbatory', 'anal', 'bestial', 'adulterous', 'incestuous'—could be lumped together as 'filth'. Take for example Thomas Gainsford's exhaustive catalogue under 'Lechery' in his miscellany *The Rich Cabinet* (1616): 'Lechery is a filthiness of such beastly variety, that men may sin with men, women with women: man may sin by himself, by and with his own wife, with beasts in abominable prostitutions: with their own bloods and kindred in incestuous manner: with other men's wives in adulterous combination: with all sorts in filthy licentiousness: and in all, both abuse God and confound [i.e., damn] themselves in body and soul'.[6]

The orifice associated most persistently with filthiness was the anus. In more ways than one, the anus figured in early modern imagination as the site of the unspeakable. A quite literal example of that circumstance can be found in the earliest printed editions of *Romeo and Juliet*. Mercutio's misogynist attacks on Juliet reach a climax in these mocking lines: 'O Romeo, that she were, O that she were / An open-arse, and thou a popp'rin' pear' (2.1.37–8). (*Poperin* was a variety of pear; it could also be heard as 'pop her in', an invitation to anal intercourse.) 'Open arse': that's what most modern editions print. When the play first appeared in print in 1597, within a year or two of its first performance, the text divulged only 'an open *Et Caetera*'. In another quarto two years later the garbled line read 'an open, or'—a bit of phonetic nonsense that has helped modern scholars reconstruct the censored original. Eighteenth-century editors like Alexander Pope and George Steevens quietly dropped the line in question.

If anal intercourse seems to be the one inadmissible form of sexual behaviour in Shakespeare's scripts, there are several reasons why. In physiological terms the anus serves, in its daily offices, as the ultimate reminder of the body's fleshly materiality. In terms of gender, the anus is disturbingly *un*gendered. Gainsford is no respecter of genders, or even of species, in his catalogue of filthy acts involving the anus. In social terms, anal intercourse is the very thing that early modern sodomy laws were set up to police. Finally, in ontological terms, in terms of its state of being, the anus presents a void, a dark vortex. As such, the anus exposes the limits of language in marking and controlling the human body, witness Bottom's transformation in *A Midsummer Night's Dream* and Aufidius's shift from mouth to anus when he moves in his welcome to Coriolanus from 'fisting each other's throat' to 'pouring war / Into the bowels of ungrateful Rome' (4.5.124, 128–9). Of all the body's parts, the anus is the fissure of deconstruction *par excellence*: it undoes all of language's pretensions to transcendental meaning.

It is this deconstructive potential that explains why so many studies of sexuality in Shakespeare's works have started with practices that have been branded as non-normative. Under close scrutiny, *hetero*sexuality turns out to be, not a thing in itself, but merely a word, a back-formation from *homo*sexuality. No better example of the instability of words with respect to sex could be found than the variety of things that 'sodomy' could mean in early modern English. In the course of the sixteenth century, the laws of the land became increasingly exact in specifying the legal definition of sodomy as an adult male forcing anal intercourse with another male, usually assumed to be a legal minor, but the term never lost its associations with Catholics, Jews, Muslims, witches, heretics, sorcerers—in effect, with all things foreign, with all things unknown, with all things uncanny.

The deconstructive potential of sexual desire and sexual acts is given a therapeutic valuation in the psychoanalytical theory of Jacques Lacan. All human beings, Lacan observes, enter the world as part of someone else's body, their mother's body. They achieve self-identity in two phases: first through a recognition of their physical separateness (which Lacan calls entering the imaginary order), then through their inculcation into language (which Lacan calls entering the symbolic order). The subjection of individuals to a particular language becomes a way of accounting for cultural differences in identity formation. The enforcement of this subjection Lacan calls 'the law of the father'. While it makes socialization possible, the symbolic order estranges individuals from their originary wholeness.

'The real' is Lacan's name for the desired but never reattainable wholeness that exists before and beyond language. Sexual desire for another person's body—particularly for access to the interior otherness that lies beyond eyes, ears, nose, mouth, vagina, and anus—becomes one way of attempting to connect with the real. Desire for the otherness that seems to lie beyond the words of fictions becomes another. Desire, for Lacan, is thus both sexual and metaphysical. To desire the illusion of interiority in another person's body and to desire the illusion of a fiction are two versions of the same impulse. The moments in works of fiction with the most power to satisfy those impulses are precisely those that exhaust language: silence, gesture, orgasm, death.

It is the relentless testing of the limits of language in expressing desire, Joel Fineman has argued, that endows Shakespeare's sonnets with such a compelling sense of interiority and hence such an irresistible power over readers in search of Lacan's real. Examples can be found in every part of the sequence. The first quatrain of sonnet 23, addressed to the fair young man, seems to ally the persona's inability to speak ('As an unperfect actor on the stage / Who with his fear is put besides his part') and his inability to perform sexually ('Or some fierce thing replete with too much rage / Whose strength's abundance weakens his own heart'). In connection with the latter two lines several commentators have called attention to the belief that ejaculation weakens a man's body. As an unperfect actor, as some fierce thing, the persona confesses that it is a 'fear of trust' that makes him 'forget to say / The perfect ceremony of love's rite' (23.1–6). Against these failures of language the persona goes on to plead the 'silent love' (23.13) witnessed by his books—in effect locating sexual desire in silence.

The sonnets may present Shakespeare's most sustained encounters with the Lacanian real, but the narrative poems and the plays derive the same power from the emptying out of language in acts of sexual desire. After her rape by Tarquin, Lucrece finds herself with *no* self precisely because patriarchal language offers a ruined wife no place to exist. 'Out, idle words', she cries in desperation, 'servants to shallow fools, / Unprofitable sounds, weak arbitrators!' (1016–17). Only the physical act of opening the veins of her body will give her release. The protracted word games of *Love's Labour's Lost* lose their sexual object when news arrives of the King's death. Biron, for one, is charged to visit 'the speechless sick' for the space of twelve months and use his wit 'to enforce the painèd impotent to smile' (5.2.828, 831). Cleopatra's 'infinite variety' (2.2.241), behaviour that beggars words, ends in the consummation of suicide. First she puts one poisonous serpent to her breast, then another, before she dies in mid sentence: 'O Antony! Nay, I will take thee too. / What should I stay—' (5.2.303–4). Charmian completes her unfinished sentence. In such moments of passion, in such failures of language, the Lacanian real seems to exist just beyond the listener's grasp.

The relationship between body and language, as deconstructionist critic Judith Butler has argued, is reciprocal: 'Language and materiality are fully embedded in each other, chiasmic in their interdependency, but never fully collapsed into one another, i.e., reduced to one another, and yet neither fully ever exceeds the other. Always already implicated in each other, always already exceeding one another, language and materiality are never fully identical nor fully different'.[7] The epistemological concerns of contemporary criticism suggest that there is likewise a reciprocal relationship between sexuality and language. *Erōs* challenges language at the same time that language constructs the forms that *erōs* takes on in different cultures. Consider Phillip Stubbes's last words: 'in their secret conclaves they play the sodomites *or worse*'. Imagining what contemporary play-goers did when they tried out in bed what they had seen on stage, Stubbes can only end by gesturing toward something beyond words.

In the last analysis, the thing that connects Stubbes with the deconstructionists is the inescapable *thereness* of the human body in the theatre. Bodies are as essential to plays in performance as electric signals are to videos. Actors have bodies, listeners/spectators have bodies, and the transactions among them in the course of a performance are energized by various forms of desire. Desire that is specifically genital seems to be a constant in the history of theatre, in Shakespeare's plays no less than in scripts by writers today. Taking genital desire as a starting point for criticism allows us to engage issues of interiority, socialization, and epistemology.

FURTHER READING

Bray, Alan. *Homosexuality in Renaissance England* (New York: Columbia University Press, 1995). The first book on male homosexuality in sixteenth- and early seventeenth-century England (it was originally published in 1982) remains essential for its treatment of social structures.

Di Gangi, Mario. *The Homoerotics of Early Modern Drama* (Cambridge: Cambridge University Press, 1997). Organized by genre (Ovidian comedy, satiric comedy, tragedy, tragicomedy), this study pays particular attention to social settings in which erotic desires were focused and deployed.

Fineman, Joel. *Shakespeare's Perjured Eye: The Invention of Poetic Subjectivity in the Sonnets* (Berkeley: University of California Press, 1986). It is Shakespeare's focus on the disjunction between seeing and hearing, between perceptions and words, Fineman argues, that makes the sonnets the first documents of modern sensibility.

Foucault, Michel. *The History of Sexuality. Vol. 1: An Introduction* trans. Robert Hurley (New York: Random House, 1978). In the course of writing two more volumes, Foucault changed his mind about just when certain paradigmatic shifts in the history of sexuality occurred, but Volume 1 lays out directions of inquiry that still govern the field today.

Laqueur, Thomas. *Making Sex: Body and Gender from the Greeks to Freud* (Cambridge, MA: Harvard University Press, 1990). Laqueur traces the full history of the idea that there is only one sex, women's organs being considered the inverse of men's. It was not until comparatively recently, Laqueur argues, that biologically essential differences between male and female have been used to create the notion of 'opposite' sexes.

Masten, Jeffrey. *Textual Intercourse: Collaboration, Authorship and Sexualities in Renaissance Drama* (Cambridge: Cambridge University Press, 1997). Starting with Plato's paradigm of artistic work as an all-male form of procreation, this book examines the erotics of male collaboration, in playwrighting practices and in the organization of acting companies as well as in fictions presented onstage.

Orgel, Stephen. *Impersonations: The Performance of Gender in Shakespeare's England* (Cambridge: Cambridge University Press, 1996). Taking anti-theatrical critics like Stubbes at their word and assuming that the fundamental appeal of drama in Shakespeare's time was indeed erotic, Orgel presents an especially interesting case for an erotics of drama that appealed to women spectators as well as men.

Smith, Bruce R. *Homosexual Desire in Shakespeare's England: A Cultural Poetics* (Chicago: Chicago University Press, 1991). Chapter Two offers an account of classical and early modern ideas about male friendship, as well as a discussion of the legal status of sodomy in the sixteenth and early seventeenth centuries.

Traub, Valerie. *Desire and Anxiety: Circulations of Sexuality in Shakespearean Drama* (London: Routledge, 1992). The 'circulations' of Traub's title refer to the multiple, often contradictory ways in which gender and sexuality—two quite distinct concepts—intersect in Shakespeare's scripts.

Traub, Valerie. *The Renaissance of 'Lesbianism' in Early Modern England* (Cambridge: Cambridge University Press, 2002). This theoretically sophisticated study specifically addresses the interplay between modern conceptual categories and the historical particulars of sixteenth- and seventeenth-century England.

NOTES

1. Philip Stubbes. *The Anatomy of Abuses in Ailgna*, ed. F. J. Furnivall (London: New Shakespeare Society, 1877–9), pp. 144–5.
2. Francis Meres. *Palladis Tamia, Wit's Treasury*, ed. D. C. Allen (New York: Scholar's Facsimiles and Reprints, 1938), fols. 280v–81.
3. Thomas Wright. *The Passions of the Mind in General*, ed. W. Webster Newbold (New York: Garland, 1986), p. 123.
4. Aristotle. *Complete Works*, ed. Jonathan Barnes (Princeton: Princeton University Press, 1984), Vol. 1, pp. 659–60.
5. Hesiod. *Theogony*, in *The Works and Days, Theogony, The Shield of Herakles*, trans. Richmond Lattimore (Ann Arbor: University of Michigan Press, 1959), p. 130.
6. Thomas Gainsford. *The Rich Cabinet Furnished with Variety of Excellent Descriptions . . . Characters . . . Discourses, and . . . Histories* (London: I.B. for Roger Jackson, 1616), sig. M2v.
7. Judith Butler. *Bodies That Matter* (London: Routledge, 1993), p. 69.

READING: *The Merchant of Venice*

On the subject of bodily desire we can approach *The Merchant of Venice* from two temporal vantage points, one grounded in sixteenth- and early seventeenth-century ideas of passion, the other in modern conceptions of sexuality.

Passion as a starting point for criticism

In numerous respects the script of *The Merchant of Venice* seems calculated to excite the audience's passions. The main plot is structured as a quest with a highly marriageable woman as its object. The rhetoric that Bassanio uses to describe that quest is borrowed from ancient Greek romances, specifically from Apollodorus's *Jason and the Argonauts*. 'In Belmont is a lady richly left', Bassanio tells Antonio, 'And she is fair, and, fairer than that word, / Of wondrous virtues'. Her renown brings suitors from the four corners of the world: 'her sunny locks / Hang on her temples like a golden fleece, / Which makes her seat of Belmont Colchis' strand, / And many Jasons come in quest of her' (1.1.161–3, 169–72). Belmont itself, whither the romantic protagonists converge toward the end of the play, is presented as a place devoted to love, the sort of place Shakespeare and his contemporaries knew as a *locus amoenus*. Lorenzo and Jessica are the first to arrive. 'The moon shines bright', Lorenzo effuses in the scene's first line (5.1.1). He goes on, however, to inaugurate with Jessica a catalogue of famous lovers, all of whom met with violence when they acted on their passions: Troilus, Thisbe, Dido, Medea. There are sinister shadows in the starlit land-scape of Belmont. Lorenzo and Jessica put themselves last in the list, exceptions, they believe, to the rule.

When music is added to the moonlight, the seduction of the senses would seem to be complete. In summoning the musicians out of the house, Lorenzo appeals to the music of the spheres, in concord with which 'the smallest orb which thou behold'st / But in his motion like an angel sings' (5.1.60–1). But darker forces are acknowledged as well. 'I am never merry when I hear sweet music', Jessica complains (5.1.68). 'Merry' carries the force here of being 'full of animated enjoyment', used in this sense in the sixteenth century chiefly in connection with feasting or sport,[1] as Lorenzo realizes when he replies, 'The reason is, your *spirits* are attentive' (5.1.69, emphasis added). 'Spirit' is being contrasted here with 'merriment', soul with body. Music has the power, Lorenzo tells Jessica, to silence the bellowing and neighing of 'a wild and wanton herd', acting on 'the hot condition of their blood' (5.1.70, 73). Even so did Orpheus charm trees, stones, and water with his lyre. In sum, 'The man that hath no music in himself, / Nor is not moved with concord of sweet sounds, / Is fit for treasons, stratagems, and spoils' (5.1.82–4). Shylock has confessed himself to be just such a man when he charges Jessica to keep his house's casements locked against the street musicians' 'sound of shallow fopp'ry' (2.5.34). The remarks exchanged between Lorenzo and Jessica at the opening of the play's last scene do more than create a pleasant atmosphere; they give visual and aural presence to an undercurrent of violence, wildness, wantonness, hot blood, treasons, stratagems, and spoils that must be quelled before the play's last line is spoken.

The mounting energy that impels all of Shakespeare's comedies toward their conclusions in marrying up and bedding down is especially forceful in *The Merchant of Venice*. It is in Act Three, Scene Two, at the very middle of the play, that Bassanio passes the casket test and claims Portia's hand. Almost immediately news arrives that Antonio's argosies have been lost and that Shylock is claiming his pound of flesh. Portia's response is decisive: 'First go with me to church and call me wife, / And then away to Venice to your friend; / For never shall you lie by Portia's side / With an unquiet soul' (3.2.302–5). Sexual consummation of their marriage will be postponed until Antonio's business with Shylock has been settled. Bassanio understands exactly what is at stake: 'till I come again', he assures Portia, 'No bed shall e'er be guilty of my stay' (3.2.322–3). The repression of sexual desire here is not unlike that in *The Taming of the Shrew*. Certainly bed is on everyone's mind when the last scene finally reaches its end. Dawn is about to break on the night that Lorenzo has filled with uneasy music. When Portia suggests that all the newly married couples—there are three of them—go into the house and ask each other questions about what has transpired, Graziano has the last word: 'Let it be so. The first inter'gatory / That my Nerissa shall be sworn on is / Whether till the next night she had rather stay, / Or go to bed now, being two hours to day' (5.2.299–302). The very design of *The Merchant of Venice* could thus be read as flirtation, foreplay, and (just beyond the play's last scene) orgasm. In that respect, it would realize Philip Stubbes's fears about the theatre.

It might, in fact, realize his *worst* fears. The play opens with the mystery of Antonio's passion. 'In sooth', Antonio says to his friends, 'I know not why I am so sad' (1.1.1). Salerio thinks Antonio's sadness is the result of anxieties about his ships. Not so, says Antonio. Salanio then hits upon another proverbial cause of melancholy: the unsatisfied love-longing that Shakespeare and his contemporaries knew as 'green sickness'. This time Antonio's response is stronger but still nonconclusive: 'Fie, fie' (1.1.46). The exact cause of Antonio's sadness is, in fact, never settled in Act One, Scene One. But the extremity to which he goes to provide for Bassanio's desires seems to confirm the opinion of many modern critics that Antonio (sad in the sixteenth-century senses of being both steadfast, firm, and constant and also trustworthy in character and judgement) is in love with his impetuous youthful friend.

Bassanio may even return the feeling. When Antonio, apparently condemned to die in yielding up his pound of flesh, enjoins Bassanio, 'Commend me to your honourable wife', Bassanio's reply is startlingly forthright:

> Antonio, I am married to a wife
> Which is as dear to me as life itself,
> But life itself, my wife, and all the world

> Are not with me esteemed above thy life.
> I would lose all, ay, sacrifice them all
> Here to this devil, to deliver you.

Portia, standing by in the guise of Balthazar, is audibly shocked: 'Your wife would give you little thanks for that / If she were by to hear you make the offer' (4.1.268, 277–84). It is, perhaps, a desire to test what Bassanio has just said that prompts Portia, later in the scene, to ask for Bassanio's engagement ring as a reward for saving Antonio's life. Sodomy, that crime not to be named among Christians, may be among the passions that animate *The Merchant of Venice*.

In the person of Shylock the script may even be staging resistance to these guilty pleasures. The Jew's insistence on payment in flesh resonates with St Paul's distinction between flesh and spirit several places in the New Testament. Christ's sacrifice has nullified the letter of Old Testament law, with its insistence on 'an eye for an eye, a tooth for a tooth' (Matthew 5:38). Christians, in contrast to Jews, 'walk not after the flesh, but after the spirit. For they that are after the flesh, savour the things of the flesh: but they that are after the spirit, the things of the spirit' (Romans 8:4–5, in the Geneva Bible, the translation used by Shakespeare). Just what does *The Merchant of Venice* invite audiences to savour? With respect to lust and passion, the play charts a carefully plotted course. At the same time that it moves toward the consummation of passion in marriage, *The Merchant of Venice* moves toward a reconciliation of flesh and spirit, exemplified in the conversion of Jessica to Christianity and her marriage to Lorenzo. Where that reconciliation leaves the triangle of Antonio-Bassanio-Portia is open to question.

Interiority

All three sets of issues implicated in modern understandings of sexuality—interiority, socialization, and epistemology—are put to the test in *The Merchant of Venice*. To modern observers it is sexual desire, precisely, that gives the principal protagonists—Antonio, Bassanio, Portia—the dramatic illusion of possessing private feelings and hence psyches that invite analysis. The mystery of Antonio's sadness has already been mentioned. Bassanio's devotion to his quest for the golden fleece in the person of Portia is just as ambiguous. Does Bassanio love Portia for herself, or is her money his real object of desire? Portia's very name suggests the 'portion' or dowry that goes with her hand. She is 'nothing undervalued', Bassanio tells Antonio, compared with Brutus's Portia. The whole world knows 'her worth'. In sum,'I have a mind presages me such thrift / That I should questionless be fortunate' (1.1.165, 167, 175–6). 'Portion', 'value', 'worth', 'thrift', and 'fortune' positively invite Freudian analysis, as unconscious signs of self-delusion, as quite conscious excuses for forsaking Antonio's love for Portia's, as an equation of money and anal eroticism in just the way Freud describes it in his papers 'From the History of an Infantile Neurosis' and 'On Transformations of Instinct as Exemplified in Anal Eroticism'. The overdetermination of the words Bassanio uses to articulate his desire heightens the sense of his possessing an interior self.

Portia, for her part, bases her very selfhood on sexual desire. She chafes under the restrictions of her father's will. 'I may neither choose who I would', she complains to Nerissa, 'nor refuse who I dislike; so is the will of a living daughter curbed by the will of a dead father' (1.2.20–2). 'Will' in sixteenth-century usage carried a strong connotation of *lustful* wilfulness, as in Shakespeare's sonnets 135 ('Whoever hath her wish, thou hast thy Will') and 136 ('If thy soul check thee that I come so near, / Swear to thy blind soul that I was thy Will'). The bawdy jokes that Portia makes about her suitors—of Monsieur le Bon she says, 'God made him, and therefore let him pass for a man' (1.2.47)—confirm that sexual desire animates her own quest in the play, a quest for self-will over her father's will.

Socialization

Sexuality in *The Merchant of Venice* is no less implicated in issues of socialization. Economics and social class are very much determinants of who feels what for whom. Bassanio's desired move from the Rialto to Belmont would, for audiences in England, represent a move up the social hierarchy from the new capitalist economy, in which rank was determined by the amount of money a man had amassed, to the traditional feudal economy, in which rank was determined by possession of land. Many capitalists in Shakespeare's England had made exactly such a move as a way of legitimizing their newly acquired wealth. Indeed, Shakespeare himself used the capital he earned as an actor and playwright to establish himself back in Stratford as a landlord.

It is not money, however, that allows Bassanio to make that desired move up the social hierarchy but his sex appeal. He has depleted his resources, he tells Antonio, 'By something showing a more swelling port / Than my faint means would grant continuance' (1.1.124–5). His dependence on Antonio can be measured, he confesses, 'in money and in love' (1.1.131). Antonio uses two alliterating [p] sounds to make the same equation of love and commerce when he replies, 'be assured / My purse, my person, my extremest means / Lie all unlocked to your occasions' (1.1.138–9).

The contested place of sexual desire in the play's economy is made patently clear in the case of Jessica, whose elopement with a casket containing her father's ducats and her mother's ring, is planned in counterpoint with Morocco and Aragon's greedy showings in the casket test set by Portia's father. Ducats and rings are, indeed, used as pawns in all the play's sexual intrigues. Even Shylock cannot make a strictly materialist separation. Of the ring that Jessica has stolen and traded for a monkey he says, 'I had it of Leah when I was a bachelor. I would not have given it for a wilderness of monkeys' (3.1.101–2). It is a ring that forces the issue of whom Bassanio loves better, Antonio or Portia. And it is the metaphor of 'Nerissa's ring' that focuses the anxieties about sexual fidelity in the play's very last words (5.1.306). The awarding of all Shylock's wealth to Jessica and Lorenzo in the courtroom scene seems to represent an attempt to make Shylock the scapegoat for the play's relentlessly 'thrifty' sexuality, in just the way he is made to serve that function for the play's anxieties about flesh and filth.

Gender figures in obvious and not-so-obvious ways in the construction of sexuality in *The Merchant of Venice*. In the love triangle of Antonio-Bassanio-Portia, the middle position is occupied, not by a woman, but by a young man, just as it is in Shakespeare's sonnets. Bassanio figures as an erotic object for both Antonio and Portia. It is Antonio's devotion to Bassanio that supplies the dominant motive of the play's opening scene. At the close of that scene Bassanio declares his desire for Portia in fifteen effusive but highly ambiguous lines (1.1.161–76). Portia's desire for Bassanio in the next scene (1.2.94–101) has, by contrast, coy understatement to vouch for its authenticity. Do you remember a certain Venetian scholar and soldier, Nerissa asks her mistress. 'Yes, yes, it was Bassanio—as I think, so was he called' (1.2.97). The way in which Portia stage manages Bassanio's trial with the caskets leaves no doubt about her desires. Once Bassanio has passed the test, Portia addresses her husband to be, for the first time, by his new patrician title of 'Lord Bassanio' (3.2.149) and submits herself and her goods to his command: 'Myself and what is mine to you and yours / Is now converted' (3.2.166–7).

That power is contingent, however, on Bassanio's keeping the ring she gives him. Failure to keep the ring will mean 'the ruin of your love / And be my vantage to exclaim on you' (3.2.173–4). 'Ruin' and 'vantage', let it be noted, are financially charged words, with a special application to Antonio. When Bassanio gives away Portia's ring, he gives away his mastery as Lord Bassanio. In the play's last scene Portia, jokingly to be sure, uses the forfeited ring as her excuse to declare 'by mine honour, which is yet mine own' (5.1.231) that she will henceforth sleep with whom she pleases. Portia ends up rather in the position of a rich widow who has married one of her servants. She can control the social upstart she has married in a way she could never have controlled Morocco or Aragon. Bassanio, with respect to both his lovers, thus ends up in the sexually ambiguous position of Adonis in *Venus and Adonis*, of 'Ganymede' in *As You Like It*, of 'Cesario' in *Twelfth Night*.

Race and ethnicity also enter into the construction of sexual desire in *The Merchant of Venice*. Although a long roll-call of Portia's suitors is provided by Nerissa in the second scene, the suitors whom the audience actually sees and hears represent the two political powers that Shakespeare's contemporaries feared most: the Muslims and the Spanish. Morocco and Aragon not only show themselves to be absolute fools; they are effectively castrated by the terms of Portia's father's will. Any suitor who chooses wrong has to promise never to marry. Morocco responds despairingly to the golden casket's advice that his suit is 'cold': 'Cold indeed, and labour lost. / Then farewell heat, and welcome frost' (2.7.73–5). When he has gone, Portia makes the racial point bluntly clear, in terms specific to Galenic medicine: 'Let all of his complexion choose me so' (2.7.79). 'Complexion' refers to the predominance of hot blood in Morocco's make-up, the product of the hot climate in which he lives. The casket test has turned the hot blood of Muslims to cold frost and eliminates them as sexual predators. Aragon, in his capitulation, is equally aware of the sterility to which he has condemned himself: 'Sweet, adieu', he tells Portia.

'I'll keep my oath / Patiently to bear my wroth' (2.9.76–7)—that is to say, his sorrow or regret.

The embroilment of race and ethnicity in sexual desire is displayed most prominently, however, in the scapegoating of Shylock. The man derided in the courtroom scene in a single contemptuous syllable, 'Jew', becomes the repository of the flesh, filth, and fetishization of money that the Christians would rather forget. He also becomes the repository of the Christians' anxieties about sodomy. It was proverbial in early modern Europe that Jews give off a foul smell, the so-called *foetor judaicus*, which helps to explain their connection in popular imagination with excrement, poison, and anal intercourse. In 1594, a year or two before Shakespeare wrote *The Merchant of Venice*, Londoners had witnessed the execution of Dr Roderigo Lopez, Queen Elizabeth's private physician—and a converted Portuguese Jew—on suspicion of having attempted to poison the queen. In an age that put much faith in purging, many medicines were administered as enemas.

Epistemology

Anxieties about sodomy in *The Merchant of Venice* point up, finally, the challenges that sexuality poses for epistemology, for testing the limits of knowledge. As human beings we know the world—or at least we *think* we know the world—through language. *Erōs* exposes the arbitrariness of language, especially when human beings attempt to control *erōs* by marking binaries like male/female, Christian/Jew, and sodomite/friend. The script of *The Merchant of Venice* manifests a keen consciousness of this process of meaning-marking, and of its undoing. The play's happy outcome depends on Portia's legal exegesis of the written bond that Shylock makes with Antonio—an exegesis that reduces the document to its most literal meaning in a way that runs counter to common sense. The play is full of other texts that demand precise interpretation: the stipulations of Portia's father's will (1.2.24–8), Shylock's citation of Genesis 27:1–40, 30:22–42, and 31:9–11 with respect to Jacob's breeding of ewes (1.3.67–92), the inscriptions contained within the three caskets (2.7.65–73, 2.9.62–71, 3.2.131–8), the hints that Portia drops in telling Bassanio 'I could teach you / How to choose *right*' (3.2.10–11, emphasis added), the additional prompts provided by the song 'Tell me where is fancy bred?' (3.2.63–72), the conditions that Portia lays down when she gives Bassanio the ring (3.2.171–4). Appropriately for Europe's greatest trading metropolis, the world of *The Merchant of Venice* depends on language, particularly on the *written* language of bonds, for its viability. That dependence on language is called into question by the falsely spoken (Bassanio's promise never to give up Portia's ring), the unspoken (Portia's hints to Bassanio in how to choose right), and the unspeakable (Antonio's sexual attachment to Bassanio).

Deconstruction as a critical practice begins with awkward silences. In such moments, so the argument runs, a text betrays the inherent contradictions out of which it is compacted (see also Chapter 34). The most prominent of such moments in *The Merchant of Venice* involve Antonio, the character for whom the play is named. Antonio is silent when he ought to speak in the play's first scene. Why *is* he, after all, so sad? He is likewise silent in the play's last scene. Portia's report of the news that his ships have come safely to port prompts this three-word response: 'I am dumb' (5.1.278). A few moments later he utters just three short lines expressing gratitude to Portia as the bearer of the good news (5.1.285–7). Otherwise, amid the couplings of Bassanio and Portia, Graziano and Nerissa, Lorenzo and Jessica, Antonio stands oddly silent. In the eyes and ears of deconstructionist critics, Antonio's apartness and his silences undermine the certitudes that the play seems to be affirming: the conclusion in heterosexual marriages, the restoration of Bassanio and Graziano to power as husbands, the triumph of Christian spirit over Jewish flesh, the suppression of sodomy.

In Early Modern English the very word 'sodomy' acted as a free radical. 'Sodomy' may have been seized upon as a way to name and hence to control a perceived threat to the social order, but in practice the word covered a host of menacing Others: heretics, papists, traitors, witches, Jews, and Italians as well as men who engage in anal penetration with one another. The first English statutes against sodomy were designed specifically to disenfranchise Catholic monks. It was Italian merchants, the seventeenth-century legal commentator Sir Edward Coke claims, who first introduced sodomy into England. Jews, as we have seen, were likewise associated with anal intercourse. With respect to *The Merchant of Venice* we may ask, 'Which is the merchant here, and which the Jew?' (4.1.169). Above all, sodomy threatened to tarnish the sterling language in which male friendship, the noblest of human bonds, was conventionally celebrated. Antonio's silences, and Antonio's sexuality, expose these slippages in meaning. The play may attempt to displace the resultant anxieties onto Shylock, but Antonio stands disconcertingly alone in the play's last scene, the binary opposite of all that the other characters stand for, and hence a reminder that making meanings by marking opposites ultimately leads nowhere.

FURTHER READING

Belsey, Catherine. 'Love in Venice', *Shakespeare Survey 44* (1992), 41–53. Economic history, gender construction, and political issues are combined with Lacanian psychoanalytical theory in this provocative essay.

Harris, Jonathan Gil. *Foreign Bodies and the Body Politic: Discourses of Pathology in Early Modern England* (Cambridge: Cambridge University Press, 1998). In a discussion of Christopher Marlowe's play *The Jew of Malta*, Harris presents the historical evidence that Jews were thought to have a peculiar smell that associated them with filth and disease.

Newman, Karen. 'Reprise: Gender, Sexuality, and Theories of Exchange'. In *The Merchant of Venice*. Theory in Practice Series (Buckingham: Open University Press, 1996). Summarizing and extending her earlier work on the construction of femininity in early modern England, Newman argues that Portia seizes the male system of women as objects of economic and sexual exchange and uses it to her own advantage.

Normand, Lawrence. 'Reading the Body in *The Merchant of Venice*', *Textual Practice* 5(1) (1991), 55–73. Normand demonstrates how human bodies are always calling into question the efficacy of words.

Sinfield, Alan. 'How to Read *The Merchant of Venice* Without Being Heterosexist'. In *Alternative Shakespeares*, Vol. 2, ed. Terrence Hawkes (London: Routledge, 1996). Through a particularly searching reading of Antonio's position in the play, Sinfield's essay exemplifies how deconstruction can be combined with materialist history.

NOTES

1. *Oxford English Dictionary*, 2nd ed. (Oxford: Clarendon Press, 1989), 'merry' 3. Further references to the *OED* are cited in the text.

31 | **Psychoanalytic criticisms**

Lynn Enterline

The history of the relationship between psychoanalysis and criticism of Shakespeare—as of Renaissance literature and culture more generally—is rich and complex. The reasons for this are several. First, as the considerable distance between popular and academic versions of 'Freud' testifies, the significance of Freud's legacy is still hotly contested between various psychoanalytic, philosophical, and political schools of thought. His work has been both influential and divisive across a number of disciplines. Readers interested in Freud's legacy, and how it intersects with the criticism of Shakespeare, confront widely divergent claims about the nature and direction of Freud's insights—and by that route, distinctly different views about the nature of human subjectivity and sexuality. Second, the way literary and cultural critics, including Shakespearians, interpret and make use of psychoanalysis today is intimately tied to debates within feminism, the intellectual/political movement for which psychoanalytic theory has been both central and controversial. Some familiarity with the history of debates within and between American and European feminism (also discussed in Chapter 29) helps one understand the various ways critics have either rejected Freud or found his work useful for cultural critique. And third, literary texts—many of them Shakespeare's—played a crucial role in the foundation of psychoanalytic thinking. For instance, Freud derived the name, 'the Oedipus Complex' from Sophocles's play. As such a derivation suggests, literature cannot be entirely disentangled from the kind of knowledge psychoanalysis created.

The title of this chapter uses the plural, 'Psychoanalytic criticisms', to suggest the wide range of interpretive work that Freud has inspired among readers of Shakespeare. The plural indicates that this kind of work does not propound a unified approach to, or method of reading, Shakespeare's texts. Indeed, because critics who bring psychoanalysis to bear on Shakespeare must negotiate several highly developed bodies of writing—psychoanalytic, literary, philosophical, political—whose aims and techniques are not always compatible, it has been an extremely contentious field of critical endeavour. It is not the aim of this chapter, therefore, to present a comprehensive account of all the kinds of interpretation that Freud, and psychoanalytic theory more generally, has inspired in criticism of Shakespeare. Rather, it will give a sense of the kinds of questions that critics today who think in a psychoanalytic manner ask about literary texts. In particular, it will describe the distinctive topics, concerns, and categories of analysis that distinguish contemporary psychoanalytic approaches from other ways of reading Shakespeare.

Literature and the unconscious

Over the course of an enormous and varied body of writing, Freud frequently refers to Shakespeare's plays, whether in the form of brief allusions or fully developed interpretations. The founder of psychoanalysis was widely conversant with the tradition of literary and visual arts in the west. His writing attests to a life-long fascination with the question of what creative work might tell us about the nature of human subjectivity and sexuality. Other sixteenth-century artists—such as Leonardo da Vinci and Rembrandt—and poets—Lodovico Ariosto and Torquato Tasso—are prominent among the many Renaissance figures who appear alongside Shakespeare in Freud's investigation of what literature and the arts reveal about the human psyche. That a turn-of-the-century physician (1856–1939) developed a theory of subjectivity that frequently draws on Renaissance examples encouraged some literary critics and historians to argue that Freud's work supports Jakob Burckhardt's famous (and much debated) contention that the Renaissance saw a turn towards 'individualism', and thus a recognizably 'modern' form of subjectivity.

The most important thing to understand about Shakespeare's place in Freud's writing, however, applies equally to the many other poets and painters who appear there. Freud alludes so frequently to literary texts, and tries his hand at his own version of literary criticism, in large part because his theories about psychic life—particularly his hypothesis of the unconscious—revolve around questions of symbolism, interpretation, and what he calls 'the conditions of representation'. The title of Freud's most famous work, *The Interpretation of Dreams*, reveals that for its founder, psychoanalysis was born out of an extended meditation on the act of interpreting. Whether discussing plays, paintings, poems, or patients' dreams, Freud looks at the human psyche by asking what it means that we are creatures who are constantly representing things, whether to ourselves (when sleeping) or to others (in every day life as well as in literary texts). If for no other reason, literary critics admire Freud's investigations and case histories for their attention to details of language and symbolization, a procedure that reminds many of the close, attentive reading that literary criticism demands.

Freud's way of reading, however, upsets common-sense notions of authorship as the controlling consciousness behind a text. Partly due to Freud's influence, the category of intention that once guided literary interpretation has lost its privileged place. His theories about what it means for human beings to be subject to language sprang from years of thinking about kinds of expression that others dismissed as insignificant: dreams, jokes, slips of the tongue, bodily symptoms and movements. In such phenomena he found not only legible signs, but also a world of meanings crucial to—yet tellingly unacknowledged by—the speakers themselves. As if he'd spent a life-time listening to the oblique yet curiously revealing gabble of a character like Dogberry in *Much Ado About Nothing*, Freud took language's trifles very seriously. As one psycho-analytic critic puts it, for Freud, in every 'infelicity of language', something else is 'quite successfully getting said'.[1] But whatever it is that is 'getting said' does not corre-spond with what the speaker believed or even wanted to say. The speaker, in fact, would be horrified could she or he but hear the repressed thought behind the infelicity.

For Freud, that is because dreams and slips of the tongue are ways of evading the internalized censor imposed on us all as we come, belatedly, to decipher the world of adult sexual meanings. He viewed shame and guilt as social precipitates rather than natural feelings, the historical after-effect of enforced taboo that organizes which desires will count as normal and acceptable in a given culture. Shame and guilt, in other words, reveal the way that the outside, social world is folded inside the self and the difference between them forgotten (relegated to the unconscious and lived as personal desire and belief). Because it is imposed from without, moreover, this internalized censor is both vigilant and yet liable to break down. One of the central tasks of psychoanalytic literary criticism, therefore, has been to investigate moments where something else gets said about gender and desire than the story we think we already know.

As the French psychoanalyst Jacques Lacan built a career from pointing out, Freud's insights into society's extraordinary pressure on human subjectivity and sexuality came from a lifetime of investigating the ways that language exceeds and masters its speakers rather than the other way around. Lacan therefore uses the term 'the speaking-subject' to refer to language's pride of place in Freud's theories about how individuals become social beings. It is no accident that such fascination with the unexpected reversal of priority between speakers and their language, which Freud shares with Shakespeare, has drawn the attention of many psychoanalytic readers of Shakespeare's plays and poems.[2] Both authors put great stock in puns, quibbles, slips of the tongue—a tendency for which they both have been criticized. A psychoanalytic critic would observe that such criticisms are born of a cherished, but poorly examined, assumption about the self: that we are the authors and controlling agents of our own discourse. It is perhaps Joel Fineman, in *Shakespeare's Perjured Eye*, who most thoroughly brought Freud's reversal of priority between language and subjectivity to bear on Shakespearian poetry. Fineman coined the phrase 'subjectivity-effect' in light of this reversal and argues that the speaker in Shakespeare's sonnets is not a re-presentation or expression of a pre-existing subjectivity. Rather, because of its experiments with the conventions of previous (Petrarchan) love poetry, the cycle *produces* a convincing (and extremely influential) fiction of personal interiority as the after-effect of its formal and rhetorical innovations.

Lacan pursued his theory of our subjection to a 'Symbolic order'—the language in which speaking-subjects come, ever precariously, into social being—by drawing on Ferdinand de Saussure's theory of semiotics. 'Semiotics' is the science of the verbal, visual, and gestural signs by which people communicate and give significance to their worlds; Lacan argued that Freud was working in the direction of modern semiotics avant la lettre [before it was invented]. Drawing extensively on de Saussure's theory of the sign, Lacan extended Freud's insights by attending to language's foundational, mediating force as well as its elusive nature as a system without positive terms. The fact that we must speak at all to get what we want is an index, for Lacan, of a foundational 'want-in-being' in speaking-subjects. Not only must words stand in for objects that are therefore by definition absent to the one who speaks of them. According to de Saussure, words themselves mean only in relation to other words that they are not, and operate according to a systemic logic of difference and deferral.

On Lacan's view, language transforms need (for this or for that thing) into desire (for some X that is always missing). Language changes our relation to the world—renders it, in a fundamental way, fugitive. Fineman argued in light of Lacan that Shakespeare's insight into this predicament, into what the 'languageness of language' does to our knowledge of the world as well as our desire for it, is most forcefully articulated in the sonnets. As the speaker tells us in the sonnets to the dark lady, the language of the poet's 'lying' tongue of 'false compare' interferes with the 'truth of vision', distorting the world through the lens of a 'perjur'd eye'.[3] On Fineman's account, the sonnets share terrain with psychoanalytic theory. Not only do they explore how language 'gives the lie to my true sight', but as poems about the language of love, they suggest that desire is produced and sustained out of this misfiring between words and the world.

If we pay attention to Freud's insight into the vicissitudes of speaking subjectivity, the centrality of Renaissance writers to Freud's work seems rather less reassuring about 'individualism' than may appear to be the case. It helps to recall a moment when Freud, commenting on the historical place of psychoanalysis, compared his discovery of the unconscious to the impact of another, sixteenth-century discovery. He wrote that the 'wound' dealt to human narcissism by psychoanalysis was comparable to the wound dealt by Copernicus when he proposed that the sun does not revolve around the earth but rather that the earth revolves around the sun.[4] As Freud saw it, when it comes to the way we view ourselves, the hypothesis of the unconscious compounds the effect of Copernicus's revolution. Where the sixteenth-century scientist asked us to question the previously accepted truth of earth's centrality, Freud asked us to question the centrality of the human mind, of conscious self-understanding. He challenged our 'narcissistic illusion' and 'self-love' because he displaced consciousness—the supposed centre of our world—with a theory of the self's foundational blindness to itself. As Freud put it, psychoanalytic inquiry shows that 'the ego is not even master in its own house'.[5] Freud's work therefore brings with it a crucial critical distance from common-sense notions of individuality, authorship, subjectivity, and intentional agency. It establishes an important critical distance from Burckhardt's claim that the Renaissance saw the birth of modern 'individualism' in so far as Burckhardt is denoting the possibility of self-determination and independence based on a complete understanding of one's thoughts and desires. In Freud's view, by contrast, we are all in some sense blind to our own history, 'strangers to ourselves'.[6]

Subjectivity and sexuality

For the purposes of a general introduction to the variety of psychoanalytic criticisms of Shakespeare practised today, there is a crucial difference between the way Freud is read and understood by two psychoanalytic schools: 'ego-psychology' or 'object-relations' theory (a school that developed in Britain and carried considerable influence in the United States) and the theories of Jacques Lacan (loosely dubbed 'the French Freud'). The difference between these two, very different ways of understanding Freud has had considerable impact upon criticism of Shakespeare.

While these differences guide the analysis below, however, it must be remembered that there is something more important at work than this divide between British ego psychology and the theories of Lacan in the way Shakespearians deploy psycho-analysis. That is, it is predominantly feminist critics (on both sides of the Anglo-American/French divide) who turned to psychoanalytic theory because they find in it a way to make gender and sexuality central categories of literary and cultural analysis. Whatever their specific affiliation, feminists who deploy psychoanalytic texts and categories find in Freud's writing revealing moments in which the question of sexual difference leads Freud (sometimes in spite of himself) not to endorse but to think his way around and through the patriarchal structures he describes.[7] Whether working within the terms of object-relations theory or Lacan's focus on symbolic structures, many Shakespearian feminists agree with Juliet Mitchell's argument that 'psycho-analysis is not a recommendation *for* a patriarchal society, but an analysis *of* one'.[8] As figures like Theseus, Lear, Hamlet senior, or Prospero suggest, 'patriarchy' in Shake-speare's plays means not simply male dominance but carries the precise sense of 'the rule of the father'. A central concern in psychoanalytic criticism of Shakespeare, therefore, has been to analyse the symbolic function and meaning of the family (whether in his plays and poems or in the social institutions which inflect those texts).

Object-relations theory, which developed from the work of Melanie Klein and D. W. Winicott, designates a psychoanalytic practice that examines the subject's inter-actions with its surroundings, especially the 'phantasies' that characterize the subject's earliest relations with its parents and that continue to influence stages of develop-ment.[9] Object-relations theory is noted for focusing on very early, 'pre-Oedipal' rela-tions between mother and child—an aspect that early feminists felt Freud overlooked in his emphasis on the Oedipus complex and the father's (socially inflected) role as the law-giver. Shakespearians allied with British object-relations theory tend to focus on either the figure of the mother in Shakespeare's works and/or on Shakespeare's characters, reading their motives, conflicts, and desires according to a theory of how the ego and sexual identity develop. The genre of psychobiography, frequently allied to object-relations theory, is evident in criticism of other major literary figures. So far it has had minimal impact on Shakespeare studies because we know so little of his life and because the collaborative nature of the Renaissance theatre vitiates a strongly author-oriented approach.

In part due to the early feminist contention that Freud's theories were derogatory to women, a number of Shakespearians embraced the work of Winicott and Klein in order to focus on the mother—or the mother-child relation—as a crucial determinant in psychological and sexual development. Such a focus seemed to redress the perceived imbalance in Freudian theory and also to explain the clearly vexed representation of maternity in Shakespeare's plays. These critics drew attention to the evident anxiety surrounding such figures as Tamora, Gertrude, Lady Macbeth, Volumnia, and the pregnant Hermione—or to complaints like that of *Cymbeline*'s Posthumus: 'Is there no way for men to be, but women / Must be half-workers?' (2.5.1–2). The most influential use of object-relations theory in relation to Shakespeare is perhaps Janet Adelman's *Suffocating Mothers*. A study of the way Shakespeare's representation of 'masculine selfhood' is 'embedded in maternal origin', Adelman's book examines the role of maternity in the shape of Shakespeare's career. She draws attention to the fact that after *The Comedy of Errors* and *Titus Andronicus*, mothers virtually disappear: in the early plays, 'masculine identity is constructed in and through the absence of the maternal'. But this 'occluded mother returns with a vengeance in *Hamlet*' and shapes the subsequent plays according to a phantasy of 'overwhelming contamination at the site' of maternal origin. Such contamination means that men in ensuing plays inherit Hamlet's tragic burden of a self reacting against such contamination and that women 'pay the price for the fantasies of maternal power invested in them'.[10]

Suffocating Mothers was published in 1992, but its powerful argument is clearly the product of the intersection between feminism and psychoanalysis articulated in and through object-relations theory. The theory on which Adelman draws, however, had already become the focus of extensive criticism in both feminist and Lacanian circles. In the late 70's and early 80's, largely due to the work of Juliet Mitchell, Gayle Rubin, and Jacqueline Rose, many feminists became critical of the impulse to privilege the mother-child relation—or at least of the tendency to focus on that relation in isolation from the father. They observed that early feminist objections to Freud's emphasis on the figure of the father—for example, his theory of the Oedipus Complex or emphasis on the fear of castration—mistook the messenger (Freud) for the message (patriarchy's foundational yet damaging psychological effects). They were also sceptical that the exclusive focus on the *body* of the mother in object-relations theory risks grounding the vicissitudes of identity and sexuality in the immutable world of anatomy and biology. As one critic objected, psychoanalytic studies treating mother-son relations in Shakespeare as the 'genetic cause' for crises of identity rather than a persuasive cultural phantasy 'obscures the extent to which social, cultural, and political circumstances influence family structure'.[11]

Current psychoanalytic work makes a concerted effort to read the impact of family structure on the subject in light of early modern social, cultural, and political circumstances. In a related move, feminists drew renewed attention to Lacan's argument that Freud (despite the occasional reductive remark) was not a biological determinist. Rather, if read carefully, Freud offers feminism an anti-foundationalist theory of sexuality—one in which the force of cultural taboo, and the contingency of particular historical experience, mean that whatever sexual 'identity' one acquires is, at best, a fragile construct liable to break down. Emphasis falls less on stages, development, and persons, as in object-relations criticism, than on the unconscious—on the distorting effects of culture and language, and thus on phantasy, prohibition, and accident on early modern subjectivity and sexuality.

The turn in object-relations theory to studying the mother-child relationship followed, in part, from the widely held position that Freud was disproportionately interested in the story of fathers and sons. His best known, and perhaps most controversial theory, was the Oedipus complex. On this theory, a son's psychic life is formed around a foundational taboo against incest. Leaning heavily on Sophocles's *Oedipus Rex* and Shakespeare's *Hamlet*, Freud argued that the cultural demand for exogamy—in other words, marriage 'outside one's social unit'—produces in a son a repressed desire for his mother and murderous rage against his father. For Freud, a son-in-the-making (only imperfectly) relinquishes incestuous desires for his mother because the father's threat of castration *forces* him to renounce it. This paternal threat—a demand for exogamy—gives rise to emotions that are inadmissible and hence relegated to the unconscious. But the fact that Freud detected an unconscious life at all meant that the threat was only ever partially successful. Prohibited desires still speak through—in dreams, jokes, and slips of the tongue. Or in Hamlet's case, in his mother's 'closet' (in 3.4).

It is crucial to understand that in Freud's work, the paternal 'threat of castration' is a culturally invested *phantasy*—not a perception of the real world, or of real bodies, but a socially-mediated imposition of hierarchical meaning upon bodily difference. It is a phantasy that eventually comes, ever imperfectly, to sustain what counts in a given culture as the difference between the sexes. In a theory that argues for the social imposition of a fear of castration, Freud writes that a 'son' learns to read female bodies in a culturally significant way. While bodies *per se* 'mean' nothing to infants, for whom gender makes no sense, a son-in-the-making slowly learns to read his own and the bodies of others retrospectively through a social lens. He learns to interpret sexual difference in light of a threat that he has slowly, imperfectly internalized as what will happen if he does not obey his father's taboo. The phantasy of castration speaks to a boy's accession to a social and familial world organized around the primacy of paternal power. It is a sex/gender system about which he must learn several things if he is to find a socially acceptable place: what it means in his culture that his mother is a 'woman'; that he must not be a woman; and that he must turn his erotic attention elsewhere.

From a feminist perspective, Freud's theory of castration speaks to the pervasive, yet oddly incoherent, place of women: undervalued and overvalued, said to be inferior yet generating tremendous desire and fear. In addition, this theory implies that women's devalued position in culture is not the result of bodily inferiority. Rather, the female body is not inferior but is *figured*, and hence perceived, as lacking or 'castrated'. An asymmetrical distribution of power between the sexes imposes a symbolic value on bodily difference that is lived and perceived as hierarchical truth.

Freud drew support for his theory from clinical practice but also from Hamlet's seemingly jealous obsession with his mother's sexual life—an obsession that nearly derails Hamlet from obeying his dead father's command. Feminists have criticized Freud's tendency to take the son's story—and thus, in some way, Hamlet's—as the model for all subjectivity. This tendency may indeed be revealing for both Freud's personal life and the prejudices of his historical moment. But given the support he found for this theory in such culturally valued texts as *Oedipus Rex* and *Hamlet*, it may be just as revealing for the longer reach of culture he was describing. Moreover, feminists and scholars of gay and lesbian studies alike have begun to point out that if one looks at Freud's work as a whole, particularly at *Three Essays on a Theory of Sexuality*, his theory was far more radical than that of the Oedipus complex.

In *Three Essays* in particular, Freud describes not merely a taboo against incest— and thus a demand for exogamy—but a simultaneous taboo against homosexuality. In this text Freud argues that the repression of love for one's parents operates across both genders and in relation to both parents. His theory of infantile sexuality argues for primary bisexuality in everyone—and therefore makes heterosexual object choice in adult life a complex social problem to be explained and not assumed. In other words, Freud is describing 'the mechanisms by which the sexes are divided and deformed, of how bisexual, androgynous infants are transformed into boys and girls'.[12] The Oedipus complex, therefore, is but one thread in a far more complex interweaving of various stories that psychoanalytic theory might have told—and might still tell—about the effects on the psyche of the social ordering of 'normal' sexual relations. Recent feminist work in Shakespeare studies therefore tries not to assume that the subject in question is male or the desire in question is necessarily, or univocally, heterosexual. At the same time, it interrogates the cultural imposition, and literary articulation, of father-power—as well as what literature has to tell us about the effects of such power on the mutable, overlapping worlds of gender, sexuality, and desire.

Whether accurately or not, Lacan argues that object-relations psychology misses the truly radical nature of Freud's insights because it relies on a notion of a given or unified self that Freud's hypothesis of the unconscious rigorously puts into question. As described earlier, Lacan's self-proclaimed 'return to Freud' analyses Freud's reflections on the 'conditions of representation' in light of contemporary semiotics. Rather than concentrate on a given subject's relation to its world of cherished objects, Lacan follows Freud to focus squarely on language, on its omnipresent mediation between the subject and the world.

In addition, Lacan also makes no apologies for Freud's focus on the figure of the father. On the contrary, he felt that attempts to redress a perceived imbalance in Freud's work—his concentration on the father—by giving equal time to the mother risks missing what is most telling about this imbalance. That is, it is the product of Freud's effort to describe the psychic effects of a deep social and cultural investment in sustaining father-power. For Lacan, Freud's focus on the father had to do with the *price* a patriarchal social order requires of its subjects. His position relies on a minimal universal axiom: that in order to become socialized, individuals are required to renounce some of their wishes. It also relies on an historical axiom: the power to enforce such renunciation has been—though it need not be—symbolized in western culture in the figure of the father.

For this social figuration of the father as the one whose prohibitions count in the sexual lives of his children, Lacan invented a variety of phrases: the Phallus, the Name of the Father, the Law of the Father. All of these phrases signify a cultural, rather than inevitable, position and are not to be confused with any particular father (who may well not live up to the social phantasy he is called upon to embody). As one psycho-analyst observes, 'the Oedipus complex is not reducible to an actual situation—to the actual influence exerted by the parental couple over the child'. Rather this theory raises an historically specific question: in a given society, 'which social role—or even which institution—incarnates the proscriptive agency'?[13]

When Lacan argues that the Father is a symbolic rather than real position as the one who usually incarnates the proscriptive agency in western culture, he draws attention to the sheer force of social convention in the production of sexuality (hence the stern, yet also the ironic, ring to the phrase 'the Law of the Father'). But because Lacan's writing is deliberately difficult, readers often miss his irony. They miss that Lacan is often subtly suggesting that force is necessary precisely because sexual identity is a ruse—a socially sanctioned construct that individuals are enjoined to adopt but never seamlessly occupy. Identity as such—both personal and sexual—is precisely what psy-choanalysis apprehends in its failure. In Lacan's reading of Freud, individuals become either masculine or feminine by learning a gender defined negatively against the other. Proposing what he called an elliptical definition of sexual difference, Lacan extended Freud's 'Copernican revolution' to include sexual identity: with no stable meaning of its own, each sex revolves around the other, defined only in negative relation to the one it is not. And so, while psychoanalytic theory interests feminist critics for making gender and sexuality central categories of analysis, it does so with a difference. Unlike sociological accounts of gender norms, which assume that such norms are roughly functional, psychoanalysis argues that they are not.

'The Law of the Father' forces its subjects to acknowledge a culturally determined notion of difference. But it is legible as a law, rather than an innate characteristic, precisely because it can be, and frequently is, disobeyed. What emerges, instead, is an ongoing, unresolved question of what precisely *is* the difference in sexual difference. One hallmark of psychoanalytic criticism, particularly criticism indebted to Lacan, is its investigation of the *failure* of gender categories—its attention to the way desire resists being reduced to or contained by conventional stories of gender and sexuality.

The future of psychoanalytic criticism

Where will psychoanalytic criticism of Shakespeare go from here? Recent trends are suggestive. Shakespearians increasingly tend to think about gender and desire as fluid, sites of struggle and contest rather than accomplished or given identities. They also challenge the either/or binary of pre-Oedipal vs. Oedipal analysis, opting instead to read the way phantasies of maternal and paternal power inflect each other and help shape Shakespeare's influential 'subjectivity-effects'. Thinking of sexual difference as an unresolved personal and historical *question* has encouraged analyses of the way his figurative language can associate not only female figures but also male ones, like Shylock and Falstaff, with 'pre-Oedipal' phantasies about symbiosis, contamination, and threats to identity.[14] Stress falls on figuration, on the way in which tropes for the mother, like those for the father, produce in Shakespeare's texts the socially inflected 'reality' they might be taken merely to describe.

In addition, psychoanalysis maintains that the nature of one's gender or the direction of one's desire attests not to identity but to an intense, unresolved, and transpersonal struggle over the meaning (and hence social value) of different bodies, dispositions, and desires. Feminist scholars as well as scholars in gay and lesbian studies are therefore increasingly forging links through psychoanalysis, analysing the power and fragility of heteronormativity in Shakespeare's texts. Not surprisingly, attention to the ways that (historically variable) sex/gender systems fail in their mission means that the material practice of cross-dressing in the early modern theatre has become newly interesting to psychoanalytic critics.

As should be clear by now, psychoanalytic criticism of Shakespeare shares with new historicist criticism the position that the self 'is not independent of or prior to its social context' (see Chapter 32). Many critics are bringing the two kinds of methodologies into productive conversation about the social and discursive production of early modern subjectivity and thus about Shakespeare's place in that production. This effort to bridge a too-rigid distinction between historicist and psychoanalytic work has produced essays that read across various kinds of early modern discourses (legal, medical, and philosophical as well as literary) to reconsider the social production of subjectivity and sexuality. But new historicist work 'often seems to assume that once [the] dependence' of the subject on its social context 'is pointed out, inwardness simply vaporizes, like the Wicked Witch of the West under Dorothy's bucket of water'.[15] Psychoanalytic theory, by contrast, maintains that however constructed or fictional, a sense of self is still something people have—and that this fiction's very tenacity and density is worth considerable analytic attention.

Psychoanalytic theory offers a rich set of tools to literary critics interested in analysing the formal mechanisms by which the norms and conventions of historically specific institutions, discourses, and practices are realized in the subject, lived not simply as belief but also in such deeply personal registers as desire, grief, or fear. Freud's speculation about the vicissitudes of speaking-subjectivity—the 'conditions of representation'—will therefore continue to play a crucial role as Shakespearians work to both historicize *and* theorize the conditions of early modern subjectivity and sexuality.

FURTHER READING

Adelman, Janet. *Suffocating Mothers: Fantasies of Maternal Origin in Shakespeare's Plays, 'Hamlet' to 'The Tempest'* (New York: Routledge, 1992). Applies object-relations theory to Shakespeare's plays and discusses their representation of mothers and maternal origin.

Buhle, Mari Jo. *Feminism and Its Discontents: A Century of Struggle with Psychoanalysis* (Cambridge, Mass.: Harvard University Press, 1998). A thorough and informative discussion of the exchange between psychoanalytic and feminist theory from the early 1900s to the present day.

Dever, Carolyn. *Skeptical Feminism In Theory* (Minneapolis: University of Minnesota Press, 2003). A detailed account of the connection between political practice and theoretical abstraction in twentieth-century feminism; contains a valuable chapter on psychoanalytic theory's role in this connection.

Enterline, Lynn. *The Tears of Narcissus: Melancholia and Masculinity in Early Modern Writing* (Stanford: Stanford University Press, 1995). Compares contemporary psychoanalytic theories of melancholia to early modern representations of the disorder, including Shakespeare's.

Fineman, Joel. *Shakespeare's Perjured Eye: The Invention of Poetic Subjectivity in the Sonnets* (Berkeley: University of California Press, 1986). Applies Freud's theories of language and subjectivity to Shakespeare's sonnets and discusses the sonnets as producing an effect that we recognise as interiority.

Finucci, Valeria and Regina Schwartz (eds.). *Desire in the Renaissance: Psychoanalysis and Literature* (Princeton: Princeton University Press, 1994). Collection of essays investigating the potential for psychoanalytic criticism across a variety of Renaissance authors and topics.

Freedman, Barbara. *Staging the Gaze: Postmodernism, Psychoanalysis, and Shakespearean Comedy* (Ithaca: Cornell University Press, 1991). Deploys psychoanalytic theory, particularly that of Lacan on the 'gaze', to analyse Shakespearian comedy in light of the Renaissance penchant for optical experiments and tricks of perception.

Laplanche, Jean and J. B. Pontalis. *The Language of Psychoanalysis*, trans. Donald Nicholson-Smith (New York: W. W. Norton, 1973). Extremely useful definitions of terms in Freud and in contemporary psychoanalysis; each entry also describes the history of the development of each term.

Mazzio, Carla and Douglas Trevor (eds.). *Historicism, Psychoanalysis, and Early Modern Culture* (New York and London: Routledge, 2000). Collection of essays by critics attempting to bring together psychoanalytic and historicist insights into early modern literature and culture.

Mitchell, Juliette and Jacqueline Rose (eds.). *Feminine Sexuality: Jacques Lacan and the École Freudienne* (New York: Norton, 1982). Translation of Lacan's major writing on the question of feminine sexuality with two influential introductions to the pertinence of psychoanalytic theory to feminist critique.

Traub, Valerie. *Desire and Anxiety: Circulations of Sexuality in Shakespearian Drama* (London: Routledge, 1992). Working between psychoanalytic and feminist theory with new historicism, charts the erotics of Shakespearian drama by 'taking heterosexuality and homoeroticism equally seriously'.

NOTES

1. Jane Gallop. 'The Monster in the Mirror: the Feminist Critic's Psychoanalysis'. In Richard Feldstein and Judith Roof (eds.). *Feminism and Psychoanalysis* (Ithaca, N.Y.: Cornell University Press, 1989).

2. See Harry Berger, Jr. *Making Trifles of Terrors: Redistributing Complicities in Shakespeare* (Stanford: Stanford University Press, 1997), Chapter 11, for an analysis of what it means to reconceive Shakespearian characters as the after-effects of the discourses available to them.

3. Joel Fineman. *Shakespeare's Perjured Eye: The Invention of Poetic Subjectivity in the Sonnets* (Berkeley: University of California Press, 1986), p. 130.

4. *The Standard Edition of the Complete Psychological Works of Sigmund Freud*, trans. James Strachey (London: Hogarth Press, 1953), Vol. 17, p. 140.

5. *The Standard Edition*, Vol. 16, p. 285.

6. The phrase is borrowed from Julie Rivkin and Michael Ryan. *Literary Theory* (Oxford: Oxford University Press), pp. 119–27.

7. See especially Gayle Rubin, 'The Traffic in Women: Notes on the "Political Economy" of Sex'. *Toward an Anthropology of Women*, ed. Rayna R. Reiter (New York: Monthly Review Press, 1975); and Carolyn Dever, *Skeptical Feminism* (Minneapolis: University of Minnesota Press, 2003).

8. Juliet Mitchell. *Psychoanalysis and Feminism* (New York: Pantheon Books, 1974), p. xiii (emphasis in original).

9. The spelling here reflects psychoanalytic usage, the effort to preserve Freud's emphasis in the German word, '*Phantasie*', on unconscious creative activity and to distinguish it from the sense of mere whimsy or trivial flight of fancy suggested by the English 'fantasy'. As J. Laplanche defines the term, a phantasy is an 'imaginary scene in which the subject protagonist represents the fulfillment of a wish (in the last analysis, an unconscious wish) in a manner that is distorted to a greater or lesser extent by unconscious processes' (Jean Laplanche and J. B. Pontalis. *The Language of Psychoanalysis*, trans. Donald Nicholson-Smith (New York: W.W. Norton, 1973), p. 314).

10. Janet Adelman. *Suffocating Mothers: Fantasies of Maternal Origin in Shakespeare's Plays, 'Hamlet' to 'The Tempest'* (New York: Routledge, 1992), p. 10.

11. Lisa Lowe. ' "Say I play the man I am": Gender and Politics in *Coriolanus*', *Kenyon Review*, n.s., 8, No. 4 (Fall 1986), 88.

12. Rubin. 'The Traffic in Women', pp. 184–5.

13. Laplanche and Pontalis. *The Language of Psychoanalysis*, p. 286.

14. On Shylock, see Lynn Enterline. *The Tears of Narcissus: Melancholia and Masculinity in Early Modern Writing* (Stanford: Stanford University Press, 1995); on Falstaff, see Valerie Traub. *Desire and Anxiety: Circulations of Sexuality in Shakespearian Drama* (London and New York: Routledge, 1992).

15. Katherine Eisaman Maus. *Inwardness and the Theatre in the English Renaissance* (Chicago: University of Chicago Press, 1995).

READING: *Venus and Adonis*

Recent psychoanalytic criticism of Shakespeare increasingly explores intersections with historicism. The following analysis of *Venus and Adonis* relies on the proposition that one such intersection occurs in the domain of rhetoric. A discipline that concentrates on language's forms and effects, rhetoric allows critics to take psychoanalytic theory's hypothesis of 'the speaking subject' seriously by taking poetic figures seriously. At the same time, it bridges two different kinds of early modern history: literary and institutional. Rhetorical analysis means attending to the specific formal issues that arise from the vogue for certain kinds of poetry and forms of expression at particular historical junctures. For the purposes of this chapter, rhetoric refers to the stylistic features attending the Renaissance habit of revisiting and revising previous literary texts and, more broadly, to the period's fascination, across various institutions, with verbal power—with a speaker's or writer's capacity to move or change an audience. When understood in light of its institutional history (i.e. the organizations in which it was either practised or taught), rhetoric also touches on questions of ideology—particularly as realized in the details of specific social transactions.

The early modern institutions most important to the rhetoric of *Venus and Adonis* are two: the Elizabethan grammar school, where Shakespeare was trained along with his peers in the art of imitating classical poetry, and London's transvestite theatre, where he put his rhetorical training to work. *Venus and Adonis* reveals the pressure of both these institutions. A classicizing work, Shakespeare's narrative poem derives its story from a Latin text Shakespeare and his contemporaries translated, and were trained to imitate at school: Ovid's *Metamorphoses*. Ovid wrote his influential epic in the first century AD; the poem remained extremely popular in Europe from the Middle Ages through the Renaissance. It eventually contributed to, and became a central source for, the sixteenth-century infatuation with Greco-Roman mythology.

Shakespeare's contemporaries, also trained in the art of classical rhetoric at school, praised him as a kind of English Ovid. And yet the classical, Ovidian flavour of *Venus and Adonis* hardly lends it dignity—a problem that frequently disconcerts modern critics despite the fact that the poem's erotic predicament and freedom with gender roles echo and amplify the overtly sexual concerns of Ovid's poem. If the protean reversals of gender in *Venus and Adonis* witness the role of the grammar school in transmitting Ovidian rhetoric, they also reveal the hand of a dramatist who was accustomed to the conventions of the English transvestite stage—and who took considerable pleasure and profit from the erotic possibilities of cross dressing. One could say that *Venus and Adonis* brings theatrical cross-dressing into the world of narrative verse, turning Ovid's story of Venus and Adonis into a poetic exploration of the effects of cross-voicing.

The following discussion describes how Shakespeare revises Ovid's epic in *Venus and*

Adonis. It also investigates what his revisions mean for the poem's famously disconcerting representation of sexuality and desire. At the same time, it explains how another important literary precursor, Petrarch, influenced this representation. Like Shakespeare after him, Petrarch drew extensively on the mythological figures of Ovid's poem to tell his story of unrequited love for his beloved Laura. Petrarch wrote his *Rime sparse*, a cycle of lyric poems addressed to Laura, in fourteenth-century Florence; the cycle spawned a virtual poetic industry of love melancholy that endured for two centuries, first on the continent and later in England. (Shakespeare's own sonnets are part of, as well as commentary on, the vogue for 'Petrarchism'.)

With regard to literary history, it is important to understand that the mix of Ovidianism and Petrarchism in *Venus and Adonis* is typical of literary representations of desire in the decade in which it was written. Former schoolboys—whether they went on to university, to the Inns of Court to study law, or to the theatre—showed a particular fondness for the figures and predicaments characteristic of both Ovid and Petrarch.

With regard to psychoanalytic criticism of Shakespeare, this reading of *Venus and Adonis* shows that the poem's literary history—its indebtedness to, and distinctive way of revising, both Ovid and Petrarch—anticipates the claims about subjectivity and desire that Lacan made in his famous 'return to Freud'. The protagonists' complex rhetorical debate suggests that we cannot fully understand the vicissitudes of sexuality, gender, and desire in *Venus and Adonis* without taking into account Lacan's hypothesis that as speaking subjects, we are the *effect* rather than cause of our own discourse.

For example, Venus draws on the language available to her—derived from the Ovidian/Petrarchan poetry in vogue in the 1590s—only to find herself trapped by it. Shakespeare's emphasis on rhetoric's transactions—on what words can or cannot *do* rather than what they mean—brings the psychoanalytic hypothesis of speaking subjectivity into precise historical focus. That is, when Ovid's story of consummated passion turns into one of unsatisfied desire, *Venus and Adonis* asks us to remember Renaissance England's fascination with rhetoric precisely because sexual disappointment becomes a matter of one lover's *failure to persuade* another. Venus fails, as an orator, to move her intended audience; and her rhetorical failure, by the end of the poem, acquires all the pathos of unrequited love.

Gender and desire

Few texts call as insistently as *Venus and Adonis* for an approach that accounts for both the tenacity and the fragility of gender categories. In little more than fifteen lines, we learn that the lovers reverse traditional roles. Venus approaches Adonis 'like a bold-faced suitor' and ''gins to woo him' while Adonis's beauty exceeds that of even the goddess of love (6). Stock Petrarchan conventions of red-and-white—which Shakespeare usually applies to female characters—characterize Adonis. Venus finds him ''Thrice fairer' than herself, 'Stain to all nymphs, more lovely than a man, / More white and red than doves or roses are' (7–10). At the same time, Venus adopts the conventionally 'masculine' position of imploring Petrarchan suitor, driven to plead a case with a reluctant object of desire she cannot win.

'Backward she pushed him, as she would be thrust' (41) is perhaps the line that best captures the erotic extension of gender reversal. The poem's rhetorical and sexual predicaments, as well as its humour, turn on precisely the question of sexual difference that first drew feminist critics to psychoanalysis. In other words, *Venus and Adonis* derives its plot, tension, and modes of address by depending on the reader's certainty about the difference between male and female bodies, identities, and desires even while it undermines those distinctions at every turn.

Exacerbating its tendency to turn sexual difference—as well as the vicissitudes of desire conventionally attached to notions of difference—into ongoing and dynamic questions, *Venus and Adonis* shifts quickly between maternal and paternal tropes to depict the goddess of love. Consonant with his attempt to ventriloquize the voice of a woman in love, Shakespeare deploys *both* parental phantasies to tell his story of desire. But the figure critics most frequently point out in the poem is that of Venus as mother. We will begin by looking at Venus's 'maternal' aspect but must consider her 'paternal' aspect as well: to assume that Venus is only, or simply, maternal risks presuming the very conventional story of gender that psychoanalysis puts into question.

The parent-child dynamic defining the protagonists' relationship distinguishes Shakespeare's story from Ovid's. He converts Ovid's story of Venus's successful relationship with Adonis into a story of unconsummated love between an older woman and a barely pubescent boy. To critics of C. S. Lewis's generation (1898–1963), this change proved distasteful: 'Certain horrible interviews with voluminous female relatives recur to mind.'[1] There are, however, plenty of incestuous overtones in the background of Ovid's story: Adonis is the offspring of a daughter-father union; he is therefore said to be a kind of 'revenge' on the goddess of love for his mother, Myrrha's, ill-fated passion. And Venus falls for Adonis, we are told, because one day she was fondling her own son, Cupid, and was accidentally pricked by his arrow. In Ovid, however, the relationship itself is not incestuous—indeed its particular texture seems unimportant—and the lovers' age of consent is assumed throughout.

Shakespeare exacerbates the hints of incest that surround Ovid's story, structuring his poem out of them. For example, he compares Venus's desire for Adonis to a mother's for her child: she mourns his absence much as 'a milch doe whose swelling dugs do ache, / Hasting to feed her fawn' (875–6). The poem's 'juxtaposition of sexuality and parenting' suggests, as one critic puts it, that 'Adonis is forced to re-enact, with generational roles reversed', the 'incestuous affair between his mother and father in the *Metamorphoses*'.[2] Several psychoanalytic critics therefore explore the poem's less than subtle hints that the protagonists are like a mother and son, noting in its figures the many 'pre-Oedipal' phantasies about overwhelming maternal power that psychoanalysis traces.[3] One of the most prominent of these occurs when Venus's caress evokes an infantile state of symbiotic fusion with a mother: 'Her arms do lend his neck a sweet embrace. / Incorporate then they seem, face grows to face' (539–40).

Such fusion is not without danger. Venus may invite Adonis to feed—'I'll be a park, and thou shalt be my deer. / Feed where thou wilt' (231–2)—but the poem soon suggests that Adonis is at risk of being devoured by a voracious mouth that feeds 'glutton-like . . . yet never filleth' (548):

> Even as an empty eagle, sharp by fast,
> Tires with her beak on feathers, flesh, and bone,
> Shaking her wings, devouring all in haste
> Till either gorge be stuffed or prey be gone,
>   Even so she kissed his brow, his cheek, his chin
>   And where she ends she doth anew begin.
>   (55-60)

Here Venus embodies the principle that Janet Adelman might call Shakespeare's 'suffocating mother'. She calls to mind a nightmare mother who at best engulfs, and at worst annihilates, her child.

But things are not quite so straightforward as that in the depiction of Venus and her desire. The simile of the hungry eagle connotes not simply a ravenous, 'maternal' force but also the entry of a powerful, phallic 'beak' into Adonis's vulnerable body. Recently, feminist critics have pointed out that maternal phantasies like the ones in *Venus and Adonis* are not unmediated expressions of the universal nature of the maternal body or mother-child relationship. Rather, they are socially invested phantasies retrospectively imposed to *interpret* a relationship that both logically and chronologically precedes any child's understanding of the difference between mother and father, male and female.[4] Such representations do not precede the Law of the Father—the imposition of sexual difference—but rather are shaped by it. They are projected back in time to explain an original state in which what it means to say 'my mother is a woman' has yet to make any sense.[5]

It is more appropriate to think about these images of Venus not as either/or—either maternal or paternal—but rather as both, as undifferentiated phantasies about *parental* power. If we read these 'pre-Oedipal' fantasies of Venus as a voracious *and* penetrating parent alongside the poem's ongoing reversals of gender roles, *Venus and Adonis* becomes particularly suggestive for an anti-foundational theory of sexuality. For psycho-analysis, there is a moment in all our lives when bodies have yet to acquire their culturally assigned meaning, when sexual difference makes no sense. Intimations of this indifference persist despite a culture's best efforts to eradicate it. Such a claim helps account for a poem about desire in which the imagery is at once rigidly differential and yet also strangely mutable.

There is a more telling moment yet when Venus takes on a conventionally 'paternal' aspect. As described in the first section, Lacan calls the threat of castration the 'Law of the Father'. Shakespeare turns his obviously maternal Venus with 'swelling dugs' into just such a castrating father figure for Adonis. First, Venus rules by sheer size: she 'courageously' 'plucks' him 'from his horse' (30). And given the poem's central problem (Adonis's impotence with Venus) and its central tragedy (Adonis's death by wound in the groin), figures for castration abound. Both in life and in death, Adonis is 'missing' something in Venus's eyes. Hints of his castration emerge first by comparison to the horse, then to the boar, and finally to Venus. By contrast to the lusty, 'well proportioned' horse that 'lacks' nothing and stamps in anticipation, ears 'up-pricked', impatient for sex with a nearby mare (271, 289–300), Adonis evades such heterosexual, phallic power. The narrator does not shy away from reminding us how his performance pales by comparison to equine potency: 'he will not manage her, although he mount her' (598).

To underscore the point of what Venus finds 'missing' in Adonis, the boar does not merely kill him. His potent tusk opens a 'wide wound' (1052) in Adonis's 'soft groin' (1116). That early modern readers interpreted Adonis's wound as a form of castration is evident in a contemporary translation of Ovid's line as a wound to Adonis's 'coddes' (a word for the stem of a plant, or overripe pods). Finally, Venus takes over the boar's castrating role: we do not read about Adonis's death, or his wound, until Venus sees it, and when she does, she compares her own desire to the effects of the boar's penetrating tusk. 'Had I been toothed like him, I must confess/ With kissing him I should have killed him first' (1117–18). Venus's mere act of looking exacerbates the boar's damage to Adonis's thigh: 'Upon his hurt she looks so steadfastly / That her sight, dazzling, makes the wound seem three' (1063–4). Venus's earlier threat to Adonis evoked the fear of being engulfed or penetrated by an omnipotent parental force. Now her 'dazzling' look magnifies and multiplies the wound caused by a boar's phallic tusk.

Language and desire

It is not, however, merely at the level of theme and imagery that we discover the pertinence of psychoanalysis's anti-foundational theory of sexuality to a poem that purports to explain the origin of love's 'perverse' nature (1157). The poem's rhetorical register also calls for a psychoanalytic account of the effects of language on desire—on what Freud would call 'the conditions of representation' and Lacan the problem of becoming a 'speaking subject'. Shakespeare's interest in the connection between sexuality and language emerges at a crucial moment characterizing Venus's sexual dilemma. She is in 'the very lists of love', yet 'all in vain' (595, 607). To capture this futility, the poem moves into one of several moments of ekphrasis. A mode of poetic invention extremely popular in late classical poetry, 'ekphrasis' literally means to 'point or designate outside of' or 'beyond' something. It was born of rhetorical training and in its original sense, *ekphrasis* designates the description of a work of visual art in verse.

Shakespeare's version of this trope manages to boast about his poem's own beauty and, at the same time, to draw attention to exactly how Adonis disappoints Venus:

> Even so poor birds, deceived with painted grapes,
> Do surfeit by the eye, and pine the maw;
> Even so she languisheth in her mishaps
> As those poor birds that helpless berries saw.
>   The warm effects which she in him finds missing
>   She seeks to kindle with continual kissing
>
> (601-6)

Here, as in the earlier ekphrasis on a painting of that lusty horse—'Look when a painter would surpass the life / In limning out a well proportioned steed'(289–90)—Shakespeare deploys the traditional language of competition between the arts to lay claim to his own form of poetic virtuosity. The simile of 'painted grapes' that deceive even the natural world suggests that Shakespeare's verses about Adonis are as beautiful and powerful as that legendary painting. The same trope that designates Adonis's impotence also makes a claim about the power of the poem's own art.

The difference between the birds' predicament and Venus's, of course, is that while they eventually fly away after realizing they are trying to consume an empty image, Venus remains fascinated.[6] She refuses to give up, tries to overcome what is 'missing' by 'continual kissing'. As Shakespeare puts it, 'worse than Tantalus' is her annoy, / To clip Elysium and to lack her joy' (599–600). Venus's tantalizing 'lack' begins to get at something like what Lacan means by saying that language separates us from the unmediated world of need and engenders the unending world of desire. The simile of painted grapes that fascinate because of their insufficiency—'helpless berries' that nonetheless 'surfeit by the eye' (602–4)—applies both to Adonis and to the poem that describes him. The attraction of each is the result of a fundamental deficiency, an absence that produces a state of infatuated longing or unending 'pining'. The poem's claims to beauty point to its own emptiness: like 'painted' grapes, the poem is a *representation* rather than the thing itself. As Lacan might say, the poem's inability to satisfy physical need—an inability modelled on Adonis's—engenders desire.

Adonis is the overt subject of the simile and the painted, 'helpless berries' carry an obvious sexual resonance. But such resonance also extends to the language of the poem, the simile's other topic. That such a sexualized, corporeal image should connect the poem's protagonist to its own language tells us something about Lacan's reason for coining the term, 'the Phallus'. By this term Lacan is suggesting that cultures have construed language's emptiness, its status as re-presentation of the world as well as its internal slippages, in decidedly gendered, hierarchical terms—in figures that reveal the historical (and hence not inevitable) pressure of father-power. And in his view, a world organized around father-power—and the threat of castration—imposes a 'symbolic reduction' on the multiple possibilities of human desire, constraining them according to a universalized image of the male body.

Beyond this provocative trope, the larger rhetorical situation of *Venus and Adonis*—the attempt by one character to persuade another to love—tells us something else about desire if we consider it according to the psychoanalytic hypothesis that subjects are the *effect* rather than the cause of their discourse. Here it is important to note that the subject in question is Venus, not Adonis. Unlike Freud's focus on the vicissitudes of male subjectivity, *Venus and Adonis* centres on the drama and contours of female desire. It is Venus's longing, her disappointment, and her mourning to which Shakespeare is trying to give a voice and which determines the constant shifts in tone for which the poem is noted. The distinctive texture of Venus's desire—first comic but finally tragic—emerges as an after-effect of two historically specific literary discourses: Ovidianism and Petrarchism. Like Shakespeare's sonnets—in which Fineman argues that a convincing fiction of personal interiority emerges as the effect of the cycle's formal and rhetorical innovations—this poem conveys Venus's desire by manipulating and satirizing previous literary convention.

First, Venus seems trapped by the Ovidian story that preexists her—and more specifically, by the *name* that defines her as the classical goddess of Love: 'She's Love; she loves; and yet she is not loved' (610). The narrator conveys the intensity of her longing by highlighting the contradiction between Venus and the classical texts that define her: 'Poor queen of love, in thine own law forlorn' (251). Second, the rhetoric of love available to Venus for wooing Adonis guarantees her disappointment. Petrarchan convention requires, and is sustained by, erotic frustration. A highly conventional diction, Petrarchism was born from the fiction of a lady's refusal to relent to the speaker's (poetic) request for love. The beloved's refusal is, in fact, the precondition for Petrarchan poetry: there would be no reason for writing poems were the speaker to receive the love he says he wants. Not only is Venus's tragic story already written for her in Ovid's *Metamorphoses*, but the Petrarchan language she inherits for wooing Adonis presumes her frustrated longing.

The trouble in Venus's case is acute: the codified figures of Petrarchan poetry developed on the presumption that the lover/speaker is male. For Venus, these figures produce not just the plot of refusal, but also the problem of Adonis's impotence. That is, Shakespeare develops the embarrassing situation implicit in Venus's command, 'thou shalt not rise' (710), into a broad parody of Petrarchan imagery. In Petrarch's figure of Laura's 'stony breast', the stone is a metaphor for the lady's refusal; the poet spends his words trying to 'soften' her stony resistance. But this conventional image of the lady as a statue or 'stone' becomes a sexual joke in *Venus and Adonis* because, as usual in Shakespeare, 'stones' also mean 'testicles'. In Venus's situation, the Petrarchan notion of softening a stone produces unhappy results. She chides, entirely conventionally, 'Fie, lifeless picture, cold and senseless stone' (211) and 'Art thou obdurate, flinty, hard as steel?/ Nay, more than flint, for stone at rain relenteth' (199–200). Pleading according to the rules of literary convention for her beloved to melt and dissolve, Venus calls for the softening of the very thing she wants to remain 'hard as steel'.

And yet the poem is not done. Petrarchan convention may turn Venus into the subject of a rather absurd desire in the poem's first half. After Adonis dies, however, the tone shifts radically. Venus speaks, again according to precedent, as if she were the loving Petrarchan subject whose melancholy desire became an extremely influential form of early modern literary autobiography. Once again, it is Venus's subjectivity that is at issue—both because of the poem's own emphasis but also because of the literary history it invokes. In fact, the conventional discourse of love that once trapped Venus now allows her to articulate a sense of aesthetic power. The melancholy Petrarchan lover gets the compensations of poetry, the figure of the laurel leaf, in lieu of his absent beloved. And so Venus gets 'a purple flower . . . chequered with white' as a sign of the dead Adonis. Access to aesthetic power, along with Petrarchan mourning, now confer a certain dignity on Venus's previously absurd desire.

This final turn to aesthetic appreciation, moreover, should remind us of the late Shakespeare, for whom things like 'pearls' in place of 'eyes' suggests consolation (*The Tempest*, 1.2.402). At once a thing of beauty and a sign, Venus's purple flower symbolizes her dead love and, more generally, the condition of human desire. Signs of lost love, Petrarch's laurel and Venus's purple flower suggest something like Lacan's notion that our entry into language, our ability to manipulate signs, involves sacrifice: because we must speak to get what we want, something is always 'missing'—both in the world and in the self.

FURTHER READING

Belsey, Catherine. 'Love as Trompe-l'Oeil: Taxonomies of Desire in *Venus and Adonis*'. *Shakespeare Quarterly*, 46 (1995), 257–76. Describes how an anachronistic distinction between love and lust informs modern moralizing critical accounts of a poem that refuses definitive statements about desire—a refusal that, in turn, marks its historical difference.

Halpern, Richard. ' "Pining their Maws": Female Readers and the Erotic Ontology of the Text in Shakespeare's *Venus and Adonis*'. In Kolin, ed. *Venus and Adonis: Critical Essays*, pp. 377–88. Beginning with the fact that early modern references indicate that the poem's primary audience was predominantly female, reconsiders the 'allegory of textual consumption' conveyed in the simile of the painted grapes.

Kolin, Philip C. (ed.). *Venus and Adonis: Critical Essays* (New York and London: Garland Publishing, 1997). A comprehensive edition of major critical essays about the poem from Coleridge to the time of its publication.

Rambuss, Richard. 'What It Feels Like For a Boy: Shakespeare's *Venus and Adonis*'. In Richard Dutton and Jean E. Howard (eds.). *A Companion to Shakespeare, Vol. IV; The Poems, Problem Comedies, Late Plays* (London: Blackwell, 2003). Questions normative assumptions about 'natural' heterosexuality that inform earlier readings of the poem and offers an analysis of desire based on the observation that Adonis is 'missing' something only if readers adopt Venus's point of view.

Schiffer, James. 'Shakespeare's *Venus and Adonis*: A Lacanian Tragicomedy of Desire'. In Kolin, ed. *Venus and Adonis: Critical Essays*. Compares Shakespeare's representation of desire to Lacan's.

NOTES

1. C.S. Lewis. *English Literature in the Sixteenth Century, Excluding Drama* (Oxford: Oxford University Press, 1954), p. 487.
2. Jonathan Bate. *Shakespeare and Ovid* (Oxford: Clarendon Press, 1993), p. 54.
3. The most prominent studies of maternal power in the poem are Coppélia Kahn. *Man's Estate: Masculine Identity in Shakespeare* (Berkeley: University of California Press, 1981); Alan Rothenberg. 'The Oral Rape Fantasy and the Rejection of the Mother in the Imagery of Shakespeare's *Venus and Adonis*'.

Psychoanalytic Quarterly, 40 (1971), 447–68; Wayne Rebhorn, 'Temptation in Shakespeare's *Venus and Adonis*'. *Shakespeare Studies*, 11 (1978), 1–19.

4. Judith Butler. *Gender Trouble: Feminism and the Subversion of Identity* (London: Routledge, 1990); Lynn Enterline. *The Tears of Narcissus: Melancholia and Masculinity in Early Modern Writing* (Stanford: Stanford University Press, 1995); Jacqueline Rose. *Sexuality in the Field of Vision* (London: Verso, 1986).

5. I borrow Constance Penley's formulation in *The Future of an Illusion: Film, Feminism, and Psychoanalysis* (Minneapolis: University of Minnesota Press, 1989), p. 27.

6. For further comment on this passage, see Catherine Belsey. 'Love as Trompe-l'Oeil: Taxonomies of Desire in *Venus and Adonis*'. *Shakespeare Quarterly*, 46 (1995), 257–76 and Richard Halpern. ' "Pining Their Maws": Female Readers and the Erotic Ontology of the Text in Shakespeare's *Venus and Adonis*'. In Kolin (ed.). *Venus and Adonis: Critical Essays*, pp. 377–87.

Materialist criticisms

Jonathan Gil Harris

Introduction

'Always historicize!'[1] This imperative, issued by Marxist literary critic Fredric Jameson in 1981, has become the watchword of a diverse array of critical methodologies that tend to be grouped under the umbrella of 'materialism'. Literary texts, the materialist critic assumes, cannot be understood in isolation; rather, they acquire meaning only in relation to their historical contexts. What exactly these contexts may be, how-ever, and how we are to understand the notion of 'history' that underwrites them, has been interpreted rather differently by materialism's three most influential strands— Marxism, new historicism, and cultural materialism.

This divergence has entailed a paradoxical convergence. Materialism's three strands have not only applied their different premises to readings of Shakespeare; they have also repeatedly found in Shakespeare the grounds for these premises. As Jameson has noted, 'the encounter between Shakespeare and radical (or Marxist) criticism and theory is a two-way street: we find ourselves asking not merely what such critical theory has to tell us about Shakespeare . . . but also what Shakespeare has to tell us about radical criticism'.[2] Inasmuch as Shakespeare has provided the ground for materialism's diverse highways, however, Jameson's 'two-way street' might seem more like a confusing spaghetti junction. Each of this junction's offramps is signposted with what seems to be the same destination ('Shakespeare Historicized!'); yet each leads in quite different directions. How, then, does each materialist path understand 'history' and its relation to Shakespeare?

Marxism

As a philosophical tradition, materialism dates back to classical Greece. As a tendency within literary criticism, however, materialism owes a significant debt to the political and economic theories of Karl Marx (1818–83). A middle-class German exiled to Britain in 1848, Marx devoted his life to analysing and strategizing against the social effects of industrial capitalism. Together with his fellow German expatriate and collaborator Friedrich Engels (1820–95), Marx denounced the misery produced by the capitalist exploitation of 'deskilled' or **alienated** workers, whom he called the **proletariat**. The latter are alienated psychologically, inasmuch as they have become automatons who perform mind-numbingly repetitive factory work. But they are alienated economically as well, having sold their labour to capitalists who also own their places of work, tools, and products. Marx's solution to this state of affairs was communism—a classless society based on common ownership of the economic **means of production**.

No matter how untenable it might seem in light of the Soviet communist experiment of the twentieth century, Marx's solution was based on a rigorous theorization and analysis of history. Many nineteenth-century Europeans understood history as the march of progress: patriotic historians tended to see this march in terms of the rise of national identity and sovereignty, while the German idealist philosopher G. W. F. Hegel (1770–1831) saw history as a progression of the spirit. Marx, however, understood history to be driven by the struggle between different social classes, irrespective of national identity, for economic and political advantage—a competition most nakedly evident in the age of capitalism. In contrast to nationalist historians, then, Marx conceived of history with an internationalist inflection (evident in his famous battlecry 'workers of the world, unite!'). And in contrast to Hegel with his notion of spiritual progress, Marx insisted on the economic basis of human history.

Even as Marx reacted against Hegel's idealism, he borrowed from him the concept of the **dialectic**, or the notion that struggle between two opposed forces produces change. Indeed, change is crucial to all of Marx's thought. In his early writings, he famously asserted that while philosophers have tried simply to understand the world, the point is to change it. But whereas Hegel saw the dialectic operating solely in the history of ideas, Marx insisted that change was largely a product of contradictions within the material realms of social organization and economic production. Hence Marx's claim that his was a philosophy of **dialectical materialism**.

The dialectical cast of Marx's thought is most visible in his analyses of different modes of production in European history. Marx devoted considerable attention to feudalism, the hierarchical system of medieval polity in which peasants worked the estates of a hereditary lord to whom they owed tribute (usually in the form of a percentage of the fruits of their labour). During the Renaissance, Marx argued, the feudal system collapsed under the weight of its internal contradictions and, in doing so, paved the way for the rise of capitalism. Marx predicted that capitalism will likewise crumble as a result of its own foundational contradiction—the bourgeoisie's need for an alienated working class, who will eventually rebel against their oppressors. Such analyses might seem to view social change simply as the inevitable consequence of structural problems within an economic system. Marx nevertheless stressed the active role people play in bringing about change. Men and women, he insisted, make their own history, even if it is not under conditions of their own choosing.

Throughout Marx's analyses of historical change persists a model of social formation founded on a division between the economic **base** (the material means of production, distribution, and exchange) and the cultural **superstructure** (religion, law, philosophy, language, literature, and art). For Marx, the latter is not free-standing, but determined (or shaped) by the base. The model seems to imply that certain systems of social and economic organization will produce certain types of literature. This assumption guides his pioneering sketches of materialist literary criticism, compiled in *Grundrisse* (1857–8). In the latter, Marx argues that Homeric epic is possible only in a society like that of classical Greece, in which humans have not tamed the forces of nature. He asks: 'is the view of nature and of social relations on which the Greek imagination and hence Greek [mythology] is based possible with self-acting mule spindles and railways and locomotives and electrical telegraphs? What chance has Vulcan against Roberts & Co., Jupiter against the lightning-rod and Hermes against the Credit Mobilier?'[3] Here are the rudiments of a Marxist literary criticism. It entails an **economic determinism** in which literature **reflects** the economic and social organization of the time and place in which it is written.

What precisely this relation of reflection entails, however, is unclear. Does 'reflection' occur at the level of literary content, or of form? Is the relation simply one of straightforward mirroring? Or is it more complex? In *The German Ideology*, Marx and Engels elaborated their notion of **ideology** as a camera obscura that reflects the world. Like the camera's image, however, ideology's reflection of reality is an inverted one: it plasters over social contradictions in order to create the illusion of a seamless, natural unity. Ideology produces not a passive or disinterested image of the world, then, but an active distortion of real tensions and conflicts. Literature, Marx might have suggested, can ideologically 'reflect' the world in just this fashion, reconciling opposed forces in fantasies of harmonious reconciliation. One might argue that this is particularly the case with the genre of Shakespearian comedy. Think, for instance, of *The Merchant of Venice*, in which the spendthrift Venetian Bassanio weds Portia, the fairy-tale princess from Belmont. This play performs an ideological resolution of social contradiction through the marriage of two historically competing classes—the mercantile bourgeoisie and the feudal aristocracy.

Marx never developed the potential connections between his theories of ideology and literature. In fact, his understanding of literature's relation to its historical contexts remained imprecise throughout his writing. If he advanced a deterministic understanding of literature in *Grundrisse*, he on occasion implied that art has a degree of autonomy from prevailing economic circumstances. The tension between a deterministic and a relatively autonomous view of literature is evident in Marx's many references to Shakespeare, in whose work he took particular delight. He often illustrated his economic theories with recourse to Shakespeare's plays, most notably *Timon of Athens* in his essay on 'The Power of Money in Bourgeois Society'. Elsewhere, he repeatedly drew on *Hamlet*'s images of ghosts and gravediggers to figure the processes of social revolution in nineteenth-century Europe. One can interpret such uses of Shakespeare as case studies of how literature is determined by the economic base (in

Shakespeare's time, a base in transition from feudalism to capitalism); or one might view them as examples of how literature is relatively autonomous from the economic conditions of its moment of production, and can thus provide an enabling vocabulary for social and ideological critique.

Although Marx laid the foundations for a materialist literary criticism, the latter did not become a fully fledged practice until the twentieth century. Lenin, the first leader of the Soviet Union, had argued that literature should become an instrument of the Communist Party. Under his successor Stalin, this goal was translated into a state-mandated 'socialist realism' in which literature was expected to reflect the 'truth' of the communist base—a policy that spawned a dreary brood of homogeneous novels, poems, and plays populated by noble proletarian heroes. Even far less programmatic Marxist literary critics of the time, such as the Hungarian Georg Lukács, championed realism for the light it could cast on the 'true' material conditions of society. In all these Marxist embraces of literary reflectionism, we can see an unresolved tension between literature as mirror and as prescription. Literature is understood to be determined by its material conditions of production; yet it is imagined to play a shaping and sometimes revolutionary role in relation to the latter.

Many Marxists outside the Soviet Union rejected the socialist realist aesthetic in order to theorize literature's revolutionary potential. A good case in point is the German playwright Bertolt Brecht (1898–1956), who proposed the theory of **epic theatre**. Unlike naturalist drama, which presents its characters' behaviour as the product of a universal, unchanging 'human nature', Brecht's epic theatre sought to impress on its audiences how all behaviour is shaped by specific material conditions that can be challenged and transformed. To this end, Brecht employed a device that he called the **alienation effect**, which interrupts a play to show how seemingly 'natural' human feelings, actions, and identities are in fact social constructs. Brecht found particular support for his theory in Shakespeare's drama, which repeatedly draws attention to the various social and theatrical conventions that shape its characters' behaviour. We might think, for example, of the Induction scenes in *The Taming of the Shrew*. These dramatize a trick played on a drunken tinker, who is made to believe he is a Lord. As part of the hoax, the tinker is dressed up in rich costumes and presented with an aristocratic 'wife', played by a page-boy. The Induction scenes thus employ alienation effects that disclose how both nobility and femininity are not natural identities, but socially scripted roles.

The class and gender inversions of *The Taming of the Shrew*'s Induction scenes resonate with the preoccupations of another materialist who, like Brecht, stressed the subversive potential of certain literary forms. The maverick Russian critic Mikhail Bakhtin (1895–1975)—who fits uneasily into any conventional Marxist pigeonhole—advanced a theory of what he termed **grotesque realism**. This genre is a world apart from socialist realism; it is instead characterized by images of comic inversion and excess. For Bakhtin, the genre was typified by works of Renaissance literature such as François Rabelais's *Gargantua and Pantagruel*, Miguel de Cervantes's *Don Quixote*, and, importantly, the plays of Shakespeare. Bakhtin claimed that these works were literary expressions of **carnival**, the popular festival that preceded Lent in much of medieval Europe. During carnival, social hierarchy was not only suspended but inverted: the village idiot became king (or Lord of Misrule), men dressed as women, children mocked adults. Both carnival and grotesque realist literature are replete with images of the **grotesque body**, an entity that is perpetually eating, boozing, fornicating, and defecating. By means of such images, Bakhtin argued, grotesque realism not only topples social hierarchies, but also insists on the common creatureliness of all human beings.

Brecht and Bakhtin's theories helped prise Marxist literary criticism from the grip of the reflectionist model and the rigid economic determinism that supported it. But the biggest philosophical challenge to the model was presented by the rise of post-structuralist theory in the 1960s and 1970s. Post-structuralism's suspicion of any theoretical system that locates the origin of meaning outside of language, as indeed the reflectionist theory of literature does, led Marxists to new understandings of the relationship between base and superstructure, and of the status of literature.

The French Marxist Louis Althusser (1918–90) mounted an extensive critique of the reflectionist model. According to Althusser, literature was determined by the economic base only in the last instance; it thus possessed a high degree of autonomy. His critique of economic determinism was accompanied by a radical reconceptualization of how power operates within capitalist societies. Althusser argued that power is exercised not only through ownership of the means of production and extraction of surplus value from alienated labour, but also through specifically ideological means. Institutions that Althusser termed **ideological state apparatuses**, including church, school, and literature, shape people's attitudes by a process of **interpellation**, in which the subject is 'hailed' or given an identity that secures a willing subjection to existing structures of power. With this analysis, Althusser developed and refined Italian Marxist Antonio Gramsci's notion of **hegemony**, the ideological means by which the bourgeoisie control the working class—that is, by controlling the means of cultural rather than economic production.

Althusser's challenge has been important for Marxist understandings of literature. According to his theory of power, literature can be an ideological state apparatus, and thus serve the interests of the dominant class. But its relative autonomy from the economic base also gives it the potential to critique and transform the latter. This shift in Marxism, from a rigid economic determinism to a post-structuralist model of power that operates within a relatively autonomous superstructure, has helped produce the two materialist tendencies that have been most influential within the last twenty years: new historicism and cultural materialism.

New historicism

The term 'new historicism' was coined by the American critic Stephen Greenblatt in the 1980s to differentiate his and others' scholarship from the older historicism of Shakespearians like E. M. W. Tillyard. Writing immediately after the Second World War, Tillyard subscribed to a kind of conservative Hegelianism, which led him to understand Renaissance literature in terms only of its intellectual contexts. In his influential works *The Elizabethan World Picture* and *Shakespeare's History Plays*, Tillyard argued that all Elizabethans believed in a hierarchically organized universe and society; good literature of the period simply reflects that belief. The historicism of Greenblatt and his peers is of a very different order from Tillyard's. Influenced by post-structuralism, they reject Tillyard's reflectionist theory of literature; influenced by Marxism, they reject Tillyard's conservative idealism. Yet they do not propose returning to the old model of the economic base as the determining ground of literary texts. Instead, new historicists seek to clarify the relations between literature and what Marxists would regard as other aspects of the cultural superstructure. Indeed, this emphasis has led to Greenblatt's subsequent embrace of the term 'cultural poetics' at the expense of 'new historicism'.

Whatever name we use to characterize it, this school has often been reluctant to theorize its assumptions. Greenblatt has himself admitted that 'my own work has always been done with a sense of just having to go about and do it, without first establishing exactly what my theoretical position is'.[4] To the extent that he has theoretically situated his work, Greenblatt—like most other practitioners of new historicism—has claimed a Marxist genealogy. Yet he is also adamant in his rejection of some of Marxism's fundamental tenets, including the notion of class struggle as the motor of history. In the process, Greenblatt has replaced traditional Marxist conceptions of history and power with ones inflected by post-structuralist theory in general, and the work of the French thinker Michel Foucault (1926–84) in particular.

In his collection of essays *Power/Knowledge*, Foucault critiques the 'economic functionality' of Marxist conceptions of power. Power, he argues, has tended to be understood as a commodity; for Marxists, this commodity is the means of production, which in capitalist societies has become the property of the bourgeoisie. By contrast, Foucault is more interested in how power can be exercised in other realms of cultural practice—not as a *thing* to be owned, but as a force that circulates impersonally through **discourse**. By the latter term, he means the systems of meaning created within institutions and disciplines devoted to the production of normative 'truths' about humans—for example, criminology, medicine, psychology, and education. Foucault's 'discourse' is thus quite close to Althusser's 'ideological state apparatus'. By creating 'the individual' as an object of knowledge that can be defined in opposition to forms of deviant behaviour and identity (madness, criminality, sexual perversity, etc.), discourse—like Althusser's ideological state apparatus—interpellates the individual within a grid of power: 'the individual', Foucault has observed, 'is not the *vis-à-vis* of power; it is, I believe, one of its prime effects'.[5] Foucault, it should be stressed, is even less of a literary critic than Marx. Yet inasmuch as his work has foregrounded the politics of discourse, it has proved immensely useful for materialist literary critics. Foucault's analysis of power has had four important consequences for the new historicism, each of which serves to differentiate it from traditional Marxist approaches to literature.

First, by taking on board Foucault's notion of discourse, new historicists insist that 'history' is itself textual. Rather than pushing outside of language to locate the origins of power (in an individual's rapacious will, say, or in a social class's ownership of the means of production), new historicists remind us that we do not have any direct access to a history that exists outside of texts. This emphasis is suggested in Louis Montrose's definition of new historicism, which he characterizes as preoccupied with 'the Textuality of History, the Historicity of Texts'.[6] Such an approach is different from the traditional Marxist conception of history, which posits an unproblematically real backdrop outside of language (the base and its contradictions) as the determining ground of the literary work. By contrast, new historicists insist that texts are not simply produced by history—they are also active productions of history as text. Hence new historicists have spoken less of 'historical background' or 'historical context', phrases that might presume a determinist model of literary reflection, than of 'historical co-texts', a coinage that assumes a more mutual, two-way relation between literature and other aspects of culture.

This shift relates to Foucault's second legacy. His insistence that power does not involve ownership but circulates through different discourses of 'truth' has resulted in one of new historicism's most characteristic gambits: parallel readings of literary and non-literary texts. A new historicist essay typically reads a work by Shakespeare in conjunction with (say) a contemporaneous account of New World exploration, or a medical text, or a treatise on witchcraft. In doing so, it endeavours to show how similar configurations of discourse and power circulate through each. For traditional critics, this parallelism is scandalous, a lamentable decentring of the literary. Some might counter, though, that new historicism expands the empire of the literary, inasmuch as it applies the skills of close reading to a host of archival documents previously considered beyond the purview of literary criticism.

The third legacy of Foucault stems from his understanding of the 'individual' as an effect of power rather than as its potential victim. In embracing the latter perspective, new historicists have by and large dispensed with the humanist accent of Marx's account of worker alienation. Much new historicist scholarship—including Greenblatt's ground-breaking *Renaissance Self-Fashioning* (1980)—is concerned instead to show how the illusion of the free individual that precedes the constraints of power is, in fact, one of power's primary effects. This is perhaps typical of a move for which new historicists, particularly Greenblatt, have often been criticized. The new historicism has been preoccupied with how seemingly **subversive** identities are

contained by the very power grid that they seem to contest. Greenblatt, for example, has examined the figure of the atheist, an identity that in Renaissance England was as subversive as any other. Rather than a free-thinking individual who undermined Christian ideals, however, the Renaissance atheist is in Greenblatt's analysis a convenient straw man invented by Christian ideology. Power thrives, therefore, on what seems to undermine it. To this extent, the containment model has something in common with the theory of the **ideological compromise formation**, proposed by the French Marxists Pierre Macherey and Étienne Balibar. This formation entails a dominant faction appropriating seemingly subversive elements of an opposing class's ideology to make itself seem more persuasive or attractive. The theories of containment and the ideological compromise formation are both somewhat pessimistic models of power, inasmuch as each pays homage to the extraordinary self-reproducing potential of structures of domination.

This relates to Foucault's last legacy, which concerns new historicists' attitudes to social change. As we have seen, Marxism is in many ways a philosophy of revolution; it attends dialectically to social contradictions and the possibility of human agency to explain why and how configurations of economic, social, and political power can be transformed. New historicists' analyses of power, like Foucault's, have a functionalist bias—that is, they tend to examine how power maintains itself, rather than how it is altered. Hence, to use a distinction from structural linguistics, if Marxism tends to encourage **diachronic** analysis, i.e., examination of how things change over time, new historicism tends to engage in **synchronic** analysis, i.e., attention to the organization of things within a single moment.

Shakespeare's privileged role as the ground for certain key materialist assumptions is even more evident with new historicism than it is with Marxism. The movement's most influential figures—Greenblatt and Montrose—are both Shakespearians. Their investment in Shakespeare has led to a recurrent interest in theatricality as a mode of power: for both critics, power is 'scripted', 'produced', 'rehearsed', 'performed'. This view owes a debt also to the work of American cultural anthropologists such as Clifford Geertz, who have analysed how rituals of performance constitute one of the principal modes of power within diverse cultures. For new historicists, Shakespeare's plays similarly exemplify the exercise of power in Renaissance culture. In the words of one of the new historicism's critics, 'all conflicts and "jostlings" among social groups become a mere show of political dissension, a prearranged theatre of struggle . . . which produces "opposition" as one of its delusive political effects'.[7] This remark not only sums up the new historicism's synchronic account of subversion and containment; it also hints at the movement's characteristically theatrical lexicon.

At its best, the new historicism's textualization of history has provided a challenging alternative to the orthodoxies of traditional Marxist criticism, not least by insisting on the more complex arrangements of power encoded in literary and non-literary language. Its reluctance to theorize its assumptions, however, has meant that the new historicism has sometimes tended to become a new antiquarianism, endlessly mining non-literary Renaissance texts to produce yet more scholarly articles about Shakespeare's plays and their cultural 'moment'. In such cases, the 'new' historicism begins to look more like its 'old' counterpart, reconstructing the Renaissance as it 'really' was without any attempt to account for processes of social change or to ground its image of the past in its present moment of production. In these two respects, at least, the tendencies of the new historicism are very much at odds with those of cultural materialism.

Cultural materialism

While the new historicism has been an almost exclusively American movement, its close counterpart, cultural materialism, is British. The resemblance is, at first glance, striking. Like the new historicism, cultural materalism has vigorously distinguished itself from the older historicism of Tillyard; it has attended to the relations between literature and politics; it has shown more interest in the cultural superstructure than the economic base; it has critiqued notions of the free individual who precedes power; and it has analysed relations of subversion and containment. Also like the new historicism, cultural materialism has elaborated many of its principal assumptions in studies of Shakespeare. Not surprisingly, the two methodologies were originally regarded as bedfellows. But after an initial, heady spring, their transatlantic romance has witnessed a decided cooling off.

One significant point of contention has concerned the attitude of each camp to the model of subversion and containment. Whereas new historicists have tended to produce pessimistic narratives of subversion's recuperation by a seemingly invincible power, cultural materialists have shown more interest in identifying subversive or 'dissident' literary voices as the agents of revolution. This has led to generalizations about the two methodologies' different attitudes to social change. New historicism, it has been quipped, cannot explain how the English Civil War could have started; cultural materialism cannot explain how it could have stopped.

Cultural materialism's investment in dissident voices has also informed its more extensive engagement with the complexities of gender, sexuality, and class. The new historicism's fascination with the operations of Renaissance authority has drawn criticism for its 'top-down' approach to culture, and for its masculinist neglect of women. By contrast, cultural materialism has shown more inclination to dialogue with feminist, gay, and Marxist theory, as is evidenced by the titles of influential essays and books such as 'The Patriarchal Bard', *Sexual Dissidence*, and 'Shakespeare and the Road-Sweepers'.

The biggest difference, though, lies in how each camp 'historicizes'. New historicists read literary texts in relation to their original moment of production in order to demonstrate the circulation of power through a historical discourse or a cultural system. By contrast, cultural materialists are far more likely to consider the ideological work done by present appropriations of past texts. So whereas new historicists 'historicize' Shakespeare by reading a play in conjunction with another Renaissance text, cultural materialists 'historicize' Shakespeare by looking at (say) present-day national heritage brochures, military advertisements, or stage productions. 'History', then, is seen very differently by the two camps. If the new historicists understand history as a past synchronic 'moment', cultural materialists tend to view it as a diachronic continuum that includes the present location of the critic.

This theoretical difference also entails differences of both style and politics. Perhaps because of the modern, flagrantly non-literary texts and institutions with which they contextualize Shakespeare, cultural materialists have tended to adopt a much more cheeky or irreverent tone than have the more 'scholarly' new historicists. They have also been much more expressly Marxist. If Michel Foucault has provided new historicists with their primary theoretical influence, British Marxist critic Raymond Williams (1921–88) has filled a similar role for cultural materialists. Roughly contemporaneous with Foucault, Williams was similarly interested in how power operates within culture and language. But his analysis of power was more dialectical and less functionalist than Foucault's. Williams theorized culture as a site of struggle, subdivided into **dominant**, **residual**, and **emergent** formations or **structures of feeling**.

The leading practitioners of this brand of materialism—Jonathan Dollimore, Alan Sinfield, and Graham Holderness—have all elaborated its assumptions through readings of Shakespeare. It is easy to see why Shakespeare has been so central to the cultural materialist project. His enduring status as the 'national poet' is sanctioned by the Royal Shakespeare Company, the secondary school English Lit. curriculum, and the holy shrine-cum-theme park of Stratford-upon-Avon (see Chapter 44). This has made him a far more ideologically loaded figure in Britain than he is in other parts of the world. In a country where images of Shakespeare appear on the £5 note and, in holographic form, on credit cards (the so-called 'Bard Card', for discerning consumers), the collusion between Shakespeare's cultural capital and forms of economic capital is more readily apparent than it is in the United States.

Yet, influenced by Williams's dialectical model of culture, cultural materialists don't see Shakespeare as simply a conservative icon. Rather, they regard his plays as present sites of ideological struggle over interpretation. Hence, to use a term devised by Alan Sinfield, cultural materialists look for ideological **faultlines** in Shakespeare's plays that will allow them to be appropriated for radical, 'dissident' readings. For cultural materialists more than for new historicists, then, the Shakespearian text is not simply a literary artefact in dialogue with its original moment of production; it is also an instrument of both cultural hegemony and resistance in the present.

Conclusion

Materialism's three camps share significant common ground. Their impulse to historicize is in most cases underwritten by a leftist political commitment. The 'left', however, is by no means a stable term; its meaning has changed substantially in the last fifty years. During this time, conventional Marxist critiques of capitalism have been supplemented by feminist, post-colonialist, and gay critiques of oppression. Each of the latter have helped reconfigure and reinvigorate the various strands of materialist literary criticism as well.

The differences between the camps, however, are salutary. In particular, each has interpreted Jameson's injunction to historicize in very different ways. Inasmuch as they understand history in terms of material conflict and transition, Marxists tend to historicize literature by reading it for its ideological engagement with larger processes of economic, social, and cultural transformation. New historicists, by contrast, historicize the literary text by reading it in relation to co-texts written in the same period; this relation illuminates a synchronic cultural system through which power circulates, often in theatrical forms. Finally, cultural materialists historize texts in more diachronic fashion; they are interested in the multiple ideological uses to which historical texts can be put in the critic's own moment, including the goal of effecting radical social change.

It is tempting to see the differences between the Marxist, new historicist, and cultural materialist camps as something of a familial dispute, with Marxism the old-fashioned parent displaced by its hipper, feuding offspring. But this is an over-simplification of both the genealogy of materialist literary criticism and the divisions between its modern-day strands. One could equally view these strands less as warring adversaries than as partners in an ongoing, productive dialogue. Cultural materialists have always explicitly located themselves within the big tent of Marxism; some of the germinal new historicist writing appeared in a volume of cultural materialist essays, *Political Shakespeare*; and many Marxists consider their work to be historicist. Indeed, this tradition of theoretical hybridity is nowadays reproduced by most materialist literary critics, who in practice tend to mix and match their methodologies from all three camps.

FURTHER READING

Bristol, Michael D. *Carnival and Theatre: Plebeian Culture and the Structure of Authority in Renaissance England* (London: Methuen, 1985). A useful application of Bakhtin's theories of carnival and the grotesque body to the drama of Shakespeare and his contemporaries.

Dollimore, Jonathan, and Alan Sinfield (eds.). *Political Shakespeare: New Essays in Cultural Materialism*, 2nd edn. (Cornell: Cornell University Press, 1994). This updated edition of a ground-breaking collection of cultural materialist essays, originally published in 1985, includes Stephen Greenblatt's essay 'Invisible Bullets', in which he first articulated the model of subversion and containment. Also of note are Margot Heinemann's essay 'How Brecht Read Shakespeare' and Raymond Williams's afterword.

Drakakis, John (ed.). *Alternative Shakespeares 1* (London: Methuen, 1985); Terence Hawkes (ed.). *Alternative Shakespeares 2* (London: Routledge, 1996). These companion volumes offer a number of materialist readings of Shakespeare, including James Kavanagh's particularly illuminating adaptation of Althusserian theory and Macherey and Balibar's 'ideological compromise formation' in Volume One, and a helpful account by Steven Mullaney of materialism's interactions with other critical methodologies in Volume Two.

Greenblatt, Stephen. *Shakespearian Negotiations: The Circulation of Social Energy in Renaissance England* (Berkeley: University of California Press, 1988). Greenblatt here develops his Foucault-influenced model of power in readings of Shakespeare's plays and culture. The book also contains a longer version of 'Invisible Bullets'.

Holderness, Graham (ed.). *The Shakespeare Myth* (Manchester: Manchester University Press, 1988). This collection, which includes essays on the Shakespeare industry and interviews with leading theatre directors, highlights the presentist perspective of cultural materialism.

Howard, Jean E. and Shershow, Scott Cutler (eds.). *Marxist Shakespeares* (New York and London: Routledge, 2001). This collection of essays presents the latest developments in Marxist criticism of Shakespeare, including materialist feminist readings of property law and women's labour. It also includes an essay by Peter Stallybrass on how Marx read Shakespeare.

Kamps, Ivo (ed.). *Material Shakespeare: A History* (London: Verso, 1995). A collation of some of the most influential materialist writing of the last two decades, though its bias is towards new historicist criticism. It is book-ended by Kamps's useful introduction and an afterword by Fredric Jameson.

Siegel, Paul N. *Shakespeare's English and Roman History Plays: A Marxist Approach* (Cranbury, New Jersey: Associated University Presses, 1986). This book, which typifies a more traditional Marxist approach to Shakespeare, offers a clear exposition of the base/superstructure model.

Veeser, H. Aram (ed.). *The New Historicism* (New York: Routledge, 1989). This collection of essays includes attempts by Greenblatt and Montrose to theorize the new historicism's assumptions, and powerful critiques by its opponents. Although not a volume on Shakespeare, it returns repeatedly to his work, thanks to the specialization of the movement's leading figures.

Wayne, Valerie (ed.). *The Matter of Difference: Materialist Feminist Criticism of Shakespeare* (Ithaca, NY: Cornell University Press, 1991). A collection of essays that showcases a variety of materialist methodologies, ranging from the Marxist to the new historicist, in the service of feminist readings of Shakespeare.

NOTES

1. Fredric Jameson. *The Political Unconscious: Narrative as a Socially Symbolic Act* (Ithaca, NY: Cornell University Press, 1981), p. 9.
2. Fredric Jameson. 'Radicalizing Radical Shakespeare: The Permanent Revolution in Shakespeare Studies'. In Ivo Kamps (ed.). *Material Shakespeare: A History* (London: Verso, 1995), p. 320.
3. Karl Marx. *Grundrisse*. In Robert Tucker (ed.). *The Marx-Engels Reader*, 2nd edn. (New York: Norton, 1978), pp. 245–6.
4. Stephen Greenblatt. 'Towards a Poetics of Culture'. In H. Aram Veeser (ed.). *The New Historicism* (Berkeley: University of California Press, 1989), p. 1.

5. Michel Foucault. *Power/Knowledge: Selected Interviews and Other Writings 1972–77*, ed. Colin Gordon (New York: Pantheon), p. 98.

6. Louis Montrose. 'The Politics and Poetics of Culture'. In Veeser (ed.). *The New Historicism*, p. 23.

7. Frank Lentricchia. 'Foucault's Legacy: A New Historicism?' In Veeser (ed.). *The New Historicism*, p. 235.

READING: *Henry IV Part One*

Shakespeare's history *Henry IV Part One* (c.1596) provides a good opportunity to think about the complexities of what it means to 'historicize'. The play dramatizes a sequence of events historically remote even to its first Elizabethan audiences: the multiple struggles—dynastic, familial, national, cultural—that preceded the battle of Shrewsbury in 1403. But Shakespeare's vision of medieval England is refracted through the prism of his own Elizabethan society. *Henry IV Part One* stages different modes of economic, social, and theatrical power that were very much in conflict in Shakespeare's England and, indeed, his own career. In the process, the play suggests how the present inescapably mediates the project of representing the past. To this extent, *Henry IV Part One* has anticipated its own history in literary criticism and on the stage, where it has served as something of a ventriloquist's dummy through which its interpreters have articulated their own ideological investments.

The title-page of the 1598 edition of *Henry IV Part One* contains two advertising blurbs: 'With the battle at Shrewsbury, between the King and Lord Henry Percy, surnamed Henry Hotspur of the North'; and 'With the humourous conceits of Sir John Falstaff'. The 1598 edition thus insists on the play's schematic division into two separate worlds, one 'high' and militaristic, the other 'low' and comic. These are by no means the only worlds depicted in *Henry IV Part One*. We catch brief glimpses of many others: the domestic world of aristocratic women, including Hotspur's wife Lady Percy; the hand-to-mouth world of the labouring classes, including the Carriers, the Chamberlain, and the Ostler; and a brace of Celtic cultures at odds with England and Henry Bolingbroke's rule, including the Wales of Owain Glyndŵr and the Scotland of Archibald Douglas. Yet the 1598 edition's division between Hotspur's and Falstaff's worlds hints at social forces that were coming into increasing conflict in Shakespeare's lifetime. The late sixteenth century witnessed considerable tension between England's ruling yet economically struggling feudal aristocracy and the commercially ascendant petty bourgeoisie. This tension helped generate new forms of economic practice, social organization, and cultural production—forms that *Henry IV Part One* both fantasizes and mystifies.

Hotspur is a character who lives—and dies—entirely by the aristocratic code of chivalric honour. King Henry praises him as 'the theme of honour's tongue' (1.1.80); the Scottish rebel Douglas calls him 'the king of honour' (4.1.10). Hotspur himself declares that

> . . . methinks it were an easy leap
> To pluck bright honour from the pale-faced moon,
> Or dive into the bottom of the deep,
> Where fathom-line could never touch the ground,
> And pluck up drownèd honour by the locks.
> (1.3.199-203)

Hotspur here imagines honour as a near-mythic treasure obtained by feats of super-human force and even violence. His self-representation harks back to the culture of feudalism, in which nobility was equated with militaristic strength. In Shakespeare's England, by contrast, knights were increasingly political appointees rather than genteel warriors. Nostalgia for the older code may have briefly boosted the popularity of figures like the Earl of Essex, the charismatic 'hero' who captured Cadiz from the Spanish. But, like Hotspur, he was later to meet his end rebelling against his monarch. Feudal honour was thus already a vanishing ideal at the time the play was written.

Its demise is lent voice by the denizens of the play's comic underworld. In particular, Falstaff questions the value of honour. At Shrewsbury, he asks: 'What is honour? A word. What is in that word "honour"? What is that "honour"? Air' (5.1.133–4). Falstaff instead professes allegiance to an altogether different moral system: the code of fellowship. He toasts his drinking companions as 'Gallants, lads, boys, hearts of gold, all the titles of good fellowship come to you!' (2.5.255–6), and he complains to Hal that 'There's neither honesty, manhood, nor good fellowship in thee' (1.2.124–5).

If Falstaff mocks honour, fellowship is conversely a virtue that the fiercely élitist Hotspur rejects: 'out upon this half-faced fellowship!' (1.3.206). This hints at the logic underwriting his honour, which can brook no equal. Hotspur's identity demands the subordination of the world to his will, a tendency evident also in his attitude to property. In particular, he insists on his feudal *droit de seigneur*, or lord's right of conquest, with respect to land. In his clash with Glyndŵr over the future division of the realm, for example, Hotspur complains about being deprived of 'the best of all my land' (3.1.96), and imperiously proposes altering the course of the river Trent so he will not be robbed 'of so rich a bottom' (3.1.102).

Falstaff's embrace of fellowship at the expense of honour—even if it is an embrace compromised by his boisterous selfishness—indicates more than just the boozy conviviality of the tavern. It hints at his indirect ties to an altogether different mode of economic production from that suggested by his knightly title: petty-bourgeois labour. Medieval and Renaissance artisans observed their own forms of hierarchy, embodied in the relationship between apprentice and master craftsman. But the egalitarian language of 'fellowship' underwrote a special type of artisanal property, known as 'skill'. The latter was not an individuated possession like Hotspur's land, but a form of public membership: one earned the right to practise a trade by belonging to a skilled community of artisanal peers, the craft-guild. Thomas Dekker's play *The Shoemaker's Holiday* (1599), for example, repeatedly presents fellowship as the *sine qua non* of the guild of shoemakers.[1] Hence the play's artisans address other members of their profession as 'brother of our trade' (10.60), 'brother of the Gentle Craft' (4.45–6), or just 'my brother' (16.95). These remarks align the property of artisanal skill with a network of unbreakable fraternal relations, an alignment most explicit in the shoemakers' concluding toast to 'incomprehensible good fellowship' (18.207).

We can glimpse the language of artisanal fellowship in the remarks of some of *Henry IV Part One*'s other characters. Gadshill may be a petty highwayman, but he understands his identity in terms of his association with the fellows to which he is 'joined' (2.1.68). Hence, perhaps, his egalitarian world view, so at odds with Hotspur's élitist one: '*homo* is a common name to all men' (2.1.87). Yet Shakespeare's presentation of artisanal language entails a curious mystification. Actual artisanal craft is cast out from the play's province of 'fellowship'; Falstaff and his fellows do not practise any skilled trade (no matter how loud his protests that 'purse taking' is a 'vocation' (1.2.91–2)). Labour is instead the property of isolated characters excluded from Falstaff's 'fellowship' of roisterers—the Ostler, who 'never joyed since the price of oats rose' (2.1.11–12); Francis the apprentice tapster, who still has five years of his bond to serve (2.5.37–8); or the tavern Hostess, who doubles as a sempstress and a wholesale purchaser of cloth (3.3.59–64).

Hal, the present rakehell and future king, fits uneasily into the opposed worlds of Hotspur and Falstaff, honour and fellowship, high feudal *droit de seigneur* and middle-class artisanal skill. He ostensibly rejects aristocratic honour ('riot and dishonour stain the brow / Of my young Harry', moans his father (1.1.84–5)) to consort with Falstaff and his crew. Yet he also praises Hotspur as the nonpareil of valour (5.1.89–92), and covets his honour. Hal speaks Falstaff's language of fellowship—'I am sworn brother to a leash of drawers' (2.5.6). Yet Hal plans to abandon his 'fellows' once he becomes king. Hence his declaration of brotherhood sounds less like an identity in which he believes than a script he has learned to speak when it suits him. Indeed, Hal displays considerable proficiency in his future subjects' languages. Later, as King Henry V, he will speak French to woo Katherine and win the throne of France. In *Henry IV Part One*, he intimates how his fluency in 'low' English ('I am so good a proficient in one quarter of an hour that I can drink with any tinker in his own language during my life' (2.5.15–17)) will be crucial to his future exercise of power: 'when I am King of England I shall command all the good lads in Eastcheap' (2.5.12–13). Hal stoops linguistically, then, to conquer.

This hints at the unique form of power to which he aspires: kingship with the common touch (not quite the late Princess Diana's 'Queen of Hearts' self-image, perhaps, but something along the same lines). Once he has redeemed himself on the battlefield, his 'honour' is draped in, even as it subtly transforms, the language of artisanal fellowship. In the process, he fashions what Marxists would term an 'ideological compromise formation'. By speaking the language of brotherhood, he secures the consent of his lower-class subjects, all the while appearing to uphold the primacy of feudal honour. This compromise is evident in his famous St Crispin's Day speech from *Henry V*:

> . . . if it be a sin to covet honour
> I am the most offending soul alive.
> . . . We would not die in that man's company
> That fears his fellowship to die with us.
> . . . We few, we happy few, we band of brothers.
> For he today that sheds his blood with me
> Shall be my brother; be he ne'er so vile,
> This day shall gentle his condition.
> (4.3.28-9, 38-9, 60-3)

Hal's yoking of the languages of honour and fellowship is hinted at as early as the second scene of *Henry IV Part One*. Alone on stage, he announces he will temporarily maintain his ties to his criminal comrades in order to make his eventual reform look all the more dramatic: 'I'll so offend to make offence a *skill*' (1.2.194; emphasis added). 'Skill' is fascinatingly multivalent here. The term points to Hal's cultivation of a talent comparable in its uniqueness to Hotspur's feudal honour. But we can also hear in it an echo of the fraternal property of artisanal 'skill'.

Hal's compromise does not simply speak the low language of artisanal culture to uphold the power of aristocracy—a version of the new historicist model of subversion contained. Crucially, his compromise also produces a new configuration of power. When apologizing to his father for his delinquency, Hal announces:

> . . . for the time will come
> That I shall make this northern youth exchange
> His glorious deeds for my indignities.
> Percy is but my factor, good my lord,
> To engross up glorious deeds on my behalf;
> And I will call him to so strict account
> That he shall render every glory up,
> Yea, even the slightest worship of his time,
> Or I will tear the reckoning from his heart.
> (3.2.144-52)

The preponderance of commercial terms in this speech—'factor', 'engross', 'account', 'reckoning'—shows how Hal regards Hotspur in much the same way a loan-shark regards his client: as capital from which he will acquire profit, here in the form of 'glorious deeds'. In the course of this exchange, however, Hotspur's 'glorious deeds' become something else— the 'commodity of good names . . . to be bought' referred to by Falstaff earlier in the play (1.2.73–4). Neither feudal honour nor artisanal fellowship is evident here. Instead, Hal sounds more like Marx's characterization of the capitalist bourgeois in *The Communist Manifesto*, who 'has drowned the most heavenly ecstasies of religious fervour, of chivalrous enthusiasm, of philistine sentimentalism, in the icy water of egotistical calculation'.[2]

Yet as with Shakespeare's treatment of artisanal culture, Hal's capitalism is a somewhat mystified phenomenon. The most oppressive aspect of capitalism as a mode of production— its extraction of surplus value from a wage-earning class who have sold their labour—is not ascribed to Hal. Instead it is displaced onto Falstaff. This formerly jovial exponent of 'fellowship' profits from the military commission he receives by recruiting the cheapest, sickest men, whom he damns as 'food for powder, food for powder' (4.2.58–9). Falstaff's property here entails not seigneurship of land, nor possession of skill, but ownership of alienated—and expendable—labour. This displacement does important ideological work. *Henry IV Part One* recognizes the potential dangers of capitalism, but in a way that safeguards Hal's version of it: unlike Falstaff, he is permitted to profit without direct exploitation of a labour force.

The three different modes of power visible in *Henry IV Part One*—feudal, artisanal, capitalist—are represented throughout the play in explicitly theatrical terms. The power of the monarch, as new historicists have often pointed out, assumed theatrical forms in

Shakespeare's time. King James wrote that 'a king is one set on a stage', and the play underscores James's view not just by literally setting a king on the stage, but also by staging scenes of self-conscious royal performance.[3] The manipulation and reproduction of the royal image as a source of power is particularly evident late in the play, with doubles 'counterfeiting' the King on the battlefield to flummox and vanquish his enemies. But theatrical performance is never uniform in its political effects. Indeed, Elizabethan audiences were familiar with different styles of performance, each of which implied different modes of power.

Hotspur and Douglas are histrionic representatives of old feudal glory. Fittingly, perhaps, their modes of theatrical performance recall the outmoded styles of playing demanded by the medieval mystery plays' stock violent characters: Hotspur is a strutting ranter whose wild fury recalls the tyrannical stage Herod; Douglas is compared to Termagant (5.4.112). Ultimately, however, Hotspur's and Douglas's old-fashioned styles of performance fail them less theatrically than politically: these plotters are histrionically impressive, but they lose the plot—and hence the battle.

As his masterful parody of King Henry in the language of antiquated stage-monarchs suggests (2.5.352), Falstaff is much more self-consciously theatrical than Hotspur. At one level, of course, he is just a melodramatic liar—whether fibbing about his feats of arms at Gad's Hill, or claiming to have given Hotspur his deathblow. Yet Falstaff's theatricality also serves a critical function. His parody of the King harnesses the subversive potential of carnival; Falstaff is a theatrical Lord of Misrule who upsets social hierarchies every bit as much as his grotesque, oversized body transgresses its own boundaries. To this extent, his embrace of fellowship is of a piece with the utopian, anti-authoritarian dimension of carnival. Yet for all the attractiveness of his powers of parody, the play does stack the deck against Falstaff theatrically. Hal associates him repeatedly with outmoded medieval dramatic roles such as 'the Vice' (2.5.413), and 'white-bearded Satan' (2.5.422); like his feudal rivals Hotspur and Douglas, then, Falstaff theatrically belongs to another era.

By contrast, Hal's is a different, new kind of theatre: more calculating, more reserved, less in thrall to old styles of playing. His style arguably anticipates that advocated by Hamlet, who advises the Players to avoid the over-the-top medieval models of 'Herod' and 'Termagant' and instead 'use all gently' (*Hamlet*, 3.2.12, 5). As we have seen, Hal 'uses all gently' in a class as well as a theatrical sense, 'using'—in the sense of profiting from—a wide array of 'low' and 'high' scripts in order to advance his royal power.

Hal's new mode of theatricality is perhaps not unconnected to the disjunctive social and economic organization of the joint-stock company to which Shakespeare belonged for much of his adult life. On the one hand, the King's Men modelled certain aspects of their structure and activity on the guilds. This is made clear by the franchise they were awarded by King James in 1603 to 'practise the art and faculty of playing'—terms that recall the language of craft-guild ordinances. Yet Shakespeare's company also made a decisive break with guild practices. This was partly because of their nominal feudal subservience to a lord. The Act of 1572 concerning the punishment of vagabonds demanded that playing companies be licensed exclusively through patronage by a nobleman or two judicial dignitaries of the realm; the subsequent statute of 1598 limited patronage to nobles alone. But the professional companies' break with craft-guild culture can be seen most clearly, perhaps, in their principals' attitudes to and use of property. The sizeable capital ventures and investments of the theatre companies' impresarios and leading actor-sharers, including Shakespeare, mark a decisive shift in priorities from those of artisanal or feudal culture. Exercising property in skill or in feudal estate had become secondary to the accumulation of convertible private assets. In the case of Shakespeare, such accumulation may have helped him to buy his way into the gentry in 1598, when he purchased a coat of arms for his family. *Henry IV Part One*, then, stages a Hal whose practices are not unlike those of his author: all the while appearing to yoke two residual codes of property and identity in the pursuit of gentility, Hal—like Shakespeare—lends voice to an emergent form of cultural practice that is no longer either feudal or artisanal.

This Hal-centred reading of the play is, without doubt, a distinctly modern one. In early nineteenth-century Britain, a time of neo-feudal nostalgia (as the huge popularity of Walter Scott's *Ivanhoe* suggests), the swashbuckling Hotspur was the play's most fascinating character, and the glittering prize of the nation's leading actors. By contrast, recent North American productions of the play have marginalized Hotspur and concentrated on Hal's rise to power. Gus Van Sant's film *My Own Private Idaho* (1992), which partially adapts *Henry IV* to represent street culture in Portland, Oregon, cuts Hotspur's character altogether to focus attention on Hal (or in this case, the Portland mayor's rich son) and his strategies of self-advancement. The film's emphasis on Hal was replicated at the 2001 Shakespeare Festival in Stratford, Ontario, where the two parts of *Henry IV* were performed alongside *Henry V* with the title 'The Making of a King'.[4] This title might seem to imply a fascination with royal psychology. But the term 'making' also suggests the entrepreneurial skill of the 'self-made man'. In the age of corporate capitalism, then, Hal's theatrical self-fashioning—so dependent on his strategic manipulation of the languages of both individual glory and company loyalty—speaks to North American audiences in a way that Hotspur's feudalistic code perhaps no longer can.

FURTHER READING

Barber, C. L. 'Rule and Misrule in *Henry IV*'. In *Shakespeare's Festive Comedy: A Study of Dramatic Form and its Relation to Social Custom* (Princeton: Princeton University Press, 1959), pp. 192–221. A reading of Falstaff's function in the play, this chapter is part of a pioneering study of Renaissance festive ritual that anticipates much recent work on the 'carnivalesque' in Shakespeare.

Campbell, Lily B. 'The Unquiet Time of Henry IV'. In *Shakespeare's 'Histories': Mirrors of Elizabethan Policy* (San Marino, CA: Huntington Library, 1947), pp. 213–54. An example of 'old' historicist criticism, this essay examines Falstaff's criticisms of honour in relation to Elizabethan ideas about rebellion.

Goldberg, Jonathan. 'Desiring Hal'. In *Sodometries: Renaissance Texts, Modern Sexualities* (Stanford: Stanford University Press, 1992), pp. 145–75. Goldberg's essay is foundational in the field of gay and lesbian approaches. It considers Hal's desire and twentieth-century critics' desire for Hal, as well as the part played by each in establishing and unravelling modern regimes of sexuality.

Greenblatt, Stephen. 'Invisible Bullets'. In *Shakespearian Negotiations: The Circulation of Social Energy in Renaissance England* (Berkeley: University of California Press, 1988), pp. 21–65. This immensely influential new historicist essay offers a double reading of New World colonist Thomas Harriot's seemingly subversive encounters with Algonquin culture and Hal's seemingly subversive encounters with London's underworld culture. In both instances, Greenblatt argues, apparent 'subversion' is 'the very condition of power'.

Hodgdon, Barbara (ed.). *The First Part of 'King Henry The Fourth': Texts and Contexts* (Boston, MA: Bedford, 1997). An invaluable edition of the play, notable for its illuminating introduction as well as its inclusion of a large number of Renaissance documents that touch on pertinent topics such as historiography, politics, 'low' culture, and chivalry.

Holderness, Graham. *Shakespeare's History* (Dublin: Gill and Macmillan, 1985). This cultural materialist analysis of Shakespeare's histories examines both the production of the genre as a response to social conflicts within Shakespeare's culture, and the role played by subsequent reproductions of the plays in the historical development of 'British' culture.

Howard, Jean, and Phyllis Rackin. *Engendering a Nation: A Feminist Account of Shakespeare's English Histories* (London: Routledge, 1997). An important feminist intervention in criticism of a genre that has been often regarded as exclusively masculine or patriarchal.

McMillin, Scott. *'Henry IV Part One': Shakespeare in Performance* (Manchester: Manchester University Press, 1991). An extensive history of the play on stage, with considerable attention devoted to the changing cultural contexts of performance and interpretation.

Traub, Valerie. 'Prince Hal's Falstaff: Positioning Psychoanalysis and the Female Reproductive Body'. In *Desire and Anxiety: Circulations of Sexuality in Shakespearian Drama* (New York: Routledge, 1992), pp. 50–70. This essay draws parallels between *Henry IV Part One*'s images of Falstaff's body and psychoanalytic understandings of the female reproductive body as 'grotesque'.

Wood, Nigel (ed.). *Theory in Practice: 'Henry IV, Parts One and Two'* (Buckingham: Open University Press, 1995). This volume usefully models a wide array of theoretical approaches to *Henry IV*, including Kiernan Ryan's application of Fredric Jameson's theory of the political unconscious, and Peter Womack's essay on parallels between Shakespeare's dramatic forms and Marxist playwright Bertolt Brecht's theory of epic theatre.

NOTES

1. All references are to Thomas Dekker. *The Shoemaker's Holiday*, ed. D. J. Palmer (New York: Norton, 1986).
2. Karl Marx and Friedrich Engels. *Manifesto of the Communist Party*. In Robert Tucker (ed.). *The Marx-Engels Reader*, 2nd edn. (New York: Norton, 1978), p. 475.
3. King James I. 'Basilikon Doron'. In Charles H. McIlwain, *The Political Works of James I* (Cambridge, MA: Harvard University Press, 1921), p. 5.
4. I owe this reference to Kim Huth, whom I thank also for her invaluable research assistance in preparing this chapter.

33 | Post-colonial criticism

Jyotsna Singh

A history of post-colonial criticism

Why did Shakespeare choose a black man, Othello, as the hero of one of his greatest tragedies? What led the dramatist who had portrayed the conventional negative stereotype of the Moor in Aaron (in *Titus Andronicus*) to break away from that image in his later play, *Othello*? Had Shakespeare and his contemporaries any direct contact with black people, with new world 'Indians', and with Jews? What was his response to the prevailing stereotypes of race and religion? Such questions have become more important since the 1980s, in large part because our society has become more sensitive to issues of racial identity and equality, and also of gender equity.

Post-colonial criticism is a method of analysis that addresses these questions via two main modes of inquiry. First, it investigates how Shakespeare's plays relate to the social codes and conventions by which early modern Europeans defined non-European and non-Christian people and races they encountered. Second, it explores the more recent history of the *reception* of Shakespearian drama within non-Western societies and settings—in Africa, India, the Caribbean, and Latin America. Thus, post-colonial criticism of a play like *Othello* not only draws our attention to Renaissance attitudes toward Moors, Africans, and Turks, among others, but it also examines how the play may have been interpreted and performed in countries involved in recent colonial and post-colonial struggles, for example in apartheid and post-apartheid South Africa. This process was, of course, a complex one. On the one hand, Shakespeare was an export to the colonies of European literature and language as a part of their policy of cultural domination. On the other hand, it also enabled the colonized groups to revise and remake Shakespeare's works in ways which related to their own social conditions.

The de-colonization movements in Africa, Asia, the Caribbean, and Latin America in the 1960s and the 1970s laid the initial groundwork for post-colonial criticism. During this period, Europe's former subjects began to free themselves not only from political rule, but also from the cultural colonization that they had experienced. The African novelist, essayist, and activist, Ngugi Wa Thiong'o, has written extensively about the ways in which English literature served as a mode of domination during British colonial rule in his country, Kenya. Thus, when Africans like him began to question this cultural domination after de-colonization, they often cited Shakespeare's role as an exemplar of English education for Africans under British rule, as Ngugi recalls: 'According to the English teachers in Kenya', he writes, 'William Shakespeare and Jesus Christ had brought light to darkest Africa' (p. 91). Ngugi's humorous look at the colonial definition of Shakespeare as 'one more English gift to the world alongside the Bible' typifies the way in which non-Europeans from the former colonies began to rethink their relationship to the works of Shakespeare. But it wasn't until the early 1980s that work like Ngugi's began to attract the attention of Anglo-American critics with the formation of post-colonial approaches in Western literary studies.

What are some of the attributes and effects of post-colonial criticism within literary studies in general and Shakespearian studies in particular? In Shakespeare (and Renaissance) studies, post-colonial criticism often emphasizes historical sources drawn from travel and 'discovery' narratives, which record the contact histories of the early modern period. In 'discovering' other lands for trade and influence, Europeans were also forced to formulate their own sense of national and cultural identity—and to distinguish between themselves and the non-European others they encountered. Furthermore, new geographical knowledge also grew out of this early modern interest in mercantile or trading ventures. While involved in travel and trade, Europeans recorded their keen awareness of changing geographical, racial, and cultural boundaries. Emerging from these historical concerns, post-colonial criticism is particularly interested in charting and interrogating the many changes and shifts in the concept of 'race' and categories of racial difference—often related to culture, religion, and nationality—from the early modern period to more recent colonial and post-colonial moments of political and economic struggle.

Representations of race

Thus, from a post-colonial perspective, images of 'black' Africans and/or Moors in early modern English culture provide a crucial context for understanding Othello's complex role in the Venetian society of Shakespeare's play. Why is a highly decorated and respected general considered an unsuitable match for a Venetian senator's young daughter? Many derogatory references to Othello's race throughout the play offer a clear explanation. Not only does Iago use bestial imagery to denote the supposedly unnatural marriage between the Moor and Desdemona, but Brabanzio also accuses Othello of wooing his daughter by witchcraft. It would otherwise be 'unnatural' for her to run to the General's 'sooty bosom'. Perhaps what is most tragic is how Othello himself internalizes some of the racist stereotypes deployed by Iago and Brabanzio, so apparent when he identifies with images of the 'turbaned Turk' and 'circumcised dog' at the end of the play (5.2.362, 364). Until the 1960s, it was not unusual to read criticism of Othello that viewed the tragedy from Brabanzio's perspective, whereby an interracial marriage was seen as an aberration of nature and tragically doomed to failure. In fact, famous nineteenth-century critics such as Samuel Coleridge and Charles Lamb even questioned whether the play could be defined as a true tragedy since it dramatized what was considered an inviolable taboo in nineteenth-century England: a white woman in the embrace of a black man.

Post-colonial criticism offers an historical explanation for the treatment of Othello by exploring the complexities of early modern racial attitudes, especially the associations between specific races and religions and their physical characteristics. If one historically examines racial attitudes of the period, one finds that in the theatre, as in the culture, the Irish, the Jews, the Welsh, Turks, 'savages', Africans, 'Indians', are often shown as distinct from one another, but yet sharing characteristic differences from the English. Although examples of light-skinned Moors and Moors who have converted to Christianity can frequently be found in the writings of the period, and although not all Muslims are seen as black, the association of blackness and Moorishness becomes increasingly common in literature, as does the association of Moors and Islam.

Even while Europeans were gaining more knowledge of other races and cultures, their confusions about exact racial and religious designations persisted. And underlying the growing acquisition of knowledge was a frequent European tendency to demonize 'black' races of people who above all *looked* different from them. These historical conditions help us to better understand how a dramatist like Shakespeare could imagine that Iago could manipulate Othello into believing in his own inferiority. By the early seventeenth century, when Shakespeare was writing *Othello*, knowledge of Africa was far more detailed than it had been at the beginning of the Elizabethan era. But English representations of sub-Saharan Africans in print and performance were increasingly though unevenly critical of Africans' bodies and beliefs, customs and character. In fact, it would be fair to assume that by this time the Africans' dark skin and unfamiliar customs and habits clearly set them apart in the English imagination as a different category of humanity. Therefore, not surprisingly, Iago's references to Othello's black inferiority could not have been understood by an audience of the time without the images, verbal and visual, that circulated in the popular imagination of Elizabethan England.

A recognition of how post-colonial criticism offers historical explanations for Othello's tragedy in terms of his race and status as an outsider in Renaissance Venice leads to one of its basic assumptions: namely, that the meanings of Shakespeare's plays are neither intrinsically stable, nor a part of an unchanging, common human experience. Post-colonial criticism particularly draws our attention to the role played by Shakespeare's plays on *different historical occasions* relating to specific political struggles in recent times. Thus, the impulse to historicize reaches toward *both* the past and the present.

For instance, post-colonial approaches have shown us how racial themes in *Othello* were repressed in apartheid South Africa, when interracial relationships were legally forbidden. In the mid-1980s, for example, during the height of apartheid in South Africa, *Othello* became a site upon which the power struggles between the white rulers and black subjects were played out, giving a poignant, contemporary urgency to the plight of a fictional Renaissance figure. Since the subject of race was taboo at the time, white South African critics generally avoided *Othello*. When they did write about the play, they generally avoided its concern with colour. Instead, they focused on abstract issues or interpreted it as a tragedy of jealousy. In fact, some would argue that the racism implicit in South African criticism of *Othello* is a part of the Western critical tradition, represented by Coleridge among others. This is the very tradition that many critics uphold as transcendent and timeless in its humanity.

Colonialism and property rights

In another, more surprising, post-colonial reading of *King Lear*, a contemporary South African critic draws an analogy between the issue of landownership in the play—initiated by King Lear's arbitrary division of lands—and a history of land appropriation in South Africa until the recent end of apartheid. He does so while emphasizing the failure of the rulers in both instances to offer redress to the homeless and landless. Such a post-colonial analogy does not collapse the divide between the early modern period and our own times, but, rather, it questions the right to private property by showing how it is asserted as an inviolable, natural right in both settings and periods, while *we* can see its arbitrariness and cruelty.

This essay by Nicholas Visser approaches the issue of landownership and distribution in *King Lear* and in the early modern period in the context of recent, post-colonial (late 1990s) South African efforts to redistribute land. While it is a critical commonplace to recognize the numerous references to deeds, portions, dowries, inheritance, debts, usurers, monopolies, and so forth that permeate the language of *King Lear*, here the critic applies this language of commerce to the specific issue of landownership in the play in order to inquire how the land is represented and contested both in the play and in wider social intercourse in South Africa. In Lear's opening descriptions of his lands—'shadowy forests', 'plenteous rivers', and 'wide-skirted meads'—there are no signs of human habitation (1.1.62–3). Thus, the king can arbitrarily divide this 'empty' land with no regard for consequences. It is only on the blasted heath that the suffering Lear discovers the existence of the 'houseless' and dispossessed.

Similar divisions would resonate among South Africans, since historical, colonial claims of 'empty lands' enabled conservative historians, until recently, to legitimize the appropriation of land by colonial white settlers. Even in today's South Africa, the large numbers of people left landless and homeless are reminiscent of the poor 'wretches' of Lear's heath. What drives this analogy is a naturalized, inviolable concept of private property that permeates both the world of the play and of contemporary, post-apartheid South Africa, while not even considering any alternative rights in property other than private ownership. If one charts the history of this attitude, one can recognize that at the dawn of the modern age, *King Lear* captures the transformation of land into private property—an idea that we take for granted today.

If one does not typically associate *King Lear* with colonial or post-colonial history, such an approach enables the play to find a new context and meaning in South African political and economic struggles. At the end of *King Lear* the status quo is restored without any redress for the poor people Lear had empathized with, not even a 'shaking' of a bit of 'superflux' (cf. 3.4.36). Similar limitations in the politics of empathy are evident in post-apartheid South Africa's failure to offer redress to the poor homeless and landless. As stated earlier, this post-colonial reading does not flatten the past to accommodate the concerns of the present. Instead it emphasizes the *specificity* and difference of the two practices of land distribution in order to make us think about the assumptions underlying the way we talk about land—and the way we think about *King Lear* as a tragedy of individuals.

Narratives of discovery and trade

Post-colonial criticism's interest in a history of early modern European 'discoveries' and mercantile ventures also affords a new context for reading some of Shakespeare's plays. In *The Merchant of Venice*, for instance, the conflict between the merchants and the money lender—or the Christians and the Jew—can be better understood in the context of a new dependence on capital in a growing, though highly unstable, mercantile economy. References to the loss of Antonio's ships filled with silks and spices in the opening scene signal an important connection between the play and extensive European trading ventures of the period. Early modern European expansion for purposes of trade and discovery resulted in a growing awareness of changing geographical, racial, religious, and cultural/national boundaries. This recognition was accompanied by an anxiety about cross-cultural encounters with non-Europeans and non-Christians, which reflected the codes and conventions of the system of differences specific to the early modern period.

Post-colonial criticism also affords a more historicized and sympathetic perspective on Shylock's role. Thus, the Venetian merchants' denigration of Shylock emerges from Christian Europe's demonization of the Jews at the time. Frequently, their religion was elided with usury, without accounting for the fact that Jews often resorted to money lending as a response to a curtailment of other professions and modes of income. Like *Othello*, *The Merchant of Venice* is strategically set in Venice, a symbolic site for Europe's boundary with the non-European, non-Christian world of the Islamic Ottoman empire. While open to the possibilities of great mercantile wealth, Venice in this play is also open to the encroachment of foreigners and a dependence on their money, which fuels the trade.

A post-colonial reading of the play would be attentive to such geo-political and cultural struggles, while trying to understand interactions between the individual characters. Thus, the seemingly simple question of the play—'who is the Christian and who is the Jew?' (cf. 4.1.169)—resonates with early modern European anxieties about fixing racial and religious boundaries in the face of growing travel, trade, and the intermingling of peoples.

From this perspective, the seemingly incidental role of the Prince of Morocco also assumes a larger historical significance. He is one of the three suitors who come to Belmont to solve the riddle of the caskets, which is laid as a condition for Portia's marriage by her dead father. It is telling that Venetian daughters like Portia must contend with suitors from outside their own religion and race—and from outside the geographical boundaries of Europe. Such a marriage would prove a threat to all certainties of European identity. Therefore, while the exotic Prince would have had a flamboyant presence on stage, Shakespeare's audiences would have understood the 'logic' of the plot whereby the alien suitor of a different 'complexion' must fail at choosing the right casket, and be rejected and ridiculed by Portia (2.7.79). Furthermore, Portia's—and the audience's—dismissal of Morocco, in contrast to her obvious attraction for Bassanio who chooses the right casket, seems to foreshadow the 'otherness' evoked by Othello the Moor in another Shakespearian play set in Venice.

Such a foregrounding of the role of the Prince of Morocco in *The Merchant of Venice* points to a broader impact of post-colonial criticism in looking afresh at Shakespeare's plays. Overall, by placing these works within the European history of trade, 'discovery', and colonization, this mode of inquiry has changed the landscape of these dramatic works—peopled more visibly now by characters previously in the shadowy margins of European critical consciousness, 'Moors', 'Jews', 'Indians', and others. It is not that the dramatic casts have changed, but that we now pay more attention to characters who were 'whited out' before.

As another instance of this phenomenon, one has only to consider a very novel reading of the minor character of the changeling 'Indian boy' in another Shakespearian comedy, *A Midsummer Night's Dream*. Conflict between the fairy king and queen, Oberon and Titania, is focused on this boy. Oberon claims the child as his own henchman, whereas Titania lavishes attention on him as a part of her retinue. All we know of this changeling boy is that his mother was an Indian votaress of Titania's order who died at his birth, and the fairy queen claims and cares for him for 'her sake' (2.1.123–37). He does not figure in the list of the *dramatis personae*, so there is no call for a real actor to represent him on stage. Yet, if one follows the performance history of this play, one discovers that the boy has been played by actors of different ages, ranging from children to adolescents. The Indian boy seems first to have been brought on stage to provide an exotic touch to some productions.

A post-colonial perspective on the role of the Indian changeling boy foregrounds images of India in the play, bringing Shakespeare's European fairyland close to European trading and colonizing interests. While at the time India was frequently imagined by people as a place of fabulous wealth and exoticism, by the early seventeenth century—in the wake of explorations and trade—it was also being defined as a real geographical and cultural space, open to acquisitive drives. Shakespeare's comedy participated in the popular imaginings of 'India' both as an exotic place and also as a land to be conquered and occupied, as Oberon and Titania struggle to stake their claims on the 'Indian boy'.

Cultural and national stereotypes

References to European mercantile drives and ambitions were implicitly linked to their concerns about national and cultural stereotypes. Thus, the European 'discoveries' of other lands and peoples always involved some aspect of self-definition. Post-colonial criticism offers new perspectives on the Roman play *Antony and Cleopatra* by interrogating the stereotypical definitions of Egypt and its Queen. Shakespeare's dramatization of the famous lovers of history, Antony and Cleopatra, depicts a complex struggle between Antony's powerful attraction for the Egyptian queen and his political duty to Roman unity and military dominance. Until recently, the Western critical tradition has interpreted the play by privileging the Roman perspective. It has represented the love affair in terms of a clash of the heroic, masculine West, namely Rome, and the feminized, decadent East embodied by Cleopatra. Such stereotypes have been the basis of European justifications for supposedly bringing order and civilization to lands they conquered and colonized. The Romans in the play express such colonizing impulses toward Egypt, representing both the land and its queen as dangerous in their decadence and seductiveness. Conversely, they promote Roman (or European) power as fixed, immutable, and inherently superior.

While generations of Western critics identified with the Roman judgement of Cleopatra as a decadent, Eastern *femme fatale*, more recent, post-colonial—and feminist— critics read the play as a dialectical struggle between two competing perspectives. Among other things, they note the Roman lapses into debauchery and drunkenness in the play. In doing so, they view Shakespeare's version of the historical power struggle between Rome and Egypt as about the Roman empire's response to the geographical, cultural, and racial encroachments of Egypt. Thus they explain how in eroticizing Egypt, the Romans are not unlike subsequent generations of European colonists who justified their military conquest over the supposedly decadent lands of the East. The personal love story of the Roman general, Antony, and the Egyptian queen recedes somewhat in the background of such historical readings.

Post-colonial criticism's historical bias not only draws attention to cultural stereotyping as a part of the European colonizing imagination, but also reveals how such stereotypes underpinned the formation of the English nation in the early modern period. As English people began to imagine themselves as a nation, the process frequently involved a contrast with other races, religions, and cultures. In fact, these included the Scots, Welsh, and Irish, who were often resistant subjects of the British rulers. This process of nation-formation brings us to the history plays—the two tetralogies, for instance—which concern themselves with the fate and glory of England while a civil war is raging.

In *Henry V*, for instance, King Henry repeatedly mobilizes his armies against the French king by evoking a cohesive British society that encompasses lords and commoners as well as the Welsh, Irish, and the Scots. The ideal, unified society imagined in the play—for instance, in the Agincourt speech before battle in France—did not reflect the actual English colonizing drives toward these territories on the margins of England. Instead it emphasized and naturalized a dominant idea of the nation as singular entity. And, as many critics and historians have noted, English nationalism was based on marginalizing the Irish and Welsh as backward peoples who needed to be 'civilized'.

Conclusion

A play most directly involved in dramatizing European 'discovery' and colonization in the early modern period was *The Tempest* (discussed below). While *The Tempest* is considered the primary text on which post-colonial criticism first took root, this critical method has spawned a growing body of work that has enlarged our understanding of the politics of race, nationalism, and colonialism in early modern England. And this mode of criticism complements—and often overlaps with—the critical work of feminist and materialist criticism. If feminist criticism examines how Shakespeare's plays relate to the codes and conventions of the gender system of the period, and materialist approaches foreground the formation of class distinctions, post-colonial criticism investigates the system of racial differentiation. Collectively, all three approaches re-examine Shakespeare's plays historically, showing how they tell us a complex story about the race, class, and gender struggles in early modern England. Intellectually and politically, these theories have given a crucial impetus to various resistance movements, encompassing feminist, anti-racist, and anti-colonial struggles, while exploring literary and cultural texts as sites of ideological and political conflicts. In doing so, they have demystified the claims of a universal and timeless Shakespeare.

FURTHER READING

Cowhig, Ruth. 'Blacks in English Renaissance Drama'. In *The Black Presence in English Literature*, ed. David Dabydeen (Manchester: Manchester University Press, 1985), pp. 1–25. An early reminder of how questions of race on the early modern stage were largely ignored by generations of Anglo-American critics.

Hall, Kim. *'Things of Darkness': Economies of Race and Gender in Early Modern England* (Ithaca: Cornell University Press, 1995). A historical and literary exploration of the black/white binary in English Renaissance culture, showing the emergence of a colour-coded power hierarchy in the early period of European colonization and the slave trade.

Hendricks, Margo. ' "Obscured by dreams": Race, Empire, and Shakespeare's *A Midsummer Night's Dream'*. *Shakespeare Quarterly*, 47 (1996), 37–60. An essay on the 'Indian boy' in *A Midsummer Night's Dream* relates images of India in the play to European trading and colonizing interests in the Renaissance.

Hendricks, Margo and Patricia Parker (eds.). *Women, 'Race', and Writing in the Early Modern Period* (London: Routledge, 1994), pp. 287–99. A volume of essays that explore, among other things, questions of race, empire, and colonialism in the early modern period.

Loomba, Ania and Martin Orkin (eds.). *Post-Colonial Shakespeares* (London: Routledge, 1998). A recent volume representing current trends in post-colonial criticism of Shakespeare. Among other things, this volume shows how Moors came to be associated with both blackness and Islam in England.

Newman, Karen. ' "And Wash the Ethiop White": Femininity and the Monstrous in *Othello'*. In *Shakespeare Reproduced: The Text in History and Ideology*, Jean E. Howard and Marion F. O'Connor (eds.). (London: Methuen, 1987), pp. 141–62. A reading of the play that explores Elizabethan and Jacobean attitudes toward women and black men as dramatized in *Othello*.

Ngugi, Wa Thiong'o. *Decolonising the Mind: The Politics of Language in African Literature* (London: James Currey, 1986). An analysis of the cultural effects of colonialism in East Africa.

Orkin, Martin. 'Othello and the Plain Face of Racism'. *Shakespeare Quarterly*, 38 (1987), 166–88. A critical and performance history of the reception of *Othello* in South Africa in recent decades—one that shows the effects of apartheid and its aftermath on interpretations of the play.

Said, Edward. *Orientalism* (New York: Vintage Books, 1979). A seminal work which produced the field of post-colonial studies.

Singh, Jyotsna G. 'Othello's Identity: Post-colonial Theory and Contemporary African Re-writings of *Othello'*. In *Women, 'Race', and Writing in the Early Modern Period*, eds. Margo Hendricks and Patricia Parker (London: Routledge, 1994), pp. 287–99. An essay that examines contemporary African re-readings of *Othello*, bringing together the early modern period and the Third World of the post-colonial era.

Vaughan, Virginia. *Othello: A Contextual History* (Cambridge: Cambridge University Press, 1994). A useful account of the historical contexts of the play, with an emphasis on visual as well as verbal images of difference in early modern England.

Visser, Nicholas. 'Shakespeare and Hanekom, *King Lear* and Land: A South African Perspective'. In Ania Loomba and Martin Orkin (eds.). *Post-Colonial Shakespeares* (London: Routledge, 1998), pp. 205–217. Visser gives a contemporary relevance to the issue of landownership in *King Lear* by relating it to the history of land appropriation in South Africa, while emphasizing in both instances the plight of the homeless and landless.

READING: *The Tempest*

Early post-colonial responses

Until the advent of post-colonial criticism, Anglo-American critics frequently read *The Tempest* as an allegory about artistic creation. Since this was once considered to be Shakespeare's final play, Prospero has been defined as a surrogate playwright, shaping the main action through his magic. Starting with the artificial tempest of the opening scene, Prospero directs, rewards, and punishes the main characters according to his master plan, which is to marry his daughter, Miranda, to Ferdinand, the son and heir to the Duke of Naples, his former enemy. This plan is considered his benevolent revenge for his forcible exile from his own kingdom. In leading to this desired union of Naples and Milan, Prospero obstructs the advances of Caliban, the native of the island where he and Miranda are exiled. Furthermore, Prospero's magical power not only ensures the enslavement of Caliban, but also demands the servitude of a sprite named Ariel to put his magical designs into action. Overall, in this commonly accepted reading of *The Tempest*, Prospero emerges as an all-knowing patriarch and artistic creator whose manipulations have benevolent and providential ends, and whose motives are beyond reproach. Since the play is a romance in terms of its genre, its plot was generally approached as a fanciful, 'mouldy tale', with little connection to the history of the period or its aftermath.

This long tradition of privileging Prospero's creative powers as beneficent and providential could not withstand the growing stature of Caliban, following the de-colonization movements of the 1960s and 1970s in Africa, the Caribbean, and Latin America. If, traditionally, Prospero's art represented the world of civility and learning in contrast to the 'natural' black magic of Sycorax, Caliban's mother, anti-colonial revisions of the play challenged this rather abstract Eurocentric division between art and nature. Instead, as Africans and Caribbeans saw that widespread national liberation was imminent—that is from 1959 onwards—they began to revise and mobilize the play in defence of Caliban's right to the island on which he is born prior to Prospero's arrival. Caliban's assertion in the play, 'This island's mine, by Sycorax my mother, / Which thou tak'st from me' (1.2.334–5), became the rallying cry for African and Caribbean intellectuals from the 1960s to the 1970s.

For instance, Aimé Césaire, a black writer and activist from Martinique, re-wrote Shakespeare's play in 1969 in French. *Une Tempête* (translated into the English *A Tempest* in 1985) celebrates Caliban's verbal attacks on Prospero and repudiates the latter's claims to the island. Set in a colony—a prototype of a Caribbean or African setting—in the throes of resistance and unrest, Césaire's play focuses initially on Caliban's resistance to Prospero's control over language. Here, Césaire is clearly sensitive to the way in which the name Caliban/Cannibal appears in Shakespeare's play and in colonial history as a cultural stereotype for the natives of the new world. Accompanying Caliban's challenge to language are

Fig. 3.3 David Suchet as a humanized, though exploited, 'third-world' Caliban in the 1978 Royal Shakespeare Company production of *The Tempest*. According to reviewers, Suchet's Caliban could be a representative African or West Indian.

the intimations of an actual guerrilla movement and an impending black independence. And Ariel, who is labelled a 'mulatto' in this play, represents the mixed races more able to accept their limited oppression. Overall, this play typifies the changes undergone by the figure of Caliban in the stage manifestations of the play: in eighteenth- and nineteenth-century European productions he was represented as a primitive or a 'missing link' from Darwin's theory. However, with the advent of national liberation of the non-European races, as in Césaire's play, Caliban was widely depicted as a defiant subject under European rule, or simply an embodiment of any oppressed group.

Such identifications with Caliban and an accompanying unease about his alien language typify numerous Latin American and Caribbean responses to the play in the wake of decolonization in the 1960s. Roberto Fernandez Retamar, for instance, notes how many writers from these regions considered Prospero a European usurper and Caliban an enslaved subject. In some instances, they explored Ariel's role as a native intellectual forced to betray those below him. In Africa too, the play became a site for anti-colonial responses, one good example of such an appropriation being the novel *A Grain of Wheat* (1967), by Kenyan Ngugi Wa Thiong'o. This work, however, does not focus on Caliban's potential resistance. Rather, it examines the nature of Prospero's colonizing drives and methods.

The central character of Ngugi's novel is a colonial functionary, John Thompson, who associates *The Tempest* with the grand moral idea of the British empire and plans to write about his experiences in Africa in a book entitled *Prospero in Africa*. However, while Thompson imagines he identifies with Prospero, Ngugi achieves an intertextual irony by also linking his rhetoric and violence to Kurtz in Conrad's *Heart of Darkness*. In focusing on Thompson as a Prospero, the writer exposes the European justifications of empire under the guise of cultural and moral superiority. Thompson, like Prospero, perceives his role and methods in terms of a necessary paternalism, but Ngugi views him as a figure representing the moral justification for the destruction of African culture.

Overall, whether one considers *The Tempest* as an allegory of Caliban's liberation or of Prospero's colonial paternalism, post-colonial readings of the play's reception in the third world clearly establish that we can no longer recuperate *The Tempest* as a historically 'innocent' text, uncorrupted by later historical readings.

The Tempest as an allegory of European discovery and colonization

Given these changing responses to Shakespeare's *The Tempest* in the former Third World, it is not surprising that by the 1980s, Anglo-American readings of the play began to join in such interrogations of Prospero's rule and in empathy for Caliban. In doing so, post-colonial criticism in the West was somewhat belated in acknowledging the significance of the play's historical background.

Since the 1980s, burgeoning post-colonial critical activity has brought new light to bear upon the play's sources in the narratives of 'discovery' and colonization of the Americas. Most critics agree that Shakespeare used Elizabethan travel writing, both for his dramatization of the opening storm and shipwreck and his depiction of the European confrontation with a 'savage', Caliban. In particular, he drew on William Strachey's account written in 1610—probably circulating in unpublished form—of the shipwreck and redemption of Sir Thomas Gates' expedition in the Bermudas in 1609, while on his way to Jamestown in the Virginia colony established by the British. Gates was wrecked in a most dreadful tempest on an island that proved to be so habitable and rich in food that his men were reluctant to leave. Thus, one strand of post-colonial criticism follows the play's journey literally to the European 'discovery' and settlement of the Americas. In that context, critics note how the figure of Caliban easily elides into the image of the cannibal, the mythical 'savage' whom many European travellers claimed to have encountered. Fantasies of real and imagined cannibals in the Renaissance gave an important impetus to European ventures of bringing 'civilization' to the natives. Images of otherness evoked by the play, however, also suggest an ambiguous geography, whereby the shipwrecked travellers in the play are supposedly traveling to North Africa, across the Mediterranean.

Such a post-colonial focus on *The Tempest's* relation to geographical exploration—with an emphasis on the colonization of the Americas—produces a reading of the play that differs radically from traditional European validations of Prospero's dominant role. It calls for a re-appraisal of Prospero's and Caliban's competing views of history and settlement of the island. According to Prospero, Caliban's mother was the 'damned witch Sycorax' who 'For mischiefs manifold, and sorceries terrible / To enter human hearing, from Algiers, . . . was banished' to this island (1.2.265–8). When Prospero recounts this story to Ariel, the sprite in his servitude, he makes sure to remind Ariel of the distinction between Sycorax's evil magic and his own supposedly benevolent arts:

> This blue-eyed hag was hither brought with child,
> And here was left by th' sailors. Thou, my slave,
> As thou [Ariel] report's thyself, was then her servant;
> And for thou wast a spirit too delicate
> To act her earthy and abhorred commands,
> Refusing her grand hests, she did confine thee
> By help of her more potent ministers,
> And in her most unmitigable rage,
> Into a cloven pine; within which rift
> Imprisoned thou didst painfully remain
> A dozen years
>
> (1.2 271-81)

Once he establishes Sycorax's supposedly evil nature, Prospero then labels her son, Caliban, as less than human—'freckled whelp, hag-born—not honoured with / A human shape' (1.2.285–6). However, even as he derides Caliban, Prospero claims to have treated him with kindness in attempts to humanize him. 'I have used thee, / Filth as thou art, with human care, and lodged thee / In mine own cell, till thou didst seek to violate / The honour of my child' (1.2.348–51). Once Prospero defines Caliban as a potential rapist of his daughter Miranda, he easily justifies taking the latter into forced servitude, as he explains in this exchange:

> MIRANDA: 'Tis a villain, sir,
>   I do not love to look on.
> PROSPERO: But as 'tis,
>   . . . He does make our fire,
>   Fetch in our wood, and serves in offices
>   That profit us.—What ho! Slave, Caliban!
>   (1.2.312-16)

Miranda also justifies their enslavement of Caliban with the assertion that they tried to civilize him but to no avail:

>   Abhorrèd slave,
>   Which any print of goodness wilt not take,
>   Being capable of all ill! I pitied thee,
>   Took pains to make thee speak, taught thee each hour
>   One thing or other. When thou didst not, savage,
>   Know thine own meaning, but wouldst gabble like
>   A thing most brutish, I endowed thy purposes
>   With words that made them known.
>   (1.2.354-61)

Miranda and Prospero's justifications of their enslavement of the 'savage' Caliban, whose 'vile race' lacks natural goodness, are strongly challenged by post-colonial criticism. Unlike generations of earlier readers, post-colonial critics view Prospero's and Miranda's relations with Caliban as an allegory of European colonialism—one that reveals Shakespeare's own ambivalence toward Prospero's power. Europeans' colonizing activities among non-European natives they encountered in the Americas, Africa, and the Caribbean were based on the premiss of the 'civilizing mission'. This mission assumed that the natives lacked any culture or formal language until the Europeans brought them the 'gifts' of Western language and culture. If the natives resisted European paternal rule, then they were labelled as 'savages', beyond redemption. It is ironic that Shakespeare makes Caliban articulate this dilemma when he exclaims to Miranda and Prospero: 'You taught me language, and my profit on't / Is I know how to curse' (1.2.366–7).

Caliban's version of history

In trying to view the conditions of Caliban's servitude from *his* perspective, post-colonial criticism gives legitimacy to his claims to the island, based on a reading of history antithetical to that narrated by Prospero to his daughter. In Caliban's account, Prospero is the intruder who betrayed the initial welcome given to him by Caliban:

> This island's mine, by Sycorax my mother,
> Which thou tak'st from me. When thou cam'st first,
> Thou strok'st me and made much of me, wouldst give me
> Water with berries in't, and teach me how
> To name the bigger light, and how the less,
> That burn by day and night; and then I loved thee,
> And showed thee all the qualities o'th' isle,
> The fresh springs, brine-pits, barren place and fertile—
> Cursed be I that did so! All the charms
> Of Sycorax, toads, beetles, bats, light on you;
> For I am all the subjects that you have,
> Which first was mine own king, and here you sty me
> In this hard rock, whiles you do keep from me
> The rest o'th' island.

(1.2.334-47)

It is this rendition of history that became the battle cry for the anti-colonial movements in Africa, the Caribbean, and Latin America—a rendition that became the staple of many revisions and appropriations of Shakespeare's play in these regions. While the play was written in seventeenth-century England, post-colonial criticism takes the play outwards towards its complicated transactions between European and African and Caribbean cultures in the succeeding centuries. Post-colonial criticism in the West has mined this new archive of the reception history of Shakespeare's *The Tempest*, questioning, once again, all normative ideas of a 'common humanity', while articulating, as Shakespeare did, the voices of the seemingly marginal characters in Prospero's grand designs.

FURTHER READING

Barker, Francis and Peter Hulme. 'Nymphs and Reapers Heavily Vanish: the Discursive Con-texts of *The Tempest*'. In *Alternative Shakespeares*, ed. John Drakakis (London: Methuen, 1985), pp. 191–205. This essay addresses the play's relation with its colonial contexts, showing how Caliban's political claims, until recently, were occluded by Western literary critics.

Brown, Paul. ' "This thing of darkness I acknowledge mine": *The Tempest* and the Discourse of Colonialism'. In *Political Shakespeare: New Essays In Cultural Materialism* (Ithaca: Cornell University Press, 1985), pp. 48–71. This (like the Barker and Hulme piece) was among the early essays that contextualized the play within the history of colonialism, though with more emphasis on Ireland than the Americas.

Bruster, Douglas. 'Local *Tempest*: Shakespeare and the Work of the Early Modern Playhouse', *The Journal of Medieval and Renaissance Studies* 25 (1995), 33–53. This essay offers a contrast to the typical post-colonial perspectives in its emphasis on local conditions of theatrical production in early modern London.

Cartelli, Thomas. 'Prospero in Africa: *The Tempest* as colonialist text and pretext'. In *Shakespeare Reproduced: The Text in History and Ideology*, ed. Jean E. Howard and Marion F. O'Connor (London: Methuen, 1987), pp. 99–115. Cartelli's approach typifies the many post-colonial readings, showing how colonized subjects in Africa and elsewhere appropriated and revised the play for political ends.

Césaire, Aimé. *A Tempest*. Trans. Richard Miller (New York: Ubu Repertory Theatre. 1969). An important dramatic revision of Shakespeare's play, which radically alters the relations and power equation between Prospero and Caliban.

Hulme, Peter and William H. Sherman (eds.). *'The Tempest' and its Travels* (Philadelphia: University of Pennsylvania Press, 2000). An important volume of essays that explores the play's travels in a variety of historical, cultural, and political settings and contexts.

Ngugi Wa Thiong'o. *A Grain of Wheat* (London: Heinemann, 1975).

Retamar, Roberto Fernandez. *Caliban and Other Essays*. Trans. Edward Baker. Foreword, Fredric Jameson (Minneapolis: University of Minnesota Press, 1989). Retamar follows *The Tempest's* 'travels' in Latin American and Caribbean culture, with an emphasis on Cuba, to show how the figure of Caliban became a symbol for anti-American sentiments.

Singh, Jyotsna G. 'Miranda versus Caliban: Race and Gender Conflicts in Post-Colonial Readings of *The Tempest*'. In *Feminist Readings of Early Modern Culture*: *Emerging Subjects*, eds. Valerie Traub, M. Lindsey Kaplan, Dympna Callaghan (Cambridge: Cambridge University Press, 1996), pp. 191–209. This essay critiques post-colonial revisions (such as Césaire's) for ignoring the gender struggles and the role of women within the play as well as within its critical history.

Vaughan, Alden T. and Virginia Mason Vaughan. *Shakespeare's Caliban: A Cultural History* (Cambridge: Cambridge University Press, 1991). An historical account of Caliban's place in cultural and literary history.

Vaughan, Virginia Mason. ' "Something Rich and Strange': Caliban's Theatrical Metamorphosis'. In *Shakespeare Quarterly* 39(4) (1985), 390–405. This essay is especially useful in showing the transformation undergone by the figure of Caliban on stage from the Renaissance to the 1980s.

34 | Deconstruction

Kiernan Ryan

Introduction

Deconstruction has much in common with several of the approaches to Shakespeare discussed in this section. It shares with the approach in Chapter 28 a commitment to the close reading of Shakespeare's texts. Like psychoanalytic criticism (see Chapter 31), deconstruction is intrigued by the conflict in the plays between what they overtly assert and what they unconsciously disclose. It unites with Marxism, new historicism, and cultural materialism (see Chapter 32) in supposing that Shakespeare's texts are tethered to their contexts, that their meaning is shaped as much by the culture that cradled them as by the interests of the present in which we encounter them. It is moved, moreover, by the same spirit of political critique that animates not only Marxist, new-historicist and cultural-materialist interpretations, but also most feminist, gay, and post-colonial readings of Shakespeare (see Chapters 29, 30 and 33). Like these approaches, deconstruction strives to expose the assumptions that preserve the oppressive divisions of Shakespeare's world and, indeed, our own. Like most of them, too, it seeks to subvert the logic of oppression by switching the spotlight from the centre to the outskirts of the work, turning accepted notions of what matters in it upside down.

However, the features that distinguish deconstruction from its rivals are no less striking than the points of resemblance. If deconstruction is, first and foremost, an exacting technique of close reading, it's also a technique that rejects the quest for coherence and completeness to which traditional close readings of Shakespeare's texts are wedded. In fact, deconstruction has no time for any critical approach that aims to discern a unifying theme or vision around which the work revolves. Nor will it tolerate interpretations that view Shakespeare's plays as the expression of some reality, philosophy, or ideology that lies beyond the precinct of the texts. Consequently, despite the common ground they share, deconstruction parts company with Marxism, new historicism and cultural materialism when they subordinate Shakespeare's texts to their historical contexts, and find the meaning of the plays in the realities in which they are rooted instead of in the words from which they are woven.

By the same token, deconstruction proves incompatible with psychoanalytic criticism in so far as the latter merely perceives in Shakespeare the validity of its theory of human motivation. Equally unsatisfactory, from a deconstructive point of view, is the tendency of feminist and gay critics to view gender and sexuality as the golden keys to the plays, just as post-colonial critics are apt to treat them as turning on race, and new historicists are prone to construe them as transfixed by power. The alternative angles offered by humanist criticism, character criticism, and source study (see Chapters 25, 26 and 27) fare no better, however, when subjected to scrutiny by deconstruction. Character criticism invites us to privilege the personality and fate of an individual as the fulcrum of the play; humanist criticism traces in Shakespeare's drama a vindication of the essential human truths and values it espouses; and source study presumes that the best way to work out what the creator of that drama had in mind is to go back to the texts he raided for plots, characters, and turns of phrase, and reconstruct his intention by analyzing what he kept and what he changed. These approaches are therefore just as vulnerable to the charge that they locate the text's meaning either in a prior system of thought or point of origin outside it, or in a central focus of interpretation within it.

Deconstruction wouldn't deny that *King Lear*, for example, raises all sorts of issues to do with gender, sexuality, power, and the hidden motives of the human heart and mind. Nor would a deconstructive account of the play get far without employing the concept of character, acknowledging *Lear*'s debt to its sources and the discourses of its day, and recognizing that the tragedy grapples with profound moral, philosophical, and ideological matters. What deconstruction objects to in other kinds of criticism is their keenness to boil the text down to one governing concern or turn it into the puppet of a standpoint anchored anywhere but in its own language. For such approaches try to deny what deconstruction regards as the innate diversity and fluidity of the text, which confounds all attempts to pin its significance down or make it the mouthpiece of a position that precedes or transcends it.

One of the most appealing aspects of deconstruction as an approach to Shakespeare is its respect for the plays' resistance to elucidation and their gift for outwitting any reading that fancies itself to be conclusive. Through its close engagement with the complexity of Shakespeare's language, deconstruction allows us to observe how the meaning of a play is always turning into something more or other than it seemed to be, making a mockery of the constructions critics have imposed on it. As opponents of deconstruction have been quick to complain, however, there's a price to be paid for this liberation of the text from the tyranny of interpretation. The downside of deconstruction is that its reluctance to settle on a reading of its own can leave us floundering in a slough of uncertainty, aware of the inadequacy of existing accounts, but bereft of any cogent view of the work to put in their place, and thus of a firm basis on which to discuss or judge it.

Deconstruction: assumptions, aims, and methods

Before we take a closer look at how deconstruction can enhance our understanding of Shakespeare, it's worth considering in more detail what this kind of criticism entails. The first point to make is that deconstruction is not a systematic methodology or procedure, which the critic dutifully applies to the interpretation of the text. To practise deconstruction is rather to command a flexible range of reading strategies and put them to work in whatever ways the text, and the situation in which it is being read, demand. The deconstructive critic inevitably addresses a text with certain assumptions and expectations in mind, but it's the text that poses the questions and sets the agenda, and its deconstruction obliges the critic to display an intellectual agility that few other forms of criticism require.

So what *are* the basic assumptions and expectations with which the critic bent on deconstruction approaches a literary text? On the face of it, the task of defining them seems daunting. This is chiefly because the founder of deconstruction, the French philosopher Jacques Derrida, and most of his followers, have made a point of writing in a wilfully obscure manner, which has led many to dismiss deconstruction as impenetrable and pretentious. This is unfortunate, because the core ideas of deconstruction are powerful and productive, and can be grasped without resorting to Derrida's arcane jargon and without losing their bite. Those who do wish to hack their way through the thorny thickets of 'différance', 'dissemination', and 'logocentrism' will find these and other terms explained with admirable clarity in the books by Christopher Norris and Jonathan Culler listed at the end of this part of the chapter.

The term 'deconstruction' itself, however, merits a second glance. It's a portmanteau word, which splices together the words '*de*struction' and '*con*struction' to form a compound term that combines their antithetical meanings. At the core of deconstruction, in other words, is a double strategy of critique and creation, of demolition and renewal. To undertake the deconstruction of a text is to undo its apparently seamless logic, to shatter its illusion of coherence, in order to open up the possibility of new and different kinds of meaning. The aim is not to replace a misconception of the work with an alternative interpretation. It's rather to complicate our understanding of it in such a way as to free us from the grip of our preconceptions, and steer us into a space in which fresh perceptions of the work can be forged.

In the case of sophisticated literary texts like Shakespeare's, however, there's an important rider to add. Such works have a habit of anticipating the moves the deconstructive critic is likely to make on them. Time and again, they turn out to have built into their language and form their own deconstruction of what they are about. So that, more often than not, when a critic sets out to deconstruct a poem, play, or novel in which language and form are being used with a high degree of self-consciousness, the task is to bring the work's self-deconstruction to the fore in order to unpack its implications. In such cases the role of the critic is to serve as a midwife to the work's most developed understanding of itself.

According to deconstruction, the nature of language is such that the meaning of a text is never single, fixed, or final, but always plural, contradictory, and incomplete. However hard the author tries to nail meaning down, the work will always give its creator the slip by disclosing other implications to the reader. Different readers in different cultures at different times expand the text's capacity to multiply its meanings, because they bring diverse concerns to bear on it, and so can perceive in the text implications which are demonstrably there, but which they alone are in a position to perceive. To read a literary text as a deconstructionist is to read with the awareness that its full and final meaning is constantly receding and impossible to grasp, that the prospect of completeness and closure is a mirage. Nothing might seem more indelibly fixed than the published text of the work on the desk before us. But no sooner have we begun to read the signs printed on its pages than we are compelled to realize how fragile and provisional is the sense we make of them, and how vain is the dream of capturing all the connotations breeding between the lines.

To arrive at a cohesive reading of a work, a critic has to repress or filter out all sorts of unruly elements that refuse to fit in, and proceed in the belief that the meaning of the work is complete at its conclusion. Deconstruction, in contrast, assumes that the meaning of the literary text will be discontinuous, self-divided, and open-ended. It therefore fastens on every feature that makes a unified interpretation impossible. The deconstructive critic proceeds on the premiss that the semantic potential of a text is, in principle, inexhaustible. The work is forever generating more meanings than any reading can quarry, and those meanings will return to plague readers who have excluded them. Far from being frustrated by the text's endless, uncontrollable play of meanings, deconstruction thrives on it.

For deconstruction, there's no point appealing to the authority of the author, how-ever precisely the latter may have defined the aim of the work, in order to arrest that endless play of meanings in a single, privileged interpretation. Authors may have many helpful things to say about their works, but they don't have the last word on what those works signify, any more than their readers do. Indeed, as far as deconstruc-tion is concerned, there is no transcendental concept outside the text and no ruling principle within it—whether it be the author, the reader, truth, history, reality, nature, God, order, or harmony—to which one can appeal in order to promote one reading as more valid than any other.

Deconstruction is thus suspicious of texts that seek to persuade us that their view of things is transparent, authoritative, and complete—a concerted verbal vision of the world within, or the world around, the author. It musters all its ingenuity to expose the cracks in the façade of such texts, the weak points at which they betray that their vision is the effect of the way they use words, and therefore open to dispute. Conversely, deconstruction prizes literary works that flaunt their fabrication from language and consequent susceptibility to reinterpretation. When a novel, poem, or play parades its construction out of words and its use of rhetorical and formal techniques, it under-scores the fact that the sense it makes of the world, and the sense we make of it, are the products of those words and techniques, and subject to a process of explication which can never be brought to a close.

For this reason, few things delight the deconstructionist more than finding a passage, chapter, or scene that mirrors in miniature the work as a whole and the issues that animate it. Such self-referential features prompt us to reflect on our own situation as readers of an artful composition, whose coded import we are engaged in construing. At their most elaborate, indeed, they can create—like Russian dolls or Chinese boxes—an effect of infinite regression: the dizzying sense that there is no solid ground of truth or reality beyond the verbal fabric of the work that can bring signification to a halt. It's a cardinal tenet of deconstruction that we have no knowledge or experience of the world that is not mediated through language and representation. What we call reality, experience, meaning, and truth are intrinsic effects of the play of signification: we can apprehend them only in and through language. Intensely self-aware fictions, which frame within themselves an epitome of their own enterprise, bring that unsettling fact home with unusual force.

Another key feature of literary works to which deconstruction is drawn is the aporia. (Examples of aporias in Shakespeare's plays are discussed below.) An aporia is a point of logical contradiction in a text where reading finds itself at an impasse, because the meaning is opaque or undecidable. It's a point at which the text admits its inability to give a watertight account of its purpose, a symptom of its covert incoherence and anxiety about what it's up to. Aporias are paradigms of the ultimately irresolvable meaning of the work that contains them. Once these knots in the fabric of the text have been located, the critic's job is to tease away at them until the rationale of the whole work is unravelled.

The aporia is one of the stoutest allies of deconstruction in its war against hierarchy. At the heart of Western thinking, deconstruction contends, lies an adherence to dubious binary oppositions, such as nature versus culture, male versus female, white versus black, heterosexual versus homosexual, body versus soul, or reason versus emotion. What's dubious about them is not merely their stark division of thought into antithetical categories, but the tendency for one of the two terms to be elevated over the other in a relationship of domination. Patriarchal culture, for example, rests on the assumption that female is subordinate to male, just as racism relies on the supposition that black is inferior to white, and heterosexuality presumes itself to be the rule to which homosexuality is the exception. This polarizing habit of mind is so deeply ingrained in our discourse that most of us are unaware of its operation, as it quietly locks the prevailing power-structures and value-systems into place, securing the sway of the status quo.

Deconstruction doesn't delude itself that it can eradicate this ubiquitous mentality. But what it *can* do is, first of all, lay its mechanisms bare and make them visible; then problematize it by inverting or blurring the hierarchical opposition in question and undermining its authority; and finally, through this process of exposure and inversion, edge us into a domain on which the foundations of a less oppressive dispensation might be laid. It's not difficult to discern the progressive political potential of deconstruction, or the reason why Marxists, feminists, post-colonial critics, and gay theorists have sought to adapt its techniques to their explicitly political objectives.

One of deconstruction's most effective methods of combating hierarchy is to home in on the marginal elements of a work. Because texts tend to expel to their periphery, or disguise as ancillary, whatever threatens the integrity of their avowed objective, deconstruction makes a beeline for these embarrassing exclusions and makes them the targets of critical attention, reversing the relationship between the major and the minor, the essential and the extraneous. In so doing, it's able to undo the authority of previous interpretations, which have taken the text's conception of its priorities at face value.

To sum up: a deconstructive reading of a literary work will use all the ruses outlined above to subvert the apparent logic of the work by unmasking its contradictions and exposing its unconscious ambitions. It will seize on instances of aporia, self-mirroring, and marginalization as allies in its assault on hierarchy and the fantasy of freezing meaning in a final interpretation. It will seek to disturb and displace the polarizing cast of mind that no text can escape, paving the way for a perspective uncontaminated by division and domination. And what it will often discover, once the reigning misconstructions of the text have been dethroned, is that the text was way ahead of it and had already deconstructed itself.

Deconstructing Shakespeare

The postmodern brainchild of a late twentieth-century French philosopher might well seem the approach least likely to shed light on a playwright who flourished four hundred years ago, at the dawn of the early modern era. But Shakespeare's drama turns out to be uncannily in tune with the assumptions and aims of deconstruction; indeed, so much so that, far from the application of deconstruction to his plays being absurdly anachronistic, it might be more appropriate to see Shakespeare's drama as foreshadowing deconstruction in poetic and theatrical terms. Derrida himself has written at length on *Hamlet* and on *Romeo and Juliet*, and would plainly be happy to concede that Shakespeare, like many a great writer, got there before him, and that all he has been able to do is formulate in the abstract discourse of theory what Shakespeare enacted in the concrete discourse of drama.

In the first place, it's hard to think of an author who revels more than Shakespeare in the multiplicity and mutability of meaning. The compulsive punning and quipping in which so many of his characters indulge expose the fluid, unfixable nature of language, and hence the instability of the structures of meaning that sustain the conventions of Shakespeare's world. By their playful misprisions and impromptu riddling, Hamlet and the gravedigger, the fools Touchstone and Feste, and witty heroines like Beatrice and Rosalind (to take just a few obvious examples) play havoc with received ideas and uses of language. They shake our confidence in familiar words and modes of speech by cutting them adrift from settled meanings and accepted realities. As Feste, Olivia's self-styled 'corrupter of words', remarks in *Twelfth Night*: 'A sentence is but a cheverel glove to a good wit, how quickly the wrong side may be turned outward'. 'Nay, that's certain', retorts Viola, 'They that dally nicely with words may quickly make them wanton' (3.1.31, 10–14). The exchange encapsulates the promiscuous, unbiddable disposition of language, its incorrigible knack of saying one thing and meaning another, or meaning several different things at the same time.

'Words, words, words', replies Hamlet to Polonius's inquiry as to what he is reading (2.2.192). Acute verbal and theatrical self-consciousness is the hallmark of Shakespeare's plays, each of which exhibits a shifting spectrum of literary and theatrical discourses. *The Winter's Tale*, for example, shuffles together the formal and idiomatic verse and prose of the aristocrats; the colloquial banter of the shepherds and the wily thief, Autolycus; and the disparate styles of the pastoral lyric, the popular ballad, and the masque. In case the poetic artifice of the play they are in escapes us, the characters make a point of bringing it to our attention: 'Nay then, God b'wi'you', exclaims a disgusted Jaques to Orlando, 'an you talk in blank verse' (*As You Like It*, 4.1.28). The effect of these strategies is to frustrate expectations of a transparent, unified dramatic discourse, and instead stress the play's discursive diversity, which in turn confirms the plural, contested character of the reality transfigured by the text. Moreover, by foregrounding its scripted status, the play emphasizes that the meanings it activates are not derived from a reality that precedes language, but are the result of a written attempt to make sense of a mutable world—a world which is as open to interpretation as the play itself: 'I am a scribbled form', observes the dying King John, 'drawn with a pen / Upon a parchment' (*King John*, 5.7.32–3).

The theatrical self-consciousness of Shakespeare's plays is intensified by their penchant for mounting an actual or virtual play, complete with audience, within the play proper, as in the 'Mousetrap' staged by Hamlet or the masque of the Muscovites and the Pageant of the Nine Worthies in *Love's Labour's Lost*. In *A Midsummer Night's Dream*, through their performance of 'Pyramus and Thisbe', Bottom's troupe treats us to a farcical travesty of the tragedy the main plot could have become; and that plot in turn is framed as a production staged by its fairy author, Oberon, whose goblin henchman, Puck, rends the veil of illusion at the end and addresses us directly about the performance we have witnessed. Characters repeatedly remind us through self-mirroring remarks that we are spectators in the theatre. 'I see the play so lies', muses Perdita in *The Winter's Tale*, 'That I must bear a part' (4.4.638–9). Perhaps the most striking instance occurs, however, in *Twelfth Night* when, after watching what amounts to a play within a play, of which Malvolio has been the unwitting star, Fabian exclaims,

'If this were played upon a stage, now, I could condemn it as an improbable fiction'
(3.4.114–15).

It's easy to see how scenes and lines like these might seem designed to strand us in a
maze of visual and verbal deception, in which the border between representation and
reality has been abolished. But what they actually imply is that both the play world
and the real world it transposes to the stage are provisional versions of experience, not
permanent definitions of what life is like. The audience are invited to test the validity
of the dramatic representation against the reality with which it begs comparison; but
they are also asked to reassess the real production in which they have been cast by
history in light of the play's account of it.

Shakespeare's plays abound in aporias, which are primed to explode the texts'
apparent logic and expose us to more perplexing issues. In *Twelfth Night*, for example,
Viola, disguised as a man, declares to the infatuated Olivia: 'I am not what I am'
(3.1.132). The duplicitous Iago uses precisely the same words to describe himself in the
opening scene of *Othello* (1.1.65). In both cases the expected statement 'I am not what
I *seem*' is usurped by a sentence that flouts common sense. The deranged wording
confounds complacent distinctions between appearance and reality, and suggests that
the sexual identity of Viola and the moral identity of Iago are much more complex and
disturbing matters, which defy the explanations offered by such trite dichotomies.
An extended instance of an aporia that requires us to rethink our conception of a
character, and consequently a whole play, is provided by *The Merchant of Venice*. The
first scene of the comedy is devoted to the vain attempt of Antonio, the merchant of
the title, and his friends to establish the source of his enigmatic sadness, and the
mystery is left unsolved by the text. Right at the outset, we are urged to ask questions of
the play and its ostensible protagonist which the latter cannot answer, because they
strike at the Venetian values that Antonio embodies and the play seems to endorse—
the values whose barbarity Shylock unmasks in the trial scene.

Hierarchy is subjected to a sustained assault at every level of Shakespearian drama.
At the most fundamental level, the multivocal composition of the plays distributes
authority across the whole spectrum of dramatis personae, ensuring that no one view-
point or set of values is privileged. This innate egalitarian impulse can be seen at work
in *Henry IV Part One*, for example, as the perspective switches back and forth between
king and commoners, the criminals in the royal court, and the outlaws in Eastcheap,
tacitly drawing the parallels, and thus dissolving the divisions, between them. The
absence of any point of view that can be identified as Shakespeare's rules out appeals to
the playwright's intention as the transcendental origin and guarantee of meaning.
Spectator and reader are thrown instead on the mercy of the text, whose elusive significance they are charged with co-creating, as the choruses and epilogues of the plays
repeatedly remind them. Even Prospero, the protagonist widely regarded as a surrogate
for the dramatist himself, concludes Shakespeare's last masterpiece by handing the
power to judge and complete *The Tempest* over to us: 'Gentle breath of yours my sails /
Must fill, or else my project fails' (Epilogue 11–12).

The sexual hierarchy on which patriarchy depends is collapsed in the comedies by cross-dressing. In the original production of *As You Like It*, for instance, a boy actor played a young woman (Rosalind), who disguises herself as a man (Ganymede), who in turn pretends to be a woman on whom Orlando can practise his courtship of Rosalind. Similarly, in *Twelfth Night* Viola assumes the identity of a male page, Cesario, in order to pursue the love of her master, Orsino, whose first love Olivia ends up, thanks to Viola's identical twin, Sebastian, 'betrothed both to a maid and man' (5.1.256). These mind-bending confusions of gender abolish the normal boundary between masculine and feminine and allow us to glimpse, beyond the horizon of patriarchy, forms of sexual identity and desire unbridled by existing definitions.

Disguise and the dissolution of identity also have a hand in the unhinging of social hierarchy in the plays. The most powerful example of this can be found in *King Lear*, when the demented monarch, marooned on the storm-battered heath, is forced to feel what the 'naked wretches' (3.4.29) of his kingdom feel, and to realize that beneath his royal robes and the homeless beggar's rags shivers the same 'poor, bare, forked animal' (3.4.99–100) that stands incarnate before him in the person of Poor Tom. We know, of course, that Tom, the insane Bedlam beggar, is actually the exiled nobleman, Edgar, who plays the part with terrifying authenticity. But the plausibility of Edgar's performance only reinforces the revelation that the strict segregations of rank, on which the unequal distribution of status, power, and wealth depends, are mere veneers, with no basis whatsoever in nature.

Finally, Shakespeare's drama offers deconstruction countless opportunities for reversing the relationship between what seems to be central to a play and what appears to be of secondary significance in its design. Three remarkable characters at once spring to mind: Shylock in *The Merchant of Venice*, Malvolio in *Twelfth Night*, and Caliban in *The Tempest*. All three are clearly assigned subordinate roles as malign foils to the protagonists, whose progress towards a benign denouement they labour to frustrate. But in performance and in critical practice, as most spectators and students have discovered, they have proved reluctant to remain on the sidelines and have loomed so much larger than the nominal heroes and heroines that they have frequently displaced them as the axis of the drama. Shylock's searing exposure of the Christians' racist hypocrisy; Malvolio's valedictory threat of revenge for his punitive humiliation; Caliban's castigation of Prospero for robbing him of his island and enslaving him: such signs of self-division at the heart of the plays are meat and drink to the deconstructive critic, who perceives in them proof of the plays' detachment from the social and racial assumptions that seem to govern them.

To deconstruct Shakespeare is to testify to the fact that the creator of Shylock, Malvolio, and Caliban was a master of deconstruction himself, since he built all these features into the language and form of his plays. It's a pretty safe bet that the last thing Shakespeare had in mind as he wrote his plays was outdoing Monsieur Derrida, whose tortuous prose would have left him as baffled as most of Derrida's modern students.

Nevertheless, that is just what Shakespeare's drama turns out to have done, as we look back on it through the eyes of deconstruction.

It's true that deconstructions of Shakespeare's plays, when they pursue their *destructive* at the expense of their *constructive* ends, can leave us adrift on a sea of indecision. But it's also true that, when a deconstructive reading of a play strikes the right balance between undermining and reconstructing, it can unlock startling insights stored in the play's poetic language and theatrical techniques. Not the least merit of deconstructive accounts of Shakespeare is that they're in no danger of regarding themselves as the last word on his works. On the contrary, they take for granted their blindness to the wealth of interpretations latent in the language of the plays, waiting to be unpacked by readers of the future, with other matters on their minds.

FURTHER READING

Atkins, Douglas and David M. Bergeron (eds.). *Shakespeare and Deconstruction* (New York, Bern, Frankfurt and Paris: Peter Lang, 1988). Includes an excellent general essay on deconstructing Shakespeare by Gary Waller, 'Decentering the Bard: The Dissemination of the Shakespearian Text', as well as essays applying deconstruction to *King Lear*, *Hamlet*, the Sonnets, *Troilus and Cressida*, and *Richard II*.

Culler, Jonathan. *On Deconstruction* (London: Routledge & Kegan Paul, 1983). Lucid introduction to the key ideas and critical implications of deconstruction. See pp. 213–15 for a concise summary of the six principal strategies employed by deconstructive critics.

Evans, Malcolm. *Signifying Nothing: Truth's True Contents in Shakespeare's Text*, 2nd edn. (Hemel Hempstead: Harvester Wheatsheaf, 1989). Explains both the challenge deconstruction offers to traditional accounts of Shakespeare and its limitations as a critical method. Includes readings of *As You Like It*, *Hamlet*, *King Lear*, *Love's Labour's Lost*, *Macbeth*, and *The Tempest*.

Felperin, Howard. 'The Dark Lady Identified, or What Deconstruction Can Do For Shakespeare's *Sonnets*'. In his *The Uses of the Canon: Elizabethan Literature and Contemporary Theory* (Oxford: Clarendon Press, 1990), pp. 56–78. Through close analysis of their insoluble enigmas and poetic self-consciousness, argues that the Sonnets 'seem to have been cunningly constructed . . . with the idea of deconstruction in mind'.

Norris, Christopher. *Deconstruction: Theory and Practice* (London and New York: Methuen, 1982). Excellent short introduction, which centres on Derrida's major texts and explains both the philosophical significance of deconstruction and its consequences for literary criticism.

Parker, Patricia and Geoffrey Hartman (eds.). *Shakespeare and the Question of Theory* (New York and London: Methuen, 1985). The first four chapters are devoted to deconstructive readings of *The Winter's Tale*, *Troilus and Cressida*, *Twelfth Night*, and *Othello* respectively. Howard Felperin's essay on *The Winter's Tale* is especially rewarding.

READING: *Romeo and Juliet*

At first glance, it's hard to imagine what fresh revelations *Romeo and Juliet* might yield to a deconstructive approach. Criticism has generally contented itself with one of three explanations of what makes the tragedy tick, and there's no obvious reason why it should go out of its way to concoct any more. The first line commonly taken by critics is to read *Romeo and Juliet* as a perennial tragedy of the human condition, a dramatization of the doom to which passionate young love is inevitably sentenced by the inscrutable nature of things. The second latches on to the failure of Friar Laurence's message to reach Romeo in Mantua and the fatal mistiming of events in the tomb of the Capulets. From these and other facts it infers that the lovers are the helpless victims of happenstance, the luckless dupes of the chance adversities to which all human beings are potentially prey. The third standard critical response is to lay the blame for the whole catastrophe on Romeo and Juliet for refusing to bridle their desires. This reading turns the tragedy into a secular morality play, depicting the fate that awaits those who ride roughshod over prudent social restraints.

The play itself, it must be confessed, offers textual corroboration for each of these accounts. Romeo believes himself to be the predestined victim of 'Some consequence yet hanging in the stars' (1.4.107). Strong support for the moralistic critic, on the other hand, is furnished by Friar Laurence, who counsels Romeo to 'love moderately' because 'These violent delights have violent ends' (2.5.14, 9). Nor is there any reason to dispute the notorious part played by sheer bad luck in consigning the lovers to an early grave. But the very inconsistency of these views of the tragedy suggests that each of them is open to question from the standpoint of its rivals. Indeed their explicit inclusion *within* the play suggests that none of them is equipped to do justice to the complexity of the text that subsumes them and sets them against each other.

Deconstruction, in contrast, takes it as given that the text as a whole has a mind of its own, a mind which cannot be so easily read, and which is apt to change as the assumptions of its readers change. It therefore expects *Romeo and Juliet* to imply far more by the way it is shaped and worded than it states overtly through the speeches and actions of its characters. It knows, in short, that the play adds up to more than the sum of its parts, and that its protean meaning is the product of a continuous engagement with the totality of the text. A deconstructive approach to *Romeo and Juliet* would consequently decline to swallow one line on the tragedy, however sensible or plausible it might seem, and embrace from the outset the text's display of contending voices and diverse discourses.

In *Romeo and Juliet*, the stately blank verse of the Prince collides with the streetwise backchat of the belligerent Capulet servants; the stilted couplets in which Romeo idealizes Rosaline fall foul of Mercutio's cynical vulgarity; the closed formality of the sonnet, to which both the Chorus and the lovers resort, contrasts sharply with the open flow of dramatic dialogue in verse and prose; and the sublime romantic arias into which Juliet pours her passion for Romeo are tested against the earthbound practicality of her plain-speaking nurse. The play advertises its literary artifice and its array of competing attitudes at every turn.

The characters are equally keen to point out the play's status as a theatrical fiction, a poetic composition for the stage. Mercutio's travesty of Romeo's posturing makes sport of his compulsion to speak in couplets:

> Romeo! Humours! Madman! Passion! Lover!
> Appear thou in the likeness of a sigh.
> Speak but one rhyme and I am satisfied.
> Cry but 'Ay me!' Pronounce but 'love' and 'dove'.
>   (2.1.7–10)

Right on the brink of the heartbreaking denouement, Juliet is given a line that keeps the fact of theatrical performance at the forefront of our minds: 'My dismal scene I needs must act alone' (4.3.19). Romeo, too, in the last scene of the tragedy, makes his peace with his slain rival, Paris, in words designed to underscore the scripted nature of their fate: 'O, give me thy hand, / One writ with me in sour misfortune's book' (5.3.81–2). Romeo's application of the book metaphor to Paris is particularly apt, because it echoes Lady Capulet's elaborate portrayal of Paris as a 'precious book of love', an 'unbound lover' (1.3.89), when she seeks Juliet's acceptance of him as her suitor earlier in the play:

> Read o'er the volume of young Paris' face,
> And find delight writ there with beauty's pen.
> Examine every married lineament,
> And see how one another lends content;
> And what obscured in this fair volume lies
> Find written in the margin of his eyes.
>   (1.3.83-8)

This passage is a gift to the deconstructive critic, because it enshrines the realization that identity cannot be divorced from language, that the self is, amongst other things, a kind of text that has to be interpreted by means of words in order to be understood. We may exist physically without words, but we acquire identities and invest our lives with meaning only by virtue of the language that links us together as a community, defines who we are, and allows us to converse with each other. The trouble is that language can become as much an instrument of imprisonment as a means of empowerment, as Romeo and Juliet discover to their cost. Nowhere in the play is the destructive potential of language expressed more forcefully than in Juliet's response to being told that her lover has taken his life:

> Hath Romeo slain himself? Say thou but 'Ay',
> And that bare vowel 'I' shall poison more
> Than the death-darting eye of cockatrice.
> I am not I if there be such an 'Ay' . . .
>   (3.2.45-8)

Here Shakespeare's homonymic pun on 'Ay', which sounds the same as 'I' and 'eye', exploits the word's semantic instability to demonstrate the power of a simple vowel to erase identity in a self-cancelling aporia: 'I am not I if there be such an "Ay"'.

Throughout the tragedy, the lovers' incarceration in the prison-house of language is heavily underlined. Words are the chains that bind Romeo and Juliet to the social imperatives and sexual norms of Verona. That's why their doomed struggle to liberate their love is dramatized as a struggle to free themselves from the way Verona has taught them to speak and the destinies to which their names have bound them. It's scarcely an accident that Romeo and Juliet meet and fall in love at the Capulet ball, while Romeo is masked and before they discover each other's name. For a fleeting moment they are unburdened by the patriarchal obligations inscribed in their surnames. They are released not only from the strict proscriptions of the family feud, but also from the codes of courtship that would normally forbid such a direct encounter between any man and woman of their class. Within seconds of this enchanted exchange, however, each of them learns the name of the other, and immediately, at the mere uttering of the words 'Montague' and 'Capulet', the festive licence of the moment expires and the tragic battle between the lovers and their world begins.

The celebrated balcony scene of Act Two makes explicit the role of language as a basic condition and a key cause of the tragedy. Unaware that she is being overheard by Romeo, Juliet meditates on the issue at the heart of their dilemma:

> O Romeo, Romeo, wherefore art thou Romeo?
> Deny thy father and refuse thy name,
> Or if thou wilt not, be but sworn my love,
> And I'll no longer be a Capulet . . .
>   . . . O, be some other name!
> What's in a name? That which we call a rose
> By any other word would smell as sweet.
> So Romeo would, were he not Romeo called,
> Retain that dear perfection which he owes
> Without that title. Romeo, doff thy name,
> And for thy name—which is no part of thee—
> Take all myself.
>   (2.1.75-8, 84-91)

And Romeo replies:

>   By a name
> I know not how to tell thee who I am.
> My name, dear saint, is hateful to myself
> Because it is an enemy to thee.
> Had I it written, I would tear the word.
>   (2.1.95-9)

These speeches capture the conflict between the unfettered potential of these two individuals and the crippling constraints to which the names they never chose compel them to submit. The appellations 'Capulet' and 'Montague' bolt Juliet and Romeo into a dungeon, whose walls are made of words. Not surprisingly, this preoccupation with the despotic power of names is what hooks Derrida's attention in his typically cryptic, but suggestive, essay on the tragedy, 'Aphorism Countertime' (see Further Reading).

So potent do words and names become in the play that they seem to acquire their own identities and independent will to kill. When Juliet hears of the sentence passed on Romeo for slaying her cousin Tybalt, she cries:

> Some word there was, worser than Tybalt's death,
> That murdered me . . .
> > . . . 'Romeo is banishèd'—
> There is no end, no limit, measure, bound,
> In that word's death. No words can that woe sound.
> > (3.2.108-9, 124-6)

Likewise, when Romeo is told of the agony he has inflicted on Juliet by killing her cousin, he replies:

> As if that name
> Shot from the deadly level of a gun
> Did murder her as that name's cursèd hand
> Murdered her kinsman. O tell me, friar, tell me,
> In what vile part of this anatomy
> Doth my name lodge?
> > (3.3.101-6)

Romeo and Juliet recognize that words have the power to wound and kill, that language can be literally lethal. But, by the very act of recoiling from this recognition, they sharpen the contradiction between their own sense of who they are and the alien selves that the language of their world is weaving round them.

Juliet and Romeo are clearly striving to shake off more than the yoke of their names and the impact of a harsh decree. There's no doubt that the tragedy is an indictment of the irrational family feud and the oppressive patriarchal law that deny them the freedom to love and marry whomever they choose. To see the play in these terms, moreover, as a vindication of the rights of the individual, is a marked improvement on viewing it as an ageless tragedy of the human condition, a cautionary tale for impetuous youth, or a terminal case of bad timing. But *Romeo and Juliet* goes much further than that, and deconstruction is better placed than most critical approaches to see why and how it does so. For it's plain to the deconstructive critic that language has locked the lovers not only into their families and the feud through their names, but also into a whole way of life warped by hierarchy. Deconstruction is therefore ideally equipped to discern the play's disclosure of a love beyond hierarchy, a love undefiled by the urge to dominate.

Before he has met Juliet, while he is still infatuated with Rosaline, Romeo is trapped inside the phoney pose and threadbare poetic tropes of the moping lover: 'She hath forsworn to love, and In that vow / Do I live dead, that live to tell it now' (1.1.216–7). He is the passive dupe of a stale scenario, which casts the woman as a sadistic goddess and her suitor as a tormented slave, obliging both parties to act out a demeaning charade of domination and subjection. Mercutio, as has been noted, mocks Romeo's submission to this masochistic fantasy, but it's soon clear that Mercutio's disenchantment offers no real alternative. On the contrary, his crude view of sex as the gratification of male lust is simply the inverted mirror-image of what he derides in Romeo: 'If love be rough with you, be rough with love. / Prick love for pricking and you beat love down' (1.4.27–8).

At this stage in the play, Juliet lives under the heel of the same mentality, which precludes the possibility of love untrammelled by subjugation. In her case, subjugation takes the form of acquiescing in her parents' choice of husband, the 'precious book of love' for which her beauty will provide the ornamental 'cover' and 'gold clasps' (1.3.89, 90, 94). The devoted Nurse aids and abets Juliet in defying her father's will for the sake of Romeo, and her homespun realism affords a salutary contrast to Juliet's rhapsodies of desire; but when catastrophe strikes and Romeo is exiled, the Nurse's pragmatic advice to ditch Romeo for Paris, swapping one husband for another, betrays her blindness to the new form of love that Juliet has discovered.

The innovative nature of that love begins to unfold from the opening of Act Two. What sets it apart is the fact that it is founded on reciprocity rather than subservience. In the words of the Chorus: 'Now Romeo is beloved and loves again [i.e. in return], / Alike bewitchèd by the charm of looks . . . / And she as much in love' (2.0.5–6, 11). Romeo uses symmetrical syntax and matching diction to define the equal exchange of desire and power that makes this relationship so different: 'one hath wounded me / That's by me wounded' (2.2.50–1); 'As mine [i.e. my heart] on hers, so hers is set on mine' (2.2.59); 'Her I love now / Doth grace for grace and love for love allow. / The other did not so' (2.2.85–7). It is, furthermore, as Juliet observes, a mutually enriching, unlimited love, whose value is beyond calculation:

> My bounty is as boundless as the sea,
> My love as deep. The more I give to thee
> The more I have, for both are infinite.
> (2.1.175-7)

In lines like these Shakespeare turns the discourse of domination against itself, recasting the language that ensnares the lovers to bring the prospect of boundless, mutual love within reach of the imagination. *Romeo and Juliet* deconstructs itself through a double-edged process of constructive critique: it lays bare the linguistic machinery of social and sexual subjection, but it also prefigures, through the creative power of poetry, a kind of love to which men and women still aspire, four centuries after the play was first performed.

To realize this is to realize how hamstrung most historicist critics are by their past-bound approach to Shakespeare. Such critics rarely tire of insisting that we cannot fully understand Shakespeare's plays unless we restore them to the world and time from which they sprang. But what purpose is served by ensconcing *Romeo and Juliet* in its Elizabethan context, if Shakespeare's art is the art of anticipation, and the point of the play is to transmit to the present a foretaste of the future? Nothing kills the appeal of Shakespeare's plays more quickly than entombing them in tomes of antiquarian scholarship, and deconstruction keeps that appeal alive by opening the plays to interpretation by readers and spectators yet to be born. In all probability, most of Shakespeare's audience found the reconciliation of the

Montagues and Capulets, and their promise to erect golden monuments to Romeo and Juliet, a satisfactory resolution to the lovers' tragedy. But the deconstructive critic knows, and can show, that this sixteenth-century view will no longer do, because the play sabotages its own conclusion, and constantly offers fresh footholds for further deconstruction.

It seems only right, therefore, to end this reading of *Romeo and Juliet* by flagging two points from which it might begin to be unravelled in its turn, and displaced by more cogent accounts. In both cases it's a matter of switching the focus to marginal figures, and using them as levers to dislodge the reading at which we have arrived, destabilizing the text once again and refusing to let it settle.

One figure who is crying out to be employed in this way is Mercutio, whose bawdy vivacity and flamboyant wit threaten to steal the show from the protagonists. Mercutio's fatal devotion to Romeo bespeaks a deep-rooted male bond, whose intimacy rivals Romeo's attachments to the opposite sex. Jonathan Goldberg, a leading exponent of gay criticism, has analysed the importance of this relationship in his essay '*Romeo and Juliet*'s Open Rs' (see Further Reading) and used it to question heterosexual preconceptions of the play. (The homoerotic undertones of the text were also picked up and amplified in Baz Luhrmann's film *Romeo + Juliet* (1996), in which Mercutio is played as an outrageous drag-queen.) Once alerted to this dimension of the tragedy, it's not difficult to imagine a gay deconstruction of *Romeo and Juliet*, which would show how the play undercuts its own endorsement of straight sexuality.

The other supporting character who might repay closer scrutiny is far less conspicuous and glamorous than Mercutio, but for that reason all the more intriguing from the standpoint of deconstruction. On the threshold of the catastrophe Romeo seeks the means of suicide from a destitute apothecary, who hesitates to oblige him for fear of incurring the death penalty prescribed for selling poison. Romeo's reply reveals a disenchantment with his society more profound than a rejection of its family codes and sexual conventions can explain:

> Art thou so bare and full of wretchedness,
> And fear'st to die? Famine is in thy cheeks,
> Need and oppression starveth in thy eyes,
> Contempt and beggary hangs upon thy back.
> The world is not thy friend, nor the world's law.
> The world affords no law to make thee rich . . ..
> There is thy gold—worse poison to men's souls,
> Doing more murder in this loathsome world,
> Than these poor compounds that thou mayst not sell.
> I sell thee poison; thou hast sold me none.
>   (5.1.68-73, 80-3)

At the climax of this tragedy of blighted love, Romeo's speech reminds us that the cruel misfortune suffered by the lovers is dwarfed by the inhumanity of 'the world's law', which deprives the poor and starving of their share of the world's wealth. To those whose eyes reflect not the light of love, but only 'need and oppression', whose cheeks are not flushed with desire but hollowed by 'famine', and whose destiny is nothing but 'contempt and beggary', the romantic agonies of the ruling class are merely another luxury they cannot afford. These lines leave us with the disturbing thought that the tragedy of Romeo and Juliet masks a darker, more devastating tragedy of institutionalized exploitation, which is the very precondition of its exquisite poetry. Nor is that, we may rest assured, the last disturbing thought that deconstructive readings of the play have in store for us.

FURTHER READING

Belsey, Catherine. 'The Name of the Rose in *Romeo and Juliet*'. In *Romeo and Juliet*: *Contemporary Critical Essays*, ed. R. S. White (Basingstoke: Palgrave, 2001), pp. 47–67. Draws on Derrida to argue that in *Romeo and Juliet* the age-old distinction between mind and body is deconstructed, and desire is shown to exceed the language used to express it.

Derrida, Jacques. 'Aphorism Countertime'. In *Acts of Literature*, ed. D. Attridge (New York and London: Routledge, 1992), pp. 414–33. A series of aphorisms on the play's defiance of the tyranny of names and conventional notions of time, turning on a close analysis of the balcony scene.

Goldberg, Jonathan. '*Romeo and Juliet*'s Open Rs'. In his *Queering the Renaissance* (Durham, NC: Duke University Press, 1994), pp. 218–35. Reading of *Romeo and Juliet* that explores its resistance to the ideology of 'compulsory heterosexuality' by focusing on relationships between men in the play, and the friendship of Romeo and Mercutio in particular.

Ryan, Kiernan. '*Romeo and Juliet*: The Murdering Word'. In his *Shakespeare*, 3rd edn. (Basingstoke: Palgrave, 2002), pp. 72–83. Expands on some of the ideas pursued in the reading of *Romeo and Juliet* sketched in this chapter, contesting conservative critical views of the play and of Shakespearian tragedy in general.

Snow, Edward. 'Language and Sexual Difference in *Romeo and Juliet*'. In *Shakespeare's 'Rough Magic'*: *Renaissance Essays in Honor of C. L. Barber* (Newark: University of Delaware Press, 1985), pp. 168–92. Traces the shifting dynamics of the lovers' relationship through the changes in their language. Especially illuminating on their verbal echoes of each other, which suggest 'two imaginations working in the same idiom' and thus 'a single world of desire encompassing the two lovers' separate longings'.

Whittier, Gayle. 'The Sonnet's Body and the Body Sonnetized in *Romeo and Juliet*'. *Shakespeare Quarterly*, 40 (1989), 27–41. Shows how the conventions of the Petrarchan sonnet serve 'the dramatic conspiracy between word and world' in the play and demonstrate 'the performative and potentially deadly power of poetry'.

35 | Performance history: Shakespeare on the stage 1660–2001

Patricia Tatspaugh

One way of learning how to interpret Shakespeare is to read and analyse what scholars and other critics have written. Another way is to investigate what actors and directors have discovered. This second method includes both performance criticism (see Chapter 36) and performance history, which draws on performance criticism as one of the tools for the reconstruction of past performances. To do performance history responsibly one needs to have some sense of changing performance spaces, changing acting styles, and developments in the various aspects of stage design that enhance (or, lamentably, distract from) the actor and the performance script. In addition to these theatre-based topics, the performance historian needs to examine the larger context of political, historical, and sociological thought influencing a production and/or its audience.

This overview of Shakespeare on the stage explores the way actors and directors shaped and staged Shakespeare's plays to make them attractive and relevant to audiences in England between 1660 and 2001. Three topics dominate the discussion. First, there are interrelated theatre-based topics: actors and directors; performance spaces; design; text; interpretation. Second, the larger context of influences on a production and/or its audience is important. Third, some sources available to the performance historian of each period are reviewed. The first two topics are, of course, also relevant to those who write reviews of contemporary productions.

A brief historical background helps to bridge the gap between the theatre in Shakespeare's time (see Chapters 3 and 5) and the quite different situation in 1660. In 1642, Puritan objections to the theatre, long a source of satire for playwrights and pamphleteers (see Chapter 4), triumphed when Parliament closed theatres and other places of public entertainment. The English Civil Wars, fought between 1642 and 1648, culminated in the trial and execution of Charles I in January 1649. Eleven years later, in May 1660, Parliament restored the monarchy and invited Charles II home from exile. Although performances did not disappear entirely between 1642 and 1660, the eighteen-year closure of the public theatres not only broke continuity with theatrical traditions but also stifled a generation of potential playwrights and actors.

1660–1741

Three months after his restoration, in August 1660, Charles II granted patents to courtiers Charles Killigrew and Sir William Davenant to establish two theatre companies that would hold the effective monopoly on 'legitimate' (i.e., spoken) performances in London until 1843, when an Act of Parliament finally revoked the exclusive warrant. Killigrew formed the King's Company with experienced actors, who brought with them their 'rights' to plays, including Shakespeare's, written before 1642. Davenant created the Duke of York's Company from young actors. Although Davenant and his company eventually gained fourteen of Shakespeare's plays, Killigrew held the apparently stronger and larger share.

Neither of the playhouses used by Shakespeare's company had survived. The new companies played in theatres that, like pre-Restoration court theatres, were indoor spaces equipped to employ changeable scenery. The basic features of the Restoration stage included a deep proscenium or apron with two doors on either side and a series of grooves upstage of the proscenium arch into which flats or 'scenes' could be fitted. With the audience on three sides, the actors performed on the proscenium. To create an appropriate backdrop for the action, scene-shifters opened and closed flats, some lavish and especially prepared for a production and others from the stock of standard scenes suitable for a number of productions. Gradual adjustments, such as shortening the proscenium, reducing the number of doors, and providing more seating, altered the relationship between actor and audience and led eventually to the picture-frame stage familiar today.

In September 1660 *Othello* became the first Shakespeare play to be staged in the Restoration era. Reviving the play two months later, Killigrew introduced as Desdemona the first woman to act on the English public stage. (Before then, women had appeared only in court masques and other private entertainments.) Davenant's adaptations of Shakespeare—with additional roles for women—and his use of changeable scenery set standards that Killigrew, with the apparent advantages of more experienced actors and a better repertoire, was forced to adopt.

Adapters adjusted Shakespeare's scripts to meet contemporary literary standards: they tidied his plots, introduced foils to or potential partners for his characters, and made the language accessible and inoffensive. Davenant's *Macbeth*, the standard acting text from 1664 to 1744, expanded the roles of the witches. His introduction of dancing, additional songs, and flying produced operatic and comic effects. Davenant also replaced Shakespeare's rudely comic Porter with a servant whose single sentence moralizes: 'Labour by day causes rest by night'. Additional scenes for Lady Macduff, including a brief passage where her presence prevents Lady Macbeth from reading Macbeth's letter, make the two women foils in debates about ambition, love and honour, and matrimonial roles. Simplification stripped imagery from Shakespeare's poetry. Macbeth's speech beginning 'Will all great Neptune's ocean wash this blood /

Clean from my hand?' (2.2.58–9) becomes 'What hands are here! can the Sea afford / Water enough to wash away the stains? / No, they would sooner add a tincture to / The Sea, and turn the green into a red' (2.2.60–3). Slain on stage, Macbeth dies denouncing ambition. Macduff wishes Malcolm a peaceful reign and the prayers of his subjects. In an era with first-hand knowledge of civil wars and regicide, Davenant's *Macbeth* carried politically charged meanings.

In the 1660s Davenant's adaptations of Shakespeare were more popular than Killigrew's revivals of Shakespeare's scripts. *The Tempest*, which Davenant adapted with John Dryden, enlarged Miranda's role and created sisters for Miranda and for Caliban. As Michael Dobson points out in *The Making of the National Poet*, it was 'the most frequently revived play of the entire Restoration' and established the importance of enhanced and additional roles for women. Other adaptations surviving at least forty years include Thomas Otway's *Caius Marius* (1679), based on *Romeo and Juliet*, Nahum Tate's *King Lear* (1681), and Colley Cibber's *Richard III* (1699). In Otway's adaptation Lavinia (Juliet) awakens before Marius (Romeo) dies (a revision Baz Luhrmann's 1996 film incorporates). Tate's *Lear* excises the Fool and creates a confidante for Cordelia; introduces a love-interest between Cordelia and Edgar, who prevents Edmund's attempted rape of her; and closes with Lear, Gloucester, and Kent retiring 'to some cool Cell' and with Edgar, to whom Lear has given both crown and Cordelia, proclaiming that he prefers the love of the 'Divine Cordelia' over 'Empire'. Cibber's *Richard III* opens with a scene from *Henry VI Part One* and expands the role of Lady Anne. Cibber's Richard orders 'Off with his head. So much for Buckingham' (a line Laurence Olivier's 1955 film version of *Richard III* retains). Thomas Betterton, the period's most important actor, created Davenant's Macbeth and Tate's Lear and acted Hamlet in an edited version for forty-eight years, giving his last performance of the Danish prince at age seventy-four.

1741–1776

At Goodman's Fields, which evaded licensing laws by offering spoken drama 'gratis' between the halves of concerts, twenty-four-year-old David Garrick, announced simply as 'a gentleman', played Cibber's Richard III and embarked upon an extraordinary career as actor and director, adapter and restorer of Shakespeare. In their critical biography of Garrick, George W. Stone, Jr. and George M. Kahrl record that between October 1741 and June 1776 Garrick gave 585 performances (more than 20 per cent of his total) in eighteen Shakespearian roles. Garrick also initiated the restoration of *Hamlet*, *Lear*, *Richard III*, *Macbeth*, *Othello*, and *Romeo*, and he had a hand in adapting five, possibly six, other plays. Garrick managed Drury Lane from 1747 until his retirement in 1776. His correspondence records his views on many roles, and editors consulted him about readings and borrowed from his library. His contemporaries, including foreign visitors, described memorable performances; paintings and engravings portrayed him as Benedick, Hamlet, Lear, Macbeth, Richard III, and Romeo. The 'age of Garrick' accurately characterizes the period.

The titles of Garrick's two most popular adaptations, *Catherine and Petruchio* and *Florizel and Perdita*, reveal his primary aim: to simplify the plots of, respectively, *The Taming of the Shrew* and *The Winter's Tale*. Reduced to three acts and shorn of troubling character traits and bawdy and obscure language, the adaptations played as afterpieces to a play presented as the main performance. A farce, *Catherine and Petruchio* concentrates on five scenes. At the close of Act 1, Catherine confides her strategy: 'Cath'rine shall tame this haggard;—or if she fails, / Shall tie her tongue up, and pare down her nails'. In the final scene, Petruchio discards his mask of 'the lordly husband'; banishes rudeness, wilfulness, and noise; and anticipates that their lives together will be 'one gentle stream / Of mutual love, compliance, and regard'. The sheep-shearing scenes are the basis of *Florizel and Perdita*, the most popular of the three eighteenth-century adaptations of *The Winter's Tale*. Recognizing the dramatic power of the statue scene (5.3), Garrick relocated it to Bohemia, where Paulina had fled with Hermione's 'effects' and the repentant Leontes sailed sixteen years later. Garrick wrote sentimental speeches for Hermione and Leontes and required Hermione to kneel to Leontes and forgive him. The cold or ambiguous closures introduced in some twentieth-century productions of *The Winter's Tale* were not an option.

Over the stage life of a production, Garrick gradually restored some of Shakespeare's language, reinstated cuts that had eliminated psychological complication of characters, and returned minor characters to their original roles and speeches to their proper order. But he also refashioned features of the Restoration adaptations. Macbeth dies on stage speaking Garrick's, not Davenant's lines. As she did in Otway's adaptation, Juliet awakens, but she shares with Romeo seventy-five lines of Garrick's dialogue before poison claims him. *Lear* closes with the happy ending, but not the speech Tate had penned for Edgar. Garrick did not reinstate Lear's Fool; he retained Cordelia's confidante and the love interest between Edgar and Cordelia. Garrick also transposed scenes and made cuts to speed up the action. He borrowed and elaborated effects such as the funeral procession to Capulet's monument, an interpolation still staged occasionally and filmed by George Cukor (1936) and Renato Castellani (1954).

The top ten of Garrick's roles, as listed by Stone and Kahrl, includes Benedick (113 performances), Hamlet (ninety), Lear (eighty-five) and Richard III (eighty-three). Played between 1742 and 1776, his Hamlet possessed subtlety, delicacy, and sentimentality; Hamlet's melancholy did not prevent his being a man of action. Garrick restored lines and speeches, such as 'How all occasions do inform against me' (4.4), which reveal Hamlet's inner conflict, a strength of Garrick's performance. In Hamlet's first encounter with his father's ghost, Garrick started back and collapsed into the arms of Horatio and Marcellus, business his successors would imitate. When the Ghost appeared in the closet scene (3.4), Garrick's hair literally stood on end, an effect achieved

with a specially designed wig. Like Betterton, Garrick played Hamlet in contemporary costume, what we today call modern dress.

1776–1843

In matters textual, John Philip Kemble, like Garrick, is full of apparent contradictions best explained by the demands of the box office. Kemble's education and library, his attention to detail in the delivery of lines, and his restoration of some passages are at variance with actions such as his reinstating passages Garrick had banished from Tate's *Lear* and Davenant and Dryden's *Tempest*, his retention of Garrick's speech for the dying Macbeth, and his cutting and reshaping texts to allow for spectacle. As actor-manager at Drury Lane and later at Covent Garden, Kemble prepared acting scripts for twenty-nine Shakespeare plays and published twenty-six of them, an innovative venture that influenced productions well into the nineteenth century. The manuscript annotations and sketches in his promptbooks testify to his attention to placing actors on stage, especially crowd management, and to his use of business; sound, music, and lighting effects; and changeable scenery to achieve continuous action between scenes. Although Kemble initiated the use of historical props, sets, and costuming, his productions, which relied also on stock sets and costumes provided by the actors, lacked a unified or historically accurate concept. They were, however, rich in crowd-pleasing, strategically placed spectacle. Promptbooks call for lavish court scenes, in which a king is discovered, enthroned under a canopy. For his first, brief appearance in *Henry VIII*, Cardinal Wolsey processed across the stage with a train of twenty-four attendants carrying symbols of the churchman's authority. A strong visual image, not the Chorus's reminder of death and loss, closed *Henry V*: ten principals and thirty-four supernumeraries centred attention on Henry's forthcoming marriage to the Princess of France.

Kemble, who played at least twenty-one Shakespeare roles, was most successful as Coriolanus, Brutus, and Macbeth, roles more suited to his formal, stately, declamatory style. In *Macbeth and the Players*, Dennis Bartholomeusz notes that Kemble's Macbeth imitated the dress of a Highland chieftain: 'chain mail, and over it a plaid in the manner of some of the clans of Scotland'.

Kemble often shared the stage with his sister, Sarah Siddons, who brought to Volumnia, Portia, and Lady Macbeth a powerfully expressive voice and carefully observed characterization that made her the foremost tragic actress of her generation. In the sleepwalking scene Siddons broke with tradition by putting the taper aside to mime washing Lady Macbeth's hands and conveyed that she did indeed smell blood on them. Paintings and engravings attest to her insistence that costumes suit the characters rather than, as had been the custom, flatter the actress or follow the fashion.

In 1814, Edmund Kean, who had appeared as a scene-stealing infant goblin in Kemble's *Macbeth* (Drury Lane, 1794), attracted considerable attention for an acting style that Samuel Taylor Coleridge famously likened to 'reading Shakespeare by flashes of lightning'. Whereas the restraint, dignity, and elocution of Kemble and Siddons has led to their being labelled 'classical', so the energy Kean invested in his most admired roles and the pathos he discovered in them fired the Romantic imagination. Hindered by his physique and his vocal limitations, Kean played a narrower range than had either Garrick or Kemble. He failed as Coriolanus, King John, and Romeo; he succeeded as Shylock, Cibber's Richard III, Othello, and Iago, outsiders whom he presented in an unconventional manner. Reviews by William Hazlitt and Leigh Hunt—Kean's debut coincided with the first great age of performance criticism—detail the power and originality, as well as the inconsistencies and limitations, of his creations. Wearing a black wig, not the traditional red one, Kean's Shylock was a nearly tragic figure, not the then familiar one-dimensional comic creation. As Cibber's Richard III he conveyed a wide range of traits. Contemporaries praised his wooing of Lady Anne; his innovative stage business, such as that in the tent scene, where he drew battle plans in the sand with his sword; and his death scene.

Credit for the first fully realized attempt at an historically accurate production belongs to Charles Kemble, younger brother of Kemble and Siddons, and his associate James Planché, whose production of *King John* (1823) drew upon careful research of effigies, monuments, artefacts, and historical studies of costumes.

During his two periods as actor-manager (Covent Garden, 1837–9; Drury Lane, 1841–3) William Charles Macready built upon the foundation of historical accuracy laid by the Kembles. Macready's lasting contribution was an emphasis on unity of concept. He insisted not only on historically accurate dress but also on the correct wearing of costumes, as the cast of *King John*, after their full day of rehearsal in armour, would have testified. John Kemble had orchestrated impressive crowd scenes, but Macready expected the extras to participate fully—and appropriately—in the scene. His promptbook for *As You Like It* cues extras to follow closely the wrestling match and to suit their responses to the changing fortunes of Orlando.

Macready restored the original text of *King Lear*, cut Davenant and Dryden's additions to *The Tempest*, and reinstated the Chorus to *Henry V*. But he yielded to the demand for spectacle by staging a pantomimic storm for *The Tempest* and by illustrating the Chorus's words with a carefully detailed diorama. In these and other productions pictures substituted for, or enhanced, Shakespeare's poetry.

1843–1900

In this period three threads intertwine: the influence of productions at the 'new' theatres; the transition from a search for historical accuracy to the dominance of pictorial realism; and the emergence of trends that would gain greater prominence in the next century.

In 1843 the Theatres Act broke the monopoly that had, since 1660, restricted the number of theatres in London that could present spoken performances. Samuel Phelps, who had acted with Macready at both Covent Garden and Drury Lane, seized the opportunity to establish a popular and successful theatre company. Between 1844 and 1862, Phelps staged thirty-one Shakespeare plays in performances that account for more than forty-five per cent of the total at Sadler's Wells Theatre. Phelps replaced the old acting editions, such as those retaining vestiges of Tate's and Cibber's adaptations, with Shakespeare's scripts; over the stage life of some productions, however, he yielded to public pressure and reinstated some passages from the adaptations. Discarding the star system, he was able to supervise the acting of all roles and attend to the total effect of productions. By the mid-1850s, he introduced a theory of stage decoration that sought to interpret the play, not to present spectacular scenic effects.

Phelps's company challenged traditional readings of roles. Polonius became an intelligent and compassionate man, not a buffoon. Comedians distinguished between roles rather than using Shakespeare's creations as a showcase for their own talents. Phelps himself played Malvolio as 'sick of self-love' (*Twelfth Night*, 1.5.77), not as a laughter-seeking comedian. His Hamlet was 'courtly, intellectual, and spiritual'. Stressing the paternal rather than the regal, he conveyed Lear's suffering but did not, as Macready, attempt to explain it as a tragic flaw.[1] Phelps's range of roles, which included Bottom, Brutus, Falstaff, Henry V, Iago, John, Leontes, Macbeth, Mercutio, and Othello, compares favourably with Garrick's.

During his nine seasons (1850–9) as manager of the Princess's Theatre, Charles Kean, the Eton-educated son of Edmund, gave precedence not to Shakespeare's scripts and characters but to historical writings and archeological artefacts that, he believed, illuminated the period of the play. Playbills detail the settings and set pieces that substituted for Shakespeare's words or for historical events the playwright had omitted, perhaps, as the Chorus explains, because Shakespeare's 'wooden o' could not contain them. Kean's theatre contained a lavish set piece of Henry V's triumphant return to London after the battle of Agincourt. To welcome their monarch a chorus of twenty boys dropped gold coins from a triumphal arch that framed Henry on horseback. Before him twenty-four angelic girls danced; on either side subjects both worthy and menial, household servants, and representations of historical kings and prophets crowded around Henry. Although Kean acted in most of his productions and appeared in Shakespeare plays around the world, he did not distinguish himself as an interpreter of roles, as did Phelps.

Only twelve of the thirty-seven plays produced by Henry Irving, whose association with the Lyceum stretched from 1871 to 1902, were Shakespeare's. But in 1895 Irving's significant contributions to the staging and acting of Shakespeare earned him the first theatrical knighthood. To his pictorially realistic productions of popular titles, Irving introduced a number of modifications. His sets were built, three-dimensional, with practicable stairs and platforms. Illustrations of the courtyard of Macbeth's castle (1888) picture a round tower with a staircase to Duncan's chamber, an outer gate for the Porter, and a staircase to a gallery. Working with more sophisticated lighting than had been available to his predecessors, he explored the effects of lighting on a scene. Composers, including Arthur Sullivan, scored incidental music to further heighten the effect. Macbeth and his spear-carrying troops crossed the stage to a wild march; music associated with the Ghost recurred as Hamlet commanded Horatio to live and tell his story.

Irving's Hamlet, like his Lear, Romeo, and Othello, suffered because the political and social orders to which the characters were committed had disintegrated. His most successful productions also offered roles for Ellen Terry. Her Portia earned praise for the 'natural and easy' manner in which she portrayed various moods: 'tenderness', 'love', 'wit', 'dignity', 'the desire to be merciful and to inspire mercy', 'wrath', 'natural play-fulness'. Audiences commiserated with Irving's Shylock, who resisted 'extravagance or eccentricity of action'. His Shylock, 'old, haggard, halting, sordid, represents the dignity and intellect of the play'.[2]

Coexistent with the various strains of nineteenth-century pictorial realism were two movements that would command greater attention in the next century. Benjamin Webster's *Shrew* (Haymarket, 1844) introduced the first, an interest in Elizabethan playing conditions. Encouraged by Planché, Webster played all but the bawdiest twenty-five lines of Shakespeare's script, did not rearrange scenes, and set the play on a stage that sought to replicate an Elizabethan one by using moveable properties, hangings at the central opening, and placards to announce place. The stage resembled a Tudor hall; the costumes were sixteenth-century Italianate. In 1881 William Poel staged the first quarto *Hamlet*; between 1895 and 1905 his Elizabethan Stage Society presented ten Shakespeare plays without scenery in Tudor halls or on a replica of the Fortune Theatre's stage. He staged *Twelfth Night* and *The Comedy of Errors* in the halls of, respectively, Middle Temple and Gray's Inn, where Shakespeare's company had played them. A sixteen-year-old played Romeo; and a fourteen-year-old, Juliet (1905).

The incentive for the second movement was a company of German actors under the patronage of the Duke of Saxe-Meiningen. Their adherence to the principle of an ensemble acting company influenced the founder of the Shakespeare Memorial Theatre in Stratford-upon-Avon, which would in the 1960s become the Royal Shakespeare Theatre and home to the Royal Shakespeare Company.

1900–1951

Two world wars, the general strike, the world-wide economic depression and post-war austerity scarred four decades of this half century. Unlike earlier periods, where names such as Garrick, Kemble, Kean, and Irving help to define an era, no single name dominates. Numerous well- and lesser-known actors and directors helped to shape productions and to lay the groundwork for the two national theatrical companies of England and for the significant productions of the second half of the century.

One of the most influential directors was Harley Granville Barker. His productions— *The Winter's Tale* (1912), *Twelfth Night* (1912), and *A Midsummer Night's Dream* (1914)— contrast sharply with those by Herbert Beerbohm Tree, the last great exponent of pictorial realism.[3] Barker, who had played Richard II and Edward II for Poel, sought to adapt modern playing conditions to Shakespeare rather than to ossify the playwright in antiquarian reproductions. Redesigning the Savoy stage to approximate an Elizabethan one, he created an inner stage, a main playing space, and a platform extending over the orchestra pit with entrances from either side. Instead of footlights, he lit both stage and audience from spots hung before the dress circle. Basic sets and a series of patterned drop curtains made scene changes seamless. Unlike Poel, Barker played nearly complete texts, his cuts being chiefly obscure or obscene passages that might temporarily distract his audience. The text and its demands, including clear and rapid delivery, guided Barker. Breaking with tradition, Barker encouraged Lillah McCarthy to play Viola's disguise (in *Twelfth Night*) as an Elizabethan boy actor might have done, rather than as a breeches part incorporated to show off the actress's legs. Business that illuminated the characters of Sir Toby and Sir Andrew replaced inappropriate comic accretions. Barker cast Feste as an Elizabethan professional entertainer and introduced on-stage musicians. The political and economic disruptions of the next decades postponed until later in the century further work along the lines Barker had initiated.

In the 1920s, Barry Jackson's Birmingham Repertory Company presented six modern-dress productions: *Cymbeline*, *Hamlet*, *All's Well That Ends Well*, *The Taming of the Shrew*, *Macbeth*, and *Othello*. Costuming the characters in the method most often employed by Shakespeare's company and largely continued through the age of Garrick—in clothes indistinguishable from those of the spectators—freed the actors to rethink their roles. In the course of his long tenure at the theatre, Jackson built an ensemble, not a star-based company, and nurtured actors, such as Peggy Ashcroft, Laurence Olivier, Ralph Richardson, and Paul Scofield, and directors, such as Peter Brook.

A year after Jackson had founded the Birmingham Rep, Ben Greet's association with the Old Vic in London (1914–18) began the transformation that would lead, in 1964, to its becoming the National Theatre. The practical Greet staged standard acting versions with scenery that met the dual objectives of attracting the neighbourhood's working-class inhabitants and of keeping within a tight budget. Robert Atkins (1920–3) staged each of the First Folio plays. Harcourt Williams (1929–33) directed John Gielgud and Richardson in a memorable series of roles: Hotspur and Hal, Richard and Bolingbroke, Prospero and Caliban, Antony and Enobarbus, Malvolio and Sir Toby, Lear and Kent. Tyrone Guthrie (1936–45) attracted stars, some of whom had made their name in earlier Old Vic seasons, and raised the profile of the company. He directed Olivier as

Hamlet, Macbeth, and Iago (to whom he gave a Freudian interpretation, discomforting Richardson's Othello) and Coriolanus, with Sybil Thorndike as Volumnia. In 1937 Olivier's *Hamlet* played at Elsinore (in a hotel ballroom, hastily rearranged from the castle's rain-soaked courtyard), and that same year his *Henry V* was billed as a 'Coronation attraction'. (Olivier's film version of the play (1944) was part of the war effort.) Released from their wartime responsibilities, Olivier and Richardson re-established the company in the West End of London, where their productions included *Richard III*, with Olivier and Richardson as Richard and Clarence (roles they would later play in Olivier's film version of the play); both parts of *Henry IV*, with Olivier's remarkable double of Hotspur and Shallow and Richardson's memorable Falstaff; Olivier's Lear, with Alec Guinness as the Fool; and *Richard II*, with Guinness in the title role.

By mid-century, the Shakespeare Memorial Theatre (SMT) in Stratford-upon-Avon, originally home to visiting companies for seasons as brief as one week, was poised to rival the Old Vic. In all but five seasons between 1886 and 1919 the company, led by actor-director Frank Benson, staged productions that drew heavily on pictorial realism. Scenes from Benson's *Richard III* (1911), available on 'Silent Shakespeare', reveal something of Benson's methods. William Bridges-Adams, director of the first resident company (1919–39), staged virtually uncut texts on a simple set—traverse curtains provided a backdrop for scenes and could be opened to reveal appropriate structures such as arches and stairs. Theodore Komisarjevsky's six productions revitalized the company. Komisarjevsky 'transformed' *The Merchant of Venice* (1932) 'into a sharp romantic comedy with, at its centre, a dark point—Randle Ayrton's harsh and unsympathetic portrait of Shylock'.[4] Ben Iden Payne (1934–42), a follower of Poel, staged *Hamlet* (1936) on a mock Elizabethan set.

Jackson's brief tenure (1945–8) most significantly introduced a new company and a young director, Peter Brook, who would revolutionize the staging of Shakespeare. Casting young actors as Romeo and Juliet (1947), Brook sought to discover the Italian flavour that Franco Zeffirelli would more successfully extract at the Old Vic (1960) and in his film (1968). In *The Stratford Festival*, T. C. Kemp and J. C. Trewin recall productions from this era. Played on a permanent set that 'suggested the material opulence of a wealthy state and the severity of the penal system by which it kept order', Brook's *Measure for Measure* (1950) 'had a vitality which derived from the riff-raff in the streets as well as from the quality at court'. Kemp and Trewin describe Scofield's post-war Henry V (1946) as a 'lyrical rather than a declamatory king'. In Michael Benthall's *Hamlet* (1948), they record, Scofield's 'youthful', 'lyrical' prince alternated with Robert Helpmann's 'more deliberate' one. The costumes were early Victorian; Elsinore, a Renaissance castle.

1951–2001

At the expense of exciting work by companies such as Cheek by Jowl, Citizens' Theatre in Glasgow, the English Shakespeare Company, and Northern Broadsides, this section highlights the contributions of the two national companies, both of which seek to redefine themselves as I write. Focusing on the earlier decades of the period sets the stage for Michael Billington's exploration of the diversity of Shakespeare today (see Chapter 39).

Opening this final discussion with productions staged as part of the Festival of Britain provides an apparently classical order to the half-century: it begins and ends with an acclaimed production by Peter Brook and a cycle of histories from Stratford. In 1951, the cycle of four histories—*Richard II, Henry IV Parts One* and *Two*, and *Henry V*—played on a permanent set. In 2001 the three parts of *Henry VI* and *Richard III* joined the first tetralogy in a series announced as 'This England'. Tellingly, there was not a unified concept. Brook's *The Winter's Tale* (1951) drew upon the work of Harley Granville Barker and played in a West End theatre with a cast led by John Gielgud. Fifty years later, at the close of an international tour, eight actors played Brook's heavily cut *Hamlet* at London's Young Vic, a butcher's shop converted to an intimate theatre in the round. As the prince, Brook cast Adrian Lester, whose early work for Cheek by Jowl, a small-scale touring company, included, in the words of Irving Wardle, 'the most breathtakingly sensuous Rosalind since Vanessa Redgrave'.

Between 1951 and 2001 the Shakespeare Revolution—the term comes from John Styan's influential study—successfully unseated traditional staging practices and achieved a more fruitful relationship between the theatre and the study, stage and page. But a second revolution, one characterized by the diversity Billington examines, has followed closely upon the first.

In 1951, Brook, as had Barker, staged *The Winter's Tale* on a flexible set that made continuous action possible and recognized the theatrical potential of the three gentlemen (5.2), a scene that other directors had cut or shortened considerably. Whereas Barker had played a nearly full text, Brook cut scenes and episodes. In '*The Winter's Tale' in Performance* Dennis Bartholomeusz describes Gielgud's Leontes as 'a man most credible in his folly and immensely moving in his repentance'. Flora Robson played Paulina as 'a force of sanity in the insane world', not, as was the tradition, as a shrew.

At Stratford-upon-Avon in 1951, Anthony Quayle defied traditional theatrical and critical interpretations of the first tetralogy, drew upon E. M. W. Tillyard's *Shakespeare's History Plays* (1944), and sought, as Sally Beauman points out in *The Royal Shakespeare Company*, to 'trace their continuing themes, their poetic structure, and their development of characters'. By dressing the bare set—it suggested an Elizabethan theatre—with flags and banners and groupings of actors, Quayle shifted scenes quickly from court to tavern to country, to France and back. Quayle mixed stars—Michael Redgrave as Richard II, himself as Falstaff—with newcomers—Richard Burton as Hal. He pursued this policy as artistic director of the SMT in the 1950s.

In the 1960s Peter Hall transformed the Stratford company into the Royal Shakespeare Company (RSC). Hall and his successors Trevor Nunn and Terry Hands created an ensemble company that played a repertory of Shakespeare and his contemporary playwrights, classics, and new plays; attended to verse speaking; redesigned the main house to narrow the gap between the actor and audience; established The Other Place (1973), an intimate, flexible theatre; and built a third theatre, the Swan (1986), with a thrust stage and galleries.

Some Stratford seasons have explored thematic links in a set of plays, such as the late plays, the Roman plays, plays about love. Seasons of histories, including those mentioned at the beginning of this section, reflect shifting political and societal ideologies. *The War of the Roses* (1963), John Barton's adaptation of the second tetralogy (with some 1,400 lines added by Barton himself) concentrated on the over-riding issues of political power and struggle. Between 1975 and 1980, Hands directed both tetralogies in fairly full texts, focused on the human aspects of the characters and, taking his cue from the Chorus (and the accountant), staged the plays with a minimum of artifice. Alan Howard followed his haunted Henry V with a Henry VI who was, in Benedict Nightingale's words, 'sensitive, conscientious and intellectually avaricious', and then anchored the cycle with Richard II and Richard III. In 1988 Adrian Noble presented the second tetralogy as *The Plantagenets*, a trilogy more faithful to the source texts than Barton's had been. Ralph Fiennes's Henry VI, whom Michael Billington described as a 'militant pacifist', presided over the disintegration of his kingdom, presented as an emblem-rich medieval England, a design contrasting with the eclecticism of the English Shakespeare Company's cycle (1986–9), *The War of the Roses*. Both the RSC and ESC *War of the Roses* cycles were filmed for television.

Important productions of the tragedies include Brook's austere *King Lear* (1962), with Scofield as an emotionally restrained monarch. Jan Kott's *Shakespeare Our Contemporary* influenced the production, which was the basis of Brook's film (1971). Deborah Warner's *Titus Andronicus* (Swan, 1987) proved the power of the nearly full text in a production that engaged the audience in political quarrels; made intensely moving the meeting between Sonia Ritter's Lavinia and her uncle, Marcus (Donald Sumpter), after she has been raped and mutilated; and made sense of the script's apparently awkward mixture of comedy and tragedy.

Some of the company's best work has originated at The Other Place. Buzz Good-body's virtually uncut modern dress *Hamlet* (1975) introduced Ben Kingsley as a prince distinguished by his intelligence. With a strong cast led by Ian McKellen and Judi Dench, Nunn staged *Macbeth* (1976) with costumes selected from stock, minimum essential hand props, and the simplest of settings: a circle of beer crates and a bare light bulb overhead. The production was filmed for television (1976). In the small space, the narrative of *Cymbeline* (1987, director: Bill Alexander) had an urgency and appeal sometimes missing in larger houses.

Of many excellent productions of the comedies in the main house, Brook's *A Midsummer Night's Dream* (1970) is the most significant (see pp. 544–6). Barton's *Twelfth Night* (1969) evoked bittersweet lyricism and filled the late-night drinking scene (2.3) with song. Setting *Much Ado About Nothing* in colonial India, Barton (1976) created a community hospitable to Shakespeare's characters. Dench contributed original readings of Viola and Beatrice.

In the 1950s, when Quayle lured stars such as Olivier and Vivien Leigh to add lustre to Stratford's company, Benthall cast newcomers at the Old Vic, built an ensemble company, and staged all the Shakespeare plays except *Pericles*. Richard Burton's roles included Hamlet, Coriolanus, and Henry V; Dench made her debut as Ophelia and played Juliet in Zeffirelli's zesty, Italianate *Romeo and Juliet* (1960). Casts included young actors—Frank Finlay, Derek Jacobi, and Maggie Smith, for example—who would form the nucleus of the National Theatre Company under Olivier's direction, and Albert Finney, whose Hamlet would inaugurate the National's new home on the South Bank. Olivier created his last two Shakespeare roles, both outsiders, both carefully rethought, both delivered with his characteristic attention to physical details. A film (1965) records Olivier's monumental Othello (and reveals the disadvantages inherent in transferring a stage production directly to film). Setting *The Merchant of Venice* (1970) in late nineteenth-century Venice, director Jonathan Miller emphasized the financial motifs of the play. To announce his assimilation, Olivier's Shylock dressed in the frock coat and top hat of the ruling Venetians and assumed their accent, faltering only under pressure. Having struggled to regain his composure after the Duke's sentence, he made a dignified exit; offstage Shylock wailed despairingly. In an all-male *As You Like It* (1967), one of the more successful creations was Anthony Hopkins's Audrey, whom Hilary Spurling found 'impassive, monumental and eternally feminine'. More warmly received, Cheek by Jowl's modern dress, minimally designed production (1991) acknowledged Kott's influence. It was, observes John Peter in *The Sunday Times*, 'so brilliant, so intelligent, so shot through with warm generous humour' that it deserves to be remembered for more than its casting.

As this overview demonstrates, performance historians have a wide and ever-increasing range of documents at their disposal. But ideally their study begins not in the library but in the theatre itself: seeing as many performances and productions as possible, examining the choices taken by actors and directors and designers, and practising the craft by recording their impressions and insights.

FURTHER READING

Bate, Jonathan and Russell Jackson (eds.). *The Oxford Illustrated History of Shakespeare on Stage* (Oxford: Oxford University Press, 2001). With carefully integrated illustrations, this volume traces the history of Shakespeare on the English stage. The authors place adaptations and productions of Shakespeare in an historical and social context.

Bratton, J. S. and Julie Hankey. *Shakespeare in Production* (Cambridge: Cambridge University Press). This series (in progress) presents the New Cambridge text of each play annotated with notes that explain how productions shape the playing script, read lines, introduce stage business and properties, and place actors on stage. A lengthy general introduction discusses staging issues, performance history, and the influence of cultural changes on performances.

Brockbank, Philip, Russell Jackson, and Robert Smallwood (eds.). *Players of Shakespeare*, 4 vols. (Cambridge: Cambridge University Press, 1985–   ). In this series in progress actors discuss the preparation and playing of roles for the Royal Shakespeare Company. Photographs supplement the text.

David, Richard. *Shakespeare in the Theatre* (Cambridge: Cambridge University Press, 1978). This book concentrates on English productions of Shakespeare during the 1970s. It describes the productions themselves, illustrates key moments with photographs, and places the productions in the larger context of contemporary theatre and historical events.

Kennedy, Dennis. *Looking at Shakespeare: A Visual History of Twentieth-Century Performance*, 2nd edn. (Cambridge: Cambridge University Press, 2001). This book explores the visual meanings conveyed by design, the ways design influences interpretation, and the impact of contemporary cultural and social events on design. Integrated with the discussion of international productions are twenty-three colour plates and one hundred and seventy-two black-and-white illustrations.

Salgādo, Gāmini. *Eyewitnesses of Shakespeare: First Hand Accounts of Performances 1590–1890* (London: for Sussex University Press by Chatto and Windus, 1975). Supplemented by fifty-four illustrations (including end papers), this book compiles, in Part 1, allusions to and accounts of performances between 1590 and 1700 and, in Part 2, critiques of English performers and performances, chiefly in London. Organized by play, Part 2 includes reviews by professional critics, such as William Hazlitt and George Bernard Shaw, as well as reviews and commentary by less well-known playgoers.

Shattuck, Charles H. *John Philip Kemble Promptbooks*, 11 vols. (Charlottesville: for The Folger Shakespeare Library by the University Press of Virginia, 1974). These volumes reproduce Kemble's promptbooks and supply plates of his theatres and his productions. A general introduction discusses Kemble's Shakespearian roles and the promptbooks; an introduction to each play discusses the playing script, staging, and performances.

Smallwood, Robert (ed.). *Shakespeare at Stratford-upon-Avon* (London: Thomson Learning, 2001–). Published in conjunction with the Shakespeare Birthplace Trust, this series (in progress) discusses productions at Stratford since 1945. Drawing on the resources of the Shakespeare Centre Library, each richly illustrated volume describes how Stratford's artistic teams and actors have met the challenges inherent in the plays and interpreted them for international audiences embracing both scholars and first-time theatregoers.

Styan, J. L. *The Shakespeare Revolution* (Cambridge: Cambridge University Press, 1977). The revolution, argues this book, is that twentieth-century critics and directors have discovered that Shakespeare knew the craft of writing plays. The book places twentieth-century criticism and productions in the context of the nineteenth century's fascination with antiquarian research and pictorial realism, and traces the gradual emergence of stage-centred criticism.

Wells, Stanley, ed. and comp. *Shakespeare in the Theatre: An Anthology of Criticism* (Oxford: Oxford University Press, 1997). Not limited to English productions, this illustrated volume compiles a wide-range of first-hand accounts of significant performances. Critics describe, for example, Hamlets from Thomas Betterton (1700) to David Warner (1965); several roles performed by leading actors (such as David Garrick's Hamlet, Macbeth, and Lear); and rarely performed works, such as the first quarto *Hamlet* and *Titus Andronicus*.

NOTES

1. Shirley Allen. *Samuel Phelps and Sadler's Wells* (Middletown, Conn.: Wesleyan University Press, 1971). For Polonius, see p. 204; for Malvolio, pp. 182–3; for Hamlet, p. 167; for Lear, pp. 173–4.

2. For Terry, see *The Saturday Review*, 8 November 1879, excerpted and reprinted in *Shakespearean Criticism* (hereinafter *ShCrit*), eds. Laurie Lanzen Harris *et al.* (Detroit: Gale Research, 1984), 12: 23. For Irving, see Dutton Cook, *Nights at the Play* (London: Chatto & Windus, 1883), rpt in *ShCrit* 12: 17. 'Great Historical Shakespeare Recordings' (NAXOS, 2000) includes Irving, Terry, and other actors referred to in this survey.

3. 'Silent Shakespeare', a videotape published by the British Film Institute, includes a scene from Tree's production of *King John*, 1899.

4. Sally Beauman. *The Royal Shakespeare Company* (Oxford: Oxford University Press, 1982), p. 127.

READING: *A Midsummer Night's Dream*

One way of approaching the performance history of *A Midsummer Night's Dream* is to explore how actors and directors have staged answers to two questions: Whose play is it? And what is it about? Over the centuries productions have answered the question 'whose play is it?' by privileging one of the four groups of characters: the court, the two young couples, the fairies, or the mechanicals. To answer the question 'what is it about?' productions have stressed an aspect of the play that had (or seemed to have) a contemporary relevance, tested readings of the script prepared by study-bound critics, or cut and shaped the text to appeal to their audiences' tastes and interests. The visual component of productions has contributed significantly to the variety of staged responses to the play's characters and meaning. Experimenting with advances in stage lighting and machinery, borrowing from the styles and conventions of other performing arts, altering the historical period signified by the sets and costumes—each has helped to shape the responses of actors and directors and their audiences to Shakespeare's *A Midsummer Night's Dream*. This performance history introduces a variety of answers to the two basic questions and considers some of the means through which actors and directors have staged their insights into Shakespeare's script. The chapter breaks into three parts: a survey of productions between 1660 and 1900; a closer consideration of two seminal twentieth-century productions; and a discussion of how twentieth-century design and casting helped convey the production's view of whose play it is and what it is about.

1660–1900: adaptations, spectacle, pictorial realism

When Shakespeare's comedy returned to the English stage after the reopening of the theatres (see p. 526), it was not well received. After a performance in 1662, Samuel Pepys confided to his diary: 'The most insipid ridiculous play that ever I saw in my life'. Shakespeare's mixture of Athenian aristocrats, courtiers, artisans, and young lovers and quarrelling fairy monarchs did not appeal to Restoration tastes, which preferred adaptations that imposed order on Shakespeare's sprawling plots and that employed advances in stage machinery to create spectator-pleasing spectacle, such as flying witches in *Macbeth*.

For nearly two hundred years after Pepys's disappointing evening in the theatre, *A Midsummer Night's Dream* was a source for adaptations that were considerably less successful than those of, for example, *Macbeth* (William Davenant, 1664), *King Lear* (Nahum Tate, 1681), and *Richard III* (Colley Cibber, 1699). In his excellent study of the performance history of *A Midsummer Night's Dream* (1997), Gary Jay Williams places the early adaptations in a contemporary context. He argues, for example, that *The Fairy Queen* (1692), an adaptation of *Dream* with Henry Purcell's music, dancing, and spectacular scenic effects, belongs in the context of seventeenth-century works honouring monarchs: it celebrates royal power and the marriage of King William and Queen Mary as a prototype for their subjects. (Quite different, the English National Opera's exuberant three-act version (1995; revived 1997–8) replaced the seventeenth-century's adapted script with dance and celebrated late twentieth-century theatrical practice and cultural trends.)

In the eighteenth century, actor-manager David Garrick, who is credited with establishing Shakespeare as England's national poet, had considerably less success with adaptations of *A Midsummer Night's Dream* than he had with his adaptations of *The Taming of the Shrew* and *The Winter's Tale*. At Drury Lane Garrick's company staged three adaptations of *Dream*, each based on the fairy plot and played as an afterpiece with songs. None was publicly acknowledged as Garrick's work. In *The Fairies* (1755), notes Williams, 'Shakespeare's unruly women are domesticated, wholly subservient to male interests' (p. 68). The next version (1763), with more lines from *Dream*, thirty-three songs, and children as fairies, failed at its only performance. Its prompter records that 'The Performers first Sang the audience to Sleep, and then went to Sleep themselves'.

A nineteenth-century adaptation enjoyed moderate success. From Shakespeare's play Frederick Reynolds and Sir Henry Rowley Bishop crafted three acts (Covent Garden, 1816), into which they incorporated at least twenty-four songs and two elaborate spectacles. The adaptation was revived, with revisions and Felix Mendelssohn's overture, in 1833. As they had in *The Fairy Queen*, the script and spectacle had a contemporary relevance. The adaptation, Williams points out, spoke 'the language of British colonial expansionism following the Napoleonic wars' (p. 77). The spectacle, carefully detailed on the playbill, included galleys returning from India, presumably laden with offerings from the sub-continent. Interpolations dramatized the duty of women to their husbands and fathers: Titania returns the Indian boy to Oberon; Hermia seeks Egeus's forgiveness.

Successful revivals of Shakespeare's comedy date from 1840, nearly two centuries after Pepys had dismissed the play as 'insipid'. Madame Vestris (who co-managed Covent Garden with her husband) and James Robinson Planché restored all but three hundred and seventy lines of Shakespeare's text and based each of thirteen songs on lines from *Dream*. Vestris's production not only initiated the restoration of Shakespeare's script but also set production standards that many of her successors would emulate. Calling upon their designers to create elaborate effects based on historical artefacts, Vestris and Planché initiated the search for a pictorially realistic setting for the comedy. From Theseus's palace guests viewed distant Athens. A diorama created a number of forest settings. Fifty-two fairies—colour-coded to announce their allegiance to Titania or Oberon—filled the forest and danced a ballet around the sleeping lovers. Playing Oberon, Vestris established a tradition that would continue, with one exception, in major productions until 1914.

The first of Vestris's successors, Samuel Phelps (Sadler's Wells, 1853), strove for ensemble productions, attention to the text, and appropriate scenic effects. Using dioramas and gas lighting effects, Phelps and his designer created a forest with moving clouds, moonlight, and fog. Forty-two lantern-bearing fairies blessed Theseus's moonlit hall. Gaslight illuminated the pillars from within. Phelps himself was a much-praised Bottom, who did not let theatrical tricks dominate his exploration of character. Translated, with the head of an ass, he assumed an uncharacteristic stillness, though his ears moved. When he returned to the human world, memory of his experience preoccupied him.

At the Princess's Theatre (1856) Charles Kean privileged the scenic designer and antiquarian research at the expense of Shakespeare's text. Designs for scenery and props reveal the extent to which visual language replaced Shakespeare's words; Kean cut almost 40 per cent of *Dream*. For the court scenes—with Theseus as a Grecian prince, not a duke—Kean and his designers recreated Pericles' Athens with a distant view of the Acropolis. The artisans met at Peter Quince's carpenter's shop, which displayed tools based on those archeologists had found at the recent excavation of Herculaneum. More elaborate than those of Phelps, Kean's woodland scenes had a non-functioning waterfall and a pool among the rocks, trees, and hills. Airborne fairies hovered over Titania and Oberon; Titania and her attendants—including children as Peaseblossom, Cobweb, Mustardseed, and Moth—danced; forty fairies danced a ballet after the young Athenians fell asleep. Puck, nine-year-old Ellen Terry, entered from a trap on a mushroom and later flew away to find Helena (3.2.101). In the final episode, ninety fairies, played by women carrying coloured lanterns and costumed as sylphs, blessed Theseus's palace. One suspects that Pepys, who had admired 'some good dancing & some handsome women' in 1662, would have approved.

Herbert Beerbohm Tree (Her Majesty's, 1900) mounted the last important production in this visual tradition. Although he played nearly as much text as Vestris and Phelps had, his greatest debt was to Kean. He openly mocked William Poel's recent experiments with Elizabethan staging: the mechanicals, for example, wore placards around their necks to announce their roles in 'Pyramus and Thisbe'. Tree's forest had mechanical birds, a fake stream in which Bottom checked his reflection, and, in the 1911 revival, real rabbits lured by food placed strategically along the woodland paths. Fairy children danced in a ring to Mendelssohn's music; forty-seven fairies, one of whom hovered above, sang Titania to sleep; some fairies glowed, their lamps powered by batteries. In the final scene the magic touch of Oberon's wand illuminated the electric lamps within the pillars of Theseus's palace. Tree's *Dream* pleased the masses, for whom its production values reaffirmed a traditional, romantic view of England.

To the question 'whose play is it?' this period answered, chiefly, 'the fairies'. The supernatural beings provided titles for seventeenth- and eighteenth-century adaptations—*The Fairy Queen*, *The Fairies*—and contributed to the spectacle in the nineteenth century. Fairies are, of course, important subjects in Victorian literature and art. Illustrations and photographs of productions record choruses of balletic fairies, who anticipate twentieth-century ballets that George Balanchine (1962) and Frederick Ashton (1964) choreographed to Mendelssohn's music. The mechanicals, most frequently played as broadly comic, were the second most important group of characters.

The period offered a number of answers to the question 'what is it about?' Productions introduced a political relevance, such as the homage to William and Mary and the allusions to Britain's expanding empire, and reinforced contemporary social mores—for example, the duty of women to their husbands and fathers. Above all, they sought to entertain, by casting popular actors and providing song and dance, spectacle, and comic business. The fairies may have appealed to Victorian tastes, but other aspects of the productions had foreign influences. Directors looked to the German composer Mendelssohn for music he had written for a German production and urged their designers to place Theseus's court in ancient Athens. Improvements in stage machinery and lighting made possible increasingly complex special effects.

New directions: Harley Granville Barker and Peter Brook

Two seminal twentieth-century productions freed *A Midsummer Night's Dream* from the restraints of the Victorian visual tradition and explored the text more carefully than had the typical nineteenth-century production.

Harley Granville Barker's *A Midsummer Night's Dream* (Savoy, 1914), the final production in his series of three Shakespeare plays, honoured the text: Barker omitted fewer than three lines and observed the order of scenes, stressed Shakespeare's poetry and speeded up delivery of lines. Unlike Tree, Barker drew upon Poel's experiments by adjusting the Savoy stage to imitate Elizabethan playing conditions and decorating it with painted curtains suggestive of place. The modifications made rapid and smooth scene changes possible. Non-realistic sets and innovative costumes revealed the influence of continental stage designers, not the Victorians' slavish imitation of archeological artefacts. For Titania and her attendants, Norman Wilkinson designed 'a green knoll, backed by silken draperies printed in greens, blues, and purples. Above its center was a large wreath of grapes, from within which descended a slender tent of green diaphanous curtains for Titania's bower. Lighted from above by colored electric bulbs, these blew in the breeze' (Williams, 151). Barker's golden fairies crowned with golden curls revealed an eastern influence quite alien to the fairy tradition their nineteenth-century counterparts both belonged to and influenced. Puck's red costume was a modified version of Elizabethan doublet and hose. Barker's casting also challenged nineteenth-century practices. Barker cast men as Oberon and Puck; both men and women attended Hippolyta and Titania, Theseus and Oberon. The restored text redressed the imbalance of plots characteristic of the nineteenth century and allowed Barker's cast to present more fully developed characters. The young lovers, especially, benefited from this restoration. Barker replaced Mendelssohn's score with authentic folk tunes compiled by Cecil Sharp from his study of English folk music; Sharp also supplied an authentic folk dance for the restored bergomask.

The text, stage, design, casting, music, and dance for Barker's production challenged audiences and directors to rethink their assumptions about staging *A Midsummer Night's Dream*. But world events intervened before the challenge could be taken up. After the First

World War, however, directors adopted some aspects of Barker's work. Harcourt Williams (Old Vic, 1929), for example, introduced swift scene changes, rapid delivery of a fairly complete text, and Sharp's music; but he read the play as an Elizabethan or Jacobean court wedding masque, evoked images of Kenilworth Castle, and imitated Inigo Jones's seventeenth-century designs in his fairy costumes. William Bridges-Adams (Stratford-upon-Avon, 1932) played a fairly full text, and Norman Wilkinson dressed the fairies in costumes reminiscent of Barker. But Bridges Adams reinstated Mendelssohn's music, and the Elizabethan costumes and set evoked Shakespeare's England. The act drop curtain, for example, featured a view of Charlecote, an Elizabethan mansion near Stratford, and Theseus's court gathered in a Tudor great hall.

Peter Brook's production (Royal Shakespeare Company, 1970), which toured the world during its three-year stage life, had a more immediate effect on directors and designers than had Barker's. A close study of Brook's *Dream* reveals a number of influences, including Barker. But the important point here is Brook's break with tradition, most notably through an austere set and minimal, suggestive hand properties; the use of acrobatics and circus properties; and his new answer to the question 'what is the play about?'

Brook's set was simple and allowed the action to flow swiftly and smoothly from scene to scene. Designer Sally Jacobs provided a brightly lit, three-sided white box with two doors flush against the upstage wall and a catwalk around the top edges of the box. Ladders in the upstage corners and in the midstage openings provided access between the two levels. From the flies four swings dropped for the fairies, cast as adult men and women; two trapezes lowered for Oberon and Puck; and, for Titania, a large, red-feathered bower. Oberon and Titania wore long satin gowns cut from the same simple pattern, in, respectively, rich purple and green. A Chinese acrobat's costume inspired Puck's baggy, bright yellow satin jumpsuit and royal blue skull cap. Demetrius and Lysander wore tie-dyed shirts and white trousers; Hermia and Helena, long white dresses faintly tie-dyed. The mechanicals wore contemporary working-class clothing, such as string vests, cloth caps, and braces. Dressed in greyish tunics and trousers, the four fairies were omnipresent, watching from their swings or the catwalk and creating the 'woods' by dangling large coiled springs (see Figure 3.4). Actors smoothly integrated circus-like tricks into a full, well-spoken text. (The National Sound Archives at the British Library holds a recording of a performance.) Swinging on a trapeze, Puck passed the 'love in idleness' blossom—a silver disc spinning on a plexi-glass rod—to the wand held by Oberon, who was also on a trapeze. The first half of the play closed on a joyfully unexpected note: as Mendelssohn's 'Wedding March' filled the auditorium, confetti and streamers rained down on Bottom and Titania, who were being flown aloft on her red feathery bower. Similarly, the show closed with a surprise emblematic of the bond that had developed between actor and audience: as Puck said 'Give me your hands, if we be friends' (Epilogue 15) the company left the stage to shake hands with the audience. The non-traditional methods of Brook's fresh staging restored magic to the *Dream*.

Influenced by Jan Kott's reading of *A Midsummer Night's Dream* in his *Shakespeare Our Contemporary* and by the 1960s sexual revolution, Brook's production addressed more fully than had his predecessors the sexuality of the four couples. By doubling Hippolyta and

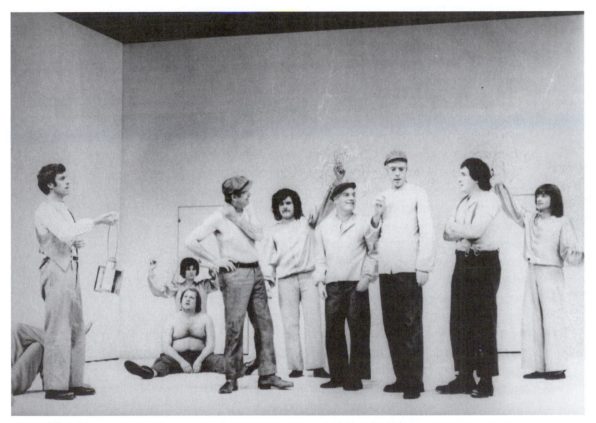

Fig. 3.4 The mechanicals rehearse their play. From left to right, they are: Terrence Hardiman as Starveling (holding lantern), Barry Stanton as Snug (seated), David Waller as Bottom, Norman Rodway as Snout, Philip Locke as Peter Quince, and Glynne Lewis as Flute. In the background three fairies look on. They hold aloft coiled springs, which were used in this production to create the impression of a wood. They are, from left to right: Celia Quicke as Peaseblossom, Hugh Keays Byrne as Cobweb, and John York as Mustardseed. *A Midsummer Night's Dream*, Royal Shakespeare Company, 1970. Director: Peter Brook. Designer: Sally Jacobs.

Titania, Theseus and Oberon, Brook freed Theseus and Hippolyta from civic responsibilities and allowed them, as Oberon and Titania, to explore the normally restrained subconscious aspects of their sexuality. In his staging of Titania's fascination with Bottom, Brook wittily exploited the sexual potency associated with the ass and pointed to a darker side of Theseus-Oberon's nature. In woods more jungle than fairyland the young couples experienced anxieties felt by many 1960s youth. The mechanicals were individuals, recognizable British working-class craftsmen, not one-dimensional comic types. One of the most important productions of Shakespeare in the twentieth century, Brook's *A Midsummer Night's Dream* was a hard act to follow.

Staging issues

The historical survey in the first section (pp. 540–3) touched lightly on staging issues, such as performance script, casting, design, and music. The second section, 'New Directions' (pp. 543–6), considered more closely how two important twentieth-century directors staged Shakespeare's early comedy. This final section focuses on design and casting, two of the many decisions directors must make, and suggests ways a decision contributes to the interpretation a production offers.

Together with their designers, Barker and Brook departed radically from their predecessors' pleasing pictures, especially in the forest scenes. Similarly startling—and more controversial—was the design for the production by the Canadian Robert Lepage, which played at London's National Theatre in 1992. Taking his queue from Titania's speech beginning 'These are the forgeries of jealousy' (2.1.81–117), in which she describes the disastrous effects that the fairy monarchs' quarrel has had on the natural world, Lepage filled the National's vast Olivier stage with a shallow pool of water surrounded by mud: 'the nine men's morris is filled up with mud' (2.1.98). Whereas Brook's actors had performed circus tricks, Lepage cast an acrobat as Puck. Critics generally agreed that her physical agility far exceeded her facility for speaking Shakespeare's verse; purists pointed out that her crab-like movement was more appropriate to Hamlet's reference to the crustacean ('if, like a crab', 2.2.202) than to the 'roasted crab', an apple, that Puck disguises as (2.1.48). Still others pondered the discomfort of acting in mud and water and the piles of dirty costumes to be laundered before the next performance. Trevor R. Griffiths explains how the mud and water illuminated the play: 'The great virtue of the set was that it placed moonlight and reflection at the centre of the staging and provided an extraordinary physical image of the quagmire of unconscious and repressed desires that lurked in its glutinous shallows' (p. 76).

John Hancock's reading (San Francisco, 1966) introduced an eclectic—and sometimes witty—mixture of popular culture and darker images. Williams records that Hancock included 'a cart full of corpses, plague victims' in the first scene; presented the fairies as 'puppet insects, hairy bats, cobwebs, and dolls with wings'; dressed Titania as Wonder

Woman, Helena in drag, and Oberon as 'a headless, faceless, menacing spirit'; and introduced 'steel-helmeted guards' to force the artisans from the palace 'while decadent courtiers cavorted to bed' (pp. 216, 217).

Instead of answering the question 'what is the play about?' with a concept that surprises and startles, many directors place the action in an historical period familiar to the audience and explore the theme of romantic love. Following in the footsteps of Franco Zeffirelli's and Kenneth Branagh's films of Shakespeare, Michael Hoffman (1998) scripted business and introduced extras to evoke sunny Italy and placed the various groups of characters in a realistic late nineteenth-century social milieu. For the BBC Shakespeare Series, Elijah Moshinsky (1981) set the play in early seventeenth-century England and created a domestic atmosphere for the Athenian scenes. As so often in the series, painters influenced filming: 'Settings, costuming, lighting, and camera angles re-create the feel of the Dutch masters in a dense, neo-romantic realism' (Williams, p. 250).

Moving the action to the recent past, Bill Alexander (RSC, 1986) contrasted a rigid, formal, male-dominated 1930s Athens with woods where the natural world—flowers, toadstools, tree trunks—grew unnaturally large and where gigantic leaves and a spider web served as seating. The contrast between Athens and the woods supported one of Alexander's dominant themes: the sexuality of Hippolyta and Titania.

John Caird (RSC, 1989) wittily evoked tradition. Mendelssohn's overture segued into a modern beat and then back again; the woods contained a pile of junk, modern 'fairy gold'; the fairies wore wings, tutus, and boots and chewed gum; Puck wore wings, a dishevelled school uniform, and Doc Martens; Oberon, like Puck, had Mr Spock ears and wore detachable wings; Puck mocked a wide range of fictional characters and actors. Stripped of sentimentality, Caird's production was witty, inventive, fun, thoughtful.

Ron Daniels (RSC 1981) set *A Midsummer Night's Dream* in the Victorian age, cast and costumed Hermia and Lysander to resemble Queen Victoria and Prince Albert, and introduced a ballet to celebrate the reunion of Titania and Oberon. The set exploited the Victorians' fascination with toy theatres: Theseus's court resembled a stage set; and the backstage area functioned as the woods. The fairies were puppets, their handlers visible. Through this technique the production encouraged the audience to consider the interrelationship between the play's theatrical metaphors and the importance of dreams.

Some directors have played *A Midsummer Night's Dream* within an interpolated framework. Perhaps alluding to the disputed assumption that *A Midsummer Night's Dream* was performed at an Elizabethan wedding (see Williams, pp. 1–37), Peter Hall (Stratford-upon-Avon, 1959) introduced an Elizabethan wedding as a framing device and staged the play as entertainment for the interpolated guests. He set *A Midsummer Night's Dream* on a mock Elizabethan stage that smoothly transformed from Theseus's palace (a Tudor great hall) to woodland, and dressed the characters in Elizabethan costumes such as those captured in Nicholas Hilliard's miniatures.

For his film of the play (1996), Adrian Noble scripted an elaborate framework. Falling asleep over an edition of *A Midsummer Night's Dream* illustrated by Arthur Rackham, a young boy dreams the events of the story. The child himself appears in most scenes as an auditor. The viewer is, apparently, meant to draw parallels between the transforming dreams of the interpolated child and those of Shakespeare's characters and also between the child's toy-stuffed bedroom and the chambers and forests and elaborate devices he imagines for Shakespeare's characters.

Illustrated throughout with various kinds of casting decisions, this chapter concentrates now on just two: doubling of roles and casting Bottom. Since Brook's seminal production, many directors have doubled Hippolyta and Titania, Theseus and Oberon. At the RSC, for example, Daniels (1981), Caird (1989) and Boyd (1999) doubled the roles. Varying the approach, Alexander (1986) doubled Hippolyta and Titania, but not Theseus and Oberon. The cast list called attention to the doubling by announcing the roles, played by Janet McTeer, as Hippolyta/Titania and Titania/Hippolyta. Uncomfortable in Athens and a reluctant bride, Hippolyta escaped to the woods where Gerard Murphy's sensual Oberon offered a tempting alternative to Richard Easton's rigid Theseus. The production closed on an ambiguous note: Hippolyta left Theseus's side to join Oberon for the song. Doubling Philostrate with Puck, productions such as Brook's and Boyd's call attention to similarities in their relationship with Theseus and Oberon. In Noble's stage production (RSC, 1994), the mechanicals, except for Bottom, doubled as fairies, a device that made them attendants on Bottom and Titania and suggested an imaginary life for them that transcended their work-a-day world and the 'tedious brief scene' (5.1.56) of 'Pyramus and Thisbe'. As part of his exploration of the subconscious, Boyd cast the same actors as cold, formal, silent attendants in Theseus's court and as lusty woodland fairies.

Although a character actor usually plays Bottom, this has not always been the case. In the nineteenth century, the company's comedian brought to the part his reputation for garnering laughter and the stage business he had borrowed, created, and honed over the years. Whether played by a comedian or character actor, Bottom is often presented as middle-aged, heavy set, and with a pleasant rather than a handsome face. Two recent productions have cast the role in unusual—and crowd-pleasing—ways. In 2001 in London's West End, television comedian Dawn French invested 'Mrs Bottom' with the personality traits of her best-known television creations. Translated, Mrs Bottom became not only an ass but masculine, a transformation that offered French an opportunity for comic business. French did not, however, capture Bottom's 'rare vision', that most crucial transformation. In equally unusual, but arguably more successful, casting, Kevin Kline was a handsome, dapper, opera-loving Bottom, attractive to the village women and inattentive to his long-suffering wife, whom Hoffman interpolated into the film. Transformed into an ass, Kline's Bottom was 'gentle' if not 'mortal' (3.1.121) and quite far from the 'vile thing' Oberon wished on Titania (2.2.40). By presenting Kline as Bottom and Michelle Pfeiffer as Titania, Hoffman demands that audiences look closely at this spell-bound couple.

Over its stage life since 1662, directors, designers, and actors have found many different answers to the questions 'whose play is it?' and 'what is it about?' Whatever their answers, their search has most often begun with the script itself: reading carefully for embedded stage directions and other clues; understanding the aural qualities in the lines; finding effective ways to convey unfamiliar words; and solving critical cruxes.

FURTHER READING

Griffiths, Trevor R. (ed.). *A Midsummer Night's Dream* (Cambridge: Cambridge University Press, 1996). In this volume of the series 'Shakespeare in Production', Griffiths provides an overview of performance history through Adrian Noble's production (1994); prefaces three scenes (1.1, 1.2, 2.1) with a lengthy description of various scenery and costume designs; and annotates the script with references to the staging practices of more than fifty directors and designers.

Halio, Jay L. *A Midsummer Night's Dream* (Manchester: Manchester University Press, 1994). In this volume of the series 'Shakespeare in Performance', Halio presents an overview of the *Dream*'s performance history; concentrates on twentieth-century productions, especially those by Peter Brook (1970), John Barton (1977), Ron Daniels (1981), Bill Alexander (1986), and Robert Lepage (1992); and discusses the films by Max Reinhardt and William Dieterle (1935) and Peter Hall (1968), as well as the television productions by Elijah Moshinsky (BBC, 1981) and Joseph Papp (1982).

Herbert, Ian (ed.). *Theatre Record*. Published every two weeks since 1981, when it was launched as *London Theatre Record, Theatre Record* compiles reviews from newspapers and periodicals of current productions in London and the regions.

Williams, Gary Jay. *Our Moonlight Revels: 'A Midsummer Night's Dream' in the Theatre* (Iowa City: University of Iowa Press, 1997). In this most thorough study of the *Dream* on the stage, Williams addresses the issue of the wedding-play myth and places more than four hundred years of performance history in cultural and historical contexts. Richly illustrated, the volume discusses performances in North America and Europe and examines also operas, ballets, and films based on Shakespeare's comedy.

Williamson, Sandra L. and James E. Person, Jr. (eds.). *Shakespearean Criticism*, Vol. 12 (Detroit: Gale Research, 1991). Focusing on *Dream* in performance, this selection presents criticism under three headings: 'Reviews and Retrospective Accounts of Selected Productions'; 'Comparisons and Overviews'; and 'Staging Issues'. The editors provide illustrations and a selected and annotated bibliography.

36 | **Performance criticism**

Miriam Gilbert

Like many other approaches to Shakespeare, performance criticism is a hybrid; it depends on textual criticism, on psychological analysis, on historical background, on cultural assumptions. But, at its centre, performance criticism involves the conversation between two kinds of 'close reading': close reading of the text in the way that actors, directors, designers read it, so as to create a performance, whether on stage or in the mind (from page to stage), and close reading of a performance so as to record it and then to see how it illuminates the text (from stage to page). Each reading enhances the other, and both extend the range of possible interpretations.

Consider the moment in Act Four, Scene Seven of *King Lear* when Lear, now in the care of his estranged daughter Cordelia instead of wandering around the heath in madness, 'fantastically dressed with wild flowers' (4.6.80), wakes up. The text reads:

> CORDELIA: Alack, alack!
>   'Tis wonder that thy life and wits at once
>   Had not concluded all. He wakes; speak to him.
> DOCTOR: Madam, do you; 'tis fittest.
>
>   (4.7.40-3)

The performance critic's first question might be utterly simple: how does Cordelia know that Lear is awake? And the obvious answer would be that the actor playing Lear has to stir or perhaps make a sound or in some way indicate that he is waking up. A second question might be: why won't Cordelia, who has just addressed twelve lines to the sleeping Lear, speak to him herself? That question asks us to think about Cordelia's emotional state at this moment, but also to think back to the first scene, when Lear banished Cordelia. Is Cordelia afraid of her father, or perhaps afraid of what he will be like when he awakes? Would an insane Lear be more distressing, or the seemingly sane but harsh father of Act One, Scene One?

A third, and much less frequently asked question, is: who is Cordelia speaking to? Most readers would assume that she is talking to the character who seems to answer her request with the reply, 'Madam, do you; 'tis fittest'. But who is that character? Depending on the version of the play used—the earlier quarto text, published during Shakespeare's lifetime, the later Folio text collected and published after Shakespeare's death, or the modern conflated text that uses material from both the quarto and Folio—the answer may vary. In the quarto text, he is a Doctor, but in the Folio he is simply a Gentleman. If, as many scholars now think, the Folio text represents Shake-speare's revisions of the quarto version, then perhaps the change from Doctor to Gentleman simply streamlines the play. Such is the opinion of editor R. A. Foakes, who notes that by using a Gentleman, 'presumably the same one who attends on Lear in 3.1 and on Cordelia in 4.4', Shakespeare gets rid of an 'unnecessary part'.[1]

But there's another man in the scene, Kent, Lear's faithful servant, still in the dis-guise he has worn since early in the play. Most of Cordelia's conversation earlier in the scene was with Kent; he defended her against Lear in the first scene, he is the one man she knows well, and she is anxious to reward his loyal service to her father. Although to a reader of the scene Kent may seemingly 'vanish', because he isn't typographically present at this moment, he's still very much present on stage. Doesn't it make just as much sense for an anxious Cordelia to turn to her staunchest ally, Kent, to ask for his help—and then for the Doctor/Gentleman, focusing just on Lear's condition, to insist that the daughter be the one to wake him?

I never imagined Cordelia's line as one addressed to Kent until I saw the National Theatre's 1990 production of *King Lear*, as Eve Matheson's Cordelia turned to Ian McKellen's Kent on 'speak to him'. Kent took one step forward, his face reflecting his happy anticipation of the moment when Lear would recognize him; when the doctor intervened, Kent stepped back, his face carefully recomposing itself into a servant's humility, but his pain still present. And this single moment—without any words—then made even more powerful Kent's scripted (but vain) attempts in the play's final scene to get Lear to recognize him. It is, after all, Kent who comes into the chaos of the last scene, asking for Lear and prompting the shocked recognition from Albany (and perhaps from the audience too) 'Great thing of us forgot' (5.3.235); it is Kent who tries to comfort Lear as the old king watches for signs of life from Cordelia; and although Lear does finally say to him, 'Are you not Kent?' (5.3.281), the sorrowing king cannot make the connection between Kent-in-disguise (as Caius) and the man he now sees. In the waking-up scene (4.7), Kent still wears his disguise, and Cordelia's request, 'Be better suited' (4.7.6), calls attention to it. But Kent insists 'Yet to be known shortens my made intent' (4.7.9)—and we may wonder what that 'intent' is. When he is invited to speak to Lear, and steps forward, we suddenly realize that he has been waiting for just this chance to achieve the recognition that he struggles for yet again in the final scene.

This moment—both on the page and on the stage—stands as a useful emblem of the way in which performance criticism can work. First of all, it's a moment that prompts basic questions: what is happening and who is speaking? Secondly, as is frequently the case when we stop and ask those seemingly basic questions, we find out that the answers aren't so simple and that we have to make choices. Thirdly, when we think about why we make the choices, we find ourselves working back and forth between page and stage in fascinating ways.

Consider the question of whether the man who says 'Madam, do you; 'tis fittest', is the Doctor or a Gentleman, a question initially raised by the fact that *King Lear* exists in two different texts, the quarto and Folio. Certainly the costume designer will want to know, but the problem is more complicated. If he is the same Gentleman who talked with Kent in Act Three, Scene One about Lear's 'contending with the fretful elements' and his 'heart-struck injuries' (3.1.14, 17), the audience will recognize him as a perceptive and sympathetic observer. Perhaps he is the same knight who, back in Act One, Scene Four, spoke with Lear about the lack of 'ceremonious affection' (1.4.50–1) he was receiving at Goneril's castle, the man who asserted 'my duty cannot be silent when I think your highness wronged' (1.4.56). Since he brings in the sleeping Lear, he may seem the logical person to speak to—and, as a servant who has always taken care of Lear, he may feel that Cordelia, Lear's daughter, should speak first to her father.

On the other hand, if he is the Doctor, who appears in the quarto first in Act Four, Scene Four, his costume and his manner, as well as his language, may create a sense of professional competence. In Act Four, Scene Four, the Doctor speaks authoritatively about the possibility of curing Lear: 'Our foster-nurse of nature is repose, / The which he lacks. That to provoke in him, / Are many simples operative, whose power / Will close the eye of anguish' (4.4.13–16). He seems to be someone who has come from France with Cordelia, who serves her and is trusted by her, since she says to him 'Be governed by your knowledge, and proceed / I' the sway of your own will' (4.7.19–20). Such a person might seem the reasonable one for Cordelia to ask to speak to Lear, which is how the scene is usually played, but equally, that professional confidence may also lead him to assume he knows best. Both choices are available—in part because we have two different texts—and both make sense.

Eventually a director will need to decide whether this character is the Doctor or the Gentleman, and here that question might well be bound up with the problem of whether Cordelia asks this person, whoever he is, or Kent, to speak to the king, and why he speaks as he does. I can see perhaps the greater likelihood of Cordelia asking the Doctor to speak, especially given her line about his knowledge. And equally I can imagine the Doctor countering Cordelia's request to Kent with his professional demeanour—the doctor knows best. The Gentleman (in the Folio) seems to me less likely as someone for Cordelia to speak to, but, if she does, then his response, 'Madam, do you; 'tis fittest', sounds exactly right, as he backs away from taking on too much responsibility.

One might ask why the choice to have Cordelia speak to Kent has been made so rarely; I've seen it once in over thirty years of playgoing—from Peter Brook and John Scofield (1962) to Tony Church (in the 1974 Buzz Goodbody production) to John Wood (1990), Robert Stephens (1993) and Ian Holm (1997), as well as the various film versions—and only with the Deborah Warner production at the National with Brian Cox did the reading arise. In large part, I'm tempted to say 'how many productions have an actor of the status of Ian McKellen in the role of Kent?' Perhaps McKellen's own magnetism on stage prompted the actress playing Cordelia to speak to him; perhaps he even suggested it? We don't know. All I know is that, having seen that choice once, it now makes so much sense to me, and is so heartbreaking a moment in terms of Kent's story, that when I now read the play, Cordelia speaks to Kent.

As you can tell from this example, performance criticism is an ongoing conversation. Many of the questions asked by a performance critic of the text are those that an actor or a director or a designer might well ask, and they stimulate thought about a performance in the mind's theatre—or, more importantly, a variety of performances. And almost always those questions begin with a specific moment, since interpretation grows out of the accumulation of details. The moment may be a gesture, implied by the text, but not given in a stage direction; when King Lear says to Cordelia, in this same scene 'Be your tears wet?' (4.7.72), he almost *has* to reach out to touch her face because 'wet' is a touch word that leads the actor to the gesture.

Or the moment may be the response to a command. Take the line 'give me your hand', which occurs, in those words, or very close to them, in about thirty-two of Shakespeare's plays. It's a line that so clearly implies a response we may be tempted to slide over the question of what that response actually is, or might be. When Duncan, welcomed by Lady Macbeth to the castle, says 'Give me your hand' (*Macbeth*, 1.6.28), we assume that she does so, acting the role of the gracious hostess. Or when Antonio, speaking what he imagines will be his last words before Shylock kills him, says to his dear friend Bassanio, 'Give me your hand' (*The Merchant of Venice*, 4.1.260) we may confidently see, in our mind, a handshake, perhaps even an embrace.

But when Petruccio spins a false account of his first meeting with Kate—'She hung about my neck, and kiss on kiss / She vied so fast, protesting oath on oath, / That in a twink she won me to her love'—and then speeds on to plan the marriage, 'Give me thy hand, Kate. I will unto Venice, / To buy apparel 'gainst the wedding day' (*The Taming of the Shrew*, 2.1.300–2, 306–7) it's unlikely that Kate will meekly extend her hand; she may have no words with which to counter Petruccio's story, but she certainly wouldn't take his hand.

In *Measure for Measure*, the same line becomes a hotly debated moment near the end of the play, as the Duke, after revealing that the muffled prisoner is none other than Claudio, alive, not dead, says to Claudio's sister, Isabella, 'Give me your hand, and say you will be mine' (5.1.486). The text offers no reply from Isabella, neither in words nor in stage directions. For many years, directors, actors, and scholarly readers assumed that because the Duke said 'Give me your hand', she did. But in John Barton's 1970 production, Estelle Kohler's Isabella confronting Sebastian Shaw's Duke, refused his offer and was left alone on stage in (to quote N. W. Bawcutt) 'obvious shock and bewilderment'.[2] A few years later, in Jonathan Miller's touring production which I saw at the National Theatre in 1974, Gillian Barge's Isabella shrank from the Duke's offer. There are other possibilities—Paola Dionisotti (RSC, 1978) flung off her veil; Juliet Stevenson (RSC, 1983) accepted the Duke's offer with real warmth, a response set up by the careful establishment of a growing relationship; Stella Gonet (RSC, 1994) slapped the Duke's face and then kissed him. My point is that because the moment is left undefined in the text, performance not only can, but *must*, make an interpretative choice for what is silent in the text.

Performance criticism values those moments of choice, and looks for them. Most of the examples I've given so far are clearly visible in the text, even if, as with Kent, one wonders why the questions haven't been asked much earlier. But performance critics often need to consider what the text really says, and here modern editions can be misleading precisely because they eliminate possibilities. Take, for instance, the opening stage direction for Act Four, Scene Six of *Troilus and Cressida*, the scene in which Cressida is brought to the Greek camp by Diomedes and Ajax engages in the abortive duel with Achilles. In both quarto and Folio, the stage direction reads: 'Enter Ajax armed, Achilles, Patroclus, Agamemnon, Menelaus, Ulysses, Nestor, Calchas, etc.' But any number of modern editors, perhaps noting that Calchas, who is Cressida's father, and a defector from Troy to the Greek army, doesn't have any lines in the scene, quietly eliminate him from the stage direction. Or perhaps, these editors take into account Diomedes's line after Cressida has been kissed by all the Greek commanders except for Ulysses, 'Lady, a word. I'll bring you to your father' (4.6.54). One can imagine the editor thinking, 'if Diomedes is going to bring Cressida to Calchas, then he can't be on stage, he must be somewhere else'. So, with a stroke of the blue pencil, Calchas is removed from the stage directions, and only a careful reader of the textual variants in the footnotes may find that, according to the two earliest texts of the play we have, Calchas was quite possibly, I would even say, quite probably, meant to be there.

But his presence raises all sorts of questions—and it's precisely those questions which become visible when you think of stage, rather than page. For a start, if he is there, why doesn't he speak to Cressida? Or she to him? If he is present, he might well be expected to speak. His non-intervention as he watches his daughter with the Greek generals—whether she is kissed or kissing—is something to consider. Perhaps he already knows what will happen to her, and certainly he seems utterly compliant with Diomedes a few scenes later. Is he then a willing accomplice, even if this scene is played as one where Cressida is kissed against her will? Or, perhaps he is shocked and surprised, but, given his status as a defector, dares not speak. Or, to take a very different view of the situation, perhaps Cressida sees her father and ignores him, turning to flirt with the Greek generals. Whatever the reading, eliminating Calchas from the scene erases a whole series of difficult questions about personal relationships, possible betrayals, and how men see women, questions that the play as a whole seems determined to raise, if not to answer.

If textual editors can make characters on the page vanish from the stage, theatrical directors can also do the reverse. What happens on stage when someone appears who isn't scripted in the scene? In 1993, David Thacker's RSC production of *The Merchant of Venice* took place in a very contemporary world of commerce and banking. David Calder's Shylock was at first supremely comfortable in this world, greeting Antonio as an equal, assured and confident. Dressed in a smart suit, identifiable as a Jew only by his yarmulke, he seemed very much an assimilated Jew rather than an outsider. And, as if to underline that point, Nick Simon's Tubal, though not textually in the scene, was sitting in the office. Wearing a long dark overcoat, he seemed much more obviously 'Jewish'. Even though he might have looked like a poor relation, Shylock referred to him ('Tubal, a wealthy Hebrew of my tribe' (1.3.52)) as if he, and not Shylock, had the ready money. This Tubal appeared again in 3.3., the short scene in which Antonio begs Shylock to listen to him. Again in the text, Tubal isn't in the scene, but in the 1993 production he was, and Shylock was extremely aware of Tubal's silent disapproval. Indeed, Shylock's first line, 'Tell not me of mercy' (3.3.1), was delivered to Tubal, rather than, as usual, to Antonio, and one imagined that Tubal might have been trying, offstage, to get Shylock to change his mind. Shylock's line, 'The Duke shall grant me justice' (3.3.8) was also spoken to Tubal, as if asking for some kind of reassurance, but when Shylock insisted 'I'll have my bond, and therefore speak no more' (3.3.13) Tubal left, underscoring Shylock's isolation.

By inserting Tubal into two scenes, the director first made us aware of the difference in social status and, it seemed, social acceptability of the two men, and then, second, used Tubal's exit as a comment on Shylock's behaviour. Similarly, Trevor Nunn brought Tubal into the trial scene of the 1999 production of *The Merchant of Venice* at the Royal National Theatre, although he's not mentioned as being there in the text. Nunn made Tubal's presence felt by creating an exit for him at a crucial moment. When Shylock insisted that he would cut off Antonio's flesh 'Nearest his heart', and Portia, after looking at the bond, agreed, 'It is so' (4.1.249, 250), Tubal left, as if unable to take any more of Shylock's attempt to kill Antonio; the surprise on Shylock's face indicated that he hadn't expected such a desertion.

These examples, of comparatively minor characters appearing but not speaking on stage, suggest the power of a silent presence to comment on the actions of a major character. But theatrical silence can also illuminate a minor character in unexpected ways. Take an example from *Hamlet*. It's difficult to imagine that actors are queueing up to play Cornelius, one of the two ambassadors sent by Claudius to Norway; he's got, at best, one line which, in the second quarto of *Hamlet* he shares with Valtemand ('In that and all things will we show our duty', 1.2.40), and which, in the Folio, is given to Valtemand alone. Indeed, the Folio change looks forward to the second scene in which the two men appear, because there Cornelius gets no lines at all. Though Claudius seems to greet both men, 'Welcome, my good friends', he then singles out Valtemand for the report: 'Say Valtemand, what from our brother Norway?' (2.2.58–9), and Valtemand responds for twenty-one lines.

Cornelius' silence probably goes unremarked in most productions, but it can also become part of a power struggle, as it did in Stephen Pimlott's 2001 production for the RSC, where Cornelius and Valtemand were clearly differentiated, by age and by race. Cornelius (young and black) began to reply to Claudius in Act One, Scene Two, but then Valtemand (middle-aged and white) jumped in and finished the line. Claudius flourished the dispatch to the King of Norway, but as Cornelius reached for it, Valtemand grabbed it. And when they returned in Act Two, Scene Two, Valtemand proudly handed over the letter from Norway, while Cornelius stood far to one side, his face expressing his disapproval and his misgivings of the 'deal' with Norway. As Valtemand left with other members of the court applauding him, Cornelius walked offstage in a different direction, alone. Given the atmosphere of Claudius's court which, in this production, seemed like the headquarters of a political party, such a power struggle made sense. Perhaps the director's idea of the world of *Hamlet* as a supremely political world generated the Cornelius/Valtemand struggle; perhaps the rehearsal experience led to the moment when the actor playing Valtemand, trying to say the first line together with his fellow actor, found himself cutting off the first one. But no matter how the staging developed, the text allows for the small, but memorable underlining of this relationship, and Cornelius and Valtemand, while not yet moving into the imagination the way that Rosencrantz and Guildenstern have done, are now in my mind more than simple functionaries.

The previous examples all demonstrate what I've called the conversation between page and stage, some growing out of a close reading of the lines, some spurred by a choice on stage. Both the play-text and the performance-text contribute to this conversation, and we need not insist on privileging one over the other; the play-text is the place where scholarship and theatrical invention begin, but not where they end. Good readers—whether writing about the play or presenting it on stage—look for every clue they can find, and intensive scrutiny of the play-text produces multiple performance-texts.

Let me focus on a familiar scene and ask a performance critic's question that can help us to imagine performance and thus open up interpretative possibilities. The scene is the 'nunnery scene' in *Hamlet* (3.1), when, after 'To be or not to be', Hamlet suddenly sees Ophelia who has, of course, been 'loosed' by Polonius for just such a meeting. There are many questions one can ask about the scene, ranging from 'does Hamlet know that he's being watched?' to 'what is the past relationship of Hamlet and Ophelia?' But starting with a seemingly trivial, but concrete, question can lead us to larger issues. Ophelia's line, 'My lord, I have remembrances of yours / That I have longèd long to redeliver' (3.1.95–6) could lead us to ask ourselves 'what are those remembrances?'

In Act One, Scene Three, Ophelia says that Hamlet has 'made many tenders / Of his affection to me' (99–100) but the phrase is tantalizingly unspecific. And in Act Two, Scene One, after Ophelia reports on Hamlet's behaviour in her closet, she tells Polonius that she 'did repel his letters' (110). We then hear one of those letters read by Polonius in Act Two, Scene Two, and Polonius, perhaps speaking of what he has heard from Ophelia, perhaps adding his own details, says that he told her she should 'receive no tokens' (2.2.144). But what are those tokens, or tenders, or remembrances? An earlier play, *A Midsummer Night's Dream*, offers us a detailed list of a lover's tokens as Egeus angrily catalogues the gifts to his daughter Hermia from her suitor Lysander: 'bracelets of thy hair, rings, gauds, conceits, / Knacks, trifles, nosegays, sweetmeats' (1.1.33–4). In *The Winter's Tale*, Autolycus's song offers a range of gifts 'for my lads to give their dears', including fabrics, masks, and jewellery, while in *Love's Labour's Lost*, the male lovers send the women they are wooing even more upscale gifts of gloves, pearls, and diamonds along with their love-verses.

Are Hamlet's gifts the same? A group of university teachers with whom I raised the question, 'what are the remembrances?', provided even more answers. For many, letters were the first choice and the ones with the greatest textual justification, since we know that Hamlet wrote letters to Ophelia. Others chose flowers (usually dried and pressed), this time looking forward in the text to Gertrude's description of Ophelia's death. Some chose jewellery, a more personal, even intimate kind of gift. As these teachers pondered the question, they saw new problems:

> I have assumed that the tokens were letters, verses, maybe a commonplace book with passages Hamlet has recorded, a speech from a play he'd seen, a description of a site visited on his travels to the university—whatever. I now realize that I have assumed that he would give or send to Ophelia what he values. His self-absorption has made it difficult for me to imagine his spending time selecting some token that Ophelia herself might like other than writing; he would trust that she values what he values, or values anything that comes from him.
>
> (Judith Clark, Stephens College)

And indeed, as soon as people started thinking concretely about the remembrances, new questions appeared. Are they visible right away? If Ophelia is returning jewellery, might she even be wearing it, perhaps concealed? If she has lots of letters, how does she manage to hold them as well as the book that Polonius gives her? The most imaginative description of the remembrances came from Professor Kirk Hendershott (Olivet College), who started with what he called the 'conventional' idea (the packet of letters), moved to the notion of a scrapbook, and then finally came up with a huge cardboard box, filled with everything Hamlet had ever sent Ophelia: travel souvenirs, postcards, poems, ticket stubs, snapshots, dried flowers, and 'the shirt Hamlet let her wear when she got soaked in that rainstorm'. Professor Hendershott even stipulated that 'the actor playing Hamlet should actually have to write the poems out and give them to his Ophelia, leaving them for her in a mailbox set up early in the rehearsal period'. That idea isn't simply a professorial speculation; Sam West, playing Hamlet for the RSC in 2001, did indeed write letters to Ophelia, building the relationship between the characters from their opening conversation at his father's funeral.

Once you start thinking so concretely, other questions emerge: what does Ophelia do with the remembrances, and, perhaps more interestingly, what does Hamlet do with them? Are they sentimental objects only to her? Or can they touch him as well? Does he even look at the remembrances? Does he toss them away? If there are letters, does he re-read them? tear them up? throw them (or anything else) at Ophelia? Any answer involves making a choice not just about the scene but about the Hamlet/Ophelia relationship, and also about the Polonius/Ophelia relationship. Even the question that would occur to any stage manager, 'how will the remembrances, whatever they are, and wherever they end up, get off stage?' has ramifications. Does Ophelia, trying to make sense of Hamlet's behaviour, pick up and take away the remembrances? Or are they as 'overthrown' as Hamlet's mind now seems to be? Obviously choices will vary, and the period in which any given production is set will help to determine what the remembrances are and how they are used. The important point to note is that there *are* choices, and the performance critic I have described works, from page to stage, and from stage to page, to discover those choices, and then to think about their implications.

My approach to performance criticism derives both from the academy (the work of J. L. Styan and John Russell Brown) and from the theatre, particularly the workshops and rehearsals of Royal Shakespeare Company actors, who developed their approach under the direction of John Barton. Barton's dictum, that the words do not 'pre-exist in the text',[3] but rather must be the words that the character finds, assumes that Shakespearian characters exist in a comprehensible, psychologically valid, and primarily realistic world. Obviously such an assumption—while helpful for many actors—is not the only one to make about Shakespeare's plays. Other versions of performance criticism exist, and stress different, though related, issues. Alan Dessen's work with Elizabethan theatrical practice cautions against 'inappropriate assumptions, conventions and expectations' and then demonstrates the usefulness of examining early modern stage conventions seriously. Steven Mullaney emphasizes both the power and the limitations of the theatre as a social/cultural institution, as he considers the placement of Elizabethan theatres outside the city of London, and across the river Thames. The social implications of the stage itself emerge in Robert Weimann's discussion of what he sees as the 'bi-fold authority' of divided representation, on a stage that both privileged certain forms of authority and yet subverted them through disguise, clowning, and frequent reminders that the audience was, after all, watching a play. Yet another approach to performance criticism deals with the afterlife of Shakespeare's plays in contemporary stage, film, and video productions (Barbara Hodgdon's work is central here), finding in our own performance practice new ways of understanding— and often challenging—Shakespeare's text. And indeed, performance criticism continues to flourish and develop precisely because the texts continue to surprise us, as productions cause us to see and hear familiar lines in new ways.

FURTHER READING

Barton, John. *Playing Shakespeare* (London: Methuen, 1984) This (edited) transcript of Barton's televised workshops with noted RSC actors demonstrates his approach to finding action and characterization through close work with the language of the plays.

Brown, John Russell. *Shakespeare's Plays in Performance* (London: Edward Arnold, 1966). *Shakespeare's Dramatic Style* (New York: Barnes and Noble, 1971). These books offer both general and specific examples of performance criticism, working first with principles that apply to many plays, and then examining individual plays or characters in more detail.

David, Richard. *Shakespeare in the Theatre* (Cambridge: Cambridge University Press, 1978). This collection of reviews written originally for *Shakespeare Survey* offers particularly fine examples of how performance criticism both preserves and interprets production choices.

Hodgdon, Barbara. 'Katherina Bound, or Play(K)ating the Strictures of Everyday Life'. In her *The Shakespeare Trade: Performances and Appropriations* (Philadelphia: University of Pennsylvania Press, 1998). Hodgdon's essay brings together a variety of productions of *The Taming of the Shrew*, from film to theatre to television parody, demonstrating how the central issues of the play have been repackaged and rewritten in the twentieth century.

Players of Shakespeare 1, ed. Philip Brockbank (Cambridge: Cambridge University Press, 1985); *Players of Shakespeare 2*, ed. Russell Jackson and Robert Smallwood (Cambridge: Cambridge University Press, 1988); *Players of Shakespeare 3*, ed. Russell Jackson and Robert Smallwood (Cambridge: Cambridge University Press, 1993); *Players of Shakespeare 4*, ed. Robert Smallwood (Cambridge: Cambridge University Press, 1998). These essays by Royal Shakespeare Company actors take an in-depth look at an individual character, showing how the actor approached the role, and, often, how the thinking about the character changed during the rehearsal process and the production's run.

Shaughnessy, Robert, ed. *Shakespeare in Performance* (London and New York: Macmillan and St. Martin's Press, 2000). This useful compendium of critical essays offers a wide spectrum of approaches to performance criticism, including essays by J. L. Styan, Alan C. Dessen, W. B. Worthen, Robert Weimann, Kathleen McLuskie, Graham Holderness, Michael D. Bristol, Alan Sinfield, Barbara Hodgdon, and Simon Shepherd, as well as a helpful bibliography.

Smallwood, Robert. 'Directors' Shakespeare'. In *Shakespeare: An Illustrated Stage History*, ed. J. Bate and R. Jackson (Oxford: Oxford University Press, 1996), pp. 176–96. By looking at questions of directorial intervention (or the lack of same), Smallwood offers not only vivid readings of individual productions but also focuses on recurring issues of performance: textual cuts and rearrangement, casting, choice of space, creation of opening and closing moments.

Styan, J. L. *Shakespeare's Stagecraft* (Cambridge: Cambridge University Press, 1967). This book offers the most basic, and still, in some ways the most comprehensive approach to mining the written text for clues to the performance-text.

NOTES

1. R. A. Foakes (ed.). *King Lear* (Thomas Nelson and Sons Ltd., 1997), footnotes, pp. 349, 352.
2. N. W. Bawcutt (ed.). *Measure for Measure* (Oxford University Press, 1991), p. 39.
3. John Barton, *Playing Shakespeare* (Methuen, 1984), p. 18.

READING: *The Taming of the Shrew*

To illustrate a more sustained application of performance criticism, first thinking from page to stage, and then from stage to page, let's turn to two scenes from *The Taming of the Shrew*. These are, not accidentally, the beginning and end of the Katherine/Petruccio story, namely their first meeting and their final public appearance. These scenes are obviously ones that raise a number of major interpretative questions about the play's central relationship; they are immensely playable in a variety of ways (the first meeting is a favourite one for acting classes); and they are also useful because they focus attention on the question of what actors must do in a scene as contrasted with what they can do, or, what is 'required' and what is 'allowed'.

The first meeting (Act Two, Scene One), between the shrew whose sharp tongue and difficult behaviour we have already seen and the blunt wooer who announces his desire to 'wive it wealthily in Padua' spans about one hundred lines, beginning with Petruccio's short soliloquy as he waits to meet Katherine, 'I'll attend her here, / And woo her with some spirit when she comes', and ending with her father's re-entrance (166–272). And what happens in those one hundred lines? Memories of Zeffirelli's exuberant 1966 film with Richard Burton and Elizabeth Taylor linger in the mind; in that version, the scene becomes an extended chase up stairs, into a loft well supplied with feathers, apples, hams, ropes, doors—and out onto the rooftop of Baptista's house. Hitting, tussling, and general struggle dominate the scene, whether one thinks of Katherine's attack on pieces of furniture at the beginning, or Petruccio's barging through doors; not once but twice does Petruccio swing across the space on a rope; not once but three times does someone fall into the feathers (which suggest a featherbed). And while one may sniff and say, 'Oh, film' or 'Oh, Zeffirelli, never one to use text when pictures are at hand', tempestuous versions of this scene are equally familiar on stage: Jonathan Pryce wrestling with Paola Dionisotti in 1978; Alun Armstrong being thrown into an onstage swimming pool by Sinead Cusack in 1982; Michael Siberry, Josie Lawrence, and the toppling sofas of 1995—just to cite several RSC productions.

Yet, when one looks at the text, what's noticeable is that there is just *one* stage direction dictating a particular action. After Petruccio's bawdy insult, 'What, with my tongue in your tail? Nay, come again' and his attempt to restart the conversation, perhaps on politer lines, 'Good Kate, I am a gentleman' (214–15) Kate, as the stage direction says, '*strikes him*' The gesture is deliberate, since she also says 'That I'll try' (215), as if testing the limits of his gentleman-like behaviour. Even if there were no printed stage direction, Petruccio's line tells us what has happened, 'I swear I'll cuff you if you strike again' (216). That single gesture must be in the scene, unless the lines are cut; *it's required*.

But when one asks, 'what is *allowed*, suggested, or implied?' the possibilities become much greater. A conservative reading finds many lines implying physical action, as the italicized words below suggest:

KATHERINE: Moved? In good time. Let him that moved you hither
   Re-move you hence. (193-4)

PETRUCCIO: Come, *sit* on me.
KATHERINE: Asses are made to *bear*, and so are you.
PETRUCCIO: Women are made to *bear*, and so are you. (196-8)

PETRUCCIO: Alas, good Kate, I will not *burden* thee. (200)

PETRUCCIO: O slow-winged turtle, shall a buzzard *take* thee? (205)

KATHERINE: If I be waspish, best beware my *sting*.
PETRUCCIO: My remedy is then to *pluck* it out. (208-9)

The text also suggests that Kate tries twice to leave the stage: 'And so farewell' (212); 'I chafe you if I tarry. Let me go' (234). The second line might imply that he's blocking her way, but the verb 'chafe,' with its connotation of irritating rubbing, could also suggest physical restraint—and 'let me go' works with either reading. Certainly Petruccio's line immediately preceding this second attempt, 'Nay, hear you, Kate. In sooth, you scape not so' (233) could set up a chase, or an attempt to keep her from 'escaping'.

Other lines (below) suggest Kate's facial responses, the first one directly (i.e. the actor playing Kate must do something to prompt Petruccio's line), the second either directly or perhaps indirectly (if Kate doesn't frown, or bite her lip, then the line seems sarcastic).

PETRUCCIO: Nay, come, Kate, come. You must not look so sour. (224)

PETRUCCIO: Thou canst not frown. Thou canst not look askance,
   Nor bite the lip, as angry wenches will. (240-1)

And Petruccio's question, 'Why does the world report that Kate doth limp?' (245) opens up a whole range of possible actions: Kate could once again try to walk away from him, and his question, addressed to a non-limping Kate, could seem so perverse as to stop her; Kate could try to leave and Petruccio could physically stop her, perhaps even by lunging forward to catch her by the leg so that the 'limp' is something he causes; often in production, an enraged Kate goes to attack Petruccio on the preceding line (when he's complimenting her on being 'soft, and affable') and winds up injuring herself, so that the limp is real.

And yet, even with all of the physical possibilities in the scene, the fact remains that there is only one scripted stage direction, '*she strikes him*'. So it's also possible to play the scene in such a way that Petruccio never touches Kate at all; 'I chafe you if I tarry. Let me go', could be spoken by Kate to a man blocking her way rather than actually holding on to her. Though in 1987, Brian Cox did indeed grab Fiona Shaw by the wrists to keep her from going, he then sat her down and let go of her hand. Anton Lesser's Petruccio, in 1992, never touched Amanda Harris's Kate in this scene; the same forbearance extended into 3.3, where Petruccio forcibly makes Kate leave the wedding (in that production Grumio picked her up and carried her out, not Petruccio). The fact that she tries to leave twice still remains, but a Petruccio can hold her there in some other way than by force. The long speech that Petruccio launches into after 'I chafe you if I tarry. Let me go', begins with 'No, not a whit. I find you passing gentle' and continues with a series of compliments:

> 'Twas told me you were rough, and coy, and sullen.
> And now I find report a very liar,
> For thou art pleasant, gamesome, passing courteous.
>
> (236-8)

If Kate is being held against her will and trying to get away, then 'rough' and 'sullen' probably suit her, and Petruccio will get an enormous laugh on 'passing courteous'. But perhaps he keeps her from leaving with 'passing gentle', because she's never had anyone describe her that way before. And perhaps she stays, rather than leaves, because the compliments—however ironic—are nonetheless nice to hear.

So, what the scene *requires* and what the scene *allows* are two points, spread over a very wide continuum of choices, and a particular production will define at least the beginning of the relationship in part by the amount of physical confrontation on stage. The ending of the play (Act Five, Scene Two), offers a similarly wide range of opportunities, although here the choices are mainly those of the actor playing Kate. Her last speech is, famously or infamously, a speech of submission, acquiescence, perhaps recognition—and it can be bitter, playful, heartfelt, or insincere. What the actor chooses to do with the speech (or what the director chooses for her to do) depends on many more factors than the playing of the first scene between Kate and Petruccio. In the first meeting, each character has less baggage to carry around; each has been seen before, but neither has seen the other before. But by the end of the play, the relationship between Kate and Petruccio is frequently quite clear; indeed, in any number of productions, the audience already knows, usually from 4.6 when Kate agrees to call the sun the moon, that Kate has decided to agree with Petruccio. Of course, she may just be playing his game with him, and with a touch of sarcasm, but she has capitulated once, at least. So we may not be surprised by what Kate is doing in the final scene—although one frequently sees Petruccios who aren't sure what she will do or say, and who wait in some anxiety at this moment. Furthermore, although the *words* of the speech are about the wife's duty to her husband, echoing lines from Ephesians and from the marriage service,[1] the *act* of speaking the words is, paradoxically, a moment of power. No other character in the play gets forty-four lines of uninterrupted text; Kate is unquestionably the centre of everyone's attention. She gets to lecture the Widow and Bianca, thereby scoring some points, in public, off the women who previously have scorned her.

The last lines of the speech are the only ones that actually require a gesture:

> Then vail your stomachs, for it is no boot,
> And place your hands below your husband's foot,
> In token of which duty, if he please,
> My hand is ready, may it do him ease.
>
> (180-3)

That gesture, significantly, is an outstretched hand. One might think of the entire play as an extended riff on 'give me your hand'—not only Petruccio's earlier request of Kate, but the whole notion of wooing a wife, whether by Petruccio, Hortensio, Gremio, Lucentio, or Tranio-in-disguise. And just as the response to that line, 'give me your hand', can vary, so too can Petruccio's response to the gesture that the line forces Kate to make. If she stoops and actually places her hand underneath his foot, as in 1978, he may look uncomfortable and quickly move his foot away, as Jonathan Pryce did. If she extends her hand to him as Fiona Shaw did to Brian Cox, it could be a gesture of equality, leading to a handshake, then a kiss. And if, as in the 1995 production, the production wants to make Petruccio horrified by what he's done (see Figure 3.5), then the director will cut his verbal response, 'Why there's a wench! Come on, and kiss me, Kate' (184), and have him stagger away, and then collapse (and, in 1995, revert to the role of Christopher Sly).

In two well-known film versions, both Kates managed to escape humiliation. Mary Pickford, the 1929 Kate had, in the previous scene, already physically vanquished Douglas Fairbanks' Petruccio, throwing a stool at him so that he collapsed moaning on the floor of their bedroom; Pickford's Kate gently cradled Petruccio's head as he looked up, dazed, asking 'The sun is shining bright?' (a line not in Shakespeare's text, though derived from Kate's line 'I know it is the sun that shines so bright' (4.6.5)). That scene is followed immediately by the banquet at Baptista's house, with Fairbanks sitting in a chair, his rakish smile of confidence contrasting noticeably with the bandage wrapped around his head, while Pickford speaks thirteen lines of Kate's speech (150–8, 165–8) in a voice dripping with fake sincerity. After proclaiming that the woman must 'serve, love, and obey', she then gives a big wink to Bianca and the camera moves in for the close-up just to make sure the film audience gets the point as well.

Zeffirelli's film (1966) uses Kate's audience even more fully. While most directors (and actors) seem to overlook Petruccio's command, 'Katherine, I charge thee tell these headstrong women / What duty they do owe their lords and husbands' (5.2.134–5), those lines, though not spoken by Richard Burton's Petruccio, serve as the central motivation for Elizabeth Taylor's Kate. Resplendent in an ornate gold headdress, long gold earrings, and a low-cut red dress, she physically forces both Bianca and the Widow into the room and then pushes them away from her, clearly relishing her opportunity to scold women who had earlier tried to humiliate her. She loves being able to cut them down in public, using a line such as 'Thy husband is thy lord, thy life, thy keeper' (150) not as a statement of feminine submission but as a weapon with which to attack these women who have defied their new husbands. Occasionally her tone of strident lecture softens, as when she explains that a wife's obedience is 'too little payment for so great a debt' (158) turning her gaze away from the women to look straight at us, and, we assume, at the offscreen Petruccio. She then turns back into the tough-minded woman, physically grabbing Bianca and the Widow, pulling them up towards the banquet table and then forcing them to kneel as she instructs them to 'place your hands below your husband's foot' (181). When she kneels, with a graceful gesture and a dewy-eyed look of love, 'may it do him ease' (183) she is still in total command of the situation: more beautiful, more assured, more comfortable, than anyone else around. Petruccio takes her hand in his, and kisses her; she eagerly returns Petruccio's kiss; and then the camera moves to focus on a smiling Petruccio, exulting in his triumph. He

Fig. 3.5 In the final scene of *The Taming of the Shrew*, Katherine (Josie Lawrence) kneels to Petruccio (Michael Siberry), her hand outstretched in submission, the money he has wagered on her visible on the floor. Though Petruccio has commanded Katherine to speak, he is clearly abashed by what she says. The 1995 Royal Shakespeare Company production was directed by Gale Edwards.

turns back to Kate, but all he can see is a crowd of wedding guests, mostly female, through whom he must push his way. So Zeffirelli's film explores a number of readings: by giving Kate almost all of the long speech (thirty-three lines), the film asserts Kate's authority; by having Kate focus most of her speech on her female audience, the film allows her to be strong, even sarcastic; by changing from the harsh Kate to the gentle one in the final lines of the speech, the film shows her as loving, not just submissive; and by undercutting that submission with her disappearance into a crowd of women, the film gives the equivalent of the Pickford wink, implying that the struggle isn't really over.

As the two previous paragraphs suggest, a performance critic can easily move from the performance implied by the text to the interpretation implied by the performance. The choices made in these two films are, thanks to videotape, easily available for viewing (and re-viewing), and thus generations of students, teachers, actors, directors, and other interested parties can watch them, argue about them, learn from them. But most choices made in the theatre can be much more ephemeral, unless a reviewer saves them through description. Look, for example, at Nicholas Shrimpton's analysis of the 1985–86 RSC touring production of *The Taming of the Shrew*, and especially his description of the two leading actors.

Casting an Anglo-Italian actor, Alfred Molina, as Petruchio made it possible to invest the *commedia dell'arte* Padua of the play with a genuinely Latin *machismo*. When Kate slaps him at 2.1.216, for example, his reply ('I swear I'll cuff you, if you strike again') had the cool menace of a man more likely to reach for a stiletto than a hairbrush. At the same time, his treatment of his wife was, if not tentative exactly, at least pondered and conscientiously discussed. 'Say that she rail' (2.1.169–80) was nervous self-inquiry. And 'Thus have I politically begun my reign' (4.1.172–95) was, for once, less the boasting of a successful know-all than a scrupulous clinical debriefing. Its climax—'He that knows better how to tame a shrew,/Now let him speak'—was a genuine challenge: quiet, authoritative, and deliberately designed to draw the audience into a shared therapeutic inquiry.

(*Shakespeare Survey 40* (1988), 171)

Shrimpton begins with one of the central realities of performance, namely that the actor chosen (true of both men and women) necessarily inflects the performance, bringing his or her own qualities to any given role. And he ties his description to particular lines, so that his many adjectives may well send one back to the text to see how that particular line or that particular speech might generate such a reading.

Shrimpton's reading of Kate starts with a more abstract description, but ends with similar specificity:

Sian Thomas played her, with unusual single-mindedness as a rejected child, fiercely distressed by the experience of being locked out of the familial conspiracy of mutual love and humour. Offered an alternative conspiracy by Petruchio, she grasped it hungrily just as soon as she realized what it was. In case this sounds too neat, I should perhaps add that her transition was charted with exceptional care. Her husband's threat to deny her a sight of her sister's wedding was clearly a far more potent inducement than any mere matter of food or clothing, and her self-abasing final speech was cunningly explained by allowing her to linger on stage after 5.2.48 long enough to overhear the terms of the bet.

(171-2)

That last sentence records the intervention of the director, Di Trevis, a way to give Kate knowledge that the text does not necessarily indicate. And yet that intervention is not, strictly speaking, contrary to the text, since the stage direction in the Folio at that point reads only *'Exit Bianca'*, even though most modern editors add 'with Katherine and Widow' in brackets.

And, of course, a perceptive Kate might get the point in other ways, as Russell Jackson's comment on the RSC's 1995 production, directed by Gale Edwards, indicates:

> In the final scene, when she first returned from the parlor, Katherina saw the stakes of the wager heaped on the floor and understood what was going on. Every preparation had been made for one of the customary 'explanations' of the play: the central couple discover a mutual sense of humor and integrity in the face of a trivial and money-grubbing Paduan society. (The harshness of this superficially benign affluent world was nicely illustrated by the demoted Tranio's appearance as a kitchen helper, with a plastic apron and two bags of garbage.) From this it was an easy step to Katherina's rounding on the widow and Bianca, but the famous speech counseling submission was oddly lacking in nuance— was she signaling her distance from its sentiments?
>
> (*Shakespeare Quarterly*, 47 (1996), 326)

The detail about Tranio—seemingly thrown away in a parenthesis—is as telling a commentary on the world of the play as one can find, even if one might wish that Jackson had listened again to Kate's speech in an effort to find the nuances he missed; my own recollection is that she was deliberately over-playing the obedient wife, as if to say 'you want submissive, I'll give you submissive and see how you like it'. More importantly, these selections demonstrate the dual process of preserving and interpreting performances. The critic first collects details, then verbally recreates the performance, and finally moves to interpretation, allowing us vivid—and convincing—glimpses of moments we would otherwise not see or hear.

FURTHER READING

Boose, Lynda E. 'Scolding Brides and Bridling Scolds: Taming the Woman's Unruly Member'. *Shakespeare Quarterly*, 42 (1991), 179–213. Looking at the severe punishments in the sixteenth century for disruptive women, Boose contextualizes the violence (and relative gentleness) of the treatment of Kate.

Dusinberre, Juliet. *'The Taming of the Shrew*: Women, Acting, and Power'. *Studies in the Literary Imagination* 26 (1993), 67–84. Since a boy-actor, who was also an apprentice to the leading actors, originally played Kate, the dynamics of performance (especially the need both for submission and approval) might well have mirrored the character's journey.

Heilman, Robert B. 'The "Taming" Untamed, or The Return of the Shrew'. *Modern Language Quarterly*, 27 (1966), 147–61. Reacting to a series of earlier articles that had defended/excused the shrew's behaviour, Heilman argues for the play first as a farce (with mechanistic behaviour from the characters) and then as something approaching comedy, with moments of real depth for Kate and Petruccio.

Kahn, Coppélia. *'The Taming of the Shrew*: Shakespeare's Mirror of Marriage'. *Modern Language Studies*, 5 (1975), 88–102. Kahn reads the play as a critique of marriage, with Kate only pretending submission, through a 'rhetoric of satirical exaggeration', especially in the final speech.

Leggatt, Alexander. *'The Taming of the Shrew'*. In *Shakespeare's Comedy of Love* (London: Methuen, 1974), pp. 41–62. Leggatt's sensible reading of the play, dealing with structure, characterization, and production choices, emphasizes both Kate and Petruccio's game-playing, and thus ultimately their power to create new games, rather than simply remain trapped in old ones.

Newman, Karen. 'Renaissance Family Politics and Shakespeare's *The Taming of the Shrew'. English Literary Renaissance* 16 (1986), 86–100. Newman uses both political and domestic sources to show how *Shrew* examines Renaissance anxieties about gender and power.

Seronsy, Cecil C. *'Supposes* as the Unifying Theme in *The Taming of the Shrew'. Shakespeare Quarterly*, 14 (1963), 15–30. Seronsy offers a thematic reading that brings together the Induction, the main plot, and the subplot, all of which turn on the notion of pretence and imagination, sometimes with positive results (i.e. Petruccio supposes that Kate has qualities that no one else has seen), sometimes with ironic consequences (the treatment of Christopher Sly).

NOTES

1. Ephesians 5:23, 'For the husband is the head of the wife, as Christ also is the head of the church' is echoed in 5.2.151, and Ephesians 5:24, 'as the church is subject to Christ, so let the wives also be to their husbands in everything', in 5.2.159–60. Kate's declaration that wives 'are bound to serve, love, and obey' sounds very close to the question in the marriage service (Book of Common Prayer), 'wilt thou obey him, and serve him, love, honour, and keep him, in sickness and in health?'.

Part IV

Shakespeare's afterlife

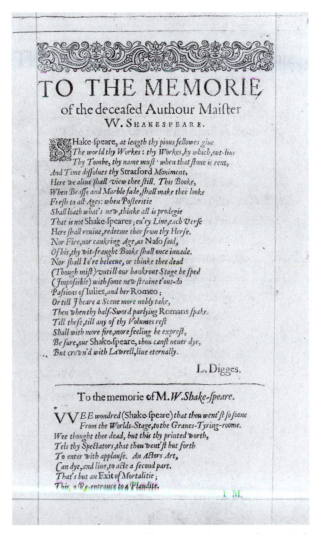

Fig. 4.1 The opening page of the memorial verses in the First Folio, of 1623, showing Leonard Digges's lines with their reference to Shakespeare's 'Stratford moniment' (for which, see Figure 4.4), and the poem by 'I. M.' – almost certainly James Mabbe (1572–1642), an Oxford scholar.

Introduction

Terence Hawkes

Bard Trek

There has never been an 'afterlife' to match it. Like some time-warping, infinitive-splitting astronaut, Shakespeare rockets beyond the grave to boldly go where no poet or playwright has ever previously ventured. No one can study his work fully without taking this phenomenon into account, and its impact on our perception of the plays is crucial. They come to us packaged and presented so as to confirm their author's remarkable status, and we have no other means of access to them. We can't 'unlearn' the fact that Shakespeare's words have been translated into virtually every language, adapted to every medium, performed before every possible sort of audience. We can't help but recognize that quotations from and allusions to the Bard litter the speeches of politicians, industrialists, bankers, statesmen, the lyrics of popular songs, and the graffiti that lap against our urban buildings. We can't fail to be aware that a well-known British radio programme routinely links his plays with the Bible as essential equipment for survival on a desert island; that his likeness underwrites banknotes and credit cards, makes votive objects of T-shirts and coffee-mugs, that you can light up a cigar called *Hamlet*. Streets named after the playwright weave their way through most of our suburbs. Replicas of the Globe Theatre sprout uncontrollably, worldwide. In Chicago, the entire fourteenth police district is called 'Shakespeare'. Even the usual terrestrial limitations no longer apply. In one of the films in the famous American science-fiction series *Star Trek*, the Klingon Chancellor Gorkon smugly informs the hero, Captain Kirk, that 'You have not experienced Shakespeare, until you've read it in the original Klingon'.[1]

What sort of work by what sort of person merits a response of this breathtaking kind? The popular view is straightforward enough. Shakespeare, it proclaims, was a 'genius', gifted with astonishing insight into and sympathy for something called 'human nature'. His plays present a wide range of individual characters across the broad spectrum of humanity, capturing our experience of love, hate, life, and death in recognizable and heart-warming detail. Such enormous scope, the ability to speak to all human beings through all the ages, at all times and everywhere, regardless of race, gender, creed, geography, or history, underwrites his work's universal validity. That's why we embrace it. The proliferating references to, hints at, and performances of the plays, the never-ending employment of their author's name and image as a kind of common coin, negotiable internationally, if not—as Chancellor Gorkon would have it—galactically, confirm as much. As no less a person than the present Prince of Wales has put it, Shakespeare's plays address 'essential truths about the meaning and significance of life', so that 'His message . . . is a universal, timeless one'.[2]

Of course, this view rests on a major presupposition: that human nature, under the surface, is indivisible, permanently one and the same, changed neither by place, time, or belief. Shakespeare's coruscating afterlife seems to signal general assent to that principle, and to the transcendental ventriloquism at which it hints: as if a single voice could speak, and has spoken, for us all, forever.

However, from the middle of the nineteenth century, if not before, serious questions have been raised about the existence of a 'given', innate, and finally unchanging 'human nature'. The work of philosophers, historians, anthropologists, and others suggests that a good deal of human behaviour, morality, religious belief, and social ordering is shaped less by cloudy generalizations of that order, than by our response to local pressures of a more material sort, involving economics, climate, historical inheritance, and the complex accumulation of beliefs, habits, and modes of perception that can be grouped under the heading of 'way of life', or 'culture'.

The evidence also suggests that, by and large, it's difficult to avoid becoming anaesthetized to our own culture's tacit impositions, so that we end up imprisoned, unaware, behind its invisible bars. Since to be human is to speak, one of the most formidable of these constraints must be language. The trouble is that our way of speaking deftly colludes with our way of seeing the world in a manner that makes both seem transparently natural, wholly appropriate, the epitome of 'common sense', and the essence of the way things are universally supposed to be. That's the stuff of which 'human nature' is made. Cultures embodying different, disconcerting concepts of what being human involves can then be safely dismissed as, at worst not genuinely human, or at best not fundamentally serious. Those who don't speak English can almost seem, in a most serious sense, to be joking.

Seen in this light, claims made for Shakespeare's 'universal' qualities, his capacity to penetrate to the core of every aspect of human life, may well come to appear faintly bogus. When, in addition, we take into account the fact that one English-speaking culture or another has for some time possessed sufficient power in the world to insist on widespread acknowledgement of its 'universality', then perhaps the game is up. This is what lends Chancellor Gorkon's observation its piquancy. *Star Trek* is recognizably an American fable about power of all kinds, from rocket propulsion to politics. It's fitting that the joke is made at the expense of that country's former colonial masters, for whom Shakespeare, if not the Prince of Wales, speaks. When Klingon can trump English as effortlessly as film and television now apparently trump theatre, then perhaps the joke is over.

An English Shakespeare

At the beginning of the twenty-first century, then, it is probably unwise to keep on ascribing Shakespeare's multifarious afterlife directly to the comforting notion of his universal genius. Things are bound to be more complicated than that. Drama, after all, is a social, communal art, rooted in the materiality of particular times, places, and people. Its very nature forces on it interests that will be as much local and specific as comprehensive and universal. Since plays consist of the performances of human beings on a stage, in front of other human beings in an audience, at a particular time and in a particular place, they cannot fail to address to some extent the concerns of a certain way of life, and to shape themselves to the contours of its 'here and now'. It's thus not unreasonable that in Shakespeare's case one of the most striking features of his afterlife should be the degree to which he comes to stand for a distinctive quality called 'Englishness'.

It's something that's not easy to define. Indeed, as the Prince of Wales perhaps unwittingly demonstrates, a kind of sublime contradiction seems to lie at the centre of Shakespeare's 'Englishness', at exactly the point where the local and the particular playwright begins mysteriously to merge into the transcendent Bard. There's evidently no doubt that he is specifically and concretely English: 'Shakespeare's language is ours, his roots are ours, his culture is ours—brought up as he was in the gentle Warwickshire countryside . . .'.[3] Yet it also transpires, as we've already noticed, that at the same time his 'message. . . is a universal, timeless one', purveying 'essential truths about the meaning and significance of life'. As a result, he ranks as 'not just our poet, but the world's'. But if Shakespeare's language, roots and culture are so firmly 'ours', how can they also simultaneously be 'the world's'? Or should the world be prepared to admit that it is—even just a little bit—'ours' too?

Of course, the roots of Shakespeare's Englishness lie deep within the English language, and his rise to global fame is linked to and fostered by its expansion as a vehicle of British power and influence in the world. But although we tend to think of Englishness as deriving from and reflecting the essence of a single, coherent, English-speaking state, it's important to remember that the country usually known as 'Britain' in fact consists of the conjunction of four distinct cultures, those of England, Wales, Scotland, and Ireland. Gradual progress towards a political union between them took place over the centuries, and one of its most significant stages occurred during the Tudor-Stuart period, when the foundations of what was to become the powerhouse of an enormous empire were laid.

Shakespeare's interest in this massive ideological project—it involved nothing less than the construction of a new nation-state—was understandably great. The so-called 'history' plays focus on the notion of national unity with consuming intensity, and the idea of a unified British civilization runs through works like *King John* and *King Lear* (where the division of the kingdom is the very source of the tragedy). It even attracts divine sanction in *Cymbeline* and *Henry VIII*.

Yet from the first there was never any doubt that the 'Britain' project would be English-dominated, and that to some degree the fate of the other three nationalities would ultimately be more a matter of incorporation than confederacy. Britain was always going to be England writ large, and its language would certainly be English. In respect of Wales, for instance, the English crown put through a series of measures between 1536 and 1543 known as the Acts of Union, whose aims seem worthy enough: 'utterly to extirp all and singular the sinister usages and customs' separating the two cultures 'and to bring the said subjects of this his realm, and of his said dominion of Wales, to an amicable concord and unity'. Concord and unity are laudable goals. But a major casualty of the process would inevitably be the Welsh language:

... from henceforth no person or persons that use the Welsh speech or language shall have or enjoy any manner office or fees within this realm of England, Wales, or other the King's dominion, upon pain of forfeiting the same offices or fees, unless he or they use and exercise the English speech or language.[4]

These are not necessarily the words of a culture which believes its language to be superior to another. They are the words of one which believes its way of speaking to be 'natural', its way of life free from 'sinister usages and customs'. It is difficult to say whether, in *Henry IV Part One*, the play's depiction of the Welsh-speaking Owen Glendower and his daughter endorses that view, or is critical of it (after all, the chief scorner of the Welsh language is the headstrong Hotspur). But the playwright's commitment to English cannot be in doubt. In fact, a later play in the sequence, *Henry V*, memorably offers us a Welshman—Fluellen—whose enthusiasm for things British has apparently led him to abandon his native tongue. And by the time he wrote *Cymbeline*, Shakespeare could locate the springs of a future British empire almost entirely in a wholly 'englished' Wales.

In other words, the dominance of Britain by England generates a new and special kind of British 'Englishness'. Shakespeare becomes one of its chief spokesmen. It is special for a number of reasons. For hundreds of years, the most effective bearers of English-speaking culture were the bullet, the bayonet, and the gallows. After all, the British colonial project aimed initially to impose its presuppositions and priorities on native languages and cultures by force. A different suggestion, that the high road to more effective subjugation might lie, less expensively, in a programme of co-option, took a somewhat longer time to develop. But it can be heard surfacing in Lord Macaulay's speech in the House of Commons in 1833, where he comments on 'how rapidly the public mind of India is advancing, how much attention is already paid by the higher classes of the natives to those intellectual pursuits on the cultivation of which the superiority of the European race principally depends.' If, as he later put it, 'To trade with civilised men is infinitely more profitable than to govern savages', then the obvious stratagem must be to propagate 'that literature before the light of which impious and cruel superstitions are fast taking flight on the banks of the Ganges . . .'[5]

It worked. Stable empires depend, as Lord Macaulay knew, not on mere military conquest, something which, in the case of the British Empire, sheer size would have made physically impossible. Rather, the process operates most efficiently by means of enlistment: that is, by persuading conquered races, not to become subservient to an 'English' way of life, but to join in a loftier enterprise: one which repeats to all colonized peoples the offer made initially to the Welsh: to 'extirp all and singular the sinister usages and customs' that separate one culture from another. As ever, 'amicable concord and unity' are on offer as a reward. If everyone, as this implies, is ultimately the same under the surface, and if this subterranean identity can be reinforced and fostered by a joining of forces, then the claim made for a conquering Englishness will be that it represents not a specific, but a general situation: that it is acting on behalf, not of a particular regime, but of nothing less than the unsullied, unsinister, human condition itself. The world, this suggests, concealed though it may be beneath all kinds of alien debris, is really *Anglia irredenta*: an England waiting to be reclaimed. The paradox that Shakespeare's work can be both comprehensive and specific, all-embracing and local, 'the world's' and 'ours', is thus neatly resolved. Englishness is no barrier to universality because the rest of the world, unless it's joking, is really English too.

An Eng. Lit. Shakespeare

In other words, Shakespeare comes to represent and speak for an English way of life at precisely the point in time when, paying the price of its imperium, 'Englishness' becomes uprooted, dislocated, the badge of a generalized, free-floating humanity. One of the most powerful engines propelling this special kind of portable, colonizer's Englishness can easily be identified: the wide-spread development and deployment in the British Empire, the United States, Canada, Australia, and ultimately in Britain itself, of the academic subject called 'English'. Shakespeare, naturally, held and continues to hold pride of place in its curriculum. It constitutes the bedrock on which his 'afterlife' rests.

In 1855, the Civil Service of the East India Company outlined plans under the provisions of the government's India Act of 1853 to open its prestigious administrative posts to competitive examination. Listing appropriate subjects for the purpose—and no doubt pursuing the idea, as someone put it, that a teacher of English is worth a regiment of dragoons—the relevant committee proposed that 'Foremost among [them] . . . we place our own language and literature'.[6] So, from the middle of the nineteenth century, courses in English literature, spearheaded by Shakespeare, grew to become part of the intellectual fabric of schools and universities from Calcutta to Quebec and from New Zealand to Nova Scotia, lending the Bard's afterlife the slight missionary inclination which has always been one of its characteristics. Thus, when Gauri Viswanathan notes 'that English literature appeared as a subject in the colonies long before it was institutionalised in the home country', she is drawing attention, not to an unheeded irony, but to one of the carefully laid stratagems of a policy of political self-interest.[7]

It would be unfair, nonetheless, to present the teaching of Shakespeare as part of a deliberate programme of cultural and linguistic cleansing aimed solely at overlaying, say, the contours of some wretched Caliban's way of life with those of a brusquely englishing Prospero. The capacity of Shakespeare's plays to enlighten, liberate, and broaden the cultural horizons of those fortunate enough to encounter them is undeniable. In any case, the process of successful subjugation is never so simple or ruthless a matter, and the sensitive 'colonizing' of a student's mind remains a perfectly proper and laudable goal for any teacher. Still, it's worth remembering that two years after the East India Company's report, the country experienced the cultural convulsion known as the Indian Mutiny. J. G. Farrell's novel, *The Siege of Krishnapur* (1973), carefully teases out some of its implicit ironies in a scene where the British, besieged in the Residency, discover that they have run out of ammunition. Hastily improvising, they cut off the heads of a number of statuettes of literary worthies for use as bullets in their muskets:

And of the heads, perhaps not surprisingly, the most effective of all had been Shakespeare's; it had scythed its way through a whole astonished platoon of sepoys advancing in single file through the jungle. The Collector suspected that the Bard's success in this respect might have a great deal to do with the ballistic advantages stemming from his baldness. The head of Keats, for example, wildly festooned with metal locks which it had proved impossible to file smooth had flown very erratically indeed, killing only a fat money-lender and a camel standing at some distance from the field of action.[8]

One central aspect of the Bard's afterlife—his use as a cultural weapon—has rarely been more graphically displayed.

A life after Shakespeare?

Of course, as the following chapters will indicate, the word 'afterlife' begs a serious question. Wherever we claim to find evidence of it (in endlessly revised editions of the plays; in controversies over authorship; in theatrical, film, or video productions; in translations; as a presence in the work of subsequent authors, painters, composers; even in the festivals, the tours, the absurd devotional bric-a-brac of mugs, ash-trays, and other paraphernalia), the same issue arises. Does any body of work genuinely possess a 'life' of its own, extending beyond its author's death?

In one sense, the answer must surely be no. Nobody's writings—not even those of Shakespeare—exist independently, as living entities, capable of doing or performing anything of their own volition. Plays above all can have no genuine 'life' of their own. They require actors, theatres, studios, rehearsals, and, importantly, financial investment to make them occur. That is, they can exist only in and as a material part of a complicated social context, to which they contribute and by which, in turn, they will to some extent be shaped. A Shakespeare performance acquires the only kind of 'life' it can enjoy as a result of decisions and actions taken by real people in concrete social and historical situations and, we must presume, for reasons and purposes which they determine. A more general truth seems to be that you can't separate the afterlife of Shakespeare in any form from the uses to which his plays are put.

One of the best-known examples of such use is Laurence Olivier's film of *Henry V*. Released in 1944 and financed by British government funds, this was conceived in great part as a propaganda exercise preparatory to the D-Day landings in Normandy, aimed at persuading its audience that a determined and united British force could defeat a ruthless enemy in pitched battle on the fields of northern France.

An earlier and very different example would be the famous production by the Negro Theater Project of the so-called 'Voodoo' *Macbeth* in Harlem, New York in 1936. Directed by the twenty-year-old Orson Welles, this was mounted, as the head of the project John Houseman, put it, less for artistic than 'for tactical reasons'.[9] Not only did Welles's astonishing and spectacular version of the play provide employment in hard times for an encouragingly large troupe of 137, including witch-doctors and African drummers. It also aimed—not without some degree of condescension—to establish black American performers as worthy interpreters of 'serious' art and thus, at a time of national crisis, as an integral part of the culture of a United States desperate to reconstruct itself after a disastrous economic depression. Reviewing the production, a journalist made the pointed comment that 'The Negro has become weary of carrying the White Man's blackface burden in the theatre. In *Macbeth* he has been given the opportunity to discard the bandanna and burnt-cork casting . . . Harlem witnessed a production in which the Negro was not lampooned or made the brunt of laughter. We attended the *Macbeth* showing, happy in the thought that we wouldn't again be reminded, with all its vicious implications, that we were niggers'.[10]

It's clear that the afterlife of the work here—Shakespeare's 'Scottish play' and one not obviously concerned to any appreciable extent with modern racial tensions—had nonetheless come to include service in the cause of American democracy and civil rights.

Perhaps something similar was at stake when Duke Ellington and his orchestra accepted an invitation to play at the Shakespeare Festival in Stratford, Ontario in 1956. For the occasion he composed a suite entitled *Such Sweet Thunder*, recalling lines from *A Midsummer Night's Dream* in which the baying of hounds in pursuit of a bear is said paradoxically to produce sounds of great beauty. It's probably an over-simplification to suggest that Ellington's sense of the occasion prompted him to present his music and his musicians as a quasi-savage, bear-like intrusion into the aesthetic niceties of mid-twentieth-century Shakespearian production (although the orchestra's lead trumpeter at this time was named 'Cat' Anderson). But certainly some notion of the reconciliation of black culture with white was clearly at stake in the *concordia discors*—harmony derived from discord—which the music achieved as it echoed the ravishing incongruities of the hounds' 'sweet thunder'.

The afterlife of a work such as *Coriolanus* is even more telling, for the play seems so often to have been used to generate political controversy. Some scholars argue that it possibly bears some imprint of the riots of 1607–8 in the Midlands, and the fundamental opposition it constructs between patricians and plebeians certainly encourages links with various aspects of modern class conflict. By the nineteenth and early twentieth centuries its political dimension was regularly used as a card that could be played by various parties. In Charlotte Brontë's novel *Shirley* (1849), Chapter VI is entitled 'Coriolanus'. Caroline Helstone and Robert Moore discuss the play against a complicated background of social unrest: that of the novel's own plot (1811–12), and that of the year of its actual composition (1848). Robert, a mill owner whose machinery has been destroyed by Luddite workers, admires and sympathizes with Coriolanus, but Caroline rebukes him; 'you sympathise with that proud patrician who does not sympathise with his famished fellow-men and insults them. . . .' Coldly, she adds 'I cannot help thinking it unjust to include all poor working people under the general and insulting name of "the mob"'.

In the twentieth century, Coriolanus's disdain of the mob further deepens the material involvement of the play's afterlife in the politics of everyday. Between December 1933 and February 1934, a production of René Louis Piachaud's version at the *Comédie Française*, sponsored by the rightwing party *Action Française*, sought to present it as a fascist denunciation of democracy, and provoked riots in the streets of Paris. School editions and performances along similar lines were popular in Nazi Germany throughout the 1930s and, together with *Julius Caesar*, *Coriolanus* was banned by the occupying American authorities in Berlin at the war's end, on the grounds that both plays constituted 'glorifications of dictatorship'. However, a famous production of *Coriolanus* planned by the Berliner Ensemble in communist East Germany in 1962–3 proposed using Bertolt Brecht's unfinished adaptation of the play for exactly the opposite purpose: as a denunciation of fascism in which the working classes, educated by their tribunes, rise to overthrow their patrician oppressors. The ironies of that, in the light of the then-situation in East Germany (where an actual rising against the rigidities of communist rule was in progress), were later explored in Günter Grass's play *The Plebeians Rehearse The Uprising* (1966).

It has been argued that one of the most significant features of Shakespeare's afterlife has been its employment as an instrument of imperial rule. Yet the so-called end of empire, together with the diminishing power of 'Englishness', has by no means meant the end of Shakespeare. Does the reason for this lie in the persistent world dominance of the English language, even though its centre of gravity is currently more likely to be New York or Los Angeles than London or Stratford? That is certainly a factor. By now, Shakespeare's words echo in the minds of all speakers of the language worldwide, and his ghost stalks the work of anyone who writes in English. As an almost-recognizable rhythm, a faintly familiar purchase on certain words and phrases, it's a quality perhaps more felt than seen in countless poems, novels, and plays. Occasionally, as in the case of T. S. Eliot's J. Alfred Prufrock ('No! I am not Prince Hamlet, nor was meant to be'), it can even be irritably, but memorably, denied.

Or does the vigour of his afterlife have more to do with the process identified above, whereby Shakespeare has somehow come to be equated, not with a firmly grounded Englishness, but with a vaguely conceived 'humanity' over and above the differences manifested by individual cultures? Of many recent instances, the film *Shakespeare in Love* (1998) perhaps most obviously trades on such presuppositions, lovingly reinforcing on their behalf a number of sentimental modern prejudices: that writers write most powerfully about what they personally 'feel', or that art's primary concern is to express the 'personality' of the artist. The afterlife of its hero then inevitably dwindles to become the story of 'Shakespeare Superwriter', an inky-fingered, golden-thighed Oscar-winning extension of ourselves, whose quill needs a good sharpening and whose verses won't flow until his bodily fluids do.

Does this mean that the plays must inevitably ratify the crass political, economic, or psychological formations that underwrite and are expressed by such a universalizing notion? After all, the world which generated and which was in turn moulded by Englishness is rapidly changing. In Britain, a massive re-negotiation of power relationships between its four constituent nations is currently underway. Not for the first time in history, but certainly for the first time concurrently and as aspects of a planned development, there are now separate parliaments or assemblies in Scotland, Wales, and Northern Ireland. Does devolution, in Britain's case, imply dissolution? The entity that Shakespeare famously depicted as a single, unified island, an 'earth' and a 'realm' called—oddly enough—'England' is undoubtedly resolving itself, five hundred years on, into its component parts. Certain questions then inevitably arise. Might the Welsh, the Scots, and the Irish, whose unity Shakespeare's plays seem to advocate, end by rejecting them as works which either explicitly or implicitly buttress exactly the structure which their new parliaments and assemblies systematically bring into question? Might similar quasi-devolutionary impulses also be at work elsewhere, in India, in Africa, in the Americas? What, in such a world, will be the future of Shakespeare's afterlife?

We can only be sure that he will have one. After all, a luminous endorsement of subsequence shines through the words said to have been inscribed over the entrance to the original Globe Theatre: *Totus Mundus Agit Histrionem*. We inhabit, they shrewdly imply, a permanently over-the-shoulder-looking, past-sifting culture, committed to wholesale recapitulation and rendition, hooked on retroactive rehearsal and performance. 'All the World's a Stage' is its perfect motto. Given that, the audacious words of Chancellor Gorkon may turn out to be oddly illuminating. For the idea of an 'original Klingon', whilst denying our Shakespeare's primacy, awards him nothing less than an eternally pre-empted *ex post facto* afterlife here on earth. And in the process, it satisfactorily confirms us as ever the bedazzled, stage-struck, history-haunted specta-tors that the Globe insists we are. No doubt the actual William Shakespeare lived and died like any mortal being. His tombstone at Stratford confirms it, adding memorably dire threats against the further rummagings of posterity. But the astonishing, prolifer-ating figment to which we have given his name is proving quite a different matter. Perhaps the truth Chancellor Gorkon brings is that an afterlife is the only sort of existence such a creature could ever have had.

FURTHER READING

Baldick, Chris. *The Social Mission of English Criticism 1848–1932* (Oxford: Clarendon Press, 1983). This gives a historical account of the promotion of English literature, including Shakespeare, as a 'civilizing' influence in educational programmes in Britain and worldwide.

Bristol, Michael D. *Shakespeare's America, America's Shakespeare* (London and New York: Routledge, 1990). This offers details of Shakespeare's extensive afterlife in the United States, and a valuable account of his growth into an American institution.

Holderness, Graham. *Cultural Shakespeare; Essays in the Shakespeare Myth* (Hatfield: University of Hertfordshire Press, 2001). These essays discuss the development of Shakespeare as a universal icon, and the cultural politics involved in the construction and institutionalizing of various forms of his afterlife.

Loomba, Ania and Orkin, Martin (eds.). *Postcolonial Shakespeares* (London: Routledge, 1998). These essays explore various aspects of the way Shakespeare's plays function in post-colonial cultures.

Sinfield, Alan. *Faultlines: Cultural Materialism and the Politics of Dissident Reading* (Oxford: Clarendon Press, 1992). This book successfully employs 'cultural materialism' to unpick Shakespeare's cultural and institutional role both in the United States and Britain.

Taylor, Gary. *Reinventing Shakespeare: a Cultural History from the Restoration to the Present* (London: Hogarth Press, 1989). A brisk and detailed account of the 'Shakespeare industry' through the ages, and a perceptive and witty guide to Shakespeare's afterlife in the form of performances, adaptations, editions, and interpretations.

Viswanathan, Gauri. *Masks of Conquest: Literary Study and British Rule in India* (London: Faber, 1990). Focuses on the ways in which English literature, including Shakespeare, has been used as a weapon of cultural subjugation.

WEB LINKS

SHAKSPER: The Global Electronic Shakespeare Conference. <http://www.shaksper.net/index.html>. This is probably the most comprehensive and useful of the websites devoted to Shakespeare. Founded, edited, and maintained by Hardy M. Cook, it offers a number of services, including a 'Guide to Shakespeare on the Internet' that is up-to-date, clearly signposted, and includes full URL details. It also gives access to a daily bulletin board.

NOTES

1. This film is significantly entitled *Star Trek VI: The Undiscovered Country*.

2. The Prince of Wales, Introduction to *The Prince's Choice; a Personal Selection from Shakespeare* (London: Hodder and Stoughton, 1995), pp. 4–5.

3. The Prince of Wales, p. 5.

4. 27 Henry VIII, c.26 (1536), excerpted in Ivor Bowen, ed., *The Statutes of Wales* (S. I.: T. Fisher Unwin, 1908), pp. 75–6; and Trevor Herbert and Gareth Elwyn Jones (eds.). *Tudor Wales* (Cardiff: University of Wales Press, 1988) pp. 149–50.

5. See Chris Baldick. *The Social Mission of English Criticism 1848–1932* (Oxford: Clarendon Press, 1983), pp. 70–1.

6. Baldick, p. 70.

7. Gauri Viswanathan. *Masks of Conquest: Literary Study and British Rule in India* (London: Faber, 1990), p. 3. See also p. 49.

8. J. G. Farrell. *The Siege of Krishnapur* (1973. Harmondsworth: Penguin Books, 1975), p. 335.

9. See John Houseman. *Unfinished Business* (London: Columbus Books, 1988), pp. 93–105.

10. Houseman, p. 104.

38 | Shakespeare published

Laurie Maguire

When we read Shakespeare's plays, we are reading something that was never meant to be read: the primary destination of drama is performance, not print. The publication of drama is inevitably a secondary concern.

But Shakespeare was also a poet, and there is reason to believe that he took an interest in publishing his non-dramatic poetry. In the sixteenth century, drama was not generally regarded as high literature: it was a commercial medium, sullied by 'filthy lucre' (because theatregoers paid to attend it), and socially promiscuous. Poetry, by contrast, was courtly and leisured. Thus it was as a narrative, rather than a dramatic, poet that Shakespeare first appeared in print (see also Chapter 22). In 1593 *Venus and Adonis* was published by Richard Field, a fellow native of Stratford-upon-Avon, who also published Shakespeare's *Rape of Lucrece* the following year. Shakespeare's sonnets, begun early in his career and revised at the start of the seventeenth century, were not published until 1609, but some of them circulated in manuscript in the 1590s. We call such circulation 'manuscript publication', a phrase that is not as oxymoronic as it sounds when one thinks of the etymology of 'publish' as simply 'make public'.

Thus, the story of 'Shakespeare published' is not one but three stories: the publication history of Shakespeare-the-dramatist; the publication history of Shakespeare-the-narrative poet; and the circulation history of Shakespeare-the-sonneteer. These three stories overlap, but this chapter focuses primarily on the first, chronicling the ways in which Shakespeare's plays were turned into books. As we shall see, the story is one of experimentation and accommodation as contrasting media—the fluidity of drama and the fixity of print—collide.

Publishing a quarto

Behind most editions of sixteenth- or early seventeenth-century plays written for the public playhouses lay a performance. This is not to say that the manuscript from which the printed text was printed was the theatre company's playbook (although this was sometimes the case) but that performance predated publication, often by several years, and was usually highlighted on the title page, if only by metonymic mention of the

IMPRESSIO LIBRORVM.

4.   *Poteſt vt vna vox capi aure plurima:*   *Linunt ita vna ſcripta mille paginas.*

Fig. 4.2 Activities in the printing workshop: compositors (with manuscript copy pinned above them) set type; someone proof-reads; an apprentice stacks paper; one man inks type, and another pulls the press. Note the newly printed sheets hanging up to dry (in reality the sheets were hung in a separate room as the air in the printing room was too dusty). The quarto pages on the table in the foreground have not yet been folded, trimmed, and gathered like those stacked on the rear table. Engraved by Jan van der Straet for *Nova Reperta* (1580).

company's name. Special occasions merited extended mention. Thus, the text of *King Lear* published in 1608 proclaimed that it had been *'played before the King's Majesty at Whitehall upon S.* Stephen's *night in Christmas Holidays. By his Majesty's servants playing usually at the Globe on the Bankside'*. The 1603 *Hamlet* 'hath been diverse times acted by his Highness's servants in the City of London: as also in the two Universities of Cambridge and Oxford, and elsewhere'.

Behind every performance lay a manuscript, what we would call a 'promptbook' but what the early modern period called simply 'the playbook' or 'the book'. The playbook may have been an annotated version of the author's original manuscript (prepared by the company's scrivener or bookholder) or, if the original manuscript was difficult in some way—illegible or heavily revised or interlined or burdened by multiple paste-ons and interleavings—it may have been copied out anew.

Other manuscripts may also have existed: an author's rough draft; a transcript made by actors for friends who had seen and enjoyed the play (some Beaumont and Fletcher plays were copied in this way); a new playbook of an abridged or adapted version of the play. With the exception of one-hundred-and-forty-seven lines believed to be by Shakespeare in the collaborative play *Sir Thomas More*, we have no Shakespeare manuscripts. The documentable history of Shakespeare's texts thus begins with publication.

Not all plays reached print. The manuscripts of those that did were released to a stationer when the play was no longer being regularly (and hence lucratively) staged. 'Stationer' is the generic term for a printer, publisher, or bookseller. Critics used to think that Elizabethan stationers were desperate to publish plays, and were consequently eager to get hold of dramatic manuscripts by fair means or foul. This is now seen as unlikely, on economic as well as practical grounds. It was much more lucrative for a publisher to publish a sermon, an almanac, a grammar book, a Bible, a volume of poetry, or ephemeral pamphlets and broadsheets containing sensational news, such as *A miraculous and monstrous but most true and certain discourse of a woman (now to be seen in London) of th[e] age of lx years in the midst of whose forehead by the wonderful work of GOD, there groweth out a crooked horn of 4 inches long.*[1] The market for these kinds of publications was steady. Shakespeare's *'Venus and Adonis'*, first published in 1593, was reprinted five times in the next six years: in 1594, 1595, 1596, and twice in 1599. *The Rape of Lucrece*, first published in 1594, was reprinted three times in the next six years: in 1598 and twice in 1600.

By contrast, the market for plays was less certain (indeed, seventeen of Shakespeare's plays did not reach print until the collected edition of 1623, published seven years after his death). *Titus Andronicus*, a box-office success at the Rose theatre and the first Shakespeare play to reach print, in 1594, had to wait until 1600 for a second edition, as did the earliest version of *Henry VI Part Two*, also first published in 1594. This discrepancy in publishing success between poetry and plays is not confined to Shakespeare: Marlowe's poem *Hero and Leander* far outsold his play *Dr Faustus*. The paucity of interest in purchasing plays may be due to their belated appearance (plays were often viewed as journalism rather than literature, and out-of-date journalism is always unattractive), but it may also be due to the change of medium from stage to page. Today, many people attend the theatre but fewer buy the contemporary drama they have seen; reading plays, now as then, is a subsidiary activity. Furthermore, in the Elizabethan period it cost more to read a play than to see it. A play quarto retailed at six pence; entrance to the Globe could cost as little as one penny (see Chapter 3).

Not only were play quartos an unreliable investment for stationers, they were technically tricky to print. Bibliographical terms like 'quarto' or 'folio' simply denote the folding process. When a large sheet of paper is folded once to make two leaves (four sides or pages), the result is a folio; when it is folded twice to make four leaves (eight sides or pages) we have a quarto; eight leaves (sixteen sides or pages) is an octavo; and so on. The quarto format favoured for plays or poems did not usually print pages in the order in which we read them. Pages 1, 8, 4 and 5 of a quarto 'gathering' of eight pages were printed on one side of the unfolded sheet, with pages 2, 7, 3 and 6 on the reverse. Calculating the number of lines that a manuscript would require in print is easy for poetry (where one verse line equals one type line) and consistent for prose. But drama uses both verse and prose in varying quantities. Anticipating where a quarto page 8 would begin on an author's manuscript, and ensuring that page 7 later matched it correctly, was a time-consuming headache. As Peter Blayney has argued, printing plays was a task that printers undertook only to fill in spare time between larger jobs.

Publishing the First Folio

In 1616 Ben Jonson engaged in an act of bibliographical and literary miscegenation: he published his plays in folio. The folio format was reserved for works of permanence and dignity: the bible (chained, for reference purposes, in parish churches), history books (Holinshed's *Chronicles of England, Scotland and Ireland* was published in three folio volumes in 1577, and enlarged in a second edition published in 1587), works of heraldry (Ralph Brooke's illustrated *Catalogue and Succession of Nobility*, published in 1619). These were reference works, serious works. When the lovestruck Don Adriano de Armado turns sonneteer in *Love's Labour's Lost* and announces that he is 'for whole volumes, in folio' (1.2.163–4), Shakespeare's joke hinges on the discrepancy between form and content: short love sonnets do not merit lavish folio publication. To the London public of 1616 Jonson's Folio must have seemed no less absurd than Armado's.

Aware of the potential for ridicule, Jonson supplemented his canon of plays and poems with more respectable material: masques (several of which had been performed at Court) and civic entertainments (one of which had a royal link, an entertainment for the coronation of King James). He also revised his plays and excised any collaborative hands. Titling the volume *Works* ('works' were different from, more serious than, 'plays'), was a further bold attempt at refashioning. In these ways Jonson self-consciously tried to turn himself from collaborative commercial playwright into author.

1616, the year in which the Jonson Folio was published, was also the year of Shakespeare's death. The Jonson Folio may have stimulated Shakespeare's fellow actors to prepare a similar volume as a tribute to their deceased colleague (books make the best memorials, as authors from Horace onwards remind us). Or the prompt may have been the later, less ambitious 'Pavier' collection of 1619.

In this year two stationers—William Jaggard, a printer, and Thomas Pavier, a publisher—produced a collection of ten plays, not all of which were by Shakespeare, although they were marketed as such. The first three plays in the volume have continuous signatures (printers 'signed' pages with alphabetical and numerical marks, an equivalent of pagination), indicating their intended publication as a single volume. This intention was clearly modified after the third play in the volume had been set up (the next seven plays are individually paginated), because of an objection by the Lord Chamberlain on behalf of the company of players called the King's Men. The stationers circumvented the objection by using falsely dated titlepages to publish the plays as if they were remaindered copies. Thus, the volume was spurious in both bibliographical and literary terms. Nonetheless, the stationers were evidently successful in selling this collection, for several bound volumes containing all ten plays survived until the late nineteenth and early twentieth centuries.

Shortly before or during the printing of the Pavier quartos, a syndicate of stationers started gathering in the copyright of Shakespeare's plays in preparation for the Shakespeare Folio of 1623. (Before the copyright act of 1709, which gave an author his own copyright, titular copyright belonged to the stationer who had first registered or printed a work.) John Heminges and Henry Condell, Shakespeare's colleagues in the King's Men, oversaw the project.

The Shakespeare Folio contained only drama, as befits the professional association of Heminges, Condell, and Shakespeare in the theatre, and was titled not *Works* or *Plays* but *Comedies, Tragedies, Histories*—a tripartite generic division of the Shakespeare canon that has persisted ever since. Although the prefatory epistle 'To the Great Variety of Readers' supplied by Heminges and Condell seems designed primarily to extol Shakespeare, it has an unmistakable fiscal tension as it enjoins us to purchase the volume: 'whatever you do, buy'. The Folio represented a hefty investment for any purchaser: its retail price of 15 shillings for unbound pages (books were presented for sale in loose sheets) would increase by as much as 5 shillings depending on the binding chosen by the individual purchaser.

Heminges and Condell's prefatory epistle promises prospective purchasers 'all his [Shakespeare's] plays'. Of course: no one wants to feel that they are getting less than 'all'. But Heminges and Condell engage in some rhetorical sleight-of-hand here (as do most advertisers), for it is clear that their editorial desire for inclusivity occasionally yielded to practical circumstance. Copyright difficulties over the acquisition of *Troilus and Cressida* were unresolved in early 1622 when printing of the Folio began. The play was dropped from the volume (it does not appear in the table of contents) and *Timon of Athens* was commandeered to take its place. The eventual resolution of the *Troilus* dispute permitted the late inclusion of this play, but not before some copies of the Folio had been sold without it.

It is clear that Heminges and Condell balanced aesthetic and practical concerns. Bibliography has enabled us to recover some of the practical concerns; the aesthetic ones are less clear-cut and merit some exploration here.

In the prefatory epistle Heminges and Condell explain the foundation of their Folio texts:

> where (before) you were abused with diverse stolen and surreptitious copies, maimed and deformed by the frauds and stealths of injurious impostors that exposed them: even those are now offered to your view cured, and perfect of their limbs; and all the rest, absolute in their numbers, as he conceived them.

As a statement of advertising, this is clear ('our edition is the best') but as a statement of editorial policy, it is highly ambiguous. Do Heminges and Condell mean to impugn all previous editions? (This interpretation is ethically awkward, since they reprint several of the early editions without alteration.) Do they mean to condemn only the textually variant versions, texts classified pejoratively by early twentieth-century critics as 'bad quartos', but now known more objectively as 'short' quartos? Or do they mean to repudiate only specific (albeit unspecified!) editions, such as the Pavier quartos? To answer these questions we need to consider the contents of those Shakespeare quartos which reached print between 1594 and 1623.

Facts and figures

In 1622–3, Heminges and Condell had, or knew of, no fewer than fifty-one Shakespeare scripts. This total of fifty-one can be adjusted by plus or minus a few depending upon one's attitude to specific textual details, which are summarized below. (Running totals showing how the total of fifty-one is reached are provided in square brackets.)

Of the thirty-six plays in the Shakespeare Folio in 1623, seventeen were appearing in print for the first time: *The Tempest, The Two Gentlemen of Verona, Measure for Measure, The Comedy of Errors, As You Like It, All's Well that Ends Well, Twelfth Night, The Winter's Tale, Henry VI Part One, Henry VIII, Coriolanus, Timon of Athens, Julius Caesar, Macbeth, Antony and Cleopatra, Cymbeline, King John* [17]. The remaining nineteen were already familiar to the reading public from individual quarto volumes and one octavo published between 1594 and 1622, but Heminge and Condell chose to print many of these nineteen in versions which differed (to varying degrees) from the texts of the first and/or second quarto or octavo editions, while excluding one of the early quarto plays altogether.

Of these nineteen, the First Folio reprinted a substantially verbatim text of eight: *Titus Andronicus, Love's Labour's Lost, Richard II, The Merchant of Venice, Henry IV Part One, Henry IV Part Two, Much Ado About Nothing,* and *A Midsummer Night's Dream* [17 + 8 = 25].[2] A further three plays were reprinted in texts which have pervasive lexical differences from the first editions, the so-called 'doubtful' quartos, thus making for two versions of each (*Richard III, Troilus and Cressida, Othello*) [25 + 3 quartos + 3 Folios = 31]. The Folio version of a fourth 'doubtful quarto', *King Lear*, not only has localized verbal variants but also alters some of the action [31 + 1 quarto + 1 Folio = 33]. Seven Folio plays were reprinted in versions which vary significantly from the texts represented in the first 'bad' quarto or octavo edition: *Henry VI Part Two* (called *The First Part of the Contention of the Two Famous Houses of York and Lancaster* in the first edition of 1594), *Henry VI Part Three* (called *The True Tragedy of Richard Duke of York* in the first edition of 1595), *The Taming of the Shrew, Romeo and Juliet, Henry V, Hamlet, The Merry Wives of Windsor* [33 + 7 Folios + 7 quartos/octavos = 47].[3]

Of the remaining plays already in print, second ('good') quarto editions of two had closely followed publication of the first ('bad') quartos (Q1 *Romeo and Juliet* 1597; Q2 *Romeo and Juliet* 1599; Q1 *Hamlet* 1603; Q2 *Hamlet* 1604/5); the title pages of these second quartos advertised that each text corrected and enlarged that of the relevant first quarto [47 + 2 second quartos = 49]. The First Folio reprints the second quarto text of *Romeo and Juliet*, but provides a third version of *Hamlet* [49 + Folio = 50]. *Pericles*, published in quarto in 1609, was not included in the First Folio [50 + 1 = 51].[4]

It is not essential to remember these details. It is necessary to remember only one thing: Heminges and Condell had choices, especially about which version of some plays to include. Had they chosen differently, our experience of Shakespeare would be quite different. For example, Heminges and Condell rejected the group of 'short quartos'. Why?

Short quartos

The standard texts of almost all Shakespeare's plays range from about 2,200 to 4,000 lines. At about 1,800 lines *The Comedy of Errors* is exceptionally short; perhaps, therefore, it was written for a special occasion. The short quartos earn their adjective by varying in length from 1,500 to 2,200 lines. But what makes a short quarto 'bad' (a qualitative rather than a quantitative adjective), since plays like *The Comedy of Errors* and *Macbeth* are short without being 'bad'?

The critics who labelled the plays 'bad' did so on the basis of apparent bluntness of language, sketchy characterization, aural errors, metrical disruption, and occasional nonsensical lines. Various theories were offered to account for these alleged imperfections: first drafts; shorthand notes; reconstruction from the notes and memory of an audience member; reconstruction from the memories of actors. This last theory, known as 'memorial reconstruction', came to dominate twentieth-century textual scholarship.

The theory of memorial reconstruction postulates a reduced company touring England when plague closed the London theatres; provincial audiences with cruder taste and poor theatrical stamina, for whom plays had to be adapted (to expand comic opportunities) and shortened (to reduce playing time); and reduced staging facilities. The company was compelled to create a new playbook, basing their text on the memories of actors who may not have played the roles they were now trying urgently, and sometimes inaccurately, to recall. In this theory, the 'bad' quartos are derivative, but they are valuable in that they preserve a link with contemporary performance. In short, they represent what Shakespeare wrote, in a text he didn't write.

We don't know why Heminges and Condell excluded all short quartos from the Folio. What we do know is that they were consistent in their exclusion policy. *Pericles* had been published in a short quarto in 1609. Presumably Heminges and Condell did not possess a longer or verbally improved version in 1622–3 since, rather than represent Shakespeare by a short quarto, they excluded *Pericles* from the Folio altogether. Not all seventeenth-century editors and publishers were so consistent. The second quarto of *Romeo and Juliet*, published in 1599 to replace the 'short' quarto of 1597, advertises its superior status on the titlepage: '*Newly corrected, augmented, and amended*'. Nonetheless, the compositor of the second quarto copied the first quarto text for portions of Act I.

In the 1980s the short quartos came to be appreciated by textual critics who believed in the theory of memorial reconstruction as well as by those who didn't. The former group renewed critical attention on the short quartos' effective staging and illuminating stage directions, such as the appearance of the ghost in *Hamlet* (3.4.93) '*in his nightgown*' (without which detail we might assume that the ghost appears, as he did in Act I, in armour). The latter group rehabilitated the short quartos' verbal quality, arguing that the difference between short quartos and their textually variant second editions was due not to memorial degeneration but to Shakespeare revising his work. The jury is still out on these competing theories, but it seems clear that neither memorial reconstruction nor authorial draft/revision provides a blanket explanation for these complicated and interesting texts. When an editor encounters a two-text or three-text play, his or her first task is to construct a theory of the relation between the versions.

Editing

An editor is a mediator. All media require editors although we know them by different names: curator, producer, director. Editing Shakespeare today is a complex technical task. It involves comparing all surviving early quartos and Folios to identify stop-press corrections, for, although proofreading took place, and corrections were made, during the Elizabethan printing process, the faulty sheets were not discarded. Thus, each buyer of a quarto purchased a (differently) mixed set of corrected and uncorrected sheets. Editors must therefore examine all surviving copies of the same edition to discover correct or corrected readings.

Editing wasn't always this thorough. Making it systematic was the achievement of a group of early twentieth-century scholars known as the New Bibliographers, whose aim was to remove 'the veil of print'. By identifying errors and practices attributable to the printing house, editors believed they could discern the lost Shakespearian manuscript which lay behind the printed version.

In the years after Shakespeare's death editing had been both more and less easy. It was easier because taste rather than evidence influenced the editor: the 1640 printing of Shakespeare's sonnets arbitrarily changed some masculine possessive pronouns to feminine, making selected sonnets more palatably heterosexual. In 1725 Alexander Pope's edition relegated to the foot of the page passages distasteful to Augustan sensibility. Instead of acknowledging that Elizabethan tastes did not accord with Augustan decorum, Pope concluded that these passages were unShakespearian.

But editing was also more difficult because fewer materials were available for comparative study. The short quarto of *Hamlet* was not discovered until 1823 (even today there are only two copies in the world, and one of them is incomplete). Editing was made even more difficult because the status of subsequent reprints was not understood as derivative. In 1709 Rowe believed that the most recent edition should be the basis of an edition, but by that date nearly a century of printing-house error had accrued.

Note the names of the early Shakespeare editors: Nicholas Rowe (1709), Alexander Pope (1725), Lewis Theobald (1733), William Warburton (1747), and Samuel Johnson (1765). These are mostly literary figures. Shakespeare editing in the eighteenth century was the property of men of letters.

It was also the property of stationers. Literacy was increasing (by 1750 at least 40 per cent of women could read and 60 per cent of men could read and write)[5]; the invention of the novel fuelled demand for reading material, and drama could be read. Jacob Tonson and his sons, the publishers who dominated the Shakespeare market in the eighteenth century, issued Shakespeare in small (octavo) multi-volume series. No longer confined to a single imposing folio volume, Shakespeare was portable, and editing was competitive.

In the nineteenth century Shakespeare editing changed its spiritual location, from the poet in the coffeehouse to the academic in the university. Three Cambridge fellows produced the influential Cambridge Shakespeare in 1863–66. Shakespeare editing was now in the hands of professional academics. In the early twentieth century the textual climate changed because of New Bibliography (see above); the projected Oxford Shakespeare (general editor R. B. McKerrow), designed as a replacement to the Oxford edition of 1891, was to be the first edition to embody New Bibliographical tenets.

This ambitious academic project was planned as an old-spelling edition. Old spelling is indeed Elizabethan spelling, but it is not necessarily Shakespearian spelling. The early modern period had not standardized orthography; compositors adjusted authors' manuscript spellings for reasons ranging from unconscious personal preference to purposeful justification. (Although 'barenes' and 'barrennesse' were pronounced the same, the variant spellings made a crucial difference to the length of a printed line.) The last Oxford editor, Alice Walker, lost faith in the value of old spelling during the forty years in which she worked sporadically on the project, and the Oxford Shakespeare, as conceived by McKerrow, was never completed. When Walker died in 1982, her will requested that all her notes for the Oxford Shakespeare be destroyed. Walker's death was, in a sense, the death of the New Bibliography.

Beginning the reconceived editorial project from scratch, and working full time, Stanley Wells, joined subsequently by Gary Taylor, John Jowett, and William Montgomery, published an Oxford *Complete Works* in 1986. The edition was very different from that first envisaged. It was based on two beliefs: (1) Shakespeare revised; (2) staging does not sully a play. Thus, the editors preferred texts adapted for stage production—versions printed from playbooks rather than from the author's longer original drafts; they provided two texts of *King Lear*; they valued stage directions from the short quartos; they published two volumes—both modern and old spelling. The edition was innovative in every conceivable way. It became a manifesto for editorial change and for a movement unofficially christened New Revisionism.

Unediting

The notion that Shakespeare revised his plays was not new when it was promulgated in the 1980s, but it had been out of favour for a long time for obvious reasons: as long as Shakespeare was viewed as a Romantic genius who 'scarce blotted a line', revision was an untenable option. Bardolatry had recreated Shakespeare as God, and God does not have second thoughts. For the current generation, which questions not just God but the very concept of an author, the notion of multiple texts poses no such problem. On the contrary, it exercises great attractions: the postmodern condition is one of plural voices.

When a Shakespeare play exists in two or three texts, which version should an editor present? The New Bibliographers believed that editors should print the version originally planned by the author, the version before theatrical exigencies intervened. Thus, a *Hamlet* editor should choose the second quarto, which is presumed to have been printed from the author's manuscript; as Philip Edwards writes in his New Cambridge edition of *Hamlet*, 'the nearer we get to the stage, the further we are getting from Shakespeare'.[6] The editors of the Oxford *Complete Works* take the opposite view to Edwards: given that a playtext is first and foremost drama, the stage version is the more appropriate editorial choice. Thus, a *Hamlet* editor should choose the shorter Folio text, which is printed from the company's playbook.

In fact, neither editorial choice is wrong (or right), because there is no definitive text of a play, just snapshots of it at different evolutionary stages. What *is* clearly wrong is to conflate different versions with separate theatrical and thematic values (e.g. Q1 merged with F *King Lear*, Q2 with F *Hamlet*) and produce an eclectic text, as was done for centuries with *King Lear* and *Hamlet*. A conflated edition is a text that Shakespeare certainly didn't write, nor was it performed in the theatre of his time.

All major publishing houses are now re-editing Shakespeare to incorporate recent advances in textual knowledge and theory. The single-volume texts in the Oxford and Cambridge series provide innovative ways of representing multiple versions to the reader: cut or revised material is italicized, printed in bold, enclosed in square brackets or added as an appendix. Although today's editors are professional scholars, not poets, they share one thing with eighteenth-century literati: their names are as prominent as Shakespeare's on the titlepage. There is no such thing as Shakespeare's text; there is only the editor's text (or what the editor says is Shakespeare's text, or *one* of Shakespeare's texts).

What we call Shakespeare

Shakespeare's first editors, Heminges and Condell, are commemorated in a modern plaque in the garden of the Church of St Mary the Virgin, in Aldermanbury in London: 'To the Memory of John Heminge and Henry Condell . . . the world owes all that it calls Shakespeare'. What Heminges and Condell called Shakespeare in 1623 is different from what the editors of the Oxford *Complete Works* called Shakespeare in 1986, not just in texts of plays but in their number.

The First Folio contained thirty-six plays; the Oxford *Complete Works* has thirty-eight (excluding the second version of *King Lear*), plus 147 lines which some believe (or want) to be by Shakespeare in the manuscript play *Sir Thomas More*. The additional Oxford plays are *Pericles* (quarto 1609), and *The Two Noble Kinsmen*, by Shakespeare and Fletcher, first published in 1634. The *Riverside Shakespeare* (1997) offers a thirty-ninth play, *The Reign of King Edward the Third*, a history play first published in 1596.

The Oxford *Complete Works* represents Shakespeare's poetry with *Venus and Adonis*, *The Rape of Lucrece*, the sonnets, *A Lover's Complaint*, and *Various Poems*, including the manuscript poem *Shall I die? Shall I fly?*, defended (controversially) as Shakespeare's by Gary Taylor in 1985 (the poem was first identified as Shakespeare's by the compiler of the manuscript in Oxford's Bodleian Library). To these poems the *Norton Shakespeare* (1997, based on the Oxford *Complete Works*) adds another: the 578-line poem *A Funeral Elegy to Master William Peter*.

As contents change, so do titles. *Henry VIII* is named *All is True* in the Oxford and

Norton editions, a change justified by contemporary references to the play under that title. Similarly, *Henry VI Part Two* and *Henry VI Part Three* appear as *The First Part of the Contention of the Two Famous Houses of York and Lancaster* and *The True Tragedy of Richard Duke of York and the Good King Henry the Sixth*, the titles under which these plays were first published in the short quartos of 1594 and 1595.

Such fluctuations in 'what we call Shakespeare' are not confined to the textually innovative and interrogative climate of the 1990s. The Second Folio edition of 1632 included *Pericles*, and the Third Folio of 1664 included six more plays, the Shakespeare 'apocrypha'. But why has *Pericles* been readily accepted whereas the apocrypha were quickly rejected? (For the textual procedures which exclude some plays from canonical status while admitting others, see Chapter 41.) Recent developments in stylometrics have put canonical judgements on a quantitative basis. Before the late twentieth century, however, such value judgements were subjective and partisan, revealing more about the tastes of a particular period than about Shakespearian authorship. The history of Shakespeare in print is thus not just a history of printing: it is a social and political history of the people and periods who read and produce him.

FURTHER READING

Berger, Thomas L. 'Looking for Shakespeare in Caroline England', *Viator* 27 (1996), 323–59. Examines the ways in which reprints subtly remake and reinterpret the Shakespearian text simply by appearing in a different historical context.

Blayney, Peter W. M. *The First Folio of Shakespeare* (Washington, D.C: Folger Library Publications, 1991). A lucid and usefully illustrated account of how the First Folio came into being.

Blayney, Peter W. M. 'The Publication of Playbooks'. In John D. Cox and David Scott Kastan (eds.). *A New History of Early English Drama* (New York: Columbia University Press, 1997), pp. 383–422. What incentive did an early modern publisher have to publish a play? This nuts-and-bolts economic analysis shows that the financial rewards were slim.

Brooks, Douglas A. *From Playhouse to Printing House: Drama and Authorship in Early Modern England* (Cambridge: Cambridge University Press, 2000). A theoretically informed analysis of the processes by which plays reach print—as accessible as it is learned.

Kastan, David Scott (ed.). *A Companion to Shakespeare* (Oxford: Blackwell, 1999). Part Seven (pp. 395–485) contains five essays covering key aspects of publishing, from manuscripts to press censorship.

Maguire, Laurie E. *Shakespearean Suspect Texts* (Cambridge: Cambridge University Press, 1996). Chapters 1–4 analyse the problems of the short quartos in relation to the rise of the New Bibliography.

Taylor, Gary. *Re-Inventing Shakespeare: A Cultural History from the Restoration to the Present* (London: Hogarth, 1990). A witty historical survey of Shakespeare's reputation in each century, dovetailing publishing and production history.

Taylor, Gary *et al.* 'General Introduction'. In Stanley Wells *et al.*, *William Shakespeare: A Textual Companion* (Oxford: Clarendon Press, 1987), pp. 1–68. A very readable survey of all aspects of textual transmission.

Taylor, Gary and Warren, Michael (eds.). *The Division of the Kingdoms* (Oxford: Clarendon Press, 1983). Thorough analysis, from many angles, of the evidence for revision in the Folio *King Lear*.

Urkowitz, Steven. *Shakespeare's Revision of 'King Lear'* (Princeton: Princeton University Press, 1980). The title serves as summary. This slightly over-polemicized book inaugurated revision theories.

Wells, Stanley. *Re-editing Shakespeare for the Modern Reader* (Oxford: Clarendon Press, 1984). Lucid explanations and illustrations of what editing involves and why it matters.

NOTES

1. Edward Arber. *A Transcript of the Registers of the Company of Stationers of London: 1554–1640*. Vol 2. (London: privately printed, 1875), p. 235v (28 October 1588).

2. I here view *A Midsummer Night's Dream* as a single text, while acknowledging that the First Folio compositors consulted a manuscript and therefore, technically, had two versions of this play; however, we do not. I similarly count *Henry IV Part Two* as a single text with a similar qualification. See Stanley Wells *et al. William Shakespeare: A Textual Companion* (Oxford: Clarendon Press, 1987), pp. 279–80 and 351–3 for detailed discussion.

3. Influenced by Stephen Miller's argument that *The Taming of a Shrew* (1594) is a deliberate, memorially derivative adaptation of *The Taming of the Shrew*, I count quarto *The Taming of a Shrew* and Folio *The Taming of the Shrew* as variant texts of one play. Although the difference between the First Folio and the quarto is not dissimilar to that between Folio *King John* and quarto *The Troublesome Reign of King John* (1591), the *Shrew* plays have more lexical links than the *King John* plays; I therefore prefer to omit the latter from this group.

4. *Love's Labour's Lost* appears to have existed in a lost edition of c.1597 to which the 1599 edition stands in the same relation as Q2 *Romeo and Juliet* to Q1 *Romeo and Juliet*; I exclude this presumed first edition of *Love's Labour's Lost* for the same reason as I exclude the alternative version of *A Midsummer Night's Dream*.

5. J. Paul Hunter. 'The novel and social/cultural history'. In *The Cambridge Companion to the Eighteenth Century Novel*, ed. John Richetti (Cambridge: Cambridge University Press, 1996), pp. 9–40. See p. 20.

6. Philip Edwards (ed.). *Hamlet* (Cambridge: Cambridge University Press, 1985), p. 32.

39 | Shakespeare and the modern British theatre

Michael Billington

Where does 'modern' Shakespeare begin? What are the key events that signify a radical shift in approaches to staging his plays? From a British perspective, theatre historians always seize on certain landmarks. One is Harley Granville Barker's seasons at the Savoy Theatre from 1912 to 1914 when he staged *Twelfth Night*, *The Winter's Tale*, and *A Midsummer Night's Dream*: productions that famously swept away scenic clutter and put the emphasis on clarity and simplicity. Everyone also agrees that Peter Hall's creation of the Royal Shakespeare Company at Stratford-upon-Avon in 1960 was a defining moment: an attempt to achieve permanence and continuity and to address standards of verse-speaking by allowing the music to emerge through the meaning. And Peter Brook's famous production of *A Midsummer Night's Dream* for the RSC in 1970 has left its mark on generations who never saw it: not least through its much-imitated white-box setting and its vision of the actor as acrobat (see Chapter 35 for more on these landmark productions).

We can all agree that, for the English-speaking world at least, these were significant events: part of a concerted drive to rescue Shakespeare from mindless Victorian spectacle, the vanity of spotlight-seeking actor-managers and euphonious but empty verse-speaking. The process of 'modernizing' Shakespeare was also accelerated by the rise of the director (initially called the producer) within the theatrical power-structure. It meant there was a controlling intelligence at work, ideally fusing performance, design, lighting, and music into one interpretative whole. In Britain the legatees of Granville Barker include such distinctive figures as Tyrone Guthrie, Peter Brook, Peter Hall, John Barton, Trevor Nunn, Terry Hands, Richard Eyre and, in a predominantly male club, Deborah Warner. In Russia there were Stanislavsky and Meyerhold. In France, Copeau and Barrault. In Germany, where the director has an almost unassailable power, Brecht and Piscator were followed by Peter Stein and Peter Zadek. Though few of them were exclusively devoted to Shakespeare, they all brought to his work a shaping individual vision.

But at the start of a new century the picture is much less clear. The director still enjoys huge authority in Western theatre. At the same time there is a growing resistance to so-called 'conceptual' productions dominated by a governing intellectual idea. And almost everything in the theatre is in a state of flux. The centrality of text is challenged by those who argue that theatre is an essentially physical, visceral experience. There is a populist appetite for spectacle, evidenced by international hit musicals such as *Cats* and *Les Misérables*, both directed alone or in part by the RSC's Trevor Nunn, which is offset by a hunger for minimalist purity. Even the idea that drama takes place in designated buildings called theatres is under threat: young directors, and audiences, delight in 'found' spaces such as converted industrial sites, garages, and warehouses. There is no consensus about what constitutes theatre: Deborah Warner, a passionate Shakespearian who has staged fine productions of *Titus Andronicus* and *King Lear*, has also created magical events in which selected spectators are guided through a disused Edwardian hotel or led to the top of an angel-frequented tower-block. Not only is there little agreement about what constitutes theatre; there is also a vocal minority that believes the very notion of live theatrical performance is outmoded in the age of television, video, and the internet.

One can look at this lack of consensus in one of two ways. One can welcome the stylistic freedom it affords; or one can say that it leads to anarchic confusion. Either way it has had a profound effect on the staging of Shakespeare. Obviously there has always been a diversity of approach to Shakespeare, but in the relatively recent past there were certain common goals: in the 1960s, for instance, there was a widespread assumption, heavily influenced by Jan Kott's seminal *Shakespeare Our Contemporary* (1964), that one had to unearth the social and political relevance of the plays. Successive British visits in 1956 and 1965 by Brecht's hugely influential Berliner Ensemble also led to a rejection of decorative, painted scenery in favour of authentic materials such as timber and steel.

Today, however, Shakespearian production provides a vivid metaphor not only for what one director, Bill Alexander, has dubbed the 'merry eclecticism' of modern theatre but for our larger social, political, and religious uncertainties. Rarely, if ever, have so many extreme Shakespearian experiences been available to the spectator. You find the plays done everywhere from Victorian proscenium theatres to converted film-studios. Texts are sometimes treated with scholarly precision; at other times ruthlessly cut and adapted. Star-oriented Shakespeare has made a comeback with Dawn French's Bottom getting top billing in a West End *A Midsummer Night's Dream*; elsewhere the director is still king. Some companies aim for standard English pronunciation; the Halifax-based Northern Broadsides use a rich Yorkshire dialect. Casting is also dictated by temperamental suitability rather than stereotypical tradition. In the course of a single twelvemonth in Britain, starting in August 2000, you could have seen *Hamlet* played by a remarkable German actress (Angela Winkler); a black, British-born actor (Adrian Lester); and a short, stout, mesmerising forty-year-old (Simon Russell Beale). Only Samuel West at Stratford-upon-Avon came remotely close to the traditional image of Hamlet as a young, tall, white male; and even the shoeless West sported black jeans and leather jacket, carried an automatic handgun, and at one point shared a joint with Rosencrantz and Guildenstern. To some extent this plurality of princes confirms Oscar Wilde's point in *The Critic as Artist* that 'there is no such thing as Shakespeare's Hamlet'; by which he meant that the role is defined by the personality of the individual interpreter. But this diversity of Hamlets, in productions ranging from a full-text, four-hour Stratford version to a two-and-a-half-hour adaptation by Peter Brook, also neatly symbolizes something larger: the total lack of any consensual approach to Shakespearian production today in terms of philosophy, politics, presentation, or practical methods of stagecraft.

Journeys through space

Space itself is obviously a determining factor in the approach to Shakespeare. There is a vast difference between watching a Shakespeare play in a 175-seat theatre such as The Pit at the Barbican Centre and sitting or standing with 1,600 spectators, partly exposed to the elements, in Shakespeare's Globe on Bankside. In the former you become an anonymous eavesdropper; in the latter a participant in a noisy public spectacle. Indeed, the opening of Shakespeare's Globe in 1996 has had a considerable effect not just on the way the plays are staged but also on the way they are received and understood.

The Globe (see Figure 4.3) was the long-cherished dream of an American actor-director, Sam Wanamaker, who could never understand why London had no lasting memorial to the world's greatest playwright. Sadly, Wanamaker died in 1993 when construction of the theatre had only just begun. And what we have today is in no sense an exact replica of the original Globe, since there is no surviving model: it is simply a 'best guess' using authentic materials such as water reed thatch for the roof and Elizabethan techniques of construction. But in the short time that the Globe has been open, several things have become clear. One is that the space dictates a 'presentational' style of acting in which speeches and emotions are shared with the audience. And another is that spectators, conditioned by illusionist theatre to sit watching plays in silence, enjoy being involved. In that sense, the Globe offers interactive Shakespeare.

At its worst, this leads to a boorish self-consciousness: it was predictable that chauvinist spectators would boo the French in the 1997 production of *Henry V*, but there was something deeply disturbing about the hissing that greeted Shylock's demand for Antonio's pound of flesh in the following year's *The Merchant of Venice*. This was Shakespeare reduced to the level of Victorian melodrama. At its best, however, the Globe can produce an eyeball-to-eyeball, two-way relationship between actor and audience. Mark Rylance, the Globe's artistic director and easily its most accomplished performer, showed this in the 2001 production of *Cymbeline*: playing the marginal role of a doctor, alongside the more substantial ones of Cloten and Posthumus, he simply turned to the audience after the exit of Cymbeline's wicked Queen and commented 'I do not like her' only to bring the house down. Mike Alfreds's production (forsaking the dubious goal of 'authenticity' and played by a cast of eight white-suited actors) also showed how the space lends itself to lightning-fast transitions. In a geographically

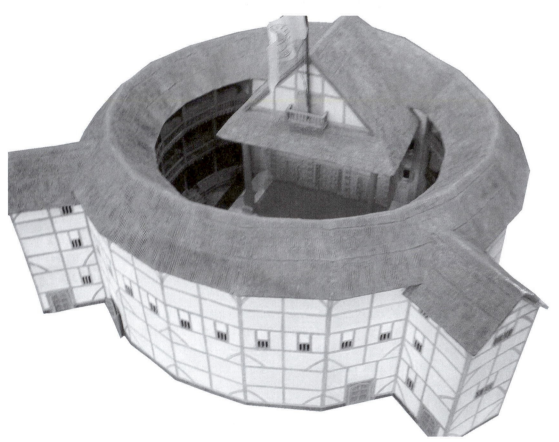

Fig. 4.3 Extensive archival and archaeological research informed the design and construction of 'Shakespeare's Globe', built on London's South Bank not far from the site of the original Globe playhouse.

restless play an actor had only to strike a gong and announce 'Rome' for us to accept the change of scene in a second.

The argument against the Globe is that, although offering a reasonable facsimile of an Elizabethan theatre, it cannot reproduce the social, physical, or intellectual climate that surrounded it. Behind the construction of the Globe also lurks the sentimental fallacy that the original building was the *ne plus ultra* in theatrical architecture rather than a phase in the natural evolution of the English playhouse. But, against that, one has to admit that the Globe has been a huge popular success. Its summer seasons are also backed up by an ambitious educational programme and by staged readings of contextual plays. In 2001, for instance, you could see Shakespeare's *King Lear* on stage and attend an afternoon reading of *King Leir and His Daughters* (1605). This anonymous chronicle play was Shakespeare's likeliest source, in which, with the help of the King of France, the hero is happily reconciled with his daughter, Cordella, and regains the English throne.

But the most vivid demonstration of the impact of space on performance and production styles is provided by the Royal Shakespeare Company. In Stratford-upon-Avon it has regularly worked in three different theatres. The largest is the 1,500-seat Royal Shakespeare Theatre, a much-modified version of a building, designed by Elisabeth Scott, that opened in 1932. Alongside that is The Swan Theatre, a galleried neo-Jacobean playhouse that opened in 1986. The third building, The Other Place, began its life as a roughly converted tin shed in 1974 but in the 1990s was successfully transformed into an elegant studio-space that mixed live performance with educational work. Each space makes its own aesthetic demands. Each yields different results, as can be seen by tracing the stage history of a single play, *Macbeth*, in the three different venues.

Macbeth is a play that invariably poses practical problems: the representation of the Witches, the casting of the title-role, the maintenance of suspense during the difficult English scene. Stratford's main theatre (then known as the Shakespeare Memorial Theatre) housed one celebrated performance by Laurence Olivier in 1955, but even that was framed by an ugly, awkward production. And, even after the creation of the Royal Shakespeare Company, the play seemed to elude most directors. Peter Hall's 1967 *Macbeth* was an acknowledged disaster with the use of real leaves from real trees from the real Birnam Wood getting unsolicited first-night laughs. Trevor Nunn's 1974 version emerged as an over-elaborate religious spectacle. And, with the arguable exception of an Adrian Noble production that highlighted the central couple's obsession with childlessness, the play continued to defeat directors in Stratford's main house.

It was only in the relatively smaller spaces that the play achieved tragic impact. In 1976 Trevor Nunn staged it in the original Other Place and used its intimacy to devastating effect. The actors, led by Ian McKellen and Judi Dench, performed the play inside a defined black circle and the audience sat a few feet away from them as if participating in an incantatory rite: when Dench's Lady Macbeth invoked evil spirits and then darted back with a stab of fear it was as if she had made contact with satanic forces. That sort of effect could be achieved only in a small space; equally, the use of a single naked light circling over Macbeth's head to convey a world gone awry depended on the setting's conspiratorial intimacy. Nunn's production become the yardstick against which future ventures were measured, and it was not matched until Gregory Doran staged the play in the Stratford Swan in 1999. Then, the voices of the witches sinisterly emerged out of total darkness. Antony Sher's Macbeth and Ken Bones's Banquo were first seen in battle-fatigues and berets, carried shoulder high by exultant soldiers rather than looking, as so often happens, as if they'd emerged from nothing more strenuous than a round of golf at St Andrews. Like Nunn, Doran also stripped the play of an interval to give it a vertiginous speed. With its echoes of bloodshed in the Balkans, Rwanda, or Iraq, it would have been a brilliant production anywhere; but there is little doubt that the sepulchral intimacy of The Swan (which Sher has dubbed the best theatre he has ever worked in) was a decisive factor in its success.

What is clear in modern Shakespeare is that space determines style. In a large theatre, with the arguable exception of The Globe, the plays become public spectacles and the actors succumb to rhetoric: in a small space it is possible to achieve both psychological intimacy and a greater verbal precision. The point was neatly proved by two productions of *Richard II* that opened within a few weeks of each other in the spring of 2000. The Almeida Theatre production, starring Ralph Fiennes, was staged in a dilapidated Edwardian power station in Shoreditch that had once served as the Gainsborough Film Studios. The setting itself was staggering: the stage-floor was a grassy carpet implying England as a demi-paradise, but the rear wall was dominated by a central fissure suggesting schismatic disintegration. But the monumental space dwarfed most of the performers and, with the exception of David Burke's John of Gaunt and Oliver Ford-Davies's Duke of York, there was much bellowing from interchangeable Shakespearian nobles. Contrast that with Steven Pimlott's production presented in an intimate white box at Stratford's Other Place. It was not simply that this version was modern rather than medieval and more concerned with political infighting than poetic tragedy. Every syllable was crystal-clear. Every character was sharply defined. And, in this stripped-down space, props acquired a symbolic resonance: a long wooden casket variously became the English throne, a vertical mirror, and Richard's coffin. It would be simplistic to argue that small is always beautiful and big is invariably bad: I have seen many fine Shakespeare productions in large theatres. But there is little doubt that the same play, *Richard II*, made a totally different aesthetic impact in these two contrasting spaces. In the Gainsborough Studios we were witnesses to an external spectacle; in The Other Place we were engaged participants.

You cannot, however, legislate for Shakespeare. Audiences flocked to the Gainsborough Studios. In particular, there is a great appetite for 'found' spaces; one of the obvious attractions of Barrie Rutter's company, Northern Broadsides, is not just that it plays in Yorkshire dialect but that its productions invariably start in the rough-hewn basement of a onetime Halifax textile-mill, Dean Clough. And the further afield you go the more you find Shakespeare being staged in everything from vast arenas to intimate spaces. During Peter Stein's tenure as theatre director of the Salzburg Festival in the 1990s, three of Shakespeare's Roman plays were staged in the huge Felsenreitschule, a performance-space actually carved out of the surrounding rock. Stein's own production of *Julius Caesar* was also one of the few in recent times to make sense of the play: employing a huge army of extras, many of them military cadets, it effectively re-created the anarchic turmoil and mob-panic that followed the assassination of Caesar. At the opposite extreme Peter Brook's *The Tragedy of Hamlet* began its life in the Bouffes du Nord (a former vaudeville house) in Paris, used only eight actors, and was based on an imaginative minimalism. Stein and Brook are two of the most lauded directors working in Europe today. But their approach to Shakespeare could hardly be more different. Stein aims for an epic realism; Brook seeks to cut through a play's historic accretions to discover its mythic roots. Stein, in Salzburg, worked on a stage of Cinerama-like proportions; Brook treats the performance-area as an empty space. Between them the two Peters neatly illustrate the irreconcilable polarities of modern Shakespearian production.

Diversities of style

Spaces, in part, dictate styles. But over the last half-century we have also witnessed an increasing fragmentation in the approach to Shakespeare. All generalizations simplify, but it would be fair to say that the 1940s and 1950s were the age of the heroic individual actor: the era of Laurence Olivier's Richard III, Macbeth, and Coriolanus; of John Gielgud's Angelo in *Measure for Measure*, Cassius, and Prospero; of Michael Redgrave's Hamlet, Lear, and Shylock; of Peggy Ashcroft's Innogen, Viola, and Portia in *The Merchant of Venice*.

Obviously there were great productions by directors of the calibre of Peter Brook and Tyrone Guthrie; but the actor was the defining presence in the immediate post-war world. Inevitably that changed, particularly in Britain, with the rise of the director and the establishment of a semi-permanent company such as the RSC. In the 1960s, through the influence of Brechtian practice, Jan Kott's theories, and an increasing political awareness, the urge was to search for Shakespeare's contemporary relevance: at the RSC that was visible in the Peter Hall–John Barton *The Wars of the Roses*, which treated the dynastic battles of York and Lancaster as a mirror for the modern world. In the 1970s, partly through the opening-up of smaller spaces and partly through the influence of Peter Brook's *A Midsummer Night's Dream* with its climactic gesture of actors and audiences linking hands, the guiding principle was to make the production of Shakespeare a shared, communal experience. Thereafter it becomes more difficult to characterize individual decades. It may, in Britain, be a result of Thatcher's notorious dictum that 'there is no such thing as society': simply a series of individual enterprises and initiatives. It may equally be a consequence of a beleaguered theatre's shift into survival-mode: for the last twenty years of the century cash-strapped companies were more concerned with appeasing bank managers and getting through to the next grant cheque than with hammering out a shared philosophy.

You can find a metaphor for the changing times (and for the dissolution of consensual approaches to Shakespeare) in two separate cycles of Shakespeare's English history plays presented by the RSC nearly forty years apart. Capitalizing on the success of *The Wars of the Roses* (a conflation of the three parts of *Henry VI* and *Richard III*) in 1963, the following year the company had the bold idea of presenting a complete seven-play history cycle. All the productions were staged in the Royal Shakespeare Theatre. All deployed the same production-team led by Peter Hall and John Barton as directors, John Bury as designer, Guy Woolfenden as composer. The company of actors was constant, so that David Warner, for instance, played Richard II and Henry VI, while Ian Holm moved through Prince Hal and Henry V to later transmogrify into Richard, Duke of Gloucester and Richard III. Above all, there was a shared philosophy. Every programme contained a note headed 'The Cycle of a Curse' which argued: 'Behind immense variety, the themes and characters are continuously developed through the cycle. As Orestes was haunted in Greek drama, so Englishmen fight each other to expunge the curse pronounced upon Bolingbroke's usurpation of the tragically weak Richard II'. And in a fascinating interview in the final programme for *Richard III*, Hall and Barton revealed their similarity of outlook and even completed each other's sentences. Hall, speaking of the histories, talks of 'the single historical awareness behind all of them . . .' while Barton goes on to talk of 'an organising political mind'. Anyone lucky enough to have seen that cycle will recall the heroic collective achievement and the molten unity of the staging, even though the chronology of the plays does not match the order in which they were written.

In 2000 the RSC, now led by Adrian Noble, went one further and staged an eight-play history cycle (with the *Henry VI* trilogy presented virtually uncut) under the collective title '*This England*'. But the differences between 1964 and 2000 were striking. In 2000 the plays were staged by four different directors—Steven Pimlott (*Richard II*), Michael Attenborough (*Henry IV Parts One and Two*), Edward Hall (*Henry V*) and Michael Boyd (*Henry VI* and *Richard III*)—in three different Stratford spaces. The final tetralogy was played by a totally separate company. And, even when there were casting links between the plays, one was aware of a deliberate discontinuity: Adam Levy's Harry Percy in *Richard II*, for instance, was a gun-toting guerrilla in a black Che Guevara beret who then turned into an equally militant but more traditionally medieval Hotspur in *Henry IV Part One*.

None of this implies criticism of the later cycle, which was a richly spectacular achievement. It brought out very clearly Shakespeare's moral ambivalence: nowhere more so than in the *Henry IV* plays, where Desmond Barrit's Falstaff was a figure of both paternal warmth and extraordinary cruelty who accepted the death of all but three of his ragamuffin recruits with casual disdain (one suspects that W. H. Auden, who once compared Falstaff to Jesus Christ, cannot have seen the plays very often in the theatre).

Sequential exposure to the plays also highlighted Shakespeare's obsessive preoccupation with fathers and sons almost matching Verdi's fascination with fathers and daughters. And the dazzlingly varied productions gave one a heightened sense of the polyphonic variety of Shakespeare's language. At a public debate about the productions the novelist Mauren Duffy ended the session with the remark that Shakespeare is 'our linguistic rainforest', a dazzling aphorism implying both multifarious variety and imminent decimation. But two key differences between the 1964 and 2000 cycles remain. The former was based on continuity; the latter on deliberate discontinuity, as if to remind audiences of the fractious tribalism that haunts both the world Shakespeare portrays and our own times. And, whereas in 1964 the cycle was played repeatedly in Stratford's largest theatre, in 2000 it was possible to view the plays in strict chronological sequence only twice, and that was in the course of their transfer from Stratford to the Royal Shakespeare Company's London home: a symbol either of commercial realism or declining confidence in the box-office appeal of Shakespeare's less familiar plays.

Methods of staging

It is true that in the modern theatre Shakespeare's plays are revived according to an assumed hierarchy of popularity: for every *King John* or *Cymbeline* there are a score of *Twelfth Night*s. It is also true that they are presented in a sometimes bewildering range of styles. But the new eclecticism also brings with it many advantages. The most immediately obvious is the casting of the plays according to talent rather than racial stereotype. Time was when the only roles a black actor could hope to play were Othello, Aaron the Moor and, if he was singularly unlucky, the Prince of Morocco in *The Merchant of Venice*. Now David Oyewolo plays Henry VI; Hugh Quarshie, Mark Antony; and Josette Simon, Rosaline in *Love's Labour's Lost*. At the National Theatre we have had a *Troilus and Cressida* in which the Trojans were black and the Greeks white, and a similar division between Montagues and Capulets in *Romeo and Juliet* with Chiweitel Ejiofor outstanding as the doomed hero. Peter Brook's company in Paris has also long been based on multi-ethnic principles, so that in *The Tragedy of Hamlet* we had a black Prince of Denmark, an Asian Ophelia, and a Japanese Rosencrantz. A few diehards occasionally mutter objections, but the battle for integrated casting has generally been won. The only loss has been the virtual impossibility, in the current climate, of any white actor ever playing Othello: Michael Gambon, in an indifferent Scarborough production, was possibly the last of a distinguished historic line.

The new eclecticism has also liberated the plays from the rigidities of gender-strict casting. There is a long tradition of women playing Hamlet, dating back to the nineteenth century and embracing France's Sarah Bernhardt, Britain's doughty Mrs Bandmann Palmer (who offstage wore tweeds and hob-nailed boots) and, more recently, Frances de la Tour and Angela Winkler. But *King Lear* has lately attracted Kathryn Hunter in Britain and Maria Casares in France; Vanessa Redgrave has played Prospero at Shakespeare's Globe; and Fiona Shaw, Richard II at the National Theatre. Conversely, Mark Rylance was a feisty, witty Cleopatra at the Globe, and Cheek by Jowl's all-male *As You Like It*, with Adrian Lester as a stunning Rosalind, captured the play's sexual mystery in a way that few conventional productions have done (certainly far better than a similar, earlier experiment at the National Theatre that looked like a second-rate drag-show). The new emphasis on cross-gender casting is not derived from any misplaced historicism: it stems, one assumes, from the age's greater openness and from the recognition that we are all a bundle of sexual contradictions. Its effects have been almost wholly positive and its possibilities are limitless.

New technology is also having its impact on the staging of Shakespeare. The incorporation of film into live action is now easily accomplished and can be beneficial or distracting according to circumstances. A recent Stratford *Hamlet*, directed by Matthew Warchus, began with film of the boy-prince playing with his father in the snow and evoked a suitably idyllic past; less happy was Trevor Nunn's device, in his National Theatre *Merchant of Venice*, of having Portia replay jerky home-movies of her previous wooers to accompany Nerissa's graphic description of them. But the director who has taken the process furthest is the American Peter Sellars in a *Merchant of Venice* that came to the Barbican Theatre in 1994.

Sellars's much-vilified production was radical in every respect. Set in modern California, it presented us with an African-American Shylock, a Chinese-American Portia and Nerissa, and an Hispanic Antonio and Bassanio. But Sellars also surrounded the stage with banks of video-monitors in which it was possible to see the actors' faces in startling close-up: during Shylock's 'Hath not a Jew eyes?' speech, the camera zoomed right in so that we were privy to the actor's emotional urgency as well as to the forensic skill of his argument. Sellars's defence of such heavy reliance on cameras and monitors was intriguing. It was partly philosophical: that technology is part of our everyday world and affects most of the decisions we make. But it was also extremely pragmatic. 'With video monitors', he said, 'people in the third balcony at *The Merchant of Venice* can really see what is happening in an actor's eyes. At the same time, when you want to get intimate on stage you don't want to have to peel the wallpaper off the back of the auditorium every time you make an utterance'. Sellars's argument under-cuts the whole history of performance in which actors have sought to combine intim-acy and audibility. At the same time, it raises an urgent question: are young audiences any longer willing to sit at the back of vast theatres having a totally different experi-ence from the privileged spectators in the stalls? It is a question clearly exercising the directorate of the Royal Shakespeare Company in their deliberations over whether to modify (or even totally abandon) their 1932 Stratford base.

But possibly the biggest debate in modern Shakespeare concerns attitudes to verse-speaking and text. At one end of the spectrum stands Peter Hall, who argues that you must present a full text and observe the rhythm of the iambic penatameter, if only to appreciate the unexpected irregularities. 'Shakespeare', says Hall, 'writes against the verse, yet always preserves it. It is about to break and never quite does—like the counterpoint in the phrasing of a great jazz musician which never quite loses the beat'. At the other end of the spectrum are directors who cut or adapt the text and who allow individual actors to shape the verse according to their psychological needs. *Hamlet*, as always, provides a living example. Peter Hall, in his most recent West End production, and Steven Pimlott, at Stratford in 2001, have played a virtually complete First Folio text. But over the years the text has been snipped and trimmed by other directors so that even Fortinbras has become expendable. The most recent example was *The Tragedy of Hamlet*, which in Peter Brook's adaptation toured the world to great acclaim. Brook cut several characters. He re-ordered the soliloquies so that 'To be or not to be' came after Hamlet had been dispatched to England. And the evening ended with Horatio speaking his lines from Act One, Scene One, in which he describes 'the morn in russet mantle clad' (1.1.147): as he did so all the lights in the theatre came up and Horatio enquired 'Who's there?' In Brook's hands the play became a cyclical study into the infinite mysteries of existence. But this in itself symbolizes the diversity of modern attitudes to Shakespeare: iambic fundamentalism and scholarly precision co-exist with a belief that text is simply one ingredient in the whole theatrical experience.

Conclusion

Shakespeare epitomizes all too accurately the dilemmas and confusions of the age. We argue over how to stage him, where to stage him, and sometimes even whether to stage him at all. Richard Eyre and Nicholas Wright in their book, *Changing Stages*, suggest 'a moratorium on public performances of his plays for two years'. It isn't likely to happen, partly because it would throw large sectors of the theatre industry out of work, but even more because the appetite for his plays remains as insatiable as ever. And this, in the end, is the single most crucial fact that underlies all the aesthetic arguments. For all the attempts to de-canonize Shakespeare academically, attack him on racial, political, or sexual grounds, or even declare him irrelevant to modern experience, the hunger to experience him in the theatre is unabated. There may be no consensus as to what constitutes the ideal approach and we may argue endlessly over the intimate versus the epic, the star-led versus the ensemble, and textual purity versus adaptation, but one salient fact persists: that the milling crowds outside Shakespeare's Bankside Globe, Stratford's Royal Shakespeare Theatre or, for that matter, New York Central Park's Delacorte Theatre in summer or the St Petersburg Maly Theatre in winter testify to the man's enduring, multi-dimensional theatrical appeal. In a godless age he remains our one surviving idol.

FURTHER READING

Bate, Jonathan. *The Genius of Shakespeare* (London: Picador, 1997). A classic study of the mythic power of Shakespeare and of his appropriation by various causes, cultures and belief-systems in the last four centuries.

Delgado, Maria and Paul Heritage (eds.). *In Contact With The Gods?* (Manchester: Manchester University Press, 1996). A series of public interviews with leading directors, including Peter Brook, Declan Donnellan, Peter Sellars, and Peter Stein, that includes much cogent, practical advice on staging Shakespeare.

Holland, Peter. *English Shakespeares* (Cambridge: Cambridge University Press, 1997). A stimulating critical survey of Shakespeare on the English stage in the 1990s that records the abundant variety of approaches and sets the work in the context of foreign productions.

Speaight, Robert. *Shakespeare on the Stage* (London: Collins, 1973). A lavishly illustrated volume that traces the history of Shakespearian performance from Burbage to Brook and that acknowledges the shifts in style in different periods and cultures.

Trewin, J. C. *The Mitchell Beazley Pocket Companion to Shakespeare's Plays* (London: Mitchell Beazley, 1981). An invaluable playgoers' vade-mecum that itemizes the plays chronologically and precisely recalls their performance history.

Wells, Stanley. *Royal Shakespeare* (Manchester: Manchester University Press, 1977). A series of lectures analysing four Stratford productions from 1959 to 1973 in considerable detail and graphically illustrating the power of the single directorial vision.

Shakespeare on film and video

Tony Howard

The history of screen Shakespeare is almost as long as that of cinema itself. For over a century, leading actors have recorded their work for posterity; directors have tried to translate their vision of particular plays into the language of cinema; and producers have dreamed of arranging a marriage between Shakespeare and the mass audience.

Silent Shakespeare

The first Shakespeare films were extracts from stage performances—the death scene from Beerbohm Tree's *King John* (1899), soon followed by Sarah Bernhardt in *The Duel Scene from Hamlet* (1900), which incorporated some form of sound accompaniment. For early filmmakers working in a disreputable industry, Shakespeare offered respectability along with familiar plots which could be compressed into short silent features based round iconic images—Juliet's balcony, *The Merchant of Venice's* trial scene, Hamlet in the graveyard. For their part, established actors were attracted by cinema's promise of unprecedented audiences, a permanent record of their work, and visual resources that would dwarf the spectacular realism of the Victorian stage. Tree's rival Frank Benson filmed several of his Stratford productions (using the stage sets), Forbes-Robertson's *Hamlet* was filmed on location, and meanwhile Tree incorporated film in his stage *Tempest* and played Macbeth in Hollywood for D. W. Griffith. Shakespearian film became an international phenomenon. Hundreds were made, though few survive in their entirety. *Hamlet*, for example, was filmed in France, Italy, Germany, Denmark, and the USA.

The American Vitagraph company produced one-reel (fifteen-minute) condensations of many plays (1908–10); later silent treatments were increasingly elaborate and ambitious. In 1916, for example, the Metro and Fox studios released rival *Romeo and Juliet*s with contrasted publicity campaigns. Metro stressed the educational value of its nine-reel version, which featured a reconstructed Renaissance town and quoted the verse extensively on caption cards. (Unusually, the cast actually learned and spoke Shakespeare's lines.) Fox's racier publicity focused on its star Theda Bara who promised, 'Juliet lived in a period of passionate abandon. Italy in the days of Romeo and Juliet was no place for a Sunday-school girl'. Filming Shakespeare is a schizophrenic activity involving both cultural pretensions and commerce. Asta Nielsen's *Hamlet* (1920) subversively linked the play to post-World War I gender politics and claimed the Prince was a woman in disguise. This witty but moving work has proved much the most enduring Shakespeare film of the period. By denying the characters speech, most silent versions reduced them to stereotypes and puppets, reacting melodramatically to arbitrary events (see Dmitri Buchovetski's *Othello*, 1922), but Neilsen's physical expressiveness translated Shakespeare into gesture to startling effect.

The coming of sound

Sound brought different challenges. Suddenly 'loyalty' to the text became an issue. So did class, nationality, and cultural ownership. Could untrained film actors speak blank verse? Should Americans play Shakespeare at all, and if so must they mimic English Received Pronunciation? Mary Pickford and Douglas Fairbanks's slapstick *Taming of the Shrew* (1929; also released as a silent) was a promising, unpretentious beginning. After a Punch-and-Judy prologue, Kate graduates from fury to manipulation and Pickford subverts her submissive last speech with a broad wink to the women. After a period of technical improvement three studios released competing Shakespearian spectaculars between 1935 and 1937: Warner Brothers' *A Midsummer Night's Dream* (Max Reinhardt, 1935), MGM's *Romeo and Juliet* (George Cukor, 1936), and the British *As You Like It* (Paul Czinner, 1936). Ornate, symphonic, and packed with stars and dances, they were made in the hope that Shakespeare's juxtapositions of tragedy, clowning, and romance would—as on the Victorian stage—attract massive mixed audiences: the *Dream*'s advertising promised 'Three Shows in One!'

In the 1930s Shakespeare signified escapism—literally for Reinhardt and Czinner, who were refugees from Nazi Germany. All three films handled comedy and love laboriously due to the directors' inexperience with English poetry and to the casting—Leslie Howard (Romeo) was forty-one, John Barrymore (Mercutio) fifty-four. However, the dark elements were extremely, even disproportionately, powerful. Czinner's Forest of Arden is a quaint pastoral zoo, but Reinhardt and Cukor's lovers stumble into nightmarish chiaroscuro worlds, plague-stricken and haunted. All three films outraged academics; worse, they failed financially, and so Hollywood largely abandoned Shakespeare for fifty years, except as plot material for genre films such as *Jubal* (1955, a western *Othello*), *Forbidden Planet* (1956, a sci-fi *Tempest*), and musicals like *Kiss Me Kate* (about a production of the *Shrew*) and *West Side Story* (*Romeo and Juliet* on the streets of New York).

Defining possibilities: Olivier and Welles

Shakespearian cinema developed elsewhere, through the commitment of two actor-directors whose careers bridged theatre and film. In 1944 Laurence Olivier achieved a revolution with his pageant-like *Henry V*. This ambitious contribution to the war effort celebrated the Allied invasion of Europe, and was the first attempt to think through the relationship between cinema and the Elizabethan stage. Olivier and his script editor Alan Dent were preoccupied with finding ways of transferring Shakespeare's theatricality and rhetoric to film. They devised an ingenious three-part structure. *Henry V* begins as an historical travelogue with a recreated afternoon performance at the Globe. Once this has acclimatized the cinema audience to stylized language, the Chorus urges them to exercise imagination and the characters reappear in stylized pastel scenery based on a medieval Book of Hours (thanks to government support, *Henry V* was the first Shakespeare film in Technicolor). Here Henry is literally larger than life. Finally the Battle of Agincourt itself is the film's climax, shot on location in a sequence modelled on the work of the Soviet director Sergei Eisenstein. Olivier turns the invading English army into a *defensive* force facing a cavalry charge that allegorizes the Battle of Britain: 'We few, we happy few' become Winston Churchill's 'first of the few'. *Henry V* recognizes that Shakespearian performances inhabit three time-frames— the characters' historical space, the Renaissance, and our own.

There was a conviction that a Shakespearian film should be a collaboration of great artists and must itself aspire to classic status. Olivier gave great scope to the composer William Walton and to the British film industry's finest designers and technicians; indeed, his films became postwar national symbols of creativity and tradition. In *Hamlet* (1948), gliding deep-focus photography and brooding sets realized his Freudian view of the play as an Oedipal case-study: the penultimate image is Gertrude's bed. In *Richard III* (1955), Richard paces a composite London set, confiding mesmerically in the camera. Olivier achieved a 'theatrical' intimacy impossible in a theatre and Richard is his masterpiece as a screen actor, but each of these films was more stagebound than the last (culminating in a flat record of Olivier's National Theatre Othello (directed by Stuart Burge in 1965)). Gracefully but blandly acted by the supporting cast, they increasingly lacked pace and moral conflict.

In total contrast Orson Welles turned Shakespeare into pure cinema. With *Macbeth* (1948), *Othello* (1952), and *Chimes at Midnight* (a.k.a. *Falstaff*, 1966) he consciously challenged Olivier's reverential approach. Welles's Shakespearian work was independent, low-budget, and deeply personal. He modestly described his *Macbeth* as a 'rough charcoal-sketch' but demanded that the film director be allowed total creative freedom. Olivier apologized for cutting *Hamlet*; Welles saw literature as raw material for a new medium (*Chimes at Midnight* draws on five plays) and, revealingly, the sound-track of all his Shakespeare films was almost inaudible. Welles reinvented Shakespeare in the cutting room, creating imaginary montage worlds where giant foolish heroes aspire and fall, and anonymous well-bred conformists—the Malcolms and Cassios—wait to inherit. *Othello* was largely shot on location: lurching camera angles and an oppressive density of visual detail and black-versus-white symbols drag the viewer into Othello's mind. *Chimes at Midnight* is an anti-war 'elegy for Merrie England' in which Welles parodied Olivier's Agincourt and created one of cinema's most appalling sequences: the Battle of Shrewsbury becomes a meaningless slaughter prefiguring the Somme and Hiroshima. Welles's last, unfinished, Shakespeare film was a *Merchant of Venice*, attacking anti-Semitism.

Despite the conscious differences, Welles's and Olivier's works have much in common. Both directors usually reduced Shakespeare's women to ciphers and cut the most articulate ones (Queen Margaret from *Richard III* and, amazingly, Portia from *The Merchant of Venice*). *Macbeth*, *Othello*, and *Hamlet* are *film noir*— claustrophobic, dream-like studies of disillusion and sexual betrayal—and utterly fatalistic: Hamlet and Othello are already dead when the films begin. Both directors failed to find funding for their later projects. Welles repeatedly tried to direct a modern-dress *Julius Caesar*, but Joseph L. Mankiewicz's sober version (1953) and Stuart Burge's inept one (1969) displaced it, whilst Olivier's plans for *Macbeth* collapsed as the British film industry declined. Nonetheless, they were the last great actor-managers, and they established Shakespearian cinema as a genre.

Contemporizing Shakespeare

A new generation inherited the classical ambitions of Olivier and Welles. Charlton Heston directed *Antony and Cleopatra* (1972) and Richard Burton and Elizabeth Taylor brought in Franco Zeffirelli to direct them in *The Taming of the Shrew* (1966), where, unlike Mary Pickford, Taylor delivered Kate's last speech as a definition of true love. With Zeffirelli, authorship in Shakespearian cinema moved from the actor-director to the director-designer. In *Romeo and Juliet* (1968) Zeffirelli combined lavish Renaissance production design with emotionalism, energy, and teeming local colour—qualities Renato Castellani's visually similar 1954 *Romeo and Juliet* lacked. More interested in *milieu* than text, Zeffirelli cast unknown teenagers as the lovers and supported them with music, choreography, and the dangerous—often homoerotic—adolescent turmoil of the street-gangs.

Zeffirelli's *Romeo and Juliet* was the first financially successful Shakespeare film. At the same time, the Royal Shakespeare Company tried to build on its radical theatre work by filming productions on location in the experimental *nouvelle-vague* style developed by such French directors as Godard and Truffaut. Peter Hall's *A Midsummer Night's Dream* (1968) was followed by Peter Brook's masterly *King Lear* (1970), with Paul Scofield. Brook's bleak Beckettian film proved the value of filming with an experienced ensemble, some of whom had worked on the production since 1962. Brook's belief that

Shakespeare should be used to explore 'contemporary' consciousness was shared by Tony Richardson's downbeat *Hamlet* (1969), shot in close-up, and Roman Polanski's *Macbeth* (1971); all were inflected with the political cynicism of the Vietnam era.

Foreign-language Shakespeare

By assuming that his function was to deal in *ideas*, Brook gave English-language screen Shakespeare a status it already enjoyed abroad. *Hamlet* and *Romeo and Juliet*, to take only the most popular examples, have been filmed more or less freely in India, Ghana, Sweden, Brazil, Germany, Turkey, Mexico, Spain, and Italy. The most significant work, however, originated in Japan and the USSR.

Soviet Shakespeare was humanistic. Directors consciously rejected Western readings: Sergei Yutkevich's *Othello* (1955) opened with a celebration of Othello's heroism and Desdemona's love, whereas Welles's prologue had showed their funeral ('He began with death, we with life'); Grigori Kozintsev's *Hamlet* (1964) replaced Olivier's Freudian inertia with social engagement, and his *King Lear* (1970) avoided Brook's pessimism. The defining metaphor of *Hamlet* becomes the prison: from Elsinore's portcullis to the iron corset locked round Ophelia as she goes insane, Kozintsev is preoccupied with freedom and tyranny. Hamlet (Innokenti Smoktunovsky), the composer (Shostakovich), and the translator (Pasternak) had all been persecuted by Stalin. Kozintsev's *Lear* sees the play as a Tolstoyan panorama of bestiality and courage—as History—where Yuri Yavet's childish king learns his humanity amongst troops of the dispossessed.

Akira Kurosawa's Shakespeare adaptations are bleaker: in his *Hamlet* set in modern corporate Tokyo (*The Bad Sleep Well*, 1960) the hero is murdered and corruption goes unpunished; his apocalyptic *Lear* (*Ran*, 1985) ends with a blind man stumbling on the edge of a cliff. *Ran* and *Throne of Blood* (1957, from *Macbeth*) transpose the tragedies to the woods and mountains of medieval Japan and stylize the protagonists by drawing on Noh and Kabuki acting conventions. Both films mourn mankind's self-destructive alienation from spirituality and nature. Kurosawa taught other directors how to reshape Shakespeare as pure cinema narrative, using speech only where absolutely necessary.

Deviant Shakespeares

In the unsympathetic economic climate of the mid-1970s and 1980s a new kind of British Shakespeare film emerged. These were defiantly experimental independent works by directors from an Art School tradition, not a theatrical one. Derek Jarman's

Tempest (1979) and *The Angelic Conversation* (the sonnets, 1985), like Celestino Coronado's *Hamlet* (1976) and *Dream* (1984), created startling images on videotape and low-grade film. They also annexed Shakespeare for gay sensibility and the spirit of nonconformity. Coronado cast twins, David and Anthony Meyer, as Hamlet, with Helen Mirren as Gertrude/Ophelia; Jarman cast comedians, magicians, and punks, and Elisabeth Welch sang 'Stormy Weather'.

Peter Greenaway's *Prospero's Books* (1991), with John Gielgud as Prospero/ Shakespeare, though superficially similar, was more elaborate and allusive, and more conservative. The Sony Corporation gave Greenaway free reign to experiment with new High Definition Video technology, resulting in unprecedented visual complexity. Greenaway's Prospero is a late-Renaissance artist surrounded by all the arcane books and great paintings that have shaped his (and Greenaway's) knowledge and imagination. Jarman's Prospero is a sullen figure in a dark house scrawled with astrological graffiti. Greenaway's *Tempest* honours tradition (Caliban saves Shakespeare's works from drowning); Jarman's ends in dissolution.

Populism versus iconoclasm

In 1989 Kenneth Branagh's *Henry V* re-established the genre within mainstream cinema. Like Zeffirelli, he aimed to make Shakespeare vivid and emotionally accessible—and did so with more conviction than Zeffirelli managed in his prosaic *Hamlet* (1990, with Mel Gibson). Branagh imported the ensemble ethic of recent British theatre, but he was also the first film director to let American stars play Shakespeare on their own terms and with their natural accents (*Much Ado About Nothing*, 1993). Branagh prioritized character—for example the network of personal dramas within *Henry V*—and his Beatrice–Benedick scenes remain the most successful attempt to film Elizabethan verbal comedy. Branagh was open equally to the influences of classical drama and popular culture, and his Shakespeare films incorporate action-film dynamics. He eagerly pastiched *The Magnificent Seven* to open *Much Ado*, whereas in 1953 Joseph L. Mankiewicz had been embarrassed by his own use of Hollywood Western conventions for the battle in *Julius Caesar*.

Like Olivier's, Branagh's style became increasingly theatrical—see his four-hour *Hamlet* (1996), and *Love's Labour's Lost* (2000) staged as a 1930s musical. Despite appearances, none of his films was unorthodox: for example the post-Falklands *Henry V* deglamorized war, but only in order to celebrate a warrior-hero's rites of passage; and *Hamlet*'s epic allusions to the fall of the Romanovs and Communism are unearned. Oliver Parker's 'erotic thriller' *Othello*, with Laurence Fishburne (1995), and Michael Hoffman's *A Midsummer Night's Dream* (1999) applied Branagh's formula exactly, but virtually all recent Shakespeare films owe their existence to his success: he is the most important *producer* in the genre's history.

For, paradoxically, Branagh's populism created an economic climate in which the Wellesian approach—cinematic, personal, iconoclastic—finally blossomed. Richard Loncraine's *Richard III* (1995), Baz Lurhmann's *William Shakespeare's Romeo + Juliet* (1996), Julie Taymor's *Titus* (1999) and Michael Almereyda's *Hamlet* (2000) all for the first time achieved the interpretative and stylistic complexity postmodern theatre takes for granted. Earlier films strained to set the plays in consistent visual worlds—providing a single framework in place of Elizabethan theatre's non-specificity—and this was still superficially true of Loncraine's 1930s London, Lurhmann's cosmopolitan Verona Beach, and Almereyda's corporate New York/Elsinore. However, these directors revelled in anachronisms and discontinuity.

Loncraine's *Richard III* stars Ian McKellen as the apparent brother-in-law of Mrs Simpson, a fascist dictator in an alternative past. Loncraine constructs a fictional London out of fragments of the real city: palaces are played by railway stations and the Tower of London by a gasometer. *Richard III* politicizes Welles's spatial montage. Lurhmann's hugely popular *Romeo + Juliet* bombards the spectator with visual and aural excitement and images that comment wryly on the play's mythic status—Juliet dresses as an angel at the ball, and Romeo as a knight errant (Tybalt plays Satan). But the film also develops coherent symbolic patterns: water, for example, is the lovers' element. Ethan Hawke's Hamlet is a student video-film-maker in a city dominated by surveillance and capitalist image-making. Ophelia is a photographer, strewing the Guggenheim museum with Polaroids of flowers. Everywhere the stress is on quotation, artifice, and irony, as in Taymor's *Titus*, which explores the extremes of violence in a composite Rome—an arena, Mussolini's public monuments, a Balkan slum. Taymor makes the armoured or mutilated bodies of the obsessed characters indistinguishable from the toys and video games of our global culture of violence.

Almereyda took Welles's irreverent 'rough charcoal sketch' approach as his direct inspiration; Al Pacino's *Looking for Richard* (1996), like Welles's *Othello* and its documentary postscript *Filming Othello* (1977), was a personal project filmed over several years. Pacino plays Richard in a film-within-a-film about New York Shakespeare, challenging the plays' possession by academics and the English. Recent Shakespearian cinema recognizes that it inhabits a mixed cultural economy, and all these films contest the right of the dominant culture—whether represented by TV newsreaders, advertising, state propaganda, or the entertainment industry—to record, shape, and define human experience. Lurhmann and his school borrow mass media forms (music videos, soap opera, etc.), but the aim is not to simplify but to provoke—and to supplement the complexity of poetic drama, based on the verbal image, with a profusion of visual associations.

Shakespeare on television

The first complete made-for-TV production was a BBC *Julius Caesar* (1938) set in fascist Italy. This sense of contemporaneity figured in several post-war American live broadcasts, including Peter Brook's sensational 1953 *King Lear* (starring Welles) and modern-dress versions of *Coriolanus* and *The Taming of the Shrew*. Major British productions included an intense *Othello* (Tony Richardson, 1955) with Gordon Heath (the first black actor to play Othello in the UK since Paul Robeson in 1930), and Philip Saville's *Hamlet at Elsinore* (1964) taped on location. But BBC Shakespeare really came of age by adjusting to the TV series format. Peter Dews's *An Age of Kings* (1960) and *The Spread of the Eagle* (1962) presented the English histories and Roman plays in one-hour episodes, quickly followed by the RSC's *Wars of the Roses*.

The result of these ambitious projects was the *BBC/Time-Life Shakespeare* (1978–84) which aimed to create 'definitive' versions of the entire canon. However, the series brief was inhibiting—modern dress was disallowed—and the founding producer Cedric Messina tried ineffectively to rival Hollywood levels of spectacle. He chose TV directors unfamiliar with Shakespeare in an attempt to prove television's independence from contemporary theatre. Only when Jonathan Miller and Shaun Sutton succeeded Messina did the series justify itself, especially with urgent productions of the less familiar plays by the (theatre-based) Jane Howell (*Henry VI*), Elijah Moshinsky (*Coriolanus*, *Cymbeline*) and David Jones (*Pericles*). Miller himself developed a thoughtful if emotionally muted aesthetic for Shakespearian television, adapting compositions from Renaissance painting.

Meanwhile, on ITV—most of whose Shakespeare output was for schools—Trevor Nunn developed a different technique, recording RSC productions in bare studios with the actors in extreme close-up. The verse was prioritized, and Nunn's casts spoke less prosaically than Miller's (e.g. *Antony and Cleopatra*, 1974). After the disappointments of the BBC cycle, little original Shakespeare was made for British TV, though stage productions including Deborah Warner's *Richard II* and Richard Eyre's *King Lear* still appeared, and the broadcasters invested in several cinema versions. The situation twenty years earlier, where the volume of television productions discouraged filmmakers, was reversed.

Shakespeare on video

When Peter Hall filmed *A Midsummer Night's Dream* in 1968, he predicted that commercially available videotapes would transform the understanding of Shakespeare: for the first time ever, the public would have easy access to the plays in performance, and to rival readings. By the year 2002, 95 per cent of the English-language sound films discussed here were on sale in the UK or USA.

Ironically the full BBC series never became readily or cheaply available, and in this respect *The Animated Tales* (1992–4) made a more enduring cultural mark. These Welsh/Russian half-hour animated versions (text edited by Leon Garfield) were designed for children, but the BBC broadcast them in both 'educational' and 'entertainment' time-slots. Artists were encouraged to visualize Shakespeare's imagery and some results, including a *Hamlet* painted on glass, were imaginative and beautiful. Several companies developed series designed for sell-through video and the schools market, including the Bard series (USA, early 1980s) of videotaped productions on a pseudo-Globe stage. Cromwell Films later produced modest British films of the tragedies (e.g. *Hamlet*, 2001). The development of CD-ROM and DVD technology has opened up important possibilities for the comparative analysis of Shakespearian performance.

Comparing comedy on film: *A Midsummer Night's Dream*

Shakespearian comedy rarely succeeds on film, where actors are stranded without audience feedback and directors often destroy the comic rhythm with forced reaction-shots. Trying to counter this, Trevor Nunn's *Twelfth Night* (1995) stressed the melancholy, and Christine Edzard tried to turn *As You Like It* (1992) into a grim discussion of homelessness and Thatcherism. However, *A Midsummer Night's Dream* has always attracted directors hoping to give cinematic form to fantasy.

There were at least eight silent versions, including Vitagraph's (1909: included in *Silent Shakespeare*, BFI Video), which made attractive use of natural locations and simple camera tricks. Puck (a little girl) flew over a spinning globe, and such stage conventions as transformations and love-at-first-sight translated naturally to the medium.

Max Reinhardt's 1935 *A Midsummer Night's Dream*, in contrast, was an advertisement for what major Hollywood studios could achieve: 'For the first time in my life I have rendered my own dreams of doing this play with no restrictions on my imagination'. In collaboration with William Dieterle, Reinhardt re-worked his famous German production using Warner Brothers contract stars including Dick Powell, Olivia de Haviland, and James Cagney (Bottom). Young Mickey Rooney played Puck as a shrieking wood-sprite, and Bronislava Njinskaya choreographed elaborate dances to Mendelssohn. Though the film is the apotheosis of the Romantic approach to the play, there are disturbing undertones on every level, from Bottom's horror at his transformation to the strange 'dawn' sequence where the Teutonic Oberon and his black bat-like army hunt Titania's silver fairies and draw them, hypnotized, into his train. Both kitsch and profound, Reinhardt's vision so dominated productions of the play for decades that most later film versions allude to it. Jiri Trnka's Czech version (1959) was a reproof to Reinhardt's monumentalism. This is a stop-motion animation film which plays charming games with ideas of scale and metamorphosis—Titania's cloak is made of living fairies, Oberon turns into animals and fruits—and Trnka honours the poetic instincts of the simple craftsmen.

Three films based on anti-traditional stage productions followed. Using a full text, Peter Hall tried to make the poetry dominate while he experimented visually with startling jump-cuts and time-disruptions: for instance, Helena appears in several locations in her bewildered Act One soliloquy to reflect her shifting moods, whilst the Fairies' body make-up constantly changes colour. Hall filmed in Warwickshire in the rain and dressed the (scowling) lovers in Carnaby Street fashions. Celestino Coronado's *Dream*—from Lindsay Kemp's mime production—was a playful riot of sexual mutability and gay desire, and focused on the Fairies' erotic pursuit of the Indian Boy, in this version a coy young adult. A prologue presents the conquest of the Amazons as military rape; Titania is a drag Queen Elizabeth; the Fairies are Victorian paintings come alive; the Mechanicals act *Romeo and Juliet* on stilts; and everything is Puck's dream.

In Adrian Noble's 1996 version, the dreamer is the Boy: this time he is an English schoolboy who falls asleep reading the play and tumbles into Noble's RSC production, luridly photographed and embellished with nostalgic allusions to children's books and films, including *The Snowman*, *Mary Poppins*, and *ET*. This sentimental framework is uncomfortably mismatched to the stage production's overt sexuality (as Julie Taymor realized: in *Titus* she reworked Noble's opening to show the same boy, Ossian Jones, in a frenzy of destructive violence—this propels him into *Titus Andronicus*, where he must learn to understand aggression and develop compassion). In Christine Edzard's *The Children's Midsummer Night's Dream* (2001) the same conceit takes on a social meaning as a cast of primary school children from a deprived London borough watch a puppet *Dream* and then enter the world of the play themselves.

Michael Hoffman's 1999 film returns to Reinhardt with film and television stars, classical music, and studio woods. His version is set in nineteenth-century Italy: Helena is a bicycling suffragette, Bottom is a dandy seeking refuge from an unhappy marriage, and the fairies are Etruscan deities haunting ruined temples. Uniting all these films is a growing self-consciousness—a preoccupation with cinema's transformative potential and with the play's own history. They are intrigued—or perplexed—by the disparity between its psychological sophistication and its status as an innocent play for children. They are all films *about* the *Dream* as well as *of* it.

Comparing tragedy on film and video: *Macbeth*

The *Macbeth*s of Welles and Polanski were both undervalued. Their interpretations, roughness, and funding (from Republic, a B-picture studio, and from Playboy) all seemed improper. Welles's *Macbeth*, filmed in three weeks with a scratch cast, will always be divisive through its combination of poetry, black comedy, and poverty, but it was an experiment in Shakespearian *film noir*, a tale of a baffled, illiterate soldier destroyed by forces he never understands. There is extensive abstract imagery/editing, but the murder is a continuous ten-minute sequence—a single 'take'—on a set designed to echo the heights and depths of the Elizabethan stage. Welles's faceless Witches control human destiny, symbolically moulding Macbeth out of mud in a pre-credits sequence simply in order to destroy him. Welles suggests a struggle between paganism and early Christianity, but presents both as superstition.

Polanski's version was dismissed as too brutal for traditionalists, insufficiently surreal for his admirers, but it is an intelligent, consistent work which seems deliberately artless. Polanski mocks 'supernatural' clichés with creaky special effects—this is a study of a corrupted generation, with contemporary associations. The Sixties folk-rock soundtrack turns cacophonous as a cast of photogenic young actors slide into affectless violence. The slaughter of the Macduffs reworks Polanski's memories of his mother's murder by the Nazis and his wife's by the Manson cult, and whereas Welles, like most directors of *Macbeth*, fantasizes operatically about evil, Polanski simply presents it: this is a numbed *Macbeth*. Lady Macbeth's cruelty is infantile; Ross is a time-server switching sides at every crisis; both look like angels. Nature veers strangely between exquisite sunsets and drizzling rain. In such an unstable world the naked ugliness of Polanski's witches—a counter-cultural coven brewing drugs—is at least honest.

Kurosawa's great *Throne of Blood* deals in visual rhythm: scenes of immobility clash with explosive action. Asaji (the Lady Macbeth) is a frozen creature from the Noh theatre; inexorably, she saps the will from Washizu, her (Kabuki-based) warrior-husband. Like Welles, Kurosawa focuses tightly on them in the long murder sequence: he follows Shakespeare's emotional graph but it is virtually silent until Kabuki music shrieks out and they are galvanized into action. They change roles—she becomes the active one, he squats in shock—and then the screen explodes into political/spiritual chaos. Men and horses hurtle back and forth on a wind-torn slope. This time the Witches become a single spirit-woman mournfully spinning at the wheel of fate. Kurosawa makes several intriguing changes to the plot. Washizu and Miki (Banquo) are appalled by the prophecy because it destroys their control of their lives, and they fear new enemies will destroy them. Miki knows Washizu is a murderer but supports him; in return his son will be Washizu's heir. It is Lady Asaji who insists Miki should die—and her sudden pregnancy provides a motive—for in Kurosawa's version characters are fixed, and the female is the source of disloyalty. Macbeth dies howling in a hail of arrows and his impregnable castle dissolves in the mists of time.

Unlike cinema, television Shakespeare prioritizes text, and Trevor Nunn's *Macbeth* exemplifies the intensive language work and ensemble spirit of his best productions. This is a microscopically detailed exploration of the play, and again its most intriguing element is the contrast between the Macbeths (Ian McKellen and Judi Dench). His commitment to evil becomes increasingly wholehearted, even grotesque, whereas she is a compassionate woman suppressing her own nature till she snaps. At the end, the survivors cluster together, appalled and exhausted, and Macduff contemplates his bloody hands.

The *Animated Tales* version (1992) offers its youthful audience reassurance here—the Old Man proclaims the rebirth of Scotland after the death of the 'butcher' and his 'fiendlike-queen'—and indeed these directors are all determined to provide closure on their terms. Welles's Witches announce the completion of their experiment ('Peace! The charm's wound up'); Polanski makes Donalbain visit them, keeping the cycle of betrayal alive; in Jeremy Freestone's version for Cromwell Films (1997), Macbeth kneels to accept death as his dead wife's voice summons him: 'Hie thee hither'.

There have also been free popularizations/modernizations of *Macbeth* which interestingly reject its Christian framework and expose saintly Duncan as a gangland boss. *Joe Macbeth* (1955) ends hopefully with the next generation (the Fleance figure) refusing to take the succession and abandoning the world of violence. But a generation later in *Men of Respect* (1990) the same character finally embraces the Mafia Family and becomes another bloody 'man of respect'. In a more sober variant on the same scenario, Penny Woolcock's brilliant TV film *Macbeth on the Estate* (BBC, 1997), the gangs fight over drugs and stolen electrical goods in a decaying Birmingham housing estate. Macbeth's wife is driven by the death of her child, to whose empty bedroom she returns before killing herself. This differs from other versions in two respects: first, the actors use Shakespeare's language but speak it almost naturalistically; second, like Edzard's *Dream*, it was the culmination of a community project to explore the role drama—specifically Shakespeare—could have for people in an inner-city estate. Many local people act alongside the professionals, and this time the epilogue is Macduff's, standing in a wasteland with tower-blocks behind him, speaking for the 'socially excluded': 'Alas, poor country, / Almost afraid to know itself'.

Encouraged by a growing critical literature, screen Shakespeare has evolved into a forum where the plays' shifting meanings and their cultural significance are the subject of deepening debate.

FURTHER READING

Anderegg, Michael. *Orson Welles: Shakespeare and Popular Culture* (Cambridge: Cambridge University Press, 2000). Orson Welles's Shakespeare films in the context of his career in all aspects of the mass media.

Boose, Lynda E. and Richard Burt (eds.). *Shakespeare the Movie* (London and New York: Routledge, 1997). Essays exploring Shakespeare's place in contemporary screen culture.

Bulman, J. C. and H. R. Coursen (eds.). *Shakespeare on Television* (Hanover: University Press of New England, 1988). A compendium of reviews and essays.

Davies, Anthony. *Filming Shakespeare's Plays* (Cambridge: Cambridge University Press, 1988). Sophisticated analyses of Laurence Olivier, Orson Welles, Peter Brook, and Akira Kurosawa.

Davies, Anthony and Stanley Wells (eds.). *Shakespeare and The Moving Image: the Plays on Film and Television* (Cambridge: Cambridge University Press, 1994). Inclusive volume with a useful filmography.

Donaldson, Peter S. *Shakespearean Films/ Shakespearean Directors* (Boston: Unwin Hyman, 1990). Provocative psychoanalytical readings.

Jackson, Russell (ed.). *The Cambridge Companion to Shakespeare on Film* (Cambridge: Cambridge University Press, 2000). Wide-ranging essays—director-based and thematic—edited by Kenneth Branagh's academic consultant.

Rothwell, Kenneth. *A History of Shakespeare on Screen* (Cambridge: Cambridge University Press, 1999). Encyclopedic survey by the foremost scholar in the field.

41 | The question of authorship

David Kathman

Just about everybody agrees that William Shakespeare was one of the greatest authors in the English language, if not the greatest of them all. But exactly what—or who—are we referring to when we talk about the author 'Shakespeare'? This question is not as simple as it might seem.

The Shakespeare authorship question that most people are aware of concerns the identity of the person who wrote *Hamlet* and *King Lear*. Scholars universally agree that this person was William Shakespeare, who lived about four hundred years ago, was born and died in Stratford-upon-Avon, and was an actor and theatrical shareholder. Yet there are some people, generally amateurs in the field, who argue that 'William Shakespeare' was actually a pseudonym for a mysterious hidden author. Why do these people believe this—and more importantly, why do Shakespeare scholars dismiss such beliefs?

A different authorship question concerns what, exactly, Shakespeare wrote. Such works as *Hamlet* and *King Lear* are recognized by everybody as being 'Shakespeare'— they form the core of the Shakespeare canon. At the other end of the spectrum are plays and poems which some scholars, but by no means all, have included under the label 'Shakespeare', such as *Edward III* and *A Funeral Elegy for Master William Peter*. How do we determine which plays and poems count as 'Shakespeare'? What are the boundaries?

Each of these authorship issues is interesting in its own way, but they're treated very differently by those who spend their lives studying Shakespeare—the first is widely dismissed as the realm of crackpots, while the second is a vibrant area of study taken very seriously by those in the field. By exploring why professional Shakespearians feel this way, we explore issues at the core of what it means to study literary history—issues that anyone studying Shakespeare should be aware of.

How we know that Shakespeare wrote Shakespeare

First, let's consider the more familiar authorship question—namely, whether William Shakespeare of Stratford (1564–1616) really did write the works commonly attributed to him. This might seem like a silly question at first, but over the past 150 years, thousands of books and articles and web sites have argued, often passionately, that he did not. These 'antiStratfordians' have formed societies, published journals, and organized conferences at which they discuss their theories. Most of them promote alternative candidates as the 'real' Shakespeare, with the most popular being the seventeenth Earl of Oxford, Francis Bacon, and Christopher Marlowe. They proudly list famous people who are sympathetic to their cause, including such luminaries as Supreme Court Justice John Paul Stevens and actor Michael York.

All this may sound impressive to a casual observer, but in fact, antiStratfordianism has remained a fringe belief system for its entire existence. Professional Shakespeare scholars mostly pay little attention to it, much as evolutionary biologists ignore creationists and astronomers dismiss UFO sightings. AntiStratfordians are fond of claiming that the tide is turning and they're on the verge of triumphing over the establishment, but similar claims have peppered antiStratfordian writings for well over 100 years, without ever coming true.

Why are professional Shakespearians—those whose job it is to study, write, and teach about Shakespeare—so dismissive of antiStratfordians? Is it, as some of the heretics claim, because these professionals have a vested interest in the traditional attribution? Actually, no. The real reason is that antiStratfordians routinely violate nearly all the methods used by historians in general, both in terms of checking their facts and in drawing conclusions from those facts. They arbitrarily discard the type of evidence that literary historians use, and the 'evidence' which they present in its place is typically distorted, taken out of context, or flat-out false. These distortions are ultimately driven by fierce élitism, a belief that a man of relatively modest origins like Shakespeare could not have written the greatest literature in the English language.

To illustrate, let's first take a look at the evidence for the traditional attribution to William Shakespeare of Stratford-upon-Avon. Despite the claims of antiStratfordians, this evidence is abundant and wide-ranging for the era in which Shakespeare lived, more abundant than the comparable evidence for most other contemporary play-wrights. Here is a brief overview of the facts.

William Shakespeare of Stratford was an actor and sharer in the leading acting company in England, known from 1594 to 1603 as the Lord Chamberlain's Men and from 1603 onward as the King's Men. He first appears with the company in March 1595, and has a prominent place in lists of company members over the next fifteen years. He was one of the original sharers in the Globe theatre in 1599 and the Blackfriars theatre in 1608, and is listed as a primary tenant of the Globe in legal documents. We know that these records refer to William Shakespeare of Stratford because, among other things, the Stratford man left bequests in his will to fellow players John Heminges, Henry Condell, and Richard Burbage, who were also sharers in the company and tenants of the Globe.

During William Shakespeare's lifetime, his name appeared in print as the author of more than twenty different plays and several poems or collections of poetry. The dedications to *Venus and Adonis* (1593) and *The Rape of Lucrece* (1594) are both signed 'William Shakespeare'. The title pages of numerous play quartos give his name as the author, and we know (both from the title pages themselves and from other records) that these plays were acted by the Lord Chamberlain's / King's Men, the same company to which William Shakespeare of Stratford belonged. This fact, by itself, would normally be enough to establish that William Shakespeare the actor and William Shakespeare the playwright were the same person.

Many people praised Shakespeare and his works, in print and in private writings, both during his lifetime and in the generation after his death. None of these people gave any indication that 'William Shakespeare' was a pseudonym, or that anybody other than Shakespeare wrote the plays and poems. In his book *Palladis Tamia* (1598), written relatively early in Shakespeare's career, Francis Meres repeatedly praised Shakespeare's poetry, mentioned his 'sugared sonnets among his private friends', and listed twelve of his plays. Ben Jonson, in addition to his famous tribute in the First Folio edition of Shakespeare's plays (1623), wrote about Shakespeare in his posthumously published *Timber* (1640), saying that 'I loved the man, and do honour his memory (on this side idolatry) as much as any'.

The First Folio and the monument in Stratford provide even more straightforward evidence. In the dedication of the Folio, John Heminges and Henry Condell of the King's Men write that they are publishing these plays 'only to keep the memory of so worthy a friend and fellow alive, as was our Shakespeare', thus explicitly stating that the actor William Shakespeare was the same person as the author. In his commendatory poem in the Folio (see Figure 4.1), Leonard Digges (who was the stepson of Shakespeare's friend Thomas Russell) refers to 'thy Stratford monument', and in fact there is a monument to Shakespeare in the Stratford church (see Figure 4.4). It depicts him with a pen in his hand, and the Latin inscription compares him to Nestor, Socrates, and Virgil.

All this is the same type of evidence used to determine any authorship question—indeed any historical question—from the Elizabethan era. It refutes the common antiStratfordian canard that there is a mysterious lack of information connecting William Shakespeare to his works. There are some playwrights of the time, such as the notorious self-promoter Ben Jonson, for whom we have more information, but many more for whom we have less.

For example, consider Christopher Marlowe and John Webster, the two playwrights from that era (besides Shakespeare) whose plays are most often performed today. No play or poem was ever attributed to Marlowe while he was alive, nor did anyone ever refer to him by name as a writer or playwright during his lifetime; there is also no explicit record associating him with any acting company or theatre. Webster's name did appear on seven plays and a few poems while he was alive, but personal information about him is so sketchy that historians could not convincingly attach the name to a real person until the 1970s. We have no letters or manuscripts by either man, in fact no handwriting of any kind except a single signature of Marlowe's. Nobody collected

Fig. 4.4 The monument to Shakespeare designed by Geerrart Janssen in Holy Trinity Church, Stratford-upon-Avon, erected a few years after the poet died in 1616. It is surmounted by the family coat of arms, and memorial verses in both Latin and English commemorate the town's greatest inhabitant.

their works or erected monuments to them; we don't even know exactly when Webster died, because nobody commemorated his death as they did Shakespeare's.

The antiStratfordians—and where they go wrong

AntiStratfordians try to discount the evidence for Shakespeare's authorship using a variety of tactics, most of which involve distorting the facts and their historical context. For example, they typically deny the most straightforward evidence—Shakespeare's name on the published plays—by claiming that the Stratford man's name was not 'Shakespeare' at all, but 'Shakspere', the spelling he himself used in his signatures. One major problem with this argument is that 'Shakespeare' and 'Shakspere' were variants of the same name, because English spelling was not yet standardized then. Christopher Marlowe's one surviving signature is spelled 'Christofer Marley', but his name was most often spelled 'Marlowe' by others; similarly, 'Shakespeare' was by far the most common spelling by which other people referred to William Shakespeare of Stratford. Many antiStratfordians also claim that the occasional hyphenation of Shakespeare's name in print was a signal that it was a pseudonym. But the idea that hyphenation has anything to do with pseudonyms is completely unsupported by the facts and unknown outside antiStratfordian literature; in fact, hyphenated real names far outnumber the occasional hyphenated pseudonym in the Elizabethan era.

AntiStratfordians also attack the monument in Stratford, since it's obviously good evidence that the man buried nearby was a writer. They point to an engraving in William Dugdale's 1656 book *Antiquities of Warwickshire* depicting a monument with a thinner face and fatter cushion, and claim that sinister, unnamed plotters replaced this 'original' monument of Shakespeare with one showing him as a writer. But this scenario, too, encounters major problems. Many of the engravings in Dugdale's book are wildly inaccurate and contain errors comparable to those in the Shakespeare engraving. More importantly, numerous observers from the 1620s onward recorded their impressions of the Shakespeare monument, and they all saw it as a monument to the great poet William Shakespeare of Stratford.

In order to discount the direct evidence of the First Folio, antiStratfordians are forced to rely on conspiracy theories in which shadowy plotters bribed Shakespeare's friends Heminges, Condell, and Jonson to lie while inserting cryptic clues to the identity of the 'real author'. Such a conspiracy is absolutely critical for any attempt to deny that William Shakespeare of Stratford wrote the plays. The abundant evidence for Shakespeare's authorship, as well as the lack of evidence for anyone else's, is explained away as the doings of seemingly all-powerful conspirators bent on hiding 'the truth'. The problem is that such an omnipotent conspiracy can be invoked to explain anything, and thus makes the notion of evidence meaningless. It's also difficult to imagine why such a massive conspiracy would continue so successfully for centuries after its original rationale was gone.

In addition to replacing evidence with conspiracy theories, antiStratfordians usually attack Shakespeare personally, sometimes quite viciously. They depict Stratford as an uncultured cesspool which could never have produced a great writer, and Shakespeare himself as a greedy, semi-literate burgher. These attacks are based on wildly biased interpretations of the records, and bear little or no resemblance to the conclusions reached by real historians. Stratford was a thriving market town which had produced an Archbishop of Canterbury and a Lord Mayor of London, and which had an excellent school. Shakespeare's father John was a prominent citizen who served as the equivalent of mayor. Even if we arbitrarily set aside all literary and theatrical records from London, Shakespeare's closest friends in Stratford were a cultured, well-connected group. To give just one example, Thomas Greene, who lived for a time in Shakespeare's house and called him 'cousin', was a lawyer prominent for many years in the Middle Temple, as well as a friend of the poets John Marston and Michael Drayton.

One of the best illustrations of the way antiStratfordians distort facts and ignore context is their discussion of William Shakespeare's death. Their attitude is summarized by Charlton Ogburn's false assertion that Shakespeare's death in 1616 'went entirely unremarked . . . in an age when the passing of noted poets called forth copious elegies from their fellows'.[1] In fact, there were many eulogies for Shakespeare, of which those in the 1623 First Folio are only the most famous. William Basse's 'On Mr. William Shakespeare' survives in more than two dozen manuscript copies, several of which specify that Shakespeare died in April 1616. Ogburn dismisses all these because they weren't printed immediately after Shakespeare's death, but he neglects to mention that only socially important people such as noblemen and church leaders received such treatment. Eulogies for poets traditionally circulated in manuscript, and often took years to reach print. The seven-year period before the first printed eulogies to Shakespeare was remarkably brief, unprecedented for a playwright, and the number of tributes written to Shakespeare was more than for any contemporary before Ben Jonson twenty years later.

Alternative 'Shakespeares'

For most antiStratfordians, these attacks on William Shakespeare of Stratford have one primary purpose: to clear the way for their own candidate as the 'real' Shakespeare. Sir Francis Bacon was the favourite candidate a century ago, although his star has faded considerably since then. Edward de Vere, seventeenth Earl of Oxford (1550–1604), is now the most popular alternate Shakespeare, but there's also a sizable contingent who believe that Christopher Marlowe faked his own death and wrote the works of

Shakespeare from hiding. Other candidates have included Queen Elizabeth I, the fifth Earl of Rutland, and an Italian named Michelangelo Crollalanza ('Shakespeare' in Italian). All in all, dozens of 'real Shakespeares' have been proposed over the years, but most of them have a few basic things in common: they were higher on the social ladder than William Shakespeare; they led more exciting and adventurous lives than Shakespeare did; and there is not a speck of direct evidence connecting them to Shakespeare's plays.

Since the Oxfordians are currently the most numerous and vocal of the antiStratfordians, let's take a closer look at their candidate and the arguments they build around him. Edward de Vere became Earl of Oxford aged twelve upon his father's death, and was brought up as a royal ward by Lord Burghley, Queen Elizabeth's chief adviser. Although he possessed some genuine talents and received a good education typical for a young nobleman, his hot temper and freespending ways got him into trouble. At the age of seventeen, he killed a servant but got off without punishment, leaving the man's family destitute. In 1575–6 he travelled to Italy with a large entourage, and ordered Burghley to sell his family estates to help pay for the trip. By the late 1580s he had completely squandered the family fortune and was in debt, so Queen Elizabeth gave him an annual pension of £1,000 to save him from bankruptcy. He spent the last fifteen years of his life unwelcome in Elizabeth's court.

What about evidence that Oxford wrote the works of Shakespeare? There is none—at least not the type of evidence literary historians use, the type we have in abundance for William Shakespeare of Stratford. Oxford wrote some poetry under his own name and was praised as a writer of comedy, but nobody at the time ever attributed any of Shakespeare's works to him, or connected him with Shakespeare in any way. Indeed, Francis Meres included both Oxford and Shakespeare in the same list of comedy writers in 1598, clearly indicating that they were two separate people. During the time when the Lord Chamberlain's Men were first staging Shakespeare's plays in the 1590s, Oxford's letters (none of which mentions plays or poetry) show that he was preoccupied with trying to get tin mining monopolies from the Queen. He died in relative obscurity in 1604, before such Shakespeare plays as *King Lear* and *The Tempest* had been written.

None of this matters to Oxfordians. They have built up a romantic picture of who they think the author must have been, and this image takes precedence over everything else. Documentary evidence (or the lack of it, in Oxford's case) becomes an annoyance to be explained away. In its place, Oxfordians seek out parallels between the plays and Oxford's life, which they use to build up an elaborate story in which Oxford wrote the plays as a sort of crypto-autobiography. Under this scenario, Oxford depicted himself as the leading man in every play, satirizing friends and enemies alike as the other characters. Oxfordians see *Hamlet* as telling Oxford's life story, and the sonnets as depicting his friendship with the young Earl of Southampton, with whom some Oxfordians (such as Joseph Sobran) believe he had a homosexual affair.

Unfortunately, there are massive problems with this scenario, however exciting it might seem at first glance. For one thing, the standard Oxfordian claim that Shakespeare's plays must have been written by a highly educated nobleman does not square with the evidence. Nobody during Shakespeare's lifetime or for a century afterward ever described him as well-educated; on the contrary, he was consistently portrayed as an unlearned natural wit, and John Dryden criticized his depiction of courtiers as unrealistic. The classical scholar J. A. K. Thomson and others have found that Shakespeare actually used remarkably few classical allusions compared to other writers of the time, and that the learning displayed in the plays corresponds to a grammar-school education such as Shakespeare would have received in Stratford.[2]

On the other side of the coin, Oxfordians typically twist the facts of Oxford's life in an attempt to make it fit Shakespeare's works. They greatly inflate his literary reputation among his contemporaries, when his social rank actually accounted for most of the praise he received. They treat unbridled speculation as though it were solid evidence, as when they imagine a close relationship between Oxford and Southampton although there is no evidence that the two men even knew each other personally. Most importantly, they ignore the fact that 'biographical parallels' to Shakespeare's works can be found for virtually any nobleman of the time. Proponents of other candidates have compiled parallels as impressive as those given by Oxfordians, and the lives of King James and the Earl of Essex mirror *Hamlet* at least as closely as Oxford's does.

The whole idea of using literary works to deduce things about the author in the absence of documentary evidence is not taken seriously by scholars, because it's so subjective as to be essentially worthless. Indeed, such a great literary figure as T. S. Eliot recognized the unreliability of these reconstructions when he wrote that he was used to 'having my personal biography reconstructed from passages which I got out of books, or which I invented out of nothing because they sounded well; and to having my biography invariably ignored in what I did write from personal experience'.[3] Certainly some literature is autobiographical, but much is not, and knowing the difference requires hard evidence of the type which has almost entirely disappeared for Shakespeare's era. By tossing aside the documentary evidence we do have and replacing it with their own dubious speculations, Oxfordians are debasing the work of all historians, abandoning the methods which allow us to know anything about what happened in the past.

How we know what Shakespeare wrote

Even if we agree that William Shakespeare did write the works of Shakespeare, a new authorship question arises: what, exactly, did this person write? The core of the Shakespeare canon is the thirty-six plays in the 1623 First Folio, plus the nondramatic poems published under Shakespeare's name during his lifetime. But some people over the years have expressed doubts that Shakespeare wrote everything in this core group, and many others have argued for Shakespeare's authorship of plays and poems outside the core group. The exact boundaries of the Shakespeare canon have continually shifted over the past four hundred years, and they are still shifting today. This is the authorship issue that Shakespeare scholars are concerned with, and it is a vital and vibrant part of Shakespeare studies.

The most important type of evidence to consider in determining what Shakespeare wrote is external evidence, such as his name on title pages. However, this evidence is not without complications. Even during Shakespeare's lifetime, he became popular enough for publishers sometimes to attach his name to works that may not have been his, presumably in an effort to drum up sales. Of the seventeen plays that had been printed individually before 1623 with Shakespeare's name on the title page, four were not included by Heminges and Condell in the First Folio: *The London Prodigal* (1605), *A Yorkshire Tragedy* (1608), *Pericles* (1609), and *Sir John Oldcastle* (1619). Heminges and Condell also excluded three plays which had been printed under the initials 'W. S.', perhaps meant to suggest Shakespeare: *Locrine* (1595), *Thomas, Lord Cromwell* (1602), and *The Puritan* (1607). These seven dubious plays form the core of what is now known as the Shakespeare apocrypha.

The exclusion of these plays from the First Folio suggests that Shakespeare's friends and fellow actors—who surely were in the best position to know—did not consider them his work. Nevertheless, in 1664, the publisher of the Third Folio added these seven plays to the original thirty-six of the First Folio, making a total of forty-three 'Shakespeare' plays. By that time, everybody involved was dead, and one title-page attribution must have looked as good as another. It took more than a century for editors to realize that not all such evidence is equally trustworthy, and to prune the doubtful plays from the canon. By the late 1700s, the First Folio had become the defining authority for what counted as Shakespeare, and it remains the most important external evidence we have for what Shakespeare wrote.

Although external evidence is certainly crucial, scholars have long supplemented it with internal evidence, or that contained in the works themselves. The oldest and most basic form of internal evidence is a work's style and quality; a disputed play or poem may simply not seem good enough to be written by Shakespeare. This was one reason why the apocryphal plays were rejected by eighteenth-century editors—in addition to the fact that they aren't in the First Folio, they simply don't 'feel' like Shakespeare, and don't fit in with the rest of the canon. (A possible exception is *Pericles*, discussed below.) While such judgements are certainly valuable, they can also be maddeningly subjective. There are no clear guidelines, and readers' opinions of a given play or poem can differ, sometimes radically.

In the late 1800s, a maverick group of scholars proposed methods for exploring authorship that were supposedly more objective than personal judgments. These methods mostly involved counting features of a disputed text, such as the percentage of rhymed lines or the average word length, and comparing them with the undisputed work of Shakespeare and other authors. Armed with these methods, a group known as disintegrators argued that other playwrights besides Shakespeare had written large parts of the First Folio, including entire plays such as *Titus Andronicus*. One famous disintegrator, J. M. Robertson, thought that the only play written entirely by Shakespeare was *A Midsummer Night's Dream*. Eventually there was a vigorous backlash, with many scholars arguing that the disintegrators had gone too far and that their methods were too subjective. By the middle of the twentieth century, internal evidence was widely distrusted, and the First Folio was again the primary authority for defining the Shakespeare canon.

The shifting boundaries of Shakespeare today

Present-day Shakespeare scholars studying questions of attribution have tried to avoid the excesses of past generations and strike a judicious balance among the various types of evidence. External evidence is seen as primary but not infallible, while internal evidence has gained increasing favour if used cautiously. For example, most scholars now believe that all the plays in the First Folio were primarily written by Shakespeare, but that he may have had collaborators on some of them. There is now widespread agreement that John Fletcher wrote parts of *Henry VIII* or *All is True*, based entirely on such internal evidence as the presence of stylistic and linguistic quirks characteristic of Fletcher. Many scholars now believe that Thomas Middleton wrote some scenes of *Macbeth*, and internal evidence has led others to argue that parts of Shakespeare's early plays were written by other playwrights.

This willingness to accept Shakespeare as a collaborator has extended beyond the First Folio. Two plays not included in the Folio but attributed to Shakespeare elsewhere—*Pericles* and *The Two Noble Kinsmen*—are now generally accepted as being at least partially written by him. As we saw earlier, *Pericles* was published in 1609 with an attribution to Shakespeare, and *The Two Noble Kinsmen* was published in 1634 as by Shakespeare and John Fletcher. Both were long excluded from the Shakespeare canon, but parts of each have also struck many people as being of Shakespearian quality. Unlike the rest of the apocrypha, both also fit stylistically and thematically with Shakespeare's late plays. Most scholars now believe that Shakespeare collaborated with an unidentified playwright (perhaps George Wilkins) on *Pericles*, and with Fletcher on *The Two Noble Kinsmen*. Both plays may have been excluded from the Folio because they contained too much non-Shakespearian matter, and thus were not seen by the editors as properly 'Shakespeare's'.

For all the plays we have discussed so far, there is some external evidence for Shakespeare's authorship. The waters become murkier when we consider plays without such evidence, but this has not stopped many people from seeking out Shakespeare's hand in anonymous plays from the era. Few of these attributions have gained much critical favour, because scholars have always been extremely wary of relying solely on internal evidence. One notable exception is *Edward III*, which was printed anonymously in 1596 and is now widely regarded as at least partly Shakespearian. Some readers since the eighteenth century have detected Shakespeare's hand in this play, particularly in scenes involving the Countess of Salisbury, but only in the past decade have some editors begun to include it among Shakespeare's works, possibly as a collaboration.

An even more interesting example is *Sir Thomas More*, a play which survives only in a manuscript written by several different hands. There is no indication in the manuscript of who wrote it, but several of the hands have been identified as those of playwrights of Shakespeare's era. Three pages of the manuscript are in a hand known as Hand D, which some scholars since the late 1800s have suggested may be Shakespeare's. The suggestion gained momentum in the first half of the twentieth century when a group of scholars presented a wide variety of evidence—from handwriting, spelling, vocabulary, and imagery—which strengthened the idea that these three pages were written by Shakespeare. Although this idea still has vigorous critics, the three pages of Hand D have been included in many recent editions of Shakespeare, and most scholars admit at least a strong possibility of Shakespeare's authorship.

So far we have only considered plays, but nondramatic poems have also been a very active area of Shakespeare attribution studies, especially in recent years. As with the plays, uncertainties in the external evidence began during Shakespeare's lifetime. The 1599 poetry collection *The Passionate Pilgrim* has Shakespeare's name on the title page, but it mixes poems known to be Shakespeare's with others known to be by other poets, plus others which might be by Shakespeare. In the centuries since then, most arguments for attributing new poems to Shakespeare have combined external and internal evidence, and have met with varying degrees of acceptance.

To give a recent example, a short poem beginning 'Shall I Die?' is preserved in two seventeenth-century manuscripts, one of which attributes it to 'William Shakespeare'. In 1985, Gary Taylor proposed on the basis of internal evidence that this attribution is correct, and the poem appeared in the 1986 Oxford edition of Shakespeare along with other short poems which may be by Shakespeare. However, Taylor's proposal met with fierce opposition from those who thought the poem is not good enough to be Shakespeare's, and the attribution has won only limited acceptance. Similarly, Donald Foster proposed in 1989 that Shakespeare might be the author of *A Funeral Elegy for Master William Peter*, a 578-line poem published in 1612 under the initials 'W. S'. Foster buttressed his argument with a wide variety of evidence involving syntax, vocabulary, and similarities to Shakespeare's known work, but many readers found it difficult to believe that Shakespeare could have written such a dull poem. While the attribution has been accepted by some editors, it continues to face much opposition from sceptics, and the poem is now widely thought to be by John Ford.

Summing up

As Shakespeare scholarship enters the twenty-first century, there is still disagreement over the precise limits of the body of literature we call 'Shakespeare', and the best ways to determine those limits. Some scholars have developed quantitative tests for distinguishing authors on the basis of vocabulary and stylistic features, helped by the increasing power of computers and the availability of electronic databases. Others have scorned such tests as attempts to reduce the uniqueness of Shakespeare to mere numbers, claiming that no quantitative methods can replace the aesthetic judgements of human beings. Intriguing questions have been raised: Is it possible to distinguish Shakespeare from other authors based on internal evidence? Could Shakespeare have sometimes written a bad poem or play? What is it about Shakespeare's works that make them so special?

Regardless of how scholars define Shakespeare as an author, they do so using a common set of basic standards and assumptions. These standards have stood the test of time and have shown their value in all areas of history and literature, not just in Shakespeare studies. In contrast, antiStratfordians toss aside these standards, ignoring both external and internal evidence in favour of romantic but ill-informed fantasies. Based on the historical evidence which has come down to us, we can confidently say that a man named William Shakespeare of Stratford-upon-Avon wrote plays and poetry four hundred years ago. Regardless of the precise boundaries we place on what Shakespeare wrote, we can be grateful for the timeless body of poetry and drama that he left us.

FURTHER READING

Churchill, R. C. *Shakespeare and his Betters* (Bloomington: Indiana University Press, 1959). The first half of this book is an excellent account of the first 100 years of antiStratfordianism; the second half explains in considerable detail why antiStratfordian claims do not hold water.

Foster, Donald. *Elegy by W. S.* (Newark: University of Delaware Press, 1989). Using a wide variety of methods and evidence, Foster explores the controversial possibility that the W. S. who wrote *A Funeral Elegy* (1612) was Shakespeare.

Gibson, H. N. *The Shakespeare Claimants* (London: Methuen, 1962). This book examines the cases for four alternative Shakespeares (Francis Bacon, the Earl of Oxford, the Earl of Derby, Christopher Marlowe) and finds them all wanting.

Hope, Jonathan. *The Authorship of Shakespeare's Plays* (Cambridge: Cambridge University Press, 1994). Hope combines linguistic evidence from the plays with historical and sociolinguistic arguments in an attempt to disentangle Shakespeare's role in writing several collaborative and apocryphal plays.

Matus, Irvin. *Shakespeare, In Fact* (New York: Continuum, 1994). This book demolishes many of the claims made by Oxfordians and other antiStratfordians, showing how they are based on factual misreadings and ignorance of historical context.

Metz, G. Harold. *Sources of Four Plays Ascribed to Shakespeare* (Columbia: University of Missouri Press, 1989). This book reprints source material for *Edward III*, *Sir Thomas More*, *Cardenio*, and *The Two Noble Kinsmen*. Its real value is in the introductions, which discuss the arguments over the authorship of these plays in great detail.

Ogburn, Charlton. *The Mysterious William Shakespeare*, 2nd edn. (McLean, Virginia: EPM, 1992). The bible of Oxfordians, this massive tome is among the most comprehensive statements of antiStratfordian arguments. However, its unreliability and extreme double standards make it essentially worthless as scholarship.

Schoenbaum, Samuel. *Shakespeare's Lives*, 2nd edn. (Oxford: Oxford University Press, 1991). A classic in the field, this book describes the bewildering array of biographies that have been written on Shakespeare over the years. A section on antiStratfordians provides a witty and informative account of the Shakespeare doubters.

Sobran, Joseph. *Alias Shakespeare* (New York: Free Press, 1997). This Oxfordian book, much more accessible than Ogburn's, emphasizes the Earl's supposed homosexuality. Though it avoids the excesses of some other Oxfordian works, it is no more reliable in its arguments.

Vickers, Brian. *Counterfeiting Shakespeare: Evidence, Authorship, and John Ford's Funerall Elegye* (Cambridge: Cambridge University Press, 2002). In this book Vickers casts a sceptical eye on the arguments that Shakespeare wrote the Funeral Elegy for William Peter, and argues instead that the author of the poem was John Ford.

Wells, Stanley and Gary Taylor. *William Shakespeare: A Textual Companion* (Oxford: Oxford University Press, 1988). This companion to the Oxford and Norton editions of Shakespeare includes one of the best and most comprehensive guides to how scholars try to determine what Shakespeare wrote. It contains extensive discussion of general methods as well as specific plays and poems.

WEB LINKS

The Shakespeare Authorship Page. <http://www.ShakespeareAuthorship.com>. This site contains the most comprehensive collection of rebuttals to Oxfordian and other antiStratfordian claims, as well as an extensive listing of links to other sites concerning the Shakespeare authorship question.

The Shakespeare Oxford Society. <http://www.shakespeare-oxford.com>. The primary online home of the Oxfordian movement, this site contains a variety of articles and news about Oxfordian activities.

Sir Francis Bacon's New Advancement of Learning. <http://www.sirbacon.org>. The most comprehensive Baconian site, containing an astonishing variety of articles arguing that Bacon wrote Shakespeare.

NOTES

1. Charlton Ogburn. *The Mysterious William Shakespeare*, 2nd edn. (McLean, Virginia: EPM, 1992), p. 112.
2. J. A. K. Thomson. *Shakespeare and the Classics* (London: Allen & Unwin, 1952); T. W. Baldwin. *William Shakspere's Small Latine & Lesse Greeke* (Urbana: University of Illinois Press, 1944).
3. T. S. Eliot. *Selected Essays, 1917–1932* (New York: Harcourt, Brace, 1932), p. 108.

42 | Shakespeare's influence

John Gross

Shakespeare has had a huge influence on other writers and artists. It began during his own lifetime, it has spread through many different cultures, and it continues today. In some cases individual plays or characters have served as an inspiration, in others it has been an aspect of his work as a whole—his freedom in handling time and space, for instance, or his skill at relating public and political themes to private lives. His own life and personality have exerted their fascination, too. They have prompted some notable poetry and fiction.

The extent of Shakespeare's influence is a measure of his greatness, but it also reflects the particular nature of that greatness. He wrote for a popular medium, the theatre. He created strong dramatic structures. His characters, however complex their inner lives, can be readily grasped in outline. His plays have a mythic quality—and myths, more than any other form of fiction, lend themselves to borrowing and adaptation.

Degrees of influence

There are many works which owe a debt to Shakespeare, but which offer not so much examples of his influence as parallels: they transpose one of his plots or his major themes to a new setting, and treat it in a new style. A celebrated instance is Leonard Bernstein's musical *West Side Story* (1957), which relocates the story of *Romeo and Juliet* among feuding teenage gangs in New York. Shakespeare provided Bernstein and his collaborators with their scaffolding, and conferred a little extra prestige. But there is nothing Shakespearian about the actual substance of the show. You could enjoy it to the full without ever having seen or read *Romeo and Juliet*. Millions of people probably have.

Some works which borrow themes or motifs from Shakespeare proclaim the fact in their titles, but that doesn't necessarily make them Shakespearian in substance either. Ivan Turgenev wrote a story entitled *A Lear of the Steppes* (1870). His fellow Russian Nikolai Leskov wrote an even more powerful story entitled *Lady Macbeth of Mtsensk* (1865). In both cases, however, Shakespeare simply provided a starting point, a roughly comparable dramatic pattern. And when the English composer Frederick

Delius wrote an opera which he called *A Village Romeo and Juliet* (1900) he didn't even use the play as a source. He took his plot from a tale by the Swiss writer Gottfried Keller.

True influence, the influence which modifies the very nature of an artist's art, is more mysterious. The deeper it goes, the more thoroughly absorbed it is likely to be, and the harder it is to measure it with any precision. By contrast, influences which can be demonstrated in detail are usually (though not always) influences which haven't been properly digested. This is especially true of similarities in style. But there is also an intermediate level of influence, one where a writer takes another writer's subject-matter—explicitly, not merely by analogy—and turns it to his own creative use. In the case of Shakespeare, that can mean writing a poem about one of his characters, for instance, or recasting scenes from one of the plays in a work of fiction, or remodelling a play with a freedom which goes beyond adaptation and leads to the creation of a new play—a work of art in its own right.

The fact that Shakespeare is so familiar also makes him an unsurpassed source of allusions. Many of the Shakespearian references in other writers are casual; many of them are jokes. (There are amusing variations on stock Shakespearian phrases scattered among the comic stories of P. G. Wodehouse, for instance.) But when T. S. Eliot's Prufrock says, 'I am not Prince Hamlet', or when a poem by Seamus Heaney alludes to Captain MacMorris, the Irish soldier in *Henry V* ('What ish my nation?'), the words reverberate. When Marcel Proust unexpectedly compares one of his greatest characters, the Baron de Charlus, to King Lear, or when the distraught hero of Saul Bellow's novel *Seize the Day* (1956) quotes from the sonnets ('. . . love that well that thou must leave ere long'), they summon up a whole world of feeling.

Plays and playwrights in English

Shakespeare exerted a strong influence on the generation of playwrights who followed him. Several of them may well have collaborated with him on some of his plays: John Fletcher undoubtedly did, and the plays which Fletcher went on to write in partnership with Francis Beaumont draw on numerous Shakespearian characters and situations. John Ford was another dramatist of the early Stuart period who frequently echoed his great predecessor. So was Philip Massinger. Elsewhere, there are striking reminiscences of Shakespeare in plays as disparate as Thomas Middleton's *A Mad World, My Masters* and *The Revenger's Tragedy* (see also Chapter 6).

However highly they esteemed him, Jacobean dramatists could still think of Shakespeare as a colleague, one of themselves. For later generations he assumed much more awesome proportions, and one consequence was that there were dangers involved in taking him as a useful model. To set out to write like him was to invite the near-certainty of being crushed by the comparison.

Still, that didn't stop people trying. In the Restoration period, for example, Thomas Otway transplanted large chunks *of Romeo and Juliet* to a Roman setting in *The History and Fall of Caius Marius* (1679), which was still being played over a hundred years later. In the eighteenth century Nicholas Rowe enjoyed considerable success with *The Tragedy of Jane Shore*, 'Written in Imitation of Shakespeare's Style' (1714). And by the nineteenth century there were few major poets who didn't aspire to write plays in the Shakespearian manner. Shelley's *The Cenci*, Byron's *Manfred*, Keats's fragment *King Stephen*, Tennyson's *Queen Mary*, Robert Browning's *Luria*, Swinburne's Mary Queen of Scots trilogy are only some of the better known examples. But most of these plays were 'closet dramas', destined never to be performed, and even those that were failed to hold the stage. Whatever their authors' gifts, they represented dead ends.

There were more possibilities, as the twentieth century was to discover, in plays which took a critical or subversive attitude towards Shakespeare. In a small way, this approach had been anticipated by the long tradition of Shakespearian burlesque, dating back to the seventeenth century and vigorously pursued by the Victorians. The most notable of these skits, *Rosenkrantz and Guildenstern* (1874), is the work of W. S. Gilbert of Gilbert and Sullivan. It makes some amusing points at the expense of actors, commentators, and Shakespeare himself. But it is simple stuff in comparison with Tom Stoppard's *Rosencrantz and Guildenstern are Dead* (1966), a play which opens up fresh perspectives by putting the spotlight on the two secondary characters who give it its title and by running a quizzical eye over the action.

Stoppard's is much the most subtle of modern British or American reworkings of Shakespeare. Many lesser efforts which excited interest at the time now seem badly dated—Barbara Garson's *MacBird!* (1965), for example, which satirizes Lyndon B. Johnson and the politics of its era in terms of *Macbeth*. Even John Osborne's *A Place Calling Itself Rome* (1973), a reworking of *Coriolanus* (with a marked bias in favour of the Patricians) now seems dismayingly crude. But Edward Bond's *Lear* (1972) has more enduring interest. It stretches the politics of *King Lear* beyond Shakespeare, in more radical directions, but its dour integrity commands respect.

There remains the special case of Samuel Beckett. He is special because his work straddles two languages (he wrote and published much of it in French, and then himself translated it into English), and also because he has absorbed a great deal of Shakespeare into his own unique and in many ways very different vision. Beckett is bleak where for Shakespeare bleakness is only one element in a rich picture. But Shakespearian echoes and motifs are nonetheless woven deep into his work. They are at their most intense in the play *Endgame* (1958: *Fin de partie* in the original French), in which the stricken central character Hamm re-embodies not only the paralysis of Hamlet, as his name suggests, but also the desolation of Lear, and the disenchantment of Prospero as well.

Plays and playwrights in the wider world

If we look beyond the English-speaking world, the quality of the drama inspired or provoked by Shakespeare is on the whole more impressive. Again and again, as his work made its way into other cultures, it acted as a tremendous liberating force.

In Germany, where a major cult of Shakespeare took root around 1770, one of Goethe's early works was a prose historical drama constructed on Shakespearian lines, *Goetz von Berlichingen* (1773), which signalled his rejection of neoclassical rules, such as the unities of time and space, and paved the way for his later masterpieces. (It also earned him a rebuke from no less a person than Frederick the Great, a staunch upholder of neoclassicism.) Goethe's younger contemporary and friend Friedrich Schiller fell under Shakespeare's spell early in his career: the lessons he learned from Shakespeare bore fruit in many of his plays, from *The Robbers* (1781), with its reminiscences of Richard III and Edmund in *King Lear*, to his trilogy about the military hero *Wallenstein* (1798–9), with its broad historical sweep.

The neoclassical resistance to Shakespeare lasted much longer in France. Its most powerful spokesman was Voltaire (even though he had originally found things to praise in the Englishman's work). The forces that were being held back eventually exploded, however, and when romanticism finally won the day in France, Shakespeare played a central role. Victor Hugo, in the preface to his play *Cromwell* (1827), praised him as a supreme master, virtually a force of nature. Alfred de Vigny produced a notable adaptation of *Othello* and introduced unprecedented Shakespearian effects, including the supernatural, into his play *La Maréchale d'Ancre* (first performed in 1831).

A little earlier, in Russia, Alexander Pushkin had written *Boris Godunov* (1825), a historical drama consciously cast in the Shakespearian mould. Pushkin, who made many penetrating remarks about Shakespeare, was impressed both by the breadth of his plays—his ability to encompass a great range of social types—and the depth of his characterization. In a later work, the narrative poem *Angelo* (1833), Pushkin offered his own version of the main action in *Measure for Measure*.

During the course of the nineteenth century, as knowledge of Shakespeare spread and translations multiplied, few major European dramatists remained untouched by his example. To take only the most famous names, Ibsen, Chekhov, and Strindberg all acknowledged his power, though in varying degrees. Ibsen's debt is most apparent in his early historical dramas, such as *Lady Inger of Östrát* (1855), in which the central character was partly inspired by Lady Macbeth. In his mature work he turned his back on verse and on artificial conventions which Shakespeare had been happy to work with, such as the soliloquy, but critics have detected buried Shakespearian parallels in his later plays even so—between *Hamlet* and *Ghosts*, for example. In Chekhov, comparisons with *Hamlet* come right out into the open—above all in The *Seagull* (1896), where characters quote directly from the earlier play. As for Strindberg, he spoke of Shakespeare as 'my teacher', and claimed to have devoured all his works (in the standard Swedish translation) by the time he was fifteen. The most striking Shakespearian parallels in his own work are those in *The Father* (1887): the hero is tormented by an obsessive jealousy which recalls that of Othello, and he also quotes at length (though without feeling obliged to give his source) from Shylock's 'hath not a Jew?' speech in *The Merchant of Venice*.

In the twentieth century—as in Britain, but to greater effect—the most notable creative responses to Shakespeare by European dramatists have been, not anti-Shakespearian, perhaps, but counter-Shakespearian. While conceding the mastery of his plays, they have revised or called in question the values they embody.

Alfred Jarry's anarchic *Ubu Roi* (1896), for instance, is one of the foundation-documents of modernism. (At its first performance in Paris, W. B. Yeats famously remarked, 'After us, the Savage God'.) To a large extent, the play takes the form of a squalid parody of *Macbeth*, with other distorted Shakespearian elements thrown into the stew. A later dramatist of the Absurd, Eugène Ionesco (Romanian-born, but writing in French), also went to work on *Macbeth* and transformed it into *Macbett* (1972). His version ends with the newly crowned Malcolm threatening to be an even worse tyrant than Macbeth, and with the prospect of oppression stretching out to the crack of doom.

In the German-speaking world, the Swiss dramatist Friedrich Dürrenmatt produced dark revisions of *King John* (1968), turning it into a tale of gang warfare, and *Titus Andronicus* (1970), making it even more grotesque than that play. But the most celebrated twentieth-century German adaptations of Shakespeare were those of Bertolt Brecht. In his lampoon of Hitler in The *Resistible Rise of Arturo Ui* (1941), he drew explicitly on *Richard III*. In *Coriolan* (1952) he produced a broadly Marxist, pro-Plebeian reading of *Coriolanus*.

Meanwhile, the middle years of the twentieth century also saw an increasing number of reworkings of Shakespeare beyond Europe and North America, in what was rapidly becoming the post-colonial world (also discussed in Chapter 33). In some of these versions, his plays were adapted to local circumstances and traditions. Others were 'appropriations', in which Shakespearian material was given a new post-colonial or anti-colonial twist—Welcome Msomi's *Umabathu*, for instance (a Zulu transposition of *Macbeth*), or Murray Carlin's *Not Now, Sweet Desdemona* (first produced in Uganda in 1968). The play which provided the principal focus for feelings about colonialism was, understandably, *The Tempest*. The Brazilian writer Augusto Boal subjected it to fierce parody in the version he wrote in 1979. Ten years earlier the Martinique-born poet Aimé Césaire had set out to 'de-mythify' (his own word) it in his play *Une Tempête*. Césaire's Prospero is an unyielding imperialist. His Caliban is a slave, but a slave who is no longer prepared to endure his servitude: the first word he utters when he appears on stage is the African liberation-cry 'Uhuru'.

Poems and poets

Shakespeare's use of language has left its mark on many later English poets. Examples of an extended debt include Milton in his early masque, *Comus*, and Keats in his 'poetic romance' *Endymion*. There are also countless instances of individual Shakespearian echoes being successfully integrated into later poetry of a very different type. They range from Wordsworth recalling Prospero's farewell speech in *The Prelude* to William Empson boldly quoting from *King Lear* ('Ripeness is all') at the start of one of his finest poems, *To an Old Lady* (1928). Nonetheless it would be foolish for other poets to try to follow such a powerful model too closely. They would be straining themselves beyond their natural resources; and in any case, as the great eighteenth-century German aphorist Georg Christoph Lichtenberg observed, 'What there was in the world to be done in Shakespearian has largely been done by Shakespeare'.

There has been more scope for later poets to make use of Shakespeare without sacrificing their independence, in poems inspired by one of his characters (or, occasionally, by an entire play). In such poems, too, foreign-language poets have been able to accomplish as much as—or more than—those writing in English.

One could compile a miniature anthology of poems suggested by *Hamlet* alone. It would include, among other items of equal interest, the Greek poet Constantine Cavafy's reappraisal of King Claudius, the Polish poet Zbigniew Herbert's *Elegy of Fortinbras*, the French poet Arthur Rimbaud's *Ophelia*, and the Russian poet Boris Pasternak's tight-packed poem about a Prince Hamlet who also takes on aspects of Christ—the first of the sequence of poems which make up the final section of Pasternak's novel *Doctor Zhivago*.

Another play which poets have built on is *The Tempest*. In Robert Browning's *Caliban upon Setebos* (1864), Caliban broods on philosophical and theological issues in a soliloquy which has its origins in his resolve at the end of the play to 'seek for grace'. W. H. Auden's *The Sea and the Mirror* (1945)—subtitled 'A Commentary on Shakespeare's *The Tempest*'—is a brilliant medley of verse and prose in which Auden pursues his own preoccupations but never loses sight for long of his Shakespearian starting point. *Nothing in Prospero's Cloak*, by the Polish poet Tadeusz Rosewicz, is a bitter cry on behalf of Caliban; Ted Hughes wrote a powerful short poem entitled *Prospero and Sycorax*. And poems inspired by other plays range from Herman Melville's *Falstaff's Lament*—the thoughts of the fat knight in old age—to Derek Walcott's *Goats and Monkeys*, the Caribbean poet's response to the racial tensions in *Othello*.

There are also innumerable poems or passages from poems about Shakespeare himself. Two noble examples are Ben Jonson's *To the memory of my beloved, The Author Mr. William Shakespeare: And what he hath left us* (one of the commendatory poems in the First Folio, 1623), and the young Milton's *What needs my Shakespear for his honoured bones* (his first poem to be published—from the Second Folio, 1632). The sonnet by Matthew Arnold, *Others abide our question* (1849), is a long-established anthology-piece; other poets who have paid tribute in verse include Henry Wadsworth Longfellow, Thomas Hardy, and Hugh MacDiarmid.

But it isn't only a question of offering homage, and some of the best poems about him go well beyond acts of celebration. Pasternak's *Shakespeare* paints a vivid imagined picture of his tavern life in London. The long dramatic soliloquy by the American poet Edwin Arlington Robinson, *Ben Jonson Entertains a Man from Stratford* (1916), sets him in the contexts of his times and of his home town. In *The Craftsman*, Rudyard Kipling traces the roots of his art back to his childhood and youth. In *When I read Shakespeare*, D. H. Lawrence comments amusingly on the gulf (as he sees it) beween the splendour of Shakespeare's language and the mediocrity of his characters. And *Everything and Nothing*, the prose-poem by the Argentinian master Jorge Luis Borges, is a memorable fable about Shakespeare's impersonality—about a playwright who has a godlike ability to fashion identities for the men and women in his plays without having a true identity of his own.

Novels and novelists

Shakespeare's indirect influence on the development of the novel is incalculable, and he impinges directly on its history at many points. *Hamlet*, for example, hovers on the edge of the first major novel which draws attention to its own fictional status, Laurence Sterne's *Tristram Shandy* (1759–67), and it plays a key role in the first great *Bildungsroman*, or novel of moral and emotional education, Goethe's *Wilhelm Meister's Apprenticeship* (1795–6). In *Tristram Shandy*, Sterne's playful alter ego is Parson Yorick, a descendant of Yorick the court jester. In *Wilhelm Meister*, the youthful hero is bowled over when he reads Shakespeare for the first time. He joins a theatrical troupe and finds himself cast as Hamlet in a new production: it is an important milestone on his road towards maturity and self-realization.

There are innumerable Shakespearian motifs elsewhere in fiction. A performance of *As You Like It* contributes to both action and atmosphere in Théophile Gautier's *Mademoiselle de Maupin* (1835). *Coriolanus* is used to teach an imperious millowner a lesson in Charlotte Brontë's *Shirley* (1849). One of the opening chapters of Dostoievsky's *The Possessed* (1872) is entitled 'Prince Harry' for the hero of the *Henry IV* plays; Stavrogin makes reference to the dissolute ways of its central character (although, as Stavrogin's mother suggests, an apter comparison would be with Hamlet). The 'rediscovery' of Shakespeare is a central theme in Aldous Huxley's *Brave New World* (1932). *Henry V* provides a frequent point of reference in David Jones's unclassifiable poem-cum-novel about the First World War, *In Parenthesis* (1937). Parallels with the Shakespearian *Tempest* are woven into Isak Dinesen's short story

Tempests, and into more recent works of fiction such as Toni Morrison's *Tar Baby* (1981). Whole novels have been devoted to individual characters, from Ludwig Lewisohn's *The Last Days of Shylock* (1931) to Robert Nye's *Falstaff* (1976).

Of all the Shakespeare plays that novelists have been drawn to, *Hamlet* remains the one that has attracted them most. Ninety years after *Wilhelm Meister*, in 1887, the poet Jules Laforgue published a remarkable short novel, *Hamlet ou les suites de la piété filiale* ('Hamlet or the consequences of filial piety') a sardonic, half-anachronistic retelling of the tale, full of narrative tricks, in which the hero is less Renaissance prince than late nineteenth-century aesthete. Vladimir Nabokov's *Bend Sinister* (1947), an even more complex work, contains a satirical account of a film-scenario for *Hamlet*; there are also elaborate discussions of the play, as in Iris Murdoch's *The Black Prince* (1973). More recently, in *Gertrude and Claudius* (1999), John Updike has traced the story of the drama at Elsinore down to the point at which Shakespeare begins.

There are recollections of *Hamlet* in the novels of Charles Dickens, too—scores if not hundreds of them; but like Dickens's other borrowings from the man he once called 'the great master who knew everything', they are more diffuse than those of the novelists who have already been mentioned. A Shakespearian echo in Dickens can serve a number of different functions. It can be used for its evocative power, or for effects of comic grandiloquence (when Mr Micawber holds forth, for example). It can reinforce an unfolding theme (the prospect of murder in *Edwin Drood* is accompanied by reminiscences of *Macbeth*), or provide an opportunity for joyous theatricality, or underline a character's reliance on cliché—often garbled cliché. The Shakespearian element in Dickens is frequently signposted, but it is also assimilated into his own creative vision.

The novels and stories in which Shakespeare himself plays a part constitute a much smaller but still varied tradition. He makes an appearance at the court of Elizabeth I in Walter Scott's *Kenilworth* (1821)—anachronistically, since the events of the novel take place in the 1570s, when Shakespeare was a small boy. Walter Savage Landor elaborated the legend of Shakespeare the youthful poacher in his jeu d'esprit *Citation and Examination of William Shakespeare Touching Deer Stealing* (1834). Oscar Wilde's theory that the Mr W. H. of the Sonnets was a boy actor, Willie Hughes, is advanced in *The Portrait of Mr W. H.* (1889), a teasing, intricately constructed story which Wilde's biographer Richard Ellman has described as anticipating Jorge Luis Borges. In one of the last stories which Rudyard Kipling wrote, *Proofs of Holy Writ* (1934), Shakespeare's help is enlisted by one of the translators entrusted with preparing the Authorized (King James) Version of the bible. He is shown revising a draft of some verses from Isaiah in the company of Ben Jonson.

While Shakespeare may not appear as a character in James Joyce's *Ulysses* (1922), his presence frequently makes itself felt. One of the book's major episodes, set in the National Library of Ireland, centres on a discussion of the relationship between his life and his work. Stephen Dedalus (the hero of Joyce's earlier, largely autobiographical *A Portrait of the Artist as a Young Man*) expounds his theory that the playwright's confidence never recovered from being seduced into marriage by Anne Hathaway, and then cuckolded by one of his brothers: he claims that the trauma left its mark on everything he wrote. Stephen, an aspiring artist, is thinking of himself as he talks, but he lacks Shakespeare's humanity—unlike his cruder but warmer-hearted opposite number in the book, Leopold Bloom. The Shakespeare allusions and quotations scattered elsewhere in *Ulysses* run into the hundreds (and there are a comparable number in *Finnegans Wake*).

In more recent times two writers, Anthony Burgess and Robert Nye, have succeeded in producing novels about Shakespeare which have lasting literary value. Burgess's theories may be debatable (especially his view that the syphilis from which Shakespeare supposedly suffered played a large part in his inspiration); but *Nothing Like the Sun* (1964) and to a lesser extent *Enderby's Dark Lady* (1984) are still notable for their gusto, wit, and linguistic exuberance. Nye is another robust writer; in *Mrs Shakespeare* (1993) he offers us an intimate and less than enraptured view of the great man through the eyes of Anne Hathaway.

Shakespeare and music

Scholars have listed over 20,000 pieces of music associated with Shakespeare—settings of songs, incidental music, general works—and the number continues to grow. Music played an integral part in his plays from the beginning: along with songs, the original productions featured 'signal' music (flourishes to mark the entrance of important figures, and so forth) and music for special or atmospheric effects. Shakespeare's own love of music, and his familiarity with it, are apparent from many passages in his work. Faced with the extraordinary wealth of later music based on his work, a note can only hope to cite a few of the more illustrious examples.

Composers who have written settings for individual songs include Franz Schubert (much-loved music for 'Hark, hark, the lark' from *Cymbeline* and 'Who is Sylvia?' from *The Two Gentleman of Verona*), Robert Schumann ('When that I was and a little tiny boy' from *Twelfth Night*), Johannes Brahms ('Come away, death' again from *Twelfth Night*) and Dmitri Shostakovich (songs from *Hamlet*). Those who have composed incidental music range from Arthur Sullivan (for half a dozen plays) to Harrison Birtwistle (for four plays), by way of such figures as Richard Strauss (for *Romeo and Juliet*) and Jean Sibelius (for *Twelfth Night* and *The Tempest*). The most celebrated of all incidental music is that composed by Felix Mendelssohn for *A Midsummer Night's Dream*. For many people, during the century or so after it was first performed (1843), it remained inseparable from the play.

Only a handful of the many operas based on Shakespeare have a firm place in the repertoire. They include Otto Nicolai's *The Merry Wives of Windsor* (1849) and Benjamin Britten's *A Midsummer Night's Dream* (1960), which draws on Shakespeare's own words for its libretto. And one name, Giuseppe Verdi, stands apart. He achieved a notable early success with *Macbeth* (1847), but his two masterpieces are *Otello* (1887), a work comparable in power to the play, and *Falstaff* (1893), a work worthy of its central character.

Although it is fine opera, *Beatrice and Benedict* (1862), the adaptation of *Much Ado about Nothing* by Hector Berlioz, is not in the same class. But Berlioz remains a towering figure in the story of Shakespeare and music none the less. His Shakespearian compositions include the incomparable dramatic symphony, *Romeo and Juliet* (1839); his great opera *The Trojans* is partly Shakespearian in inspiration; his writings reveal how soaked he was in Shakespeare, and how well he understood him.

The list of other works which deserve to be mentioned is as impressive in its variety as in its quality. Franz Joseph Haydn's setting of 'She never told her love' (from *Twelfth Night*), Sergei Prokofiev's ballet music for *Romeo and Juliet*, William Walton's music for Laurence Olivier's film of *Henry V*, Ralph Vaughan Williams' cantata *Serenade to Music* (with words from The *Merchant of Venice*) are a mere sampling. Jazz has paid its respects, too, most notably in Duke Ellington's suite of twelve pieces suggested by Shakespearian characters, *Such Sweet Thunder* (1957—the title comes from *A Midsummer Night's Dream*). And there are two classic Broadway musicals based on Shakespeare. *The Boys from Syracuse* (1938), by Rodgers and Hart, is a reworking of *The Comedy of Errors*; in *Kiss Me Kate* (1948) Cole Porter not only rings witty changes on *The Taming of the Shrew* but also discovers lyric possibilities in such lines from the play as 'I come to wive it wealthily in Padua'.

Shakespeare and the visual arts

Shakespeare has provided work for innumerable illustrators, and during the eighteenth and nineteenth centuries his plays were a favourite source of subject-matter for academic painters. Most of this work is now forgotten, but some of it must have had a considerable effect in shaping readers' conceptions of his characters.

In the course of the eighteenth century he also began to attract more significant artists. The earliest of them was William Hogarth, with his vivid depiction of Falstaff reviewing his troops (1728) and a celebrated portrait of David Garrick as Richard III (1745). Johann Zoffany painted an equally famous picture of Garrick as Macbeth; Joshua Reynolds ventured into Shakespearian territory with paintings of Puck, of Macbeth and the Witches, and of the death of Cardinal Beaufort in *Henry VI*.

In the later eighteenth century Henry Fuseli began producing hundreds of intense but often melodramatic depictions of scenes from Shakespeare, many of them drawings or watercolours. William Blake, who admired Fuseli, also created a series of Shakespeare drawings, though the link between their ostensible subjects and Blake's idiosyncratic treatment isn't always apparent. Other leading British artists of the Romantic period, including Turner and Constable, occasionally took their subjects from the plays. But the most Shakespearian of Romantic artists was undoubtedly a Frenchman, Eugène Delacroix. He produced a powerful series of lithographs of subjects from *Hamlet* (1843), while dozens of entries in his journal make it clear that his imaginative involvement with Shakespeare was deep and lasting.

Back in Britain, the Pre-Raphaelites produced some striking portrayals of Shakespearian scenes. (The best known of them is John Everett Millais's *Ophelia*.) Later, in the early twentieth century, Walter Sickert painted some fine theatrical portraits, and Wyndham Lewis published a portfolio of harsh geometrical drawings inspired by *Timon of Athens*. But after that, with the decline of figurative art in general, the story tails off.

One Shakespearian image continues to hold its own, however. The Martin Droeshout engraving which was used as a frontispiece in the First Folio (see Figure 1.1) may not be a particularly distinguished work of art, but that hasn't stopped it making its way across the world on posters and tee-shirts and in a hundred other forms. Today it must be as instantly recognizable an icon as the Mona Lisa or Marilyn Monroe.

FURTHER READING

Cohn, Ruby. *Modern Shakespeare Offshoots* (Princeton: Princeton University Press, 1976). This book provides an invaluable guide to creative adaptations and appropriations in English, French, and German. While the main emphasis is on twentieth-century authors, their nineteenth-century predecessors are also well covered.

Gager, Valerie. *Shakespeare and Dickens* (Cambridge: Cambridge University Press, 1996). This is a remarkably thorough study of Dickens's interest in Shakespeare, and of the ways in which that interest helped to shape his art. It contains an annotated catalogue of around a thousand references to Shakespeare in the novelist's writings.

Gross, John. *After Shakespeare* (Oxford: Oxford University Press, 2002). An anthology presenting a wide range of responses to Shakespeare from many periods and countries. Along with fiction, poetry, and other imaginative writing, it includes comments and reactions going far beyond the conventional limits of literary and dramatic criticism.

Hartnoll, Phyllis (ed.). *Shakespeare and Music* (London: Macmillan, 1964). This is the handiest general treatment of its subject. It contains essays by experts on the music of the Elizabethan stage, on Shakespeare's songs, on Shakespeare and opera, and on Shakespeare in the concert-room, along with a select catalogue of musical works.

LeWinter, Oswald (ed.). *Shakespeare in Europe* (Harmondsworth: Penguin Books, 1970). This wide-ranging selection of European reactions to Shakespeare is not just an anthology of criticism. The authors represented—they include Stendhal, Heine, and Tolstoy—are all major literary figures in their own right.

Merchant, W. Moelwyn. *Shakespeare and the Artist* (Oxford: Oxford University Press, 1959). This account of Shakespeare and the visual arts takes in scene designers as well as painters and illustrators. Along with its general survey it includes detailed studies of a number of individual plays.

Schmidgall, Gary. *Shakespeare and Opera* (Oxford: Oxford University Press, 1990). This is a lively and entertaining account of operas based on Shakespeare, both major and minor, which also uses opera to raise some interesting questions about the plays.

Shutte, William. *Joyce and Shakespeare* (New Haven: Yale University Press, 1957). This study is primarily concerned with the presence of Shakespeare in *Ulysses*, though it also throws a good deal of incidental light on Joyce's earlier work.

43 | Shakespeare and translation

Ton Hoenselaars

'One hears a thousand things through other tongues'

Shakespeare is easily the world's most popular poet and playwright. Especially to those who cherish him as a consummate master of the English language, it might come as a surprise that the majority of Shakespearian consumption around the globe takes place in a language other than early modern English. In most educational contexts where today's common language is taught, Shakespeare may indeed be read and discussed in English, but extracurricular Shakespeare, on the page and on the stage, exists by virtue of translation. This chapter provides a number of contexts within which to appreciate the fortunes of 'Shakespeare without his language'. It introduces relevant concepts used in this area of overlap between Shakespeare studies and Translation studies. In addition, it provides a brief survey of Shakespeare in translation from the sixteenth century to the present day. It traces views of translation from the time of the strolling players whose performances on the European continent gave rise to the first crude translations, to the current state of affairs in which the art of translation, though still practised with painstaking devotion by some, has also been taken up by writers whose political agendas seem to warrant considerable liberties. Others who support substantial deviations explain their pervasive iconoclasm from a perspective of cultural relativism.

Translation may mean many things. In Shakespeare's plays and poems, translation often means a change, in a broad sense, of an individual's convictions. By extension, it also means metamorphosis, a transmutation of species. This is what Quince in *A Midsummer Night's Dream* means when, on seeing Bottom wearing the ass-head, he exclaims: 'Thou art translated' (3.1.105). In sonnet 96, such a translation takes place not between a human and an animal, but between two animals:

> Some say thy fault is youth, some wantonness;
> Some say thy grace is youth and gentle sport.
> Both grace and faults are loved of more and less;
> Thou mak'st faults graces that to thee resort.
> As on the finger of a thronèd queen
> The basest jewel will be well esteemed,
> So are those errors that in thee are seen
> To truths translated and for true things deemed.

> *How many lambs might the stern wolf betray*
> *If like a lamb he could his looks translate!*
> (1-10; emphasis added)

A closer look at the sonnet shows that these lines really represent an analogy to the 'errors' which, seen in the beloved, look like 'truths translated' (7–8), thus alluding to the way in which translation may improve on the original. Only on rare occasions, as here, does Shakespeare seem to associate translation with the art of transcoding words and messages from one language to another. This is not to say, however, that he was not familiar with the practice. Many of Shakespeare's dramatic sources were translations from other languages: the Geneva Bible, Plutarch's Greek *Lives of the Noble Grecians and Romans* (tr. Sir Thomas North), the *Essays* of Montaigne (tr. from the French by John Florio), and the very poem that captured the translatability of the gods, of men, and of animals, Ovid's *Metamorphoses* (tr. from the Latin by Arthur Golding). Not only did Shakespeare use existing translations; translation in our modern sense of the term is also a standard routine within the plays themselves. Holofernes excels at self-translation in *Love's Labour's Lost*:

The deer was, as you know—*sanguis*—in blood, ripe as the pomewater who now hangeth like a jewel in the ear of *caelo*, the sky, the welkin, the heaven, and anon falleth like a crab on the face of *terra*, the soil, the land, the earth.

(4.2.3-6)

Also, Owen Glendower in the first part of *Henry IV*, on behalf of his daughter, interprets into English the Welsh she speaks to Mortimer. There are numerous instances of translation in the other plays, in *Henry V*, but also sardonically in *All's Well That Ends Well*, with one of the soldiers appointed as interpreter to turn a nonsense language into fluent English for Parolles.

Kinds of translation

For an appreciation of Shakespeare's afterlife in translation, it seems appropriate briefly to consider the views of the art and craft of translation as these have developed since the seventeenth century. Particularly useful for this purpose is Roman Jakobson's identification of three main types of translation. The first is *intralingual translation*, or the rewording of a text within the same language. *Intralingual translation* is considered rather unproblematic when it serves to modernize Geoffrey Chaucer's *Canterbury Tales*, but when the principle is applied to produce modern English versions of Shakespeare, many Shakespearians still prefer staunchly to ignore them. The second type of translation, labelled *interlingual translation*, is really the same process, but rather than taking place within a single language, it occurs between two languages. This is translation proper, as most people would define it. Thirdly, there is *intersemiotic translation*, whereby the source-text signs appertaining to a specific verbal system are converted or recoded into a nonverbal sign system, for example, because the limits of *interlingual translation* have been reached. *Intersemiotic translation* involves the transfer from word to image, from speech to acting, or from word to gesture. Since *intersemiotic translation* exploits Shakespeare's extra-linguistic potential, we encounter it in translations prepared for the stage or the screen rather than for the study or the armchair. An exceptional mode of *intersemiotic translation* is the practice of theatre companies to 'sign' several performances of each production for the benefit of the deaf and the hard of hearing.

Early translations of Shakespeare

Translating Shakespeare is not a recent practice. The earliest translations of his plays and poems date from the late sixteenth and the early seventeenth centuries. At this time, the travelling players, seeking their fortunes on the continent of Europe, would originally perform the London repertoire of Marlowe, Kyd, and Shakespeare in English. However, the English language was not yet widely spoken abroad. English, as John Florio, the Italian translator and probable friend of Shakespeare put it, was 'a language that will do you good in England, but pass Dover, it is worth nothing'. As a consequence, the improvised performances of the wandering actors soon prompted the first German translations of such plays as *Hamlet* (as *Der bestrafte Brudermord*, or 'Fratricide Punished', 1603), and *Titus Andronicus* (which became *Eine sehr klägliche Tragaedia von Tito Andronico und der hoffertigen Kayserin*, 'A Very Lamentable Tragedy of Titus Andronicus and the Proud Empress', in 1620). The strolling players' performances in the Low Countries led Abraham Sybant to undertake the first Dutch translation of *The Taming of the Shrew* as *De dolle bruyloft* (or 'The Mad Wedding', 1654).

Studying these early foreign versions—none of which, like the early English quartos, as yet carries the trade name of Shakespeare—one is soon convinced that the translator's desire to produce equivalence between the text in his source language and the target (or receptor) language, did not feature highly in the business of literature. In the case of early modern bible translations, a mistake might be interpreted as a sign of the translator's heresy, and thus become a matter of life and death. However, the anonymous compiler-cum-translator of the first German *Hamlet*, based on a 1603 performance by English players in Germany, seems to have had no such qualms. The opening of the play, here retranslated into English, leaves one in little doubt:

> *1. Sentinel:* Who's there?
> *2. Sentinel:* A friend!
> *1. Sentinel:* What friend?

2. Sentinel: Sentinel.

1. Sentinel: Ho! comrade, you come to relieve me. I wish the hours may not be so long to you as they have been to me.

2. Sentinel: Nay, comrade, 'tis not so bitter cold.

1. Sentinel: Cold or no, I have had an infernal fright.

Something similar may be said of Abraham Sybant's decision to translate most of *The Taming of the Shrew* rather accurately, but at the same time to dispense, among other things, with the play's famous Induction. In the case of Sybant we seem to be crossing what we would now call the borderline between translation proper and adaptation.

However, caution is called for here since the parameters for translation and adaptation during the seventeenth and eighteenth centuries were different from those of our postmodern present. What we witness in the early *Hamlet*, *Titus*, or *Shrew* does not betoken that their translators were incapable of appreciating the true value of Shakespeare; it must be recognized as part of the same normative, neoclassical tendency which, around the middle of the seventeenth century, also led John Dryden and William Davenant to make Shakespeare fit for the Restoration stage. In neoclassical poetics, translation occupied a vital principle in the creative process, where it was considered to inspire imitation and lead on to an emulation of the original. Given a poetic system that conflated the art of translation with the investment of creative and emulative energies, and hence also associated the translation process with the target rather than the source, the individual imprint of the translator was bound to be more conspicuous, and the end result of his labours likely to differ more from the original.

Second-hand translation in the eighteenth and nineteenth centuries

Normative, neoclassical French poetics were to mark Shakespearian translation during the eighteenth century and beyond, if only because in many European countries the source text for translation would not be an original English quarto or Folio version of the plays, but the French prose translations by Pierre-Antoine de la Place or Pierre le Tourneur, or the French translations-cum-adaptations produced by Jean-François Ducis. Ducis's curious reworkings of Shakespeare, in particular, found their way into many languages, including Dutch, Italian, Polish, Portuguese, Russian, and Spanish.

This phenomenon of the indirect or second-hand translation explains the spread throughout Europe and into Turkey of the final scene of *Othello* in which Desdemona, now named Hédelmone, was stabbed to death by her jealous husband Othello at the foot of the bed. As Ducis remarked about his revision:

My final scene was accepted with some difficulty in Paris; in London, the English endure that of Shakespeare quite well. In their theatre, Othello does not murder his innocent victim with a dagger; he smothers her in bed as, with force, he repeatedly stops her mouth with a pillow, until she finally dies. This is something a French audience could never endure.

The influence of Ducis' assumptions about French squeamishness here are still visible in Francesco Berio di Salsa's operatic libretto for Rossini's *Otello* (1816).

It was only slowly that such target-oriented translation, pandering to assumed audience sensibilities and taste, began to make way for source-oriented translation and greater respect for the original playwright. It was only in the 1880s, therefore, when Arrigo Boito wrote the libretto for Giuseppe Verdi's opera about the Moor of Venice, that the fatal pillow was effectively restored, and Desdemona smothered to death in bed. It nearly seems as if Otello's repeated kissing of Desdemona in Verdi's operatic rendering of the tragedy served to restore, with a vengeance, the physical intimacy of which the lovers had been deprived for over a century: '*Un bacio, un bacio ancora ... ah! un altro bacio ...*' (A kiss, another kiss ... ah! and yet another kiss).

Translation for equivalence

While Ducis's French Shakespeare continued to be read and performed well into the nineteenth century, a new type of translation developed in Germany. During the late eighteenth century, Chr. M. Wieland, J. J. Eschenburg, F. L. Schröder, Friedrich Schiller, August Wilhelm Schlegel, and Ludwig Tieck developed a mode of translation that set out to be as true as possible to the Shakespeare text as established by the eighteenth-century editors in England. In the age that effectively raised Shakespeare to the status of a divine genius who deserved a translation pursued with a degree of devotion to the letter that had so far been reserved mainly for the bible, the German translators freed Shakespeare from the straitjacket of rules to which he had long been forced to adhere, and fashioned him into the Romantic champion of anti-classicism. The so-called Schlegel-Tieck translation, which appeared between 1797 and 1833, and to which also Tieck's daughter Dorothea and her husband Count Wolf von Baudissin made a significant contribution, was to be a model in many countries on the European continent. Thanks to revisions undertaken over the years, the Schlegel-Tieck translation continues to enjoy canonical status in the German-speaking world, although this has not prevented new translations from being made.

From the Romantic period onwards, Shakespearian translation increasingly came to be judged by the newly introduced criterion of equivalence between the source text and the target text. Since every language represents a reality of its own and is part of a separate cultural system, equivalence is really a phantom, certainly in the field of translation. In fact, as we see it now, if equivalence existed, translation would cease to exist. By extension, the Romantic tradition is responsible for the widely held view that a translation is, nearly automatically, a reduction or an emasculation of the original.

The translator's a priori failure explains the popularity of the Italian proverb that the translator (or *traduttore*) was really a born deceiver (*tradittore*).

Living language

Against the background of such views on equivalence and reliability, one might be tempted to think that Ulrich Erckenbrecht's collection of one hundred and thirty-two German verse translations of sonnet 66 ('Tired with all these, for restful death I cry'), confirms this view. In 1826, Dorothea Tieck began her translation of the sonnet with the phrase '*Satt alles dies*' ('Tired with all these'), but surprisingly few other translators chose this solution. Instead, for nearly two centuries, they seem to have been engaged in an untiring search for alternative options, producing approximately eighty variants to Shakespeare's original combination of four words. Significantly, though, this plethora of German renderings neither undermines the notion of equivalence, nor does it challenge the translator's reliability. Instead, it drives home the fact that when speaking of Shakespeare and translation we are really thinking of a transfer from a fixed, historical text to a modern, foreign language that is still in flux. This explains why in the course of so many years so many individuals have been able to suggest valid new readings of the Shakespearian original. Shakespeare here manifests himself as a force that continues to activate the potential of other languages, like the developing German language, in terms of grammar, vocabulary, register, rhythm, and tone. Beyond the early modern English language area, now fixed in the past and receding ever further into it, Shakespeare presents a continuing challenge to translators world-wide, who, in turn, speak to new readers and new theatre audiences in their own modern vernaculars.

The view of the translator-as-traitor—fed by the devout Romantic search for equivalence and reliability, and developed further as those who studied translations from a distance were really policing the transfer of the literary canon from one language to another—has lost most of its relevance. The serious translator continues to check and check again the Shakespeare editions, the dictionaries, and other existing translations gathered on his desk. But it has also become common practice for the translator to rethink his traditionally subservient role. Over the years, therefore, he has really become the cultural ambassador who, treading a linguistic minefield, sets out to explore and develop new modes of expression that are also politically correct.

Translating language varieties

Some of these preoccupations may be illustrated with reference to *Henry V*, a play that contains more language varieties, native as well as foreign, than any other Shakespeare play, including standard early modern English, broken English ('I cannot speak your England'), early-modern French (*'Il faut que j'apprenne à parler'*), broken French (*'Je quand suis le possesseur de France . . .'*), as well as Latin (*Te deum, Laudamus*). No doubt some of the more intriguing language varieties in this Babylonian play are the Welsh stage dialect of Fluellen the Scottish lilt of MacMorris, and the Irish brogue of Jamy. Over the centuries, the translation of these British varieties has led to some idiosyncratic results, and a closer look at the attempts to reproduce these dialects and their hierarchical relation to English, in a new language construct, is indicative of the changing role of the translator.

Around the middle of the nineteenth century, François-Victor Hugo, the son of the famous French poet and novelist, produced a prose translation of *Henry V*. Surprisingly, in this version of the play the Irish Jamy was made to speak with a Creole accent:

By the mess, ere these eyes of mine take themselves to slumber, ay'll de gud service, or I'll lig i'th' grund for it. Ay owe Got a death, and I'll pay't as valorously as I may, that sall I suirely do, that is the brief and the long. Marry, I wad full fain heard some question 'tween you twae.

(3.3.54-8)

Par la messe, avant que ces yeux-là se livrent au sommeil, ze fehai de la besogne ou je sehai poté en terre; oui-da! ou je sahai mort; paiehah de ma personne aussi vaillamment que ze pouhai, ze m'y engaze, en un mot, comme en mille. Mobleu! ze sehais bien aise d'ouïr use discussion entre vous deux.

Like J. B. Fort, editing the Hugo translation, some readers might be tempted to describe as 'not felicitous' the implicit suggestion that the relationship between English and Scots should equal that between French and Creole. However, F.-V. Hugo's attempt to render some of the dialects in *Henry V* into French is innocent in comparison with Sylvère Monod's translation of the play, dating from 1957. In Monod's version, regional stereotypes are invoked to buttress linguistic otherness, not just of Jamy, but also of Fluellen and MacMorris:

to give the French reader, at least by approximation, an impression corresponding to that produced by the original text, we think that the phonetic and psychological traits of Fluellen recall those of a Frenchman from the eastern part of the country, that MacMorris recalls someone from the Mediterranean area, and Jamy one from Normandy.

The dubious transposition of the speech of the British eccentrics to that of French citizens from beyond the Île de France might one day invite the province to strike back, and one is happy to learn that more recently, translating *Henry V* for the Avignon Festival (which was also the French première of the play after 400 years of understandable neglect by the French), Jean-Michel Déprats has limited himself to copying consistently Shakespeare's distortions into the French text, though eschewing the option of creating speech styles that might be recognized as somehow regional.

The regional characters only represent part of the problem posed by a multilingual text like *Henry V*. The dialects may present serious problems, but how about the other language varieties? Some of these are French, and Shakespeare's use or appropriation of French here really represents a linguistic conquest that particularly the French translator cannot undo. Translation, as Jacques Derrida has put it, 'can do everything except mark this linguistic difference inscribed in the language, this difference of language systems inscribed in a single tongue'. Armed with this sobering thought—which also applies to Germano-Roman hybrid expressions like Macbeth's 'multitudinous seas incarnadine' (2.2.60)—Déprats emphasizes the importance of his search beyond the limitations of *interlingual* translation by exploring the notion of translation in terms of the play's *intersemiotic* potential on stage. With the appropriate intonation, diction, and bodily gesture it proves possible to find an attractive equivalent in French even of the courtship scene in the final act of *Henry V*.

Since Shakespeare was first and foremost a man of the theatre, this argument about the text's rich performance potential makes good sense. Déprat's recognition of an *intersemiotic* dimension to the art of translation owes much to Bertolt Brecht's beguiling *Gestus*-theory, which is central also to the work of the German Shakespeare translator, Maik Hamburger. On numerous occasions, Brecht stressed how a line of dramatic verse contained not only a certain vocal energy, but also cues for stage action. These *gestic* qualities of a word or a phrase were implicit suggestions, profound hints with regard to the actor's gesture, his attitude towards others, his physical bearing, or bodily movement. In their work for the stage, Déprats and Hamburger seek primarily to recreate this theatrical nucleus, and yield a Shakespeare in foreign garb who charms theatre audiences while seeming to silence detractors. Theatre-oriented practitioners like Déprats and Hamburger have effectively given the lie to the claim that the translator might be a traitor.

Political translation/tradaptation/adaptation

With this vindication of the art and craft of translation so well achieved, it is certainly ironic to note that alongside translators like Déprats and Hamburger, a new school of practitioners has emerged who extend the traditional privileges of the translator by creatively adapting and rewriting the Shakespearian source text to fit certain projected performance conditions. Unlike Dryden and Davenant, who set out to fit Shakespeare into the straitjacket of existing neoclassical rules, these modern manufacturers of translations, tradaptations, and adaptations create their own rules in accordance with the agenda that the play is to serve. This new kind of appropriation of Shakespeare in unexpected ways represents an attempt to forge new political or cultural identities worldwide.

A case in point is the Shakespearian activity in Quebec. Since the 1960s, this Canadian province has been seeking to achieve a sense of self-identity vis-à-vis both the original English and French colonizers, by discreetly though markedly adapting Shakespeare's plays. Instead of playing Shakespeare in Canadian English or in official French, playwrights originally opted for the distinctive dialect of French Canada known as *jouval* (named after the pronunciation of the French word *cheval* in that dialect). At the beginning of what might nearly be termed a movement, Montreal playwright Robert Gurik's *Hamlet, Prince du Québec* (1968) was a powerful call for the province to claim self-determination, rather than hesitate like Shakespeare's protagonist, unable to decide the question: '*Être ou ne pas être libre*' ('To be or not to be independent'). Once Hamlet had been presented as the impersonation of Quebec— trying to realize Charles de Gaulle's 'Vive le Québec libre' as pronounced from the balcony of Montreal's town hall—it was only a matter of time for Michel Garneau to produce a Quebec *Macbeth* (1978). Garneau chose an artificial but recognizable dialect, and called the result a 'tradaptation' of Shakespeare, thus introducing a term that has since gained worldwide currency. In both of these isolated cases that make up one of the most interesting phenomena in late twentieth-century theatre history, tradaptation was a potent post-colonial means of subordinating extraneous discourse, like Shakespeare's plays, to the immediate reality of Quebec.

Politico-cultural concerns also explain Tom Lanoye's Flemish translation-cum-adaptation of Shakespeare's two tetralogies of history plays as *Ten Oorlog* (*Into Battle*, 1997). On the one hand, delving deeply into the chaos of civil war that Shakespeare depicts, Lanoye addresses Belgium's political anxieties at a time when, among other things, the nation's pious King Baudouin died, and, soon after, an unparalleled net-work of child abuse was uncovered that helped demonstrate the ineptitude of the nation's juridical system. *Ten Oorlog* conveys the increasing political and moral chaos in Shakespeare's histories (with their pious king, Henry VI, and their child abuse in Richard II's choice of an infant bride, the Yorkist and Lancastrian hunt for young heirs, and the sad fate of the princes in the Tower) by means of a spreading multilingualism. The elegant, somewhat archaic Dutch of the Richard II sequence slowly disintegrates into a fair share of French and broken French, and slowly also into the pervasive Tarantino-like, American hiphop lingo used by the sons of York, most notably by Richard III himself ('Gimme a break! / Spreek niet dooreen and show me some respect! / You're talking here to God's numero uno').

Despite the useful model that the tetralogies provide to capture the moral and political divisions in Shakespeare's kingdom as well as present-day Belgium, Lanoye's association with the English playwright is deeply problematic. To put it in Frank McCourt's terms, quoted by Lanoye: 'Shakespeare is like mashed potatoes. You can never get enough of him'. Lanoye has a love-hate relationship with the Bard. He is wary of Shakespeare as a cultural icon, and therefore destroys the icon to produce his own version of medieval history, paradoxically, as a tribute to Shakespeare. In *Ten Oorlog*, the words of Richard III are, therefore, of great relevance also for the iconoclastic translation project itself:

> One thing I'll teach de wereld, willens nillens;
> There is tremendous poetry in killings.

A final example of the way in which Shakespeare has been translated with specific political objectives may be found in Great Britain itself, during the period leading up to the political devolution of Scotland during the early 1990s. It seems not to have been a coincidence that as, politically speaking, England's northern neighbour was preparing for the foundation of a Scottish Parliament with extensive though not unlimited powers (ultimately realized in May 1999), both David Purves and Robin L. C. Lorimer completed the difficult task of translating Shakespeare's *Macbeth* into Scots (both in 1992). Reappropriating Shakespeare's 'Scottish' play, they achieved, among other things, a linguistic victory, demonstrating that Scots was not a dialect but a language in its own right, a language eminently capable of making its own king speak again with force and elegance (compare *Macbeth* 2.1.33–9):

> What's this I see afore my een—a bítyach
> heftit towart my haund? Come, let me cleik ye—
> I grip ye no, but ey can see ye yet!
> Ar ye, weird vísion, oniething at may
> as weill be titcht as seen? Or ar ye but
> a bítyach o the mind, a fenyit craitur
> ingenrit o the heat-afflickit harns?

Translation: a creative act

From an English perspective, Shakespearian translation may on occasion seem like a shady intervention required to enable non-English-speaking people to appreciate Shakespeare. In foreign contexts, however, translating Shakespeare is recognized as both a demanding and a challenging task that has long attracted figures with literary reputations in their own right. The German-speaking world prides itself on Wieland, Schiller, Schlegel, and Tieck, not to mention the long list of writers who have tackled the sonnets, like Stefan George, Karl Kraus, and Paul Celan. In France, too, creative writers have successfully tried their hand at Shakespeare: Marcel Schwob, Alfred Vigny, Marcel Pagnol, André Gide, Jean Anouilh, and Yves Bonnefoy. In Russia, Boris Pasternak, perhaps better known as the author of *Doctor Zhivago*, produced formidable translations of *Romeo and Juliet*, *Hamlet*, *Othello*, *Henry IV*, *King Lear*, and *Antony and Cleopatra*; and one of Japan's prominent Shakespeare translators, Tsubouchi Shoyo, was himself a Kabuki writer. Shakespearian translation has even had its royal practitioners. During the nineteenth century, the Portuguese King D. Luís de Bragança (a relative of Queen Victoria's) translated *Richard III, The Merchant of Venice, Hamlet*, and *Othello* into his own Iberian tongue.

Given the status accorded to the art of Shakespeare translation in these international contexts, it may come as a surprise that this form of cultural practice does not command a more conspicuous position in world Shakespeare studies, and, instead, continues to haunt its periphery. Inga-Stina Ewbank—supporting the view expressed by Dirk Delabastita and Lieven D'hulst in their epoch-making *European Shakespeares*—has wondered if the examination of translations might not be 'a stepchild' in Shakespeare studies. The individual, national Shakespeare societies are in the habit of including translation seminars in their programmes. Also, the larger Shakespeare gatherings, particularly those flying the international flag, tend to make special arrangements for Shakespeare translators and translation specialists to attend and exchange ideas. Much of what is discussed there, however, fails to attract the attention of the larger industry. One is tempted to read as portentous the fact that Quince's famous exclamation in *A Midsummer Night's Dream*—'Bless thee, Bottom, bless thee. Thou art translated' (3.1.105)—is immediately followed by his *exit* cue. As a consequence, despite sustained attempts over the last two decades to approach Shakespeare from a number of new angles, translation has not yet been fully recognized as one of the so-called alternative Shakespeares.

This marginal position may to a certain extent be due to a very real language barrier between the hub of the Shakespeare industry, still made up by the English-speaking worlds of Britain and the United States, and the other language areas worldwide. In this sense, the current state of affairs might seem inherent to the art of translation itself. This attractive explanation, however, hides more than it reveals, because the real language barrier is not to be found between native speakers of English and the representatives of other nations admiring the same playwright, but, rather, between the present-day speaker of English and his Shakespeare, speaking early modern English.

In recent years, Dennis Kennedy and Michael Billington have championed a multicultural approach to Shakespeare which, among other things, boldly oversteps the perennial language barrier. Billington has shared with his British *Guardian* readership the view that '[w]e cannot help but see Shakespeare in terms of our own language, history and culture; but we need urgently to widen that definition of culture'. Billington's plea to work towards an appreciation of Shakespeare in cultural contexts other than the familiar, native British condition is echoed in Kennedy's emphasis on the calibre of foreign Shakespeare, Shakespeare as practised and performed in non-English-speaking contexts, 'without his language'. One of Kennedy's contentions in *Foreign Shakespeare* is that easily the most portentous developments in terms of Shakespeare on stage since the Second World War have been of foreign origin, deriving largely from continental Europe, where Shakespeare was practised in languages other than English. In translation, Shakespeare had managed to escape the immediate British cultural context from which he had emerged with the status of a high-culture superscribe. Translation was really a form of liberation, thus facilitating experiment, and valuable new engagements. Moreover, the loss of Shakespeare's 'verbal' nuance in a foreign language, which is nearly inevitable in *interlingual* translation, proved an incentive to *intersemiotic* translation with the exploration of new scenographic and physical modes in ways unparalleled in Britain.

As the ideas of Bertolt Brecht and Jan Kott began to spread across Europe and beyond, the profound irony was that their ideas had been inspired by Shakespeare in a foreign tongue. But, of course, to them, Shakespeare had been speaking a more or less modern version of that language. Shakespeare was more intelligible, captured in a language that had a recognized contemporary status, than to the average twentieth-century Englishman, saddled with Shakespeare's original early modern English which had really become a foreign language, a language belonging to the past, which is another country.

Conclusion

The dictionary has always been one of the most important tools on the translator's desk, but the translator's goals have continually shifted. Before Shakespeare became a canonical author, the translator's creativity was allowed free play. As Shakespeare became a literary saint whose work was sacrosanct like the bible, however, the translator became one of the apostles, too easily charged with treason in a Judas-like fashion. In recent years, as the traditional, literary canon has been coming under fire, and as Shakespeare is appropriated and rewritten more boldly than ever before, the translator has found a new rival in the adaptor, or the tradaptor, who, like himself, appropriates the master text, though in a seemingly more radical and hence more accessible fashion. We must not forget, however, that as tradaptation and adaptation reach the headlines, translation remains the brightest kid in class. As Shakespeare scholars continue to study the multiple mechanisms that determine the playwright's posthumous cult or culture, it is therefore to be hoped that more attention will be devoted also to Shakespeare in translation which, as Derrida has argued, is really 'a child' of the original 'with the power to speak on its own'. The profit from it might be, as he put it on another occasion, that 'one hears a thousand things through other tongues'.

FURTHER READING

Accents Now Known: Shakespeare's Drama in Translation, ed. José Roberto O'Shea. Special issue of *Ilha do desterro: A Journal of English Language, Literatures in English, and Cultural Studies* 36 (Florianópolis: Editore da Universidade Federal de Santa Catarina, 1999). An attractive collection of essays on Shakespeare and translation worldwide. Topics include: translation in history; translating for the stage and the screen; rewriting and tradaptation; translation in a post-colonial context.

Bassnett, Susan. *Translation Studies*. Rev. edn. (London and New York: Routledge, 1991). An intelligent theoretical and historical introduction to the subject of translation out of and into English.

Brisset, Annie. *A Sociocritique of Translation: Theatre and Alterity in Quebec, 1968–1988*, translated by Rosalind Gill and Roger Gannon (Toronto: University of Toronto Press, 1996). Translation of the epoch-making 1990 study of translation and the development of the Québecois theatre's sense of self-destiny.

Cohn, Albert. *Shakespeare in Germany in the Sixteenth and Seventeenth Centuries: An Account of English Actors in Germany and The Netherlands and of the Plays Performed by them during the same Period* (1865. Rpt. New York: Haskell House Publishers, 1971). A detailed history of the earliest Anglo-German theatrical relations, together with a parallel (re)translation of a selection of the German plays that have a bearing on English Renaissance drama.

Derrida, Jacques. 'Des Tours de Babel', trans. Joseph F. Graham, in *Difference in Translation*, ed. Joseph F. Graham (Ithaca and London: Cornell University Press, 1985), pp. 165–207. Influential essay whose original French title has curiously remained untranslated: using metaphors that have been rightly criticized as sexist, Derrida proposes that we look at a translation as a literary work in its own right.

Derrida, Jacques. *The Ear of the Other: Otobiography, Transference, Translation*, ed. Christie V. McDonald, trans. Peggy Kamuf (New York: Schocken Books, 1985). In part the translated record of a roundtable on translation. Derrida is challenged by various speakers: this occasionally yields fine new insights, but Derrida also repeats some of his views expressed elsewhere.

European Shakespeares: Translating Shakespeare in the Romantic Age, ed. Dirk Delabastita and Lieven D'hulst (Amsterdam and Philadelphia, PA: John Benjamins, 1993). A most valuable and influential collection of international essays on translation as a cultural act of appropriation, with contributions by Yuri Levin, Péter Dávidházi, Werner Habicht, Kristian Smidt, and Maria João da Rocha Afonso.

Ewbank, Inga-Stina. 'Shakespeare Translation as Cultural Exchange'. *Shakespeare Survey 48* (1995), 1–12. Represents the voice of the 1990s, as it pleads for greater recognition of 'Shakespeare and translation' within the ranks of the largely Anglocentric Shakespeare industry.

Foreign Shakespeare: Contemporary Performance, ed. Dennis Kennedy (Cambridge: Cambridge University Press, 1993). Ground-breaking collection of essays. It explores Shakespeare performed in languages other than English, and illustrates the creative energies released by Shakespeare 'without his language'. Foreign productions challenge Anglocentric standards of Shakespeare interpretation.

Henry V, trans. Sylvère Monod. With a Preface and notes by R. G. Cox (Paris: Flammarion, 1991).

Lanoye, Tom and Luk Perceval, *Ten Oorlog*. 3 vols. (Amsterdam: Prometheus, 1998).

Routledge Encyclopedia of Translation Studies, ed. Mona Baker (London and New York: Routledge, 1998). Useful manual on translation in general, with an intelligent entry on Shakespeare and translation by Dirk Delabastita.

Shakespeare sechsundsechzig: Variationen über ein Sonett, ed. Ulrich Erckenbrecht. 2nd rev. edn. (Kassel: Muriverlag, 2001). Compelling collection of 132 German versions of Shakespeare's Sonnet 66.

Steiner, George. *After Babel: Aspects of Language and Translation*, 2nd edn. (Oxford: Oxford University Press, 1992). The revised version of Steiner's systematic investigation of the theory and processes of translation of 1975. An erudite guide to developing views of language, multilingualism, and translation.

44 | Commemorating Shakespeare

Georgianna Ziegler

Not marble nor the gilded monuments
Of princes shall outlive this poworful rhyme.
  (Sonnet 55)

Where in the world is Shakespeare? Where would you go if you went out looking for traces of him or memorials to him? Stratford-upon-Avon in England, his birthplace, is an obvious location, but what about Germany, or Japan, or New Zealand, or even Odessa, Texas in the United States? Shakespeare himself evidently did not think much of monuments, as he says in his Sonnet 55 quoted above. He believed that the best memorial was in his plays and poems; as long as they continued to be performed and read, he would be remembered. Nevertheless, Shakespeare's popularity has grown so much since the eighteenth century that people all over the world have wanted to honour him with more tangible monuments such as statues, theatres, and libraries. This chapter begins with a brief survey of how Shakespeare first became a figure of popular culture. Then it examines places around the world that are dedicated to honouring him and his work.

The movement to honour Shakespeare began in the eighteenth century, when a committee headed by poet and editor Alexander Pope, among others, assisted by the Shakespeare Ladies' Club, raised money to erect a monument to him in Westminster Abbey. The full-length statue of Shakespeare was unveiled in 1741. The actor David Garrick, that tireless promoter of Shakespeare, wrote, 'It was You Ladies that restor'd Shakespeare to the Stage . . . and Erected a Monument to his and your own honour in Westminster Abbey'. Garrick delivered this praise on the occasion of his own Jubilee festival honouring Shakespeare in 1769 at Stratford-upon-Avon. At that time he also presented a copy of the Westminster statue to the new Stratford Town Hall, where it is still displayed on the exterior of the building. In addition, Garrick had commissioned the French sculptor Louis-François Roubiliac to create a full-length statue of Shakespeare for Garrick's Temple of Shakespeare at his villa on the Thames. Completed in 1758, the statue now resides in the British Museum, to which Garrick bequeathed it in 1779.

By the beginning of the nineteenth century, the house in which Shakespeare was probably born had become a pilgrimage site. When the American author Washington Irving visited in 1815, he could already write that 'the walls of its squalid chambers are covered with names and inscriptions in every language, by pilgrims of all nations, ranks, and conditions . . . and present a simple, but striking instance of the spontaneous and universal homage of mankind to the great poet of nature'. For the celebration of Shakespeare's three-hundredth birthday in 1864, the Great Western Railway ran to Stratford and produced a special timetable for the two weeks of events. By this time, Shakespeare idolatry had spread to Europe and America. The Germans, who had loved Shakespeare for years, established in 1864 their own society to study his works—the Deutsche Shakespeare Gesellschaft. Across the Atlantic in the same year, the three acting brothers—Junius Brutus, Edwin, and John Wilkes Booth—starred in a production of *Julius Caesar* at the Winter Garden Theatre in New York to raise money for a statue of Shakespeare in Central Park, where it still stands. Designed by J. Q. A. Ward, the statue was unveiled in 1873. In 1888 a statue of Shakespeare designed by Paul Fournier was placed on the Boulevard Haussmann in Paris. In the same year, Sir Ronald Gower's monumental seated figure of Shakespeare surrounded by four of his characters (Prince Hal, Falstaff, Lady Macbeth, and Hamlet) was situated outside the Memorial Theatre in Stratford-upon-Avon (it now stands near the gardens close to the canal basin). The homage accorded to Shakespeare is well-summarized by the writer Thomas Carlyle, in his popular work *On Heroes, Hero Worship, and the Heroic in History* (1841). Shakespeare, he wrote, 'is the grandest thing we have yet done. . . . We can fancy him as radiant aloft over all the Nations of Englishmen, a thousand years hence'.

Carlyle's fantasy of a far-flung, English-speaking world held together by 'King Shakespeare', however, was the creation of nineteenth-century British imperialism. What actually happened to Shakespeare's influence is a much more complicated story, some of which is revealed in the multitude of Shakespearian productions, translations, and sites around the world. In the present context it is possible to look at only a selection of major sites that attempt to preserve or recreate physically some aspects of Elizabethan England as memorials to Shakespeare.

Great Britain

Stratford-upon-Avon

The complex of buildings and grounds associated with Shakespeare in the town of his birth was slowly restored in the latter half of the nineteenth century. First among them was the half-timbered Birthplace on Henley Street. The property originally consisted of living quarters and a shop, purchased separately by John Shakespeare in 1556 and 1575. Shakespeare was born in 1564 before the shop was acquired. Eventually the two buildings were joined to form what we now know as 'the Birthplace'. The house was owned by private individuals until it was acquired for national preservation in 1847 and restored in time for the 1864 tercentenary celebration, when almost 9,000 people visited the site. The talkative old lady named Mrs Hornby, who had shown the house to Washington Irving, was gone; the surrounding buildings had been demolished for fire protection; and a collection of Elizabethan relics was assembled to make the Birthplace into a museum. J. O. Halliwell-Phillipps, the antiquarian, was much involved in collecting historical documents pertaining to the site and recording the process of restoration.

Shakespeare himself had no need for his birthplace when he inherited it from his father in 1601, because he had already purchased the second-largest house in town, known as New Place, in 1597. This house had been built by Hugh Clopton, Lord Mayor of London, on the corner of Chapel Street and Chapel Lane, as an investment property. Since the Clopton family was from the Stratford area, ownership passed back to them in the late seventeenth century, but the house was eventually demolished by a later owner, the Reverend Francis Gastrell, in 1759. In the mid-nineteenth century, Halliwell-Phillipps organized the purchase of the land with surrounding plots, so that by 1891 the whole property was under the care of the Shakespeare Birthplace Trust. Today an Elizabethan knot garden (flowerbeds laid out in intricate designs) borders the site of New Place, and an adjoining house once owned by Thomas Nash, first husband of Shakespeare's granddaughter, has been preserved. Another large Stratford house associated with Shakespeare's family is Hall's Croft, the home of Shakespeare's daughter Susanna and her husband, the physician John Hall. They lived there from around the time of their marriage in 1607 until Shakespeare's death in 1616, when they moved into New Place. Thereafter, Hall's Croft was owned by various private individuals, including American sisters, until 1949 when the last owner sold it to the Trust.

Two other houses near the town of Stratford are associated with Shakespeare's wife and mother. Anne Hathaway's Cottage, located in the village of Shottery, was the home of Shakespeare's wife, daughter of a prosperous farmer. The house was built in the 1460s, but later additions made it into a grander structure than the word 'cottage' suggests. The house of Shakespeare's mother has also survived a few miles outside of Stratford, but it has only recently been identified. For over two hundred years, it was assumed that she lived in a place now known as Palmer's House (named after its sixteenth-century owner). But an old list of rent payments proves that her actual home was a place long known as Glebe Farm. This farm has been renamed Mary Arden's House.

The town of Stratford on the banks of the River Avon, with its market square, schoolhouse, and Holy Trinity Church, still holds much of the feeling of Shakespeare's time, in spite of inroads by tourism. Holy Trinity Church, where Shakespeare was baptized and where he and certain members of his family are buried, dates back to 1210. As a substantial contributor to the upkeep of the chancel and hiring of a priest, Shakespeare earned the right to be buried in the sanctuary. The site is marked by a colourful bust, designed by Gheerart Janssen (see Figure 4.4), presumably by commission from Shakespeare's family, which makes it one of the two really authentic portraits of Shakespeare (the other being the engraving by Martin Droeshout in the

First Folio; see Figure 1.1). A stone with the familiar curse beginning, 'Good Friend for Jesus's sake forbear, / To dig the dust enclosed here', marks the grave itself. The graves of Shakespeare's wife Anne, daughter Susanna, her husband John Hall, their daughter Elizabeth, and Elizabeth's first husband Thomas Nash lie next to Shakespeare's grave.

The Stratford Grammar School had its origins also in the thirteenth century as an establishment sponsored by the Guild of the Holy Cross. Upon the dissolution of this religious Guild with Henry VIII's breakup of the monasteries in the sixteenth century, the school was re-endowed in 1553 under Protestant King Edward VI as the King's New School. It was here, in the upper floor of the old Guildhall, that Shakespeare learned his Latin. The school flourishes to this day with over four hundred boys.

Shakespeare's most important memorials in Stratford, however, are the productions of his plays that bring thousands of visitors to the town every year. The first permanent theatre (the Shakespeare Memorial Theatre) was designed by William Frederick Unsworth and opened on 23 April 1879 with a production of *Much Ado About Nothing*. This grand structure burned in 1926, but the Library and Museum wing survived to become the entrance to the smaller thrust-stage Swan Theatre, which opened in 1986. The Swan brings audiences and actors closer together to create an Elizabethan-like theatrical experience. Meanwhile, a new main theatre, designed by Elisabeth Scott, was dedicated in 1932. Around 1971, a small space in a rehearsal shed was adapted for more experimental productions and dubbed 'The Other Place'. The success of this small theatre led to its replacement by a more permanent building in 1991.

The town of Stratford is also a mecca for Shakespearian scholars from around the world who come to use the resources of its three specialized libraries. The Shakespeare Centre Library, next to Shakespeare's Birthplace, houses its own archives as well as those of the Royal Shakespeare Company. Collections include a video archive of RSC productions since 1982; the Bram Stoker Collection documenting the careers of actors Henry Irving and Ellen Terry; and a large picture collection. In the same building, the Shakespeare Birthplace Trust Records Office contains an important archive of historical and genealogical records relating to Stratford and its surrounding areas. At the other end of town, the Shakespeare Institute Library is housed in a new building on the grounds of the novelist Marie Corelli's old house, Mason Croft, on Church Street. It serves as the library for the Shakespeare Institute (a research department of the University of Birmingham) and contains the university's primary collection of English Renaissance materials. The distinguished annual journal *Shakespeare Survey* has had a long association with the Institute.

Birmingham

The Shakespeare Institute, under the auspices of the Department of English at the University of Birmingham, was founded in 1951 by theatre historian Allardyce Nicoll to foster postgraduate study of Shakespeare and his contemporaries. Classes are held at Mason Croft, the home of the Institute in Stratford-upon-Avon.

As an important city of the Industrial Revolution, Birmingham supported a Shakespeare Club. In honour of the 1864 tercentenary of Shakespeare's birth, the club presented a large collection of Shakespearian literature to the public Central Library, housed in a special room, with funds to purchase more books. Though about 6,500 volumes were destroyed in a disastrous fire that struck the Library in 1879, the Shakespeare collection was rebuilt, and contained 4,000 volumes when it reopened in 1882. It now houses one of the major Shakespeare collections in the world, especially strong in translations of Shakespeare into over ninety languages and in theatrical materials: playbills, posters, programmes, hundreds of scrapbooks, and thousands of illustrations.

London

As the centre for English theatre from Elizabethan times to the present, London has a long tradition of Shakespearian performance, including, in the twentieth century, companies such as the Old and Young Vic, the National Theatre, and the Royal Shakespeare Company in residence first at the Aldwych and then at the Barbican. What the city did not have, however, until the end of the twentieth century, was a centre specifically for Shakespeare, a place that would focus primarily on his works and the theatre of his time. Such a place came into being with the official opening of the new Globe Theatre by Queen Elizabeth II on 12 June 1997 (see Figure 4.3).

Shakespeare's *The Two Gentlemen of Verona* was the first play to be performed at this new venue in 1996. The large complex on the south bank of the Thames, near the site of the original Globe, was the dream of an American actor and entrepreneur, Sam Wanamaker. He established the Shakespeare Globe Playhouse Trust in 1970, but construction did not begin until 1987. Fortuitously, a small portion of the original Globe Theatre was discovered during a nearby construction site dig in 1989, providing more actual evidence for theatre historians such as John Orrell and Andrew Gurr, who had been trying to establish the shape and size of the original Globe from evidence in contemporary drawings.

Central to the new Globe site is the theatre itself, thirty-three feet high, 100 feet in diameter, with a capacity for an audience of 1,600, including 700 standing. Following the Elizabethan style of half-timbered construction with thatched roof over the galleries, the building attempts to reproduce an open-air Elizabethan theatre, complete with painted stage wall, pillars, and heavens, but with modern security measures such as fireproofing. The new Globe has two theatre companies performing in repertory, and stages productions over a twenty-week period during the summer. A second theatre, used for workshops, replicates an early seventeenth-century indoor stage, similar to that at the Blackfriars. Its construction is based on plans by Inigo Jones for what was probably the Cockpit theatre in Drury Lane. The Globe site also features an exhibition highlighting theatre design, costume, music, and printing in Shakespeare's England. Educational outreach includes programmes for schools and universities in addition to lectures, tours, and children's programmes for the public, and, in conjunction with Reading University, a research database on Shakespeare in Performance. The International Shakespeare Globe Centre complex, along with the National Theatre and the new Tate Modern art museum, forms part of the cultural renaissance on the South Bank of the Thames at the turn of the twentieth century.

In 1989, archaeologists from the Museum of London discovered remains of the 1587 Rose Theatre, as enlarged in 1592, at a site planned for a new office building in Southwark, not far from the original Globe Theatre. They uncovered two thirds of the ground-plan of the original Rose. After an appeal from the public and theatre world, the site was put under the protection of English Heritage in 1992 as an Ancient Monument. Now part of the Imry Merchant office complex and currently covered by a concrete shell, the site will be further excavated, but its history is represented by a sound-and-light show.

Germany

Weimar

Germany welcomed Shakespeare from the seventeenth century, when a group of travelling actors performed versions of his plays there. In the eighteenth century, several writers and scholars, including August Schlegel, began translating Shakespeare's works into German. In the nineteenth century, German scholars turned to serious study of Shakespeare and founded the Deutsche Shakespeare Gesellschaft (German Shakespeare Society) in 1864. The Society and its publication, the *Jahrbuch* (*Yearbook*), survived the political divisions of the twentieth century to be reunited in 1993. A rich theatrical history stretches from the realistic productions of Schröder, the Saxe-Meiningen company, and Max Reinhardt to the avant-garde work of Heiner Müller.

Eighteenth-century Weimar was the home of the great writers Goethe and Schiller and the cultural circles around the local countess, Herzogin Anna Amalia. It was thus a fitting location for the founding of the German Shakespeare Society and its library in 1864, with the aim of bringing together in one place all the important materials for Shakespeare study. The Library is still housed in the Herzogin Anna Amalia Bibliothek and comprises some 10,000 volumes, including ninety collected and 350 single-play translations into German, as well as important secondary materials from the mid-nineteenth to the early twentieth century.

Munich

After World War II, when Germany was divided into Soviet and non-Soviet sectors, the German Shakespeare Society split into East and West branches. Distinguished scholar Professor Wolfgang Clemen organized a new Shakespeare library in 1964 at the University of Munich in the west. The collection now numbers some 16,200 volumes of Shakespearian criticism, reception history, English drama of the period, and background material. Its most important collection is an archive documenting Shakespeare production history in German-speaking countries from 1960. The library produces an annual bibliography of these productions, and sponsors workshops for teachers.

Neuss

In 1987, theatre director Reinhard Schiele had the idea of constructing a mobile Renaissance stage, patterned somewhat on the 1599 Globe, that could be quickly dismantled and reassembled in market squares. The original wooden model was abandoned because of fire hazard and replaced in 1991 by a more substantial twelve-sided, open-air theatre that seats 600 in Neuss, near Dusseldorf. German and international companies perform at the Globe Neuss during the annual Shakespeare Festival.

Japan

Tokyo

Shakespeare has a long and fascinating history in Japan, beginning with a Kabuki adaptation of *The Merchant of Venice* in 1885 and reaching to over fifty productions in the 1990s. Japanese interest in Shakespeare has been heightened by several complete translations of the works; by incorporation into the rich tradition of Japanese theatre and film; and by the founding of the Shakespeare Society of Japan, first in 1930, then after World War II renewed in 1961. Admiration of Shakespeare has also led the Japanese to construct three sites as living memorials to his art.

The earliest site, the Tsubouchi Memorial Theatre Museum at Waseda University, opened in 1928 to honour Professor Tsubouchi Shoyo, a longtime scholar at the university. His passion was theatre history; he founded a Literary Society (1906) to train actors in performing Shakespeare, and he himself translated the works of Shakespeare. His students and friends acknowledged his lifelong interest with this museum of Japanese and world theatre history, housed in a structure modelled on the Fortune Theatre of Shakespeare's London. The library and museum collections containing stage plans, model stages, costumes, books, and other items form an important resource for the study of theatre history, especially Japanese. The building itself serves as a study model for one type of Elizabethan stage.

In 1973, Meisei University in Tokyo acquired a major collection of Shakespearian works (close to 4,000 items) purchased as duplicates from the Folger Shakespeare Library in Washington, D.C. Subsequent additions include important collections from the libraries of theatre historian Allardyce Nicoll and from Shakespeare scholars Alice Walker and Jiro Ozu. The library now houses an impressive collection of approximately 16,000 titles, including eleven copies of the 1623 First Folio edition of Shakespeare's plays (only about 240 are known to exist).

The great popularity of Shakespeare in Japan was confirmed by the decision to build a new theatre as part of a Tokyo development project. Designed by the architect Arata Isozaki, based on ideas of the circular and the rectangular in Frances Yates's book, *Theatre of the World*, the Tokyo Globe was the first thrust-stage theatre in Japan. Other than the thrust stage, however, it is really a modern theatre, not a replica of Shakespeare's Globe. The theatre supports a variety of productions, some by its core company of Shakespearian actors, and others from outside groups such as the Royal Shakespeare Company, the English Shakespeare Company, and the Royal National Theatre.

Canada

Stratford, Ontario

This charming Victorian town on the banks of another Avon River is the site of the Stratford Festival of Canada. Conceived in the 1930s by native journalist Tom Patterson, the idea reached fruition in July of 1953 with a production of *Richard III*, directed by Tyrone Guthrie and designed by Tanya Moiseiwitsch. Guthrie and Moiseiwitsch also designed the innovative open thrust stage with balcony and trap doors (a modernization of an Elizabethan theatre) that was first housed within a large tent. A more permanent building was dedicated in 1957, followed by a complete renovation that officially opened in June of 1997. The original influential thrust stage is still at the heart of the theatre, where no audience member is ever more than sixty-five feet from it, though the theatre's capacity is 1,820. Behind the stage is a large work area where all the costumes and props are made.

Two smaller theatres within the town (the Avon and the Tom Patterson, formerly the Third Stage) also provide venues for Shakespearian as well as other plays. The Stratford Festival now produces more than a dozen plays and musicals a season, ranging from Shakespeare (still the core of the offerings) to Albee and Chekhov. In addition, the Festival supports an educational programme of workshops and courses on acting, teaching Shakespeare, Elizabethan costuming, and set design.

Victoria, British Columbia

This western Canadian city contains replicas of Anne Hathaway's thatched Cottage and Shakespeare's Birthplace on a five-acre garden site that provides a setting for the commercial enterprise of the Olde English Inn.

Australia

Perth

The University of Western Australia is home to an outdoor performance space named the New Fortune Theatre that was built in 1964. It reconstructs the auditorium and stage dimensions of the 1600 London Fortune Theatre, providing a working environment in which to study the relationship between audience and performance during Shakespeare's time. Another attempt to recreate the feel of an Elizabethan theatre has been undertaken by the Sydney Theatre Company at the Wharf Theatre, where the indoor space was made to duplicate that of the Blackfriars Theatre.

New Zealand

Stratford

Situated among dairy and sheep farms on the Patea River, this town of 6,000 grew up as a monument to English culture during the age of Victorian imperialism. Once the town was dubbed 'Stratford' in 1877, planners followed through by naming the streets after Shakespearian characters and historic places. In 1899 a Shakespeare Society was formed, but it was not until 1964 that the town held its first Shakespeare Festival. The Festival is now held every other year and attracts people from around the world. It is a community-organized event, involving Elizabethan crafts and food as well as theatrical and musical performances.

United States

The United States adopted Shakespeare in the nineteenth century, with performances in east-coast theatres and in western mining camps, and with Shakespeare clubs and public readings. At last count there were over 114 Shakespeare festivals in the United States. There's Shakespeare On the Rocks (Texas), On the Sound (Connecticut), Under the Stars (Texas), In Paradise (California), In the Park (Texas and Minnesota), and In the Park(ing) Lot (New York). San Francisco sports an all-female company, Woman's Will, and a national Young Shakespeare Players has performers aged from seven to eighteen. Shakespeare in Central Park originated in 1957 when Joseph Papp, founder of the New York Shakespeare Festival, produced plays on a mobile stage. In 1962 this stage was replaced by the Delacourt Theater, where Shakespeare's plays are still presented for free every summer. Other important companies include the New Jersey Shakespeare Festival at Monmouth College, dating from the early 1960s; Shakespeare & Company, formed in 1978 by British director Tina Packer at Edith Wharton's estate, The Mount, in Lenox, Massachusetts; and the Alabama Shakespeare Festival, given a permanent home in Montgomery by Carolyn and Wynton Blount in the mid 1980s. The American Shakespeare Theatre was active in Stratford, Connecticut from 1955 to 1982. Since it is impossible to discuss all Shakespeare-related festivals and activities in the US, this account focuses on those places that are important research centres or have recreated an Elizabethan-style building.

Washington, D.C.

The nation's capital is a city steeped in Shakespeare. Lawyers and members of Congress quote from his works; justices of the Supreme Court hold mock trials based on Shakespearian characters; Michael Kahn directs a repertory company at the Lansburgh Shakespeare Theatre with over 13,000 subscribers and offers free summer performances in the park; and a number of other local theatre companies perform Shakespeare's plays. Physically, Shakespeare is situated at the heart of the city, for the Folger Shakespeare Library stands one block from the Capitol and across the street from the Supreme Court and the Library of Congress.

Opened in 1932, the library was a gift to the nation from Henry Clay and Emily Jordan Folger. Like many American collectors of the period, Mr Folger made his fortune in industry (he was chairman of Standard Oil of New York). Book collecting was a serious hobby for both Folgers, and, without children, they had the time and means to devote to it. When they decided to build a research library to house their large collection, they chose Paul Cret as the architect, and Washington as the city that 'belongs to all the people', in Mrs Folger's words. Today the library houses about 256,000 books, including 55,000 published in English before 1700, over 35,000 continental books, and 55,000 manuscripts. The largest part of the collection comprises editions of Shakespeare (including seventy-nine copies of the First Folio and over 200 quartos) in addition to playbills, promptbooks, paintings, engravings, photographs, and secondary material on Shakespeare and the theatre of his age. The replica of an Elizabethan inn-yard stage at one end of the building offers a venue for productions of Shakespeare's plays, programmes for area schools, and early music by the Folger Consort. About 900 scholars come every year from all over the world to use the Folger Library's resources. The library's publications include the New Folger Library Shakespeare edition and *Shakespeare Quarterly*.

Ashland, Oregon

The Oregon Shakespeare Festival (the oldest in the United States) is an offshoot of the Chautauqua movement of the late nineteenth century, designed to bring culture to outlying regions of the United States. During the Depression of the 1930s, a local professor, Angus L. Bowmer, had an Elizabethan-style stage built inside the walls of the old Chautauqua auditorium, and sponsored the first Shakespearian productions there in 1935. The stage was rebuilt in the late 1940s and then again in the late 1950s to meet fire regulations. At that time a more elaborate open-air Elizabethan Theatre was designed by Richard L. Hay, based on models by artist C. Walter Hodges and theatre scholar John Cranford Adams. In 1992, this theatre was improved with better acoustics, sight-lines, and entry for actors. Hay also designed two smaller indoor theatres that opened in 1970 and 1977: the 600-seat Angus Bowmer, and the 140-seat Black Swan. The popularity of the Festival is indicated by a continually growing audience that topped 380,000 in 2000. In addition to the theatres, the Festival's Education Office maintains an active programme in many schools and universities.

Odessa, Texas

This 1881 west Texas camp for the crews building the Texas and Pacific Railroad seems an unlikely site for a reconstruction of the Globe Theatre. But sometime in the 1950s, after the town of Odessa was established at the site, a boy brought a model of the Globe to his high school English teacher, Marjorie Morris. Mrs Morris became fired with the idea of building a full-scale replica of the theatre. After many years of research and fundraising on her part, the Globe of the Great Southwest opened with a full season in 1968. Mrs Morris worked with British theatre historian Allardyce Nicoll to perfect the design. The octagonal building with an 1,800 square foot thrust stage seats 418. While the exterior and general design are based on Shakespeare's Globe, the interior is distinctly modern. The repertory has included plays by authors from Shakespeare to Thornton Wilder, as well as musicals. A special programme links performances of Shakespeare to plays being read in the Texas schools. In 1988, a replica of Anne Hathaway's Cottage was built across the courtyard from the theatre.

Philadelphia, Pennsylvania

A statue of Hamlet designed by Alexander Calder in 1928 sits in the centre of this city, where the first American edition of Shakespeare was published in 1795. The oldest continuous Shakespeare group (the Shakspeare [sic] Society of Philadelphia) was founded here in 1852 by a group of lawyers and others. In 1860 they were joined by Horace Howard Furness who, with his son, H. H. Furness, Jr., instituted and edited the New Variorum Shakespeare. This great edition (still being produced and used by scholars today) includes on each page lines of Shakespeare's text followed by a summary of the criticism on those lines. They bequeathed their working library of 12,000 volumes to the University of Pennsylvania, where it opened as the Furness Memorial Library in 1932. The library is housed in an English gothic-style room as part of the Department of Special Collections. The Furness Library comprises a large collection of editions of

Shakespeare and his contemporary dramatists, as well as much secondary criticism, theatrical materials (including promptbooks, photographs, and manuscripts), and dissertations on Shakespeare and English drama. It contains copies of all four Folios and a dozen quartos of Shakespeare's plays. This working collection supports an active programme in Renaissance studies at the university, as well as research by international scholars. A number of the rare Shakespearian items have been scanned and are publicly available on the university library's web site.

San Diego, California

The original Old Globe Theater was built in Balboa Park in this southern California city in 1935. After it was destroyed by arson in 1972, it was rebuilt and reopened in 1982. The indoor theatre with thrust stage seats 543 to 649, depending on the arrangement for the production. Two other theatres (the intimate Cassius Carter Centre Stage and the modern outdoor Lowell Davis Festival Theatre) have been added to form The Globe Theaters site, presenting fourteen productions a year, which no longer necessarily include Shakespeare. The theatres offer educational programmes for schools, while older students can enrol in the Master of Fine Arts programme for classical theatre with the University of California at San Diego.

Staunton, Virginia

In 1999, this city in the Shenandoah Valley became home to the young and lively Shenandoah Shakespeare company. Founded by Ralph Cohen and Jim Warren in Harrisonburg, Virginia in 1988, the Shenandoah Shakespeare Express became a popular touring company in US cities and in London, performing plays in conditions similar to those of Shakespeare's theatre. The move to Staunton enabled the group to embark on an ambitious plan for a permanent home base, consisting of working models of the Blackfriar's indoor and the 1613 Globe outdoor theatres, as well as a partnership with Mary Baldwin College for a Masters programme in Shakespeare in performance. The 300-seat Blackfriars Playhouse opened in September 2001 with productions of *A Midsummer Night's Dream* and *Hamlet*. Shenandoah Shakespeare continues to support two touring companies ('Elizabeth' and 'James') along with their local productions.

Where in the world can you find Shakespeare? The answer seems to be, almost anywhere that people have remained actively interested in his life and works. The survey provided here of Shakespeare sites does not pretend to be exhaustive; it would be impossible to mention all the various Shakespeare festivals and other related programmes. But the survey *is* meant to serve as a brief overview of the historic development of popular interest in Shakespeare, and to provide a basic introduction to surviving buildings from Shakespeare's time, to modern reconstructions, and to important centres of Shakespeare study. Most of all it documents the worldwide attempts to keep his life and works alive for every new generation of students and playgoers.

FURTHER READING

Bristol, Michael. *Shakespeare's America, America's Shakespeare* (London and New York: Routledge, 1990). Discusses Shakespeare in the American imagination, and the traditions of the Shakespearian archive and of editing.

Day, Barry. *This Wooden O: Shakespeare's Globe Reborn* (London: Oberon Books, 1996). A popular and lively account of Sam Wanamaker's project to reconstruct Shakespeare's theatre in London.

Eccles, Christine. *The Rose Theatre* (New York: Routledge, 1990). A basic book detailing the history of the original Rose Theatre, the 1989 archaeological excavation, and the campaign for its preservation.

Engle, Ron, Felicia H. Londré, and Daniel J. Watermeier (eds.). *Shakespeare Companies and Festivals: An International Guide* (Westport, CT: Greenwood Press, 1995). A guide to the major Shakespeare festivals and companies in the United States, Europe, and Asia. Includes histories, production histories, budgets, other statistics, and short bibliographies.

Hodgdon, Barbara. 'Stratford's Empire of Shakespeare; Or, Fantasies of Origin, Authorship, and Authenticity: The Museum and the Souvenir'. In Barbara Hodgdon. *The Shakespeare Trade*. (Philadelphia: University of Pennsylvania Press, 1998), pp. 191–240. A lively illustrated article discussing the materiality of the tourist trade and 'bardolatry' at Stratford-upon-Avon.

Mulryne, J.R., Margaret Shewring, and Andrew Gurr (eds.). *Shakespeare's Globe Rebuilt* (Cambridge: Cambridge University Press, 1997). A series of scholarly essays discussing the reconstruction of the Globe based on archaeological research, and the impact of this stage on acting.

Taylor, Gary. *Reinventing Shakespeare: A Cultural History from the Restoration to the Present* (New York: Weidenfeld & Nicolson, 1989). Provides a lively history of the growth of interest in Shakespeare and the ways he has been received over the centuries.

Wilson, Jean. *The Archaeology of Shakespeare: The Material Legacy of Shakespeare's Theatre* (Far Thrupp, Glos.: Alan Sutton, 1995). Inspired by the Rose Theatre find, this accessible and well-illustrated book provides information on the theatricality of Elizabethan life, on costume, and on the types of playhouses. A final chapter summarizes information on the Rose and Globe excavations.

SUPPLEMENTARY READING LIST

Brown, John Russell. *New Sites for Shakespeare: Theatre, the Audience, and Asia* (London and New York: Routledge, 1999).

Guntner, J. Lawrence and Andrew M. McLean (eds.). *Redefining Shakespeare: Literary Theory and Theater Practice in the German Democratic Republic* (Newark: University of Delaware Press; London: Associated University Presses, 1998).

Hattaway, Michael, *et al.* (eds.). *Shakespeare in the New Europe* (Sheffield: Sheffield Academic Press, 1994). Includes articles on Shakespeare in Bulgaria, Croatia, the Czech Republic, Poland, Romania, Russia, and Spain.

Hortmann, Wilhelm. *Shakespeare on the German Stage: The Twentieth Century* (Cambridge: Cambridge University Press, 1998). A fine illustrated history of the richness of Shakespearian productions in modern Germany, east and west.

Kennedy, Dennis (ed.). *Foreign Shakespeare: Contemporary Performance* (Cambridge: Cambridge University Press, 1993). A series of essays on Shakespeare performance in various countries, including the Czech Republic, France, Germany, Israel, Japan, and Russia.

Kennedy, Dennis. *Looking at Shakespeare: A Visual History of Twentieth-Century Performance* (Cambridge: Cambridge University Press, 1993). Discusses productions in Great Britain, Europe, and the United States; illustrated with many photographs.

Kerr, Heather, *et al.* (eds.). *Shakespeare: World Views* (Newark: University of Delaware Press; London: Associated University Presses, 1996). Includes articles on staging Shakespeare in Australia, the Czech Republic, France, Germany, India, Japan, and Sweden.

Klein, Holger and Jean-Marie Maguin (eds.). 'Shakespeare and France', *Shakespeare Yearbook*, Vol. 5. (Lewiston: Edwin Mellen Press, 1995).

Leiter, Samuel L. *et al.* (eds.). *Shakespeare around the Globe: A Guide to Notable Postwar Revivals* (New York: Greenwood Press, 1986). Organized by play, provides production information, cast list, and description of performance.

Quince, Rohan. *Shakespeare in South Africa: Stage Productions during the Apartheid Era* (New York: Peter Lang, 2000).

Ryuta, Minami, *et al.* (eds.). *Performing Shakespeare in Japan* (Cambridge: Cambridge University Press, 2001). Includes articles on Shakespeare in the traditional Japanese theatrical traditions of Kabuki, Noh, and Kyogen, as well as modern stagings.

Stríbrný, Zdenek. *Shakespeare and Eastern Europe* (Oxford: Oxford University Press, 2000). A basic and informative introduction to the subject.

Williams, Simon. *Shakespeare on the German Stage, 1586–1914* (Cambridge: Cambridge University Press, 1990). Complements Hortmann's book (above).

Zhang, Xiao Yang. *Shakespeare in China: A Comparative Study of Two Traditions and Cultures* (Newark: University of Delaware Press; London: Associated University Presses, 1996). One of the few studies available in English on Shakespeare in China.

WEB LINKS

Birmingham Shakespeare Library. <http://www.birmingham.gov.uk>. Select 'A–Z Index' at top of page; select 'S' and then 'Shakespeare Library'. Page for the Shakespeare collection of the City of Birmingham Central Library. Gives information about the collection and a contact for reference services.

Deutsche Shakespeare Gesellschaft. <http://www.shakespeare-gesellschaft.de>. Provides information on the Society and its archives with links to other Shakespeare sites and to the German Shakespeare libraries in Munich and Weimar. Site available in English.

Folger Shakespeare Library. <http://www.folger.edu>. The homepage of the Library with links to library holdings, online catalogue, reference services, the Folger Institute programs, public programs, and exhibitions.

Fortune Theatre, University of Western Australia. <http://www.theatres.uwa.edu.au/intro. html>. The site has information, including photographs, on all seven university theatres.

Furness Shakespeare Library. <http://dewey.library.upenn.edu>. Select 'SCETI' Provides access to the online digitized items from the Furness Library at the University of Pennsylvania, through the Schoenberg Center for Electronic Text and Image.

Globe Theatre, London:

- for season and tickets: <http://www.shakespeares-globe.org/>
- for history of the original and new Globe theatres and images: <http://www.rdg.ac.uk/globe/>

Herzogin Anna Amalia Bibliothek. <http://www.weimar-klassik.de/dehaab/index.html>. The homepage of the Library housing the large German Shakespeare collection in Weimar. Links to online catalogue. Site available in English.

Rose Theatre, London. <http://www.rdg.ac.uk/rose/>. Information about the original Rose Theatre, and its discovery in 1989. Includes pictures and a bibliography.

Shakespeare Birthplace Trust. <http://www.shakespeare.org.uk/>. Official site of the organization responsible for all the Shakespeare buildings in Stratford-upon-Avon and environs. Offers information about those sites, about the Shakespeare Centre Library and Archives, and about Shakespeare's life.

Shakespeare Festivals. <http://shakespeare.palomar.edu/festivals.htm>. Major listing of over 100 sites worldwide for Shakespeare festivals and productions.

Shakespeare in Japan. <http://www.latrobe.edu.au/drama/multi/mndjapan/HOMEPAGE. HTM>. Sponsored by Latrobe University in Australia, this site provides information on the history of Shakespeare in Japan and focuses on several major productions.

Shakespeare Institute and Library. <http://www.is.bham.ac.uk/shakespeare>. The homepage for the Shakespeare Institute Library in Stratford with links to the Institute and its programs in Birmingham and to the online catalogue. Also gives information on current and forthcoming Shakespeare and Renaissance drama productions in the UK, and provides a Shakespeare Performance Archive for the UK since 1999.

Stratford, New Zealand. <http://shell.world-net.co.nz/~kennydog/>. A Worldnet site that gives information on the Shakespearian history of the town.

Tsubouchi Memorial Theatre Museum, Waseda. <http://www.waseda.ac.jp/intl-ac/bulletin/tsubouchi.html>. Official site of the Museum, in English. Provides information on the founding, the collections, and special exhibitions.

45 | Internet and CD ROM resources

Michael Best

Nets and webs are uncomfortable images in the works of Shakespeare. Webs threaten, as they are inescapably associated with the spider at the centre: Iago gloats, 'With as little a web as this will I ensnare as great a fly as Cassio' (*Othello* 2.1.169). If the image is that of an (inter)net, the associations become no more positive, since nets are devices for snaring game—and people. Later in the same act of *Othello*, Iago changes from spider to gamekeeper, netting birds (or to Vulcan, ensnaring Mars):

> So will I turn her virtue into pitch,
> And out of her own goodness make the net
> That shall enmesh them all.
>
> (2.3.334-6)

In recent years, these images have become complicated by their association with the electronic net, the Web, which itself stimulates mixed responses. The Internet provides immediate access to an increasing range of information that would otherwise be difficult or impossible to find, but at the same time there are many sites that are questionable in quality or subject matter, and irritating in their commercialism. Scholars and educators have also questioned the nature of the medium itself, where sites can change without warning or disappear altogether, and where the basic structure of data is in the process of becoming noticeably different from works published in print.

Hypertext—the capacity to link by a click of the mouse between different texts and extensions of the text—is the crucial way in which the electronic medium differs from print, and has the potential to change the way we think about texts. Writers on the theory of hypertext have argued that the medium has the potential to give a practical expression to the theories of postmodern critics, who point out that all texts can be seen as branching networks of meaning. But hypertext is still in its developmental stage; on the Internet, most resources either reproduce the linear structures of print, through the publishing of texts in an approximation to their print form, or they provide access to databases of specific kinds of information, much as a dictionary or encyclopaedia does in print. The electronic medium can go beyond print in allowing for rapid searches of large quantities of data, but thus far there have been only tentative experiments in the kinds of laterality and multilinearity an Internet multimedia text makes possible.

Nets and snares

It is both a disadvantage and an advantage of the Internet that sites are continually changed and updated. The advantage is that sites can be kept up to date after publication; the disadvantage is that sites disappear, or reorganize, so that links no longer work. The rate of change means that specific sites will change between the writing of this chapter and its appearance in print. My response to this problem is threefold: I concentrate on sites that have proven to be stable; I discuss general strategies for finding sites not mentioned in this survey; and I shall be maintaining an up-to-date list of recommended sites (a 'metasite'—see the discussion below) on the Internet.

Though it does have nets and snares, the Internet is a much more positive space than is suggested by Iago's words quoted at the beginning of this chapter. The electronic medium is only beginning to show how it can enhance the experience of research. Most linear reading—of narrative or of extended argument—is still more comfortable and more convenient in book format; perhaps there will in due course be e-books or computer pads that are as light and convenient as print books, but in the meantime the computer is most useful for searching through large quantities of material and locating specific kinds of information. In this chapter, I shall focus on the Internet as a resource for the study of Shakespeare, with the addition of a brief discussion of research-oriented CD ROMs. I shall also suggest some strategies for narrowing searches for information so that you spend less time visiting sites that are only marginally relevant to an enquiry, and I will propose some techniques for checking on the quality of the information you do find.

The Internet is a remarkably convenient resource for research. It is available from the same keyboard and screen that you use for writing research papers, so it is a simple activity to go to one of the major search engines, enter a few key words, and find a list of sites that offer promise of providing answers. It is as if you were able to click on a catalogue entry at your local library, and see the entire text of a book, ready to download, or to provide you with passages ready to copy, paste, and reference into your current essay.

But if the Internet-library is convenient, it is also very new, and suffers some of the difficulties of any new library, together with some that are the result of the nature of the medium. New libraries often find it difficult to build up a collection, since books are expensive, and many are out of print. The Internet provides one answer to this problem in that it can be seen as an enormous collaborative project, where individual scholars and enthusiasts around the world work on separate parts of the collection. In one way, however, the Internet is faced with a difficulty that is almost the opposite of the development of a new library: it is the out-of-print books that are most likely to be transcribed and posted. The laws of copyright are such that it is very difficult for someone to post recent scholarship, since the copyright will be retained by a university press or journal—and these are precisely the kinds of works that you will wish to consult. Many sites on the Internet have a cheerful (or scandalous) disregard for copyright, but in general, sites that provide unauthorized works are unlikely to be reliable. Most universities, for example, have strict regulations that require sites on their servers to conform to copyright law. In some fields—the sciences particularly—a considerable amount of current research is posted on the Internet in 'pre-publication' format. Thus, the information will be available even if it is not presented in exactly the form in which it appears in final publication. Unfortunately, however, this method of disseminating research has not yet been accepted in the humanities, though the 'electronic seminar' *Early Modern Culture* may be a sign that this resistance is diminishing.

Reader beware

The result of copyright law is that most criticism relating to Shakespeare on the Internet is of largely historical interest, and does not provide up-to-date approaches to the plays. There are some good sites that provide such texts as the classic work by A. C. Bradley on Shakespeare's tragedies, first published almost a century ago, but an essay limited to sources of such advanced age is unlikely to be on the cutting edge of critical awareness. There are indeed more modern pieces posted on the Internet, but a wise reader will be careful in assessing their reliability, since—for better or for worse— the standard of excellence in scholarship remains publication by the established presses and journals.

It is a corollary of the structure of the Internet, where everything is connected to everything, that it is often difficult to judge the value of the materials you do find. If you pick up a book in your library, you can be sure that someone has decided that it is worth buying: it has been recommended by an expert, or the press that produced it is considered to be reliable. There is no such guarantee when you arrive at a site on the Internet: it is as if the catalogue in the library included, alongside scholarly texts, all the kinds of publications that you find beside the check-out at the supermarket. To be sure, there are many books in a university library that are dated, eccentric, or even inept. Mature students will seek widely enough among critical resources to be able to see the often widely differing views of the critics they read; an often effective strategy is to take two such critics and metaphorically bang their heads together in an essay, to show that your own view is independent and well researched. This kind of careful criticism of the critics is essential when assessing Internet resources. Reader beware.

There is, however, one very positive way in which the informality of the Internet has enhanced the resources available to students and scholars of the Renaissance. The same ease of publication that makes it necessary for the reader to be cautious allows skilled and passionate non-professionals to publish on the subjects that interest them; this discussion of resources on the Internet will recommend a number of fine sites maintained by gifted non-professionals.

Checking on the credibility of a site

Once you have found a site that offers you something that seems of value, it is important to establish its academic credibility. The most reliable Web pages will provide information about the author and the date of composition. If there is no such assurance on the page there are a number of ways in which you can find out more. Often there is an 'about' link, or its equivalent, that will take you to a page with information about the author or the site. If you are an experienced Internet user, you will know that you can look at the structure of the 'URL' (Universal Resource Locator) or address, where the domain (the first section of the address after the 'http://') can give some clues. If it ends in '.edu' it will be a North American educational site, usually associated with a university. In some countries the '.edu' comes before the final denomination of the country (<http://www.usyd.edu.au> for the University of Sydney), and in many countries the letters '.ac' (academic) are used instead (<http://www.kcl.ac.uk>) for King's College London. To complicate matters, there are some countries which have neither '.edu' nor '.ac' (France, Ireland, Canada, and others); in these the best technique is to go to the 'root' domain—just the first section—to look at the home site of the institution. There are other domain types you will come across: '.org' and '.net' are used by non-profit organizations, some of which are very distinguished, and there is the ubiquitous '.com' which may signal a site as impressive and useful as Britannica.com, or one of many commercial sites of dubious quality. Cautious checking of the site and the writer is important no matter where the page originates. In addition, check the date of the page or the site, if there is one, since many pages will be put up in a burst of activity, then left to gather dust.

When you do find something that is useful, it is important to record all the details you can about the page you are quoting or using, exactly as you would when referring to a book: the author of the page, the date of its creation, and the name and place of publication—as I have just suggested, you may have to dig in order to find this information. You should also record the URL and the date of your access to the site, since the content or the address of the page may change after your visit. One complication is that an increasing number of major sites on the Internet are being managed by databases rather than individual pages; links within a site of this kind are often very long, and contain symbols rather than file names. If the URL is absurdly long and complicated, you may choose to cite the main address only, with an indication of the links to follow from it. You will find a brief guide to the accurate citation of Internet resources on the supporting web site for this chapter.

Shakespeare's popularity means that there will be many sites that are enthusiastic rather than accurate. And there are the enormously energetic activities of the conspiracy theorists: those who believe that someone other than Shakespeare wrote the plays. Be wary of sites that have specific agendas of this kind; because conspiracies make for good reading, some of them are popular, and therefore rank in the early pages of a search. The best that can be said for this curious activity is that it has led to the creation of one of the most informative and scholarly sites on Shakespeare, *The Shakespeare Authorship Page*, maintained by Terry Ross and David Kathman, who has contributed the chapter on the authorship controversy in this volume (Chapter 41). His Internet site is 'dedicated to the proposition that Shakespeare wrote Shakespeare'.

Searching for information on the Web

A fundamental puzzle for those using the Internet for research is its size and complexity. When you do reach some material that provides opinion or facts that may be of use, you are often unsure of the quality or validity of the information. If the Internet is somewhat like a huge electronic library, it is a library where the books are shelved in no discernible order, and where there is no catalogue.

Sites that list other sites

The first step is to look for a good 'metasite'—a site that lists other sites. Also known as 'gateways' or 'portals', the best sites of this kind are maintained by an expert in the field who collects links to content that is reliable. In Shakespeare studies, Terry Gray's *Master William Shakespeare and the Internet* is the most popular. It is comprehensive, attractive, and the individual links are intelligently annotated, so that a user knows whether it is worth following the link. Amongst other good metasites, the *Internet Shakespeare Editions* (*ISE*) provide a list of links for both Shakespeare studies and more general sites on Renaissance materials that may be useful for those interested in Shakespeare. The electronic journal *Early Modern Literary Studies* offers an extensive list of links to electronic texts. You will certainly come across—and bookmark—additional useful metasites; in general, it is best not to rely on just one of these sites, since the complexity of the Internet means that updating is likely to be erratic, and some valuable sites will be missed by any one metasite.

Search engines

The advantage of comprehensive search engines is that they continuously index new pages; the problem is that they have a habit of returning far too many results, most of which are of only the most remote usefulness. Few computer users are willing to go beyond the first two or three pages of links from a search, and the logic by which the search engine ranks its results is often biased towards commercial sites. The best use a measure of popularity in their rankings, but scholarship is not known for being popular, so this criterion will mean that the more useful sites may be buried several pages deep. Perhaps not surprisingly there is a flourishing industry for those who sell software that is alleged to put a site in the top pages of popular search engines.

A simple illustration: on the day I entered the term 'Hamlet' in the major search engines I was confronted by listings of between 400,000 (Lycos) and 738,000 (Google); in each case the first page was dominated by sites that try to sell papers to students unwilling to do their own research and writing. Papers from these sites cost between $3.00 and $8.99 (US). Prospective buyers should be aware that the increasing sophistication of instructors, who can use the same search engines, makes the activity of plagiarism on the Internet if anything more risky than it is when pirating print materials.

If you have experimented with the 'advanced' feature of search engines, you will know that there are several strategies that will produce more meaningful results. A concept worth learning is what is called a 'boolean' search: one that allows you to specify several words that must all be found (hamlet AND delay), or words that are not to be found (hamlet NOT essay). Google, for example, allows you to enter multiple words that must all be found. Thus, on the day I was on a quest for material on *Hamlet*, adding the word 'delay' reduced the number of sites from 738,000 to a mere 13,400. Google allows a simple way of telling it to avoid a word by using the minus sign: thus 'hamlet delay –essay –buy' suddenly weeded out the greedy sites, and reduced the number to 7,100. Google at least guessed that I was looking for sites on Shakespeare's play or character, and put the sites that mention 'hamlet' as a village, or as the name of a town, well down on the list, but the one really distinguished essay on the topic that I have found on the web, by Margreta de Grazia, was nowhere to be seen.

Even, however, with the search narrowed, the actual materials at the end of the links in this example were of only marginal use. Many links point to chat groups, to course outlines, or to the enthusiastic but amateur offerings of a Shakespeare lover or fellow student rather than to substantial or useful criticism. In some measure this is an outcome of the use of simple keywords for searching, since the inevitable result is that old-fashioned thematic or character-criticism will be found by single words. It should be clear that the Internet is at best a very approximate and uncertain place to find stimulating or reliable criticism. Notable exceptions are two fine electronic journals that include articles on Shakespeare: *Early Modern Literary Studies*, and *Renaissance Forum*. Metasites will also point you to the few really useful sites that provide helpful introductions to individual plays.

It is also true that most texts of Shakespeare's plays on the Internet are at present of limited usefulness. There are many sites that provide public domain texts, some with useful search facilities, some with hypertext annotations, but all are derived from texts old enough to be out of copyright, and therefore out of date. In due course texts that embody the major advances in editorial practice over the last century will appear from sites like the *Internet Shakespeare Editions*; in the meantime, there are some excellent facsimiles of the First Folio, and the *ISE* offers accurate and searchable transcriptions of the original texts. Though not a complete text, the shape of things to come may perhaps best be seen in *Hamlet on the Ramparts*, from MIT and the Folger Shakespeare Library.

What the Web does well

Textual resources

In many areas outside criticism and the texts of the plays, the Internet provides much more effective and reliable materials. There are many sites that publish primary sources: Shakespeare's sources, documents of historical interest, and anthologies of early poetry are all available in accurate—and sometimes attractive—transcriptions or images. These resources will be especially useful in research projects that involve source studies, comparative studies between Shakespeare and his contemporaries, close readings of his text, and New Historicist approaches. Probably because original-spelling editions are seldom seen as commercially viable, the Internet is now the best place to find good old-spelling editions of many texts.

The sources from which Shakespeare developed many of his plays are beginning to be posted online. Many are on the fine site at the University of Pennsylvania, where the Furness Library has mounted images of much useful material on Shakespeare. The disadvantage is that, as images, they are not easy to use on a slower Internet connection, and they will be difficult to read for those unused to early modern typography and spelling. There are an increasingly large number of freely available sources in various locations on the Internet: refer to metasites, or the special page maintained in support of this chapter.

Many of Shakespeare's predecessors and contemporaries are well represented in online texts. Some of the richest resources are in what may seem at first an unexpected area: women writers of the early modern period. A valuable result of the surge of interest in the writings of women in the last decade has been the publication in electronic format of texts that have been reclaimed from an undeserved neglect. The major collection of women's writing at Brown University is available by subscription only (see below), but there are many other women's works freely available online; the best way to access these is through Georgianna Ziegler's admirably annotated metasite. Shakespeare's male contemporaries are well represented on the Internet, with sites celebrating the works of writers, if not from A to Z, at least from Bacon to Webster. Some are represented by selections only, but there are excellent sites on Shakespeare's fellow dramatists (Marlowe, Beaumont and Fletcher, Jonson, and Middleton) and poets (Sidney, Spenser, and Donne). You will find links to works by Shakespeare's contemporaries, and to important writers from the medieval and classical periods on the supporting site for this chapter.

Although the sheer mass of data they must analyse makes general search engines approximate and sometimes unhelpful, the electronic medium is especially good at indexing and retrieving data from databases or textbases. Useful concordances of Shakespeare's works are available online, the best offering 'proximity' searching, where you can search for 'love' near 'death', for example. One especially valuable database is Ian Lancashire's *Early Modern English Dictionaries Database* (*EMEDD*) at the University of Toronto. This database makes it possible to explore how different words were defined in the period: though the first modern English dictionary did not appear until forty years after Shakespeare's death, there were many dictionaries that provided translations for words in other languages, and lists of 'hard words'. By cross-referencing these definitions, the *EMEDD* can give insight into the usage of many words that are either unfamiliar, or which were used in ways rather different from their modern counterparts. It is important to remember, when searching original-spelling texts, to use older forms of spelling, and to try several times with variant ways of spelling a given word.

The verbal world Shakespeare inhabited was permeated by the language of the bible, but few are now equipped to hear the allusions and make the connections that his original audience would have been sensitive to. The Internet provides a number of sites that allow for searches on various versions of the bible; most provide the King James version, which appeared in 1611 after Shakespeare's writing career was effectively over, but which retains much of the language of the bible Shakespeare would have known. *Renaissance Electronic Texts*, at the University of Toronto, has published an edition by Ian Lancashire of *The Elizabethan Homilies* that were read in church each Sunday, and which accordingly provide a useful repository of theological teaching and religious commonplaces in the period.

Historical resources

Historians have developed a wide range of resources that are useful in research, especially for a New Historicist approach to the plays. Enter 'renaissance legal history documents' in Google, and you will find that it returns several distinguished academic sites near the top of the list; from these it is possible to browse through extensive transcriptions of legal documents that may illuminate the play you are reading. It took only a brief exploration to find a document that records a law concerning Gypsies ('Egyptians'). This is of considerable interest for its frank racism, for the incentive to administrators to pursue personal gain (Falstaff's comrade in corruption in *Henry IV Part Two*, Justice Shallow, comes to mind), and for the insight it gives into the power of the insult levelled at Cleopatra by the Romans in the play, from the minor character Philo to Antony himself (see *Antony and Cleopatra*, 1.1.10 and 4.13.28):

Every Justice of Peace, Sheriff, and Escheator [an officer appointed by the Lord Treasurer to ensure that land due to the Crown was duly handed over] may seize all the goods of any outlandish persons, calling themselves Egyptians, that shall come into this Realm, within one month after their arrival, and may also keep the one moiety [half] thereof to his own use, making account to the King in the Exchequer for the other moiety.

(Vincent, *Passages*; spelling has been modernized)

Introductions to Shakespeare's life and the stage he wrote for are well covered on the Internet. As with many other Internet resources, these are best treated as starting points for study rather than as complete works. The new Globe Theatre in London has stimulated a great deal of research and some controversy; their web site, and those associated with it, provide extensive graphic materials and some continuing scholarly discussions of the staging of the plays. Several sites post biographies; the most extensive treatment of Shakespeare's life and the contexts of his plays is 'Shakespeare's Life and Times', on the site of the *Internet Shakespeare Editions*.

Several museums and libraries generously make sections of their collections available. The Folger Shakespeare Library archives some interesting exhibitions, mainly concerned with its collection, stage history, and the popular culture of the period. The Shakespeare Birthplace Trust has an attractive site that gives samples of their extensive resources, and the Furness Library at the University of Pennsylvania provides some excellent graphic resources. There is also a delightful, if uneven, array of sites that explore the popular and courtly culture of the Renaissance—music, cookery, costumes, fencing, duelling, and more—created by the enthusiastic members of the Society for Creative Anachronism (SCA). From these you can learn not only how such activities were carried out in Shakespeare's time, but how to re-create them today.

Performance

The Internet offers some rich resources in information about the performance of his plays. There are many web sites devoted to Shakespeare movies, current and not-so-current; some provide clips and useful commentary (once the advertising has been stripped away). More interesting than the movies, perhaps, are the many sites maintained by theatre companies and festivals that perform Shakespeare regularly. On some of these you will find extensive discussions of the plays, images of recent performances, and other materials that the director found useful. In the near future, databases that allow for exploration of multiple performances of the same play will come online, providing an excellent opportunity for the exploration both of the plays themselves, and of evolving attitudes towards them, as expressed in performance: watch for their appearance on the metasites.

Sites available by subscription

'Free' Internet sites of the kind discussed thus far in this chapter are financed either by the enthusiasm of the individual, or by public institutions and granting agencies. The general culture of the Internet is such that users expect to be able to get access to sites without paying; thus at present there are only a limited number of successful commercial sites that have invested in scholarly materials, recouping their expenses from subscriptions. If you are fortunate enough to have access to a library that does subscribe to these resources, there are some valuable scholarly databases, texts, and some criticism in the form of journal articles.

Two immensely valuable sites provide searchable bibliographies. The *Shakespeare Bibliography Online*, edited by James Harner, is an invaluable aid to the serious scholar; it is a meticulous and comprehensive compilation, providing world-wide coverage of Shakespeare studies, summaries of the works it lists, and sophisticated methods of searching its database. *Iter* ('Gateway to the Middle Ages and Renaissance') at the University of Toronto is 'an electronic bibliography of interdisciplinary journal literature pertaining to the Middle Ages and Renaissance (400–1700)'. The strength of *Iter* is that it indexes full runs of journals, not simply the most recent scholarship. A database of a different kind is the online version of the *Oxford English Dictionary*. This deservedly famous pillar of scholarship is made more up-to-date and more powerful in its electronic manifestation; its historical documentation of word usage remains unparalleled.

Early modern texts by subscription are available through some major scholarly and commercial ventures. I have already mentioned the Brown University *Women Writers Project*, which makes available an extensive range of women's writing from 1400 to 1850. There is a special section of the site devoted to the writings of women contemporary with Shakespeare: *Renaissance Women Online*. The texts are prepared under careful scholarly supervision, and are searchable. Two major commercial sites provide access to a huge range of early modern texts. *Literature On Line* (*LION*) has electronic, original-spelling texts of a large number of works written by major and minor writers in the early modern period; in drama alone there are 'over 4,000 works of English and American drama by authors from the late thirteenth century to the early twentieth century'. It is possible to search the entire corpus, or to restrict the search to periods or genres. The same publisher also offers *Editions and Adaptations of Shakespeare*, an extensive textbase that ranges from the First Folio of 1623 to the late nineteenth century. *Early English Books Online* (*EEBO*) offers images of early books rather than electronic transcriptions, though the works will in due course be searchable as transcriptions are completed. *EEBO* has some free offerings; at the time of writing, these included some sections of Shakespeare's sources: Holinshed, and the anonymous play *King Leir*.

For criticism, *Project Muse*, developed by Johns Hopkins University, puts online the full text of journals that also appear in print. Their list of journals does not yet include any that focus exclusively on Shakespeare, but they do have recent issues of several major journals of interest to students in English literature.

CD ROMs

As the extent of Internet resources increases, and as the speed of connection improves, the main convenience of a CD ROM—that it provides faster access to data—is becoming less important. The main advantage for publishers of CD ROMs is that many individuals and institutions are more willing to make copyright material available on the limited medium of a CD than they are on the more open (and seemingly less disciplined) medium of the Internet. Perhaps because of the expense of developing a complex multimedia resource that meets scholarly standards, there are only a few CD ROMs of a quality that makes the cost of acquiring them worthwhile. Your library may have purchased the recently published *King Lear: Text, Performance* from Cambridge University Press, a CD which will be of real value to an advanced student interested in the history of performance of the play. A more encyclopaedic work is the *Arden Shakespeare CD ROM*, which contains the complete plays, as edited in what is known as the 'Arden 2' series. The CD comes with some useful supplementary materials on Shakespeare and each play.

There are also some CDs of individual plays that can be used as a valuable addition to a reading of the play, as they provide a text, notes, and some video-clips of performance. These tend to be priced at a level that a school library or individual can afford. The *Internet Shakespeare Editions* has published a CD ROM of an enhanced version of its site, with the addition of a program that allows a student to 'block' a scene from one of three tragedies.

What's next?

Shakespeare's prophets and soothsayers tend to be uncannily accurate, no doubt because Shakespeare was writing their parts centuries after their prophecies had been fulfilled. The future of the electronic text is less comfortably predictable. As a library, the Internet—or whatever it becomes—will increase its holdings at a remarkable rate; as a web it will become less threatening to a new generation of students and scholars who will accept it, use it, and contribute to it. New technologies will very possibly change the way we work with the electronic text; speed of connection is increasing, and storage media are making trivial the use of high quality video and sound. Already film on DVD is beginning to seem more like a hypertext as it offers extra information—alternative footage, or interviews with the director.

The speed of change makes it inevitable that this chapter will seem dated within a short time of its publication. The associated web site, however, will ensure that the information and links it provides will be both current and reliable. As with many web sites, it will also include an opportunity for visitors to comment on it, and to suggest new links: the electronic medium makes possible interactions that are simply impossible in print.

FURTHER READING

Some of these readings deal with the theory of hypertext and the Internet; for additional sites of relevance to Shakespeare studies, visit the site maintained in support of this chapter at <http://www.uvic.ca/shakespeare/Library/guide.html>.

Bolter, Jay David. *Writing Space: The Computer, Hypertext, and the History of Writing* (Hillsdale, NJ: Lawrence Erlbaum Associates, 1991). A classic introduction to hypertext in theory and practice.

Early Modern Culture: An Electronic Seminar. E-Journal. eds. Crystal Bartolovich and David Siar. 2001. <http://eserver.org/emc/>. An electronic space for discussions of academic research in progress.

Ess, Charles. 'We are the Borg: the Web as Agent of Assimilation or Cultural Renaissance?' *PhilTech* (October 2000). <http://www.ephilosopher.com/120100/philtech/philtech.htm>. Challenges the view that the Internet is creating an ideal 'global village' by pointing out the ways in which the electronic discourse as it is currently constituted threatens to embody a kind of '"McWorld", a global but homogeneous culture, one resulting from the inexorable power of a Western, democratizing technology wiring the planet and reshaping all human cultures along a single set of cultural values and communicative preferences'.

Farrow, James Matthew. *The Works of the Bard* (Sydney: Department of Computer Science, University of Sydney, 1993). <http://www.cs.usyd.edu.au/~matty/Shakespeare/>. The strength of this site is its searching capability, which allows for sophisticated combination searches, once you learn to use the symbols.

Foster, Donald. 'A Romance of Electronic Scholarship, with the True and Lamentable Tragedies of *Hamlet, Prince of Denmark*. Part 1: The Words'. *EMLS* 3.3 / Special Issue 2 (January, 1998): 5.1–42. <http://www.shu.ac.uk/emls/03–3/fostshak.html>. An example of criticism which uses the resources of electronic text, in this case to explore textual problems and indeterminacies in the variant first printed versions of *Hamlet*.

Isser, Edward *et al*. *The Interactive Shakespeare Project*. 'Study Guide for *Measure for Measure*'. College of the Holy Cross: Worcester, MA, 1998–1999. <http://sterling.holycross.edu/departments/theatre/projects/isp/measure/mainmenu.html>. An excellent example of what the electronic multimedia text/classroom can offer. The site provides a modern, annotated edition of the play, extensive reviews of performance, some movie clips, and current critical discussions.

Landow, George P. (ed.). *Hyper / Text / Theory* (Baltimore, MD: Johns Hopkins University Press, 1994). A collection of essays that explores the intersection between the electronic media and recent literary theory.

Michigan Early Modern English Materials. Compiled by Richard W. Bailey *et al*. (Ann Arbor, MI: University of Michigan, Humanities Text Initiative, 1992–94). <http://www.hti.umich.edu/m/memem/index.html>. Allows for searches on the materials generated for the Oxford English Dictionary, principally the verbs, though other words will be seen in context.

Renascence Editions. General ed. Richard Bear. Eugene, OR: University of Oregon, 1994–2001. <http://darkwing.uoregon.edu/~rbear/ren.htm>. Offers a wide range of works between 1477 and 1799 by both major and minor writers; well-represented authors include Milton, Spenser, Sidney, and the prolific Anonymous.

Smith, Alastair G. 'Testing the Surf: Criteria for Evaluating Internet Information Resources'. *The Public-Access Computer Systems Review*, 8.3 (1997). <http://info.lib.uh.edu/pr/v8/n3/smit8n3.html>. Provides additional helpful suggestions for separating reliable sites from the rest.

SITES AND REFERENCES

An up-to-date listing of sites and references will be found on the site maintained in support of this chapter at <http://www.uvic.ca/shakespeare/Library/Criticism/guide.html>.

Arden Shakespeare CD ROM. Thomas Nelson,1997. Contains the Arden 2 critical edition of Shakespeare, supplemented by reference and supporting materials: facsimiles, sources, and bibliography.

Best, Michael. 'Shakespeare's Life and Times'. *Internet Shakespeare Editions*. Victoria, BC: University of Victoria, 1996–2001. <http://www.uvic.ca/shakespeare/Library/SLT/>.

Bradley, A. C. *Shakespearean Tragedy: Lectures on 'Hamlet', 'Othello', 'King Lear', 'Macbeth'*. 2nd edn. (London: Macmillan, 1905). *Shakespeare Navigators*. 29 Aug. 2001 <http://www.clicknotes.com/bradley>.

Britannica.com. The electronic version of the *Encyclopædia Britannica*. Chicago, IL, 2001. Much information is freely available; subscriptions provide additional services.

Brown University Women Writers Project. Director, Julia Flanders. Brown University, Providence, RI, 2001. <http://www.wwp.brown.edu/wwp_home.html>. A long-term research project devoted to early modern women's writing and electronic text encoding. Access by subscription only.

de Grazia, Margreta. 'Hamlet's Thoughts and Antics'. Draft version. *Early Modern Culture*. 2001. <http://eserver.org/emc/1–2/degrazia.html>.

Early Modern Literary Studies (*EMLS*). ed. Lisa Hopkins. Sheffield: Sheffield Hallam University, 1995–2001. <http://purl.oclc.org/emls/emlshome.html>.

Editions and Adaptations of Shakespeare. CD ROM and Internet site available by subscription. Executive eds. Anne Barton and John Kerrigan. Chadwyck-Healey: Bell & Howell Information and Learning Company, 1997–2000. Contains editions and adaptations from the First Folio (1623) to the late nineteenth century.

EEBO (*Early English Books Online*). University of Michigan, Oxford University, Council on Library and Information Resources, and ProQuest Information and Learning, 2001. <http://wwwlib.umi.com/eebo>.

Elizabethan Homilies 1623. ed. Ian Lancashire. *RET Editions* 1.2. 1994, 1997. <http://www.library.utoronto.ca/utel/ret/homilies/elizhom.html>.

Folger Shakespeare Library. 'Home Page' (Washington, DC: 2001). <http://www.folger.edu>.

Furness Library. 'Home Page'. Philadelphia: Schoenberg Center for Text and Image, University of Pennsylvania, 2001. <http://www.library.upenn.edu/etext/furness>.

Hamlet on the Ramparts. Peter S. Donaldson, Director (MIT and the Folger Shakespeare Library, Accessed August 2001). <http://shea.mit.edu/ramparts2000/index.htm>. A full multimedia exploration of *Hamlet*; includes the opportunity to compare editions, to view film clips, and to explore lesson plans and tutorials.

Internet Shakespeare Editions. 'Old-spelling Texts: Transcriptions'. Coordinating ed. Michael Best (Victoria, BC: University of Victoria, 1996–2001). <http://www.uvic.ca/shakespeare>. Facsimiles of Folios 1–4 are available from the same site.

Iter: Gateway to the Middle Ages and Renaissance. University of Toronto: 1997–2001. Updated daily. <http://iter.library.utoronto.ca/iter/index.htm>. Access by subscription only.

Kathman, David, and Terry Ross. *The Shakespeare Authorship Page*. Accessed 28 August 2001. <http://www.clark.net/pub/tross/>.

Lancashire, Ian (ed.). *Early Modern English Dictionaries Database* (*EMEDD*) (Toronto: University of Toronto, 1999). <http://www.chass.utoronto.ca/english/emed/emedd.html >.

Literature On Line (*LION*). Chadwyck-Healey (ProQuest Information and Learning Company), 1996–2001. <http://lion.chadwyck.com/>. Access by subscription only.

Renaissance Forum: an Electronic Journal of Early-Modern Literary and Historical Studies. ed. Andrew Butler. Hull: University of Hull, 1996–2001. <http://www.hull.ac.uk/Hull/EL_Web/renforum/index.html>.

RET (*Renaissance Electronic Texts*). General ed. Ian Lancashire (Toronto: University of Toronto Library, 1997).<http://www.library.utoronto.ca/utel/ret/ret.html>.

Shakespeare Birthplace Trust. 'Home Page' (Stratford: 2001). <http://www.shakespeare.org.uk>.

Shakespeare, William. *King Lear: Text, Performance*. CD ROM. ed. Jackie Bratton and Christie Carson (Cambridge: Cambridge University Press, 2001).

Society for Creative Anachronism. 'Home Page' (Society for Creative Anachronism, Inc.: 1996–2001). <http://www.sca.org>.

Vincent, T. *Passages and Quotes Relating to Justices of the Peace in 16th and 17th Century England*. Source: *The Country Justice*, by Michael Dalton, from a facsimile of the 1655 edition. <http://www.commonlaw.com/CoJust.html>. Copyright 1999–2001; visited 25 July 2001.

World Shakespeare Bibliography Online. ed. James L. Harner. The Folger Shakespeare Library. <http://www-english.tamu.edu/wsb>. Updated 'regularly throughout the year'. Access by subscription only.

Shakespeare's Globe Research Database. Reading: Renaissance Texts Research Centre, University of Reading, 2000. <http://www.reading.ac.uk/globe>. A site that includes extensive research materials on both the original Globe, and the New Globe now built close to the original site.

Search Engines (selected)

Altavista. AltaVista Company: Palo Alto, CA, 2001. <http://www.altavista.com>.

Dmoz: Open Directory Project. Netscape: California, 1998–2001. <http://dmoz.org>. Recommended.

Google. Google: San Francisco, CA, 2001. <http://www.google.com>. Recommended.

Lycos. Lycos, Inc.: Barcelona, Spain, and Waltham, MA, 2001. <http://www.lycos.com>.

Yahoo. Yahoo Inc.: Sunnyvale, CA: 2001. <http://www.yahoo.com>.

Metasites (selected)

Best, Michael. 'Sites on Shakespeare and the Renaissance'. *Internet Shakespeare Editions* (Victoria, BC: University of Victoria, 2001). <http://www.uvic.ca/shakespeare/Annex/ShakSites1.html>.

Gray, Terry A. *Mr. William Shakespeare and the Internet*. San Marcos, CA: Palomar College, 1995–2001. <http://shakespeare.palomar.edu/>. Recommended.

Liu, Alan. *Voice of the Shuttle* (Santa Barbara: English Department, University of California: 2001). <http://vos.ucsb.edu/>.

Ziegler, Georgianna. *Early Modern Women Online: An Annotated Bibliography*. <http://chnm.gmu.edu/emw/bibliography.htm>. A comprehensive and informative gateway to women's writing, art, and society.

Zurcher, Andrew. *CERES (Cambridge English Renaissance Electronic Service)*. 'Page of Links' (Cambridge: Faculty of English, University of Cambridge, 2000). <http://www.english.cam.ac.uk/ceres/links.htm>.

Chronology

(a) Shakespeare's works

A few of Shakespeare's plays can be fairly precisely dated. An allusion to the Earl of Essex in the chorus to Act 5 of *Henry V*, for instance, could only have been written in 1599. But for many of the plays we have only vague information, such as dates of publication (which may have occurred long after composition), dates of performances (which may not have been the first), or inclusion in Francis Meres's list (which tells us only that the plays listed there must have been written by 1598, when his book *Palladis Tamia* was published). The chronology of the early plays is particularly difficult to establish. The following table is based on the 'Canon and Chronology' section in *William Shakespeare: A Textual Companion*, by Stanley Wells and Gary Taylor, with John Jowett and William Montgomery (Oxford, 1987), where more detailed information and discussion may be found.

The Two Gentlemen of Verona	1590–1
The Taming of the Shrew	1590–1
The First Part of the Contention (Henry VI Part Two)	1591
Richard Duke of York (Henry VI Part Three)	1591
Henry VI Part One	1592
Titus Andronicus	1592
Richard III	1592–3
Venus and Adonis	1592–3
The Rape of Lucrece	1593–4
The Comedy of Errors	1594
Love's Labour's Lost	1594–5
Richard II	1595
Romeo and Juliet	1595
A Midsummer Night's Dream	1595
King John	1596
The Merchant of Venice	1596–7
Henry IV Part One	1596–7

The Merry Wives of Windsor	1597–8
Henry IV Part Two	1597–8
Much Ado About Nothing	1598
Henry V	1598–9
Julius Caesar	1599
As You Like It	1599–1600
Hamlet	1600–1
Twelfth Night	1600–1
Troilus and Cressida	1602
The Sonnets	1593–1603
A Lover's Complaint	1603–4
Sir Thomas More	1603–4
Measure for Measure	1603
Othello	1603–4
All's Well that Ends Well	1604–5
Timon of Athens	1605
King Lear	1605–6
Macbeth	1606
Antony and Cleopatra	1606
Pericles	1607
Coriolanus	1608
The Winter's Tale	1609
Cymbeline	1610
The Tempest	1611
All is True (Henry VIII)	1613
Cardenio (by Shakespeare and Fletcher; lost)	1613
The Two Noble Kinsmen (by Shakespeare and Fletcher)	1613–14

(b) Shakespeare's life and career: an outline chronology

1564
26 April: baptism of William Shakespeare in Stratford-upon-Avon.

1582
28 November: issue of marriage licence bond to William Shakespeare and
Anne Hathaway.

1583

26 May: baptism in Stratford-upon-Avon of their daughter Susanna.

1585

2 February: baptism in Stratford-upon-Avon of their twin son and daughter, Hamnet and Judith.

1592

First printed reference to Shakespeare, in *Greene's Groatsworth of Wit*, by Robert Greene, where Shakespeare is called an 'upstart crow'.

1593

Shakespeare's first published work, the poem *Venus and Adonis*, dedicated to the Earl of Southampton.

1594

Publication of Shakespeare's poem *The Rape of Lucrece*, also dedicated to Southampton.

Founding of the Lord Chamberlain's Men, the acting company of which Shakespeare was to be a member as shareholder, actor, and writer for the rest of his life.

1595

Shakespeare named as joint payee of the Lord Chamberlain's Men for performances at court.

1596

11 August: Shakespeare's son Hamnet buried in Stratford-upon-Avon.

October: draft grants of coat of arms to Shakespeare's father, John, giving him and his descendants the status of gentlemen.

1597

May: Shakespeare buys the large and impressive New Place as his home in Stratford-upon-Avon.

15 November: Shakespeare listed in Bishopsgate Ward, London, for non-payment of taxes.

1598

Shakespeare listed as one of the 'principal comedians' acting in Ben Jonson's play *Every Man in His Humour*.

Shakespeare's name first appears on title pages of plays: second quartos of *Richard II* and *Richard III*, and first (surviving) quarto of *Love's Labour's Lost*.

Francis Meres, in his book *Palladis Tamia*, praises Shakespeare as 'among the English . . . the most excellent' in comedy and tragedy 'for the stage', and refers to his 'sugared sonnets among his private friends.'

15 October: the only surviving letter addressed to Shakespeare, from his fellow-Stratfordian Richard Quiney, asking for a loan of £30.

1598–1601

References to Shakespeare in *The Pilgrimage to Parnassus* and *The Return to Parnassus*, anonymous university plays acted at St John's College Cambridge.

1599

16 May: the newly built Globe Theatre named as being in the occupation of 'William Shakespeare and others'.

1601

7 February: the Lord Chamberlain's Men give a special performance of *Richard II* at the Globe the day before the Earl of Essex leads an abortive rebellion against the Queen, for which he is executed.

8 September: Shakespeare's father John buried in Stratford-upon-Avon.

1602

13 March: a law student, John Manningham, records a scurrilous anecdote about Burbage and Shakespeare (p. 13).

2 February: John Manningham records seeing *Twelfth Night* at the Middle Temple.

1 May: Shakespeare buys additional land worth £320 in Stratford-upon-Avon.

1603

24 March: death of Queen Elizabeth I and accession of King James I; the Lord Chamberlain's Men are soon afterwards renamed the King's Men.

Shakespeare listed among 'the principal tragedians' acting in Ben Jonson's tragedy *Sejanus*.

1604

15 March: Shakespeare and his fellow members of the King's Men granted scarlet cloth for livery to walk in King James's coronation procession.

1605

24 July: Shakespeare pays £440 for an interest in the tithes—taxes administered by the Corporation—of Stratford-upon-Avon.

1607

5 June: marriage of Shakespeare's older daughter Susanna to Dr John Hall in Stratford-upon-Avon.

1608

The King's Men take over the indoor Blackfriars theatre but continue to use the Globe as well.

9 September: burial of Shakespeare's mother, Mary, in Stratford-upon-Avon.

1609

Publication of *Shakespeare's Sonnets*.

1610

10 March: Shakespeare buys the Blackfriars Gatehouse, a residential property in London.

1612

Shakespeare testifies as a witness in Stephen Belott's court case against Christopher Mountjoy in London concerning a marriage contract made in a house in which he was a lodger eight years earlier.

1613

31 March: Shakespeare and Richard Burbage each paid 44 shillings for respectively designing and painting an *impresa* (emblematic design on a shield) for the Earl of Rutland.

29 June: the Globe burns down during a performance of *Henry VIII* (*All is True*). It is rebuilt within a year.

September: documents recording Shakespeare's involvement in the process of enclosing (privatizing) common pasture land at Welcombe, near Stratford-upon-Avon.

1616

10 February: Shakespeare's younger daughter Judith marries Thomas Quiney in Stratford-upon-Avon.

25 March: Shakespeare's will drawn up in Stratford-upon-Avon.

25 April: Shakespeare's death in Stratford-upon-Avon (his memorial says that he died on 23 April).

1623

Publication of the First Folio by Shakespeare's colleagues, collecting his plays.

8 August: Shakespeare's wife Anne buried in Stratford-upon-Avon.

1632

Publication of the Second Folio.

1649

16 July: Shakespeare's daughter, Susanna Hall, buried in Stratford-upon-Avon.

1662

9 February: burial of Shakespeare's daughter Judith Quiney in Stratford-upon-Avon.

1670

Death of Shakespeare's last descendant, his granddaughter Elizabeth, who married Thomas Nash in 1626 and John (later Sir John) Bernard in 1649.

Index

Note: entries are listed alphabetically, with the exception of the three *Henry VI* plays, which are listed numerically.